The Law And Practice In Ejectment

THE

LAW AND PRACTICE

IN

EJECTMENT,

UNDER

The Common Law Procedure Acts

OF

1852 & 1854:

ALSO

IN ACTIONS FOR MESNE PROFITS—FOR DOUBLE VALUE
AND DOUBLE RENT—AND FOR POSSESSION IN
THE COUNTY COURTS:

SUMMARY PROCEEDINGS BEFORE JUSTICES TO RECOVER POSSESSION OF
SMALL TENEMENTS, DESERTED PREMISES, OR PARISH PROPERTY;
AND UNDER THE STATUTES AGAINST FORCIBLE ENTRIES
AND DETAINERS:

WITH

AN APPENDIX OF FORMS.

By W. R. COLE, Esq.,
OF THE MIDDLE TEMPLE, BARRISTER AT LAW.

LONDON:

H. SWEET, 3, CHANCERY LANE, FLEET STREET,
Law Bookseller and Publisher.

1857.

LONDON:

PRINTED BY C. ROWORTH AND SONS, BELL YARD,
TEMPLE BAR.

PREFACE.

—◆—

THE Common Law Procedure Acts of 1852 and 1854, and the New Rules, have rendered all previous Treatises of Ejectment of little or no value.

Having practised as a Common Law Barrister and Conveyancer for eighteen years, I hope I may, without presumption, venture to offer to the Profession a New Treatise of Ejectment, &c. I have taken great pains to render it as complete and accurate as possible. As a general rule no case is cited at second-hand, or with reference only to the Marginal Note; but I have read and maturely considered every case and authority cited, with few exceptions.

This Book treats fully—1. Of divers preliminary matters, ex. gr., the Statutes of Limitation, Notices to Quit, Demand of Possession, and various other points to be considered *before* the commencement of the Action. 2. Of the Law and Practice in Ejectment generally. 3. The like, as between particular persons. 4. Of Actions of Trespass for Mesne Profits; Actions for Double Value and Double Rent; Actions for Possession in the County Courts; Summary Proceedings before Justices under the Acts relating to Small Tenements, Deserted Premises, and Parish Property: also of Indictments, Inquisitions, and Summary Proceedings under the Acts relating to Forcible Entries and Detainers.

The Appendix of Forms contains all those authorized by any Statute or Rule: also many others prepared by myself: these have been drawn with great care, and will, I trust, be found safe and useful in practice. It should be observed, that to the heading or title of each Form is added a reference to the page of the Treatise wherein the Form is mentioned.

Particular care has been taken to make the General Index as perfect as possible: under the heads of " Statutes cited," or " Rules of Court cited," any Enactment or Rule comprised in this Book may be readily found.

W. R. COLE.

4, Paper Buildings, Temple,
November, 1856.

TABLE OF CONTENTS.

PART I.

PRELIMINARY MATTERS.

PART II.

PROCEEDINGS IN EJECTMENT IN ORDINARY CASES.

PART III.

PROCEEDINGS IN EJECTMENT BY AND AGAINST PARTICULAR PERSONS.

PART IV.

ACTIONS OF TRESPASS FOR MESNE PROFITS—FOR DOUBLE VALUE AND DOUBLE RENT—FOR RECOVERY OF SMALL TENEMENTS IN THE COUNTY COURTS—SUMMARY PROCEEDINGS BEFORE JUSTICES FOR THE RECOVERY OF SMALL TENEMENTS, DESERTED PREMISES, OR PARISH PROPERTY—FORCIBLE ENTRY AND DETAINER.

APPENDIX.

TABLE OF CASES.

b

d

d 2

e

THE

ıW AND PRACTICE

IN

C T M E N T, &c.

PART THE FIRST.

RELIMINARY MATTERS.

CHAPTER I.

IN EJECTMENT BEFORE 15 & 16 VICT. C. 76.

ȝ of the Common Law Procedure Act, 1852, actions
ı point of form pure fictions, but in substance and
ȝrious realities (*a*).   The action was commenced
by a declaration, *every word of which was untrue:*
`rom the claimant to the nominal plaintiff (*John*
ɪ by him under and by virtue of such lease; and
ȝr by the nominal defendant (*Richard Roe (b)*)):
Jeclaration was a notice addressed to the *tenants in*
them, that, unless they appeared and defended the
ȝified time, *they would be turned out of possession.*
ɔmprehensible part to a non-professional person: it
he tenants sufficiently to send them to their attorney,
object of the proceeding was attained: but the
ɼmitted to defend the action, nor to substitute their
ɪ in lieu of that of the casual ejector (*Richard Roe*),
ng into a " consent rule," whereby they bound
t the alleged *lease, entry* and *ouster,* and to plead
` not guilty," and to insist on the title only.   The

` *Ten Thousand a Year,*" by Warren, Q. C., is a popular
ıtion of the proceedings in such actions, and of their

mes might have been, and frequently were used, *ex.*
tle, *Goodright* v. *No-right, Peaceable* v. *Thrustout,* and the

B

effect of this was that they were bound to admit the truth of all the fictions in the declaration; and (curiously enough) the only matter in issue was a fact or point *not alleged in the declaration*, viz. whether the claimant on the day of the alleged demise, and from thence until the service of the declaration, was *entitled to demise* the property claimed or any part thereof; *i. e.* whether he was himself then legally entitled to actual possession, and consequently to dispose of such possession: if not, it is obvious that the defendants might very safely admit that he did *in fact* make the alleged demise, and that his lessee entered, and was afterwards ousted by the defendants. Such admissions (however contrary to the truth) could not prejudice the defendants, except upon the supposition that the claimant really was entitled to the possession of the property claimed, or some part thereof, on the day of the alleged demise, *Doe* d. *Graves* v. *Wells*, 10 A. & E. 427; 2 P. & D. 396; *Roe* d. *Wrangham* v. *Kersey*, 3 Wils. 274, and from thence until the declaration was served, *Doe* d. *Gardner* v. *Kennard*, 12 Q. B. 244; *Doe* d. *Newby* v. *Jackson*, 1 B. & C. 454, which was the real question to be decided.

The whole proceeding was an ingenious fiction, dexterously contrived so as to raise in every case the only real question, viz. the claimant's title or right of possession, and to exclude every other, and whereby the delay and expense of special pleadings and the danger of variances by an incorrect statement of the claimant's title or estate were avoided. But it was objectionable, on the ground that fictions and unintelligible forms should not be used in courts of justice; especially when the necessity for them might be avoided by a simple writ so framed as to raise precisely the same question in a true, concise, and intelligible form. This has been attempted with considerable success in The Common Law Procedure Act, 1852.

The First Report of the Common Law Commissioners, made in the year 1851, contains the following concise outline of the proceedings in an ordinary action of ejectment, according to the practice before the passing of the above-mentioned act, viz.—

" They are commenced by the delivery to the person in possession of the property to be recovered of a written statement, purporting to be a declaration in an action of trespass and ejectment, alleged to have been previously commenced in one of the superior courts at the suit of a fictitious person, generally called *John Doe* (and styled the nominal plaintiff), against another fictitious person, generally called *Richard Roe* (styled the casual ejector). It states that the person in whom the title really is (styled the *lessor of the plaintiff*), on a day named, made a lease for a certain number of years to the nominal plaintiff *John Doe* of the property in question, which is described in terms so vague as to give no clue to its identity. *John Doe* is then stated to have entered and remained in possession until the imaginary defendant *Richard Roe* ousted or ejected him; and it is then alleged that *John Doe* has sustained damage by such ejectment to a certain amount, for which he brings his action. At the foot of that statement is a letter from *Richard Roe* to the person in possession, informing him that he, *Richard Roe*, is sued as a casual ejector only, and advising the actual possessor to appear in court and procure himself to be made defendant in the stead of *Richard Roe*, or that he will be turned out of possession.

" The above statement must, as a general rule, be served upon the

session, either personally or in such a way as to
it has come to his possession or knowledge before
rm in which proceedings are to be taken.
ossession does not appear within the time allowed
e court, viz. the first four days of the following
ty is in London or Middlesex, or the entire term
ny other county, judgment is pronounced against
hn Doe recover his term, and upon that judgment
and the possession delivered to the lessor of the

d with the declaration in ejectment, or, by leave
ord, may, however, appear within the time above
himself to be substituted as defendant instead of
ntering into a rule of court (called 'the consent
hich is, that the substituted defendant pleads the
ty, and agrees upon the trial of the cause to admit
ments in the declaration to be true, and also that
at the time of the service of the original declara-
on the title only.' The rule further provides for
he defeated party, and that in case the defendant
ve admission at the trial, the plaintiff shall have
a against the casual ejector.
oy reason of the real plaintiff and defendant being
oint tenants, or coparceners, an actual ouster must
er to found an action of trespass, the consent rule
ng the substituted defendant to admit the fictitious
an actual ouster of the lessor of the plaintiff is

rt, the consent rule ought to specify the property
taken, but in practice this rule is wholly disre-
ect is occasionally supplied by particulars of the
e recovered being delivered under a judge's order

ed to trial upon the issue joined upon the plea of
aration, which, pursuant to the consent rule, is
laration by the nominal plaintiff against a real

e defendant does not appear, or appears and does
us statements to be true, according to his agree-
e consent rule, the plaintiff is nonsuited, but is
erms of the consent rule, entitled to a judgment
e lessor of the plaintiff is entitled to receive his
fendant.
appears and makes the admission according to the
stion is then tried upon its merits, whether the
on the day when he is alleged to have made the
id from thence until the service of the original
tled to the property in question; and judgment
vs upon a verdict in the affirmative. In case of
ndant, he is entitled, under the consent rule, to
the lessor of the plaintiff." Pp. 54—56.
ctment before 15 & 16 Vict. c. 76, is fully stated
nent (4th ed.), 2 Chit. Arch. Prac. 914—983

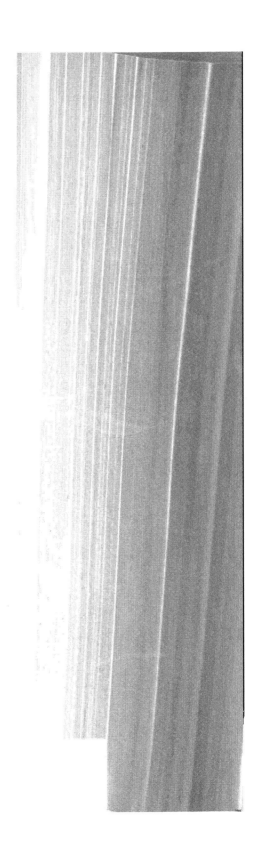

CHAPTER II.

THE STATUTES OF LIMITATION (3 & 4 WILL. 4, C. 27; 7 WILL. 4 AND 1 VICT. C. 28).

---

n action of ejectment must be brought within the
allowed by the stat. 3 & 4 Will. 4, c. 27, intituled
Limitation of Actions and Suits relating to Real
simplifying the Remedies for trying the Rights
twenty years next after the time at which the right
shall have *first accrued.* *Post,* 7.

ierally is to determine *from what event or period*
ins to run in the particular case. To ascertain this
ssary to consider several sections of the statute, par-
14, 35; and in cases of disabilities, sects. 16—19.

gagee, or person claiming under a mortgagee, may
long after the mortgagor's title is barred. 7 Will.
Doe d. *Palmer* v. *Eyre,* 17 Q. B. 366; *Doe* d.
10 Q. B. 486. A purchaser from the mortgagor
person "claiming under" a mortgage within the
t-mentioned act. *Doe* d. *Baddely* v. *Massey,* 17

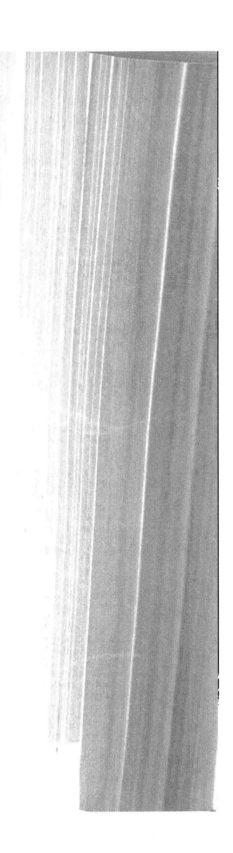

ion under 21 *Jac.* 1, *c.* 16, *ss.* 1, 2.]—Before pro-
fully the stat. of 3 & 4 Will. 4, c. 27, it appears
ncisely the previous law. The 21 Jac. 1, c. 16, s.
ia), "that no person or persons shall at any time
entry into any lands, tenements, or hereditaments,
ears next after his or their right or title which shall
nd or accrue to the same;" with a proviso for per-
y when their right or title first accrued. Sect. 2.
to make an entry ceased, the right to maintain
d.

d, that the statute could only operate as a bar of an
in case of an *adverse possession for twenty years;*
s to what was an adverse possession was partly a
partly a question of fact for the jury. *Fairclaim*
tleton, 5 Burr. 2604; 2 W. Blac. 690; *S. C. Doe*
r, Cowp. 217; *Doe* d. *Tranter* v. *Wing,* 6 C. & P.
it very nice and difficult questions frequently arose.
ted in 2 Smith, L. C. 396; and see Ros. Ev. 477
Parker v. *Gregory,* 2 A. & E. 14; 4 N. & M. 308;
tees, 5 B. & A. 687; 1 D. & R. 340; *Doe* d. *Mil-*
Bing. N. C. 498; *Doe* d. *Linsey* v. *Edwards,* 5 A.
d. *Millett* v. *Millett,* 11 Q. B. 1036; *Faussett* v.
), 5 Bligh, N. S. 76; 2 Dow. & Cl. 232. Fifty
possession would have been no bar to an ejectment.
larbrow, 3 A. & E. 767, n.

ion-*adverse possession,* with all the questions and
h it gave rise, was abolished by the 3 & 4 Will. 4,

c. 27, s. 2; *Culley* v. *Doe* d. *Taylerson* (in error), 11 A. & E. 1008, 1015; 3 P. & D. 539, 549; *Holmes* v. *Newlands*, 11 A. & E. 44; 3 P. & D. 128; *S. C.* in error, 3 Q. B. 679; *Nepean, Bart.* v. *Doe* d. *Knight* (in error) 2 M. & W. 894; 2 Smith, L. C. 396; except as to cases within sect. 15, *i. e.* where the possession was not adverse at the time of the passing of the act, and the ejectment was commenced before the 24th July, 1838. *Post*, 19. The question of adverse possession cannot arise in an action commenced after that day. *Doe* d. *Dayman* v. *Moore*, 9 Q. B. 555.

Statute never pleaded in Ejectment.]—There are no special pleadings in ejectment; and the Statute of Limitations, when it applies, not only bars the remedy, but extinguishes the title. *Post*, 25. Consequently the statute is never pleaded in ejectment, but the claimant must always prove a legal title to possession *not barred by the statute.* *Taylor* d. *Atkyns* v. *Horde*, 1 Bur. 60; 2 Smith, L. C. 324, 389; 6 Bro. P. C. 633, *S. C.*; *Nepean, Bart.* v. *Doe* d. *Knight* (in error), 2 M. & W. 894; 2 Smith, L. C. 307, *S. C.* "The necessity to plead a Statute of Limitations applies to cases where the remedy only is taken away, and in which the defence is by way of confession and avoidance; not where the right and title to the thing is extinguished and gone, and the defence is by denial of that right." *Per cur.* in *De Beavoir* v. *Owen* (in error), 5 Exch. 177. In actions of trespass quare clausum fregit, it may sometimes be necessary or expedient for the plaintiff *to reply* the statute specially; *Jones* v. *Jones*, 16 M. & W. 699; 4 Dowl. & L. 494; but nothing of this sort can happen in an ejectment.

How construed generally.]—Statutes of Limitation ought not to be construed strictly, but beneficially with a view to the mischief intended to be remedied. In *Tolson* v. *Kaye*, 3 Brod. & Bing. 222, Dallas, C. J., said, "I cannot agree in the position that statutes of this description ought to receive a strict construction; on the contrary, I think they ought to receive a beneficial construction, with a view to the mischief intended to be remedied, and this is pointed out by the very first words of the statute [21 Jac. 1, c. 16], which are 'For quieting of men's estates and avoiding of suits.' It is, therefore, that this statute, and all others of this description, are termed by Lord Kenyon Statutes of Repose, and long before and since the passing of this statute this has been the principle which has guided the courts in the construction of them."

3 & 4 *Will.* 4, *c.* 27.]—We now proceed to consider fully the present Statute of Limitations and the decisions thereon, so far as the same apply to actions of ejectment.

Definitions.]—Sect. 1 enacts, "that the words and expressions hereinafter mentioned, which in their ordinary signification have a more confined or a different meaning, shall in this act, except where the nature of the provision, or the context of the act, shall exclude such construction, be interpreted as follows; (that is to say) the word 'land' shall extend to manors, messuages, and all other corporeal hereditaments whatsoever, and also to tithes (other than tithes belonging to a spiritual or eleemosynary corporation sole), and also to any share, estate or

any of them, whether the same shall be a freehold
and whether freehold or copyhold, or held according
:; and the word 'rent' shall extend to all heriots,
and suits for which a distress may be made, and to
periodical sums of money charged upon or payable
except moduses or compositions belonging to a
synary corporation sole); and the person, through
son is said to claim, shall mean any person by,
, or by the act of whom, the person so claiming
the estate or interest claimed, as heir, issue in tail,
:sy of England, tenant in dower, successor, special
at, executor, administrator, legatee, husband, as-
levisee, or otherwise, and also any person who was
te or interest to which the person so claiming, or
gh whom he claims, became entitled as lord by
/ord 'person' shall extend to a body politic, cor-
e, and to a class of creditors or other persons, as
al; and every word importing the singular number
and be applied to several persons or things as well
thing; and every word importing the masculine
extend and be applied to a female as well as a

." does not include a share of turnpike tolls ; *Mel-*
eavan, 22 ; but it does include a right or easement
Wright v. *Williams,* 1 M. & W. 77 ; Tyr. & Gr.
rent" does not include rent reserved on a lease for
s incident to the reversion; but only fee farm and
a distinct estate may be had. *Grant* v. *Ellis,* 9 M.
Ex. 179 ; *Humfrey* v. *Gery,* 7 C. B. 567. The
es not extend to arrears of tithes due as chattels
to the tithe owner; *Dean and Chapter of Ely* v.
. 617 ; but it does extend to tithes belonging to
rations aggregate. *Dean and Chapter of Ely* v.

ion fixed.]—Sect. 2 enacts, "that after the 31st
1833, no person shall make an entry or distress, or
ecover any land or rent, but *within twenty years*
at which the right to make such entry or distress,
:ion, shall have *first accrued to some person through*
if such right shall not have accrued to any person
laims, then *within twenty years* next after the time
to make such entry or distress, or to bring such
first accrued to the person making or bringing the

blishes, as a general rule, that the action must be
nty years *after the right first accrued.* But the
is to ascertain *when the right first accrued* within
act. This is explained by section 3, and several
Others qualify the above rule, and create excep-
rly where there has been any written acknowledg-
14), or payment of rent (sect. 35), or any disability
ght first accrued, and continuing thenceforth without

interruption for more than ten years (sect. 16) ; disabilities for less than that period make no difference.

The effect of this section is to put an end to all questions and discussions whether the possession of the lands, &c. be adverse or not; and if one party has been in the actual possession for twenty years, whether adversely or not, without any payment of rent or written acknowledgment of title, the claimant whose original right of entry accrued above twenty years . before bringing the ejectment, and any person claiming through him, is barred by this section. *Culley* v. *Doe* d. *Taylerson* (in error), 11 A. & E. 1008—1015 ; 3 P. & D. 539, 549. The doctrine of *non-adverse possession* is done away with, except in cases provided for by sect. 15; and an ejectment must be brought within twenty years after the original right of entry of the plaintiff (or of the party under whom he claims) accrued, whatever be the nature of the defendant's possession. *Ante*, 5 ; *Nepean, Bart.* v. *Doe* d. *Knight* (in error), 2 M. & W. 894 ; 2 Smith, L. C. 396 ; *Holmes* v. *Newlands*, 11 A. & E. 44 ; 3 P. & D. 128 ; *S. C.* (in error), 3 Q. B. 679 ; *Culley* v. *Doe* d. *Taylerson, supra.*

When a long term becomes vested in a trustee who does not enter for twenty years, but suffers other persons to remain in possession, his right to enter or maintain ejectment is gone. *Doe* d. *Jacobs* v. *Phillips*, 8 Q. B. 158.

The statute does not apply to cases of want of actual possession by the plaintiff, but to those cases only where he has been out of it, and *another party has been in possession for the prescribed time ;* for there must be both absence of possession by the person who has the right, and *actual possession by another, whether adverse or not, to be protected,* to bring the case within the statute. *Smith* v. *Lloyd,* 9 Exch. 562, 572. Thus where the owner of the fee simple of a close, with minerals under it, conveys the surface, reserving the minerals with the right of entry to get them, and he afterwards grants the minerals with such right, *mere non-user for more than forty years,* no other person having worked, or having been in possession of the minerals, is not sufficient to bar the grantee's right of entry to get the minerals. *S. C.*, *M'Donnell* v. *M'Kinty,* 10 Ir. L. Rep. 514 ; Sugd. Real Prop. Stats. 31. "The act does not extinguish the right of entry where no other party has ever had the possession." *Per Parke,* B., in *Smith* v. *Lloyd,* 9 Exch. 571.

The word "rent," as used in this section, does not apply to a rent reserved in a demise, but only to rents in which a distinct estate may be claimed ; *Grant* v. *Ellis,* 9 M. & W. 113, cited 5 Exch. 179 ; *e. g.* an ancient fee farm rent; *Owen* v. *De Beavoir,* 16 M. & W. 547 ; *S. C.* (in error), 5 Exch. 166 ; a fee farm rent reserved in letters patent or otherwise. *Humfrey* v. *Gery,* 7 C. B. 567. The amount of a rent-charge may be recovered in an action on a covenant for its payment, although the charge has ceased by more than twenty years' non-payment. *Manning* v. *Phelps,* 24 L. J., N. S., Exch. 62.

The word "land" includes "tithes;" sect. 1 ; but this statute does not operate to prevent the tithe owner from recovering tithes *as chattels* from the occupier, although none has been set out for twenty years. This section is confined to cases where there are two parties, each claiming an adverse *estate* in the tithes. *Dean and Chapter of Ely* v. *Cash,* 15 M. & W. 617.

! *be deemed to have first accrued.*]—Sect. 3 enacts,
'uction of this act, the right to make an entry or
action to recover any land or rent, shall be deemed
l at such time as hereinafter is mentioned (that is
the person claiming such land or rent, or some
m he claims, shall, in respect of the estate or inte-
een in possession or in receipt of the profits of such
f such rent, and shall, *while entitled thereto, have
· have discontinued such possession or receipt*, then
leemed to have first accrued at the time of such
continuance of possession, or at the last time at
ofits or rent were or was so received; (2) and
iming such land or rent shall claim the estate or
:ceased person who shall have continued in such
in respect of the same estate or interest until the
nd shall have been the last person entitled to such
ho shall have been in such possession or receipt,
l be deemed to have first accrued at the time of
l when the person claiming such land or rent shall
n estate or interest in possession granted, appointed,
. by any instrument (other than a will) to him, or
ı whom he claims, by a person being, in respect of
ıterest, in the possession or receipt of the profits of
·eceipt of the rent, and no person entitled under
all have been in such possession or receipt, then
leemed to have first accrued at the time at which
ʒ as aforesaid, or the person through whom he
:led to such possession or receipt by virtue of such
d when the estate or interest claimed shall have
ıterest in reversion or remainder, or other future
ınd no person shall have obtained the possession or
; of such land, or the receipt of such rent in respect
erest, then such right shall be deemed to have first
at which such estate or interest became an estate
iion; (5) and when the person claiming such land
ison through whom he claims, shall have become
f any forfeiture or breach of condition, then such
:d to have first accrued when such forfeiture was
ıdition was broken."
be divided into five distinct branches, which explain
ion to sect. 2, as to the time at which the right first
es in which doubt or difficulty might occur; leaving
ainly falls within the general words of the second
:luded amongst the instances given by the third, to
operation of the second. *James* v. *Salter*, 3 Bing.
Scott, 168; 5 Dowl. 496; Sugd. Real Prop. Stat.
'. 253 (5th ed.); 2 Smith, L. C. 401.
applies where the claimant, or the person through
:s *been dispossessed, or has discontinued possession
nts,* as in *Reading* v. *Rawsterne*, 2 Ld. Ray. 829.
y where a lessor permits his lessee during the con-
se to pay no rent for twenty years. Such a case
:he *fourth* branch of this section. *Doe* d. *Davy* v.
W. 131; *Grant* v. *Ellis*, 9 M. & W. 113; *Doe* d.

B 5

Newman v. *Gopsall*, 4 Q. B. 608 ; *Chadwick* v. *Broadwood*, 3 Beav.
308 ; 5 Jur. 359.

An estate tail having been discontinued by a feoffment made by the
tenant in tail more than twenty years before his death : held, that the
issue in tail could not maintain ejectment ; sect. 21 ; *Doe* d. *Cannon*
v. *Rucastle*, 8 C. B. 876 ; but might bring a writ of formedon at any
time within twenty years next after the death of the tenant in tail.
Sect. 38 ; *Cannon*, dem., v. *Rimington*, ten., 12 C. B. 1 ; *S. C.*
(in error), 12 C. B. 18. In this case the court said, "We are all
of opinion that the discontinuance of possession here referred to [sect. 3]
means the quitting possession of land, *to the possession of which he was
entitled.* The right of entry begins the moment the possession has
been discontinued by the party entitled to it ; and if not exercised in
twenty years from that time, it is barred. The principle of the act,
generally speaking, is to bar a person who has a right to enter, if he
does not exercise that right in a certain time, not to bar those who
cannot exercise that right. *Contrà non valentem agere non currit
præscriptio.* To this rule there are express enactments to the contrary,
as in sects. 21, 22, &c., which must of course prevail where they apply.
But it is a strong thing to deprive a man of a right who has had no
opportunity of exercising it ; and the general principle of the act is to
extinguish rights which those who possess them have suffered to lie
dormant." *Id.* 33.

If a tenant for life execute a conveyance in fee, and the purchaser
has undisturbed possession under such conveyance for above twenty
years, the remainderman, or his assigns, may maintain ejectment within
twenty years after the death of the tenant for life. *Doe* d. *Souter* v.
Hull, 2 D. & R. 38.

Under the *second* branch of this section, the following case may be
mentioned :—A. was possessed of lands for more than twenty years,
and died in 1817. His widow had possession from that time until her
death in 1838. B., who was the eldest son of A. and his wife, brought
ejectment soon after the death of his mother : held, that he could not
recover as heir of his father, because more than twenty years had
elapsed since his father's death ; but that he might recover as heir of
his mother, if the jury should infer and find (as they might do) that
the property originally belonged to the mother, and survived to her on
her husband's death. *Doe* d. *Bennett* v. *Long*, 9 C. & P. 773, Coleridge, J.

In a recent case, tried before Parke, B., at Newcastle-on-Tyne, on
28th February 1855, the plaintiff sought to recover lands worth
10,000*l.* per annum as heir of Dorothy Windsor, who died in 1757.
His counsel relied on a fraud committed in the year 1782 on the
plaintiff's grandfather, who was then imbecile, which fraud had only
recently been discovered by the plaintiff ; and he contended that the
statute was not retrospective. But Parke, B., held that the plaintiff's
title was barred, and a nonsuit was entered. *Manby* v. *Craster*, The
Times, 2nd March, 1855, p. 10. And see *Doe* d. *Corbyn* v. *Bramston*, 3 A. & E. 63 ; 4 N. & M. 664.

The *third* branch of this section applies to claims to land or rents
under any instrument (*other than a will*). In the case of an annuity
or rent-charge created by will, an action must be commenced or
distress made within the time limited by sect. 2, which is general, and
not confined to the particular classes of cases mentioned in sect 3.

3 Bing. N. C. 544. Only six years' arrears can be
42. Even such arrears cannot be recovered after the
uity or rent-charge is barred by sect. 2. *James* v.
N. C. 544, 555 ; *Humfrey* v. *Gery*, 7 C. B. 567 ;
woir, 16 M. & W. 547 ; *S. C.* (in error), 5 Exch. 166.
cured by a *covenant* stands on a different footing in
te, 8.

anch of this section, which relates to estates in re-
sion expectant on the determination of a particular
construed with reference to sect. 5 (*infra*). It
uses where *another person* than the remainderman or
titled to the particular estate. If the same person
rights to both estates, sect. 20 applies ; and therefore
pect to the particular estate, he, or any person claim-
e remainder or reversion, is barred as to *that* also :
Moulsdale, 16 M. & W. 689, 698 : unless indeed
entitled to an intervening estate has by ejectment or
possession of such estate. *Doe* d. *Johnson* v. *Lever-
V.* 517, 526.

life execute a conveyance in fee to a purchaser, who
possession under such conveyance for above twenty
derman or his assigns may maintain ejectment within
r the death of the tenant for life. *Doe* d. *Souter* v.
38.

ch of this section applies to ejectments founded on
breach of condition : but where no advantage is at-
en of the forfeiture sect. 4 applies.

Sect. 4 provides, " that when any right to make an
or to bring an action to recover any land or rent by
eiture or breach of condition, shall have first accrued
estate or interest, in reversion or remainder, and the
not have been recovered by virtue of such right, the
entry or distress, or bring an action to recover such
be deemed to have first accrued, in respect of such
at the time when the same shall have become an
in possession, as if no such forfeiture or breach of
pened."

bound to take advantage of the first or any other
ted during the term. *Doe* d. *Boscawen* v. *Bliss*, 4
d. *Shepherd* v. *Allen*, 3 Taunt. 78 ; *Doe* d. *Bryon* v.
401 ; *Doe* d. *Baker* v. *Jones*, 5 Exch. 498. There-
ce to an ejectment commenced after the expiration
a forfeiture and right of entry thereon accrued under
an twenty years before the commencement of the
Doe d. *Allen* v. *Blakeway*, 5 C. & P. 563 ; *Doe* d.
7 East, 299.

eiture is relied on, ejectment must be brought within
by the fifth branch of sect. 3 (*ante*, 9).

-Sect. 5 provides, " that a right to make an entry or
ng an action to recover any land or rent, shall be
rst accrued, in respect of an estate or interest in re-
me at which the same shall have become an estate or

interest in possession, by the determination of any estate or estates in respect of which such land shall have been held, or the profits thereof, or such rent shall have been received, notwithstanding the person claiming such land, or some person through whom he claims, shall, at any time *previously to the creation of the estate or estates which shall have been determined*, have been in possession or receipt of the profits of such land or in receipt of· such rent."

This section is materially affected by sections 9 and 20, in cases to which those sections respectively apply. A reversioner after a long term of years must generally bring ejectment within twenty years after the expiration of the term. Sects. 3, 5. He is not bound to sue within twenty years after rent was last received under the lease. *Doe* d. *Davy* v. *Oxenham*, 7 M. & W. 131 ; *Grant* v. *Ellis*, 9 M. & W. 113 ; *Doe* d. *Newman* v. *Gopsall*, 4 Q. B. 603, note ; *Chadwick* v. *Broadwood*, 3 Beav. 308. So any person claiming through him is not bound to show any receipt of rent under the lease by either of the parties through whom the claimant makes out his pedigree : *Orrell* v. *Maddox*, Runn. Eject. 458 : but if any person wrongfully claiming the reversion has been permitted wrongfully to receive the rent reserved by the lease (amounting to 20*s*. per annum or upwards) for more than twenty years, the case falls within sect. 9, and no fresh right of entry will accrue under sect. 5 on the expiration of the lease.

Encroachments made by a tenant during his term are generally presumed to have been made for the benefit of the landlord ; *Doe* d. *Lewis* v. *Rees*, 6 C. & P. 610 ; *Doe* d. *Harrison* v. *Murrell*, 8 C. & P. 134 ; *Andrews* v. *Hailes*, 3 E. & B. 349 ; who may recover the same by ejectment within twenty years after the expiration of the term, although the encroachment has been made for thirty or forty years. *Doe* d. *Croft* v. *Tidbury*, 14 C. B. 304 ; *Doe* d. *Earl of Dunraven* v. *Williams*, 7 C. & P. 332.

Copyholds were surrendered in 1798 to husband and wife for their joint lives, *with remainder to the heirs of the husband*. In 1805 the husband absconded and went abroad, and was never afterwards heard of. In 1807 a commission of bankruptcy issued against him, and the usual assignment of his estate was made by the commissioner to his assignee, whose title then first accrued. In 1812 the husband would be presumed to be dead, and the wife's title as survivor commenced. She occupied till her death in 1841, when the assignee was admitted : held, that an ejectment by the assignee brought after her death was in time, for that the husband's *reversion in fee was a future estate* within the meaning of this section, and that the wife had sufficiently *recovered* possession of her intervening estate to satisfy sect. 20. *Doe* d. *Johnson* v. *Leversedge*, 11 M. & W. 517, 526.

A reversioner after a tenancy at will must bring ejectment within the time allowed by sect. 7 (*post*, 13). A reversioner after a tenancy from year to year must bring ejectment within the time allowed by sect. 8 (*post*, 14).

Administrator.]—Sect. 6 enacts, " that, *for the purposes of this act*, an administrator claiming the estate or interest of the deceased person of whose chattels he shall be appointed administrator, shall be deemed to claim as if· there had been no interval of time between the death of such deceased person and the grant of the letters of administration."

istration *may* be obtained almost immediately after
ı; any delay in obtaining them is to make no
e time within which the administrator may bring
Prop. Rep. 48. In such action the right of pos-
imed on any day after the intestate's death, even
of administration were granted. Selw. N. P. 716
f *Patten* v. *Patten*, 1 Alcock & Napier (Irish) Rep.
v. *Inhabitants of Horsely*, 8 East, 410; *Bratt* v.
287, *per* Bayley, J.; 2 Man. & Ry. 350, *S. C.*

]—Sect. 7 enacts, " that when any person shall be
receipt of the profits of any land, or in receipt of
t at will, the right of the person entitled, subject
erson through whom he claims, to make an entry
g an action to recover such land or rent, shall be
rst accrued either at the determination of such
expiration of one year next after the commence-
cy, at which time such tenancy shall be deemed to
provided always, that no mortgagor or cestui que
ed to be a tenant at will within the meaning of this
agee or trustee."
ı not apply to tenancies at will which *ceased* before
act (24th July, 1833). *Doe* d. *Thompson* v. *Thomp-*
; 2 N. & P. 656. In such cases the action must be
twenty years after the tenancy ceased. *Doe* d. *Evans*
'67; *Doe* d. *The Birmingham Canal Company* v.
7, 130. But see *Doe* d. *Bennett* v. *Turner*, 7 M. &
ı error), 9 M. & W. 643; explained in *Randall* v.
647.
course applies to tenancies at will which com-
ı act and were in existence on the 31st December,
ıancy be determined by either party, and no fresh
ı ejectment must be commenced within twenty years
ı of the first year of the tenancy at will. *Doe* d.
ı Q. B. 863; *Doe* d. *Dayman* v. *Moore*, *Id.* 555.
tenancies at will which commenced after the passing
ı established by this section is, that if the tenancy
ng the first year of its existence, an ejectment must
twenty years next after such determination; but if
termined at any later period, an ejectment must be
renty years from the expiration of one year next
ement of the tenancy, *i. e.* within twenty-one years
rst commenced. *Doe* d. *Dayman* v. *Moore*, 9 Q. B.
pson v. *Thompson*, 6 A. & E. 721; 2 Smith, L. Cas.

ıncy *at will* has been created after the determination
at will, the twenty-one years will begin to run from
nmencement of such new tenancy, and the creation
cy is a question of fact for the jury. *Doe* d. *Bennett*
ı W. 226; *S. C.* (in error), 9 M. & W. 643; *Doe*
k, 4 Man. & Gr. 30; Car. & Mar. 549, *S. C.*; *Doe*
es, 10 Q. B. 486.
enter and take *actual possession* before his right is
ıte, he will thereupon become legally seised or pos-
ıo the nature of his title); and if the tenant at will

subsequently enter and retake possession, even on the same day, the landlord will thereupon have a *new right of entry commencing at that time*, and may maintain ejectment within twenty years afterwards, although more than twenty-one years after the tenant was first let into possession. *Randall* v. *Stevens*, 2 E. & B. 641.

The concluding proviso, that no cestui que trust shall be deemed a tenant at will within the meaning of this clause to his trustee, only applies to *express trusts*, not to cases where a trust is implied by any rule of law or equity. *Doe* d. *Stanway* v. *Rock*, 4 Man. & Gr. 30. A purchaser let into possession under an agreement to purchase is not a cestui que trust within the meaning of the proviso, but a tenant at will; and, in case the purchase is not completed, the vendor must bring ejectment within twenty years after the expiration of the first year of the tenancy at will. *Doe* d. *Counsell* v. *Caperton*, 9 C. & P. 112.

Although a cestui que trust is not to be deemed a tenant at will to his trustee *for the purposes of this act*, yet he is tenant at will for other purposes, and such tenancy must be determined *before* ejectment can be commenced and maintained by the trustee. *Doe* d. *Jacob* v. *Phillips*, 10 Q. B. 130; 16 Law J., N.S., Q. B. 269; 2 Smith, L. C. 411. Such tenancy will continue until actually determined by the parties, and not at the end of the twenty-first year from its commencement. The object of the stat. 3 & 4 Will. 4, c. 27, was to settle the rights of persons adversely litigating with each other; not to deal with cases of trustees and cestui que trust, where there is but one single interest, viz. that of the person beneficially entitled. *Garrard* v. *Tuck*, 8 C. B. 232. A cestui que trust, who enters into possession of land, becomes at law tenant at will to the trustee; where, therefore, the equitable owner of an estate, a term in which has been assigned to attend the inheritance, is in possession, the right of entry under sect. 2 accrues only upon the determination of the tenancy at will resulting from such possession; and the 3rd section does not apply to the case of a cestui que trust holding possession of land under the trustee. *Garrard* v. *Tuck, supra.* But this doctrine applies only where the cestui que trust is the actual occupant. If he be merely allowed to receive the rents, or otherwise deal with the estate in the hands of the occupying tenant, he stands in the relation of an agent or bailiff of the trustee. If, therefore, the actual occupier be permitted under such circumstances to occupy for more than twenty years without paying rent, or acknowledging title, the trustee is barred by the statute. *Melling* v. *Leak*, 24 Law J., N. S., C. P. 187; 16 C. B. 652.

According to the previous law, possession of the cestui que trust was *not adverse* to the title of the trustee. *Smith* d. *Dennison* v. *King*, 16 East, 283; *Keene* v. *Deardon*, 8 East, 248 (3rd point); *Fausett* v. *Carpenter*, 2 Dow. & Cl. 232; 5 Bligh, N. S. 76; 2 Smith, L. C. 409—412.

Tenancy from Year to Year.]—Sect. 8 enacts, " that when any person shall be in possession or in receipt of the profits of any land, or in receipt of any rent, as tenant from year to year or other period, *without any lease in writing*, the right of the person entitled, subject thereto, or of the person through whom he claims, to make an entry or distress, or to bring an action to recover such land or rent, shall be deemed to have first accrued at the determination of the first of such years or other periods, or at the last time when any rent payable in ιncy shall have been received (which shall *last* hap-

lies to tenancies from year to year created before
ɔ passing of the act. *Doe* d. *Jukes* v. *Summer*, 14
d see *Doe* d. *The Birmingham Canal Company* v.
7.

operation of this section there must have been a
mere memorandum as to the terms of holding, signed
(not being a counterpart lease), and which does not
y estate from the lessor, is not sufficient. *Doe* d.
, 17 Q. B. 589; 21 Law J., N. S., Q. B. 57. An
form of a lease under seal, but which is not ex-
ɔr, does not operate as a lease nor create any term :
ry, 3 Exch. 4; *Swatman* v. *Ambler*, 8 Exch. 72 :
ɪerein named execute the deed and enter into pos-
ιy part of the rent therein expressed to be reserved,
accept such rent, the law will from such circum-
ιancy from year to year upon the terms of the in-
ɾ as the same are or may be applicable to a yearly
ιpra ; *Doe* d. *Thompson* v. *Amey*, 12 A. & E. 476;
ʹest v. *Fritche*, 3 Exch. 216; *Doe* d. *Davenish* v.
. 257, 265; 19 Law J., N. S., Q. B. 438; 14 Jur.
theless, the tenant does not hold under a *lease in*
ɓre an ejectment must be brought within the time
tion. *Doe* d. *Lansdell* v. *Gower*, 17 Q. B. 589; 21
B. 57.

been paid to the claimant, or to the person under
n ejectment may be maintained within twenty years
ιent. The payment may be proved by an oral ad-
ɪson who was in actual possession at the time of
ɪsion, which will be good evidence as against him
nts or assigns. *Doe* d. *Earl Spencer* v. *Beckett*, 4

: two cottages by churchwardens and overseers, it
lefendants had within twenty years swept the church
ːch bell : held, that these were services for which a
ɪ been made, and consequently that the statute was
ιent. *Doe* d. *Edney* v. *Benham and Billett*, 7 Q. B.
ι poor person occupied for twenty years, paying no
ι grindstone on the premises for the convenience of
that the statute was a bar. *Doe* d. *Robinson* v.
Rob. 441.

Rent.]—Sect. 9 enacts, "that when any person
ɪion or in receipt of the profits of any land, or in
t, by virtue of a lease in writing, by which a rent
ɾearly sum of *twenty shillings* or upwards shall be
rent reserved by such lease shall have been *received*
ɪngfully claiming to be entitled to such land or rent
ɪately expectant on the determination of such lease,
ɪ respect of the rent reserved by such lease shall
ɛen made to the person rightfully entitled thereto,
ιerson entitled to such land or rent, subject to such
ɪson through whom he claims, to make an entry or

distress, or to bring an action after the determination of such lease, shall be deemed to have first accrued at the time at which the rent reserved by such lease was first so received by the person wrongfully claiming as aforesaid; and no such right shall be deemed to have first accrued upon the determination of such lease to the person rightfully entitled."

This section applies only where the rent reserved by the lease amounts to 20*s*. per annum or upwards and another person wrongfully claiming to be entitled to such rent has been permitted to receive it for more than twenty years. *Doe* d. *Angell* v. *Angell*, 9 Q. B. 328, 358. A rent less than 20*s*. is considered as only *nominal*. 1 Real Prop. Rep. 47; 2 Smith, L. C. 407. If no rent be reserved, this section does not apply. *Ex parte Jones, Re St. Philip's Bridge Company*, 4 You. & Coll. 466. Before this act, even the adverse receipt of rent (however large) for more than twenty years did not deprive the reversioner of his right of entry on the determination of the lease, because the possession of the land was not adverse during the term. *Doe* d. *Cook* v. *Danvers*, 7 East, 299, 312; 2 Smith, L. C. 407.

Entry.]—Sect. 10 enacts, "that no person shall be deemed to have been in possession of any land within the meaning of this act *merely* by reason of having made an entry thereon."

Before this enactment, a mere entry upon lands was of no force to satisfy the then Statute of Limitations (21 Jac. 1, c. 16), or to avoid a fine levied of lands, unless an action were thereupon commenced within one year after, and prosecuted with effect. 4 & 5 Anne, c. 16, s. 16; *Rex* v. *Inhabitants of Wooburn*, 10 B. & C. 846, 848, Bayley, J.; *Rex* v. *Inhabitants of Pensax*, 3 B. & Ad. 815. The entry of cestui que trust (followed by an action in due time) was sufficient to avoid the statute. *Gree* v. *Rolle*, 1 Ld. Raym. 716.

Section 10 applies only to *mere entries pro formâ*; not where actual possession is taken and the tenant turned out. *Randall* v. *Stevens*, 2 E. & B. 641. It "evidently applies to a *mere entry*, as for the purpose of avoiding a fine, which may be made by stepping on any corner of the land in the night time and pronouncing a few words, without any attempt or intention or wish to take possession. In the present case possession was actually taken by the overseers *animo possidendi*; and whether possession was retained by them an hour or a week must for this purpose be immaterial. They were lawfully in of their fee simple title; and by nothing that had previously happened could their right, in respect of the Statute of Limitations, be at all prejudiced." *Id*. 652, *per* Lord Campbell, C. J.

The defendant being in adverse possession of a hut and piece of land, the lord of the manor entered in the absence of the defendant, but in the presence of his family said he took possession in his own right, and he caused a stone to be taken from the hut, and a portion of the fence to be removed: held, that these acts were not sufficient to disturb the defendant's possession, but a mere entry within the meaning of sect. 10. *Doe* d. *Baker* v. *Combes*, 19 Law J., N. S., C. P. 306.

Continual Claim.]—Sect. 11 enacts, "that no continual or other claim upon or near any land shall preserve any right of making an entry or distress, or of bringing an action."

As to the previous law, see Litt. ss. 414—443; Co. Litt. 250 a—264 a.

]—Sect. 12 enacts, " that when any one or more
ntitled to any land or rent as coparceners, joint-
ɔ common, shall have been in possession or receipt
iore than his or their undivided share or shares of
profits thereof, or of such rent, for his or their own
benefit of any person or persons other than the
ntitled to the other share or shares of the same
possession or receipt shall not be deemed to have
ɔr receipt of or by such last-mentioned person or
ɪem."

: the possession of coparceners, joint-tenants, and
separate from the commencement of the tenancy,
m the time of the act passing. *Doe* d. *Holt* v.
: K. 566 ; *Culley* v. *Doe* d. *Taylerson* (in error),
); 11 A. & E. 1008 ; *O'Sullivan* v. *M'Swiney,*
s. (Irish) Rep. 118, 119.

: previous law, the possession of one of several
would not prevent the Statute of Limitations (21
ɪ operating against the rest. *Earl of Essex* v.
rm. 310. The bare perception of all the rents and
: in common was no ouster of his co-tenants.
:, 2 Salk. 423 ; 2 Lord Raym. 830 ; *Fairclaim* d.
:ton, 5 Burr. 2604 ; 2 W. Black. 690. But after
:ssion had continued without any interruption or
·ty-seven years : held, that the jury might from
infer and find an actual ouster. *Doe* d. *Fishar* v.
l7. The disability of a coparcener for more than
ot preserve the right of entry of the other copar-
ɪgdon v. *Rowlston,* 2 Taunt. 441.

:nger Brother, &c.]—Sect. 13 enacts, " that when
: other relation of the person entitled as heir to the
of the profits of any land, or to the receipt of any
ɔ the possession or receipt thereof, such possession
be deemed to be the possession or receipt of or by
s heir."

s law, see Litt. s. 396 ; Com. Dig. " Abatement"
:er v. *Lawley,* 3 N. & M. 331 ; 13 Q. B. 954.

:dgment of Title.]—Sect. 14 provides and enacts,
knowledgment of the title of the person entitled
hall have been given to him or his agent, *in writing,*
ɪ in possession or in receipt of the profits of such
ɔf such rent, then such possession or receipt of or
hom such acknowledgment shall have been given
ording to the meaning of this act, to have been the
: of or by the person to whom or to whose agent
ɪt shall have been given at the time of giving the
: of such last-mentioned person, or any person
m, to make an entry or distress, or bring an action
or rent, shall be deemed to have first accrued at
time at which such acknowledgment or the last
ments, if more than one, was given."
ɪent of title within the meaning of this section

must be *in writing: see a Form, Appendix, No. 9.* It must be signed by the person then in possession or in receipt of the profits of the land. It seems that a signature by his agent is not sufficient. *Hyde* v. *Johnson*, 2 Bing. N. C. 778, 780; 3 Scott, 289. The 40th and 42nd sections are differently worded in this respect, and see 3 & 4 Will. 4, c. 42, s. 5. The acknowledgment may be given to the person entitled "or his agent." Sect. 14. A written acknowledgment made or given to a third person (not being such agent) is not sufficient. *Grenfell* v. *Girdlestone*, 2 You. & Coll. 676; *Forsyth* v. *Bristowe*, 22 L. J., N. S., Exch. 255. So a recital in a deed to which the person entitled is no party would seem insufficient. *Batchelor* v. *Middleton*, 6 Hare, 75; but see *Mountstephen* v. *Brooke*, 3 B. & A. 141. It may be sufficient where he is a party. *Cheslyn* v. *Dolby*, 4 You. & Coll. 238; *Forsyth* v. *Bristowe, supra.* In such case the acknowledgment will operate from the time when the deed is executed, and not from its date, provided the time of such execution be proved. *Jaynes* v. *Hughes*, 24 L. J., N. S., Exch. 115.

An attornment in writing to the person entitled is sufficient. If it be a mere attornment, and do not amount to a new demise, it will not require a stamp. *Doe* d. *Linsey* v. *Edwards*, 5 A. & E. 95. But an instrument in writing professing to be an attornment, which does in fact create a new tenancy upon different terms, does require a stamp, either as a lease or as an agreement. *Cornish* v. *Searle*, 8 B. & C. 471. An instrument in these terms, "I hereby certify, that I remain in the house No. 3, Swinton-street, belonging to W. G., on sufferance only, and agree to give him immediate possession at any time he may require," does not amount to an agreement for a tenancy, so as to require a stamp. *Barry* v. *Goodman*, 2 M. & W. 768.

Where, in answer to an application for arrears of rent, the tenant by letter complained of having been put to much expense with respect to the land, and said it was reasonable that the lords of the fee should make him recompense accordingly, and that F. (the party applying) should vindicate his right to the land, rather than that the expenses should fall upon the tenants, and concluded his letter by begging "compassion, mercy and pity and recompense in a satisfactory manner:" held, that such letter in effect admitted that rent was due to F., and, therefore, amounted to a sufficient admission of F.'s title to satisfy this section. *Fursdon, Executrix, &c.* v. *Clogg*, 10 M. & W. 572. A correspondence by a party in possession of property with the solicitor of a society, by which he merely professed to hold the estates until an account, on the foot of charges to which he was entitled, should be closed, and offered to refer to arbitration all questions touching such account, as the only matter in dispute, was held to amount to a sufficient acknowledgment of the society's title. *Incorporated Society* v. *Richards*, 1 Con. & L. (Irish) Rep. 86; 1 Dru. & War. 290, *S. C.* But where a person in possession adversely of land, being applied to by the party claiming title to it to pay rent, and offered a lease of it, wrote as follows,— "Although, if matters were contested, I am of opinion that I should establish a legal right to the premises, yet, under all circumstances, I have made up my mind to accede to the proposal you made of paying a moderate rent, on an agreement for a term of twenty-one years," but the bargain subsequently went off, and no rent was paid or lease executed: held, that this letter was not an acknowledgment of title within this section. *Doe* d. *Curzon* v. *Edmonds*, 6 M. & W. 295.

Whether a writing amounts to an acknowledgment of title within

estion for the judge, and not for the jury, to decide.
Edmands, 6 M. & W. 295 ; 2 Smith, L. C. 412 ;
. *Frith,* 3 M. & W. 402 ; *Routledge* v. *Ramsay,* 8
I. & P. 319 ; *Edmands* v. *Goater,* 21 L. J., N. S.,

of the contents of a written acknowledgment may
tted. *Haydon* v. *Williams,* 7 Bing. 168 ; 4 Moo.

bal admission is admissible, not as an " acknowledg-
in the meaning of this section, but as *proof of a*
ayment of rent to the claimant or to some person
claims. *Doe* d. *Earl Spencer* v. *Beckett,* 4 Q. B.
Rowe, 1 A. & E. 114 ; *Doe* d. *Daniel* v. *Coulthred,*
7. Thus, where it was proved that within twenty
brought, H., being in possession, declared, that he
ent to the lessor of the plaintiff ; and that after-
ction brought, the defendant had said that he was
t appeared that H. had died before the trial : held,
was not barred by 3 & 4 Will. 4, c. 27, s. 2 ; pay-
g duly proved by H.'s admission, so as to satisfy
fendant being bound by the evidence, which was
    Doe d. *Earl Spencer* v. *Beckett, supra.*

ion enlarged—Possession not adverse at passing of
ovides and enacts, " that when no such acknow-
id shall have been given before the passing of this
ssion or receipt of the profits of the land, or the
shall *not at the time of the passing of this act have*
right or title of the person claiming to be entitled
person, or the person claiming through him, may,
e period of twenty years, hereinbefore limited, shall
e an entry or distress, or bring an action to recover
est, at any time *within five years next after the*
"

applicable to any action of ejectment commenced
rs after the 24th July, 1833, when the act passed.
Moore, 9 Q. B. 555.
enced before the expiration of the above period, it
—1. That, if the possession were *not adverse* at the
of the act, the action might be supported. *Doe* d.
5 A. & E. 291 ; *Culley* v. *Doe* d. *Taylerson,* 11 A. &
. 551 ; *Doe* d. *Burgess* v. *Thompson, Id.* 532 ; *Doe*
9 Q. B. 328 ; *Lessee of O'Sullivan* v. *M'Sweeney,*
Moore, 89 ; 1 Jones & Carey, 295, S. C.
ion were *adverse* at the time of the passing of the
not apply. *Nepean, Bart.* v. *Doe* d. *Knight* (in
911 ; *Ex parte Hasell, In re Manchester Gas Act,*
; 3 Jur. 1101, *S. C. ; Holmes* v. *Newland,* 11 A.
. 128 ; *S. C.* (in error), 3 Q. B. 679.

ect. 16 provides and enacts, "that if at the time
: of any person to make an entry, or distress, or
ecover any land or rent, shall have first accrued as
son shall have been under any of the disabilities

hereinafter mentioned (that is to say), infancy, coverture, idiotcy, lunacy, unsoundness of mind, or absence beyond seas, then such person, or the person claiming through him, may, notwithstanding the period of twenty years, hereinbefore limited, shall have expired, make an entry or distress, or bring an action to recover such land or rent, at any time *within ten years* next after the time at which the person to whom such right shall have first accrued as aforesaid shall have ceased to be under any such disability, or shall have died (which shall have *first* happened)."

This and the next three sections must be read with reference to each other.

It is to be observed : 1. That a disability makes no difference unless it *continue for more than ten years next* after the right of entry first accrues. 2. That when once the statute begins to run, no subsequent disability will stop it. *Doe* d. *Count Duroure* v. *Jones,* 4 T. R. 300, 310; *Doe* d. *George* v. *Jesson,* 6 East, 80; *Cotterell* v. *Dutton,* 4 Taunt. 826. 3. No further time is allowed for a succession of disabilities in different persons. Sect. 18. 4. Imprisonment is not a disability within the meaning of this act. 5. In no case can ejectment be brought more than forty years after the right of entry first accrued. Sect. 17. This limit is never reached except where a disability which existed when the right of entry first accrued has uninterruptedly continued for thirty years afterwards. An occasional hardship in such cases is of less consequence than the want of certainty in titles generally after forty years' possession. *Lex vult potius malum quam inconveniens.*

Where a father entered as guardian on behalf of his infant child: held, that a trust was thereby created in equity, and that the statute did not begin to run until the infant attained his full age. *Thomas* v. *Thomas,* 25 L. J., N. S., Chanc., 159, Wood, V. C. In this case the remedy *at law* was barred by the statute.

Extreme Period of Limitation fixed—Forty Years.] —Sect. 17 provides and enacts, "that no entry, distress or action shall be made or brought by any person who, at the time at which his right to make an entry or distress, or to bring an action to recover any land or rent, shall have first accrued shall be under any of the disabilities hereinbefore mentioned, or by any person claiming through him, but within forty years next after the time at which such right shall have first accrued, although the person under disability at such time may have remained under one or more of such disabilities during the whole of such forty years, or although the term of ten years, from the time at which he shall have ceased to be under such disability, or have died, shall not have expired."

See the observations on sect. 16 (*supra*).

An heir of a married woman deceased cannot maintain ejectment as heir more than forty years after she was dispossessed or discontinued the possession or receipt of the rents within the meaning of the first branch of sect. 3 (*ante,* 9). *Doe* d. *Corbyn* v. *Bramston,* 3 A. & E. 63; 4 N. & M. 664; *Manby* v. *Craster* (*ante,* 10). Formerly fifty years of *non-adverse* possession was no bar to an ejectment. *Doe* d. *Roffey* v. *Harbrow,* 3 A. & E. 767, n.

Successive Disabilities.] —Sect. 18 provides and enacts, "that when any person shall be under any of the disabilities hereinbefore men-

t which his right to make an entry or distress, or to
recover any land or rent, shall have first accrued,
is life without having ceased to be under any such
to make an entry or distress, or to bring an action
l or rent beyond the said period of twenty years
of such person to make an entry or distress, or to
ecover such land or rent, shall have first accrued,
f ten years next after the time at which such person
all be allowed by reason of any disability of any

he previous law. *Doe* d. *George* v. *Jesson,* 6 East,
Cotterel v. *Dutton,* 4 Taunt. 826, 830; *Tolson* v.
ing. 217; 6 Moor. 542. A succession of disabilities
(without any intermission) would entitle such per-
iming through him or her, to bring an action within
iects. 16 and 17. Thus where A., a minor, having
1787, married in 1794, and, being a feme covert,
ge in 1796, and died in 1827: held, that an eject-
er heir within ten years after her death was main-
Supple v. *Raymond,* 1 Hayes (Irish) R. 6. But
ction must now be brought within forty years after
ied. Sect. 17.

.]—Sect. 19 enacts, " that no part of the united
Britain and Ireland, nor the islands of Man,
Alderney, or Sark, nor any islands adjacent to any
t of the dominions of his majesty,) shall be deemed
ithin the meaning of this act."

ts.]—Sect. 20 enacts, " that when the right of any
entry or distress, or bring an action to recover any
iich he may have been entitled for an estate or
n, shall have been barred by the determination of
ore limited, which shall be applicable in such case,
ll, *at any time during the said period,* have been
r estate, interest, right or possibility, in reversion,
vise, in or to the same land or rent, no entry, dis-
be made or brought by such person, or any person
im, to recover such land or rent in respect of such
t, right or possibility, unless in the meantime such
ave been recovered by some person entitled to an
ght which shall have been limited or taken effect
e of such estate or interest in possession."
ies where a person having two estates in the same
ime allows his estate in possession to be barred by
i case his estate in remainder or reversion will be
. *Hall* v. *Moulsdale,* 16 M. & W. 689, 698: unless
erson entitled to an intervening estate has recovered
nd. In the latter case a new right of entry will
nainder or reversion first becomes an estate in pos-
; *Doe* d. *Johnson* v. *Leversedge,* 11 M. & W. 517.
that the person entitled to the intervening estate
possession by an action of ejectment: an entry and

enjoyment of the property by virtue of such estate is a sufficient "recovery" within the meaning of this section. *Id.* 526, *per cur.*

Estates Tail—Where Time has run against Tenant in Tail.]—Sect. 21 enacts, " that when the right of a tenant in tail of any land or rent to make an entry or distress, or to bring an action to recover the same, shall have been barred by reason of the same not having been made or brought within the period hereinbefore limited, which shall be applicable in such case, no such entry, distress or action shall be made or brought by any person claiming any estate, interest or right, which such tenant in tail might lawfully have barred."

This section is retrospective. *Goodall* v. *Skerratt,* 25 Law Times R. 6, Kindersley, V. C. Whenever the statute bars the tenant in tail it also bars his issue in tail and all remainders and reversions which he might have barred by a disentailing deed. Sug. Real Prop. Stat. 89; *Goodall* v. *Skerratt, supra.* In ejectment the plaintiff proved that A., being seised in fee of the land in question, devised it to the father of the plaintiff in tail general, and died in 1799. The plaintiff's father received the rents and profits from 1799 to 1807, at which time he was succeeded by a person through whom the defendant obtained possession : held, that as the tenant in tail was barred, his issue was also barred. *Austin* v. *Llewellyn,* 9 Exch. 276. " If a tenant in tail remains out of possession for twenty years, his neglect bars the issue in tail, the same as if he had executed a disentailing deed, and conveyed away the estate." *Id.* 278, Alderson, B.; and see *Cannon* v. *Rucastle,* 8 C. B. 876; *Goodall* v. *Skerratt, supra.* But according to the previous law the issue in tail would have had a fresh right of entry, commencing on the death of the tenant in tail. *Doe* d. *Smith* v. *Pike,* 3 B. & Adol. 738; 1 N. & M. 385.

Where Time has commenced running against Tenant in Tail.]— Sect. 22 enacts, " that when a tenant in tail of any land or rent entitled to recover the same shall have died before the expiration of the period hereinbefore limited, which shall be applicable in such case, for making an entry or distress, or bringing an action to recover such land or rent, no person claiming any estate, interest or right which such tenant in tail might lawfully have barred, shall make an entry or distress, or bring an action to recover such land or rent, but within the period during which if such tenant in tail had so long continued to live, he might have made such entry or distress or brought such action."

The *neglect* of the tenant in tail will bar all those—issue in tail and remaindermen—whom the tenant in tail himself might have barred; and if the whole time has not run against him, the persons, issue or remaindermen, whom he could have barred, have only the time which remains to run within which to prosecute their right; and thus, claiming as it were to stand in his place, they cannot claim the benefit of the savings of the act in regard to their own disabilities. Sug. Real Prop. Stat. 89; *Austin* v. *Llewellyn,* 9 Ex. 276; *Goodall* v. *Skerratt,* 25 Law Times R. 6, Kindersley, V. C. Under the 21 Jac. 1, c. 16, a remainderman in fee, after an estate tail, might maintain ejectment within twenty years after the failure of the issue in tail, notwithstanding any length of adverse possession against the tenant in tail or his issue. *Taylor* v. *Horde,* 1 Burr. 60; Cowp. 689; 1 Ld. Ken. 143, *S. C.* So the issue in tail had a right of entry, commencing from the

in tail. *Doe* d. *Smith* v. *Pike*, 3 B. & Adol. 738,
ed.

tail in remainder, with the consent of the tenant
of the settlement, bars the estate tail, and converts
exhausting the fee simple, any person claiming
he same time to bring ejectment as the tenant in
if his estate tail had not been barred, viz. twenty
of the tenant for life (not twenty years from the
of the deed). *Doe* d. *Curzon* v. *Edmonds*, 6

Defective Conveyance by Tenant in Tail.] — Sect. 23
a tenant in tail of any land or rent shall have
hereof, which shall not operate to bar an estate or
after or in defeasance of his estate tail, and any
e of such assurance, at the time of the execution
ime afterwards, be in possession or receipt of the
l, or in the receipt of such rent, and the same
r person whatsoever (other than some persons en-
ion or receipt in respect of an estate which shall
ter or in defeasance of the estate tail), shall con-
ossession or receipt for the period of twenty years
iencement of the time at which such assurance, if
ecuted by such tenant in tail, or the person who
titled to his estate tail if such assurance had not
l, without the consent of any other person, have
estate or estates as aforesaid, then, at the expira-
of twenty years, such assurance shall be, and be
n, effectual as against any person claiming any
ght to take effect after or in defeasance of such

irtue of this section twenty years' possession under
ice by a tenant in tail renders such conveyance
gainst all persons whom the tenant in tail might
Prop. Rep. 46, 79; *Doe* d. *Cannon* v. *Rucastle*,
0. But see 12 C. B. 12, in which this point was
guendo. A conveyance by a tenant in tail may
during his life, although defeasible by the issue in
l v. *Woodruffe*, 10 M. & W. 624; and see *Doe*
nds, 6 M. & W. 295; *Goodright* d. *Tyrrell* v.

tail brought ejectment (before this act) against a
een in receipt of the rents thirty years during the
in tail, and seven years after his death, and the
sin: held, that such possession by the defendant
ion, and that the lessor of the plaintiff was not
resumption arising from such possession, by show-
r had not conveyed by fine or recovery. *Doe* d.
& Adol. 738. A conveyance in fee by lease and
a tail conveys a base fee voidable by the entry of
)oe d. *Neville* v. *Rivers*, 7 T. R. 276; *Goodright*
3 Burr. 1703; and see 2 Smith, L. C. 406.

-Sects. 24, 25, 26 and 27 relate only to suits in

equity, not to actions of ejectment. For the cases on these sections see Shelford's Real Property Statutes, 185 to 196 (4th edit.).

Mortgagor and Mortgagee—Time of Limitation fixed—Twenty Years.]—Sect. 28. This section does not apply to actions of ejectment, but to suits in equity to redeem a mortgage. Such suits must be commenced within twenty years after the mortgagee entered into possession or into receipt of the rents and profits, unless indeed there has since been a sufficient acknowledgment as to all or part of the land within the meaning of this section. *Batchelor* v. *Middleton,* 6 Hare, 75; *Trulock* v. *Robey,* 15 Sim. 265 ; 5 Jur. 1101. But see *Hyde* v. *Dallaway,* 2 Hare, 528.

Where no interest has been paid under a mortgage, the mortgagee must generally bring ejectment to recover possession of the mortgaged property within twenty years next after the date and execution of the deed, although no default was made till a later period. Sects. 2, 3 ; *Doe* d. *Roylance* v. *Lightfoot,* 8 M. & W. 553. In *Doe* d. *Jones* v. *Williams,* 5 A. & E. 295, 297, doubts were expressed whether a mortgagee who had not been in possession or in receipt of rents for more than twenty years was not barred by sects. 2 and 3, notwithstanding the payment of any interest on the mortgage within that period. This led to the passing of the 7 Will. 4 & 1 Vict. c. 28, whereby, after reciting such doubts, and that it was expedient to remove them, "it is declared and enacted, that it shall and may be lawful for any person entitled to or claiming under any mortgage of land, being land within the definition contained in the first section of the said act, to make an entry or bring an action at law or suit in equity to recover such land at any time *within twenty years next after the last payment* of any part of the principal money or interest secured by such mortgage, although more than twenty years may have elapsed since the time at which the right to make such entry or bring such action or suit in equity shall have first accrued, anything in the said act notwithstanding."

According to the old law, payment of interest on a mortgage prevented the operation of the Statute of Limitations. *Hatcher* v. *Fineaux,* 1 Lord Raym. 740 ; and see *Loftus* v. *Smith,* 2 Scho. & Lef. (Irish) R. 642. Even where no interest was proved to have been paid, yet if it appeared that the mortgagor remained in possession by the permission of the mortgagee, even for more than twenty years, there was *no adverse possession,* and consequently no bar by the statute. *Hall* v. *Doe* d. *Surtees* (in error), 5 B. & A. 687 ; 1 D. & R. 340; *Doe* d. *Jones* v. *Williams,* 5 A. & E. 291 ; 2 Smith, L. C. 409.

By virtue of the 7 Will. 4 & 1 Vict. c. 28, a mortgagee, or person claiming under a mortgage, may sometimes maintain ejectment against the mortgagor's tenants long after the mortgagor himself is barred, provided any interest on the mortgage has been paid within twenty years. *Doe* d. *Palmer* v. *Eyre,* 17 Q. B. 366. A purchaser from the mortgagor and mortgagee is a person "claiming under" a mortgage within the meaning of this act. *Doe* d. *Baddeley* v. *Massey,* 17 Q. B. 373. This enactment is not confined to cases where the mortgagor has been in possession of the mortgaged premises, but its object was to protect mortgagees generally, and to make mortgages available securities wherever they are valid in their inception ; and the mortgagee having received payment of his interest cannot be charged with any laches. *Doe* d. *Palmer* v. *Eyre, supra.*

Eleemosynary Corporations Sole—Time of Limitation
) provides and enacts, "that it shall be lawful for any
op, dean, prebendary, parson, vicar, master of hospital,
l or eleemosynary corporation sole, to make an entry
bring an action or suit to recover any land or rent
od as hereinafter is mentioned next after the time at
of such corporation sole, or of his predecessor, to make
stress, or bring such action or suit, shall first have
to say), the period during which two persons in suc-
e held the office or benefice in respect whereof such
ll be claimed, and six years after a third person shall
nted thereto, if the times of such two incumbencies
f six years taken together shall amount to the full
years; and if such times taken together shall not
full period of sixty years, then during such further
in addition to such six years as will, with the time of
ich two persons and such six years, make up the *full
ears;* and after the said 31st day of December, 1833,
istress, action or suit shall be made or brought at any
determination of such period."
actment, adverse possession for twenty years was not
or vicar, except as against the same incumbent who
:h possession. *Runcorn* v. *Doe* d. *Cooper* (in error),
8 D. & R. 450.

-Sects. 30, 31, 32 and 33 relate to advowsons and
ation, but do not apply to actions of ejectment. See
Property Statutes, 209—217 (4th ed.).

tion of Right.]—Sect. 34 enacts, "that at the deter-
)eriod limited by this act to any person for making an
or bringing any writ of *quare impedit*, or other action
and title of such person to the land, rent or advowson,
whereof such entry, distress, action or suit respectively
made or brought within such period, shall be *extin-
s* v. *Jones,* 16 M. & W. 699; 4 Dowl. & L. 494.
ict only barred the remedy, but did not extinguish the
where A., whose right of entry had been barred by
lverse possession of B., entered into possession on the
:ld, that C., the devisee of B., could not maintain
t A., he being in possession under his old lawful title.
h and Wife v. *Reade,* 8 East, 353.
it rent, in respect whereof no payment or acknow-
:n made for twenty years, is at the end of that period
wen v. *De Beavoir,* 16 M. & W. 547; *S. C.* (in error),
umfrey, a lunatic, v. *Gery,* 7 C. B. 567. But although
ise as a charge on the land, yet if there be a covenant
, an action may be maintained on such covenant.
lps, 24 Law J., N.S., Ex. 62.
iid by high authority that, at the end of the period
ct, this enactment *operates as a parliamentary con-
rson then in possession. Per* Sugden, L. C., in *The
:iety* v. *Richards,* 4 Ir. Eq. Rep. 177, 197; 1 Dru. &
nnor & Lawson, 84, 85, *S. C.;* and *per* Parke, B.,

C

in *Doe* d. *Jukes* v. *Sumner*, 14 M. & W. 39, 42. But this seems to be incorrect. Sect. 34 merely *extinguishes* the right and title of the person who has permitted the limited time to elapse, and of those claiming through or under him; *Jones* v. *Jones*, 16 M. & W. 699; 4 Dowl. & L. 494; but it does not *transfer* such right or title to the person who happens then to be in possession, nor to any other person. *Doe* d. *Carter* v. *Barnard*, 13 Q. B. 945, 952.

If the person whose right and title is extinguished by the statute were the only person then having any right or title to the land, besides the tenant in actual possession, such tenant will in effect acquire the fee simple. 2 Smith, L. C. 416. The maxim being—*Possessio contra omnes valet præter eum cui jus sit possessionis.* Lofft. maxims, No. 265. But if such tenant then occupied as tenant to any third person, such third person will be deemed to have been in possession. *Possessio terminum tenentis, possessio reversionarii est habenda.* Lofft. maxims, No. 588; *Bushby* v. *Dixon*, 3 B. & C. 307, Littledale, J. Upon the expiration or determination of such tenancy, the reversioner may enter or eject the tenant, who will not be permitted to dispute his landlord's title. *Post*, Chap. XXI., "Title by Estoppel."

It may sometimes happen, that the party whose right and title is extinguished by the statute had only a particular estate; and that, although he, and all persons claiming through or under him, may be barred, yet remaindermen or reversioners may not be barred. *Vide* sects. 5, 14, 35; *Doe* d. *Baverstock* v. *Rolfe*, 8 A. & E. 650; 3 N. & P. 648. But, generally speaking, when a tenant in tail is barred, his issue in tail, and all subsequent remaindermen and reversioners, are barred also. *Ante*, 22.

Receipt of Rent.]—Sect. 35 enacts, "that the receipt of the rent payable by any tenant from year to year, or other lessee, shall, as against such lessee, or any person claiming under him (but subject to the lease), be deemed to be the receipt of the profits of the land for the purposes of this act."

Where a cottager occupied a piece of land inclosed from the waste on the side of a turnpike road for more than thirty years, without paying any rent, and at the end of that time paid six pence on four several occasions to the owner of the adjoining land: held (before the passing of this act), that this was conclusive evidence of a permissive occupation only, so as to entitle the owner to maintain ejectment. *Doe* d. *Jackson* v. *Wilkinson*, 5 D. & R. 273.

The performance, within twenty years, of services for which a distress might have been made is equivalent to the payment of rent, and bars the statute. *Doe* d. *Edney* v. *Benham and Billett*, 7 Q. B. 976. But keeping a grindstone on the premises for the convenience of the parish is not sufficient. *Doe* d. *Robinson* v. *Hinde*, 2 Moo. & Rob. 441.

Proof in ejectment, that the claimant or his agent received rent from the persons from time to time in actual occupation, is admissible against the defendant, although he does not claim under such previous occupiers. *Doe* d. *Earl of Litchfield* v. *Stacey*, 6 C. & P. 139, Tindal, C. J.; and see *Daintry* v. *Brocklehurst*, 3 Exch. 207, 210; *Doe* d. *Stansbury* v. *Arkwright*, 5 C. & P. 575, 578.

The acts and admissions of occupiers during their occupation, such as payment of rent, &c., are, even after their occupation has ceased,

ae parties under whom such occupier came into pos-
Iantin v. *Austin,* 9 Bing. 41.

˙ rent may be proved by the *oral admission* of the
i, which will be admissible against him or his under-
d. *Earl Spencer* v. *Beckett,* 4 Q. B. 601. Such
as a proof of a fact, and not as an acknowledgment
meaning of section 14. *S. C.*

:d *Actions abolished.*]—Sect. 36 abolishes all real
a, and plaints of the like nature, after the 31st De-
cept writs of right of dower, writs of dower *unde*
ats for freebench or dower, *quare impedit,* and

real actions to be brought before 1st June, 1835,
of ejectment was barred on 31st December, 1834.
the rights of persons entitled to real actions only
835. *Cannon, dem.* v. *Rimington, ten.,* 12 C. B.,
Gilbert v. *Ross,* 7 M. & W. 102; 2 Sugd. V. & P.
writ of right sued out after the time allowed by the
y. *Davies* v. *Lowndes,* 6 M. & G. 529; 8 Scott,
wl. & L. 272.

Discontinuance and Warranty.]—Sect. 39 enacts,
at cast, discontinuance or warranty, which may
le after the said 31st day of December, 1833, shall
˙ight of entry or action for the recovery of land."
extends the remedy by ejectment to many cases in
to the previous law, the remedy by entry or eject-
and the party was driven to a real action. Shelf.
227 (4th ed.); Roscoe on Real Actions, 81; 2 Chit.
).

:gacies—Time of Limitation fixed, Twenty Years.]
ı section does not apply to actions of ejectment,
as and suits for the recovery of money secured by
herwise. *Per* Littledale, J., in *Doe* d. *Jones* v.
E. 296. For the cases upon this section, see Shelf.
. 228—253 (4th ed.); *Adams* v. *Barry,* 2 Coll.

:er—Time of Limitation fixed, Six Years.]—Sect.
loes not apply to actions of ejectment.

or Interest—Time of Limitation fixed, Six Years.]
"that after the 31st day of December, 1833, no
of interest in respect of any sum of money charged
at of any land or rent, or in respect of any legacy,
ı respect of such arrears of rent or interest, shall be
distress, action or suit, but within six years next
pectively shall have become due, or next after an
ıf the same in writing shall have been given to the
:reto or his agent, signed by the person by whom
.ble or his agent : provided, nevertheless, that where
:ee or other incumbrancer shall have been in pos-

session of any land, or in the receipt of the profits thereof, within one year next before an action or suit shall be brought by any person entitled to a subsequent mortgage or other incumbrance on the same land, the person entitled to such subsequent mortgage or incumbrance may recover in such action or suit the arrears of interest which shall have become due during the whole time that such prior mortgagee or incumbrancer was in such possession or receipt as aforesaid, although such time may have exceeded the said term of six years."

This section does not apply to actions of ejectment. It is materially affected, but not entirely repealed, as to arrears of rent, &c., by the 3 & 4 Will. 4, c. 42, s. 3, which enacts, " that all actions of debt for rent upon an indenture of demise, all actions of covenant or debt upon any bond or other specialty, shall be commenced and sued *within twenty years* after the cause of such actions or suits, but not after." The 3 & 4 Will. 4, c. 27, s. 42, takes away from an incumbrancer upon land, in all cases, the right of recovery *as against the land* more than six years' arrears of rent or interest; and the statute 3 & 4 Will. 4, c. 42, s. 3, merely restores the *personal remedy against the debtor on the covenant.* *Hunter* v. *Nockold,* 1 Mac. & Gord. 640; 1 Hall & Tw. 644; 19 L. J., N. S., Chanc., 177; *Humfrey* v. *Gery,* 7 C. B. 567.

Covenant for rent arrear may be brought within twenty years, and is not limited to six years. *Paget* v. *Foley,* 2 Bing. N. C. 679; 3 Scott, 135; and see *Du Vigier* v. *Lee,* 2 Hare, 326; *Dearman* v. *Wyche,* 9 Sim. 570. So debt upon a covenant contained in an indenture granting an annuity or rent-charge to issue out of land, may be brought within twenty years, and more than six years' arrears may be recovered. *Strachan* v. *Thomas,* 12 A. & E. 536; 4 P. & D. 229. The second and third sections do not apply to rent reserved on a demise (which is a mere incident to the reversion), but to rents wherein a distinct estate may be had, independently of any title to the land out of which the rent issues; *Grant* v. *Ellis,* 9 M. & W. 113, cited 5 Exch. 179; *e. g.,* an ancient quit-rent; *Owen* v. *De Beavoir,* 16 M. & W. 547; *S. C.* (in error), 5 Exch. 166; a fee farm rent reserved in letters patent. *Humfrey* v. *Gery,* 7 C. B. 567. Not more than six years' arrears of such a rent can be recovered by distress, action or suit. *S. C.*

It is to be observed that this section has no proviso in favour of persons under disabilities. *Per cur.* in *De Beavoir* v. *Owen* (in error), 5 Exch. 182.

CHAPTER III.

NOTICE TO QUIT.

Nature of.]—A notice to quit is a certain reasonable notice required by law, or by custom, or by special agreement, to enable either the landlord or tenant, or the assignees or representatives of either of them, *without the consent of the other*, to determine a tenancy from year to year, or from two years to two years, or for other like indefinite period. Without such notice, or an actual or implied surrender (which involves mutual consent), a tenancy of the above nature would never determine, but the term would continue in the tenant and his assigns or representatives; *Mackay* v. *Mackrell*, 4 Doug. 213; *Doe* d. *Shore* v. *Porter*, 3 T. R. 13; *Rex* v. *Inhabitants of Stone*, 6 T. R. 295, 298; *Doe* d. *Read* v. *Ridout*, 5 Taunt. 519; *Doe* d. *Hull* v. *Wood*, 14 M. & W. 682; Ad. Eject. 87; and would be prolonged from year to year as part of the original term or tenancy; 3 Prest. Conv. 76, 77; *Legg* v. *Strudwick*, 2 Salk. 413; *Birch* v. *Wright*, 1 T. R. 390, Buller, J.; 3 Man. & Gr. 510, n.; *Oxley* v. *James*, 13 M. & W. 209; and the

m would continue in the landlord and his assigns
Maddon d. *Baker* v. *White*, 2 T. R. 159, until ex-
Statute of Limitations, 3 & 4 Will. 4, c. 27. *Doe* d.
r, 17 Q. B. 589.
ermine a tenancy from year to year by a notice to
t *incident* to such tenancy. Ad. Eject. 73. Any
. such notice being given by one party or by the
: to the nature of the tenancy, and therefore void,
ge. *Doe* d. *Warner* v. *Browne*, 8 East, 165. The
rally be determined by a half-year's notice, expiring
first or any subsequent year of the term. *Doe* d.
e, 7 Q. B. 957; *Doe* d. *Plumer* v. *Mainby*, 10 Q.
parties may expressly stipulate for a longer or shorter
n that usually required by law; *Doe* d. *Pitcher* v.
. 555; 2 Camp. 78, *S. C.*; *Doe* d. *Green* v. *Baker*,
ve d. *Robinson* v. *Dobell*, 1 Q. B. 806; 1 Gale &
. notice expiring at some other period of the tenancy
' the first or some other year; *ex. gr.* at the end of
p v. *Derrett*, 3 Camp. 510; *Rex* v. *The Inhabitants*
:, 7 B. & C. 551; 1 Man. & Ry. 426; *Collett* v.
. 785; *Bird* v. *Defonville*, 2 Car. & K. 415, 418;
ilar quarter; *Doe* d. *Rigge* v. *Bell*, 5 T. R. 471; 2
or at any time of the year, upon the expiration of a
previous notice. *Doe* d. *Green* v. *Baker*, 8 Taunt.
: v. *Grafton*, 18 Q. B. 496; 21 Law J., N. S., Q. B.

But as the power of determining the tenancy at any
is generally attended with inconvenience to one or
language conferring such power must be clear and
re on a letting from year to year " to quit at a
such notice must expire *at the end* of the first or
f the tenancy, and not at any other part of the year.
Donovan, 1 Taunt. 555; 2 Camp. 78, *S. C.*; *Brown*
D. & R. 603; and see *Doe* d. *Robinson* v. *Dobell*,
ale & Dav. 218; *Doe* d. *Chadborn* v. *Green*, 9 A.
: D. 454. Where the tenant is " *always* to be sub-
ree months' notice" he will be deemed a quarterly
otice to quit must expire with some quarter, and not
of the year. *Kemp* v. *Derrett*, 3 Camp. 510. Where
t so much a quarter (not saying for what period),
a quarterly tenancy, and not a yearly tenancy at a
rterly. *Wilkinson* v. *Hall*, 3 Bing. N. C. 508; 4
re premises are let not for any definite period, but
ive up possession at any time on one month's notice,
nancy from month to month. *Doe* d. *Lansdell* v.
589. Where premises are let for an indefinite period,
ayable weekly, with power to determine the tenancy
notice from any quarter day, that creates a yearly
The Inhabitants of Herstmonceaux, 7 B. & C. 551;
3. The parties to a demise may expressly stipulate
rent the tenant may quit *without any notice*. *Bethell*
an. & Gr. 119; 3 Scott, N. R. 568.
was held that the usual half-year's notice to quit
d with by parol, and that a less notice given by the
ted to by the landlord or his agent, was sufficient.

Shirley v. *Newman*, 1 Esp. 266, Lord Kenyon, C. J.; and see *Redpath* v. *Roberts*, 3 Esp. 225; *Aldenburg* v. *Peaple*, 6 C. & P. 212, Parke, J. It has since been decided that an insufficient notice to quit given by the tenant, and assented to by the landlord, will not determine the tenancy,· nor operate as a surrender, on the expiration of such notice. *Doe* d. *Huddlestone* v. *Johnstone*, 1 M'Clel. & You. 141; *Johnstone* v. *Huddlestone*, 4 B. & C. 922; *Doe* d. *Murrell* v. *Milward*, 3 M. & W. 328; *Bessell* v. *Landsberg*, 7 Q. B. 638. "The cases in *Espinasse* are consistent with the supposition of an original agreement to determine at less than six months' notice." *Id.* 640, Lord Denman, C. J. An agreement for a new lease upon different terms (not amounting to an actual demise) will not be sufficient, without a notice to quit, to determine a previous yearly tenancy. *John* v. *Jenkins*, 1 Cr. & Mee. 227; 3 Tyr. 170; and see *Jones* v. *Reynolds*, 1 Q. B. 506. A tenancy from year to year, created by parol, is not determined by a parol licence from the landlord to the tenant to quit in the middle of a quarter, and the tenant quitting the premises accordingly. *Mollet* v. *Brayne*, 2 Camp. 103.

Upon the expiration of a notice to quit duly given by either party *the tenancy ceases*, and, unless a fresh tenancy be afterwards created, the landlord cannot distrain for subsequent rent, notwithstanding the tenant continues in possession for a year after the expiration of the notice. *Alford* v. *Vickery*, Car. & Mar. 280, Coleridge, J. The remedy in such case is by action for use and occupation (*S. C.*), or for double rent, or double value. *Post*, Chap. LXIX.

In what Cases necessary — 1. *By Special Agreement.*]—Where there is any express stipulation as to the notice to be given by either party to determine the tenancy, such notice, whether more or less than that usually required by law, must be given, and will be sufficient. *Doe* d. *Green* v. *Baker*, 8 Taunt. 241; *Doe* d. *Robinson* v. *Dobell*, 1 Q. B. 806; 1 Gale & D. 218; *ante*, 31.

In such cases the usual notice required by law, or by local custom, if less than that expressly stipulated for, will not be sufficient. Thus, where an implied tenancy from week to week is created by the payment of rent weekly, pursuant to the terms of an agreement for a demise for a year (never executed), under which the defendant entered, and which stipulated for *four week's notice* : held, that an ejectment brought after a week's notice to quit could not be maintained. *Doe* d. *Peacock* v. *Raffan*, 6 Esp. 4, Lord Ellenborough, C. J.; and see *Richardson* v. *Giffard*, 1 A. & E. 52; *Doe* d. *Davenish* v. *Moffatt*, 15 Q. B. 257.

Where a three months' notice is stipulated for, such notice must expire at the end of some current year of the tenancy, unless the contrary be specially provided. *Brown* v. *Burtinshaw*, 7 D. & R. 603; *Doe* d. *Pitcher* v. *Donovan*, 2 Camp. 78; 1 Taunt. 555; *ante*, 31.

2. *By Local Custom.*]—Where the lease or agreement creating a tenancy from year to year, or from quarter to quarter, or from month to month, or from week to week, or for any other indefinite period, is silent as to any notice to quit, and there is a special local custom regulating the notice to be given under such circumstances, such custom will be deemed to be part of the contract, as an *implied* term or condition thereof. Arch. L. & T. 86; Ad. Eject. 103; *Tyley* v. *Seed*,

Henderson v. *Charnock*, Peake, N. P. C. 6. But
such custom lies on the party asserting its existence;
Vilkinson, Co. Lit. 270 b (note 228); *Caldecott* v.
. 808; and the witnesses must speak, not to opinion,
Henderson v. *Charnock*, Peake, N. P. C. 4. A
ot extend to another place some miles distant, unless
: to extend to that place also. *Roe* d. *Brown* v.
270 b (note 228).

n ordinary weekly tenancy a week's notice to quit
art of the contract, unless there be a usage to that
ampbell, 3 C. B. 921; *post*, 37; but in the absence
:ekly tenant who enters on a fresh week may be
intil the expiration of that week, or pay the week's
Armitstead, 7 C. & P. 56. But a weekly tenant,
menced on a Saturday, may quit on a Saturday,
e to another week's rent: " I cannot say a week
ıy holding for six days and two fractions of a day."

" I am not aware that it has ever been decided
an ordinary monthly or weekly tenancy a month's
to quit must be given." *Id.* 58, Parke, B. If
required by law, the consequence would be that in
ıcy would almost unavoidably continue for a double
e very inconvenient to one, if not both of the parties.
taken by the month, and a month's notice is given,
ficient, in the absence of a special stipulation to the
arry v. *Hazell*, 1 Esp. 94. Where a week's notice
ıt expire on the proper day, *i. e.* at the end of some
y. *Doe* d. *Finlayson* v. *Bayley*, 5 C. & P. 67.

ıon Law.]—Where a tenancy from year to year
ss agreement, and there is no special stipulation
ıviding for the determination of the tenancy, the
required by law, *i. e.*, half a year's notice to quit
ıt or some other year of the tenancy, must be given.
v. *Constable*, 3 Wils. 25; *Right* d. *Flower* v.
; *Doe* d. *Pitcher* v. *Donovan*, 1 Taunt. 555; *Roe*
son, Co. Lit. 270 b, note (1); 2 Arch. N. P. 394;
M. & W. 198. So where a tenancy from year to
aw, from the payment and acceptance of rent, or
tances. 2 Arch. N. P. 394; *Doe* d. *Wawn* v.
833; *Doe* d. *Cater* v. *Somerville*, 6 B. & C. 126,
).·

question whether such a tenancy is to be implied,
ıat period. If a remainderman accept money, or
·ved as rent in a lease granted by the previous
h became void on the death of such tenant for life,
ı new tenancy from year to year as between him
he old terms, and the tenant is entitled to the usual
e d. *Martin* v. *Watts*, 2 Esp. 501; 7 T. R. 83,
ıer v. *Morse*, 1 B. & Adol. 365; *Doe* d. *Potter* v.
'. 531; *Bell* v. *Nangle*, 2 Jebb & Symes (Irish)
v. *Sherwood*, Alcock & Napier (Irish) R. 217:
:ent received be so grossly inadequate, with refer-
·alue of the property, that the jury ought to pre-

sume and find that no such new tenancy was intended to be created. *Doe* d. *Brune* v. *Prideaux*, 10 East, 158; *Denne* d. *Brune* v. *Rawlins*, 10 East, 261; and see *Doe* d. *Lord* v. *Crago*, 6 C. B. 90; *Right* d. *Dean and Chapter of Wells* v. *Bawden*, 3 East, 260, 275. Any such new tenancy will be deemed to have commenced from the same day of the year as the original term, and the notice to quit should be given accordingly. *Roe* d. *Jordan* v. *Ward*, 1 H. Blac. 96; *Doe* d. *Collins* v. *Weller*, 7 T. R. 478.

So where a tenant for a term of years holds over after the expiration of his lease, and continues to pay rent as before, which the landlord accepts, a new tenancy from year to year is thereby created upon the same terms and conditions as those contained in the original lease, so far as the same are applicable to a yearly tenancy. *Doe* d. *Hollingworth* v. *Stennett*, 2 Esp. 717, Lord Kenyon, C. J.; *Bishop* v. *Howard*, 2 B. & C. 100; *Doe* d. *Thompson* v. *Amey*, 12 A. & E. 476; 4 P. & D. 177; *Hyatt* v. *Griffiths*, 17 Q. B. 505. Such new tenancy will be deemed to have commenced at the same time of the year as the original term, and notice to quit should be given accordingly. *Doe* d. *Castleton* v. *Samuel*, 5 Esp. 173, Lord Ellenborough, C. J.; *Doe* d. *Spicer* v. *Lea*, 11 East, 312.

Where a person is let into possession under an agreement for a future lease, *and pays rent*, he thereby becomes tenant from year to year upon the terms of such intended lease, so far as they are applicable to a yearly tenancy; *Doe* d. *Thompson* v. *Amey*, 12 A. & E. 476; 4 P. & D. 177; and he is entitled to the usual notice to quit. But, at the expiration of the term mentioned in such agreement, the implied tenancy from year to year will cease without any notice to quit. *Post*, 36.

So where a person is let into possession under a lease for more than three years, not made by deed, and pays part of the rent therein expressed to be reserved, he becomes tenant from year to year upon the terms mentioned in such void lease, so far as the same may be applicable to a yearly tenancy, and a notice to quit must expire at that period of the year at which the tenant is to quit, according to the terms of the lease. *Doe* d. *Rigge* v. *Bell*, 5 T. R. 471; 2 Smith, L. C. 72; *Richardson* v. *Gifford*, 1 A. & E. 52; *Beale* v. *Saunders*, 3 Bing. N. C. 850.

Where a tenancy is created for "one year certain, and so on from year to year," it enures as a tenancy for two years at the least, and cannot be determined by notice to quit at the end of the first year; *Doe* d. *Chadborn* v. *Green*, 9 A. & E. 658; 1 P. & D. 454; *Birch* v. *Wright*, 1 T. R. 380; *White* v. *Darley*, 1 T. R. 159; *Bellasis* v. *Burbrick*, 1 Salk. 413; *Legg* v. *Strudwick*, 2 Salk. 414; but it may be determined by due notice to quit at the end of the second or any subsequent year of the tenancy. *S. C.*

A tenancy "from year to year, so long as both parties please," is determinable at the end of the first as well as of any subsequent year, unless, in creating such tenancy, the parties use words showing that they contemplate a tenancy for two years at least. *Doe* d. *Clark* v. *Smaridge*, 7 Q. B. 957; *Doe* d. *Plumer* v. *Nainby*, 10 Q. B. 473.

A tenancy "for twelve months certain, and six months' notice afterwards," may be determined by notice to quit at the end of the first year; *Thompson* v. *Maberley*, 2 Camp. 573; but a demise "not for one year only, but from year to year," constitutes a demise for two

. cannot be determined by a notice to quit at the end
Dean d. *Jacklin* v. *Cartwright*, 4 East, 31.
ix months, and so on from six months to six months
by either party, is a tenancy for one year at least.
ts of Chawton, 1 Q. B. 247; 4 P. & D. 525.
 years, and so on from three years to three years,
for six years. *Per* Bridgman, C. J., in *Henning* v.
. 45. Such tenancy may be determined by a half
uit, expiring at the end of the first six years, or of
riod of three years, but not at any other time. It is
nancy for one year, and so on from year to year.
. Conv. 76.
two years to two years, or from three years to three
 may be determined by half a year's notice to quit,
d of any period of two or three years (as the case
at the end of any intervening year, nor at any other
ee v. *Lees*, 2 W. Blac. 1171; *Henning* v. *Brabason*,
an, C. J.; Ad. Eject. 99. Leases from three years
analogous to leases for year to year, the only differ-
the one case three years, and in the other case one
of computation. 3 Prest. Conv. 76. In one case a
o hold " from seven years to seven years for and
 forty-nine years." *Richards* v. *Sely*, 2 Mod. 80.
it is not rendered unnecessary by the death of the
eing a tenant for his own life only); *Maddon* d.
2 T. R. 159; or of the tenant; *Doe* d. *Shore* v.
; *Doe* d. *Hull* v. *Wood*, 14 M. & W. 682; *Mackey*
oug. 213; *Gulliver* d. *Tasker* v. *Burr*, 1 W. Blac.
signment of the term; *Doe* d. *Castleton* v. *Samuel*,
the reversion. *Birch* v. *Wright*, 1 T. R. 378; *Bur-*
1 Dowl. & L. 213; *Id.* 218, Wightman, J. But in
e to quit should be given by or to the person or per-
eing legally entitled to the term or to the reversion,
. Ad. Eject. 87.
not maintain ejectment for his wife's lands, let from
 his express or implied assent, without first giving
Doe d. *Leicester* v. *Biggs*, 1 Taunt. 367.
t becomes entitled to the reversion of an estate leased
 he cannot eject the tenant without giving the same
or must have given. *Maddon* d. *Baker* v. *White*,
when an infant becomes of age, he cannot, without
 quit, eject a tenant who has attorned to him during
 previous ejectment in his name. *Doe* d. *Miller* v.
), Lord Kenyon, C. J. Generally speaking, a lease
 an infant is presumed to be for his benefit (in the
o the contrary), and shall bind him when of age.
5 Bro. P. C. 570.
quit is duly given by the landlord, or other person
ntitled to the reversion, and he afterwards assigns his
nee may avail himself of the notice. *Doe* d. *Earl*
rwood, 3 Q. B. 627.
ardens and overseers of a parish may avail them-
 to quit duly given by their predecessors. *Doe* d.
 A. & E. 274; *Doe* d. *Hobbs* v. *Cockell*, *Id.* 478.

A proper notice to quit given to the tenant or his assignee will operate against any subsequent assignee. *Doe* d. *Castleton* v. *Samuel,* 5 Esp. 173.

A tenant of apartments is not justified in quitting without notice, merely from a fear, however reasonable, that his goods may be seized for his landlord's rent. *Rickett* v. *Tullick,* 6 C. & P. 66. But there may be an express stipulation, reserving to him leave to quit at any time without notice, "if he finds any thing that may at all lead him to suspect that there is any embarrassment in his landlord." *Bethell* v. *Blencowe,* 3 Man. & Gr. 119; 3 Scott, N. R. 568.

In what Cases unnecessary.]—Where the demise or agreement specifies the term or event upon which the tenancy is to determine, no notice to quit is necessary, because both parties are equally apprised of the determination of the term. *Per* Lord Mansfield, C. J., in *Right* d. *Flower* v. *Darby,* 1 T. R. 162; *Id.* 54; *Doe* d. *Leeson* v. *Sayer,* 3 Camp. 8; 2 Arch. N. P. 395. Thus where the demise is for one year. *Cobb* v. *Stokes,* 8 East, 358, 361; *Johnstone* v. *Huddlestone,* 4 B. & C. 937, Bayley, J.; *Wilson* v. *Abbott,* 9 B. & C. 88; *Strickland* v. *Maxwell,* 2 Cr. & Mee. 539; 4 Tyr. 346. Or for any certain number of years. *Messenger* v. *Armstrong,* 1 T. R. 54, Lord Mansfield, C. J.; *Doe* d. *Godsell* v. *Inglis,* 3 Taunt. 54; *Roberts* v. *Hayward,* 3 C. & P. 432. Or till a particular day. *Doe* d. *Leeson* v. *Sayer,* 3 Camp. 8.

Where a tenant entered under an agreement for a lease for seven years, which lease was never executed: held, that at the end of the seven years his tenancy from year to year, created by the payment and acceptance of rent during that period, determined without any notice to quit. *Doe* d. *Tilt* v. *Stratton,* 3 C. & P. 164; 4 Bing. 446; 1 Moo. & Pay, 153, *S. C.*; *Berrey* v. *Lindley,* 3 Man. & Gr. 498; *Id.* 514, Maule, J.; *Doe* d. *Davenish* v. *Moffatt,* 15 Q. B. 257, 265; *Tress* v. *Savage,* 4 E. & B. 36.

Where there is a lease, or an agreement for a lease, "during the joint lives of A. and B.," upon the death of either of them the term determines, without any notice to quit. *Doe* d. *Bromfield* v. *Smith,* 6 East, 530. So where a house, or part of a house, is occupied by one of several partners "during the continuance of the partnership," upon a dissolution thereof, he may be ejected without any notice to quit. *Doe* d. *Waithman* v. *Miles,* 1 Stark. R. 181, Lord Ellenborough, C. J.; *Doe* d. *Colnaghi* v. *Bluck,* 8 C. & P. 464, Tindal, C. J. So where premises are occupied by a servant and his family, as part of the remuneration for his services, whenever such service is determined an ejectment may be maintained against the servant, without any notice to quit. *Doe* d. *Hughes* v. *Corbett and Derry,* 9 C. & P. 494, Parke, B. The vendor of a term, before the whole of the purchase money is paid, agrees with the purchaser that the latter shall have possession of the premises till a given day, paying the reserved rent in the meantime, and that if he does not pay the residue of the purchase money on that day he shall forfeit the instalments already paid, and shall not be entitled to an assignment of the lease. The purchaser being thus put into possession, if the residue of the purchase money is not paid at the day appointed, the vendor may maintain an ejectment, without any notice to quit or demand of possession. *Doe* d. *Leeson* v. *Sayer,* 3 Camp. 8; and see *Doe* d. *Parker* v. *Boulton,* 6 M. & S. 148.

ssly stipulated that the tenant may quit *without*
upon the happening or discovery of a particular
hell v. *Blencowe*, 3 Man. & Gr. 119; 3 Scott, N. R.

lly or other tenancy of lodgings or apartments will
the term, without any notice to quit, unless there
m or special stipulation to the contrary. *Ante*, 33.
ead, 7 C. & P. 56, Parke, B.; *Towne* v. *Camp-*
Wilson v. *Abbott*, 9 B. & C. 88. They form an ex-
leral rule, and the necessity for notice (if any)
express or implied contract between the parties.
. *Darby*, 1 T. R. 162, Lord Mansfield, C. J. The
ly local custom lies on the party asserting its exist-
on v. *Wilkinson*, Co. Lit. 270 b, note (1); *Calde-*
C. & P. 808. If there be any such local custom or
notice to quit must be given accordingly. *Doe* d.
, 6 Esp. 4; *ante*, 32; *Doe* d. *Finlayson* v. *Bayley*,
d such notice will of course be sufficient. *Doe* d.
l Esp. 94; *Doe* d. *Campbell* v. *Scott*, 6 Bing. 362;

is unnecessary to determine a tenancy *at will*. *Doe*
erlaine, 5 M. & W. 14; *Doe* d. *Milburn* v. *Edgar*,
; *Doe* d. *Jones* v. *Jones*, 10 B & C. 718; *Doe* d.
M. & W. 682 (2nd point); *Doe* d. *Hollingsworth*
717. But such tenancy must be duly determined
possession," or by entry, or by something equiva-
he date of the plaintiff's alleged title in an eject-
l. *Galloway* v. *Herbert*, 4 T. R. 680; *Denn* d.
10 East, 261; *Doe* d. *Jacobs* v. *Phillips*, 10 Q. B.
oll v. *M'Kaeg*, 10 B. & C. 721; 5 M. & R. 620.
remembered that in many instances estates, which
ied to be estates at will only, are now construed to
year to year. Ad. Ejec. 75; *Clayton* v. *Blakey*, 8
imple permission to occupy, or a mere general let-
. tenancy at will, unless there are circumstances to
to create a tenancy from year to year; as for in-
it to pay rent by the quarter, or some other aliquot
ichardson v. *Langridge*, 4 Taunt. 128, Chambre, J.;
od, 14 M. & W. 687, Parke, B.

possession as an intended purchaser, who has never
a mere tenant at will, and may be ejected. after a
on, without any notice to quit. *Right* d. *Lewis* v.
11; *Doe* d. *Rogers* v. *Pullen*, 2 Bing. N. C. 749.
n the land for the purpose of resuming possession
ithout any notice to quit. *Doe* d. *Moore* v. *Lawder*,
Lord Ellenborough, C. J. Even a threat of legal
ver possession if certain monies claimed be not paid
so paid), is sufficient to determine a tenancy at will.
ice, 9 Bing. 356. But there must be a demand of
thing equivalent to such demand, before an eject-
ained. *Doe* d. *Newby* v. *Jackson*, 1 B. & C. 448;

agreement for sale from A. to B., to be completed
B. agreed with C. to let the premises to him, to

commence from that day, and C. was let into possession before that day by the permission of A.; but B. failed to complete the purchase on the appointed day: held, that C. merely represented B., and occupied as his tenant, and therefore was not entitled to any notice to quit, or even to a demand of possession before ejectment by A. *Doe d. Parker* v. *Boulton*, 6 M. & S. 148.

If a man get into possession of a house to be let, without the privity of the landlord, and they afterwards enter into negociations for a lease, but differ upon the terms, the landlord may maintain ejectment to recover possession of the premises, without giving any notice to quit. *Doe* d. *Knight* v. *Quigley*, 2 Camp. 505.

A tenant *at sufferance* is not entitled to any notice to quit, nor even to a demand of possession, before an ejectment can be maintained against him. *Doe* d. *Moore* v. *Lawder*, 1 Stark. R. 308; *Doe* d. *Leeson* v. *Sayer*, 3 Camp. 8; *Doe* d. *Roby* v. *Maisey*, 8 B. & C. 767. Thus where a tenant for years, without the consent of his landlord, holds over after the expiration of the term: but if he hold over *with the consent* of his landlord, during a negociation for a further lease, he thereby becomes tenant at will; and although not entitled to any notice to quit, yet he cannot be ejected without a previous demand of possession, or something equivalent to such demand, as an entry for the purpose of resuming possession. *Doe* d. *Hollingsworth* v. *Stennett*, 2 Esp. 717; *Doe* d. *Moore* v. *Lawder*, 1 Stark. R. 308.

If any rent has been paid and accepted in respect of the possession subsequent to the expiration of the lease, a new tenancy from year to year will be implied, and the usual notice must be given to determine such new tenancy. *Doe* d. *Hollingsworth* v. *Stennett*, 2 Esp. 717, Lord Kenyon, C. J.; *Bishop* v. *Howard*, 2 B. & C. 100; *Doe* d. *Thompson* v. *Amey*, 12 A. & E. 476; 4 P. & D. 177. Such notice must expire at the same time of the year as the original tenancy commenced. *Doe* d. *Castleton* v. *Samuel*, 5 Esp. 173, Lord Ellenborough, C. J.; *Doe* d. *Spicer* v. *Lea*, 11 East, 312.

If a man get into possession of a house to be let, without the privity of the landlord, and they afterwards enter into negociations for a lease, but differ upon the terms, the landlord may maintain ejectment to recover possession of the premises without giving any notice to quit. *Doe* d. *Knight* v. *Quigley*, 2 Camp. 505.

Generally speaking a mortgagor who is suffered to remain in possession, or in receipt of the rents and profits of the property mortgaged, is *not a tenant* thereof to the mortgagee, but in the nature of a bailiff to receive the rents, and thereout to pay the interest, and to keep the surplus for his own use, without any liability to account for the same at law or in equity; *Ex parte Wilson*, 2 Ves. & Bea. 252; and with an authority *implied by law* to distrain for the rents, when in arrear, as bailiff of the mortgagee. *Trent* v. *Hunt*, 9 Exch. 14. A mortgagor is not even a tenant at will, but at most a tenant at sufferance, and may be treated as such, or as a trespasser, at the election of the mortgagee. *Moss* v. *Gallimore*, 1 Doug. 279; 1 Smith, L. C. 310, 314, *per* Lord Mansfield, C. J. Consequently he is not entitled to any notice to quit, nor even to a demand of possession before ejectment. *Doe* d. *Roby* v. *Maisey*, 8 B. & C. 767; *Doe* d. *Fisher* v. *Giles*, 5 Bing. 421; 2 M. & P. 749.

Where T. mortgaged land to B., and by the mortgage deed attorned to B. as tenant at a quarterly rent, which was stated to be done

securing the principal and interest, and in contem-
ischarge thereof: the mortgage deed also gave B.
n default of payment: held, that B. or his assignee
lefault bring ejectment against T., without giving
juit. *Doe* d. *Snell and Short* v. *Tom*, 4 Q. B. 615;
rrod v. *Olley*, 12 A. & E. 481; 4 P. & D. 275.
for arrears of interest, " as for rent," made in pur-
ral power in that behalf contained in the mortgage
unt to a recognition of the mortgagor as tenant so
mortgagee from bringing ejectment without any
ое d. *Wilkinson* v. *Goodier*, 10 Q. B. 957; but see
Exch. 216.
ar to year, who were let into possession *before* the
vere mortgaged by their landlord, are entitled to the
t, because the mortgagee is only an assignee of the
fuller, J., in *Birch* v. *Wright*, 1 T. R. 379—381;
n, 1 Dowl. & L. 213; *Id.* 218, Wightman, J.
а year to year of a mortgagor in possession, whose
ced *after* the execution of the mortgage, may be
rtgagee, or his assignee, without any notice to quit
ssion. *Keech* v. *Hall*, 1 Doug. 21; 1 Smith, L. C.
Weaver v. *Belcher*, 3 East, 450; *Doe* d. *Parker* v.
3. 148. Unless indeed something has been done by
· his assignee, and the tenant in possession, from
l imply the creation of a new tenancy from year to
иem. *Doe* d. *Hughes and Rising* v. *Bucknell*, 8 C.
where the mortgagee, or his assignee, has demanded
nt" from the tenant. *Doe* d. *Whittaker* v. *Hales*,

ce of the mortgagee, requiring the tenant to pay his
gee or his assignee, *not assented to by the tenant*, is
ause a new tenancy cannot be created without the
assent of both parties. *Evans* v. *Elliott*, 9 A. & E.
56; *Partington* v. *Woodcock*, 6 A. & E. 690; 5 N.
. *Higginbotham* v. *Barker*, 11 A. & E. 307; 3 P. &

y a mortgagee, the mere fact of his having received
rtgage down to a time later than the day on which
ed in the writ, does not amount to a recognition by
agor or his tenant was in lawful possession of the pre-
when such interest was paid, and consequently is no
tment. *Doe* d. *Rogers* v. *Cadwallader*, 2 B. & Adol.
tress for arrears of interest " as for rent" made in
wer in that behalf contained in the mortgage deed
Doe d. *Wilkinson* v. *Goodier*, 10 Q. B. 957; *Doe*
y, 12 A. & E. 481; 4 P. & D. 275.
tice to quit need not be given by or to a corporation
here has been no demise *under seal*, and that either
ine the tenancy at any time without notice. *Finlay*
l *Exeter Railway Company*, 7 Exch. 409; *The Go-*
any *of Copper Miners of England* v. *Fox*, 16 Q. B.
e d. *Pennington* v. *Tanıere*, 12 Q. B. 998. A lease
e granted by or to a corporation, so as to bind them,
r common seal; *Tredyman* v. *Wodry*, Cro. Jac. 110,

cited 7 Exch. 413, Parke, B.; but a tenancy from year to year may of course be created by deed. A corporation aggregate may sue or be sued for use and occupation without any contract under seal, because the consideration has been executed, and the compensation in respect thereof is given by the stat. 11 Geo. 2, c. 19, s. 14. *Dean and Chapter of Rochester* v. *Pierce*, 1 Camp. 466; *The Mayor and Burgesses of Stafford* v. *Till*, 4 Bing. 75; 12 Moore, 260; *The Mayor and Burgesses of Carmarthen* v. *Lewis*, 6 C. & P. 608; *The Mayor, &c. of Thetford* v. *Tyler*, 8 Q. B. 95; *The Drury Lane Theatre Company* v. *Chapman*, 1 Car. & Kir. 14. A notice to quit (when necessary) may be given by the steward of the corporation without his being authorized so to do under the common seal. *Roe d. Dean and Chapter of Rochester* v. *Pierce*, 2 Camp. 96; *Doe d. The Birmingham Canal Company* v. *Bold*, 11 Q. B. 127. If given to the corporation it must be directed to them, and not to their head officers. *Doe d. Earl of Carlisle* v. *Woodman*, 8 East, 228.

Where the plaintiff claims by a *title paramount* to the tenancy from year to year, notice to quit is unnecessary. Thus where a mortgagee claims under a mortgage executed *before* the creation of the tenancy from year to year by the mortgagor. *Ante*, 39. So where a tenant had come into possession of the premises in 1816, and the lessor of the plaintiff claimed under a writ of elegit and inquisition thereon issued in 1818, but founded on a judgment recovered prior to 1816: held, that no notice to quit was necessary. *Doe d. Putland* v. *Hilder*, 2 B. & A. 782. Had the tenancy commenced prior to the judgment, the tenant by elegit would have been only an assignee of the reversion, and might, without any attornment, have distrained for subsequent rent; *Lloyd* v. *Davies*, 2 Exch. 103; but he could not have maintained ejectment without first giving a proper notice to quit. *Doe d. Da Costa* v. *Wharton*, 8 T. R. 2.

The incumbent of a living may maintain ejectment for the glebe lands against tenants from year to year of the previous incumbent, without giving them any notice to quit; *Doe d. Kirby* v. *Carter*, Ry. & Moo. 237, Littledale, J.; but where a rector had suffered persons, who were in possession as tenants prior to his incumbency, to continue in quiet and undisturbed possession for eight months after his institution: held, that he must be presumed to have assented to the continuance of their tenancy (or, rather, to the creation of a new tenancy as between him and them) under the terms of their previous holding; and, therefore, that he could not eject them without the usual notice to quit. *Doe d. Cates* v. *Somerville*, 6 B. & C. 126. This is the only case in which a mere permission (or, rather, "sufferance") by the owner to occupy premises, without some positive act of acknowledgment, has been held sufficient to create a tenancy requiring a regular notice to quit. Ad. Eject. 82. But an inclosure made from the waste, and seen by the steward of the manor from time to time, without any objection being made, may, after twelve or fourteen years' possession, be presumed by a jury to have been made by licence of the lord; and ejectment cannot be brought against the tenant as a trespasser without previous notice to throw it up; *Doe d. Foley* v. *Wilson*, 11 East, 56; or something equivalent to such notice, as entering and breaking down the fences, &c. *Doe d. Beck* v. *Heakin*, 6 A. & E. 495 (3rd point).

A disclaimer by a tenant from year to year of the title of his landlord, or of the person for the time being entitled to the immediate

ee, heir, devisee, executor or administrator of the
te as a waiver by the tenant of the usual notice to
ffect, determine the tenancy at the election of the
rson so entitled. *Doe* d. *Bennett* v. *Long*, 9 C. & P.
bb v. *Grubb*, 10 B. & C. 816; *Doe* d. *Phillips* v.
88; *Doe* d. *Davies* v. *Evans*, 9 M. & W. 480; *Doe*
ver, 17 Q. B. 589 (1st point); 2 Arch. N. P. 395;
d.). " Because a notice to quit is only requisite
admitted on both sides, and if a defendant denies
an be no necessity to end that which he says has no
lest, C. J., in *Doe* d. *Calvert* v. *Frowd*, 4 Bing.
480; *Doe* d. *Phillips* v. *Rollings*, 4 C. B. 188, 200;
Whittich, Gow. 195, Holroyd, J. The law upon
be founded on the doctrine of estoppel, rather than
otice by consent. The tenant, by denying the
ancy as between him and the claimant, and thereby
ent necessary, is estopped from afterwards proving
ancy from year to year existing between them, and
ve been duly determined by notice to quit before
seems that there cannot be an effectual waiver of
even by mutual consent, unless possession of the
aken at the same time. *Ante*, 32. But there may
disclaimer: thus where the landlord distrains for
Doe d. *David* v. *Williams*, 7 C. & P. 322.

a nice question whether what has taken place does
to a disclaimer of the tenancy. It is difficult, if
econcile all the cases on this point. But the result
be, that if a tenant from year to year use any ex-
ng reasonably construed with reference to the cir-
which they were uttered or written, amount to a
nce of any tenancy as between him and the claim-
as amount to a disclaimer, and render a notice to
Doe d. *Calvert* v. *Frowd*, 4 Bing. 560; 1 Moo. &
rubb v. *Grubb*, 10 B. & C. 816; 8 M. & R. 666;
Long, 9 C. & P. 773; *Doe* d. *Hughes* v. *Bucknell*,
e d. *Whitehead* v. *Pittman*, 1 N. & M. 673; *Doe*
s, 9 M. & W. 48; *Doe* d. *Phillips* v. *Rollings*, 4
ee d. *Landsdell* v. *Gower*, 17 Q. B. 589 (1st point).
, if the expressions used cannot, under the cir-
onably construed to amount to such a denial, they
a disclaimer, nor render a notice to quit unneces-
s v. *Earl Cawdor*, 1 Cr. Mee. & Ros. 398; 4 Tyr.
ns v. *Cooper*, 1 Man. & Gr. 135; *Doe* d. *Williams*
, N. P. C. 259 (3rd ed.).

a verbal or written disclaimer sufficient, it must
epudiation of the relation of landlord and tenant;
a to hold possession of the estate upon a ground
with that relation, which by necessary implication
it. *Per cur.* in *Doe* d. *Gray* v. *Stanion*, 1 M. &
& Gr. 1066; *Doe* d. *Williams* v. *Cooper*, 1 Man.
rery slight matter, not really intended as a repudia-
be construed as a repudiation, in order to defeat an
nical nature. *Doe* d. *Davies* v. *Evans*, 9 M. &

Where a disclaimer is relied on, it must appear to have been made *before or on* the day mentioned in the writ of ejectment as the time when the claimant was entitled to possession. *Doe* d. *Lewis* v. *Earl Cawdor*, 1 Cr. Mee. & Ros. 389; 4 Tyr. 852; *Doe* d. *Bennett* v. *Long*, 9 C. & P. 773. But where the defendant, by his agent, on the 26th June, 1813, answered an application for rent by saying that "his connection as tenant with the late John Grubb, Esq. (through whom the plaintiff derived title), has *ceased for several years*, and that he now pays his rent to his brother:"—held, evidence of a disclaimer of title *before the 1st May*, 1813 (on which day the demise was laid in the ejectment), and rendered any notice to quit unnecessary. *Doe* d. *Grubb* v. *Grubb*, 10 B. & C. 816; 8 M. & R. 666.

A denial by parol of a landlord's title does not incur a forfeiture of a lease for a *term certain*, whether under seal or not. *Doe* d. *Graves* v. *Wells*, 10 A. & E. 427; 2 P. & D. 396; *Rees* d. *Powell* v. *King*, Forrest. R. 19. Nor will payment to a third person of the rent reserved by such lease. *Doe* d. *Dillon* v. *Parker, Knt.* Gow. 180, Richardson, J. But where a tenant for five years delivered up possession of the premises and of the lease, *in fraud* of his landlord, to a person claiming under a hostile title, with the intention of enabling him to set up such title, and not to hold under the lease: held, that the term was thereby forfeited. *Doe* d. *Ellerbrock* v. *Flynn*, 1 Cr. Mee. & Ros. 137; 4 Tyr. 619. But that case turned upon the fraud of the tenant, and can only be sustained on that ground. All the other cases in the books of forfeiture by disclaimer have been by matter of record. *Per* Lord Denman, C. J., in *Gregg* v. *Wells*, 2 P. & D. 402; *S. C.* 10 A. & E. 427.

An attornment by a tenant from year to year to a third person amounts to such a disclaimer of the landlord's title as will enable him to maintain ejectment without any notice to quit. *Throgmorton* v. *Whelpdale*, Bull. N. P. 96; Ad. Eject. 86. "I have no rent for you, because A. B. has ordered me to pay none." This is evidence of a disclaimer of the tenancy. *Doe* d. *Whitehead* v. *Pittman*, 1 N. & M. 673.

A tenant or his assignee, who brings ejectment against his landlord, and attempts to prove a freehold title, thereby disclaims to hold of the landlord, and is not entitled to any notice to quit. *Doe* d. *Jefferies* v. *Whittick*, Gow. 195, Holroyd, J.

A disclaimer may be waived by any act of the landlord acknowledging the party as his tenant at a later period, as by a distress for subsequent rent. *Doe* d. *David* v. *Williams*, 7 C. & P. 322.

By whom given.]—A notice to quit may be given either by the landlord or by the tenant, or by the authorized agent of either party. Any special stipulation that either of them shall not give such notice is repugnant to the nature of the tenancy, and therefore void, and mere surplusage. *Doe* d. *Warner* v. *Browne*, 8 East, 165. If the notice be duly given by the landlord, and the tenant does not quit pursuant to such notice, he will be liable to pay *double value* during the time he holds over. 4 Geo. 4, c. 28, s. 1; *post*, Chap. LXIX. s. 1. On the other hand, if the notice be duly given by the tenant, and he does not quit accordingly, he will be liable to pay *double rent* during the time he holds over. 11 Geo. 2, c. 19, s. 18; *post*, Chap. LXIX. s. 2. Any person for the time being *legally entitled to the immediate reversion* of and in the demised premises, *ex. gr.* as assignee, devisee, heir,

trator of the landlord, may give notice to quit.
subsequent owner deriving title through or under
notice may avail himself of it. *Doe* d. *Earl of*
7s, 6 Jur. 821, Q. B.; *Doe* d. *Earl of Egremont*
627; *Doe* d. *Higgs* v. *Terry,* 4 A. & E. 274. A
ry from year to year cannot be assigned without a
Vade, M'Clel. 664; *Pleasant* d. *Hayton* v. *Ben-*
A mortgagee whose mortgage is *subsequent* to the
tenancy from year to year created by the mort-
of the reversion, and he may give the tenant the
. *Burrowes* v. *Gradin,* 1 Dowl. & L. 213, 218;
A. & E. 451; 2 N. & P. 423. Even an infant
such notice, and indeed must do so before he can
against a tenant from year to year. *Maddon* d.
. R. 159; *ante,* 35.
id overseers of a parish may give notice to quit
under a void lease upon an implied tenancy from
ir successors may avail themselves of such notice.
ry, 4 A. & E. 274; *Doe* d. *Hobbs* v. *Cockell,* 4 A.
gal estate be vested in trustees for the benefit of
tees should give notice to quit, or sue for use and
urchwardens, &c. of St. Nicholas, Deptford v.
. 394, overruling *Rumball* v. *Munt, Id.* 382. If
ch party the legal estate is vested, all should join
. *Whayman* v. *Chaplin,* 3 Taunt. 120; or a sepa-
given by the churchwardens and overseers, and
ees. In a recent case the notice purported to be
ehalf of the late churchwardens (who had demised
the present churchwardens and overseers; but it
n the possession was to be delivered: held suffi-
y v. *Foster,* 3 C. B. 215. A notice to quit and
to the churchwardens and overseers *for the time*
Brooks v. *Fairclough,* 6 M. & S. 40.
emised to a publican upon a yearly tenancy, de-
ie by three months' notice, after which the brewer
irtners, and the subsequent receipts for rent were
f the firm: held, that a notice to quit given by
a name only was sufficient, and that it was not to
e receipts that the *legal* estate in the reversion had
Doe d. *Green* v. *Baker,* 8 Taunt. 241; 2 Moore,

to a mining company, and afterwards becomes a
any, he may nevertheless give the company notice
ie expiration thereof maintain ejectment against
y v. *Francis,* Cornw. Sum. Ass. 1837, Patteson, J.;
I. & W. 331.
recutors or administrators is competent to give
alf of all. But a notice to determine a lease for
the end of the first seven or fourteen years, in
iso therein contained, must be signed by *all* the
as of the proviso so require. *Right* d. *Fisher* v.
; 2 Smith, 83.
its jointly demise from year to year, such of them
ait may severally recover their respective shares.

Doe d. *Whayman* v. *Chaplin*, 3 Taunt. 120. Where joint lessors are partners in trade, a notice to quit in the names of all, signed by one only, is valid. *Doe* d. *Elliott* v. *Hulme*, 2 Man. & R. 433. A notice to quit, signed by one of several joint tenants on behalf of himself and the others (whether authorized by them or not), is sufficient to determine a tenancy from year to year as to all; because the tenant holds *the whole premises of all* so long as he and all shall please, and a notice to quit given by any one effectually puts an end to that tenancy. *Doe* d. *Aslin* v. *Summersett*, 1 B. & Ad. 135, 140 ; *per* Parke, B., in *Doe* d. *Kindersley* v. *Hughes*, 7 M. & W. 141 ; *Alford* v. *Vickery*, Car. & Mar. 280, Coleridge, J. So a notice to quit given on behalf of several joint tenants by a person authorized by one of them to give such notice is sufficient to determine the tenancy as to all. *Doe* d. *Kindersley* v. *Hughes, supra.*

A notice to quit given by one of several tenants in common may be to quit his undivided part or share. *Cutting* v. *Derby*, 2 W. Blac. 1075 ; *Doe* d. *Roberton* v. *Gardiner*, 12 C. B. 323 ; Chit. Forms, 529 (7th ed.). Where several tenants in common *demise jointly*, it would seem that a notice to quit given by any one of them on behalf of himself and the others (whether authorized by them or not) will be sufficient to determine the tenancy as to all, upon the same principle as a notice given by one of several joint tenants will have that effect. *Supra.* But where, after a demise from year to year, the reversion vests in several persons as tenants in common, it would seem that a notice to quit given by either of them, without the authority of the other, would only operate as to his undivided share or proportion of the demised premises. Ad. Eject. 88. Unless indeed the tenant, knowing of an agreement for a partition between them, pays his whole rent, or submits to a distress by one of them, and so estops himself from disputing his sole title to the demised premises. *Doe* d. *Pritchitt* v. *Mitchell*, 1 Bro. & Bing. 11 ; 3 Moore, 229.

Where a notice to quit is given by an agent of the landlord, the agent ought to have authority to give it *at the time when it begins to operate:* a mere recognition of the authority of the agent at a subsequent period will not make the notice good. *Doe* d. *Mann* v. *Walters*, 10 B. & C. 626 ; 5 Man. & R. 357. The notice must be such that the tenant may safely act upon it at the time of receiving it ; therefore a notice by an unauthorized agent cannot be made good by an adoption of it by the principal after the proper time for giving it: *Doe* d. *Lyster* v. *Goldwin*, 2 Q. B. 143, 146 ; *Doe* d. *Rhodes* v. *Robinson*, 3 Bing. N. C. 677 ; 4 Scott, 396 ; *Doe* d. *Fisher* v. *Cuttell*, 5 East, 491, 498 ; 2 Smith, 83 ; Ad. Eject. 88 ; and see *Doe* d. *Pulker* v. *Walker*, 14 Law J., N. S., Q. B. 181 ; *Bird* v. *Brown*, 4 Exch. 786 (a case of stoppage in transitu): were it otherwise, the principal would in effect have the option of continuing or determining the tenancy at the expiration of the notice. And on the other hand, a corresponding inconvenience would accrue to the landlord, where the notice to quit was given by a person professing to act as agent for the tenant, but not having his authority.

A notice to quit given by an agent should purport to be given in the name or on behalf of the principal. If given in the agent's name, and on his own behalf, that is not sufficient, and no subsequent adoption or ratification of such notice by the principal will make it valid. *Doe* d. *Lyster* v. *Goldwin*, 2 Q. B. 143, 146 ; *Buron* v. *Denman*, 2 Exch. 188,

see *Wilson* v. *Tumman*, 6 Man. & Gr. 236, Tin-
N. R. 894; 1 Dowl. & Low. 516, *S. C.*; *Heath*
W. 632, 638.

ven by an agent in the names of W. and B., "*and*
notice from W. and B. only. *Doe* d. *Bailey* v.

given by an *agent of an agent* (*ex. gr.*, a person
ncipal's attorney) is not sufficient, without proof
ority or recognition by the principal. *Doe* d.
3 Bing. N. C. 677.
ed by the Court of Chancery, or by a private in-
ral authority to let the lands to tenants from year
also implied authority to determine such tenancies
o quit. *Wilkinson* v. *Colley*, 5 Burr. 2696, 2698;
Read, 12 East, 57; *Doe* d. *Manvers* v. *Mizem*,
atteson, J. But a person authorized to manage
r during his absence abroad, and to receive his
ity, implied by law, to determine a tenancy by
is a question of fact for the jury whether he had
d. *Mann* v. *Walters*, 10 B. & C. 626. "A mere
uch, has no authority to determine a tenancy;"
Doe d. *Rhodes* v. *Robinson*, 3 Bing. N. C. 677;
distrain as bailiff of the landlord; for that might
personally liable for irregularities, &c. connected
Ward v. *Shew*, 9 Bing. 608; 2 Moo. & Sc. 756;
t, 9 Exch. 14.

-A notice to quit given by the landlord should be
te tenant, or to his assignee, &c. in whom the term
ot to a mere undertenant. *Pleasant* d. *Hayton*
234; 2 Arch. N. P. 396; Ad. Eject. 92. A notice
ant, but served upon the undertenant upon the
nt. *Doe* d. *Mitchell* v. *Levi*, Ad. Eject. 92,
orough, C. J. A landlord may however seriously
giving notice to quit to an undertenant. *Burn* v.
4. The notice should be directed to the tenant,
d to his attorney or agent. *Doe* d. *Prior* v.
, 34. If served upon the tenant personally, it
to him by name. *Doe* d. *Matthewson* v. *Wright*-
Kenyon, C. J. The tenant, on being served with
e a similar notice to his undertenant, and will be
t if his undertenant hold over. *Roe* v. *Wiggs*,
30. If due notice to quit be given to the tenant,
maintained by the landlord against the under-
but it seems that a tenant cannot by a surrender
is undertenant, without any notice to quit given
is tenant, nor by the tenant to his undertenant.
v. *Benson*, 14 East, 232. Where A. had been
nises, and upon his leaving them B. *took posses*-
he absence of evidence to the contrary, it might
came in *as assignee* of A., and not as his under-
ugh B. had never paid any rent to the landlord,
ejectment as landlord of B.: held also, that a
y the landlord to B. was sufficient, in the ab-

sence of evidence showing that B. was a mere undertenant, and not the assignee of A. *Doe* d. *Morris* v. *Williams*, 6 B. & C. 41; 9 D. & R. 30; and see *Roe* d. *Blair* v. *Street and Fairbanks*, 2 A. & E. 329, 331; *Hindley* v. *Rickerby*, 5 Esp. 4. Upon the death of a tenant from year to year, his widow remained in possession, and a notice to quit was given to her: held sufficient in the absence of any evidence of a probate or letters of administration granted to some other person. *Rees* d. *Mears* v. *Perrot*, 4 C. & P. 230, Littledale, J.

A tenant from year to year died leaving a widow and an only son an infant; the widow remained in possession, and subsequently married; her second husband obtained a lease of the premises so held by the deceased, for a term of seven years, during the minority of the infant: held, on the expiration of that term, that the landlord was entitled to maintain an ejectment without notice to quit. *Armstrong* v. *Loughnane*, 2 Irish Law R., N. S., 72.

A notice to quit given by the tenant should be given *to his immediate landlord,* and not to the ground landlord or other person through whom the immediate landlord derives his title. Arch. L. & T. 89; 2 Arch. N. P. 396. If the landlord who demised to the tenant be dead, or have assigned his reversion, the notice should be given to the person or persons for the time being *legally entitled to the immediate reversion, ex. gr.* to the heir, executor, administrator, devisee or assignee of such landlord, as the case may be. Or it may be given to the attorney or agent, duly authorized in that behalf, of such landlord or other person so entitled as aforesaid. *Doe* d. *Prior* v. *Ongley*, 10 C. B. 25 (last point).

Where there are two or more joint lessees, a notice to quit given to one of them, even by parol, is sufficient for all. *Doe* d. *Lord Macartney* v. *J. & W. Crick*, 5 Esp. 196 (the marginal note of this case is incorrect); *Doe* d. *Lord Bradford* v. *Watkins and another*, 7 East, 551; 3 Smith, 517.

When a corporation aggregate is the tenant, the notice should be addressed to the corporation, and not to its officers. *Doe* d. *Lord Carlisle* v. *Woodman*, 8 East, 228. But it seems that no notice need be given unless the tenancy were created by an instrument under seal. *Ante*, 39.

Form and Substance of Notice, and when it should expire.]—A parol notice to quit is generally sufficient, whether given by or on behalf of the landlord; *Doe* d. *Lord Macartney* v. *Crick*, 5 Esp. 196; 2 Car. & K. 420, note (*d*); or the tenant; *Timmins* v. *Rowlinson*, 3 Burr. 1603; 1 W. Blac. 533; *Bird* v. *Defonvielle*, 2 Car. & K. 415; and even when given on behalf of a corporation aggregate by their steward or agent, *Roe* d. *Dean and Chapter of Rochester* v. *Pierce*, 2 Camp. 96; 7 Q. B. 577, if any notice to quit be necessary in such case. *Ante*, 39.

A good parol notice will not be waived by a subsequent insufficient notice in writing. *Doe* d. *Lord Macartney* v. *Crick*, 5 Esp. 196; and see *Smith* v. *Young*, 1 Camp. 440; Phil. Ev. 665, note (2) (8th ed.).

Generally speaking notice to quit is given *in writing*. No particular form is necessary. Ros. Ev. 451 (7th ed.). But if given by or on behalf of the landlord, it must in substance and effect request the tenant, or other the person for the time being legally entitled to the term (not

t, *ante,* 45) to quit and deliver up possession of *all*
es *at the proper time.* 2 Arch. N. P. 397; *see
ix, No.* 1. If given by or on behalf of the
substance and effect inform the landlord, or other
s for the time being legally entitled to the imme-
t the tenant will quit and deliver up possession of
mises *at the proper time.* 2 Arch. N. P. 397; *see
r, No.* 3.
t the end of the current year of the tenancy, " on
hall require you to pay me double former rent or
you detain possession," is an unqualified notice to
;ive the tenant an option. *Doe* d. *Lyster* v. *Gold-
1 Gale & D.* 463; *Doe* d. *Matthews* v. *Jackson,*
where the notice really does give the tenant an
continue tenant at an increased rent, it will not be
t an ejectment. Ad. Eject. 95; Ros. Ev. 452

r that a notice to quit given by the landlord should
mant by name. If proved to have been delivered
:ient. *Doe* d. *Matthewson* v. *Wrightman,* 4 Esp.
. J.
uit be directed to a tenant by a wrong christian
ps it without objection, the mistake is thereby
iller, 6 Esp. 70, Lord Ellenborough, C. J.
directed to the bailiffs or head officers of a cor-
, instead of to the corporation itself, is bad. *Doe*
v. *Woodman,* 8 East, 228. But no such notice
y generally. *Ante,* 39.
;iven by an agent should be expressed to be given
or on behalf of his principal, otherwise it will be
l. *Lyster* v. *Goldwin,* 2 Q. B. 143, 146; *ante,* 44.
en by an agent of an agent is not sufficient with-
by the principal. *Doe* d. *Rhodes* v. *Robinson,* 3

tenant of lands originally devised to the rector and
parish and their successors in trust, and signed by
chwardens, requiring him to deliver up the pre-
and churchwardens *for the time being,* is ill. *Doe
'ough,* 6 M. & S. 40. But a notice given by an
d present churchwardens and overseers of a parish,
it of parish property to quit and deliver up posses-
time (*not saying to whom*), is sufficient. *Doe* d.
3 C. B. 215.
·equire the tenant to quit all the demised premises,
ly, otherwise it will be bad. *Right* d. *Fisher* v.
98, Grose, J.; *Doe* d. *Rodd* v. *Archer,* 14 East,
rt will, if possible, construe the notice as a good
:, rather than as a bad notice for part, *ut res majis
t.* Therefore a notice to quit "Town Barton,
for Town Barton and other lands and tenements
es held therewith. *S. C.* So a notice to quit "all
ment or dwellinghouse, farm, lands and premises,
1ces, which you rent of me in the parish of S.," is
e the *great and small tithes* held therewith under

a parol demise. *Doe* d. *Morgan* v. *Church,* 3 Camp. 71, Le Blanc, J.
A misdescription of the demised premises in a notice to quit is not
fatal, if the tenant be not misled by it. Thus, where the premises were
fully and correctly described, except that they were called "The
Waterman's Arms" instead of "The Bricklayer's Arms." *Doe* d.
Cox v. ——, 4 Esp. 185, Lord Ellenborough, C. J. So when the
premises were described as situate in the parish of *Dunnington* (instead
of the parish of *Haslington*), in the county of York : held, sufficient, the defendant not appearing to have been misled by it. *Doe* d.
Armstrong v. *Wilkinson,* 12 A. & E. 743 ; 4 P. & D. 323.

A notice to quit given by one of several tenants in common may be
to quit his undivided part or share. *Cutting* v. *Derby,* 2 W. Blac.
1075 ; *Doe* d. *Roberton* v. *Gardiner,* 12 C. B. 323 ; Chit. Forms,
529 (7th ed.) ; *see the Form, Appendix, No.* 2.

The notice must require the tenant to quit, or give notice of his
intention to quit, *at the proper time.* This is the point with respect to
which mistakes are most frequently made ; and such mistakes are
usually fatal to the validity of the notice. *Ante,* 32 ; *Doe* d. *Castleton*
v. *Samuel,* 5 Esp. 173 ; *Doe* d. *Spicer* v. *Lea,* 11 East, 312 ; *Doe*
d. *Finlayson* v. *Bayley,* 5 C. & P. 671 ; *Doe* d. *Daniel* v. *Williams,* 7
C. & P. 322 ; *Doe* d. *Murrell* v. *Milward,* 3 M. & W. 328 ; *Goode*
v. *Howells,* 4 M. & W. 198 ; 2 Arch. N. P. 397.

Where there is no special stipulation, or local custom, providing
what notice shall be given, the law requires *half a year's notice to quit
at the end of the first or some other year of the tenancy,* and not at
any other period. *Parker* d. *Walker* v. *Constable,* 3 Wils. 25 ; *Right*
d. *Flower* v. *Darby,* 1 T. R. 159 ; *Doe* d. *David* v. *Williams,* 7
C. & P. 322 ; *Doe* d. *Murrell* v. *Milward,* 3 M. & W. 328 ; *Roe* d.
Brown v. *Wilkinson,* Co. Litt. 270 b. (note 228) ; *Leighton* v. *Theed,*
1 Ld. Ray. 707 ; 2 Arch. N. P. 394, 397. This has been settled ever
since a case in the Year Book, 13 Hen. 8, 15. *Throgmorton* d.
Wandby v. *Whelpdale,* Bull. N. P. 96 ; Ad. Eject. 74. It makes no
difference in this respect whether the demised premises consist of land
or houses. *Roe* d. *Brown* v. *Wilkinson, supra ; per* Ashhurst, J., in
Right d. *Flower* v. *Darby,* 1 T. R. 162. So with respect to a composition for tithes ; *Goode* v. *Howells,* 4 M. & W. 198 ; *Hulme* v. *Pardoe,* 1 C. & P. 93 ; M'Clel. 393 ; but the case of " lodgings" depends
upon a particular contract (express or implied), and is an exception to
the general rule. *Right* d. *Flower* v. *Darby,* 1 T. R. 162, *per* Lord
Mansfield, C. J. ; *ante,* 37.

A customary half year's notice to quit, expiring on one of the usual
quarter days, is sufficient, although it may happen to be less than a
full half year's notice. Thus a notice served on or before Michaelmas
Day to quit on the following Lady Day (from which day the tenancy
commenced) is sufficient. *Roe* d. *Durant* v. *Doe,* 6 Bing. 574 ; 4 Moo.
& P. 391 ; *Doe* d. *Matthewson* v. *Wrightman,* 4 Esp. 5 ; *Doe* d. *Harrop*
v. *Green,* 4 Esp. 198, 199 ; Ad. Eject. 100 ; *Doe* d. *Lord Bradford*
v. *Watkins,* 7 East, 551 ; 3 Smith, 517. A notice to quit on the 24th
June, served on the preceding Christmas Day, is sufficient. *Doe* d.
Buddle v. *Lewis,* 11 Q. B. 402. But where the tenancy commenced
from some day in the year other than one of the usual quarter days,
a full half year's notice (183 days), expiring on such day, must be
given. *Doe* d. *Spicer* v. *Lea,* 11 East, 312 ; *Mills* v. *Goff,* 14 M. &

ᴛ L. 23; *Doe* d. *Cornwall* v. *Matthews*, 11 C. B.
)0.

ᴉancy from year to year is *implied* upon the terms of
ᴉe notice to quit must generally expire at that period
:he previous lease commenced. *Ante*, 34; *post*, 50.
ʳ-tenant holds over and pays rent after the expira-
fourteen and a half years, commencing at Christmas
ᴹidsummer, a notice requiring him to quit at Mid-
Doe d. *Buddle* v. *Lines*, 11 Q. B. 402.

ing, a notice to quit should expire on the *last day*
ᴉe tenancy, and not on the same day on which the
ᴇd. *Poole* v. *Warren*, 8 A. & E. 587, 588. Thus
ʳom Lady Day, the notice should expire on Lady
ᴉe 26th of March. A lease for years *from* the 25th
; that day, and does not expire until the last minute
of the 25th day of March in the last year of the
. *Lutley*, 9 A. & E. 879; 1 P. & D. 636; *Haths* v.
Anon., Lofft. 275; *Gorst* v. *Lowndes*, 5 Jur. 458,
But when the defendant entered as tenant, under a
;, on the 7th May, 1850, and paid no rent: held,
notice to quit, expiring on the 7th May, 1851, was
ʰoe d. *Cornwall* v. *Matthews*, 11 C. B. 675. In this
ᴉtended that the notice ought to have expired on the
but at Midsummer, 1851. It seems to have been
tenancy commenced *from* the 7th May, 1850 (ex-
although not so expressed in the report; or the above
ᴇen overlooked. When a term of years commences
ne, it expires on the 19th of June. *Clayton's case*,
ᵉsolution). If a term expire on the 25th June, a
the 24th June is bad; *Poole* v. *Warren*, 8 A. & E.
ᴉew trial will not be granted on such a point. *Cut-*
ᴺ. Blac. 1076, 1077. In ejectment against a weekly
proved was to quit on Wednesday the 4th of August.
was called to prove that Wednesday was the expira-
ᴉt week of the tenancy, said "that he guessed the
ᴉn about a Tuesday or Wednesday, but he had no
:" held insufficient. *Doe* d. *Finlayson* v. *Bayley*,
ᴉdal, C. J.

ᴛ on the proper day, *at twelve o'clock at noon*, is bad.
; Q. B. 684.

"at Michaelmas next," *primâ facie*, means Michael-
29th Sept.); but it will be sufficient for a tenancy
ᴉichaelmas, old style (11th Oct.), because the tenant
misled or prejudiced by it. *Doe* d. *Hinde* v. *Vince*,
ʰoe d. *Willis* v. *Perrin*, 9 C. & P. 467, Parke, B.
ᴉit "on the 11th of October, Old Michaelmas Day,"
ᴉᴉcy commenced at New Michaelmas. *Doe* d. *Spicer*
312. Upon a written agreement to demise from the
Day," a notice to quit on the 6th of April is good,
ᴉce that by "Lady Day" the parties meant Old Lady
ᴉᴉce is admissible where the written agreement is *not*
ᵉ d. *Peters* v. *Hopkinson*, 3 Dowl. & Ry. 507; *Doe*
ᴉ, 4 B. & A. 588. A notice to quit on "Lady Day"
ʳ New or Old Lady Day, according to the holding, if

D

served in due time. *Denn* d. *Willan* v. *Walker*, Peake, Add. Cases, 194. A notice to quit " on the 25th day of March, *or* the 6th day of April next," if served in sufficient time, is good for New or Old Lady Day, according as the tenancy actually commenced. *Doe* d. *Matthewson* v. *Wrightman*, 4 Esp. 6, Lord Kenyon, C. J.

Formerly it was held that a notice to quit upon a particular day was *primâ facie* evidence that the tenancy commenced on that day, and threw upon the defendant the onus of proving that it commenced on some other day. *Matthewson* v. *Wrightman*, 4 Esp. 7, Lord Kenyon, C. J. But that doctrine was afterwards exploded, and it is now settled that such a notice is not *primâ facie* evidence that the tenancy commenced on the day therein mentioned; *Doe* d. *Ash* v. *Calvert*, 2 Camp. 388; unless it be proved that the notice was served personally upon the tenant, who read it, or had it read to him, *and made no objection to it*. *Thomas* d. *Jones* v. *Reece*, 2 Camp. 647; *Doe* d. *Clarges, Bart.*, v. *Forster*, 13 East, 405; *Doe* d. *Leicester* v. *Biggs*, 2 Taunt. 109. Even such proof will not prevent the defendant from showing that the tenancy actually commenced at a different part of the year. *Oakapple* d. *Green* v. *Copous*, 4 T. R. 361; and see *Cadby* v. *Martinez*, 11 A. & E. 720; 3 P. & D. 386.

If the tenant, in answer to an application by the landlord or his agent, state that the tenancy commenced on a particular day, and a notice is thereupon given to quit on that day, the tenant will be estopped from afterwards proving that the tenancy actually commenced on a different day. *Doe* d. *Eyre* v. *Lambly*, 2 Esp. 625, Lord Kenyon, C. J.; but see *Doe* d. *Murrell* v. *Milward*, 3 M. & W. 331, Alderson, B.

Generally speaking, an implied tenancy from year to year, created by the payment and acceptance of rent after the end or determination of a previous term, will be deemed to have commenced at the same time of the year as the original term; and notice to quit should be given accordingly. *Roe* d. *Jordan* v. *Ward*, 1 H. Blac. 96; *Doe* d. *Martin* v. *Watts*, 7 T. R. 83; *Doe* d. *Collins* v. *Weller*, 7 T. R. 478; *Doe* d. *Castleton* v. *Samuel*, 5 Esp. 173; *Doe* d. *Spicer* v. *Lea*, 11 East, 312; *Doe* d. *Tucker* v. *Morse*, 1 B. & Adol. 365. And this rule prevails even where the original term did not cease at the same time of the year as it commenced. Thus where premises were originally demised for five and a half years, and an implied tenancy from year to year was afterwards created. *Berrey* v. *Lindley*, 3 Man. & Gr. 498; *Doe* d. *Robinson* v. *Dobell*, 1 Q. B. 806; *Kemp* v. *Derrett*, 3 Camp. 510. There seems, however, to be some difference in this respect between a holding over by the original tenant, and by an *undertenant*, after the expiration of a term of fourteen and a half years. *Doe* d. *Buddle* v. *Lines*, 11 Q. B. 402.

Where a tenant enters in the middle of a quarter, and *pays rent for the broken period* to the next regular quarter day, and subsequently pays his rent from quarter to quarter, his tenancy will be deemed to have commenced, not when he first entered, but at the ensuing quarter day, and notice should be given accordingly. *Doe* d. *Holcomb* v. *Johnson*, 6 Esp. 10; *Doe* d. *Savage* v. *Stapleton*, 3 C. & P. 275; *Doe* d. *King* v. *Grafton*, 18 Q. B. 496; 21 Law J., N. S., Q. B. 276; 16 Jur. 833. But if he has not paid any rent, the tenancy will be deemed to have commenced on the day when he entered, and notice to

will be good. *Doe* d. *Cornwall* v. *Matthews,* 11
e the tenant entered in the middle of a quarter upon
pay rent quarterly, and for the half quarter," it was
say whether the party was tenant from the quarter
ne when he entered, or from the succeeding quarter
:he direction of Lord Ellenborough, C. J., the jury
ancy commenced with the preceding quarter. *Doe*
lwyn, H. T. 47 Geo. 3; Ad. Eject. 107; Ros. Ev.

mise by parol for seven years on the terms that the
at Lady Day and *quit at Candlemas,* though the
e Statute of Frauds as to the duration of the term,
other respects the implied tenancy from year to year
yment and acceptance of the rent reserved; and,
lord or tenant can determine the tenancy by a notice
: Candlemas, but not by a notice expiring at Lady
ye v. *Bell,* 5 T. R. 471; and see *Doe* d. *Peacock* v.
(*ante,* 32); *Richardson* v. *Gifford,* 1 A. & E. 52;
v. *Amey,* 12 A. & E. 476; 4 P. & D. 177; *Doe* d.
itt, 15 Q. B. 257.
parts of the demised premises were entered upon at
notice should be to quit at corresponding periods, or
of the year of the tenancy which will expire next after
alf-a-year from the delivery of this notice." *Doe* d.
. 5 A. & E. 350. Such notice will be sufficient for
remises if served in time for the principal subject of
l. *Dagget* v. *Snowdon,* 2 W. Black. 1224; *Doe* d.
ce, 6 East, 120; 2 Smith, 255; *Doe* d. *Lord Brad-*
l East, 551; 3 Smith, 517; cited fully in *Doe* d.
les, 11 M. & W. 602, 603. If any doubt arise as
rincipal and which the accessorial subject of the
lestion of fact for the jury: but if the judge assumes
, and decides accordingly that the notice to quit is,
, the party against whom he so decides should ex-
:o leave the question of fact to the jury: otherwise
pon any application for a new trial, &c., that he
fact assumed by the judge as the ground of his
Heapy v. *Howard,* 11 East, 498; *Doe* d. *Kindersley*
: W. 141, Parke, B.
lown, and cannot be ascertained or proved, at what
he tenancy actually commenced, the notice should
pecified quarter day, "or at the expiration of the
ur tenancy which shall expire next after the end of
the service of this notice." *See the form, Ap-*
Camp. 257, 258, note; *Doe* d. *Digby* v. *Steel,* 3
. v. *Horn,* 6 M. & W. 393. If the ejectment be
ir the claimant alleged in the writ to be entitled to
me day *after the third quarter day succeeding that*
iotice, such notice will certainly be sufficient, sup-
)e payable on the usual quarter days. This is the
pursued under such circumstances.
ekly tenant, whose tenancy commenced on a *Wed-*
in Friday the 2nd day of October next, provided
ienced on a Friday, or otherwise at the end of your

tenancy next after one week from the date hereof," is sufficient to support an ejectment brought after the Wednesday following the 2nd October. *Doe* d. *Campbell* v. *Scott*, 6 Bing. 362; 4 Moo. & Pay. 20. In ejectment against a weekly tenant, the notice proved was to quit on Wednesday the 4th of August. The witness, who was called to prove that Wednesday was the expiration of the current week of the tenancy, said " that he guessed the defendant came in about a Tuesday or Wednesday, but he had no recollection which :" held insufficient. *Doe* d. *Finlayson* v. *Bayley*, 5 C. & P. 67, Tindal, C. J.

The notice *need not mention the particular day* on which the tenant is required to quit. Thus a notice to quit " at the expiration of the current year of the tenancy which shall expire next after the end of one half-year from the date hereof " is sufficient. *Doe* d. *Phillips* v. *Butler*, 2 Esp. 589; *Doe* v. *Williams* v. *Smith*, 5 A. & E. 350. A notice on 22nd March to quit " at the expiration of the current year," is sufficient for the 29th September, if the tenancy commenced on that day. *Doe* d. *Baker* v. *Wombwell*, 2 Camp. 559. A notice on 27th September to quit " at the expiration of the term for which you hold the same," is sufficient for Lady Day, if the tenancy commenced at that time. *Doe* d. *Milnes* v. *Lamb*, Ad. Ejec. 272, Holroyd, J. A notice to quit " at the expiration of the present year's tenancy" is sufficient, although it does not appear *on the face of it* that it was given six months before the period therein specified for quitting. *Doe* d. *Gorst* v. *Timothy*, 2 Car. & Kir. 351, Rolfe, B.

The day or time mentioned in the notice to quit should always be *correct with reference to the date of the notice.* Any mistake in this respect is generally fatal to the validity of the notice. But a notice given at Michaelmas, 1795, to quit " at Lady Day, which will be in the year 1795," was held a good notice for Lady Day, 1796. *Doe* d. *Duke of Bedford* v. *Kightley*, 7 T. R. 63. So a notice dated 27th September, 1822, to quit " at Lady day next, or at the end of your current year," was held a good half-year's notice for the year ending at Lady Day, 1823, rather than a bad two days' notice for the current year ending 29th September, 1822. *Doe* d. *Lord Huntingtower* v. *Culliford*, 4 Dowl. & Ry. 248. In this case the tenancy must have been determinable at the end of any quarter or half-year, upon six months' notice, although that is not mentioned in the report. But the case itself is now of no authority, having been expressly overruled in *Doe* d. *The Mayor, Aldermen and Burgesses of Richmond* v. *Morphett*, 7 Q. B. 577. There a notice was served on 21st October, 1842, to quit " on the 13th day of May next, or upon such other day or time as the *current* year for which you now hold will expire." The tenancy commenced at Martinmas (20th September): held, a bad notice for Martinmas, 1842, and not a good one for Martinmas, 1843. *S. C.* So where a tenancy commenced on the 11th October, and on the 17th June, 1840, a notice was given to quit " on the 11th day of October now next ensuing, or such other day or time as your said tenancy may expire on :" held a bad notice for the 11th October, 1840, and not a good one for the 11th October, 1841. *Mills* v. *Goff*, 14 M. & W. 72; 2 Dowl. & L. 23. But where lands and buildings were held by a yearly tenant, the land from 2nd February to 2nd February, and the buildings from 1st May to 1st May ; and the landlord, on the 22nd October, 1833, served the tenant with a notice to quit the land and buildings " at the expiration of half a year from the delivery of this

other time or times as your *present* year's holding of
nises, or any part or parts thereof respectively, shall
xpiration of half a year from the delivery of this
at as to the land (which was the principal subject of
)tice was to be considered, not as a bad notice for the
34, but as a good notice for the 2nd February, 1835,
support ejectment on a demise dated 4th February,
'illiams v. *Smith*, 5 A. & E. 350: there the word
;jected, "because the notice necessarily referred to
ie expiration of half a year from the notice." Per
Doe d. *Mayor of Richmond* v. *Morphett*, 7 Q. B.

otice to quit at Midsummer instead of Christmas,
at and assented to by the landlord, will not be suffi-
the tenancy at Midsummer, and cannot operate as a
effect at that time, for there cannot be a surrender *in*
Murrell v. *Milward*, 3 M. & W. 328; *Bessell* v.
3. 638 (*ante*, 32); and see *Cadby* v. *Martinez*, 11 A.
: D. 386.
: need not be attested: formerly an attestation some-
fficulty in proof of the notice. *Doe* d. *Sykes* v. *Durn-*
2; but now see 17 & 18 Vict. c. 125, s. 26.

ice.—1. *When.*]—We have already fully considered
it should be given, and at what period, or time of the
)ught to expire (*ante*, 46 to 52). Generally speaking
e served *half a year* before the time when the tenant
possession. *Right* d. *Flower* v. *Darby*, 1 T. R. 159.
ice, if less than half a year, or 183 days, is not suffi-
luller, J.; *Johnstone* v. *Huddlestone*, 4 B. & C. 932,
t customary half-year's notice is sufficient where the
me of the usual quarter days. Therefore a notice
e Michaelmas Day is sufficient for the ensuing Lady
;y commenced at that time. *Doe* d. *Matthewson* v.
). 5; *Doe* d. *Harrop* v. *Green*, 4 Esp. 198, 199; *Roe*
e, 6 Bing. 574.
less notice than that usually required by law be ex-
'or, such notice must be given, and will be sufficient.

iotice to quit *need not be served personally* on the
:ient to leave it at his dwelling-house with his wife or
. *Clarke*, 9 Dowl. 202; *Jones* d. *Griffiths* v. *Marsh*,
· d. *Blair* v. *Street and Fairbanks*, 2 A. & E. 329;
)oe d. *Neville* v. *Dunbar*, Moo. & Mal. 10, Abbott,
istices of North Riding of Yorkshire*, 7 Q. B. 154.
icient, although the notice does not reach the tenant's
half-year has commenced. *Doe* d. *Neville* v. *Dun-*
merely leaving the notice at the tenant's house,
mation, and without proof that the person to whom
as the tenant's wife or servant, or that it ever came
ot sufficient. *Doe* d. *Buross* v. *Lucas*, 5 Esp. 153.
ce upon a relation of the *undertenant*, upon the pre-
:ient, although the notice was properly addressed to

the tenant. *Doe* d. *Michell* v. *Levi*, Ad. Eject. 92 (note b), Lord Ellenborough, C. J. But putting the notice under the door of the tenant's house, or any other mode of service, will be deemed sufficient, if it be shown that the notice came to the tenant's hands before the commencement of the six months. *Alford* v. *Vickery*, Car. & Mar. 280, Coleridge, J. Service on the wife of the tenant, not at the premises, appears to be insufficient; *Roe* d. *Blair* v. *Street*, 2 A. & E. 328, 331; unless it be shown that the service took place at the husband's residence, where the wife was then living with him. *Ante*, 53.

A notice to quit, if not served personally on the tenant, is no evidence to prove that the tenancy commenced on the day mentioned in the notice. *Doe* d. *Ash* v. *Calvert*, 2 Camp. 388. But if the notice require the tenant to quit on a particular day, and it is served upon him personally, and he reads it, or it is read to him, and he makes no objection to the time when he is required to quit, that will constitute *primâ facie* evidence as against him, from which the jury may infer and find that the tenancy commenced at that period. *Doe* d. *Clarges, Bart.*, v. *Forster*, 13 East, 405; *Thomas* d. *Jones* v. *Reece*, 2 Camp. 647; and see *Doe* d. *Baker* v. *Wombwell*, 2 Camp. 559. But the tenant may rebut such evidence by proof that the tenancy actually commenced at another time of the year than that mentioned in the notice. *Oakapple* d. *Green* v. *Copous*, 4 T. R. 361; and see *Cadby* v. *Martinez*, 11 A. & E. 720; 3 P. & D. 386. Unless, indeed, he has estopped himself from so doing by stating to the landlord or his agent before the notice to quit was given, that the tenancy commenced on the particular day afterwards mentioned in the notice. *Doe* d. *Eyre* v. *Lambly*, 2 Esp. 635, Lord Kenyon, C. J.; but see *Doe* d. *Murrell* v. *Milward*, 3 M. & W. 331, Alderson, B.

3. *Proof of Service.*]—A notice to quit may be proved by the copy retained, although there has been no notice given to produce the original. *Doe* d. *Fleming* v. *Somerton*, 7 Q. B. 58. The principle is, that a notice to produce a notice is always unnecessary; for that might go on *ad infinitum*. If there be an attesting witness to the notice, he need not be called; 17 & 18 Vict. c. 125, s. 26; but it was formerly otherwise. *Doe* d. *Sykes and Benyon* v. *Durnford*, 2 M. & S. 62; *Poole* v. *Warren*, 8 A. & E. 582.

The service must be proved to have been made in due time, and in proper form and manner (*ante*, 53); but a verbal notice is sufficient (*ante*, 46).

If the witness who served the notice be dead, but has indorsed on the notice a memorandum of the service, proof thereof and of his death, and that such indorsement was made in the usual course of business, is sufficient. *Doe* d. *Patteshall* v. *Turford*, 3 B. & Adol. 890; and see *Poole* v. *Dicas*, 1 Bing. N. C. 649. But an oral statement of the deceased person as to the mode of service, not made in the ordinary course of business, is inadmissible. *Stapylton* v. *Clough*, 2 E. & B. 933.

The regular service of a notice to quit, held to have been properly inferred from the circumstance of the tenant speaking about " the notice to quit which he had received," and engaging a valuer to value his rights as an outgoing tenant. *Doe* d. *Simpson* v. *Hall*, 5 Man. & Gr. 795.

It is not necessary to prove that the signature to the notice served

writing of the party giving the notice, because it is
notice were given on his behalf, and with his autho-
Dawes, 1 Car. & Mar. 127.

ice.]—A notice to quit can be waived, and a new or
y created, only by the express or implied consent of
There is this difference between a determination of a
ice to quit and a forfeiture: in the former case the
end to by the agreement of the parties, which deter-
enancy cannot be waived without the assent of both;
a forfeiture, the lease is voidable only at the election
the one case the estate continues, though voidable;
tenancy is at an end." Per Maule, J., in *Blyth* v.
. 180.
me by the landlord with the express or implied assent
ich is inconsistent with a determination of the tenancy
of the notice to quit, amounts to *evidence for the jury*
notice to quit, and of an express or implied agreement
ies for a continuation of the tenancy, or the creation
between them. It is, however, a question of *inten-*
of evidence only, and not a conclusion of law. *Doe*
en, Cowp. 243. If the landlord expressly state that
at in lieu of double rent, or double value, or that he
waive the notice, or if there be any fraud or con-
art of the tenant in paying the subsequent rent, such
ft to the jury. *S. C.*
nt, stipulating that acceptance of the rent shall not
ver of a previous notice to quit, does not require an
under 55 Geo. 3, c. 184. *Doe* d. *Wheeble* v. *Fuller*,
Generally speaking, if the landlord accept rent which
- the expiration of a notice to quit, it is a waiver of
odright d. *Charter* v. *Cordwent*, 6 T. R. 219. But
rent which became *due before or on* the expiration of
it, is not a waiver of such notice. Ad. Eject. 116;
t, 13 C. B. 178, *per* Jervis, C. J. Where rent is
ie landlord's bankers, who, without any knowledge
; having been given, and without any special autho-
due after the expiration of the notice to quit, such
by waived. *Doe* d. *Ash* v. *Calvert*, 2 Camp. 387.
of *double value* given by 4 Geo. 2, c. 28, s. 1, will
raiver of the notice to quit, it being in the nature of
or the trespass by holding over after the determination
Soulsby v. *Newing*, 9 East, 310. But the acceptance
ven by 11 Geo. 2, c. 19, s. 18, or a distress for such
an acknowledgment of the existence of the tenancy
n of the notice to quit, and consequently as a waiver
ntry which accrued on the expiration of such notice.

of *subsequent single rent* may amount either to a
ice to quit, or to a waiver of double rent or double
to the intention of the parties, which is a question for
l. *Cheny* v. *Batten*, Cowp. 243; *Ryal* v. *Rich*, 10
l see *Doe* d. *Digby* v. *Steel*, 3 Camp. 114.
for rent accrued *after* the expiration of a notice to

quit is a waiver of the notice; *Zouch* d. *Ward* v. *Willingale*, 1 H. Black. 311; *Doe* d. *David* v. *Williams*, 7 C. & P. 322; provided such distress be not replevied. *Blyth* v. *Dennett*, 13 C. B. 180, Jervis, C. J. But a distress taken before or after the expiration of the notice to quit for rent *due before or at* the time of the expiration of such notice, is no waiver of the notice, because such distress may be made within six months after the expiration of the tenancy, pursuant to 8 Ann. c. 14, ss. 6, 7. 1 H. Black. 312, Wilson, J.; Ad. Eject. 116. That statute does not apply where the tenancy is terminated by the wrongful disclaimer of the tenant. In such case a subsequent distress amounts to a waiver of the disclaimer. *Doe* d. *David* v. *Williams*, 9 C. & P. 322, Patteson, J. A distress for rent after verdict in ejectment is no waiver of any previous notice to quit, but a mere wrongful act, which may be disputed by the tenant. *Doe* d. *Holmes* v. *Darby*, 8 Taunt. 538; 2 Moore, 581. If the tenant replevy a distress made for rent which became due *after* the expiration of a notice to quit, such distress does not necessarily amount to a waiver of the notice to quit, and the creation of a new implied tenancy; because a new tenancy can be created only by the express or implied assent of both parties. *Blyth* v. *Dennett*, 13 C. B. 180, *per* Jervis, C. J.

A *demand* of rent accruing subsequently to the expiration of a notice to quit is not necessarily a waiver of the notice. It is a question of intention, which must be left to the jury. *Blyth* v. *Dennett*, 13 C. B. 178.

A fresh notice to quit at Michaelmas, 1811, operates as a waiver of a previous notice to quit at Michaelmas, 1810. *Doe* d. *Brierly* v. *Palmer*, 16 East, 53. But where a landlord gave a notice to quit, and after the expiration thereof commenced an ejectment, pending which the witness who served the notice became dangerously ill, and the landlord fearing to lose his evidence, and so to be unable to support that action, by way of precaution gave the defendant a fresh notice to quit the premises *then held under him* in the following year: held, that he did not thereby waive his first notice. *Doe* d. *Williams* v. *Humphreys*, 2 East, 237. So where, after the expiration of a notice to quit, the landlord gave the tenant a fresh notice to quit the premises *then held under him* in fourteen days, *otherwise he should require double value:* held, that such second notice was not a waiver of the first, unless it was given with that intent, and not merely to entitle the landlord to double value; and it was left to the jury to say *quo animo* the second notice was given. *Doe* d. *Digby* v. *Steel*, 3 Camp. 117; and see *Doe* d. *Godsell* v. *Inglis*, 3 Taunt. 54; *Blyth* v. *Dennett*, 13 C. B. 178; *Messenger* v. *Armstrong*, 1 T. R. 53. To prevent doubts and questions of the above nature, it is advisable to express on the face of the second notice that it is given *without prejudice* to the previous notice. See the forms in *Wilkinson* v. *Hall*, 3 Bing. N. C. 520, 521.

A landlord of premises about to sell them gave his tenant notice to quit on the 11th October, 1806, but promised not to turn him out, *unless they were sold;* and not being sold till February, 1807, the tenant refused, on demand made after the sale, to give up possession. On ejectment brought after such refusal: held, that the promise (which was performed) was no waiver of the notice, nor operated as a licence to be on the premises, *otherwise than subject to the notice. Whiteacre* d. *Boult* v. *Symonds*, 10 East, 13. And *per* Lord Ellenborough, C. J.,

d, in answer to the tenant's application, that he would
until the place were sold; that is in effect saying that
ere sold he would suspend the exercise of his right
to quit; but it could not have been intended to give
licence as would vacate the notice, and be destructive
h the landlord was so anxious to retain." *Id.* 16.

t gave notice of his intention to quit at Michaelmas,
that time offered to continue tenant at a reduced rent,
rd agreed to, provided he could not find another
r rent before the 12th day of August then next; but
le tenant refused to permit a third person (who con-
the farm) to go over it: held, that the conditional
new tenancy was thereby determined, and that the
Michaelmas, 1835, remained in force, and would sup-
. *Doe* d. *Marquis of Hertford* v. *Hunt*, 1 M. & W.
1028.

ord gave his tenants a good parol notice to quit at
but at the same time said that, if it would be any
em, he would permit them to occupy till Christmas,
uld pay no rent; and one of the tenants expressed
ified and grateful for the indulgence; after which a
is served on the tenants to quit at Christmas: held,
t commenced after Christmas might be maintained
itice to quit at Old Michaelmas. *Doe* d. *Lord Mac-*
5 Esp. 196, Lord Ellenborough, C. J.

t from year to year holds over after the expiration of
iven by him, it is a question for the jury (in an action
ibsequent rent) whether he did so with the intention
otice to quit, and continuing the tenancy. *Jones* v.
E. 832. If he holds over, and *pays one quarter's*
that is evidence of a new tenancy on the old terms;
rd, 2 B. & C. 100; unless the quarter's rent be paid
l. *Freeman* v. *Jury*, Moo. & Mal. 19, Abbott, C. J.
ig over after the expiration of a notice to quit given
is liable to an action for double value, or for use and
an ejectment, but not to a distress for rent, without
a renewal of the tenancy. *Jenner* v. *Clegg*, 1 Moo.
ke, J.

idlord proposed to the tenant after the expiration of
should continue tenant at a certain increased rent,
vithout expressly assenting or dissenting to such pro-
to occupy: held, that he must be presumed to have
proposal, and consequently that the landlord might
int. *Roberts* v. *Hayward*, 3 C. & P. 432, Best, C. J.;
. *Storey*, 1 Man. & Gr. 117, 126.

CHAPTER IV.

DEMAND OF POSSESSION.

When necessary before Action.]—Sometimes a demand of possession is necessary before an ejectment can be maintained, although the defendant is not entitled to the usual notice to quit. This happens where the defendant is, by construction of law or otherwise, a *tenant at will* to the plaintiff, and such estate has not been legally determined by entry or otherwise. *Goodtitle* d. *Gallaway* v. *Herbert*, 4 T. R. 680; *Doe* d. *Jacobs* v. *Phillips*, 10 Q. B. 130; *Doe* d. *Hull* v. *Wood*, 14 M. & W. 682; *Doe* d. *Loscombe* v. *Clifford*, 2 Car. & K. 448. Thus, if a party be let into possession of land under a contract for the purchase of it, which afterwards goes off; *Right* d. *Lewis* v. *Beard*, 13 East, 210; *Doe* d. *Newby* v. *Jackson*, 1. B. & C. 448; 2 D. & R. 514; *Doe* d. *Hiatt* v. *Miller*, 5 C. & P. 595; *Doe* d. *Milburn* v. *Edgar*, 2 Bing. N. C. 498; *Doe* d. *Stanway* v. *Rock*, 4 Man. & Gr. 30; *Doe* d. *Gray* v. *Stanion*, 1 M. & W. 700, Parke, B.; or under an agreement for a lease which is never granted, and no rent has been paid; *Doe* d. *Hollingsworth* v. *Stennett*, 2 Esp. 716, 717; *Doe* d. *Lambourn* v. *Pedgriph*, 4 C. & P. 312; or under a defective conveyance; *Denn* d. *Warren* v. *Fearnside*, 1 Wils. 176; or without a deed of partition, where that is necessary; *Doe* d. *Loscombe* v. *Gifford*, 2 Car. & K. 448; or under a conveyance which is void under the Mortmain Act, 9 Geo. 2, c. 36; *Doe* d. *Pulker* v. *Walker*, 14 Law J., N. S., Q. B., 181; or under a void lease, and no rent has been paid. *Goodtitle* d. *Gallaway* v. *Herbert*, 4 T. R. 680; *De Medina* v. *Polson*, Holt, N. P. C. 47. So where a tenant, after the expiration of his term, continues in possession *with the assent* of the landlord, negociating for a new lease; *Doe* d. *Hollingsworth* v. *Stennett*, 2 Esp. 716; or for the purchase of the landlord's estate. *Doe* d. *Gray* v. *Stanion*, 1 M. & W. 695. So where a tenant is permitted to remain in possession after his lease has become void. *Denn* d. *Brune Clerk* v. *Rawlins*, 10 East, 261. (If merely *suffered* to remain in such possession, see *Doe* d. *Biggs* v. *White*, 2 D. & R. 716; *Doe* d. *Thomas* v. *Roberts*, 16 M. & W. 778.) So where a dissenting minister, upon his election, is put into possession of a chapel and dwellinghouse by the trustees. *Doe* d. *Jones* v. *Jones*, 10 B. & C. 718; 5 Man. & Ry. 616; *Doe* d. *Nicholl* v. *M'Kaeg*, 10 B. & C. 721; 5 Man. &

ıese and the like cases the party is either strictly tenant
events is in lawful possession, and cannot be treated
r ejected until *after* such possession has been deter-
d of possession, breaking off the treaty, entry or other
f the will. Ros. Ev. 447 ; *ante,* 58. " It is not,
greement, but the *letting into possession,* that creates
for the person suffered so to occupy cannot, on the one
ered as a trespasser when he enters, and, on the other
ave more than the interest of a tenant at will, the
ıown to the law." *Per* Parke, B., in *Doe* d. *Gray*
. & W. 700 ; *Doe* d. *Hull* v. *Wood,* 14 M. & W. 682,

ts in 1825 were put in possession of land by the owner,
:cuted a conveyance of it to them, which was void by
atute of Mortmain, 9 Geo. 2, c. 36. The devisees of
ıght an action of ejectment in 1843. A demand of
ıade by the attorney, who afterwards brought the
 written authority, purporting to be signed by the
aintiff, but the attorney being unacquainted with their
vitness stated that he had a few days before the trial
ısors and showed them the authority, when they ac-
signatures to be theirs : held, first, that a demand of
ıecessary (*sed quære,* whether the implied tenancy at
:e on the vendor's death ?) Secondly. That the recog-
mand by bringing the action was insufficient. And,
e acknowledgment of the signatures by the lessors
itimate evidence that it was signed by them. *Doe* d.
:r, 14 Law J., N. S., Q. B., 181.

sary.]—A demand of possession is unnecessary where
ll has been determined by entry, or by anything
. Litt. 55 b, 57 b, 245 b, cited 9 M. & W. 646, *per*
ullimore, 2 Cr. M. & R. 120 ; 5 Tyr. 753 ; 1 Gale,
: d. *Davies* v. *Thomas,* 6 Exch. 854, 857 ; *Doe* d.
, 7 Exch. 89 ; *Pinhorn* v. *Souster,* 8 Exch. 763 ; *post,*

eement stipulates that the intended purchaser or lessee
ısion *until a specified day,* an ejectment may be main-
t day without any previous demand of possession.
v. *Sayer,* 3 Camp. 8 ; *Doe* d. *Moore* v. *Lawder,* 1
Doe d. *Parker* v. *Boulton,* 6 M. & S. 148. No de-
sion is necessary before commencing an ejectment
ıant at sufferance. *Doe* d. *Leeson* v. *Sayer,* 3 Camp.
: v. *Maisey,* 8 B. & C. 767 ; *Doe* d. *Fisher* v. *Giles,*
Moo. & P. 749 ; *Doe* d. *Moore* v. *Lawder,* 1 Stark.
Briggs v. *White,* 2 D. & R. 716. Although it seems
bly be turned out of possession without a previous
l. *Harrison* v. *Murrell,* 8 C. & P. 134, Lord Abinger,
intruder must be civilly requested to depart before
ly be used to turn him out.
is granted by a tenant for life, not in pursuance of a
lessor dies, the remainderman may maintain ejectment
vious notice to quit or demand of possession. *Doe* d.
rts, 16 M. & W. 778.

Where a rent-charge is granted, with a power to the grantee to enter, &c. in case of nonpayment for a specified time, the grantee may after the expiration of such time maintain ejectment, without any previous demand of the arrears. *Doe* d. *Biass* v. *Horseley*, 1 A. & E. 766; 3 N. & M. 567; *post,* Chap. LVII.

Demand of Possession pursuant to 15 & 16 *Vict. c.* 76, *s.* 213.] —It is generally advisable for a landlord to make a written demand of possession pursuant to sect. 213, and to obtain the tenant's refusal to comply therewith, *before* commencing an ejectment against a tenant who held under a lease or agreement in writing for any term or number of years certain, which has expired; or against a tenant from year to year under a lease or agreement in writing whose tenancy has been determined either by the landlord or tenant by a regular notice to quit. The necessity or advantage of such a demand, and the mode of proceeding, will be more fully considered in Chapter XXXVI. Such a demand may also prove useful in a subsequent action for double rent or double value. See Chapter LXIX.

Proof of Demand.]—Where a demand in writing is necessarily made, it must be admitted in the cause in the usual manner, or proved to have been signed by the claimants, *Doe* d. *Pulker* v. *Walker*, 14 Law J., N. S., Q. B., 181, or by their agent duly authorized in that behalf. The bringing of an ejectment, founded on such demand, is not sufficient evidence of the agent's authority, or of the demand having been signed by or on behalf of the claimants. *S. C.*

CHAPTER V.

...RAL REMEDIES FOR THE RECOVERY OF THE
POSSESSION OF LAND.

...lies for the recovery of *the possession* of any land,
...poreal hereditaments, situate in England, Wales, or
...weed, are : 1. By entry (*post*, Chap. VII.). 2. An
...nt, pursuant to the Common Law Procedure Act,
...p. VIII. *et seq.*): besides which, in some cases of
..., a summary remedy is provided, *ex. gr.* 3. An ac-
...n in the County Courts, by a landlord against his
...expiration or determination of the tenancy, in cases
...9 & 10 Vict. c. 95, s. 122 (*post*, Chap. LXX.). 4.
...cation to justices of the peace, by a landlord against
...the expiration or determination of the tenancy, in
...in the 1 & 2 Vict. c. 74, s. 1 (*post*, Chap. LXXI.).
...plication to justices, by a landlord against his tenant,
...es have been deserted, in cases falling within the 11
...16, as amended by 57 Geo. 3, c. 52 (*post*, Chap.
...summary application to justices, for parish or union-
...ursuant to 59 Geo. 3, c. 12, ss. 24, 25, or 5 & 6 Will.
...st, Chap. LXXIII.). 7. After a forcible entry or
...egal entry and forcible detainer, the possession may
...overed upon an indictment, or inquisition before jus-
...post, Chap. LXXIV.). 8. Under an arbitration and
...*orris* v. *Rosser*, 3 East, 11), with a rule of court for
...int to 17 & 18 Vict. c. 125, s. 16, and a writ of habere
...n thereon, pursuant to Reg. Gen., Mich. Vac., 1854,
...wer may be recovered by a writ of dower *unde nihil*

habet, or a writ of right of dower ; 3 Chit. Pl. 575—587 (7th ed.) ;
Roper on Husband and W. c. 9, s. 5 ; Roscoe on Real Actions, 29, 39 ;
Com. Dig. tit. "Dower;" 2 Wms. Saund. 43, 45d, notes ; *Garrard*
v. *Tuck*, 8 C. B. 231 ; *Watson* v. *Watson*, 10 C. B. 3 ; or by a bill or
claim in equity ; 1 Story, Eq. Jur. ch. xii.; *Mundy* v. *Mundy*, 2 Ves.
jun. 122 ; *D'Arcy* v. *Blake*, 2 Scho. & Lefroy (Irish), R. 391 ; *Bamford* v. *Bamford*, 5 Hare, 203 ; *Fry* v. *Noble*, 24 Law J., N. S.,
Chanc., 591 ; 25 *id.* 144 ; but not by ejectment until after it has been
duly assigned by metes and bounds. *Doe* d. *Nutt* v. *Nutt*, 2 C. & P.
430, Garrow, B. The reason is that a widow legally entitled to
dower has *no estate* in an undivided third part of the land, but *only a
right* to have a divided third part assigned to her by metes and bounds
according to law : after that has been done, she may, by entry or
ejectment, recover possession of her third part so assigned. *Doe* d.
Nutt v. *Nutt, supra.* Sometimes a widow is entitled to maintain
ejectment for her freebench in copyholds (*post*, Chap. LXVII. s. 6).

All *real* and *mixed* actions for the recovery of the possession of land,
or of any estate or interest therein (except as above mentioned, and
quare impedit), were abolished by 3 & 4 Will. 4, c. 27, s. 36.

The crown may recover lands by an information of intrusion ex-
hibited by the Attorney-General ; Manning's Exch. Prac. 198 ; *At-
torney-General* v. *Parsons*, 2 M. & W. 23 ; 5 Dowl. 165 ; *Attorney-
General* v. *Donaldson*, 7 M. & W. 422 ; 10 *id.* 117 ; 9 Dowl. 319 ;
Attorney-General v. *Churchill*, 8 M. & W. 171 ; *Attorney-General* v.
Hallett, 1 Exch. 211 ; 5 Dowl. & L. 87 ; or the grantee or lessee of the
crown may recover possession by ejectment. *Doe* d. *King Will.* 4 v.
Roberts, 13 M. & W. 520.

But an ejectment cannot be maintained against the crown, or any of
its immediate officers or servants in possession of land, &c. on behalf of
the crown. The proceedings in any such action may be stayed upon a
summary application by the Attorney-General on behalf of the crown.
Doe d. *Legh* v. *Roe*, 8 M. & W. 579. The remedy is by a petition
of right. *S. C.*; *The Warden and Commonalty of Sadlers' Company*,
4 Co. R. 55 a.

CHAPTER VI.

S AND PROCEEDINGS WHEREIN THE TITLE TO LAND
MAY COME IN QUESTION.

possession of land, &c. cannot be recovered except by
nt, or by some other mode of proceeding mentioned in
e, 61), yet the *right and title* to land may come in ques-
ided in various ways; *ex. gr.*—
on of trespass *quare clausum fregit*, with a plea that
ch, &c. was not the plaintiff's as alleged. 3 Chit. Pl.
Jones v. Chapman (in error), 2 Exch. 803; *Slocombe*
h. 119; 2 Low. M. & P. 33; *Murley v. M'Dermott,*
Browne v. Dawson, 12 A. & E. 624; 4 P. & D. 355;
lestone, 13 M. & W. 358; *Wright v. Burroughes,* 3
. & L. 438; *Barton v. Dawes,* 10 C. B. 261; *Rivett*
ling. 7; 2 Moo. & P. 12; *The Earl of Dunraven v.*
. B. 791; *Keyse v. Powell,* 2 E. & B. 132. Or a
tenementum. 3 Chit. Pl. 359 (7th ed.); *Brest v.*
W. 593; *S. C.* nom. *Grice v. Lever,* 9 Dowl. 246;
m, 8 M. & W. 381; 1 Dowl. N. S. 124; *Slocombe v.*
Ryan v. Clark, 14 Q. B. 65; 7 D. & L. 8; *Barton*
. B. 261. Or a plea of justification of the acts com-
irtue of some lawful right or title to the *locus in quo.*
(7th ed.); *Mayhew v. Suttle,* 4 E. & B. 347, 348;
land, 11 A. & E. 44; 3 P. & D. 128; *S. C.* (in error),
avanagh v. Gudge, 5 Man. & Gr. 726; 6 Scott, N. R.
. 928; *Wright v. Burroughes,* 3 C. B. 685; 4 D. &
. *Dixon,* 3 C. B. 776; *Smith v. Adkins,* 8 M. & W.
. S. 129; *Playfair v. Musgrove,* 14 M. & W. 239;
2.
n of trespass or trover for taking the plaintiff's cattle,

with a plea of justification that the defendant or his employer was lawfully possessed of a close, in which the cattle were *damage feasant;* wherefore he took them as a distress: replication, traversing the alleged possession of the close, or putting in issue the whole plea. 3 Chit. Pl. 351; *Id.* 290 (7th ed.); *Bond* v. *Downton,* 2 A. & E. 26; *Wormer* v. *Biggs,* 2 Car. & Kir. 31.

3. In an action of trespass or trover for taking the plaintiff's goods, with a plea that they were encumbering a close whereof the defendant or his employer was lawfully possessed, wherefore he removed them, &c.: replication, traversing the alleged possession of the close, or putting in issue the whole plea. 3 Chit. Pl. 352, 7th ed ; *Rea* v. *Sheward,* 2 M. & W. 424; *Ackland* v. *Lutley,* 9 A. & E. 879; 1 P. & D. 636; *Drewell* v. *Towler,* 3 B. & Adol. 735; or a plea of not guilty (by statute), or a plea of justification, as a distress for rent. *Brawley* v. *Wade,* M'Clel. 664; *Lloyd* v. *Davies,* 2 Ex. 103; *Moss* v. *Gallimore,* 1 Doug. 279; 1 Smith, L. C. 310. So in trover for sand, tin ore and gravel obtained by the plaintiff under a mining licence, whether granted by parol or under seal, with a plea of not guilty, and not possessed. *Northam* v. *Bowden,* 11 Exch. 70; 24 Law J., N. S., Ex., 237; *Rowe* v. *Brenton,* 8 B. & C. 737; 3 M. & R. 133.

4. In an action of trespass for an assault and battery, or for false imprisonment, with a plea of justification in defence of a messuage, &c. whereof the defendant or his employer was lawfully possessed, and into which the plaintiff intruded, and made a disturbance: wherefore, &c.: replication, putting in issue the whole plea, or traversing the alleged possession of the messuage, &c. 3 Chit. Pl. 323 (7th ed.); *Piggott* v. *Kemp,* 1 Cr. & Mee. 197; *Monks* v. *Dyke,* 4 M. & W. 567; *Fenn* v. *Grafton,* 2 Bing. N. C. 217; 3 Scott, 56; *Hayling* v. *Okey* (in error), 8 Exch. 531.

5. In an action of trespass for a forcible entry and detainer, founded on 8 Hen. 6, c. 9. *Cole* v. *Eagle,* 8 B. & C. 409.

6. In an action on the case for an injury to the plaintiff's reversion in buildings or land in the possession of his tenants, with special pleas denying his alleged title. *Hosking* v. *Phillips,* 3 Exch. 168; *Daintry* v. *Brocklehurst, id.* 207; *Wallis* v. *Harrison,* 5 M. & W. 142; 7 Dowl. 395.

7. In an action of debt or covenant for rent. *Franklin* v. *Carter,* 1 C. B. 750; 3 D. & L. 213; *Simons* v. *Farren,* 1 Bing. N. C. 126; *Hill* v. *Saunders* (in error), 4 B. & C. 529; 7 D. & R. 17: especially where the plaintiff sues as heir, executor or administrator of the lessor, or as assignee of the reversion; *Webb* v. *Russell,* 3 T. R. 393; *Russell* v. *Stokes,* 1 H. Blac. 562; *Burton* v. *Barclay and Perkins,* 7 Bing. 745; 5 Moo. & P. 785; *Baker* v. *Gosling,* 1 Bing. N. C. 19; 1 Scott, 58; *Robertson* v. *Norris,* 11 Q. B. 916; or as a tenant by the curtesy. *Voller* v. *Carter,* 4 E. & B. 173.

8. In an action for use and occupation. *Steele* v. *Mart,* 4 B. & C. 272; 6 D. & R. 392; *Phillips* v. *Pearce,* 5 B. & C. 433; 8 D. & R. 43; *Cornish* v. *Searell,* 8 B. & C. 471; 1 Man. & R. 703; *Fursdon, Executrix, &c.* v. *Clogg,* 10 M. & W. 572; *Selby* v. *Browne,* 7 Q. B. 620; *Rawson* v. *Eicke,* 7 A. & E. 451; 2 N. & P. 423; Arch. L. & T. 156.

9. In an action of replevin with a special avowry or cognizance for rent. 3 Chit. Pl. 475 (7th ed.); *Richmond* v. *Butcher,* Cro. Eliz. 217; *Rogers* v. *Pitcher,* 6 Taunt. 202; 1 Marsh, 541; *Staniland* v. *Lud-*

9; 7 D. & R. 484; *Neave* v. *Moss*, 1 Bing. 360;
.dges v. *Smith*, 5 Bing. 410; 2 Moo. & P. 740;
.ombe, 5 Q. B. 373; 1 D. & M. 406; *Hitchins* v.
.h. 50; *Foster* v. *Hayes*, 2 E. & B. 27; *Pluck* v.
Cl. 180; or for a rent-charge; *Beaumont* v. *Squire,*
.gowe's case, 1 Co. R. 146 b; or for damage feasant,
.; 2 Saund. 206 a, note 22; *Fraunce's case*, 8 Co. R.
277; *Wade* v. *Baker and Cole*, 1 Ld. Ray. 130;
., 7 T. R. 431; *Evans* v. *Rees*, 2 Q. B. 334; *Wil-*
15 Q. B. 782.

or trover for title deeds. *Slater* v. *Dangerfield,* 15
.bertson v. *Showler*, 13 M. & W. 600; 2 Dowl. &
. Administratrix, &c. v. *Baker*, 4 T. R. 229; *Goode*
. 189; *Lord* v. *Wardle*, 3 Bing. N. C. 680; 4 Scott,
.Dorrein, 9 Bing. 76; 2 Moo. & Sc. 114; *Harring-*
.& Adol. 170; *Lightfoot* v. *Leane*, 1 M. & W. 745;
. Davis v. *Vernon*, 6 Q. B. 443; *Foster* v. *Crabb,*
.stin v. *Croome*, Car. & M. 653. Trover does not
.t lessee to obtain possession of the indenture of lease
.n of the term by forfeiture or otherwise. *Ball* v.
R. 577; 3 M. & G. 242.

n by a vendor against the purchaser for not com-
.ase, with a plea denying the plaintiff's ability to
title. *Wheeler* v. *Wright*, 7 M. & W. 359; *Wilson*
*.*3. 616; *Watson* v. *Pearson*, 2 Exch. 581; *Martin*
*.*555; *Souter* v. *Drake*, 5 B. & Adol. 992; 3 N. &
v. *Keatley*, 1 Cr. M. & R. 117; 4 Tyr. 571.

.t by a purchaser against the vendor to recover back
.r without expenses, the defendant not being able to
.ccording to the contract or the conditions of sale.
*.*Taunt. 334; *Maberley* v. *Robins*, 5 Taunt. 625; 1
.er v. *Coombes*, 6 B. & C. 534; 9 D. & R. 562;
.es, 2 Bing. N. C. 252; 2 Scott, 411; *Barnett* v.
*.*W. 364; *Blake* v. *Phinn*, 3 C. B. 976; *Penniall* v.
B. 368; *Wilson* v. *Wilson*, 14 C. B. 616; *Forster*
. B. 155; *Blackburn* v. *Smith*, 2 Exch. 783; *Mon-*
Exch. 507.

.t without any pleadings, with a special case stated
.& 16 Vict. c. 76, s. 46. *Carpenter* v. *Dunsmac*, 3
.ler v. *Carter*, 4 E. & B. 173: *Alexander* v. *Alex-*
.); 24 Law J., N. S., C. P., 150. Or a special case
*.*3 & 4 Will. 4, c. 42, s. 25. *Doe d. Pemberton* v.
*.*W. 553; Tyr. & Gr. 1006; *Sadd* v. *The Maldon,*
.ntree Railway Company, 6 Exch. 143.

.ler of removal of a pauper, or an appeal against such
.r Law, tit. "Settlement by Estate," pp. 608—641
. Inhabitants of Burgate, 3 E. & B. 823; *Reg.* v.
.lifax, 4 E. & B. 647.

ther proceedings, both civil and criminal, including
.ts in equity, and proceedings in bankruptcy and
to land may come in question and be decided. But
or ejectment, or by an action or summary proceed-
in Chapter V., that the *possession can be recovered*

CHAPTER VII.

ENTRY.

Meaning of " Right of Entry."]—A right of entry (as the name imports) means a *legal right to enter and take actual possession* of land, &c. as incident to some estate or interest therein, not barred or extinguished by the Statute of Limitations (3 & 4 Will. 4, c. 27; *ante*, Chap. II.). Tomline's Law Dict. tit. " Entry;" 2 Arch. N. P. 304.

The right must be a *legal* right: a mere equitable title is not sufficient. *Goodright d. Lord Grosvenor* v. *Swymmer*, 1 Lord Ken. 385; *Doe d. Da Costa* v. *Wharton*, 8 T. R. 2; *Doe d. Hodsden* v. *Staple*, 2 T. R. 684; *Doe d. Shewin* v. *Wroot*, 5 East, 132; id. 138; 1 Smith, 363; *Doe d. Lloyd* v. *Passingham*, 6 B. & C. 305; *Doe d. Barker* v. *Goldsmith*, 2 Cr. & Jer. 674; 2 Tyr. 710; *Doe d. North* v. *Webber*, 3 Bing. N. C. 922; Ad. Eject. 28. A husband may be entitled in equity to curtesy in his deceased wife's equitable estate; but he cannot by virtue of such right maintain ejectment. *Doe d. Rees* v. *Williams*, 2 M. & W. 749.

The right must be a legal right *to actual possession* of the property. A right to the rent is not sufficient; *Doe d. Da Costa* v. *Wharton*, 8 T. R. 2; *Hill* v. *Saunders*, 2 Bing. 112; 9 Moore, 238; *Doe d. Fellowes* v. *Alford*, 1 Dowl. & L. 470; the remedy in such case being by distress; *Lloyd* v. *Davies*, 2 Exch. 103; *Moss* v. *Gallimore*, 1 Doug. 279; 1 Smith's L. C. 310; or action for the rent. *Voller* v. *Carter*, 4 E. & B. 173; *Rawson* v. *Eicke*, 7 A. & E. 451; 2 N. & P. 423.

A reversion or other future estate is not sufficient, unless coupled with some forfeiture or defeazance of the previous estate in possession. *Doe d. Wilson* v. *Phillips*, 2 Bing. 13; 9 Moore, 46; *Doe d. Wilson* v. *Abel*, 2 M. & S. 541. But after the expiration of a term or other estate, the immediate remainder or reversion becomes an estate in possession, and will warrant an actual entry.

An outstanding term is sufficient to defeat a right of entry or ejectment. *Doe d. Hodsden* v. *Staple*, 2 T. R. 684; *Goodtitle d. Jones* v.

es (in error), 7 T. R. 43; *Cotterell* v. *Hughes,* 15 C. B. 532; *Doe*
Earl of Egremont v. *Langdon,* 12 Q. B. 711; 18 Law J. (N. S.)
3. 17. Even a mere tenancy from year to year implied from proof
ayment of rent, and not shown to have been duly determined by a
ce to quit or otherwise, is sufficient to defeat an ejectment, although
defendants do not pretend to derive any title through or under such
nts, nor to defend on their behalf; *Doe* d. *Waxon* v. *Horn,* 3 M.
7. 333; *Doe* d. *Fellowes* v. *Alford,* 1 Dowl. & L. 470; unless
ed the defendant be estopped from setting up such outstanding
ncy. *Doe* d. *Manners* v. *Mizem,* 2 Moo. & Rob. 56; *Phipps* v.
thorpe, 1 B. & A. 50; *Doe* d. *Gaisford* v. *Stone,* 3 C. B. 176;
d. *Fellowes* v. *Alford, supra.*

ny person having a right of entry (as above described) may either
g an action of ejectment, or he may, by himself or his agent, *enter*
take actual possession of the property. *Davis* v. *Burrell and*
, 10 C. B. 821; *Brown* v. *Dawson,* 12 A. & E. 624; 4 P. & D.
; *Randall* v. *Stevens,* 3 E. & B. 641; *Wildboar* v. *Rainforth,* 8
c C. 4; 2 Man. & R. 185; *Davis* v. *Eyton,* 7 Bing. 154; 4 Moo.
'. 820; *Turner* v. *Meymott,* 1 Bing. 158; 7 Moo. 574; *Doe* d.
on v. *Phillips,* 2 Bing. 17, Best, C. J.; *Wright* v. *Burroughes,*
B. 699; 4 Dowl. & L. 438; *Doe* d. *Hanley* v. *Wood,* 2 B. & A.
741 (3rd point); *Mayhew* v. *Suttle,* 4 E. & B. 347. For this
ose he may employ an attorney, a house agent, a broker, a sheriff's
er, or any other person or persons; *Doe* d. *Wilson* v. *Abel,* 2 M.
543, 547; or he may grant a new lease. *Doe* d. *Hanley* v.
d, 2 B. & A. 724, 741. A mere verbal request or authority is
cient, or any unstamped note or writing. A power of attorney
r seal is not necessary. *Fitchett* v. *Adams,* 2 Stra. 1128, 1129,
cur. An entry by a stranger on behalf of the party entitled, but
out his authority, if subsequently ratified by him, operates as a
l entry. *Fitchett* v. *Adams (supra).* An entry by one of two
ons jointly entitled amounts, in contemplation of law, to an entry
oth. *Hingen* v. *Payn,* Cro. Jac. 475.

lawful entry into any part of the property in the name of the
le enures as an entry into every part; Litt. s. 417; *Richard Cot-*
case, Cro. Eliz. 189; unless the land lie in different counties, in
h case a separate entry must be made in each county. Co. Litt.
b. So if there be two or more disseisors, as their seisin is distinct,
so must be the act which divests that seisin. Id. 252 b.

ie moment the party having a right of entry enters, either by
elf or his agent, on any part of the property for the purpose of
1g possession, he thereupon becomes *legally seised or possessed*
ording to the nature of his title), and any previous tenants in pos-
on and all other persons, who afterwards remain on the property
out his leave or licence, and against his will, become trespassers,
as such liable to an action of trespass *quare clausum fregit. But-*
v. *Butcher,* 7 B. & C. 309; 1 M. & R. 220; *Hey* v. *Moorhouse,*
ng. N. C. 52; 8 Scott, 156; Co. Litt. 245.

1 the other hand, if the party so entering, or his agent, be sued in
ass by the previous tenant, he may plead *liberum tenementum,*
ander it justify an entry even with strong hand, whilst the plaintiff
intruder) and his family were actually in the house; *Burling* v.
l, 11 Q. B. 904; *Davison* v. *Wilson,* id. 890; *Meriton* v. *Coombes,*
w., M. & P. 510; *Harvey* v. *Bridges,* 14 M. & W. 442,

Parke, B.; *S. C.* 3 Dowl. & L. 60; or he may plead a lease to himself from the freeholder, by virtue whereof he entered and became possessed, and afterwards ceased to have the actual possession thereof; and that afterwards, in order to regain possession (the demise and tenancy still subsisting), he broke and entered, &c.; *Mayhew* v. *Suttle,* 4 E. & B. 347; or he may plead that the close in which, &c. was not *at the said time when, &c.* the close of the plaintiff, as alleged; and under such plea the defendant may show that he entered by virtue of a lawful right to the possession of the close, either in himself or in some other person, under whose authority he acted. *Jones* v. *Chapman* (in error), 2 Exch. 803; *Browne* v. *Dawson,* 12 A. & E. 624; 4 P. & D. 355.

Actual entry with sufficient title changes the legal possession in an instant. *Randall* v. *Stevens,* 2 E. & B. 641; *Davis* v. *Burrell,* 10 C. B. 821. The reason for this is well explained by Maule, J., in *Jones* v. *Chapman* (in error), 2 Exch. 820, 821, as follows:—" I agree with the exception of the plaintiff in error, that the question raised by the issue of 'not possessed' is, whether the plaintiff was in *actual possession* or not; but it seems to me that as soon as a person is entitled to possession, and enters in the assertion of that possession, or, which is exactly the same thing, any other person enters by command of that lawful owner so entitled to possession, the law immediately vests the actual possession in the person who has so entered. If there are two persons in a field, each asserting that the field is his, and each doing some act in the assertion of the right of possession, and if the question is, which of these two is in actual possession, I answer, the person who has the title is in actual possession, and the other person is a trespasser. They differ in no other respects. You cannot say that it is *joint* possession; you cannot say it is a possession as tenants in common. It cannot be denied that one is in possession, and the other is a trespasser. Then that is to be determined, as it seems to me, by the fact of the *title,* each having the same apparent actual possession. The question as to which of the two really is in possession is determined by the fact of the possession following the title; that is, by the law, which makes it follow the title." There are many other authorities to the same effect, but none in which the law is so clearly laid down. *Anon.,* 1 Salk. 246; *Doe* d. *Barney* v. *Adams,* 2 Cro. & Jer. 235, Lord Lyndhurst, C. B.; id. 236, Bayley, B.; *S. C.* 2 Tyr. 289; *Browne* v. *Dawson,* 12 A. & E. 624; 4 P. & D. 355.

Immediately upon entry the party is by law *remitted* to his previous estate; (that is to say) he becomes seised or possessed of the land for such an estate therein (if any) as was legally vested in him before and at the time of the entry. Lit. ss. 653—696; *Taylor* d. *Atkins* v. *Horde,* 1 Burr. 114; *Id.* 90; *Doe* d. *Daniell* v. *Woodroffe,* 10 M. & W. 632; 2 H. L. Cas. 811; *Spotswood* v. *Barrow,* 5 Exch. 113, Rolfe, B.; Ad. Eject. 286, 308. "If he has a freehold, he is in as a freeholder; if he has a chattel interest, he is in as a termor; and in respect of the freehold, his possession enures according to right. If he has no title, he is in as a trespasser; and, without any re-entry by the true owner, is liable to account for the profits." *Per cur.* in *Taylor* d. *Atkyns* v. *Horde,* 1 Burr. 114; *Id.* 90.

A surrenderor of copyholds who lawfully re-enters for a condition broken shall be reinstated in his former estate, free from the sur-

Simonds v. *Lawnd,* Cro. Eliz. 239. So a person who *law-*
ers and avoids a lease under a provision for re-entry, or for
f a condition, thereupon becomes legally entitled to possession,
ι the lease and the term thereby granted. *S. C.*
ctment for nonpayment of rent may sometimes be maintained
e 15 & 16 Vict. c. 76, s. 210, where an entry without a pre-
ctment would not be lawful, no demand of payment having
y made according to the provisions of the common law.
a lawful and peaceable entry has been made by the person
ntitled to actual possession, or his agent, he may proceed to
of possession the previous tenants and their servants, &c. This
lone, without violating the law or any of the statutes against
:ntries and detainers, in the following manner:—1. He should
quest one of them to depart. 2. In case of refusal or neglect,
l gently lay hands upon him, and turn him out: a very slight
ufficient, if it be continued and no actual or passive resistance
. 3. In case of any resistance, so much force may be used as
ably necessary to overcome the resistance; but excessive vio-
ιuld be avoided. The like course should be adopted towards
:on separately. If an action or actions of trespass be afterwards
the defendant may plead a justification. *See the forms, Ap-*
Vos. 402, 403; *Smith* v. *Adkins,* 8 M. & W. 362; 1 Dowl. N. S.
the party complain of being turned out of his dwellinghouse
with a strong hand, &c., the defendant (being owner of the
or his servant may plead " *liberum tenementum ;*" *Davison*
n, 11 Q. B. 890; *Burling* v. *Read,* id. 904; *Meriton* v.
, 1 Low. M. & P. 510; or that it was not the plaintiff's
close. *Jones* v. *Chapman* (in error), 2 Ex. 803. "Formerly
was entertained whether a landlord was justified in entering
lling the tenant on the expiration of his term; but that doubt
set at rest ever since the case of *Taunton* v. *Costar* (7 T. R.
ιject, of course, to any question of excess." *Per* Wilde, C. J.,
ιt v. *Burroughes,* 3 C. B. 685, 699; 4 D. & L. 438; and see
:e, B., in *Harvey* v. *Brydges,* 14 M. & W. 442; 3 D. & L.
med in error, 1 Exch. 261. If the plaintiff complain of an
the defendant may plead that he was lawfully possessed of a
ιat the plaintiff was on it against the defendant's will; that
ιdant requested the plaintiff to leave, which he refused to do,
ιn the defendant gently laid his hands on the plaintiff, and
im off, which is the alleged assault, &c. 3 Chit. Pl. 323—326
; *Roberts* v. *Tayler,* 1 C. B. 117; 3 Dowl. & L. 1; *Jelly* v.
, Car. & Mar. 270. But *liberum tenementum* is not sufficient
· (*inter alia*) an assault. *Roberts* v. *Tayler, supra.*
indictment for a forcible entry be preferred, the defence will
That the prosecutor was not legally seised at the time of the
offence, and consequently is not entitled to restitution. *Cole*
, 8 B. & C. 409. 2. As to the force, &c., that the defendant
ιeaceably, and not with strong hand or multitude of people;
the force proved was *after the lawful and peaceable entry,*
: the legal seizin or possession thereby acquired; and that
:e was occasioned by the prosecutor's own misconduct; and
prosecutor is the party really liable to an indictment for what
:e. Hawk. P. C. c. 64, ss. 23, 34, 53; *per* Parke, J., in *Rex*
y, 4 B. & Adol. 312; 1 N. & M. 58; *post,* Chap. LXXIV.

If an indictment for a forcible detainer be preferred, the defence will be that the defendant's *entry was lawful*, and there cannot be a forcible detainer within the meaning of the statute, except after an unlawful entry. *Rex* v. *Oakley*, 4 B. & Adol. 307; 1 N. & M. 58; *Rex* v. *Wilson*, 3 A. & E. 817; 5 N. & M. 164; *post*, Chap. LXXIV.

If the right of entry be *clear, and free from all doubt*, the remedy by entry is in many cases preferable to an action of ejectment, because the possession is thereby obtained immediately and without any expense; whereas the remedy by ejectment is always attended with more or less delay and expense, and sometimes the defendant may not be able to pay the costs: besides which, *extra costs* are not uncommon as between attorney and client, although not recognized by law as between party and party. *Doe* d. *Drax* v. *Filliter*, 11 M. & W. 80; 2 D. & L. 186; *Hodges* v. *The Earl of Lichfield*, 1 Bing. N. C. 500; 1 Scott, 492; *Grace* v. *Morgan*, 2 Bing. N. C. 534; 2 Scott, 790.

On the other hand, if the right of entry be not clear, it is generally more advisable to bring ejectment, and to have the right determined in the first instance; because, if the party or his agent enter and take possession, he may be sued in trespass; *Kavanagh* v. *Gudge*, 5 Man. & Gr. 726; 6 Scott, N. S., 508; 1 Dowl. & L. 928, *S. C.*; *Watson* v. *Waltham*, 2 A. & E. 485; 4 N. & M. 537; *Smallman* v. *Agborow*, Cro. Jac. 417; *Turner* v. *Meymott*, 1 Bing. 158; 7 Moore, 574; and perhaps have vindictive damages awarded against him, especially if any force were used in taking possession; *Merest* v. *Harvey*, 5 Taunt. 442; 1 Marsh. 139; *Williams* v. *Currie*, 1 C. B. 841; *Huxley* v. *Berg*, 1 Stark. R. 98; *Martin* v. *Parker*, 5 M. & W. 351; *Wild* v. *Holt*, 9 M. & W. 672; 1 Dowl., N. S., 876; or he may have his cattle distrained upon for damage feasant, and so be obliged to replevy and find sureties for double their value, and afterwards to bring a plaint in replevin in the County Court, and to remove it into one of the superior courts; *Taunton* v. *Costar*, 7 T. R. 431; and ultimately, if successful, recover only the expense of the replevin bond and costs, without any damages for the annoyance and inconvenience occasioned by the distress. Ros. Ev. 486 (7th ed.); *Phillips* v. *Berryman*, 3 Doug. 286. Sometimes an ejectment is maintainable (under 15 & 16 Vict. c. 76, s. 210) where an entry without ejectment would be unlawful, *ex. gr.*, for nonpayment of rent, where half a year's rent is in arrear, and no sufficient distress on the premises to satisfy the arrears, and the landlord has power to re-enter for nonpayment of rent; but no demand of the rent was made on the last day for saving the forfeiture pursuant to the strict rules of the common law. *Post*, Chap. XXXIX., Sect. 2.

If the right of entry be clear and free from all doubt, but the tenant in possession is a strong resolute man, or an obstinate litigious person, it is generally more advisable to proceed by ejectment than by entry. It is not easy to turn out such a person and his family and servants and their respective goods and chattels in a legal manner, without being guilty of a breach of the peace, or of any excess of force and violence. A timid person would be afraid to make the attempt, either on his own behalf or as agent for another. A person not well acquainted with the law would not know how to do it in a proper or legal manner. *Ante*, 69.

The law relating to forcible entries and forcible detainers is by no means clear, but open to much misconstruction, and very few persons are acquainted with it. See *post*, Chap. LXXIV. The general ι seems to be that no force whatever can be legally used; hich there is always the danger of being guilty of some force and violence where resistance is offered. Ros. Ev. 502; . 491, 505, 519 (7th edit.); *Weaver* v. *Bush*, 8 T. R. 78; *Pol- . Wright*, 8 Q. B. 197; *Penn* v. *Ward*, 2 Cr. M. & R. 338; . *Burroughes*, 3 C. B. 699, *per* Wilde, C. J. Neither judges ι favour persons who, instead of proceeding by ejectment, ι take the law into their own hands, and use force and vio- effect their object. An erroneous verdict or judgment is ι given in such cases. *Hillary* v. *Gay*, 6 C. & P. 284, Lord t, C. B.; *Newton and Wife* v. *Harland*, 1 Man. & Gr. 644; ν. R. 474. (These two cases have in effect been overruled ecisions.)

nes considerable advantages may be obtained by proceeding ent rather than by entry, *ex. gr.* as between landlord and here there has been a lease or agreement *in writing*, and the ιnded, or been duly determined by a regular notice to quit, the ιy be compelled to find sureties to pay the damages and costs will be permitted to defend the action. 15 & 16 Vict. c. 76, In ejectment for a forfeiture by nonpayment of rent, six months after execution is executed the landlord will hold d from the lease both at law and in equity. S. 210. So it lly more advisable for a mortgagee to proceed by action of , rather than by entry. Ss. 219, 220. Lastly.—The title to . is much less likely to be called in question after an eject- ι after an entry, and a second ejectment to try the same title ζenerally be permitted until the costs of the previous action ι paid; *post*, 77; and sometimes security for the defendant's he subsequent action will be ordered. 17 & 18 Vict. c. 125, *st*, 81.

CHAPTER VIII.

POINTS TO BE CONSIDERED BEFORE COMMENCING AN EJECTMENT.

BEFORE commencing an action of ejectment, the following points should be considered, viz. :—

1. Whether the property claimed is of such a nature and so situate, that an ejectment will lie for it, *i. e.* does it consist of any land, tenements or *corporeal* hereditaments situate in England or Wales, or the town of Berwick-upon-Tweed, or of any undivided part or share of any such land, &c.? For a particular statement of the various sorts of property for which an ejectment may be brought, and how it should be described in the writ, see *post*, Chap. IX.

2. Who is or are *legally entitled to actual possession* of such property? An *interesse termini*, although a mere right and no estate before entry, is sufficient to support an ejectment after the day appointed for the commencement of the term. *Post*, Chap. XLIII. ; *Doe* d. *Parsley* v. *Day*, 2 Q. B. 156, *per cur.*; *Ryan* v. *Clark*, 14

3. 73; 7 Dowl. & L. 8; Co. Lit. 46 b; Shep. Touch. 269. As to nature of an *interesse termini*, and how it may be released, sur-[?]ered, merged or assigned, see *Doe* d. *Rawlings* v. *Walker*, 5 B. & [?]11; 7 D. & R. 487. In ejectment a legal title is sufficient, not-[?]standing the defendant has an equitable title. *Doe* d. *Hughes* v. [?], 9 M. & W. 372; *Id.* 377, Alderson, B.; *S. C.* 1 Dowl. N. S. ; *Goodtitle* d. *Estwick* v. *Way*, 1 T. R. 735; *Keene* v. *Deardon*, [?]st, 248; *Fenny* d. *Eastham* v. *Child*, 2 M. & S. 255; 2 Arch. P. 306. An equitable defence cannot be pleaded in ejectment. [?]ve v. *Avery*, 16 C. B. 328. A lease from *cestui que trust* cannot [?]et up against the trustee in any case without the aid of a [?]t of equity. *Baker* v. *Mellish*, 10 Ves. 554; Ad. Eject. 68; and *Doe* d. *Davies* v. *Evans*, 9 M. & W. 48. Generally speaking, a [?]ly equitable title to the land, or a legal right to the rents and [?]its, is not sufficient to support an ejectment. *Ante*, 66. But a by estoppel will sometimes do, as against any tenant or other [?]on subject and liable to such estoppel. *Francis* v. *Doe* d. *Harvey* [?]error), 4 M. & W. 331, 336; 7 Dowl. 193; *post*, Chap. XXI. [?]tle by Estoppel."

Whether such legal or other title has been barred or extinguished [?]he Statute of Limitations, 3 & 4 Will. 4, c. 27. *Ante*, Chap. II.

Whether the claimant has in his possession or power, or can [?]pel the production of sufficient legal evidence of his title? See [?]p. XV. "Advice on Evidence." The title deeds, or an abstract [?]eof, should be carefully examined so far as may be necessary. The [?]t or question (if any) likely to arise in the action should be ascer-[?]ed and duly considered. By the Directions to the Masters of the [?]rt, dated 27th January, 1853, they are to allow in ejectment for [?]structions to sue and examining deeds, 13s. 4d.—if a question of , 1l. 1s." 1 Ell. & Blac. lxxi.

Whether any notice to quit or demand of possession is necessary [?]re action? And if so, whether it has been duly given or made? [?]etimes a demand of possession in writing is necessary, or at all [?]ts expedient. 15 & 16 Vict. c. 76, s. 213; *ante*, 60.

Whether the remedy by entry be not more advisable than an [?]ment? *Ante*, 70. After such entry, if actual possession be not [?]eby effectually obtained, an action of trespass *quare clausum fregit* be maintained against the tenant, or any other person who con-[?]es in possession. *Butcher* v. *Butcher*, 7 B. & C. 399; 1 Man. & [?]220; *Hey* v. *Moorhouse*, 6 Bing. N. C. 52; 8 Scott, 156; Co. [?]245. A person may sometimes maintain trespass *quare clausum* [?]it where he could not prove sufficient title to support an ejectment. [?]ham v. *Peat*, 1 East, 244; *Doe* d. *Crisp* v. *Barber*, 2 T. R. 749; [?]d. *Carter* v. *Barnard*, 13 Q. B. 945; *Barton* v. *Dawes*, 10 C. B. ; *Matson* v. *Cook*, 4 Bing. N. C. 392; 6 Scott, 179; *Catteris* v. [?]per. 4 Taunt. 547; *Woodcock* v. *Gibson*, 4 B. & C. 462; *Harper* [?]harlesworth, *Id.* 574; 6 D. & R. 572; *Crosby* v. *Wadsworth*, 6 [?], 602; 2 Smith, 559. So he may maintain trover for minerals, ore, sand, and gravel, obtained by him under a mining licence, [?]ther granted by parol or under seal, and which has been *taken* [?] him by the defendant; *Northam* v. *Bowden*, 11 Exch. 70; 24 [?] J., N. S., Exch., 237; whereas he could not maintain ejectment. [?]d. *Hanley* v. *Wood*, 2 B. & A. 724. If the tenant or other person [?]t the entry with strong hand and in a forcible manner, the claimant may maintain an action of trespass under 8 Hen. 6, c. 9, and thereby recover treble damages, with full costs, charges and expenses, as between attorney and client; *post*, Chap. LXXIV. s. 5; provided the claimant be a freeholder, but not otherwise; *Cole* v. *Eagle*, 8 B. & C. 409: or instead of such action, the claimant, whether a freeholder, leaseholder or copyholder, may indict the tenant for a forcible detainer, and under such indictment obtain restitution of possession. *Post*, Chap. LXXIV. s. 6. But it is in the discretion of the court to award restitution or not under such indictment. *Reg.* v. *Harland*, 2 Moo. & Rob. 141; 8 A. & E. 826; 1 P. & D. 93, *S. C.* Or instead of an indictment, the claimant may complain before a justice or justices of the forcible detainer, and obtain restitution in a summary manner. *Post*, Chap. LXXIV. s. 8. But if the justices decline to hear and determine such complaint, or to award restitution, the Court of Queen's Bench will not compel them to do so. *Ex parte William Davy*, 2 Dowl. N. S. 24.

An entry is not generally so advantageous as an ejectment, where a tenant under a lease or agreement *in writing* wrongfully holds over after his term has expired, or been determined by a regular notice to quit; 15 & 16 Vict. c. 76, s. 213; *post*, Chap. XXXVI. s. 1; nor as between mortgagee and mortgagor or a subsequent mortgagee. *Id.* ss. 219, 220; *post*, Chap. XLIV. s. 1.

7. Whether an action for possession in the County Court (*post*, Chap. LXX.), or a summary remedy before justices (*post*, Chap. LXXI.), be not practicable and more expedient than an ejectment.

8. Whether the question of law or fact (if any) likely to arise, may not be more conveniently, or more advantageously for the claimant, raised in some other form of action or proceeding (*ante*, Chap. VI.), although, perhaps, *the possession* of the property cannot be thereby recovered. Sometimes the *onus* of proof as to the title, &c. may be thrown on the opposite party, by adopting some other mode of proceeding, *ex. gr.* an action of trespass (*ante*, 73); *Catteris* v. *Cowper*, 4 Taunt. 547; *Matson* v. *Cook*, 4 Bing. N. C. 392; 6 Scott, 179; *Barton* v. *Davies*, 10 C. B. 261; *Brest* v. *Levy*, 7 M. & W. 593; *S. C.* nom. *Grice* v. *Lever*, 9 Dowl. 246; *Woodcock* v. *Gibson*, 4 B. & C. 462; or an action of trover for minerals, tin ore, gravel, and sand, obtained by the plaintiff under a mining licence, and taken from him by the defendant. *Northam* v. *Bowden*, 11 Exch. 70; 24 Law J., N. S., Exch., 237.

9. If an ejectment be determined on, the next thing to consider is, in whose name or names the action should be brought? Generally speaking, it should be brought by the person or persons *legally entitled to actual possession* of the property (*ante*, 66). But sometimes from the state of the title, or the evidence thereof, or the absence of complete information on the subject, it is doubtful in whom the legal estate is vested, and therefore it may be expedient to bring the action in the names of several persons, the legal estate certainly being in some or one of them, which will be sufficient to support the action. 15 & 16 Vict. c. 76, s. 180; *Doe* d. *Danson* v. *Parke*, 4 A. & E. 816. So where a title by estoppel can be proved in one or more of the claimants as against the intended defendant or defendants, but the legal estate is vested in some other claimant or claimants, all should join. *See Index,* tit. "*Estoppel.*" Sometimes proof of the title of a particular claimant is short and clear, and can only be disproved by evidence showing the

n another claimant. In such case both names may be used
tage. *Doe* d. *Danson* v. *Parke*, 4 A. & E. 816 ; *Roe* d.
Urry v. *Harvey*, 4 Burr. 2484.

ral estate be vested in trustees, but the action is brought by
ue trust, he should, if possible, first obtain their authority or
their names being used as claimants ; but if they unreason-
. the *cestui que trust* should offer to indemnify them against
f the action (including the defendant's costs), and after-
lout their consent, use their names, *together with his own*,
:s. The trustees will not be able to discontinue or defeat
, except with leave of the court or a judge. 15 & 16 Vict.
1 (*post*, Chap. XXXIII.) ; *Doe* d. *Hurst* v. *Clifton*, 4 A.
Archard v. *Coulstrong*, 6 Man. & Gr. 75 ; *Doe* d. *Prosser*
Dowl. 580 ; *Doe* d. *Vine* v. *Figgins*, 3 Taunt. 440 ; *Doe* d.
. Roe, 2 Chit. R. 171 ; *Doe* d. *Hammick* v. *Fellis, Id.*

nt subsequent mistakes and disputes, the claimant's attorney
e a *retainer in writing* from the person or persons to whom
to look for payment of his costs. *See the Form, Appendix,*
But this is not absolutely necessary : an oral retainer is suf-
it may be implied by a jury upon proof of the party at-
the attorney's office from time to time, and giving direc-

next thing to be considered is, who should be named in the
efendant or defendants ? The general rule on this subject
e action should be brought against *all the tenants in pos-*
'. every person who occupies, as a tenant or undertenant,
f the property. *Doe* d. *Smith* v. *Roe*, 5 Dowl. 254 ;
'liamson v. *Roe*, 10 Moore, 493 ; *Doe* d. *Lord Darlington*
B. & C. 259 ; *Doe* d. *Turner* v. *Gee*, 9 Dowl. 612. Even
ho has the exclusive use of certain rooms and apartments
the property claimed) for a short term may be included ;
ncson v. *Roe*, 1 D. & L. 657 ; *Doe* d. *Thready* v. *Roe*, 1
3. 261 ; and see *Brawley* v. *Wade*, M'Clel. 664 ; but this
l, because under a writ of *habere facias possessionem* the
ld, upon being requested so to do, turn everybody out of
and if the lodger afterwards brought trespass against the
nd the sheriff and his officer, or any or either of them, the
might justify, *without the aid of the judgment and writ:*
its by virtue of their title and right to possession, and the
his officer, as the servants and by the command of the
3 Chit. Pl. 360—363 (7th ed) ; *Jones* v. *Jones*, 16 M. &
D. & L. 494 ; *Ewer* v. *Jones*, 9 Q. B. 623. The fact that
r his officer professed at the time to act under and by virtue
: would not negative the above defence, because if he *did*
he was *legally entitled to do*, it matters not *what he said*, or
ofessed to do. *Crowther* v. *Ramsbottom*, 7 T. R. 654, 657 ;
unt, 9 Exch. 14 ; *Wootley* v. *Gregory*, 2 You. & Jer. 536 ;
lle v. *The College of Physicians*, 12 Mod. 386 ; *Holt*, C. J.,
1. 658 ; *Blessley* v. *Sloman*, 3 M. & W. 40 ; and see 11 M.
16 M. & W. 154 ; 1 Wms. Saund. 347 c, n. (4). But see
vens v. *Lord*, 7 A. & E. 610 ; 2 N. & P. 604 ; 6 Dowl. 256.
seldom, if ever, that a mere lodger ventures to bring an

action against the sheriff, &c. for anything done on the execution of a writ of possession. His interest in the property is generally too trifling to make it worth his while to incur the trouble, risk, and expense, more especially as in most cases he would probably fail in the action, for the reasons above mentioned.

Mere friends and visitors of the tenant in possession, and his wife, children, and servants, do not *occupy as tenants*, and therefore should not be included in the writ as defendants. The possession of a servant is in contemplation of law the possession of his master; *Bertie* v. *Beaumont*, 16 East, 33; *Mayhew* v. *Suttle*, 4 E. & B. 347; but a servant may so act as to render himself personally liable to be sued in ejectment. *Doe d. James* v. *Staunton*, 1 Chit. R. 113; *Doe d. Atkins* v. *Roe*, 2 Chit. R. 179.

Any third person under whom any tenant in possession holds, but who does not himself occupy as a tenant, need not be named in the writ; but the tenant in possession may be left to give him notice of the writ, pursuant to 15 & 16 Vict. c. 76, s. 209.

Lunatics or criminals in confinement do not occupy as tenants any part of the building in which they are confined.

Ejectment will not lie against the crown or any of its immediate officers or servants in possession of land, &c. on behalf of the crown; therefore, if an ejectment be brought, the court will stay it, upon a summary application by the Attorney-General. *Doe d. Legh* v. *Roe*, 8 M. & W. 579. The remedy is by a petition of right. *S. C.*; *The Warden and Commonalty of Sadlers' Case*, 4 Co. R. 55 a.

When the tenements claimed, and the tenants thereof, are numerous, it is frequently advisable to bring two or more distinct ejectments, rather than one action against all of them for the whole of the property. The exercise of a sound discretion and judgment on this point may sometimes save much trouble.

11. In what manner the property should be described in the writ (see *post*, Chap. IX.). Generally speaking, it should be described " with reasonable certainty," *i.e.* as accurately as conveniently may be, and not in the loose and exaggerated manner which prevailed before the Common Law Procedure Act, 1852; but at the same time care should be taken to *state enough*.

12. Whether possession should be claimed from the date of the teste and issuing of the writ, or from any and what previous day. *Post*, Chap. IX.

13. In which of the superior courts the action should be brought? Sometimes a good deal may depend upon this, especially where there has been a recent decision upon the point or question likely to arise.

14. Whether the writ should issue in the usual form (*Appendix, No.* 15); or pursuant to 15 & 16 Vict. c. 76, s. 217 (*Appendix, No.* 17); or with a notice for bail, pursuant to sect. 213 (*Appendix, No.* 16).

15. *Effect of a Judgment in Ejectment.*]—By 15 & 16 Vict. c. 76, s. 207, " The effect of a judgment in an action of ejectment under this act shall be the same as that of a judgment in the action of ejectment heretofore used."

By a judgment in ejectment the claimant recovers *only the possession* of the land claimed, or some part thereof (with or without costs), but *not any particular estate or interest therein.* His right and title to

ie land are precisely the same as if he had never been disseised or
dispossessed. "If he has a freehold, he is in as a freeholder; if he has
a chattel interest, he is in as a termor; and in respect of the freehold,
his possession enures *according to right.* If he has no title, he is in
as a trespasser; and, without any re-entry by the true owner, is liable
to account for the profits." *Per cur.* in *Taylor* d. *Atkyns* v. *Horde,* 1
Burr. 114; *Id.* 90; Ad. Eject. 286, 308. Upon obtaining possession
under an ejectment, or by entry, the party is *remitted* to his old estate
(if any), and cannot by a disclaimer or otherwise repudiate such title.
Id. ss. 659—696; *Doe* d. *Daniell* v. *Woodroffe,* 10 M. & W. 632;
H. L. Cas. 811; *Spotswood* v. *Barrow,* 5 Exch. 113; *ante,* 68.
As a general rule a judgment in ejectment does not conclude the
title. Run. Eject. 12; *Doe* d. *Strode* v. *Seaton,* 2 Cr. M. & R. 728,
731, 732; *infra.* Therefore an unsuccessful claimant may imme-
ately commence another ejectment in the same or another court; *Doe*
Davis v. *Evans,* 9 M. & W. 48; or a defendant against whom judgment has been obtained (whether by default or after verdict) may immediately commence an ejectment against the previous claimant or his
tenant in possession to recover back possession of the land. Ad. Eject.
308; *Foster* v. *The Earl of Derby,* 1 A. & E. 783, 784, 791, note (b);
Doe d. *Hutchins* v. *Lewis,* 1 Burr. 614, 619; 2 Ld. Ken. 320, *S. C.*
Indeed this is frequently done. The judgment in the first action is
admissible in evidence as between the same parties and their privies in
estate, and of course has some weight with the jury, especially after a
verdict. *Doe* d. *Strode* v. *Seaton,* 2 Cr. M. & R. 728, 731, 732. But
it is not conclusive, because a party may have a title to possession at
one time and not at another. *Id.* 732, *per* Lord Abinger, C. B. A judgment is in no case conclusive unless pleaded by way of estoppel. It
cannot be pleaded in ejectment, for no such plea is permitted in that
form of action. *Id.* 732, Parke, B. But in trespass for mesne profits,
&c., if the defendant plead *liberum tenementum,* or that the close was
not the plaintiff's as alleged, the plaintiff may reply the judgment by
way of estoppel, as to the time covered by such judgment. See *Appendix, Nos.* 397, 398, 399; *Aslin* v. *Parker,* 2 Burr. 665; 1 Smith,
L. C. 264; *Vooght* v. *Winch,* 2 B. & A. 662; *Doe* v. *Huddart,* 2 Cr.
M. & R. 316; 5 Tyr. 846; 4 Dowl. 437, *S. C.; Doe* v. *Wellsman,* 2
Exch. 368; 6 Dowl. & L. 179; *Matthews* v. *Osborne,* 13 C. B. 919;
Wilkinson v. *Kirby,* 15 C. B. 430. A judgment in ejectment is admissible in evidence between the same parties and their respective
privies in estate, *ex gr.,* their heirs, executors, administrators and assigns. Ros. Ev. 137 (7th ed.). But a judgment in ejectment, obtained
against a mortgagor by a second or subsequent mortgagee, is not admissible evidence against a prior mortgagee. *Doe* d. *Smith* v. *Webber,*
8 A. & E. 119. The evidence of a deceased witness, examined on a
previous ejectment between the same parties (or their *subsequent* privies
in estate) relating to the same title, whether for the same land or not,
is admissible in a subsequent ejectment, upon proof of his death. *Earl*
of Derby v. *Foster,* 1 A. & E. 791, note (b); *Sherwin* v. *Clarges,* 12
Mod. 343. But if either of the parties be different, and there be no
subsequent privity of estate, such evidence is inadmissible. *Doe* d.
Foster v. *The Earl of Derby,* 1 A. & E. 783.

16. *Stay of Proceedings until Costs of a previous Ejectment on the
same Title are paid.*]—In order to lessen, and to prevent as much as

possible, the annoyance and vexation of repeated ejectments to try *the same title*, the courts have by degrees established, as a general rule, that the proceedings in a subsequent action of ejectment will be stayed, upon the application of the defendant, until the costs of a previous ejectment are paid, provided both actions were brought to try the *same title*; *Keene* d. *Angel* v. *Angel*, 6 T. R. 740; *Doe* d. *Feldon* v. *Roe*, 8 T. R. 645; *Doe* d. *Cotterell* v. *Roe*, 1 Chit. R. 195; Ad. Eject. 312; but not otherwise. *Doe* d. *Bailey* v. *Bennett*, 9 Dowl. 1012; *Doe* d. *Henry* v. *Gustard*, 4 Man. & Gr. 987; 2 Dowl. N. S. 615; *Doe* d. *Evans* v. *Snead*, 2 Dowl. & L. 119. The rule applies, notwithstanding the two actions were brought in different courts: *Anon.*, 1 Salk. 255; *Doe* d. *Walker* v. *Stevenson*, 3 Bos. & Pul. 22; *Holdfast* d. *Hattersley* v. *Jackson*, Barnes, 133; *Doe* d. *Hamilton* v. *Atherley*, 7 Mod. 420: or by different claimants, provided they respectively claim through or under the same title: *Doe* d. *Feldon* v. *Roe*, 8 T. R. 645; *Doe* d. *Mudd* v. *Roe*, 8 Dowl. 444; *Doe* d. *Duchess of Hamilton* v. *Hatherley*, 2 Stra. 1152; *Doe* d. *Brayne* v. *Bather*, 12 Q. B. 941; *Doe* d. *Rees* v. *Thomas*, 4 A. & E. 348: or against different defendants, provided the title in question be in substance the same: *Keene* d. *Angel* v. *Angel*, 6 T. R. 740; *Doe* d. *Feldon* v. *Roe*, 8 T. R. 645; *Doe* d. *Mudd* v. *Roe*, 8 Dowl. 444; *Doe* d. *Brayne* v. *Bather*, 12 Q. B. 941: or for different land, provided it be part of the same estate, or held under the same title. *Keene* d. *Angel* v. *Angel*, 6 T. R. 740; *Doe* d. *Heighley* v. *Harland*, 10 A. & E. 761; *Doe* d. *Brayne* v. *Bather*, 12 Q. B. 941.

"The only question in these cases is, whether the second ejectment is *in substance brought to try the same title*; if so, the rule is of course to stay the proceedings until the costs of the former ejectment have been paid." *Per* Lord Kenyon, C. J., in *Keene* d. *Angel* v. *Angel*, 6 T. R. 740. As to the defendants being different, "that must be the case upon every change of tenants, and is no manner of importance, any more than the ejectment being brought for a different part of the same estate. If it were otherwise the rule itself would be nugatory, as nothing would be more easy than to evade it." *Id.* 741. In *Doe* d. *Lawson* v. *Law*, cited 8 T. R. 646; Hullock on Costs, 452, Lord Mansfield, C. J., said, "That the court had arrived by degrees at this practice. It was adopted to prevent the hardship of frequent ejectments on the same title; and was the more reasonable, as in real actions all representatives of the party were concluded for ever from setting up the same title." And see *per* Lord Kenyon, C. J., in *Doe* d. *Feldon* v. *Roe*, 8 T. R. 647. "One of the reasons for this rule is, that the verdict in one action of ejectment cannot be pleaded in bar of another action for the same premises." *Per* Wilmot, J., in *Gravenor* v. *Cape*, Say on Costs, 247.

The rule applies, notwithstanding the position of the parties is reversed. Thus, if a defendant in ejectment, having been evicted, afterwards bring ejectment to recover the same premises, the proceedings in such second action will be stayed until the costs of the previous ejectment have been paid. *Thrustout* d. *Williams* v. *Holdfast*, 6 T. R. 223; *Doe* d. *Walker* v. *Stevenson*, 3 Bos. & Pul. 22; *Doe* d. *Thomas* v. *Shadwell*, 7 Dowl. 527; Ad. Eject. 313.

The rule applies although the first action was discontinued, or the plaintiff nonsuited, or determined otherwise than after a trial on the merits. *Doe* d. *Langdon* v. *Langdon*, 5 B. & Adol. 864; *Smith* d.

nger v. *Barnardiston*, 2 W. Black. 904. *Doe* d. *Mudd* v. *Roe*, 8)wl. 444.

The rule extends to the payment of the *costs* in a subsequent action trespass for mesne profits, &c., arising out of the former ejectment : *ie* d. *Pinchard* v. *Roe*, 4 East, 585 ; *Doe* d. *Church* v. *Barclay*, 13 *st*, 233 ; *Doe* d. *Bailey* v. *Bennett*, 9 Dowl. 1012 : but not to the *mages* in such action, however vexatious or improper the conduct of *e* defendant in that action may appear to have been : *Doe* d. *Church Barclay*, 13 East, 233 : nor to the costs of a suit in equity brought the same party for recovery of the same premises. *Doe* d. *Williams Winch*, 3 B. & A. 602.

The following cases illustrate the general rule before mentioned. *nte*, 78.) A. brought ejectment against B. in the Common Pleas, and tained a verdict and judgment ; B. paid the costs of that action, and erwards brought ejectment against A. in the King's Bench and reco-red : A., without paying the costs of that action, brought a third eject-nt against B. in the Common Pleas ; whereupon that court stayed the)ceedings until the costs of the second ejectment were paid. *Doe* d. *alker* v. *Stevenson*, 3 Bos. & Pul. 22. Ejectment by the heir of : proceedings therein stayed until the defendant's costs in a third tion of ejectment by R. were paid, although R. had, in two previous ctments, recovered upon the same title. *Doe* d. *Rees* v. *Thomas*, 4 & E. 348. Where the claimant is the son and heir of the claimant a former ejectment, and claims under the same title and against the ne defendant, but brings his action for different premises, the court ll stay the proceedings until the costs of the first action are paid : d this, although the claimant in the first action has been discharged an insolvent debtor whilst in custody under an attachment for non-yment of such costs. *Doe* d. *Heighley* v. *Harland*, 10 A. & E. 761. , having brought an ejectment, had judgment of nonsuit against n ; afterwards he was discharged under the Insolvent Debtors Act, : costs of the ejectment being inserted as a debt in his schedule. The ignee of his estate having brought a second ejectment upon the insol-at's original title, the court stayed the proceedings in it until the costs the first were paid. *Doe* d. *Standish* v. *Roe*, 5 B. & Ad. 878 ; 2 N. M. 468. But if the claimant be in custody under an execution or achment for the costs of a previous ejectment, the court will not y the proceedings in a second ejectment at his suit until such costs : paid. *Benn* d. *Denn* v. *Mortimer*, Barnes, 180 ; cited 10 A. & E. 2. Where the defendant is heir-at-law of a former tenant, against iom several ejectments were brought, but in no case was a trial had, d the costs of such previous actions belong to the executors or admi-trators of the previous tenant, and not to the defendant, the court ll not stay the ejectment against him until such costs are paid. *Doe* Blackburn v. *Standish*, 2 Dowl. N. S. 26. Where A., the defendant ejectment for land in the county of C., had attorned and paid rent B., who recovered, but did not pay costs ; and A. afterwards suc-ided in a second action brought by B. upon the same title, for lands the county of G., the costs of which had also not been paid, the irt would not stay proceedings in a subsequent action of ejectment)ught by A. against the heirs of B., for the land in the county of , till the costs of the former ejectment were paid, unless B.'s heir uld undertake not to rely on his ancestor's title, save by estoppel y. *Doe* d. *Evans* v. *Snead*, 2 Dowl. & L. 119. The court will not stay proceedings in a second ejectment until the costs of a prior ejectment are paid, where the second ejectment is founded upon a fresh forfeiture, *e. g.* the non-payment of a subsequent quarter's rent. *Doe* d. *Henry* v. *Gustard,* 4 M. & Gr. 987; 2 Dowl. N. S. 615. So the rule nisi will be discharged if the claimant swear generally that his claim is not founded on the same title as was previously in question, but upon another and different title, although he does not state the nature or particulars of such other title. *Doe* d. *Bailey* v. *Bennett,* 9 Dowl. 1012. The affidavit must, however, clearly swear to the existence of a distinct title. *Harvey* d. *Beal* v. *Baker,* 2 Dowl. N. S. 75, 77. The court may, however, if they think fit, allow new affidavits in reply, or direct the production of documents, and a *vivâ voce* examination of the parties and their witnesses. 17 & 18 Vict. c. 125, ss. 45, 46, 47.

The application to stay, &c., must be made to the court in which the last ejectment is brought, or in vacation to a judge at chambers. *See form of summons and rule nisi, Appendix, Nos.* 75, 77. It must be supported by an affidavit or affidavits entitled in the proper court and cause, and showing specially the material facts. See the form, 12 Q. B. 942. The main points to be attended to are :—1. That the costs of the previous ejectment have been taxed, and not paid. 2. That the subsequent ejectment is *founded upon the same title in substance* as that called in question in the previous action. It makes no difference whether the title was tried and determined in the first action or not. Thus, where the defendant delivered a plea, together with a proper consent rule, but the lessor of the plaintiff omitted to enter into such rule, and was non-prossed for want of a replication, *Smith* d. *Ginger* v. *Barnardiston,* 2 W. Black. 904; *Doe* d. *Langdon* v. *Langdon,* 5 B. & Adol. 864; 2 N. & M. 848; and see *Doe* d. *Mudd* v. *Roe,* 8 Dowl. 444.

It will be no answer to the application, that in the first action the title was not tried by reason of the claimant therein relying upon an estoppel, if it appear that the defendant in that action improperly obtained possession from a previous tenant on purpose that he might become a defendant rather than a plaintiff in an ejectment. *Doe* d. *Thomas* v. *Shadwell,* 7 Dowl. 527. But the rule is not inflexible : therefore, if it be clearly made out that the verdict in the former ejectment has been obtained by fraud and perjury, the court will not stay the proceedings in a second ejectment until the costs of the previous ejectment have been paid. *Doe* d. *Rees* v. *Thomas,* 2 B. & C. 622; 4 D. & R. 145. But the poverty of the claimant in the pending action will be no answer to the application; *Doe* d. *Green* v. *Packer,* 2 Dowl. 373; nor even his discharge from the costs of the previous action, under an act for the relief of insolvent debtors; *Doe* d. *Standish* v. *Roe,* 5 B. & Adol. 878; 2 N. & M. 468; *Doe* d. *Chambers* v. *Law,* 2 W. Black. 1180; nor the large amount of the costs of the previous action. In *Doe* d. *Rees* v. *Thomas,* 4 A. & E. 348, such costs amounted to £1,198 : 17s. 8d. The court does not order payment of the previous costs, but merely that the proceedings in the subsequent action be stayed until such costs are paid : " We are not going to order the Duchess to pay costs, but only preventing her from being vexatious, which, in 4 Mod. 349, is said to be the foundation of these rules." *Per cur.* in *Doe* d. *Duchess of Hamilton* v. *Hatherley,* 2 Stra. 1252.

The lateness of the application to stay, &c., is seldom (if ever) an answer to it. *Keene* d. *Angel* v. *Angel,* 6 T. R. 740. Thus, where the costs of the first action were not taxed until notice of trial was given in the second action, and the application to stay, &c., was not made until the day before the trial of the second action. *Doe* d. *Chadwick* v. *Law*, 2 W. Black. 1158. So where a term had elapsed since the commencement of the second action, in which notice of trial had been given before the application. *Doe* d. *Green* v. *Packer*, 2 Dowl. 373. Where several actions of ejectment were unsuccessfully brought, contesting the title to certain premises, and afterwards possession was obtained as upon a vacant possession in a subsequent ejectment founded on the same title, the court set aside the judgment and execution, and stayed all further proceedings until the costs of the previous actions were paid. *Harvey* d. *Beal* v. *Baker*, 2 Dowl. N. S. 75.

17. *Security for Defendant's Costs after a previous Ejectment.* — By 17 & 18 Vict. c. 125, s. 93, "If any person shall bring an action of ejectment after a prior action of ejectment *for the same premises* has been or shall have been unsuccessfully brought by such person, or by any person through or under whom he claims, against the same defendant, or any person through or under whom he defends, the court or a judge may, if they or he think fit, on the application of the defendant, at any time after such defendant has appeared to the writ, order that the plaintiff shall give to the defendant *security for the payment of the defendant's costs*, and that all further proceedings in the cause shall be stayed until such security be given, whether the prior action has been or shall have been disposed of by discontinuance or by nonsuit, or by judgment for the defendant."

This section affords an additional protection to defendants against repeated actions of ejectment for the *same premises*. It enables the defendant to apply for security for costs of the subsequent action then pending, whereas the previous rule (*ante*, 78), related to the costs of the previous action only; and whether those had been paid or not, no security for the costs of the subsequent action could be obtained. *Doe* d. *Selby* v. *Alston, Bart.*, 1 T. R. 491.

Whether an application can be made to stay proceedings until the costs of a previous ejectment have been paid, and until security be given for the defendant's costs in the pending action; or whether the defendant must elect between the one and the other, remains to be decided. Such an application seems as reasonable as an application for the latter purpose only, after the costs of the previous action have been paid.

PART THE SECOND.

PROCEEDINGS IN EJECTMENT IN ORDINARY CASES.

CHAPTER IX.

THE WRIT IN EJECTMENT.

Preliminary Points.]—Before suing out a writ in ejectment the various points mentioned in Chap. VIII. should be duly considered. By bringing an ejectment the plaintiff elects to consider the defendant as a trespasser, and not as tenant, from the day on which the right of possession is claimed in the writ; and he cannot distrain or sue for any subsequent *rent. Birch* v. *Wright*, 1 T. R. 378; *Bridges* v. *Smith*, 5 Bing. 410; 2 Moo. & P. 740; *Jones* v. *Carter*, 15 M. & W. 718; *Francklin* v. *Carter*, 1 C. B. 750; 3 Dowl. & L. 213. Nor for an apportioned part of the current quarter's rent (where the rent is reserved payable quarterly) calculated from the last quarter day to the day on which possession is claimed in the writ. *Aldershaw* v. *Holt*, 12 A. & E. 590; 3 P. & D. 307.

Form.]—By 15 & 16 Vict. c. 76, ss. 168—170, actions of ejectment shall be commenced by a writ in the form contained in the Schedule (A.) to that act annexed, marked No. 13, *or to the like effect :* such form is as follows : —

"Victoria, &c., to X. Y. Z. and all persons entitled to defend the possession of —— [*describe the property with reasonable certainty*], in the parish

ounty of ——, to the possession whereof A., B. and C., some
claim to be [*or* to have been on and since the —— day of
] entitled, and to eject all other persons therefrom : these
command you, or such of you as deny the alleged title,
ays after service hereof, to appear in our Court of —— to
property, or such part thereof as you may be advised ; in
judgment may be signed, and you turned out of possession.
See the Form, Appendix, No. 15.

Defendants.]—By 15 & 16 Vict. c. 76, s. 168, "In-
resent proceeding by ejectment, a writ shall be issued,
persons in possession by name, and to all persons entitled
ossession of the property claimed, which property shall
the writ with reasonable certainty."
roperty consists of several tenements in the possession of
its, it may sometimes be expedient to bring two or more
than one action against all of them for the whole of the

i name and surname of each person in possession of all
the property claimed in the writ, whether as a tenant or
ereof, should be correctly stated. *Doe* d. *Smith* v. *Roe,*
Doe d. *Williamson* v. *Roe,* 10 Moore, 493. *Doe* d.
ton v. *Cock,* 4 B. & C. 259 ; *Doe* d. *Turner* v. *Gee,*
But the court will not set aside the writ, or the copy
reason only of a misnomer. *Doe* d. *Stainton* v. *Roe,*
; *Wells* v. *Lord Suffield,* 4 C. B. 750 ; 5 Dowl. & L.
ig to the previous practice judgment would be given
ual ejector, notwithstanding a misnomer in the notice at
le declaration, provided it appeared that the persons
ose intended to be sued, and were the tenants in pos-
d. *Folkes* v. *Roe,* 2 Dowl. 567 ; *Doe* d. *Frost* v. *Roe,*
Doe d. *Peach* v. *Roe,* 6 Dowl. 62 ; *Doe* d. *Smart* v.
340. So where the christian name was omitted ; *Doe* d.
2 Dowl. 517 ; or stated thus, "Mrs. Martin and Mrs.
e d. *Smith* v. *Roe,* 6 Dowl. 629. But a notice directed
ind served on the wife of another, was insufficient. *Doe*
e, 5 Dowl. 254. Where the tenant was lying dead in
claration and notice addressed *to him,* and served on
re, was held insufficient. *Doe* d. *Crouch* v. *Roe,* 13
Q. B., 80. The action should have been against his
ministrators. *Post,* 84, 85.
ame of the tenant in possession was unknown, and he
e it, but stated that he was the tenant, whereupon the
ginal lessee was introduced into the notice at the foot of
, and a copy served, the court granted a rule nisi. *Doe*
v. *Roe,* 2 Dowl. N. S. 672.
ignity is part of the name of the person who has it.
John Germain, 2 Lord Ray. 859 ; 3 Salk, 235, *S. C.* ;
)., c. 25, s. 69. Therefore a duke, marquis, earl, vis-
laronet or knight, should be described as such in the
a writ of summons described the defendant as "The
ble *Baron* Suffield," his true description being "The
ole Edward Vernon Harbord, Baron Suffield," the court
aside the process, saying that "Baron" might possibly

be his christian name, and if so, it was a mere misnomer which might be amended. *Wells* v. *Lord Suffield*, 4 C. B. 750; 5 Dowl. & L. 177. Upon the same principle, when the christian name of a tenant in possession cannot readily be ascertained, he may be described as *Mister*.

It is sufficient to describe a company by its name, without stating it to be a corporation, or how it became one. *Woolf* v. *The City Steam Boat Company*, 7 C. B. 103; 6 Dowl. & L. 606.

If there be a tenant in possession who occupies by a sub-tenant, the former *may be* included in the writ as a defendant; *Roe* v. *Wigg*, 2 B. & P., New R., 330; but it is sufficient to name the sub-tenant, leaving him to give notice of the writ to his immediate landlord. *Post*, Chap. XI. s. 1.

An under-tenant may sometimes have a good defence, although his immediate landlord (the tenant) has none. *Pleasant* d. *Hayton* v. *Benson*, 14 East, 232; *Doe* d. *Beaden* v. *Pyke*, 5 M. & S. 146; *Bramley* v. *Wade*, M'Clel. 664; *Toriano* v. *Young*, 6 C. & P. 8; *Clarke* v. *Ardern*, 16 C. B. 227. He should be named as a defendant in the writ, and is entitled to defend for his part. *Doe* d. *Turner* v. *Gee*, 9 Dowl. 612. Occupiers of apartments or lodgings are generally under-tenants of part, and may be named in the writ; *Doe* d. *Henson* v. *Roe*, 1 Dowl. & L. 657; *Doe* d. *Threader* v. *Roe*, 1 Dowl. N. S. 261; but they are usually omitted for the reasons before stated. *Ante*, Chap. VIII. p. 75. The names of wives, children, servants, friends and visitors of tenants or under-tenants should not be mentioned, for they do not *occupy as tenants*, and are not "persons in possession" within the meaning of sect. 168. Generally speaking, the occupation of a servant is construed as the possession of his master. *Mayhew* v. *Suttle*, 4 E. & B. 347; *Becke* v. *Beaumont*, 16 East, 33. Therefore a mere servant of a tenant in possession cannot properly be made a defendant; nor be truly described as a "tenant in possession" in the affidavit of service of the writ: but if he appear to the writ and defend the action, it will be no defence that he occupied merely as servant of another person. *Doe* d. *Cuff* v. *Stradling*, 2 Stark. R. 187; *Doe* d. *James* v. *Stanton*, 2 B. & A. 371; 1 Chit. R. 113. So if the servant of a deceased tenant continue in possession, and prevent the landlord from taking or obtaining possession, the latter may thereupon treat him as a tenant, and maintain ejectment against him. *Doe* d. *Atkins* v. *Roe*, 2 Chit. R. 179. Where a tenant lay dead in the house, and a declaration in ejectment with notice addressed *to him* was served there on his widow: held insufficient. *Doe* d. *Crouch* v. *Roe*, 13 Law J., N. S., Q. B., 80. In such case the writ should be directed to the executors or administrators of the deceased tenant, or other the person or persons in actual possession as tenant. *Doe* d. *Pamphilon* v. *Roe*, 1 Dowl., N. S., 186. If any tenant in possession has become bankrupt or an insolvent debtor, his assignees may be necessary parties; especially if they have assented to take the property. *Doe* d. *Johnson* v. *Roe*, 1 Dowl. N. S. 493; *Doe* d. *Wyatt* v. *Roe*, 6 Jur. 781. Where the assignees of a bankrupt had not repudiated or claimed, judgment was given against the casual ejector with leave for the assignees to come in and defend. *Doe* d. *Rowley* v. *Roe*, 11 Jur. 309, Erle, J. It need scarcely be said that lunatics and criminals in custody are not tenants in possession of any part of the building in which they are confined.

If the name of any tenant in possession be omitted as a defendant,

se parts of the premises which are in his occupation cannot be reco-
ed in that action. On the other hand, if the name of any person be
:rted as a defendant, who is not actually a tenant in possession of
/ part of the property claimed, it will probably be necessary to
ain a judge's order to amend the writ by striking out his name,
l to amend the writ accordingly. *Post*, Chap. XII. To avoid this,
s sometimes expedient to bring two or more actions instead of one.
[f the possession of the premises be vacant, the writ should be
:ected to the person who would have been tenant in possession if he
l not abandoned the possession. If he be dead the writ should be
:ected, not to him, but to his executors or administrators. *Doe* d.
ouch v. *Roe*, 13 Law J., N. S., Q. B., 80; *Doe* d. *Pamphilon* v.
e, 1 Dowl. N. S. 186. If there be no rightful executor or admi-
trator, an executor de son tort who has taken possession may be
d. *S. C.*

Description of the Property claimed.]—By 15 & 16 Vict. c. 76,
168, the property claimed "shall be described in the writ *with rea-
able certainty.*" *Ante*, 83. But by s. 175, "want of reasonable
tainty in the description of the property or part of it in the writ or
ice [*i. e.* the notice to defend for part only, s. 174], shall not nullify
m, but shall only be ground for an application to a judge for better
ticulars of the land claimed or defended, which a judge shall have
ver to give in all cases." An order for such particulars will not be
de except under special circumstances. *Doe* d. *Saxton* v. *Turner*,
C. B. 896.
t has been most usual in practice since the above act to describe the
perty claimed *with such certainty as to identify it*; or as in a grant
demise (omitting the boundaries and abuttals); and this seems gene-
ly advisable when practicable, but in many cases such precision is
really necessary, and sometimes it is not advisable.
[t is difficult to say what does, or rather what *does not*, amount to
easonable certainty " within the meaning of the above enactments.
may be laid down as a general rule, that whatever description would
've been sufficient before the act is sufficient since. But the converse
s not hold; for it cannot be doubted that many of the old cases,
erein the descriptions have been held insufficient, would not now be
ognized as law. Ad. Eject. 21. "There are many cases in eject-
nt which have gone very far indeed; and therefore the doctrine of
se cases ought not to be extended." *Per* Lord Mansfield, C. J.,
Massey v. *Rice*, Cowp. 350. The Common Law Procedure Act,
i2, will be found to have very materially narrowed and restricted
above-mentioned doctrine. Besides which, it is to be observed that
time and mode of raising the objection, and the consequences of
r defect, are altogether different. Formerly, if the premises were
described with sufficient legal certainty, the defendant might have
ved in arrest of judgment. *Ford* v. *Lerke*, Noy, 109; *Hexham* v.
niers, 3 Mod. 238; *Knight* v. *Syms*, 1 Salk. 254; 4 Mod. 97;
th. 204; *S. C.*; *Doe* d. *Bradshaw* v. *Plowman*, 1 East, 441. Or
judgment might have been reversed upon a writ of error. *Rochester*
{eckhouse, Noy, 86; *Sprigge* v. *Rawlinson*, March. 96; Cro. Eliz.
:; *S. C.*; *Challenor* v. *Thomas*, Yelv. 143. But if *part* of the
mises were sufficiently described, the judgment would not have
n arrested, because the plaintiff might have cured the defect by

entering up judgment for that part only, and remitting the damages (which included the costs). *Hancock* v. *Price*, Hard. 57; *Ashworth* v. *Stanley*, Styles, 364. Or he might have obtained leave to enter up the verdict, according to the judge's notes, for the premises actually recovered, without remitting the damages. *Goodtitle* d. *Wright* v. *Otway*, 8 East, 357. Or sometimes the defect might after verdict be cured by an amendment upon payment of costs. *Doe* d. *Rogers* v. *Bath*, 2 N. & M. 440; 7 A. & E. 246, note (*d*). In a recent case where ejectment was brought for a messuage *and tenement*, and judgment was entered up generally for the plaintiff, and a writ of error brought, it was decided that the judgment could not be reversed because it was good for the messuage, and the costs were to be referred to the good cause of action and not to the residue. *Doe* d. *Lawrie* v. *Dyeball*, 8 B. & C. 70. Since the above act, no objection of the above nature can be taken either in arrest of judgment or upon a writ of error; but only upon an application to a judge for better particulars. Sect. 175, *ante*, 85.

It is not necessary to describe the premises in the writ with such certainty that the defendant, or the sheriff, or any other person, may be able to *identify* them, or to distinguish them from other property in the same parish. With respect to the defendant he may defend for part only, and he must be taken to know whether all the premises as described in the writ, or any and what parts thereof are in the possession of himself or his tenants. If, under special circumstances, an order for particulars of the premises claimed be really necessary, it may be obtained; but not otherwise. *Doe* d. *Saxton* v. *Turner*, 11 C. B. 896. So far as the sheriff is concerned, the settled practice for a long period has been and still is for the claimant or his attorney or agent to attend upon the execution of the writ of *habere facias possessionem* to receive the possession, and then at his peril to point out to the sheriff the property recovered and to be delivered under the writ, and for the sheriff to deliver possession accordingly. 1 Burr. 629; 5 Burr. 2673; Saville, 28 (Case 67). If no person attend on behalf of the claimant to point out the particular premises, the sheriff may make a return to that effect as an excuse for not having executed the writ. Watson's Sheriff, 322, 486; *see Form of Return, Appendix, No.* 282. If the claimant obtain under the writ possession of more than he actually recovered in the action, the court will, upon a summary application founded upon affidavits, compel him to make restitution of the excess. *Roe* d. *Saul* v. *Dawson*, 3 Wils. 49; and see 1 Burr. 629; 5 Burr. 2673.

It always was and still is necessary to *claim enough* to cover and include every thing which the claimant seeks to recover. There is little, if any, harm in claiming too much, but great prejudice may arise from claiming too little, or from omitting anything which ought to be specially named; because, although the claimant may recover less, he cannot recover more than he has claimed. *Denn* d. *Burges* v. *Purvis*, 1 Burr. 327; *Doe* d. *Bryant* v. *Wipple*, 1 Esp. 330; *Goodwin* v. *Blackman*, 3 Lev. 334. Thus, if he claim one hundred acres, he may recover any less number, but not more. *Guy* v. *Rand*, Cro. Eliz. 12. If he claim certain messuages, lands, &c. (*i. e.* the whole of them), he may recover one moiety, or three-fifths, or any other part, share or proportion thereof respectively. *Doe* d. *Roper* v. *Lonsdale*, 12 East, 39; *Denne* d. *Bowyer* v. *Judge*, 11 East, 288. So if he claim one moiety, he may recover one-third. *Denn* d. *Burges* v.

vis, 1 Burr. 327. If he claim one-fourth, he may recover one-
l of one-fourth. *Ablett* d. *Glenham* v. *Skinner*, 1 Sid. 229. If
claim "one acre of land," he may recover two or more distinct
es not exceeding in the whole one acre. *Goodtitle* d. *Chester* v.
er, 1 Burr. 133. If he claim a house he may recover any part of
:cording to the evidence; *Doe* d. *Coyle*, *Clerk*, v. *Cole*, 6 C. & P.
; but whatever may be the quantity, part, share or proportion
:med he cannot recover more. So in actions for the recovery of
:s or damages, the plaintiff cannot recover more than he has claimed
iis declaration. *Tomlinson* v. *Blacksmith*, 7 T. R. 132; *Tebbs* v.
:ron, 4 Man. & Gr. 844; *Watkins* v. *Morgan*, 6 C. & P. 661.
.s, however, the defendant may defend for part only, and as the
lict is to be entered distributively according to the evidence, viz.
:o part for the claimant, and as to the residue for the defendant, it
: be expected that in future the premises claimed will be described
:e nearly according to the truth, rather than in the exaggerated
iner which previously prevailed.

iny undivided part, share or proportion of messuages, lands, &c.
: be claimed in and by the writ. Thus "one undivided moiety (the
)le into two equal moieties to be divided) of and in —— messuages,"
Tidd's Appendix, 646; *Denn* d. *Burges* v. *Purvis*, 1 Burr. 326.
ne undivided [third, fourth *or* fifth, &c.] part (the whole into ——
al parts to be divided) of and in —— messuages," &c. *Rawson*
Maynard, Cro. Eliz. 286. "Six undivided fifty-sixth parts (the
)le into fifty-six equal parts to be divided) of and in —— mes-
zes," &c. *Doe* d. *Clift* v. *Birkhead*, 4 Exch. 110. "Nineteen
ivided three hundred and thirty-sixth parts (the whole into three
dred and thirty-six equal parts to be divided) of and in ——
suages," &c. *S. C.*
:o one undivided moiety of two undivided fifths, or one undivided
d of one undivided fifth, or two undivided thirds of one undivided
:rth, or any other part, share or proportion, may be claimed by
ropriate words. *Ablett* d. *Glenham* v. *Skinner*, 1 Sid. 229; *Culley*
Doe d. *Taylerson* (in error), 11 A. & E. 1008; 3 P. & D. 539, 540.
any such part may be recovered under a writ claiming either a
ier part or the whole of the lands, &c. *Ante*, 86.

'he property claimed may be described in the writ in general terms
follows:—(*Stating enough of each, but omitting anything clearly
vplicable*), viz. —— messuages, —— cottages, —— barns, ——
)les, —— coachhouses, —— outhouses, —— yards, —— gardens,
- orchards, —— acres of arable land, —— acres of meadow land,
- acres of pasture land, —— acres of woodland, —— acres of land
ered with water, and —— acres of other land, with the appurte-
ces, situate and being in the parish of ——, in the county of ——.
hit. Pl. 671.

t is, however, more usual in practice, since the Common Law Pro-
ure Act, 1852, to give a more precise and accurate description of
property claimed; *ante*, 85; so as to identify it, or as in a convey-
:e or lease, but omitting the boundaries and abuttals. Thus in
:tment for a dwelling-house it may be described as follows, viz.:—
: messuage, with the [yard, garden and] appurtenances, situate and
ig in —— street, in the parish of ——, in the county of ——, and
wn as No. ——, in the said street. In *Durley* v. *Martin*, 13 C. B.
, the property was described thus:—"A leasehold messuage and

premises, known as No. 48, Dorset street, in the parish of Saint Mary-lebone, in the county of Middlesex, and another leasehold messuage and premises, known as No. 42, Beaumont street, in the same parish and county." But it is not always possible to describe the premises with such precision, especially when they are numerous. The person who prepares the writ may not be sufficiently informed of the exact particulars of the property claimed, and there is always more danger of variance and mistake where the description is precise than where it is framed in general terms.

Unless there be some special object in so doing, the property should not be described as freehold, leasehold or copyhold.

The word "tenements" should generally be avoided, because it comprises many *incorporeal* hereditaments, for which an ejectment will not lie. Formerly the use of this word was held to create such an uncertainty as to render the proceedings substantially defective and erroneous. *Goodtitle* v. *Walton*, 2 Stra. 834; *S. C.* 1 Barnard. 155, 164; *Copleston* v. *Piper*, 1 Lord Raym. 191, note (*a*); *Sprigge* v. *Rawlinson*, March. 96, *per cur.* A messuage *or* tenement has been held bad. *Rochester* v. *Keckhouse*, Noy, 86; *Hexham* v. *Coniers*, 3 Mod. 238; *Goodright* d. *Welch* v. *Flood*, 3 Wils. 23. "A messuage or tenement, and forty acres of land," has been held good as to the land only. *Wood* v. *Payne*, Cro. Eliz. 186. "Three messuages or tenements and a toft," good only as to the toft. *Ashworth* v. *Stanley*, Styles, 364. But "a messuage or tenement, called the Black Swan," was held sufficient. *Burbury* v. *Yeomans*, 1 Sid. 295; *Hexham* v. *Coniers*, 3 Mod. 238. And even "a messuage or tenement, with the appurtenances and a garden," &c. has been held sufficient, because the other words show that "messuage or tenement" are two words for the same thing, and that both mean a dwelling-house. *Massey* v. *Rice*, Cowp. 350, Lord Mansfield, C. J.

A "messuage or burgage" in a borough is good. *Davers* v. *Wellington*, Hardres, 173. A messuage *and* tenement has been held bad. *Doe* d. *Bradshaw* v. *Plowman*, 1 East, 441; overruling *Doe* d. *Stewart* v. *Denton*, 1 T. R. 11. But it was afterwards held sufficient for the messuage only. *Goodtitle* d. *Wright* v. *Otway*, 8 East, 357; *Doe* d. *Laurie* v. *Dyeball*, 1 Moo. & P. 330; *S. C.* (in error), 8 B. & C. 70; and see *Wood* v. *Payne*, Cro. Eliz. 186; *Ashworth* v. *Stanley*, Styles, 364.

The term "a dwelling-house" or "a house" is unobjectionable. *Royston* v. *Eccleston*, Cro. Jac. 654; Palmer, 337; *Rawson* v. *Maynard*, Cro. Eliz. 286. But the word "messuage" is generally used, and is the more correct expression. The word "messuage," with the appurtenances, may include the curtilage and gardens. *Bettisworth's case*, 2 Co. R. 31 b; *Smith* v. *Martin*, 2 Saund. 400. A stable, a barn or a chapel may be described as a messuage. 1 Wms. Saund. 7. The word "cottage" is usual and proper. *Hill* v. *Giles*, Cro. Eliz. 818; *Lady Dacre's case*, 1 Lev. 58; *Hammond* v. *Ireland*, Styles, 215; *Doe* d. *Young* v. *Sotheron*, 2 B. & Adol. 628.

Other buildings and parts of buildings may be described as follows:—"The fourth part of a house in N." *Rawson* v. *Maynard*, Cro. Eliz. 286. "Part of a house called A. in B." (not saying what part). *Sullivan* v. *Seagrave*, 2 Stra. 695. "A chamber in the second story" of a house, situate, &c. "A place called a passage room" in a house, situate, &c. *Bindover* v. *Sindercombe*, 2 Lord Raym. 1470. "A

tain place called the vestry." *Per cur.* in *Hutchinson* v. *Puller,*
Lev. 96. "A kitchen" has been held bad, because of the supposed
certainty, as any room in the house might be appropriated to that
rpose. *Ford* v. *Lerke,* Noy, 109. But it would clearly be suffi-
nt in modern times; Ad. Eject. 24; because the claimant may,
ien necessary, point out to the sheriff which room was recovered by
it name. *Ante,* 86. So with respect to the words "cellar and wine
ults;" *Doe* d. *Freeland* v. *Burt,* 1 T. R. 701; "shop," "ware-
use" and the like; although in former times these words appear to
ve been insufficient. *Sprigge* v. *Rawlinson,* Cro. Car. 554; March.
, *S. C.* "Four mills," situate, &c. is sufficient without saying
wind-mills" or "water-mills." *Fitzgerald* v. *Marshall,* 1 Mod. 90;
Ventr. 206; 3 Keb. 44, *S. C.* A church or chapel may be reco-
red under the name of a messuage. *Hollingsworth* v. *Brewster,* 1
lk. 256; *Harpur's case,* 11 Co. R. 25 b; *Martin* v. *Davis,* 2 Stra.
4; 2 Barnard. 27; 1 Wms. Saund. 7. "The rectory of the parish
urch of K. in the county of N., with the appurtenances," is a proper
scription. *Doe* d. *Watson* v. *Fletcher,* 8 B. & C. 25; *Hutchinson*
Puller, 3 Lev. 95; *Snow* d. *Crawley* v. *Phillips,* 1 Sid. 220; *Heath*
Pryn, 1 Ventr. 14.
Where land has been built upon by the defendant, or by any person
rough whom he obtained the possession, it is sufficient if the writ claim
e land, without mentioning the buildings. *Goodtitle* d. *Chester* v.
ker, 1 Burr. 133, 137, 144.
In describing land, the words "a close" or "closes," or "a piece
land" (without further description, except as to the parish and
inty), should be avoided. In several old cases the word "close"
s been held insufficient. *Savil's case,* 11 Co. R. 55 a; *Hammond* v.
vill, 1 Roll. R. 55; *Ablett* d. *Glenham* v. *Skinner,* 1 Siderf. 229.
"a piece of land," not stating the name or contents or number
acres, has been held bad. *Palmer's case,* Owen, 18; *Martyn* v.
chols, Cro. Car. 573; *Jordan* v. *Cleabourne,* Cro. Eliz. 339; *Pemble*
Sterne, 1 Lev. 213. But "a close of land called A.," or "a piece
land called B.," or "two closes of land containing three acres," is
ficient. *Wykes* v. *Sparrow,* Cro. Jac. 435; *Id.* 654; *Lady Dacre's*
se, 1 Lev. 58; 3 Lev. 97.
In ejectment for several closes each being *named* or otherwise suffi-
ntly described, it is not necessary to state the number of acres.
ans v. *Hoel,* Cro. Eliz. 235. The third part of a close called Gut-
use close (not mentioning the quantity), is good. *Jordan* v. *Clea-*
erne, Cro. Eliz. 339.
Generally speaking, the word "land," when used alone, means
ible land. Therefore when meadow or pasture or other land is
imed, the species should be mentioned; 3 Chit. Pl. 671, note (*o*);
l. Eject. 25; and when divers sorts are claimed, the *quantity of each*
uld be stated. *Knight* v. *Syms,* 1 Salk. 254; Carthew, 204; 4
od. 97, *S. C.* An ejectment for "one messuage and two acres of
adow and pasture" has been held bad after verdict. *Goodier* v.
att, Cro. Car. 471. So an ejectment for "a messuage and forty
res of land, meadow and pasture thereto appertaining" (not saying
w much of each), has been held bad. *Martyn* v. *Nichols,* Cro.
r. 573. But no advantage can now be taken of such inaccuracies.
te, 85, 86.
Other property (not being buildings) for which an ejectment will lie

may be named or described in the writ as follows:—The manor of
——, in the county of ——; *Hems* v. *Stroud*, Latch. 61; *Doe* d.
Lushington v. *Bishop of Llandaff*, 2 B. & P. New R. 491; the rectory
of the parish church of K., in the county of ——, with the appurtenances, and also the rectory manor of K., otherwise called the rectory
manor, with the rights, members, and appurtenances to the said manor
belonging; *Doe* d. *Watson* v. *Fletcher*, 8 B. & C. 25; 2 M. & R. 104;
the manor of R., &c., and the rectory appropriate of the parish church
of R., with the appurtenances, and the tithes, obventions, oblations,
pensions, and portions to the said rectory belonging; *Doe* d. *Lushington* v. *Bishop of Llandaff*, 2 B. & P. New R. 491; " —— acres of
land covered with water;" 2 Bl. Com. 18.   But it would be improper
to say " a watercourse," " a river," or " a rivulet."   *Challenor* v.
Thomas, Yelv. 143; Ad. Eject. 18.   "A piscary" and "a fishery"
seem improper.   *Herbert* v. *Laughluyn*, Cro. Car. 492; *Molineaux* v.
Molineaux, Cro. Jac. 144; *Waddy* v. *Newton*, 8 Mod. 275, 277; but
see 1 T. R. 361, *per* Ashhurst, J.; 2 Arch. N. P. 303; Ad. Eject. 18.
"A pool" or "a pit of water" is sufficient, because it includes the
land.   Co. Lit. 5; Yelv. 143; Ad. Eject. 19.   "A yard" is correct.
"A garden" may be described by that name; *Royston* v. *Eccleston*,
Cro. Jac. 654; *Smith* v. *Martin*, 2 Saund. 400; 3 Keb. 44; or as so
much "land," or "garden ground," or "garden land."   2 Arch. N.
P. 329; Godb. 6, pl. 7; *Burton* v. *Brown*, Cro. Jac. 648.   "An
orchard" is a proper description. *Wright* v. *Wheatley*, Cro. Eliz. 854;
Noy, 37, *S. C.*   So is a "hop-yard;" Ad. Eject. 20; a "toft;"
Ashworth v. *Stanley*, Styles, 364; " fifty acres of wood, and fifty acres
of underwood;" *Warren* v. *Wakeley*, 2 Roll. R. 482; "five acres of
alder carr" (land covered with alders), in Norfolk; *Barnes* v. *Peterson*, 2 Stra. 1063; "ten acres of peas" (land sown with peas); *Oding-
sall* v. *Jackson*, 1 Brownl. 149; "fifty acres of gorse and furze;"
Fitzgerald v. *Marshall*, 1 Mod. 90; 1 Ventr. 206; 3 Keb. 44, *S. C.*;
"fifty acres of furze and heath, and fifty acres of moor and marsh;"
Connor v. *West*, 5 Burr. 2762; " —— acres of hay, grass, and aftermath," or "herbage;" *Wheeler* v. *Toulson*, Hardres, 330; Ad. Eject.
19; "500 acres of bog and 500 acres of mountain" (in Ireland);
Macduncoh v. *Stafford*, 2 Roll. R. 166; Palmer, 100, *S. C.*   But it
has been held insufficient to say, " 3,000 acres of waste," because that
might include several sorts of land.   *Hancocke* v. *Price*, Hard. 57.
An ejectment lies for a beast-gate (land and common for one beast) in
Suffolk; *Bennington* v. *Goodtitle*, 2 Stra. 1084; Andr. 106, *S. C.*;
"cattle-gates" in Yorkshire; *Barnes* v. *Peterson*, 2 Stra. 1063, *per
cur.*; and see *Rex* v. *The Inhabitants of Whixley*, 1 T. R. 137; "a
tin bound" in Cornwall; *Rogers* v. *Brenton*, 10 Q. B. 26; 17 Law J.,
N. S., Q. B., 34; but see *Doe* d. *Earl of Falmouth* v. *Alderson*, 1 M.
& W. 210; 4 Dowl. 701; *Doe* d. *Hanley* v. *Wood*, 2 B. & A. 724,
737; a "salt-pit," or a "boilery of salt;" *Comyn* v. *Kyneto*, Cro.
Jac. 150; *Sanders* v. *Patridge*, Noy, 132; Ad. Eject. 17; a "coal
mine;" *Comyn* v. *Kyneto*, Cro. Jac. 150; *Comyn* v. *Wheatley*, Noy,
121; or "coal mines" in Durham (not mentioning the number of
them); *Whittingham* v. *Andrews*, 1 Salk. 255; Carthew, 277; 1 Show.
364; other "mines;" *Doe* d. *Earl of Falmouth* v. *Alderson*, 1 M. &
W. 210; 4 Dowl. 701; Collier on Mines, 103 (2nd ed.); for "land,
and a coal-pit in the same land;" *Harebottle* v. *Placock*, Cro. Jac. 21.
It seems doubtful whether ejectment can be maintained for an *un-*

:d mine, as the sheriff could not deliver possession of it. *Sayer* v.
:, 1 Ves. sen. 234; Collier on Mines, 105 (2nd ed.). A mere
see to work mines (not being a lessee) cannot maintain ejectment.
d. *Hanley* v. *Wood*, 2 B. & A. 724; *Mushet* v. *Hill*, 5 Bing. N.
)4; Collier on Mines, 105. A mortgage by a railway company of
 undertaking, and all and singular the rates and tolls, and other
 arising by virtue of the act," does not convey the land, and will
upport an ejectment; *Doe* d. *Myatt* v. *St. Helen's and Runcorn
 Railway Company*, 2 Q. B. 364; but a mortgage or demise of
olls, houses, and toll gates, &c., passes the land, and will support
jectment. *Doe* d. *Banks* v. *Booth*, 2 Bos. & P. 219; *Doe* d.
ipson v. *Lediard*, 4 B. & Adol. 137; *Doe* d. *Butt* v. *Rous*, 1 E.
419. Tithes may be recovered in ejectment, by virtue of 32 Hen.
7, s. 7; *Baldwin* v. *Wine*, Cro. Car. 301; Sir W. Jones, 321, *S.
Partridge* v. *Ball*, 1 Lord Raym. 136; *Camel* v. *Clavering*, 2 *Id.
Doe* d. *Butcher* v. *Musgrove*, 1 Man. & Gr. 639, *Tindal*, C. J.;
the particular species of them should be mentioned; *Harpur's*
11 Co. R. 25 b; *Worrall* v. *Harper*, 1 Roll. R. 65, 68; Dyer,
5; thus, " all and singular the tithes of corn, grain, hay, wood,
, wool, lambs, and calves, arising, growing, renewing, increasing,
happening, within the parish of ——, in the said county, and
n the bounds, limits, and titheable places of the said rectory," *or
e case may be*; Tidd's App. 644; but ejectment does not lie for a
subtraction of tithes by the tenant or occupier; Runn. Eject. 134;
Eject. 59; and see *The Dean and Chapter of Ely* v. *Cash*, 15 M.
. 617; nor where the tithes are not taken in kind, but an annual
is paid in lieu thereof. Dyer, 116(*b*). Common of pasture, common
rbary, and other commonable rights appendant or appurtenant to
 &c., may be recovered, together with the land to which they are
rtenant. *Newman* v. *Holdmyfast*, 1 Stra. 54; Andr. 107; *Baker
)e* (in error), Cas. temp. Hardw. 127. They may be specially
ioned in the writ thus : " with common of pasture thereunto be-
ng and appertaining," or they will be included under the general
s " with the appurtenances."
ectment does not lie for any *incorporeal* hereditaments; 2 Arch.
. 303; except as appendant or appurtenant to something corpo-
and together with it. Per *Holroyd*, J., in *Crocker* v. *Fothergill*,
& A. 661, *ex. gr.* for rents common in gross; Cro. Jac. 146; an
wson in gross; Cro. Jac. 146; nor for a river, a rivulet, or a
rcourse; Yelv. 143; except by the description of so much " land
ed with water (*ante*, 90); nor, as it seems, for a " piscary" or
ery" (*ante*, 90); nor for a canonry, that being only an eccle-
cal office; *Doe* d. *Butcher* v. *Musgrave*, 1 Man. & Gr. 625,
 nor for a prebendary stall, or the house for the time being allot-
) the canon or prebendary for his residence, and to enable him to
rm his official duties; *S. C.*; nor for land in the possession of the
a or its immediate officers or servants, the remedy being by a pe-
of right. *Doe* d. *Leigh* v. *Roe*, 8 M. & W. 579(*a*). But it is
)jection to the recovery of land that there is a public highway
it, because the soil is vested in the legal owner, subject to the pub-

---

The crown or its lessee may maintain ejectment. *Doe* d. *King
m the Fourth* v. *Roberts*, 13 M. & W. 520.

lic right of passage over it, and possession of the land may be delivered
by the sheriff to the claimant, without interfering with or prejudicing
such public right. *Goodtitle* d. *Chester* v. *Alker*, 1 Burr. 133, 136,
143, 145; *Dovaston* v. *Payne*, 2 H. Black. 527; 2 Smith, L. C. 90;
Lade v. *Shepherd*, 2 Stra. 1004.

It seems that ejectment cannot be maintained for setting up a stall
in a public street, the remedy being an action of trespass by the owner
of the soil. *Doe* d. *The Churchwardens and Overseers of St. Julian,
Shrewsbury* v. *Cowley*, 1 C. & P. 123, Hullock, B. So for erecting
stalls in a market. *The Mayor of Northampton* v. *Ward*, 2 Stra.
1238.

Ejectment does not lie for dower which has not been assigned; *Doe*
d. *Nutt* v. *Nutt*, 2 C. & P. 430, Garrow, B.; for it is a mere *right* to
have one-third part of the land, &c. assigned, and not an estate in one
undivided third part of the land. The remedy is by a writ of *dower
unde nihil habet*, or a writ of *right of dower*; Co. Lit. 32 b; 2 Car. &
Pay. 431, note; 3 Chit. Pl. 575—587 (7th ed.); Roscoe on Real Actions, 29, 39; Roper's Husband and Wife, c. 9, s. 5; *Garrard* v. *Tuck*,
8 C. B. 231; *Watson* v. *Watson*, 10 C. B. 3; or more frequently by a
bill or claim in equity. 1 Story, Eq. Jur., Chap. XII.; *Mundy* v.
Mundy, 2 Ves. jun. 122; *D'Arcey* v. *Blake*, 2 Sch. & Lef. (Irish),
R. 391; *Bamford* v. *Bamford*, 5 Hare, 203.

No ejectment will lie for wrongfully preventing the patron of a
living from presenting to it on a vacancy. The remedy is by a writ of
quare impedit. 3 Chit. Pl. 568; *Stone* v. *The Bishop of Winchester*,
9 C. B. 62. But possession of a rectory, &c. may be recovered in
ejectment by the person legally entitled thereto. *Doe* d. *Watson* v.
Fletcher, 8 B. & C. 25; 2 M. & R. 104 (*post*, Chap. LXV.).

Parish and County.]—The parish and county in which the lands
lie should generally be mentioned. The prescribed form of the writ
in ejectment says, "in the parish of ——, in the county of ——."
(*Ante*, 82.)

Before the 15 & 16 Vict. c. 76, the usual practice was to state the
name of the parish, township or ville, and also the county, wherein the
premises were situated. But in a late case it was held sufficient to
mention the county, without any parish, township or ville. *Doe* d.
Edwards v. *Gunning*, 7 A. & E. 240, 253; 2 N. & P. 260. It seems,
however, to have been incorrect to omit all mention of the locality of
the premises. *Doe* d. *Rogers* v. *Bath*, 2 N. & M. 440; 7 A. & E.
246, note (*d*). But where the place of the *ouster* was mentioned that
was held sufficient. *Goodright* d. *Smallwood* v. *Strother*, 2 W. Black.
706.

The name of the parish, township or ville should be *correctly* stated,
otherwise a variance will arise, which may be fatal unless amended.
Goodtitle d. *Pinsent* v. *Lammiman*, 2 Camp. 274; *Doe* d. *Marriott*
v. *Edwards*, 1 Moo. & Rob. 319; 6 C. & P. 208, Parke, B. But an
amendment will, generally, be permitted at the trial unless the defendant
appear to have been actually misled or prejudiced by the misdescription.
S. C.

Where the premises were stated to be "in the parish of Farnham,"
and the evidence showed them to be in the parish of "Farnham
Royal:" held, that the variance was immaterial. *Doe* d. *Tollet* v.
Salter, 13 East, 9. So where the premises were described as situate in
the parish of *Westbury*, in the county of Gloucester, and it appeared

were two parishes of Westbury in that county, viz. *Westbury-on-*
and *Westbury-on-Severn*, and that the premises were situated in
itter parish : held, that there was no variance. *Doe* d. *James* v.
is, 5 M. & S. 326. So where the premises were laid to be in the
h of *Saint Luke*, in the county of Middlesex, and it appeared at
ial that there were two parishes of St. Luke in that county, viz.
uke, Chelsea, and *St. Luke, Old Street*, or, more commonly, *St.*
, in which latter parish the premises were : held, that there was
uiance. *Doe* d. *Boys* v. *Carter*, 1 You. & Jer. 492.

hen the property is situate in two or more parishes, it is sufficient
y, "in the several parishes of A., B. and C., in the county of
" without attempting to distinguish the property in each parish.
Eject. 175. But it would formerly have been erroneous to say
he parishes of A., B. and C., *or one of them.*" *Goodright* d. *Griffin*
woson, 7 Mod. 457 ; Barnard. 184 ; 2 Barnes, 150, *S. C.*

the property be stated to be in the several parishes of A. and B.,
he evidence shows all the property to be in parish A., the variance
ierally immaterial. *Goodwin* v. *Blackman*, 3 Lev. 334.

hen two parishes, A. and B., are united by act of parliament for
ticular purpose only, they should not be described in an ejectment
he *united* parishes of A. and B." *Goodtitle* d. *Pinsent* v. *Lammi-*
2 Camp. 274 ; 6 Esp. 128, *S. C.*

mes of the Claimants.]—By 15 & 16 Vict. c. 76, s. 169, "The
shall state the names of all the persons in whom the title is alleged
, and command the persons to whom it is directed to appear within
n days after service thereof, in the court from which it is issued,
'end the possession of the property sued for, or such part thereof
ey may think fit, and it shall contain a notice that in default of
irance they will be turned out of possession ; and the writ shall
teste of the day on which it is issued, and shall be in force for
months, and shall be in the form contained in the Schedule (A.)
is act annexed, marked No. 13 (*ante*, 82), or to the like effect ;
:he name and abode of the attorney issuing the same, or, if no
iey, the name and residence of the party shall be indorsed thereon,
e manner as hereinbefore enacted with reference to the indorse-
i on a writ of summons in a personal action ; and the same pro-
ngs may be had to ascertain whether the writ was issued by the
irity of the attorney whose name was indorsed thereon, and who
vhat the claimants are, and their abode, and as to staying the
edings upon writs issued without authority, as in the case of writs
rsonal actions."

the above section the writ shall state "*the names of all the per-*
n whom the title is alleged to be," i. e. the correct christian name
urname of each of the claimants. *King* v. *King*, Cro. Eliz. 776 ;
r v. *West*, Freem. 116 ; *Doe* d. *Miller* v. *Rogers*, 1 Car. & Kir.

Also the title of dignity, if any, of each claimant, such title form-
art of his name (*ante*, 83) ; but the writ need not attempt to dis-
ish whether all or any of the parties claim jointly or severally.
title is to be stated thus : "to the possession whereof A., B. and
ime or one of them claim [to be entitled," *or* "to have been on
ince the —— day of ——, A.D. ——, entitled], and to eject all
persons therefrom." Such form is equally applicable whether
laimants sue as joint tenants, tenants in common, coparceners, or
wise.

If the legal estate in possession be vested in trustees, their names should be used as co-plaintiffs in the writ; but not without first obtaining their authority or consent, unless they unreasonably refuse to permit their names to be used, after an offer to indemnify them against the costs. The name of a claimant used without his consent may sometimes be struck out upon application to the court or a judge. 2 Chit. Arch. 955 (9th ed.); *Doe d. Shepherd* v. *Roe*, 2 Chit. R. 171. But where substantial justice and equity require his name to be used without his consent, the court or a judge will refuse to strike it out, and only order an indemnity to be given him against all costs. *Doe d. Vine* v. *Figgins*, 3 Taunt. 440; *Doe d. Prosser* v. *King*, 2 Dowl. 580; *Spicer* v. *Todd*, 2 Cr. & Jer. 165. *See form of Order, Appendix, No.* 332; *Bond of Indemnity, Id. No.* 333.

Assignees of a bankrupt, or of an insolvent debtor, may, but need not, be described as such assignees in the writ; so with respect to executors and administrators.

Churchwardens and overseers must be named in the writ, and also described as churchwardens and overseers of the parish. *Doe d. Churchwardens and Overseers of Llandesilio* v. *Roe*, 4 Dowl. 222; *Ward* v. *Clarke*, 12 M. & W. 747; 1 Dowl. & L. 1027. Thus "A. B. and C. D., churchwardens of the parish of ——, in the county of ——, and E. F. and G. H. overseers of the said parish." *Doe d. Webster* v. *Norton*, 4 P. & D. 270; 12 A. & E. 442. Or thus: "A. B., C. D., E. F. and G. H., churchwardens and overseers of the parish of ——, in the county of ——." *Doe d. Bowley* v. *Barnes*, 8 Q. B. 1037.

Corporations aggregate should be described by their corporate name; *Doe d. Mayor, &c., of Maldin* v. *Miller*, 1 B. & A. 699; *Woolf* v. *The City Steam Boat Company*, 7 C. B. 103; 6 Dowl. & L. 606; but a corporation sole should be described by his christian name and corporate name. *Carter* v. *Cromwell*, Sav. 128, cited Dyer, 86; Ad. Eject. 169.

"The principal officers of her majesty's ordnance" might formerly have maintained ejectment by that description without mentioning their names; 5 & 6 Vict. c. 94, s. 34. But now all the property vested in them is transferred to "her majesty's principal secretary of state for the war department;" 18 & 19 Vict. c. 117. "The commissioners for executing the office of lord high admiral of the united kingdom of Great Britain and Ireland," may sue or be sued by that description, without mentioning their names; 1 & 2 Geo. 4, c. 93, s. 9; *Williams* v. *The Lords Commissioners of the Admiralty*, 11 C. B. 420.

Date of Claimant's Title.—The *date* of the claimants' right or title to possession, as stated in the writ, is sometimes of considerable importance. *Ante*, 82. If they simply claim "to be entitled," &c., that means on the day of the teste and issuing of the writ; and this is the most common and usual form: but a verdict and judgment for the claimants, upon a writ so framed, will not be available, in a subsequent action of trespass for mesne profits, &c., in proof of the plaintiff's title or right to possession on any day *prior* to the teste and issuing of the writ in ejectment; nor can such verdict and judgment be used by way of estoppel to prevent the defendants in the action for mesne profits from pleading *liberum tenementum*, or by way of traverse of the plaintiff's title, except as to the period between the date of the writ and the date of final judgment in the ejectment, both inclusive. *Doe* v. *Wells-*

1, 2 Exch. 368; 6 Dowl. & L. 179; *see Appendix, No.* 397; *Scott* v.
ynall, 26 Law Times R. 256, Q. B. Nor can the plaintiffs (if more
n one) jointly recover mesne profits for any previous period, without
ving a joint title and right of possession during such earlier period,
which the verdict and judgment in the ejectment will be no evi-
ce. *Post,* Chap. LXVIII. It may, therefore, frequently be ma-
al to claim possession in the writ of ejectment from some previous
', and not merely on the day the writ issues.

)n the other hand, it is dangerous and improper to claim possession
and from too early a day; because when by the writ the plaintiffs
im to have been entitled on and since a specified day, they cannot
intain such action without proof of a right of possession in them, or
ie or one of them, *on that day; Doe* d. *Lewis* v. *Earl Cawdor,* 1
M. & R. 398; *Roe* d. *Wrangham* v. *Hersey,* 3 Wils. 274; *Doe* d.
nnett v. *Long,* 9 C. & P. 773; *Doe* d. *Graves* v. *Wells,* 10 A. & E.
'; 2 P. & D. 396; *Doe* d. *Esdaile* v. *Mitchell,* 2 M. & S. 446; and
m thence until the commencement of the action. *Doe* d. *Gardner*
Kennard, 12 Q. B. 244; *Doe* d. *Newby* v. *Jackson,* 1 B. & C. 454,
yley, J.; 2 D. & R. 514, *S. C.* Whereas the right of possession
y have accrued after the day named and before action brought,
ier by the expiration of a notice to quit; *Doe* d. *Lloyd* v. *Ingleby,*
M. & W. 91; or upon a demand of possession made; *Doe* d. *Los-*
ibe v. *Clifford,* 2 Car. & Kir. 448; *Goodtitle* d. *Galloway* v. *Her-*
t, 4 T. R. 680; *Doe* d. *Newby* v. *Jackson,* 1 B. & C. 448; 2 D.
R. 514; *Doe* d. *Jacobs* v. *Phillips,* 10 Q. B. 130; or upon some
v act or omission of the tenant creating a forfeiture; or upon some
er act done, as actual entry, when that was necessary to avoid a
e with proclamations. *Berrington* d. *Dormer* v. *Parkhurst,* 4 Bro.
C. 85; 2 Stra. 1086; Andr. 125, *S. C.* But a mistake as to the
e may sometimes be cured by an amendment at the trial, provided
ie not material to the real merits, and the defendants appear not to
re been misled or prejudiced by it in their defence. Thus, where in
ctment for a forfeiture by non-payment of rent, the demise was laid
the 15th, instead of the 16th January, 1841, on which latter day
right of entry for the forfeiture was complete, and the action was
nmenced after the 16th: held, that the date might be amended.
e d. *Edwards* v. *Leach,* 3 Man. & Gr. 229; 3 Scott, N. R. 509; 9
wl. 877; and see *Doe* d. *Simpson* v. *Hall,* 5 Man. & Gr. 795; 1
wl. & L. 49; *Doe* d. *Bennett* v. *Long,* 9 C. & P. 773, 777. But
h an amendment will not always be permitted. Thus, where several
thers and sisters divided certain property between them at their
ther's death, supposing it to have been hers, and verbally allotted a
ise to a sister. The property really had been their deceased father's:
d, in ejectment by the father's devisee (one of the brothers) that he
ild not recover without a demand of possession; and the demand of
session being after the day of the demise, the judge would not allow
amendment by altering the day of the demise, as the arrangement
s equitable. *Doe* d. *Loscombe* v. *Clifford,* 2 Car. & Kir. 448,
lerson, B.

The titles of the several claimants may have accrued at different
es, or it may be doubtful whether the title of the claimants, or some
ine of them, accrued at an earlier or later period. In such cases
old practice used to be to insert several counts in the declaration,
ting the demises on different days. The new form of writ in eject-

ment does not provide for such a difficulty, and therefore it seems that in such cases the claimants should only claim " to be entitled" to the possession, or at all events they should not claim to have been entitled on and since a day so remote as to exclude the right or title of any or either of them.

In a recent case the writ was thus framed:—"To the possession whereof A., B. and C., some or one of them, claim to have been on and since the 30th day of November, A.D. 1852, entitled, *or to be entitled,* and to eject all other persons therefrom." The defendants suffered judgment for want of appearance: held, in a subsequent action of trespass for mesne profits, &c., that the defendants were not estopped by the judgment in ejectment from denying the plaintiff's title prior to the date and teste of the writ in ejectment. *Scott* v. *Reynall,* 26 Law Times R. 256, Q. B.

But as *a verdict* in ejectment finds that the claimant " on the —— day of ——, A.D. 18—, was and still is entitled to the possession, &c." it may frequently be useful and advantageous to frame the writ in ejectment in the alternative. *See the Form, Appendix, No.* 15. It is, however, not clear that the writ may be framed in that manner. 2 Chit. Arch. 954 (9th ed.).

Teste.]—The writ must be tested in the name of the chief justice or chief baron of the court out of which it issues, or, in case of a vacancy in that office, in the name of the senior puisne judge of the court for the time being. It must also be tested on the day on which it actually issues, whether in term or vacation. It is immaterial whether the teste mentions the year of our Lord, or the year of the queen's reign.

Notice for Bail.]—In actions by a landlord against a tenant, where the writ issues pursuant to 15 & 16 Vict. c. 76, s. 213 (*post,* Chap. XXXVI.), it should be subscribed with the following notice:—

" Take notice, that you will be required, if ordered by the court or a judge, to give bail by yourself and two sufficient sureties conditioned to pay the costs and damages which shall be recovered in this action." This must be written or printed at the foot of the writ (not indorsed). It may as well be entitled in the cause, and directed to the defendant, and subscribed with the name of the plaintiff or his attorney, until decided to be unnecessary. *See the Form, Appendix, No.* 16.

Indorsements.]—By sect. 169 (*ante,* 93), the writ in ejectment is to be indorsed with the name, &c. of the attorney or party issuing it, in like manner as a writ of summons. This refers to sect. 6, which is as follows:—" Every writ of summons shall be indorsed with the name and place of abode of the attorney actually suing out the same, and in case such attorney shall not be an attorney of the court in which the same is sued out, then also with the name and place of abode of the attorney of such court in whose name such writ shall be taken out; and when the attorney actually suing out any writ shall sue out the same as agent for an attorney in the country, the name and place of abode of such attorney in the country shall also be indorsed upon the said writ; and in case no attorney shall be employed to issue the writ, then it shall be indorsed with a memorandum expressing that the same has been sued out by the plaintiff in person, mentioning the city, town or parish, and also the name of the hamlet, street and number of the ouse of such plaintiff's residence, if any such there be." *See the form, Appendix, No.* 15.

Practical Directions.]—A printed form of the writ in ejectment may be bought at any law stationer's. It should be properly filled up as above directed), and then taken to the Master's Office, together vith a *præcipe* for the writ, written on a slip of paper. *See the form, lppendix, No.* 14. The master will thereupon file the *præcipe*, and eal the writ.

If the plaintiff sue *in person*, he must at the time of issuing the writ nter in the book kept for that purpose at the Master's Office an *ad- 'ress within three miles from the General Post Office,* at which all roceedings not requiring personal service may be left for him. Reg. 'rac. H. T. 1853, No. 166.

At any time after issuing the writ "in person," the plaintiff may mploy an attorney, and give notice thereof to the defendant. *Id.* No. 167; *see the form, Appendix, No.* 100.

F

CHAPTER X.

SERVICE OF THE WRIT.

Service of the Writ.]—By 15 & 16 Vict. c. 76, s. 169 (*ante*, 93), " the writ shall bear teste on the day on which it is issued, and shall be in force for three months" (*i. e.* three calendar months. 13 & 14 Vict. c. 21, s. 4). And by sect. 170, " the writ shall be served in the same manner as an ejectment has heretofore been served, or in such manner as the court or a judge shall order, and in case of vacant possession by posting a copy thereof. upon the door of the dwellinghouse or other conspicuous part of the property."

By the Practice Rules of H. T. 1853, No. 112, " no judgment in ejectment for want of appearance or defence, whether limited or otherwise, shall be signed without first filing an affidavit of the service of the writ, according to the Common Law Procedure Act, 1852, and a copy thereof, or where personal service has not been effected, without first obtaining a judge's order or a rule of court authorizing the signing such judgment, which said rule or order, or a duplicate thereof, shall be filed, together with a copy of the writ."

It is generally better, when practicable, to serve the writ on each defendant *personally* ; but where that cannot be managed, it should be served in the best manner practicable, and upon affidavit thereof the judge will order in what other manner (if any) service shall be effected. 2 Chit. Arch. 965 (9th ed.).

The service must be made whilst the writ is in force, *i. e.* within three calendar months. *Supra.* It would seem that the day on which the writ issues and is tested should be *included* in the computa-

ion, as the service may be made on that day. It is to be observed
hat the first day is included in writs of summons and other writs issued
or served pursuant to the Common Law Procedure Act, 1852; and
that the Practice Rule of H. T..1853, No. 174 (excluding the first
lay), does not apply where the time is prescribed by act of parliament,
and not by the rules or practice of the courts. The service may be
made at any hour before twelve o'clock at night on the last day. *Doe*
1. *Kenrick* v. *Roe*, 5 Dowl. & L. 578; *Priddee* v. *Cooper*, 1 Bing.
36; *Maud* v. *Barnard*, 2 Burr. 812. By Reg. Prac. H. T. 1853, No.
164, "service of pleadings, notices, summonses, orders, rules and other
proceedings, shall be made before seven o'clock, p.m. If made after
that hour, the service shall be deemed as made on the following day."
But this rule does not apply to a writ in ejectment served on the last
lay allowed for that purpose by the statute. The service must not be
made on a Sunday. 29 Car. 2, c. 7, s. 6; *Doe* d. *Hine* v. *Roe*, 4 Man.
& Gr. 766; *Doe* d. *Warren* v. *Roe*, 8 D. & R. 342; *Doe* v. *Roe*, 5 B.
& C. 764; 8 D. & R. 592. If the last day happen to fall on a Sunday,
care should be taken to serve the writ on or before the Saturday
preceding.

There are no provisions in the act for renewing the writ, or continuing it by *alias* or *pluries;* therefore it would seem that, if not served
within the time limited, the claimants can only commence a fresh action, before which their right of entry may perhaps be barred by the
Statute of Limitations.

Where the writ is served after it has ceased to be in force, the defendant should not treat it as a nullity, but should apply to the court
or a judge to set aside the copy and service for irregularity with costs;
at least, this is so in personal actions. *Hamp* v. *Warren*, 11 M. & W.
103; 2 Dowl. N. S. 758.

The writ is generally to be " served in the same manner as an ejectment has heretofore been served." *Ante*, 98. But if not served on
each tenant in possession *personally*, a judge's order or rule of court
must be obtained for leave to sign judgment for want of appearance or
defence. *Ante*, 98. Such rule or order will not be made except upon
proof by affidavit of such a service as would have been deemed sufficient before the above act, except perhaps where the possession of the
premises is " vacant," having been utterly deserted by the tenant.
We now proceed to consider fully the various modes of service.

1. *On the Tenant personally.*]—A writ of ejectment may be served
personally on the tenant in possession, not only on the premises in
question, but in any other place or county; *Anon.*, Lofft. 301;
Savage v. *Dent*, 2 Stra. 1064; even in prison; *Doe* d. *Mann* v. *Roe*,
11 M. & W. 77; or in a lunatic asylum; *Doe* d. *Gibbard* v. *Roe*, 3
Man. & G. 87; 3 Scott, N. R., 363; 9 Dowl. 844; or abroad; *Doe*
d. *Daniel* v. *Woodroffe*, 7 Dowl. 494.

The writ is to be served " in the same manner as an ejectment has
heretofore been served." 15 & 16 Vict. c. 76, s. 170; *ante*, 98. Formerly it was necessary to explain the object and meaning of the service, the declaration being incomprehensible to most persons. *Doe*
v. *Roe*, 1 Dowl. 428; *Doe* v. *Roe*, 2 Dowl. 199; *Doe* d. *Wade* v.
Roe, 6 Dowl. 551. But if the tenant read the declaration and notice,
and said that he understood their nature and object, no explanation
was necessary. *Doe* d. *Jones* v. *Roe*, 1 Dowl. 518; *Doe* d. *Thompson* v. *Roe*, 2 Chit. R. 186. So where the tenant was an attorney.

Doe d. *Duke of Portland* v. *Roe*, 3 Man. & Gr. 397 ; 1 Dowl. N. S. 183. As the writ in ejectment now clearly expresses what is meant, no explanation of the service need be made. There have been several decisions to this effect at chambers. And see Lush, Prac. 768 (2nd ed.) ; Chit. Forms, 534 (7th ed.); *Edwards* v. *Griffith*, 16 C. B. 397. *Cessat ratione, cessat ipsa lex.*

Where the tenant in possession (Mrs. Magdalen Campbell) was at the time of service of the ejectment personated by another woman, who said that her name was Magdalen Campbell, the court granted a rule to show cause why such service should not be deemed sufficient, with special directions as to the mode of service, and which rule was afterwards made absolute. *Fenn* d. *Tyrrell* v. *Denn*, 2 Burr. 1181. The assizes would have been lost if this course had not been pursued.

On the other hand, where a tenant in possession, upon being served with the declaration and notice in ejectment, denied his own identity, the court granted a rule absolute in the first instance, there appearing to be good reason for believing that the person served really was the tenant in possession. *Doe* d. *Hunter* v. *Roe*, 5 Dowl. 553. In this case the person served at first said that his name was Cooper. But when the declaration in ejectment was delivered to him he said that his name was William Cooper, and that the declaration was addressed to and intended for Mr. William Henry Cooper, who was from home. The deponent immediately afterwards made inquiries at the adjoining house, and described the man he had served to the person resident there. The latter then said that he had no doubt that the person who received the declaration was William Henry Cooper, the tenant in possession. Rule absolute granted.

Service on a Welchman who did not understand English, with proof that another person who understood Welch explained to the tenant the intent and meaning of the declaration and notice, was held sufficient, although such other person did not join in the affidavit of service. *Doe* d. *Probert* v. *Roe*, 3 Dowl. 335. So where the tenant was a foreigner who did not understand English, explanation through the medium of an interpreter (who did not join in the affidavit of service) was held sufficient. *Doe* d. *Cuttell* v. *Roe*, 9 Dowl. 1023.

If the tenant in possession be a lunatic, and confined in a lunatic asylum, a writ in ejectment may be served on him personally there. *Doe* d. *Gibbard* v. *Roe*, 3 Man. & Gr. 87 ; 3 Scott, N. R. 363 ; 9 Dowl. 844. But if he has been found lunatic under an inquisition, and a committee of his estate appointed, service may be made on such committee. *Anon.*, Lofft. 401. Service on his daughter or servant who carries on his business for him on the premises in question during his absence is not sufficient. *Doe* d. *Brown* v. *Roe*, 6 Dowl. 270. But in a case where C., who lived with the lunatic and transacted his business, would not permit the deponent to have access to her, whereupon he delivered the declaration in ejectment to C., the court granted a rule nisi. *Doe* d. *Lord Aylesbury* v. *Roe*, 2 Chit. R. 163. Service on the wife of a lunatic, the doctor having refused permission to serve the lunatic himself, is sufficient. *Doe* d. —— v. *Roe*, 7 Jur. 725, Wightman, J. So is service upon the keeper of the asylum, and upon the lunatic's sister-in-law on the premises. *S. C.* In other actions against lunatics, see *Humphreys* v. *Griffiths*, 6 M. & W. 89 ; *Banfield* v. *Darell*, 2 Dowl. & L. 4 ; *Limbert* v. *Hayward*, 13 M. & W. 480 ; 2 Dowl. & L. 406 ; *Mutter* v. *Foulkes*, 5 Dowl. & L. 557.

The copy writ must be *left* with the tenant or other person on whom

is served ; otherwise only a rule or order *nisi* will be granted. *Doe
Forbes* v. *Roe*, 2 Dowl. 452; *Doe* d. *Mann* v. *Roe*, 11 M. & W.
7.

The writ of ejectment need not be produced at the time the copy is
rved. But if the tenant then demands to see the writ, and it be not
roduced, the *service* may, perhaps, be set aside as irregular with costs
pon an application made promptly to the court or a judge. *Thomas
Pearce*, 2 B. & C. 761; 4 D. & R. 317; *Petit* v. *Ambrose*, 6 M. &
. 274.

2. *On Tenant's Wife.*]—Service of a writ in ejectment may be made
a the tenant's wife, either on the premises sought to be recovered, or
t her husband's dwelling-house elsewhere, she residing there with him.
)oe d. *Morland* v. *Bayliss*, 6 T. R. 765; *Doe* d. *Baddam* v. *Roe*,
Bos. & P. 55; *Doe* d. *Briggs* v. *Roe*, 2 Cr. & Jer. 202; 1 Dowl.
12; *Doe* d. *Lord Southampton* v. *Roe*, 1 Hodges, 24; *Smith* d.
ord Stourton v. *Hurst*, 1 H. Blac. 644; *Doe* d. *Wingfield* v. *Roe*, 1
)owl. 693; *Doe* d. *Graef* v. *Roe*, 6 Dowl. 456; *Doe* d. *Boullott* v.
?oe, 7 Dowl. 463. But the affidavit of such service must show *where*
took place. *Oates* d. *Chatterton* v. *Cotes*, cited 6 T. R. 765; *Doe*
. *Bomsall* v. *Wrong*, 2 D. & R. 84; *Doe* d. *Williams* v. *Roe*, 2
)owl. 89; *Doe* d. *Mingay* v. *Roe*, 6 Dowl. 182; *Doe* d. *Royle* v. *Roe*,
C. B. 256. And if the service were made, not on any part of the
remises in question, but at the tenant's dwelling-house elsewhere, the
ffidavit must show that she was living with him there at the time.
)oe d. *Briggs* v. *Roe*, 2 Cr. & Jer. 202; 1 Dowl. 312; *Doe* d. *Boul-
att* v. *Roe*, 7 Dowl. 463; *Jenny* d. *Preston* v. *Cutts*, 1 B. & P.,
I. R., 308. Service on the tenant's wife *on the premises* sought to
e recovered is sufficient, notwithstanding the tenant has left the king-
om and settled abroad with no intention to return. *Doe* v. *Roe*, 1 D.
 R. 514; but see *Doe* d. *Harrison* v. *Roe*, 10 Price, 30. Service on
he tenant's wife in a shed where the husband carried on his business,
ot on the premises in question, but closely adjoining them, has been
eld sufficient. *Doe* v. *Roe*, 1 Dowl. 67. Service on the tenant's
rife " near the premises " is sufficient for a rule nisi. *Doe* d. *Mar-
uess of Bath* v. *Roe*, 7 Dowl. 692.

Service on the premises in question on a woman who there represented
erself to be the tenant's wife, is sufficient for a rule or order absolute
' the affidavit state the deponent's belief that such representation was
rue. *Doe* d. *Grange* v. *Roe*, 1 Dowl. N. S. 274. If the affidavit
o not state such belief, or says that the woman served merely lives
nd cohabits with the tenant as his wife, only a rule or order *nisi* will
e granted. *Doe* d. *Bremner* v. *Roe*, 8 Dowl. 135; *Doe* d. *Croley* v.
?oe, 2 Dowl. N. S. 344; *Doe* d. *Walker* v. *Roe*, 4 Moo. & P. 11. In
ne case of this nature the court refused even a rule nisi. *Doe* d. *Sim-
tons* v. *Roe*, 1 Chit. R. 228.

Service on the tenant's wife should be effected in the same manner
s service on the tenant himself. *Ante*, 99. Where a declaration in
jectment was delivered to the tenant's wife, and the attorney was
bout to read and explain the notice at the foot of it (according to the
hen practice); but she took it from him, and said she could read it
erself, and ran her eye over it as if she read it: held that such service
ras sufficient. *Goodright* d. *Waddington* v. *Thrustout*, 2 W. Blac.
00. Where the tenant's wife refused to receive a declaration in
jectment, or to hear it read or explained, and said that she would

have nothing to do with it, and immediately left the shop, whereupon the attorney left the declaration in the shop, but did not read it aloud or explain it there : held, that only a rule nisi could be granted. *Doe* d. *Neale* v. *Roe*, 2 Wils. 263. Where the tenant's wife refused to take the declaration, whereupon the attorney left it on the table, and explained the nature and object of it, and the wife flung it after him as he was leaving, whereupon he took it up and affixed it on the most conspicuous part of the premises : held, that such service was sufficient. *Doe* d. *Courthorpe* v. *Roe*, 2 Dowl. 441 ; and see *Doe* d. *Visger* v. *Roe*, 2 Dowl. 449. Where the tenant's wife refused to take the declaration, and ran in and shut the door, whereupon the attorney's clerk read it aloud and explained it outside, and then stuck it on the door : held sufficient for a rule nisi. *Doe* d. *Nash* v. *Roe*, 8 Dowl. 305. Where the declaration was given to the tenant's wife through a window, which she immediately shut down and went away, and so prevented any explanation being given : held, that such service was sufficient. *Doe* d. *George* v. *Roe*, 3 Dowl. 541.

3. *On Tenant's Servant, or some Member of his Family.*—Generally speaking, service of a writ in ejectment on the tenant's servant, or on his son, or daughter, or any other member of his family residing with him (except his wife) is insufficient, unless a subsequent acknowledgment by the tenant himself, or other special circumstances, be proved by affidavit. *Doe* d. *Halsey* v. *Roe*, 1 Chit. R. 100 ; *Doe* d. *Ginger* v. *Roe*, 9 Dowl. 336 ; *Doe* d. *Lord Dinorben* v. *Roe*, 2 M. & W. 374 ; *Doe* d. *Emerson* v. *Roe*, 6 Dowl. 736 ; *Doe* d. *George* v. *Roe*, 3 Dowl. 9 ; *Doe* d. *Smith* v. *Roe*, 1 Dowl. 614 ; *Doe* d. *Harris* v. *Roe*, 1 Dowl. N. S. 704 ; *Doe* d. *Fowler* v. *Roe*, 4 Dowl. & L. 639. Service on a servant of the tenant *left in care of the premises* is insufficient, even for a rule nisi. *Doe* d. *Read* v. *Roe*, 1 M. & W. 633 ; 5 Dowl. 85. Service on the tenant's servant, coupled with proof that the premises have since been deserted, is not sufficient for a rule nisi. *Doe* d. *Dobler* v. *Roe*, 2 Dowl. N. S. 383. Service on the tenant's female servant, upon the premises, coupled with a subsequent explanation to the tenant himself, elsewhere, of the meaning of the service, has been held insufficient. *Doe* d. *Ginger* v. *Roe*, 9 Dowl. 336 ; *Doe* d. *Shepherd* v. *Roe*, 10 Law J. (N. S.) Q. B. 129. Service on the tenant's daughter on the premises is not sufficient for a rule nisi, although the tenant's wife is shown to be aware of the proceeding, and to have avoided service. *Doe* d. *George* v. *Roe*, 3 Dowl. 9. Service on the tenant's son, coupled with proof of a statement by the tenant's wife that she had taken care to keep her husband out of the way to avoid being arrested or annoyed, is not sufficient. *Doe* d. *Wilson* v. *Smith*, 3 Dowl. 379. Service on the tenant's sister, coupled with the acknowledgment of another tenant of part (also served), that the tenant had handed the papers over to him as his landlord, is not sufficient. *Doe* d. *Harris* v. *Roe*, 1 Dowl. N. S. 704. Service on the tenant's foreman, coupled with a subsequent admission by the tenant's wife that she had communicated the declaration and notice to her husband, is not sufficient for a rule nisi. *Doe* d. *Tucker* v. *Roe*, 4 Moo. & Sc. 165 ; 2 Dowl. 775. But see *Doe* d. *Chaffey* v. *Roe*, 9 Dowl. 100 ; *Doe* d. *Governors of Grey Coat Hospital* v. *Roe*, 7 Man. & Gr. 537 ; 8 Scott, N. R. 274 ; *Doe* d. *Morgan* v. *Roe*, 1 Dowl. N. S. 543 ; *Doe* d. *Wetherall* v. *Roe*, 2 Dowl. 441. Service on a sister of the tenant, who undertakes to accept service on his behalf, is insufficient, even for a

ule nisi, unless her authority as agent be proved. *Doe* d. *Tibbs* v.
Roe, 3 Dowl. 380 ; and see *Doe* d. *Nottidge* v. *Roe*, 3 Man. & Gr. 28 ;
: Scott, N. R. 706 ; 1 Dowl. N. S. 750.

On the other hand, service of a writ in ejectment on the tenant's
ervant, or son, or daughter, or other member of his family, either on
he premises sought to be recovered, or at his dwelling-house elsewhere,
:oupled with proof of a subsequent acknowledgment by the tenant, or
iy the party served, or with proof of other special facts, from which it
nay reasonably be inferred that the copy writ reached the tenant's
iands, is sufficient for a rule or order nisi. Thus where the tenant
iimself acknowledges the receipt of the copy writ. *Doe* d. *Smith* v.
Roe, 4 Dowl. 265 ; *Doe* d. *Figgins* v. *Roe*, 2 Man. & Gr. 294 ; Ad.
Eject. 199. Service on the turnkey of a prison in which the tenant
was confined, coupled with a subsequent admission by the tenant that
ie had received it, has been held sufficient. *Doe* d. *Harris* v. *Roe*, 2
Dowl. 607. Service on the tenant's daughter, coupled with an admission by the tenant's wife that she had delivered the declaration to
ier husband, has been held sufficient for a rule nisi. *Doe* d. *Chaffey*
r. Roe, 9 Dowl. 100; but see *Doe* d. *Tucker* v. *Roe*, 4 Moo. & Sc. 165 ;
2 Dowl. 775. Service on a stranger on the premises, coupled with
)roof of an admission by the tenant's wife that *she* had received the
ieclaration, has been held sufficient for a rule nisi. *Doe* d. *Governors*
)f *Grey Coat Hospital* v. *Roe*, 7 Man. & Gr. 537 ; 8 Scott, N. R. 274 ;
Doe d. *Morgan* v. *Roe*, 1 Dowl. N. S. 543. Service on the tenant's
ion, with a subsequent acknowledgment by him that he had given it
:o his father, has been held sufficient for a rule nisi, the affidavit stating
:he deponent's belief that what the son said was true. *Doe* d. *Overy* v.
Roe, 6 Man. & Gr. 754 ; 7 Scott, N. R. 519 ; 1 Dowl. & L. 808 ; and
see *Doe* d. *Farnecombe* v. *Roe*, 10 Jur. 525. But if the affidavit do
not state such belief, the service, or the affidavit of service, will be
leemed insufficient. *Doe* d. *Hine* v. *Roe*, 4 Man. & Gr. 766. There
are, however, cases in which this has been overlooked, or deemed unnecessary. *Doe* d. *Timmins* v. *Roe*, 6 Dowl. 765 ; *Doe* d. *Threader*
v. *Roe*, 1 Dowl. N. S. 261 ; *Doe* v. *Roe*, 2 D. & R. 12 ; *Doe* d. *Cock-
'urn* v. *Roe*, 1 Dowl. 692 ; *Doe* d. *James* v. *Roe*, 1 Moo. & Sc. 597 ;
Doe d. *Sykes* v. *Roe*, 7 Scott, 121. Service on the daughter of a bed-
ridden tenant, on the premises, who afterwards stated that she had
lelivered the declaration to her mother : held sufficient for a rule nisi.
Doe d. *Frost* v. *Roe*, 8 Dowl. 301 ; *Doe* v. *Roe*, 2 D. & R. 12 ; *Doe*
d. *Messer* v. *Roe*, 5 Dowl. 716 ; *Doe* d. *Cockburn* v. *Roe*, 1 Dowl.
692 ; *Doe* d. *Tucker* v. *Roe*, 1 Harr. & Woll. 671. Service on the
tenant's niece, on the premises, the tenant being too ill to be seen,
coupled with an *affidavit from the niece* that she had delivered the
declaration to the tenant : held sufficient for a rule absolute. *Doe* d.
Eaton v. *Roe*, 7 Scott, 124. Service on a nephew of the tenant, on
the premises, who stated that the tenant refused to be seen : held sufficient for a rule nisi. *Doe* d. *Moody* v. *Roe*, 8 Dowl. 306. Service
on a servant of the tenant, who admits that his master is at home, but
refuses to see the deponent unless he first sends in his name and address :
held sufficient for a rule nisi. *Doe* d. *Hervey* v. *Roe*, 2 Price, 112.
Service on tenant's daughter, on the premises, with proof of subsequent
attempts at a compromise by the tenant, who said that he knew that
the time was approaching when something must be done : held sufficient for a rule absolute. *Doe* d. *Agar* v. *Roe*, 6 Dowl. 624. But,
in a subsequent case, where the service was on the tenant's son, on the

premises, and the attorney afterwards met the tenant and told him what he had done, whereupon the tenant said, then he had no time to lose, only a rule nisi was granted. *Doe* d. *Brickfield* v. *Roe,* 1 Dowl. N. S. 270. Service on the tenant's servant, who afterwards said that she had delivered it to her master, coupled with proof of a refusal by the tenant to make any admission as to the service, and referring the deponent to his attorney, who also refused to make any admission : held sufficient for a rule nisi. *Doe* d. *Elderton* v. *Roe,* 1 Dowl. N. S. 585. Service on the tenant's son-in-law, *near* the premises, coupled with proof of a summons for particulars of the premises sought to be recovered taken out by the tenant : held sufficient for a rule nisi. *Doe* d. *Evans* v. *Roe,* 2 Dowl. N. S. 334. Service on the tenant's servant, with proof of the declaration having since been seen in the hands of the tenant's attorney : held sufficient for a rule nisi. *Doe* v. *Roe,* 2 Dowl. 184 ; *Doe* d. *Mortlake* v. *Roe,* 2 Dowl. 444. Service on the tenant's daughter, on the premises, coupled with proof of a letter from the tenant's attorney, stating that the tenant had put the declaration in his hands : held sufficient for a rule nisi. *Doe* d. *Gibbard* v. *Roe,* 3 Man. & Gr. 87 ; 9 Dowl. 844 ; *Doe* d. *Teverell* v. *Snee,* 2 D. & R. 5 ; *Tenny* d. *Mills* v. *Cutts,* 1 Scott, 52. But in such cases the affidavit should distinctly show that the attorney is the attorney for the tenant in the matter. *Doe* d. *Reynolds* v. *Roe,* 1 C. B. 711. Service on the clerk of the tenant (an attorney) at his office, who stated that his employer was out of town, but that he, the clerk, would accept service for him, has been held sufficient, without any subsequent acknowledgment by the tenant. *Doe* d. *Gowar* v. *Roe,* 5 Man. & Gr. 375 ; 6 Scott, N. R. 41. There the clerk was deemed to be the authorized agent. *Per* Erle, J., in *Doe* d. *Fowler* v. *Roe,* 4 Dowl. & L. 639.

Where lodgers in a house cannot be served, service on the keeper of the house is sufficient for a rule or order nisi. *Doe* d. *Threader* v. *Roe,* 1 Dowl. N. S. 261.

4. On Tenant's Attorney, Agent or Bailiff.]—Generally speaking, service of a writ in ejectment on the tenant's attorney, agent, or bailiff, is insufficient, even for a rule nisi, unless the authority of such attorney, &c., to accept such service on behalf of the tenant be sufficiently proved. *Doe* d. *Collins* v. *Roe,* 1 Dowl. 613 ; *Doe* d. *Nottidge* v. *Roe,* 4 Man. & Gr. 28 ; 4 Scott, N. R. 706 ; 1 Dowl. N. S. 750. Service on the attorney of a mortgagee in possession, who undertook to accept the same and appear for his client : held insufficient, without proof of the attorney's authority, or a subsequent acknowledgment by the mortgagee. *Doe* d. *Collins* v. *Roe,* 1 Dowl. 613. Service on the tenant's sister, who undertook to accept service on her behalf, was held insufficient for a rule nisi, her authority to accept service as the tenant's agent not being proved. *Doe* d. *Tibbs* v. *Roe,* 3 Dowl. 380. Service on a person appointed by the Court of Chancery to manage an estate for an infant is not sufficient, "It amounts to no more than service on a gentleman's bailiff." *Goodtitle* d. *Roberts* v. *Badtitle,* 1 Bos. & P. 385. But service on the tenant's bailiff, with proof of an acknowledgment by the tenant's attorney that the declaration had come to his hands, and that he would appear for the tenant, has been held sufficient for a rule nisi. *Tenny* d. *Mills* v. *Cutts,* 1 Scott, 52 ; and see *Doe* d. *Teverell* v. *Snee,* 2 D. & R. 5 ; *Doe* d. *Reynolds* v. *Roe,* 1 C. B. 711. Service on the clerk of the tenant in possession (an attorney) at his office, who stated that his employer was out of town, but that he, the

erk, would accept service for him, has been held sufficient, without
·oof of the clerk's authority to accept service, or of any subsequent
:knowledgment by the tenant. *Doe* d. *Gowar* v. *Roe*, 5 Man. & Gr.
'5 ; 6 Scott, N. R. 41 ; *S. C. nom. Doe* d. *Bowar* v. *Roe*, 2 Dowl.
. S. 923. There the clerk was deemed to be an authorized agent.
'er Erle, J., in *Doe* d. *Fowler* v. *Roe*, 4 Dowl. & L. 639.

Service of a writ in ejectment on the tenant's agent, &c., which
ould of itself be insufficient, will frequently be deemed sufficient for
rule nisi, upon proof of other special facts, *ex. gr.* that the tenant has
›sconded, or keeps out of the way to avoid service, or has gone
›road, leaving the premises sought to be recovered in the care or pos-
ssion of his agent or servant. *Infra ; post,* 107.

5. *Where the Tenant absconds or keeps out of the Way to avoid
·rvice.*]—If it be proved to the satisfaction of the court or a judge
·at the tenant has absconded, or keeps out of the way to avoid ser-
·ce, or refuses to be seen, or being at home is denied, a service on his
rvant, or his son or daughter, or other member of his family, or by
fixing a copy of the writ on the outer door or other conspicuous part
' the property, will be deemed sufficient for a rule or order nisi. Thus
here it was proved by affidavit that the tenant had absconded, leaving
·e key of the house in the hands of his broker, with instructions to
t the house: held, that service on the broker, and by sticking a copy
·t the door of the house, was sufficient. *Doe* d. *Scott* v. *Roe*, 6 Bing.
. C. 207; 8 Dowl. 254. So where the tenant had absconded, leaving
·e key of the premises with his attorney, to whom he by letter re-
·rred the landlord : held, that service on such attorney, and by affix-
·g a copy on the outer door of the premises, was sufficient. *Doe* d.
·ovaston v. *Roe*, 4 Man. & Gr. 765. Where the tenant had ab-
·onded, leaving his niece to manage the house during his absence,
·rvice on the niece on ·the premises, and by affixing a copy on the
·ter door, was held sufficient for a rule nisi, to be served in like
·anner. *Sprightly* d. *Collins* v. *Dunch*, 2 Burr. 1116. Where the
·nant of a public-house kept out of the way to avoid being served :
·ld, that service on her foreman, who carried on her business for her,
·t the premises, was sufficient for a rule nisi. *Doe* d. *Morpeth* v.
·oe, 3 Dowl. 577; and see *Doe* d. *Knight* v. *Roe*, Barnes' Notes, 192;
·oe d. *Potter* v. *Roe*, 1 Hodges, 216. So service on the tenant's son
·t the premises, with proof that the tenant is keeping out of the way
· avoid service, is sufficient for a rule nisi, to be served in like manner.
·oe d. *Luff* v. *Roe*, 3 Dowl. 575. But the deponent must pledge his
·lief that the tenant keeps out of the way to avoid being served. *Doe
· Batson* v. *Roe*, 2 Chit. R. 176; *Doe* d. *Lowe* v. *Roe, Id.* 177. He
·ust also state the facts specially, so that the court or a judge may be
·abled to come to the conclusion that such belief is well founded.
·oe d. *Tarluy* v. *Roe*, 1 Chit. R. 506.

Proof that the tenant's *wife* keeps out of the way to avoid being
·rved, and of a service on the tenant's daughter on the premises, is
·t sufficient for a rule nisi. *Doe* d. *George* v. *Roe*, 3 Dowl. 9. Ser-
·:e on the tenant's female servant on the premises, who said that she
·ew all about it, as former attempts had ·been made to serve the de-
·tration, but without success, and by sticking a copy on the outer door,
·ıs held sufficient for a rule nisi ; which rule was afterwards made
·solute, upon proof of service thereof on the same servant in a yard

attached to the tenant's house, and near to the premises in question. *Doe* d. *Wright* v. *Roe*, 6 Dowl. 455.

Service on lodgers, by delivering the declaration and notice to the keeper of the house, with proof of several previous ineffectual attempts to serve them personally, has been held sufficient for a rule nisi. *Doe* d. *Threader* v. *Roe*, 1 Dowl. N. S. 261. Service on the tenant's nephew on the premises, who stated that the tenant refused to be seen: held sufficient for a rule nisi. *Doe* d. *Moody* v. *Roe*, 8 Dowl. 306. Service on the tenant's servant, who admitted that his master was at home, but refused to see the deponent, unless he first sent in his name and message: held sufficient for a rule nisi. *Doe* d. *Hervey* v. *Roe*, 2 Price, 112. Service on the tenant's servant, at his house on the premises in question, the servant denying that his master was at home, but the affidavit showing that such denial was probably false: held sufficient for a rule nisi. *Doe* d. *Turnercoft* v. *Roe*, 1 Harr. & Woll. 871. An affidavit of service stated that the deponent went to the premises and knocked at the door; that he received no answer, but shortly afterwards he heard some one, whom he believed was the tenant, come to the door and apparently listen; that he then read the declaration aloud, and explained the object of it; that he then thrust a copy of it through a pane in the window close to the entrance door, and there left it; and that the deponent verily believed that the tenant was in the house at the time: held sufficient for a rule nisi. *Doe* d. *Frost* v. *Roe*, 3 Dowl. 314; and see *Doe* d. *Lowndes* v. *Roe*, 7 M. & W. 439. In another case the affidavit stated the following service, viz.:—The deponent had gone to the premises, and knocked and called loudly at the door of the house, which he found shut up. Voices were heard conversing inside. Shortly afterwards the window was opened by some person, who, to the best of the deponent's belief, was the tenant in possession, and a quantity of filth thrown over him. The deponent then read very loudly the notice at the foot of the declaration, and gave the usual explanation. The deponent again called very loudly, but could get no answer. He then stuck a copy of the declaration on the door. The affidavit then went on to state that the tenant had been for some time keeping within the house, in order to avoid being served: held sufficient for a rule nisi, to be served on the tenant personally, or by sticking it up on the outside of the door, which rule was afterwards made absolute on an affidavit of service, by sticking the rule outside the house. *Doe* d. *Wills* v. *Roe*, 3 Dowl. 582. In another case the affidavit stated that the tenant was keeping out of the way to avoid service; that the deponent went to the house sought to be recovered, and having been informed that the tenant was at home, he put a ladder against the drawing-room window, and got up to it. While there, believing that the tenant was in the room, he explained at the window the nature of the proceeding, and a copy was stuck up on the door: held sufficient for a rule nisi, to be served at the dwellinghouse personally if possible, but if not, then in the same way as the copy of the declaration was served. *Doe* d. *Colson* v. *Roe*, 6 Dowl. 765. Where tenants lock themselves up in the premises sought to be recovered, and refuse to open the door, and a copy declaration or writ in ejectment is read aloud and explained outside, and immediately afterwards put under the door, a rule or order nisi will be granted. *Doe* d. *Summers* v. *Roe*, 5 Dowl. 552. Service by putting the declaration and notice under the door, the tenant being in the house at the time, but refusing to open the door, or to listen to the explanation given of the object and nature of the service, was held sufficient. *Doe* d. *Lowndes* v. *Roe*, 7 M. & W. 439. Where the tenants had rendered the premises inaccessible by a high wall, and evaded personal service: held, that service on a clerk at their counting-house adjoining the premises was sufficient for a rule nisi. *Doe* d. *Barrow* v. *Roe*, 1 Man. & Gr. 238.

6. *When the Tenant is abroad.*]—A declaration and notice in ejectment might formerly have been served on the tenant personally anywhere, even in a foreign country; *Doe* d. *Daniel* v. *Woodroffe*, 7 Dowl. 494; and it seems that a writ in ejectment may be served abroad on the tenant personally, as it is to be served "in the same manner as an ejectment has heretofore been served." Sect. 170; *ante*, 98. An affidavit of personal service need not mention where such service took place.

But where the tenant has gone abroad, and left the property in the care of his servant or agent, service of the writ in ejectment on such servant or agent, on the premises sought to be recovered, coupled with proof of the tenant being abroad, is sufficient for a rule or order nisi, to be served in like manner, and by sticking a copy on the door or other conspicuous part of the property. *Doe* d. *Robinson* v. *Roe*, 3 Dowl. 11; *Doe* d. *Treat* v. *Roe*, 4 Dowl. 278; *Doe* d. *Mather* v. *Roe*, 5 Dowl. 552; *Doe* v. *Roe*, 4 B. & A. 653. Where the tenant and his family had gone to America, service of a declaration in ejectment by affixing it on the outer door, and by leaving a copy with a servant of the tenant of *other* parts of the premises, has been held sufficient for a rule nisi. *Doe* d. *Osbaldiston* v. *Roe*, 1 Dowl. 456. Where it was believed that the tenant had gone to America, and there appeared reasonable grounds for such belief, service on his agent on the premises (who was left there to take care of them, and keep them in repair), and by sticking a copy on the outer door, was held sufficient for a rule nisi, to be served in like manner. *Doe* d. *Tabay* v. *Roe*, 1 Dowl. & L. 118. Service on the wife of the tenant's son, the tenant himself being in America, and the son managing his business during his absence, has been held sufficient for a rule nisi, to be served on the son. *Doe* d. *Potter* v. *Roe*, 2 Scott, 378; 1 Hodges, 316; and see *Doe* d. *Morpeth* v. *Roe*, 3 Dowl. 577.

On the other hand, it has been decided that where the tenant is abroad, and the service is made on his agent on the premises, such service is not sufficient, *unless the agency be distinctly sworn to*. *Doe* d. *Nottidge* v. *Roe*, 4 Man. & Gr. 28; 1 Dowl. N. S. 750. It is not sufficient that the party serving the writ swears that he was informed by the person served, and verily believes, that such person is the tenant's agent. *S. C.* In another case it was decided, that the affidavit of service on the agent must show that the tenant went or remains abroad *to avoid service* of the ejectment. *Roe* d. *Fenwick* v. *Doe*, 3 Moore, 576. It has even been decided that proof of service on the tenant's servant on the premises, and that the tenant had gone to France *to avoid service*, was insufficient. *Doe* d. *Jones* v. *Roe*, 1 Chit. R. 213. But these cases are contrary to many others of later date, before mentioned.

Service on the tenant's wife on the premises is sufficient, notwithstanding he had previously left this kingdom, and settled abroad, with no intention of returning. *Doe* v. *Roe*, 1 D. & R. 514; but see *Doe d. Harrison* v. *Roe*, 10 Price, 30.

7. *Where there are several Tenants.*]—Generally speaking, when there are several persons in possession of all or any part of the property sought to be recovered, all of them should be named in the writ. *Ante*, 83; *Doe* d. *Williamson* v. *Roe*, 10 Moore, 493; *Doe* d. *Lord Darlington* v. *Cock*, 4 B. & C. 259; *Doe* d. *Hewson* v. *Roe*, 1 Dowl. & L. 657. And each must be separately served. *Doe* d. *Levi* v. *Roe*, 7 Dowl. 102; *Doe* d. *Slee* v. *Roe*, 8 Dowl. 66; *Doe* d. *Cock* v. *Roe*, 6 Man. & Gr. 273; 6 Scott, N. R. 961. But if the parties are proved to be *in possession as joint tenants*, service on any one of them will be deemed sufficient for a rule or order nisi against all. *Doe* d. *Clothier* v. *Roe*, 6 Dowl. 291; *Doe* d. *Field* v. *Roe*, 2 Chit. R. 174; *Doe* d. *Bailey* v. *Roe*, 1 Bos. & P. 369. Thus in ejectment for copper works held by a trading firm under a lease, proof of a service on one of the partners, and also upon the manager of the works, is sufficient for a rule nisi against the firm, the affidavit stating them to be joint tenants in possession of the premises. *Doe* d. *Bennet* v. *Roe*, 7 C. B. 127; *Doe* d. —— v. *Roe*, 1 Dowl. & L. 873; *Doe* d. *Overton* v. *Roe*, 9 Dowl. 1039.

Service on one of two or more co-executors of a deceased lessee, who are proved to be *in possession*, is sufficient for a rule or order nisi against all, the affidavit showing them to be joint tenants in possession. *Doe* d. *Strickland* v. *Roe*, 4 Dowl. & L. 431; 1 Bail C. C. 210. But the affidavit must show them to be "in possession." *Doe* d. *Paul* v. *Hurst*, 1 Chit. R. 162; *Doe* d. *Governors of the Hospital of St. Margaret, Westminster* v. *Roe*, 1 Moore, 113.

Service on the official assignee of a bankrupt lessee, and on the messenger in possession, without any other service on the creditors' assignees, or on the bankrupt, is sufficient for a rule nisi against all the assignees, the affidavit showing them to be in possession as joint tenants. *Doe* d. *Baring* v. *Roe*, 6 Dowl. 456; *Doe* d. *Johnson* v. *Roe*, 1 Dowl. N. S. 493. If *all* the assignees be served, and also the messenger in possession, the rule or order will be absolute in the first instance. *Doe* d. *Chadwick* v. *Roe*, 9 Dowl. 492.

Churchwardens and overseers are not considered as joint tenants of parish property, therefore each must be separately served. *Doe* d. *Weeks* v. *Roe*, 5 Dowl. 405. If they occupy the property by placing some of the parish poor in it, that is sufficient to constitute them tenants "in possession." *Tupper* d. *Mercer* v. *Doe*, Barnes, 181.

Where a sole surviving joint tenant has been served, and the other is shown to have died since the commencement of the ejectment, the rule or order for leave to proceed will be made against the survivor only. *Doe* d. *Hewson* v. *Roe*, 5 Dowl. 404.

8. *On Companies and Public Commissioners.*]—By the Companies Clauses Consolidation Act, 1845 (8 & 9 Vict. c. 16, s. 135), "any summons or notice, or any writ, or other proceeding at law or in equity, requiring to be served upon the company, may be served by the same being left at, or transmitted through the post directed to the principal office of the company, or one of their principal offices where there shall be more than one, or being given personally to the secretary, or in case there be no secretary, then by being given to any one

lirector of the company." There is a similar enactment in the Railways
Clauses Consolidation Act, 1845 (8 & 9 Vict. c. 20, s. 138). By the
Commissioners' Clauses Act, 1847 (10 Vict. c. 16, s. 99), "any summons or notice, or any writ or other proceeding at law or in equity,
required to be served upon the commissioners, may be served by the
same being left at or sent through the post office, directed to the commissioners at their principal office, or one of their principal offices
where there shall be more than one, or by being given personally to
the clerk, or in case there be no clerk, then by being given to any
one commissioner."

Many acts of parliament incorporating railway or other companies,
or commissioners for executing undertakings of a public nature, before
the passing of the above acts, contain special provisions of the like
nature. In all such cases, if the writ in ejectment be served in the
manner prescribed, such service will be sufficient for a rule or order
for leave to proceed absolute in the first instance. *Doe* d. *Bromley* v.
Roe, 8 Dowl. 858.

Personal service on the secretary of a railway company, not on the
and sought to be recovered, nor at the office at the company, is sufficient for a rule absolute. *Doe* d. *Bayes* v. *Roe*. 16 M. & W. 98;
S. C., *nom. Doe* d. *Burgess* v. *Roe*, 4 Dowl. & L. 311. So service
of a writ of summons in London upon the secretary of a Scotch and
English railway company has been held regular. *Wilson* v. *The Cale-
donian Railway Company*, 5 Exch. 822; 1 Low. M. & P. 731. But
service of a writ of summons in Westminster upon the director of an
Irish railway company has been held null and void. *Evans* v. *The
Dublin and Drogheda Railway Company*, 14 M. & W. 142; 2 Dowl.
& L. 865; 3 Rail. C. 760. Service upon a clerk of the secretary, at
the company's office, is insufficient. *Walker* v. *The Universal Salvage
Company*, 16 M. & W. 438; 4 Dowl. & L. 558.

Service on a book-keeper of a railway company on a part of the
premises which he occupied and where he slept, has been held sufficient
for a rule absolute. *Doe* v. *Roe*, 1 Dowl. 23. So also, service at the
London station upon an officer of a railway company, who was sworn
to be in possession of the premises sought to be recovered, was held
sufficient. *Doe* d. *Martyn* v. *Roe*, 6 Scott, 610.

In ejectment against a canal company for part of the bed of the
canal, service on a clerk of the company at their office has been held
sufficient for a rule nisi. *Doe* d. *Fisher* v. *Roe*, 10 M. & W. 21; 2
Dowl. N. S. 225; 3 Rail. C. 145—in this case Lord Abinger, C. B.,
asked, "Why did you not serve the directors?" Service on the clerk
of an incorporated canal company (not authorized to sue or be sued by
their clerk), on a portion of the premises sought to be recovered, has
been held sufficient for a rule nisi, although the clerk did not reside
there. *Doe* d. *Ross* v. *Roe*, 5 Dowl. 157; and see *Doe* d. —— v. *Roe*,
1 Dowl. & L. 873.

Service on the secretary of the East India Company at his office
(not on the premises sought to be recovered) is sufficient. *Doe* d.
The Coopers' Company v. *Roe*, 8 Dowl. 134.

The affidavit of service upon a railway or other company, or upon
the commissioners of a public undertaking, must unequivocally state
that such company or commissioners are "tenants in possession" of the
land sought to be recovered, and must proceed to show a sufficient
service on them. An affidavit of service on one of several road commissioners and their clerk, not stating them to be "tenants in posses-

sion," but that the land sought to be recovered had been illegally taken into their road, and that the road was vested in them under their act of parliament, has been held insufficient. *Doe* d. *White* v. *Roe*, 8 Dowl. 71.

9. *For Chapels, School-Houses, &c.*]—In ejectment for recovery of a chapel, proof of service on the minister and on one of the trustees, and that a copy had been stuck up on the door, was held sufficient. *Doe* d. *Smith, Bart.*, v. *Roe*, 8 Dowl. 509. So service on the surviving lessees, and on the sextoness, has been held sufficient. *Doe* d. *Kirschner* v. *Roe*, 7 Dowl. 97. In ejectment for a Baptist Chapel with a school-room attached, service on a person who was in the occupation of the school-room, and on another person who paid the rates and taxes for the chapel, whereof there was no fixed minister, was held sufficient for a rule nisi. *Doe* d. *Earl Somers* v. *Roe*, 8 Dowl. 292. In ejectment for a chapel, the tenant having quitted the country, and not being likely to return: held, that service upon the tenant's wife, and on his servant, and on the person in whose custody the keys of the chapel were placed, was sufficient. *Doe* d. *Dickens* v. *Roe*, 7 Dowl. 121; and see *Doe* d. *Scott* v. *Roe*, 5 Scott, 732; 6 Bing. N. C. 207; 8 Dowl. 254.

In ejectment to recover buildings used as a free school, service may be made on the master, or other person in occupation of the school, and by sticking a copy on the outer door. *Doe* d. *Earl Somers* v. *Roe*, 8 Dowl. 292; *Doe* d. *Smith, Bart.*, v. *Roe*, *1d*. 509.

Where the premises in question were in the possession of a charitable institution as tenants, service on the matron upon the premises, and upon the secretary, coupled with a subsequent acknowledgment by the solicitor to the Association of the copy having reached his hands, is sufficient. *Doe* d. *Fishmongers' Company* v. *Roe*, 2 Dowl. N. S. 689.

10. *Where the possession is vacant.*]—Service of a writ in ejectment may be made "in case of vacant possession by posting a copy thereof upon the door of the dwelling-house or other conspicuous part of the property." 15 & 16 Vict. c. 76, s. 170; *ante*, 98.

Where this mode of service is resorted to, it will be necessary to satisfy the court or a judge that it is a "case of vacant possession," within the meaning of the act. It is to be observed that the writ in ejectment must be directed to "the persons in possession by name." Sect. 168, *ante*, 83. If the possession be vacant the writ must be directed to the person who would be tenant in possession if he had not abandoned the possession; or if he be dead to his executors or administrators. *Ante*, 85. The claimants will have to satisfy the court or a judge upon two points, which at first sight appear somewhat irreconcilable,—viz. 1. That the person mentioned by name in the writ as a defendant, or tenant in possession, was properly so named therein. 2. That the possession was vacant within the meaning of the act.

It must not be supposed that premises are *vacant*, merely because nobody happens to be in or upon them at the time of the issuing or service of the writ. 2 Chit. Arch. 965 (9th ed.); *Doe* d. *Burrowes* v. *Roe*, 7 Dowl. 326. That frequently happens when there is a tenant in possession. There may be a legal or constructive possession without any actual occupation, or during the tenant's absence. *Doe* d. *Johnson* v. *Roe*, 12 Law J. (N. S.) Q. B. 97. If he have left any of his goods or chattels on the premises, or any part thereof, *ex. gr.* beer in a cellar or hay in a barn, he thereby virtually retains possession of the premises, and it would be improper to proceed in ejectment as in case of a vacant possession, especially if his place of residence be known. *Savage* v. *Dent*, 2 Stra. 1064; 1 Chit. R. 506, note. But if the court or a judge be satisfied by affidavit that the person named in the writ was recently tenant in possession of the premises sought to be recovered, and that he has since *abandoned and deserted the possession* of them, and cannot be served personally, or otherwise, with a copy of the writ, and that nobody was in or upon the premises or any part thereof at the time when a copy of the writ was posted upon the door of the dwelling-house, or other conspicuous part of the property (*see the form of such Affidavit, Appendix, No.* 37), a rule or order nisi will be granted, with special directions as to the service thereof. *See form of Order, Appendix, No.* 38. Under such circumstances the former practice was to refuse even a rule nisi, and to leave the claimant to proceed as in case of a vacant possession. *Doe* d. *Norman* v. *Roe*, 2 Dowl. 399, 428; *Doe* d. *Showell* v. *Roe*, 2 Cr., M. & R. 42; *S. C. nom. Doe* d. *Schovell* v. *Roe*, 3 Dowl. 691; *Doe* v. *Roe*, 4 Dowl. 173; *Doe* d. *Burrows* v. *Roe*, 7 Dowl. 326; *Doe* d. *Darlington* v. *Cock*, 4 B. & C. 259; *Doe* d. *Lovell* v. *Roe*, 1 Chit. R. 505; *Doe* d. *Lowe* v. *Roe*, 2 Chit. R. 177. But the decisions on that point were not uniform; and sometimes a rule nisi was granted. *Doe* d. *Osbaldiston* v. *Roe*, 1 Dowl. 456; *Doe* d. *Hindle* v. *Roe*, 3 M. & W. 279; 6 Dowl. 393; *Doe* d. *Timothy* v. *Roe*, 8 Scott, 126; *Doe* d. *Pope* v. *Roe*, 8 Scott, N. R. 321; 7 Man. & Gr. 602; *Doe* d. *Chippendale* v. *Roe*, 7 C. B. 125; *Doe* d. *Tarluy* v. *Roe*, 1 Chit. R. 506; *Fenn* d. *Buckle* v. *Roe*, 1 Bos. & Pul. New R. 293. The mode of proceeding in case of a vacant possession was formerly distinct from the ordinary mode, and somewhat peculiar. Ad. Eject. Chap. V.; Woodf. Land. & Ten. 858 (5th ed.); 2 Chit. Arch. 964 (8th ed.). Now, however, the only difference seems to be in the mode of serving the writ and in the affidavit of service.

Affidavit of Service.]—By the Practice Rules of H. T. 1853, No. 112, "no judgment in ejectment for want of appearance or defence, whether limited or otherwise, shall be signed *without first filing an affidavit of service* of the writ according to the Common Law Procedure Act, 1852, and a copy thereof, or, *where personal service has not been effected*, without first obtaining a judge's order or a rule of court authorizing the signing such judgment; which said rule or order, or a duplicate thereof, shall be filed, together with a copy of the writ."

If the affidavit upon which judgment is signed be insufficient, an application may be made to set aside the judgment and execution, and for a writ of restitution. But in answer to such application the plaintiff may show that the irregularity has been waived; especially if the objection be of a technical nature. *Edwards* v. *Griffith*, 15 C. B. 397.

If the affidavit state a service of a copy of the writ on each tenant *personally*, no rule or order will be necessary to authorize the claimants to sign judgment for want of appearance or defence. *See the form of such Affidavit, Appendix, No.* 29. But in all other cases a rule or order must be obtained. *Reg.* 112, *supra.* Such rule or order will be granted upon an *ex parte* application made to the court, or to a judge at chambers, and supported by an affidavit or affidavits showing a sufficient service upon the tenant or tenants in possession. We have already considered fully what does or does not amount to a sufficient service. *Ante*, 98—111. The affidavits of service, &c., will of course vary in each case, according to the mode of service and the special facts. *See the forms, Appendix, Nos.* 30—37.

The affidavit should be entitled in the proper court, and with the proper title of the cause *at full length*, *i. e.* with the names of all the claimants, as plaintiffs; *Doe* d. *Barles* v. *Roe*, 5 Dowl. 447; *Doe* d. *Cousins* v. *Roe*, 4 M. & W. 68; *Doe* d. *Neville* v. *Lloyd*, 2 Dowl. N. S. 330; and with the names of all the persons to whom the writ is directed by name, as defendants. Chit. Forms, 534 (7th ed.); *see post, Appendix, No.* 19, *notes* (*b*) *and* (*c*). It should not be abbreviated thus: " Between A. B. *and another*" (*or* " others") " plaintiffs, and C. D. *and another*" (*or* " others") " defendants." *Doe* d. *Pryme* v. *Roe*, 8 Dowl. 340.

Generally speaking the person who served the copy writ should make, or join in, the affidavit of service; but a person who saw the copy writ served may make the affidavit. *Goodtitle* d. *Wanklen* v. *Badtitle*, 2 Bos. & P. 120. A person who merely acts as an interpreter need not join in the affidavit. *Ante*, 100. Where the copy writ was delivered to the tenant's servant, or to some member of his family, who afterwards delivered it to the tenant, if such servant, &c., can be induced to join in the affidavit a rule or order absolute in the first instance will be granted. *Doe* d. *Eaton* v. *Roe*, 7 Scott, 124. Otherwise only a rule or order nisi, to be served in such manner as the court or a judge shall direct. *Ante*, 103.

The affidavit must state *positively* that the person served (whether personally or otherwise) was the " tenant in possession" of the premises, or of part of the premises, sought to be recovered. *Doe* d. *Dolby* v. *Hitchcock*, 2 Dowl. N. S. 1. An affidavit merely stating the deponent's *belief* that the person served was tenant in possession, &c., is insufficient. *Doe* d. *George* v. *Roe*, 3 Dowl. 22; *Doe* v. *Badtitle*, 1 Chit. R. 215. It is not sufficient to swear that the copy writ was served on the party therein named, being the " person in possession," &c. *Doe* d. *Robinson* v. *Roe*, 1 Chit. R. 118, note (*a*); *Doe* d. *Fraser* v. *Roe*, 5 Dowl. 720. An affidavit of service on " two women in possession," mentioning their names, but not stating them to be tenants in possession, or servants of tenants, is insufficient. *Doe* d. *Story* v. *Roe*, 4 Man. & Gr. 843. An affidavit of service on C. D., " the occupier" of the premises in question, is insufficient. *Doe* d. *Jackson* v. *Roe*, 4 Dowl. 609. An affidavit of service on one of several road commissioners, and their clerk, not stating them to be joint tenants in possession, but that the premises sought to be recovered formed part of a road which was vested in them by a local act of parliament, is not sufficient. *Doe* d. *White* v. *Roe*, 8 Dowl. 71.

Where a constructive service is relied on, the affidavit must state that the deponent *served the tenant in possession* with a copy of the writ, by delivering the same to and leaving it with the person to whom it was actually delivered, at such a place, &c., showing specially why such service should be deemed good service on the tenant. *Doe* d. *Piggot* v. *Roe*, 4 Dowl. & L. 88.

An affidavit of service on the *wife* of a tenant in possession must state *where* such service took place. *Ante*, 101; *see the form, Appendix, No.* 30. It must show either a service on the premises in

estion, or at some place adjoining, or very near to them. *Ante,* 101.
r at the tenant's residence elsewhere, and that she then resided with
m-there. *Ante,* 101. It should also state that the person to whom
e copy writ was delivered was the tenant's wife, or that she so repre-
nted herself at the time, and that the deponent verily believes such
presentation to be true. *Ante,* 101. But if such belief cannot be
orn to, or if the woman served merely cohabited with the tenant as
a wife, only a rule or order nisi will be granted. *Ante,* 101.

An affidavit of service on the tenant's servant, or on his son or
ughter, or other member of his family on the premises in question,
residing with him elsewhere, must not only state such service, but
ust go on to show a subsequent acknowledgment by the tenant him-
lf that the copy writ reached his hands, or to that effect; *ante,* 102;
a subsequent statement by the servant or other person to whom the
py writ was delivered, that he or she had given it to the tenant, and
at the deponent verily believes such statement to be true. *Ante,*
3; *see the form, Appendix, No.* 31. If the servant, &c. can be
duced to join in the affidavit, so much the better. *Doe* d. *Eaton* v.
oe, 7 Scott, 124; *ante,* 103. But where there has not been any such
bsequent acknowledgment or statement, other special facts must be
posed to, from which the court or a judge may reasonably infer
at the copy writ has reached the tenant's hands; *ante,* 103, 104;
that he has absconded, or keeps out of the way to avoid service;
te, 105; or that he has gone abroad. *Ante,* 107. Where the
fidavit states the deponent's *belief* on the above points, it should
so state the facts upon which such belief is founded, so that the court
a judge may see that such belief is reasonable, and may be able to
me to the same conclusion. *Doe* d. *Jones* v. *Roe,* 1 Chit. R. 213.

An affidavit of service on the tenant's agent should distinctly show
e authority of the agent to accept service on the tenant's behalf, or
cts from which such authority may be implied. *Ante,* 104; *see the
rm, Appendix, No.* 32. So where a subsequent acknowledgment by
e attorney of the tenant is relied on to aid an otherwise insufficient
rvice, the affidavit must distinctly show that such attorney is the
torney for the tenant in the particular business or matter. *Doe* d.
eynolds v. *Roe,* 1 C. B. 711.

Where several persons are named in the writ as defendants or tenants
possession, the affidavit of service must show a sufficient service on
ch; *ante,* 108; *Doe* d. *Levi* v. *Roe,* 7 Dowl. 102; *Doe* d. *Slee* v.
e, 8 Dowl. 66; *Doe* d. *Cock* v. *Roe,* 6 Man. & Gr. 273; 6 Scott,
R. 961; or that they or some of them were in possession of all or
rt of the property *as joint tenants. Ante,* 108; *see the forms, Ap-
ndix, Nos.* 34, 35.

The affidavit of service on a company, or upon a public body of
mmissioners, should show a service exactly in accordance with the
ovisions of some statute. *Ante,* 109; *see the form, Appendix, No.*
. The judge's attention should be drawn to the particular section
ied on, or to some case in which a service similar to that sworn to
s been decided to be sufficient. *Ante,* 108, 109. So also where a
apel or free school is sought to be recovered. *Ante,* 110.

Where the affidavit states a service only by posting a copy of the
it upon the door of the dwellinghouse or other part of the property,
nust go on to state specially the facts showing a "case of vacant
ssession" within the meaning of the statute. *Ante,* 110. It must,

amongst other things, show that the tenant named in the writ as a
defendant has *abandoned and deserted the possession. Ante,* 111; *see
the form, Appendix, No.* 37.

Rule or Order for Judgment for want of Appearance.]—It is entirely in the discretion of the court or a judge to grant a rule or order
absolute in the first instance, or only a rule or order nisi, and, in the
latter case, to direct in what manner such rule or order shall be served.
See the form, Appendix, No. 38. A copy must be served as directed,
and an affidavit of such service made. It will be no sufficient answer
to the application to disprove by affidavit some of the facts upon which
the rule or order nisi was obtained. Thus where a rule nisi was granted
upon affidavit of service on the tenant's son, and upon proof of facts
showing that the tenant was keeping out of the way to avoid service;
in answer to which it was clearly proved by the affidavit of the tenant
and his two sons that the tenant was at the time absent from home on
business, and not to avoid service of the ejectment: but the affidavit
did not show that the son had not given the declaration to his father
on his return: held insufficient; and *per* Parke, B., " The father does
not swear that he did not get the declaration before the first day of
term. The affidavits do not exclude the possibility of the son having
given it to him; and if he did, we should not interfere. He had better
appear." *Doe* d. *Protheroe* v. *Roe,* 4 Dowl. 385. In another case,
counsel for the tenant in possession objected that the service as sworn
to was insufficient; but as he had no affidavit that the notice and
declaration had not come to the hands of the tenant, the court made
the rule absolute. *Doe* d. *Fowler* v. *Roe,* 4 Dowl. & L. 640. When
an explanation of the service was necessary, it was no answer to a rule
or order nisi to deny that the declaration or writ in ejectment was
read over or explained at the time of service. *Doe* d. *Kenrick* v. *Roe,*
5 Dowl. & L. 578.

An application to set aside the service of a writ in ejectment for
irregularity must be made within a reasonable time, and before the
party applying has taken a fresh step after knowledge of the irregularity.
Reg. Prac. H. T. 1853, No. 135; *Doe* d. *Parr* v. *Roe,* 1 Q. B. 700.
In answer to such application it may be shown that the irregularity
(if any) has been waived. *Edwards* v. *Griffith,* 15 C. B. 397.

CHAPTER XI.

PROCEEDINGS BY DEFENDANT ON BEING SERVED WITH THE WRIT.

1. *Notice of Ejectment to Defendant's Landlord.*] — By 15 & 16 Vict. c. 76, s. 209, " every tenant to whom any writ in ejectment shall be delivered, or to whose knowledge it shall come, shall *forthwith give notice thereof* to his landlord, or his bailiff or receiver, under penalty of forfeiting the value of *three years' improved or rack rent* of the premises demised or holden in the possession of such tenant, to the person of whom he holds, to be recovered by action in any court of common law having jurisdiction for the amount."

The main object of the above enactment is to secure to the landlord a reasonable opportunity of applying to the court or a judge for leave to appear and defend the action for those parts of the property claimed, which are in the possession of his tenants named in the writ. *Post,* Chap. XII.

Where the tenant omits to give his landlord notice of the writ, and suffers judgment by default, the court will not, *after execution executed,* set aside such judgment and the subsequent proceedings, and let in the landlord to defend the ejectment, unless collusion between the plaintiff and the tenant in possession be proved. *Doe d. Thompson* v. *Roe,* 4 Dowl. 115; *Goodtitle* v. *Badtitle,* 4 Taunt. 820. But they will do so if such collusion be proved. *Doe d. Grocers' Company* v. *Roe,* 5 Taunt. 205. In other cases they will leave the landlord to his remedy against his tenant under the above act, and to bring a new ejectment. *Goodtitle* v. *Badtitle, supra;* but see *Doe* d. *Meyrick* v. *Roe,* 2 Cr. & Jer. 682; *Doe* d. *Stratford* v. *Shail,* 2 Dowl. & L. 161. Too much strictness in this respect may sometimes occasion serious injustice. " A man's title may depend entirely upon his possession, and he may be unable, if once turned out of possession, to show such a title as would justify him in bringing an action to recover back the land; to say nothing of the additional expense, trouble and anxiety that might be cast upon him." *Per* Pollock, C. B., in *Butler* v. *Meredith,* 11 Exch. 91; and see *per* Martin, B., *Id.* 99. There may be collusion between the tenant and the claimant without the landlord being able to prove it, especially by affidavit.

The above section is a re-enactment of 11 Geo. 2, c. 19, s. 12. It is considered as remedial to the landlord, rather than as penal to the tenant, and therefore it ought to be construed liberally. *Crocker* v. *Fothergill,* 2 B. & A. 652. The improved or rack rent does not mean the rent actually reserved by the lease, but such a rent as the landlord and tenant might fairly agree on *at the time of the service of the writ in ejectment. S. C.* Consequently if the lease were made in consideration of a large fine or premium and a small rent; or if the demised premises have since been built upon, and the annual value thereof greatly increased, the improved or rack rent for the time being, when the writ in ejectment is served, is the measure of damages recoverable by the landlord. *S. C.* If the premises recovered in the ejectment do not include *all the premises comprised in the lease,* the landlord may nevertheless recover the improved or rack rent of *all the premises demised, with the appurtenances,* and not merely of those so recovered. *S. C.* If the lease were granted to two or more persons as lessees, or it has been assigned to two or more persons, and *one* of such lessees or assignees, being in possession together with the others of the demised premises, and served with a writ in ejectment, omits to give notice thereof to his landlord forthwith pursuant to sect. 209, he will thereby render himself liable to the whole penalty in respect of all the demised premises. *S. C.* "The remedy given by the act is not confined to cases where the ejectment proceeds to a writ of possession, but will include a case where the landlord, after a writ in ejectment delivered to his tenant, and before judgment signed, discovers the fraud, and is let in to defend the ejectment. In such a case he would be clearly entitled to maintain this action." *Id.* 660, *per* Holroyd, J. On the other hand, it has been decided that a tenant to a mortgagor, who does not give him notice of an ejectment brought by the mortgagee to enforce an attornment, is not liable to a penalty for secreting the ejectment. *Buckley* v. *Buckley,* 1 T. R. 647. "The court were of opinion that this case did not come within the statute, for that it only extended to cases where ejectments were brought *which were inconsistent with the landlord's title.* They observed likewise that the ejectment was brought for the purpose of compelling the tenant to attorn to the mortgagee, which the act expressly permitted him to do." *Id.* 648.

The notice must be given *forthwith. Ante,* 115; *see the form, Appendix, No.* 58. As to the meaning of the word "forthwith," see *per* Holroyd, J., in *Crocker* v. *Fothergill, supra; Spenceley* v. *Robinson,* 3 B. & C. 658; *S. C.* Moo. & Mal. 300; *Reg.* v. *Justices of Worcestershire,* 7 Dowl. 789; *Ex parte Lowe,* 3 Dowl. & L. 737; *Reg.* v. *Robinson,* 12 A. & E. 672; 4 P. & D. 391; *Tennant* v. *Bell,* 9 Q. B. 684, 690; *Doe* d. *Pittman* v. *Sutton,* 9 C. & P. 706. "There is no doubt the word *forthwith* means with all reasonable celerity." *Per* Tindal, C. J., in *Burgess* v. *Boetefeur,* 7 Man. & Gr. 494.

If a copy of the writ in ejectment be forthwith delivered to the landlord, or his bailiff or receiver, that will probably be deemed sufficient, without any written notice accompanying it. But it is safer and more prudent to give a written notice. By Reg. Prac. H. T. 1853, No.

1, "all notices required by these rules or by the practice of the court ill be in writing;" but a notice of the above nature does not appear fall within that rule.

A penal action under sect. 209 (*ante*, 115) may be brought in the unty court, where the penalty or sum claimed does not exceed 50*l*. *othecaries' Company* v. *Burt*, 5 Exch. 363; 1 Low. M. & P. 405; d see *Izaac* v. *Wylde*, 7 Exch. 163; 2 Low. M. & P. 676. But if : penalty exceed 20*l*., and in some other cases falling within the k 10 Vict. c. 95, s. 128, the action may be brought in one of the perior courts, which have concurrent jurisdiction. The writ of mmons may be specially indorsed pursuant to 15 & 16 Vict. c. 76, 25. Such indorsement may be as follows:—

"The following are the particulars of the plaintiff's claim:—A nalty of £—— (being the value of three years' [improved *or* rack] it of certain demised premises held by and in the possession of the fendant as tenant thereof to the plaintiff), under the statute 15 & 16 ct. c. 76, s. 209."

If the plaintiff claim by the indorsement too much, that will not :vent him from recovering what he is actually entitled to. If the fendant do not appear in due time, final judgment may be signed by fault for the whole sum claimed. 15 & 16 Vict. c. 76, s. 27. If the fendant appear, the plaintiff must declare and proceed to trial in the ial manner. *See form of declaration, Appendix, No.* 59; *Crocker Fothergill*, 2 B. & A. 652; 7 Wentw. Pl. 359.

The defendant may plead *nil debet* or not guilty "by statute" 21 :. 1, c. 4, s. 4. *Jones* v. *Williams*, 4 M. & W. 375; 7 Dowl. 206; *the form, Appendix, No.* 60. In the margin of such plea he must ert the words "by statute 21 Jac. 1, c. 4, s. 4—public act;" other- se such plea shall be taken not to have been pleaded by virtue of y act of parliament; and such memorandum shall be inserted in the rgin of the issue, and of the nisi prius record." Reg. Pl. H. T. 53, No. 21.

With respect to the evidence, the plaintiff must prove all the material ts stated in the declaration. The tenancy of the defendant must be ived in the same manner as in ejectment by a landlord against his ant after the expiration of the term. See *post*, Chap. XXXVII. e service of the writ in ejectment must also be proved by the person o served it, or otherwise. The defendant should have notice to duce the copy writ in ejectment if it remain in his possession or ver. The omission of the defendant forthwith to give notice of the it to the landlord, or his bailiff or receiver, should be proved. Some- es it may be necessary to call both of them, or the defendant him- ', to prove such omission. Perhaps the defendant could not be npelled to give evidence against himself in such a case, as no man be compelled to give evidence which may criminate or tend to cri- nate himself, or to subject himself to any forfeiture or penalty. *Boyle Cardinal Wiseman*, 10 Exch. 647. The improved annual value or k rent of all the demised premises at the time the writ in ejectment s served should be proved by a sufficient number of competent wit- ses, *ex. gr.* surveyors, land agents, architects, builders, &c. In *ker* v. *Fothergill*, 2 B. & A. 652, 655, Garrow, B., "stated to the y that the improved rack rent of the premises was that which the llord could obtain from a respectable tenant at the time the grievance nplained of was committed; that in determining that, they were not bound by the estimate given by the witnesses, but might act upon their own judgment, and were at liberty to give a lower sum if they thought fit." And the court in banc held that the directions of the learned judge, with respect to estimating the improved or rack rent, were quite correct. The reserved rent could not be considered as the improved rent, the latter being what the landlord granting and the tenant taking might fairly agree on at the time. It is true that it must not be any fanciful rent, nor one which a person having peculiar facilities would pay, but it must be such as a stranger might fairly be expected to give." *Id.* 656. In this case the rent reserved by the lease was 134*l.* per annum; the jury found a verdict for the plaintiff for 4,500*l.* which the court refused to disturb. Several other points were decided in this case, which we have fully noticed, *ante*, 116.

The plaintiff, being "the party grieved," is entitled to recover not only the penalty, but also his costs of suit. Bull. N. P. 333; *North* v. *Wingate*, Cro. Car. 559; *Ward* v. *Snell*, 1 H. Black. 10; *Tyte* v. *Glode*, 7 T. R. 267. He is, however, only entitled to the ordinary costs as between party and party. *Crocker* v. *Fothergill*, 2 B. & A. 622, note (*a*). If he recover only 20*l.*, or less, he is not entitled to any costs, without a certificate of the judge pursuant to 13 & 14 Vict. c. 61, s. 12; or a judge's order under 15 & 16 Vict. c. 54, s. 4. It would seem, however, that a certificate for costs on the "higher scale" is not necessary, the action not being "on contract" within the meaning of the directions to taxing officers of H. T. 1853, No. 7. 13 C. B. 97; 1 E. & B. lxvi. It will, however, be prudent to obtain such certificate, if possible, until it be decided to be unnecessary.

If the plaintiff be nonsuited, or the defendant obtain a verdict, the defendant is entitled to costs as in other actions.

2. *Address and Description of the Claimants, how obtained.*]—By 15 & 16 Vict. c. 76, s. 169, "the same proceedings may be had to ascertain whether the writ was issued by the authority of the attorney whose name was indorsed thereon, and who and what the claimants are, and their abode, and as to staying the proceedings upon writs issued without authority, as in the case of writs in personal actions." This refers to sect. 7, which is as follows : " every attorney whose name shall be indorsed on any writ issued by authority of this act shall, on demand in writing, made by or on behalf of any defendant, declare *forthwith* whether such writ has been issued by him, or with his authority or privity ; and if he shall answer in the affirmative, then he shall also, in case the court or a judge shall so order and direct, declare in writing, within a time to be allowed by such court or judge, the profession, occupation or quality, and place of abode of the plaintiff, on pain of being guilty of a contempt of the court from which such writ shall appear to have been issued ; and if such attorney shall declare that the writ was not issued by him, or with his authority or privity, all proceedings upon the same shall be stayed, and no further proceedings shall be taken thereupon without leave of the court or a judge."

The Uniformity of Process Act, 2 Will. 4, c. 39, contained a clause to the like effect. Sect. 17.

The first step is to serve a demand in writing on the plaintiff's attorney, whether the writ in ejectment has been issued by him or with his authority or privity. *See the form, Appendix, No.* 61. This, it would seem, should be served on the attorney *personally*, or it should be erwards ascertained *from him* that it reached his hands : otherwise attachment will be granted for non-compliance with it. To this he st "forthwith" give an answer in the affirmative or negative. the form, *Appendix, No.* 62. As to the meaning of the word 'orthwith," see *ante,* 116. If he give no answer it seems that he ll thereby be guilty of a contempt of court, and an attachment may moved for. Sect. 169. Or, perhaps, an order may be obtained to y all further proceedings in the action until an answer be given ; and t the plaintiff's attorney do pay the costs of such application, to be ted. If the answer be in the *negative* a judge's order may thereupon obtained to stay all further proceedings in the action. *See form of mnons and Order, Appendix, Nos.* 63 *and* 64. If the answer be in affirmative, a summons and order may be obtained for particulars the profession, occupation or quality, and place of abode of the plain- or plaintiffs. *See forms of Summons and Order, Appendix, Nos. and* 66. No such order will be made if it appear to the judge that real object of the defendant is to arrest the plaintiff upon a criminal arge. *Harris* v. *Holler,* 7 Dowl. & L. 319. The order will, if so rded, operate as a stay of proceedings until the required particulars given. *See form of such Particulars, Appendix, No.* 67. If in- ficient or incorrect particulars be delivered, the defendant should tain a summons and order for further and better particulars. *Smith Bond,* 11 M. & W. 326; 1 Dowl. & L. 287. If the plaintiff's orney omit to deliver particulars within the time allowed by the lge's order, or knowingly deliver false particulars, an attachment y be moved for against him without making the judge's order a rule court. Sect. 169, *ante,* 118; *Smith* v. *Bond,* 13 M. & W. 594, 3 ; 2 D. & L. 460. And it seems that if the plaintiff wilfully cause attorney to deliver a false particular he may be punished by attach- nt. *S. C.*

3. *Particulars of the Land claimed.*]—The property claimed in an ctment must be described in the writ "with reasonable certainty." & 16 Vict. c. 76, s. 168. Any defendant may, by a written notice, it his defence to a part only of the property mentioned in the writ, cribing that part "with reasonable certainty" in the notice. Sect. 4. Want of "reasonable certainty" in the description of the pro- ty, or part of it, in the writ or notice, shall not nullify them, but ll only be ground for an application *to a judge* for better particulars the land claimed or defended, which a judge shall have power to e in all cases." Sect. 175. The application for better particulars of the land claimed should be de to a judge at chambers ; and not in the first instance to the court. forms of *Summons and Order, Appendix, Nos.* 69 *and* 70. The plication may be made by or on behalf of any defendant named in writ, before he has entered an appearance. *Doe* d. *Vernon* v. *Roe,* . & E. 14 ; *Doe* d. *Roberts* v. *Roe,* 13 M. & W. 691; 2 Dowl. & L. 3 ; 2 Chit. Arch. 984 (9th ed.). The judge must be satisfied, by davit or otherwise, that there is some real necessity for an order for ticulars of the property claimed. *See form of Affidavit, Appendix,* . 68. It is only under special circumstances that such an order will made ; because the defendant has the means of knowing what pre- ses are in the possession of himself and his tenants, and he may spe- lly defend for his own, limiting his defence to that part only for

which he intends to defend. *Doe* d. *Saxton* v. *Turner*, 11 C. B. 896. It may, however, sometimes happen that a defendant really is ignorant whether the plaintiffs claim all the property in the possession of himself and his tenants, or only some, and what part thereof; and, under such circumstances, it may be deemed more advisable to obtain a summons and order for particulars of the property claimed, than to appear and give a notice of defence for all the property in the possession of the defendant and his tenants situate in the parish named. *See forms of Affidavit, Summons and Order, Appendix, Nos.* 68, 69, 70.

An order for particulars of the land claimed does not operate as a stay of proceedings in the meantime, unless it contain a clause to that effect. *Doe* d. *Roberts* v. *Roe*, 13 M. & W. 691 ; 2 Dowl. & L. 673.

4. *Particulars of Breaches.*]—In an ejectment for a forfeiture of a lease, the court, or a judge at chambers, will, upon the application of the defendant, compel the plaintiff to deliver a particular of the breaches of covenant on which he intends to rely, with dates ; and that he shall not be permitted to give evidence at the trial of anything not contained in such particulars; *Doe* d. *Birch* v. *Phillips*, 6 T. R. 597 ; 2 Chit. Arch. 984 (9th ed.) ; with a stay of proceedings in the meantime until the particulars are delivered. *Doe* d. *Roberts* v. *Roe*, 23 Law J. (N. S.) Exch. 102 ; *Doe* d. *Child* v. *Roe*, 1 E. & B. 279. *See form of Summons, Order and Particulars, Appendix, Nos.* 72, 73, 74. Upon the same principle, where a remainderman brings ejectment to avoid a lease, granted by a previous tenant for life, as not being a due execution of the power of leasing vested in him, the court will order a particular of the alleged defects in the execution of the power. *Doe* d. *Earl of Egremont* v. *Williams*, 7 Q. B. 686. If unsatisfactory particulars be delivered, an application may be made for further and better particulars, and so from time to time until sufficient particulars are delivered. It would seem that an order for particulars of breaches may be made before appearance. *Doe* d. *Roberts* v. *Roe*, *supra* ; and see Reg. Prac. H. T. 1853, No. 20. The order for particulars may be used at the trial to prevent the plaintiff from recovering in respect of any breach not mentioned in such particulars. Thus, under particulars "for selling hay and straw off the land, removing manure, *and non-cultivation*," evidence of a breach of covenant by mismanagement in over-cropping, or by deviating from the usual rotation of crops, is inadmissible. *Doe* d. *Winnall* v. *Broad*, 2 Man. & Gr. 523. But where the particulars were for nonpayment of seven quarters' rent, and the evidence showed that only six quarters were in arrear: held, that the variance was immaterial. *Tenny* d. *Gibbs* v. *Moody*, 3 Bing. 3 ; 10 Moo. 252.

5. *Inspection of Lease.*]—When ejectment is brought for an alleged forfeiture, and the lessee, or any person claiming through or under him (not being a mere trespasser), has no duplicate or copy, the court or a judge will, upon proof or admission of the above facts, order that the defendant be permitted to inspect and take a copy of the lease ; and that in the meantime all further proceedings in the ejectment be stayed. Such an order may be made by virtue of the common law jurisdiction, and without the aid of stat. 14 & 15 Vict. c. 99, s. 6. *Doe* d. *Child* v. *Roe*, 1 E. & B. 279. On the other hand, where a lease is executed by both the landlord and the tenant, the lessor, not having a counterpart, is entitled, on bringing ejectment for a forfeiture, to demand an inspection

ıd copy of the lease from the lessee, or from a person to whom it has
ıen assigned by way of mortgage. *Doe* d. *Morris* v. *Roe,* 1 M. & W.
)7 ; Tyr. & Gr. 545.

6. *Stay of Proceedings until Costs of prior Ejectment paid.*]—
⁷hen a second ejectment is brought, founded substantially on the *same
tle,* before the costs of the first ejectment are paid, the court or a
ıdge will, upon the application of the defendant, stay the proceedings
ıtil the costs of the prior action are paid. *See forms, Appendix, Nos.*
ɔ—78. This has been already fully considered, *ante,* 77—81.

7. *Security for Defendant's Costs.*]—When a second ejectment is
:ought for the *same premises,* after a previous unsuccessful action,
ıe court or a judge may order all further proceedings to be stayed,
ıtil security be given for the payment of the defendant's costs. 17
 18 Vict. c. 125, s. 93. *Ante,* 81 ; *see forms of Summons and Order,*
⁷os. 79, 80.

For the cases in which such security might have been ordered before
ıe above act, see 2 Chit. Arch. 945 (8th ed.).

G

CHAPTER XII.

Appearance—15 & 16 Vict. c. 76, *ss.* 171—177.]—The Common Law Procedure Act, 1852, contains a series of enactments relating to appearances in actions of ejectment, viz.—

Sect. 171, " the persons *named* as defendants in such writ, or either of them, shall be allowed to appear within the time appointed."

Sect. 172, " any other person *not named* in such writ shall, by leave of the court or a judge, be allowed to appear and defend on filing an affidavit showing that he is in possession of the land either by himself or his tenant."

Sect. 173, " any person appearing to defend as landlord in respect of property, whereof he is in possession only by his tenant, shall state in his appearance that he appears *as landlord;* and such person shall be at liberty to set up any defence which a landlord appearing in an action of ejectment has heretofore been allowed to set up, and no other."

Sect. 174, " any person appearing to such writ shall be at liberty to *limit his defence to part only* of the property mentioned in the writ, describing that part with reasonable certainty in a notice intituled in the court and cause, and signed by the party appearing, or his attorney; such notice to be served within four days after appearance upon

he attorney whose name is indorsed on the writ, if any, and if none,
hen to be filed in the master's office ; and an appearance without such
otice confining the defence to part shall be deemed an appearance to
efend for the whole."

Sect. 175, "want of 'reasonable certainty' in the description of the
roperty, or part of it, in the writ or notice shall not nullify them,
ut shall only be ground for an application to a judge for better par-
iculars of the land claimed or defended, which a judge shall have
ower to give in all cases."

Sect. 176, "the court or a judge shall have power to strike out or
onfine appearances and defences set up by persons not in possession
y themselves or their tenants."

Sect. 177, "in case no appearance shall be entered into within the
ime appointed, or if an appearance be entered but the defence be
imited to part only, the plaintiffs shall be at liberty to sign a judgment
hat the person whose title is asserted in the writ shall recover posses-
ion of the land, or of the part thereof to which the defence does not
pply, which judgment, if for all, may be in the form contained in the
chedule (A.) to this act annexed, marked No. 14, or to the like
ffect [*Appendix, No.* 123] ; and if for part, may be in the form con-
ained in the Schedule (A.) to this act annexed, marked No. 15, or
o the like effect." *Appendix, No.* 124.

Sect. 188, relates to appearances and defences by joint tenants,
enants in common, and coparceners. *Post,* 130.

Sect. 31, directs the mode and form of entering appearances to
ctions generally, including actions of ejectment. *Post,* 125.

By whom — 1. *Defendants named in the Writ.*] — Any person
amed as a defendant in the writ shall be allowed to appear within the
ime appointed. Sect. 171, *ante,* 122. His right to do so cannot be
uestioned upon a summary application to strike out or set aside the
ppearance, founded upon an affidavit stating that he is not in possession
y himself or his tenants of any part of the property claimed. *Doe* d.
urner v. *Gee,* 9 Dowl. 612. For, if so, why was he made a defend-
nt ? But if he defend for more than he is in possession of by himself
r his tenants, an application may be made to confine his appearance
nd defence pursuant to sect. 176. *Post,* 129.

Any person named in the writ may defend not only for the land in his
wn possession, but also for other land claimed in the writ, and in the
ossession of his tenants, whether the latter be named in the writ
r not.

A landlord cannot compel his tenants on whom the writ is served to
ppear and defend the action, nor to allow him to do so in their names.
Chit. Arch. 966 (9th ed.) ; *Right* v. *Wrong,* Barnes, 173 ; *Doe* d.
urner v. *Gee,* 9 Dowl. 612. But with their consent he may appear
nd defend the action in their names for his own benefit. *Doe* d.
ocke v. *Franklin,* 7 Taunt. 9. He will not thereby escape liability
o the plaintiff for the costs of the action, but may be made to pay
hem upon a summary application. *Hutchinson* v. *Greenwood,* 4
. & B. 324 ; *Doe* d. *Masters* v. *Gray,* 10 B. & C. 615 ; *Thrustout*
. *Jones* v. *Shenton, Id.* 110. The affidavit in support of such appli-
ation must clearly show that the ejectment was *defended by the land-
rd* for his own benefit, and not merely that he was interested in the

property, and endeavoured to make terms with the plaintiff for the settlement of the action. *Anstey* v. *Edwards*, 16 C. B. 212.

If a mere servant, bailiff or other person having no title be served with a writ in ejectment wherein he is named as a defendant, he should not appear, otherwise he may render himself personally liable as a trespasser, and his capacity of servant, &c. will afford no defence. *Doe* d. *Cuff* v. *Stradling*, 2 Stark. R. 187 ; *Doe* d. *James* v. *Stanton*, 2 B. & A. 371. A servant or bailiff when so served should hand the copy writ to his employer, leaving *him* to apply to the court or a judge for leave to appear and defend the action as tenant in possession " by himself" (*infra*), or to take such other steps as he may think fit. If judgment be signed for want of an appearance, no costs will be payable; Gray on Costs, 196 ; *post*, Chap. XXX. ; except as damages in a subsequent action for mesne profits, &c. Nor will the judgment be any evidence in such subsequent action that the party served with the writ, and who suffered judgment by default, was in *actual possession* of the land at the time of such service or judgment. *Doe* d. *James* v. *Stanton*, 2 B. & A. 373, Bayley, J.; *post*, Chap. LXVIII.

2. *Persons not named in the Writ.*]—A person not named in the writ cannot enter an appearance in his own name (either as landlord or tenant) without leave of the court or a judge, to be obtained on filing an affidavit showing that he is in possession either by himself or his tenant. *Ante*, 122 ; *see form of Affidavit, Appendix, No.* 89. If the affidavit show the deponent to be in possession "by himself," he will be allowed to defend as tenant in possession. But if the affidavit show him to be in possession "by his tenant," he will be allowed to defend as landlord of such tenant. *See form of Order, Appendix, No.* 90. And, in the latter case, he must describe himself as such landlord in the appearance. *Post*, 127.

It seems that only a rule nisi or summons will be granted in the first instance. *Croft* v. *Lumley*, 4 E. & B. 608 ; 24 Law J., N. S., Q. B., 78. Upon such application the court or a judge will not consider nice questions as to the party's title as landlord, or as to his right of possession. *S. C.*, 2 Chit. Arch. 967 (9th ed.). Nevertheless "there ought to be a discretion exercised by the court or a judge in granting such permission." *Per* Parke, B., in *Butler* v. *Meredith*, 11 Exch. 94. "The statute does not provide for striking out an appearance by a person who has satisfied the court or a judge that he is in possession as landlord either by himself or others." *Id.*, 89, Pollock, C. B. The word "landlord" extends to all persons claiming title, *consistent with the possession of the occupier*, whether he has actually received any rent or not. *Lovelock* d. *Norris* v. *Dancaster*, 4 T. R. 122 ; *Doe* d. *Heblethwaite* v. *Roe*, cited 3 T. R. 783. It seems that a mortgagee may defend as landlord of the mortgagor in possession. *Doe* d. *Tilyard* v. *Cooper*, 8 T. R. 645 ; but see *Doe* d. *Pearson* v. *Roe*, 6 Bing. 613 ; 4 Moo. & P. 437. For some purposes a mortgagee may elect to consider the mortgagor who remains in possession as his tenant. *Post*, Chap. XLIV., Sect. 1. But a mortgagee who has no interest in the result of an ejectment ought not to be put forward merely to serve the purposes of the mortgagor, or the tenant in possession. *Doe* d. *Pearson* v. *Roe*, *supra*. Where it is shown that the tenant obtained possession from the claimant, a third person claiming adversely will not be permitted to defend as landlord of such tenant. *Doe* d. *Horton* v. *Rhys*, 2 You. & Jer. 88; 2 Chit. Arch. 967 (9th ed.). In an action by a lessor against a lessee for a forfeiture for breaches of covenant, an elegit creditor of the lessee, who has not obtained actual possession under the writ, will not be permitted to appear, he not being in possession either by himself or his tenant within the meaning of the act. *Croft* v. *Lumley*, 4 E. & B. 614; 24 Law J., N. S., Q. B., 78, 80; *Thompson* v. *Tomkinson*, 11 Exch. 442. Two persons *claiming separately* will not be permitted to defend as landlords of the same tenant for the same land. *Doe* d. *Lloyd* v. *Roe*, 15 M. & W. 431. But in *Chester* v. *Wortley and Cole*, 17 C. B. 410, the defendant Wortley defended as landlady for the whole of the premises, and the defendant Cole defended as landlord for part of the premises, as assignee of an underlease. Where a person claims *in opposition to the title of the tenant* in possession, he can in no light be considered as landlord. *Per* Lord Mansfield, C. J., in *Fairclaim* d. *Fowler* v. *Shamtitle*, 3 Burr. 1295; Ad. Eject. 216.

A person who is in possession by himself or his tenant will be allowed to defend without giving any security for costs, notwithstanding he resides abroad. *Butler* v. *Meredith*, 11 Exch. 85; 24 Law J., N. S., Exch., 239, overruling *Doe* d. *Hudson* v. *Jameson*, 4 Man. & Ry. 570.

When.]—Appearances are to be entered "within the time appointed" (sect. 171, *ante*, 122), *i. e.* within sixteen days after service of the writ in ejectment; unless the writ be issued pursuant to sect. 217, in which case the defendant must appear within ten days after service. In either case the day of service may be *excluded.* The writ commands the defendant to appear "within sixteen days *after* service hereof," not saying "inclusive of the day of such service," as in the forms, Nos. 1, 2, 3, contained in the schedule of the same act, 15 & 16 Vict. c. 76.

If the last day for appearing happen to fall on a *Sunday*, it seems that the defendant is not entitled to the whole of the following Monday to appear, notwithstanding the Rule of H. T. 1853, No. 174. *Rowberry* v. *Morgan*, 9 Exch. 730. When the last day for appearing falls on any day between the Thursday before and the Wednesday after Easter Day, then the Wednesday after Easter Day is considered as the last day for appearing, and the plaintiff may sign judgment for want of appearance on the next day. *Harrison* v. *Robinson*, 2 C. B. 908; 3 Dowl. & L. 813.

Appearances may be entered at any time before judgment is signed for want of appearance or defence, although after "the time appointed." See 15 & 16 Vict. c. 76, s. 29. The judgment says that "no appearance *has been* entered or defence made to the said writ" (*i. e.* at the time of signing the judgment), not that there was no appearance within the time appointed, or within the sixteen days mentioned in the writ. *See the form, Appendix, No.* 123.

How.]—By 15 & 16 Vict. c. 76, s. 31, "the mode of appearance to every such writ of summons, *or under the authority of this act*, shall be by delivering a memorandum in writing, according to the following form, *or to the like effect :—*

"A., plaintiff against C. D.,
     or
against C. D. and another,
     or
against C. D. and others.
} The defendant C. D. appears in person.
E. F., attorney for C. D., appears for him.

[*If the defendant appears in person, here give his address.*]
"Entered the —— day of —— 18—."

Such memorandum to be delivered to the proper officer or person in that behalf, and to be dated on the day of the delivery thereof." *See forms of Appearances, Appendix, Nos.* 92—96.

The form of appearance is precisely the same, whether the defendant intends to defend for all or part only of the premises claimed in the writ. But in the latter case a notice to defend for part only should be given within four days after the appearance, pursuant to sect. 174. *Post,* 128. As to defences by joint-tenants, tenants in common or coparceners, see *post,* 130.

As the memorandum of appearance constitutes a record of the court, the practice is to write it on parchment. It is to be filed with the proper officer or person in that behalf; *i. e.* at the office of the masters of the particular court in which the action is brought (a).

Any defendant named in the writ, or other person duly authorized to appear, may do so in person or by attorney; but infants should defend by guardian. *Post,* Chap. LXII.

By the Practice Rule of H. T. 1853, No. 2, " if two or more defendants in the same action shall appear by the same attorney and at the same time, the names of all the defendants so appearing shall be inserted in one appearance." The main object of this rule is to save the unnecessary expense of separate appearances, when one would be sufficient.

Appearance in Person.]—By 15 & 16 Vict. c. 76, s. 30, " every appearance by the defendant in person shall give an address, at which it shall be sufficient to leave all pleadings and other proceedings not requiring personal service; and if such address be not given, the appearance shall not be received; and if an address so given shall be illusory or fictitious, the appearance shall be irregular, and may be set aside by the court or a judge, and the plaintiff shall be permitted to proceed by sticking up the proceedings in the master's office without further service." *See forms of Summons and Order, Appendix, Nos.* 110, 111.

By Reg. Prac. H. T. 1853, No. 166, " in all cases where a party sues or defends *in person,* he shall, upon issuing any writ of summons or other proceeding, or entering an appearance, enter in a book to be kept for that purpose at the master's office an *address within three miles from the General Post Office,* at which all pleadings, notices, summonses, orders, rules or other proceedings not requiring personal service shall be left; and if such address shall not be entered in the said book, or if such address shall be more than three miles from the General Post

---

(a) The Master's Office in Q. B. is at No. 2, Mitre Court Buildings, Inner Temple; in C. P., in Serjeants' Inn, Chancery Lane; in Exch., at No. 7, Stone Buildings, Lincoln's Inn.

Office, then the opposite party shall be at liberty to proceed by sticking up all pleadings, notices, summonses, orders, rules or other proceedings in the master's office, without the necessity of any further service."

The General Post Office, mentioned in the above rule, means that in Saint Martin's-le-Grand, near Saint Paul's Cathedral, London.

The address given must be within the above limits, and not illusory or fictitious, *i. e.* one not in existence, as No. 500, Fleet Street, London, or one at which the defendant is not known, or where he has no authority or permission to have papers left for him; *ex. gr.*, at the Treasury Office, Whitehall, or the like. But an address at a club-house, hotel, coffee-shop, or the like, where papers will be taken in for the defendant, is sufficient, although he does not sleep or live there.

The appearance must be entered at the master's office. *Ante*, 126. It must give a proper address, as above mentioned. *See the form, Appendix, No.* 93. At the time it is entered, a proper address should be entered in the " Address Book" kept at the master's office. Reg. 166, *ante*, 126. Notice of such appearance need not be given, if the defendant be *named in the writ* and appears within the time appointed : otherwise it must be given forthwith to the plaintiff's attorney, or to the plaintiff himself if he sue in person. *Post*, 128. The notice, when necessary, must be in writing. Reg. Prac. H. T. 1853, No. 161 ; *see the form, Appendix, No.* 97.

By Reg. Prac. H. T. 1853, No. 167, " in all cases where a plaintiff shall have sued out a writ in person, *or a defendant shall have appeared in person*, and either party shall, by an attorney of the court, have given notice in writing to the opposite party, or to the attorney or agent of such party, of such attorney being authorized to act as attorney for the party on whose behalf such notice is given, all pleadings, notices, summonses, orders, rules and other proceedings which, according to the practice of the courts, are to be delivered to or served upon the party on whose behalf such notice is given, shall thereafter be delivered to or served upon such attorney." *See form of notice, Appendix, No.* 100.

Appearance by Landlord.]—By Reg. Prac. H. T. 1853, No. 113, " where a person *not named* in the writ in ejectment has obtained leave of the court or a judge to appear and defend, he shall enter an appearance according to the Common Law Procedure Act, 1852, entitled in the action against the party or parties named in the writ as defendant or defendants, and shall forthwith give notice of such appearance to the plaintiff's attorney, or to the plaintiff if he sues in person."

By 15 & 16 Vict. c. 76, s. 173, " any person appearing to defend *as landlord* in respect of property, whereof he is in possession only by his tenant, shall state in his appearance that he appears as landlord [*see the forms, Appendix, Nos.* 94, 95]; and such person shall be at liberty to set up any defence which a landlord appearing in an action of ejectment has heretofore been allowed to set up, and no other."

We have already considered how leave of the court or a judge is to be obtained; *ante*, 124; thereupon an appearance may be entered at the master's office. *Ante*, 126; *see the forms, Appendix, Nos.* 94, 95, 96. Notice of such appearance must be given forthwith. Reg. Prac. H. T. 1853, No. 113; *see the forms, Appendix, Nos.* 98, 99.

The appearance as landlord must be entered specially in the issue. 15 & 16 Vict. c. 76, s. 188; *see the forms, Appendix, Nos.* 135, 136.

When a person appears "as landlord" of a particular tenant in possession, he is at liberty to set up any defence which such tenant might have set up had he appeared to the action, except the want of a notice to quit from the claimant to the tenant in possession, who has suffered judgment by default. *Doe* d. *Davis* v. *Creed,* 5 Bing. 327 ; 2 Moo. & P. 648. The reason for this exception is that the want of such notice is inconsistent with the defendant's title as landlord. The latter can only *defend his tenant's possession,* and is bound by the same admissions and estoppels as the tenant himself. *Doe* d. *Mee* v. *Sutherland,* 4 A. & E. 784. Therefore if the tenant be estopped from disputing the claimant's title, so will any person defending "as his landlord." *Doe* d. *Knight* v. *Lady Smythe,* 4 M. & S. 347 ; *Doe* d. *Manners* v. *Mizem,* 2 Moo. & Rob. 56, Patteson, J. ; *Doe* d. *Willis* v. *Birchmore,* 9 A. & E. 662 ; 1 P. & D. 448 ; sect. 173, *ante,* 127. But where a defendant in ejectment by mistake defended "as landlord" instead of as owner, or as tenant in possession : held, that he was not thereby estopped from relying on a tenancy from year to year to the plaintiff outstanding in a third person. *Doe* d. *Fellowes* v. *Alford,* 1 Dowl. & L. 470.

Notice of Appearance.]—It does not appear to be necessary for defendants *named in the writ* to give any notice of an appearance entered by them, or on their behalf, within the time appointed. Nevertheless it is usual, as a matter of courtesy, to give such notice. *See the form, Appendix, No.* 97. It is the duty of the claimant or his attorney to search for such appearance without any notice thereof. But persons named in the writ who appear after the time appointed, and before judgment has been signed against them, should forthwith give notice of such appearance.

Persons *not named* in the writ, who appear in pursuance of leave of the court or a judge, are bound forthwith to give notice of such appearance to the plaintiff or his attorney. Reg. Prac. H. T. 1853, No. 113 ; *ante,* 127.

Notice to defend for Part only.]—We have already seen that the form of appearance is exactly the same whether the defendant intends to defend for the whole or only for part of the property mentioned in the writ. *Ante,* 126. But in the latter case he should *within four days after appearance* (exclusive of the day of appearance) give a notice limiting his defence, pursuant to sect. 174. *Ante,* 122 ; *see the forms, Appendix, Nos.* 101, 102, 103. An appearance without such notice confining the defence to part shall be deemed an appearance to defend for the whole. 15 & 16 Vict. c. 76, s. 174, *ante,* 122. The defendant has no right to describe the part for which he defends as freehold or copyhold, unless it be so described in the writ, for the whole question may turn upon the point whether the land is freehold or copyhold. *Doe* d. *Baggaley* v. *Jones,* 1 Camp. 367 ; and see *Davies* v. *Pierce,* 2 T. R. 53. In ejectment for a chapel, &c., the parson will not be permitted to defend only for "a right to enter and perform divine service." *Martin* v. *Davis,* 2 Stra. 914 ; 2 Barnard. 27, *S. C.*

If one of several defendants, who has a good title to part only, join in defending for the whole, he will thereby render himself liable to the general costs of the suit if the claimants recover any part.

Doe d. *Bishton* v. *Hughes,* 5 Tyr. 957; 4 Dowl. 412; Gray on
Costs, 202; 2 Chit. Arch. 969 (9th ed.); Bull. N. P. 335, 336. It is
therefore most important for such a defendant to give a proper notice
in due time. The notice is afterwards to be stated in the issue, so that
it may therein appear for what defence is made. 15 & 16 Vict. c. 76,
i. 188; *see the forms, Appendix, Nos.* 132, 133, 134.

Application for better Particulars of the Land defended.]—An
application for better particulars of the land defended may frequently
be necessary on behalf of the plaintiff, especially where the defendant
does not by notice limit his defence as to part *with sufficient certainty*
to enable the plaintiff to know for what the defendant really intends to defend. A defendant has no legal right to appear and defend
for more than the lands, &c. *in the possession of himself and his
tenants.* The court or a judge has power to strike out or confine appearances and defences set up by persons not in possession by themselves or their tenants. Sect. 176, *infra.* To enable such an application to be made, and also proper affidavits in support thereof, it may
frequently be necessary first to obtain a judge's order for particulars
of the land defended. *See forms of Summons and Order, Appendix,*
Nos. 108, 109.

Application to strike out or confine Appearances and Defences.]—
By 15 & 16 Vict. c. 76, s. 176, " the court or a judge shall have
power to strike out or confine appearances and defences set up by
persons not in possession by themselves or their tenants."
If several persons be named as defendants in the writ, and any one
of them being in possession, by himself or his tenants, of part only
of the property claimed enter an appearance, and do not within four
days afterwards (exclusive of the day of appearance) limit his defence,
by a notice to defend for part only, pursuant to sect. 174 (*ante,* 128),
whereby in effect he defends for the whole, and prevents the plaintiff
from obtaining judgment for the part not in the possession of such
defendant or his tenant, an application may be made to the court or a
judge to confine the appearance and defence of such defendant to that
part of the property claimed which is in the possession of himself and
his tenant. *See forms of Summons and Order and Affidavit in support
of the Application, Appendix, Nos.* 112, 113, 114. It would be improper to apply to *strike out* the appearance under such circumstances,
the appearance itself being perfectly regular. *Ante,* 126.
If any person *not named* in the writ obtain leave of the court or a
judge to appear and defend for all or part of the property claimed,
and it can be shown by affidavit or otherwise to the satisfaction of the
court or a judge, that the plaintiffs do not claim possession of any
part of the property for which such person defends, but only other
and different property, a rule *nisi* or summons may be obtained to
rescind or set aside the previous rule or order, and any appearance
entered in pursuance thereof. *See forms of Summons and Order,
Appendix, Nos.* 118, 119. If the application be made to the court, a
short affidavit will be necessary. But, perhaps, this would not be
required upon an application to a judge at chambers. It is to be observed that the form of the summons and order precludes the possibility of prejudice to the person against whom the application is made.
If, however, the plaintiff do claim *part,* but not the whole, of what

such third person defends for, the application should be to confine the
appearance and defence to the part so claimed. *See forms of Summons,
Order and Affidavit, Appendix, Nos.* 115, 116, 117.

Defence of Joint Tenants, Tenants in Common, or Coparceners.]—
By 15 & 16 Vict. c. 76, s. 188, "in case of such an action being
brought by some or one of several persons entitled as joint tenants,
tenants in common, or coparceners, any joint tenant, tenant in common or coparcener in possession may, *at the time of appearance, or
within four days after, give notice,* in the same form as in the notice of
a limited defence, that he or she defends as such, and admits the right
of the claimant to an undivided share of the property (stating what
share), but denies any actual ouster of him from the property [*see
forms of Notice, Appendix, Nos.* 104, 105], and may, *within the same
time, file an affidavit* stating with reasonable certainty that he or she
is such joint tenant, tenant in common, or coparcener, and the share
of such property to which he or she is entitled, and that he or she has
not ousted the claimant [*see form of Affidavit, Appendix, No.* 106] ;
and such notice shall be entered in the issue in the same manner as the
notice limiting the defence [*see forms, Appendix, Nos.* 137, 138], and
upon the trial of such an issue the additional question of whether an
actual ouster has taken place shall be tried."

By sect. 189, "upon the trial of *such issue* as last aforesaid, if it
shall be found that the defendant is joint tenant, tenant in common or
coparcener with the claimant, then the question whether an actual
ouster has taken place shall be tried, and unless such actual ouster
shall be proved the defendant shall be entitled to judgment and costs ;
but if it shall be found either that the defendant is not such joint
tenant, tenant in common, or coparcener, or that an actual ouster has
taken place, then the claimant shall be entitled to such judgment for
the recovery of possession and costs."

The above enactments do not apply to a defendant who occupies *as
tenant* of one of several joint tenants, tenants in common or coparceners. *Doe* d. *Wills* v. *Roe,* 4 Dowl. 628.

We shall consider fully hereafter what does or does not amount to
an *actual ouster,* and what is or is not sufficient evidence thereof.
Chap. XXIV. In the meantime it is to be observed, that to entitle a
defendant to avail himself of the provisions of sections 188 and 189,
he must *at the time of appearance, or within four days afterwards*
(exclusive of the day of appearance, *infra*), give the notice and file
the affidavit mentioned in section 188 : *see the forms, Appendix,
Nos.* 104, 105, 106 : in default whereof the ejectment will be tried as
in ordinary cases, and the claimant will recover any part or share of
the property to which he proves a sufficient title and right of possession, although it appear by the evidence that the defendant is a joint
tenant, or tenant in common, or coparcener with the claimant, and has
never in any manner ousted him from the possession or enjoyment
thereof. The very act of appearing to and defending the action,
otherwise than according to section 188, sufficiently shows that the
defendant is in possession of the property for which he defends to the
exclusion of the claimant, who must be taken to have been ousted
therefrom, if legally entitled thereto.

The notice must be given to the plaintiff's attorney, or to the plaintiff if he sue in person, within four days after the day of appearance,

exclusive of such day. Reg. Prac. H. T. 1853, No. 174. If served on the last day, the service must be made before seven o'clock, p.m. *Id.* No. 164.

The affidavit must be *filed* at the master's office, *ante*, 126, with the officer with whom the appearance was entered. Notice of the filing thereof need not be given to the plaintiff or his attorney. He should search for it after the expiration of the four days. If none be then filed, he should treat the notice served on him as a nullity, and not enter it on the issue. If an affidavit be filed he should obtain an office copy, which may be useful at the trial.

When the issue is delivered the defendant should take care to see that the notice is entered in it pursuant to sect. 188. *Ante*, 130; *see the forms, Appendix, Nos.* 137, 138. If omitted, he should forthwith take out a summons to set aside the issue for irregularity, with costs. *See the forms, Appendix, Nos.* 139, 140. In answer to which the plaintiff may show for cause, that no affidavit, or no sufficient affidavit, was filed in due time pursuant to sect. 188. *Ante*, 130.

Judgment for want of Appearance or Defence.]—By 15 & 16 Vict. c. 76, s. 177, " in case no appearance shall be entered into within the time appointed (*ante*, 125), or if an appearance be entered, but the defence be limited to part only, the plaintiff shall be at liberty to sign a judgment that the person whose title is asserted in the writ shall recover possession of the land, or of the part thereof to which the defence does not apply ; which judgment, if for all, may be in the form contained in the Schedule (A.) to this act annexed, marked No. 14 [*post, Appendix, No.* 123]; and if for part, may be in the form contained in the Schedule (A.) to this act annexed, marked No. 15 [*post, Appendix, No.* 124], or to the like effect."

By Reg. Prac. H. T. 1853, No. 112, "no judgment in ejectment for want of appearance or defence, whether limited or otherwise, shall be signed without first filing an affidavit of service of the writ, according to the Common Law Procedure Act, 1852, and a copy thereof [*i. e.* of the writ], or, where personal service has not been effected, without first obtaining a judge's order or a rule of court authorizing the signing such judgment ; which said rule or order, or a duplicate thereof, shall be filed, together with a copy of the writ."

If the affidavit of service show a *personal* service on each tenant in possession named as a defendant in the writ, no rule or order will be necessary for leave to sign judgment for want of appearance or defence ; but such judgment may be signed (after the time allowed for appearing has expired) upon filing a copy of the writ in ejectment, and the affidavit of service. *Supra.* Where *personal service* has not been effected a rule or order must be obtained (*ante*, 99); and such rule or order, together with a copy of the writ, must be filed at the time of signing judgment.

An appearance entered *after the appointed time*, but before any judgment for want of appearance, is sufficient to prevent such judgment being afterwards signed. *Ante*, 125.

Where any defendant defends for the whole, but other defendants do not appear, judgment by default should be signed *as against the latter for the whole* of the property claimed. *See the forms, Appendix, Nos.* 125, 126.

No costs are recoverable upon a judgment for want of appearance or defence; Gray on Costs, 196; 2 Chit. Arch. 973 (9th ed.); but the amount may generally be recovered in a subsequent action of trespass for mesne profits, &c., if the declaration be properly framed. *See forms of Declaration, Appendix, Nos.* 390, 391.

Setting aside Judgment for want of Appearance.]—If a judgment for want of appearance be signed *irregularly*, it may be set aside by the court or a judge upon an application made within a reasonable time. Reg. Prac. H. T. 1853, No. 135; *Doe* d. *Parr* v. *Roe*, 1 Q. B. 700; *Doe* d. *Williams* v. *Williams*, 2 A. & E. 381. The application may (if necessary) include a direction to the plaintiff to restore the possession; and the rule in that behalf (or the judge's order, when made a rule of court) may be enforced by attachment. *Anon.*, 2 Salk. 588; *Davies* d. *Povey* v. *Doe*, 2 W. Blac. 892. But the sheriff should not be directed to restore the possession; nor can a writ of restitution issue, unless expressly ordered. *Doe* d. *Williams* v. *Williams*, 2 A. & E. 381.

Formerly the court would not, *before appearance entered* by the tenant in an action of ejectment, entertain an application to set aside the judgment signed against the casual ejector on the ground of irregularity. *Doe* d. *Williamson* v. *Roe*, 3 Dowl. & L. 328.

A *regular* judgment for want of appearance may sometimes be set aside on payment of costs and other equitable terms; *ex. gr.*, where the tenant duly instructed his attorney to appear and defend the action, but the latter omitted to do so, owing to matters personally affecting himself, which prevented his attending to it. *Doe* d. *Shaw* v. *Roe*, 13 Price, 260. So where the attorney in the country inadvertently omitted to instruct his London agents. *Doe* d. *Mullarky* v. *Roe*, 3 P. & D. 316; 11 A. & E. 333. Such an order is by no means uncommon at chambers in proper cases; *Id.* 334; *per* Coleridge and Littledale, Js.; especially where the application is made before execution executed. Ad. Eject. 211; *see forms of Affidavit, Summons and Order, Appendix, Nos.* 128, 129, 130.

Where the tenant in possession *neglects* to appear, or to instruct an attorney to do so on his behalf, and judgment by default is signed against him, the court will not (except under special circumstances) set aside the judgment and execution, and let him in to defend upon payment of costs, &c., although he swears distinctly to a good title; but they will generally leave him to bring a subsequent ejectment. *Doe* d. *Ledger* v. *Roe*, 3 Taunt. 506. Even where the tenant omits to give his landlord notice of the writ, and suffers judgment by default, the court will not let in the landlord to defend, unless collusion between the plaintiff and the tenant be proved. *Ante*, 115. But too much strictness in this respect may sometimes occasion serious injustice. "A man's title may depend entirely upon his possession, and he may be unable, if once turned out of possession, to show such a title as would justify him in bringing an action to recover back the land; to say nothing of the additional expense, trouble and anxiety that might be cast upon him." *Per* Pollock, C. B., in *Butler* v. *Meredith*, 11 Exch. 91; and see *per* Martin, B., *Id.* 99; *see form of Summons, Appendix, No.* 91.

Ancient Demesne—Equitable Defences.]—Formerly a defendant in ejectment might, with leave of the court, have pleaded that the lands were ancient demesne; Arch. Pl. & Ev. 280, 277; 2 Arch. N. P. 334; *Williams* v. *Keen,* 1 W. Blac. 197; *Doe* d. *Rust* v. *Roe,* 2 Burr. 1046; *Hatch* v. *Cannon,* 3 Wils. 51; *Denn* d. *Wroot* v. *Fenn,* 8 T. R. 474; *Doe* d. *Morton* v. *Roe,* 10 East, 523; and if issue were joined on the plea, it was tried by Domesday Book. But now there are no pleadings whatever in ejectment, and the plea of ancient demesne is in effect abolished. Even an equitable defence cannot be pleaded pursuant to 17 & 18 Vict. c. 125, s. 83. *Neave* v. *Avery,* 16 C. B. 328; 25 Law Times R. 181.

CHAPTER XIII.

———

Issue.]—By 15 & 16 Vict. c. 76, s. 178, " in case an appearance shall be entered, an issue may [at] once be made up, without any pleadings, by the claimants or their attorney, setting forth the writ, and stating the fact of the appearance, with its date, and the notice limiting the defence, if any, of each of the persons appearing, so that it may appear for what defence is made, and directing the sheriff to summon a jury ; and such issue, in case defence is made for the whole, may be in the form contained in Schedule (A.) to this act annexed, marked No. 16, or to the like effect [*Appendix, No.* 131] ; and in case defence is made for part, may be in the form contained in the Schedule (A.) to this act annexed, marked No. 15, or to the like effect." *Appendix, No.* 132.

In case of an appearance entered *by all the defendants,* the issue may " at once" be made up. *Supra.* But where there is time to do so, without losing the assizes or sitting, the plaintiff should abstain from making up the issue until the four days have elapsed, during which any of the defendants may give notice to defend for part only, because such notice materially affects the form of the issue. 2 Chit. Arch. 974 (9th ed.) ; *see Appendix, Nos.* 131—138. Where, however, such a delay would occasion the loss of the assizes or sitting, the plaintiff may make up the issue " at once ;" and afterwards, if necessary, obtain an order for leave to amend it, without prejudice to the notice of trial. *See forms of Summons and Order, Appendix, Nos.* 141, 142.

When several defendants appear and defend separately for different parts, which together comprise the whole property claimed, the issue must be framed accordingly. *See the form, Appendix, No.* 133.

In case of an appearance and defence by some of the defendants who defend for the whole, *i. e.* do not give notice that they defend for part only, and no appearance entered by the other defendants, the plaintiffs should file an affidavit of personal service of the writ, or obtain and file a judge's order or rule of court for leave to sign judgment against such other defendants, and also file a copy of the writ, and thereupon sign judgment *as against them* for all the property claimed. *See the forms, Appendix, Nos.* 125, 126.

It must sometimes happen that all the defendants named in the writ have not been served personally or otherwise ; so that no affidavit of personal service can be made, nor a judge's order or rule of court obtained, as to some of them ; but the claimants desire to proceed in the action, without delay, as against the other defendants. It is not clear what course the claimants ought to pursue under such circumstances. In Chitty's Forms, 547 (7th ed.), it is suggested that the claimants may elect to abandon all further proceedings against those defendants who have not been served with the writ, and enter a memorandum to that effect on the roll. *See the form, Appendix, No.* 134. This mode of proceeding, if allowable, is very convenient. But I rather think that the proper course would be to apply to a judge at chambers *ex parte* for an order for leave to amend the writ by striking out the names of the defendants who have not been served. *See the form, Appendix, No.* 144. Such application should be founded on a short affidavit, stating that the particular defendants have not been served with the writ, and have not appeared. *See the form, Appendix, No.* 143. A copy of the order, and of the writ (as amended), should be served on the defendants who have appeared, or their attorneys or agents, if the order so directs. The subsequent proceedings would be the same as if the writ had originally issued in its amended form.

In case of an appearance and defence *as to part only* entered by some or one of the defendants, and no appearance by the others, the plaintiff should *sign judgment for the residue* of the property, upon filing an affidavit of personal service of the writ on the other defendants, or a judge's order or rule of court for leave to sign judgment as against them for want of appearance. *See form of Judgment, Appendix, No.* 124. But if no such affidavit can be made, or order or rule obtained, as to some of them, it would rather seem that an order to amend the writ should be applied for, as above suggested.

When any person appears and defends *as landlord*, that must be specially mentioned in the issue. Sect. 188; *see the forms, Appendix, Nos.* 135, 136.

When any defendant defends as a joint tenant, tenant in common, or coparcener with the claimants, or any or either of them, and gives a notice, and makes an affidavit pursuant to sect. 188 (*ante,* 130), " such notice shall be entered on the issue in the same manner as the notice limiting the defence." *Ante,* 130; *see the forms, Appendix, Nos.* 137, 138. If the notice only be given, but a proper affidavit be not made and filed pursuant to sect. 188, it seems that the claimants may treat the notice as a nullity, and omit all mention of it in the issue.

If the plaintiff improperly omit to state in the issue any notice to defend for part only, or as a landlord, or as a joint tenant, tenant in common, or coparcener, the defendant should apply *promptly* to the court or a judge to set aside the issue for irregularity : *see forms of Summons and Order, Appendix, Nos.* 139, 140 : so if the venue be improperly laid.

The venue should be laid in the county wherein the lands lie as described in the writ, the action being of a local nature. *Anon.,* 6 Mod. 222; *Mostyn* v. *Fabrigas,* Cowp. 176; Run. Eject. 154 ; Ad. Eject. 165; 2 Chit. Arch. 920 (8th ed.). In Lancashire the venue should be laid thus : " Lancashire, Northern Division (to wit)," or " Lancashire, Southern Division (to wit)," according as the lands lie. *Thompson* v. *Hornby,* 9 Q. B. 978 ; *Atkinson* v. *Hornby,* 2 Car. & K. 335. Formerly Warwickshire was divided into the " Warwick Division" and the " Coventry Division" (5 & 6 Vict. c. 110); but it is now otherwise, and the venue in that county must be laid in the usual manner. 17 & 18 Vict. c. 35. After verdict, any mistake as to the venue will be cured by the Statute of Jeofails, 16 & 17 Car. 2, c. 8, s. 1. *The Mayor, &c. of London* v. *Cole,* 7 T. R. 583; *The Bailiffs, &c. of Lichfield* v. *Slater,* Willes, 431, cited by Parke, B., 8 Exch. 439;

Planche v. *Hooper*, 6 Q. B. 877, note (*b*). And execution may issue into the proper county, although the venue be laid elsewhere. 15 & 16 Vict. c. 76, s. 121. The plaintiffs may therefore lay their venue in any county at the risk of an application by the defendants to set aside the issue for irregularity, or to amend it at the plaintiff's expense by changing the venue to the proper county. Unless such application be made in due time, no advantage can be taken of the mistake. In *Doe* d. *Goodwin* v. *Roe*, 3 Dowl. 323, Patteson, J., held, that, if the county stated in the body of the declaration were correct, the venue in the margin was immaterial: and see *Simmins* v. *Lillystone*, 8 Exch. 431, 441.

The proper course, however, is to lay the venue in the county where the lands lie, and afterwards, if necessary, apply to the court or a judge to change the place of trial, pursuant to 15 & 16 Vict. c. 76, s. 182 (*post*, 142).

Time allowed for Proceeding to Trial.]—By the Common Law Procedure Act, 1852 (15 & 16 Vict. c. 76), sect. 202, "if, *after appearance entered*, the claimant, without going to trial, allow the time allowed for going to trial by the practice of the court in ordinary cases after issue joined to elapse, the defendant in ejectment may give twenty days' notice to the claimant to proceed to trial at the sittings or assizes next after the expiration of the notice [*form, Appendix, No.* 176]; and if the claimant afterwards neglects to give notice of trial for such sittings or assizes, or to proceed to trial in pursuance of the said notice given by the defendant, and the time for going to trial shall not be extended by the court or a judge, the defendant may sign judgment in the form contained in the Schedule (A.) to this act annexed, marked No. 19, and recover the costs of defence." *Form, Appendix, No.* 181.

The time allowed for proceeding to trial in ordinary cases is regulated by sect. 101, as follows : " Where any issue is or shall be joined in any cause, and the plaintiff has neglected or shall neglect to bring such issue on to be tried, that is to say, in town causes where issue has been or shall be joined in, or in the vacation before, any term, for instance, *Hilary* Term, and the plaintiff has neglected or shall neglect to bring the issue on to be tried during or before the following term and vacation, for instance, *Easter* Term and vacation, and in country causes, where issue has been or shall be joined in, or in the vacation before, *Hilary* or *Trinity* Term, and the plaintiff has neglected or shall neglect to bring the issue on to be tried at or before the second assizes following such term, or if issue has been or shall be joined in, or in the vacation before, *Easter* or *Michaelmas* Term, then, if the plaintiff has neglected or shall neglect to bring the issue on to be tried at or before the first assizes after such term, whether the plaintiff shall in the mean time have given notice of trial or not, the defendant may give twenty days' notice to the plaintiff to bring the issue on to be tried at the sittings or assizes, as the case may be, next after the expiration of the notice, and if the plaintiff afterwards neglects to give notice of trial for such sittings or assizes, or to proceed to trial in pursuance of the said notice given by the defendant, the defendant may suggest on the record that the plaintiff has failed to proceed to trial, although duly required so to do (which suggestion shall not be traversable, but only be subject to be set aside if untrue), and may sign judgment for his costs ;

provided that the court or a judge shall have power to extend the time for proceeding to trial, with or without terms."

The time allowed under this section is exactly the same as under the previous practice where no notice of trial had been given; *Heeles* v. *Kidd*, 10 M. & W. 76; 1 Dowl. N. S. 663; but according to the previous practice, where notice of trial was given earlier than was necessary, and the plaintiff did not proceed to trial in pursuance of such notice, he thereby made default in proceeding to trial according to the course and practice of the court, within the meaning of 14 Geo. 2, c. 17. *Howell* v. *Powlett*, 8 Bing. 272; 1 Moo. & Sc. 355; 1 Dowl. 263; *May* v. *Husband*, 5 M. & W. 493; 7 Dowl. 867. But the 14 Geo. 2, c. 17, is now repealed; 15 & 16 Vict. c. 76, s. 100; and the time for proceeding to trial (whether notice of trial has been given or not) is now regulated by sects. 101, 202 (*ante*, 136).

In other actions than ejectment the time allowed for going to trial counts from the time *when issue is joined*, and issue is not considered as joined until the last similiter or joinder of issue is delivered, and the cause completely at issue. *Wright* v. *Oldfield*, 8 Dowl. 899; *Knaggs* v. *Knaggs*, 2 Low. M. & P. 465. In ejectment, the time for proceeding to trial counts from the time *when an appearance is entered*. *Ante*, 136. The reason is, that issue may be delivered immediately after such appearance. Sect. 178, *ante*, 134. If there be several defendants named in the writ, it would seem that any defendant who has duly appeared, whether he defends for the whole or only for part, may in due time after such appearance give the twenty days' notice, whether the other defendants named in the writ have or have not appeared: because the claimant might have signed judgment for want of appearance by the other defendants, unless he had been guilty of some neglect or default in not serving the writ, or otherwise. In other actions than ejectment one of several defendants may proceed pursuant to sect. 101. *Sawyer* v. *Hodges*, 1 Dowl. N. S. 16; *Rhodes* v. *Thomas*, 2 D. & L. 553; *Bridgford* v. *Wiseman*, 16 M. & W. 439.

The plaintiff must proceed to trial at the sittings or assizes next after the expiration of the twenty days mentioned in the notice; and for that purpose he must, if necessary, give notice of trial before the expiration of such twenty days. *Judkins* v. *Atherton*, 3 E. & B. 987.

If the twenty days' notice be given *prematurely*, the claimant should not treat it as a nullity, but should apply to a judge to set it aside for irregularity, with costs. *See forms of Summons and Order, Appendix, Nos.* 177, 178.

If the notice be regular, but by reason of special circumstances the claimant cannot comply with it, he should apply to the court or a judge to extend the time for proceeding to trial, upon a special affidavit of the facts. *Farthing* v. *Castles*, 1 Bail C. C. 142; *see forms of Summons and Order, Appendix, Nos.* 179, 180.

CHAPTER XIV.

SPECIAL CASE, WITHOUT PROCEEDING TO TRIAL.

———

By 15 & 16 Vict. c. 76, s. 179, " by consent of the parties and by leave of a judge, a special case may be stated according to the practice heretofore used."

The previous practice was established by 3 & 4 Will. 4, c. 42, s. 25, whereby it was enacted, that " it shall be lawful for the parties in any action or information after issue joined, by consent and by order of any of the judges of the said superior courts, to state the facts of the case in the form of a special case for the opinion of the court, and to agree that a judgment shall be entered for the plaintiff or defendant by confession, or of *nolle prosequi*, immediately after the decision of the case, or otherwise as the court may think fit ; and judgment shall be entered accordingly."

In other actions than ejectment a special case will not be ordered until "after issue joined;" 3 & 4 Will. 4, c. 42, s. 25; Jerv. N. R. 411, note (*b*); and so it seems that in ejectment a special case will not be ordered until the issue has been made up. 15 & 16 Vict. c. 76, ss. 178, 179, 180.

An order for a special case may be obtained " by consent," *either before or after* the draft special case has been settled by counsel on both sides. *See forms of Summons and Order, Appendix, Nos.* 146, 147. The latter course seems preferable, because if an order for a special case be drawn up in the first instance, and the parties cannot afterwards agree upon the terms of the special case, another summons and order to rescind the first order must be obtained before the plaintiff can regularly proceed to trial. 15 & 16 Vict. c. 76, s. 180.

The draft special case is usually drawn by the plaintiff's counsel, and settled by the defendant's counsel, or *vice versâ*, as may be deemed most expedient. *See the forms, Appendix, Nos.* 148, 149. It should, when finally settled and agreed on, be copied on brief paper, and signed by counsel for each party. A judge's order having been obtained, as before mentioned, the case may be set down for argument in the special paper, at the request of either party, four clear days before the day on which the same is to be argued, and notice thereof shall be given forthwith by such party to the opposite party. Reg. Prac. H. T. 1853, No. 15; *see form of Notice, Appendix, No.* 150.

Four *clear* days before the day appointed for argument each party must deliver two copies of the special case, with the points intended to be insisted on, to the judges, pursuant to Reg. Prac. H. T. 1853, No. 16. In case of default by either party, the other should, *on the day next after such default*, deliver copies for the party in default. See *post*, Chap. XXVI.

The brief for counsel, and subsequent proceedings, will be the same as after a "verdict subject to a special case." *Post,* Chap. XXVI.; *see form of Judgment after Argument on a Special Case, Appendix, No.* 151.

The court will not entertain a case where there is reason to believe that the action is *not bond fide* brought for the purpose of determining a matter in controversy between the parties. *Doe d. Duntze* v. *Duntze,* 6 C. B. 100. If they entertain any suspicion, from the frame of the case or the nature of the question, that the proceeding is only a friendly and colourable one for the mere purpose of obtaining the opinion of the court, they will require an affidavit as to the facts, &c.; and if such affidavit be not satisfactory, and such as to remove their suspicions, they will decline to give any opinion on the case. *S. C.* Under such circumstances the judge's order for the case should be rescinded or set aside, to enable the plaintiff to proceed to trial. 15 & 16 Vict. c. 76, s. 180.

Where there is a real question between the parties, *but the facts are not disputed,* a special case is much more advisable than proceeding to a trial at Nisi Prius, because the unnecessary expense of a trial will be thereby avoided. If the parties proceed to trial, any difficult point of law will in all probability be "reserved" for the opinion of the court in banc, or a verdict taken "subject to a special case," or a special verdict given, or a bill of exceptions tendered.

CHAPTER XV.

PROCEEDINGS BY CLAIMANTS AFTER APPEARANCE AND BEFORE GIVING NOTICE OF TRIAL.

BY the Common Law Procedure Act, 1852, 15 & 16 Vict. c. 76, s. 180, "the claimants may, if no special case be agreed to, proceed to trial upon the issue, *in the same manner as in other actions;* and the particulars of the claim and defence, if any, or copies thereof, shall be annexed to the record by the claimants."

We have already considered when and how the issue is to be made up and delivered. *Ante,* 134. Notice of trial is usually indorsed upon it, or such notice may be given afterwards in a separate form (*post,* Chap. XVI.); but before notice of trial is given certain steps should sometimes be taken, and these we now propose to consider.

Retainer to Counsel.]—At this stage of the proceedings, if not before, it is generally advisable to retain some leading counsel on behalf of the claimants, especially in country causes. This is done by delivering to his clerk a written retainer (*see the forms, Appendix, Nos.* 152, 153), together with the fee, 1*l.* 3*s.* 6*d.*

Advice on Evidence.]—Before giving notice of trial, a full statement of the claimant's case, and of the proposed proofs, should be laid before counsel, in the shape of a draft brief or otherwise, with instructions for him " to advise on evidence." In contested actions this should seldom or never be omitted; and the reasonable expense of obtaining such advice will be allowed on taxation, as costs in the cause. In many cases it would be prudent to take this step before commencing the action; but perhaps the expense of so doing would not be allowed on taxation, as " costs in the cause." By the directions to the masters of the courts of H. T. 1853, they are to allow in ejectment, for " instructions to sue and examining deeds, 13*s.* 4*d.*: if a question of title, 1*l.* 1*s.*" I E. & B. lxxi.

In subsequent parts of this work we shall consider fully the law and practice with respect to notices to admit (Chap. XVII.); notices to produce (Chap. XVIII.); *subpœnas ad testificandum,* and *subpœnas duces tecum* (Chap. XIX.); also as to the discovery of evidence, and inspection of documents before the trial (Chap. XX.); evidence on particular points frequently in question in actions of ejectment (Chap. XXI.); also evidence for the plaintiffs generally in ejectment (Chap. XXIV.); evidence and points for the defendant (Chap. XXIV.); also evidence and points for both parties in actions of ejectment between particular parties (Chaps. XXXVII.–LXVII.). See the "Table of Contents" (*ante*), and the "General Index" (*post*).

Counsel, when instructed to advise on evidence, will of course consider, and, if necessary, advise on the following points, viz.:—

1. Whether the claimants, or any and which of them, are necessary or material witnesses on their own behalf; also whether any and which of the defendants should be subpœnaed and examined on behalf of the claimants.

2. What other persons should be subpœnaed on behalf of the claimants, and whether with a *subpœna ad testificandum*, or a *subpœna duces tecum.*

3. What deeds and other documents, letters, papers and writings, should be proved by or on behalf of the claimants, and by what evidence.

4. What "notice to produce" should be given, and what particular documents should be mentioned in such notice.

5. What "notice to admit" should be given, and what particular documents should be mentioned in such notice. Generally speaking the notice should include (*inter alia*) any notice to produce; also some of the original documents therein mentioned, and copies thereof.

6. With what evidence (if any) the claimants should be prepared to prove the execution of the respective documents necessary to be produced on their behalf, and particularly those mentioned in the above notices respectively.

7. With what *secondary* evidence the claimants should be prepared to prove the contents of the respective documents mentioned in the notice to produce, in case the same be not produced at the trial when called for in pursuance of such notice; and the preliminary evidence necessary to render such secondary evidence admissible.

8. Whether the notice to produce, and any "admissions" made, should be proved *by affidavit* pursuant to 15 & 16 Vict. c. 76, ss. 118, 119 (*post*, Chap. XVII.), or how otherwise.

9. Whether any application should be made to compel the discovery and production of documents before the trial pursuant to 17 & 18 Vict. c. 125, s. 50. *Post*, Chap. XX., Sects. 1, 2.

10. Whether it is expedient to examine the opposite party upon interrogatories before the trial, pursuant to 17 & 18 Vict. c. 125, ss. 51 to 57. *Post*, Chap. XX., Sect. 3.

12. Whether the cause should be tried by a special jury, or by a common jury in the usual manner, or by a judge without a jury. *Post*, 143.

13. Whether an inspection of the property in question should be had by the jury, or by the claimants, or by any of their witnesses before the trial, pursuant to 17 & 18 Vict. c. 125, s. 58 (Chap. XX., Sect. 4): or whether a view should be had in the usual manner. Chap. XXII.

14. What other facts and points are material for the claimants, and by whom or in what manner they should be proved.

In many cases a full opinion upon each of the above points is un-necessary, and must not be expected.

Counsel's opinion or advice on the evidence should generally be *copied verbatim* into the brief. More attention is usually paid to it in that form by the leading counsel, than when the substance or effect of it is incorporated in the brief as part of the attorney's instructions or observations. But the latter course is frequently pursued because on taxation the attorney will be allowed for so much "drawing and copy-ing," instead of so much "copying" only.

Change of Place of Trial.]—By 15 & 16 Vict. c. 76, s. 182, "the court or a judge may, on the application of either party, order that the trial shall take place in any county or place other than that in which the venue is laid, and such order being suggested on the record, the trial may be had accordingly." *See forms of Summons, Order and Suggestion, Appendix, Nos.* 154, 155, 156.

Ejectment is a local action, and therefore the venue must be laid in the county wherein the lands lie, as described in the writ (*ante*, 135); otherwise the issue may be set aside for irregularity, or amended at the plaintiff's expense by altering the venue to the proper county, upon an application made promptly. *Ante*, 136.

An order made in pursuance of section 182 does not change the venue, but merely directs the trial to take place in some other county or place. *Doe* d. *Mayor, &c. of Bristol* v. ——, 1 Wils. 77. "No two things can be more different than changing the venue and con-tinuing it as it was, with such a suggestion on the roll as is now pro-posed." *Per* Lord Mansfield, C. J., in *Rex* v. *Harris*, 3 Burr. 1333; and see *Reg.* v. *Mitchell*, 2 Q. B. 636.

An order of the above nature will not be made until after issue joined. *Bell* v. *Harrison*, 2 Cr. M. & R. 733; 4 Dowl. 181; *Tolson* v. *The Bishop of Carlisle*, 7 C. B. 79.

After issue joined the order may be obtained almost as a matter of course "by consent:" but where the opposite party, whether plaintiff or defendant, will not consent, special grounds must be shown by affida-vit in support of the application. The affidavits must clearly show that from local causes, or other specified reasons, an impartial trial cannot be had in the county in which the venue is laid: *Rex* v. *Harris*, 3 Burr. 1333; *Rex* v. *Hunt*, 3 B. & A. 444; 2 Chit. Arch. 1270 (9th ed.): or that he has a large number of witnesses to examine, and that it will be a great saving of expense to him, and no great inconvenience to the opposite party, to have the action tried in some other county or place. *Doe* d. *Baker* v. *Harmer*, 1 Har. & Wool. 80; *Harris* v. *Pawlett*, 5 Dowl. & L. 780; *Hodge* v. *Churchyard*, *Id.* 514; 5 C. B. 495; *Pashley* v. *The Mayor, &c. of Birmingham*, 14 C. B. 421. The place of trial will be changed where justice and convenience mani-festly require it. *Robertson* v. *Hayne*, 16 C. B. 560. Sometimes the applicant will be made to pay the costs of the application and the extra expense (if any) occasioned to the opposite party by the change of the place of trial, whatever may be the result of the cause. *Att-wood* v. *Ridley*, 2 Man. & Gr. 893; *Pashley* v. *The Mayor, &c. of Birmingham*, 14 C. B. 421, 425.

If the venue be laid in any city or place, where no assizes or sittings at nisi prius are held, an order may be made, as of course, to try the action in the next adjoining county. *Cole* v. *Gane*, 3 Dowl. & L.

169; *Mayor of Berwick* v. *Ewart*, 2 W. Blac. 1636; *Reg.* v. *Holden*, C. & P. 606.

Trial by Judge without a Jury.]—By the Common Law Procedure Act, 1854 (17 & 18 Vict. c. 125), sect. 1, "the parties to any cause may, by consent in writing signed by them or their attorneys, as the case may be, leave the decision of any issue of fact to the court : provided that the court, upon a rule to show cause, or a judge on summons, shall in their or his discretion think fit to allow such trial, or provided the judges of the superior courts of law at Westminster shall, in pursuance of the power hereinafter given to them, make any general rule or order dispensing with such allowance, either in all cases or in any particular class or classes of cases to be defined in such rule or order, and such issue of fact may thereupon be tried and determined, and damages assessed where necessary, in open court, either in term or vacation, by any judge who might otherwise have presided at the trial thereof by jury, either with or without the assistance of any other judge or judges of the same court, or included in the same commission at the assizes, and the verdict of such judge or judges shall be of the same effect as the verdict of a jury, save that it shall not be questioned upon the ground of being against the weight of evidence ; and the proceedings upon and after such trial, as to the power of the court or judge, the evidence and otherwise, shall be the same as in the case of trial by jury."

A trial before a judge without a jury cannot be obtained without the consent in writing of all parties, or of their attorneys. *See the form, Appendix, No.* 157. It would seem that defendants named in the writ, who have suffered judgment against them for want of appearance, are not necessary consenting parties ; but this has not yet been decided. The signatures to the consent should be verified by affidavit. *See the form, Appendix, No.* 158. Thereupon a judge's summons or rule may be obtained to show cause why such trial should not be allowed. *See form of Summons, Appendix, No.* 159. Upon the hearing of such application the court or judge may exercise their or his discretion whether it is fit to allow such a trial, considering the nature of the action and the points to be decided. Such a trial will generally be allowed in ejectment. *See form of Order, Appendix, No.* 160. The issue should then be made up and delivered. *See the form, Appendix, No.* 161. Notice of trial may be indorsed in the usual form. *Appendix, Nos.* 168, 169, 170. The nisi prius record is a mere copy of the issue. *See Appendix, No.* 163. Subpœnas to testify, &c. are in the usual form, omitting the words "by a jury." Reg. Mic. Vac. 1854, Sched. No. 2 ; *see Appendix, No.* 162. At the trial the judge acts both as judge and jury, with the same powers of amending the record and of certifying, &c. as upon a trial before a jury. Either party may move the court in banc to set aside the verdict and for a new trial, on the ground of the reception of improper evidence, or of the rejection of proper evidence, or for any other *mistake in law*, but not on the ground that the verdict was against the weight of evidence. *Supra.* The forms of postea and judgment are prescribed by the Rule of Mic. Vac. 1854, Nos. 4, 5, 6. *See Appendix, Nos.* 164, 165, 166. The form of execution is the same as in ordinary cases. *Appendix, No.* 167.

Trial at Bar.]—If the property in question be of great value, and it be shown by affidavit that difficult questions are likely to arise at the trial, the court will sometimes grant a trial at bar. 1 Chit. Arch. 345 (9th ed.). The land must be of the yearly value of 100*l.* at the least; but the mere value, however great, is not of itself sufficient. *Goodright* v. *Wood,* 1 Barnard. 111. The nature of the expected difficulties must be shown by affidavit. Ad. Eject. 284; *Rex* v. *Burgesses of Carmarthen,* Sayer, 79; Andr. 271, *S. C.*

The application for a trial at bar may be made by either party. In ejectment it may be moved for before issue joined; *Anon.,* Sayer, 155; but not in other actions. It must be moved for in the term previous to that in which the cause is intended to be tried, unless the action be for lands in Middlesex. *Turner* v. *Barnaby,* 2 Salk. 649. It cannot be moved for in an issuable term; *Dimes* v. *Lord Cottenham,* 5 Exch. 311; 1 Low. M. & P. 318; *Rex* v. *Foley,* 1 Stra. 52; unless the crown be interested, and the application be made by the attorney-general *ex officio.*

The rank of the parties, or the value of the property in question, or the probable length of the trial, are not of themselves sufficient to induce the court to grant a trial at bar, especially in modern times. *Dimes* v. *Lord Cottenham,* 5 Exch. 311; 1 Low. M. & P. 318.

The court may impose any terms and conditions they think reasonable on granting a trial at bar. *Holmes* v. *Brown,* 2 Doug. 437.

Ten days' notice of trial at bar is sufficient. 15 & 16 Vict. c. 76, s. 97. "Notice of trial at bar shall be given to the masters of the court before giving notice of trial to the party." Reg. Prac. H. T. 1853, No. 41. Notice of trial at bar may be countermanded as in other cases; but it seems that no fresh notice of trial at bar can be given without another rule obtained for that purpose, and no second rule will be granted in the same term. 1 Chit. Arch. 347 (9th ed.).

A trial at bar takes place in Westminster Hall before the full court, and a special jury of the county in which the venue is laid. If twelve jurors do not attend the trial must be adjourned, and a *decem* or *octo tales* awarded as at common law. *Denn* v. *Cadogan,* 1 Burr. 273; 2 Saund. 349 a; *Buron* v. *Denman,* 1 Exch. 769; 1 Chit. Arch. 347 (9th ed.).

In other respects the trial is similar to that at nisi prius. A bill of exceptions may be tendered. *Rowe* v. *Brenton,* 3 M. & R. 266; 8 B. & C. 737.

CHAPTER XVI.

NOTICE OF TRIAL.

When to be given.]—Before giving notice of trial, the claimants should obtain " advice on evidence" (*ante*, 140), or otherwise satisfy themselves that they are in a condition to prove their title and right to possession, by sufficient legal evidence.

Notice of trial cannot be given before the issue is made up pursuant to sect. 178 (*ante*, 134). It should be given at the latest within such time after appearance entered as is allowed by the practice of the court in other actions after issue joined. Sect. 202, *ante*, 136.

Previous Month's Notice—when necessary.]—By Reg. Prac. H. T. 1853, No. 176, "in all causes in which there have been no proceedings for one year from the last proceeding had, the party, whether plaintiff or defendant, who desires to proceed, shall give a calendar month's notice to the other party of his intention to proceed. The summons of a judge, if no order be made thereupon, shall not be deemed a proceeding within this rule. Notice of trial, though afterwards countermanded, shall be deemed a proceeding within it."

Ten Days' Notice sufficient.]—By 15 & 16 Vict. c. 76, s. 97, "ten days' notice of trial or inquiry shall be given, and shall be sufficient in all cases, whether at bar or nisi prius, in town or country, unless otherwise ordered by the court or a judge."

The ten days are to be reckoned exclusively of the day on which the notice is given, but inclusively of the commission day at the assizes, or of the first day of the particular sitting in London or Middlesex. Reg. Prac. H. T. 1853, No. 174.

" The days *between* Thursday next before, and the Wednesday next after Easter-day, and Christmas-day and the three following days, shall not be reckoned or included in any rules, notices, or other pro-

H

ceedings, *except notices of trial,* or notices of inquiry." Reg. Prac. H. T. 1853, No. 175; *Charnock* v. *Smith,* 3 Dowl. 607.

If the notice be served on the last day for giving it, the service must be made before 7 o'clock, p.m., on that day, unless it be Saturday, or before 2 o'clock, p.m., on Saturday; otherwise it will be deemed to have been made on the following day, or if that be Sunday, then on the following Monday; Reg. E. T. 1856, *post,* 147; and consequently insufficient.

A notice of trial in due time, according to the practice of the court, is regular, although a previous notice has been given which is void, and has not been countermanded. *Fell* v. *Tyne,* 5 Dowl. 246; *Ranger* v. *Bligh, Id.* 235; *Tyte* v. *Steventon,* 2 W. Black. 1298.

Effect of irregular or insufficient Notice.]—The court or a judge will not generally set aside a notice of trial for irregularity or insufficiency, but will leave the plaintiffs to proceed thereon at their peril; and the defendants to treat it as a nullity at their peril. *Burton* v. *Fitch,* 21 Law J., N. S., Q. B., 266; but see *Nicholl* v. *Forshall,* 15 Law J., N. S., Q. B., 203; 1 Chit. Arch. 297 (8th ed.).

An insufficient notice of trial is something more than a mere irregularity. It is a nullity at election, and may be so treated, and no notice whatever taken of it. The defendant is not bound to return it (except perhaps as a matter of courtesy), nor will he by retaining it waive the defect or insufficiency. *Wood* v. *Harding,* 3 C. B. 968; *Dignam* v. *Ibbotson,* 3 M. & W. 431; *S. C., nom. Dignam* v. *Mostyn,* 6 Dowl. 547; *Fell* v. *Tyne,* 5 Dowl. 246; *Ranger* v. *Bligh, Id.* 235. The giving of a proper and sufficient notice of trial is in the nature of a condition precedent to the trial, and without which the trial itself will be irregular, and may be set aside with costs. *Wood* v. *Harding,* 3 C. B. 968. No affidavit of merits is necessary upon such application, the trial itself being irregular. *Williams* v. *Williams,* 2 Dowl. 350; *Dignam* v. *Ibbotson,* 3 M. & W. 451; 6 Dowl. 547; *Slatter* v. *Painter,* 8 M. & W. 672; 1 Dowl. N. S. 35. But if the defendant appear at the trial, and take his chance of the verdict, he will thereby waive any defect in the notice of trial, or even the total absence of any such notice. *Thermolin* v. *Cole,* 2 Salk. 646; *Figg* v. *Wedderburne,* 11 Law J., N. S., Q. B., 45; *Doe* d. *Antrobus* v. *Jepson,* 3 B. & Adol. 402.

Form of Notice.]—Notice of trial must be given *in writing;* Reg. Prac. H. T. 1853, No. 161; but no particular form is necessary. Therefore a notice framed and intended as a notice by way of continuance may operate as a new original notice if served in sufficient time. *Tyte* v. *Steventon,* 2 W. Black. 1298; *Ginger* v. *Pycroft,* 5 Dowl. & L. 554; *Cory* v. *Hotson,* 1 Low. M. & P. 23. The notice may either be indorsed on the issue, or afterwards delivered separately. *See the Forms, Appendix, Nos.* 168—170. It should mention the particular sitting or assizes, and also the place of trial, correctly; but any inaccuracy not calculated to mislead a reasonable person will be deemed immaterial; *Young* v. *Fisher,* 4 Man. & Gr. 814; 2 Dowl. N. S. 637; unless, indeed, the defendant swear to facts showing that he was actually misled by it. *Cross* v. *Long,* 1 Dowl. 342. But a notice of trial dated and delivered on the first day of Hilary Term, for trial at the second sittings in *next* Hilary Term, was held insufficient, though it appeared that the defendant could not have been misled by it. *Benthall* v. *West,* 1 Dowl. & L. 599, Lord Abinger, C. B., *dissentiente.*

Service.]—The notice of trial must be served "in town," *i.e.*, on the ondon agent, and not on the country attorney. Reg. Prac. H. T. 153, No. 34. It must be served on each attorney who defends for ie or more defendants; also on each defendant who defends personly. In the latter case the notice may be left for the defendant at his ldress as entered in the master's "Address Book" (*ante*, 127); or, no such entry has been made, the notice of trial may be stuck up in e masters' office, which will be good service as to that defendant *nte*, 127).

Notice of a trial at bar shall be given to the masters of the court fore giving notice of trial to the party. Reg. Prac. H. T. 1853, No.

By Reg. E. T. 1856, "it is ordered, that in lieu of rule 164 of the ractice Rules of Hilary Term, 1853, the following be substituted:— "Service of pleadings, notices, summonses, orders, rules and other 'oceedings shall be made before 7 o'clock, p.m., except on Saturdays, hen it shall be made before 2 o'clock, p.m. If made after 7 o'clock, m., on any day except Saturday, the service shall be deemed as made i the following day. And if made after 2, p.m., on Saturday, the rvice shall be deemed as made on the following Monday."

The object of this rule is to give the profession a half-holiday on iturday.

Short Notice.]—"The expression 'short notice of trial,' or 'short itice of inquiry,' shall in all cases be taken to mean *four days*." eg. Prac. H. T. 1853, No. 35. The four days are to be reckoned clusively of the day on which the notice is given, but inclusively of e commission day at the assizes, or of the first day of the particular :ting in London or Middlesex. Reg. Prac. H. T. 1853, No. 174.

The form and mode of service of short notice of trial is exactly the me as where full notice is given (*ante*, 146). The only difference is to the time of service.

A defendant who is under terms to take short notice of trial "*if cessary*" *for a particular sitting*, is entitled to full notice of trial for at sitting, if the plaintiff be in a condition to give such notice when e issue is delivered. *Drake* v. *Pickford*, 15 M. & W. 607; *Flowers Welch*, 9 Exch. 272. Such a defendant is not bound to take short itice of trial for any subsequent sitting, either in or after the same rm, or any other term. *White* v. *Clarke*, 8 Dowl. 730; *Slatter* v. *ainter*, 8 M. & W. 672; 1 Dowl. N. S. 35; *Wood* v. *Harding*, 3 C. 968; *Dignam* v. *Mostyn*, 6 Dowl. 547; *S. C.*, *nom. Dignam* v. *Ibtson*, 3 M. & W. 431. On the other hand, the plaintiff is not bound join issue before the usual time, and thereby to enable himself to ve full notice of trial. *Flowers* v. *Welch*, 9 Exch. 272.

A short notice of trial may be "continued" (in London or Middlex) by a *two days'* notice before the time mentioned in the short notice trial. Reg. Prac. H. T. 1853, No. 36, *post*, 148. It may also be countermanded" by a two days' notice. 15 & 16 Vict. c. 76, s. 98, *st*, 148.

Monday for Wednesday is a two days' notice within the meaning of e above rules; but a notice on Saturday for Monday is insufficient. *se* v. *M'Gregor*, 12 M. & W. 517; 1 Dowl. & L. 583; *Wardle* v. :*kland*, 4 Tyr. 819; 2 Dowl. 28; *Grosjean* v. *Manning*, 2 Cro. & r. 635.

Continuance of Notice.]—In London or Middlesex (but not in any other county), if the plaintiff be not prepared to try at the particular sitting for which notice of trial has been duly given, he may continue such notice to a subsequent sitting by a further notice. *Ranger* v. *Bligh*, 5 Dowl. 235; *see the form, Appendix, No.* 171. This is in effect a countermand of the notice of trial, combined with a new short notice of trial for the subsequent sitting, or in the nature of an amendment of the previous notice of trial. A notice of trial can be continued only once in the same term; *Wyatt* v. *Stocken*, 6 A. & E. 803; but a bad notice of continuance may operate as a good original notice of trial, if served in sufficient time. *Cory* v. *Hotson*, 1 Low., M. & P. 23; *ante*, 146. A notice by continuance cannot be given after a *ne recipiatur* has been duly entered; *Fitch* v. *Burton*, 2 Dowl. N. S. 958; nor after the plaintiff has countermanded his notice of trial; *Smith* v. *Hoff*. Barnes, 301; nor after a bad and insufficient notice of trial. *Brown* v. *Wildbore*, 1 Man. & Gr. 276.

Notice of continuance of trial shall be given *in town*, unless otherwise ordered by the court or a judge. Reg. Prac. H. T. 1853, No. 34.

" Notice of trial or inquiry may be continued *to any sitting in or after term* on giving a notice of continuance *four days* before the time mentioned in the notice of trial or inquiry, unless short notice of trial or inquiry has been given; in which cases two days' previous notice shall be sufficient, unless otherwise ordered by the court or a judge, or by consent." Reg. Prac. H. T. 1853, No. 36.

A notice of trial by continuance from the sittings in term to the sitting after term, in London, may be given, although the cause cannot be tried until the adjournment day. *Toulmin* v. *Elgie*, 3 Dowl. & L. 558.

The notice must be served within the hours prescribed by the rule of E. T. 1856. *Ante*, 147.

Countermand.]—If the claimants find that they will not be prepared to try at the particular sitting or assizes for which notice of trial has been given, they should in due time countermand such notice, except where they are entitled to continue it (*ante*, 147), and such continuance will allow them sufficient time to be fully prepared.

A countermand of notice of trial must be in writing. Reg. Prac. H. T. 1853, No. 161; *see the form, Appendix, No.* 172.

By 15 & 16 Vict. c. 76, s. 98, " a countermand of notice of trial shall be given four days before the time mentioned in the notice of trial, unless short notice of trial has been given, and then two days before the time mentioned in the notice of trial, unless otherwise ordered by the court or a judge, or by consent."

Notice on Saturday, countermanding the trial on the following Monday, is not a two days' notice. *Rose* v. *M'Gregor*, 12 M. & W. 517; 1 Dowl. & L. 583. Where countermand of notice of trial is given after the commission day, and the record is not withdrawn, the proper course is, on the cause being called on, to nonsuit the plaintiff. *Howarth* v. *Whalley*, 1 Car. & K. 586. A plaintiff cannot countermand notice of trial after the case has been made a remanet in London or Middlesex. *Tempany* v. *Rigby*, 10 Exch. 476.

Countermand of notice of trial " may be given either in town or country, unless otherwise ordered by the court or a judge." Reg. Prac. H. T. 1853, No. 34. It may be given either by the claimant's attorney in the country, or by his agent in town; *Cheslyn* v. *Pearce*, 1 M. & W. 56; 4 Dowl. 693; and it may be served either on the defendant's attorney in the country, or on his agent in town; Reg. Prac. H. T. 1853, No. 34; *Margettson* v. *Rush*, 8 Dowl. 388; but not on the defendant himself, who appears or defends by an attorney. *S. C.* It must be served within the hours prescribed by the rule of E. T. 1856 (*ante*, 147).

By countermanding notice of trial *in sufficient time*, a rule for costs of the day will be prevented; *May* v. *Husband*, 5 M. & W. 493; but a countermand after the cause has been made a remanet is ineffectual. *Tempany* v. *Rigby*, 10 Exch. 476.

By 15 & 16 Vict. c. 76, s. 99, "a rule for costs of the day for not proceeding to trial pursuant to notice, or countermanding in sufficient time, may be drawn up on affidavit, without notice." *See forms of Affidavit and Rule, Appendix, Nos.* 173, 174, 175.

Fresh Notice.]—When a cause is made a remanet from one sitting to another in London or Middlesex, no fresh notice of trial is necessary; *Jacks* v. *Meyer*, 8 T. R. 245; *Ham* v. *Greig*, 6 B. & C. 125; 9 Dowl. & Ry. 125; *Gibbons* v. *Phillips*, 8 B. & C. 437; but where a cause is made a remanet at the assizes, a fresh notice of trial for the subsequent assizes is necessary. *Gains* v. *Bilson*, 4 Bing. 414; 1 Moo. & P. 87. So where a trial is postponed from one term to another by rule of court. *Jacks* v. *Meyer*, 8 T. R. 245; *Ellis* v. *Trusler*, 2 W. Blac. 798. But if the trial be postponed to a subsequent sitting by an order of nisi prius, no fresh notice of trial is necessary. *Shepherd* v. *Butler*, 1 Dowl. & Ry. 15. So where the trial is stayed by injunction from the Court of Chancery, the cause may be tried after such injunction is dissolved without any fresh notice of trial. *The Stockton and Darlington Railway Company* v. *Fox*, 6 Exch. 127; 2 Low., M. & P. 141.

There must always be a notice of trial *for the particular assizes* at which the cause is tried, notwithstanding the plaintiff is under a peremptory undertaking to try at those assizes. *Ifield* v. *Weeks*, 1 H. Blac. 222; *Sulsh* v. *Cranbrook*, 1 Dowl. 148. But in London or Middlesex a notice of trial for a particular sitting operates as a notice for any subsequent sitting to which the cause may be made a remanet. *Ham* v. *Greg*, 6 B. & C. 125; 9 Dowl. & Ry. 125. When the trial is postponed from one term to another by a rule of court, fresh notice of trial should be given. *Jacks* v. *Meyer*, 8 T. R. 245.

CHAPTER XVII.

NOTICE TO ADMIT.

By 15 & 16 Vict. c. 76, s. 117, " either party may call on the other by notice to admit any document, saving all just exceptions; and in case of refusal or neglect to admit, the costs of proving the document shall be paid by the party so neglecting or refusing, whatever the result of the cause may be, unless at the trial the judge shall certify that the refusal to admit was reasonable ; and no costs of proving any document shall be allowed unless such notice be given, except in cases where the omission to give the notice is, in the opinion of the master, a saving of expense."

By Reg. Prac. H. T. 1853, No. 29, " the form of notice to admit documents, referred to in the Common Law Procedure Act, 1852, sect. 117, *may be* as follows." *See Appendix, No.* 184.

By 15 & 16 Vict. c. 76, s. 118, " an affidavit of the attorney in the cause, or his clerk, of the due signature of any admissions made in pursuance of such notice, and annexed to the affidavit, shall be in all cases sufficient evidence of such admissions." *See form of Admissions and Affidavit, Appendix, Nos.* 187, 188, 189.

Sect. 119. "An affidavit of the attorney in the cause, or his clerk, of the service of any notice to produce, *in respect of which notice to admit shall have been given,* and of the time when it was served, with a copy of such notice to produce annexed to such affidavit, shall be sufficient evidence of the service of the original of such notice, and of the time when it was served." *See form of Notice and Affidavit, Appendix, Nos.* 182, 183.

The above enactment (sect. 117) extends to all documents intended to be given in evidence by either party. *Spencer* v. *Brough,* 9 M. & W. 425. It is not confined to documents in their custody or control. *Rutter* v. *Chapman,* 8 M. & W. 388; 1 Dowl. N. S. 118. It applies to charters and other documents of a public nature deposited in the privy council office; *S. C.;* also to original wills deposited in any ecclesiastical court; also to title deeds, &c. in the possession of any third person, whether he will or will not permit them to be inspected; also to documents which are not in this kingdom. *Story* v. *Houlditch,* 1 Scott, N. R. 211, *per* Bosanquet, J.

When unnecessary.]—A notice to admit documents is unnecessary in the following cases:—

1. "Where the omission to give the notice is, in the opinion of the master, a saving of expense." Sect. 117, *ante,* 150. But the master's opinion cannot be obtained before taxation. The parties, or their legal advisers, must, at their peril, exercise their own judgment and discretion in the first instance.

2. Where the document can be proved by some witness who must necessarily attend to prove some other material fact. *Story* v. *Houlditch,* 1 Scott, N. R. 206, 211; *Bastard* v. *Smith,* 10 A. & E. 213; 2 P. & D. 453.

3. Where it is important to avoid disclosing to the opposite party the nature or contents of some document on which reliance is placed, and with reference to which it would be preferable to bear the expense of proof.

4. In any other case the only consequence of not giving the notice is, that the costs of proving the document cannot be recovered from the opposite party.

Form of Notice.]—The form is prescribed by Reg. Pr. H. T. 1853, No. 29, *ante,* 150; *see Appendix, No.* 184; but any necessary variations may be made therein. *Rutter* v. *Chapman,* 8 M. & W. 394; 1 Dowl. N. S. 118. No advantage can be gained by omitting the words, "saving all just exceptions to the admissibility of all such documents as evidence in this cause." *Sharpe* v. *Lambe,* 11 A. & E. 805; 3 P. & D. 454. The documents should be described as correctly as possible, but an error in this respect will not always have the effect of rendering the documents inadmissible without further proof at the trial. *Field* v. *Hemming,* 7 C. & P. 619; 5 Dowl. 450, *S. C.; Moillet* v. *Powell,* 6 C. & P. 233. Sometimes an advantage may be gained over the opposite party (if he be not sufficiently on his guard) by describing the documents in such a manner as to involve an admission of something more than their execution, or than their being what on the face of them they purport to be. *Wilkins* v. *Hopkins*, 1 C. B. 737; 3 D. & L. 184. Thus, if the defendant admit a document described in the notice as a *counterpart* of a lease dated, &c., he will thereby be precluded from objecting at the trial, that the document really is a lease and ought to have been stamped as such, and not merely as a counterpart. *Doe* d. *Wright* v. *Smith*, 8 A. & E. 255; 3 N. & P. 335; 2 Moo. & Rob. 7, *S. C.* So where the date of a document is written on an erasure, but it agrees with the description of it in the notice to admit, the party making such admission cannot require proof at the trial as to the time when or the circumstances under which the alteration was made. *Poole* v. *Palmer*, 1 Car. & Mar. 69, Rolfe, B.; *Freeman* v. *Steggall*, 14 Q. B. 202. Where a deed or will appears to have been altered, and no such admission is made, see *Doe* d. *Tatum* v. *Catomore*, 16 Q. B. 745; *Doe* d. *Shallcross* v. *Palmer*, *Id.* 747. In a recent case it was held, that the admission of a document described in the usual notice to admit is not the admission of *a fact stated in the description*; it may be some evidence of the fact, which may be rebutted by evidence to the contrary. *Pilgram* v. *The Southampton and Dorchester Railway Company*, 18 Law J., N. S., C. P., 338; *S. C.* (on other points), 8 C. B. 25. Where a document is admitted to have been "signed, sealed and executed as it purports to be," and the attestation mentions only the signing and sealing but not the *delivery*, yet such admission, coupled with the production of the instrument by the proper party, is evidence from which the jury may and ought to find that it was duly signed, sealed and *delivered as a deed*. *Hall* v. *Bainbridge*, 12 Q. B. 699.

The notice to admit should generally include the notice to produce. Sect. 119, *ante*, 151. It may be served immediately after the parties are at issue: *ante*, 134: or at any time before the trial which will allow of sufficient time for an inspection, and forty-eight hours afterwards for the opposite party to make the required admission. *Tymm* v. *Billingsley*, 2 Cr. M. & R. 253; 5 Tyr. 788; 3 Dowl. 810, *S. C.* It should be served within the hours prescribed by the rule of E. T. 1856. *Ante*, 147.

A party called upon to inspect and admit documents should examine the *description of the documents* in the notice very carefully, and with some jealousy; for sometimes it would seriously prejudice him to make *such* admissions as are specified in the notice. *Ante*, 151. He should also carefully inspect the documents required to be admitted, and compare each of them with its description in the notice. If, without doing this, he consent to make the required admissions, he must take the consequences: the admission, when made, will have the same effect as if made after the most careful examination of the documents. *Doe* d. *Wright* v. *Smith*, 8 A. & E. 263—265.

The admission must be made *within forty-eight hours* after the last hour mentioned in the notice, and not afterwards, except by consent of the opposite party or his attorney, or by order of a judge. *See forms of Summons and Order, Appendix, Nos.* 185, 186. It may frequently happen that more time than forty-eight hours is necessary to make inquiries and obtain instructions, before any admission can be safely made, especially in agency cases.

The admission may be written on the notice to admit, or on a fair copy. *See the form, Appendix, No.* 187. It should be signed in the presence of the attorney for the opposite party or his clerk, so that an affidavit of the signature may be made pursuant to section 118.

Ante, 150; *see form of Affidavit, Appendix, No.* 188. If the attorney or his clerk can swear to the signature, although he did not see it written, that is sufficient to enable him to make the necessary affidavit. *See the form, Appendix, No.* 189. But where no affidavit can be made in either of the above forms *by the attorney or his clerk*, some communication should be made to the opposite party or his attorney on the subject; and if a further admission or signature cannot be obtained, probably the expense of proving the admission by some third person acquainted with the signature, or the expense of proving the execution of the documents to which the admission relates, would be allowed on taxation.

Formerly, when either party consented to make any admission of documents, a judge's order was thereupon drawn up for such admission. Reg. H. T. 4 W. 4, No. 20; 1 Chit. Arch. 213 (7th ed.). But no such order is now necessary; in lieu thereof, and for the purpose of saving expense, an affidavit is substituted. Sect. 118, *ante*, 150. Such affidavit should be forthwith made. *See the forms, Appendix, Nos.* 188, 189.

When an admission is once made, it cannot be retracted except by consent, or by leave of the court or a judge, which will be granted only under special circumstances and upon equitable terms. *Elton* v. *Larkins*, 1 Moo. & Rob. 96; 5 C. & P. 385, 386; *Doe* d. *Wetherell* v. *Bird*, 7 C. & P. 6; *Wilkes* v. *Hopkins*, 1 C. B. 737; 3 D. & L. 184. It will be available not only for the first trial, but upon any new trial which may be granted. *Langley* v. *Earl of Oxford*, 1 M. & W. 508; and see *Hope* v. *Beadon*, 17 Q. B. 509; 2 Low. M. & P. 593.

Effect of Admission at the Trial.]—An admission may be proved at the trial by affidavit. Sect. 118, *ante*, 150. It may include any notice to produce. Sect. 119, *ante*, 151. The omission of the usual words, "saving all just exceptions to the admissibility of all such documents as evidence in this cause," will make no difference. *Sharpe* v. *Lambe*, 11 A. & E. 805; 3 P. & D. 454. The admission does not preclude an objection that any document therein mentioned is not duly stamped. *Vane* v. *Whittington*, 2 Dowl. N. S. 757; Car. & Mar. 484, *S. C.* But it does admit that the nature of the instrument is correctly described in the notice. Therefore where a deed was described and admitted as a *counterpart*, whereas it was in reality a lease: held, that it was admissible in evidence if duly stamped as a counterpart, although the stamp was insufficient for a lease. *Doe* d. *Wright* v. *Smith*, 8 A. & E. 255; 3 N. & P. 335; 2 Moo. & Rob. 7, *S. C.* So where a document appears to have been altered in its date, but has been admitted as altered, no evidence is necessary to explain when or under what circumstances such alteration was made. *Poole* v. *Palmer*, 1 Car. & Mar. 69, Rolfe, B.; *Freeman* v. *Steggall*, 14 Q. B. 202. Where a deed or will appears to have been altered, and no such admission is made, see *Doe* d. *Tatum* v. *Catomore*, 16 Q. B. 745; *Doe* d. *Shallcross* v. *Palmer*, *Id.* 747. Where certain bills of exchange were described in the notice and admitted as having been respectively accepted, drawn and indorsed *by one H. B. for the defendants*: held, that the defendants could not dispute the authority of H. B. to bind them by such bills, although that was the very question in issue in the action. *Wilkes* v. *Hopkins*, 1 C. B. 737; 3 D. & L. 184. Where it was admitted that a certain agreement "was signed, sealed and executed as it purports to be," and the attestation witnessed the signing and sealing (but not the delivery): held, that such admission, coupled with production of the instrument by the proper party, was evidence from which the jury might and ought to find that it was duly delivered as a deed. *Hall* v. *Bainbridge*, 12 Q. B. 699. But the admission of any document merely dispenses with proof of its execution, or that it is a true copy as described in the notice. It does not render a copy admissible in evidence when the original ought to be produced, or its nonproduction satisfactorily accounted for. Therefore, an admission by the plaintiff of a copy of a letter from himself to the defendant, with a notice given to produce the original letter, will not supersede the necessity of accounting for the original before such copy can be used in evidence. *Sharpe* v. *Lambe*, 11 A. & E. 805; 3 P. & D. 454.

If the documents, when produced, agree with the description of them in the notice and admission, no further evidence as to their identity appears to be necessary. *Doe* d. *Wright* v. *Smith*, 8 A. & E. 265; but see *Doe* d. *Tindal* v. *Roe*, 5 Dowl. 420; *Clay* v. *Thackrah*, 9 C. & P. 47, 53. If the documents do not exactly agree with the admission, some evidence may be necessary to show that they are the documents which were produced for inspection, and intended to be admitted. If the variance be not material, nor calculated to mislead the opposite party, the document may sometimes be admitted without any further proof. Thus, where an *ambiguous* document was described as a bill of exchange instead of a promissory note. *Moillet* v. *Powell*, 6 C. & P. 233, Alderson, B. So where a promissory note was in all respects described correctly, except as to the time of payment, which was erroneously stated to be on the 10th October instead of the 10th November. *Field* v. *Hemming*, 7 C. & P. 619, Lord Abinger, C. B.; 5 Dowl. 450, *S. C.*

Judge's Certificate.]—Generally speaking no certificate is necessary. The exception is where there has been a *refusal* to admit some particular document, which has been proved at the trial, and the party who so refused wishes to escape the costs of proof on the ground that such refusal was *reasonable*. *Ante*, 150; *see form of Certificate, Appendix, No.* 191. The certificate must be made "at the trial." *Ante*, 150. Sometimes an affidavit may be necessary, showing why and under what circumstances the party refused to admit the document, so as to satisfy the judge that the refusal was reasonable. Unless the document be *actually proved* at the trial no certificate is necessary. *Doe* d. *Peters* v. *Peters*, 1 Car. & M. 279; *Doe* d. *Meredith* v. *Sapsford*, 2 Car. & K. 30; *Freeman* v. *Rosher*, 6 Dowl. & L. 517.

CHAPTER XVIII.

NOTICE TO PRODUCE.

When necessary.]—If any deed or writing be in the possession or power of the opposite party, secondary evidence of the contents will not be admitted, unless notice to produce the original has been duly given, or the document happens to be in court at the trial. *Dwyer* v. *Collins*, 7 Exch. 639; *Doe* d. *Loscombe* v. *Clifford*, 2 Car. & K. 448.

If the original document be in the possession of a third person, not being the agent for the opposite party, such third person must be served with a *subpœna duces tecum* to produce it: a mere notice to produce it is not sufficient. *Hibbert* v. *Knight*, 2 Exch. 11; *Robinson* v. *Brown*, 3 C. B. 754, 762. A justice's summons to parish officers to produce their rate books, on an application for an order of removal, is not equivalent to a *subpœna duces tecum*, and cannot operate as a notice to produce. *Reg.* v. *The Inhabitants of Orton*, 7 Q. B. 120. The parish officers are not considered as parties to such application. *Reg.* v. *Greenaway*, 7 Q. B. 126, 135.

Before the 14 & 15 Vict. c. 99, a party to any suit or proceeding could not be *compelled* to produce or give evidence against himself; *Reg.* v. *Hawkins*, 2 Car. & K. 823, 826, Coltman, J.; Phil. Ev. 157 (8th ed.); but he may now be served with a *subpœna ad testificandum*, or *subpœna duces tecum*, in the same manner as any other witness: *Boyle* v. *Cardinal Wiseman*, 10 Exch. 647: nevertheless, a notice to produce has precisely the same operation and effect since the above act as it had previously. It does not exactly *compel* the party to produce the document, but it gives him an opportunity of doing so, and in case of non-compliance it lets in secondary evidence of the contents of the document withheld. *Dwyer* v. *Collins*, 7 Exch. 639. In many cases it has the effect of *indirectly* compelling the party to produce the document, for fear of prejudicing his case with the judge or jury. When there are several plaintiffs or several defendants, and certain documents are known to be in the custody, possession or power of some or one of them, or of some other person as their attorney or agent, but it is not known *exactly* who has actual possession thereof, a notice to produce will often prove more effectual than a *subpœna duces tecum*, because the notice has a wider and more sweeping operation; and as it requires to be served only on the attorney or agent in the cause, there is little or no danger of serving the wrong person. Moreover, the conduct money payable on the service of a subpœna is avoided; and secondary evidence is admissible if the notice be not complied with. The following are instances of the necessity of a notice to produce, viz. in an ejectment, the defendant relied on a will devising all the testator's property, except a pecuniary legacy.

In answer, the plaintiff proved that after the execution of such will a document which he alleged to have been a will was signed by the testator and delivered to a woman whom the defendant afterwards married, since which the witness who prepared it had heard nothing of it. It was then asked, on behalf of the plaintiff, whether the deceased had declared that paper to be his will, and whether the witness and others had signed it in his presence : held, that the questions could not be put, no notice having been given to produce the last-mentioned document. *Doe* d. *Phillips* v. *Morris,* 3 A. & E. 46 ; 4 N. & M. 598. In trover against a carrier, where the defendant relies on a general lien, he cannot prove the contents of bills (partly printed) delivered to the plaintiff from time to time, stating that all goods carried by the defendant were to be subject to such general lien ; unless he give notice to the plaintiff to produce such bills. *Jones* v. *Tarleton,* 9 M. & W. 675 ; 1 Dowl. N. S. 25. To make a defendant's card evidence against him, to show that he carried on a certain trade or business, the plaintiff must give him notice to produce his cards and put in one as a copy ; unless the one to be put in can be proved to have been given to the witness by the defendant or his agent. *Clark* v. *Capp,* 1 C. & P. 199, Abbott, C. J. In actions on bills and notes, if there be no plea on the record rendering it necessary for the plaintiff to produce the bill or note in support of his own case, he should have due notice to produce it at the trial ; otherwise the defendant will not be able to establish any special defence ; *Read* v. *Gamble,* 5 N. & M. 433 ; 10 A. & E. 597, note ; *Goodered* v. *Armour,* 3 Q. B. 956 ; *Lawrence* v. *Clark,* 14 M. & W. 250 ; 3 Dowl. & L. 87 : *Lane* v. *Mullins,* 2 Q. B. 254 ; 1 Gale & Dav. 712 ; 1 Dowl. N. S. 562 ; unless indeed the bill or note happen to be in court at the trial. *Dwyer* v. *Collins,* 7 Exch. 639. Upon an appeal against an order of removal, it is the duty of the appellants to produce the original order ; and if it be in the hands of the respondents, the appellants cannot put in evidence the copy which has been served upon them by the respondents, unless they have given the latter notice to produce the original order. *Reg.* v. *Justices of Sussex,* 9 Dowl. 125 ; *Reg.* v. *Justices of Peterborough,* 6 Dowl. & L. 512. But it is otherwise where by the practice of the sessions a copy of the order is required to be filed with the clerk of the peace. *Reg.* v. *The Inhabitants of Townstal,* 3 Q. B. 357, 365. In debt for rent by the assignee of the reversion against the assignee of the term, the plaintiff's attorney was called by his client to prove the execution of a deed. On cross-examination he admitted that there had been another deed between the same parties relating to the demised premises executed after the former, and that he had that deed in court, but he refused to produce it, relying on his privilege as an attorney of not disclosing the contents of his client's title deeds. The defendant then offered to produce evidence of the contents of the deed, without stating what evidence : no notice to produce had been given ; parol evidence was rejected : held, that such evidence was rightly rejected. *Bate* v. *Kinsey,* 1 Cr. M. & R. 38 ; 4 Tyr. 662. But "that decision proceeded upon the ground that the defendant was not entitled to use as secondary evidence that which he had obtained or would obtain out of the mouth of the plaintiff's own attorney ; for it did not appear that the defendant was prepared with any other secondary evidence, and an attorney cannot be compelled to state the contents of his client's deed." *Per* Parke, B., in *Dwyer* v. *Collins,* 7 Exch. 643, 644 ; and see *Davies* v.

Waters, 9 M. & W. 608 ; 1 Dowl. N. S. 651 ; *Lloyd* v. *Mostyn,* 10 M. & W. 478 ; 2 Dowl. N. S. 476.

It was formerly held that the circumstance of the document happening to be in court at the trial, in the possession of the opposite party or his attorney, did not render a notice to produce it unnecessary, for that such party ought to have an opportunity of producing the attesting witness or other evidence to do away with the effect of the written instrument. *Doe* d. *Wartney* v. *Grey,* 1 Stark. R. 283, Lord Ellenborough, C. J. ; *Cook* v. *Hearn,* 1 Moo. & Rob. 201, Patteson, J. ; *Bate* v. *Kinsey,* 1 Cr. M. & R. 38 ; 4 Tyr. 662. But under such circumstances less than the usual notice was deemed sufficient ; *Lloyd, Administrator, &c.* v. *Mostyn,* 10 M. & W. 478 ; 2 Dowl. N. S. 476 ; especially if such notice mentioned (according to the fact) that the document required was then in the possession of the attorney at the assize town. *Reg.* v. *Hankins,* 2 Car. & Kir. 823, 826. It has, however, since been decided that the true principle on which a notice to produce is required, is not to give the opposite party notice that such a document will be used in order to enable him to prepare evidence to explain or do away with the effect of the document, but is *merely to give him a sufficient opportunity to produce it,* and thereby to secure, if he pleases, the best evidence of the contents ; and therefore, where a document is shown to be in court, a request then and there made to produce it, without any previous notice, is sufficient to let in secondary evidence of the contents. *Dwyer* v. *Collins,* 7 Exch. 639.

When a document is proved to have come into the hands of a party to the cause, it can in no case be presumed to have been lost or destroyed, so as to let in secondary evidence of the contents, without notice to produce the original. It even seems doubtful whether the loss or destruction of the original instrument could be proved so as to let in secondary evidence of the contents, without a notice to produce ; *Doe* d. *Phillips* v. *Morris,* 3 A. & E. 46 ; 4 N. & M. 498 ; for the instrument might perhaps be found just before the trial, or it might be produced in a cancelled state. But if it can be shown that the original document is *not in existence,* then evidence of the contents may be given without any notice to produce ; *Foster* v. *Pointer,* 9 C. & P. 718, Gurney, B. ; for in such case the reason for requiring the notice fails. Phil. Ev. 662, note (3), (8th ed.). The principle is, that evidence of a secondary nature shall not be received where evidence of a primary nature might be produced.

A counterpart of a lease is admissible in evidence against the lessee or any person claiming through or under him, without any notice to produce the lease. *Burleigh* v. *Stibbs,* 5 T. R. 465 ; *Roe* d. *West* v. *Davis,* 7 East, 363. The reason is, that such counterpart is *primary* evidence of the contents of the lease, being an *admission* thereof under the lessee's hand and seal. Even an oral admission of the contents of a deed amounts to primary evidence of such contents as against the person making the admission. *Slatterie* v. *Pooley,* 6 M. & W. 664 ; *Howard* v. *Smith,* 3 Man. & Gr. 254 ; 3 Scott, N. R. 574. And see *Hall* v. *Ball,* 3 Man. & Gr. 242 ; 3 Scott, N. R. 577 ; *Doe* d. *Gilbert* v. *Ross,* 7 M. & W. 102. A notice signed by partners, stating that the partnership "has been dissolved," is evidence against them of the dissolution, though the partnership was by deed. *Doe* v. *Miles,* 1 Stark. R. 181 ; 4 Camp. 373, *S. C.* A recital of a deed in a subsequent written instrument, whether under seal or not, is primary evidence, in the nature of an admission, as against the parties to the subsequent instrument; *Carpenter* v. *Buller*, 8 M. & W. 209; and also against all persons claiming through or under any of them. *Doe* d. *Gaisford* v. *Stone*, 3 C. B. 176. But a declaration at law, or a bill in equity, is mere special pleading, and no evidence of any of the facts therein alleged. *Boileau* v. *Rutlin*, 2 Exch. 665.

There are some exceptions to the general rule which requires notice to produce, viz.: 1. In trover and other actions where, from the nature of the proceeding, the party has notice that he is to be charged with possession of the documents. *How* v. *Hall*, 14 East, 274; *Colling* v. *Treweek*, 6 B. & C. 399, Bayley, J.; *Whitehead* v. *Scott*, 1 Moo. & Rob. 2; *Minshall* v. *Lloyd*, 2 M. & W. 450. 2. A notice to produce a notice is unnecessary, for that might go on *ad infinitum*. This exception is not confined to notices to produce, but extends to notices of every description relating to any matter in question, and given to the opposite party or his attorney or agent. *Doe* d. *Fleming* v. *Somerton*, 7 Q. B. 58; *Reg.* v. *Mortlock*, 7 Q. B. 459. But not to notices given to third persons; *Robinson* v. *Brown*, 3 C. B. 754, 762; nor to notices relating to collateral matters. *Lanauze* v. *Palmer*, Moo. & Mal. 31. 3. Where a party to a suit has, in fraud of a *subpœna duces tecum*, obtained possession of a document after the commencement of the action, even before the subpœna was served: this is *in odium spoliatoris*. *Leeds* v. *Cook*, 4 Esp. 256, Lord Ellenborough, C. J.; and see *Doe* d. *Pearson* v. *Ries*, 7 Bing. 724. 4. In actions by seamen to recover their wages. *Bowman* v. *Manzelman*, 3 Camp. 315, cited 7 Man. & Gr. 476, note (*a*); *Johnson* v. *Lewellin*, 6 Esp. 102.

Form of Notice.]—A notice to produce must be in writing. Reg. Prac. H. T. 1853, No. 161. But no particular form is necessary. *Lawrence* v. *Clark*, 14 M. & W. 251. *See a form, Appendix, No.* 182. It should be entitled correctly in the cause. *Harvey* v. *Morgan*, 2 Stark. R. 17. But any mistake which does not actually mislead the opposite party will be deemed immaterial. *Lawrence* v. *Clark, supra.* The notice must mention, *with reasonable certainty*, the documents required to be produced, and it is for the judge to decide whether the notice is or is not sufficiently certain with reference to any particular document called for at the trial. Matters of a preliminary nature, upon which the admissibility of evidence depends, are always heard and decided by the judge alone, without the assistance of the jury. *Bartlett* v. *Smith*, 11 M. & W. 486; *Smith* v. *Sleap*, 1 Car. & Kir. 48; *Painter* v. *Hill*, 2 Id. 924; *Doe* d. *Jenkins* v. *Davies*, 10 Q. B. 323; *Rees* v. *Walters*, 3 M. & W. 531; *Doe* d. *Fryer* v. *Coombs*, 3 Q. B. 687; *Cleave* v. *Jones*, 7 Exch. 425, Parke, B.; *Boyle* v. *Wiseman*, 11 Exch. 360.

A notice to produce "all letters and copies of letters, also all books relating to this cause," is too general to let in secondary evidence of the contents of a letter written nine years previously, and not produced. *Jones* v. *Edwards*, M'Clel. & You. 139. So a notice to produce "all letters, papers and documents, touching or concerning the bill of exchange mentioned in the declaration, and the debt sought to be recovered," is too general. *France* v. *Lucy*, Ry. & Moo. 341, Best, C. J. But if the notice mention by whom and to whom the letters were written, *ex. gr.* by the plaintiff or his attorney to the defendant or his attorney, that will be sufficient without mentioning the dates of the letters. *Jacob* v. *Lee*, 2 Moo. & Rob. 33, Patteson, J. A notice served by the defendants on the plaintiffs, giving them notice to produce "all letters written to and received by you between the years 1837 and 1841, both inclusive, and from the said defendants, or either of them, during the time aforesaid, or by or to any person on their or your behalf respectively," is good, and is not too general, although it does not specify the date of each particular letter. *Morris* v. *Hannen*, Car. & M. 29 ; 2 Moo. & Rob. 392, Lord Denman, C. J. So in an action for work done, a notice to produce "all accounts relating to the matters in question in this cause," but not mentioning any particular account by date or otherwise, has been held sufficient to let in secondary evidence of an account for work done given by the plaintiff to the defendant. *Rogers* v. *Custance*, 2 Moo. & Rob. 179, Lord Denman, C. J. On a motion for a new trial in this case, the lord chief justice said : "the court did not mean to lay down any general rule as to what the notice ought to contain ; that much must depend on the particular circumstances of each case ; but where enough was stated on the notice to leave no doubt that the party must have been aware the particular instrument would be called for, the notice must be considered sufficient to let in secondary evidence. The court thought the defendant must have been aware in the present case that this account was one of those required." *S. C.*

In drawing the notice it may sometimes be advisable to describe the nature or contents of a particular document fully, or even to set it out *verbatim*, adding "or to that effect." For the party giving a notice to produce is *entitled to have it read at the trial*, although the other side offer to admit that a notice to produce the document called for has been duly given. *Whitehead* v. *Scott*, 1 Moo. & Rob. 2, Lord Tenterden, C. J. Such notice will not be evidence of any facts therein stated, but only that the defendant was so informed. *S. C.* Nevertheless it would probably have some effect with the jury where the defendant refuses to produce a document proved to be in his possession or power. They get an idea of the contents of the instrument withheld, and draw their inferences from its non-production : moreover they are satisfied with very slight secondary evidence as to the contents.

Sometimes a notice to produce which would, in the ordinary form, be deemed insufficient because served too late, may be made sufficient by going on to state (if the fact be so) that the document required is then in the assize town in the possession of the defendant's attorney, at such an hotel, &c. *Reg.* v. *Hankins*, 2 Car. & Kir. 826, Coltman, J.

*Service—*1. *On whom.*]—A notice to produce may be served on the party himself, though he has employed an attorney ; and if such notice be sufficient it will not be affected by a subsequent bad notice served upon the attorney. *Hughes* v. *Budd*, 8 Dowl. 315. But the general practice is to serve notices to produce on the attorney in the cause, if there be one. *Houseman* v. *Roberts*, 5 C. & P. 394, Gurney, B. It is sufficient to give such notice to the attorney even in a *qui tam* action. *Cates* v. *Winter*, 3 T. R. 306. And where the attorney in the cause has been changed, a notice to produce, served on the first attorney before the change, is sufficient, without any fresh notice to the second attorney. *Doe* d. *Martin* v. *Martin*, 1 Moo. & Rob. 242, Tindal, C. J.

Generally speaking notices do not require personal service, but they may be left at the dwellinghouse of the person to whom directed, with his servant, or some member of his family. *Reg.* v. *Justices of North Riding, Yorkshire*, 7 Q. B. 154; *Macgregor* v. *Keily*, 3 Exch. 794; 6 Dowl. & L. 635; and *per* Lord Kenyon, C. J., and Buller, J., in *Jones* d. *Griffiths* v. *Marsh*, 4 T. R. 465.

2. *When.*]—A notice to produce must not be served on a Sunday. *Hughes* v. *Budd*, 8 Dowl. 315. It must be served within the hours prescribed by the rule of E. T. 1856. *Ante*, 147. The notice applies not only to the first, but to any subsequent trial of the same cause, and need not be repeated. *Hope* v. *Beadon*, 17 Q. B. 509; 2 Low. M. & P. 593.

As a general rule, both in town and country causes, a notice to produce must be served *a reasonable time before the trial.* What amounts to such reasonable time depends upon the particular circumstances in each case; *Firkin* v. *Edwards*, 9 C. & P. 478, Williams, J.; amongst which must be taken into consideration,—1. Whether the trial is to be had in London or Middlesex, or at the assizes. 2. The place where the notice was served, especially with reference to its distance from the place of trial. 3. The place where the party in the cause resides; its distance from his own attorney, and from the place of trial, and particularly whether the party resides abroad, or in England. *Ehrensperger* v. *Anderson*, 3 Exch. 148. 4. The nature of the documents required to be produced, whether they are such as a client usually hands over to an attorney employed by him to conduct or defend an action, or such as he would retain in his own possession. *Atkins* v. *Meredith*, 4 Dowl. 658; *Gibbons* v. *Powell*, 9 C. & P. 634.

A very short notice is usually deemed reasonable and sufficient. The cases on this point may be conveniently arranged under two heads,— 1. Where the trial takes place at the assizes. 2. In London or Middlesex.

At the Assizes.]—A notice to produce must generally be served *before the commission-day* on parties living away from the assize town. *Trist* v. *Johnson*, 1 Moo. & Rob. 259, Parke, B.; *Rex* v. *Ellicombe, Id.* 260, Littledale, J.; *Reg.* v. *Kitson*, 17 Jur. 422. But a notice to produce served at Liverpool on the commission-day, the trial taking place fourteen days afterwards, is sufficient. *Doe* d. *Rowlandson* v. *Wainwright*, 5 A. & E. 520. Service at noon on the commission-day has been held sufficient where the notice mentioned (as the fact was) that the document required was then in the possession of the defendant's attorney, at a particular hotel in the assize town, the trial taking place on the next day. *Reg.* v. *Hankins*, 2 Car. & K. 823, Coltman, J. Notice to produce an agreement, served upon the defendant's attorney at five o'clock on the commission-day of the assizes, held too late, the defendant's attorney having then left home for the assize town, which was nine miles distant from his office, and the opposite party refusing to furnish him with a conveyance. *George* v. *Thompson*, 4 Dowl. 656. Service of notice to produce on the attorney in the cause on the day before the trial, at a distance from his place of business, is bad. *Hughes* v. *Budd*, 8 Dowl. 315; and see *Howard* v. *Williams*, 9 M. & W. 725; 1 Dowl. N. S. 877. A notice to produce deeds was served on the defendant's attorney in Essex on Saturday, the commission-day of the assizes being Monday; the attorney went to London and fetched them: a further notice was served on the Monday evening to produce another deed; the attorney thereupon stated that he had been to town to fetch the deeds, and if the plaintiff would pay the expenses of sending for this from town where it was, it should be had; no offer was made to pay, and the trial was on Thursday: held, that under the special circumstances of this case the plaintiff was not entitled to give secondary evidence of the last-mentioned deed; Lord Tenterden, C. J., saying, " I think the defendant was justified in not complying with the notice, and was not bound to have his title deeds sent by a coach if the other party refused to be at the expense of a special messenger." *Doe* d. *Curtis* v. *Spitty*, 3 B. & Ad. 182.

Sometimes a notice served *after the commission-day* is sufficient. Thus where the attorney and his client lived in the assize town, the commission-day was on Thursday, a notice to produce was served on the following Saturday, the cause was tried on Monday: held, that the service was not too late; and that the question in such cases is whether, under all the circumstances, reasonable notice has been given. *Firkin* v. *Edwards*, 9 C. & P. 478, Williams, J. Where the document required was in court at the trial in the possession of an attorney for both parties, who refused to produce it under a *subpœna duces tecum*, and the defendant's attorney had been served on the day previous to the trial (but after the commission-day) with a notice to produce it: held, that the service of the notice was in sufficient time to let in secondary evidence. *Lloyd, Administrator, &c.* v. *Mostyn*, 10 M. & W. 478; 2 Dowl. N. S. 476. Where the document was at the assize town in the possession of the defendant's attorney, notice to produce it, served at noon on the commission-day, the trial taking place the next day, was sufficient, the notice specially mentioning where the document then was. *Reg.* v. *Hankins*, 2 Car. & Kir. 823, Coltman, J. It has been decided that a notice to produce cannot be served at the time of the trial, although the attorney then has the document with him in court. *Cook* v. *Hearn*, 1 Moo. & Rob. 201, Patteson, J. But it has since been held that no notice to produce is requisite when the document happens to be in court at the trial. *Dwyer* v. *Collins*, 7 Exch. 638, *ante*, 158. Therefore in every case where an insufficient notice to produce has been served, counsel should endeavour to ascertain at the trial that the document wanted is then in court.

In London or Middlesex.]—A notice to produce must be served before seven o'clock p.m., otherwise the service will be considered as made on the next day. Reg. Prac. H. T. 1853, No. 164. A notice served on the evening before the trial is generally insufficient. *Sims* v. *Kitchen*, 5 Esp. 46; *Atkins* v. *Meredith*, 4 Dowl. 658; *Holt* v. *Miers*, 9 C. & P. 191; *Byrne* v. *Harvey*, 2 Moo. & Rob. 89; *Howard* v. *Williams*, 9 M. & W. 725; 1 Dowl. N. S. 877; *Lawrence* v. *Clarke*, 14 M. & W. 250; 3 Dowl. & L. 87. Except where the document required is of such a nature that it will be presumed to be in the possession of the attorney; *ex. gr.* the copy writ of summons in the action; *Gibbons* v. *Powell*, 9 C. & P. 634, Gurney, B.; the attorney's letter before action for payment of the debt or compensation claimed. *Leaf* v. *Butt*, Car. & M. 451; *Meyrick* v. *Woods*, *Id.* 452. A letter from defendant to plaintiff, touching the bill of exchange upon which the action is brought, is not such a document. *Holt* v. *Miers*, 9 C. & P. 191, Lord Abinger, C. B.; but see *Sturm* v. *Jeffree*, 2 Car. & K., 442.

When the Party resides Abroad.]—In case either party resides abroad, and sues or defends by attorney, it will be presumed that he has left with his attorney all the documents in his possession or power relating to the matters in question; consequently, the usual notice to produce, served on such attorney on the evening next but one before the trial, will be deemed sufficient. *Bryan* v. *Wagstaff*, Ry. & Moo. 327, Abbott, C. J. But it is otherwise where the party resides in England, and is temporarily absent in Scotland or elsewhere. *Vice* v. *Lady Anson*, 3 C. & P. 19, Moo. & Mal. 96, *S. C.*, Lord Tenterden, C. J. A notice to produce certain letters written by the plaintiff to the defendant (a foreigner) eighteen years previously, and directed to him abroad, was served on the defendant on the 10th April: held in sufficient time for the 14th April, although it was objected that he might probably have left the letters behind him on coming to this country. *Drabble* v. *Donner*, 1 C. & P. 188; Ry. & Moo. 47, Abbott, C. J.; but see *Ehrensperger* v. *Anderson*, 3 Exch. 148.

Affidavit of Service.]—By 15 & 16 Vict. c. 76, s. 119, "an affidavit of the attorney in the cause, or his clerk, of the service of any notice to produce, *in respect of which notice to admit shall have been given,* and of the time when it was served, with a copy of such notice to produce annexed to such affidavit, shall be sufficient evidence of the service of the original of such notice, and of the time when it was served." *See the form of such Affidavit, Appendix, No.* 183.

If the notice to produce be not mentioned in the notice to admit, it must be proved by *vivâ voce* evidence in the usual manner.

Effect of the Notice at the Trial—1. When the Document is produced.]—If the counsel for the party giving the notice to produce *merely calls for* the documents therein mentioned, but when they are produced he *declines to inspect them or to make any use of them,* although that is matter of observation for the jury, yet he is not bound to give them in evidence, nor does it entitle the opposite party to use them as evidence on his own behalf. *Sayer* v. *Kitchen*, 1 Esp. 209, Lord Kenyon, C. J. But where the counsel calls for a document and *inspects it,* he is bound to give it in evidence if it be material to the matters in issue; for he has no right to call for and inspect a document in order to ascertain if it makes in his favour, and then, finding it does not, to decline using it. *Wharam* v. *Routledge,* 5 Esp. 235, Lord Ellenborough, C. J.; *Calvert* v. *Flower,* 7 C. & P. 386, Lord Denman, C. J. If the plaintiff's counsel calls on the other side to produce a paper, *and reads it,* he is bound to give it in evidence if it be material to the issue (which the judge will decide); but if it be not material, the plaintiff's counsel need not give it in evidence, though required to do so by the other side. *Wilson* v. *Bowie,* 1 C. & P. 10, Park, J.

Where a tradesman's day book is called for and produced, and the plaintiff reads one or more of the entries therein contained, the defendant is not thereupon entitled to read other distinct entries in the same book, unconnected with and not referred to by those read by the plaintiff. *Catt* v. *Howard*, 3 Stark. R. 3, Abbott, C. J. So where a merchant's letter book is produced pursuant to notice, and some of the letters entered in it are read by the plaintiff, the defendant has no right to read on his own behalf other letters upon the same subject copied in the same book, but not referred to in those read by the plaintiff. He may, however, read any others that are so referred to. *Sturge* v. *Buchanan*, 10 A. & E. 598; 2 P. & D. 573. Upon the same principle, when certain parts only of a book containing proceedings in bankruptcy are put in by one party, the opposite counsel have no right to refer to other parts of it. *Whitfield* v. *Aland*, 2 Car. & K. 1015, Wilde, C. J. Under a notice to produce a letter, which is produced and mentions that it covers other papers, these papers are not thereby made evidence unless they are referred to in the letter. *Johnson* v. *Gibson*, 4 Esp. 21. " If the letter refers to the papers which it covers, that is, refers to them in such a way that it is necessary to incorporate the papers inclosed with the body of the letter in order to make it intelligible, or the sense complete, in that case the papers inclosed would be by the note made evidence, and admissible; and the party who produced the letter and the inclosure would have a right to have the whole read; but independent papers, not referred to by the letter, but which it only covers, such papers are not thereby made evidence." *Id.*, *per* Lord Kenyon, C. J. Where a promissory note is called for, and used in evidence by the plaintiff, he is bound, if required, to read an indorsement written thereon. *Richards* v. *Frankum*, 9 C. & P. 221, Gurney, B.

A document produced by the opposite party, in pursuance of a notice to produce, cannot be read in evidence unless it be legally stamped, nor can the defect be supplied by parol evidence. *The Fishmongers' Company* v. *Robertson*, 1 C. B. 60, 73; *Doe* d. *St. John* v. *Hore*, 2 Esp. 724; *Doe* d. *Frankis* v. *Frankis*, 4 Jur. 273, Patteson, J. But an application may be made before the trial to have the document produced at the Stamp Office to be stamped, at the expense of the party making the application; and this even in cases where such party would not be entitled to an *inspection* of the document: *Neale* v. *Swind*, 2 Cr. & Jer. 278; 2 Tyr. 318; 1 Dowl. 314; *Hall* v. *Bainbridge*, 3 Dowl. & L. 92: or the duty and penalty, with 1*l.* extra, may be paid at the trial, pursuant to 17 & 18 Vict. c. 125, ss. 28, 29 (*post*, Chap. XXIV.), and thereupon the document will be admissible. An unstamped part of an agreement, produced pursuant to notice, may be read as secondary evidence of the original, upon proof that the latter was duly stamped, and has been lost. *Munn* v. *Godbold*, 3 Bing. 298. If the document be not produced pursuant to notice, it will be presumed to have been properly stamped. *Crisp* v. *Anderson*, 1 Stark. R. 35, Lord Ellenborough, C. J.; *Pooley* v. *Godwin*, 4 A. & E. 94.

As a general rule, when a document is produced in pursuance of notice by a person who has not derived, and does not claim under it any beneficial estate or interest *in question in the cause*, the execution of it must be proved in the usual manner before it will be admissible in evidence. *Gordon* v. *Secretan*, 8 East, 548; *Johnson* v. *Lewillin*, 6 Esp. 101, Lord Ellenborough, C. J.; *Rearden* v. *Minter*, 5 Man. & Gr. 204; *Collins* v. *Bayntum*, 1 Q. B. 117; 4 P. & D. 544. It makes no difference in this respect whether the document be under seal or not; *Wetherston* v. *Edgington*, 2 Camp. 94, Heath, J.; nor that it has been cancelled. *Breton* v. *Cope*, 1 Peake, N. P. C. 44, Lord Kenyon, C. J. Formerly it was necessary to call the attesting witness, whenever there was one to any document whatever. *Cases supra; Richards* v. *Frankum*, 9 C. & P. 221; *The Fishmongers' Company* v. *Robertson*, 1 C. B. 69, 70. This rule applied even to a mere notice to quit. *Doe* d. *Sykes* v. *Durnford*, 2 M. & S. 62. But now, by 17 & 18 Vict. c. 125, s. 26, "it shall not be necessary to prove by the attesting witness any instrument *to the validity of which attestation is not requisite;* and such instrument may be proved by admission, or otherwise, as if there had been no attesting witness." Since the above act, wills, codicils, and deeds or writings executed in pursuance of powers requiring attestation by one or more credible witnesses, and the like, must be proved by one or more of the attesting witnesses; but other instruments may be proved by any person who can speak to the handwriting, &c. An indorsement on a feoffment (purporting to have been made by the attorney thereby appointed to deliver seisin), that he had done so in the presence of A., is not evidence of that fact, although the deed is produced by the defendant upon notice from the plaintiff; unless the defendant claims under it. *Doe* d. *Wilkins* v. *Cleveland*, 9 B. & C. 864; 4 M. & R. 666.

Where the party producing a document pursuant to notice has derived, or claims under it, a beneficial estate or interest in any of the matters in question in the cause, it is unnecessary to prove its execution; for, as against him, it must be taken to have been duly executed. *Pearce* v. *Hooper*, 3 Taunt. 60. Thus, in an action by lessee against his assignee, founded upon the defendant's implied undertaking to indemnify the plaintiff from the rent and covenants in the lease, if the defendant, upon notice, produced such lease, the plaintiff need not prove the execution of it. *Knight* v. *Martin*, Gow. 26, Dallas, C. J.; and see *Burnett* v. *Lynch*, 5 B. & C. 589; 8 Dowl. & Ry. 368. The assignees of a bankrupt producing under notice the deed of assignment to them of the bankrupt's effects, and under which it appeared they occupied: held, that it was not necessary for the plaintiff to prove the execution of such deed by the attesting witness. *Orr* v. *Morrice*, 3 Brod. & B. 139; 6 Moore, 347. In an action against the vendor of an estate to recover the deposit on a contract for the purchase, if the defendant, on notice, produce the contract, the plaintiff need not prove its execution. *Bradshaw* v. *Bennett*, 1 Moo. & Rob. 143; 5 C. & P. 48, Lord Tenterden, C. J. Where the defendants claimed title to certain goods under an assignment, and in pursuance of notice produced it at the trial when called for by the plaintiffs: held, that the plaintiffs were entitled to read it in evidence without calling the attesting witness to prove the execution, although they impugned the validity of the assignment on the ground of fraud. *Carr* v. *Burdiss*, 1 Cr. M. & R. 782; 5 Tyr. 309. Where, in ejectment, the attorney for the claimant obtained from one of the defendants (the tenant in possession) a lease of the premises granted to him for a term not then expired, in order to prevent the defendants from setting it up to defeat the action: held, that he thereby recognized it as a valid instrument, and that when produced in pursuance of notice from the defendants it might be read in evidence without calling the subscribing witness to prove the execution by the grantor of the lease. *Doe* d. *Tyndale* v. *Heming*, 6 B. & C. 28; 9 Dowl. & Ry. 15; 2 C. & P. 462, S. C.

In an action by a servant against his master for not employing him for one year pursuant to a written agreement, the agreement was produced under notice : held that it was not necessary for the plaintiff to call the subscribing witness to prove the execution. *Bell* v. *Sir W. Chaytor*, 1 Car. & K. 162, Cresswell, J. But the propriety of this decision may perhaps be doubted, for the mere circumstance of a person being party to an agreement, containing stipulations in his favour, is not sufficient to make such agreement evidence against him when produced by himself under notice, unless he derives or has derived under it some title or interest to real or personal property in question in the cause ; his mere interest in the contract as such is not sufficient to render proof of the execution of the contract unnecessary. *Collins* v. *Bayntum*, 1 Q. B. 117 ; 4 P. & D. 544. In an action by an agent for commission for procuring an apprentice, the defendant produced (pursuant to notice) the deed of apprenticeship to which there was an attesting witness : held, that such witness must be called by the plaintiff. *Rearden* v. *Minter*, 5 Man. & Gr. 204 ; but now see 17 & 18 Vict. c. 125, s. 26, *ante*, 165.

Proof of the execution of a document produced by the opposite party upon notice is unnecessary where such party is a sheriff or other public officer, who, in the discharge of his official duties, was bound to take a bond or other instrument duly executed ; for as against him the instrument so taken and produced must be presumed to be valid. *Scott* v. *Waithman*, 3 Stark. R. 168.

2. *When the Document is not produced.*] — The party giving a notice to produce should be prepared with an admission or proof of the service thereof. Sometimes it may be proved by affidavit. *Ante*, 163.

The party giving the notice is *entitled to have it read* at the trial, although the other side offer to admit that a notice to produce the document called for has been duly given. *Whitehead* v. *Scott*, 1 Moo. & Rob. 2, Lord Tenterden, C. J. Such notice will not be evidence of any of the facts therein stated, but only that the defendant was so informed. *S. C., ante*, 160.

The regular time for calling for the production of books, papers, &c. is not until the party who requires them has entered upon his case ; till that period arrives the other party may refuse to produce them, and there can be no cross-examination as to their contents, although the notice to produce them is admitted. Therefore a defendant cannot in the course of the plaintiff's evidence cross-examine the plaintiff's witnesses as to the contents of written instruments, although notice has been given to the plaintiff to produce them, and he refuses to produce them in that stage of the cause. *Sideways* v. *Dyson*, 2 Stark. R. 49, Lord Ellenborough, C. J.; *Graham* v. *Dyster, Id.* 21 ; but see *Calvert* v. *Flower*, 7 C. & P. 386, Lord Denman, C. J. To prevent any point of the above nature, the plaintiff should not admit the notice to produce, and should object to its being proved prematurely.

When the opposite party is regularly called upon to produce a document pursuant to notice, he must produce it *then or not at all* : after having once refused to do so, he cannot (except by consent) be permitted to produce it at any subsequent part of the trial for any purpose whatever. *Jackson* v. *Allen*, 3 Stark. R. 74 ; *Edmunds* v. *Challis*, 7 C. B. 413, 439 ; 6 Dowl. & L. 581. Thus, he cannot afterwards put it into the hands of a witness to ask him at what time an interlineation was made in it: *Doe* d. *Higgs* v. *Cockell*, 6 C. & P. 525, Alderson, B.: nor can a defendant put a document in evidence as part of his own case, which he has refused to produce in the course of the plaintiff's case when regularly called for pursuant to notice. *Doe* d. *Thompson* v. *Hodgson*, 2 Moo. & Rob. 283 ; 12 A. & E. 135; 4 P. & D. 143, *S. C.*; and see *Lewis* v. *Hartley*, 7 C. & P. 405.

It is perfectly *optional* with the party on whom notice to produce has been served to comply with such notice or not. No inference as to the contents of any document not produced can legitimately be drawn from its nonproduction, the only consequence is to let in *secondary* evidence of the contents. *Cooper* v. *Gibbons*, 3 Camp. 363, Gibbs, J.; *Lawson* v. *Sherwood*, 1 Stark. R. 314. But it is matter of observation to the jury, that the party would not have withheld the document unless it made against him. *Bate* v. *Kinsey*, 1 Cr. M. & R. 41, Lord Lyndhurst, C. B.; *Roe* v. *Harvey*, 4 Burr. 2484, Lord Mansfield, C. J. The jury generally draw most unfavourable inferences when a document is withheld, and will be satisfied with slight secondary evidence of the contents.

Proof of Possession of the Original.]—Before secondary evidence can be admitted it must be proved to the satisfaction of the judge (not the jury), that the document called for is in the possession or power of the party required to produce it. For if it be in the possession of any third person (not being the agent or under the control of such party), he should be served with a *subpœna duces tecum*. *Robinson* v. *Brown*, 3 C. B. 754; *Hibbert* v. *Knight*, 2 Exch. 11; *ante*, 156. Thus, if the document be in the possession of a stakeholder: *Parry* v. *May*, 1 Moo. & Rob. 279, Littledale, J.: or of a third independent person under whom the defendant justifies: *Evans* v. *Sweet*, Ry. & Moo. 83; 1 C. & P. 277, Best, C. J.: or of one of the committee of a charitable institution. *Whitford* v. *Tutin*, 4 Moo. & Sc. 166; 10 Bing. 395; 6 C. & P. 228. The law presumes the written appointment of overseers to be in the custody of some of the overseers who are responsible for the acts done under it—not that it is in the possession of the parish officers for the time being, and therefore it is not sufficient (to let in parol evidence upon an appeal) to give notice to the parish officers for the time being, but the former overseers should be subpœnaed. *Rex* v. *Inhabitants of Stoke Golding*, 1 B. & A. 173.

If a document be traced into the hands of an agent of the party to whom notice to produce it has been given, and it be not produced when called for pursuant to the notice, secondary evidence of the contents is admissible, without calling the agent. *Sinclair* v. *Stephenson*, 1 C. & P. 582; 2 Bing. 514; 10 Moore, 46, *S. C.* Thus, where a check drawn by the defendant has been paid by his bankers and remains in their hands, and he has had notice to produce it. *Partridge, q. t.* v. *Coates*, Ry. & Moo. 156; 1 C. & P. 534, Abbott, C. J.; *Burton* v. *Payne*, 2 C. & P. 520, Bayley, J. So where an order relating to a ship has been delivered to the captain by the shipowner (the defendant). *Baldney* v. *Ritchie*, 1 Stark. R. 338, Lord Ellenborough, C. J. Where a sheriff's warrant to levy execution had, after the levy, been returned by the bailiff to the undersheriff, while the sheriff was yet in office, and the bailiff being called as a witness did not produce it: held, in an action against the sheriff, that upon proof of a notice to produce the warrant served on the defendant's attorney, secondary evidence of the contents was admissible. *Taplin* v. *Atty*, 3 Bing. 164; 10 Moore, 564; and see *Coates* v. *Mudge*, 2 Q. B. 252; 1 Dowl. N. S. 540.

Where a letter, which had been in the possession of the defendant, was filed in the Court of Chancery pursuant to an order of that court: held, that a notice to produce it was insufficient to let in secondary evidence of the contents: an order for its production might have been obtained by either party. *Williams* v. *Munnings*, Ry. & Moo. 18, Abbott, C. J. But where the defendant has presented a petition to the Vice-Chancellor to allow the plaintiff's books deposited in the master's office to be produced at the trial, which petition was opposed by the plaintiffs, and dismissed with costs: held, that under such circumstances a notice to produce was sufficient to let in secondary evidence of the contents of the books. *The Mayor, Aldermen and Burgesses of Ludlow* v. *Charlton*, 9 C. & P. 242, Gurney, B. A document deposited in a court of equity by a party to a suit there, but which remains with an officer of that court *after an order to deliver it up to the party*, is sufficiently in the control and power of such party to let in secondary evidence of the contents upon proof of notice to produce. *Bush* v. *Peacock*, 2 Moo. & Rob. 162, Lord Denman, C. J.

The degree or quantum of evidence necessary to prove that an instrument, not produced upon notice, is in the possession or power of the party on whom the notice was served, must of course depend very much on the nature of the transaction, and the particular circumstances of each individual case; and it is for the judge (not the jury) to decide whether such evidence is or is not sufficient. Slight evidence (such as on other points ought to be left to the jury) will do where the document belongs exclusively to the party, or ought in the regular course of business to be in his possession or power. *Robb* v. *Starkey*, 2 Car. & Kir. 143, Cresswell, J. Thus, a notice by a tenant to his landlord of his intention to cut down trees pursuant to a power in the lease will be presumed to have been delivered by the lessor, together with the other title deeds, to a purchaser of the reversion. *Goodtitle* d. *Luxmore* v. *Saville*, 16 East, 87 (2nd point); *Id.* 91, note (*a*). So where the solicitor to a commission of bankruptcy proved that he had been employed by the defendant to solicit his certificate, and that, looking at his entry of charges, he had no doubt that the certificate was allowed; this was held to be sufficient proof of the certificate having come to the defendant's hands. *Henry* v. *Leigh*, 3 Camp. 502. *Primâ facie* it must be presumed that the books of a corporation, which existed before the Municipal Reform Act, are in the possession or power of the new corporation which succeeded them under the act: but if it be shown that the old corporation, before their dissolution, deposited them with a banker, and that from his hands they passed into the master's office of the Court of Chancery, this rebuts the presumption. *The Mayor, Aldermen and Burgesses of Ludlow* v. *Charlton*, 9 C. & P. 242, Gurney, B. The written appointment of overseers will be presumed to be in the custody of some or one of them, rather than of their successors in office. *Rex* v. *Inhabitants of Stoke Golding*, 1 B. & A. 173. In an action against the directors of an intended company, it was proved (in order to let in secondary evidence of their minute book called for under a notice to produce) that *four months* before the trial the late secretary had the books in a desk at the office of the company, and that he then gave up the key of the desk to the manager of the company, who acted for the directors : held sufficient. *Bell* v. *Francis*, 9 C. & P. 66, Lord Denman, C. J.

Although the plaintiff has inspected and admitted in the usual manner the copy of a letter from himself to one of the defendants, and has also had notice to produce the original, the copy cannot be read unless some evidence be given to show that the original is in the possession or power of the plaintiff ; *Sharpe* v. *Lamb*, 11 A. & E. 805 ; 3 P. & D. 454 ; for if not the co-defendant should be served with a *subpœna duces tecum* to produce the letter. *Colley* v. *Smith*, 4 Bing. N. C. 285 ; 6 Dowl. 399.

It must frequently happen that a notice to admit documents given pursuant to 15 & 16 Vict. c. 76, s. 117, and the Practice Rule of H. T. 1853, No. 29, will afford sufficient evidence of a document therein mentioned being in the possession of the party giving such notice, or of his attorney or agent. But the opposite party wishing to use the notice for such purpose, should be prepared with proof that it was served upon him or his attorney, by the other party or his attorney or agent in the progress of the cause. *Thomas* v. *Williams*, 1 Dowl. & L. 624.

Proof of an answer received to a letter is sufficient to show that such letter is in the possession of the party who wrote the answer. *Overston* v. *Wilson*, 2 Car. & K. 1 ; *Id.*, 3, Pollock, C. B.

The attorney for a party is not privileged from answering whether a document is in the possession of his client, or of himself as attorney in the cause, the object of such question being merely to let in secondary evidence of the contents of the instrument. *Bevan* v. *Waters*, Moo. & Mal. 235 ; *Coates* v. *Mudge*, 2 Q. B. 252 ; 1 Dowl. N. S. 540.

Whenever sufficient *primâ facie* evidence is given to satisfy the judge that the document is in the possession of the party required to produce it, such party may thereupon interpose with contradictory evidence of himself or any other witness on that point, showing that the document really is not in his possession or power. This is a *collateral issue*, to be decided by the judge *before* secondary evidence of the contents of the instrument is admitted. *Harvey* v. *Mitchell*, 2 Moo. & Rob. 366 ; and see *Cleave* v. *Jones*, 7 Exch. 421, 425 ; *Bartlett* v. *Smith*, 11 M. & W. 483 ; *Doe* d. *Fryer* v. *Coombs*, 3 Q. B. 687 ; *Doe* d. *Jenkins* v. *Davies*, 10 Q. B. 323, Lord Denman, C. J. ; *Painter* v. *Hill*, 2 Car. & K. 924, note, Erle, J. ; *Boyle* v. *Wiseman*, 11 Exch. 360.

Secondary Evidence.]—The principal object of a notice to produce is to give the opposite party an opportunity to produce the original document at the trial, and, in case of its nonproduction, *to let in secondary evidence of the contents. Ante*, 156.

There are no degrees of secondary evidence. Therefore, where a party is entitled to give secondary evidence (in lieu of primary evidence), he may give any species of it within his power, although not the most satisfactory that might be produced. Thus, where a defendant has given notice to the plaintiff to produce a letter, of which the defendant kept a copy, he may, if the letter be not produced, give parol evidence of its contents, and he is not bound to put in the copy.

I

Brown v. *Woodman*, 6 C. & P. 206, Parke, J.; *Kensington* v. *Inglis*, 8 East, 273. So, where a duplicate notice of distress is proved to have been lost, parol evidence of the contents may be given, without producing or accounting for the copy delivered to the party distrained on. *Doe* d. *Morse* v. *Williams*, 1 Car. & M. 615, Patteson, J. So, where either party has an attested copy of a deed, which copy is not admissible in evidence for want of a stamp, he may nevertheless give parol evidence of the contents of the deed. *Doe* d. *Gilbert* v. *Ross*, 7 M. & W. 102; 8 Dowl. 389; and see *Doe* d. *Rowlandson* v. *Wainwright*, 3 A. & E. 520. In an action by lessor against lessee, the plaintiff may give parol evidence of the contents of the lease where the defendant declines to produce it upon due notice, and that without accounting for the nonproduction of the counterpart. *Hall* v. *Ball*, 3 Scott, N. R. 577; 3 Man. & Gr. 242. The counterpart itself would be primary evidence. *Burleigh* v. *Stibbs*, 5 T. R. 465; *Roe* d. *West* v. *Davis*, 7 East, 363; *Paul* v. *Meek*, 2 You. & Jer. 116. But the copy of a copy is not secondary evidence of the original; the first copy must be produced: *Leibman* v. *Pooley*, 1 Stark. R. 167, Lord Ellenborough, C. J.; *Everingham* v. *Roundell*, 2 Moo. & Rob. 138, Alderson, B.: or parol evidence given of the contents by some one who has seen the original. An abstract of a deed, which has been examined with the deed by the witness called, is admissible as secondary evidence of the contents of the deed. *Doe* d. *Rowlandson* v. *Wainwright*, 5 A. & E. 520. A copy of a letter made by the plaintiff, or by the defendant, in his own hand in his letter book, is not, without further proof, admissible as secondary evidence of the contents of the letter sent. *Fisher* v. *Samuda*, 1 Camp. 193, Lord Ellenborough, C. J.

The *admissions* of a party to a suit, whether they relate to the contents of a deed or other writing, are *primary evidence as against him* of the contents of the document so far as such admissions extend. *Slatterie* v. *Pooley*, 6 M. & W. 664; *Newhall* v. *Holt*, 6 M. & W. 662. Thus, in replevin the admissions of the plaintiff are evidence to show the terms upon which he held the premises, though he held under an agreement in writing that is not produced. *Howard* v. *Smith*, 3 Scott, N. R. 574; 3 Man. & Gr. 254; see also *Lord Trimleston* v. *Kemmis*, 9 Cl. & Fin. 784. So a recital or other admission contained in a deed is primary evidence of the fact so recited or admitted as against a party to the deed: *Carpenter* v. *Buller*, 8 M. & W. 209: or against any other person claiming through or under him. *Doe* d. *Gaisford* v. *Stone*, 3 C. B. 176. But such evidence may sometimes be rebutted by evidence showing the real facts. *Carpenter* v. *Buller*, *supra*. The counterpart of a lease or other deed or writing executed by the defendant, or by any person through whom he derives title, is admissible against him as an admission of the contents of the original, without any notice to produce. *Burleigh* v. *Stibbs*, 5 T. R. 465; *Roe* d. *West* v. *Davis*, 7 East, 363. A lessee who executes a counterpart of a lease cannot dispute the admissibility in evidence of such counterpart, nor its validity, by producing the original lease, and showing that it was not duly stamped. *Paul* v. *Meek*, 2 You. & Jer. 116. Where there are two parts of a written agreement both executed at the same time, but the one stamped and the other unstamped, the unstamped part is receivable (after due notice to produce) as secondary evidence of the contents of the stamped part. *Waller* v. *Horsfall*, 1

Camp. 501, Lord Ellenborough, C. J.; *Gurnons* v. *Swift*, 1 Taunt. 506. And under such circumstances an unstamped counterpart may be considered as a mere copy. *Munn* v. *Godbolt*, 3 Bing. 292. An *attested* copy cannot be received unless duly stamped as such. *Doe* d. *Gilbert* v. *Ross*, 7 M. & W. 102; 8 Dowl. 389. But an unstamped attested copy may be used to refresh the memory of the attesting witness as to the contents of the deed, and when proved by him to be a true copy, it may be read as secondary evidence of the contents of the deed (due notice having been given to produce the original), although not as an attested copy. *Braythwayte* v. *Hitchcock*, 10 M. & W. 494; 2 Dowl. N. S. 444. The duty on attested copies applies only to copies which are evidence *per se.* Tilsley's Stamp Laws, 313 (2nd ed.) By cutting off the memorandum of attestation the copy ceases to be an attested copy, and may be used as a plain copy to refresh the memory of the witness who has seen the original, and has to prove the contents; but such evidence is admissible only after due notice to produce the original document.

Generally speaking, when a document is not produced pursuant to notice, it will be presumed to have been *duly stamped; Crisp* v. *Anderson*, 1 Stark. R. 35, Lord Ellenborough, C. J.; *Pooley* v. *Goodwin*, 4 A. & E. 94; *Hart* v. *Hart*, 1 Hare, 1, Wigram, V. C.; for otherwise the document might be produced and the objection taken. *Ante*, 164. But after having once refused to produce the original, the party would not afterwards be permitted to produce it in support of the objection, or for any other purpose. *Ante*, 166. If, however, the witness who gives evidence of the contents of the instrument, state on examination or cross-examination that it was unstamped, the presumption that it is duly stamped is rebutted, and parol evidence of the contents will be rejected. *Crowther* v. *Solomon*, 6 C. B. 758; *Crisp* v. *Anderson*, 1 Stark. R. 35. Whether the duty and penalty, with 1*l.* extra, can be paid at the trial pursuant to 17 & 18 Vict. c. 125, ss. 28, 29, although the document be *not there produced,* remains to be decided; probably it may. But before the above act, if it appeared that the unstamped document had been *lost,* or even *fraudulently destroyed,* by the party who objected to the want of a stamp, parol evidence of the contents would have been inadmissible. *Rappinier* v. *Wright*, 2 B. & A. 478; *Rex* v. *Castle Morton*, 3 B. & A. 588; *Rankin* v. *Hamilton*, 15 Q. B. 187; Chit. Stamp Laws, sect. IX. The court or a judge might before the trial have ordered the original to be produced before the Commissioners of Inland Revenue to be stamped, even where the party applying was not entitled to an *inspection* of the document. *Hall* v. *Bainbrigge*, 3 Dowl. & L. 92; *Neale* v. *Swynd*, 2 Cr. & Jer. 278; 1 Dowl. 314; 2 Chit. Arch. 1025 (7th ed.). But the judge could not order that if the party did not produce the document to be stamped (as ordered) a duly stamped copy should be read in evidence at the trial, and that the original should not then be produced on the other side, nor objection taken to the want of a stamp on the original. *Rankin* v. *Hamilton*, 15 Q. B. 187, overruling *Bousfield* v. *Godfrey*, 5 Bing. 418. The proper course was to apply to the court or a judge to disallow or strike out the defendant's plea, which rendered proof of the original document necessary, unless the defendant produced the original document to be stamped. *Per cur.* in *Rankin* v. *Hamilton*, 15 Q. B. 196, 199.

CHAPTER XIX.

SUBPŒNAS.

I. SUBPŒNA AD TESTIFICANDUM.

Nature and Effect of, and when necessary.]—This writ is a judicial process to compel witnesses to attend and give evidence on a trial or other legal inquiry. It commands the witnesses by name to appear before the judge, at the time and place where the trial is to be had, and then and there to testify, &c. under the penalty (*sub pœná*) of £100. *See the forms, Appendix, Nos.* 192, 193. The penalty is merely nominal ; disobedience of the writ is considered a contempt of court, and punished as such by attachment ; the witness also thereby subjects himself to an action of debt on the stat. 5 Eliz. c. 9, s. 12, or to an action on the case by the party grieved, who may thereby recover all the damages he has sustained by reason of the non-attendance of the witness pursuant to his subpœna. *Couling* v. *Coxe,* 6 C. B. 703 ; 6 Dowl. & L. 399. But of this more fully hereafter.

Generally speaking, a writ of subpœna has no operation out of the jurisdiction of the court from which it issues. But writs of subpœna issued pursuant to 17 & 18 Vict. c. 34, may be served in any part of the United Kingdom. *Post,* 197.

Formerly no party to a cause could be compelled by a subpœna to give or produce evidence against himself. *Reg.* v. *Hankins,* 2 Car. & K. 823, 826. But it is otherwise since the stat. 14 & 15 Vict. c. 99. *Boyle* v. *Wiseman,* 10 Exch. 647.

No person can be compelled to give evidence on the trial of an action at nisi prius unless regularly subpœnaed, even though he happen to be in court at the time of the trial. *Bowles* v. *Johnson,* 1 W. Blac. 36 ; 3 Bac. Abr. Evid. (D.); 1 Chit. Arch. 327 (8th ed.); Lush, Prac. 459. A mere stander-by may refuse to be examined, and a person who has not been properly subpœnaed is looked upon only as a stander-by. *Per* Wright, J., in *Bowles* v. *Johnson, supra.* But it is otherwise in the county courts. 9 & 10 Vict. c. 95, s. 86. It would seem sufficient to serve in court (at nisi prius) a copy of the subpœna upon any person named therein who happens to be present accidentally. *Per* Williams, J., in *Pitcher* v. *King,* 2 Dowl. & L. 758. Or as one of the parties to the cause, or as attorney for either party. *Doe* v. *Andrews,* Cowp. 845. In no case should the form of subpœnaing the witnesses be omitted, even where they are disposed to attend voluntarily. *Austin* v. *Evans,* 2 Man. & Gr. 430 ; 9 Dowl. 408 ; *Robinson* v. *Brown,* 3 C. B. 754.

Form.]—The form of a subpœna to testify has been long settled.
See Appendix, Nos. 192, 193. A printed form on parchment, and
also printed copies on paper, may be obtained from any law stationer.

It seems that the writ may issue with a blank for the names of the
witnesses, which may afterwards be filled up at any time before the
copies are served. *Wakefield* v. *Gall,* Holt, N. P. C. 526; 2 Tidd,
855 (8th ed.). This is constantly done in practice, but the strict propriety of it is questionable. See 1 Chit. Arch. 327 (8th ed.); and *per*
Lord Abinger, C. B., in *Barber* v. *Wood,* 2 Moo. & Rob. 172. Not
more than four names can properly be introduced into one subpœna.
2 Tidd, 855 (8th ed.); Chit. Gen. Prac. 703 (3rd ed.); *Doe* v. *Andrews,* Cowp. 846.

The writ should mention the title of the cause at full length; *i. e.,*
the names of all the plaintiffs and of all the defendants. It should not
abbreviate them thus, "John Nokes and another," or "Joseph Styles
and others." *Doe d. Clarke* v. *Thomson,* 9 Dowl. 948.

The writ must specify the *place* at which the cause is to be tried,
ex. gr., "at Westminster Hall, in the county of Middlesex," or "at ·
the Guildhall of the city of London," or "at [*name of assize town*]
—— in the county of ——." *Milsom* v. *Day,* 3 Moo. & P. 333.
Where a subpœna required the witness to attend at Westminster Hall,
but the cause was actually tried in a detached building, called The
Westminster Sessions House, to which place witnesses were referred
by notices affixed to the walls of the court in Westminster Hall: held
sufficient for an attachment. *Chapman* v. *Davis,* 1 Dowl. N. S. 239;
3 Man. & Gr. 609; 3 Scott, N. R. 319, *S. C.* So in the city of London the courts of Queen's Bench and Common Pleas are held in a
building adjoining the Guildhall, and not in the Guildhall itself, as
was formerly the case; and yet a subpœna in the usual form commanding the witness to appear before the proper judge "in the Guildhall of the city of London," would clearly be sufficient, and, indeed,
is the ordinary form.

The writ should require the witnesses to appear on the commission-
day of the assizes, or on the first day of the particular sitting in
London or Middlesex. Even when issued after such day, the writ
should be in the same form in this respect. The witnesses may be
apprised at the time of service that the cause has not been tried, and
the time when they are actually required to attend. *Davis* v. *Lovell,*
4 M. & W. 678; 7 Dowl. 178. The writ should not only mention a
particular day (as above), but it should go on to say, "and so from day
to day until this cause be tried," or to that effect. Sometimes the
omission of these words will prevent an attachment; thus, where the
trial in a town cause was postponed for several days. *Vaughton* v.
Brine, 9 Dowl. 179. But probably, in this case, the trial stood over
to a subsequent sitting. Each particular sitting in London or Middlesex, although adjourned for several successive days, and the assizes for
each county elsewhere, although actually lasting several days, is considered in law as one day only. And, therefore, as a general rule the
witnesses must attend from day to day until the cause be tried, notwithstanding those words are omitted in the subpœna. *Scholes* v.
Hilton, 10 M. & W. 15; 2 Dowl. N. S. 229; *Swanne* v. *Taaffe,* 8
Ir. Law R. 101.

The writ must be *tested* in the name of the chief judge, or chief
baron, of the court out of which it issues; or if he be dead, then in the

name of the senior puisne judge of that court. 1 Chit. Arch. 328 (8th ed.). It must be tested in term time and not in vacation, otherwise it will be void. *Edgell* v. *Curling*, 7 Man. & Gr. 958; 8 Scott, N. R. 663; 2 Dowl. & L. 600. When issued in term time it is usually tested on the first day of the term; when issued in vacation it is usually tested in the last day of the previous term; 1 Chit. Arch. 328 (8th ed.); but any other day in term time will do equally well. There seems to be no legal objection to the subpœna being tested or sued out before the cause is at issue. *Reg.* v. *Vickery*, 12 Q. B. 478; 17 Law J., N. S., M. C., 129. It might *then* be too late to meet with the witnesses, especially when short notice of trial is given.

The writ should be indorsed with the attorney's name, address and date of issuing. When properly filled up it must be taken (with a precipe for the writ) to the Master's Office, and there sealed.

Service.]—A true copy of the writ of subpœna should be served on each witness personally, and at the time of such service the writ itself should be produced to the witness, and a proper sum for his expenses paid or tendered to him. All this should be done a reasonable time before the trial. We propose now to consider fully each of the above requisites.

1. The copy served must be a *true copy;* any material variance will render the service inoperative. *Doe* d. *Clarke* v. *Thomson*, 9 Dowl. 948. But if the writ be directed to A. B., C. D., E. F. and G. H., a copy served on A. B., directed to him alone (however ungrammatical it may read), or to him "and John Doe," or to him "and others" (although no such words are in the writ) will be sufficient; for so far as A. B. is concerned the variance is immaterial. A copy of so much of the writ as relates to the particular witness is all that need be served upon him, the object being merely to give him due *notice of the writ*. *Masterman* v. *Judson*, 8 Bing. 224; *Mullett* v. *Hunt*, 1 Cr. & Mee. 752. And this course is generally advisable, for it is often dangerous to let an adverse witness know the names of the other witnesses named in the subpœna; for he might perhaps give them notice to keep out of the way; or he might communicate their names to the opposite party. And although each witness, when served, may require to inspect the writ; *Mullett* v. *Hunt, supra;* yet this is very seldom done.

2. The service on each witness must be *personal,* otherwise the court will not grant an attachment. *Smalt* v. *Whitmill*, 2 Stra. 1054; *Thorpe* v. *Gisbourne*, 11 Moore, 55. Difficulty in serving a subpœna will not induce the court to dispense with personal service. *Barnes* v. *Williams*, 1 Dowl. 615. Whether an action could be maintained for non-attendance of a witness who has not been served personally, but who actually received the copy with his reasonable expenses in due time, has not yet been decided. There is no instance of an action against a witness under these circumstances. *Per cur.* in *Barnes* v. *Williams*, 1 Dowl. 615. But upon principle it would rather seem that such action would be maintainable. See *per* Bayley, J., in *Mullett* v. *Hunt*, 1 Cr. & Mee. 756. "The plaintiff may have a perfect cause of action against the witness for not attending, and yet the circumstances may not justify an attachment for contempt." *Per* Jervis, C. J., in *Marshall* v. *The York, Newcastle and Berwick Railway Company*, 11 C. B. 403.

Generally speaking, the service must be made within the jurisdiction of the court out of which the writ issues. But if the writ issue pur-

suant to 17 & 18 Vict. c. 34, the service may be made in Scotland or
Ireland. See *post*, 197.

3. At the time of serving the copy, *the writ itself should be produced*
to the witness, whether he require to see it or not; otherwise the court
will not grant an attachment. 1 Chit. Arch. 328 (8th ed.); *Wadsworth* v. *Marshall*, 1 Cr. & Mee. 87; *Rex* v. *Wood*, 1 Dowl. 509;
Rex v. *Sloman, Id.* 618; *Jacob* v. *Hungate*, 3 Dowl. 456; *Garden*
v. *Creswell*, 2 M. & W. 319; 5 Dowl. 461; *Smith* v. *Truscott*, 6
Man. & Gr. 267; 6 Scott, N. R. 808; 1 Dowl. & L. 530; *Pitcher* v.
King, 2 Dowl. & L. 755; *Marshall* v. *The York, Newcastle and Berwick Railway Company*, 11 C. B. 398; and see *Lloyd* v. *Harris*, 8
C. B. 63, 71, 75. But an *action* may be supported against the witness
for his non-attendance, although the writ was not produced to him at
the time the copy was served, unless indeed he then required to see
the writ. *Mullett* v. *Hunt*, 1 Cr. & Mee. 752; *Id.* 756, *per* Bayley,
B.; and see *Marshall* v. *The York, Newcastle and Berwick Railway
Company*, 11 C. B. 403, 404.

4. A proper sum for the reasonable expenses (if any) of the witness
in *going to, staying at, and returning from* the place of trial, must be
paid or tendered to the witness at the time the copy subpœna is served.
Fuller v. *Prentice*, 1 H. Blac. 49. Or, at all events, a reasonable
time before the trial; *Whiteland* v. *Grant*, 4 Jur. 1061; 2 Harr. Dig.
2764 (3rd ed.); 1 Chit. Arch. 329 (8th ed.); otherwise no attachment
will be granted against the witness; *Ashton* v. *Haigh*, 2 Chit. R. 201;
although he goes to the assizes, and there refuses to be sworn; *Bowles*
v. *Johnson*, 1 W. Blac. 36; or goes there, but neglects to appear in
court. *Newton* v. *Harland*, 1 Man. & Gr. 956; 1 Scott, N. R. 502;
9 Dowl. 16. Nor can any action be maintained against him for not
going. *Per* Tindal, C. J., in *Betteley* v. *M'Leod*, 3 Bing. N. C. 407.
If a witness refuse to attend except upon payment of an unreasonable
sum for his expenses, a proper sum should nevertheless be tendered.
Newton v. *Harland, supra.* A witness may, however, waive his
right to have a proper sum paid or tendered to him for his expenses,
or may consent to take part, with a promise as to the residue. *Goodwin* v. *West*, Cro. Car. 522, 540; and see *per* Tindal, C. J., in *Newton* v. *Harland, supra.* Where an insufficient sum is tendered to a
witness, and he makes no objection to the amount, but declines to take
it, saying he will pay his own expenses, an attachment will be granted
for his non-attendance. *Goff* v. *Mills*, 2 Dowl. & L. 23. The court
have refused an attachment where the witness resided twenty-four
miles from the assize town, and his expenses were tendered only the
previous evening. *Holme* v. *Smith*, 1 Marsh. 410; *S. C. nom. Horne*
v. *Smith*, 6 Taunt. 9; but see *Goff* v. *Mills, supra.* The expenses
must be paid or tendered either when the copy subpœna is served
(which is most usual), or afterwards a reasonable time before the trial;
not later than the last moment when the copy subpœna might properly
be served. If the witness be a married woman, the conduct money
must be paid or tendered to her, and not to her husband. 1 Chit.
Arch. 329 (8th ed.); Phil. Ev. 782 (8th ed.).

What is a sufficient and proper sum to pay or tender to any particular witness must of course depend upon a due consideration of all the
circumstances. The amount will be more or less, according to his station in life, the distance he will have to travel, and the length of time
he is likely to be engaged from home. As a general rule, the calcu-

lation should be made thus: viz., a reasonable sum for travelling expenses by railway, &c. to the assize town or other place where he is required to attend, and back again, *not exceeding one shilling per mile one way*, or sixpence per mile for the whole distance the witness will have to travel: to this add his *other expenses, at so much per day*, for the number of days he is likely to be detained in going to, staying at, and returning from the place of trial, at the rate mentioned in the following scale:—

Allowance to Witnesses.

	If resident in the town in which the cause is tried.			If resident at a distance from the place of trial.		
	£	s.	d.	£	s.	d.
Common witnesses, such as labourers, journeymen, &c. per diem	0	5	0	0 to 0	5 7	0 6
Master tradesmen, yeomen and farmers, per diem, from	0 to 0	7 10	6 0	0 to 0	10 15	0 0
Auctioneers and accountants, per diem	0 to 1	10 1	6 0	0 to 1	10 1	6 0
Professional men, per diem	1	1	0	1	1	0
Ditto, inclusive of all except travelling expenses, per diem	.	.		2 to 3	2 3	0 0
Attorney's or other clerks, per diem	0	10	6	0 to 1	15 1	0 0
Engineers and surveyors, per diem	1	1	0	1 to 3	1 3	0 0
Notaries, per diem	1	1	0	1	1	0
Gentlemen . . . . . Esquires . . . . . Bankers . . . . . Merchants	1 1 0 with subpœna; but no daily allowance except after the first day, and then a reasonable sum for refreshment and conveyance.			1 1 0 per diem.		
Females, according to station in life, per diem, from	0 to 0	5 10	0 0	0 to 1	5 0	0 0
Police inspector, per diem	0	5	0	0 to 0	7 10	6 0
Police constable	0	3	0	0 to 0	5 7	0 6

" If the witnesses attend in one cause only, they will be entitled to the full allowance. If they attend in more than one cause, they will be entitled to a proportionate part in each cause only.

" The travelling expenses of witnesses shall be allowed according to the sums reasonably and actually paid, but in no case shall exceed

1*s.* per mile one way."—*Directions to Taxing Officers, H. T.* 1853; 13 C. B. 110; 1 E. & B. lxxv.

The above is what is usually allowed upon taxation. It is, however, somewhat dangerous to be too nice in calculating the expenses of a witness; for if the sufficiency of the sum tendered appear doubtful, the court will sometimes refuse an attachment, and leave the party to his remedy by action. 13 East, 16, note (*a*); *Dixon* v. *Lee,* 3 Dowl. 259; 1 Cr. M. & R. 645. Besides which, witnesses are very apt to feel offended, if not treated liberally, rather than otherwise.

No person is entitled to any compensation for his *loss of time* in attending as a witness, but only to his *expenses.* Even an express promise to pay a witness for his loss of time, will not support an action. *Willis* v. *Peckham,* 1 Brod. & B. 515; 4 Moore, 300. It makes no difference that the witnesses come from abroad on purpose to attend the trial. *Moor* v. *Adams,* 5 M. & S. 156. But as medical men and attornies are more frequently called upon to give evidence than the rest of the community, compensation for their loss of time is allowed. *Per* Park, J., in *Willis* v. *Peckham,* 1 Brod. & B. 516; 4 Moore, 302. This, however, is done *indirectly,* viz., by a more liberal allowance for their expenses. Even an attorney cannot maintain an action for his loss of time in attending as a witness. *Collins* v. *Godefroy,* 1 B. & Adol. 950; 1 Dowl. 326. A broker is not entitled to compensation for loss of time. *Lopes* v. *De Tastet,* 3 Brod. & B. 292; 7 Moore, 120. But a witness, who is called to depose to a matter of *opinion,* depending on his skill in a particular trade, has a right, before he is examined, to demand from the party calling him a compensation for his loss of time; and there is a distinction between a witness thus called and a witness who is called to depose to *facts* which he saw. *Webb* v. *Page,* 1 Car. & K. 23, Maule, J. The senior clerk of the Petty Bag Office, who attends (or sends his clerk) with original rolls in Chancery, pursuant to a subpœna *and an order from the Master of the Rolls* (which is necessary), is entitled to recover the usual fees allowed by the general orders of the court for such attendance. *Bentall* v. *Sydney,* 10 A. & E. 162; 2 P. & D. 416.

In *criminal* cases, a reasonable allowance may be made to a witness for his "trouble and loss of time" (in addition to his necessary expenses), where he attends pursuant to a recognizance or subpœna, and appears to the court to be in poor circumstances. 18 Geo. 3, c. 19, s. 8; and see 27 Geo. 2, c. 3, s. 3; 58 Geo. 3, c. 70, s. 48; Phil. Ev. 788 (8th ed.). But, generally speaking, a witness must obey a subpœna in a criminal case at his own expense. It is a duty of a public nature, although it is otherwise in civil cases. *Pell* v. *Daubney,* 5 Exch. 958.

In *town causes,* where the witnesses reside within the bills of mortality, it is usual to pay or tender *one shilling* to each of them with his copy subpœna. 3 Bl. Com. 369; 2 Chit. R. 201, note (*a*); 1 Chit. Arch. 328 (8th ed.); *Smalt* v. *Whitmill,* 2 Stra. 1054. And this seems to be sufficient, even where the witness is an attorney. *Jackson* v. *Seager,* 2 Dowl. & L. 13. Strictly speaking, in such cases no conduct money is necessary; *Jacob* v. *Hungate,* 3 Dowl. 456; for the witness is not supposed to incur any expenses in attending the trial. 3 Chit. Gen. Prac. 705 (3rd ed.); but see *Betteley* v. *M'Leod,* 3 Bing. N. C. 405; 4 Scott, 131; 5 Dowl. 481. One guinea is generally given to esquires, bankers, merchants, professional men and persons of higher rank (*ante,* 177), and a similar compliment to other respectable witnesses is not unusual, and sometimes very advisable.

Where a witness is subpœnaed on both sides, he is not entitled to be paid his expenses twice over. Therefore, where a witness residing at Camberwell, upon being served with a subpœna to attend a trial at the Guildhall, London, stated that he had previously been subpœnaed by the opposite side, and had received one guinea, and the party serving the subpœna gave him one shilling, to which he made no objection: held, in an action for disobeying the subpœna, upon an issue whether a reasonable sum for conduct money had been paid, that the plaintiff was entitled to the verdict. *Betteley* v. *M'Leod,* 3 Bing. N. C. 405; 4 Scott, 131; 5 Dowl. 481. Where a witness conceals the fact of his having been previously subpœnaed and paid by the opposite party, the usual conduct money should be paid him, and will be allowed on taxation. *Benson* v. *Schneider,* 1 Moore, 76; 7 Taunt. 337. Whether the unsuccessful party can recover back from the witness either of the sums so paid, and if so, in what form of action, seems doubtful; certainly not in an action for money had and received. *Crompton* v. *Hutton,* 3 Taunt. 230. Perhaps redress might be obtained in the county court. A witness who is subpœnaed by both parties in a cause, but whose expenses are not paid by either of them, is entitled to have all his expenses paid by the party who calls him at the trial, although the other party may be the first who subpœnaed him. *Allen* v. *Yoxall,* 1 Car. & K. 315, Rolfe, B. But a witness from the country, subpœnaed there by the defendant, without receiving sufficient for his expenses, and *afterwards, when in London, subpœnaed by the plaintiff,* and called by him on the trial, is bound to give his evidence both in chief and on cross-examination, and must seek to obtain his expenses in some other way than by objecting to be examined. *Edmonds* v. *Pearson,* 3 C. & P. 113, Gaselee, J.

A witness may maintain an action to recover the amount of his reasonable *expenses* in attending a trial, although he was not examined in consequence of his refusal to give any evidence until his expenses were paid. *Hallet* v. *Mears,* 13 East, 15. Such action should be brought against the party on whose behalf the witness was subpœnaed; *Pell* v. *Daubney,* 5 Exch. 995; not against the attorney who issued and served the writ. *Robins* v. *Bridge,* 3 M. & W. 114; 6 Dowl. 140; unless, indeed, the attorney has rendered himself personally liable by an I O U, or some other express agreement with the witness. *Evans* v. *Phillpotts, Gent., one, &c.,* 9 C. & P. 270, Gurney, B. No action will lie to recover compensation for *loss of time* in attending as a witness; *Willis* v. *Peckham,* 1 Brod. & B. 515; 4 Moore, 300; *Pell* v. *Daubney, supra;* even where the witness is an attorney. *Collins* v. *Godefroy,* 1 B. & Adol. 950; 1 Dowl. 326.

5. The subpœna must be served and the conduct money paid or tendered *a reasonable time before the trial.* Lush, Prac. 461; 1 Chit. Arch. 330 (8th ed.). The service should not be made on a Sunday. 2 C. B. 76, Maule, J. The service will be good although made after the day of trial mentioned in the subpœna, if there be then sufficient time for the witness to attend, and he is informed that the cause has not been tried, and of the time when his attendance will be required. *Davis* v. *Lovell,* 4 M. & W. 678; 7 Dowl. 178. But no attachment will be granted if the writ be served after the day therein mentioned, and the witness be not informed that the cause has not been tried. *Alexander*

v. *Dixon*, 8 Moore, 387 ; 1 Bing. 366, cited and explained in *Davis* v. *Lovell, supra.*

The question what is a reasonable time before the trial for service of a subpœna, must depend upon the circumstances of each particular case. *Maunsell* v. *Ainsworth*, 8 Dowl. 869. And it seems to be a question for the judge to decide, rather than the jury. *Barber* v. *Wood*, 2 Moo. & Rob. 172, Lord Abinger, C. B. ; *ante*, 159. Gene-rally speaking, a very short time is considered sufficient, especially if it appear that the witness could have attended, if he had chosen so to do. Therefore, where a witness was served on the steps of the court house at twelve o'clock, and was told that the trial would come on that day, to which he answered "Very well," and the trial took place at five o'clock, but the witness did not appear : held, that the service was sufficient. *Maunsell* v. *Ainsworth*, 8 Dowl. 869. So where the defendant's attorney was served at Chelsea, just before ten o'clock at night, with a *subpœna duces tecum*, commanding him to appear at Westminster the next morning at nine o'clock, and then and there to produce certain documents which were at his office in Symond's Inn : held, that the service was sufficient, it appearing that he omitted to obey the writ principally because he thought he should have time first to attend a meeting of the board of guardians at Chelsea, as their vestry clerk, and that he made his appearance at Westminster as soon as possible after such meeting was over. *Jackson* v. *Seager*, 2 Dowl. & L. 13. So where a subpœna to attend at Norwich on the 15th February was served on the 13th, and the conduct money tendered on the 14th. The witness resided eighteen miles from Norwich, and the place where the conduct money was tendered was twenty-six miles from Norwich. The witness was servant of a maltster, and at the time in question was employed in watching green malt, with strict orders from his master not to leave it by night or day, as considerable damage might ensue : held, that the service was in sufficient time, although it was too late to afford the witness a reasonable time for communicating with his master ; *Goff* v. *Mills*, 2 Dowl. & L. 23 ; and, *per* Wightman, J., "The duty of attending a court of justice, in pursuance of a subpœna, is one paramount to that of obeying a master, however urgent his commands may be ; and as it is clear that this wit-ness had sufficient time to have enabled him to attend if he had pleased, the rule for an attachment against him must be made absolute." *Id.* 28. It seems that a person sitting in court merely as a spectator may be served with a subpœna to give evidence in an action then pending. *Per* Williams, J., in *Pitcher* v. *King*, 2 Dowl. & L. 758. So either party, or his attorney, may be served in court during the trial. *Doe* v. *Andrews*, Cowp. 845.

On the other hand, it has been decided that service on a person living close to the place of trial at half-past eleven o'clock in the morning, for a cause called on at two o'clock, is not in sufficient time. *Barber* v. *Wood*, 2 Moo. & Rob. 172, Lord Abinger, C. B. ; and see *Hammond* v. *Stewart*, 1 Stra. 510. So where a witness, who was managing clerk to an attorney, was served with a subpœna in court about an hour before the trial came on, and whilst he was attending to the winding up of a cause in which he was engaged, and which stood next but one on the list before the cause in question, it was doubted by Williams, J., whether such service was sufficient. *Pitcher* v. *King*, 2 Dowl. & L. 755. And the court have refused an attach-ment where the witness resided twenty-four miles from the assize town, and his expenses were tendered only the previous evening. *Holme* v. *Smith,* 1 Marsh. 410; *S. C. nom. Horne* v. *Smith,* 6 Taunt. 9. Generally speaking, witnesses ought to have a reasonable time to put their own affairs in such order, that their attendance may be as little prejudicial to themselves as possible. *Hammond* v. *Stewart,* 1 Stra. 510.

The writ may be served on any day except Sunday, and at any hour of the day or night. 1 Chit. Arch. 331 (8th ed.).

6. *By whom served.*]—The subpœnas are usually served by the attorney or his clerk, or some other person employed by him. But service by a party in the cause is sufficient.

Re-service—when necessary.]—If a cause be made a *remanet* from one assize to another, or from one sitting to another in London or Middlesex, the subpœnas must be altered and resealed, and copies served as before. 1 Chit. Arch. 331 (8th ed.); 2 Tidd. 855; (8th ed.). A mere written notice to a witness previously subpœnaed to attend at such subsequent sitting, will not be sufficient. *Sydenham* v. *Rand,* 3 Doug. 429; 2 Tidd, 855; Phil. Ev. 782 (8th ed.). And if the subpœna be altered without being resealed, it will be inoperative. *Barber* v. *Wood,* 2 Moo. & Rob. 172, Lord Abinger, C. B.

If a cause be merely *adjourned* to a subsequent day of the same sitting, it is not necessary to alter, reseal, and again serve the subpœnas; but in such case it will be prudent to give the witnesses express notice of the time when their further attendance will be required; otherwise the court may perhaps be induced to refuse an attachment. *Blandford* v. *De Tastet,* 5 Taunt. 260; 1 Marsh. 42; *Vaughton* v. *Brine,* 9 Dowl. 179.

Evading Service.]—A defendant who keeps a material witness for the plaintiff out of the way, and thereby impedes the service of a subpœna, and so obstructs the course of justice, is liable to an attachment. *Clements* v. *Williams,* 2 Scott, 814. But where the defendant does not prevent the subpœna from being served, but merely endeavours to persuade the witness not to give evidence, or not to produce a document at the trial pursuant to the subpœna, no attachment will be granted. *Schlesinger* v. *Flersheim,* 2 Dowl. & L. 737. It would be otherwise in criminal cases. *Rex* v. *Stevenson,* 2 East, 362; *Rex* v. *Lawley,* 2 Stra. 904; Hawk. P. C. Book I. ch. 1, sect. 15. Where an attorney improperly evades service of a subpœna, the court will discharge *without costs* a rule for an attachment against him, if the service be insufficient. *Smith* v. *Truscott,* 6 Man. & Gr. 267; 6 Scott, N. R. 808; 1 Dowl. & L. 530. It seems that the court will not by rule dispense with personal service of a subpœna where the witness keeps out of the way to avoid being served: certainly not, because there appear to be difficulties in the way of personal service. *Barnes* v. *Williams,* 1 Dowl. 615.

Calling Witnesses on their Subpœna.]—The plaintiff (or his counsel) has a right to have his witnesses called on their subpœnas *before the jury are sworn,* and to withdraw the record in case any material witness does not appear. *Hopper* v. *Smith,* Moo. & Mal. 115, Lord Tenterden, C. J.; *Pope* v. *Fleming,* 3 Car. & K. 146, Wilde, C. J. He will thereby avoid a nonsuit, but will generally be liable to the costs of the day, and to be served with a notice to proceed to trial pursuant to 15 & 16 Vict. c. 76, ss. 101, 202. Having withdrawn the record for the reason above mentioned, he may afterwards maintain an action against any material witness who was duly subpœnaed, and being so called did not appear : *Mullett* v. *Hunt*, 1 Cr. & Mee. 752 (overruling *Bland* v. *Swafford*, Peake Cas. 60, Lord Kenyon, C. J.); *Lamont* v. *Crook*, 6 M. & W. 615; 8 Dowl. 737; *Needham* v. *Fraser*, 1 C. B. 815; 3 Dowl. & L. 190; *Couling* v. *Coxe*, 6 C. B. 703; 6 Dowl. & L. 399: or he may obtain an attachment against the witness. *Barrow* v. *Humphreys*, 3 B. & A. 598; *Rex* v. *Fenn*, 3 Dowl. 546. But it is not always safe and proper to withdraw the record under the above circumstances. *Chapman* v. *Davis*, 3 Man. & Gr. 609; 1 Dowl. N. S. 239.

When a witness does not appear upon being called by counsel in the usual manner, the practice is to have him *formally called* on his subpœna three times in open court, by the proper officer, who makes a memorandum on the back of the writ of the witness's neglect to appear. A witness cannot be called upon his subpœna without the writ being then and there produced. *Langley* v. *Faircross*, C. P., 8th November, 1844, Cresswell, J. But the officer need not hold the subpœna in his hand when the witness is called, provided the writ be then produced in court. *Rex* v. *Fenn*, 3 Dowl. 546. It is sufficient, even for an attachment, that the witness be called three times in open court, although not on his subpœna. *Dixon* v. *Lee*, 3 Dowl. 259; 1 Cr. M. & R. 645; *Rex* v. *Stretch*, 3 A. & E. 503; 4 Dowl. 30. It is not essentially necessary to call the witness in open court, if it can be *clearly proved* that he was not in attendance at the trial, and therefore could not have appeared if called. *Lamont* v. *Crook*, 6 Mee. & Wel. 615; 8 Dowl. 737; *Goff* v. *Mills*, 14 M. & W. 72; 2 Dowl. & L. 23. "Calling out the name of a party who is not in attendance would be perfectly useless." *Per* Alderson, B., in *Dixon* v. *Lee*, 3 Dowl. 261. "The calling of the witness upon the subpœna is only for the purpose of obtaining clear evidence of his having neglected to appear; but that is not necessary if it can be clearly shown by other means that the party has disobeyed the order of the court." *Per* Best, J., in *Barrow* v. *Humphreys*, 3 B. & A. 600, cited by Wightman, J., in *Goff* v. *Mills*, 2 Dowl. & L. 28.

Consequences of Disobedience. 1. *To the parties in the cause.*]— If a material witness for the plaintiff do not appear when called on his subpœna, the plaintiff may withdraw the record, provided the jury have not been sworn; *ante*, 181; otherwise he must submit to a nonsuit, or take his chance of obtaining the verdict without the evidence of that witness.

The defendant is not so well off in this respect, for he cannot withdraw the record, nor in any other manner avoid a *verdict* against him, unless he can manage to establish his defence without the evidence of the absent witness. Perhaps, however, the court might be induced to grant a new trial (a) upon payment of costs and other special terms, if satisfied by affidavit that the witness was duly subpœnaed,

---

(a) See *per* Lord Abinger, C. B., in *Scholes* v. *Hilton*, 2 Dowl. N. S. 231; 10 M. & W. 17.

and that there really was a good defence to the action, which the witness could probably have established, especially if the circumstances of the witness appear at all doubtful, so that no adequate remedy could be obtained against him: but even then the defendant would have to take his chance of the witness again disobeying the subpœna, or of procuring other witnesses to prove his defence.

In an action on a bond, to which there was an attesting witness, tried before 17 & 18 Vict. c. 125, s. 26, it was proved that all due means had been adopted to procure the attendance of such witness, but without effect, he having been purposely kept out of the way by the defendant, whereupon Mr. Justice Wightman allowed another witness to prove the handwriting of the attesting witness and of the defendant, and directed the jury to find a verdict for the plaintiff. *Collett* v. *Curling,* Q. B., Guildhall, London, 4th July, 1848; see also *Spooner* v. *Payne,* 4 C. B. 328.

It seems that neither party ought to be allowed to go into evidence at the trial to show why he could not procure the attendance of a particular person as a witness, or to show what steps he has taken to procure such person's attendance at the trial. *Turpin* v. *Heald,* 1 Car. & K. 264, Lord Denman, C. J.

2. *To the witness.*]—There are three ways of proceeding against a witness for not obeying a subpœna. 1. By attachment. 2. By action on the case. 3. By action of debt under the statute 5 Eliz. c. 9, s. 12.

Attachment.]—This is the most usual remedy, although generally a fruitless one, so far as the party injured is concerned. The object of it is not to compensate the party for the loss he has sustained (except perhaps in an indirect manner (a)), but *to vindicate the authority of the court,* and to compel obedience to its process.

The application for an attachment must be made *promptly,* and at all events before the end of the term next succeeding the trial. *Rex* v. *Stretch,* 3 A. & E. 503; 4 Dowl. 30; *Thorpe* v. *Gisbourne,* 11 Moore, 55; 3 Bing. 223. A clear case of contempt must be made out. *Holme* v. *Smith,* 1 Marsh. 410; *S. C. nom. Horne* v. *Smith,* 6 Taunt. 9; *Reg.* v. *Lord John Russell and Fox Maule,* 7 Dowl. 693. The affidavit in support of the application should be entitled in the action in which the subpœna issued; *Whitehead* v. *Firth,* 12 East, 165; and should show the due issuing of the writ, and that a copy of it was served on the witness personally; *ante,* 175; and that the writ itself was then produced to him; *ante,* 176; and that a sufficient sum for his expenses was paid or tendered to him; *ante,* 176; and that all this was done a reasonable time before the trial; *ante,* 179; and that the witness was duly called on his subpœna at the trial and did not appear: *Re Jacobs,* 1 Har. & Woll. 123: or if not so called, it must be made to appear very clearly that he was absent and could not have appeared if called. *Ante,* 182. Any special facts tending to show that his absence was *voluntary,* and that he could and might have attended if he had chosen, will of course strengthen the application. *Scholes* v. *Hilton,* 10 M. & W. 15; 2 Dowl. N. S. 229; *Marshall* v.

(a) See *Reg.* v. *Hemsworth,* 3 C. B. 753; *Doe* v. *Andrews,* Cowp. 846.

The York, Newcastle and Berwick Railway Company, 11 C. B. 398. It should also be sworn that he was a material witness. *Taylor* v. *Willans*, 4 Moo. & P. 59; *Tinley* v. *Porter*, 2 M. & W. 822; 5 Dowl. 744; but see *Scholes* v. *Hilton*, *supra*, where it is said that there is a difference in this respect between an attachment and an action.

Of course only a rule nisi will be granted in the first instance, 2 Chit. Arch. 1522 (8th ed.); Corner's Crown Office Prac. 26, which rule must (as in other cases of attachment) be served *personally*. *Id.* 26.

If the affidavits in support of the application be in any respect defective, or if the witness can by affidavit or otherwise satisfy the court that the subpœna was not in all respects duly served; *ante,* 175; or that he was, not guilty of a *wilful contempt* of the process of the court, the rule will be discharged. *Blandford* v. *De Tastet*, 1 Marsh. 42; 5 Taunt. 259; *Chapman* v. *Davis*, 3 Man. & Gr. 609; 4 Scott, N. R. 319; 1 Dowl. N. S. 239; *Scholes* v. *Hilton*, 10 M. & W. 15; 2 Dowl. N. S. 229; *Reg.* v. *Lord John Russell and Fox Maule*, 7 Dowl. 693; *Marshall* v. *The York, Newcastle and Berwick Railway Company*, 11 C. B. 398; *Netherwood* v. *Wilkinson*, 17 C. B. 226. It should, however, be remembered that the duty of attending a court of justice in pursuance of a subpœna, is one paramount to that of obeying a master however urgent his commands may be. And, therefore, where the servant of a maltster was employed in watching green malt, with strict orders not to leave it by night or day, as considerable damage might ensue, but that by neglecting such orders he could and might have attended in obedience to the subpœna, an attachment was granted. *Goff* v. *Mills*, 14 M. & W. 72; 2 Dowl. & L. 23, 28; and see *Jackson* v. *Seager*, 2 Dowl. & L. 13.

If it appear from the judge's report, or otherwise to the satisfaction of the court, that the evidence required from the witness was utterly immaterial to the matters in issue, a rule for an attachment will not be granted. *Dicas* v. *Lawson*, 1 Cr. M. & R. 934; 3 Dowl. 427; and see *Taylor* v. *Willans*, 4 Moo. & P. 59; *Tinley* v. *Porter*, 2 M. & W. 822; 5 Dowl. 744. So where it appears that the documents required by a *subpœna duces tecum* would have been inadmissible in evidence. *Reg.* v. *Lord John Russell and Fox Maule*, 7 Dowl. 693. It is a sufficient excuse that the witness was too ill to attend: *Re Jacobs*, 1 Harr. & Woll. 123: or that he was absent with leave of the attorney who served the subpœna. *Farrah* v. *Keat*, 6 Dowl. 470; *Netherwood* v. *Wilkinson*, 17 C. B. 226.

The court will sometimes permit a rule for an attachment to be discharged upon payment by the witness of the costs of the nonsuit, and of the costs of the application against him, otherwise the attachment to issue. *Doe* v. *Andrews*, Cowp. 846. If there appear to have been "some approximation" towards a wilful contempt, the court, on discharging the rule nisi for an attachment, will refuse the witness his costs of showing cause against it. *Marshall* v. *The York, Newcastle and Berwick Railway Company*, 11 C. B. 398; *Netherwood* v. *Wilkinson*, 17 C. B. 226.

The proceedings upon an attachment are fully detailed in Corner's Crown Office Prac. 23—44; 2 Chit. Arch. 1523—1528 (8th ed.); and see *Reg.* v. *Hemsworth*, 3 C. B. 745. The following is a concise outline of them :—

Upon the rule being made absolute, an attachment issues under which the witness is taken into custody, and compelled to answer upon oath interrogatories exhibited to him touching his alleged contempt. Thereupon the master reports to the court, whether he has or has not cleared himself of the contempt. If the master report in his favour, he will of course be discharged, but may afterwards be indicted for perjury. If the master report him guilty of a contempt, the court will thereupon sentence him to pay a fine, or to imprisonment, or both, according to their discretion, in the same manner as after a conviction for misdemeanor. In *Reg.* v. *Hemsworth*, 3 C. B. 753, the Court of Common Pleas sentenced a defendant to two years' imprisonment for his contempt in not performing an award; the object being to compel him to act justly towards the plaintiff, by performing the award and paying the costs of the attachment, &c. If the witness be willing to make compensation to the party grieved for the loss he has sustained by his non-attendance, including the costs of and incident to the attachment, the court will usually permit a reference to the master to ascertain the amount; and, upon payment thereof, inflict only a nominal fine for the contempt. As to the mode of proceeding upon such a reference see Cole, Crim. Informations, 106.

Where a witness is attached and sentenced to imprisonment for contempt, and suffers such imprisonment, that will not exonerate him from an action. *Reg.* v. *Hemsworth*, 3 C. B. 745.

Action on the Case.]—It is the duty of a witness to attend and give evidence in obedience to a writ of subpœna; and if, without lawful excuse, he neglect to perform such duty, and damage thereby ensue, an action on the case may be maintained by the party grieved, provided he had a good cause of action or defence (as the case may be) in the original suit, or was entitled to succeed and recover costs under any of the issues joined, and the party subpœnaed was a material and necessary witness on his behalf, and was duly subpœnaed; all of which facts must, with more or less distinctness, be alleged in the declaration, and (if traversed) sufficiently proved. *Cowling* v. *Coxe*, 6 C. B. 703; 6 Dowl. & L. 399; *Needham* v. *Fraser*, 1 C. B. 815; 3 Dowl. & L. 190; *Mullett* v. *Hunt*, 1 Cr. & Mee. 752; *Masterman* v. *Judson*, 8 Bing. 224; 1 Moo. & Sc. 367; *Davis* v. *Lovell*, 4 M. & W. 678; 7 Dowl. 178; *Lamont* v. *Crook*, 6 M. & W. 615; 8 Dowl. 737; *Maunsell* v. *Ainsworth*, 8 Dowl. 869. Where there are *several issues* in a cause, the fact that the plaintiff had no good cause of action is immaterial (except as to the amount of damages) in a subsequent action against a witness for not attending a subpœna, if it be shown that he might have succeeded in recovering the costs of *some* of the issues had the defendant attended, his evidence being material as to those issues. It is, however, essential for the plaintiff to prove that he has sustained some damage by the absence of the defendant. *Cowling* v. *Coxe*, 6 C. B. 703; 6 Dowl. & L. 399.

In many cases an action is maintainable against a witness where the court would refuse or discharge an attachment, because of a clear wilful contempt not having been committed. Indeed, where that does not clearly appear, it is usual to leave the party grieved to his remedy by action. *Ante*, 175.

Action of Debt.]—By stat. 5 Eliz. c. 9, s. 12, it is provided and enacted, "that if any person or persons, upon whom any process out of any of the courts of record within this realm or Wales, shall be served to testify or depose concerning any cause or matter depending in any of the same courts, and having tendered unto him or them, according to his or their circumstance or calling, such reasonable sums of money for his or their costs and charges, as, having regard to the distance of the places, is necessary to be allowed in that behalf, do not appear according to the tenor of the said process, having not a lawful and reasonable let or impediment to the contrary; that then the party making default, to lose and forfeit for every such offence ten pounds, and to yield such further recompense to the party grieved, as by the discretion of the judge of the court out of which the said process shall be awarded, according to the loss and hindrance that the party which procured the said process shall sustain, by reason of the non-appearance of the said witness or witnesses; the said several sums to be recovered by the party so grieved against the offender or offenders, by action of debt, bill, plaint or information, in any of the Queen's Majesty's Courts of Record, in which no wager of law, essoin or protection to be allowed."

The further recompense to be recovered under the above statute must be assessed not by the judge at nisi prius, nor by a jury, but by the court out of which the process issued. *Pearson* v. *Isles*, Doug. 556. This must be done by a rule of court, to be made upon motion supported by proper affidavits. "Upon such an adjudication or assessment, there is no doubt but debt might be brought. But it has never been done. Why? Because there is a preferable remedy by attachment." *Per* Lord Mansfield, C. J., in *Pearson* v. *Isles*, Doug. 561. Or by action on the case. *Ante*, 185. In point of fact, the necessity for an assessment of damages by the court in banc, before the commencement of an action of debt against the witness, has rendered the above enactment a dead letter. It does not appear how the expenses of such assessment could be recovered. In an old case it was decided that the declaration must show the plaintiff to be a "party grieved" within the meaning of the statute. *Goodwin* v. *West*, Cro. Car. 522, 540; Sir W. Jones, 430.

II. Subpœna duces tecum.

Nature and Effect of, and when necessary.]—This writ takes its name from the principal operative words, "*duces tecum*," bring with you, "*sub pœnâ*," under a penalty. It commands the party to whom it is addressed, to appear before the judge, at the time and place where the trial is to be had, and to bring with him and produce at the time and place aforesaid certain documents (*describing them*), and then and there to testify, &c., under the penalty of 100*l*. *See the form, Appendix, No*. 194. The penalty is merely nominal. The consequences of disobeying the writ are similar to those of disobeying a *subpœna ad testificandum. Ante*, 173; *Amey* v. *Long*, 9 East, 473.

The writ has a double operation. It commands the witness to bring with him and produce at the trial the documents therein mentioned, and also to testify, &c. Under it he may be called upon to do both *or either*. *Summers* v. *Mosely*, 2 Cr. & Mee. 477; 4 Tyr. 158; *Evans* v. *Moseley*, 2 Cr. & Mee. 490; 4 Tyr. 109; 2 Dowl. 364; *Perry* v. *Gibson*, 1 A. & E. 48; *Rush* v. *Smith*, 1 Cr. M. & R. 94; 2 Dowl. 687.

In *Lamont* v. *Crook*, 8 Dowl. 737, the action was for not attending *to testify* in obedience to a *subpœna duces tecum*. It is of compulsory obligation on a witness to produce the papers thereby demanded, which he has in his possession, and which he has no lawful or reasonable excuse for withholding; of the validity of which excuse the court, and not the witness, is to judge. *Amey* v. *Long*, 9 East, 473. Therefore, if the witness do not appear at all, or do not bring with him the documents required, or such of them as are in his possession, the court will grant an attachment against him, notwithstanding he was advised and believed that he was not legally bound to produce them. *Reg.* v. *Greenaway and Carey*, 7 Q. B. 126, 135. A person served with a writ of *subpœna duces tecum* is bound to attend as a witness, and to bring the paper called for in obedience to the writ. Whether he is bound to produce it, and permit it to be examined and given in evidence at the trial, is a question altogether different. *Per* Lord Denman, C. J., in *Reg.* v. *Greenaway, supra*. "If a *subpœna duces tecum* is served, the party *must bring* his deeds into court in obedience to the subpœna; but if he states that they are his title deeds, no judge will ever compel him *to produce* them." *Per cur.* in *Pickering* v. *Noyes*, 1 B. & C. 262; and see 1 C. & P. 179, note (a); *post*, 189. If the witness appear pursuant to the subpœna, but instead of bringing with him the document required, he *untruly* swears that he has it not in his possession, and knows nothing of it, he will not only be liable to an indictment for perjury, but also to an action for the non-production. *Amey* v. *Long*, 1 Camp. 14; 6 Esp. 116, Lord Ellenborough, C. J.; 9 East, 473, *S. C.*

The witness must, at all events, attend to testify, &c., although he has not in his possession any of the documents mentioned in the subpœna; *Reg.* v. *Greenaway, supra;* for he will probably be able to give some evidence relating to them. *Wilson* v. *Rastall*, 4 T. R. 753, 754. And if it appear that he has, in fraud of the subpœna, parted with any of the documents to one of the parties in the cause, or his attorney, after action brought, and whether before or after being served with the subpœna, the court will permit secondary evidence to be given of the contents, without any notice to produce. This is *in odium spoliatoris*. *Leeds* v. *Cook*, 4 Esp. 256, Lord Ellenborough, C. J.; but see *Todd* v. *Emly*, 11 Mee. & W. 2.

If the witness, at the time of being served with the subpœna, had not in his custody or possession any of the documents therein mentioned, and has not obtained them subsequently, that will, of course, furnish a sufficient excuse to him for their non-production, "no man being obliged, according to any sense of the effect of such a subpœna, to sue and labour in order to obtain the possession of any instrument from another for the purpose of its production afterwards by himself in obedience to the subpœna." *Per* Lord Ellenborough, C. J., in *Amey* v. *Long*, 9 East, 483. But it seems that he may be required "diligently to search for, and examine and inquire after all such deeds, documents, instruments, papers and writings," as are mentioned in the writ, and which may happen to be in his own possession. 3 Chit. Gen. Prac. 702 (3rd ed.).

A witness *being sworn* to give evidence, and having then in court a document in his possession which he might have been compelled to produce under a *subpœna duces tecum*, may be ordered to produce it at the trial; for he is just as much under the control of the court in this respect as if he had brought the document under a *subpœna duces tecum.* *Snelgrove* v. *Stevens*, Car. & M. 508, Cresswell, J.; and see *Dwyer* v. *Collins*, 7 Exch. 639. If a deed be in the possession of a third person as mortgagee, and he, *having the deed in court*, though not subpœnaed in the cause, decline to produce it, secondary evidence may be given of its contents; but if the deed be not in court, and he has not been subpœnaed to produce it, it is otherwise. *Doe d. Loscombe* v. *Clifford*, 2 Car. & K. 448, Alderson, B.

The mere chance of a witness bringing the document with him, without being served with a *subpœna duces tecum*, should never be relied on; for the consequences of its non-production may be most disastrous. Even when he is willing to bring it, and promises to do so, the form of serving him with a *subpœna duces tecum* should not be omitted. If the plaintiff do not regularly subpœna the proper witnesses, and is, consequently, nonsuited for want of a document, the court will not grant a new trial on the ground of surprise. *Austin* v. *Evans*, 2 Man. & Gr. 430; 9 Dowl. 408. In *Robinson* v. *Brown*, 3 C. B. 754, the court set aside a verdict for the plaintiff, and directed a nonsuit to be entered, because he had not subpœnaed a third person to produce a necessary document, which was not forthcoming at the trial. On the other hand, where an attorney was duly subpœnaed to produce a deed, and promised that it should be forthcoming at the trial, but there objected to produce it, and the objection was allowed, and a verdict passed against the party, who was not prepared with secondary evidence of the contents, the court granted a new trial on affidavits of surprise, &c. *Cocks* v. *Nash*, 4 Moo. & Sc. 162.

If the document required be in the possession of one of the parties to the suit, or his attorney (whether such attorney be employed in the particular suit, or not), the proper course is to serve such party or his attorney in the cause, with a "notice to produce." *Ante*, 156; *Reg.* v. *Hankins*, 2 Car. & K. 823, 826, Coltman, J.; *Lloyd* v. *Mostyn*, 10 M. & W. 478; 2 Dowl. & L. 476. But a *subpœna duces tecum* may be served on a party to the suit in like manner as on any other witness, 14 & 15 Vict. c. 99, s. 6. And this may sometimes be expedient, especially where the party is also required to give parol evidence.

If a written contract be in the possession of a stakeholder, on behalf of the defendant *and some third person*, such agent must be subpœnaed to produce it. A mere notice to produce served on the defendant will not be sufficient to let in secondary evidence. *Parry* v. *May*, 1 Moo. & Rob. 279, Littledale, J.

If any document be *abroad*, and in the possession of a third person, who refuses to part with it, or if for any other reason its production cannot be enforced by a *subpœna duces tecum*, upon proof of those facts, secondary evidence of the contents will be admissible. *Boyle* v. *Wiseman*, 10 Exch. 647; *Sayer* v. *Glossop*, 2 Exch. 409. But subpœnas may be issued for service in Scotland or Ireland, pursuant to 17 & 18 Vict. c. 34. *Post*, 197.

Form.]—For the form of a writ of *subpœna duces tecum*, see *Appendix, No.* 194. A printed copy on parchment, and also printed copies on paper, may be obtained from any law stationer. It must be filled up in like manner as a subpœna to testify. *Ante*, 174. The mode of describing the documents is shown in the form above referred to.

Service.]—The writ should be served in the same manner as a writ of *subpœna ad testificandum. Ante,* 175. Everything hereinbefore stated on that subject will equally apply to a writ of *subpœna duces tecum.*

Excuses for not producing Documents—1. *Parties to the suit.*] Before the 14 & 15 Vict. c. 99, s. 6, parties to a suit could not be compelled by subpœna to give or produce evidence against themselves. *Reg.* v. *Hankins,* 2 Car. & K. 823, 826. But a co-defendant who had suffered judgment by default might have been served with a *subpœna duces tecum* to produce a document in his possession, on behalf of another defendant who had pleaded. *Colley* v. *Smith,* 4 Bing. N. C. 285; 6 Dowl. 399. Now any plaintiff or defendant in ejectment may be served with a *subpœna duces tecum* in like manner as another witness.

2. *Title Deeds.*]—No person, whether a party to the suit or not, can by means of a *subpœna duces tecum,* or by rule of court, or otherwise, be compelled to produce his *title deeds. Pickering* v. *Noyes,* 1 B. & C. 262. "If a *subpœna duces tecum* is served the party must bring his deeds into court in obedience to the subpœna, but if he states that they are his title deeds no judge will ever compel him to produce them." *Id.* 263, *per cur.* He may, however, be ordered to let another witness *see the outside* of a deed to enable him to identify it; *Phelps* v. *Prew,* 3 E. & B. 430; unless that cannot be done without thereby disclosing the contents. *Brard* v. *Ackerman,* 5 Esp. 119. The witness may also be compelled to state on oath the date of the deed, and the names of the parties to it, for the purpose of identifying it. *Doe* d. *Loscombe* v. *Clifford,* 2 Car. & K. 448, Alderson, B. The judge has no right to inspect the document to see if the objection to produce it, or to disclose the contents, be well founded or not. *Doe* d. *Carter* v. *James,* 2 Moo. & Rob. 47, Lord Denman, C. J.; *Volant* v. *Soyer,* 13 C. B. 231. But evidence may be produced to show that the excuse is false. This was done successfully in *Doe* d. *Courtail* v. *Thomas,* 9 B. & C. 288.

A lessee cannot be compelled to produce his lease, nor a lessor his counterpart. *Mills* v. *Oddy,* 6 C. & P. 730, Parke, B. But a lessor, or his attorney, may be compelled to produce a lease on behalf of the lessee, notwithstanding the deed is in a cancelled state. *Doe* d. *Courtail* v. *Thomas,* 9 B. & C. 288. A devisee cannot be compelled to produce the will under which he derives his title, although such will relates to personalty as well as realty, and, therefore, ought to be deposited in the proper ecclesiastical court. *Doe* d. *Carter* v. *James,* 2 Moo. & Rob. 47, Lord Denman, C. J. A mortgagee cannot be compelled to produce his mortgage; *Doe* d. *Earl of Egremont* v. *Langdon,* 12 Q. B. 711; *Doe* d. *Loscombe* v. *Clifford,* 2 Car. & Kir. 448; nor a will through which his title is derived. *Doe* d. *Bowdler* v. *Owen,* 8 C. & P. 110, Lord Abinger, C. B. A person with whom a lease has been deposited, by way of equitable mortgage for money lent, cannot be compelled to produce such lease. *Mills* v. *Oddy,* 6 C. & P. 732, Parke, B.; *Schlencker* v. *Moxsy,* 1 C. & P. 178; 3 B. & C. 791; 5 D. & R. 747. A person who has merely a lien upon a document cannot be compelled to produce it on behalf of the party against whom he has such lien. *Kemp* v. *King,* Car. & M. 396; 2 Moo. & Rob. 473, Lord Denman, C. J. But a lien as against other parties furnishes no sufficient objection, because such production will not directly or indirectly prejudice the lien. *Thompson* v. *Mosley*, 5 C. & P. 501, Lord Lyndhurst, C. B.; *Croft, Bart.* v. *Lyster*, 24 Dec. 1829, Tindal, C. J. A broker who has effected a policy, and has a lien on it for his premiums, may be compelled to produce it on the trial of an action by the assured against the underwriters. *Hunter* v. *Leathley*, 10 B. & C. 151. The solicitors for a railway company, having a lien on the subscribers' agreement and parliamentary contract, may be compelled to produce them in an action by an allottee of shares against a member of the committee of management for recovery of the plaintiff's deposit. *Ley* v. *Barlow*, 5 Dowl. & L. 375. In this case, Parke, B., said, "with respect to the lien of the attornies, they will not be deprived of it by the production of the deed, which they will still retain." *Id.* 377. "The question is, whether the right of the attorney against A. can interfere with the course of justice between B. and C.? *per* Knight Bruce, Lord J., in *Hope* v. *Liddell*, 25 Law Times R. 231, where it was decided, on appeal, that the lien of a solicitor upon a deed belonging to his client does not entitle him to refuse to produce the deed as evidence between third persons; and see *Brassington* v. *Brassington*, 1 Sim. & Stu. 455. A mere trustee cannot be compelled to produce his title deeds. *Roberts* v. *Simpson*, 2 Stark. R. 203, Richards, C. B.

The above rule does not appear to be strictly confined to what are commonly called title deeds. Thus a company or their solicitor cannot be compelled to produce a deed of composition between themselves and their creditors, in a suit between other parties. *Harris* v. *Hill*, 3 Stark. R. 140, Abbott, C. J. A co-contractor who has been released, or his attorney, cannot be compelled to produce such release on behalf of the defendant. *Cocks* v. *Nash*, 4 Moo. & Sc. 162. A person who has seized a ship under and by virtue of a power of attorney, cannot be compelled to produce that document. *Miles* v. *Dawson*, 1 Esp. 405, Lord Kenyon, C. J. The assignees of a bankrupt, or their solicitor, cannot be compelled to produce the proceedings under the fiat in an action against the bankrupt or any third person. *Bateson* v. *Hartsink*, 4 Esp. 43, Lord Kenyon, C. J.; *Laing* v. *Barclay*, 3 Stark. R. 38, Abbott, C. J.; but see *Corsen* v. *Dubois*, Holt, N. P. C. 239, Gibbs, C. J.

It has, however, been decided that "rent books," containing entries by a deceased steward of rents received by him, do not so far partake of the nature of title deeds that their production cannot be compelled under a *subpœna duces tecum*. *Doe* d. *Earl of Egremont* v. *Date*, 3 Q. B. 609, 610, Rolfe, B. So with respect to accounts of rents received by a deceased tenant for life. *Doe* d. *Rowcliffe* v. *Earl of Egremont*, 2 Moo. & Rob. 386, Rolfe, B. But the minute book of a projected railway company has been held privileged. *Newton* v. *Chaplin*, 10 C. B. 356.

Where a lease or other deed forms no part of the title of the party having possession of it, he or his attorney may be compelled to produce it. *Doe* d. *Courtail* v. *Thomas*, 9 B. & C. 288, 293; *Copeland* v. *Watts*, 1 Stark. R. 95, Gibbs, C. J.

The owner of a title deed, or his attorney, may withdraw his objection to its production, and thereupon it may be given in evidence; *Mills* v. *Oddy*, 6 C. & P. 733, 734, Parke, B.; *Doe* d. *Earl of Egremont* v. *Langdon*, 12 Q. B. 711; or he may refuse to do so, and thereupon secondary evidence of the contents will be admissible. *Newton* v. *Chaplin*, 10 C. B. 356, 358; *Volant* v. *Soyer*, 13 C. B. 231.

Where a draft conveyance is prepared by the vendor's solicitor on behalf of both parties, and is settled by the purchaser's solicitor, and after the completion of the purchase the draft is permitted to remain in the possession of the solicitor who prepared it, he holds it for both parties, and will not be permitted to produce it against the purchaser, even with the vendor's consent. *Doe* d. *Strode* v. *Seaton*, 2 A. & E. 171, 179, 181. A draft deed settled by counsel, with his notes or opinion thereon, although not made in contemplation of any legal proceedings afterwards commenced, is a privileged document. *Manser* v. *Dix*, 25 Law Times Rep. 113, Wood, V. C.

3. *Documents tending to criminate.*]—No person can be compelled to give or produce any evidence which may criminate, or tend directly or indirectly to criminate himself, or to expose him to any penalty or forfeiture; *Sir John Friend's case*, 13 Howell, St. Tr. 16; *Cates* v. *Hardacre*, 3 Taunt. 424; *Paxton* v. *Douglas*, 16 Ves. 239, 242; *Parkhurst* v. *Lowten*, 2 Swanston, 214, 215, *per* Lord Eldon, C.; *Reg.* v. *Garbett*, 2 Car. & K. 474; 1 Den. C. C. 236; unless, indeed, the time limited for recovering any such penalty be past. *Roberts* v. *Allatt*, Moo. & Mal. 192, Lord Tenterden, C. J. It seems, however, that a stockbroker is bound to produce under a *subpœna duces tecum* his "broker's book," kept pursuant to 7 Geo. 2, c. 8, s. 9, although it contain entries which may subject him to penalties. *Rawlings* v. *Hall*, 1 C. & P. 11. The reason is, that the statute requires him to produce such book "when thereunto lawfully required," *per* Coltman, J., in *Pritchett* v. *Smart*, 7 C. B. 629. But in an action by a stockbroker he cannot be compelled to produce such book upon a summary application; *Pritchett* v. *Smart*, 7 C. B. 625; 6 Dowl. & L. 702; nor even in equity by a bill of discovery. *Bullock* v. *Richardson*, 11 Ves. 373.

By stat. 46 Geo. 3, c. 37, it was *declared* "that a witness cannot by law refuse to answer a question relevant to the matter in issue, the answering of which has no tendency to accuse himself, or to expose him to penalty or forfeiture of any nature whatsoever, by reason only, or on the sole ground, that the answering of such question may establish or tend to establish that he owes a debt, or is otherwise subject to a civil suit, either at the instance of his majesty, or of any other person or persons." This act was passed to remove doubts upon the above points, and merely *declares* the law on the subject. The principles of it equally apply to written evidence. Holt, N. P. C. 241, note, *Summers* v. *Moseley*, 2 Cr. & Mee. 485, *per* Bayley, B.

4. *Attorneys and Solicitors.*]—An attorney or solicitor cannot be compelled to produce under a *subpœna duces tecum* any written instrument intrusted to him in his professional capacity, or to disclose the contents; *Volant* v. *Soyer*, 13 C. B. 231; *Newton* v. *Chaplin*, 10 C. B. 356; *Reg.* v. *Hankins*, 2 Car. & K. 823; provided the client himself could not have been compelled to produce it, if in his own custody. *Doe* d. *Courtail* v. *Thomas*, 9 B. & C. 293, Lord Tenterden, C. J.; *Doe* d. *Carter* v. *James*, 2 Moo. & Rob. 47; *Mills* v. *Oddy*, 6 C. & P. 730; *Harris* v. *Hill*, 3 Stark. R. 140; *Laing* v. *Barclay*, *Id.* 38; *Bateson* v. *Hartsink*, 4 Esp. 43; *Doe* d. *Earl of Egremont* v. *Langdon*, 12 Q. B. 711; *Cocks* v. *Nash*, 4 Moo. & Sc. 162. This is the privilege of the client and not of the attorney; 4 T. R. 753; who ought

not (if so disposed) to be permitted to violate it to his client's prejudice. *Rex* v. *Smith*, Phil. Ev. 171 (9th ed.); *Doe* d. *Strode* v. *Seaton*, 2 A. & E. 171, 181 ; *Reg.* v. *Tylney and others*, 18 Law J., N. S., M. C., 36. It has, however, been recently held, that where an attorney is *not compellable* to produce his client's title deed, or to disclose the contents, yet if he *willingly* do so his evidence is admissible. *Hibbert* v. *Knight*, 2 Exch. 11. But it does not follow that an attorney will in all cases be permitted to betray his client. *Per* Maule, J., in *Newton* v. *Chaplin*, 10 C. B. 362 ; and see *Doe* d. *Strode* v. *Seaton*, 2 A. & E. 179, 181. A court of equity would restrain him by injunction. *Lewis* v. *Smith*, 1 Mac. & Gor. 417. An attorney may properly waive the objection where the judge thinks he can do so without prejudicing his client. *Mills* v. *Oddy*, 6 C. & P. 733, 734, Parke, B.; *Doe* d. *Earl of Egremont* v. *Langdon*, 12 Q. B. 711. Indeed the judge would under such circumstances order him to produce the document. *Corsen* v. *Dubois*, Holt, N. P. C. 239, Gibbs, C. J.

An attorney is not compellable to state, when examined as a witness, whether a document shown to him by his client in the course of a professional interview was then in the same state as when produced at the trial, *ex. gr.*, whether it was then stamped or not. *Wheatley* v. *Williams*, 1 M. & W. 533. An attorney's privilege in this respect extends to all knowledge that he obtains, which he would not have obtained but for his being consulted professionally by his client. *Id.* 541, Alderson, B.; *Volant* v. *Soyer*, 13 C. B. 231. But he cannot refuse to answer whether an original document is at the time of the trial *in the possession* of himself or his client, the object of such question being merely to let in secondary evidence of the contents. *Bevan* v. *Walters*, Moo. & Mal. 235, Best, C. J.; *Coates* v. *Birch, Bart.*, 2 Q. B. 252 ; 1 Gale & Dav. 647 ; 1 Dowl. N. S. 54 ; *Dwyer* v. *Collins*, 7 Exch. 639, 644. And he will, if necessary, be ordered to produce the deed, in order that the *indorsement on the outside of it* may be inspected by another witness for the purpose of *identification*; *Phelps* v. *Prew*, 3 E. & B. 430 ; unless, indeed, that cannot be done without thereby disclosing the contents of the document. *Brard* v. *Ackerman*, 5 Esp. 119. The judge has no right to inspect the document to see if the objection to produce it, or to disclose the contents, be well founded or not. *Volant* v. *Soyer*, 13 C. B. 231 ; *Doe* d. *Carter* v. *James*, 2 Moo. & Rob. 47, Lord Denman, C. J. But the witness may be compelled to state on oath the date of the deed, and the names of the parties to it, for the purpose of identifying it. *Doe* d. *Loscombe* v. *Clifford*, 2 Car. & K. 448, Alderson, B.

Where documents are intrusted to an attorney, *not in his professional capacity*, he is not privileged from producing them. *Wilson* v. *Rastall*, 4 T. R. 753 ; and see *Reg.* v. *Hayward*, 2 Car. & K. 234, Pollock, C. B. So, where the documents are of such a nature that the client could not have refused to produce them if in his own possession ; *Doe* d. *Courtail* v. *Thomas*, 9 B. & C. 288, 293 ; for otherwise any person might prevent a document being given in evidence, by merely depositing it with his attorney : but see *Volant* v. *Soyer*, 13 C. B. 231 ; *Newton* v. *Chaplin*, 10 C. B. 356. So, where it appears that production of the document cannot possibly operate to the prejudice of the client. *Copeland* v. *Watts*, 1 Stark. R. 95, Gibbs, C. J. Where a solicitor attends with document in lieu of his client, he must, of course, produce whatever his client would have been bound to produce. *Doe*

d. *Earl of Egremont* v. *Date*, 3 Q. B. 609; *Doe* d. *Earl of Egremont* v. *Langdon*, 12 Q. B. 711.

Professional communications, made with a view to secure the title of the client against all claimants, are protected from production, although made *ante litem motam;* and where the solicitor is privileged from disclosing them, the client himself will also be protected in like manner; for the privilege is that of the client, and not of the attorney. This is so even in a court of equity. *Manser* v. *Dix*, 24 Law J., N. S., Chan., 497.

The privilege of withholding documents on the ground of professional confidence is confined to the cases of counsel, solicitor, and attorney; *Wilson* v. *Rastall*, 4 T. R. 753; *Id.* 759, *per* Buller, J.: but the clerk of an attorney or solicitor stands in the same situation as his master. *Mills* v. *Oddy*, 6 C. & P. 731, Parke, B.; *Rex* v. *The Inhabitants of Upper Boddington*, 8 D. & R. 732, *per* Bayley, J.; *Taylor* v. *Forster*, 2 C. & P. 195, Best, C. J. And an interpreter employed by an attorney has been considered as "the organ of the attorney." *Madame du Barre's case*, cited 4 T. R. 756, Lord Kenyon, C. J.

An agent, or steward, or servant, or an intimate friend, with whom documents are intrusted, cannot refuse to produce them when required to do so under a *subpœna duces tecum*. 2 Atk. 524; 4 T. R. 758, 759. It is no objection to such production that the legal right and property in the document belongs to another person. The party having the actual possession of it is the proper person to be served with the subpœna. *Corsen* v. *Dubois*, Holt, N. P. C. 239, Gibbs, C. J.; *Amey* v. *Long*, 1 Camp. 14; 6 Esp. 116. If a written contract be in the possession of a stakeholder on behalf of the defendant and some third person, such agent must be subpœnaed to produce it. A mere notice to produce, served on the defendant, will not be sufficient to let in secondary evidence. *Parry* v. *May*, 1 Moo. & Rob. 279, Littledale, J.

5. *Original Records and Public Documents.*]—By Reg. Gen. H. T. 1853, No. 32, "no subpœna for the production of an original record shall be issued, unless a rule of court or the order of a judge shall be produced to the officer issuing the same, and filed with him, and unless the writ shall be made conformable to the description of the documents mentioned in such rule or order." 13 C. B. 11. The court or judge will require to be satisfied that there is good reason for requiring the original record rather than an examined office copy.

Before the above rule it was decided that the original rolls of the Court of Chancery could not be taken out of court to be given in evidence as a matter of course; neither the Master of the Rolls, nor the senior clerk of the Petty Bag Office, would be compellable to produce them on a subpœna alone, but there must have been an order of the Master of the Rolls for that purpose, and the usual fees paid as allowed by the General Orders of that court. *Bentall* v. *Sydney*, 10 A. & E. 162; 2 P. & D. 416.

A person having the lawful custody of an original register of marriages cannot be compelled to produce it under a *subpœna duces tecum*. But an examined copy may be given in evidence in any case, whether civil or criminal. *Sayer* v. *Glossop*, 2 Exch. 409.

It seems that documents of a public nature in the possession of a secretary of state, or other public officer in his official capacity (except

K

as above), must be produced in obedience to a *subpœna duces tecum.* *Reg.* v. *Lord John Russell and Fox Maule,* 7 Dowl. 693. But it would not be sufficient to subpœna a mere clerk in the Legacy Duty Office to produce accounts filed there, and which are in the legal custody of the comptroller. *Austin* v. *Evans,* 2 Man. & Gr. 430; 9 Dowl. 408.

Excuses, how decided, and the Consequences of such Decision.]—It is for the judge at nisi prius to decide as to the validity of any objection or excuse made by a witness to the production of any documents which he has brought with him in obedience to a writ of *subpœna duces tecum.* *Amey* v. *Long,* 9 East, 473, 486; *Reg.* v. *Greenaway,* 7 Q. B. 126, 135. If the judge improperly allow the objection, the court will grant a new trial, even in a penal action. *Wilson* v. *Rastall,* 4 T. R. 753; *Newton* v. *Chaplin,* 10 C. B. 356. But it seems otherwise where the judge improperly overrules the objection and compels the witness to produce the document. *Doe* d. *Earl of Egremont* v. *Date,* 3 Q. B. 609, *per* Patteson, Williams and Coleridge, JJ., *dubitante* Lord Denman, C. J. The reason for the distinction is, that in the former case proper evidence is erroneously excluded, to the prejudice of one of the parties in the cause; but in the latter case no injustice is done, except perhaps to the witness; only legitimate evidence has been admitted, of which the party against whom it was produced has no right to complain. *S. C.*; and see *Marston* v. *Downes,* 1 A. & E. 31, 34; *Doe* d. *Earl of Egremont* v. *Langdon,* 12 Q. B. 711; *Id.* 714, note (*b*); *Phelps* v. *Prew,* 3 E. & B. 430.

The counsel engaged in the cause frequently attempt to support the objection of the witness; but this is irregular. They have no right to interfere for the purpose of excluding evidence, to which, as against their client, there is no legal objection. *Mills* v. *Oddy,* 6 C. & P. 733, Parke, B.; *Rex* v. *Adey,* 1 Moo. & Rob. 94, Lord Tenterden, C. J.; *Doe* d. *Earl of Egremont* v. *Langdon,* 12 Q. B. 714, note (*b*). Nor has the witness himself any right to have the question of his liability to produce the document argued by counsel retained on his behalf. *Doe* d. *Earl of Egremont* v. *Date,* 3 Q. B. 621, *per* Coleridge, J., citing a decision of Park, J., on the western circuit; *Doe* d. *Rowcliffe* v. *Earl of Egremont,* 2 Moo. & Rob. 386, Rolfe, B. "The course has always been for the witness himself to state to the judge the grounds upon which he contends he is not bound to produce the document required, and the judge is to decide on the validity of those grounds, and to give the witness the protection claimed if he finds him entitled to it." *Id.* 387, *per* Rolfe, B. There would seem to be no objection to the witness reading or handing in to the judge a *written statement* of his objection, and of the grounds upon which he relies in support of it; and this of course might be prepared beforehand by his counsel or attorney.

Counsel engaged in the cause may of course argue *against* the witness's objection; for they have a legal right on behalf of their clients to insist upon the production of legal evidence.

If it appear that the document mentioned in the *subpœna duces tecum* has been destroyed, or if the witness prevaricate as to its existence, secondary evidence of the contents may be admitted. *Doe* d. *Manton* v. *Austin,* 9 Bing. 45, Tindal, C. J.

If the judge disallow the witness's objection, and order him to produce the document, which he nevertheless *refuses* to do, the judge may at once commit him for contempt of court for the remainder of the assizes or sittings; or the court in banc may be moved for an attachment against him for contempt of its process, and he will also be liable to an action. But the wrongful refusal of a witness to produce a document when ordered to do so, will not let in secondary evidence of the contents. 1 Stark. Ev. 90 (3rd ed.); Ros. Ev. 4 (7th ed.); *Jesus College* v. *Gibbs*, 1 You. & Coll. 156; *Phelps* v. *Prew*, 3 E. & B. 430; *Reg.* v. *The Inhabitants of Llanfaethly, Id.* 940. This is much to be regretted. Upon principle it would seem, that where a party proves that he has done all in his power to compel production of an original document, by issuing and duly serving a writ of *subpœna duces tecum* to produce it (which is the only legal process for the purpose), he ought to be permitted to give secondary evidence of the contents. *Hibberd* v. *Knight*, 2 Exch. 12; *Newton* v. *Chaplin*, 10 C. B. 356; *Doe* d. *Loscombe* v. *Clifford*, 2 Car. & K. 451, Alderson, B. The rule is, that secondary evidence is not admissible unless primary evidence cannot be procured; and before it can be admitted, it must be shown that reasonable efforts have been made, and have proved unavailing to procure the primary evidence." *Per* Parke, B., in *Boyle* v. *Wiseman*, 11 Exch. 362. It might be impossible for a defendant to establish his defence without such evidence; *Augustien* v. *Challis*, 1 Exch. 279; and his remedy over against the witness would in many cases be merely illusory. A new trial would not afford an adequate remedy, for, to say nothing of the expense, the witness might again disobey the subpœna: besides which, what remedy would there be in criminal cases? Possibly, the practice on this point is different in criminal cases and penal actions. Thus, when a witness had been served with a writ of *subpœna duces tecum* to produce a bill of exchange in his possession, upon the trial of an indictment for stealing such bill preferred against the party for whom he received it, and the witness *did not appear*; Heath, J., allowed parol evidence to be given of the contents; and the twelve judges afterwards decided that such evidence had been properly received. *Rex* v. *Aickles*, 1 Leach's C. C. 294 (1st point); so in a penal action it was determined that parol evidence might be given of letters which were not produced pursuant to a *subpœna duces tecum. The Attorney-General* v. *Le Merchant*, cited 4 T. R. 759. But if these cases be law, they show what *ought* also to be the practice in civil cases. It seems unreasonable that a defendant should be excluded from proving a valid defence founded on a deed or other document which may have been designedly placed in the hands of an insolvent person, to ensure its non-production, and against whom any remedy by action or otherwise would be worse than useless.

Where the objection is allowed, and the witness excused from producing a document in his possession, secondary evidence may be given of the contents. *Ditcher* v. *Kenrick*, 1 C. & P. 161; *Mills* v. *Oddy*, 6 C. & P. 732; *Doe* d. *Gilbert* v. *Ross*, 7 M. & W. 102; 8 Dowl. 389; *Doe* d. *Loscombe* v. *Clifford*, 2 Car. & K. 448; *Newton* v. *Chaplin*, 10 C. B. 356; *Wilson* v. *Rastall*, 4 T. R. 753, 754, Thompson, B.; *Rex* v. *The Inhabitants of Upper Boddington*, 8 D. & R. 732; *Cocks* v. *Nash*, 4 Moo. & Sc. 163; *Hibberd* v. *Knight*, 2 Exch. 12. If the attorney for either party be so excused (whether engaged in the cause or not), there should be a notice to produce the document, otherwise secondary evidence cannot be received. *Lloyd* v. *Mostyn*,

10 M. & W. 478; 2 Dowl. N. S. 476; *Bate* v. *Kinsey*, 1 Cr. M. & R. 38. Unless, indeed, the attorney claim and be allowed to withhold the document by virtue of a lien thereon, or in some other right than as attorney for one of the parties in the cause. *Doe* d. *Gilbert* v. *Ross*, and *Doe* d. *Loscombe* v. *Clifford*, *supra*. If the attorney for a third person (*ex. gr.*, a mortgagee), be excused from producing a document, secondary evidence will be admissible, although the client has not been subpœnaed; *Phelps* v. *Prew*, 3 E. & B. 430; especially if it appear that the client has advised his attorney not to produce the document; but this does not appear to be essential. *S. C.*

When a witness objects to produce a deed, and such objection is allowed, he cannot be *compelled* to give parol evidence of the contents; for that would render the protection illusory. *Davies* v. *Waters*, 9 M. & W. 608; 1 Dowl. N. S. 651; *Rex* v. *Inhabitants of Upper Boddington*, 8 D. & R. 726, 732; *Doe* d. *Earl of Egremont* v. *Langdon*, 12 Q. B. 711. It makes no difference that the witness happens to be the attesting witness to the deed, for his knowledge of the contents would not be acquired in that capacity. *Mills* v. *Oddy*, 6 C. & P. 731, 733, Parke, B. But the attorney for either party may be interrogated as to his *possession* of the document required, for the purpose of letting in secondary evidence (due notice to produce having been given), although he obtained it from his client only in the course of communication with reference to the cause. *Coates* v. *Birch*, 2 Q. B. 252; 1 Dowl. N. S. 540. He may also be compelled to show *the indorsement* or outside of the deed or document to enable another witness to *identify* it. *Phelps* v. *Prew*, 3 E. & B. 430. Unless, indeed, the document be of such a nature that it cannot be produced for identification without disclosing the contents. *Brard* v. *Ackerman*, 5 Exch. 119. The judge has no right to look at the instrument to see if the objection to produce it, or to disclose its contents, be well founded or not. *Volant* v. *Soyer*, 13 C. B. 231; *Doe* d. *Carter* v. *James*, 2 Moo. & Rob. 47, Lord Denman, C. J. The witness, although excused from producing the deed, may be compelled to state on oath the date of the deed, and the names of the parties to it, in order to identify it. *Doe* d. *Loscombe* v. *Clifford*, 2 Car. & K. 448. "The witness says, I decline to produce *this deed*, and then I must know what 'this deed' is, so as to identify it." *Id.* 451, Alderson, B. If the attorney be willing to state the contents of the deed (though not compellable to do so), his evidence is admissible. *Hibberd* v. *Knight*, 2 Exch. 11; *Marston* v. *Downes*, 6 C. & P. 381; 1 A. & E. 31; 4 N. & M. 861, *S. C.* "From the reports of *Marston* v. *Downes* it would seem as if the attorney was compelled against his will to state the contents of his client's deed; whereas the real decision in that case was, that if he willingly do so the court will receive his evidence, not that he would be punished for refusing." *Per* Alderson, B., in *Hibberd* v. *Knight*, *supra*; see also *Doe* d. *Earl of Egremont* v. *Langdon*, 12 Q. B. 711. But query, whether an attorney will in all cases be permitted to betray his client. *Ante*, 192.

If Documents produced.]—When a witness brings with him the documents mentioned in his subpœna, and makes no valid objection to their production, they must be *proved* in the usual manner before they can be given in evidence. It makes no difference in this respect that the deed has been cancelled. *Breton* v. *Cope*, 1 Peake, N. P. C.

44, Lord Kenyon, C. J. Where no parol evidence is required from a witness who produces a document in obedience to a *subpœna duces tecum*, he need not be sworn. *Summers* v. *Moseley*, 2 Cr. & Mee. 477; 4 Tyr. 158; *Evans* v. *Moseley*, 2 Cr. & Mee. 490; 4 Tyr. 109; 2 Dowl. 364; *Perry* v. *Gibson*, 1 A. & E. 48. If sworn by mistake, but not examined, he cannot be cross-examined. *Rush* v. *Smith*, 1 Cr. M. & R. 94; 2 Dowl. 687.

Consequences of Disobedience. 1. To the Parties in the Cause.]— When the witness does not appear, or does not bring with him the documents (having them in his possession), or refuses to produce them, although ordered to do so by the judge, it seems that secondary evidence cannot be given of the contents. *Ante*, 195. Where the witness is *excused* from producing them, secondary evidence may be given, *ante*, 195, except, perhaps, where the witness holds the documents as attorney for a party to the suit, and notice to produce has not been duly served. *Lloyd* v. *Mostyn*, 10 M. & W. 478; 2 Dowl. N. S. 476; *Bate* v. *Kinsey*, 1 Cr. M. & R. 38; but see *Phelps* v. *Prew*, 3 E. & B. 430.

A witness for the plaintiff may be called on his *subpœna duces tecum before the jury are sworn*, in the same manner and with the like consequences as upon a *subpœna ad testificandum. Ante*, 181.

2. *To the Witness.*]—The witness may be punished by attachment in the same manner as for not obeying a *subpœna ad testificandum: ante*, 183; *Reg.* v. *Lord John Russell and Fox Maule*, 7 Dowl. 693; *Reg.* v. *Greenaway and Carey*, 7 Q. B. 134: or an action on the case may be maintained against him either for not attending to testify: *Lamont* v. *Crook*, 8 Dowl. 737: or for not producing the documents required. *Amey* v. *Long*, 9 East, 473; *Barber* v. *Wood*, 2 Moo. & Rob. 172; *Davis* v. *Lovell*, 4 M. & W. 678; 7 Dowl. 178. As to the form of declaration, see 2 Chit. Pl. 570 (7th ed.); *Davis* v. *Lovell*, and *Lamont* v. *Crook*, *supra;* also the cases cited, *ante*, 185. It would, however, seem that an action of debt on the statute 5 Eliz. c. 9, s. 12, would not lie for not producing documents in obedience to a *subpœna duces tecum, but only for not attending to testify, &c.; ante*, 186; and even in such case the remedy is so defective that it is never resorted to.

III. Subpœnas for service in Scotland or Ireland.

By 17 & 18 Vict. c. 34, s. 1, "if, in any action or suit now or at any time hereafter depending in any of her majesty's superior courts of common law at *Westminster* or *Dublin*, or the court of session or exchequer in *Scotland*, it shall appear to the court in which such action is pending, or, if such court is not sitting, to any judge of any of the said courts respectively, that it is proper to compel the personal attendance at any trial of any witness who may not be within the jurisdiction of the court in which such action is pending, it shall be lawful for such court or judge, if in his or their discretion it shall so seem fit, to order that a writ called a writ of *subpœna ad testificandum*, or of *subpœna duces tecum*, or warrant of citation, shall issue in special form, commanding such witness to attend such trial wherever he shall be within the United Kingdom, and the service of any such writ or process in any part of the United Kingdom shall be as valid and effectual to all intents and purposes as if the same had been served within the jurisdiction of the court from which it issues."

2. "Every such writ shall have at foot thereof a statement or notice that the same is issued by the special order of the court or judge, as the case may be, and no such writ shall issue without such special order."

3. "In case any person so served shall not appear according to the exigency of such writ or process, it shall be lawful for the court out of which the same issued, upon proof made of the service thereof, and of such default, to the satisfaction of the said court, to transmit a certificate of such default under the seal of the same court, or under the hand of one of the judges or justices of the same, to any of her majesty's superior courts of common law at *Westminster*, in case such service was had in *England*, or in case such service was had in *Scotland* to the court of session or exchequer at *Edinburgh*, or in case such service was had in *Ireland*, to any of her majesty's superior courts of common law at *Dublin*, and the court to which such certificate is so sent shall and may thereupon proceed against and punish the person so having made default, in like manner as they might have done if such person had neglected or refused to appear in obedience to a writ of subpœna or other process issued out of such last-mentioned court."

4. "None of the said courts shall in any case proceed against or punish any person for having made default by not appearing to give evidence in obedience to any writ of subpœna or other process issued under the powers given by this act, unless it shall be made to appear to such court that a reasonable and sufficient sum of money to defray the expenses of coming and attending to give evidence, and of returning from giving such evidence, had been tendered to such person, at the time when such writ of subpœna or process was served upon such person."

5. "Nothing herein contained shall alter or affect the power of any of such courts to issue a commission for the examination of witnesses out of their jurisdiction, in any case in which, notwithstanding this act, they shall think fit to issue such commission."

6. "Nothing herein contained shall alter or effect the admissibility of any evidence at any trial where such evidence is now by law receivable, on the ground of any witness being beyond the jurisdiction of the court, but the admissibility of all such evidence shall be determined as if this act had not passed." *For the forms of Writs and Proceedings under this Act, see Appendix, Nos.* 195 *to* 198.

According to the previous law, if it appeared at the trial that an attesting witness was in Ireland or Scotland, proof of his handwriting was sufficient in like manner as if he were dead. *Doe* d. *Counsell* v. *Caperton*, 9 C. & P. 112, Alderson, B.

IV. Habeas Corpus for Debtors to Testify.

If the witness be in custody under civil process an application must be made to a judge at chambers (not to the court, *Brown* v. *Gisborne*, 21 Law J., N. S., Q. B., 297) for a writ of *habeas corpus ad testificandum;* such application must be founded upon an affidavit, stating that the party in custody is a material witness and willing to attend. *See the form, Appendix, No.* 199. The judge will thereupon grant his fiat for the writ. Engross the writ on parchment. *See the form, Appendix, No.* 200. Take it to the judge's chambers and obtain his signature on the back. *Rex* v. *Roddam,* Cowp. 672. Make out a precipe for the writ. *Form, Appendix, No.* 201. Take it and the writ to the masters' office and get the writ sealed, then leave it with the officer to whom it is directed, and pay or tender him his reasonable fees.

V. WARRANT OR ORDER FOR CRIMINALS TO TESTIFY.

By 16 Vict. c. 30, s. 9, "it shall be lawful for one of her majesty's principal secretaries of state, or any judge of the Court of Queen's Bench or Common Pleas, or any baron of the Exchequer, in any case where he may see fit to do so, *upon application by affidavit* to issue a warrant or order under his hand for bringing up any prisoner or person confined in any gaol, prison or place under any sentence or under commitment for trial or otherwise (except under process in any civil action, suit or proceeding), before any court, judge, justice or other judicature to be examined as a witness in any cause or matter, civil or criminal, depending, or to be inquired of, or determined in or before such court, judge, justice or judicature ; and the person required by any such warrant or order to be so brought before such court, judge, justice or other judicature shall be so brought under the same care and custody, and be dealt with in like manner in all respects, as a prisoner required by any writ of *habeas corpus* awarded by any of her majesty's superior courts of law at Westminster, to be brought before such court to be examined as a witness in any cause or matter depending before such court is now by law required to be dealt with."

CHAPTER XX.

DISCOVERY OF EVIDENCE BEFORE THE TRIAL.

1. *Inspection of Documents before the Trial.*]—By 14 & 15 Vict. c. 99, s. 6, "whenever any action or other legal proceeding shall henceforth be pending in any of the superior courts of common law at *Westminster* or *Dublin,* or in the Court of Common Pleas for the county palatine of *Lancaster,* or the Court of Pleas for the county of *Durham,* such court and each of the judges thereof may respectively, on application made for such purpose by either of the litigants compel the opposite party to allow the party making the application *to inspect all documents* in the custody or under the control of such opposite party *relating to such action* or other legal proceeding, and, if necessary, to take examined copies of the same, or to procure the same to be duly stamped, in all cases in which previous to the passing of this act *a discovery might have been obtained* by filing a bill, or by any other proceeding in a court of equity, at the instance of the party so making application as aforesaid to the said court or judge."

This section has not given the courts of common law the power of compelling a *discovery,* but only of allowing an *inspection* of documents, subject to the following limitations :—first, there must be an action or other proceeding pending ; secondly, the document must relate to such action or other proceeding ; and thirdly, the case must be one in which a discovery could be obtained in a court of equity. *Hunt* v. *Hewitt,* 7 Exch. 236. The affidavits must be positive and sufficient as to the facts necessary to bring the case within the statute. *Pepper* v. *Chambers,* 7 Exch. 226 ; *Sneider* v. *Mangino, Id.* 229.

Besides the authority given by this act the courts possess a common law jurisdiction of an extensive nature, to order the production of deeds and writings, where it is shown that the party applying has any interest in them, and has no copy. *Bluck* v. *Gompertz,* 7 Exch. 67 ; 2 Low, M. & P. 597 ; *Doe d. Child* v. *Roe,* 1 E. & B. 279 ; *Webb* v. *Adkins,* 14 C. B. 401 ; 2 Chit. Arch. 1347 (9th ed.). They have also further jurisdiction under the 17 & 18 Vict. c. 125, s. 50 (*post,* 201).

In an ejectment for a forfeiture the defendant will not be compelled, *under this act,* to produce the lease or any other document tending to establish the forfeiture. *May* v. *Hawkins*, 11 Exch. 210; but see *Doe* d. *Morris* v. *Roe*, 1 M. & W. 207; Tyr. & Gr. 545; *Chester* v. *Wortley*, 17 C. B. 410. Nor where the defendant's act would render him liable to a criminal prosecution. *Cartwright* v. *Green*, 8 Ves. 405.

A party is not entitled to search his adversary's deeds and writings *to find out a flaw in his title;* but if the documents sought to be inspected can be shown to afford evidence in support of the applicant's case, by recitals or otherwise, the circumstance that they are the title deeds of the opposite party will afford no objection. *Smith* v. *Duke of Beaufort*, 1 Phil. R. 209, 219; *Hunt* v. *Hewitt*, 7 Exch. 236; *Scott* v. *Walker*, 2 E. & B. 555; *Riccard* v. *The Inclosure Commissioners*, 4 E. & B. 329. Thus, in ejectment, the deeds which constitute the title of the defendant may be inspected as evidence for the plaintiff, if it appear by the affidavits in support of the application that the recitals tend to support the plaintiff's case by showing his pedigree. *Coster* v. *Baring*, 2 Com. Law R. 811, C. P.; and see *Riccard* v. *The Inclosure Commissioners*, 4 E. & B. 329. Where a lease is executed by both the landlord and tenant, the lessor, not having a counterpart, is entitled on bringing ejectment for a forfeiture, to demand an inspection and copy of the lease from a mortgagee to whom it has been assigned by way of mortgage. *Doe* d. *Morris* v. *Roe*, 1 M. & W. 207; Tyr. & Gr. 545; but see *May* v. *Hawkins*, 11 Exch. 210. Whatever advances the plaintiff's case may be inquired into by the plaintiff, though it may at the same time bring out matter which the defendant relies upon for his defence; but the plaintiff cannot inquire into that which is exclusively matter of defence—that which is common to both the plaintiff and defendant may be inquired into by either. Wigram on Discovery, 13—15, recognized by Lord Campbell, C. J., in *Whateley* v. *Crawford*, and *Carew* v. *Davis*, 26 Law Times R. 104; and see 17 C. B. 425. Inspection may be granted at the instance of the plaintiff for obtaining any evidence necessary to support the plaintiff's original case, or to meet the defendant's case; though not for information, showing how the defendant's case will be supported. *Scott* v. *Walker*, 2 E. & B. 555.

2. *Discovery and Production of Documents before the Trial.*]—By 17 & 18 Vict. c. 125, s. 50, "upon the application of either party to any cause or other civil proceeding in any of the superior courts, upon an affidavit by such party of his belief that any document, *to the production of which he is entitled for the purpose of discovery or otherwise,* is in the possession or power of the opposite party, it shall be lawful for the court or judge to order that the party against whom such application is made, or if such party is a body corporate that some officer to be named of such body corporate, shall *answer on affidavit,* stating what documents he or they has or have in his or their possession or power relating to the matters in dispute, or what he knows as to the custody they or any of them are in, and whether he or they objects or object (and if so on what grounds) to the production of such as are in his or their possession or power; and upon such affidavit being made the court or judge may make such further order thereon as shall be just."

Where a discovery as to the *contents* of any document is wanted, the application must be made under this section, and not under sect. 51. *Infra; Scott* v. *Zygomala*, 4 E. & B. 483.

Sect. 50 is not confined to cases wherein a discovery might previously have been obtained by filing a bill in equity. It extends to any document, "to the production whereof he is entitled for the purpose of discovery *or otherwise.*" *Per* Parke, B., in *Osborne* v. *The London Dock Company*, 10 Exch. 702. The 14 & 15 Vict. c. 99, s. 6, is differently worded in this respect. *Ante*, 200.

The attorney for the party need not join in the affidavit in support of an application under sect. 50, though he must do so under sect. 51. *See form of Affidavit, Appendix, No.* 202. It would seem that if the party swear to his belief that any particular document, to the production of which he is entitled for the purpose of discovery or otherwise, is in the possession or power of the opposite party, an application of a *general nature* may be made. *Ante*, 201; *see forms of Summons and Order, Appendix, Nos.* 203—207.

An application under sect. 50 may be made by a defendant in a personal action *before* plea pleaded. *Forshaw* v. *Lewis*, 10 Exch. 712. But a discovery under sect. 51 cannot be obtained by a defendant in a personal action before plea pleaded, except under special circumstances of extreme urgency. *Martin* v. *Hemming*, 10 Exch. 478.

It is no answer to an application under sect. 50, that the documents are such as the party is privileged for producing; if that be so, the fact may be shown in the affidavit to be made in obedience to the rule, as a ground or excuse for their non-production. *Forshaw* v. *Lewis*, 10 Exch. 712. An affidavit of the party's attorney, stating his belief that the documents if produced will criminate, or tend to criminate, his client, is no answer to the application; the party himself may state *that* on oath, as a ground or excuse for objecting to the production of the documents. *Osborne* v. *The London Dock Company*, 10 Exch. 698. The objection should be so stated in the affidavit in answer, that the court or judge may be able to decide as to its validity upon the subsequent application for production of the documents. *S. C.*

It does not appear by sect. 50, that the party is bound to answer as to any documents not in his possession or power, nor to state his objections (if any) to their production.

The affidavit when made must be filed at the masters' office, but no notice of its having been filed need be given, except as a matter of courtesy. The opposite party or his attorney should search for the affidavit, and obtain an office copy; after which the court or a judge "may make such further order thereon as shall be just." *Ante*, 201.

3. *Examination upon Interrogatories of the opposite Party.*]—By 17 & 18 Vict. c. 125, s. 51, "in *all causes* in any of the superior courts, by order of the court or a judge, the plaintiff may, with the declaration, and the defendant may, with the plea, or either of them *by leave of the court or a judge may at any other time*, deliver to the opposite party or his attorney (provided such party, if not a body corporate, *would be liable to be called and examined as a witness upon such matter*) *interrogatories in writing upon any matter as to which discovery may be sought*, and require such party, or in the case of a body corporate any of the officers of such body corporate, within ten days to answer the questions in writing by affidavit, to be sworn and filed in the ordinary way; and any party or officer omitting, *without just cause*, sufficiently

to answer all questions as to which a discovery may be sought within the above time, or such extended time as the court or a judge shall allow, shall be deemed to have committed a contempt of the court, and shall be liable to be proceeded against accordingly."

By sect. 52, "the application for such order shall be made upon an affidavit of the party proposing to interrogate, *and* his attorney or agent, or, in the case of a body corporate, of their attorney or agent, stating that the deponents or deponent believe or believes that the party proposing to interrogate, whether plaintiff or defendant, *will derive material benefit in the cause from the discovery* which he seeks, that there is a good cause of action or defence *upon the merits,* and if the application be made on the part of the defendant, that the discovery is not sought for the purpose of delay; provided, that where it shall happen, from unavoidable circumstances, that the plaintiff or defendant cannot join in such affidavit, the court or judge may, if they or he think fit, upon affidavit of such circumstances by which the party is prevented from so joining therein, allow and order that the interrogatories may be delivered without such affidavit."

Sect. 51 extends to "all causes," and consequently to actions of ejectment, wherein a discovery before the trial may frequently be material. *Flitcroft* v. *Fletcher,* 11 Exch. 543 ; *Chester* v. *Wortley,* 17 C. B. 410. But as there are no pleadings in ejectment the interrogatories can be delivered by either party only within a time to be specially allowed in that behalf by the court or a judge. The court or a judge will exercise a discretion in allowing or refusing interrogatories to be exhibited. The court has refused such permission in an ejectment for a forfeiture, where the object of the interrogatories was to discover whether a forfeiture had been committed, and to obtain evidence of such forfeiture. *May* v. *Hawkins,* 11 Exch. 210. But in a more recent case it was decided that such interrogatories might be delivered, and that the defendant might perhaps decline to answer them, stating on oath his reason or excuse for not answering each question. *Chester* v. *Wortley,* 17 C. B. 410; *Osborne* v. *The London Dock Company,* 10 Exch. 698; *Doe* d. *Morris* v. *Roe,* 1 M. & W. 207 ; *Tyr.* & *Gr.* 545. The court or a judge will order the plaintiff to answer interrogatories, notwithstanding he is a foreigner residing abroad. *Pohl* v. *Young,* 25 Law J., N. S., Q. B., 23.

The interrogatories should be drawn or settled by counsel. *See the forms, Appendix, Nos.* 213, 214. They need not be confined to matters as to which a discovery might previously have been obtained in a court of equity ; but may extend to "any matter as to which discovery is sought," and with respect to which the party interrogated "would be liable to be called and examined as a witness upon such matter." *Ante,* 202 ; *per* Parke, B., in *Osborne* v. *The London Dock Company,* 10 Exch. 702 ; *Thöl* v. *Leask, Id.* 704 ; *Martin* v. *Hemming, Id.* 478. They should not inquire as to the contents of any written instrument, nor require a copy of it to be set forth. But they may inquire as to the *possession* of the document, and whether the party objects (and if so, on what grounds) to its production and inspection by the interrogating party, and his attorney or agent, &c.; and afterwards an application may be made for such production and inspection pursuant to sect. 50. *Ante,* 201 ; *Scott* v. *Zygomala,* 4 E. & B. 483.

As a party examined in court as a witness would not be bound to answer any question tending to criminate himself, or to subject him to any forfeiture or penalty, he is not bound to answer written interrogatories of that nature; but, nevertheless, it seems that such questions may be put, and the party may, if he think fit, state on oath his reason or excuse for not answering each question. *Osborne* v. *The London Dock Company*, 10 Exch. 702; *Chester* v. *Wortley*, 17 C. B. 410.

It is not yet clearly settled whether the defendant in ejectment may interrogate the plaintiff as to the nature of his title, and how and by what evidence he proposes or intends to establish it. In *Flitcroft* v. *Fletcher*, 11 Exch. 543, the Court of Exchequer allowed interrogatories as to the plaintiff's pedigree, &c. *See the form, Appendix, No.* 214. But in a more recent case at chambers, Wightman, J., refused to act upon that decision; and held that the defendant could not interrogate the plaintiff as to his own pedigree or title, but only as to matters tending to establish the defendant's title, &c. *Morgan* v. *Nicholl*, 18 Feb. 1856, MSS. It would seem, however, that either party ought to be permitted to interrogate the other as to the nature and particulars of his pedigree or title, but not as to the evidence by which he intends to support it. *Selby* v. *Selby*, 4 Bro. C. C. 11; *Attorney-General* v. *The Corporation of London*, 2 Mac. & Gor. 247, Lord Cottenham, C.; *Metcalf* v. *Hervey*, 1 Ves. sen. 248; all cited in *Flitcroft* v. *Fletcher, supra*. Each party ought to be able to ascertain with precision what case he has to meet, but not to know on what evidence his opponent relies; for that might enable him in an unscrupulous manner to deprive his opponent of such evidence, or some material part of it.

The application for leave to deliver interrogatories must be supported by an affidavit of the party proposing to interrogate, *and* his attorney. *Ante*, 203; *see the forms, Appendix, Nos.* 211, 212. The affidavit must state not merely a good cause of action upon the merits, but a good cause of action of ejectment upon the merits. *May* v. *Hawkins*, 25 Law Times R. 185; 11 Exch. 210. A summons for leave to deliver interrogatories should be obtained and served in the usual manner, together with a copy of the affidavit and proposed interrogatories. *See forms of Summons, Appendix, Nos.* 208, 209. The opposite party is entitled to see the proposed interrogatories upon the hearing of the application, and to object to such of them as may appear improper or informal. The judge will, if necessary, settle them upon hearing the application for leave to deliver them. But there have been conflicting decisions at chambers on this point. When counsel attend on both sides the judge usually expects *them* to settle the draft interrogatories, except as to those parts (if any) upon which they cannot agree. The judge's order is drawn up in the usual manner. *See the form, Appendix, No.* 210. If the judge decline to make an order, an application may be made to the court. *Thöl* v. *Leask*, 10 Exch. 704, 705. Only a rule nisi will be granted in the first instance. *Id.* 704, note (*a*). It is afterwards argued and discharged, or made absolute in the usual manner. It will be no answer to such application that the attorney for the party to be interrogated swears he believes that the questions proposed will criminate his client; such objection ought to be made by the party himself in his answer to the interrogatories. *Osborne* v. *The London Dock Company*, 10 Exch. 698; and see *Forshaw* v. *Lewis, Id.* 712; *Boyle* v. *Wiseman, Id.* 647; *Chester* v. *Wortley*, 17 C. B. 410.

When a judge's order or rule has been obtained, the interrogatories should be copied on paper and delivered to the party to be interrogated or to his attorney, indorsed with a notice requiring such party to answer them by affidavit within ten days. *See forms of Notice, Appendix, Nos.* 213, 214. A copy of the order or rule should be annexed.

An affidavit in answer must be filed at the masters' office within ten days after the interrogatories are delivered, or an order for further time must be obtained. *See forms of Summons and Order, Appendix, Nos.* 215, 216.

If the party interrogated do not, within the limited or extended time, file his answer to the interrogatories, he will thereby be guilty of a contempt of court, and an attachment may be moved for upon an affidavit of the facts. *Scott* v. *Zygomala,* 4 E. & B. 483. The judge's order for leave to deliver the interrogatories need not be made a rule of court: the contempt is not for disobeying *that,* but is created by the act of Parliament. *Ante,* 203. So where the defendant omits to answer sufficiently any particular question "without just cause." *S. C.* In the latter case, instead of moving for an attachment, an application may be made under sect. 53 for an oral examination.

The answer to the interrogatories should be prepared with great care, and be generally settled by counsel. *See the form, Appendix, No.* 217. It should *answer fully all* the questions, or show "just cause" for any omission. *Scott* v. *Zygomala,* 4 E. & B. 483 ; *Forshaw* v. *Cox,* 10 Exch. 712 ; *Boyle* v. *Wiseman, Id.* 647 ; *Osborne* v. *The London Dock Company, Id.* 698 ; *Chester* v. *Wortley,* 17 C. B. 410. But a very evasive or insufficient answer will frequently be allowed to pass without objection, especially where an oral examination could not be obtained in time for the assizes or sitting ; or where from the answer already put in, it is evident that the further discovery when obtained could not safely be used as evidence at the trial, taken in conjunction with the answer already put in. The answer should be filed within the limited or extended time at the masters' office ; but no notice of its having been so filed need be given, except as a matter of courtesy. It is the duty of the interrogating party or his attorney to search for the affidavit.

Oral Examination.]—By 17 & 18 Vict. c. 125, s. 53, "in case of omission, *without just cause,* to answer sufficiently such written interrogatories, it shall be lawful for the court or a judge, at their or his discretion, *to direct an oral examination* of the interrogated party, as to such points as they or he may direct, *before a judge or master;* and the court or judge may by such rule or order, or any subsequent rule or order, command the attendance of such party or parties before the person appointed to take such examination, for the purpose of being orally examined as aforesaid, or the production of any writings or other documents to be mentioned in such rule or order, and may impose therein such terms as to such examination, and the costs of the application, and of the proceedings thereon, and otherwise, as to such court or judge shall seem just."

Sect. 54, "such rule or order shall have the same force and effect, and may be proceeded upon in like manner, as an order made under the said hereinbefore-mentioned act, passed in the first year of the reign of his late majesty King William the Fourth." 1 Will. 4, c. 22, *post,* 206.

Generally speaking, counsel should be instructed to advise on the sufficiency of the affidavit as an answer to the interrogatories; and if necessary to draw the "points" upon which an oral examination should be applied for. *See the form, Appendix, No.* 219. If the answer on any material point be evasive or otherwise insufficient, a summons should be taken out for an oral examination. *See forms of Summons and Order, Appendix, Nos.* 218, 220. It will frequently be advisable to attend this summons by counsel. On hearing the application, the judge will consider the various "points," and he must be satisfied not only that the affidavit does not answer the interrogatories upon the points objected to, but also that the *omission is without just cause.* Sect. 53, *ante,* 205. A party is not bound to answer any matter as to which he could not be called and examined as a witness at the trial, *ex. gr.,* the contents of his title deeds, or of any other document; *Scott* v. *Zygomala,* 4 E. & B. 483; matter tending to criminate himself; *Osborne* v. *The London Dock Company,* 10 Exch. 698; or to render him liable to any penalty or forfeiture; *May* v. *Hawkins,* 11 Exch. 210; *Chester* v. *Wortley,* 17 C. B. 410; matter intrusted to him in professional confidence as an attorney. Facts irrelevant to the matters in question in the cause, and the like.

By 17 & 18 Vict. c. 125, s. 55, "whenever, by virtue of this act, an examination of any witness or witnesses has been taken before a judge of one of the said superior courts, or before a master, the depositions taken down by such examiner shall be returned to and kept in the masters' office of the court in which the proceedings are pending; and office copies of such depositions may be given out, and the depositions may be otherwise used in the same manner as in the case of depositions taken under the hereinbefore-mentioned act, passed in the first year of the reign of his late majesty King William the Fourth." 1 Will. 4, c. 22, *infra.*

Sect. 56, "it shall be lawful for every judge or master named in any such rule or order as aforesaid for taking examinations under this act, and he is hereby required to make, if need be, a special report to the court in which such proceedings are pending touching such examination, and the conduct or absence of any witness or other person thereon or relating thereto; and the court is hereby authorized to institute such proceedings and make such order and orders upon such report as justice may require, and as may be instituted and made in any case of contempt of the court."

Sect. 57, "the costs of every application for any rule or order to be made for the examination of witnesses by virtue of this act, and of the rule or order and proceedings thereon, shall be in the discretion of the court or judge by whom such rule or order is made."

4. *Examination of Witnesses upon Interrogatories.*] — If any material witness for either party be *out of the jurisdiction* of the court, a rule or order may be obtained after issue joined upon proper affidavits for a mandamus or commission to examine witnesses, pursuant to 1 Will. 4, c. 22; *Dye* v. *Bennett,* 1 Low, M. & P. 92; unless, indeed, the witness be in a hostile country. *Barrick* v. *Buba,* 16 C. B. 492. If the witness be *within the jurisdiction,* but unable to attend the trial, a rule or order may be obtained for his examination before one of the masters. *Id.* s. 4. The mode of proceeding in each case is fully stated in 1 Chit. Arch. 312—327 (8th ed.). The application cannot be made before issue joined, except in extreme cases where justice would be

defeated by the exclusion of material evidence. *Finney* v. *Beesley*, 17 Q. B. 86; but see *Braun* v. *Mollett*, 16 C. B. 514. It is not enough to entitle a plaintiff to a mandamus to examine a witness in Australia, to show a mere *probability* that he can give useful evidence. *Lane* v. *Bagshaw*, 16 C. B. 576.

Sect. 10 enacts, "that no examination or deposition to be taken by virtue of this act shall be read in evidence at any time without the consent of the party against whom the same may be offered, unless it shall appear *to the satisfaction of the judge* that the examinant or deponent is beyond the jurisdiction of the court, or dead, or unable from permanent sickness, or other permanent infirmity, to attend the trial; in all or any of which cases the examination and depositions certified under the hands of the commissioners, master, prothonotary or other person taking the same, shall and may without proof of the signature to such certificate be received and read in evidence, *saving just exceptions*."

The judge (not the jury) must be satisfied by evidence at the trial that the witness is then out of the jurisdiction, or dead, or unable from permanent sickness or other permanent infirmity, to attend the trial, before the examination or deposition will be admissible. *Supra.* The fact of the witness being abroad must be shown by somebody who can speak to it of his own knowledge. *Robinson* v. *Markis*, 2 Man. & Ry. 375. Statements in the depositions, or proof of inquiries made at the residence of the witness, and of the answers given, is not sufficient. *Proctor* v. *Lainson*, 7 C. & P. 629; *Robinson* v. *Markis, supra*; but see *Austin* v. *Rumsey*, 2 Car. & K. 736. Proof that on the evening before the trial the witness was with his luggage on board a ship bound for Montreal, the ship being then three quarters of a mile below Gravesend, waiting for her captain to come on board, is not sufficient. *Carruthers* v. *Graham*, Car. & M. 1. But where the witness had actually sailed on his voyage, and the vessel was at the time of the trial driven back into port by contrary winds, his depositions were allowed to be read. *Fonsick* v. *Agar*, 6 Esp. 92; and see *Varicas* v. *French*, 2 Car. & K. 1008; *Ward* v. *Wells*, 1 Taunt. 461; *Falconer* v. *Hanson*, 1 Camp. 172. Whether pregnancy or imminent delivery at the time of the trial constitutes a permanent sickness or other permanent infirmity, within the meaning of the act, is not clear. *Abraham* v. *Newton*, 8 Bing. 274; 1 Moo. & Sc. 384; 1 Dowl. 266, *S. C.* But where a witness is so unwell that there is no probability of his recovering so as to be able to attend the trial, and that is proved by a medical man, the examination may be received. *Pond* v. *Dimes*, 3 Moo. & Sc. 161; 2 Dowl. 730; *Davis* v. *Lowndes*, 7 Dowl. 101.

The depositions may be used as evidence by either party. *Proctor* v. *Lainson*, 7 C. & P. 629.

An office copy of the depositions is admissible without proof of its correctness. *Duncan* v. *Scott*, 1 Camp. 100. The whole of the answers, both to the interrogatories and cross-interrogatories, must be read as part of the party's case who is desirous of making any use of them. *Temperley* v. *Scott*, 5 C. & P. 341; *Wheeler* v. *Atkins*, 5 Esp. 216. But a paper produced to the witness, and upon which he was cross-examined and re-examined, and which is annexed to the depositions, need not be read as part of them. *Stephens* v. *Foster*, 6 C. & P. 280. The contents of a letter (not produced) will be excluded, notwithstanding such letter appears to be abroad. *Steinkeller* v. *Newton*, 9 C. & P.

313. The depositions are admissible notwithstanding it appears that on the examination the witness referred to papers which he refused to allow the commissioners to see. *S. C.* Objectionable questions and depositions, or any part of an objectionable question or deposition, may be excluded from the jury on the trial; but not so by the party who put them. *Hutchinson* v. *Bernard,* 2 Man. & Ry. 1; *Tufton* v. *Whitmore,* 9 Law J., N. S., Q. B., 405; *Williams* v. *Williams,* 4 M. & S. 497. All "just exceptions" to the examinations and depositions are saved by 1 Will. 4, c. 22, s. 10. *Ante,* 207.

The costs of the rule or order and proceedings thereon are usually costs in the cause, "unless otherwise directed either by the judge making such rule or order, or by the judge before whom the cause may be tried, or by the court." *Prince* v. *Samo,* 4 Dowl. 5; *Clay* v. *Stephenson,* 3 A. & E. 307; 5 N. & M. 318. No such costs will be allowed unless the examination or depositions be used at the trial. *Curling* v. *Robertson,* 7 Man. & Gr. 525; 2 D. & L. 307.

5. *Inspection of the Property in question by Jury, the Parties or their Witnesses.*]—By 17 & 18 Vict. c. 125, s. 58, "either party shall be at liberty to apply to the court or a judge for a rule or order for the inspection by the jury, or by himself, or by his witnesses, of any real or personal property, the inspection of which may be material to the proper determination of the question in dispute; and it shall be lawful for the court or a judge, if they or he think fit, to make such rule or order, upon such terms as to costs and otherwise as such court or judge may direct: Provided always, that nothing herein contained shall affect the provisions of the Common Law Procedure Act, 1852, or any previous act, as to obtaining a view by jury: Provided also, that all rules and regulations now in force and applicable to the proceedings by view under the said last-mentioned act shall be held to apply to proceedings for inspection by a jury under the provisions of this act, or as near thereto as may be." *See forms of Summons and Order, Appendix, Nos.* 233, 234.

6. *View.*]—For the mode of proceeding to obtain a view by the jury in the usual manner, see *post,* Chap. XXII.

CHAPTER XXI.

EVIDENCE ON PARTICULAR POINTS FREQUENTLY IN QUESTION IN ACTIONS OF EJECTMENT.

1. *Seisin in Fee.*]—Proof that A. B. was in actual possession of land, or in receipt of the rents and profits thereof, is *primâ facie* evidence that he was then seised in fee-simple. 1 Tayl. Ev. s. 108 (2nd ed.); Ros. Ev. 460 (7th ed.); Ad. Eject. 240; Bull. N. P. 103; 2 Arch. N. P. 340; *Doe d. Graham* v. *Penfold,* 8 C. & P. 536; *Jayne* v. *Price,* 5 Taunt. 326. But in actions of ejectment there seems to be a material difference between proof of possession within twenty years and proof of receipt of rent within twenty years. Payment of rent by an occupier of land is an *act done apparently against his own interest;* and evidence thereof is admissible even as against subsequent tenants in possession or other persons, whether deriving title through or under such occupier or not. *Doe* d. *Manton* v. *Austin,* 9 Bing. 41; *Doe* d. *Earl of Lichfield* v. *Stacey,* 6 C. & P. 139, Tindal, C. J. Proof of payment of rent to the plaintiffs by the person in possession is evidence of their title to the reversion as against all the world, except the person who can prove that he then was legally entitled to the property. *Daintry* v. *Brocklehurst,* 3 Exch. 207. Even a verbal admission of payment of rent made by the person in possession is evidence of such payment as against the person making such admission, or any other claiming through or under him. *Doe* d. *Earl Spencer* v. *Beckett,* 4 Q. B. 601. So receipts for rent produced from the papers of a deceased tenant are admissible evidence of the landlord's seisin in fee. *Doe* d. *Blayney* v. *Savage,* 1 Car. & K. 487. The principle is, that any *act done* by a person in possession, which in effect admits the title of another person, is admissible evidence as against all persons whomsoever. Thus, if a person is seen felling timber in a wood, it is *primâ facie* evidence that he is the owner of it; and therefore anything he says at that or any other time as to any one else being the owner of it is a declaration to cut down his own apparent title, and consequently evidence even as against third persons. *Doe* d. *Stansbury* v. *Arkwright,* 5 C. & P. 575, 578, Park, J.; *Davies* v. *Pierce,* 2 T. R. 53. So payment of rent by the person in possession is an act done. " It is a fact." *Per* Tindal, C. J., in *Doe* d. *Earl of Lichfield* v. *Stacey,* 6 C. & P. 139.

To prove the seisin of an alleged former owner of an estate, the counterpart of a lease of part of the estate was produced from the muniment room of the estate, which counterpart was executed by the lessee, and purported to be a lease granted by the person whose seisin was to be established, and who had died about 100 years before the trial. No possession was proved under the lease: held, admissible in evidence in an ejectment against a party who neither claimed under the lease, nor was privy to it. *Doe* d. *Earl of Egremont* v. *Pulman,* 3 Q. B. 622. Proof of possession of A. B., and of a conveyance from him in fee, is *primâ facie* evidence that at the time of such conveyance he was seised in fee. *Doe* d. *Graham* v. *Penfold,* 8 C. & P. 536, Patteson, J.; and see *Doe* d. *Hindmarch* v. *Oliver,* 1 Car. & K. 543.

Proof of mere possession by the plaintiff, or of the person through whom he claims, within twenty years before action, is not generally sufficient to support an ejectment, because the defendants in such action are *sued as tenants in possession ;* and their possession is presumed to be lawful, in the absence of proof of title in the claimants. *Possessio contra omnes valet præter eum cui jus sit possessionis.* Lofft, Maxims, No. 265. "The plaintiff cannot recover but upon the strength of his own title. He cannot found his claim upon the weakness of the defendant's title ; for possession gives the defendant a good title against every man who cannot show a good title." *Per* Lord Mansfield, C. J., in *Roe* d. *Haldane* v. *Urry and Harvey,* 4 Burr. 2487. The question is, whether the plaintiff is legally entitled to actual possession? Not whether the defendant has any title. *Doe* d. *Oliver* v. *Powell,* 1 A. & E. 531 ; *Doe* d. *Dand* v. *Thompson,* 13 Q. B. 674, 679. If the title be in any third person, the defendant is entitled to the verdict, although he does not pretend to claim under or on behalf of such third person ; *Doe* d. *Wawn* v. *Horn,* 3 M. & W. 333 ; *Doe* d. *Fellowes* v. *Alford,* 1 Dowl. & L. 470 ; *Culley* v. *Doe* d. *Taylerson* (in error), 3 P. & D. 539, 557 ; 11 A. & E. 1008 ; *Doe* d. *Lloyd* v. *Passingham,* 6 B. & C. 305 ; unless indeed the defendant be estopped from disputing the title of the plaintiff. *Post,* 213.

Proof of possession *for twenty years* and upwards is sufficient *primâ facie* evidence of a seisin in fee, even in an action of ejectment. *Doe* d. *Harding* v. *Cooke,* 7 Bing. 346 ; 5 Moo. & P. 181 ; *Denn* d. *Tarzwell* v. *Barnard,* 2 Cowp. 595 ; *Stokes* v. *Berry,* 2 Salk. 421 ; *S. C. nom. Stocker* v. *Berry,* 1 Lord Raym. 741. And this is so especially since the 3 & 4 Will. 4, c. 27, whereby any outstanding right of entry is *extinguished* when the period of twenty years limited by that act is determined. *Ante,* 25. In ejectment the plaintiff proved twenty years' possession, ending about ten years before the commencement of the action, and it appeared that the defendant had been in possession for ten years next before action : held, that the plaintiff was entitled to recover. *Doe* d. *Harding* v. *Cooke,* 7 Bing. 346 ; 5 Moo. & P. 181. In ejectment, if it appear by the record of a special verdict that the plaintiff has a priority of possession, and no title is found for the defendant, the plaintiff shall have judgment. *Allen* v. *Rivington,* 2 Saund. 110 a ; 2 Keb. 606 ; 1 Sid. 445, *S. C.* But, generally speaking, proof of priority of possession for a less period than twenty years is insufficient in ejectment, for the reasons above mentioned. Thus, in ejectment by a widow, proof of possession by her for thirteen years next after her husband's death is insufficient, it appearing that for eighteen years prior to and at the time of his death he was in possession ; because such evidence shows *primâ facie* that he died seised, and his estate would descend to his son and heir ; not to his widow. *Doe* d. *Carter* v. *Barnard,* 13 Q. B. 945.

Possession of land for any less period than twenty years is not presumptive evidence of livery of seisin. *Doe* d. *Wilkins* v. *Marquis of Cleveland,* 9 B. & C. 864 ; *Doe* d. *Lewis* v. *Davies,* 2 M. & W. 503. But after twenty years of possession livery of seisin may be presumed. *Rees* d. *Chamberlain* v. *Lloyd,* Wightw. 123. A plea of *liberum tenementum* to an action of trespass *quare clausum fregit* is not supported by proof of the exercise of acts of ownership by the defendant for a less period than twenty years, where it appears that before the commencement of that period, and also within twenty years, the estate was in a third person. *Brest* v. *Lever*, 7 M. & W. 593; *S. C. nom. Grice* v. *Lever*, 9 Dowl. 246.

If the defendant be shown to be a *mere wrongdoer*, proof of prior possession, and of the wrongful act of the defendant, whereby the plaintiff was deprived of such possession, is sufficient *primâ facie* evidence of title. *Doe* d. *Hughes* v. *Dyeball*, Moo. & Mal. 346; 3 C. & P. 610, Lord Tenterden, C. J. Thus, proof that the plaintiff was in actual possession for one year under a lease, and that the defendant then entered, and turned him out by force, is sufficient to throw upon the defendant the onus of proving his title. *S. C.* In ejectment to recover five houses, it was proved that the claimant had received the rents of some of them for four quarters, and of others for five quarters, down to March, 1841, and that in that month the claimant's receiver of rents found the door of one of the houses *secured by a chain, and the defendant in it, who said that it was his freehold:* held, that this was evidence to go to the jury of title in the claimant; and if there was no evidence of title on the part of the defendant, it would be for the jury to consider whether they were satisfied upon this evidence that the property really belonged to the claimant. *Doe* d. *Humphrey* v. *Martin*, Car. & Mar. 32, Lord Denman, C. J. Where a widow being in possession of a house and garden, the defendant (her stepdaughter) asked leave to get vegetables in the garden, and borrowed the keys for that purpose, and then fraudulently took possession of the house: held, in an action of ejectment by the widow, that the defendant having so obtained possession was estopped from disputing the widow's title, and was bound to restore to her the possession before her title could be questioned. *Doe* d. *Johnson* v. *Baytup*, 3 A. & E. 188; 4 N. & M. 837.

Although seisin in fee may be proved *primâ facie* by showing actual possession or receipt of rent, as before mentioned, *ante*, 211, it is frequently more advisable in an ejectment to prove it by producing the deed or will, whereby the fee is granted or devised, and proving the execution thereof in the usual manner: also that the grantor or testator was in actual possession, or receipt of the rents; *Doe* d. *Graham* v. *Penfold*, 8 C. & P. 536; or a subsequent possession under and by virtue of the deed or will. It is not generally advisable to rely on a mere *primâ facie* case, where a good title can be proved by conclusive evidence, unless there be some special reason for so doing, *ex. gr.*, the difficulty of proof; or the great expense, and the poverty of the defendant; or the wish to avoid disclosing the real title, and the contents of the deeds, &c.; or the impossibility of the defendant rebutting a *primâ facie* case by evidence on his behalf.

2. *Title by Estoppel.*]—1. *As between Landlord and Tenant.*—It is a well-established rule or maxim of law, that a tenant cannot dispute his landlord's title. Lit. s. 58; Co. Lit. 47 b. He will not be allowed to plead or prove that at the time of such demise the lessor *nil habuit in tenementis*, or to that effect. *Blake* v. *Foster*, 8 T. R. 487; *Parker* v. *Manning*, 7 T. R. 537; *Wilkins* v. *Wingate*, 6 T. R. 62. And according to many modern decisions the above maxim is not confined to demises *under seal* (*post*, 214). *Agar* v. *Young*, Car. & M. 78. "The principle is, that a tenant shall not contest his landlord's title; on the contrary, it is his duty to defend it. If he objects to such title let him go out of possession." *Per* Tindal, C. J., in *Doe* d. *Manton* v. *Austin*, 9 Bing. 45; 2 Moo. & Sc. 107; *Agar* v. *Young*, Car. & M. 78,

Erskine, J. The court will not endure a lessee to defend an ejectment against his landlord, or those claiming under him, on a supposed defect of title; *Driver d. Oxenden* v. *Lawrence*, 2 W. Black. 1259; therefore, so long as the tenant, or any person claiming through or under him, *retains possession*, he is estopped from proving that at the time of the demise the lessor had no legal right or title to dispose of such possession. *Barwick* d. *The Mayor and Aldermen of Richmond* v. *Thompson*, 7 T. R. 488; *Driver* d. *Oxenden* v. *Lawrence*, 2 W. Black. 1259; *Francis* v. *Doe* d. *Harvey* (in error), 4 M. & W. 331, 336; 7 Dowl. 193. Thus, he will not be permitted to prove that at the time of the demise the lessor had only an equitable estate; *Blake* v. *Foster*, 8 T. R. 487; *Francis* v. *Doe* d. *Harvey*, *supra*; *Doe* d. *Nepean* v. *Budden*, 5 B. & A. 626; *Doe* d. *Marriott* v. *Edwards*, 6 C. & P. 208; 5 B. & Adol. 1065; 3 N. & M. 193, *S. C.*; or that he had previously let the property to a tenant from year to year, who had absconded, but whose tenancy had never been determined by notice to quit, surrender, or otherwise; *Phipps* v. *Sculthorpe*, 1 B. & A. 50; *Doe* d. *Manners* v. *Mizem*, 2 Moo. & Rob. 56, Parke, J.; and see *Bringloe* v. *Goodson*, 4 Bing. N. C. 726; 6 Scott, 502; or that he had mortgaged the property, and such mortgage had become forfeited before the demise; *Alchorne* v. *Gomme*, 2 Bing. 54; 9 Moo. 143; *Doe* d. *Leeming* v. *Skirrow*, 7 A. & E. 157; unless, indeed, he goes on to show that the mortgagee, by the threat of an ejectment, has since compelled him to attorn and become his tenant; *Doe* d. *Higginbotham* v. *Barton and Warburton*, 11 A. & E. 307; 3 P. & D. 194; nor can a tenant of glebe land, who has paid rent to the incumbent, be permitted to prove a simoniacal presentation of the plaintiff, in order to avoid his title. *Cooke* v. *Loxley*, 5 T. R. 4. A person who holds possession under B. cannot dispute B.'s title (in an ejectment by his assignees in bankruptcy), on the ground that the lease to B. from the crown was illegal and void. *Doe* d. *Biddle* v. *Abrahams*, 1 Stark. R. 305, Lord Ellenborough, C. J. Where the plaintiffs " as trustees of the joint estate of A. & B. deceased" (by their agents in that behalf) demised certain premises to the defendant: held, that he could not dispute their title by showing that they were not trustees of the joint estate of A. & B. deceased, but only of the separate estate of B. *Fleming* v. *Gooding*, 10 Bing. 549; 4 Moo. & Sc. 455; and see *Doe* d. *Bord* v. *Burton*, 16 Q. B. 807. Where a lessee accepted a lease and executed a counterpart, which purported to be made in exercise of a power contained in the will of P. S.: held proof as against the lessee of the due execution of the will. *Bringloe* v. *Goodson*, 5 Bing. N. C. 738; 8 Scott, 71.

The rule is not confined to actual tenancies for a definite term, but extends to constructive or implied tenancies at will; and even to tenancies at sufferance; *per* Cresswell, J., in *Doe* d. *Bailey* v. *Foster*, 3 C. B. 229. Thus, where A. lets B. into possession of land, &c., under a contract for the sale of it, and the purchase afterwards goes off for want of a sufficient title, or for any other reason, whereupon A. demands possession and brings ejectment, B. cannot dispute A.'s title. *Doe* d. *Bord* v. *Burton*, 16 Q. B. 807. So, where B. is let into possession by A. under an agreement for a lease, which is never executed, nor any rent paid, and the implied tenancy at will is determined by a demand of possession or otherwise, A.'s title cannot be disputed. *Agar* v. *Young*, Car. & M. 78; *Doe* d. *Bailey* v. *Foster*, 3 C. B. 215, 229. If possession be taken under a mere parol license, that is sufficient to estop the party from afterwards disputing the licensor's right to dispose of the possession. Thus, where a widow, being in possession of a house and garden, the defendant (her stepdaughter) asked leave to get vegetables in the garden, and borrowed the keys for that purpose, and then fraudulently took possession of the house, and set up a claim of title: held, in an action of ejectment by the widow, that the defendant, having so obtained possession, was estopped from disputing the widow's title, and was bound to restore to her the possession before her title could be questioned. *Doe d. Johnson* v. *Baytup,* 3 A. & E. 188; and see *Doe* d. *Willis* v. *Birchmore,* 9 A. & E. 662; 1 P. & D. 448.

A title by estoppel is established by proof of the lease, or agreement, or licence (whether in writing or otherwise), and of the entry or *possession by virtue thereof.* If it be in writing it must be produced properly stamped, and admitted in the cause (*ante,* 150), or proved in the usual manner.

Where the state of the title appears by recital or otherwise on the face of the deed, neither party is estopped by any other part of the deed from taking advantage of the truth. Co. Lit. 352 b; Vin. Abr. Estoppel, A. 2; *Doe* d. *North* v. *Webber,* 3 Bing. N. C. 922, 925; *Pargeter* v. *Harris,* 7 Q. B. 708; *Right* d. *Jefferys* v. *Bucknell,* 2 B. & Adol. 278; *Doe* d. *Barker* v. *Goldsmith,* 2 Cr. & Jer. 674; 2 Tyr. 710; *Hermitage* v. *Tomkins,* 1 Ld. Ray. 729.

An estoppel on a tenant from denying his landlord's title may be met by a counter estoppel on the landlord from denying the tenant's right to hold under another person. *Downs* v. *Cooper,* 2 Q. B. 256.

An estoppel ends with the lease, and *then* both parts of the deed belong to the lessor. Co. Lit. 48 a; *Rawlyn's case,* 4 Co. R. 52 a; 4 Leon, 116; Golds. 89, 93; *James* v. *Landon,* Cro. Eliz. 36; Moore, 181, *S. C.* But it seems that the estoppel will continue so long as the tenant or any person claiming under him retains possession of the land after the expiration of the lease. *Doe* d. *Manton* v. *Austin,* 9 Bing. 41; 2 Moo. & Sc. 107. In a recent case it was decided, that a lease belongs to the tenant after the expiration of the term, and not to the landlord.

The rule that a tenant cannot dispute his landlord's title extends to all persons who claim or obtain *possession through or under the tenant.* They are respectively estopped in like manner and to the same extent as the tenant himself. *Cooper* v. *Blandy,* 1 Bing. N. C. 45; 4 Moo. & Sc. 562; *Doe* d. *Milburn* v. *Edgar,* 2 Bing. N. C. 498; 2 Scott, 581; *Doe* d. *Manton* v. *Austin,* 9 Bing. 41; 2 Moo. & Sc. 107; and see 4 Q. B. 368, note. Thus, an assignee of the term is so estopped; *Taylor* v. *Needham,* 2 Taunt. 278; also an undertenant; *Barwick* d. *The Mayor and Aldermen of Richmond* v. *Thompson,* 7 T. R. 488; *Doe* d. *Higginbotham* v. *Barton and Warburton,* 11 A. & E. 307; 3 P. & D. 194; *Doe* d. *Manton* v. *Austin,* 9 Bing. 41; 2 Moo. & Sc. 107; *Doe* d. *Earl Spencer* v. *Beckett,* 4 Q. B. 601; *Id.* 605, per Lord Denman, C. J.; *Atkinson* v. *Coatsworth,* 1 Stra. 512; 8 Mod. 33; so is any person who obtained possession from the tenant or undertenant by an arrangement made with him, whether by collusion or otherwise, but without any deed of assignment or underlease.—He will not be permitted to defend such possession by proof of a title *aliunde.* Doe d. *Buller* v. *Mills,* 2 A. & E. 17; 4 N. & M. 25; *Doe* d. *Haden* v. *Burton,* 9 C. & P. 254, Gurney, B.; *Doe* d. *Thomas* v. *Shadwell,* 7

Dowl. 527. Previous to 1812, a person built a house on a piece of waste ground, and before he acquired a title to it, gave up possession to the tenant of the adjoining land, who held under a lease granted in 1812. The latter let the premises to the defendant: held, in ejectment by the landlord of the adjoining land, that the defendant was estopped from denying the title of the tenant, and the tenant from disputing that of the landlord. *Doe* d. *Wheeble* v. *Fuller,* Tyr. & Gr. 17. The widow of a tenant, who remains in possession after his death, is estopped from denying the landlord's title, in like manner as the tenant himself would have been had he lived. *Doe* d. *Leeming* v. *Skirrow,* 7 A. & E. 157; *Doe* d. *Nepean* v. *Budden,* 5 B. & A. 626. So is a devisee of the tenant. *Doe* d. *Willis* v. *Birchmore,* 9 A. & E. 662; 1 P. & D. 448. So is an undertenant, or any person who obtained possession from him upon or after the expiration of the lease. *Doe* d. *Manton* v. *Austin,* 9 Bing. 41; 2 Moo. & Sc. 107. If the defendant be shown to have come into possession after the tenant entered, and during the continuance of the demise, he will be presumed, in the absence of proof to the contrary, to have obtained such possession as assignee of the term. *Doe* d. *Morris* v. *Williams,* 6 B. & C. 41; 9 D. & R. 30; and see *Roe* d. *Blair* v. *Street and Fairbanks,* 2 A. & E. 329, 331; *Hindley* v. *Rickerby,* 5 Esp. 4; *Rees* d. *Mears* v. *Perrott,* 4 C. & P. 230. Proof of payment of rent to the plaintiff by a previous occupier, then in possession, is admissible evidence of the plaintiff's title as against any subsequent tenant in possession, whether claiming through or under such occupier or not. *Doe* d. *Earl of Lichfield* v. *Stacey,* 6 C. & P. 139; *Doe* d. *Manton* v. *Austin,* 9 Bing. 41; *Doe* d. *Earl Spencer* v. *Beckett,* 4 Q. B. 601; *Daintry* v. *Brocklehurst,* 3 Exch. 207.

Where the tenant in possession is estopped from disputing the claimant's title, any third person let in to defend *as his landlord* will be estopped in like manner, and will not be permitted to prove a distinct title in himself to defeat the action. *Doe* d. *Knight* v. *Lady Smythe,* 4 M. & S. 347; *Doe* d. *Manvers* v. *Mizem,* 2 Moo. & Rob. 56, Patteson, J.; *Doe* d. *Willis* v. *Birchmore,* 9 A. & E. 662; 1 P. & D. 448; *Doe* d. *Mee* v. *Litherland,* 4 A. & E. 784. The principle is that the tenant, &c. must first restore the possession to the person from whom it was obtained, and then if he, or any one claiming by him, has a title *aliunde,* that title may be tried in a subsequent ejectment, in which the onus of proof will lie upon the then claimant. *Doe* d. *Knight* v. *Lady Smythe,* 4 M. & S. 347. But a defendant who defends *as landlord of* L. cannot contend that L. was in possession only as his servant, and not as a tenant, because it is L.'s right of possession as tenant which he defends; and if L. be estopped from denying the claimant's title, the defendant who defends as landlord of L. is estopped in like manner. *Doe* d. *Willis* v. *Birchmore,* 9 A. & E. 662; 1 P. & D. 448; *Doe* d. *Mee* v. *Litherland,* 4 A. & E. 784; 15 & 16 Vict. c. 76, s. 173. If, however, the tenant himself be not estopped, there will be no estoppel on any person defending as his landlord. *Doe* d. *Plevin* v. *Brown,* 7 A. & E. 447. If the tenant has suffered judgment by default, the landlord cannot insist that the tenant was entitled to a notice to quit from the claimant. *Doe* d. *Davis* v. *Creed,* 5 Bing. 327.

The rule that a tenant cannot dispute his landlord's title, extends to persons *claiming the reversion through or under the landlord.* *Driver*

d. *Oxenden* v. *Lawrence,* 2 W. Blac. 1259. Their title cannot be defeated by showing that at the time of the demise the lessor had no right to demise. *Palmer* v. *Ekins,* 2 Ld. Ray. 1550 ; 2 Stra. 817 ; 11 Mod. 407, *S. C.* ; *Parker* v. *Manning,* 7 T. R. 537 ; *Doe* d. *Willis* v. *Birchmore,* 9 A. & E. 662 ; 1 P. & D. 448 ; *Bringloe* v. *Goodson,* 4 Bing. N. C. 726 ; 6 Scott, 502. Thus, in an action by an assignee of the reversion, the defendant will not be permitted to prove that the lessor had no legal reversion to assign, because at the time of the demise the property was vested in the trustees of his marriage settlement for the separate use of his wife : *Rennie* v. *Robinson,* 1 Bing. 147 ; 7 Moore, 539 : or that the lessor was then a bankrupt, and that all his estate had vested in his assignees : *Parker* v. *Manning,* 7 T. R. 537 : or that the lessor had only an equitable estate, and consequently no *legal* reversion. *Rennie* v. *Robinson,* 1 Bing. 147 ; 9 Moore, 539. A reversion by estoppel is a legal estate which will continue during the tenancy, and may be assigned. *Doe* d. *Marriott* v. *Edwards,* 6 C. & P. 208, Parke, J. ; 5 B. & Adol. 1665 ; 3 N. & M. 193, *S. C.* ; *Sturgeon* v. *Wingfield,* 15 M. & W. 224 ; but see *Noke* v. *Awder,* Cro. Eliz. 373, 436, 437.

Although a tenant, or any person claiming or obtaining possession through or under him, cannot dispute the lessor's right to demise, yet he may show that *since the demise* the lessor's title has expired, or been duly determined or defeated ; or that he has since assigned it by way of sale, mortgage or otherwise. And this is obviously founded on good sense and justice, because if such evidence were not permitted the tenant might be compelled to pay the amount of his rent twice over. *Fenner* v. *Duplock,* 2 Bing. 10 ; *Id.* 11, Best, C. J. ; 9 Moore, 38, *S. C.* ; *Mountnoy* v. *Collier,* 1 E. & B. 630 ; *Id.* 636, *per* Coleridge, J. ; *Id.* 640, *per* Erle, J. ; *Agar* v. *Young,* Car. & M. 78 ; *Harmer* v. *Bean,* 3 Car. & K. 307. Therefore a tenant, &c. may prove that at the time of the demise the lessor was possessed only for a term of years which has since expired : *England* d. *Syburn* v. *Slade,* 4 T. R. 682 : or only as tenant for his own life, and that he is dead : *Neave* v. *Moss,* 1 Bing. 360 ; 8 Moore, 389 : or only as tenant for the life of another person, who has since died : *Blake* v. *Foster,* 8 T. R. 487 ; *Roe* d. *Jackson* v. *Ramsbottom,* 3 M. & S. 516 ; *Fenner* v. *Duplock,* 2 Bing. 10 ; 9 Moore, 38 ; *Hill* v. *Saunders,* 2 Bing. 112 ; 9 Moo. 238 ; affirmed in error, 4 B. & C. 529 ; 7 D. & R. 17, *S. C.* ; *Doe* d. *Strode* v. *Seaton,* 2 Cr. M. & R. 728 ; Tyr. & Gr. 19 : or only as tenant from year to year, and that such tenancy has since been determined by a regular notice to quit : *Mountnoy* v. *Collier,* 1 E. & B. 630 : or only as tenant at will, or tenant at sufferance, and that such tenancy has since been duly determined, and that the real owner has relet the premises to the defendant, with the actual or implied acquiescence of the claimant : *Neave* v. *Moss,* 1 Bing. 360 : or that the lessor was only a mortgagor in possession, and that the mortgagee has since given the defendant notice of his title, and requested the defendant to attorn and pay the rent to him, threatening in case of refusal to eject the defendant, or to " put the law in force ;" and that the defendant did accordingly attorn to the mortgagee before the commencement of the action ; because such evidence only shows that at the time of the demise the lessor had a defeasible title, which has since been legally defeated. *Doe* d. *Higginbotham* v. *Barton and Warburton,* 11 A. & E. 307 ; 3 P. & D. 194. The defendant may also

L

prove that since the demise the lessor has parted with his reversion by way of sale, mortgage or otherwise: *Doe* d. *Lowden* v. *Watson*, 2 Stark. R. 230, Lord Ellenborough, C. J.; cited 4 Man. & Gr. 152, *per* Tindal, C. J.; *Doe* d. *Marriott* v. *Edwards*, 6 C. & P. 208, Parke, J.; 5 B. & Adol. 1065; 3 N. & M. 193, *S. C.*; *Agar* v. *Young*, Car. & M. 78; *Harmer* v. *Bean*, 3 Car. & K. 307: or that he has taken the benefit of the act for relief of Insolvent Debtors, and assigned his reversion, &c. to the provisional assignee. *Doe* d. *Palmer* v. *Andrews*, 4 Bing. 348.

Where a tenant after the expiration of his term enters into a new agreement with the same landlord for a further term, and continues in possession, he is thereby estopped from disputing the *then* right or title of the landlord to dispose of such possession. *Doe* d. *Bord* v. *Burton*, 16 Q. B. 807. But if the landlord's previous title had then expired, and the tenant was ignorant of that fact, the new agreement made under such circumstances is not equivalent to a fresh letting into possession, so as to estop the tenant from proving all the facts, or from showing that the landlord's title had previously expired, and that he (the tenant) renewed the tenancy in ignorance and mistake. *Claridge* v. *Mackenzie*, 4 Man. & Gr. 143; but see *Doe* d. *Marlow* v. *Wiggins*, 4 Q. B. 367, 375, 377; *post*, 219. A tenant may show that his landlord was entitled only *pur autre vie*, and that *cestui que vie* is dead, notwithstanding he has since paid rent, or submitted to a distress for rent by his landlord, with knowledge that a third person claimed the property, but without knowing the precise nature of the adverse claim, nor the manner in which the lessor's title had expired. *Fenner* v. *Duploek*, 2 Bing. 10; 9 Moore, 38. It has been held at nisi prius, that where the defendant came in under the plaintiff, he cannot show that the plaintiff's title has since expired, unless he then solemnly renounced the plaintiff's title, and commenced a fresh holding under another person. *Balls* v. *Westwood*, 2 Camp. 11, Lord Ellenborough, C. J. But there are many subsequent decisions the other way. *Ante*, 217; *Mountnoy* v. *Collier*, 1 E. & B. 630.

If the claimant be not the person from whom the possession was originally obtained, but there has been an attornment to him, or a renewed tenancy, or a payment of rent, or a distress submitted to, the defendant may sometimes show that the claimant really had no title, and that the attornment or payment, &c. was by mistake or in ignorance of material facts. *Rogers* v. *Pitcher*, 6 Taunt. 202; *Brook* v. *Briggs*, 2 Bing. N. C. 572; *Hughes* v. *Hughes*, 15 M. & W. 703, *per cur.*; 2 Smith, L. C. 459. Thus, where A. demised to B., and afterwards committed an act of bankruptcy, and then assigned to the plaintiffs as trustees for his creditors, and induced B. to attorn to them and pay 1*s.* on account of rent: held, in an ejectment by the plaintiffs against B., which was defended by the assignees in bankruptcy as the landlords of B., that neither B. nor the assignees were estopped from disputing the validity of the assignment to the plaintiffs, B. not having obtained the possession from them, and having been induced to attorn under the supposition that the assignment to the plaintiffs was valid, and in ignorance that A. had previously committed an act of bankruptcy. *Doe* d. *Plevin* v. *Brown*, 7 A. & E. 447. Where a lessee for years attorned to the plaintiffs as sequestrators of the estate of the lessor, to hold for such time and upon such terms as might be subsequently agreed on: held, that as he had not obtained possession from the plaintiffs, he was not estopped from denying their title, or their legal estate as sequestrators, nor from using his lease as a defence to an action by them for use and occupation. *Cornish* v. *Searell,* 8 B. & C. 471. Where A., being tenant to B., who died, afterwards attorned to C. as heir of B. in ignorance that C.'s title as heir was disputed : held, that A. was not thereby estopped from showing that C. really had no title to the property, and that the attornment to him was a mistake. *Gregory* v. *Dioge,* 3 Bing. 474.

On the other hand, where the tenant had attorned and paid rent to a devisee of the landlord, and no fraud or misrepresentation had been practised towards him : held, that he could not afterwards dispute the devisee's title by evidence showing that the testator was incompetent to make a will. *Doe* d. *Marlow* v. *Wiggins,* 4 Q. B. 367. So, where a tenant of glebe land has paid rent to the subsequent incumbent, he will not be permitted to dispute his title by evidence of a simoniacal presentation of the incumbent. *Cooke* v. *Loxley,* 5 T. R. 4 ; and see *Doe* d. *Biddle* v. *Abrahams,* 1 Stark. R. 305. A. and B., tenants in common, having agreed to divide their property, and that *Blackacre* should belong to A. ; the occupier of Blackacre who, after this agreement, had paid his whole rent to A., cannot, in an ejectment brought against him by A., object that the partition deed between A. and B. is not executed. *Doe* d. *Pritchett* v. *Mitchell,* 1 Brod. & B. 11 ; 3 Moore, 229. Where an attornment was made to the claimants in an ejectment, who derived their title under a will, the tenant was held to be estopped in a subsequent action from contending that upon the true construction of the will the claimants had no title ; *Gravenor* v. *Woodhouse,* 2 Bing. 71 ; although on a previous occasion it had been decided that the tenant might show the attornment to have been made by mistake, and under suspicious circumstances, and that it had not been acted on for seven years ; and a conveyance to himself made by the real owner. *Gravenor* v. *Woodhouse,* 1 Bing. 38.

Where there has been no attornment, or payment of rent to the claimant, who claims through or under the landlord, the tenant will not be estopped from disputing the *derivative* title of the claimant, *ex. gr.* that he was assignee of the reversion, heir, executor, administrator, devisee or legatee, &c. *Hughes* v. *Hughes,* 15 M. & W. 703, *per cur.* ; *Doe* d. *Grundy* v. *Clarke,* 14 East, 488 ; *Phillips* v. *Pearce,* 5 B. & C. 433 ; *Doe* d. *Higginbotham* v. *Barton,* 11 A. & E. 307 ; 3 P. & D. 194. Thus, if the claimant sue as assignee of the reversion, the defendant may dispute the assignment. But he cannot object that the lessor had no legal reversion to assign. *Rennie* v. *Robinson,* 1 Bing. 147. For a reversion by estoppel is a legal reversion, which will continue during the tenancy, and may be assigned. *Doe* d. *Marriott* v. *Edwards,* 6 C. & P. 208, Parke, J. ; 5 B. & Adol. 1065, *S. C.* ; *Sturgeon* v. *Wingfield,* 15 M. & W. 224 ; but see *Noke* v. *Awder,* Cro. Eliz. 373, 436, 437. If the claimant sue as heir, the defendant may dispute the pedigree or legitimacy of the claimant, or show that the lessor was possessed only for a term of years, or for his own life. *Doe* d. *Strode* v. *Seaton,* 2 Cr. M. & R. 728. If the claimant sue as executor of the lessor the probate is conclusive evidence as to the contents of the will and the mental capacity of the testator ; but the defendant may contend that it is not sufficiently stamped ; *Doe* d. *Richards* v. *Evans,* 10 Q. B. 476 ; or not granted by the proper court ; or that the reversion was not a mere term, but an inheritance not devised by the will ; or

L 2

that the will itself ought to be produced, and not the probate only; or that the reversion, being a mere term, was bequeathed by the will to a third person (not being one of the claimants), and that the executor has assented to such bequest. But the assent of an executor is a matter of fact to be proved to the satisfaction of a jury. *Mason* v. *Farnell,* 12 M. & W. 674; 1 Dowl. & L. 576; *Doe* d. *Chidgey* v. *Harris,* 16 M. & W. 517, 520; 2 Wms. Exors. 1087 (3rd ed.). If the claimant sue as legatee the defendant may raise similar points to those above mentioned, and may insist (*inter alia*) that the assent of the executor to the bequest is not sufficiently proved. *Cases supra.* But no such assent is necessary to a devise of the reversion in fee. To prove *that,* the original will (not the probate) must be produced, and either admitted in the cause or proved in the usual manner. And the defendant may show that the testator was possessed only for his own life. *Doe* d. *Strode* v. *Seaton,* 2 Cr. M. & R. 728. Or for a term of years (no probate or assent of the executors being proved). Where the overseers of a parish put B. in possession of a cottage, which was repaired from time to time at the expense of the parish, but no rent was ever paid in respect thereof. Forty years afterwards B. disposed of the cottage to C.: held, that neither the then overseers, nor the subsequent overseers for the time being, could maintain ejectment against C., their title not having been recognized by payment of rent or otherwise, and it not appearing to be sufficiently connected with that of the overseers from whom possession was originally obtained. *Doe* d. *Grundy* v. *Clarke,* 14 East, 488; *Doe* d. *Lansdell* v. *Gower,* 17 Q. B. 589. Land belonging to a parish was occupied by A., and he paid rent to the churchwardens. They executed a lease of the same land to B. for a term of years, and gave notice to A. of the lease: held, in an action for use and occupation by B. against A., that A. was not estopped from disputing B.'s title because he had paid rent to the churchwardens, and that B. could not derive a valid title from the churchwardens, the property being vested in them and the overseers as a *quasi* corporation by 59 Geo. 3, c. 12, s. 17. *Phillips* v. *Pearce,* 5 B. & C. 433.

The landlord is estopped by the lease from denying that he had any estate in the land at the time the lease was executed by him, or that he had no right to dispose of the possession during the term thereby expressed to be granted. *Darlington* v. *Pritchard,* 4 Man. & Gr. 783; 2 Dowl. N. S. 664; *Green* v. *James,* 6 M. & W. 656. But he may (whether plaintiff or defendant) show that the term has since expired, or been determined by notice to quit, surrender, forfeiture, or otherwise. Persons claiming title through the landlord are estopped in like manner as the landlord himself. But where *cestui que trust* grants a lease his trustee may maintain ejectment. *Doe* d. *Kay* v. *Day,* 10 East, 427, 429. Where A. B., having *no estate* in certain land, demises it by indenture to C. D. for a term of twenty-one years, he thereby creates (as against himself) an estate for years by estoppel, and a reversion in himself by estoppel, which, in the absence of evidence to the contrary, must be presumed to be a reversion in fee. If A. B. afterwards procure to himself a lease for 100 years of the land, such term operates to *feed* the lease for twenty-one years, and to create a lease, not by estoppel only, but in interest for the residue of that time. If A. B. afterwards conveys the land to E. F. for the residue of the term of 100 years, and all his estate and interest therein, he thereby conveys (*inter alia*) his reversion by estoppel, and a privity of estate is created as between E. F. and C. D. *Sturgeon* v. *Wingfield*, 15 M. & W. 224; and see *Doe* d. *Marriott* v. *Edwards*, 6 C. & P. 208; 5 B. & Adol. 1065, *S. C.*; *Palmer* v. *Ekins*, 2 Ld. Raym. 1550; 2 Stra. 817; 11 Mod. 407; 1 Barnard, 103, *S. C.*; *Green* v. *James*, 6 M. & W. 656. If a lessor had only a contingent estate at the time of the demise, but afterwards acquired the fee, or any other estate in possession, the demise would at first operate by estoppel only; but the subsequent estate, when acquired, would feed the estoppel, and enable the tenant to maintain ejectment, even against third persons. *Doe* d. *Christmas* v. *Oliver*, 5 Man. & R. 202; 2 Smith, L. C. 417. When an estoppel works on the interest in the land it runs with it, and is a title. *Trevivian* v. *Lawrence*, 1 Salk. 276 (2nd Resolution); 2 Smith, L. C. 435, 436.

2. *In other Cases.*—It is a general rule or maxim of law that "no man shall derogate from his own grant." 2 Prest. Conv. 42. Neither the grantor, nor any person subsequently claiming possession under him, can dispute the grantee's title, whether the conveyance be by way of mortgage or otherwise. *Doe* d. *Gaisford* v. *Stone*, 3 C. B. 176; 15 L. J., N. S., C. P., 234. A grantor cannot impeach his own deed by proof that it was fraudulent. *Doe* d. *Roberts* v. *Roberts*, 2 B. & A. 367. For though fraudulent and void as against creditors or purchasers, it may, nevertheless, be valid and binding as between the parties themselves. *S. C.* The vendor of land, or his widow, cannot impeach a conveyance in fee by proof that he had previously mortgaged the property for a long term. *Doe* d. *Leeming* v. *Skirrow*, 7 A. & E. 157. An attorney who draws and attests a deed conveying land from A. to B. is not allowed afterwards to say that the property in the land and deed did not pass. *Lord* v. *Wardle*, 3 Bing. N. C. 680; 4 Scott, 402. So a mortgagor cannot impeach a security made by him by evidence, showing that he then had no legal title or power to mortgage. *Doe* d. *Hurst* v. *Clifton*, 4 A. & E. 813; *Doe* d. *Gaisford* v. *Stone*, 3 C. B. 176; *Lindsey* v. *Lindsey*, Bull. N. P. 110. It makes no difference in this respect that the parties acted in a public capacity, *ex. gr.* as commissioners under a turnpike act. *Doe* d. *Levy* v. *Horne*, 3 Q. B. 757, 766; overruling *Fairtitle* d. *Mytton* v. *Gilbert*, 2 T. R. 169; and see *Horton* v. *The Westminster Improvement Commissioners*, 7 Exch. 780. An estoppel binds not only the parties, but their privies in estate. 2 Smith, L. C. 442. In ejectment by a mortgagee, a defendant, not being the mortgagor, but, in reality, defending for his benefit, cannot set up a prior mortgage executed by him. *Doe* d. *Hurst* v. *Clifton*, 4 A. & E. 813. But a purchaser for value from the mortgagor, who first acquired the legal estate after the mortgage to the plaintiff (wherein the mortgagor was recited to be legally or equitably entitled) is not estopped from proving the real state of the title, and the subsequent conveyance from the mortgagor to him. *Right* d. *Jefferys* v. *Bucknell*, 2 B. & Adol. 278. There can be no estoppel where an interest passes. *Walton* v. *Waterhouse*, 2 Wms. Saund. 418; 2 Smith, L. C. 457. In defence to an action of ejectment it may be shown that the parties under whom the plaintiff claims had no title when they conveyed to him, although the defendant himself claims by a conveyance from the same parties, if the latter conveyance was subsequent to that which the defendant seeks to impeach. *Doe* d. *Oliver* v. *Powell*, 1 A. & E. 531; 3 N. & M. 616.

Where the parties to an ejectment referred their right to the land to an arbitrator, who awarded in favour of the claimant, but the defendant, being dissatisfied with the award, made an unsuccessful application to the court to set it aside, and afterwards retained possession, to recover which another ejectment was brought : held, that the reference and award estopped the defendant from disputing the claimant's title. *Doe* d. *Morris* v. *Rosser,* 3 East, 11 ; and see *Allason* v. *Stark,* 9 A. & E. 255 ; 1 P. & D. 183, 192. In such a case a rule for possession might be obtained pursuant to 17 & 18 Vict. c. 125, s. 16, and a writ of *habere facias possessionem* thereon. Reg. Mic. Vac. 1854, Form 17, *post, Appendix No.* 291.

3. *Lease or Agreement.*]—This question is not often of much consequence in an ejectment since the 8 & 9 Vict. c. 106. *Tress* v. *Savage,* 4 E. & B. 36; *Doe* d. *Bromfield* v. *Smith,* 6 East, 530. Except where a point is raised as to the sufficiency of the stamp. *Doe* d. *Estwick* v. *Way,* 1 T. R. 737 ; *Doe* d. *Marlow* v. *Wiggins,* 4 Q. B. 367 ; *Doe* d. *Morgan* v. *Amos,* 2 Man. & Ry. 180 ; *Mayfield* v. *Robinson,* 7 Q. B. 486. But in other forms of action it may be most material. *Stratton* v. *Pettit,* 16 C. B. 420 ; *Swatman* v. *Ambler,* 8 Exch. 72 ; *Tarte* v. *Darby,* 15 M. & W. 601 ; *Brashier* v. *Jackson,* 6 M. & W. 549 ; 8 Dowl. 784.

By 8 & 9 Vict. c. 106, s. 3, "a lease *required by law to be in writing* of any tenements or hereditaments," made after the 1st October, 1845, shall be "*void at law, unless made by deed.*"

By the Statute of Frauds (29 Car. 2, c. 3, ss. 1, 2), all leases of lands, &c. must be *in writing,* signed, &c., "except, nevertheless, all leases not exceeding the term of three years from the making thereof, whereupon the rent reserved to the landlord, during such term, shall amount unto two-third parts at least of the full improved value of the thing demised."

An *agreement* for a lease exceeding three years may be valid as an agreement, and enforced in a court of equity by a bill for a specific performance ; or damages for its non-performance may be recovered at law ; but it will *not create any term. Doe* d. *Morgan* v. *Powell,* 7 Man. & Gr. 980 ; 8 Scott, N. R. 687 ; *Doe* d. *Estwick* v. *Way,* 1 T. R. 735. If, however, the intended lessee be permitted to enter and take possession, and to pay part of the agreed rent, a tenancy from year to year will be thereby created, upon the terms of the agreement so far as they may be applicable to a yearly tenancy ; which tenancy may be determined at the end of any year thereof, by a regular notice to quit. *Doe* d. *Thomson* v. *Amey,* 12 A. & E. 476 ; 4 P. & D. 177. Or it will expire at the end of the term mentioned in the agreement, without any previous notice to quit. *Ante,* 36.

A *lease* is void at law unless made by deed ; or for a term not exceeding three years from the making thereof, and reserving a rent amounting to two-thirds of a rack-rent during the whole term. But if the lessee be permitted to enter under a void lease, and to pay part of the rent therein expressed to be reserved, a tenancy from year to year will be thereby created, upon the terms of the void lease, so far as they may be applicable to a yearly tenancy. *Doe* d. *Rigge* v. *Bell,* 5 T. R. 471 ; 2 Smith, L. C. 74 ; *Richardson* v. *Giffard,* 1 A. & E. 52 ; 3 N. & M. 325 ; *Lee* v. *Smith,* 9 Exch. 662 ; *Doe* d. *Pennington* v. *Taniere,* 12 Q. B. 998, 1013. Such tenancy may be determined at the end of any year thereof by a regular notice to quit. *Ante,* 34. And it will cease, without any notice to quit, at the end of the void term mentioned in the lease. *Tress* v. *Savage,* 4 E. & B. 36.

Whether a particular writing amounts to a void lease, or only to an agreement for a lease, depends upon the intention of the parties, to be collected from the terms of the instrument. Chitty on Contracts, 282 (5th ed.); Woodf. L. & T. 130—146 (7th ed.); *Poole* v. *Bentley,* 12 East, 168; *Morgan* d. *Dowding* v. *Bissell,* 3 Taunt. 65; *Perring* v. *Brook,* 1 Moo. & Rob. 510; 7 C. & P. 360; *Curling* v. *Mills,* 6 Man. & Gr. 182, Tindal, C. J.; *Stratton* v. *Pettit,* 16 C. B. 420, 435. And the court will if possible put such a construction upon it, as will effectuate the intention of the parties, rather than defeat it. *Stratton* v. *Pettit, supra*; Shep. Touch. 86—89. If words of present demise be used, they will generally amount to a lease, notwithstanding a stipulation for a future lease; that being regarded merely by way of further assurance. *Jones* v. *Reynolds,* 1 Q. B. 517; *Chapman* v. *Towner,* 6 M. & W. 100, 104; Chitty on Contracts, 283 (5th ed.). But words of present demise will not create a lease against the intention of the parties, to be collected from the whole instrument. *Id.* 284; *Perring* v. *Brook,* Moo. & Rob. 510; 7 C. & P. 360. The question is, whether the parties intended the relation of landlord and tenant to commence before the execution of any further document. If so the instrument amounts to a lease; otherwise only to an agreement. *Jones* v. *Reynolds,* 1 Q. B. 516; *Doe* d. *Bromfield* v. *Smith,* 6 East, 530.

4. *Assignments and Underleases.*]—Whether a particular instrument amounts to an assignment or to an underlease is sometimes a question in an action of ejectment. *Doe* d. *Wilkins* v. *Kemeys,* 9 East, 371, 375. But more frequently in other forms of action. *Poultney* v. *Holmes,* 1 Stra. 405; *Preece* v. *Corrie,* 5 Bing. 24; *Parmenter* v. *Webber,* 8 Taunt. 593; *Pollock* v. *Stacy,* 9 Q. B. 1033; *Barrett* v. *Rolph,* 14 M. & W. 348; *Cottee* v. *Richardson,* 7 Exch. 143.

The Statute of Frauds (29 Car. 2, c. 3, s. 3) required that all assignments of leases or terms of years should be by deed or note in writing, duly signed. *Hodges* v. *Drakeford,* 1 B. & P. New R. 270. But by 8 & 9 Vict. c. 106, s. 3, " an assignment of a chattel interest, not being copyhold, in any tenements or hereditaments," made after 1st October, 1845, shall be " void at law unless made *by deed.*"

Whenever a tenant for life or years grants *less than the whole* of his estate, reserving to himself rent and a reversion even for a single day, hour or minute, it amounts to an underlease, although purporting to be an assignment. 2 Pres. Conv. 124, 125.

On the other hand, when a tenant for years grants *his whole estate,* it amounts to an assignment, whatever may be the form of words used. *Thorne* v. *Wollicombe,* 3 B. & Adol. 595, *per* Lord Tenterden, C. J.; and see 4 Man. & Gr. 145, note, citing 5 Man. & Ry. 157—162; *Palmer* v. *Edwards,* 1 Doug. 187; 2 Pres. Conv. 124. Unless indeed the grant be made to the lessor, his heirs or assigns, in which case it will amount to a surrender. *Smith* v. *Mapleback,* 1 T. R. 441; *Cottee* v. *Richardson,* 7 Exch. 143. In either case no reversion being left in the termor, he cannot *distrain* for any rent reserved to himself in the deed; *Preece* v. *Corrie,* 5 Bing. 24; 2 Moo. & P. 57; *Parmenter* v. *Webber,* 8 Taunt. 593; *Pascoe* v. *Pascoe,* 3 Bing. N. C. 898; unless in pursuance of some express power reserved to him in that behalf. But he may maintain an action founded on the deed to recover the rent thereby reserved; *Baker* v. *Gostling*, 1 Bing. N. C. 19; *Id.* 246; 4 Moo. & Sc. 539; or an action for use and occupation if the instrument be not under seal. *Pollock* v. *Stacy*, 9 Q. B. 1033. In this case the court held that an instrument purporting to demise for the whole term which the lessor had, at a rent payable weekly, should not be construed as an assignment against the intention of the parties, who evidently intended to create the relation of landlord and tenant. But see *Barrett* v. *Rolph*, 14 M. & W. 348; *Cottee* v. *Richardson*, 7 Exch. 143, 147, 151. To carry into effect the obvious intention of the parties the court will, if possible, construe the instrument as a valid *underlease for the time* therein mentioned, rather than as a void assignment of *the term* vested in the grantor. *Cottee* v. *Richardson*, 7 Exch. 151.

When the plaintiff claims as assignee of an old term, it is not always necessary to prove all the mesne assignments; but upon proof of the original lease, and of some of the most recent assignments, and of possession thereunder, the intermediate assignments will be presumed. *Earl* d. *Goodwin* v. *Baxter*, 2 W. Black. 1222; 3 Stark. Ev. 914 (3rd ed.); but see *Doe* d. *Woodhouse* v. *Powell*, 8 Q. B. 576.

When the plaintiff in ejectment sues as assignee of the reversion and relies on a right of re-entry for a forfeiture, it must appear that the forfeiture accrued after he became assignee. *Hunt* v. *Bishop*, 8 Exch. 675, 680; 9 Exch. 635, *S. C.* And also that notice of the assignment was given to the defendant before the forfeiture accrued. *Fraunce's case*, 8 Co. R. 89 b; 2 Brownl. 277; *Hingen* v. *Payne*, Cro. Jac. 476.

If a defendant in ejectment be shown to have come into possession after the original tenant entered under a demise, and during the term thereby granted, he will be presumed (in the absence of proof to the contrary) to have obtained possession as assignee of the term. *Doe* d. *Morris* v. *Williams*, 6 B. & C. 41; 9 D. & R. 30; and see *Roe* d. *Blair* v. *Street and Fairbanks*, 2 A. & E. 329, 331; *Hindley* v. *Rickerby*, 5 Esp. 4. Upon the death of a tenant from year to year his widow remained in possession: held, that she must be presumed to hold under an assignment, in the absence of any evidence of a probate or letters of administration. *Rees* d. *Mears* v. *Perrot*, 4 C. & P. 230, Littledale, J.

Proof that defendant in ejectment came into possession under or after the lessee, during the term, is generally sufficient without proof of any assignment. *Humphrey* v. *Damion*, Cro. Jac. 300; *ante*, 215. But proof of an assignment was erroneously supposed to be necessary in *Doe* d. *Hemmings* v. *Durnford*, 2 Cro. & Jer. 667.

An underlease will not be prejudiced by a subsequent surrender of the original term. *Post*, 226.

5. *Surrenders.*]—By the Statute of Frauds (29 Car. 2, c. 3, s. 3), no leases, estates or interests, either of freehold or terms of years, or any uncertain interest, not being copyhold or customary interest, of, in, to or out of any messuages, manors, lands, tenements or hereditaments, shall be assigned, granted or *surrendered*, unless it be by deed or note in writing, signed by the party so assigning, granting or surrendering the same, or their agents thereunto lawfully authorized by writing, *or by act and operation of law.* 1 Wms. Saund. 236.

By 8 & 9 Vict. c. 106, s. 3, " a surrender in writing of an interest in any tenements or hereditaments, not being a copyhold interest, and not being an interest which might by law have been created without writing, made after the first day of October, 1845, shall be *void at law, unless made by deed.*"

Although a term may sometimes be created without any writing, *ex. gr.* a term not exceeding three years from the making thereof, or a tenancy from year to year, yet a surrender of such term must be by deed or note in writing, signed pursuant to the Statute of Frauds, or by act and operation of law. 1 Wms. Saund. 236 c, note (*n*). Where the term could not have been created otherwise than by a deed (8 & 9 Vict. c. 106, s. 3), it cannot be surrendered except by deed, or by act and operation of law.

Any instrument in writing used as evidence of a surrender must be duly stamped as a surrender. 13 & 14 Vict. c. 97, Sched. part I. tit. "Surrender;" *Williams* v. *Sawyer*, 3 Brod. & B. 70; 6 Moore, 226; *Doe* d. *Wyatt* v. *Stagg*, 5 Bing. N. C. 564.

No particular words are necessary to make a surrender; but where a deed is not required by 8 & 9 Vict. c. 106, s. 3 (*ante*, 224), any instrument in writing, duly signed, and expressing an *immediate* purpose of giving up the estate on the part of the tenant, if accepted by the landlord, will be sufficient. Shep. Touch. 306; *Weddall* v. *Capes*, 1 M. & W. 50; *Smith* v. *Mapleback*, 1 T. R. 441. Thus a receipt by a mortgagee for his mortgage money, concluding thus, "and I do hereby release and discharge the within premises of the said mortgage money," was holden a valid surrender to the mortgagor. *Farmer* v. *Rogers*, 2 Wils. 26. A notice to quit at a *future* day cannot operate as a surrender. *Doe* d. *Murrell* v. *Milward*, 3 M. & W. 328; *Bessell* v. *Lansberg*, 7 Q. B. 638. But a written request by the tenant to his landlord to relet the premises to some other person may, when acted on, amount to a surrender by act and operation of law. *Nickells* v. *Atherstone*, 10 Q. B. 944.

A term or tenancy may be determined by a surrender "by act and operation of law." 29 Car. 2, c. 3, s. 3; *ante*, 224; 1 Wms. Saund. 236; Woodf. L. & T. 253 (7th ed.). A surrender by act and operation of law takes place when the tenant of a particular estate becomes party to an act having some other object than that of a surrender, but which object cannot be effected whilst the particular estate continues. See the cases collected, Com. Dig. tit. "Surrender I.;" 20 Vin. Abr. tit. "Surrender F, G." In these cases the presumed surrender is also presumed to have *preceded* the act to which the tenant is party. 9 C. B. 634, note (*a*). The term "surrender by operation of law" is properly applied to cases where the owner of a particular estate has been a party to some act, the validity of which he is by law afterwards estopped from disputing, and which would not be valid if his particular estate continued to exist. Thus, where lessee for years accepts a new lease from his lessor, he is estopped from saying that his lessor had not the power to make the new lease; and as the lessor could not grant the new lease until the prior one had been surrendered, the acceptance of such new lease is of itself a surrender of the former one. Such surrender is *the act of the law*, and takes place independently of, and even in spite of the intention of the parties. *Lyon* v. *Reed*, 13 M. & W. 285, 306; 2 Taylor, Ev. 675; and see *Bessell* v. *Lundsberg*, 7 Q. B. 640, Patteson, J. So where the landlord, with the consent of his tenant, relets the premises to a new tenant, who enters, a surrender of the previous tenancy takes place by act and operation of law. *Nickells* v.

Atherstone, 10 Q. B. 944; *Thomas* v. *Cook,* 2 B. & A. 119; *Wilson* v. *Sewell,* 4 Burr. 1975; *Stone* v. *Whiting,* 2 Stark. R. 235; *Hall* v. *Burgess,* 5 B. & C. 332; *Walls* v. *Atcheson,* 3 Bing. 462; *Woodcock* v. *Nuth,* 1 Moo. & Sc. 317; 8 Bing. 170. At all events, the new tenant is estopped from disputing the landlord's right to demise to him, by showing the continued existence of the previous tenancy. *Phipps* v. *Sculthorpe,* 1 B. & A. 50. A., being a tenant to B. of rooms for a term of years, upon the bankruptcy of B. sent the key to his official assignee, and quitted possession. The key was not returned: held not to amount to a surrender by act and operation of law. *Cannan* v. *Hartley,* 9 C. B. 634.

Any new lease inconsistent with the previous one, although for a shorter period, will, if accepted, work a surrender by operation of law; Roll. Abr. tit. "Surrender;" *Crowley* v. *Vitty,* 21 Law J., N. S., Exch., 136, Parke, B.; 7 Exch. 319, *S. C.;* and the accruing rent will sink and be entirely lost. *Grimman* v. *Legge,* 8 B. & C. 324; 2 M. & R. 438; *Slack* v. *Sharp,* 8 A. & E. 366; 3 N. & P. 390; *Dodd* v. *Achlom,* 6 Man. & Gr. 673; 7 Scott, N. R. 415; *Doe* d. *Philip* v. *Benjamin,* 9 A. & E. 644; 1 P. & D. 440. The new lease must be one *valid in law; Roe* d. *Earl of Berkeley* v. *Archbishop of York,* 6 East, 86; *Davison* d. *Bromley* v. *Stanley,* 4 Burr. 2210; 3 Prest. Conv. 164, 165; or, at all events, voidable only; and if avoided contrary to the intention of the parties, it will not operate as a surrender of the previous lease, notwithstanding express words of surrender therein contained. *Doe* d. *Earl of Egremont* v. *Courtenay,* 11 Q. B. 702; *Doe* d. *Biddulph* v. *Poole, Id.* 713; overruling *Doe* d. *Earl of Egremont* v. *Forwood,* 3 Q. B. 627. A mere agreement for a new lease is not sufficient to create an implied surrender of the previous one; *John* v. *Jenkins,* 1 Cr. & Mee. 227; 3 Tyr. 170; especially if such new agreement be not in writing and signed pursuant to the Statute of Frauds. *Foquet* v. *Moor,* 7 Exch. 870. So a mere oral agreement to reduce the rent previously paid will not create a new demise. *Crowley* v. *Vitty,* 7 Exch. 319(¹) So an agreement by the tenant to pay an additional sum yearly, in consideration of his landlord's making certain improvements in the demised premises, does not create a new demise. *Donnellan* v. *Read,* 3 B. & Adol. 899; *Foquet* v. *Moor,* 7 Exch. 870. Merely cancelling a lease does not determine the term, nor revest the estate in the lessor. *Roe* d. *Earl of Berkeley* v. *The Archbishop of York,* 6 East, 86; *Woolley* v. *Gregory,* 2 You. & Jer. 536. The production of a lease by the lessor or his attorney in a cancelled state is not *primâ facie* evidence that such lease has been surrendered by deed, or note in writing, or by act and operation of law. *Doe* d. *Courtail* v. *Thomas,* 9 B. & C. 288; 4 Man. & R. 218.

If a lessee for years accept a new lease by indenture of *part* of the lands, it is a surrender of that part only, and not of the whole. Woodf. L. & T. 255 (7th ed.); *Earl of Carnarvon* v. *Villebois,* 13 M. & W. 342, Alderson, B.; *Morrison* v. *Chadwick,* 7 C. B. 266; 6 Dowl. & L. 567. The surrender of a lease will not affect or prejudice an underlease previously granted. *Doe* d. *Beaden* v. *Pyke,* 5 M. & S. 146; *Pleasant* d. *Hayton* v. *Benson,* 14 East, 232; *Torriano* v. *Young,* 6 C. & P. 8. So where a copyhold tenant commits a forfeiture after a demise made with licence of the lord. *Clarke* v. *Ardern,* 16 C. B. 227. So a tortious alienation by a tenant for life (whilst such aliena-

(1) nor shall the acceptance of a higher rent, along is Doe v Geldere 5 QB 841. Doe d Bedford Kenbrick. MS. Adams on Ejectment 107. 3 edition.

tions were possible) did not defeat derivative estates or charges. *Archer's case*, 1 Co. R. 66 b; Cro. Eliz. 453; 2 And. 37, *S. C.*

6. *Satisfied Terms.*]—By 8 & 9 Vict. c. 112, intituled "An Act to render the Assignment of satisfied Terms unnecessary," after reciting that "whereas the assignment of satisfied terms has been found to be attended with great difficulty, delay and expense, and to operate in many cases to the prejudice of the persons justly entitled to the lands to which they relate," it is enacted (sect. 1), "that every *satisfied* term of years which, *either by express declaration, or by construction of law*, shall upon the 31st day of December, 1845, be attendant upon the inheritance or reversion of any lands, shall on that day absolutely cease and determine as to the land upon the inheritance or reversion whereof such term shall be attendant as aforesaid, *except* that every such term of years which shall be so attendant as aforesaid *by express declaration*, although hereby made to cease and determine, shall afford to every person the same *protection* against every incumbrance, charge, estate, right, action, suit, claim and demand, as it would have afforded to him if it had continued to subsist, but had not been assigned or dealt with after the said 31st day of December, 1845, and shall *for the purpose of such protection* be considered in every court of law and equity to be a subsisting term."

Sect. 2 enacts, "that every term of years now subsisting, or hereafter to be created, *becoming satisfied after* the said 31st day of December, 1845, and which either by express declaration or by construction of law shall after that day become attendant upon the inheritance or reversion of any lands, shall *immediately upon the same becoming so attendant absolutely cease and determine* as to the land upon the inheritance or reversion whereof such term shall become attendant as aforesaid."

Sect. 3 enacts, "that in the construction and for the purposes of this act, unless there be something in the subject or context repugnant to such construction, the word 'lands' shall extend to all freehold tenements and hereditaments, whether corporeal or incorporeal, and to all such customary land as will pass by deed, or deed and admittance, and not by surrender, or any undivided part or share thereof respectively."

Before the above act it was the practice to direct the jury to presume the surrender of a term, where it clearly appeared that all the purposes for which it was created had been fully satisfied, and that the term *ought* in justice and equity to have been reassigned or surrendered to the owner of the inheritance, especially if there had been any subsequent dealing with the property of such a nature as would not have happened with reasonable men, supposing the term had not been put an end to, or there was other express evidence (beyond the mere lapse of time) from which such a presumption might have been made. *Doe* d. *Hodson* v. *Staple*, 2 T. R. 684; *England* d. *Syburn* v. *Slade*, 4 T. R. 682; *Doe* d. *Bowerman* v. *Syburn*, 7 T. R. 2; *Doe* d. *Burdett* v. *Wrighte*, 2 B. & A. 710; *Doe* d. *Putland* v. *Hilder*, *Id.* 782; *Bartlett* v. *Downes*, 3 B. & C. 616; 5 D. & R. 526; 1 C. & P. 522, *S. C.*; *Doe* d. *Lloyd* v. *Passingham*, 6 B. & C. 305; 9 D. & R. 416; *Doe* d. *Blacknell* v. *Plowman*, 2 B. & Adol. 573; *Doe* d. *Rees* v. *Williams*, 2 M. & W. 749; *Garrard* v. *Tuck*, 8 C. B. 231, 237, 242, 248; Ad. Eject. 66; Ros. Ev. 439 (7th ed.). But the mere lapse of time was not sufficient; *Doe* d. *Earl of Egremont* v. *Langdon*, 12 Q. B. 711, 719; *Doe* d. *Fenwick* v. *Read*, 5 B. & A. 232; especially if there had been any dealing with the term, or the owner of the inheritance was interested in upholding it. *Doe* d. *Graham* v. *Scott*, 11 East, 478. The presumption of a surrender would have arisen only where a title was shown by the party who called for the presumption, or the possession was shown to have been consistent with the existence of the surrender required to be presumed. *Doe* d. *Harrop* v. *Cooke*, 3 Moo. & P. 411; 6 Bing. 174. Such presumptions were made in favour of the possession, not against it. *Doe* d. *Rees* v. *Williams*, 2 M. & W. 749, 758; *Doe* d. *Brandon* v. *Calvert*, 5 Taunt. 170. The jury might presume an old satisfied term surrendered to the *cestui que use* in order to substantiate a lease executed by him. *Doe* d. *Bowerman* v. *Sybourn*, 7 T. R. 2. But no surrender or reconveyance from trustees would be presumed, where it would have amounted to a breach of trust. *Keene* v. *Deardon*, 8 East, 248. And in no case whatever would the court in banc have presumed the surrender of an outstanding term. That must have been done (if at all) by the jury as an inference of fact. *Cottrell* v. *Hughes*, 15 C. B. 532.

It is to be observed, that the act applies only to *satisfied* terms. See the cases decided on " provisoes for cesser of terms," Sugd. V. & P. Chap. XV. p. 770 (11th ed.). Where a term was assigned upon trust to secure the amount of a mortgage, and afterwards to be reconveyed as C. and H. should direct; but C. and H. were not then legally entitled to the inheritance or reversion, as was erroneously supposed; and C. afterwards paid off the mortgage: held, that the term was not put an end to by the 8 & 9 Vict. c. 112, s. 2, inasmuch as it was not made attendant upon the inheritance by express declaration, nor by construction of law, being expressly assigned in trust for parties not legally entitled to the inheritance, although erroneously supposed to be so. *Doe* d. *Clay* v. *Jones*, 13 Q. B. 774; and see *Doe* d. *Jacobs* v. *Philips*, 10 Q. B. 130; *Haskett* v. *Strong*, 2 Stra. 689.

The act in effect divides satisfied attendant terms into two classes, viz., 1. Those which were satisfied on or before the 31st day of December, 1845; 2. Terms which since that day have become satisfied. The latter are absolutely determined and extinguished for all purposes; but the former, if attendant *by express declaration*, may, *for the purpose of protection* to the person for whose benefit the assignment or declaration was made, be "considered to be a subsisting term," notwithstanding its extinction for all other purposes. It will enable such person to defend an ejectment. *Cottrell* v. *Hughes*, 15 C. B. 532. A term assigned before the 31st December, 1845, to a trustee for a *bonâ fide* purchaser for value without notice, will continue to exist *for his protection*, if necessary, but not for the benefit of the owner of the inheritance. *S. C.*; *Doe* d. *Cadwaller* v. *Price*, 16 M. & W. 603. It may be used as a shield, but not as a sword. *Id.* 609, *per* Alderson, B. As to the previous law, see *Goodtitle* d. *Norris* v. *Morgan*, 1 T. R. 755; *Doe* d. *Earl of Egremont* v. *Langdon*, 12 Q. B. 711. If such owner use the name of the trustee of the term as one of the claimants in the writ, an application may be made to the court or a judge to strike it out, provided the defendant really wants the protection of the term for his defence. 16 M. & W. 614, Parke, B. A satisfied term will afford no defence against the owner of the inheritance for the time being, unless the defendant be *equitably entitled* to the benefit of the

.term. *Doe* d. *Hall* v. *Mousdale*, 16 M. & W. 689. Where the claimants and defendants are respectively entitled to the benefit of the term (supposing it to exist), there must be a *demand of possession* by the trustee of the term before an ejectment can be maintained in his name, especially where the *cestuis que trusts* have been in actual possession for above twenty years before action. *Doe* d. *Jacobs* v. *Phillips*, 10 Q. B. 130.

The Ecclesiastical Court will not grant limited letters of administration of a *satisfied* attendant term. 16 M. & W. 690.

The reason for restricting the operation of the act to freehold hereditaments and customary *land* passing by deed, or deed and admittance, is not obvious. The proper course would seem to have been to have included hereditaments of any tenure, for satisfied attendant terms are as great an evil to lands of one tenure as of another. It is true that satisfied terms in copyholds are of very rare occurrence, but they are not incompatible with the tenure, and may occasionally exist; see *Earl of Bath* v. *Abney*, 1 Burr. 206; Burton's Comp. Art. 1314; and lands passing by deed, and surrender and admittance, which seem to be customary freehold; see *Bingham* v. *Woodgate*, 1 Russ. & Myl. 32, 750; and are therefore liable, it is presumed, to be infected with attendant terms, are apparently excluded from the benefit of the act. So too, it would seem, are customary hereditaments (if such there be) which are *not land*, and which pass by deed, or deed and admittance. These anomalies seem to have been introduced without sufficient consideration. Davidson's Concise Prec. 77 (2nd ed.).

7. *Attornment.*]—Where the original landlord parts with his estate, and transfers it to another, and the tenant consents to hold of that other, the tenant is said to attorn to the new landlord. The attornment is the act of the tenant's putting one person in the place of another as his landlord. The tenant who has attorned continues to hold upon the same terms as he held of his former landlord. *Per* Holroyd, J., in *Cornish* v. *Searell*, 8 B. & C. 476; Co. Lit. 309 *a*. The assignee of a lease, to whom an under-lessee has attorned, may enter upon such under-lessee for a condition broken. *Davy* v. *Matthew*, Cro. Eliz. 649.

Generally speaking an attornment is unnecessary. 4 Anne, c. 16, s. 9; Woodf. L. & T. 221 (7th ed.). An assignee of the reversion may sue or distrain for the rent without any attornment. *Lumley* v. *Hodgson*, 16 East, 99; *Rivis* v. *Watson*, 5 M. & W. 255; *Lloyd* v. *Davies*, 2 Exch. 803. An attornment to a stranger is void, unless made " pursuant to and in consequence of some judgment at law, or decree or order of a court of equity; or made with the privity and consent of the landlord or landlords, lessor or lessors; or to any mortgagee after the mortgage is become forfeited." 11 Geo. 2, c. 19, s. 11.

An actual attornment is sometimes advisable; for it is an *act done by the tenant in possession*, and consequently evidence even as against third persons. Thus an attornment to A. by B., the tenant or under-tenant in possession, is evidence of A.'s ownership at the time of the attornment against future occupiers, whether they claim through B. or not. *Doe* d. *Linsey* v. *Edwards*, 5 A. & E. 95, 102. When a mortgage is forfeited, the tenants of the mortgagor whose leases or tenancies commenced *after the mortgage* must attorn to the mortgagee before the latter can distrain or sue for the rent. *Evans* v. *Elliott*, 9 A. & E.

342; 1 P. & D. 256; *Partington* v. *Woodcock*, 6 A. & E. 690; 5 N. & M. 672; *Rogers* v. *Humphreys*, 4 A. & E. 313; 5 N. & M. 513. After an attornment the mortgagee may distrain for the arrears of rent thereby admitted to be due. *Gladman* v. *Plumer*, 15 Law J., N. S., Q. B., 79. Such attornment may be made "after the mortgage is become forfeited," without the assent of the mortgagor. *Ante*, 229. The assignee of a lease, to whom an under-tenant has attorned, may enter under upon such under-tenant for breach of a condition in the under-lease. *Davy* v. *Matthew*, Cro. Eliz. 649. Attornment by tenant to heir, upon a threat of eviction, is tantamount to entry by the heir. *Hill* v. *Saunders* (in error), 4 B. & C. 529; 7 D. & R. 17. A. and B., tenants in common, having agreed to divide their property, and that *Blackacre* should belong to A.; the occupier of *Blackacre*, who after this agreement had paid his whole rent to A., cannot, in an ejectment brought against him by A., object that the partition deed between A. and B. is not executed. *Doe* d. *Pritchett* v. *Mitchell*, 1 Brod. & B. 11; 3 Moore, 219.

An instrument in writing professing to be a mere attornment, but which is in fact an agreement to create a fresh tenancy on new terms, requires a stamp as a lease or as an agreement. *Cornish* v. *Searell*, 8 B. & C. 471; 1 M. & R. 703; *Doe* d. *Frankis* v. *Frankis*, 11 A. & E. 792; 3 P. & D. 565; *Eagleton* v. *Gutteridge*, 11 M. & W. 465; 2 Dowl. N. S. 1053. But a mere memorandum of attornment, not creating any new tenancy, or fresh terms, but merely substituting one landlord for another, does not require a stamp either as a lease or as an agreement. *Doe* d. *Linsey* v. *Edwards*, 5 A. & E. 95, 102; *Doe* d. *Wright* v. *Smith*, 8 A. & E. 255; 3 N. & P. 335; *see form of Attornment after Judgment in Ejectment, Appendix, No.* 269. An instrument in these terms, "I hereby certify that I remain in the house No. 3, Swinton Street, belonging to W. G., on sufferance only, and agree to give him possession at any time he may require:" held, not to amount to an agreement for a tenancy so as to require a stamp. *Barry* v. *Goodman*, 2 M. & W. 768.

An attornment generally estops the party making it from denying the title of the person to whom the attornment is made. Thus where an attornment was made to the claimants in an ejectment, who derived their title under a will, the tenant was held to be estopped from contending in a subsequent action that upon the true construction of the will the claimants had no title; *Gravenor* v. *Woodhouse*, 2 Bing. 71; although on a previous occasion it had been decided that the tenant might show the attornment to have been made by mistake, and under suspicious circumstances, and that it had not been acted on for seven years, and a conveyance to himself made by the real owner. *Gravenor* v. *Woodhouse*, 1 Bing. 38. Where a tenant had attorned and paid rent to a devisee of the landlord, and no fraud or misrepresentation had been practised towards him: held, that he could not afterwards dispute the devisee's title by evidence showing that the testator was incompetent to make a will. *Doe* d. *Marlow* v. *Wiggins*, 4 Q. B. 367. Attornment by tenant to heir upon threat of eviction, is tantamount to entry by the heir, and prevents the tenant from afterwards disputing his title. *Hill* v. *Saunders* (in error), 4 B. & C. 529; 7 D. & R. 17. So where a tenant of glebe land has attorned and paid rent to the subsequent incumbent, he will not be permitted to dispute his title by evidence of a simoniacal presentation of the incumbent. *Cooke* v. *Loxley*, 5 T. R. 4.

Sometimes, however, a tenant who has attorned will be allowed to prove that such attornment was procured by fraud, covin or misrepresentation; or that it was made by mistake, and in ignorance of material facts, and that the person to whom the attornment was made really had no title. *Rogers* v. *Pitcher*, 6 Taunt. 202; *Brook* v. *Briggs*, 2 Bing. N. C. 572; *Doe* d. *Plevin* v. *Brown*, 7 A. & E. 447; *Cornish* v. *Searell*, 8 B. & C. 471; *Hughes* v. *Hughes*, 15 M. & W. 703, *per cur.* Thus where A., being tenant to B., who died, afterwards attorned to C. as heir of B., in ignorance that C.'s title as heir was disputed: held, that A. was not thereby estopped from showing that C. really had no title to the property, and that the attornment to him was a mistake. *Gregory* v. *Doidge*, 3 Bing. 474.

If an attornment be relied on to defeat the Statute of Limitations, it must be made before action brought. *Doe* d. *Mee* v. *Litherland*, 4 A. & E. 784; 6 N. & M. 313. And the defendant may contend that the person making such attornment did so without any intention to admit the party's right or title, and in ignorance that it would have that effect. In a recent case such a defence was established, no rent having been paid for many years before or after the alleged attornment. *Kearns* v. *Genner*, 25 July, 1855, *coram* Cresswell, J., at Lewes (see "The Times," 26 July, 1855, p. 11, col. 4); and see *Doe* d. *Linsey* v. *Edwards*, 5 A. & E. 95, 106.

8. *Acts of Occupiers.*]—The acts of occupiers during their occupation (other than mere admissions) are evidence, even after their occupation has ceased, against all persons who subsequently hold or claim the property. *Doe* d. *Manton* v. *Austin*, 9 Bing. 41; 2 Moo. & Sc. 107. Thus payment of rent by the tenant in possession to A. B. is an act done, "it is a fact," and therefore admissible evidence of A. B.'s title as against third persons. *Doe* d. *Earl of Lichfield* v. *Stacey*, 6 C. & P. 139, Tindal, C. J.; *Doe* d. *Manton* v. *Austin*, 9 Bing. 41; 2 Moo. & Sc. 107; *Dainty* v. *Brocklehurst*, 3 Exch. 207. Proof of payment of rent to the common clerk or agent of several trustees is *primâ facie* evidence of their seisin in fee as joint tenants; and evidence that they were appointed trustees at different times is not sufficient to rebut such *primâ facie* proof. *Doe* d. *Clark* v. *Grant*, 12 East, ·209. Receipts for rent given from time to time by M. P. to the tenant in possession, and *coming out of the tenant's possession*, are (after the deaths of both parties) admissible evidence of M. P.'s seisin in fee. *Doe* d. *Blaney* v. *Savage*, 1 Car. & K. 487. A verbal admission of the payment of rent to A. B. is evidence of A. B.'s title against the party making such admission, and all persons claiming through or under him. *Doe* d. *Earl Spencer* v. *Beckett*, 4 Q. B. 601. But an *act done* stands on a different footing to a mere declaration, and is evidence even against strangers. Many things which pass by words only are really acts; thus where leave is applied for and granted for the doing of something on or relating to land. *Wakeman* v. *West*, 8 C. & P. 99. An attornment by the tenants or under-tenants in possession to A. B., with payment of 1s. on account of the rent, is an act done, and evidence thereof is admissible against subsequent occupiers, notwithstanding they do not claim through or under the persons making such attornment. *Doe* d. *Linsey* v. *Edwards*, 5 A. & E. 95, 102; *Doe* d. *Mee* v. *Litherland*, 4 A. & E. 784; 6 N. & M. 313. Acts of ownership done on land are *primâ facie* evidence against all the world that the person doing such acts was then seised of the land in fee simple. Thus in ejectment, evidence that the shutters of the house claimed were repaired, and a washhouse built on the premises, and that this was paid for by W. L. is evidence to go to the jury of the seisin of W. L. *Doe* d. *Loscombe* v. *Clifford,* 2 Car. & K. 448, Alderson, B. So where a person is seen felling timber in a wood, that is *primâ facie* evidence that he is the owner of it, although probably only a mere labourer. *Doe* d. *Stansbury* v. *Arkwright,* 5 C. & P. 575, 578, Parke, J. Perambulations of a manor by or on behalf of the lord may be proved. *Woolway* v. *Rowe,* 1 A. & E. 114; 3 N. & M. 849. To prove a right to the soil, acts of ownership exercised by one party are conclusive evidence against a supposed title from boundaries, which have never been ascertained. *Curzon* v. *Lomax,* 5 Esp. 60; *Jones* v. *Williams,* 2 M. & W. 326. Proof that A. B., being in possession of land, executed a conveyance thereof to C. D. in fee simple, is good *primâ facie* evidence of the title of C. D. or his assigns. *Doe* d. *Graham* v. *Penfold,* 8 C. & P. 536, Patteson, J.

A verbal statement of the *intent* with which an act is done (although made at the time) is inadmissible against strangers. *Reg.* v. *Bliss,* 7 A. & E. 550; but see *Doe* d. *Stansbury* v. *Arkwright,* 5 C. & P. 575, 578, Parke, J.

Proof that the occupier, at the time he did the act proved, was merely a tenant of the defendant, or of some person through whom the defendant claims, will destroy the inference to be drawn from the act proved; because a tenant cannot by any act of his, without the landlord's consent, derogate from the rights of his landlord. *Papendick* v. *Bridgwater,* 24 Law J., N. S., Q. B., 289; 25 Law T. R. 144, Q. B.; *Wood* v. *Veal,* 5 B. & A. 454; *Daniel* v. *North,* 11 East, 372; *Scholes* v. *Chadwick,* 2 Moo. & Rob. 507.

9. *Declarations of deceased Occupiers.*]—An occupier of land is presumed to be *seised in fee* in the absence of proof to the contrary. *Ante,* 211; 1 Taylor, Ev. 122 (2nd ed.); *Doe* d. *Hall* v. *Penfold,* 8 C. & P. 536. Therefore declarations made by a deceased occupier, showing that he held merely for his own life, or for a certain term, or as tenant of A. B., are *apparently against his own interest,* whether made orally, or by writing, or by a deed, and consequently are receivable in evidence after his death, even as against third persons then holding or claiming the property. *Peaceable* d. *Uncle* v. *Watson,* 4 Taunt. 16; *Id.* 17, *per* Lord Mansfield, C. J.; *Davies* v. *Pierce,* 2 T. R. 53; *Carne* v. *Nicoll,* 1 Bing. N. C. 430; 1 Scott, 466; *Doe* d. *Majoribanks* v. *Green,* Gow. 227; *Doe* d. *Pritchard* v. *Jauncy,* 8 C. & P. 99; *Doe* d. *Daniel* v. *Coulthred,* 7 A. & E. 235, 239; 2 N. & P. 165; *Mountnoy* v. *Collier,* 1 E. & B. 630, 640, Erle, J.; *Lord Trimlestown* v. *Kemmis,* 9 Cl. & Fin. 780, 784, 785; Tayl. Ev. s. 617 (2nd ed.). But it must first be proved that the party making any such declaration was then or previously in possession of the property to which his statement relates. *Peaceable* d. *Uncle* v. *Watson,* 4 Taunt. 17, Lord Mansfield, C. J.; *Crease* v. *Barrett,* 1 Cr. M. & R. 919, 931; 5 Tyr. 458, 473, S. C. But see *Doe* d. *Pritchard* v. *Jauncy,* 8 C. & P. 99. Slight evidence on this point is generally sufficient; thus where a person (probably a mere labourer) was seen felling timber in a wood, this was held sufficient to raise the presumption that he was seised in fee of the wood, so as to let in a statement made by him at

that or any subsequent time as to whom the wood belonged. *Doe* d. *Stansbury* v. *Arkwright*, 5 C. & P. 575, Parke, J. It is also necessary to prove that the party making any such declaration is dead. *Davies* v. *Pierce*, 2 T. R. 53; *Carne* v. *Nicoll*, 1 Bing. N. C. 430; 1 Scott, 466; *Phillips* v. *Cole*, 10 A. & E. 111, Lord Denman, C. J.; Taylor, Ev. ss. 603, 617; and see *Reg.* v. *Inhabitants of Milton*, 1 Car. & K. 58. It is not sufficient that he is unable to attend the trial from serious indisposition, and lies without hope of recovery. *Harrison* v. *Blades*, 2 Camp. 457, Lord Ellenborough, C. J. "All statements made by a *deceased* person, while in the possession of property, are in themselves original evidence, if they go to cut down his interest in it." *Per* Parke, B., in *Doe* d. *Welsh* v. *Langfield*, 16 M. & W. 514; *per* Erle, J., in *Mountnoy* v. *Collier*, 1 E. & B. 640. The statements of a deceased occupier touching the party under whom he held, are admissible evidence of that party's seisin in fee, and not merely to negative the seisin in fee of such occupier. *Carne* v. *Nicoll*, 1 Bing. N. C. 430; 1 Scott, 466; *Davies* v. *Pierce*, 2 T. R. 53; *Peaceable* d. *Uncle* v. *Watson*, 4 Taunt. 16. The declarations of a widow in possession of premises, that she held them only for her life, and that after her death they would go to the heirs of her husband, are admissible evidence of the heir's title after her death. *Doe* d. *Human* v. *Pettett*, 5 B. & A. 223; *Doe* d. *Roffey* v. *Harbrow*, 3 A. & E. 767, n. In ejectment by S., evidence is admissible to show that a deceased party, being then in receipt of the rents, executed a deed charging the land with an annuity, in which he stated S. to be the legal owner of the fee, and himself to hold for the term of his natural life by permission of S. *Doe* d. *Daniel* v. *Coulthred*, 7 A. & E. 235; 2 N. & P. 165. A memorandum signed by a person deceased, who had been owner of a copyhold tenement, and had occupied a slip of garden ground adjoining, stating that no part of the garden ground belonged to the copyhold, but that he paid rent for the whole of it, is admissible evidence for the plaintiff in an ejectment for this garden ground, to show that it is not a part of the copyhold tenement. *Doe* d. *Baggaly* v. *Jones*, 1 Camp. 367. The party "charged himself, by this representation, with the payment of rent, to which he would not have been liable had the garden ground been parcel of his own tenement." *Id.* 367, Lord Ellenborough, C. J.; and see *Mountnoy* v. *Collier*, 1 E. & B. 630; *Davies* v. *Pierce*, 2 T. R. 53.

The statements of a deceased occupier of land, which do not tend to limit or abridge his presumed estate or rights, but *rather to extend them*, are not admissible. *Per cur.* in *Lord Dunraven* v. *Llewellyn*, 15 Q. B. 812; *Doe* d. *Sweeting* v. *Webber*, 1 A. & E. 733; 3 N. & M. 586. The declarations of the lord of a manor, as to the boundaries of the manor, are evidence after his death, but not as to the extent of his rights over the waste. *Crease* v. *Barrett*, 5 Tyr. 458; 1 Cr. M. & R. 919.

Declarations of a deceased occupier, which merely affect the land itself, and not his own estate or interest in it, are not admissible, except as against himself and persons claiming through or under him. Thus, if he admit that a certain person (a neighbour) has an easement in or upon the land, or that there is a public highway over it, such admissions will not be evidence against his landlord, or a stranger. *Reg.* v. *Bliss*, 7 A. & E. 550; *Scholes* v. *Chadwick*, 2 Moo. & Rob. 507; Tayl. Ev. s. 620 (2nd ed.). The declarations of a deceased tenant *which derogate from the rights of his landlord,* are not admissible against the landlord or his subsequent tenants or assigns. *Papendick* v. *Bridgwater,* 24 Law J., N. S., Q. B., 289 ; 25 Law T. R. 144, Q. B. Otherwise it would be in the power of the tenant to destroy any easement to which the premises might be entitled, or to impose any servitude upon them ; which would be extremely inconvenient. *S. C. per* Lord Campbell, C. J. A lessee for ninety-nine years cannot dedicate a right of way to the public, without the assent of the reversioner. *Wood* v. *Veal,* 5 B. & A. 454.

10. *Entries by deceased Stewards, &c.*]—Entries made by deceased stewards, bailiffs, &c., *charging themselves* with sums received on behalf of their employers, are admissible upon the principle that such entries are *primâ facie against the interest* of the persons making them. Tayl. Ev. 534 (2nd ed.) ; *Barry* v. *Bebbington,* 4 T. R. 514. It is not necessary that the accounts should be wholly in the handwriting of the deceased steward, &c., or signed by him. *Doe* d. *Sturt* v. *Mobbs,* Car. & M. 1 ; *Doe* d. *Bodenham* v. *Colcombe, Id.* 155 ; *Doe* d. *Graham* v. *Hawkins,* 2 Q. B. 212. The entry is admissible to prove not merely the payment of the money, but by whom and on what account, and *in respect of what property* it was paid. *Percival* v. *Nanson,* 7 Exch. 1 ; *Bradley* v. *James,* 13 C. B. 822 ; *Doe* d. *Kinglake* v. *Beviss,* 7 C. B. 456, 481, 486 ; *Davies* v. *Humphreys,* 6 M. & W. 153, 166, Parke, B. ; *Doe* d. *Reece* v. *Robson,* 15 East, 32 ; *Barry* v. *Babbington,* 4 T. R. 514 ; *Brune* v. *Thompson,* Car. & M. 34 ; *The Mayor, Aldermen and Burgesses of Exeter* v. *Warren,* 5 Q. B. 773 ; 1 Dav. & Mer. 524. In an ejectment between the representatives of a deceased landlord and a person claiming under a deceased tenant, upon a question of parcel or no parcel of the demised premises, such evidence may turn the scale in favour of the plaintiff, and prove that his ancestor was seised in fee of the property in question. *Doe* d. *Sturt* v. *Mobbs,* Car. & M. 1.

Entries which *do not charge* the deceased steward, &c., are not admissible. *Dean and Chapter of Ely* v. *Caldecott,* 7 Bing. 434 ; *Doe* d. *Padwich* v. *Skinner,* 3 Exch. 84 ; *Doe* d. *Kinglake* v. *Beviss,* 7 C. B. 456. But entries which do charge him are admissible, although contained in an account, the balance of which is in his favor. Tayl. Ev. 534 (2nd ed.).

11. *Hearsay Evidence of Pedigree.*]—The oral and written declarations of deceased members of a family, made *ante litem motam,* are admissible to prove or disprove a pedigree. Ros. Ev. 28, 30 (7th ed.) ; 1 Tayl. Ev. 503 (2nd ed.). They constitute an exception to the general rule of law that hearsay evidence is inadmissible. *Id.*

Before such evidence will be admitted the judge (not the jury) must be satisfied, 1. That the person who made the declaration is dead. *Pendrell* v. *Pendrell,* 2 Stra. 925 ; *Rex* v. *Inhabitants of Milton,* 1 Car. & K. 58. 2. That such person was related to the family *de jure* by blood or marriage. *Doe* d. *Davies* v. *Davies,* 16 Law J., N. S., Q. B. 218 ; *Whitelock* v. *Baker,* 13 Ves. 514 ; 1 Tayl. Ev. 503, 506 (2nd ed.). The declarations of deceased servants or intimate acquaintances are inadmissible. *Johnson* v. *Lawson,* 2 Bing. 86 ; 9 Moo. 183. So are declarations of illegitimate relations. *Doe* d. *Bamford* v. *Barton,* 2 Moo. & Rob. 28. But declarations of a deceased husband as to the legitimacy of his wife, and as to the pedigree of her family, are evidence. *Vowles* v. *Young*, 13 Ves. 140; *Doe* d. *Northey* v. *Harvey*, Ry. & Moo. 297. The declarations of a deceased person as to the fact of his own marriage are evidence. Bull. N. P. 112; *Rex* v. *Bramley*, 6 T. R. 330. But the declarations of a person as to his own illegitimacy, or place of birth, seem inadmissible, except against himself or those claiming under him. *Rex* v. *Inhabitants of Rishworth*, 2 Q. B. 476; 1 Tayl. Ev. 504 (2nd ed.). The declarations of a deceased husband or wife as to access or non-access are inadmissible on grounds of public policy. *Rex* v. *Luffe*, 8 East, 193; *Goodright* d. *Stevens* v. *Moss*, 2 Cowp. 594. 3. That the declarations were made *ante litem motam.* 1 Tayl. Ev. 495 (2nd ed.). Declarations made after a controversy had arisen with regard to the point in question are inadmissible. *Berkeley Peerage case*, 4 Camp. 401. The evidence will be excluded, although it be not shown that the party who made the declaration knew of the controversy. *Id.* 417. The word controversy does not necessarily mean an existing suit. *Monkton* v. *Attorney-General*, 2 Russ. & Myl. 161; *Walker* v. *Beauchamp*, 6 C. & P. 552. It is not necessary that the declarations should be contemporaneous with the matters declared; therefore a person's declaration that his grandmother's maiden name was A. B. is admissible. *Monkton* v. *Attorney-General*, 2 Russ. & Myl. 158, *per* Lord Brougham, C.

Declarations of deceased parents are admissible to prove the legitimacy of their children. Ros. Ev. 28 (7th ed.). But the declarations of a deceased husband or wife as to access or non-access are inadmissible on grounds of public policy. *Rex* v. *Luffe*, 8 East, 193; *Goodright* d. *Stevens* v. *Moss*, 2 Cowp. 594. The written memoranda of a deceased parent are good evidence to prove the *time* of the birth of a child; *Herbert* v. *Tuckal*, T. Raym. 84, cited in *Roe* d. *Brune* v. *Rawlings*, 7 East, 290; but not the *place*, upon a question of settlement depending on locality rather than pedigree. *Rex* v. *Inhabitants of Erith*, 8 East, 542; *Reg.* v. *Inhabitants of Rishworth*, 2 Q. B. 476. Such evidence appears admissible on a question of genealogy, and with a view to identify ancestors. *Shields* v. *Boucher*, 1 De Gex & Sm. 40, Knight Bruce, V. C. The declarations of a deceased parent and another relation were admitted to show which of several children born at a birth was the eldest. 12 Vin. Abr. 247, Reynolds, C. B.; 4 Camp. 401; Phil. Ev. 225 (8th ed.). Declarations of deceased relations are admissible to prove who was a person's grandfather; when he married; what children he had; the death of a relation beyond sea. Bull. N. P. 294, 295. A minute book of a visitation, signed by the heads of the family, has been admitted, though produced from a private library. *Pitton* v. *Walter*, 1 Stra. 162. So a pedigree hung up in a family mansion is good evidence. *Goodright* d. *Stevens* v. *Moss*, 2 Cowp. 594. So a paper in the handwriting of a deceased member of the family, purporting to give a genealogical account of the family, was held admissible, though never made public by the writer, though erroneous in many particulars, and professing to be founded *partly* on hearsay. *Monkton* v. *Attorney-General*, 2 Russ. & Myl. 147. But an old pedigree, professing on the face of it to be "collected from registers, wills, monumental inscriptions, family records and history," is not evidence, though proved to be signed by members of the family; *Davies* v. *Lowndes*, 5 Bing. N. C. 161; *S. C.* in error, 6 Man. & Gr. 476; except so far as it relates to persons presumably known to the

party signing it, or respecting whom such party may have obtained
information from other members of the family. *S. C.* Whether the
mere recognition of a pedigree by a deceased ancestor will make it
admissible seems doubtful. *S. C.* A ring, stating the date of the death
of the party whose name is engraved on it, if worn publicly by a relation, since deceased, is admissible evidence. *Monkton* v. *Attorney-
General,* 2 Russ. & Myl. 162. An inscription on a tombstone, stating
the death of a party at the age of ninety, has been admitted as evidence
of the age. *Kidney* v. *Cockburn,* 2 Russ. & Myl. 167; Ros. Ev. 29.
So an old tracing from an effaced monument has been admitted. *Slaney*
v. *Wade,* 7 Sim. 595. A recital in a family conveyance by a trustee
is evidence of parentage. *S. C.* An old and cancelled will has been
allowed as evidence of the existence and relative ages of certain deceased members of the family from whom both parties derived title.
Doe d. *Johnson* v. *Pembroke,* 11 East, 504. But a probate is not
admissible for this purpose; *Doe* d. *Wild* v. *Ormerod,* 1 Moo. & Rob.
466; nor a copy of the register of a will. *Dike* v. *Polhill,* 1 Ld. Raym.
744; but see Bull. N. P. 246. Declarations in a family, descriptions
in wills, inscriptions upon monuments, in bibles, and in registry books,
are all admitted, upon the principle that they are the natural effusions
of a party who must know the truth, and who speaks upon an occasion
where the mind stands in an even position, without any temptation to
exceed or fall short of the truth. *Whitelock* v. *Baker,* 13 Ves. 514,
per Lord Eldon, C.; *Higham* v. *Ridgway,* 10 East, 120; *Slane
Peerage case,* 5 Cl. & Fin. 23; *Vaux Peerage case, Id.* 526.

12. *Marriage.*]—In actions for criminal conversation, and on indictments for bigamy, a valid marriage must be strictly proved. *Morris* v. *Miller,* 4 Burr. 2057; 1 W. Black. 632; *Birt* v. *Barlow,* 1
Doug. 171, 174; *Catherwood* v. *Caslon,* 13 M. & W. 261, 265,
Parke, B.; 1 Tayl. Ev. 150, 455 (2nd ed.). But in every other civil
case, including actions of ejectment, evidence of general reputation,
the acknowledgments of the parties, and reception of their friends, &c.,
as man and wife, is sufficient. *Leader* v. *Barry,* 1 Esp. 353, Lord
Kenyon, C. J.; *Hervey* v. *Hervey,* 2 W. Black. 877; *Kay* v.
Duchesse de Pienne, 3 Camp. 123; *Read* v. *Passer,* 1 Esp. 214; *per*
Patteson, J., in *Reg.* v. *Inhabitants of Totley,* 7 Q. B. 599; 1 Tayl.
Ev. 455. In an ejectment, where the plaintiff sought to recover as
heir of his deceased brother (before 3 & 4 Will. 4, c. 106, s. 5): held,
that evidence of reputation of his parents having lived together as man
and wife was sufficient, notwithstanding the parents were then living.
Doe d. *Fleming* v. *Fleming,* 4 Bing. 266. In an action against husband and wife on a promissory note made by the female defendant
before marriage, the only evidence to prove the marriage was, that of
a person who did not appear to be related to the parties, or to live near
them, or to know them intimately; and he proved that he knew the
defendant *Jane Morris* when she was *Jane Rees,* and that *he had
heard that she had since married Morris.* This witness was not cross-
examined: held sufficient *primâ facie* proof of the marriage. *Evans*
v. *Morgan and Morris and wife,* 2 Cr. & Jer. 453.

A marriage is usually proved by an examined copy of the register of
marriage, with some evidence of the identity of the parties, or by a
certified copy made pursuant to 14 & 15 Vict. c. 99, s. 14; 2 Tayl. Ev.
1233 (2nd ed.), together with evidence of identity. The original re-

gister need not be produced, nor any of the attesting witnesses, nor the minister who performed the ceremony, nor the parish clerk, nor any other person who was present on the occasion. *Birt* v. *Barlow*, 1 Doug. 171 ; *Doe* d. *Woollaston* v. *Barnes*, 1 Moo. & Rob. 388 ; *Doe* d. *Blayney* v. *Savage*, 1 Car. & K. 487 ; *Sayer* v. *Glossop*, 2 Car. & K. 694 ; 2 Exch. 409. " Registers are in the nature of records, and need not be produced, nor proved by subscribing witnesses. A copy is sufficient, and is proof of a marriage in fact between two parties describing themselves by such and such names and places of abode, though it does not prove the identity." " As to the proof of identity, whatever is sufficient to satisfy a jury is good evidence. If neither the minister, nor the clerk, nor any of the subscribing witnesses, were acquainted with the married couple, in such a case none of them might be able to prove the identity. But it may be proved in a thousand other ways. Suppose the bell-ringers were called, and proved that they rung the bells, and came immediately after the marriage and were paid by the parties ; suppose the handwriting of the parties were proved ; suppose persons called who were present at the wedding dinner, &c., &c." *Per* Lord Mansfield, C. J., in *Birt* v. *Barlow*, 1 Doug. 174. Proof that the wife was called by her maiden name (as mentioned in the register), until the day of the marriage, and from that time by her married name (as also mentioned in the register), is good evidence of identity. *Id*. 173, *per* Buller, J. The identity of the parties to a marriage may be proved by a person who knows their handwriting, and has inspected the original register, although such register be not produced, but only an examined copy. *Sayer* v. *Glossop*, 2 Exch. 409; 2 Car. & K. 694.

An examined or duly certified copy of a register of marriage is receivable in evidence, although the entry purports to be attested by one witness only, the words " in the presence of " being followed by one name only. *Doe* d. *Blayney* v. *Savage*, 1 Car. & K. 487. The act (26 Geo. 2, c. 33, s. 15) is *directory* only, in requiring the entry to be attested by two witnesses. *S. C.*

An examined or duly certified copy of the registry of a marriage is evidence *of the time* of the marriage, even as against strangers. *Doe* d. *Woollaston* v. *Barnes*, 1 Moo. & Rob. 386.

A marriage may be proved by any person who was present on the occasion ; and in such case it is not necessary to prove a copy of the entry in the register, nor the licence or bans. *Rex* v. *Allison, alias Wilkinson*, Russ. & Ry. C. C. 109; *St. Devereux* v. *Much Dew Church*, 1 W. Black. 367 ; Burr. Set. Cas. 509, *S. C.* Either the husband or wife is a competent witness to prove or disprove the marriage. *Standen* v. *Standen*, Peake, N. P. C. 33 ; *Henley* v. *Chesham*, 2 Bott. 81 ; *Goodright* d. *Stevens* v. *Moss*, 2 Cowp. 591, 593 ; *Rex* v. *Bathwick*, 2 B. & Adol. 639.

A marriage by special licence in a private house may sometimes be proved *without producing the licence*. *Doe* d. *Earl of Egremont* v. *Grazebrook*, 4 Q. B. 406 ; 3 Gale & D. 334 ; *Piers* v. *Piers*, 2 H. L. Cas. 331 ; 13 Jur. 569. Such a marriage, being valid, the law will presume it to have been duly celebrated in the absence of clear proof to the contrary. *S. C.*

It is impossible to state concisely the law relating to the validity of marriages. The statutes, with notes thereon, are collected in 3 Chit. Stat. 204—244 (2nd ed.) ; and see Shelford on Marriage and Divorce ;

2 Arch. N. P. 361—368. The following points of frequent occurrence may be mentioned.

The law will presume that a marriage *de facto* was a valid marriage, unless the contrary be clearly proved; *Piers* v. *Piers*, 2 H. L. Cas. 331; 1 Tayl. Ev. 150 (2nd ed.); except perhaps on an indictment for bigamy. *Reg.* v. *Millis*, 10 Cl. & Fin. 534; 8 Jur. 717.

A marriage between English subjects, celebrated according to the rites of the church of England, but not in the presence of a priest in holy orders, is invalid at common law. *Catherwood* v. *Caslon*, 13 M. & W. 261.

A marriage celebrated after the 31st August, 1835, between persons within the prohibited degrees of consanguinity or affinity, is *null and void.* 5 & 6 Will. 4, c. 54, s. 2. The prohibited degrees are those mentioned in the Book of Common Prayer, and in the stat. 28 Hen. 8, c. 7, s. 11. Therefore the marriage of a man with the sister of his deceased wife is absolutely null and void. *Reg.* v. *Chadwick* (in error), 11 Q. B. 173, 227. This law extends to an illegitimate as well as a legitimate child of the late wife's parents. *S. C.*

The validity of a marriage by bans cannot be questioned on the ground that neither of the parties lived in the parish in which the bans were published. *Free* v. *Quin*, 2 Phil. Ecc. R. 14; *Dobbyn* v. *Corneck*, 2 *Id.* 104; *Didder* v. *Faucit*, 3 *Id.* 581; *Ray* v. *Sherwood*, 1 Curt. 193, 235; *Rex* v. *Hind*, Russ. & Ry. C. C. 253. In order to render a marriage void by reason of undue publication of bans (in false names or otherwise) *both* parties must be shown to have been cognizant of the undue publication, before the celebration of the marriage. *Wiltshire* v. *Prince*, 3 Hagg. Ecc. R. 332; *Rex* v. *Inhabitants of Wroxton*, 4 B. & Adol. 640; *Wright* v. *Ellwood*, 1 Curt. 662. But on sufficient evidence of such knowledge by both parties, the marriage may be declared void. *Tongue* v. *Allen*, 1 Curt. 38; *Tongue* v. *Tongue*, 1 Moore, P. C. C. 90; *Brealy* v. *Reed*, 2 Curt. 833; *Rex* v. *Tibshelf* 1 B. & Adol. 190. The uncorroborated evidence of either party will not be deemed sufficient. If the bans were in the incorrect names by which the parties were usually known, the marriage is valid. *Rex* v. *Inhabitants of Billinghurst*, 3 M. & S. 250; *Rex* v. *St. Faith's*, *Newton*, 3 Dowl. & Ry. 348.

A marriage by licence is valid, notwithstanding a misnomer of either of the parties in the licence, provided the marriage takes place between the parties to whom the licence was intended to apply. *Clowes* v. *Clowes*, 3 Curt. 185; *Rex* v. *The Inhabitants of Burton-upon-Trent*, 3 M. & S. 537; *Lane* v. *Godwin*, 4 Q. B. 361; 3 Gale & D. 610. But if the licence were obtained for a marriage between A. and B., and knowingly used by *other* persons, such marriage would be void. *S. C.* The marriage of a minor by licence without the consent required by 4 Geo. 4, c. 75, s. 16, is valid, the enactment requiring such consent being directory only. *Rex* v. *Inhabitants of Birmingham*, 8 B. & C. 29; 2 M. & R. 230.

Evidence that a marriage was solemnized in Scotland or in a foreign country, *according to the laws of that country*, will be sufficient. *Dalrymple* v. *Dalrymple*, 2 Hagg. Ecc. R. 54; *Ilderton* v. *Ilderton*, 2 H. Blac. 145; *Lacon* v. *Higgins*, 3 Stark. R. 178; 2 Arch. N. P. 366. But some witness conversant with the Scotch or foreign law must be called. *Reg.* v. *Povey*, 22 Law J., N. S., M. C., 19; 17 Jur. 120; 2 Tayl. Ev. 1106 (2nd ed.). A marriage between a British subject domiciled in England and a female ward of Chancery was celebrated at Antwerp in the English Church, by the British Chaplain, in the presence of the British Consul; but certain ceremonies prescribed by the law of Belgium were not observed: held, that the marriage was invalid. *Kent* v. *Burgess*, 11 Simon, 361; 5 Jur. 166; *Lacon* v. *Higgins*, 3 Stark. R. 178.

A marriage of Jews must be proved by the written contract of marriage: it is not sufficient to prove the performance of the religious ceremony. *Horn* v. *Noel*, 1 Camp. 61. But it would seem that evidence of reputation, &c. would be sufficient as in other cases. 2 Arch. N. P. 360; *ante*, 236.

13. *Birth and Baptism.*]—A birth or baptism is usually proved by an *examined* copy of the register, with evidence of the identity of the party; 2 Arch. N. P. 368; or by a *certified* copy, made pursuant to 14 & 15 Vict. c. 99, s. 14; 2 Tayl. Ev. 1233 (2nd ed.); together with evidence of identity. But it may be proved by parol evidence, without the aid of the register, or any copy of the entry. *Id.* 360.

The *time* of birth is matter of pedigree, and therefore may be proved by hearsay evidence. *Ante*, 234; 2 Arch. N. P. 368; Phil. Ev. 225 (8th ed.); *Herbert* v. *Tuckal*, Sir T. Ray. 84, cited 7 East, 290; *Goodright* v. *Moss*, 2 Cowp. 593; *Johnston* v. *Parker*, 3 Phillimore R., 42; *Figg* v. *Wedderburne*, 11 Law J., N. S., Q. B., 45. But in settlement cases, where the question is one rather of locality than of pedigree, hearsay evidence as to the *place* of birth is not admissible. *Rex* v. *Inhabitants of Erith*, 8 East, 542; *Reg.* v. *Inhabitants of Rishworth*, 2 Q. B. 476. Such evidence appears admissible on a question of genealogy, and with a view to identify ancestors. *Shields* v *Boucher*, 1 De Gex & Sm. 40, K. Bruce, V. C.

14. *Death.*]—A death is usually proved by an *examined* copy of the register, with evidence of the identity; 2 Arch. N. P. 369; or by a *certified* copy made pursuant to 14 & 15 Vict. c. 99, s. 14; 2 Tayl. Ev. 1223 (2nd ed.); together with evidence of identity. But it may be proved by parol evidence, without the aid of the register, or of any copy of the entry; *Id.* 360; *ex. gr.*, by any person who saw him dead, or who saw or attended his funeral, and can give reasonable evidence of his identity. 2 Arch. N. P. 369. So evidence of reputation in the family, of the death of any member of it, is admissible. *Id.* 369; Bull. N. P. 294; *ante*, 236.

Registers of births and deaths under the Registration Act, 6 & 7 Will. 4, c. 86, s. 38, are evidence not only of the births and deaths to which they relate, but also of the time and place when and where those events occurred, if mentioned in the entry pursuant to 7 Will. 4 & 1 Vict. c. 22, s. 8. 2 Tayl. Ev. 1361 (2nd ed.). But a register of baptism, made before the Registration Act, was no evidence of the exact date of the birth, although mentioned therein. *Rex* v. *Clapham*, 4 C. & P. 29; *Burghart* v. *Angerstein*, 6 C. & P. 690, 696; *Wihen* v. *Law*, 3 Stark. 63. When an examined copy of a register is produced, the witness must prove that the original was in the proper custody. *Doe* d. *Lord Arundel* v. *Fowler*, 14 Q. B. 700; *Doe* d. *France* v. *Andrews*, 15 Q. B. 756.

Letters of administration are not *primâ facie* evidence of the death of the intestate. 2 Tayl. Ev. 1295 (2nd ed.); *Thompson* v. *Donaldson*,

3 Esp. 63; *Moorus* v. *De Bernales*, 1 Russ. 301; *French* v. *French*,
1 Dick. 268.

When a party has been absent seven years without having been
heard of by members of his family likely to have heard of or from him,
if living, the presumption of law arises that he is *then dead*; but there
is no legal presumption as to the *time* of his death. *Doe* d. *Knight* v.
Nepean, 5 B. & Adol. 86; *S. C.* (in error), 2 M. & W. 894. Therefore where he had a life estate, an ejectment by the remainderman or
reversioner must be brought within thirteen years after the expiration of the seven years, or within twenty years after he was last heard
of alive; if commenced after that time evidence must be produced by
the plaintiff as to the *time* of his death. *S. C.* To raise the presumption of his death after seven years' absence inquiries should be made of
those persons who would naturally have heard of him, had he been
alive; or that search had been ineffectually made to find such a person. *Doe* d. *France* v. *Andrews*, 15 Q. B. 756.

Where a person is once shown to have been living, the law, in the
absence of proof that he has not been heard of for seven years, will in
general presume that he is still alive; unless after a lapse of time considerably exceeding the ordinary duration of human life. 1 Tayl. Ev.
166; *Doe* d. *France* v. *Andrews*, 15 Q. B. 756. The deposition of
a witness taken sixty years before the trial has been rejected, no
account being given of him, and no search having been made for him.
Benson v. *Olive*, 2 Stra. 920; *Manby* v. *Curtis*, 1 Price, 225. On
the other hand, the accounts of a steward charging himself with rents
received, and signed fifty-four years before the trial, were allowed to
be read without any proof of his death, that being presumed. *Doe* d.
Earl of Ashburnham v. *Michael*, 17 Q. B. 276.

Proof by one of a family, that many years before a younger brother
of the person last seised had gone abroad, and that the report of the
family was that he had died there, and that the witness had never
heard in the family of his having been married, is *primâ facie* evidence
that the party is *dead without lawful issue*, so as to entitle the next
claimant by descent to recover in ejectment. *Doe* d. *Banning* v.
Griffen, 15 East, 293. Members of a family named in a marriage
settlement 100 years old, and not mentioned in subsequent wills, &c.
may be presumed to be *dead without issue. Doe* d. *Oldham* v. *Wolley*,
8 B. & C. 22. But, generally speaking, proof of the death of a person
is not *primâ facie* evidence of his death *without issue.* The failure of
issue is a distinct fact, which must be proved by evidence of reputation
or otherwise. *Richards* v. *Richards*, 15 East, 294, note (*a*).

15. *Parcel or no Parcel.*]—Sometimes this is the only question to
be decided. *Doe* d. *Renow* v. *Ashley*, 10 Q. B. 663; *Doe* d. *Davies*
v. *Williams*, 1 H. Blac. 25; *Doe* d. *Freeland* v. *Burt*, 1 T. R. 701;
Doe d. *Smith* v. *Galloway*, 5 B. & Adol. 43; *Bartlett* v. *Wright*, Cro.
Eliz. 299; *Williams* v. *Morgan*, 15 Q. B. 782; *Dyne* v. *Nutley*, 14
C. B. 122. It is a question of fact for the jury so far as the identity
of the land depends upon parol evidence. Such evidence is generally
admissible *to apply the words used* in a deed or writing, and to identify
the property therein comprised. *Paddock* v. *Fradley*, 1 Cro. & Jer.
90; *Doe* d. *Freeland* v. *Burt*, 1 T. R. 701; *Id.* 704, Buller, J.;
Dyne v. *Nutley*, 14 C. B. 122. So with respect to the words used in
a will. *Doe* d. *Beach* v. *The Earl of Jersey*, 3 B. & C. 870, 873; *Doe*

d. *Renow* v. *Ashley*, 10 Q. B. 663; *Nightingall* v. *Smith*, 1 Exch. 879, 885; *Doe* d. *Hemming* v. *Willetts*, 7 C. B. 709; *Ricketts* v. *Turquand*, 1 H. L. Cas. 473. But parol evidence is not admissible to show that the words were *intended* to be used so as to comprise other property; *Doe* d. *Oxenden* v. *Chichester*, 3 Taunt. 147; 4 Dow. Parl. C. 65; or that they were *intended* to include a particular close or parcel of land. Where a contract for the purchase of land is afterwards carried into effect by a deed of conveyance wherein the property is described, the original written contract for the purchase is not admissible to show that a particular close is comprised, or was intended to be comprised, in the conveyance. *Williams* v. *Morgan*, 15 Q. B. 782. But *collateral facts*, from which the meaning of the words used may be collected, may be proved, so as to include or exclude a particular tenement, the words used being capable of either construction. *Doe* d. *Freeland* v. *Burt*, 1 T. R. 701, 704; *Doe* d. *Renow* v. *Ashley*, 10 Q. B. 663; *Nightingall* v. *Smith*, 1 Exch. 879, 885; *Doe* d. *Hemming* v. *Willetts*, 7 C. B. 709.

Evidence of *reputation* as to the ownership of private property is inadmissible. *Doe* d. *Didsbury* v. *Thomas*, 14 East, 323; *Clothier* v. *Chapman, Id.* 331 n.; *The Earl of Dunraven* v. *Llewellyn*, 15 Q. B. 791; *Williams* v. *Morgan, Id.* 782, 785; but see *Davies* v. *Lewis*, 2 Chit. R. 535, where evidence of reputation was admitted whether the place in question was parcel of a sheep-walk. Evidence of reputation as to particular land being parcel of a manor or parish has been held admissible. *Doe* d. *Jones* v. *Richards*, Peake, Add. Cas. 180; *Plaxton* v. *Dare*, 10 B. & C. 17.

Where the description of the property is substantially correct, but not in all its details, the latter may be rejected upon the principle *falsa demonstratio non nocet.* Plow. 191; cited 1 Exch. 886; 2 Pres. Conv. 449; Com. Dig. Fait, E. 4; *Goodtitle* d. *Radford* v. *Southern*, 1 M. & S. 299; *Down* v. *Down*, 7 Taunt. 343; *Marshall* v. *Hopkins*, 15 East, 309; *Preedy* v. *Halton*, 4 A. & E. 76. In such cases evidence is admissible of the facts showing in what respects the description is accurate and in what inaccurate; also of any other collateral facts from which the intention may be inferred. *Doe* d. *Renow* v. *Ashley*, 10 Q. B. 663; *Nightingall* v. *Smith*, 1 Exch. 885. But direct evidence of what the testator intended is inadmissible. If premises be described in general terms, and a particular description of them be added, the latter will control the former. *Per* Parke, J., in *Doe* d. *Smith* v. *Galloway*, 5 B. & Adol. 51; *Dyne* v. *Nutley*, 14 C. B. 122; *Doe* d. *Hubbard* v. *Hubbard*, 15 Q. B. 227; *Thomas* v. *Thomas*, 6 T. R. 671; *Doe* d. *Parkin* v. *Parkin*, 5 Taunt. 321; *Morrell* v. *Fisher*, 4 Exch. 591; *Llewellyn* v. *Earl of Jersey*, 11 M. & W. 183. Where premises are particularly enumerated or described by names, abuttals or otherwise, the addition of subsequent general words will not extend to *other* property, *expressio unius est exclusio alterius.* *Hare* v. *Horton*, 5 B. & Adol. 715; *Doe* d. *Meyrick* v. *Meyrick*, 2 Cr. & Jer. 223; 2 Tyr. 178; *per* Alderson, B., in *Doe* d. *Spilsbury* v. *Burdett*, 9 A. & E. 953; 1 P. & D. 682. A conveyance by lease and release of a mill and of all lands, &c. used or occupied therewith, will pass not only freeholds, but also leaseholds which fall within the description. *Doe* d. *Davies* v. *Williams*, 1 H. Blac. 25. A devise of a *freehold* farm in a particular parish will not include two pieces of leasehold held as part of that farm. *Hall* v. *Fisher*, 1 Collier, 47,

M

K. Bruce, V. C.; but see *Doe* d. *Dunning* v. *Lord Cranstown*, 7 M.
& W. 1. A conveyance of certain messuages and lands in Wootton
(describing them), and of *all other* the grantor's messuages, &c., in
Wootton or elsewhere, will pass other lands, &c. in Wootton held by
the grantor under a distinct title. *Doe* d. *Pell* v. *Jeyes*, 1 B. & Adol.
593 ; and see *Doe* d. *Campton* v. *Carpenter*, 16 Q. B. 181 ; 20 Law
J., N. S., Q. B., 70.

Maps.]—In ejectment the only case in which a map of property is
receivable in evidence is, where it is undisputed that at the time the
map was made the property belonged to the person from whom both
parties claim. *Doe* d. *Hughes* d. *Lakin*, 7 C. & P. 481, Patteson, J.

16. *Boundaries of Estates, &c.—A Wall.*]—Where two properties,
whether houses or lands, are separated by a wall, and it cannot be
proved on whose land the wall was originally built, the presumption is
that the owners of the land on each side are tenants in common of the
wall, and of the land on which it is built. *Wiltshire* v. *Sidford*, 8 B.
& C. 259, note. The common user of a wall separating adjoining
lands belonging to different owners is *primâ facie* evidence that the
wall and the land on which it stands belong to the owners of those
adjoining lands in equal moieties as tenants in common. *Cubitt* v.
Porter, 8 B. & C. 257 ; 2 M. & Ry. 267. Where such an ancient
wall was pulled down by one of the two tenants in common, with the
intention of rebuilding the same, and he built a new wall (before
action) of a greater height than the old one : held, that this was not
such a total destruction of the wall as to entitle the other tenant in
common to maintain trespass against him. *Cubitt* v. *Porter, supra*.
But if it be proved that the wall was originally built at the joint expense of both proprietors, and that it stood on the boundary line, so
that part of the wall was on the ground of each proprietor, they will
not be deemed tenants in common of the wall, or of the land on which
it is built; but each will be considered as separately entitled to his
moiety of the wall, &c., and he may maintain an action against the
other for pulling down, or building on his part of the wall. *Matts* v.
Hawkins, 5 Taunt. 20 ; and see *Taylor* v. *Stendall*, 7 Q. B. 634 ; 3
Dowl. & L. 161. In contemplation of law, a party-wall built partly
on the land of A. and partly on the land of B. constitutes two distinct
walls, and must be so described in pleading. *Murly* v. *M'Dermott*,
8 A. & E. 138, 142; 3 N. & P. 356. Either party may at any time
make a severance by splitting the wall (supposing that to be physically
possible), taking down the half which stood on his land, and resuming
his own moiety of the soil, bricks and mortar; although perhaps the
consequence will be that the other half of the wall will fall down, not
being thick enough to support itself. *Wigford* v. *Gill*, Cro. Eliz. 369;
5 Taunt. 22, note (*a*); *per* Bayley, J., in *Cubitt* v. *Porter*, 8 B. & C.
264; 2 Man. & Ry. 267. Trespass does not generally lie by one part-
owner of a party-wall against the other part-owner. *Wiltshire* v. *Sidford*, 1 Man. & Ry. 404.

Hedge and Ditch.]—Where two estates adjoin each other, but
are separated by a hedge and ditch, the presumption of law (in the
absence of proof to the contrary) is, that both the hedge and ditch
belong to the owner of the land on the side on which the hedge is;

because it is presumed that the person who dug the ditch did so on his own land, and threw the soil dug out on his own side, and which formed the mound on which the hedge was planted. 1 Arch. N. P. 439. Proof of the ancient width of the ditch is evidence that the owner's land did not extend beyond the outer edge thereof; and he has no right to cut away his neighbour's land for the purpose of widening the ditch. *Vowles* v. *Miller*, 3 Taunt. 137. In this case the defendant directed his evidence to prove that the fence had immemorially been a bank with a ditch on the outside of it; and he contended that consequently he was entitled at common law to have a width of eight feet as the reasonable width for the base of his bank and the area of his ditch together, admitting that, if the fence were a bank only, he was entitled only to four feet. *Sed per* Lawrence, J., "The rule about ditching is this; no man making a ditch can cut into his neighbour's soil, but usually cuts it to the very extremity of his own land. He is of course bound to throw the soil which he digs out upon his own land; and if he likes, he plants a hedge on the top of it; therefore if he afterwards cuts beyond the edge of the ditch, which is the extremity of his land, he cuts into his neighbour's land, and is a trespasser. No rule about four feet and eight feet has anything to do with it. He may cut the ditch as much wider as he will, if he enlarges it into his own land." *Id.* 138. At present we are considering only where the ditch lies between the lands of two proprietors: when it adjoins a slip of waste on the side of a highway, see *per* Holroyd, J., in *Doe* d. *Pring* v. *Pearsey*, 7 B. & C. 307, 308; *post*, 244.

Hedge with a Ditch on each Side, or Hedge only.]—Where two estates adjoin each other, but are separated by a hedge with a ditch on each side, or by a hedge only (or by a ditch only), then the presumption of law (in the absence of proof to the contrary) is, that the owners of the land on either side are tenants in common of the hedge; 1 Arch. N. P. 439; (or ditch); not that each is separately entitled to one moiety of the hedge, and of the land on which it grows. Therefore if either party clip the hedge, the other cannot maintain trespass against him; but for grubbing it up, or otherwise wholly destroying it, he may. *Voyce* v. *Voyce*, Gow. 201.

Road or Highway.]—Where two estates are separated by a road or public highway, the origin of which cannot be proved, the presumption is, that the proprietors of such estates respectively are owners of the soil *usque ad medium filum viæ*. *Cooke* v. *Green*, 11 Price, 736; 2 Smith, L. C. 94. And the presumption also is, that the waste land which adjoins to the road belongs to the owner of the adjoining freehold on that side of the road, and not to the lord of the manor. *Steel* v. *Prichett*, 2 Stark. R. 463, Abbott, C. J. And it makes no difference in this respect whether such owner be a freeholder, leaseholder or copyholder. *Doe* d. *Pring* v. *Pearsey*, 9 Dowl. & Ry. 908; 7 B. & C. 304. And *per* Bayley, J., "It is very desirable that there should be one certain and definite rule applicable to all cases of this description. Now it is a *primâ facie* presumption that waste land on the sides, and the soil to the middle of a highway, belongs to the owner of the adjoining freehold land. The rule is founded on a supposition that the proprietor of the adjoining land at some former period gave up to the public for passage all the land between his inclosure and the middle

M 2

of the road. I think that rule applies not only to freehold, but to
copyhold lands also." *Id.* 306. And *per* Holroyd, J., "I see no
reason for confining the rule to cases where the person in possession of
the adjoining land is a freeholder. It applies equally whether the party
occupying the adjoining land be a freeholder, leaseholder or copyholder.
As to the property granted, a copyholder stands in the place of the
lord; the leaseholder in the place of the lessor. It is very improbable
that when a lease or grant is made of land near the high road, and
there is between the highway and the land inclosed a small quantity of
uninclosed land, of little or no use to the lord or lessor, that he should
separate it from the rest, or reserve to himself such land. When a
grant of land near to a road is made (even when it is inclosed and
separated from the land adjoining), it appears to me that the *primâ
facie* presumption is, that the land on that side of the fence on which
the road is, passes likewise with it. Generally speaking, where an
inclosure is made, the party making it erects his bank and digs his
ditch on his own ground on the outside of the bank. The land which
constitutes the ditch in point of law is part of the close, though it be
on the outside of the bank; and if something further is done for his
own convenience when that which constitutes the fence is dug out
from his land, as, for instance, if a small portion of uninclosed land
near a public or private way is left out of the inclosure to protect and
secure the occupation of that part of the land which is inclosed, that
in point of law is a part of the close on which the inclosure is made.
If any grant of such land, being copyhold, had been made before the
inclosure, the subsequent grants would probably continue to be made
in the same way, notwithstanding the inclosure, and all the land, both
within and without the inclosure, would therefore pass by these grants.
It seems to me, therefore, that the rule that waste land near a highway
is to be presumed *primâ facie* to belong to the owner of the inclosed
land next adjoining, is not confined to a case where the owner of that
land is a freeholder, but extends equally to cases where the owner is a
leaseholder or a copyholder. In either case evidence may be given to
rebut the *primâ facie* presumption. But it is of considerable importance that the *primâ facie* presumption should be constant and uniform, and not left to depend on a variety of particular circumstances,
some of which may be beyond the time of actual memory, although
not beyond the time of legal memory." *Id.* 307, 308. The presumption, however, arises only where the original dedication of the road
cannot be shown by positive evidence. *Headlam* v. *Headley*, 1 Holt,
N. P. C. 463. If the road be proved to have been made within the
memory of living witnesses on part of the common or waste land of
the manor previously used by commoners for feeding their cattle, &c.,
the presumption in favour of the owner of the adjoining land is rebutted. *S. C.* Evidence of acts of ownership in the lord of the manor
is admissible to repel the presumption. *Anon.*, Lofft, 358. When the
question was, whether a slip of land between some old inclosures and
the highway belonged to the lord of the manor, or to the owner of the
adjoining freehold: held, that evidence ought to be received of acts of
ownership by the lord of the manor on similar slips of land not adjoining his own freehold in various parts of the manor. *Doe* d. *Barrett*
v. *Kemp*, 7 Bing. 332; 5 Moo. & P. 173; *S. C.* (in error), 2 Bing.
N. C. 102; 2 Scott, 9. If the slip of land communicate with open
commons or other larger portions of land, the presumption in favour of

the owner of the adjoining land is either done away, or considerably narrowed; for the evidence of ownership, which applies to the larger portions, applies also to the narrow slip which communicates with them. *Grove* v. *West*, 7 Taunt. 39; and see *Doe* d. *Harrison* v. *Hampson*, 4 C. B. 267; *Headlam* v. *Headley*, 1 Holt, N. P. C. 463; *Doe* d. *Barrett* v. *Kemp*, *supra*; *Jones* v. *Williams*, 2 M. & W. 326; *Stanley* v. *White*, 14 East, 332; *Taylor* v. *Parry*, 1 Man. & Gr. 605; 1 Scott, N. R. 576; *Wild* v. *Holt*, 9 M. & W. 672. But the evidence must show a continuity or one entire thing, and not several. *Tyrwhitt* v. *Wynne, Bart.*, 2 B. & A. 554; *The Earl of Dunraven* v. *Llewellyn*, 15 Q. B. 791.

In *Steel* v. *Prichett*, 2 Stark. R. 469, Abbott, C. J., explained the origin of waste pieces of land on the sides of highways thus:—" In remote and ancient times, when roads were frequently made through uninclosed lands, and when the same labour and expense was not employed upon roads, and they were not formed with that exactness which the exigences of society now require, it was part of the law that the public, where the road was out of repair, might pass along the land by the side of the road. This right on the part of the public was attended with this consequence, that although the parishioners were bound to the repair of the road, yet if an owner excluded the public from using the adjoining land, he cast upon himself the onus of repairing the road. If the same person was the owner of the land on both sides, and inclosed both sides, he was bound to repair the whole of the road. If he inclosed on one side only, the other being left open, he was bound to repair to the middle of the road; and where there was ancient inclosure on one side, and the owner of lands inclosed on the other, he was bound to repair the whole. Hence it followed as a natural consequence, that when a person inclosed his land from the road, he did not make his fence close to the road, but left an open space at the side of the road to be used by the public when occasion required. This appears to be the most natural and satisfactory mode of explaining the frequency of wastes left at the sides of roads. The object was to leave a sufficiency of land for passage by the side of a road when it was out of repair, is the general presumption of law; but this presumption is capable of being rebutted."

It seems that no such presumption in favour of the owners of the adjoining lands applies with reference to roads set out under an Inclosure Act. *Rex* v. *Inhabitants of Edmonton*, 1 Moo. & Rob. 24, 32, Lord Tenterden, C. J.; but see *Cooke* v. *Green*, 11 Price, 736. Nor as between the owners of adjoining lands separated by a road, and both deriving title through the same person. *White* v. *Hill*, 6 Q. B. 487; 2 Dowl. & L. 537; and see *Noye* v. *Reed*, 1 Man. & R. 63.

A River.]—Where two estates are separated by a river, if it be a navigable river the presumption is, that the soil of the bed of the river belongs to the crown, and the banks of the river (above high water mark) form the boundaries on each side. 1 Arch. N. P. 438. But if the river be fresh water and not navigable, the presumption is, that the lands of the proprietors on each side extend *usque ad medium filum aquæ*. 1 Arch. N. P. 438. This, however (like the other presumptions before mentioned), may be rebutted by evidence showing that one owner is entitled to the whole bed of the river. This is usually proved by acts of ownership exercised on the other side of the river. Thus in trespass *quare clausum fregit*, the plaintiff claimed the whole bed of the river flowing between his land and the defendant's, the defendant contending that each was entitled *ad medium filum aquæ*: held, that evidence of acts of ownership exercised by the plaintiff upon the bed and banks of the river on the defendant's side lower down the stream, and where it flowed between the plaintiff's land and a farm of C. adjoining the defendant's land, and also of repairs done by the plaintiff to a fence which divided C.'s farm from the river, and was in continuation of a fence dividing the defendant's land from the river, was admissible evidence for the plaintiff. *Jones* v. *Williams*, 2 M. & W. 326; *Id.* 327, 331, Parke, B., who explains the principles upon which such evidence is admissible. Proof of acts of ownership on different parts of a continuous or entire thing is admissible evidence in proof of the title and right to possession of the whole thing, *ex. gr.*, a woody belt surrounding the plaintiff's land; *Stanley* v. *White*, 14 East, 332; a piece of waste by a highway leading to a common; *Grose* v. *West*, 7 Taunt. 39; *Doe* d. *Barrett* v. *Kemp*, 7 Bing. 332; 5 Moo. & P. 173; *S. C.* (in error), 2 Bing. N. C. 102; 2 Scott, 9; a river; *Jones* v. *Williams*, 2 M. & W. 326; a continuous hedge or fence; *id.*; a mountain; *Taylor* v. *Barry*, 1 Man. & Gr. 605; 1 Scott, N. R. 576; a coal mine; *Wild* v. *Holt*, 9 M. & W. 672; a ridge of hills forming the boundary between two or more manors. *Brisco* v. *Lomax*, 8 A. & E. 198; 3 N. & P. 308; the boundary of two hamlets and of two estates. *Thomas* v. *Jenkins*, 6 A. & E. 525; 1 N. & P. 587; and see *Rowe* v. *Brenton*, 8 B. & C. 675; 3 Man. & Ry. 143; cited 9 M. & W. 556; *Jewinson* v. *Dyson*, 9 M. & W. 540. But the evidence must appear to relate to one continuous and entire thing, and not to several distinct ones. *Tyrwhitt* v. *Wynne, Bart.*, 2 B. & A. 554; *The Earl of Dunraven* v. *Llewellyn*, 15 Q. B. 791. Where a private river runs through a manor, the presumption of law is, that each owner of land within the manor and on the bank of the river has the right of fishing in front of his land; and if the lord claim a several fishery, he must make out that claim by evidence, and *primâ facie* evidence thereof may be rebutted. *Lamb* v. *Newbiggin*, 1 Car. & K. 549.

Unascertained Boundaries.]—Where the boundaries between two manors or estates have never been ascertained, or the evidence thereof is lost, and the question is, to which of them the *locus in quo* belongs, evidence of acts of ownership thereon by either party is most material, and conclusive, if not met by similar evidence. *Curzon* v. *Lomax*, 5 Esp. 60, Lord Ellenborough, C. J.; *Smith* v. *Royston*, 8 M. & W. 381; 1 Dowl. N. S. 124. In the year 1848, Earl Cawdor lost a valuable mountain in Wales by evidence of this sort, which had been designedly manufactured for the purpose during a period of from twenty to thirty years. In trespass for breaking and entering the plaintiff's mine and taking coals, evidence of working by the plaintiff in another part of the same mine, within eighty yards of the place of the alleged trespass, coupled with a statement by the defendant that he had got the coal, and was willing to pay such amount as should be settled by arbitration, was held to be evidence of the plaintiff's being in possession of the place where the trespass was committed, although they had failed in an attempt to prove their title under certain leases. *Wild* v. *Holt*, 9 M. & W. 672. Where the plaintiffs were lessees under certain persons, called the Lords of Mold, of all mines and minerals under a large tract of waste land called Mold Mountain; in trover for ore wrongfully extracted by the defendants from a spot which the plaintiffs alleged to be part of Mold Mountain: held, that it was not necessary for the plaintiffs to prove the title or seisin of their lessors, but that it was enough for them as against the defendants, who were wrongdoers, to show a possession and enjoyment by themselves under the lease, and that for this purpose *acts of ownership* exercised by the plaintiffs, by working mines in *other parts* of the mountain, were evidence of their right under the spot in question, being part of the waste. *Taylor* v. *Parry,* 1 Man. & Gr. 605; 1 Scott, N. R. 576.

Evidence of Reputation.]—The boundaries of *manors and parishes* may be proved by evidence of reputation, on the ground of the publicity of the rights affected by the boundary. *Nicholls* v. *Parker,* 14 East, 331, note; *Weeks* v. *Sparke,* 1 M. & S. 679; *Crease* v. *Barrett,* 1 Cr. M. & R. 919; 5 Tyr. 458. Hearsay is admissible to show that a particular spot was within a parish boundary, but not that houses stood on any given spot. *Ireland* v. *Powell,* Peake's Ev. 13; cited 2 A. & E. 795. An old survey of two manors is good evidence of the boundaries of each *inter se,* if both manors belonged at the time when the survey was taken to the person who took it, or caused it to be taken; otherwise not. *Bridgeman* v. *Jennings,* 1 Lord Raym. 734; and see *Doe* d. *Hughes* v. *Lakin,* 7 C. & P. 481. A county history describing the boundaries between two manors is not admissible. *Evans* v. *Getting,* 6 C. & P. 586. Where a legal manor has once existed, declarations of persons deceased as to its boundaries are admissible in evidence, though the manor has ceased to exist otherwise than by reputation. *Doe* d. *Molesworth, Bart.,* v. *Sleeman,* 9 Q. B. 298.

On a question of boundary between *two estates,* evidence of reputation as to the boundaries is generally inadmissible, because it relates to private and not public rights. *Doe* d. *Didsbury* v. *Thomas,* 14 East, 323; *Clothier* v. *Chapman, Id.* 331, note; *The Earl of Dunraven* v. *Llewellyn* (in error), 15 Q. B. 791, 812. But if it be proved that the boundary of the estates is the same as that between two hamlets or parishes, or other public districts, evidence of reputation as to the boundary of the latter may be adduced for the purpose of proving that of the estates; and the jury may be desired to take into consideration the latter evidence, if they are satisfied with the first. *Thomas* v. *Jenkins,* 6 A. & E. 525; 1 N. & P. 587. Where the boundary between two manors is formed by a ridge of hills, which runs beyond those manors, and on an issue as to the boundary between one of those manors and a third manor, one of the parties wishes to prove that the same ridge is the boundary between the two latter manors, evidence of its being the boundary of the other two is admissible for this purpose, the three manors being contiguous. *Brisco* v. *Lomax,* 8 A. & E. 198; 3 N. & P. 308.

17. *Encroachments by Tenants.*]—Encroachments made by a tenant during his term from the adjoining waste, &c., are generally presumed to have been *added to the demised premises, and to form part thereof,* with the implied assent of the landlord, for the benefit of the tenant during the term, and afterwards for the landlord. *Doe* d. *Lewis* v.

Rees, 6 C. & P. 610, Parke, B.; *Doe* d. *Earl of Dunraven* v. *Williams*, 7 C. & P. 332, Coleridge, J.; *Doe* d. *Harrison* v. *Murrell*, 8 C. & P. 134, Lord Abinger, C. B.; *Bryan* v. *Winwood*, 1 Taunt. 208; *Doe* d. *Lloyd* v. *Jones*, 15 M. & W. 580; *Andrews* v. *Hailes*, 2 E. & B. 349; *Doe* d. *Croft* v. *Tidbury*, 14 C. B. 304. "It is clearly settled that encroachments made by a tenant are for the benefit of his landlord, unless it appear clearly by some *act done at the time* of the making of the encroachments that the tenant intended the encroachments for his own benefit, and not to hold them as he held the farm to which the encroachments were adjacent." *Per* Parke, B., in *Doe* d. *Lewis* v. *Rees*, 6 C. & P. 610. It makes no difference in this respect that the encroachment does not immediately adjoin the demised premises. *Doe* d. *Challnor* v. *Davies*, 1 Esp. 461, Thompson, B.; *Doe* d. *Lloyd* v. *Jones*, 15 M. & W. 580. The mere intervention of a road does not rebut the *primâ facie* presumption. *Andrews* v. *Hailes*, 2 E. & B. 349. It is not necessary that the soil of the waste should have belonged to the lessor. *Doe* d. *Lloyd* v. *Jones* and *Andrews* v. *Hailes*, *supra*; *Doe* d. *Croft* v. *Tidbury*, 14 C. B. 304. The presumption is, not that the tenant *stole* the land for the benefit of his landlord, but that it belonged to his landlord, and that the tenant held it as part of the demised premises during the term, with the implied assent of the landlord. *Andrews* v. *Hailes*, *supra*. If it be proved that the waste really did belong to the landlord, that will strengthen the presumption in his favour. *Bryan* d. *Child* v. *Winwood*, 1 Taunt. 208, Graham, B.; and see *Doe* d. *Lloyd* v. *Jones*, 15 M. & W. 580. On the other hand, the presumption may be rebutted by proof of some *act done at the time* of the making of the encroachment, clearly showing the intention of the tenant to encroach for his own benefit, and not to hold the encroachments in the same manner as the demised premises. *Doe* d. *Badeley* v. *Massey*, 17 Q. B. 373; 20 Law J. (N. S.) Q. B. 434; *Doe* d. *Lewis* v. *Rees*, 6 C. & P. 610, Parke, B. The fact that the lessee, during the lease, made a conveyance of the encroachments to his son in fee, which, however, was not delivered to the son, nor followed by any possession, is not sufficient to rebut the usual presumption. *Doe* d. *Lloyd* v. *Jones*, 15 M. & W. 580.

Upon the expiration of the lease, or other determination of the tenancy, the encroachments made by the tenant during his term may generally be recovered by the landlord, together with and as part of the demised premises. *Cases*, *supra*. But if all the premises originally demised have been given up to the landlord, he may maintain ejectment for the encroachments alone; *Andrews* v. *Hailes*, 2 E. & B. 349; and they may be recovered at any time within the period limited for the recovery of any other part of the demised premises, *i. e.* within twenty years after the expiration of the lease. *Doe* d. *Croft* v. *Tidbury*, 14 C. B. 304; *Doe* d. *Earl of Dunraven* v. *Williams*, 7 C. & P. 332.

After the expiration of the period prescribed by the Statute of Limitations (3 & 4 Will. 4, c. 27) has elapsed from the making of an inclosure, neither the lord of the manor, nor any commoner, can lawfully deprive the party of his encroachment; *Hawke* v. *Bacon*, 2 Taunt. 156; *Creach* v. *Wilmot*, *Id.* 160, note; *Tapley* v. *Wainwright*, 5 B. & Adol. 395; unless, indeed, the lord of the manor happen to be the lessor or landlord. *Doe* d. *Croft* v. *Tidbury*, 14 C. B. 304; *Doe* d. *Earl of Dunraven* v. *Williams*, 7 C. & P. 332.

An encroachment made by a tenant in fee, who dies within twenty years afterwards, will descend to his heir and not go to his executor. *Doe* d. *Pritchard* v. *Jauncey*, 8 C. & P. 99, Coleridge, J.

18. *Custom of the Country.*]—It frequently happens that by the custom of the country, that is to say, of the neighbourhood where the demised premises are situate, an outgoing tenant is entitled to the way-going crop, or some portion thereof, with liberty to cut and carry it away. *Wigglesworth* v. *Dalison*, 1 Doug. 201; 1 Smith, L. C. 300; *Boraston* v. *Green*, 16 East, 81, Bayley, J.; *Griffiths* v. *Pulestone*, 13 M. & W. 358. Or to the use of the barns, or some of them, for a certain period after the end of the term, for the purpose of threshing his crops; in which case the right will, in effect, *operate as a prolongation of the term as to such part;* and the outgoing tenant, or his assignee, may maintain trespass for acts done during such period on that part; *Beatty* v. *Gibbons*, 16 East, 116; *Griffiths* v. *Pulestone*, 13 M. & W. 358; and during such period the landlord may distrain on that part for rent; *Beavan* v. *Delahay*, 1 H. Black. 5; *Knight* v. *Bennett*, 3 Bing. 364; 11 Moore, 227; and during such period the outgoing tenant cannot remove any of the straw, &c., which he has covenanted not to remove "during the leased term." *Earl of St. Germains* v. *Willan*, 2 B. & C. 216. Sometimes, also, the outgoing tenant is entitled by the custom to allowances for tillages, seeds, manure, work done on the farm, &c.; *Wilkins* v. *Hood*, 17 Law J., Q. B., 319; *Faviell* v. *Gaskoin, Executor, &c.*, 7 Exch. 273; *Wigglesworth* v. *Dalison*, 1 Doug. 201; 1 Smith's L. C. 300; or to a proportion of the expense of drainage. *Mousley* v. *Ludlam* (on appeal from the county court), 21 Law J., Q. B., 64. But the onus of proving any such custom lies upon the tenant or other person alleging its existence. *Caldecott* v. *Smythies*, 7 C. & P. 808. Where any such custom is sufficiently proved it will prevail in all cases to which it is applicable, whether the tenant held under a verbal demise, *Wilkins* v. *Hood*, 17 Law J., Q. B., 319, or under a written agreement, or even by deed. *Wigglesworth* v. *Dalison*, 1 Doug. 201; 1 Smith's L. C. 300. But if the lease or agreement contain terms or stipulations which are inconsistent with the custom of the country, such custom will be thereby excluded, upon the principle *expressum facit cessare tacitum*. *Webb* v. *Plummer*, 2 B. & A. 746; *Roberts* v. *Barker*, 1 Cr. & Mee. 808; *Clarke* v. *Roystone*, 13 M. & W. 752. If, however, the custom and the stipulations of the lease or agreement are not wholly inconsistent with each other, both of them may sometimes prevail. *Hutton* v. *Warren*, 1 M. & W. 466; *Holding* v. *Pigott*, 7 Bing. 465; 5 M. & P. 427; *Sutton* v. *Temple*, 12 M. & W. 63, Parke, B.; *Faviell* v. *Gaskoin*, 7 Exch. 273.

19. *Land Tax Books.*]—Assessments of commissioners of land tax, by which it appears that at a certain time property was assessed in the name of "Strode" (without any christian name), are evidence to show, *in connection with other facts*, that at such time the property was occupied by a particular individual of the Strode family. *Doe* d. *Strode* v. *Seaton*, 2 A. & E. 171; 4 N. & M. 81. In this case the entries corresponded to some extent with entries in the steward's book, wherein he charged himself with rents received in respect of the property and allowances made to the tenant in respect of land tax. It is not clear

whether the appearance of a party's name in the land tax assessments in respect of certain property is, *of itself,* sufficient *primâ facie* evidence that he was seised of that property at the time ; it would rather seem not. *Doe* d. *Stansbury* v. *Arkwright,* 5 C. & P. 575 ; 1 A. & E. 182 ; 1 N. & M. 731. But where it was proved to be a common practice to continue the same name in the assessment so long as the property remained in the same family: held, that an assessment of " Mr. S." was not admissible to prove that Mr. S. S. was then seised. *S. C.* The assessment to the land tax, if it appears doubtful on the face of the rate whether it be on the landlord or tenant, is presumed to be on the tenant. *Rex* v. *Inhabitants of St. Lawrence,* 4 Doug. 190.

Entries in the land tax collector's books, stating A. B. to be rated for a particular house, and his *payment of the sum rated,* are admissible evidence to show that A. B. was in the occupation of the premises at the time mentioned. *Doe* d. *Smith* v. *Cartwright,* Ry. & Moo. 62 ; 1 C. & P. 218, Abbott, C. J. ; and see *Plaxton* v. *Dare,* 10 B. & C. 17.

An examined copy of an assessment of land tax is admissible, it being a public document. *Rex* v. *King,* 2 T. R. 234. If the assessment be deposited in the public record office, pursuant to 1 & 2 Vict. c. 94, an office copy certified and stamped with the seal of the record office, pursuant to sect. 12, is admissible " without any other or further proof thereof, in every case in which the original record could have been received as evidence." Sect. 13.

20. *Prior Judgment in Ejectment.*]—A prior judgment in ejectment is *admissible* evidence in a subsequent action between the same parties or their respective privies in estate, *ex. gr.* their heirs, executors, administrators and *subsequent* assigns. Ros. Ev. 137 (7th ed.) ; *Doe* d. *Strode* v. *Seaton,* 2 Cr. M. & R. 728, 731, 732. But not as against other persons ; *Neal* d. *Athol* v. *Wilding,* 2 Stra. 1151 ; *Doe* d. *Bacon* v. *Brydges,* 6 Man. & Gr. 282 ; 1 Dowl. & L. 954 ; for it would be unjust to bind any person who could not be admitted to make a defence, or to examine witnesses, or to appeal from a judgment he might think erroneous. Bull. N. P. 233 ; *Duchess of Kingston's case,* 2 Smith, L. C. 424, 440. A previous judgment in ejectment, when admitted in evidence, will of course have some weight with the jury ; but it is not conclusive in a subsequent ejectment. *Per* Lord Abinger, C. B., and Parke, B., in *Doe* d. *Strode* v. *Seaton,* 2 Cr. M. & R. 732. A judgment in ejectment obtained since the Common Law Procedure Act, 1852, has the same effect as a judgment obtained before the passing of that act. *Ante,* 76. It may be replied by way of estoppel to a plea of *liberum tenementum,* or to a plea denying the plaintiff's title, in an action of trespass for mesne profits, &c. *See the Forms, Appendix, Nos.* 397, 398, 399. But unless so replied it is not conclusive as an estoppel. *Aslin* v. *Parker,* 2 Burr. 665 ; 1 Smith, L. C. 264 ; *Vooght* v. *Winch,* 2 B. & A. 662 ; *Doe* v. *Huddart,* 2 Cr. M. & R. 316 ; 5 Tyr. 846 ; 4 Dowl. 437, *S. C.; Doe* v. *Wellsman,* 2 Exch. 368 ; 6 Dowl. & L. 179 ; *Matthews* v. *Osborne,* 13 C. B. 919 ; *Wilkinson* v. *Kirby,* 15 C. B. 430. A judgment in ejectment obtained against a mortgagor by a second or subsequent mortgagee, is not admissible evidence against a prior mortgagee ; *Doe* d. *Smith* v. *Webber,* 1 A. & E. 119 ; and see *Doe* d. *Foster* v. *The Earl of Derby, Id.* 783. A mother

and son were in possession of a house for which a declaration in ejectment was served on both; the son suffered judgment by default, but the mother defended : held, that an examined copy of a judgment, in an action by the plaintiff against the son for use and occupation of the house, was not receivable in evidence against the mother. *Doe* d. *Morse* v. *Williams*, Car. & M. 615. A special verdict in a former cause, to which present defendants were not parties, was rejected, when offered to prove some descents. *Neal* d. *Athol* v. *Wilding*, 2 Stra. 1151; and see *Doe* d. *Bacon* v. *Bridges*, 6 Man. & Gr. 282; 7 Scott, N. R. 333.

A judgment in ejectment (when admissible) must be proved by an office copy, either admitted in the usual manner (*ante*, 150), or proved to have been examined at the proper office with the original judgment roll. The witness must prove either that he compared the copy line for line with the original, or that the officer of the court, or some other person, *read to him* the entry on the judgment roll, and that he, at the same time, examined the copy; but it is not necessary that the original and the copy should be examined alternately by both parties. *Rolf* v. *Dart*, 2 Taunt. 52; *Reid* v. *Margison*, 1 Camp. 469; Phil. Ev. 615 (8th ed.). The witness must be able to state that the document with which he examined the copy was the judgment roll, kept at the proper office or place where it ought to be deposited. *Adamthwaite* v. *Synge*, 4 Camp. 372; 1 Stark. R. 183. If the copy contain *abbreviated* words, which are not so abbreviated in the judgment roll, it is not a true copy, and will be rejected. *Reg.* v. *Christian*, Car. & M. 388.

A certified copy of any judgment deposited with the Master of the Rolls pursuant to 1 & 2 Vict. c. 94, and stamped with the seal of the Record Office, pursuant to sect. 12, is admissible " without any further or other proof thereof, in every case in which the original record could have been received as evidence." Sect. 13.

21. *Evidence of deceased Witnesses given in a previous Ejectment.*] —The evidence of witnesses examined in a previous ejectment between the same parties, or their *subsequent* privies in estate, in which the same title was in issue, whether for the same or different land, is admissible in a subsequent ejectment, upon proof of the previous proceedings and of the death of the witness. Bull. N. P. 242; *The Earl of Derby* v. *Foster*, 1 A. & E. 791, note (*b*); *Wright* v. *Doe* d. *Tatham* (in error), 1 A. & E. 3, 18. If the parties are substantially the same, and the party against whom the evidence is tendered had an opportunity of cross-examining the witness at the time the evidence was given, that is sufficient. *Id.* 19; Phil. Ev. 353 (8th ed.); *Doe* d. *Hulin* v. *Powell*, 3 Car. & K. 323. But where the parties are not the same, and no *subsequent* privity of estate appears, the evidence given in the previous action is inadmissible. *Doe* d. *Foster* v. *The Earl of Derby*, 1 A. & E. 783; *Id.* 790, Littledale, J.; *Lock* v. *Norborne*, 3 Mod. 141.

If the verdict and judgment in the previous ejectment be inadmissible, *ante*, 250, the evidence of any witness then examined, and since dead, will be inadmissible. Bull. N. P. 242; Phil. Ev. 354 (8th ed.). In order to let in the evidence an office copy of the judgment, or the original record of nisi prius, with the postea indorsed, must be given in evidence. Gilb. Ev. 68; *Pitton* v. *Walter*, 1 Stra.

162. It must also be proved that the witness was duly sworn, and that he is dead.

The evidence of the deceased witness must be proved either by the judge's notes, or by a shorthand-writer's notes, or by the evidence of some person present at the former trial who can repeat the words of the witness, with or without the aid of notes made by him at the time. *Mayor of Doncaster* v. *Day*, 3 Taunt. 262; *Strutt* v. *Bovingdon*, 5 Esp. 56; Gilb. Ev. 68, 69. It is not sufficient for the witness to swear generally *to the effect* of the evidence of the deceased witness. *Lord Palmerston's case*, cited 4 T. R. 290. He should prove the precise words used as nearly as possible. Phil. Ev. 354 (8th ed.). On an indictment for perjury it is sufficient if a witness state from recollection the evidence which the defendant gave, though he cannot say with certainty that it was all the evidence the defendant gave, if he can say with certainty that it was all he gave on that point, and that there was nothing to qualify it. *Rex* v. *Rowley*, 1 Moody, C. C. 111; *Rex* v. *Munton*, 3 C. & P. 498.

Where the verdict in a prior ejectment is impeached on the ground that it was obtained by false and fabricated evidence, the opposite party may show what *other* evidence was then given in support of the verdict. *Doe* d. *Lloyd* v. *Passingham*, 2 C. & P. 440, Burrough, J.

22. Copies, Duplicates and Counterparts. — Attested Copies.]— It is very seldom, if ever, that an attested copy is admissible in evidence as *primary* evidence of the contents of a deed. *Brindley* v. *Woodhouse*, 1 Car. & K. 647; Sug. V. & P. 477 (11th ed.). But when so used on behalf of any party to the deed, it must be stamped with the same duty as the original instrument. 13 & 14 Vict. c. 97, Sched. I., tit. "Copy." If so used on behalf of any other person, it must be stamped with a 1s. stamp for every entire 720 words. *Id.* When used only as *secondary* evidence (after a notice to produce) it does not require any stamp. *Ditcher* v. *Kenrick*, 1 C. & P. 161, Abbott, C. J.; *Braythwayte* v. *Hitchcock*, 10 M. & W. 494; 2 Dowl. 444. For it is only used in point of law to refresh the witness's memory as to the contents of the deed. *S. C.*

The contents of a lost deed cannot be proved by an attested copy, without calling some or one of the persons who examined it with the original and attested it; it is not admissible on proof of their deaths and handwriting to the attestation. *Brindley* v. *Woodhouse*, 1 Car. & K. 647, Pollock, C. B.

Conveyancers place much reliance upon attested copies, especially when coupled with a covenant for the production of the original documents. Sug. V. & P. ch. ix. sect. 6. But attested copies appear to be of little use in courts of justice, except as examined copies used to refresh the memory of the attesting witness, when secondary evidence of the contents of the deed is admissible.

Examined Copies.]—An examined copy of a deed or other private writing is not generally admissible, except as *secondary* evidence. The original document should be produced or its absence accounted for to the satisfaction of the judge; after which an examined copy or other secondary evidence of the contents may be received.

An examined copy of a judgment, writ, return or other *public* document, may generally be proved in lieu of the original. 1 Tayl. Ev. 438 (2nd ed.); *Lynche* v. *Clerke*, 3 Salk. 154; *Reg.* v. *Lord Geo. Gordon*, Doug. 591, 593, note (3). The witness should swear that he compared the copy line for line with the original; or that the officer of the court, or some person acting for him, read the original whilst the witness examined the copy, and that it is correct; the parties need not examine it both ways alternately. *Reid* v. *Margison*, 1 Camp. 469; *Gyles* v. *Hill, Id.* 471, note; *M'Neil* v. *Perchard*, 1 Esp. 263; *Rolf* v. *Dart*, 2 Taunt. 51; *Fyson* v. *Kemp*, 6 C. & P. 71; Tayl. Ev. 1195 (2nd ed.). The copy *must not contain any abbreviations*, not in the original, otherwise it will not be received in evidence. *Reg.* v. *Christian*, Car. & M. 388. If the original be written in an ancient or foreign charac-ter, the witness must prove that he was able to read and understand the original. *Crawford* v. *Lindsay*, 2 H. L. Cas. 534, 544. It must also be shown that the original was in the custody of the proper officer, or kept at the proper place. *Adamthwaite* v. *Synge*, 1 Stark. 183; 4 Camp. 372; *Doe* d. *Lord Arundel* v. *Fowler*, 14 Q. B. 700; *Doe* d. *France* v. *Andrews*, 15 Q. B. 756; Tayl. Ev. 1195 (2nd ed.).

An examined copy of a register of marriage is admissible, although the entry does not exactly follow the directions of the statute, as where it is attested by only one witness. *Doe* d. *Blaney* v. *Savage*, 1 Car. & K. 487.

Office Copies.]—These are admissible in the *same court and cause*, without proof of their examination with the original; *Doe* d. *Lucas* v. *Fulford*, 2 Burr. 1179; 2 Phil. Ev. 131 (9th ed.); but not in any other court or cause; 2 Tayl. Ev. 1190; *Ritcher* v. *King*, 1 Car. & K. 655; unless, indeed, the copy be made by an officer who is bound by the common law or by some statute to furnish copies. 2 Tayl. Ev. 1191. The rules of the superior courts of common law may be proved by an office copy. *Id.* 1192. A copy of depositions sworn at a judge's chambers, and delivered out by his clerk, and attested by his signature, is admissible evidence, without proof of its having been examined with the original. *Duncan* v. *Scott*, 1 Camp. 100. So are office copies of records and documents made pursuant to 12 & 13 Vict. c. 109. 2 Tayl. Ev. 1192 (2nd ed.). And certified copies of books and documents of a public nature, or of extracts therefrom, made pursuant to 14 & 15 Vict. c. 99, s. 14. 2 Tayl. Ev. 1233. And certified extracts of births, marriages and deaths made by the registrar-general, and sealed and stamped pursuant to 6 & 7 Will. 4, c. 86, s. 38. 2 Tayl. Ev. 1236. And office copies of the acknowledgment of deeds by married women, made pursuant to 3 & 4 Will. 4, c. 74, s. 88; 8 & 9 Vict. c. 113, s. 1.

Duplicates and Counterparts.]—These are *primary* evidence, and therefore admissible without any notice to produce the original. *Ante*, 158; *Colling* v. *Trewick*, 6 B. & C. 398, Bayley, J.; *Philipson* v. *Chace*, 2 Camp. 110; *Roe* d. *West* v. *Davies*, 7 East, 363; *Hughes* v. *Clark*, 10 C. B. 905. When two or more parts of a deed are exe-cuted by each party they are called duplicates, and one of them must be stamped with a denoting stamp unless the full duty be paid on each. 13 & 14 Vict. c. 97, Sched. part I., tit. "Duplicate or Counterpart." But when a lease is executed by the lessor only, and the other part by the lessee only, the latter is called a counterpart, and must be stamped as such (or as a lease), but no *denoting* stamp is necessary. 16 & 17

Vict. c. 59, s. 2.   A lessee who executes the counterpart of a lease, or any person claiming under him, cannot dispute its admissibility in evidence, or impeach its validity on the ground of the original lease not being properly stamped.   *Paul* v. *Meek*, 2 You. & Jer. 116.

A *machine* copy is not considered as a duplicate or counterpart, but only as a plain copy; and admissible only after due notice to produce the original, and upon proof of its having been examined or compared with the original and found to be correct. *Nodin* v. *Murray*, 3 Camp. 228; *Simpson* v. *Thoreton*, 2 Man. & Ry. 433.

CHAPTER XXII.

COMMON AND SPECIAL JURIES—CHALLENGES—AND VIEWS.

1. *Qualification of Jurors.*]—By 6 Geo. 4, c. 50, intituled "*An Act for consolidating and amending the Laws relative to Jurors and Juries,*" it is enacted, sect. 1, "that every man, except as hereinafter excepted, between the ages of 21 years and 60 years, residing in any county in England, who shall have in his own name or in trust for him, within the same county, £10 by the year above reprises, in lands or tenements, whether of freehold, copyhold or customary tenure, or of ancient demesne; or in rents issuing out of any such lands or tenements; or in such lands, tenements and rents taken together; in fee simple, fee tail, or for the life of himself or some other person; or who shall have within the same county £20 by the year above reprises in lands or tenements held by lease or leases for the absolute term of 21 years, or some longer term, or for any term of years determinable on any life or lives; or who being a householder shall be rated or assessed to the poor rate, or to the inhabited house duty in the county of Middlesex on a value of not less than £30, or in any other county on a value of not less than £20; or who shall occupy a house containing not less than 15 windows, shall be *qualified and liable to serve on juries* for the trial of all issues joined in any of the king's courts of record at Westminster, and in the superior courts, both civil and criminal, of the three counties palatine, and in all courts of assize, nisi prius, oyer and terminer, and gaol delivery, such issues being respectively triable in the county in which every man so qualified respectively shall reside." Also on grand and petty juries at sessions. In Wales three-fifths of any of the foregoing qualifications is sufficient.

Exemptions from serving on Juries.]—Sect. 2, provides, "that all peers, all judges of the king's courts of record at Westminster, and the courts of Great Session in Wales [now abolished]; all clergymen in holy orders; all priests of the Roman Catholic faith who shall have duly taken and subscribed the oaths and declarations required by law; all persons who shall teach or preach in any congregation of Protestant Dissenters, whose place of meeting is duly registered, and who shall follow no secular occupation except that of a schoolmaster, producing a certificate of some justice of the peace of their having taken the oaths and subscribed the declaration required by law; all serjeants and barristers at law actually practising; all attornies, solicitors and proctors duly admitted in any court of law or equity, or of ecclesiastical or admiralty jurisdiction, in which attornies, solicitors and proctors have usually been admitted, actually practising, and having duly taken out their annual certificates; all officers of any such courts actually exercising the duties of their respective offices; all coroners, gaolers and keepers of houses of correction; all members and licentiates of the Royal College of Physicians in London actually practising; all surgeons being members of one of the Royal Colleges of Surgeons in

London, Edinburgh or Dublin, and actually practising; all apothecaries certified by the court of examiners of the Apothecaries' Company and actually practising; all officers in his majesty's navy or army on full pay; all pilots licensed by the Trinity House of Deptford Stroud, Kingston-upon-Hull, or Newcastle-upon-Tyne, and all masters of vessels in the buoy and light service, employed by either of those corporations, and all pilots licensed by the lord warden of the Cinque Ports, or under any act of Parliament or charter for the regulation of pilots in any other port; all the household servants of his majesty, his heirs and successors; all officers of customs and excise; all sheriffs' officers, high constables and parish clerks; shall be and are hereby *absolutely freed and exempted* from being returned, and from serving upon any juries or inquests whatsoever, and shall not be inserted in the lists to be prepared by virtue of this act as hereinafter mentioned: Provided also, that all persons exempt from serving upon juries in any of the courts aforesaid, by virtue of any prescription, charter, grant or writ, shall continue to have and enjoy such exemption in as ample a manner as before the passing of this act, and shall not be inserted in the lists hereinafter mentioned.''

Aliens, Felons, &c., disqualified.]—Sect. 3 provides, "that no man, not being a natural born subject of the king, is or shall be qualified to serve on juries or inquests, except only in the cases hereinafter expressly provided for (*i. e.* juries *de medietate linguæ*, sect. 47); and no man who hath been or shall be attainted of any treason or felony, or convicted of any crime that is infamous, unless he shall have obtained a free pardon, nor any man who is under outlawry or excommunication, is or shall be qualified to serve on juries or inquests in any court, or on any occasion whatsoever.''

The Jurors' Book.]—Sect. 12 provides for the preparation in each year of a book to be called "The Jurors' Book for the year 18—,'' which shall be used for one year next following the first day of January after it is prepared and delivered to the sheriff as therein mentioned. Sect. 14 enacts, that the sheriff, &c., shall return as jurors the "names of men contained in the jurors' book for the then current year, and no others;'' "provided always, that if there be no jurors' book in existence for the current year, it shall be lawful to return jurors from the jurors' book for the year preceding.''

Qualification of Special Jurors.]—Sect. 31 enacts, "that every man who shall be described in 'The Jurors' Book' in any county in England or Wales, or for the county of the city of London, as an *esquire or person of higher degree, or as a banker or merchant*, shall be qualified and liable to serve on special juries in every such county in England and Wales, and in London respectively; and the sheriff of every county in England and Wales, or his under-sheriff, and the sheriffs of London or their secondary, shall within ten days after the delivery of the jurors' book for the current year to either of them, take from such book the names of all men who shall be described therein as esquires or persons of higher degree, or as bankers or merchants, and shall respectively cause the names of all such men to be fairly and truly copied out in alphabetical order, together with their respective places of abode and additions, in a separate list, to be subjoined to the jurors' book, which list shall be called 'The Special Jurors' List,' and shall prefix to every name in such list its proper number, beginning the numbers from the first name, and continuing them in a regular arithmetical series down to the last name, and shall cause the said several numbers to be written upon distinct pieces of parchment or card, being all as nearly as may be of equal size; and, after all the said numbers shall have been so written, shall put the same together in a separate drawer or box, and shall there safely keep the same, to be used for the purpose hereinafter mentioned."

Qualification of Jurors in London, and in other Cities and Franchises.]—Sect. 50 enacts, " that the qualification hereinbefore required for jurors, and the regulations for procuring lists of persons liable to serve on juries, shall not extend to the jurors or juries in any liberties, franchises, cities, boroughs, or towns corporate, not being counties, or in any cities, boroughs or towns being counties of themselves, which shall respectively possess any jurisdiction, civil or criminal; but that in all such places the sheriffs, bailiffs or other ministers having the return of juries, shall prepare their panels in the manner heretofore accustomed: provided always, that no man shall be impannelled or returned by the sheriffs of the city of London as a juror to try any issue joined in his majesty's courts of record at Westminster, or to serve on any jury at the sessions of oyer and terminer, gaol delivery or sessions of the peace to be held for the said city, who shall not be a *householder*, or the *occupier* of a shop, warehouse, counting-house, chambers or office for the purpose of trade or commerce, within the said city, *and have lands, tenements or personal estate of the value of* 100*l.*; and that the lists of men resident in each ward of the city of London, who shall be so qualified as herein mentioned, shall be made out, with the proper quality or addition and the place of abode of each man, by the parties who have heretofore been used and accustomed in each ward to make out the same respectively; and that such shop, warehouse, counting-house, chambers or office as aforesaid, shall, for the purposes of this act, be respectively deemed and taken to be the place of abode of every occupier thereof: provided also, that no man shall be impannelled or returned to serve on any jury for the trial of any capital offence in any county, city or place, who shall not be qualified to serve as a juror in civil causes within the same county, city or place; and the same matter and cause being alleged by way of challenge and so found, shall be admitted and taken as a principal challenge, and the person so challenged shall and may be examined on oath of the truth of the said matter."

2. *Jury—how nominated and summoned.*]—*Jury Process abolished.* —By 15 & 16 Vict. c. 76, s. 104, " the several writs of *venire facias juratores*, and *distringas juratores*, or *habeas corpora juratorum*, and the entry *jurata ponitur in respectu*, shall no longer be necessary or used."

Common Jury at the Assizes.]—Sect. 105 enacts, that " the precept issued by the judges of assize to the sheriff to summon jurors for the assizes shall direct that the jurors be summoned for the trial of all issues, whether civil or criminal, which may come on for trial at the assizes; and the jurors shall thereupon be summoned in like manner as at present."

Panel of Jurors.]—Sect. 106 enacts, that "a printed panel of the jurors summoned shall, seven days before the commission day, be made by the sheriff, and kept in the office for inspection; and a printed copy of such panel shall be delivered by the sheriff to any party requiring the same, on payment of one shilling; and such copy shall be annexed to the nisi prius record."

Generally speaking, *each party* (not the plaintiff only) should obtain a printed copy of the panel of jurors, and should carefully examine it to ascertain if it contain the names of any objectionable jurors, *ex. gr.* enemies of the party, or friends of the opposite party, or of his attorney, or persons known to have an adverse opinion, political or otherwise, upon the point or matter in question, and the like. At the trial the associate will, upon the request of counsel on either side, pass over the name of any juror objected to, and obtain a full jury without him, if possible; or any juror may be challenged for cause. *Creed* v. *Fisher*, 9 Exch. 472, 474, Parke, B. But the above precautions (which might often save or secure a verdict) are very seldom attended to in practice.

Common Jury in London and Middlesex.]—By 15 & 16 Vict. c. 76, s. 107, "the sheriffs of *London* and *Middlesex* respectively shall, pursuant to a precept under the hand of a judge of any of the said superior courts, and without any other authority, summon a sufficient number of common jurors for the trial of all issues in the superior courts of common law, in like manner as before this act; and seven days before the first day of each sittings a printed panel of the jurors so summoned for the trial of causes at such sittings shall be made by such sheriffs, and kept in their offices for public inspection, and a printed copy of such panel shall be delivered by the said sheriffs to any party requiring the same, on payment of one shilling; and such copy shall be annexed to the nisi prius record; and the said precept shall and may be in like form as the precept issued by the judges of assize, and one thereof shall suffice for each term, and for all the superior courts; and it shall be the duty of the sheriffs respectively to apply for and procure such precept to be issued in sufficient time before each term to enable them to summon the jurors in manner aforesaid; and it shall be lawful for the several courts, or any judge thereof, at any time to issue such precept or precepts to summon jurors for disposing of the business pending in such courts, and to direct the time and place for which such jurors shall be summoned, and all such other matters as to such judge shall seem requisite."

Each party, and not the plaintiff only, should obtain a printed copy of the panel of jurors, and examine it carefully, as above suggested.

Special Jury at Assizes.]—By 15 & 16 Vict. c. 76, s. 108, "the precept issued by the judges of assize as aforesaid shall direct the sheriff to summon a sufficient number of special jurymen, to be mentioned therein, not exceeding forty-eight in all, to try the special jury causes at the assizes, and the persons summoned in pursuance of such precept shall be the jury for trying the special jury causes at the assizes, *subject to such right of challenge* as the parties are now by law entitled to; and a printed panel of the special jurors so summoned shall be made, kept, delivered and annexed to the nisi prius record, in like time and manner and upon the same terms as hereinbefore provided with reference to the panel of common jurors; *supra;* and upon the trial the special jury shall be ballotted for and called in the order in which they shall be drawn from the box, in the same manner as common jurors : provided that the court or a judge in such case, as they or he may think fit, may order that a special jury be struck according to the present practice, and such order shall be a sufficient warrant for striking such special jury, and making a panel thereof for the trial of the particular cause."

When it is wished to have a special jury nominated and struck according to the old practice, and reasonable grounds can be shown, an application may be made to the court or a judge pursuant to the concluding proviso of sect. 108. *See forms of Summons and Order, Appendix, Nos.* 226, 227. The mode of proceeding on such order is similar to that under sect. 110. *Post,* 261, 262.

Mode of obtaining a Special Jury in Country Causes.]—By 15 & 16 Vict. c. 76, s. 109, "in any county, except *London* and *Middlesex*, the plaintiff in any action, except replevin, shall be entitled to have the cause tried by a special jury, upon giving notice in writing to the defendant, *at such time as would be necessary for a notice of trial,* of his intention that the cause shall be so tried ; and the defendant, or plaintiff in replevin, shall be so entitled, on giving the like notice *within the time now limited for obtaining a rule for a special jury :* provided that the court or a judge may at any time order that a cause shall be tried by a special jury, upon such terms as they or he shall think fit."

The plaintiff in ejectment must give a ten days' notice. *See the form, Appendix, No.* 222. But whether a less notice is sufficient when short notice of trial is given is not clear. It must be given " at such time as would be necessary for a notice of trial." Sect. 109. Six clear days' notice must also be given to the sheriff. Sect. 112, *post,* 264. A plaintiff, who is compelled by a twenty days' notice to try at a particular sitting in term, must try the cause by a common jury, if a special jury cannot be obtained at that sitting. *Levy* v. *Moylan,* 10 C. B. 657 ; 2 Low. M. & P. 172. The defendant in ejectment must give notice for a special jury either before notice of trial has been given, or six days at least before the commission day. *See the form, Appendix, No.* 222. The notice must be given *six clear days,* exclusive of the day the notice is served, and of the commission day. If such notice cannot be given a rule of court or judge's order must be obtained. *Sayer* v. *Dufaur,* 9 Q. B. 800 ; 5 D. & L. 313 ; *Sayer* v. *Dufaur,* 7 C. B. 800. Six days' notice must also be given to the sheriff. *Post,* 264.

The subject's right to try a case by a special jury is not affected by any suggestion of the attorney or solicitor-general, *without affidavit,* that the crown is interested in the property, though that suggestion would be sufficient to obtain a trial at bar. *Dunn* v. *Cox,* 16 M. & W. 439.

By Reg. Prac. H. T. 1853, No. 47, "sheriffs, other than the sheriffs of London and Middlesex, shall, seven days before the commission day, make and keep at their offices, for inspection, a printed copy of the panel of the special jurymen to try the special jury causes at the assizes, as directed by the Common Law Procedure Act, 1852 ; *ante,* 259 ; but such special jury need not be summoned except notice be given as provided for by the 112th section of the said act." *Post,* 264.

Each party should take care to examine this list carefully before the trial, to ascertain if it contain the names of any jurors who ought to be challenged, or otherwise objected to. *Ante*, 259.

Special Jury in Town Causes.]—By 15 & 16 Vict. c. 76, s. 110, "in *London* and *Middlesex* special juries shall be nominated and reduced by and before the under-sheriff and secondary respectively, in like manner as by the master before this act, upon the application of either party entitled to a special jury, and his *obtaining a rule for such purpose;* and the names of the jurors so struck shall be placed upon a panel, which shall be delivered and annexed to the nisi prius record, in like manner and upon the same terms as hereinbefore provided with reference to the panel of common jurors; and upon the trial the special jury shall be ballotted for, and called in the order in which they shall be drawn from the box, in the same manner as common jurors."

The rule for a special jury in London or Middlesex is drawn up as a matter of course on behalf of the plaintiff, upon the production of a motion paper signed by counsel (fee 10s. 6d.) *See form of Rule, Appendix, No.* 225.

By Reg. Prac. H. T. 1853, No. 44, "no rule for a special jury shall be granted on behalf of the defendant (or plaintiff in replevin), except on an affidavit, either stating that no notice of trial has been given, or, if it has been given, then stating the day for which such notice has been given; *see the form, Appendix, No.* 224; and in the latter case no such rule is to be granted unless such application is made for it *more than six days before that day;* provided that a judge may, on summons, order a rule for a special jury to be drawn up at any time."

A defendant cannot, without special application to the court or a judge, have a rule for a special jury *before issue joined*, although, being under terms to take short notice of trial, he would not, if he waited till joinder, be in time to move for a special jury a sufficient number of days before trial. *Sayer* v. *Dufaur*, 9 Q. B. 800; 5 D. & L. 313; 7 C. B. 800.

The application must be made at least six clear days before the day of the particular sitting, *exclusive* of the day of the application and of the sitting day. *Ante*, 260.

By Reg. Prac. H. T. 1853, No. 45, "no cause shall be tried by a special jury in Middlesex or London, unless the rule for such special jury be served, and the cause marked in the associate's book as a special jury cause, on or before the day preceding the day appointed in Middlesex and London respectively for the trial of special juries."

Having obtained the rule for a special jury the under-sheriff of Middlesex, or the secondary of London (as the case may require) will, upon application, write upon it an appointment to nominate the jury: serve a copy of the rule and appointment on the attorney or agent for the opposite party: attend at the time and place appointed, when the under-sheriff or secondary will produce the special jurors' list, and numbers written on pieces of parchment or card corresponding with the names in such list; the under-sheriff or secondary then puts the numbers into a box, and, having shaken them together, draws out forty-eight of them one after another, and, as each number is drawn, he refers to the corresponding number in the special jurors' list, and reads aloud the name, address and title of the person designated by such number; at the time of reading each name, either party or his attorney, may object to such person named as being incapacitated from serving on the jury, and if he prove such incapacity to the satisfaction of the under-sheriff or secondary, that name shall be set aside and another number drawn instead thereof, which may in like manner be challenged; and so on, until forty-eight names shall be chosen.

The opportunity of objecting to a disqualified juror *at the time of nomination* is frequently lost by reason that a common clerk, who knows nothing of the gentry of the county, is sent to attend the appointment to nominate; but this is not generally of much consequence.

The under-sheriff or secondary will, if required, furnish each party with a copy of the names, addresses and additions or titles of the forty-eight jurors nominated as above mentioned.

No time should be lost by either party in obtaining proper instructions or information for reducing the list. Each party may strike out twelve names, and the result of the cause may often depend upon whether this is done judiciously or otherwise. Immediately after the jury have been nominated, inquiries should be made from experienced persons, of sound judgment and well acquainted with the gentry of the county, and particularly with the jurors named in the list, or as many of them as possible, to ascertain which of them are objectionable, either by reason of their being relations or friends of the opposite party, or of his attorney, or enemies of the party on whose behalf the inquiries are made, or opposed to him politically or otherwise, or known to entertain opinions adverse to his interests on the point or matter in question; and the like.

Each party should be prepared to strike out a dozen of the most objectionable names; *also three or four more*, distinguishing in what order each of the latter should be struck out. The reason for this is, that the opposite party may perhaps strike out some of your twelve objectionable names; besides which, if no instructions be given as to the others, the most desirable names to be retained may be struck out by mistake, to make up the full number to be struck out.

When either party is prepared to reduce the list, he may obtain an appointment for that purpose from the under-sheriff or secondary, and serve a copy on the attorney or agent for the other party. Such appointment is peremptory, and the sheriff or secondary is entitled to proceed *ex parte*, if either party fail to attend. 1 Chit. Arch. 338 (9th ed.). But he will adjourn the appointment, if so required, where it appears to him just and reasonable so to do.

Attend at the time appointed: then in the presence of the under-sheriff or secondary, one party strikes a name out of the list of forty-eight, and the opposite party another, and so on alternately until each party has struck out twelve names. If either party do not attend, the under-sheriff or secondary, upon being satisfied that due notice of the appointment has been given, will strike out *the last twelve names* on behalf of the absent party, and the other party will strike out such other twelve names as he may think fit.

The remaining twenty-four names "shall be placed upon a panel." *Ante*, 261. This is prepared by the under-sheriff or secondary, and must afterwards be annexed to the nisi prius record. *Ante*, 261. A common jury panel should also be obtained, and annexed to the record.

" Upon the trial the special jury shall be ballotted for, and called in the order in which they shall be drawn from the box, in the same manner as common jurors." *Ante*, 261.

If a full special jury do not appear, those making default may be fined, upon proof that they were duly summoned. 6 Geo. 4, c. 50, ss. 38, 51; 1 Chit. Arch. 401 (9th ed.). Sometimes a fine of 50*l.* is imposed. *Carne* v. *Nicoll*, 3 Dowl. 116; *Wood* v. *Thompson*, Car. & M. 178, note (*b*). In the case of a viewer the fine must not be less than 10*l.*, unless some reasonable excuse shall be proved by oath or affidavit. 6 Geo. 4, c. 50, s. 38. The sheriff's bailiffs who served the summonses always attend the trial to prove the same. If *none* of the jury appear, the cause cannot regularly be tried by a common jury (except by consent), for the common jury panel is intended merely to supply *a tales*, if necessary. *Holt* v. *Meadowcroft*, 4 M. & S. 467; *Hague* v. *Hall*, 5 Man. & Gr. 693; 6 Scott, N. R. 705; 1 D. & L. 83. If any one or more of the special jury appear, either party may pray a tales, which will be granted as of course, without the consent of the opposite party. *Gatliffe* v. *Bourne*, 2 Moo. & Rob. 100; overruling *The British Museum Trustees* v. *White*, 3 C. & P. 289. If a full special jury do not appear, and neither party will pray a tales, the trial must be postponed for want of jurors; *Jenkins* v. *Purcel*, 1 Stra. 707; 2 Wms. Saund. 349, note (1); after which the defendant may proceed to a trial by proviso, but cannot compel the plaintiff to proceed to trial by a twenty days' notice, pursuant to sect. 202. *Phillips* v. *Dance*, 9 B. & C. 769. Although perhaps he may be entitled to a rule for the costs of the day. Tidd's Prac. 759 (9th ed.).

Upon the trial of an issue *devisavit vel non*, directed by the Court of Chancery, neither party can pray a tales unless the order for the trial gives leave so to do. *Wood* v. *Thompson*, Car. & M. 171. The order usually contains special directions in that behalf.

Remedy for Delay by Special Jury in Town Causes.]—By 15 & 16 Vict. c. 76, s. 111, "where the defendant in any case, or plaintiff in replevin, gives notice of his intention to try the cause by a special jury, and the venue is in *London* or *Middlesex*, the court or judge, *if satisfied that such notice is given for the purpose of delay*, may order that the cause be tried by a common jury, or make such other order as to the trial of the cause as such court or judge shall think fit."

If the court be satisfied that the rule was obtained merely to delay the trial, they will order that the cause be tried by a special jury in its order, if the defendant then have one in attendance, and in default thereof that the cause be then tried by a common jury. *Gray* v. *Knight*, 16 C. B. 143.

The court or a judge used sometimes to make an order of the above nature before this enactment. *Bush* v. *Pring*, 9 Dowl. 180; 16 M. & W. 439, note (*a*); *Breach* v. *O'Brien*, 9 C. B. 227; *Devanoge* v. *Borthwick*, 2 Low. M. & P. 277; *Dawson* v. *Smith*, 1 Low. M. & P. 151. But the propriety of this was doubtful, especially after the special jury had been *struck*, because the stat. 6 Geo. 4, c. 50, s. 30, was imperative that "every jury so struck *shall be the jury* returned for the trial of the issue." *Newman* v. *Graham*, 11 C. B. 153; *White* v. *The Eastern Union Railway Company*, 11 C. B. 875; *Haldane* v. *Beauclerk*, 3 Exch. 658; 6 D. & L. 642; *Wilson* v. *Butler*, 2 Moo. & Rob. 78; *Hague* v. *Hall*, 5 Man. & Gr. 693; 6 Scott, N. R. 705; 1 D. & L. 83.

Notice to Sheriff of Special Jury (Town or Country).]—By 15 & 16 Vict. c. 76, s. 112, " where notice has been given to try by special jury, either party may, *six days before the first day* of the sittings in London or Middlesex, or adjournment day in London, or commission day of the assizes, give notice to the sheriff that such cause is to be tried by a special jury (*see the form, Appendix, No.* 223); and in case no such notice be given, no special jury need be summoned or attend, and the cause may be tried by a common jury, unless otherwise ordered by the court or a judge."

Sect. 113 enacts, that " in all cases where notice is not given to the sheriff that the cause is to be tried by a special jury, and by reason thereof a special jury is not summoned or does not attend, the cause may be tried by a common jury, to be taken from the panel of common jurors, in like manner as if no proceedings had been had to try the cause by a special jury."

According to the previous law the jurors were to be summoned three days at the least before the day on which they were required to attend, except in London and Middlesex, where one clear day's notice was sufficient. 6 Geo. 4, c. 50, s. 25. It was the duty of the plaintiff to summon the special jury, even where the rule was obtained by the defendant. Nevertheless it was the defendant's jury, and he was liable to pay their fees, &c. *Wilson* v. *Butler*, 2 Moo. & Rob. 78, Tindal, C. J. The cause could not be tried by a common jury after a special jury had been *struck*. *Ante*, 263.

Special Rule or Order for summoning Jury.]—By 17 & 18 Vict. c. 125, s. 59, " the several courts, or any judge thereof, may make all such rules or orders upon the sheriff or other person as may be necessary to procure the attendance of a special or common jury for the trial of any cause or matter depending in such courts, at such time and place and in such manner as they or he may think fit."

Powers of Jury—same as before.]—By 15 & 16 Vict. c. 76, s. 115, " the jurors contained in such panels as aforesaid shall be the jurors to try the causes at the assizes and sittings for which they shall be summoned respectively ; and all such proceedings may be had and taken before such juries in like manner, and with the like consequences in all respects, as before any jury summoned in pursuance of any writ or writs of *venire facias juratores, distringas juratores* or *habeas corpora juratorum*, before this act."

3. *Costs of Special Jury.*]—By 6 Geo. 4, c. 50, s. 34, " the person or party, who shall apply for a special jury, shall pay the fees for striking such jury, and all expenses occasioned by the trial of the cause by the same, and shall not have any further or other allowance for the same upon taxation of costs than such person or party would be entitled unto in case the cause had been tried by a common jury, unless the judge before whom the cause is tried *shall, immediately after the verdict, certify under his hand upon the back of the record* that the same was a cause proper to be tried by a special jury." *See the form of such Certificate, Appendix, No.* 228.

The certificate must be granted "immediately after the verdict." But a reasonable construction must be put upon the word "immediately ;" and it must be taken to mean within a short reasonable time. *Christie* v. *Richardson,* 10 M. & W. 688; 2 Dowl. N. S. 503. If not actually drawn up and signed within that time, the omission cannot afterwards be supplied. *Grace* v. *Church,* 4 Q. B. 606; 3 Gale & D. 591; *Leach* v. *Lamb,* 11 Exch. 437.

By 3 & 4 Will. 4, c. 42, s. 35, the above enactment was extended to causes in which the plaintiff is *nonsuited.*

4. *Challenges of Jurors.*]—By 6 Geo. 4, c. 50, s. 27, "if any man shall be returned as a juror for the trial of any issue in any of the courts hereinbefore mentioned, who shall not be qualified according to this act (*ante,* 256, 258), *the want of such qualification shall be good cause of challenge,* and he shall be discharged upon such challenge if the court shall be satisfied of the fact; and that if any man returned as a juror for the trial of any such issue shall be qualified in other respects according to this act, the want of *freehold*(a) shall not on such trial in any case, civil or criminal, be accepted as good cause of challenge, either by the crown or by the party, nor as cause for discharging the man so returned upon his own application; any law, custom or usage to the contrary notwithstanding: *provided that nothing herein contained shall extend in anywise to any special juror.*"

Sect. 28 enacts, "that no challenge shall be taken to any panel of jurors for want of a knight's being returned in such panel, nor any array quashed by reason of any such challenge; any law, custom or usage to the contrary notwithstanding." As to the previous law, see Co. Lit. 156 a, note (*g*).

Sect. 13 provides, that "the want of hundredors shall be no cause of challenge, any law, custom or usage to the contrary notwithstanding." As to the previous law, see Co. Lit. 157 a, 125 a; 6 Co. R. 14 b.

As to the law of challenges of jurors generally, see Co. Lit. 155 b— 158 b; 1 Chit. Arch. 402—407 (9th ed.).

Challenges are either to the array or to the polls. Each of these may be subdivided into principal challenges and challenges for favour. 1 Chit. Arch. 402 (9th ed.).

A principal challenge is so called because, if it be found to be true, it standeth sufficient of itself without leaving anything to the conscience or discretion of the triers. Co. Lit. 156 b. The challenge and proceedings thereon are entered upon the record, and the cause made a remanet. *Rex* v. *Dolby,* 1 Car. & Kir. 238; 2 B. & C. 104. But a challenge for favour, if found to be true, "must be left to the conscience and discretion of the triers, upon hearing their evidence, to find him favourable or not favourable." Co. Lit. 157 b. If the juror be found impartial, he should be admitted, notwithstanding what is alleged against him as a challenge for favour is found to be true.

Challenge to the Array.]—A challenge to the array is an objection made to all the jurors collectively, not for any defect in them, but for some partiality or default in the sheriff, or his under-sheriff, or deputy who arranged the panel. 3 Bl. Com. 359. It is either a principal challenge or a challenge to the favour. *Supra.*

(a) Formerly a 40s. freehold, situate within the particular county, was necessary, Co. Lit. 157 a.

N

The causes of *principal* challenge to the array are such as the following, viz. :—That the sheriff or other returning officer is of kindred or affinity to either party, if the affinity continue. Co. Lit. 156 a. That one or more of the jury are returned at the nomination of either party. Co. Lit. 156 a. That the sheriff, &c. holds land depending upon the same title with that in litigation between the parties. Co. Lit. 156 a. That the sheriff, &c. is counsel, attorney, officer, servant or gossip of either party ; Co. Lit. 156 a ; or a member of the corporation suing ; *The Mayor, &c. of Carmarthen* v. *Evans*, 10 M. & W. 274 ; 2 Dowl. N. S. 296 ; or that litigation is pending between the sheriff and either party, except an action on contract by the sheriff *against* either party. Co. Lit. 156 a. That the sheriff, &c. has acted as an arbitrator for either party touching the matter in question ; Co. Lit. 156 a ; and the like. 1 Chit. Arch. 402 (9th ed.).

The causes of challenge to the array *for favour* are of an inferior nature. They imply a probability of bias or partiality in the sheriff, &c. ; *ex. gr.* that either party is tenant to the sheriff ; that the son of the sheriff has married the daughter of either party, or the like. Co. Lit. 156 a. If such challenge be found to be true, the triers must thereupon decide whether the sheriff has in fact been influenced by the cause alleged, or whether he has impartially returned the panel. *Ante*, 265.

It is not clear that the array of a special jury can be challenged ; 1 Chit. Arch. 403 (9th ed.) ; but see 15 & 16 Vict. c. 76, s. 108 ; *ante*, 259 ; *Creed* v. *Fisher*, 9 Exch. 472 ; and a challenge to the array of a common jury is very unusual in practice. 1 Chit. Arch. 403 (9th ed.). But it sometimes happens in criminal cases. *Rex* v. *Dolby*, 1 Car. & K. 238 ; 2 B. & C. 104 ; *Reg.* v. *Hughes*, 1 Car. & K. 235. An application to change the place of trial, pursuant to 15 & 16 Vict. c. 76, s. 182 (*ante*, 142), should be made when the circumstances are such as would support a principal challenge to the array. *The Mayor, &c. of Carmarthen* v. *Evans*, 10 M. & W. 274 ; 2 Dowl. N. S. 296 ; *Rex* v. *Edmonds*, 4 B. & A. 471.

Challenge to the Polls.]—A challenge to the polls is an objection to one or more of the jurors who have appeared individually ; and it is either a principal challenge or a challenge to the favour. *Ante*, 265. Every challenge must be for cause ; a peremptory challenge not being allowed in civil cases, except as a matter of courtesy. *Creed* v. *Fisher*, 9 Exch. 472 ; *Id.* 474, Parke, B.

Principal.]—If a juryman do not possess the qualification required by 6 Geo. 4, c. 50 (*ante*, 256, 258), he may be challenged on that ground. *Ante*, 265 ; *In re The Chelsea Water Works Company, Ex parte Phillips*, 10 Exch. 731. So if he be disqualified under sect. 3. *Ante*, 257. But if he be merely exempt from serving on juries under sect. 2 (*ante*, 256), that does not authorize either of the parties to challenge him, but he may himself claim his exemption ; and upon the court being satisfied of it, he will be discharged from attendance, unless indeed a sufficient number of jurors cannot be obtained without him. 2 Hawk. P. C. c. 43, s. 26 ; 1 Chit. Arch. 403 (9th ed.).

If a juryman appearing be not the person named in the panel, he may be challenged. *In re The Chelsea Water Works Company, Ex parte Phillips*, 10 Exch. 731 ; *Earl of Falmouth* v. *Roberts*, 9 M. &

W. 469; 1 Dowl. N. S. 633. So if he be named therein incorrectly. *Wray* v. *Thorns*, Willes, 488; *Hill* v. *Yates*, 12 East, 229. If the mistake be not discovered until after the verdict, the court will grant a new trial, if any injustice appear to have been done, but not otherwise. *In re The Chelsea Water Works Company, Ex parte Phillips,* 10 Exch. 731; *Earl of Falmouth* v. *Roberts,* 9 M. & W. 469; 1 Dowl. N. S. 633.

A principal challenge to the polls may be made *propter affectum, i. e.,* by reason of some supposed bias or partiality. 1 Chit. Arch. 404 (9th ed.). As where the juror is of kin to either party ; Co. Lit. 157; 3 Bl. Com. 363; Finch, L. 401; *Barrett* v. *Long,* 3 H. L. Cas. 395; or there is affinity or alliance by marriage between the juror and one of the parties, if such affinity continue, or there be issue of the marriage alive ; for otherwise it would only be a challenge to the favour. Co. Lit. 157. That the juror is godfather to the party's child, or the party godfather to the juror's child. Co. Lit. 157. That the juror has land which depends upon the same title as the land in question. Co. Lit. 157 ; and see *Craig* v. *Fenn,* 1 Car. & M. 43 ; *Bailey* v. *Macauley,* 13 Q. B. 815. Or, in a cause where the parson of a parish is a party, and the right to the church comes in debate, that the juror is a parishioner. Co. Lit. 157. So in all other cases where the juror has an interest in the action, direct or collateral. Co. Lit. 157 ; *Bailey* v. *Macauley,* 13 Q. B. 815. Or has acted as arbitrator for either of them with reference to the matters in question. Co. Lit. 157. That the juror is of the same society or corporation with either party. Gilb. C. B. 95 ; *The Mayor, &c. of Carmarthen* v. *Evans,* 10 M. & W. 274 ; 2 Dowl. N. S. 296. But that he is his fellow-servant is only a challenge to the favour. Co. Lit. 157. That the juror has taken information in the cause before he is sworn. 2 Hale, P. C. 306. That he has declared his opinion of the case beforehand. 2 Hawk. P. C. c. 43, s. 28. That since he has been returned as one of the jury he has eaten or drunk at the expense of one of the parties. Co. Lit. 157. But that one of the parties has lately been entertained by the juror at his house is only matter of challenge to the favour. *Anon.,* 3 Salk. 81. That the juror has been bribed, or tampered with by either of the parties. Co. Lit. 157. But if merely requested to appear and act conscientiously that is no matter of challenge whatever. Co. Lit. 157. That an action implying malice or displeasure is pending between the juror and one of the parties ; but if not implying malice or displeasure it is only matter of challenge to the favour. Co. Lit. 157. In an action against an insurance office on a life policy, it is no objection to a special juror being sworn that he is a director of another insurance office, unless that office has granted a policy on the life in question, and the amount of that policy is unpaid. *Craig* v. *Fenn,* 1 Car. & M. 43.

Challenges for Favour.]—A challenge to the polls for favour is of the same nature with a principal challenge, *propter affectum,* but of an inferior degree. *Supra;* 1 Chit. Arch. 405 (9th ed.). Thus, if there has been affinity or alliance by marriage between the juror and one of the parties, but it has ceased, and there is no issue of the marriage alive. Co. Lit. 157. That the juror is fellow-servant with one of the parties. Co. Lit. 157. That the juror has since his nomination entertained one of the parties. *Anon.,* 3 Salk. 81. That an action, not implying malice or displeasure, is pending between the juror and one of the parties. Co. Lit. 157. In all such cases the triers have to determine not merely whether the matter of challenge is true, but also whether the juror is impartial notwithstanding such matter. *Ante,* 265.

How made.]—No challenge whatever can be made until a full jury have appeared in the jury box. *Rex* v. *Edmonds,* 4 B. & A. 471. The objection must be made when the jury come to the book to be sworn and not afterwards, except under special circumstances of surprise, &c. *Brunskill* v. *Giles,* 9 Bing. 13; 2 Moo. & Sc. 41. The right to challenge peremptorily, and without cause, does not exist in civil cases. *Creed* v. *Fisher,* 9 Exch. 472. The party must therefore be prepared to state and prove his cause of challenge. It is immaterial which party challenges first, but the party who begins must make *all* his challenges in the first instance; otherwise he will be precluded from making any further challenge: the challenges made by him shall be first tried. 1 Chit. Arch. 405 (9th ed.); Tr. per Pais, 144. But challenges to the poll may be made after a challenge to the array has been disposed of. Co. Lit. 156 b. After a challenge to the poll has been made by one party and overruled, the other party may afterwards challenge the same juror. Co. Lit. 158 ; 1 Chit. Arch. 405 (9th ed.).

A challenge to the array must be made in writing. 1 Chit. Arch. 406 (9th ed.); *see the form, Appendix, No.* 229. A challenge to the array stating that the sheriff "has not chosen the panel indifferently and impartially as he ought to have done, and that the panel is not an indifferent panel," is too general, and bad on demurrer. *Reg.* v. *Hughes,* 1 Car. & K. 235. The cause of challenge should be particularly stated, as in *Rex* v. *Dolby,* 1 Car. & K. 238; 2 B. & C. 104, *S. C.* A challenge to the polls is made *ore tenus ;* and the party need not immediately declare his cause of challenge, unless there be not a sufficient number of jurors remaining on the panel. Tr. per Pais, 143; 1 Chit. Arch. 405 (9th ed.). Or unless he has previously challenged the array. Co. Lit. 158. But in strictness there is no right to challenge peremptorily, and without cause, in civil cases. *Creed* v. *Fisher,* 9 Exch. 472. "In practice it has been usual as a matter of courtesy to allow peremptory challenges in civil cases and misdemeanors, but it is not matter of right." *Id.* 474, Parke, B.

A challenge to the array or to the polls ought to be propounded in such a way at the trial, that it may then be entered on the record of nisi prius ; so that the other party may either demur, or counterplead, or deny the matter of challenge : and unless the challenges are so put upon the record, the party is not in a condition, as a matter of right, to insist upon them. *Mayor, &c. of Carmarthen* v. *Evans,* 10 M. & W. 274 ; 2 Dowl. N. S. 290 ; *Rex* v. *Edmonds,* 4 B. & A. 471. If a challenge duly made be disallowed, a bill of exceptions may be tendered. *Cort* v. *Bishop of St. David's,* Cro. Car. 342 ; T. Jon. 331, *S. C.; per* Tindal, C. J., in *Strother* v. *Hutchinson,* 4 Bing. N. C. 90; 5 Scott, 346 ; 6 Dowl. 238, *S. C.* But, generally speaking, a new trial will not be granted where the party was aware of the cause of challenge to the array before the trial, and might have applied to change the place of trial, pursuant to 15 & 16 Vict. c. 76, s. 182. *The Mayor, &c. of Carmarthen* v. *Evans, supra.*

How decided.—1. *Challenge to the Array.*]—The opposite party may demur to a challenge to the array, and thereupon the judge at nisi prius will, after hearing counsel on both sides, decide whether the challenge is sufficient in law. *Reg.* v. *Hughes,* 1 Car. & K. 235. Or the challenge may be traversed *ore tenus,* and in such case it is entirely in the discretion of the court how it shall be tried. 1 Chit. Arch. 406 (9th ed.). Sometimes it is tried by two of the coroners; sometimes by two of the jury. 2 Hale, P. C. 275; *Rex* v. *Dolby,* 1 Car. & K. 238; 2 B. & C. 104, *S. C.* If, however, the challenge be a principal challenge, it may be tried by the court itself without the aid or intervention of triers. 1 Chit. Arch. 406 (9th ed.). If the array be quashed, a jury shall be summoned by the coroner, or, in his default, by elisors; Co. Lit. 158; and the cause must be made a remanet for that purpose. *Rex* v. *Dolby,* 1 Car. & K. 240; 2 B. & C. 104, *S. C.* If the challenge to the array be disallowed, the party may thereupon make his challenges to the polls. Co. Lit. 156 b; 1 Chit. Arch. 406 (9th ed.).

2. *Challenges to the Polls.*]—A *principal* challenge to the polls is tried by the court without the aid or intervention of triers. 1 Chit. Arch. 407 (9th ed.). But a challenge to the polls *for favour* is tried by two of the jurors already sworn, or by two other indifferent persons appointed for that purpose by the court and called triers. 1 Chit. Arch. 406 (9th ed.). The following oath is administered to the triers, " You shall well and truly try whether J. S. [*the juror challenged*] stand indifferent between the parties to this issue: So help you God." *Anon.,* 1 Salk. 152. Witnesses are then called to prove and disprove the matter of challenge. The juror himself may be examined on the subject, provided it do not tend to his dishonour or discredit. Co. Lit. 158; *Anon.,* 1 Salk. 153; 1 Chit. Arch. 407 (9th ed.). If the triers find the matter of challenge *for favour* to be true, they should also consider and decide whether the juror is in fact impartial, notwithstanding the matter alleged. *Ante,* 265. Immediately the juror is decided to be indifferent, he should be sworn on the jury; but if found otherwise, he is thereupon desired to leave the jury-box, and he cannot afterwards be sworn in the same cause even as a talesman. *Parker* v. *Thornton,* 2 Ld. Raym. 1410; 1 Stra. 640, *S. C.* If the triers (not being sworn jurors) try one juror, and he be found indifferent, he shall be sworn, and then he and the two triers shall try the next: when another is found indifferent the two triers shall be superseded, and the first two so sworn on the jury shall try the next. Co. Lit. 158; 1 Chit. Arch. 406 (9th ed.).

It is very seldom, if ever, that the court, in the exercise of its discretion, will grant a new trial on any ground which might have been the subject of a challenge to a juryman; especially where it is not expressly sworn that the objection was unknown at the trial, and first discovered afterwards. *Earl of Falmouth* v. *Roberts,* 9 M. & W. 469; 1 Dowl. N. S. 633; but see *Bailey* v. *Macauley,* 13 Q. B. 815.

5. *View.*]—By 15 & 16 Vict. c. 76, s. 114, "a writ of view shall not be necessary or used, but whether the view is to be had by a common or special jury, it shall be sufficient to obtain a rule of the court or judge's order, directing a view to be had; and the proceedings upon the rule for a view shall be the same as the proceedings heretofore had under a writ of view; and the sheriff, upon request, shall deliver to either party the names of the viewers, and shall also return their names

to the associate for the purpose of their being called as jurymen upon the trial."

By Reg. Prac. H. T. 1853, No. 48, "the rule for a view may, in all cases, be drawn up by the officer of the court, on the application of the party, without a motion for that purpose." *See form of Rule, Appendix, No.* 232.

No. 49. Upon any application for a view, there shall be an affidavit stating the place at which the view is to be made, and the distance thereof from the office of the under-sheriff; [*see the form, Appendix, No.* 230;] and the sum to be deposited in the hand of the under-sheriff shall be 10*l.* in case of a common jury, and 16*l.* in case of a special jury, if such distance do not exceed five miles; and 15*l.* in case of a common jury, and 21*l.* in case of a special jury, if it be above five miles. And if such sum shall be more than sufficient to pay the expenses of the view, the surplus shall forthwith be returned to the attorney of the party who obtained the view; and if such sum shall not be sufficient to pay such expenses, the deficiency shall forthwith be paid by such attorney to the under-sheriff. And the under-sheriff shall pay and account for the money so deposited according to the scale following; (that is to say)—

	£	*s.*	*d.*
For travelling expenses to the under-sheriff, showers and jurymen, expenses actually paid, *if reasonable.*			
Fee to the under-sheriff, when the distance does not exceed five miles from his office	1	1	0
Where such distance exceeds five miles	2	2	0
And in case he shall be necessarily absent more than one day, then for each day after the first a further fee of	1	1	0
Fee to each of the showers the same as the under-sheriff, calculating the distance from their respective places of abode.			
Fee to each common juryman, per diem	0	5	0
For each special juryman, per diem	1	1	0
Allowance for refreshment to the under-sheriff, showers and jurymen, whether common or special, each, per diem	0	5	0
To the bailiff for summoning each juryman whose residence is not more than five miles distant from the office of the under-sheriff	0	2	6
And to each whose residence does exceed five miles of such distance	0	5	0

Practical Directions.]—The mode of obtaining a view is as follows: First prepare an affidavit stating where the view is to be had, and its distance from the office of the under-sheriff. *Supra; see the form, Appendix, No.* 230. Next prepare a precipe or memorandum for the rule. *See the form, Appendix, No.* 231. Obtain from the opposite party the name and place of abode of his shower. If there be any difficulty in this, obtain an appointment from the master on the precipe for the rule " to nominate a shower for the [plaintiff *or* defendant]." *Stone* v. *Menham,* 2 Exch. 382. Serve such appointment on the attorney or agent for the opposite party. If he do not attend the appointment, the master upon being satisfied as to the service thereof will nominate a shower on his behalf. This is written on the precipe for the rule. Then draw up a side bar rule. *See the form, Appendix,*

No. 232. Serve a copy on the attorney or agent of the opposite party. Leave with the under-sheriff the original rule, together with a panel of the jurors, whether special or common. Deposit the expenses as *ante,* 270. The sheriff will thereupon summon the proper jurors.

At the time and place mentioned in the rule, the sheriff and jurors attend. Also the showers. The latter point out to the viewers the place in question; and, if necessary, draw their particular attention to any dilapidations, boundaries, or the like; but no evidence is given on either side.

At the trial, the jurors who have taken the view are called first, and as many of them as appear form part of the jury. 6 Geo. 4, c. 50, s. 22. Any one neglecting to attend at the trial may be fined not less than 10*l.* *Id.* ss. 38, 51. The other jurors are then called, and the full number obtained in the ordinary way.

The expenses of the view are in the first instance paid out of the deposit or otherwise, pursuant to the rule of H. T. 1853, No. 49. *Ante,* 270. But the costs of a view are ultimately costs in the cause, like the costs of any other proceeding in a cause. Gray on Costs, 371.

6. *Inspection of Property (in lieu of a view).*]—As to this see 17 & 18 Vict. c. 125, s. 58. *Ante,* 208.

CHAPTER XXIII.

Nisi Prius Record.]—"The nisi prius record will be a *copy of the issue as delivered in the action.* It must be engrossed on parchment, and a more convenient shape than that heretofore in use must be adopted." Reg. Prac. H. T. 1853, Sched. No. 2 ; *see the form, Appendix, No.* 221. It is now usually written on one or more skins of parchment of a particular size, fastened together (if more than one) at the top corner on the left side. Formerly any sized skins might have been used, and they were sewn together so as to form one large sheet, which was very inconvenient.

The particulars of the claim and defence, if any, or copies thereof, shall be annexed to the record by the claimants; 15 & 16 Vict. c. 76, s. 180; also a printed copy of the panel of jurors. *Id.* ss. 106, 107. The latter must be obtained from the sheriff of the county in which the venue is laid, or his under-sheriff, or deputy (*ante*, 259).

By 15 & 16 Vict. c. 76, s. 102, "the record of nisi prius shall not be sealed or passed, but may be delivered to the proper officer of the court in which the cause is to be tried, to be by him *entered as at present*, and remain until disposed of."

By sect. 103, "records of the superior courts of common law shall be brought to trial, and entered and disposed of in the counties palatine in the same manner as in other counties ;" and see 18 & 19 Vict. c. 45, for further assimilating the practice in the county palatine of *Lancaster* to that of other counties with respect to the trial of issues from the superior courts at Westminster.

Entry of Cause for Trial.]—By Reg. Prac. H. T. 1853, No. 43, "all causes to be entered for trial in London and Middlesex shall be entered as follows; that is to say, if notice of trial shall be given for any sitting *within term*, two days before the day of sitting; and if for a sitting *after term*, before eight o'clock p. m. of the day before the first day of such sitting; and if the same shall not be so entered for such sittings respectively, a *ne recipiatur* may be entered." As to a *ne recipiatur*, see *infra*.

In country causes the record, &c. must be entered, and the cause set down for trial, with the judge's associate, at the judge's lodgings in the assize town. This cannot be done before the commission day; nor, indeed, until the commission of assize has been formally opened. It must be done *before the court sits on the following day*, except in Yorkshire, where the entry may be made at any time before the sitting of the court on the *second* day after the commission day. On the Oxford Circuit the practice is, that whenever the commission day of an assize is on any day except Saturday, the time for the entry of causes extends to twelve o'clock at noon, on the day after the commission day; but where the commission day is on a Saturday, the parties must enter their causes before the sitting of the court on the following Monday, at whatever hour on that day the court may sit, the usual hour being nine o'clock. And where the commission day announced is Saturday, but from pressure of business at another town the commission day is postponed till Monday, under the stat. 3 Geo. 4, c. 10, parties ought to be prepared to enter and try their causes at the sitting of the court on Monday. *In re Stafford Assizes*, 1 Car. & K. 394.

By a little diligence and management, the claimant's attorney can generally enter a common jury cause for trial *either early or late* in the cause list, as may best suit the convenience of himself and his witnesses; and it will come on for trial accordingly. On the other hand, the defendant's attorney should take care to have the cause *marked as defended* (by entering his name as the defendant's attorney, in the cause list, at the judge's lodgings), otherwise the cause may be tried out of its turn as "undefended."

Entry by Proviso.]—By 15 & 16 Vict. c. 76, s. 116, "nothing herein contained shall affect the right of a defendant to take down a cause for trial, after default by the plaintiff to proceed to trial, according to the course and practice of the court; and if records are entered for trial both by the plaintiff and the defendant, the defendant's record shall be treated as standing next in order after the plaintiff's record in the list of causes, and the trial of the cause shall take place accordingly."

By Reg. Prac. H. T. 1853, No. 42, "no trial by proviso shall be allowed in the same term in which the default of the plaintiff has been made, and no rule for a trial by proviso shall be necessary."

Ne recipiatur.]—If the record, &c. be not entered within the proper time in that behalf (*ante*, 272), the defendant may enter with the associate a *ne recipiatur*. *See the form, Appendix, No.* 235. This will prevent the record being entered for trial at a later period upon a special application to the judge for that purpose. *Pope* v. *Fleming*, 3 Car. & K. 146; 5 Exch. 249; 1 Low. M. & P. 272. So, where the record is entered in due time, but withdrawn at nisi prius, in consequence of the non-arrival of a material witness, the defendant may immediately enter with the associate a *ne recipiatur*, which will prevent the cause being re-entered, and tried on the arrival of the witness. *Pope* v. *Fleming, supra*.

A *ne recipiatur* duly entered will prevent a subsequent notice of trial by continuance in London or Middlesex, and compel the plaintiff to give a fresh notice of trial. *Fitch* v. *Burton,* 2 Dowl. N. S. 958. Where a *ne recipiatur* is not entered, the judge at nisi prius may in his discretion allow the record to be entered after the usual time has elapsed, under special circumstances proved to his satisfaction upon affidavit or by the statement of counsel; but this will seldom be permitted if it appear that the plaintiff or his attorney or agent has been guilty of any negligence.

Briefs for Counsel.]—The draft brief should not be prepared by either party until notice of trial has been given; at all events, it will not be allowed for on taxation if the action be discontinued or otherwise settled before notice of trial; *Doe* d. *Postlethwaite* v. *Neale,* 2 M. & W. 732; 6 Dowl. 166; nevertheless it may frequently be prudent in important cases to prepare the draft brief, before the notice of trial is given. It may be used as instructions for counsel to advise on evidence (*ante,* 140).

The draft brief is usually prepared by the attorney (not the London agent), or by some competent clerk. It should include a fair copy of the nisi prius record, and of any particulars of claim and defence annexed thereto. The facts should be stated concisely, and as nearly as possible chronologically. Long documents should not be copied verbatim, unless absolutely necessary. Where any thing turns upon particular words they should be set out verbatim. Letters and correspondence (if material) should be copied verbatim. When any opinion or advice on evidence has been taken, it should generally be copied verbatim, for the reasons before suggested (*ante,* 142). The "proofs" should be written with a quarter margin on each side. The evidence which each witness will give should be stated as correctly as possible. The witnesses should be carefully examined beforehand, and their evidence taken down from their own lips where that is practicable: for want of this precaution it too frequently happens that the evidence as stated in the brief is very different from that given by the witnesses in court. The age of each witness may as well be mentioned, also his profession, trade, or business, and whether he is favourable or adverse. Sometimes also his general character or reputation, so that counsel may be able to judge whether to call him, or to endeavour to dispense with his evidence.

To the "proofs" may be added "hints or suggestions for cross-examination" of the witnesses for the opposite party. In many cases it must be known, and in others it may be guessed, who are likely to be called as witnesses on the other side. The probable nature and effect of their evidence may often be anticipated, and many facts may be ascertained respecting the witnesses which would be useful on cross-examination, but which will not occur to counsel at the trial without some previous suggestion.

The brief should be fair copied on brief paper with a quarter margin on the left side, and written on one side only, leaving the other for the notes of counsel at the trial. They should be properly indorsed and delivered to counsel *a reasonable time before the trial.* It too frequently happens that they are delivered only the evening before the trial, or so late as to render it impossible for counsel to give the case full consideration. On the other hand, fair copies of the brief should not be made too soon, *i.e.,* a long time before there is any necessity to deliver them to counsel; otherwise, if the action be discontinued or settled before trial, the master may perhaps disallow them as unnecessary.

Sometimes it is advisable to have a consultation between counsel, in order that they may discuss the points or questions likely to arise, and the cases or authorities bearing upon the subject; also, to consider in what manner the case should be presented to the jury, and what documents produced, and what witnesses called, and in what order.

As a general rule the masters will not allow on taxation for more than two briefs, on either side, *unless ten witnesses are examined* at the trial ; but this rule is not inflexible, and the masters are bound to exercise their discretion in each particular case. *Sharp* v. *Ashby*, 12 M. & W. 732; 1 Dowl. & L. 998; *Stewart* v. *Steele*, 4 Man. & Gr. 669; 5 Scott, N. R. 517. The court will not usually interfere with the master's discretion on this point ; *Grindall* v. *Godman*, 5 Dowl. 378 ; but they will do so under very special circumstances, as where only one brief is allowed for the defendant in a difficult and important case, *S. C.* The master is not bound by the certificate of counsel upon the subject, but must exercise his own discretion. *May* v. *Tarn*, 12 M. & W. 730 ; 1 Dowl. & L. 997. When the plaintiff employs a Queen's counsel or other member of the inner bar, he must also employ a junior to open the pleadings ; consequently two briefs at least should be allowed for the plaintiff in such case. The defendant may employ two or more Queen's counsel, without any junior.

By the Directions to the Taxing Masters of H. T. 1853, No. 2, "in order to diminish as much as possible the costs arising from the copying of documents to accompany the briefs of counsel, the masters are to allow only the copying of such documents, or such parts of documents, *as they may consider necessary* for the instruction of counsel, or for use at the trial." Gray on Costs, 502, 551. This rule leaves it entirely in the discretion of the master as to what copies of documents are necessary. *Pilgrim* v. *The Southampton and Dorchester Railway Company*, 8 C. B. 25. Sometimes where three counsel are allowed, only one copy of documents will be allowed for the use of all of them. *Stewart* v. *Steele*, 4 Man. & Gr. 669; 5 Scott, N. R. 517. The master is not bound by the certificate of counsel as to the necessity for more than one copy, but must exercise his own discretion. *May* v. *Tarn*, 12 M. & W. 730 ; 1 Dowl. & L. 997.

Notices to produce, notices to admit, and any admissions made thereon, and affidavits verifying the same (or copies thereof), should be annexed in front of each brief.

Cause List.]—In London and Middlesex there is a *general printed list* of all the causes set down for trial, and remaining undisposed of; also a *daily written list* of the causes appointed for trial on the particular day. The latter is prepared by the associate immediately after the rising of the court on the previous day, and stuck up in his office (*a*), and also outside the court. The fact of a cause being in such daily list is deemed notice to the counsel and attorneys concerned in it that the cause may be tried at any time of the day, either in or out of its regular turn, as may appear most convenient for the ends of justice and the economy of the public time. *Fourdrinier* v. *Bradbury*, 3 B.

(*a*) Nos. 18 & 19, Chancery Lane.

& A. 328; *Banks* v. *Newton*, 4 Dowl. & L. 632. An undefended cause may be taken out of its turn at the sitting of the court. *Banks* v. *Newton*, 2 Saund. & Cole, 1; *Cottam* v. *Banks*, 1 Saund. & Cole, 302. The presiding judge at nisi prius has the entire conduct of the cause list, and may appoint any cause therein to be taken on any day of the sittings at his discretion; and the court in banc will not interfere with such discretion. *Dunn* v. *Coutts*, 17 Jur. 347; Bail Court, Coleridge, J. Where a cause stood in the printed cause list below the last cause mentioned in the daily written list affixed outside the court, and the plaintiff's counsel applied to have it tried, saying that there was no substantial defence, and that there were witnesses for the plaintiff remaining in town on purpose, whose residence was in Lancashire; but the defendant's counsel objected to the cause being tried out of its turn, and declined to appear; whereupon the judge permitted the cause to be tried as undefended: the court held that such trial was regular and refused a new trial, there being no affidavit of merits. *Blackhurst* v. *Bulmer*, 5 B. & A. 907; and *per* Abbott, C. J., "with respect to the general rule, it may be doubted whether the modern practice of putting up written lists has not done more harm than good; but at all events it cannot be permitted that a defendant in any case shall prevent a judge from trying a cause in the printed paper, that he may think proper, merely for the purpose of delay, or at least without showing some substantial ground either of justice or convenience." *Id.* 908.

At the assizes a cause list is published as soon as possible after the usual time for entering causes has elapsed (*ante*, 273).

It seems that the court in banc or a judge at chambers has no jurisdiction over the cause list. *Jacob* v. *Rule*, 1 Dowl. 349; 1 Chit. Arch. 349 (9th ed.). That is left entirely to the discretion of the judge at nisi prius, and the court in banc will not interfere with the exercise of such discretion. *Dunn* v. *Coutts*, 17 Jur. 347, Bail Court, Coleridge, J.

When a cause is tried *in its regular turn*, as entered in the cause list, either in town or at the assizes, in the absence of the defendant's counsel or attorney, the court will seldom grant a new trial, except under special circumstances, and then only upon an affidavit of merits, and payment of costs, and other equitable terms. *Doe* d. *Cooling* v. *Appleby*, 3 P. & D. 538; 9 Dowl. 556. If it appear that the defendant's attorney neglected to instruct counsel in due time, a new trial will not be granted on any terms whatever. *Gwilt* v. *Crawley*, 8 Bing. 144; *Watson* v. *Reeve*, 5 Bing. N. C. 112. "It would be a gross injustice to the plaintiffs if we were to listen to the application, as it would enable the defendants to lie by, and after learning the particulars of the plaintiff's case, to harass him with a new trial, and evidence got up in answer." *Per* Tindal, C. J., in *Gwilt* v. *Crawley*, *supra*. Where a cause had been tried in its regular turn, in the absence of the defendant's counsel, who had been duly instructed, but it appeared to the court that the defence intended to be set up was without equity (although perhaps valid in law), the court refused to grant a new trial upon any terms. *Blogg* v. *Bousquet*, 6 C. B. 75.

Where a cause is tried as undefended *out of its regular turn*, and in the absence of the defendant's counsel, a new trial will sometimes be granted. Thus, if at the assizes a cause be *marked as defended* (*ante*, 273), but is taken out of its regular turn, and tried as undefended, in the absence of the defendant's counsel, who was duly instructed, a new

trial will be granted. *Aust* v. *Fenwick*, 2 Dowl. 246. So, in London
or Middlesex, if a cause be taken out of its regular turn, and in the
absence of the defendant's counsel, upon a representation of the plaintiff's counsel that the cause is undefended, whereas in fact counsel was
duly instructed for the defendant, a new trial will be granted without
any affidavit of merits, and the costs of the application (not of the
previous trial) will be directed to abide the event of the cause. *Dorrein*
v. *Howell*, 6 Bing. N. C. 245; 8 Scott, 508; 8 Dowl. 277, *S. C.; De
Medina* v. *Shrapnell*, 21 Law J., C. P., 37. But a new trial will not
be granted merely because a cause in the daily list in London or Middlesex is taken out of its turn, and tried as undefended, upon a representation reasonably and bonâ fide made by the plaintiff's counsel that
he believes the action is undefended. *Banks* v. *Newton*, 4 Dowl. &
L. 632. To prevent any mistake of this sort, the defendant's counsel
should inform the plaintiff's counsel that he is instructed to defend.
After such notice it would be considered almost a breach of faith to try
the cause as undefended, out of its regular turn, or during the mo-
mentary absence of the defendant's counsel. *Chapwys* v. *Derby*, C.
P. 8th May, 1856. If the plaintiff's attorney so acted with notice of
the cause being defended, the court would not only grant a new trial,
but probably make him *personally* pay the costs of the first trial, *S. C.*
If a cause be tried as undefended at the last sitting in Middlesex, in
the absence of the defendant's counsel (who should appear and state
that the action is defended), a new trial will be granted only on payment of costs, and other equitable terms. *Bland* v. *Warren*, 7 A. &
E. 11; 6 Dowl. 21; *Doe* d. *Cooling* v. *Appleby*, 8 P. & D. 538; 9
Dowl. 556. Such costs will generally be taxed as between party and
party; not as between attorney and client; *S. C.;* and the court will
not fix a time within which they must be paid. *Bland* v. *Warren*,
supra. The defendant may be prevented from setting up on the subsequent trial an outstanding term to defeat the action contrary to the
merits. *Doe* d. *Cooling* v. *Appleby*, 4 P. & D. 538.

CHAPTER XXIV

PROCEEDINGS AT THE TRIAL.

Entry of the Cause and Nisi Prius Record.]—We have already considered when and how the record of nisi prius is prepared, and the cause entered for trial at the assizes, and in London or Middlesex. *Ante,* 272.

Cause List to be watched.]—The attornies and counsel for the respective parties must, at their peril, watch the "cause list," and be prepared for trial when the cause is called on, whether in or out of its regular turn. *Ante,* 275. To prevent the cause being called on and tried as undefended, out of its regular turn, and in the absence of the defendant's counsel, the latter should inform the plaintiff's counsel that he has been instructed to defend. *Ante,* 277.

Cause called on.]—When the cause is reached in the cause list the associate usually asks the plaintiff's counsel or attorney "Are you ready?" and upon receiving an answer in the affirmative he proceeds to call and swear the jury.

Challenge of Jurors.]—When a full jury have appeared, and before any of them are sworn, either party may challenge the array; *Ante,*

265, 268 ; or he may challenge the polls, and so object to any one or more of the jurors named in the panel. *Ante,* 266, 268. But the usual practice is, for counsel, by a note or memorandum in writing, or otherwise, before the jury are called, to request the associate to pass over any objectionable name on the panel, and, if possible, to obtain a full jury without such juror. This will accordingly be done, as a matter of course. If the juror be already in the box (having served in a previous case) he will be requested to withdraw, and another juror called. In this manner a formal challenge to the polls may generally be avoided.

Withdrawing Record.]—At any time before the jury are *sworn* (but not afterwards), the plaintiff, or his attorney or counsel, may withdraw the record, and so avoid a nonsuit, or a verdict for the defendant. 1 Chit. Arch. 349 (9th ed.). A barrister who has been merely *retained* for the plaintiff, but to whom no brief has been delivered, has no authority to withdraw the record. *Abitbol* v. *Beneditto,* 2 Camp. 487 ; *S. C. nom. Ahitbol* v. *Benedetto,* 3 Taunt. 225 ; *Doe* d. *Crake* v. *Brown,* 5 C. & P. 315, Gurney, B. But the plaintiff's counsel, to whom a brief has been delivered, may withdraw the record in the absence of the plaintiff and his attorney ; and he is entitled to have the plaintiff's witnesses called on their subpœna before the jury are sworn, and, in case of their non-appearance, to withdraw the record. *Hopper* v. *Smith,* Moo. & Mal. 115, Lord Tenterden, C. J. ; *ante,* 181. But this course is not always expedient. *Chapman* v. *Davis,* 3 Man. & Gr. 609 ; 3 Scott, N. R. 319 ; 1 Dowl. N. S. 239, *S. C.* By withdrawing the record at the trial the plaintiff renders himself liable to pay the defendant's costs of the day. Gray on Costs, 371. He also loses the costs of entering the cause for trial, and of the attendance of his witnesses on the first occasion. 1 Chit. Arch. 350 (9th ed.). He also *makes default* in proceeding to trial, if then under a twenty days' notice to try. *Ante,* 136. But if no such notice has been given he does not, before the expiration of the usual time allowed for proceeding to trial, become liable to a *non pros,* or judgment as in case of nonsuit ; as was formerly the case. *May* v. *Husband,* 5 M. & W. 493 ; 7 Dowl. 867 ; *ante,* 136, 137.

Appearance of the Parties.]—If neither party appear at the trial, in person or by counsel, the jury should not be sworn, but the judge should order the case to be struck out of the list. 1 Chit. Arch. 350 (9th ed.) ; *Allott* v. *Bearcroft,* 4 Dowl. & L. 327. If, however, the jury be sworn by mistake, the judge should discharge them from giving any verdict ; it would be incorrect to direct a nonsuit to be entered. *Arnold* v. *Johnson,* 1 Stra. 267. The defendant, being equally in fault with the plaintiff, is not entitled to any costs of the day. *Morgan* v. *Fernyhough,* 25 Law J., N. S., Exch., 52.

By 15 & 16 Vict. c. 76, s. 183, " if the defendant appears, and the claimant does not appear, at the trial, the claimant shall be nonsuited ; and if the claimant appears, and the defendant does not appear, the claimant shall be entitled to recover as heretofore, without any proof of his title."

The words "as heretofore" are inaccurate, because, prior to the above enactment, if the defendant did not appear to confess lease, entry and ouster, the plaintiff was *nonsuited,* and afterwards recovered possession against the casual ejector, and his costs under the consent rule. *Turner* v. *Barnaby*, 1 Salk. 259. But the mistake has been rectified by two rules of court, viz. :—

By Reg. Prac. H. T. 1853, No. 114, " if the plaintiff in ejectment appears at the trial, and the defendant does not appear, the defendant shall be *taken to have admitted the plaintiff's title*, and the verdict shall be entered for the plaintiff, without producing any evidence, and the plaintiff shall have judgment for his costs of suit as in other cases."

By Reg. Pl. H. T. 1853, No. 30, " if the plaintiff in ejectment appear at the trial, and the defendant does not appear, the plaintiff shall be *entitled to a verdict without producing any evidence*, and shall have judgment for his costs of suit, as in other cases."

If a defendant who defends as a joint tenant, tenant in common, or coparcener with the plaintiff, do not appear at the trial, it seems that an actual ouster need not be proved. 2 Chit. Arch. 977 (9th ed.).

In ejectment by a landlord against a tenant, when the defendant does not appear, and the plaintiff wishes to recover not only possession of the demised premises, but also mesne profits, he should not take a verdict as of course without producing any evidence, but should prove : 1. His right to recover the whole or part of the premises mentioned in the writ. 2. That the defendant or his attorney has been served with due notice of trial. 3. The value of the mesne profits from the day of the expiration or determination of the defendant's interest in the premises down to the time of the verdict, or to some preceding day to be specially mentioned therein. 15 & 16 Vict. c. 76, s. 214; *post*, 292, Chap. XXXVI. Sect. 2.

By appearing at the trial and taking his chance of obtaining the verdict, the defendant in effect admits that he has had *due notice of trial*, and he cannot afterwards object to the trial as irregular for want of a proper and sufficient notice, or on the ground that no notice whatever was given. *Thermolin* v. *Cole*, 2 Salk. 646 ; *Doe* d. *Antrobus* v. *Jepson*, 3 B. & Adol. 402 ; *Figg* v. *Wedderburne*, 11 Law J., N. S., Q. B., 45. To avail himself of such objection he must, at his peril, abstain from appearing at the trial, and afterwards rely entirely upon the supposed irregularity.

Appearance in Person or by Counsel.]—Either party may appear at the trial in person or by counsel ; but not by an attorney or agent, except by special leave of the court, which is seldom or never granted where the assistance of counsel might be obtained. The wife of a party in custody will not be permitted to act as an advocate on his behalf. *Cobbett* v. *Hudson*, 15 Q. B. 988.

It does not appear to be clearly settled whether, in a *civil* case, if a party conduct his own cause and examine the witnesses, he can be allowed to have the assistance of counsel to argue points of law, *ex. gr.* as to the admissibility or non-admissibility of evidence, or the like. It would rather seem that he cannot. *Moscati* v. *Lawson*, 7 C. & P. 32, Alderson, B.

There is no positive rule of law, or of practice of the courts, which prevents a defendant who has entered an appearance in person to the action from having in the conduct of the cause the assistance of counsel *instructed by himself*, instead of by an attorney ; and, therefore, where the judge at nisi prius refused to allow a counsel so instructed to address the jury for the defendant, the Court of Queen's Bench made absolute a rule for a new trial. It is, however, for the benefit of suitors, and for the satisfactory administration of justice, that the understanding in the profession that a barrister ought not to accept a brief in a civil suit except from an attorney, should be acted upon, and the almost uniform usage which has prevailed in this respect should be adhered to. *Doe* d. *Bennett* v. *Hale*, 15 Q. B. 171; 19 Law J., N. S., Q. B., 353. The etiquette of the bar will prevent counsel from accepting a brief in a civil case from any person except an attorney.

A party to a suit, who conducts his own case at the trial, has, in strictness, a legal right to address the jury as an advocate, and afterwards to give evidence as a witness on his own behalf. But that is a most objectionable mode of proceeding, and much discouraged. *Cobbett* v. *Hudson*, 1 E. & B. 14. It would, however, be erroneous to reject his evidence as inadmissible. *S. C.*

When plaintiffs employ a queen's counsel, or a serjeant-at-law, they must also employ a member of the outer bar as a junior, to open the pleadings, &c. ; or, rather, in ejectment (where there are no pleadings), to state to the jury the contents of the record of nisi prius, and otherwise to assist in the conduct of the case. *Ante*, 275. There is, however, one exception, viz. where the plaintiff sues *in formâ pauperis*. *James* v. *Harris*, 7 C. & P. 257, Williams, J. The rule is founded entirely on the etiquette of the bar, and not on any positive rule of law or practice. *Per* Lord Campbell, C. J., 15 Q. B. 175. It does not apply to defendants; they may employ one or more counsel within the bar, without any junior; on the other hand, either party may employ a junior only, without any queen's counsel or serjeant.

Only one counsel will be allowed to address the jury on behalf of the plaintiffs, whether they claim under the same or distinct titles; *Doe* d. *Fox* v. *Bromley*, 6 Dowl. & Ry. 292, 294; 2 Chit. Arch. 975 (9th ed.) ; but one may open the case, and another sum up the evidence.

Only one counsel will be allowed to address the jury on behalf of the defendants, except where they appear to the action and defend *separately* in respect of different parts of the property, or under distinct titles. *Doe* d. *Hogg* v. *Tindal*, 3 C. & P. 565; Moo. & Mal. 314, Lord Tenterden, C. J. But the counsel for each defendant who defends separately may cross-examine the plaintiff's witnesses, and may also produce and examine witnesses for his own client. *S. C.* 2 Chit. Arch. 975 (9th ed.). In an action for false imprisonment, where the defendants had pleaded a *joint plea* of not guilty, the judge would not allow the counsel of each defendant either to cross-examine separately, or to address the jury separately. *Seale* v. *Evans*, 7 C. & P. 593, Lord Denman, C. J. Where several defendants appear at the trial by different counsel, it is generally matter *for the discretion of the judge* whether he will allow more than one counsel to address the jury on behalf of the defendants; *Nicholson* v. *Brooke*, 2 Exch. 213; 17 Law J., N. S., Exch. 229 ; and if so, in what order they shall cross-examine the plaintiff's witnesses and address the jury. The order of seniority is not imperative. *Fletcher* v. *Crosbie*, 2 Moo. & Rob. 417; and see *Reg.* v. *Barber*, 1 Car. & K. 434. In trover, where two defendants appear and plead jointly by one attorney, but at the trial counsel appear only for one defendant, and the other defendant appears in person, the counsel only will be allowed to address the jury, but the defendant who has no counsel may cross-examine the witnesses. *Perring* v. *Tucker*, 4 C. & P. 70, Tindal, C. J. Where several defendants appear by separate attorneys, and have separate counsel, if they are in the *same interest* only one counsel can be heard to address the jury, and the witnesses are to be examined by one counsel on the part of all the defendants, in the same manner as if the defence were joint. *Chippendale* v. *Mason*, 4 Camp. 174, Lord Ellenborough, C. J. Where two defendants *pleaded separately*, and by different attorneys, it was held at the trial that the counsel for each defendant had a right to cross-examine the witnesses, and to address the jury separately; and on Mr. Kelly, for the plaintiff, observing that this practice had been held to be incorrect, Mr. Baron Parke said, "it has been so ruled; but it is not calculated to further the ends of justice. I think the proper course was pursued in the present case." *Ridgway* v. *Philip*, 1 Cr. M. & R. 415.

Ordering Witnesses out of Court.]—Either party, at any period of a cause, has a right to require that the unexamined witnesses be ordered out of court. *Southey* v. *Nash*, 7 C. & P. 632, Alderson, B. In revenue causes, such order is peremptory, and a witness who violates it will not be permitted to be examined. *Attorney-General* v. *Bulpit*, 9 Price, 4. So, in criminal cases, the witness will not generally be admitted; *Rex* v. *Wylde*, 6 C. & P. 380, Park, J.; but the judge may (even in a criminal case) allow him to be examined, subject to observation on his conduct in disobeying the order. *Rex* v. *Colley and Sweet*, Moo. & Mal. 329, Littledale, J. In civil cases, the witness has sometimes been admitted and sometimes rejected, according to the discretion of the judge; *Parker* v. *M'William*, 6 Bing. 683; 4 Moo. & P. 480; *Beamon* v. *Ellice*, 4 C. & P. 585; *Thomas* v. *David*, 7 C. & P. 350; but the better opinion seems to be, that it is no ground for rejecting a witness's evidence that he remained in court after an order for all the witnesses to leave the court: it is merely matter of observation on his evidence. *Cook* v. *Nethercote*, 6 C. & P. 741, Alderson, B.; *Chandler* v. *Horne*, 2 Moo. & Rob. 423. "With respect to ordering the witnesses out of court, although this is clearly within the power of the judge, and he may fine a witness for disobeying his order, the better opinion seems to be, that his power is limited to the infliction of the fine, and that he cannot lawfully refuse to permit the examination of the witness." *Per cur.* in *Cobbett* v. *Hudson*, 1 E. & B. 14; citing *Cook* v. *Nethercote*, *Thomas* v. *David*, and *Rex* v. *Colley*, supra. In *Doe* d. *Good* v. *Cox*, 6 C. & P. 743, note, Gould, J., would not allow a witness for the defendant to be examined because he had remained in court after the witnesses had been ordered to leave it: but the Court of King's Bench were of opinion that the witness ought to have been heard, and granted a new trial. However, as the defendant had been negligent in not keeping his witnesses out of court, when ordered to do so, the court made him pay the costs of the trial.

The usual order for witnesses to go out of court does not apply to the attorney in the cause for either party, because his attendance is in most cases absolutely necessary for the purposes of the cause. *Pomeroy* v. *Baddeley*, Ry. & Moo. 431, Littledale, J.

The judge cannot order any plaintiff or defendant to leave the court; *Charnock* v. *Dewings*, 3 Car. & K. 378; unless he be intended to be called as a witness; *Reg.* v. *Newman*, *D.D.*, 3 Car. & K. 252; or improperly interrupts the proceedings.

"There is always a great deal of time lost by sending the witnesses out of court, and I think that, in general, it does not answer any good purpose." *Per* Taunton, J., in *Beamon* v. *Ellice*, 4 C. & P. 587. But it is sometimes expedient, *ex gr.*, where several witnesses are to be examined on some very material point, and the opposite party wishes to extract from them, upon cross-examination, statements at variance with each other, and so to discredit their testimony with the jury; whereas, if they hear each other examined, their evidence will probably coincide.

Right to begin.]—In ejectment, the plaintiff is generally entitled to begin, because the onus lies on him to prove his title. But the defendant will be allowed to begin, *upon admitting the whole of the plaintiff's case* (*i.e.* each and every link of his title), and relying upon a totally distinct title. *Doe* d. *Bather* v. *Brayne*, 5 C. B. 655. Thus, where the plaintiff claims as heir-at-law, and the defendant as devisee of A. B. deceased, the defendant will be entitled to begin, upon admitting that A. B. died seised of the property, and that the plaintiff is his heir-at-law. *Goodtitle* d. *Revett* v. *Braham*, 4 T. R. 497; *Doe* d. *Woollaston* v. *Barnes*, 1 Moo. & Rob. 386, Lord Denman, C. J.; *Doe* d. *Smith* v. *Smart*, 1 Moo. & Rob. 476, Gurney, B.; 1 Car. & K. 123, note, *S. C.*; *Doe* d. *Peters* v. *Peters*, 1 Car. & K. 279, Lord Denman, C. J. But if the heirship be not admitted without qualification, the plaintiff is entitled to begin. Thus where each party claimed as heir-at-law, and the real question was as to the legitimacy of the defendant, who was clearly heir, if legitimate, he proposed to admit that, *unless he were legitimate*, the lessor of the plaintiff was the heir-at-law: held, that this admission did not give him the right of beginning. *Doe* d. *Warren* v. *Bray*, Moo. & Mal. 166, Vaughan, B. In ejectment by the heir-at-law, the defendant is not entitled to begin by admitting the heirship and seisin, *unless defeated by a conveyance* made by the ancestor under which the defendant claims. *Doe* d. *Tucker* v. *Tucker*, Moo. & Mal. 536, Bolland, B.; *Doe* d. *Lewis* v. *Lewis*, 1 Car. & K. 122, Maule, J. The principle is, that to entitle the defendant to begin, the plaintiff's whole *prima facie* case must be admitted. *S. C.* Where the plaintiff claims under a will, and the defendant under another will of later date, the plaintiff is entitled to begin, because an admission of the will under which the plaintiff claims, without admitting it to be the testator's *last* will, is insufficient. *Doe* d. *Bather* v. *Brayne*, 5 C. B. 655, overruling *Doe* d. *Corbett* v. *Corbett*, 3 Camp. 368.

The court in banc will seldom grant a new trial because of an erroneous ruling as to the right to begin. *Brandford* v. *Freeman*, 5 Exch. 734; *Cannam* v. *Farmer*, 3 Exch. 700, Rolfe, B.; *Edwards* v. *Matthews*, 16 Law J., N. S., Exch. 291; 11 Jur. 398. But if it appear to the court that the party entitled to begin at the trial has been deprived of that right, *and that his cause has been thereby substantially prejudiced*, a new trial will be granted. *Doe* d. *Bather* v. *Brayne*, 5 C. B. 655; *Ashby* v. *Bates*, 15 M. & W. 589; 4 Dowl. & L. 33.

Speeches to the Jury.]—By 17 & 18 Vict. c. 125, s. 18, "upon the trial of any cause, the addresses to the jury shall be regulated as follows: the party who begins, or his counsel, shall be allowed, in the event of his opponent not announcing, at the close of the case of the party who begins, his intention to adduce evidence, to address the jury a second time at the close of such case, for the purpose of summing up the evidence; and the party on the other side, or his counsel, shall be allowed to open the case, and also to sum up the evidence (if any); and the right to reply shall be the same as at present." The practical importance of this clause is so great, that it has been extended to Ireland by an act passed for that sole purpose. 18 & 19 Vict. c. 7.

It is matter for the discretion of counsel, and of arrangement between themselves, whether the senior or junior shall *sum up the evidence.* Some leaders act upon the principle that it is their duty to do so, especially in important cases, and generally more satisfactory to their client and his attorney: but others have so much business, requiring their attendance in divers places, as to render it impossible for them to sum up the evidence in each case, and therefore leave it to their junior, whenever it suits their own convenience, especially if the junior be, in their judgment, fully competent to the task. Whoever performs it must necessarily remain in court during the whole trial, or the greater part of it, and must pay particular attention to the evidence, and watch especially for those points which make in his client's favour.

The object of an opening speech is to give the jury a general notion of what will be given in evidence, so as to enable them to understand the evidence when it is given: but the statement so made will not operate as an admission of the facts stated, so as to render proof thereof unnecessary on behalf of the defendant who relies upon them. *Machell* v. *Ellis,* 1 Car. & K. 682, Pollock, C. B.

Questions at the Trial.]—By 15 & 16 Vict. c. 76, s. 180, "the question at the trial shall, except in the cases hereafter mentioned, be, whether the statement in the writ of the title of the claimants is true or false, and if true, then which of the claimants is entitled, and whether to the whole or part; and if to part, then to which part of the property in question: and the entry of the verdict may be made in the form contained in the Schedule (A) to this act annexed, marked No. 17, or to the like effect, with such modifications as may be necessary to meet the facts." *See forms, Appendix, Nos.* 242—248.

The writ in ejectment merely alleges the claimant's title thus: "to the possession whereof A., B. and C., some or one of them, claim to be entitled [*or* 'to have been on and since the —— day of ——, A.D. 18—, entitled'], and to eject all other persons therefrom." *Ante,* 82. This equally applies, whether the plaintiffs claim as joint tenants, tenants in common, coparceners, executors or otherwise. *Lloyd* v. *Davies,* 15 C. B. 78, 79. Proof of a sufficient title in any one or more of the claimants will support the action, either for the whole or for part of the property, according to the evidence. *Doe* d. *Rowlanson* v. *Wainwright,* 5 A. & E. 520. But where a title is shown to less than the whole, the evidence for the claimants must show to what particular part or share of the property they are entitled: the onus of proof on this point lies on them. *Doe* d. *Hellyer* v. *King,* 6 Exch. 791; 2 Low. M. & P. 493.

Before the above act, *tenants in common* could not recover in ejectment under a count alleging a joint demise by them to the nominal plaintiff: *Doe* d. *Poole* v. *Errington,* 1 A. & E. 750; *Mantle* v. *Woollington,* Cro. Jac. 166; *Hatherley* d. *Worthington* v. *Weston,* 2

Wils. 232; *Gyles* v. *Kemp*, 1 Freem. 235; *Fursden* v. *Moor*, Carth. 224: unless it appeared by the evidence that they had a *joint right of re-entry* under a lease made by them. *Doe* d. *Campbell* v. *Hamilton*, 13 Q. B. 977. But any one or more of them (without the others) might have recovered his undivided share, or their respective shares and proportions, under a separate or several demises. Bull. N. P. 107; Ad. Eject. 167; *Doe* d. *Thorn* v. *Phillips*, 3 B. & Adol. 753. And under a count claiming the whole, any undivided part or share to which the claimant appeared by the evidence to be entitled might have been recovered. *Denn* d. *Burges* v. *Purvis*, 1 Burr. 327; *Roe* d. *Saul* v. *Dawson*, 3 Wils. 49. But it was, and still is, necessary to prove the claimant's title to some specific part or share of the property claimed; otherwise he could not recover a verdict for any part, certainly not for the whole. *Doe* d. *Hellyer* v. *King*, 6 Exch. 791; 2 Low. M. & P. 493; *Doe* d. *Bowman* v. *Lewis*, 13 M. & W. 241; 2 Dowl. & L. 667.

Joint tenants are seised (or possessed) *per my et per tout*, that is to say, of the whole and every part, but not of any undivided part or share. See a learned note on this subject, 7 C. B. 455. They might have recovered the whole property under a count on a joint demise by them, or under several counts on separate demises by each. *Doe* d. *Marsack* v. *Reed*, 12 East, 57; *Doe* d. *Lulham* v. *Fenn*, 3 Camp. 190; *Doe* d. *Whyman* v. *Chaplin*, 3 Taunt. 120: or any one of them (without the others) might have recovered his share or proportion on his sole demise. *Roe* d. *Roper* v. *Lonsdale*, 12 East, 39. The reason was, that any demise by one of several joint tenants operated as a severance *pro tanto* of the joint tenancy. *Denne* d. *Bowyer* v. *Judge*, 11 East, 288; Ad. Eject. 167. But under a count on a joint demise by four, any three, two, or one of them, could not have recovered. *Doe* d. *Blight* v. *Pett*, 11 A. & E. 842; 4 P. & D. 278; *Right* d. *Phillips* v. *Smith*, 12 East, 455, 463; *Doe* d. *Wilton and Ux.* v. *Beck*, 13 C. B. 329. So several persons, not being joint tenants, could not have recovered under a count alleging a joint demise by them. *Doe* d. *Barney and others* v. *Adams*, 2 Cro. & Jer. 232; 2 Tyr. 289; *King* v. *Berry*, Pop. 57. But under a count upon the single demise of one of several joint tenants claiming the whole property, or a larger share or proportion than the claimant was entitled to, one of several joint tenants might have recovered so much, or such part or share, as the evidence showed him to be actually entitled to. *Roe* d. *Roper* v. *Lonsdale*, 12 East, 39; *Denn* d. *Burges* v. *Purvis*, 1 Burr. 327.

Coparceners might have sued either jointly or severally, and recovered so much as the evidence showed them or her entitled to. *Bover* v. *Juner*, 1 Ld. Ray. 726; *Doe* d. *Gill* v. *Pearson*, 6 East, 173, 181; *Doe* d. *Roper* v. *Lonsdale*, 12 East, 39. But under a count on a joint demise by four, any three, two or one of them could not have recovered. *Doe* d. *Blight* v. *Pett*, 11 A. & E. 842; 4 P. & D. 278.

Executors are for some purposes joint tenants, and for others tenants in common. Two of three executors might have recovered *the whole* of their testator's leaseholds in an ejectment on their joint demise. *Doe* d. *Stace* v. *Wheeler*, 15 M. & W. 623; and see *Parnell* v. *Fenn*, Cro. Eliz. 347; Moore, 350; 1 Gould, 185, *S. C.*; *Heath* v. *Chilton*, 12 M. & W. 632. One of several executors may demise. *Doe* d. *Hayes* v. *Sturges*, 7 Taunt. 217; 2 Marsh. 505.

Evidence for Plaintiffs.]—The plaintiffs must either prove a title by estoppel (*ante*, 209; *Doe* d. *Bord* v. *Burton*, 16 Q. B. 807), or a *legal title to actual possession* of the property claimed (*ante*, 66, 72, 73), or some part or share thereof (*ante*, 86); and it must appear that such title was vested in them or some or one of them (*ante*, 285), on the day mentioned in the writ (*ante*, 94; *post*, 288), and from thence until the writ was served. *Doe* d. *Gardner* v. *Kennard*, 12 Q. B. 244; *Newby* v. *Jackson*, 1 B. & C. 454, Bayley, J.; 2 D. & R. 514, *S. C.* If such title has expired since the writ was served, the verdict may so find, and thereupon the plaintiff will be entitled to a judgment for his costs of suit. *Post*, 289.

The plaintiff's evidence must show a *legal right to actual possession.* *Ante*, 66, 72, 73. A mere equitable title is not sufficient; *Goodright* d. *Lord Grosvenor* v. *Swymmer*, 1 Lord Ken. 385; *Doe* d. *Da Costa* v. *Wharton*, 8 T. R. 2; *Doe* d. *Hodsden* v. *Staple*, 2 T. R. 684; *Doe* d. *Shewen* v. *Wroot*, 5 East, 132, 138; *Doe* d. *Lloyd* v. *Passingham*, 6 B. & C. 305; *Doe* d. *Barker* v. *Goldsmith*, 2 Cr. & Jer. 674; 2 Tyr. 710; *Doe* d. *North* v. *Webber*, 3 Bing. N. C. 922; Ad. Eject. 28; nor a legal right to the rent; *Doe* d. *Da Costa* v. *Wharton*, 8 T. R. 2; *Hill* v. *Saunders*, 2 Bing. 112; 9 Moore, 238; the remedy for *that* being by distress; *Lloyd* v. *Davies*, 2 Exch. 103; or by action of debt, covenant, or use and occupation. *Voller* v. *Carter*, 4 E. & B. 173; *Rawson* v. *Eicke*, 7 A. & E. 451; 2 N. & P. 423. But when a remainder falls into possession, the remainderman or his lessee (although the lease was granted during the continuance of the prior estate) may maintain or defend an ejectment. *Doe* d. *Agar* v. *Brown*, 2 E. & B. 331. A mere *interesse termini* after the day appointed for the commencement of the term is sufficient to support an ejectment. Co. Lit. 46 b; Shep. Touch. 269; *Doe* d. *Parsley* v. *Day*, 2 Q. B. 156, *per cur.*; *Ryan* v. *Clark*, 14 Q. B. 73, *per cur.*; 7 Dowl. & L. 8, *S. C.* But not an action of trespass, because actual possession, and not merely the right to possession, is necessary to support that form of action. Co. Lit. 296 b; Com. Dig. Trespass, B. 1, 2; *Wheeler* v. *Montifiore*, 2 Q. B. 133, 156; *Turner* v. *Cameron's Coalbrook Steam Coal Company*, 5 Exch. 932; *Lichfield* v. *Ready*, 5 Exch. 939; *Lowe* v. *Ross*, *Id.* 553. As to the nature of an *interesse termini*, see *Doe* d. *Rawlings* v. *Walker*, 5 B. & C. 111, 118; 7 D. & R. 487. A demise by a remainderman during the prior life estate will operate as a grant *pro tanto* of the remainder, and will not create an *interesse termini*. *Doe* d. *Agar* v. *Brown*, 2 E. & B. 331.

In ejectment the plaintiff must generally recover upon the strength of his own title, and not upon any weakness or defect in the defendant's title. Ad. Eject. 28, 232; *Martin* d. *Tregonwell* v. *Strachan*, 5 T. R. 107, note (*b*); *Doe* d. *Dand* v. *Thompson*, 13 Q. B. 674, 679; *Doe* d. *Oliver* v. *Powell*, 1 A. & E. 531; *Doe* d. *Crisp* v. *Barber*, 2 T. R. 749. "The plaintiff must remove every possibility of title in another person before he can recover, no presumption being to be admitted against the person in possession." *Per cur.* in *Richards* v. *Richards*, 15 East, 294, note (*a*). The fact of the defendant being tenant in possession of itself amounts to *primâ facie* proof that he is seised in fee, or otherwise legally entitled to the possession, until the contrary be proved. *Ante*, 211; *Roe* d. *Haldane and Urry* v. *Harvey*, 4 Burr. 2487, Lord Mansfield, C. J. If it appear by the evidence that neither party is entitled to possession, but that the right is vested in some third person, not a party to the record, the defendant is entitled to the verdict, although he does not pretend to claim under or on behalf of such third person. *Doe* d. *Wawn* v. *Horn*, 3 M. & W. 333; *Culley* v. *Doe* d. *Taylerson* (in error), 3 P. & D. 539, 557; 11 A. & E. 1008; *Doe* d. *Lloyd* v. *Passingham*, 6 B. & C. 305. It makes no difference that such third person is a trustee for the plaintiff. *Doe* d. *Leicester* v. *Biggs*, 2 Taunt. 109. An outstanding term is sufficient to defeat a right of entry or ejectment. *Doe* d. *Hodsden* v. *Staple*, 2 T. R. 684; *Goodtitle* d. *Jones* v. *Jones* (in error), 7 T. R. 43; *Doe* d. *Oliver* v. *Powell*, 1 A. & E. 531; *Cotterell* v. *Hughes*, 15 C. B. 532. Even a mere tenancy from year to year, not shown to have been determined by notice to quit or otherwise, is sufficient. *Doe* d. *Wawn* v. *Horn*, 3 M. & W. 333. The reason is, that it shows the plaintiffs were not entitled to actual possession of the property claimed, or any part thereof, at the time stated in the writ, and from thence until the writ was served; which is the real question to be decided, and not whether the defendant then had any such title. *Doe* d. *Oliver* v. *Powell*, 1 A. & E. 531; *Doe* d. *Dand* v. *Thompson*, 13 Q. B. 674, 679; 7 Q. B. 897, *S. C.* But the defendant may sometimes be estopped from setting up an outstanding term or tenancy; *Doe* d. *Leeming* v. *Skirrow*, 7 A. & E. 157; *Doe* d. *Manners* v. *Mizem*, 2 Moo. & Rob. 56; *Phipps* v. *Sculthorpe*, 1 B. & A. 50; or that the legal estate is outstanding in a trustee for the plaintiff. *Doe* d. *Nepean* v. *Budden*, 5 B. & A. 626. A title by estoppel is generally sufficient (*ante*, 209); and sometimes a *primâ facie* title may be proved (*ante*, 211), which will throw upon the defendant the onus of proving his title. *Daintry* v. *Brocklehurst*, 3 Exch. 207; *Doe* d. *Bord* v. *Burton*, 16 Q. B. 807.

A person who has the legal estate must prevail in a court of law; and it makes no difference in this respect whether the plaintiff be a trustee for the defendant or not. *Roe* d. *Reade* v. *Reade*, 8 T. R. 118, 121, 122; *Goodtitle* d. *Estwick* v. *Way*, 1 T. R. 735; *Keene* v. *Deardon*, 8 East, 248; *Fenny* d. *Eastham* v. *Child*, 2 M. & S. 255; *Doe* d. *Hughes* v. *Jones*, 9 M. & W. 372; *Id.* 377, Alderson, B.; 1 Dowl. N. S. 352, *S. C.*

The plaintiff's title to actual possession must be shown to have accrued *on or before the day on which possession is claimed in the writ.* *Ante*, 95; *Doe* d. *Lloyd* v. *Ingleby*, 14 M. & W. 91; *Doe* d. *Lawrence* v. *Shawcross*, 3 B. & C. 752; *Berrington* d. *Dormer* v. *Parkhurst*, 13 East, 489; *Doe* d. *Lee Compere* v. *Hicks*, 7 T. R. 433; *Id.* 727; *Doe* d. *Esdaile* v. *Mitchell*, 2 M. & S. 446. Therefore where the defendant was tenant at will, it must appear that the will was determined on or *before* the day mentioned in the writ. *Goodtitle* d. *Galloway* v. *Herbert*, 4 T. R. 680; *Doe* d. *Jacobs* v. *Phillips*, 10 Q. B. 130. So where the defendant became lawfully possessed under a contract for purchase, or the like, it must appear that such possession was legally determined by a demand of possession or otherwise on or before the day mentioned in the writ. *Right* d. *Lewis* v. *Beard*, 13 East, 210; 2 Arch. N. P. 391; Ros. Ev. 437; *Doe* d. *Newby* v. *Jackson*, 1 B. & C. 448; 2 D. & R. 514. It is, however, sufficient that the plaintiff's right of entry accrued on the very day on which possession is claimed in the writ; *Roe* d. *Wrangham* v. *Hersey*, 3 Wils. 274; *Doe* d. *Bennett* v. *Long*, 9 C. & P. 773, 795; *Doe* d. *Nicholl* v. *M'Kaeg*, 10 B. & C. 721; 5 Man. & Ry. 620; even in an action for a forfeiture. *Doe* d. *Graves* v. *Wells*, 10 A. & E. 427; 2 P. & D. 396. But it must be shown to have continued down to and until the service of the writ. Sect. 181, *infra*; *Doe* d. *Gardner* v. *Kennard*, 12 Q. B. 244; *Doe* d. *Newby* v. *Jackson*, 1 B. & C. 454, Bayley, J.; 2 D. & R. 514, *S. C.*

If the day be erroneously stated in the writ prior to that on which the claimant's title accrued, the judge at nisi prius may, if he think fit, allow the date to be amended; 15 & 16 Vict. c. 76, s. 222; even in an ejectment for a forfeiture. *Doe* d. *Edwards* v. *Leach*, 3 Man. & Gr. 229; 3 Scott, N. R. 509; 9 Dowl. 877; *Doe* d. *Simpson* v. *Hall*, 5 Man. & Gr. 795; 1 D. & L. 49. Where the year of the demise was omitted: held, that it might be supplied by an amendment at the trial. *Doe* d. *Parson* v. *Heather*, 8 M. & W. 158; 1 Dowl. N. S. 64. Any amendment of the above nature must be made before the verdict. *Doe* d. *Bennett* v. *Long*, 9 C. & P. 773, 777, Coleridge, J. No such amendment will be permitted except in furtherance of substantial justice and equity. Thus, where several brothers and sisters divided certain property between them at their mother's death, supposing it to have been hers, and verbally allotted a house to a sister: the property really had been their deceased father's: held, in ejectment by the father's devisee (one of those brothers), that he could not recover without a demand of possession; and the demand of possession being after the day of the demise, the judge would not allow an amendment by altering the day of the demise, as the arrangement was equitable. *Doe* d. *Loscombe* v. *Clifford*, 2 Car. & Kir. 448, Alderson, B. Probably an amendment would not be permitted where an unfair advantage appears to have been attempted, by claiming the possession from too early a day. But on the other hand, it is to be remembered that, according to the old practice, two or more counts stating the demises on different days might have been inserted as a matter of course.

The *locality* of the premises, as described in the writ, should be proved, and any material variance will be fatal unless amended. *Goodtitle* d. *Pinsent* v. *Lammiman*, 2 Camp. 274; *Doe* d. *Marriott* v. *Edwards*, 1 Moo. & Rob. 319; 6 C. & P. 208, Parke, B. But an amendment will generally be permitted when necessary, unless the defendant appear to have been actually misled or prejudiced by the misdescription. *S. C.* Generally speaking, an inaccuracy in the name of the parish is immaterial. *Ante*, 92, 93. In ejectment for a house situate in parish M., proof that the watchmen of that parish always watch the court in which the house stands, as being within the parish, is sufficient *primâ facie* evidence that the house is in that parish; but proof of information obtained by inquiries in the neighbourhood just before the commencement of the action is not sufficient. *Doe* d. *Gunson* v. *Welch*, 4 Camp. 264, Lord Ellenborough, C. J.

Proof of particular Facts.]—We have already considered the evidence on many points frequently in question in actions of ejectment. Chap. XXI. *ante*, 209.

Proofs by or against particular Parties.]—These will be fully considered in *Part the Third* of this work. *Post*, Chap. XXXVI. to LXVII.

Where Title expired before Trial.]— By 15 & 16 Vict. c. 76, s. 181, "in case the title of the claimant shall appear to have existed as alleged in the writ, and at the time of service thereof, but it shall also appear

O

to have expired before the time of trial, the claimant shall notwithstanding be entitled to a verdict according to the fact that he was so entitled at the time of bringing the action and serving the writ, and to a judgment for his costs of suit." *See the form, Appendix, No.* 245 (*b*).

If the claimant's title ceased before the writ was *served* (whether before or after the writ issued), the jury should find a verdict for the defendant. Before the above enactment, if it appeared that any lessor's title had ceased before the service of the declaration in ejectment, the action could not be supported on his demise. *Doe* d. *Gardner* v. *Kennard,* 12 Q. B. 244; *Doe* d. *Newby* v. *Jackson,* 1 B. & C. 454, Bayley, J.; 2 D. & R. 514, *S. C.* If the demise, as stated in the declaration, expired after service of the declaration, and before the trial, the plaintiff might recover his damages and costs without the possession. *Thrustout* d. *Turner* v. *Grey,* 2 Stra. 1056; *Doe* d. *Morgan* v. *Bluck,* 3 Camp. 447; *Doe* d. *Butt* v. *Rous,* 1 E. & B. 419. But to enable him to recover possession, it became necessary to amend the declaration by altering the term of the alleged demise, on payment of costs. Ad. Eject. 180; *Doe* d. *Lewis* v. *Coles,* 1 Ry. & Moo. 380; *Doe* d. *Manning* v. *Hay,* 1 Moo. & Rob. 243; *Doe* d. *Rabbits* v. *Welch,* 4 Dowl. & L. 115. As the objection might be cured by an amendment, it could not be successfully taken at nisi prius. *Peaceable* d. *Uncle* v. *Watson,* 4 Taunt. 16. Before it became the practice to permit such an amendment, the lessor was obliged, under the above circumstances, to resort to a new ejectment, in order to recover possession. Ad. Eject. 180. This, however, seldom happened, because the length of the demise, as stated in the declaration, had no reference to the nature of the title of the claimant, and might be of longer duration than his interest in the land. *Doe* d. *Shore* v. *Porter,* 3 T. R. 13; *Havergill* v. *Hare,* Cro. Jac. 510 (3rd point); Ad. Eject. 172. Consequently the practice was to state a demise for seven, fourteen or twenty-one years, even where the lessor's title was only for a year, or any other short period; *Doe* d. *Shore* v. *Porter,* 3 T. R. 13; and this was not productive of any practical injustice. Ad. Eject. 173.

Actual Ouster: when to be proved.]—By 15 & 16 Vict. c. 76, s. 188, joint tenants, tenants in common or coparceners, when sued in ejectment by their co-tenants, may give a notice and file an affidavit admitting the right of the claimant to an undivided share of the property (stating what share), and denying any actual ouster of him from the property. *Ante,* 130. "And such notice shall be entered in the issue in the same manner as the notice limiting the defence." *See the forms, Appendix, Nos.* 137, 138. "And upon the trial of such an issue the additional question of *whether an actual ouster has taken place* shall be tried." Sect. 188, *ante,* 130.

By sect. 189, "upon the trial of *such issue as last aforesaid,* if it shall be found that the defendant is joint tenant, tenant in common or coparcener with the claimant, then the question whether an actual ouster has taken place shall be tried, and unless such actual ouster shall be proved the defendant shall be entitled to judgment and costs; but if it shall be found either that the defendant is not such joint tenant, tenant in common or coparcener, or that an actual ouster has taken place, then the claimant shall be entitled to such judgment for the recovery of possession and costs."

In a recent case, the defendant admitted the plaintiff's title to one-third of the property claimed, and successfully defended for the residue. *Lloyd* v. *Davis*, 15 C. B. 76. In another case, four sisters, as tenants in common, recovered against their brother (the other tenant in common) four undivided fifth parts of certain property, to the whole of which the brother claimed to be entitled as tenant in tail. *Doe* d. *Strong* v. *Goff*, 11 East, 668; and see *Doe* d. *Hellings* v. *Bird*, 11 East, 49; *Oates* d. *Wigfall* v. *Brydon*, 3 Burr. 1898.

It is to be observed, that the question whether there has been an actual ouster does not arise unless the defendant appear at the trial; 2 Chit. Arch. 977 (9th ed.); and the issue and record be framed specially pursuant to sect. 188 : *ante*, 130; *Oates* d. *Wigfall* v. *Brydon*, 3 Burr. 1897-8; cited 4 C. B. 197; *Doe* d. *White* v. *Cuff*, 1 Camp. 174 : nor unless it appear to the jury, and be found by them, that the defendant is a joint tenant, tenant in common or coparcener with the claimant. Sect. 189, *ante*, 290.

What amounts to an actual Ouster.]—If one of several joint tenants, tenants in common or coparceners occupy all, and put the other out of possession and occupation, he which is put out shall have against the other a writ of *ejectione firmæ* of the moietie, &c. Lit. s. 322. But there must be an actual disseisin, as turning him out, or hindering him to enter, &c. A bare perception of profits is not enough. *Per cur. in Reading's case*, 1 Salk. 392 ; Co. Lit. 199 b. The remedy in such case is by an action of account under the stat. 4 Ann. c. 16, s. 27, if the party receive *more than his just share;* but not otherwise ; *Henderson, Executor, &c.* v. *Eason* (in error), 17 Q. B. 701 ; *Sturton* v. *Richardson*, 13 M. & W. 17 ; 2 D. & L. 182 ; *Wheeler* v. *Horn*, Willes, 208 ; *Thomas* v. *Thomas*, 5 Exch. 28 ; *Beer* v. *Beer*, 12 C. B. 60 : or by a bill in equity. *Denys* v. *Shuckburgh*, 4 You. & Col. 42. Mere occupation by one of several tenants in common of an estate, if unaccompanied by exclusion, does not make him liable for rent to his co-tenants, even in a court of equity. *M'Mahon* v. *Burchell*, 2 Phil. R. 127. *Aliter* where the occupation has been by consent, and upon the understanding that an occupation rent should be paid. *Henderson* v. *Eason*, 15 Simon, 303 ; 2 Phil. R. 308. In one case, where a tenant in common remained for thirty-six years in sole and uninterrupted possession without any account to, or demand made, or claim set up by his companion : held, that under such circumstances the jury might presume and find an actual ouster of the co-tenant. *Doe* d. *Fishar* v. *Taylor*, 1 Cowp. 217. But a bare perception of the whole profits for twenty-six years by one tenant in common was not sufficient. *Fairclaim* d. *Empson* v. *Shackleton*, 5 Burr. 2604. Where one tenant in common levied a fine, and received all the rents for more than five years afterwards, without any entry or claim made to avoid the fine : held, that no actual ouster of his co-tenant could be presumed. *Peaceable* d. *Hornblower* v. *Read*, 1 East, 568 ; and see *Roe* d. *Truscott* v. *Elliott*, 1 B. & A. 85. A demand of possession by one tenant in common, and a refusal by the other, *stating that he claimed the whole*, is evidence of an actual ouster of his companion. *Doe* d. *Hellings* v. *Bird*, 11 East, 49. Where three tenants in common (without the fourth) demised the whole property for a long term to a railway company, who thereupon pulled down the houses and made a railway over the land : held, that such user of the property necessarily excluded the fourth tenant in common from the use and enjoyment of his undivided share, and amounted to an actual ouster thereof. *Doe* d. *Wawn* v. *Horn*, 3 M. & W. 333; 5 M. & W. 564, *S. C.* Not only ejectment but trespass *quare clausum fregit* lies by one of several tenants in common against his co-tenant where there has been an actual expulsion : *Murray* v. *Hall*, 7 C. B. 441 : or a destruction of the subject matter of the tenancy : *Wilkinson* v. *Haygarth*, 12 Q. B. 837 : but not for any common trespasses however aggravated. *Bennington* v. *Bennington*, Cro. Eliz. 157.

Damages and Mesne Profits.] — No damages are recoverable in ejectment, except as between landlord and tenant, and then only at the option of the landlord, pursuant to 15 & 16 Vict. c. 76, s. 214. *Post*, Chap. XXXVI., sect. 2. Such option may be exercised at the trial, without any previous notice. *Smith* v. *Tett*, 9 Exch. 307. If the defendant do not appear at the trial, the landlord may recover possession without any proof of his title. *Ante*, 280, 281. But to recover mesne profits he must prove :— 1. His right to recover possession of the whole or part of the premises mentioned in the writ. 2. That the defendant or his attorney has been served with due notice of trial. (This is unnecessary where the defendant appears at the trial. *Doe* d. *Thompson* v. *Hodgson*, 2 Moo. & Rob. 283; 12 A. & E. 135; 4 P. & D. 142.) 3. The value of the mesne profits from the day of the expiration or determination of the defendant's interest in the same, down to the time of the verdict, or to some preceding day to be specially mentioned therein. 15 & 16 Vict. c. 76, s. 214; *post*, Chap. XXXVI., Sect. 2.

It is generally advisable for a landlord to take a verdict for the mesne profits where the tenant has given bail "to pay the costs *and damages*, which shall be recovered by the claimants in the action," pursuant to 15 & 16 Vict. c. 76, s. 213. *Post*, Chap. XXXVI. But in other cases, if the defendant be a solvent man, the landlord should consider whether a subsequent action for double value or double rent is not preferable. *Post*, Chap. LXIX. It can seldom happen that a subsequent action of trespass for mesne profits is preferable to taking a verdict for the amount on the trial of the ejectment, except where the landlord is not then prepared with the necessary proofs above mentioned.

Affirmation instead of Oath in certain Cases.]—By 17 & 18 Vict. c 125, s. 20, "if any person called as a witness, or required or desiring to make an affidavit or deposition, shall refuse or be unwilling from alleged conscientious motives to be sworn, it shall be lawful for the court or judge, or other presiding officer, or person qualified to take affidavits or depositions, *upon being satisfied of the sincerity of such objection*, to permit such person, instead of being sworn, to make his or her solemn affirmation or declaration in the words following, videlicet :—

'I, A. B., do solemnly, sincerely and truly affirm and declare, that the taking of any oath is, according to my religious belief, unlawful ; and I do also solemnly, sincerely and truly affirm and declare, &c.'

Which solemn affirmation and declaration shall be of the same force and effect as if such person had taken an oath in the usual form."

By sect. 21, "if any person making such solemn affirmation or declaration shall wilfully, falsely and corruptly affirm or declare any matter or thing which, if the same had been sworn in the usual form, would have amounted to wilful and corrupt perjury, every such person so offending shall incur the same penalties as by the laws and statutes of this kingdom are or may be enacted or provided against persons convicted of wilful and corrupt perjury."

Quakers and Moravians may in all cases give evidence upon their solemn affirmation instead of upon oath ; 3 & 4 Will. 4, c. 49 ; and the privilege has been extended to all persons who have been Quakers or Moravians, but have ceased to belong to either of those sects ; 1 & 2 Vict. c. 77 ; also to the sect called Separatists. 3 & 4 Will. 4, c. 82.

How far a Party may discredit his own Witness.]—By 17 & 18 Vict. c. 125, s. 22, " a party producing a witness shall not be allowed to impeach his credit by general evidence of bad character, but he may in case the witness shall, *in the opinion of the judge, prove adverse*, contradict him by other evidence, or, *by leave of the judge*, prove that he has made at other times a statement inconsistent with his present testimony ; but before such last-mentioned proof can be given, the circumstances of the supposed statement, sufficient to designate the particular occasion, must be mentioned to the witness, and he must be asked whether or not he has made such statement."

A party ought not to be permitted to produce to the court and jury any person as a witness worthy of credit, and upon finding his evidence to be different from what was expected, to turn round and prove that he was unworthy of belief, by general evidence of bad character. For if his character be known to be so bad as to render him unworthy of belief on his oath, why call him as a witness?

On the other hand, a party ought not to be " sold," or otherwise tricked, by the evidence of an *adverse* witness, who has perhaps pretended to be a friend, and given a different statement of the evidence he would give if called. Therefore a discretionary power is now vested in the judge, to allow proof of a prior inconsistent statement made by the witness, or to allow the party to produce contradictory evidence. Before this act the counsel calling a witness, who gave adverse testimony, could not, on re-examination, ask whether the witness had not given a different account to the attorney. *Winter* v. *Butt*, 2 Moo. & Rob. 357.

Proof of Contradictory Statements of Adverse Witness.]—By 17 & 18 Vict. c. 125, s. 23, "if a witness, upon cross-examination as to a former statement made by him relative to the subject matter of the cause, and inconsistent with his present testimony, does not distinctly admit that he has made such statement, proof may be given that he did in fact make it, but before such proof can be given, the circumstances of the supposed statement, sufficient to designate the particular occasion, must be mentioned to the witness, and he must be asked whether or not he has made such statement."

Cross-examination as to previous Statements in Writing.]—By 17 & 18 Vict. c. 125, s. 24, "a witness may be cross-examined as to previous statements made by him in writing, or reduced into writing, relative to the subject matter of the cause, without such writing being shown to him; but if it is intended to contradict such witness *by the writing*, his attention must, before such contradictory proof can be given, be called to those parts of the writing which are to be used for the purpose of so contradicting him: provided always, that it shall be competent for the judge, at any time during the trial, to require the production of the writing for his inspection, and he may thereupon make such use of it for the purposes of the trial as he shall think fit."

Proof of previous Conviction of a Witness.]—By 17 & 18 Vict. c. 125, s. 25, "a witness in any cause may be questioned as to whether he has been convicted of any felony or misdemeanor, and, upon being so questioned, if he either denies the fact, or refuses to answer, it shall be lawful for the opposite party to prove such conviction, and a certificate containing the substance and effect only (omitting the formal part) of the indictment and conviction for such offence, purporting to be signed by the clerk of the court, or other officer having the custody of the records of the court where the offender was convicted, or by the deputy of such clerk or officer (for which certificate a fee of five shillings and no more shall be demanded or taken), shall, upon proof of the identity of the person, be sufficient evidence of the said conviction, without proof of the signature or official character of the person appearing to have signed the same."

Attesting Witness.]—By 17 & 18 Vict. c. 125, s. 26, "it shall not be necessary to prove by the attesting witness any instrument *to the validity of which attestation is not requisite;* and such instrument may be proved by admission, or otherwise, as if there had been no attesting witness thereto."

If the party's handwriting to a deed (not requiring attestation) be proved, the jury may presume the sealing and delivery, *Grellier* v. *Neale*, Peake, N. P. C. 198, especially if the deed purport to have been signed, sealed and delivered by the party, or contains an attestation to that effect. *Talbot* v. *Hodson*, 7 Taunt. 251; 2 Marsh. 527.

Many instruments are invalid and inoperative unless duly attested by one or more witnesses; 2 Taylor, Ev. 1408 (2nd ed.); *ex. gr.* wills, codicils and appointments in pursuance of powers requiring to be attested in some prescribed manner. *Doe d. Daniel* v. *Keir*, 4 Man. & Ry. 101; *Doe d. Mansfield* v. *Peach*, 2 M. & S. 576. Such instruments must be proved by some or one of the attesting witnesses, unless admitted in the cause in the usual manner. *Ante*, 150. It would not be sufficient to examine at the trial the party himself who executed the deed; but the attesting witness must be called. *Whyman* v. *Garth*, 8 Exch. 803; 2 Taylor, Ev. 1410.

Comparison of disputed Writing.]—By 17 & 18 Vict. c. 125, s. 27, "comparison of a disputed writing with any writing *proved to the satisfaction of the judge* to be genuine shall be permitted to be made by witnesses, and such writings, and the evidence of witnesses respecting the same, may be submitted to the court and jury as evidence of the genuineness, or otherwise, of the writing in dispute."

This has become a common mode of proving or disproving a signature. Other documents, not in issue in the cause, may be put in and proved for the mere purpose of letting in evidence of this nature.

The comparison may be made by skilled or other witnesses, or by the court and jury, with or without the assistance of witnesses. 2 Taylor Ev. 1429 (2nd ed.).

Provisions for Stamping Documents at the Trial.]—By 17 & 18 Vict. c. 125, s. 28, " upon the production of any document as evidence at the trial of any cause, it shall be the duty of the officer of the court, whose duty it is to read such document, to call the attention of the judge to any omission or insufficiency of the stamps; and the document, if unstamped, or not sufficiently stamped, shall not be received in evidence until the whole, or (as the case may be) the deficiency of the stamp duty, and the penalty required by statute, together with the additional penalty of one pound, shall have been paid."

By sect. 29, " such officer of the court shall, upon payment to him of the whole, or (as the case may be) of the deficiency of the stamp duty payable upon or in respect of such document, and of the penalty required by statute, and of the additional penalty of one pound, give a receipt for the amount of the duty or deficiency which the judge shall determine to be payable, and also of the penalty, and thereupon such document shall be admissible in evidence, saving all just exceptions on other grounds; and an entry of the fact of such payment, and of the amount thereof, shall be made in a book kept by such officer; and such officer shall, at the end of each sittings or assizes (as the case may be) duly make a return to the commissioners of the Inland Revenue of the monies, if any, which he has so received by way of duty or penalty, distinguishing between such monies and stating the name of the cause and of the parties from whom he received such monies, and the date, if any, and description of the document for the purpose of identifying the same; and he shall pay over the said monies to the receiver-general of the Inland Revenue, or to such person as the said commissioners shall appoint or authorize to receive the same, and in case such officer shall neglect or refuse to furnish such account, or to pay over any of the monies so received by him as aforesaid, he shall be liable to be proceeded against in the manner directed by the eighth section of an act passed in the session of parliament holden in the thirteenth and fourteenth years of the reign of her present majesty, intituled ' *An Act to repeal certain Stamp Duties, and to grant others in lieu thereof, and to amend the Laws relating to the Stamp Duties ;*' [13 & 14 Vict. c. 97]; and the said commissioners shall, upon request and production of the receipt hereinbefore mentioned, cause such documents to be stamped with the proper stamp or stamps in respect of the sums so paid as aforesaid: provided always, that the aforesaid enactment shall not extend to any document which cannot now be stamped after the execution thereof on payment of the duty and a penalty.'

Sect. 30, "no document made or required under the provisions of this act shall be liable to any stamp duty."

Sect. 31, " no new trial shall be granted by reason of the ruling of any judge that the stamp upon any document is sufficient, or that the document *does not require* a stamp." When the judge holds the document admissible, and the stamp sufficient, he ought not to reserve the point. *Siordet* v. *Kuczynski*, 17 C. B. 251 ; 25 Law J., N. S., C. P., 2; *Tattersall*, App., *Fearnley*, Resp., 17 C. B. 368. The judge's decision is deemed sufficient protection to the revenue. If the judge erroneously decide that a stamp *is necessary*, or that the stamp *is insufficient*, and on that ground the document is rejected, the party grieved may tender a bill of exceptions ; or ask the judge to reserve the point with leave to move to enter a verdict in his favour, or a nonsuit; or (without any such leave) move for a new trial. *Gurr* v. *Scudds*, 11 Exch. 190.

Cross-examination of Witnesses.]—When a witness has been called *and sworn* (unless by mistake) the opposite party has a right to cross-examine him although he has not been asked a single question in chief. *Phillips* v. *Eamer*, 1 Esp. 357, Lord Kenyon, C. J.; 2 Tayl. Ev. 1113 (2nd ed.). But if the witness be sworn under a mistake, whether on the part of the officer of the court or of counsel, and the mistake be discovered before the examination in chief has substantially begun, no cross-examination will be allowed. *Id.* 1113 ; *Wood* v. *Mackinson*, 2 Moo. & Rob. 273, Coleridge, J. So, where the examination in chief is stopped by the judge after answering an immaterial question. *Creevy* v. *Carr*, 7 C. & P. 64, Gurney, B. If a witness be called merely to produce a document under a *subpœna duces tecum*, he need not be sworn, and if unsworn, cannot be cross-examined. *Summers* v. *Moseley*, 2 Cr. & Mee. 477 ; 4 Tyr. 158 ; *Perry* v. *Gibson*, 1 A. & E. 48 ; 3 N. & M. 462 ; *Davis* v. *Dale*, Moo. & Mal. 514 ; 4 C. & P. 335. If sworn by mistake, and a question is put to him which he does not answer, the opposite party is not entitled to cross-examine him. *Rush* v. *Smith*, 1 Cr. M. & R. 94.

When the examination in chief of a witness is closed, the opposite party has a right to cross-examine him. 2 Tayl. Ev. 1111 (2nd ed.). The cross-examination is not limited to the matters upon which the witness has been examined in chief, but extends to the whole case. *Id.* 1116; *Lord* v. *Colvin*, 24 Law J., N. S., Chanc., 517. When a witness is examined in chief on behalf of one or more of the defendants, not only the plaintiff but the other defendants have the right to cross-examine him. *S. C.* "Cases may arise in which intentionally or unfairly one of several co-defendants, who are supposed *primâ facie* to have a common case against the plaintiff, although as between themselves there might be matters in controversy, might call a witness and ask him some indifferent questions, in order that his co-defendant might cross-examine that witness, and so both the defendants get an advantage against the plaintiff which they ought not to have. On the other hand, it might be that one defendant is in the same interest as the plaintiff, and he might call a witness, and affect by the evidence of that witness another defendant who theoretically is supposed not to know, but in reality does know, of that evidence, and that might prejudice the co-defendant if he were not allowed to cross-examine that witness. It appears to me that justice would be best worked out, and there would be less expense on examination, if it were open to all parties, as if each had a separate interest." *Per* Kindersley, V. C. ; *Id.* 519. If the plaintiff calls a witness and examines him, whether that witness is cross-examined or not by the defendant, and after that witness is done with, the defendant may still call the same witness as his own witness, and the plaintiff has a right to cross-examine that witness just as much as if he had never called him. *Id.* 517, 518.

Leading questions may generally be asked on cross-examination ; but the very words required ought not to be put into the witness's mouth, especially if he be friendly. 2 Tayl. Ev. 1115 (2nd ed.). Great latitude is allowed on cross-examination as to collateral facts. *Id.* 1117. Many questions may be put which the witness is not legally bound to answer.

On cross-examining a witness the following rules should be observed, viz. : —

1. Consider well whether it would not be more prudent *to comment on the defects and omissions* of your adversary's case, rather than to run the risk of a cross-examination and re-examination, which may supply or explain them.

2. Never attempt to prove by your adversary's witness what you are prepared to prove by your own, especially if you have only one witness to speak to the point.

3. Never ask a question without having a good reason to assign for asking it.

4. Never hazard a critical question without having good ground to believe that the answer *must* be in your favour.

5. Proceed guardedly, and by degrees; be perfect master of yourself; never appear surprised or dissatisfied; keep your countenance on the most trying occasions; remember there is always "the chance of war."

6. Never appear to treat a witness roughly, rudely or with injustice; if you attempt it every hearer (including the jury) feels offended in the person of the witness; you make your work more difficult; the witness shuts himself up and considers you as his enemy, and stands upon his defence.

For want of a due observance of some or one of the above rules, it frequently happens that a cross-examination does more harm than good to the party on whose behalf it is had.

Re-examination of Witnesses.]—After a witness has been cross-examined he may be re-examined on those points and facts as to which he has been cross-examined, but not as to other unconnected facts. 2 Tayl. Ev. 1147 (2nd ed.); *Prince* v. *Samo*, 7 A. & E. 627; 3 N. & P. 139; *Sturge* v. *Buchanan*, 10 A. & E. 605. If any material question was forgotten or overlooked when the witness was examined in chief, the judge will generally allow it to be put at a later period, during or after the cross-examination; or he will himself put the question, if necessary for furthering the ends of substantial justice.

The object of a re-examination is generally to explain and correct inaccurate expressions used by the witness on cross-examination, and to supply any additional or omitted facts which qualify or do away with the effect of those extracted on cross-examination. The motives and reasons of the witness for acting as he did, or for using particular expressions, may frequently be very material, but would probably not be asked on his cross-examination.

Evidence and Points for Defendants.]—Unless the defendants be estopped from disputing the plaintiff's title (*ante*, 209), they may contend that the plaintiff's evidence does not show a sufficient legal title to actual possession of the property claimed, or any part thereof; and they may produce contradictory evidence on any material point, or evidence showing a distinct title in themselves, or in some or one of them, or in some third person. If it appear, by the evidence produced by either party, that the legal estate in possession is vested in a third person, that constitutes a good defence, although the defendants do not defend on behalf of such person, nor pretend to derive any right or title through or under him. *Culley* v. *Doe* d. *Taylerson* (in error), 11 A. & E. 1008; 3 P. & D. 539, 557; *Doe* d. *Wawn* v. *Horn*, 3 M. & W. 333; *Doe* d. *Fellowes* v. *Alford*, 1 Dowl. & L. 470; *Doe* d. *Lloyd* v. *Passingham*, 6 B. & C. 305; *Goodtitle* d. *Parker* v. *Baldwin*, 11 East, 488; *Doe* d. *Carter* v. *Barnard*, 13 Q. B. 945. An outstanding term, not barred by the Statute of Limitations, is sufficient. *Doe* d. *Hodsden* v. *Staple*, 2 T. R. 684; *Goodtitle* d. *Jones* v. *Jones* (in error), 7 T. R. 43; *Doe* d. *Oliver* v. *Powell*, 1 A. & E. 531; *Cotterell* v. *Hughes*, 15 C. B. 532. It makes no difference in this respect that such outstanding term is vested in a trustee for the plaintiff. *Doe* d. *Leicester* v. *Biggs*, 2 Taunt. 109. The question is, whether the plaintiffs, or any or either of them, are or is legally entitled to actual possession of the property claimed, or any part thereof. *Ante*, 285. The onus of proof lies on the plaintiffs, because the defendants, being *tenants in possession*, are *primâ facie* entitled to such possession. *Ante*, 287. Indeed they are absolutely and legally entitled to such possession as against all the world except the real owner; and if any third person be shown to be the real owner, or entitled to actual possession, it follows that the plaintiffs are not entitled, and that a nonsuit, or a verdict for the defendants, should be entered. *Doe* d. *Fellowes* v. *Alford*, 1 Dowl. & L. 470; *possessio contra omnes valet præter eum cui jus sit possessionis*; Lofft, Max. No. 265.

If the plaintiff prove a legal title, and possession under such title within twenty years, that will throw upon the defendant the onus of proving a legal title to possession vested either in himself or in some third person; proof of a subsequent possession by the defendant for less than twenty years is not sufficient. Thus, where the plaintiff proves title by possession or receipt of rents for twenty-three years, ending within twenty years next before the commencement of the action, and the defendant proves possession for ten years next after such twenty-three years, that is not sufficient; he must prove a legal title. *Doe* d. *Harding* v. *Cooke*, 7 Bing. 346; 5 Moo. & P. 181. A title having been proved in A., who continued in possession from 1809 to 1814, and from whom the plaintiff derived title in 1815, it is not sufficient for the defendant to prove a bare possession by himself during the year 1814. *Doe* d. *Pitcher* v. *Anderson*, 1 Stark. R. 262.

It is a good defence that the plaintiff's title did not accrue until after the day on which possession is claimed in the writ; *ante*, 95; unless, indeed, the mistake be cured by an amendment before or at the trial, which will sometimes be permitted. *Ante*, 95; *post*, 302. So it is a good defence that the plaintiff's title ceased before the service of the writ. *Ante*, 95, 290. But if it ceased subsequently, and before the trial, the plaintiff will be entitled to a verdict and judgment *for his costs* (*ante*, 289), but not for the property claimed.

If the defendant be merely a tenant *at will* to the plaintiff, and such estate has not been determined in any manner before the commencement of the action, or, rather, before the day on which possession is claimed in the writ, *that* is sufficient to defeat the action. *Ante*, 58; *post*, Chap. XLI. So if the defendant be a tenant from year to year to the plaintiff, and such tenancy has not been determined by notice to quit, surrender or otherwise, before the day mentioned in the writ. *Post*, Chap. XL. So if the defendant be tenant to the plaintiff, for a term of years, which has not expired, nor become forfeited, nor otherwise determined. *Post*, Chaps. XXXVII., XXXVIII., XXXIX. But a tenancy at sufferance is not sufficient. *Post*, Chap. XLII.

Generally speaking, when it appears that the defendant obtained possession of the property from the plaintiff, either as a tenant, or by means of any fraud or misconduct, he (the defendant) is estopped from disputing the plaintiff's title to dispose of the possession; *ante*, 213; so if the defendant came in under any person who obtained possession from the plaintiff as above mentioned; *ante*, 215; or from any person through or under whom the plaintiff derives title. *Ante*, 216. The defendant may, however, show that *after the demise* the plaintiff's title expired, or otherwise ceased; *ante*, 217; or that he assigned it either absolutely or by way of mortgage. *Ante*, 217.

If the defendant did not originally obtain possession of the property from the plaintiff, but has since attorned to him, or paid rent, or submitted to a distress made by him, he may sometimes prove that he so acted in ignorance and mistake, and that the plaintiff really had no title. *Ante*, 218. Where that cannot be shown the defendant may dispute the plaintiff's derivative title. *Ante*, 219.

As to estoppels in other cases than as between landlord and tenant, and their respective assigns, see *ante*, 221.

It will be no defence (except as to the defendant's undivided part or share) that the defendant is a joint tenant, tenant in common, or co-parcener with the plaintiff, unless he has given notice and made an affidavit pursuant to 15 & 16 Vict. c. 76, s. 188; *ante*, 130; and an entry of such defence has been made on the roll. *Ante*, 291. But where that has been done, the plaintiff must prove an actual ouster; *ante*, 290; otherwise the defendant will be entitled to the verdict.

The defendant may contend that the deed under which the plaintiff claims is void under the Mortmain Act (9 Geo. 2, c. 36); and that, notwithstanding the defendant is a party to the deed. *Doe* d. *Preece* v. *Howels*, 2 B. & Adol. 744. But a limitation void under this act will not affect another valid limitation contained in the same deed. *Doe* d. *Thompson* v. *Pitcher*, 6 Taunt. 359; 2 Marsh. 61. Whilst the laws against usury were in force the defendant might have contended that the deed was void for usury. *Doe* d. *Haughton* v. *King*, 11 M. & W. 333.

In ejectment for lands in Middlesex or Yorkshire the defendant may contend that the plaintiff's deed is fraudulent and void as against a subsequent conveyance to the defendant, the latter having been first registered; and that notwithstanding the defendant had, at the time of the conveyance to him, full knowledge of the prior conveyance to the plaintiff. *Doe* d. *Robinson* v. *Allsop*, 5 B. & A. 142; *Westbrook* v. *Blythe*, 3 E. & B. 737; *Hughes* v. *Lumley*, 4 E. & B. 274.

When the plaintiff claims under a deed which is fraudulent and void as against creditors on grounds of public policy, the defendant, being a creditor, may rely on the illegality as a defence, notwithstanding he is a party to the deed. *Higgins* v. *Pitt*, 4 Exch. 312. But where the deed is fraudulent and void as against creditors, under 13 Eliz. c. 5, (made perpetual by 29 Eliz. c. 5), it will be valid as against those creditors who were privy and consenting to it. *Steel* v. *Brown and*

Parry, 1 Taunt. 381 ; *Doe* d. *Roberts* v. *Roberts*, 2 B. & A. 367 ; *Robinson* v. *M'Donnel, Id.* 134.

When the plaintiff claims under a voluntary settlement or conveyance, the defendant may show that it was void under the stat. 27 Eliz. c. 4 (made perpetual by 30 Eliz. c. 18), as against subsequent purchasers for value from the grantor, and that he, the defendant, is such a purchaser. *Doe* d. *Baverstock* v. *Rolfe*, 8 A. & E. 650 ; 3 N. & P. 648 ; *Doe* d. *Otley* v. *Manning*, 9 East, 59 ; *Doe* d. *Parry* v. *James*, 16 East, 212 ; *Johnson* v. *Legard*, 6 M. & S. 60 ; *Doe* d. *Bothell* v. *Martyr*, 1 B. & P. New R. 332 ; note to *Twine's case*, 1 Smith's L. C. 13. Copyholds are within the statute. *Doe* d. *Tunstill* v. *Bottriell*, 5 B. & Adol. 131 ; 2 N. & M. 64. A mortgagee is a purchaser within the meaning of the above act. *Doe* d. *Barnes* v. *Rowe*, 4 Bing. N. C. 737 ; 6 Scott, 525 ; *Doe* d. *Sweeting* v. *Webber*, 1 A. & E. 733 ; 3 N. & M. 586 ; *Chapman* d. *Hamerton* v. *Emery*, 1 Cowp. 278. But not an equitable mortgagee by deposit of title deeds ; *Kerrison* v. *Dorrien*, 9 Bing. 76 ; 2 Moo. & Sc. 114 : nor a judgment creditor. *Beavan* v. *Lord Oxford*, 25 Law J., N. S., Chanc., 299. Limitations in a settlement made *before* marriage, in favour of the issue of a second marriage by the settlor, are good as against a subsequent purchaser for valuable consideration. *Clayton* v. *The Earl of Wilton*, 6 M. & S. 67, note. But limitations to the use of the brothers or sisters of the settlor, and their respective issue, are void as against a subsequent purchaser with notice ; *Johnson* v. *Legard*, 6 M. & S. 60 ; unless there be some other consideration besides the marriage to support such limitations. *Roe* d. *Hamerton* v. *Mitton*, 2 Wils. 356. A settlement made for a good consideration, as for the provision of children, will, if made with power of revocation in the settlor, be void against a purchaser for valuable consideration. *Cross* v. *Faustenditch*, Cro. Jac. 180. When the plaintiff claims under an appointment made pursuant to a power contained in a deed or will, the defendant may show, by evidence or otherwise, that it was not a due execution of the power. *Doe* d. *Salt* v. *Carr*, Car. & M. 123.

The "evidence and points for defendant" in many actions of ejectment, as between particular parties, are stated fully in the third part of this work (Chaps. XXXVI. to LXVII.).

Evidence in reply.]—As a general rule the claimant must produce in the first instance all the evidence upon which he relies in support of his own case; he cannot be permitted to prove a mere *primâ facie* title, and when that is controverted by evidence for the defendant, produce further evidence in reply, to strengthen and confirm his *primâ facie* case. 1 Taylor, Ev. 336 (2nd ed.) ; *Jacobs* v. *Tarleton*, 11 Q. B. 421 ; *Osborne* v. *Thompson*, 2 Moo. & Rob. 254. Where, however, the evidence in reply is offered *to disprove the defendant's title or ground of defence*, it seems to be in the discretion of the judge to allow the evidence to be received, notwithstanding it has a tendency to support the plaintiff's original case. *Doe* d. *Sturt* v. *Mobbs*, Car. & M. 1 ; *Briggs* v. *Aynsworth*, 2 Moo. & Rob. 168 ; *Doe* d. *Nicoll* v. *Bower*, 16 Q. B. 805 ; *Wright* v. *Willcox*, 9 C. B. 650. Where the plaintiff relies upon a deed, and the defendant produces evidence to show that the deed was fraudulent and void, the plaintiff may call evidence in reply to prove a *bonâ fide* consideration, or otherwise to negative the alleged fraud. *Shaw*, App., *Beck*, Resp., 8 Exch. 392 ; and see *Doe*

d. *Nicoll* v. *Bower*, and *Wright* v. *Willcox*, *supra.* Where the plaintiff claims as heir of A. B., and the defendant proves a will of A. B., the plaintiff may, by evidence in reply, dispute the validity of the will, or show it to have been revoked. *Doe* d. *Gosley* v. *Gosley*, 2 Moo. & Rob. 243 ; 9 C. & P. 46, Lord Denman, C. J. So where the plaintiff claims as devisee, and the defendant as devisee under a subsequent will or codicil of the same testator. Where the plaintiff and defendant respectively claim as heir of A. B. deceased, the plaintiff must, in the first instance, produce all his evidence in support of his own pedigree, and he may afterwards produce evidence in reply to negative the defendant's pedigree, but not further evidence to support or confirm his own.

When the plaintiff and defendant rely on distinct titles, the plaintiff may in the first instance not only prove his own title, but also anticipate and negative that of the defendant; or he may reserve his evidence on the latter point as evidence in reply ; but if he produce any of it in the first instance for the purpose of negativing or defeating the intended defence, he must then produce all, and not part only in the first instance, and the residue as evidence in reply. 1 Taylor, Ev. 335 (2nd ed.) ; Phil. Ev. 843 (8th ed.) ; *Brown* v. *Murray*, Ry. & Moo. 254, Abbott, C. J. ; *Roe* d. *Barry* v. *Day*, 7 C. & P. 707, Park, J.

The plaintiff may generally call evidence in reply *to contradict* the defendant's witnesses upon any material point. *Cope* v. *The Thames Haven Dock Company*, 2 Car. & K. 758 ; *Doe* d. *Sturt* v. *Mobbs*, Car. & M. 1 ; *Greswolde* v. *Kemp*, *Id.* 635.

Reply on further Evidence of Plaintiff.]—When the plaintiff calls evidence in reply, the defendant's counsel is entitled to reply upon such evidence ; *ante*, 285 ; but not upon the whole case. *Furze* v. *Asker*, 3 Car. & K. 73.

General Reply.]—Where the evidence is conflicting, a powerful and dexterous reply will frequently secure the verdict. We have already seen in what cases the plaintiff is entitled to the general reply. *Ante*, 284. When evidence is given on behalf of any one or more of the defendants, the plaintiff's counsel is entitled to a general reply on the whole case as against *all* the defendants. *Reg.* v. *Blackburn*, 3 Car. & K. 330, Talfourd, J.

Where counsel for a defendant *opens facts* to the jury, but does not go into any evidence, the counsel for the plaintiff has not an absolute right to reply, but it is in the discretion of the judge ; the object of allowing a reply in such cases being, that injustice should not be done by facts being improperly opened when the defendant's counsel has no intention of proving them. *Nash* v. *Brown*, 2 Car. & K. 219, Pollock, C. B. ; *Crerar* v. *Sodo*, Moo. & M. 85, Lord Tenterden, C. J.

Summing up by the Judge to the Jury.]—After all the evidence has been given and commented on by the counsel on both sides, the judge proceeds to sum up the case and evidence to the jury. He generally explains to them what is the precise point or question of fact they have to determine, and the law touching or relating to it, so far as that appears to be necessary. He then either reads his notes of the evidence with comments, or states the substance and effect of it in a compendious manner, and concludes by directing them to find their verdict upon the question or point submitted to them according to their view of the evidence.

Each party should take care that the point or question of fact (if any) upon which he relies is properly submitted to the jury, and that no misdirection upon any point of law be made to the prejudice of his client. If necessary, a bill of exceptions should be tendered. *Post,* Chap. XXV.

Amendments.]—The Common Law Procedure Act, 1852 (15 & 16 Vict. c. 76), s. 222, after reciting that "whereas the power of amendment now vested in the courts and the judges thereof is insufficient to enable them to prevent the failure of justice by reason of mistakes and objections of form," enacts, that "it shall be lawful for the superior courts of common law, and every judge thereof, and any judge sitting at nisi prius, at all times to amend all defects and errors in any proceeding in civil causes, whether there is anything in writing to amend by or not, and whether the defect or error be that of the party applying to amend or not; and all such amendments may be made with or without costs, and upon such terms as to the court or judge may seem fit; and all such amendments as may be necessary for the purpose of determining in the existing suit the *real question in controversy* between the parties *shall be so made.*"

This section "enables the court or judge to make the amendment in the cases provided for, whether it be in a matter that is material to the merits of the case or not. Now whether or not a particular amendment is a matter material to the merits is matter of law; but whether or not the proposed amendment is necessary for the purpose of determining the real question in controversy between the parties is matter of fact to be decided by the judge. It often happens that, there being a controversy, the parties are unable to try that controversy properly, because the pleadings between them do not correctly show upon the record what that controversy is. It was to obviate that inconvenience that this section was framed." *Per* Maule, J., in *Wilkin* v. *Reed,* 15 C. B. 205.

The previous act, 3 & 4 Will. 4, c. 42, s. 23, only allowed amendments in case of variances between the proof and the record; *Doe* d. *Parson* v. *Heather,* 8 M. & W. 158; 1 Dowl. N. S. 64; and where such variances were "not material to the merits of the case." *Doe* d. *Wilton and Wife* v. *Beck,* 13 C. B. 329. The 15 & 16 Vict. c. 76, s. 222, *supra,* is much more extensive.

A misnomer of one of the claimants may, if necessary, be amended, or his christian or first name (if it cannot be proved) may be struck out. *Doe* d. *Miller* v. *Rogers,* 1 Car. & K. 390. So the name of the parish may be amended. *Doe* d. *Marriott* v. *Edwards,* 1 Moo. & Rob. 319; 6 C. & P. 208. But frequently any such amendment is unnecessary. *Ante,* 92. Parties must not come down to trial on the ground that there is a variance on the record, which they suppose a judge will not rectify. *Per* Parke, J., in *Doe* v. *Edwards, supra.* In ejectment for a forfeiture the demise was laid on a day prior to that on which the right of entry for the forfeiture accrued: held, that the date might be amended. *Doe* d. *Edwards* v. *Leach,* 3 Man. & Gr. 229; 3 Scott, N. R. 509; 9 Dowl. 877. When necessary, an *earlier* day may be inserted. *Doe* d. *Simpson* v. *Hall,* 5 Man. & Gr. 795; 1 Dowl. & L. 49. An amendment will not generally be refused on the ground of the hardness of the action. *Doe* d. *Marriott* v. *Edwards*, 1 Moo. & Rob. 319; 6 C. & P. 208. But where several brothers and sisters divided certain property between them at their mother's death, supposing it to have been hers, and verbally allotted a house to a sister, the property really had been their deceased father's: held, in ejectment by the father's devisee (one of the brothers), that he could not recover without a demand of possession; and the demand of possession being after the day of the demise, the judge would not allow an amendment by altering the day of the demise, *as the arrangement was equitable*. *Doe* d. *Loscombe* v. *Clifford*, 2 Car. & K. 448, Alderson, B.

An amendment cannot be made at nisi prius *after* the verdict; *Doe* d. *Bennett* v. *Long*, 9 C. & P. 777, Coleridge, J.; nor can leave to amend after the verdict be reserved at the trial, except by consent.

Power to adjourn the Trial.]—By 17 & 18 Vict. c. 125, s. 19, "it shall be lawful for the court or judge at the trial of any cause, where they or he may deem it right for the purposes of justice, to order an adjournment for such time, and subject to such terms and conditions as to costs and otherwise, as they or he may think fit."

An adjournment may be ordered as above, either before or after the jury have been sworn, and the cause partly heard. *Morgan* v. *Pike*, 14 C. B. 477.

Bill of Exceptions.]—If improper and inadmissible evidence be received (although duly objected to), or proper and admissible evidence be rejected, or the judge misdirect the jury upon any point of law material to the matters in issue, a bill of exceptions may be tendered. *Post*, Chap. XXV. But frequently the point is reserved, or otherwise raised in a manner somewhat less offensive to the judge. *Post*, Chap. XXVI.

Withdrawing a Juror.]—Sometimes a juror is withdrawn by consent upon terms mutually agreed on. *Doe* d. *Rankin* v. *Brindley*, 4 B. & Adol. 84. But this does not often happen in ejectment. When a juror is withdrawn, the rest of the jury are thereupon discharged from giving any verdict. Each party pays his own costs; *Stodhart* v. *Johnson*, 3 T. R. 657; *Burdin* v. *Flower*, 7 Dowl. 786; Gray on Costs, 290; and no further proceedings can be had *in that action*, unless the parties agree to the contrary. *Harries* v. *Thomas*, 2 M. & W. 32. In other actions than ejectment, if after the withdrawal of a juror by consent a subsequent action be brought for the same cause, the court will generally stay the proceedings, upon a summary application, as being against good faith; *Moscati* v. *Lawson*, 4 A. & E. 331; *Gibbs* v. *Ralph*, 14 M. & W. 804; but it constitutes no legal defence by way of plea or otherwise to the subsequent action. *Saunderson* v. *Nestor*, Ry. & Moo. 402, Abbott, C. J. A subsequent ejectment may be brought for the same forfeiture, after the withdrawal of a juror by consent, upon terms not duly performed by the defendant. *Doe* d. *Rankin* v. *Brindley*, 4 B. & Adol. 84.

Discharging Jury without a Verdict.]—Sometimes when the jury cannot agree, they are discharged by consent, or by order of the judge, from giving any verdict. *Reg.* v. *Newton*, 3 Car. & K. 85. When that happens, each party has to pay his own costs of the abortive trial, whatever may be the result of a subsequent trial. *Bostock v. The North Staffordshire Railway Company*, 18 Q. B. 777.

Nonsuit.]—At any time before the jury have actually given their verdict (even at the last moment) the plaintiff may elect to be non-suited, and insist on such right, and so avoid a verdict against him. 3 Bl. Com. 376; *Vacher v. Cocks*, 1 B. & Adol. 145; *Munn v. Love-joy*, Ry. & Moo. 357; *Outhwaite v. Hudson*, 7 Exch. 380; *Robinson v. Lawrence, Id.* 123; *see the forms of Entry on the Postea, Appendix, Nos.* 246, 247; and of the judgment thereon; *Id., No.* 265. Upon a nonsuit the plaintiff is liable to the costs of the action in like manner as on a verdict for the defendant. *Cameron v. Reynolds*, Cowp. 407; 2 Bos. & P. 376; *Davila v. Herring*, 1 Stra. 300. And the judge may certify for the costs of a special jury obtained by the defendant. 3 & 4 Will. 4, c. 42, s. 35.

On the other hand, when the plaintiff appears at the trial, he cannot be nonsuited except with his own consent, express or implied. It is entirely optional with him to take his chance of obtaining the verdict, or to submit to a nonsuit. *Minchin v. Clement*, 1 B. & A. 252; *Lumley v. Allday*, 1 Cr. & Jer. 301; *Stancliffe*, App., *Clarke*, Resp., 7 Exch. 439; 1 Wms. Saund. 195 d, note. When formally called upon to appear, he may appear and refuse to be nonsuited, and claim the verdict. *Boyes v. Hewetson*, 2 Bing. N. C. 576, Tindal, C. J.; *Dewar v. Purday*, 3 A. & E. 170, Lord Denman, C. J.; *Corsar v. Reed*, 17 Q. B. 542, Lord Campbell, C. J.; *Hughes v. The Great Western Railway Company*, 17 C. B. 637. If there be no legal evidence to go to the jury in support of his case, the judge should thereupon direct the jury to find a verdict for the defendant. *Rennie v. Wynn* (in error), 4 Exch. 698; *Stancliffe v. Clarke*, 7 Exch. 446, Parke, B. Whereupon the plaintiff may tender a bill of exceptions for misdirection. *Minchin v. Clement*, 1 B. & A. 252; *Corsar v. Reed*, 17 Q. B. 540, 544. But if the judge persist in directing a nonsuit to be entered, the plaintiff may *on that ground* tender a bill of exceptions; *Corsar v. Reed, supra; Strother v. Hutchinson*, 4 Bing. N. C. 83; 5 Scott, 346; 6 Dowl. 238; or the court in banc will set aside the nonsuit, and grant a new trial. *Sadler v. Evans*, 4 Burr. 1984; *Alexander v. Barker*, 2 Cr. & Jer. 133; *Elsworthy v. Bird*, M'Clel. 69; *Outhwaite v. Hudson*, 7 Exch. 380. And in such case the nonsuit being *irregular*, it would seem that the defendant cannot rely on the point on which the nonsuit proceeded as an answer to the application. *Dewar v. Purday*, 3 A. & E. 166; 4 N. & M. 633.

The time at which a nonsuit is usually applied for is at the close of the plaintiff's case. The defendant then submits to the judge that there is no evidence to go to the jury upon some essential point; but if there be any such evidence (however slight and insufficient), the judge usually overrules the objection, and decides upon leaving the question to the jury, sometimes reserving the point, with liberty for the defendant to move upon it (if necessary) to set aside the verdict, and enter a nonsuit. *Mortimer v. Wright*, 6 M. & W. 482; *Rawlings v. Chandler*, 9 Exch. 687. But unless such leave be expressly reserved at the trial, the court in banc cannot direct a nonsuit to be entered. *Ricketts v. Burman*, 4 Dowl. 578. Where there is any doubt whether such leave was duly reserved or not, the rule nisi should be in the alternative, viz., to set aside the verdict and enter a nonsuit, *or* for a new trial. *Watkins* v. *Towers*, 2 T. R. 276. Such leave cannot be reserved at the trial except with the consent of the plaintiff, express or implied. *Dewar* v. *Purday*, 3 A. & E. 166; 4 N. & M. 633. If such consent be refused improperly, the judge may direct the jury to find 'a verdict for the defendant, with or without liberty for the plaintiff to move to set aside such verdict, and to enter one in his favour. *Rennie* v. *Wynn* (in error), 4 Exch. 698. But this is rather a strong measure, especially since the 17 & 18 Vict. c. 125, s. 35. The judge will not nonsuit a plaintiff on the ground, that, to make out a *primâ facie* case in his favour, part of the testimony of his own witnesses must be disbelieved. *Briers* v. *Rust*, 3 Car. & K. 294.

If the plaintiff elect to be nonsuited, to avoid a verdict against him, he cannot move to set aside the nonsuit, and for a new trial, however strong may have been the opinion expressed by the judge as to the effect of the plaintiff's evidence. *Simpson* v. *Clayton*, 2 Bing. N. C. 467; 2 Scott, 691; *Barnes* v. *Whiteman*, 2 Man. & Gr. 430; 9 Dowl. 409; *Wilkinson* v. *Whalley*, 5 Man. & Gr. 590; 1 Dowl. & L. 9. Where the judge, in summing up a case, directed the jury, if they came to a certain conclusion, to give their verdict for the plaintiff; but if they came to either of two other conclusions, which he pointed out, to find for the defendant, and state on what ground their judgment was formed, and the plaintiff then elected to be nonsuited : held, that he was not entitled to a new trial on account of misdirection, if either of the two latter points was rightly put to the jury. *Vacher* v. *Cocks*, 1 B. & Adol. 145. If the judge tells the plaintiff's counsel that he will nonsuit him *on a point of law*, the latter does not by mere acquiescence lose his right to move ; but if the judge says he will nonsuit the plaintiff, *because there is no evidence to leave to the jury*, the plaintiff's counsel, if he means to object, should insist upon going to the jury, or he cannot afterwards complain. *Hughes* v. *The Great Western Railway Company*, 17 C. B. 637.

If the plaintiff submit to be nonsuited upon a point of law, in deference to an incorrect opinion of the judge at the trial, he may move the court to set aside the nonsuit, and for a new trial. *Law* v. *Wilkin*, 6 A. & E. 718; 1 N. & P. 697; *Ward* v. *Mason*, 9 Price, 291; *Alexander* v. *Barker*, 2 Cr. & Jer. 133 ; *Elsworthy* v. *Bird*, M'Clel. 69; *Sadler* v. *Evans*, 4 Burr. 1984; *Wilkinson* v. *Whalley*, 5 Man. & Gr. 591; 6 Scott, N. R. 631; 1 Dowl. & L. 9 ; or to set aside the nonsuit and enter a verdict in his favour, provided leave to that effect be expressly reserved to him at the trial; but not otherwise. *Minchin* v. *Clement*, 1 B. & A. 252; *Matthews* v. *Smith*, 2 You. & Jer. 426; *Russell* v. *Briant*, 8 C. B. 849; *Ricketts* v. *Burman*, 4 Dowl. 478.

When any such leave is reserved, care should be taken to have it entered on the judge's notes. *Beverley* v. *Walker*, 8 Dowl. 418; *Gibbs* v. *Pike*, 9 M. & W. 351; 1 Dowl. N. S. 409.

Retirement of the Jury to consider their Verdict.]—If the jury cannot agree as to their verdict, they usually retire to an adjoining room to consider their verdict, and they should be locked up there, under the charge of a bailiff, without meat, drink, fire or candle, until they agree. Co. Lit. 227 b. They should not be permitted to speak to anybody except the bailiff, and with him only when they are agreed; Co. Lit. 227 b ; unless they wish to communicate with the judge in open court. The judge cannot discharge them without giving a verdict, except under very special circumstances; *Reg.* v. *Newton*, 3 Car. & K. 85; or by consent of both parties, or their counsel. When so discharged, whether by consent or otherwise, each party has to pay his own costs of that trial, whatever may be the result of a subsequent trial. *Bostock* v. *The North Staffordshire Railway Company*, 18 Q. B. 777.

If either of the jury eat or drink at his own cost, whilst locked up, he may be fined; Co. Lit. 227 b; *Mounson* v. *West*, 1 Lev. 132; Bac. Abr. Verdict, H.; but it shall not avoid the verdict. If the jury, before they agree on their verdict, eat or drink at the expense of either party, it will avoid a verdict in his favour, but not a verdict for the opposite party. Co. Lit. 227 b. It is, however, in the discretion of the court in banc whether they will set aside a verdict on this ground. *Morris* v. *Vivian*, 10 M. & W. 137; 2 Dowl. N. S. 235.

If the plaintiff, after evidence given and the jury departed from the bar, or any for him, do deliver any letter from the plaintiff to any of the jury concerning the matter in issue, which was not given in evidence, it shall avoid the verdict, if it be found for the plaintiff, but not if it be found for the defendant, *et sic è converso*. But if the jury carry away any writing unsealed which was given in evidence in open court, this shall not avoid their verdict, albeit they should not have carried it with them. Co. Lit. 227 b.

The jury, when agreed, usually give their verdict in open court; but if necessary, a privy verdict may be given in civil cases. Co. Lit. 227 b. When the judge adjourns the court to his lodgings, and the jury give their verdict there, it is a public, and not a privy verdict.

Verdict.]—The jury must find, according to the evidence, whether the plaintiffs, or any or either and which of them, are or is entitled to all or any and what part of the property claimed. (*Ante*, 285); *see Appendix, No.* 243. If it appear that the plaintiffs are entitled to some undivided part or share of the property claimed, the verdict should find accordingly. (*Ante*, 86.) If the jury find for the plaintiffs, or any or either of them, *for part only* of the property claimed, or for some undivided part thereof, they should find as to the residue for the defendants. *Doe* d. *Bowman* v. *Ellis*, 13 M. & W. 241; 2 Dowl. & L. 667; *Doe* d. *Hellyer* v. *King*, 6 Exch. 791; 2 Low. M. & P. 493; *see the form, Appendix, No.* 243. A verdict for either party as to part, which says nothing as to the residue, is altogether bad and insufficient in law. Co. Lit. 227 a; *Rochel* v. *Stedle*, Hardres, 166; *Miller* v. *Tretts*, 1 Ld. Raym. 32; 2 *Id.* 1521; *Cattle* v. *Andrews*, 3 Salk. 372; and see *Finymore* v. *Sanky*, Cro. Eliz. 133; *Hooper* v. *Shepherd*, Stra. 1089; *Loveday's case*, 8 Co. R. 65 b; Cro. Jac. 210, *S. C.*; *Bishop* v. *Kaye*, 3 B. & A. 605. In *Rowe* v. *Huntington*, Vaughan, R. 66, the jury found, except as to two hundred acres for the defendants, and as to those two hundred acres a special verdict.

It seems that a verdict may be found as to part of the property for some or one of the plaintiffs, and as to other part for another plaintiff. *Doe* d. *Simpson* v. *Simpson*, 4 Bing. N. C. 348; 5 Scott, 770; and as to the residue (if any) for the defendants.

In no case can the jury find a verdict for the plaintiff for more property, or for a larger undivided part or share than that claimed in the writ. (*Ante*, 86.) But the verdict may be for any less undivided part or share, according to the evidence. (*Ante*, 86.) So where the plaintiff claims the whole of certain premises, the jury may give a verdict in his favour for any divided or undivided part or share thereof (*ante*, 87), and for the defendants as to the residue.

As between landlord and tenant, the jury may be required to find the amount of the damages for mesne profits to which the plaintiff is entitled, either down to the day of the trial, or to some previous day. *Ante*, 292; *post*, Chap. XXXVI., Sect. 2.

If the plaintiff's title expired after the service of the writ, the jury should find a verdict to that effect. *Ante*, 289; *see the form, Appendix, No.* 245 b. But if it expired before such service, the verdict should be for the defendants.

"By consent" the jury may find a verdict for either party, subject to a reference: Chap. XXVI., Sect. 1: or to a point reserved: Chap. XXVI., Sect. 2: or to a special case: Chap. XXVI., Sect. 3: or (without any such consent) they may find a special verdict: Chap. XXVI., Sect. 4: or a general verdict as to part, and a special verdict as to the residue. *Rowe v. Huntingdon*, Vaughan, R. 66.

Verdict by Lot.]—If the jury, not being able to agree, toss up for the verdict, or decide it by lot, and that fact can be sufficiently proved without any affidavit from either of the jury, the court will set aside the verdict, although it be according to the evidence and the opinion of the judge: *Fry v. Ward*, T. Jon. 33; *Hall v. Cove*, 1 Stra. 642. Thus where the bailiff having charge of the jury overheard them agree to decide by lot. *Harding v. Hewitt*, 8 Dowl. 598; *Addison v. Williamson*, 5 Jurist, 166; *Fry v. Ward*, *supra*. But the court will not receive the affidavit of any of the jury upon the above point. *Owen v. Warburton*, 1 B. & P. New R. 326; *Vaise v. Deleval*, 1 T. R. 11; *Jackson v. Williamson*, 2 T. R. 281: nor the affidavit of the attorney as to an *admission* made to him by one or more of the jury on this point. *Straker v. Graham*, 4 M. & W. 721; 7 Dowl. 223; *Burgess v. Langley*, 5 Man. & Gr. 722; 6 Scott, N. R. 518; 1 Dowl. & L. 21. "If such evidence was admissible, what verdict would be safe? If one of the jury is displeased at the verdict, he may say they tossed up for it, and if that be false he is subject to no punishment." *Per* Alderson, B., in *Straker v. Graham*, *supra*. Affidavits of jurors, as to what took place in open court on delivering their verdict, are receivable. *Roberts v. Hughes*, 7 M. & W. 399; 1 Dowl. N. S. 82. So where a new trial is moved for on affidavits of misconduct and partiality on the part of the jury, affidavits of any of the jury in denial or explanation of the alleged misconduct are receivable. *Standewick v. Hopkins*, 2 Dowl. & L. 502. An affidavit of the attorney of what a juryman stated in open court when the verdict was delivered, but not in the hearing of the judge or associate, is not admissible. *Burgess v. Langley*, *supra*.

Entry of the Verdict.]—Immediately the verdict is given, the associate makes a short note of it on the back of the panel of jurors, thus: —

1. Verdict for plaintiffs.
2. Verdict for defendants.
3. Verdict for plaintiffs [A. B., I. K. and L. M.] as to —— [*describe the part*], and for defendants as to the residue.

4. Verdict for plaintiff, with £—— for mesne profits from —— to ——.

5. Verdict for plaintiffs [as to —— *describe the part*], subject to a special case; and for defendants as to the residue.

6. Verdict for defendants [as to —— *describe the part*]; and for plaintiffs as to the residue, subject to a special case.

7. Special verdict [as to —— *describe the part*]; and for defendants as to the residue.

8. Nonsuit.

9. A juror [*name*] withdrawn by consent.

From the above note or memorandum, the *postea* is afterwards prepared. *See post*, Chap. XXVIII.

Certificate for Special Jury.]—As to this, see *ante*, 264.

Certificate that refusal to admit Documents was reasonable.]—As to this, see *ante*, 154.

Order to stay Judgment or Execution.]—If no order be made by the judge before whom the cause is tried to stay judgment or execution, judgment may be signed and execution issue on the fifth day in term after the verdict, or within fourteen days after such verdict, *whichever shall first happen.* 15 & 16 Vict. c. 76, ss. 185, 186, *post*, Chap. XXIX. When the trial takes place at the assizes, or at the sittings after term in London or Middlesex, if the defendant wish to move for a new trial, &c., he should generally apply to the judge, immediately after the verdict, for an order to stay judgment and execution until the fifth day of the next term; because fourteen days after the verdict will elapse before the application can be made to the court in banc.

When a landlord obtains a verdict in ejectment against a tenant who has found security for the costs and damages, pursuant to 15 & 16 Vict. c. 76, s. 213, the judgment or execution cannot be stayed by order of the judge, except under the circumstances and in manner provided by sect. 215. *Post*, Chap. XXXVI., Sect. 3.

CHAPTER XXV.

BILL OF EXCEPTIONS.

By the Statute of Westm. 2 (13 Edw. 1, c. 31), "when one that is impleaded before any of the justices doth allege an exception, praying that the justices will allow it, which if they will not allow, if he that alleged the exception do write the same exception, and require that the justices will put their seals for a witness, the justices shall so do; and if one will not, another of the company shall; and if the king, upon complaint made of the justices, cause the record to come before him, and the same exception be not found in the roll, and the plaintiff show the exception written, with the seal of a justice put to, the justice shall be commanded that he appear at a certain day, either to confess or deny his seal; and if the justice cannot deny his seal they shall proceed to judgment according to the same exception, as it ought to be allowed or disallowed." 2 Inst. 426.

By 15 & 16 Vict. c. 76, s. 184, "either party may tender a bill of exceptions" in an ejectment.

Sometimes a bill of exceptions is tendered on both sides. *Nepean, Bart.* v. *Doe* d. *Knight*, 2 M. & W. 894, 897, 911.

Must be on Matter of Law.]—A bill of exceptions must be upon some *point of law*, but it is not confined to errors in directing the jury. *Bridgman* v. *Holt*, Show. P. C. 120. It extends to any mistake of the judge upon matter of law during the progress of the trial, 3 Blac. Com. 372 (except on *collateral* points, *post*, 311), *ex. gr.* :—

1. In erroneously allowing or disallowing a challenge of jurors, or a demurrer to evidence. *Ante*, 268; *Cort* v. *Bishop of Saint David's*, Cro. Car. 342; T. Jon. 331, *S. C.*; *per* Tindal, C. J., in *Strother* v. *Hutchinson*, 4 Bing. N. C. 90; 5 Scott, 346; 6 Dowl. 238, *S. C.*

2. In the reception of inadmissible parol evidence, although objected to. *Tennant* v. *Hamilton*, 7 Cl. & Fin. 122; *Bradley* v. *Pilots of Newcastle*, 2 E. & B. 427, 437.

3. In the reception of inadmissible written evidence, although objected to. *Hammond* v. *Bradstreet*, 10 Exch. 390; *The Irish Society* v. *The Bishop of Derry*, 12 Cl. & Fin. 641. But by 17 & 18 Vict. c. 125, s. 31, "no new trial shall be granted by reason of the ruling of any judge that the stamp upon any document is sufficient, or that the document does not require a stamp." Therefore it seems that a bill of exceptions and trial *de novo* would not be permitted on such grounds. It is otherwise where the judge erroneously decides that a stamp is necessary, or that the stamp impressed is insufficient; and on that ground rejects the document. *The Fishmongers' Company* v. *Dimsdale*, 12 C. B. 557; *Gurr* v. *Scudds*, 11 Exch. 190. If a document be admissible in evidence *for any purpose*, a bill of exceptions cannot be supported for its reception in evidence. *The Irish Society* v. *The Bishop of Derry*, 12 Cl. & Fin. 641. See the converse of this case, where admissible evidence was rejected, being tendered only for a purpose for which it was not admissible. *Rex* v. *Grant*, 3 Nev. & M. 106.

4. In the rejection of proper and admissible evidence, whether oral or in writing. *Doe* d. *Beach* v. *The Earl of Jersey*, 3 B. & C. 870; *Bent* v. *Baker*, 3 T. R. 27; *Davies* v. *Pierce*, 2 T. R. 53, 54, 125; *Doe* d. *Oxenden* v. *Sir A. Chichester*, 4 Dow. Parl. C. 65; *Lord Dunraven* v. *Llewellyn*, 15 Q. B. 791, 795; *Doe* d. *Padwick* v. *Wittcomb*, 6 Exch. 601. A bill of exceptions on this ground is frequently preferable to a motion for a new trial, because, upon such application, the court will consider whether the evidence was really material, and whether the fact proposed to be proved was sufficiently proved by other evidence. *Doe* d. *Welsh* v. *Langfield*, 16 M. & W. 497, 515; *Doe* d. *Lord Teynham* v. *Tyler*, 6 Bing. 561; 4 Moo. & P. 377; *Crease* v. *Barrett*, 1 Cr. M. & R. 919; 5 Tyr. 458, 475. Whereas a court of

error cannot look beyond the bill of exceptions, but must decide on that alone. *Bain* v. *The Whitehaven and Furness Junction Railway Company*, 3 H. L. Cas. 1; *The Household Coal and Iron Company* v. *Neilson*, 9 Cl. & Fin. 788.

5. Where the judge erroneously leaves to the decision of the jury a question of law. *Doe* d. *Strickland* v. *Strickland*, 8 C. B. 724; *Bradley* v. *Pilots of Newcastle*, 2 E. & B. 427, 437; *Cheveley*, App., *Fuller*, Resp., 13 C. B. 122.

6. Where the judge erroneously refuses to leave to the jury a question of fact. *Runcorn* v. *Doe* d. *Cooper* (in error), 5 B. & C. 696, 698; *Graham* v. *The Van Diemen's Land Company*, 11 Exch. 108. But if the judge take upon himself, without objection, to decide a question of fact, or assume the fact to be one way, it will (in the absence of proof to the contrary) be assumed that he did so with the express or implied assent of both parties. *Doe* d. *Heapy* v. *Howard*, 11 East, 498; *Doe* d. *Kindersley* v. *Hughes*, 7 M. & W. 141, Parke, B.; *Doe* d. *Strickland* v. *Strickland*, 8 C. B. 724. If the judge allow the matter to be evidence, but not conclusive, and so refer it to the jury; as for instance, where the probate of a will is produced to prove a devise of a term of years, and the judge leaves it to the jury, a bill of exceptions will not lie. *Chichester* v. *Phillips*, T. Raym. 405; 2 Jones, 146, *S. C.* So where the question is not as to the admissibility, but as to the sufficiency of the evidence. *Bulkeley* v. *Butler*, 2 B. & C. 434; *Id.* 444, *per* Holroyd, J.

7. Where the judge erroneously leaves to the jury a question of fact upon which there is no evidence which ought to be left to them, that amounts to a misdirection. *Bulkeley* v. *Butler* (in error), 2 B. & C. 434; *Drouet* v. *Taylor*, 16 C. B. 671; *Smith* v. *Cannan*, 2 E. & B. 35; *Giles* v. *The Taff Vale Railway Company*, *Id.* 822; *Briers* v. *Rust*, 3 Car. & K. 298; *The Great Northern Railway Company* v. *Harrison*, 10 Exch. 376.

8. Where the judge puts an erroneous construction upon a document produced and given in evidence to the jury. *Cook* v. *Bishop of Elphin*, 2 Dow. & Cl. 247.

9. Where the judge in his summing up to the jury misdirects them upon some point of law touching the matter in question. *Hickell* v. *Money*, Bull. N. P. 317 (where see a good form); *Money* v. *Leach*, 3 Burr. 1742, 1750; *Francis* v. *Doe* d. *Harvey*, 4 M. & W. 331, 333; 7 Dowl. 193; *Rowe* v. *Power* (in error), 2 Bos. & P. New. R. 1, 5; *Ball* v. *Mannin*, 1 Dow. & Cl. 380; 3 Bligh, N. S. 1, *S. C.*; *The Househill Coal and Iron Company* v. *Neilson*, 9 Cl. & Fin. 788; or directs them to find a verdict for the wrong party; *Davenport* v. *Tyrrell*, 1 W. Black. 676; *Vines* v. *The Corporation of Reading*, 1 You. & Jer. 4, 8; *Warre* v. *Miller*, 4 B. & C. 538, 540; 7 D. & R. 1; *Money* v. *Leach*, 3 Burr. 1746; *Minchin* v. *Clement*, 1 B. & A. 252; *Corsar* v. *Reed*, 17 Q. B. 540, 544; or erroneously tells them that there is no evidence which would authorize them to find a verdict for the plaintiff; *Heath* v. *Unwin*, 12 C. B. 522; *Graham* v. *The Van Diemen's Land Company*, 11 Exch. 108; *post*, 312.

A bill of exceptions will not lie for a misdirection upon any *collateral* point. *Black* v. *Jones*, 6 Exch. 213. Thus, where a judge expresses an opinion upon a point of law, not for the purpose of directing the jury as to the matter immediately before them, but merely adverts to the point for some collateral purpose, and in order to explain and give effect to other evidence, such expression of opinion cannot be made the subject of a bill of exceptions, because a bill of exceptions can only be tendered in respect of those matters of law on which a judge is bound to instruct the jury, in order that, he telling them the law, and they deciding the fact, a just conclusion may result from the labours of both. *Id.* 216. So a bill of exceptions will not lie for a mere *non-direction*, but only for a misdirection. *Anderson* v. *Fitzgerald*, 4 H. L. Cas. 484 ; *Gregory* v. *Cotterell*, 25 Law J., N. S., Q. B., 33 ; *M'Alpine* v. *Mangnall*, 3 C. B. 517, Parke, B.

10. Where the judge decides that there is no evidence for the jury in favour of the plaintiff, and directs the plaintiff to be called, the latter may appear when so called, and object to be nonsuited ; whereupon the judge should direct the jury to find a verdict for the defendant ; but if the judge then persists in directing a nonsuit to be entered, notwithstanding the plaintiff's appearance, the plaintiff may, on that ground, tender a bill of exceptions. *Strother* v. *Hutchinson*, 4 Bing. N. C. 83 ; 5 Scott, 346 ; 6 Dowl. 238, *S. C.* But if the plaintiff submit to be nonsuited, he cannot tender a bill of exceptions. *Corsar* v. *Reed*, 17 Q. B. 540. He should refuse to submit to a nonsuit, and put the judge to express his opinion by way of direction to the jury, and thereupon tender a bill of exceptions to such direction. *Doe* d. *Tolson* v. *Fisher* (in error), 2 Bligh, N. S. 9.

Only available in Error.]—A bill of exceptions can only be made use of in a court of error. *Davenport* v. *Tyrrel*, 1 W. Black. 675, 679 ; Lofft, 84, *S. C.* ; *Gawley* v. *Baker*, 7 Cl. & Fin. 379 ; West, 467. At nisi prius the case is always left to the jury, who give their verdict as though no bill of exceptions had been tendered. *Miller* v. *Warre*, 1 C. & P. 237, 239, Park, J. ; *Warre* v. *Miller*, 4 B. & C. 538 ; 7 D. & R. 1. The court in banc afterwards give judgment for the successful party without taking any notice of the bill of exceptions. *Davenport* v. *Tyrrel* and *Gawley* v. *Baker*, *supra* ; *Gardner* v. *Baillie*, 1 Bos. & P. 32, *per cur.* ; *Rex* v. *Higgins*, Ventr. 366. Where proceedings in error will not lie there can be no bill of exceptions. Bull. N. P. 316 ; *Rex* v. *Preston-on-the-Hill*, Cas. temp. Hardw. 249 ; 2 Stra. 1040, *S. C.* ; 1 Chit. Arch. 410 (9th ed.). It does not lie in cases of treason or felony ; *Sir H. Vane's case*, 1 Lev. 68 ; Bull. N. P. 316 ; *Rex* v. *Barkshead*, T. Raym. 486 ; 1 Sid. 85 ; 1 Bac. Abr. tit. " Bill of Exceptions ;" but upon indictments for offences not capital a bill of exceptions may be allowed. *Id.* ; 2 Hawk. P. C. c. 46, s. 1 ; *Reg.* v. *Alleyne*, 4 E. & B. 186. It does not lie on a feigned issue ; *King* v. *Simmonds*, 7 Q. B. 289, 311 ; *Armstrong* v. *Lewis*, 3 Myl. & K. 52 ; Car. & M. 175, note ; nor, as it seems, for a misdirection upon the execution of a writ of inquiry before a judge, because he then acts merely as assessor for the sheriff. *Price* v. *Green*, 16 M. & W. 346, 350.

When expedient.]—When the cause is tried before a judge of the court out of which the record issues (whether a chief or puisne judge), and he is very positive upon the point decided, and not likely to change his opinion, a bill of exceptions is generally preferable to a motion for a new trial ; for such motion would fail unless *all* the other judges were satisfied that the judge at nisi prius decided erroneously. *Doe* d. *Mudd* v. *Suckermore*, 5 A. & E. 703 ; *Doe* d. *Campbell* v. *Hamilton*,

13 Q. B. 977, 985; *Thomas* v. *Cross*, 7 Exch. 728. There would, however, generally be an appeal from the decision on such application. 17 & 18 Vict. c. 125, s. 35.

Sometimes the court in banc exercises a discretion upon an application for a new trial, which a court of error would not exercise on hearing a bill of exceptions argued. *Ante,* 310; *post,* 330. Where it is desired to exclude the exercise of any such discretion, a bill of exceptions should be tendered.

A bill of exceptions may be tendered on a trial at bar. *City of London* v. *The Unfree Merchants,* 2 Show. 146; *Thruston* v. *Slatford,* 3 Salk. 155; *Davies* v. *Lowndes,* 4 Bing. N. C. 478; 5 Bing. N. C. 161; 7 Scott, 21; *S. C.* in error, 6 Man. & Gr. 471, 475; 7 Scott, N. R. 141; *Rowe* v. *Brenton,* 3 Man. & Ry. 266; 8 B. & C. 765. Indeed it is then most useful, as there would be little chance of success upon an application for a new trial after a trial at bar.

When and how tendered, prepared and sealed.]—The bill of exceptions, or rather a short note of it, must be *tendered at the trial.* See *the form, Appendix, No.* 236. The statute, indeed, appoints no time, but the nature and reason of the thing requires the exception should be reduced to writing when taken and disallowed, like a special verdict, or a demurrer to evidence; not that they need be drawn up in form, but the substance must be reduced to writing while the thing is transacting, because it is to become a record. *Wright* v. *Sharp,* 1 Salk. 288; 11 Mod. 175, *S. C.;* Bull. N. P. 315. A judge is not obliged to seal a bill of exceptions unless the exception be tendered in writing at the trial, and the bill of exceptions be drawn up according to the minutes. *Pochlington* v. *Hatton,* 8 Mod. 221. By consent a bill of exceptions may be tendered and sealed *nunc pro tunc,* long after the trial, to avoid the expense of a new trial. *Willoughby* v. *Willoughby,* 9 Q. B. 935. The decision of the court in banc, on a motion for a new trial for misdirection, may, by consent, be embodied in a bill of exceptions as the ruling of the judge at nisi prius. *Hart* v. *Baxendale,* 6 Exch. 782, 788.

The usual practice is to tender at the trial a short note in writing of the exception. *See the form, Appendix, No.* 236. Afterwards, and before final judgment is entered up, the bill of exceptions should be prepared, or settled and signed by counsel, and then engrossed on parchment, and tendered to the judge for his seal thereto. 1 Chit. Arch. 410, 412 (9th ed.). It is not unusual for the draft bill of exceptions to be settled on behalf of both parties in like manner as a special verdict, or a special case after verdict. *Post,* Chap. XXVI.; 1 Chit. Arch. 410 (9th ed.); *Willans* v. *Taylor,* 4 Moo. & P. 257; 6 Bing. 512, *S. C.; Taylor* v. *Willans,* 2 B. & Adol. 846; *Reg.* v. *Rowley,* 2 Dowl. N. S. 335.

The costs of settling a bill of exceptions are costs in the court of error, not in the court below. *Gardner* v. *Baillie,* 1 Bos. & P. 32; *Doe* d. *Harvey* v. *Francis,* 4 M. & W. 331; 7 Dowl. 193; *Francis* v. *Doe* d. *Harvey,* 5 M. & W. 273; 7 Dowl. 523. Where the plaintiff in error succeeds on a bill of exceptions, he cannot recover any of his costs in error. *Bell* v. *Potts,* 5 East, 49; *Wyvil* v. *Stapleton,* 1 Stra. 615. Where the defendant in error succeeds he is only entitled to single costs. Reg. Pl. H. T. 1853, No. 25.

There should be no unnecessary delay in preparing a bill of excep-

P

tions and getting it sealed by the judge. This should, if possible, be done before the time when the opposite party is entitled to enter up judgment on the verdict. If judgment be signed, and proceedings in error brought before the bill of exceptions is completed, the party will be deemed to have waived it, and will not afterwards be permitted to annex it to the record. *Dillon* v. *Doe* d. *Parker*, 1 Bing. 17; 11 Price, 100, *S. C.* But where the defendant had sent the plaintiff a copy of the draft bill of exceptions, in order to his concurring in the statement of facts, and at the same time sued out a writ of error, the court held that the plaintiff had no right to retain the bill of exceptions in order to frustrate the writ of error, on the ground that the defendant had waived it by suing out such writ. *Willans* v. *Taylor*, 4 Moo. & P. 257; 6 Bing. 512, *S. C.* And where the defendant below tendered a bill of exceptions, and afterwards brought error, the bill of exceptions not having been ready when the writ of error was returned, the court, on consideration of the circumstances, allowed it to be tacked to the record afterwards. *Taylor* v. *Willans*, 2 B. & Adol. 846; and see *Reg.* v. *Rowley*, 2 Dowl. N. S. 335. As a general rule "the postea is not to be delivered out until the bill of exceptions is sealed, but the party who obtains the verdict is at liberty to sign judgment, whether the bill of exceptions is sealed or not; but it is not the practice to do so without an order of a judge of the court." *Per* Wilde, C. J., in *The Fishmongers' Company* v. *Robertson*, 4 D. & L. 659; *Id.* 657; 3 C. B. 970, *S. C.* Where delay takes place in the settling of a bill of exceptions, and the plaintiff or defendant, or one of several plaintiffs or defendants, dies, and more than two terms elapse subsequent to the verdict and before judgment signed thereon, the court will not give leave to enter judgment *nunc pro tunc* unless the delay has arisen from the act of the court, and not of the parties or their attornies. *S. C.*

The bill of exceptions may set out the whole record, &c.; *see the forms, Appendix, Nos.* 237, 238; or it may omit the proceedings previous to the trial. Bull. N. P. 319; 1 Chit. Arch. 411 (9th ed.). But in the latter case it must be tacked to the record, which the statute plainly shows may be done, by saying, *if the exceptions be not in the roll.* Bull. N. P. 319. Indeed, this is the most usual course; but as in actions of ejectment the proceedings are very concise, it seems better to state them in the bill of exceptions.

When exceptions are taken to the direction of the judge in his summing up to the jury, the bill of exceptions must set out in terms what his direction was. It is not sufficient to state that the counsel requested the judge to leave certain questions to the jury, and that he refused to do so. *M'Alpine* v. *Mangnall*, 3 C. B. 496. "It is misdirection, and not non-direction, that is the proper subject of a bill of exceptions." *Id.* 517, Parke, B.; *Anderson* v. *Fitzgerald*, 4 H. L. Cas. 484; *Gregory* v. *Cottrell*, 25 Law J., N. S., Q. B., 33. But nevertheless the whole of the charge to the jury ought not to be set out at length. The precise point upon which the summing up is sought to be impugned should be stated with so much only of the context as is necessary (if any be necessary) to explain the direction of the judge, and no more. The statement of the charge *at length* tends much to embarrass the question, and adds greatly to the expense of the proceedings in error. *Per cur.* in *Soares* v. *Glyn*, 8 Q. B. 25. "A bill of exceptions is not to draw the whole matter into examination again; it is only for a single point, and the truth of it can never be doubted after the bill is sealed; for the adverse party is concluded from averring the contrary, or supplying an omission in it." Bull. N. P. 316. *Bridgman* v. *Holt*, Show. P. C. 120. If a deed be not fully set out in a bill of exceptions, it cannot be looked at, although the bill says, "as by the said indenture of release will appear." *Galway* v. *Baker*, 5 Cl. & Fin. 457. A court of error cannot look beyond the bill of exceptions, but must decide on that alone. *Bain* v. *The Whitehaven and Furness Junction Railway Company*, 3 H. L. Cas. 1; *Warre* v. *Miller*, 4 B. & C. 540, Abbott, C. J.; *Bulkeley* v. *Butler*, 2 B. & C. 445, Holroyd, J. A bill of exceptions need not contain a statement made by the jury of that which they were not called upon by law to find. *Davies* v. *Lowndes*, 1 Man. & Gr. 473; 1 Scott, N. R. 328.

A bill of exceptions should state that the exceptions were made *before* the giving of the verdict; *Armstrong* v. *Lewis*, 4 Moo. & Sc. 1; 2 Cr. & Mee. 275, *S. C.*; but if framed erroneously in this respect, it may be amended according to the fact. *Culley* v. *Doe* d. *Taylerson*, 11 A. & E. 1008; 3 P. & D. 539, 542.

Judge's Seal.]—If the exceptions be truly stated in the bill, the judge should affix his seal to it; but otherwise, if the bill contains matters false or erroneously stated, or matters wherein the party was not overruled. *Bridgman* v. *Holt*, Show. P. C. 120; 1 Chit. Arch. 412 (9th ed.). So where the jury do not act according to the direction complained of. *Archer* v. *Williams*, 2 Car. & K. 28, Cresswell, J.

If the judge refuse to seal a proper bill of exceptions, the party grieved by the denial may have a writ upon the statute commanding the same to be done *juxta formam statuti*. It recites the form of an exception taken and overruled, and it follows *vobis præcipimus quod si ita est, hinc sigilla vestra apponatis;* and if it be returned *quod non ita est*, an action will lie for a false return, and thereupon the surmise will be tried; and if found to be so, damages will be given; and upon such a recovery, a peremptory writ commanding the same. Bull. N. P. 316; 1 Chit. Arch. 412 (9th ed.). In such case the bill of exceptions may be sealed after final judgment. 2 Inst. 427.

If the judge at nisi prius *die before sealing* a bill of exceptions to his ruling, it is not competent for any other judge to seal it (even by consent), nor for the executors of the deceased judge to affix their testator's seal to it. In such a case the court can only grant a new trial; *Nind* v. *Arthur*, 7 Dowl. & L. 252; which they will do long after the usual time for moving for a new trial has elapsed. *Newton* v. *Boodle*, 3 C. B. 795; 4 Dowl. & L. 664; *Benet* v. *The Peninsular and Oriental Steam Boat Company*, 16 C. B. 29. If the judge *die after sealing* the bill of exceptions, a *scire facias* may issue directed to his executors, requiring them to appear in the court of error to confess or deny their testator's seal. 2 Inst. 428; *The Fishmongers' Company* v. *Dimsdale*, 6 C. B. 904; 2 Wms. Exors. 1387 (3rd ed.).

Proceedings in Error.]—Formerly the judge was called upon to confess or deny his seal in the court of error upon the return of the writ of error. Rast. Ent. 293; *Money* v. *Leach*, 3 Burr. 1693; *Davies* v. *Pierce*, 3 T. R. 54. If he confessed it, the proceedings were entered upon the record, and the party assigned his errors. 1 Arch. Chit. 412 (9th ed.). But now writs of error are abolished, and a more summary mode of proceeding in error substituted. 15 & 16 Vict. c. 76, ss. 146—167; 1 Chit. Arch. 505 (9th ed.). The judgment roll is taken into the court of error, and the judge there acknowledges his seal to the bill of exceptions. If necessary, a writ of *scire facias* may issue directed to him for that purpose. *See the Form; Money* v. *Leach,* 3 Burr. 1693. On the bill of exceptions being so acknowledged, it is then for the first time annexed to the record; *per cur.* in *Garden* v. *Baillie,* 1 Bos. & P. 32; and it becomes *evidence of record* in the court of error as to what took place at the trial. No other evidence is admissible in that court. Therefore a deed not fully set out in a bill of exceptions cannot be looked at, although the bill says, "as by the said indenture of release will appear." *Galway* v. *Barker,* 5 Cl. & Fin. 457. No objection not appearing on the face of the bill of exceptions can be taken in the court of error. *Warre* v. *Miller,* 4 B. & C. 540, Abbott, C. J.; *Bulkeley* v. *Butler,* 2 B. & C. 445, Holroyd, J.; *Rutter* v. *Chapman,* 8 M. & W. 1. A court of error cannot look beyond the bill of exceptions, but must decide on that alone. *Bain* v. *The Whitehaven and Furness Junction Railway Company,* 3 H. L. Cas. 1.

If, upon a bill of exceptions to the judge's charge to the jury, the court of error sees that there was a misdirection calculated to mislead the jury in their verdict, the court has no discretion, but must allow the exception, and direct a trial *de novo,* even though the verdict be right. *Secus,* in the case of a motion for a new trial on the ground of misdirection. *The Househill Coal and Iron Company* v. *Neilson,* 9 Cl. & Fin. 788; *ante,* 310, 311; *post,* 330.

If the judge deny his seal, the plaintiff in error may take issue thereon. Rast. Ent. 293; 2 Inst. 428.

The defendant in error cannot plead specially that there is no record of the bill of exceptions, or that the judge did not put his seal to the bill, or that he did not duly acknowledge his seal, or the like. *The Fishmongers' Company* v. *Dimsdale,* 6 C. B. 896. Any defect or irregularity in or relating to the bill of exceptions can be taken advantage of only by an application to take the bill of exceptions off the record. *Id.* 908, *per* Alderson, B.

The proceedings in error upon a bill of exceptions in an ejectment are the same as in ordinary cases. 1 Chit. Arch. 505 (9th ed.); *post,* Chap. XXXIV. The bill of exceptions merely forms evidence in the court of error of what took place at nisi prius. If the plaintiff in error succeed, he obtains no costs in error. *Bell* v. *Potts,* 5 East, 49; *Wyvil* v. *Stapleton,* 1 Stra. 615. If the defendant in error succeed, he is generally entitled only to single costs; Reg. Pl. H. T. 1853, No. 25; including the costs of settling the bill of exceptions, which form part of the costs in error. *Gardiner* v. *Baillie,* 1 Bos. & P. 32; *Doe* d. *Harvey* v. *Francis,* 4 M. & W. 331; 7 Dowl. 193; *Francis* v. *Doe* d. *Harvey,* 5 M. & W. 273; 7 Dowl. 523.

If the Court of Exchequer Chamber decide in favour of the bill of exceptions, and award a trial *de novo,* the unsuccessful party may proceed in error in parliament. *Harrison* v. *Stickney,* 2 H. L. Cas. 114; *Jeffreys* v. *Boosey,* 24 Law J., N. S., Exch., 81. So, if they decide against the bill of exceptions, error may be brought in parliament. *Rowe* v. *Power* (in error), 2 B. & P. New R. 1; *Doe* d. *Beach* v. *The Earl of Jersey,* 3 B. & C. 870; *Doe* d. *Oxenden* v. *Sir A. Chichester,* 4 Dow. Parl. C. 65.

Motion for a new Trial after a Bill of Exceptions tendered.]—
Where a bill of exceptions is tendered at the trial, the court in banc
will not hear a motion for a new trial upon any point which is or *might
have been* included in the bill of exceptions, unless the bill of exceptions be first abandoned. *Doe* d. *Roberts* v. *Roberts*, 2 Chit. R. 272;
2 B. & A. 367, *S. C.*; *Adams* v. *Andrews*, 15 Q. B. 1001. But a
new trial may be moved for (without abandoning the bill of exceptions)
upon any point or ground which could not have been included in the
bill of exceptions; *ex. gr.*, that the verdict was against evidence, or the
damages excessive; *Gregory* v. *Cotterill*, 1 E. & B. 360, 363; or upon
an affidavit of facts subsequently discovered. *Crotty* v. *Price*, 15 Q. B.
1003, note. It is sometimes advisable to abandon a bill of exceptions,
and move for a new trial. 7 C. B. 481, note (*b*); *Davenport* v. *Tyrrell*,
1 W. Black. 678, *per cur.*; *Vines* v. *The Corporation of Reading*, 1
You. & Jer. 7, Best, C. J.

CHAPTER XXVI.

VERDICTS SUBJECT TO A REFERENCE; OR TO A POINT RESERVED;
OR TO A SPECIAL CASE; SPECIAL VERDICTS; AND PROCEEDINGS
THEREON.

1. *Verdict subject to a Reference.*]—In ejectment, when the facts are not fully admitted or proved at the trial, a verdict is sometimes taken by consent, subject to a reference to a legal arbitrator to find the facts, and state the points of law for the opinion of the court; the verdict and judgment to be entered thereon as the court shall direct. *Doe* d. *Phillips* v. *Rollings,* 2 C. B. 842. When the arbitrator is merely to state a case, the death of either party will not revoke his authority. *James* v. *Crane,* 15 M. & W. 379 ; 3 Dowl. & L. 661. A case when settled and signed by a legal arbitrator need not be signed by counsel on both sides. *Price* v. *Quarrell,* 12 A. & E. 784 ; 2 Gale & D. 632. Sometimes a verdict is taken for the plaintiff subject to a reference of the cause *and all matters in difference* between the parties to a barrister, who is to determine what shall be done by either party respecting the matters in dispute, and is empowered to order a verdict to be entered for the plaintiff or for the defendant, as he shall think proper, *with liberty* also to state facts for the opinion of the court. *Doe* d. *Pennington* v. *Taniere,* 12 Q. B. 998. In such case it is in the discretion of the arbitrator whether he will state any facts for the opinion of the court, or take upon himself to decide finally all the matters referred. *Miller* v. *Shuttleworth,* 7 C. B. 105 ; *Wood* v. *Hotham,* 5 M. & W. 674 ; *Jones* v. *Nicholls,* 6 Exch. 373 ; 2 Low. M. & P. 335. Care should be taken that the order of reference be correctly worded, otherwise one or other of the parties may be precluded from raising before the arbitrator the very point or question intended to be submitted to him. *Doe* d. *Lord Carlisle* v. *Bailiff and Burgesses of Morpeth,* 3 Taunt. 378. If the arbitrator is to have "all such and the like powers as a judge at nisi prius," or any other special powers, they should be expressly mentioned· in the order. *Toby* v. *Lovibond,* 5 C. B. 770 ; 5 Dowl. & L. 768. The order may be made a rule of court without any clause to that effect. *Harrison* v. *Smith,* 1 Dowl. & L. 876 ; *Millington* v. *Claridge,* 3 C. B. 609.

An attorney authorized to prosecute or defend an action has incidentally an implied authority to refer it, without obtaining fresh authority to that effect from his client. Watson on Awards, 79 (3rd ed.) ; *Filmer* v. *Delber,* 3 Taunt. 486 ; *Buckle* v. *Roach,* 1 Chit. R.

193; *Smith* v. *Troup,* 7 C. B. 757; *Faviell* v. *The Eastern Counties Railway Company,* 2 Exch. 344; 6 Dowl. & L. 54. But he has no such implied authority to refer *other matters in difference.* Sometimes an order of reference is made by consent before the trial. *See the form, Appendix, No.* 145.

When the arbitrator is to decide *what shall be done* by either party, and he makes an award accordingly, the court will, if possible, support such award. *Mays* v. *Carnell,* 15 C. B. 107; *Law* v. *Blackburrow,* 14 C. B. 77. But this is sometimes impossible. *Stonehaver* v. *Farrar,* 6 Q. B. 730; *Doe* d. *Madkins* v. *Horner,* 8 A. & E. 235; 3 N. & P. 344. An award may, however, be bad as to part, and good as to the residue, if the two parts be distinct and separable. *Doe* d. *Body* v. *Cox,* 4 Dowl. & L. 75; 2 Chit. Arch. 1575 (9th ed.). When the award directs the defendant to *execute a conveyance.* to the plaintiff of the property in question, that may be enforced by attachment. *Doe* d. *Williams* v. *Howell,* 5 Exch. 299; *Doe* d. *Clarke* v. *Stilwell,* 2 Dowl. N. S. 18; *Reg.* v. *Hensworth,* 3 C. B. 745. The proceedings to enforce an award in this manner are stated in Watson on Awards, Chap. X.; 2 Chit. Arch. 1590—1596 (9th ed.).

Rule or Order to deliver Possession pursuant to an Award.]—By 17 & 18 Vict. c. 125, s. 16, "when any award made on any such submission, document or order of reference as aforesaid directs that possession of any lands or tenements capable of being the subject of an action of ejectment shall be delivered to any party, either forthwith or at any future time, or that any such party is entitled to the possession of any such lands or tenements, it shall be lawful for the court, of which the document authorizing the reference is ôr is made a rule or order, to order any party to the reference who shall be in possession of any such lands or tenements, or any person in possession of the same claiming under or put in possession by him since the making of the document authorizing the reference, to deliver possession of the same to the party entitled thereto, pursuant to the award; and such rule or order to deliver possession shall have the effect of a judgment in ejectment against every such party or person named in it, and execution may issue, and possession shall be delivered by the sheriff as on a judgment in ejectment."

The form of a writ of *habere facias possessionem* on a rule to deliver possession of land pursuant to an award, is prescribed by Reg. Mic. Vac. 1854, Sched. No. 17. *See the form, Appendix, No.* 291.

2. *Verdict subject to a Point reserved.*]—It frequently happens at nisi prius, that during a trial some difficult question of law arises, upon which the judge entertains doubts, but which he is obliged then to decide one way or other, unless a special case be agreed on, or a special verdict be given. Under such circumstances the usual course is for the judge to decide in favour of that party whom he thinks is right, reserving to the opposite party leave to move to set aside the verdict, and instead thereof to enter a verdict in his favour, or a nonsuit, on the point so decided. *Doe* d. *Campbell* v. *Hamilton,* 13 Q. B. 977; *Lloyd* v. *Davies,* 16 C. B. 79; *Greenway* v. *Hart,* 14 C. B. 348. Where such leave is reserved, it is considered as done with the express or implied consent of both parties, and particularly of the party in whose favour the point is decided at nisi prius. *Dewar* v. *Purday,* 3

A. & E. 166; 4 N. & M. 633; 1 Harr. & Woll. 227; but see *Treacher* v. *Hinton*, 4 B. & A. 413. If such party refuse his consent, and object to any such leave being reserved, the judge, if he thinks such refusal unreasonable, will sometimes reverse his decision, and direct the jury (contrary to his own opinion) to find against the party so objecting, leaving him to tender a bill of exceptions, or to move for a new trial; or perhaps giving him leave to move to set aside the verdict, and to enter a verdict in his favour, or a nonsuit; or the judge may direct the jury to find a special verdict, if the point in question can be conveniently raised in that form. *Post*, 326.

Where any mistake upon matter of law, or with respect to the admission or rejection of evidence, is made by the judge at nisi prius, the party prejudiced by it may thereupon tender a bill of exceptions (*ante*, Chap. XXV.); or he may afterwards move the court in banc for a new trial; but he cannot move to set aside the verdict, and enter a verdict in his favour or a nonsuit, unless leave to that effect was expressly reserved at the trial. *Minchin* v. *Clement*, 1 B. & A. 252; *Rickets* v. *Burman*, 4 Dowl. 578; *Tippetts* v. *Heane*, 4 Tyr. 772; *Beverley* v. *Walker*, 8 Dowl. 418; 1 Chit. Arch. 415; 2 *Id.* 1435 (9th ed.).

A motion for a rule nisi to set aside the verdict, and to enter a verdict or nonsuit pursuant to leave reserved, must be made (if it all) within the same time as a motion for a new trial. Reg. Prac. H. T. 1853, No. 50; 2 Chit. Arch. 1441 (9th ed.); *post*, Chap. XXVII. If a rule nisi be granted, "the grounds upon which such rule shall have been granted shall be shortly stated therein." 17 & 18 Vict. c. 125, c. 33; *see the forms, Appendix, Nos.* 253, 254. A copy of the rule nisi must be forthwith served on the attorney or agent for the opposite party, and an affidavit of such service made. *See the forms, Appendix, Nos.* 26, 27. The rule is entered by the master in the "new trial paper" at the time it is granted, and comes on for argument in its turn. The judge's notes are thereupon read, after which counsel show cause against the rule, and afterwards, if necessary, counsel are heard in support of it. Two or more counsel on each side may be heard. The court then, or after taking time to consider, make absolute or discharge the rule.

If the rule be made absolute, it should be drawn up and served. *See the form, Appendix, No.* 255. Upon production of the rule to the associate, and delivering to him a copy, he will alter the entry of the verdict (if necessary), and deliver the record of nisi prius to the attorney or agent for the successful party. Such party will be entitled to the costs of the trial at nisi prius in the same manner as if he had obtained the verdict there; *Tobin* v. *Crawford*, 10 M. & W. 602; 2 Dowl. N. S. 541; also the costs of and incident to the application as part of his costs of the cause. If the rule nisi be discharged, the successful party will be entitled to the costs of showing cause against it as part of his costs in the cause. *Eyre* v. *Thorpe*, 6 Dowl. 768; *Delisser* v. *Towne*, 1 Q. B. 333; 4 P. & D. 644; Gray on Costs, 386.

Appeal.]—"In all cases of rules to enter a verdict or nonsuit upon a point reserved at the trial, if the rule to show cause be refused, or granted and then discharged or made absolute, the party decided against may appeal." 17 & 18 Vict. c. 125, s. 34. "The court of error, the Exchequer Chamber, and the House of Lords shall be courts of appeal for the purposes of this act." *Id.* s. 36. The Court of Queen's Bench, being the court of error from the Court of Common Pleas at *Lancaster*, and Court of Pleas at *Durham* respectively, shall also be the court of appeal from the said respective courts for the purposes of this act." *Id.* s. 102.

Notice of Appeal.]—"No appeal shall be allowed unless notice thereof be given in writing to the opposite party or his attorney, *and* to one of the masters of the court, within four days after the decision complained of, or such further time as may be allowed by the court or a judge." 17 & 18 Vict. c. 125, s. 37; *see the forms of Notice, Appendix, Nos.* 256, 257, 258.

Bail.]—"Notice of appeal shall be a *stay of execution, provided bail to pay* the sum recovered and costs, or to pay costs where the appellant was plaintiff below, be given, in like manner and to the same amount as bail in error, within eight days after the decision complained of, or before execution delivered to the sheriff." 17 & 18 Vict. c. 125, s. 38. Bail is not necessary to enable the party to prosecute his appeal, but only to make such appeal a stay of execution. *Newlands* v. *Holmes* (in error), 4 Q. B. 858; *Sutherland* v. *Wills*, 5 Exch. 980.

Case to be stated.]—By 17 & 18 Vict. c. 125, s. 39, "the appeal hereinbefore mentioned shall be upon a case to be stated by the parties (and in case of difference to be settled by the court or a judge of the court appealed from), in which case shall be set forth so much of the pleadings, evidence, and the ruling or judgment objected to, as may be necessary to raise the question for the decision of the court of appeal." *See the forms, Appendix, Nos.* 259, 260, 261.

Appeal from refusal of Rule Nisi.]—By 17 & 18 Vict. c. 125, s. 46, "when the appeal is from the refusal of the court below to grant a rule to show cause, and the court of appeal grant such rule, such rule shall be argued and disposed of in the court of appeal."

Judgment on Appeal.]—By 17 & 18 Vict. c. 125, s. 41, "the court of appeal shall give such judgment as ought to have been given in the court below; and all such further proceedings may be taken thereupon as if the judgment had been given by the court in which the record originated." By sect. 42, "the court of appeal shall have power to adjudge payment of costs, and to order restitution; and they shall have the same powers as the court of error in respect of awarding process and otherwise."

3. *Verdict subject to a Special Case.*]—By consent of both parties, or their counsel, a verdict may be entered for the plaintiff "subject to a special case." This is frequently done when it appears at nisi prius that the matter in dispute turns mainly upon some *point of law, ex. gr.,* the construction to be put upon an act of parliament, deed, will or other instrument in writing, the estate (if any) taken by a particular person under a certain limitation or demise in the events which have happened, and the like. *Bancks* v. *Ollerton*, 10 Exch. 168. But

the express or implied consent of both parties is always necessary to authorize a verdict, subject to a special case.

To prevent any difficulty in settling the special case, *all the material facts on both sides should be proved, or distinctly admitted in open court before the verdict is entered.* The judge and counsel on both sides should carefully take notes of what is so admitted and proved. If necessary, the opinion of the jury may be taken upon any disputed fact. If it be intended that the judgment of the court in banc shall be final, and without any appeal to a court of error, that should be expressly stipulated, otherwise error may be brought by the unsuccessful party. 17 & 18 Vict. c. 125, s. 32 ; *post,* 326. The verdict is entered for the claimants generally, or for some or one of them, either for the whole or some specified part of the premises sought to be recovered, " subject to a special case," and as to the residue (if any), for the defendants. A memorandum to that effect is written by the associate on the back of the jury panel. *Ante,* 308. In a recent action a verdict was found for one of the plaintiffs (H.), subject to a special case, for the purpose of determining whether the verdict ought to stand for the plaintiff H., or ought to be entered for the other plaintiffs, or any and which of them, or whether the verdict ought to be entered for the defendants. *Hughes and others* v. *Lumley and Fish,* 4 E. & B. 274.

A special case should (when conveniently practicable) be dictated in court at the trial, and signed by the counsel on both sides before the jury are discharged ; and the opinion of the jury should be taken as to any fact in dispute between the parties. 1 Burr. Rep. Pref. iv. But this is very seldom done, and in most cases is impracticable, there not being time to prepare and settle at nisi prius a long special case. The practice, therefore, is for the counsel on both sides to agree in court as to the material facts proved and admitted, especially those upon which the question mainly depends, and, if necessary, to take the opinion of the jury upon any disputed fact. 1 Chit. Arch. 422 (9th ed.). Afterwards the junior counsel for the plaintiff, upon being instructed to do so, prepares the draft special case. *See forms, Appendix, Nos.* 251, 252. A fair copy of such draft is submitted to the defendant's junior counsel, with instructions to settle it on behalf of the defendant. If any alterations be made by him, they are submitted to the counsel who prepared the draft. If he disapprove of and dissent to any of the alterations, the two counsel usually meet in consultation, and endeavour to arrange the points in difference between them, and finally to settle the draft. If they cannot agree, or if no consultation be had as above mentioned, then the course is for either party to take out a summons returnable before the judge who tried the cause " to settle the draft special case." The judge's notes should be bespoken. Upon the summons being attended, the judge, after hearing the counsel or attorneys on both sides, and referring to his notes, will finally settle the draft special case. 1 Chit. Arch. 422 (9th ed.).

The draft, as finally settled by the counsel on both sides, or by the judge (as the case may be), should be fairly copied on brief paper, and signed by counsel on both sides. *De la Branchardiere* v. *Elvery,* 4 Exch. 380; *Doe* d. *Phillips* v. *Rollins,* 2 C. B. 842. But if either party act personally on his own behalf, and intends to argue the case in person, it is sufficient if the special case, when finally settled, be signed by him, and by counsel for opposite party. *Udney* v. *The East*

India Company, 13 C. B. 742. Where a verdict is taken subject to a special case to be stated by a legal arbitrator, such case, when settled and signed by him, need not be signed by counsel on both sides. *Price v. Quarrell*, 12 A. & E. 784 ; 2 Gale & D. 632.

A special case signed by counsel on both sides, may be used as evidence on a subsequent trial of the same action. *Van Wort v. Woolley*, Ry. & Moo. 4 ; 1 Moo. & Mal. 520, Lord Tenterden, C. J.

Where a verdict is taken for the plaintiff subject to a special case, and the defendant afterwards refuses to settle such case, or to get it signed by counsel on his behalf, the court will order him to do so within a limited time, otherwise the plaintiff to be at liberty to sign judgment on his verdict. *Jackson v. Hall*, 2 B. Moo. 478 ; 8 Taunt. 421 ; *Rex v. Smith*, 2 Chit. R. 398 ; and see *Taylor v. Gregory*, 2 B. & Adol. 774 ; *Wilkinson v. Time*, 4 Dowl. 37. But where the plaintiff refuses or neglects to proceed with the special case, the court can only order that the verdict entered for him be set aside, with liberty for the defendant to proceed to a new trial. *Medley v. Smith*, 6 B. Moo. 53 ; *Cottam v. Partridge*, 2 Man. & Gr. 843 ; 3 Scott, N. R. 174 ; 9 Dowl. 629 ; Tidd's Prac. 899 (9th ed.).

Where the lessor of the plaintiff died after obtaining a verdict subject to a special case, and the case was not settled before his death : held, that the verdict ought not on that ground to be set aside, but security for costs was ordered. *Doe* d. *Earl of Egremont v. Stephens*, 2 Dowl. & L. 993. The costs of an abortive special case are not costs in the cause. *Foley v. Botfield*, 16 M. & W. 65 ; 4 Dowl. & L. 328.

By Reg. Prac. H. T. 1853, No. 15, " no motion or rule for a concilium shall be required ; but demurrers, as well as all special cases, special verdicts, and appeals from county courts, shall be set down for argument in the special paper, at the request of either party, four clear days before the day on which the same are to be argued, and notice thereof shall be given forthwith by such party to the opposite party."

16. " Four clear days before the day appointed for argument, the plaintiff shall deliver copies of the demurrer book, special case, special verdict, or appeal cases, *with the points intended to be insisted on*, to the Lord Chief Justice of the Queen's Bench or Common Pleas, or the Lord Chief Baron, as the case may be, and the senior puisne judge of the court in which the action is brought ; and the defendant shall deliver copies to the other two judges of the court next in seniority ; and in default thereof by either party, the other party may, *on the day following*, deliver such copies as ought to have been so delivered by the party making default ; and the party making default shall not be heard until he shall have paid for such copies, or deposited with the master a sufficient sum to pay for such copies. If the statement of the points have not been exchanged between the parties, each party shall, in addition to the two copies left by him, deliver also his statement of the points to the other two judges, either by making the same in the margin of the books delivered, or on separate papers."

Copies of the special case must be delivered by each party pursuant to the above rule *four clear days* (*i. e.* both exclusive) before the special paper day for which the case is set down to be heard. In case of default by either party, the other should *on the next day* after such default, deliver copies for the party in default. If delivered punctually on that day (but not otherwise) the party in default will not be heard to argue the case until he has paid for such copies, or deposited with the master a sufficient sum to pay for them. *Sandall* v. *Bennett*, 2 A. & E. 204; *Hooper* v. *Woolmer*, 10 C. B. 370; *Dorsett* v. *Aspdin*, 11 C. B. 651; *Wilton* v. *Scarlett*, 1 Dowl. & L. 810; *Scott* v. *Robson*, 2 Cr. M. & R. 29. If either party has neglected to deliver copies, and the other has not delivered them for him, before the case comes on for argument, the case will not be heard. *Sheddon* v. *Butt*, 11 C. B. 27; *Allan* v. *Waterhouse*, 1 Dowl. & L. 787.

The brief for counsel should contain a copy of the special case, and of the points intended to be insisted on, with perhaps a few " observations" referring to the authorities. Only one counsel on each side will be heard to argue the case; but it is not unusual to employ another " to take notes." Either the junior may argue, and the senior take notes, or *vice versâ*, as may be deemed most expedient.

On hearing a special case argued, the court will not presume any material fact which is not expressly stated, unless power be reserved to the court to draw inferences from the facts stated, and that power be accepted by them. *Doe* d. *Taylor* v. *Crisp*, 8 A. & E. 779; 1 P. & D. 37; 7 Dowl. 584. The 17 & 18 Vict. c. 125, s. 32 (*post*, 326), does not seem to alter the law on this point. Where no such power is reserved, the court may draw such inferences as are reasonable, and obviously arise out of the facts that are stated. There is a difference in this respect between a special case and a special verdict. See *per* Maule, J., in *Manning* v. *Irvine*, 1 C. B. 176; *Bailey* v. *Culverwell*, 8 B. & C. 455, Littledale, J.; *Rex* v. *Leake*, 5 B. & Adol. 481, Parke, J.; *Doe* v. *Danvers*, 7 East, 307. Where express power to draw inferences is reserved, that perhaps enlarges the power which the court would otherwise have, and the court will exercise such power with greater freedom and liberality. *Cases supra.*

The court will not presume the surrender of an outstanding term, even under circumstances which might authorize a jury to do so. *Cottrell* v. *Hughes*, 15 C. B. 532, 547, 559.

The court will not allow a special case to be amended, by raising a point which the parties have not raised for their consideration. *Hills* v. *Hunt*, 15 C. B. 2, 30.

Immediately after the decision of the court upon a special case, the successful party may draw up a rule for judgment in his favour. Upon production of that rule to the associate, and delivering to him a copy, he will, if necessary, amend the entry of the verdict (according to the rule), and deliver the record and postea to the attorney or agent for the successful party. Final judgment may be thereupon signed forthwith. *See the form, Appendix, No.* 268. A mere *incipitur* of the judgment is usually entered in the first instance. *See the form, Appendix, No.* 122. Upon this the costs may be taxed and execution issued in the usual manner. *Post*, Chap. XXXI.

The costs of the special case, and of the argument thereon, will be allowed as costs in the cause to the successful party. *Robertson* v. *Liddell*, 10 East, 416; Gray on Costs, 406. A defendant who succeeds on a special case is entitled to the costs of the trial at nisi prius. So, where a special case is turned into a special verdict, and the defendant obtains judgment on such verdict. *Tobin* v. *Crawford*, 10 M. & W. 602; 2 Dowl. N. S. 541. But the costs of an abortive special case are

not costs in the cause; *Foley* v. *Botfield,* 16 M. & W. 65; 4 Dowl.
& L. 328; nor the costs of the previous trial, which becomes abortive
by reason of a defect in the special case. *Hankey* v. *Smith,* 3 T. R.
507; *Smith* v. *Haile,* 6 T. R. 71; *Joliffe* v. *Mundy,* 4 M. & W. 502;
7 Dowl. 229.

By 17 & 18 Vict. c. 125, s. 32, "error may be brought upon a
judgment upon a special case in the same manner as upon a judgment
upon a special verdict, *unless the parties agree to the contrary;* and
the proceedings for bringing a special case before the court of error
shall, as nearly as may be, be the same as in the case of a special verdict; and the court of error shall either affirm the judgment, or give
the same judgment as ought to have been given in the court in which
it was originally decided, the said court of error being required to draw
any inferences of fact from the facts stated in such special case which
the court where it was originally decided ought to have drawn."

4. *Special Verdict.*]—By 15 & 16 Vict. c. 76, s. 184, "the jury may
find a special verdict" in ejectment. *See the forms, Appendix, Nos.*
249, 250.

The consent of both parties is not necessary to enable the jury to
find a special verdict; whereas it is necessary to enable them to find a
verdict subject to a special case (*ante,* 322), or a verdict subject to a
point reserved for the opinion of the court in banc (*ante,* 320).

In no case is a jury bound to find a special verdict; Lit. s. 368; but
they usually do so when both parties wish it, or the judge so directs.
Ricketts v. *Salvey,* 1 Chit. R. 108, 115. It is very seldom, if ever,
that the jury insist upon giving a special verdict, without being requested so to do. But if the question turn upon matter of law, they
may, if they will find the facts specially, leaving the conclusion of
the law to be decided by the court. Co. Lit. 226 b, 155 b; *Downman's case,* 9 Co. R. 11 b. Although the jury find an issue in special
terms, the parties are not entitled to have it entered as a special verdict,
unless disputed questions of law are raised by the finding; therefore,
where upon the traverse of an immemorial custom stated in the return
to a mandamus, the jury found that the custom had existed from time
immemorial down to 1689: held that this amounted to a verdict that
the custom still existed, no determination of it being shown; and that
a general verdict should be entered for the defendants. *Scales* v. *Key,
Bart.,* 3 P. & D. 505. Generally speaking, conditions annexed to a
verdict, or given as part thereof, are rejected as surplusage; *Taylor* v.
Willis, Cro. Car. 219; *Hewett* v. *Ferneley,* 7 Price, 234; *Burgess* v.
Langley, 5 Man. & Gr. 722, 726; 1 Dowl. & L. 21; unless made by
consent. *Tucker* v. *Neck,* 4 Bing. N. C. 113; 6 Dowl. 231.

A special case is sometimes preferable to a special verdict, because
the real point in dispute may be presented more concisely and at less
expense. *Gybson* v. *Searls,* Cro. Jac. 84. Formerly the principal
difference between a special case and a special verdict was, that upon
the latter a writ of error might be brought by the party against whom
judgment was given, the facts appearing on the record by the special
verdict as entered; whereas no proceeding in error could be had after
judgment upon a special case, the facts therein stated not being entered
upon the record. But now, by 17 & 18 Vict. c. 125, s. 32, error may
be brought upon a judgment upon a special case in the same manner
as upon a judgment upon a special verdict, *unless the parties agree to
the contrary. Supra.*

A special verdict should (when conveniently practicable) be dictated by the court at the trial, and signed by counsel on both sides, before the jury are discharged; and if any difference arise about a fact, the opinion of the jury should be taken upon it, and the fact stated accordingly. 1 Burr. R., Preface, iv. But this is very seldom practicable. Few things require more care on both sides than the preparation of a special verdict. An inaccurate expression, or the omission of a material fact, may operate to 'defeat substantial justice, and entitle the wrong party to judgment in his favour (*vide infra*). Therefore, the usual practice is to have *all the material facts on both sides either admitted or proved at the trial*, and full notes thereof taken by the judge, and by counsel on both sides. 1 Chit. Arch. 420 (9th ed.). Great care should be taken by each party to have every fact which makes in his favour distinctly admitted or proved, and a note thereof taken by the judge. If any fact be disputed the opinion of the jury should be taken upon it.

The draft special verdict is afterwards prepared and settled by counsel on both sides, and, if necessary, by the judge, in like manner as a special case (*ante*, 323). When finally settled and signed by counsel on both sides, it is indorsed on the record of nisi prius by the associate, and signed by him. It should then be set down with the master for argument, and copies delivered to the judges, pursuant to the rules of H. T. 1853, Nos. 15 and 16 (*ante*, 324). It is argued in like manner as a special case. 1 Chit. Arch. 421 (9th ed.). Only one counsel will be heard on each side, but another may be employed " to take notes." The plaintiff's counsel is entitled to begin and reply.

A special verdict should state all the *material facts* proved or admitted at the trial, and not merely *the evidence* as to such facts; otherwise it will be deemed imperfect, and a trial *de novo* awarded. *Bird* v. *Appleton*, 1 East, 111, note (*a*); *Parker* v. *Wells*, 1 T. R. 783; *The Maidstone case*, cited 1 Wils. 56; *Hubbard* v. *Johnstone*, 3 Taunt. 209, Wood, B.; 1 Chit. Arch. 420 (9th ed.). Thus, in trover, if the jury find a special verdict that the goods were demanded of the defendant by the plaintiff, and the defendant refused to deliver them, a trial *de novo* should be directed, because the jury have found only the evidence of a fact, which they ought to have determined; for demand and refusal are only evidence of a conversion, and they ought to have found a conversion. 1 Wils. 56; and see *Acraman* v. *Cooper*, 10 M. & W. 585; 2 Dowl. N. S. 495. Although on a special verdict the jury find such facts as would well have warranted them to have inferred fraud, yet if they do not expressly find the fraud the court cannot presume it. *Crisp* v. *Pratt*, Cro. Car. 549.

Upon a special verdict the court will not infer any facts, or conclusions of fact, not expressly found by the jury, even where, from the other facts stated in the verdict, such an inference or conclusion may be reasonably drawn. *Sanders* v. *Vanzeller*, 4 Q. B. 260, 272; *Lyon* v. *Haynes*, 5 Man. & Gr. 542; *Dowman* v. *Williams* (in error), 7 Q. B. 108, *per* Tindal, C. J.; *Tancred* v. *Christy*, 12 M. & W. 316; *Crisp* v. *Pratt*, Cro. Car. 549.

If the verdict be perfect on the face of it, the court will not award a trial *de novo* upon a suggestion that an important fact, which would make all the difference, has been wholly omitted; but they will give judgment against the party to whom such fact, if found, would have been material. *Allen* v. *Hill*, Cro. Eliz. 238. Thus where a recovery is found, but no seisin under it. *Earl of Derby* v. *Witham*, 2 Stra. 1185; *S. C.* (in error), 1 Wils. 55. So in ejectment where an outstanding term is found, but no surrender. *Goodtitle* d. *Jones* v. *Jones*, 7 T. R. 43, 48. If the jury find an *entry on the plaintiff*, by the defendant, without finding any title or possession in the defendant, the plaintiff shall have judgment. *Bateman* v. *Allen*, Cro. Eliz. 438; and see *Doe* d. *Earl of Egremont* v. *Langdon*, 12 Q. B. 711, 719; *Cottrell* v. *Hughes*, 15 C. B. 532. In assumpsit, where the jury specially found that the defendant promised in a letter thus—"I undertake (*on behalf of Messrs. Esdaile & Co.*) to pay," &c.: held, that such letter imported only an undertaking by the defendant as agent for Messrs. Esdaile & Co., and that in default of the special verdict directly stating, or finding facts from which it resulted by necessary implication that there was a want of authority in the defendant to give such undertaking, or any excess of his authority in giving it, the defendant was entitled to judgment. *Downman* v. *Williams* (in error), 7 Q. B. 103. So where the question is whether the defendant contracted to pay freight for the carriage of certain goods, and the jury find facts from which such a contract might be implied as a matter of fact, but from which no contract or promise would be implied by law, the court will give judgment for the defendant, and not award a trial *de novo*. *Sanders* v. *Vanzeller*, 4 Q. B. 260, 272, 296; 2 Gale & Dav. 244, *S. C.*; and see *Kemp* v. *Clark*, 12 Q. B. 647; *Lyon* v. *Haynes*, 5 Man. & Gr. 542; 6 Scott, N. R. 371; *Tancred* v. *Christy*, 12 M. & W. 316; *Id.* 321, Cresswell, J. "Upon well recognized principles of law, the court, or a court of error, is strictly restrained to the facts found by the jury, and stated in the special verdict." *Per* Tindal, C. J., in *Downman* v. *Williams* (in error), 7 Q. B. 108. They are also confined to the points raised and submitted by the special verdict. *Mowatt* v. *Lord Londesborough*, 4 E. & B. 1.

In a special verdict it is not necessary to state that any particular fact was not proved; because the negative will be assumed as to any fact not found—*De non apparentibus et de non existentibus eadem est ratio*. *Per cur.* in *The Mayor, &c. of Nottingham* v. *Lambert*, Willes, 117; *Witham* v. *Earl of Derby*, 1 Wils. 57 (2nd point); *Martin* v. *Jenkin*, 2 Stra. 1145; *Doe* d. *Kenrick* v. *Lord W. Beauclerk*, 11 East, 657, 662. If it appear by the record of a special verdict in ejectment that the claimant has a priority of possession, and no title is found for the defendant, the plaintiff shall have judgment. *Allen* v. *Rivington*, 2 Saund. 110 a; 2 Keb. 606; 1 Sid. 445; *Bateman* v. *Allen*, Cro. Eliz. 438. On the other hand, if it appear by the verdict that there is an outstanding term vested in a trustee, who is not one of the claimants, the defendant is entitled to judgment. *Goodtitle* d. *Jones* v. *Jones* (in error), 7 T. R. 43. But where an objection was made to a special verdict that A. B. was not found to be son and heir of Sir R. B., and then his fine conveys nothing to Sir G. Brown; and although he be found to be son to Sir R. B. and his wife, that may be true if he be his second son; and so there is not a sufficient title found for the plaintiff. All the court resolved, that this being a verdict is well enough; for being found to be son, and none other found to be heir, he may well be intended to be son and heir of Sir R. B. Wherefore it was adjudged for the plaintiff. *Lynch* v. *Spencer*, Cro. Eliz. 513, 515.

"If in a special verdict the jury find that one joint-tenant *granted* his estate to another joint-tenant, yet the court will adjudge that he *released*, which is the proper conveyance for one joint-tenant to pass his estate to another. But if the party in pleading had pleaded that he granted, the plea would be bad, for every one must order his plea according to the rules of law; but it is otherwise of a verdict, because it is the saying of laymen." 2 Wms. Saund. 97. A special verdict found that J. S., being seised of land in fee, being upon the land *demised it to the plaintiff for life. Et quod nulla alia deliberatio seisinæ facta fuit*: held, that there was no livery, and therefore no lease for life, notwithstanding the express words of the verdict. *Sharp* v. *Sharp*, Cro. Eliz. 482; 6 Co. Rep. 26; 2 Wms. Saund. 97. So where the jury find the effect of a deed, and also set it out *in hæc verba*, the court will judge of the effect of the deed as set out, rather than from the effect of it as collected by the jury. *Rowe* v. *Huntington*, Vaughan, 77; Cro. Eliz. 515; 2 Wms. Saund. 97 e, note (3).

Where an indispensable fact is not sufficiently stated either way in a special verdict, so that the court cannot properly give any judgment upon such verdict for or against either party, the court will award a trial *de novo*. If, under such circumstances, the court give judgment for either party, a court of error will reverse the judgment and direct a trial *de novo*. *Hodgson* v. *Repton, Clerk* (in error), 7 Q. B. 101; *Trafford* v. *The King* (in error), 2 Cr. & Jer. 265, 274, 278; 8 Bing. 204; 1 Moo. & Sc. 401, *S. C.; Tancred* v. *Christy*, 12 M. & W. 316, 324, cited 15 M. & W. 168, Parke, B.; *Doe* d. *Beach* v. *The Earl of Jersey*, 3 B. & C. 870, 875; *Parker* v. *Wells* (in error), 1 T. R. 783.

In personal actions, if a special verdict in effect find that the facts as stated in a special plea in confession and avoidance are true, but the court in banc, or a court of error, is of opinion that the facts as pleaded are not sufficient in law, the proper course is to give judgment for the plaintiff *non obstante veredicto*, and not to enter a verdict for the plaintiff on that plea. *Cook* v. *Pearce*, 8 Q. B. 1044.

The pleadings cannot be amended after a special verdict (except by consent). *Warwick* v. *Rogers*, 5 Man. & Gr. 340, 358; 6 Scott, N. R. 1. Nor will the court direct the verdict itself to be amended, after it has given judgment for the defendant. *Sanders* v. *Vanzeller*, 4 Q. B. 260, 273. But the court will sometimes, as a great favour, give the plaintiff leave to discontinue his action after a special verdict. *Price* v. *Parker*, 1 Salk. 178, cited 6 Q. B. 613. The plaintiff will not be permitted to discontinue the action after a general verdict for the defendant, although leave be reserved to him to move to set aside such verdict and to enter one for himself. *Goodenough* v. *Butler*, 3 Dowl. 751. The distinction is between a special and a general verdict, the latter being final, and the former not. *Per* Coleridge, J., and Lord Denman, C. J., in *Young* v. *Hichens*, 6 Q. B. 614; 2 Chit. Arch. 1389 (9th ed.).

When judgment is pronounced on a special verdict a rule is drawn up in favour of the successful party, and judgment signed thereon with the Master. *See the forms, Appendix, Nos.* 266, 267. A mere *incipitur* of the judgment is usually entered in the first instance. *See the form, Appendix, No.* 122. Thereupon execution may issue. 15 & 16 Vict. c. 76, s. 206; *post*, Chap. XXXI.

CHAPTER XXVII.

NEW TRIAL. .

In what Cases granted.]—If the judge admit improper evidence (although duly objected to); or reject proper evidence ; or misdirect the jury upon any point of law material to the matters in issue, a new trial will generally be granted. So where there appears to have been a substantial failure of justice by reason of any misconduct of the jury ; or of the successful party, or his attorney ; or a sufficient notice of trial was not duly given, and the defendant did not appear at the trial. For particular instances see 2 Chit. Arch. 1423 (9th ed.). If any mistake be made at the trial, for which a bill of exceptions *might* have been tendered (*ante*, 309), and a note of the point or objection was then and there taken, the court will usually grant a new trial, which is a practical substitute for a bill of exceptions and proceedings in error thereon. *Bernasconi* v. *Farebrother*, 3 B. & Adol. 372. "The granting a new trial, strictly speaking, is in the discretion of the court, although the court regulates its discretion as nearly as possible by the rules applicable to bills of exceptions. Where evidence has been improperly rejected or admitted the court will not grant a new trial, if with the evidence rejected a verdict given for the party offering it would be clearly against the weight of evidence, or if without the evidence received there be enough to warrant the verdict." *Per* Alderson, B., in *Hughes* v. *Hughes*, 15 M. & W. 704, citing *Doe* d. *Lord Teignham* v. *Tyler*, 6 Bing. 561 ; 4 Moo. & P. 377 ; *Crease* v. *Barrett*, 1 Cr. M. & R. 919 ; 5 Tyr. 458, 475 ; and see *Doe* d. *Welsh* v. *Langfield*, 16 M. & W. 497, 515. But upon a bill of exceptions, the court of error does not exercise any such discretionary power. *Ante*, 310, 316.

Before the 17 & 18 Vict. c. 125, s. 34 (which gives a right of appeal), the courts would seldom grant a new trial in ejectment, when the verdict was *for the defendant* ; because all parties remaining in the situation they were previously to the commencement of the action, the claimant might bring a second ejectment without subjecting himself to additional difficulties. Ad. Eject. 286; 2 Chit. Arch. 1336 (8th ed.). Sometimes, however, a new trial was granted at the instance of the plaintiff; and in case of his death before the disposal of such rule the court would not compel his representatives to give security for costs. *Doe* d. *Cozens* v. *Cozens*, 1 Q. B. 503; 9 Dowl. 1040. Unless, indeed, the plaintiff claimed only as tenant for life. *Throustout* d. *Turner* v. *Grey*, 2 Stra. 1056.

The circumstance of the judge having left an immaterial question to the jury, with a direction that if they find it one way they must return a verdict for the defendant, does not entitle the plaintiff to move for a new trial, if upon all the other facts of the case the defendant is clearly entitled to the verdict. *Clarke* v. *Arden*, 16 C. B. 227. So where the judge misdirects the jury upon a collateral point. *Black* v. *Jones*, 6 Exch. 213, 216.

If the verdict pass *for the plaintiff* a new trial may be granted in a proper case, because the verdict and judgment in ejectment affect the possession, and change the relative situation of the parties, and the onus of proof. *Goodtitle* d. *Alexander* v. *Clayton*, 4 Burr. 2224; *Wright* d. *Clymer* v. *Littler*, 3 Burr. 1244; 1 W. Blac. 345. "Ejectments are substituted in the place of real actions, in which the title appeared upon the pleadings, and gave no room for surprise. We should, therefore, rather lean to new trials on behalf of defendants, in the case of ejectments, especially on the footing of surprise. Another good rule for granting or refusing new trials, is, that upon the whole substantial justice has not been, or has been, done to the parties." *Id.* 348, *per* Lord Mansfield, C. J.; and see *Roe* d. *Thorne* v. *Lord*, 2 W. Blac. 1099; *Doe* d. *Angell* v. *Angell*, 9 Q. B. 360; *Doe* d. *Cooling* v. *Appleby*, 9 Dowl. 556. "A new trial ought not to be granted, merely for the sake of turning the party round; but where substantial justice cannot otherwise be obtained. And in the case of *Smith* d. *Dormer* v. *Fortescue*, 2 Stra. 1106, the court under such circumstances refused to grant a new trial." *Per* Lord Mansfield, C. J., in *Doe* d. *Foster* v. *Williams*, 2 Cowp. 621, 622.

In a recent action of ejectment there was a verdict for the plaintiff, with leave for the defendant to move to set it aside and enter a nonsuit instead, if the title set up should be deemed insufficient. A rule nisi was accordingly obtained, and after argument the court thought that there were fatal defects in the plaintiff's title; but as it appeared probable that upon another occasion the plaintiff might be able to supply these defects, which had no bearing on the merits of the case, and as it would have been an useless expense to the parties to direct a nonsuit to be entered, they made the rule absolute for a new trial upon payment by the plaintiff of the costs of the previous trial. *Doe* d. *North* v. *Webber*, 3 Bing. N. C. 922, 927. For the converse of this case see *Doe* d. *Angell* v. *Angell*, 9 Q. B. 332, 360.

On a motion for a new trial counsel cannot present a point which does not appear by the judge's notes to have been raised at the trial. *Gibbs* v. *Pike*, 1 Dowl. N. S. 409; 9 M. & W. 223, *S. C.* The court will not grant a new trial for an objection either to the admission or rejection of evidence, or to the direction of the judge at the trial, unless such objection was distinctly raised at the trial. 2 Chit. Arch. 1425 (9th ed.).

Motion for, within what time.]—By Reg. Prac. H. T. 1853, No. 50, "no motion for a new trial, or to enter a verdict or nonsuit, motion in arrest of judgment, or for judgment *non obstante veredicto,* shall be allowed after the expiration of four days from the day of trial, nor in any case after the expiration of the term, if the cause be tried in term, or after the expiration of the first four days of the ensuing term when the cause is tried out of term, unless entered in a list of postponed motions by leave of the court."

No. 51, "no suitor who appears in person shall be at liberty to set down any motion in such list of postponed motions, without the special permission of the court for that purpose."

No. 52, "no affidavit shall be used in support of a motion for a new trial in any case, unless such affidavit shall have been made within the time limited for the making such motion, without the special permission of the court for that purpose."

No. 53, " if such motion as above mentioned be entered in such list of postponed motions, or if such motion be postponed by leave of the court, in the case of a cause tried in term, the attorney who has instructed counsel to make the motion shall give notice of it to the attorney of the opposite party, otherwise judgment signed on behalf of the opposite party shall be *deemed regular,* and every suitor who appears in person shall give a similar notice."

If a regular judgment be signed (no such notice having been given) the application for a new trial must include a motion to set aside the judgment, upon an affidavit of merits or special circumstances; and that part of the rule must first be disposed of before the application for a new trial can be argued. *Doe* d. *Whitty* v. *Carr,* 16 Q. B. 117; *Doe* d. *Howe* v. *Taunton, Id.* 117, note (*b*).

Rule Nisi.]—By 17 & 18 Vict. c. 125, s. 33, "in every rule nisi for a new trial such rule shall have been granted, shall be shortly stated therein." *See the forms, Appendix, Nos.* 253, 254. The grounds must be *specifically* stated: it is not sufficient to say "on the grounds set forth in the affidavit." *Drayson* v. *Andrews,* 10 Exch. 472. But sometimes the court may order the rule to be amended on cause being shown against it. *S. C.* The counsel who obtains the rule should take care to indorse his brief correctly, stating the grounds upon which it was granted, so that the proper officer may copy them in the rule nisi.

Where in an action against several defendants a verdict has been found against some of them, and for others, and the former apply for a new trial, the rule nisi should call not only upon the plaintiff, but also upon the other defendants, to show cause why a new trial should not be granted. *Doe* d. *Dudgeon* v. *Martin,* 13 M. & W. 811; 2 Dowl. & L. 678; *Belcher* v. *Magnay,* 13 M. & W. 815, note; 3 Dowl. & L. 70; *Haddrick* v. *Heslop,* 12 Q. B. 289, Lord Denman, C. J. Where a new trial is granted *ex debito justitiæ* on one of several issues, the rule for a new trial opens the whole record. *The Earl of Macclesfield* v. *Bradley,* 7 M. & W. 570; 9 Dowl. 312.

Appeal.]—By 17 & 18 Vict. c. 125, s. 34, "in all cases of rules *to enter a verdict or nonsuit* upon a point reserved at the trial, if the rule to show cause be refused, or granted and then discharged or made absolute, the party decided against may appeal."

Sect. 35, "in all cases of motions *for a new trial,* upon the ground that the judge has not ruled according to law, if the rule to show cause be refused, or if granted be then discharged or made absolute, the party decided against may appeal, provided any one of the judges dissent from the rule being refused, or, when granted, being discharged or made absolute, as the case may be, or, provided the court in its discretion think fit that an appeal should be allowed; provided, that where the application for a new trial is upon matter of discretion only, as on the ground that the verdict is against the weight of evidence or otherwise, no such appeal shall be allowed." *Jenkins* v. *Betham*, 15 C. B. 191.

Sect. 36, " the court of error, the Exchequer Chamber, and the House of Lords shall be courts of appeal for the purposes of this act."

Sect. 37, " no appeal shall be allowed unless notice thereof be given in writing to the opposite party or his attorney, and to one of the masters of the court, within four days after the decision complained of, or such further time as may be allowed by the court or judge." *See forms of Notice, Appendix, Nos.* 256, 257, 258.

Sect. 38, " notice of appeal shall be a stay of execution, provided *bail to pay* the sum recovered and costs, or to pay costs where the appellant was plaintiff below, be given, in like manner and to the same amount as bail in error, within eight days after the decision complained of, or before execution delivered to the sheriff." No bail is necessary except to make the notice of appeal a stay of execution.

Sect. 39, " the appeal hereinbefore mentioned shall be upon a case to be stated by the parties (and in case of difference, to be settled by the court or a judge of the court appealed from), in which case shall be set forth so much of the pleadings, evidence and the ruling or judgment objected to as may be necessary to raise the question for the decision of the court of appeal." *See forms, Appendix, Nos.* 259, 260, 261.

Sect. 40, " when an appeal is from the refusal of the court below to grant a rule to show cause, and the court of appeal grant such rule, such rule shall be argued and disposed of in the court of appeal."

Sect. 41, " the court of appeal shall give such judgment as ought to have been given in the court below ; and all such further proceedings may be taken thereupon as if the judgment had been given by the court in which the record originated." The form of judgment is given in the rule of Mic. Vac. 1854, Sched. No. 21. *See Appendix, No.* 261 (*b*).

Sect. 42, " the court of appeal shall have power to adjudge payment of costs, and to order restitution; and they shall have the same powers as the court of error in respect of awarding process and otherwise." *See Appendix, No.* 261 (*b*).

Sect. 43, " upon an award of a trial *de novo* by any one of the superior courts or by the court of error, upon matter appearing upon the record, error may at once be brought; and if the judgment in such or any other case be affirmed in error, it shall be lawful for the court of error to adjudge costs to the defendant in error."

Costs of previous Trial.]—By 17 & 18 Vict. c. 125, s. 44, " when a new trial is granted, on the ground that the *verdict was against evidence,* the costs of the first trial shall abide the event, unless the court shall otherwise order."

By Reg. Pr. H. T. 1853, No. 54, " if a new trial be granted without any mention of costs in the rule, the costs of the first trial shall not be allowed to the successful party, though he succeed on the second." *Evans* v. *Robinson,* 11 Exch. 40.

CHAPTER XXVIII.

THE POSTEA.

By whom and how prepared.]—In country causes, the postea is prepared by the associate, who will deliver it to the attorney or agent of the successful party, when he is entitled to sign judgment upon it. In town causes it is prepared by the attorney or agent of the successful party. *See the forms, Appendix, Nos.* 242, 250. It must agree in substance and effect with the entry of the verdict as made at the trial. *Ante,* 307. The successful party has no right to frame the postea in such a manner as to add to or modify the finding of the jury. Thus, where a declaration in ejectment contained two counts, in each of which "one pasture gate and one cattle gate" were sought to be recovered. The cause having been referred, the arbitrator awarded that the lessor of the plaintiff was entitled to recover "three certain pasture gates." The lessor of the plaintiff entered up the verdict for "three certain pasture gates, sometimes known as pasture gates, sometimes as cattle gates:" held, that it was not competent to the lessor of the plaintiff to make such an alteration; although it was sworn, on the part of the lessor, that the names "pasture gate" and "cattle gate" were indiscriminately used for the same thing. *Doe* d. *Hoxby* v. *Preston,* 5 Dowl. & L. 7. But sometimes an incorrect verdict may be cured by entering a *remittitur* as to part and taking judgment for the residue only. 2 Chit. Arch. 1422 (9th ed.). Where the objection cannot be cured in this manner, the proper course is to apply to the judge to amend the postea according to his notes. *Post,* 385.

Who entitled to.]—The plaintiffs are entitled to the postea, if they, or any or either of them, recover a verdict for all *or any part* of the property claimed. But the defendants are entitled to the postea if they obtain a general verdict in their favour, or the plaintiff be non-suited. Where the plaintiff succeeds as to a small part only, and the defendants as to the residue, if the plaintiff *will not* enter up judgment on the postea, he may be ordered to deliver it to the defendants, who will thereupon be entitled to enter up a proper judgment, according to the verdict. *Taylor* v. *Nesfield,* 4 E. & B. 462.

Amendment of Postea.]—The postea is in the nature of a return made by the judge who tried the cause of what has been done before him under the record of nisi prius. If any mistake be made in the postea, an application to amend it must be made to the judge who tried the cause, and not to the court in banc. *Roe* d. *Blair* v. *Street and Fairbanks*, 2 A. & E. 329; 4 N. & M. 42; *Newton* v. *Harland*, 1 Man. & Gr. 958. If the judge refuse to make the amendment, the court in banc will not interfere. *Cases supra.* So where the judge orders an amendment. *Sandford* v. *Alcock*, 10 M. & W. 689; 2 Dowl. N. S. 463; *Daintry* v. *Brocklehust*, 3 Exch. 691; but see *Empson* v. *Griffin*, 11 A. & E. 186; 3 P. & D. 160. Sometimes an application may be made to the judge in court, in order that he may have the benefit of the assistance of the other judges. *Harrison* v. *King*, 1 B. & A. 161, 163, Abbott, C. J.; *Doe* d. *Haxby* v. *Preston*, 5 Dowl. & L. 7. But in such case the other judges can act only as his assessors or advisers in the matter. *Per* Maule, J., in *Jackson* v. *Galloway*, 1 C. B. 296. In no case will a court of error consider the propriety of any such amendment. *Mellish* v. *Richardson*, 1 Cl. & Fin. 224; 6 Bligh, N. S. 70, 84, 86; 9 Bing. 125, *S. C.*; *Scales* v. *Cheese*, 12 M. & W. 685; 1 Dowl. & L. 657; *Salter* v. *Slade*, 1 A. & E. 608; 3 N. & M. 717.

The postea should be amended (if at all) according to the judge's notes. He ought not to act upon his recollection of what took place. *Reg.* v. *Sarah Verrier*, 12 A. & E. 317; 4 P. & D. 161; *Jackson* v. *Galloway*, 1 C. B. 280; *Gould* v. *Oliver*, 2 Scott, N. R. 636; but see *Bowers* v. *Nixon*, 12 Q. B. 546, 556; *Gregory* v. *The Queen* (in error), 15 Q. B. 957, 967.

The postea may be amended according to the judge's notes *at any time*, even after final judgment and error brought. *Doe* d. *Church* v. *Perkins*, 3 T. R. 749; *Wallis* v. *Goddard*, 2 Man. & Gr. 912; *Richardson* v. *Mellish*, 3 Bing. 346; 11 Moore, 104; 7 B. & C. 819; 1 Cl. & Fin. 228, 232; 6 Bligh, N. S. 70, 84, 86, *S. C.*; *Bowers* v. *Nixon*, 12 Q. B. 546; *Gregory* v. *The Queen* (in error), 15 Q. B. 957. Sometimes the court of error will postpone their judgment to enable such an application to be made; *Bowers* v. *Nixon*, 12 Q. B. 546, 552; *Gregory* v. *The Queen* (in error), 15 Q. B. 957; and will afterwards permit the proceedings in error to be amended in a corresponding manner. *Mellish* v. *Richardson*, 7 B. & C. 819. But after final judgment has been reversed in error, it is too late to correct the mistake by an amendment of the postea; and the court below has then no jurisdiction in that behalf. *Jackson* v. *Galloway*, 1 C. B. 280; 2 Dowl. & L. 839.

The principle is, that a *mere misprision* may be cured at any time before the judgment has been actually reversed in error. The postea not being drawn up pursuant to the judge's notes is considered as a mere misprision of the officer of the court; and the judgment not being entered up according to the postea (as amended) is considered as another misprision. *Per* Erle, J., in *Bowers* v. *Nixon*, 12 Q. B. 558.

CHAPTER XXIX.

JUDGMENT AFTER VERDICT.

When Judgment may be signed.]—By 15 & 16 Vict. c. 76, s. 185, "upon a finding for the claimant judgment may be signed, and execution issue for the recovery of possession of the property, or such part thereof as the jury shall find the claimant entitled to, and for costs, within such time, not exceeding the fifth day in term after the verdict, as the court or judge before whom the cause is tried shall order; and if no such order be made, then on the fifth day in term after the verdict, *or within fourteen days after such verdict, whichever shall first happen.*"

By sect. 186, "upon a finding for the defendants, or any of them, judgment may be signed and execution issue for costs against the claimants named in the writ, within such time, not exceeding the fifth day in term after the verdict, as the court or judge before whom the cause is tried shall order; and if no such order be made, then on the fifth day in term after the verdict, or *within fourteen days after such verdict, whichever shall first happen.*"

In other actions than ejectment, "when a plaintiff or defendant has obtained a verdict *in term,* or in case a plaintiff has been nonsuited at the trial in or out of term, judgment may be signed and execution issue thereon in fourteen days, unless the judge who tries the cause, or some other judge, or the court, shall order execution to issue at an earlier or later period, with or without terms." Reg. Prac. H. T. 1853, No. 57. But this rule does not apply to actions of ejectment wherein another time is expressly limited by statute. *Supra.*

Order to stay Judgment or Execution.]—Generally speaking, when the trial takes place at the assizes, or at the sittings after term in London or Middlesex, if the defendant wish to move for a new trial, &c., he should apply to the judge for an order to stay judgment and execution until the fifth day of the next term; because *fourteen days after the verdict* will elapse before the motion can be made.

When a landlord obtains a verdict in ejectment against a tenant who has found security for the costs and damages, pursuant to 15 & 16 Vict. c. 76, s. 213, the judgment or execution cannot be stayed by order of the judge, except under the circumstances and in manner provided by s. 215. *Post*, Chap. XXXVI. Sect. 3.

Rule for Judgment unnecessary.]—By Reg. Prac. H. T. 1855, No. 55, "no rule for judgment shall be necessary."

Date of Judgment.]—"All judgments, whether interlocutory or final, shall be entered of record of the day of the month and year, whether in term or vacation, *when signed*, and shall not have relation to any other day; but it shall be competent for the court or a judge to order a judgment to be entered *nunc pro tunc*." Reg. Prac. H. T. 1853, No. 56; Reg. Pl. H. T. 1853, No. 32.

The court or a judge will seldom or never permit judgment to be entered *nunc pro tunc*, except where the delay has been occasioned by the act of the court, as where they take time to consider their judgment. 2 Chit. Arch. 1474 (9th ed.).

Incipitur of Judgment.]—By 15 & 16 Vict. c. 76, s. 206, "it shall not be necessary, before issuing execution upon any judgment under the authority of this act, to enter the proceedings upon any roll, but an *incipitur* thereof may be made upon paper, shortly describing the nature of the judgment according to the practice heretofore used, and judgment may thereupon be signed, and costs taxed, and execution issued, according to the practice heretofore used: provided nevertheless, that the proceedings may be entered upon the roll whenever the same may become necessary for the purpose of evidence, or of bringing error, or the like." For the form of an *incipitur*, *see Appendix, No.* 122; entry of final judgment, *Appendix, Nos.* 262—268.

When the plaintiff obtains a general judgment in his favour he may enter it up as to part for himself, and as to the residue for the defendant. *Harnidge* v. *Wilson*, 8 Dowl. 417.

Judgment is considered as entered up when an *incipitur* thereof is entered at the master's office. *Fisher* v. *Dudding*, 3 Man. & Gr. 238; 3 Scott, N. R. 516; 9 Dowl. 872; *Newton* v. *The Grand Junction Railway Company*, 16 M. & W. 139; *Reg.* v. *Gordon*, Car. & M. 410. But see *Pierce* v. *Derry*, 21 Law J., N. S., Q. B., 277.

Delay in signing Judgment.]—The party entitled to judgment may postpone signing it as long as he pleases. 1 Chit. Arch. 485 (9th ed.). Where more than four terms have elapsed since the trial, it is not necessary to give a term's notice before signing judgment. *Id.*; *May* v. *Wooding*, 3 M. & S. 500; *Deacon* v. *Fuller*, 1 Dowl. 675; *Newton* v. *Boodle*, 3 C. B. 795; 4 Dowl. & L. 664.

If the plaintiff succeeded as to part, and failed as to the residue, and delays signing judgment, whereby the defendant sustains any prejudice, he may apply to the court or a judge for the postea, with liberty to sign judgment upon it, according to the verdict. *Taylor* v. *Nesfield*, 4 E. & B. 462.

Q

Revival of Judgment.]—Six years after the date of a judgment in ejectment it must generally be revived by a *scire facias* before execution can regularly issue upon it. 15 & 16 Vict. c. 76, s. 128 ; 2 Chit. Arch. 979 (9th ed.); *Doe* d. *Stevens* v. *Lord,* 7 A. & E. 610 ; 2 N. & P. 604 ; 6 Dowl. 255. The want of such revival is not a mere irregularity, of which advantage must be taken promptly, but a defect of a substantial nature, for which the execution will be set aside at a later period. *Goodtitle* d. *Murrell* v. *Badtitle,* 9 Dowl. 1009. A scire facias is necessary after six years, although the judgment was obtained by default : and notice of it should be served on *all* the tenants in possession. *Doe* d. *Ramsbottom* v. *Roe,* 2 Dowl. N. S. 690. But the necessity for a *scire facias* may be dispensed with by express agreement between the parties, even by parol. *Morgan* v. *Burgess,* 1 Dowl. N. S. 850; *Sherran* v. *Marshall,* 1 Dowl. & L. 689.

CHAPTER XXX.

COSTS.

1. *On a Judgment for Non-appearance.*]—Upon a judgment for non-appearance against all or any of the defendants named in the writ, no costs are recoverable. *Ante*, 131. But such costs may generally be recovered in a subsequent action of trespass for mesne profits, if the declaration be properly framed. *Doe* v. *Davis*, 1 Esp. 358; *Doe* v. *Huddart*, 2 Cr. M. & R. 316; 5 Tyr. 846; 4 Dowl. 437; *Grace* v. *Morgan*, 2 Bing. N. C. 534; 2 Scott, 790; *see Forms of Declaration, Appendix, Nos.* 390, 391.

2. *On a Judgment by Confession.*]—After appearance, any defendant may confess the action, as to all or part of the property claimed, and for which he defends; and thereupon the plaintiffs may sign judgment against such defendant, for the whole or part (as the notice may be), with costs. 15 & 16 Vict. c. 76, ss. 203, 204, 205; *post*, Chap. XXXIII.

3. *On a Discontinuance.*]—The claimant may at any time discontinue his action as to any one or more of the defendants by a notice in writing; and thereupon such defendant or defendants will be entitled to judgment and costs. 15 & 16 Vict. c. 76, s. 200; *post*, Chap. XXXIII.

4. *On a Judgment for not Proceeding to Trial.*]—Where judgment is obtained against the claimant for not proceeding to trial in pursuance of a twenty days' notice, the defendant is entitled to his costs of defence. 15 & 16 Vict. c. 76, s. 202; *ante*, 136.

5. *Costs of the Day.*]—If the claimants give notice of trial, and do not countermand it in due time, the defendants may obtain a side-bar rule for the costs of the day, on the usual affidavit, and without any motion. 15 & 16 Vict. c. 76, s. 99; Reg. Prac. H. T. 1853, No. 39, *ante*, 149; *see forms of Affidavit and Rule, Appendix, Nos.* 173, 174, 175. By countermanding notice of trial *in due time*, the plaintiff

Q 2

avoids being liable to pay the costs of the day. *Ante,* 149. So where the notice of trial is duly continued. *Ante,* 148.

Costs of the day mean such costs as are properly incurred in preparing for trial according to the notice, but which must be incurred over again on a trial at any subsequent assizes, or sitting in or after another term. Gray on Costs, 371. Notice to admit and notice to produce may be used on a trial at a later period; and therefore are not costs of the day. The briefs and fees to counsel will do again; but an allowance should be made for alterations, and refreshers to counsel. Subpœnas for witnesses will do again; but the expense of altering and resealing them, and the costs of copies and service, and witnesses' expenses on the first occasion, should be allowed as costs of the day. So with respect to any other expenses properly incurred, which will not be useful on a trial at a later period.

6. *Nonsuit.*]—"If a plaintiff in ejectment be nonsuited at the trial the defendant shall be entitled to judgment for his costs of suit." Reg. Pl. H. T. 1853, No. 29, *ante,* 304; *see forms of Postea and Judgment, Appendix, Nos.* 246, 247, 265.

7. *On a Verdict for the Plaintiffs.*]—If the claimants obtain a verdict for *the whole* of the property claimed, whether by reason of the defendant's non-appearance at the trial, or upon the merits, they are entitled to costs. 15 & 16 Vict. c. 76, s. 185; Reg. Pr. H. T. 1853, No. 114; Reg. Pl. H. T. 1853, No. 30.

Any defendants who have suffered judgment for want of appearance, or confessed the action before trial, are not liable for the costs of the trial, &c. But only those who defend, and against whom the verdict passes. *Doe* d. *Bishton* v. *Hughes,* 2 Cr. M. & R. 281; 5 Tyr. 957; 4 Dowl. 412.

Where some defendants defend for part, and others for the residue, and the plaintiff obtains a verdict generally, it seems that only one set of costs can be taxed for the plaintiffs, and not separate costs as against each set of defendants; and that all the defendants are liable for the whole. *Thrustout* d. *Wilson* v. *Foot,* Barnes's Notes, 149; Bull. N. P. 335. This must sometimes operate very harshly. But the defendants are all trespassers and wrong-doers, otherwise the verdict would not pass against them. The action is *for a tort,* viz. an unlawful possession of the plaintiff's land against his will.

If the plaintiffs or any of them obtain a verdict for *any part* of the property claimed, they are entitled to judgment against all the defendants who defend *for such part* with costs. *Doe* d. *Bishton* v. *Hughes,* 2 Cr. M. & R. 281; 5 Tyr. 957; 4 Dowl. 412. But the defendants are entitled to their costs of defence as to the residue of the property claimed. 15 & 16 Vict. c. 76, s. 186; Gray on Costs, 200; *Doe* d. *Errington* v. *Errington,* 4 Dowl. 602; *Doe* d. *Smith* v. *Webber,* 2 A. & E. 448; *Doe* d. *Bowman* v. *Lewis,* 13 M. & W. 241, 251; 2 Dowl. & L. 667.

A party succeeding on an issue in a personal action, which entitles him to the postea, and to the general costs of the cause, is entitled to the costs of all witnesses attending to prove that issue, whether their evidence applies to any other issue or not. But the opposite party is entitled only to the costs of such witnesses as attend solely to prove the issue on which he succeeds, and if they also attend to prove an issue on which he fails, he is not entitled to any costs in respect of them. *Welby* v. *Brown*, 5 Dowl. & L. 746; 1 Exch. 770; *Clothier* v. *Gann*, 13 C. B. 220; Gray on Costs, 81; but see *Jewell* v. *Parr*, 17 C. B. 636. It is not however clear that the above would apply to an ejectment wherein the verdict is as to part for the claimants, and as to the residue for the defendants, especially where the defendants defend separately for different parts of the land. *Doe* d. *Smith* v. *Webber*, 2 A. & E. 448; Gray on Costs, 78. Where the plaintiff's title to possession expires after service of the writ in ejectment, and before the trial, he is entitled to a verdict according to the fact, that he was entitled to possession at the time of bringing the action and serving the writ; and to a *judgment for his costs of suit*. 15 & 16 Vict. c. 76, s. 181, *ante*, 289. In such a case the court will not stay the proceedings before trial, except on payment of the plaintiff's costs.

8. *On a Verdict for Defendants.*]—If the verdict pass for the defendants, they are entitled to judgment against all the claimants named in the writ, with costs. 15 & 16 Vict. c. 76, s. 186, *ante*, 336. If the verdict be, as to part of the property, for the plaintiffs, or some or one of them, and as to the residue for the defendants, the plaintiffs who succeed as to part are entitled to the general costs of the cause (*ante*, 340), but the defendants are entitled to their costs of defence as to the residue. Sect. 186; *Doe* d. *Errington* v. *Errington*, 4 Dowl. 602; *Doe* d. *Smith* v. *Webber*, 2 A. & E. 448; Gray on Costs, 78; *Id*. 200. Where any defendant defends separately for part only, and obtains a verdict as to such part, he is entitled to his costs of defence (including the costs of his witnesses, *ante*, 340), notwithstanding the plaintiffs recover a verdict as to other parts for which the defendant did not defend.

If to avoid or delay payment of any defendant's costs, the plaintiffs abstain from entering up judgment on the postea, such defendant may apply to the court or a judge for the delivery to him of the postea, with liberty to sign judgment upon it according to the verdict. *Taylor* v. *Nesfield*, 4 E. & B. 462. But generally speaking, a party entitled to judgment may postpone signing it as long as he pleases. *Ante*, 337.

Where several defendants are jointly entitled to costs, the claimant may pay them to which of the defendants he pleases. *Jordan* v. *Harper*, 1 Stra. 516.

9. *After a Suggestion.*]—The costs of a suggestion are usually costs in the cause and abide the result. *Benge* v. *Swaine*, 15 C. B. 784. But where the suggestion is made after trial, and the new claimant fails, it seems that he is not liable to the costs of the suit prior to the application for leave to enter the suggestion. Gray on Costs, 199. It would be unreasonable and contrary to all principle to give the defendant the costs of the action in which the *verdict passed against him*. On the other hand, if the new claimant succeed he is only entitled to judgment for possession "and for the costs of and occasioned by such suggestion." 15 & 16 Vict. c. 76, s. 194; Gray on Costs, 199. The previous costs were in effect lost by the death of the original claimant. According to the previous law the consent rule in an ejectment created only a *personal liability*, which ceased upon the death of either party. *Doe* d. *Harrison* v. *Hampson*, 4 C. B. 745; 5 Dowl. & L. 484.

CHAPTER XXXI.

EXECUTIONS.

BY 15 & 16 Vict. c. 76, s. 187, "upon any judgment in ejectment for recovery of possession and costs, there may be either one writ or separate writs of execution for the recovery of possession and for the costs, at the election of the claimant." *See the forms, Appendix, Nos.* 270—278.

Sometimes separate writs are absolutely necessary, because the *habere facias possessionem* can be executed only by the sheriff of the county wherein the lands lie; whereas the persons of the defendants, or their goods and chattels, may be in other counties. A separate writ of *fi. fa.* or *ca. sa.* for the costs may issue into any county, without any previous writ into the county where the venue is laid. 15 & 16 Vict. c. 76, s. 121.

By Reg. Prac. H. T. 1853, No. 70, "it shall not be necessary before issuing execution upon any judgment whatever, to enter the proceedings upon any roll." A mere *incipitur* of the judgment is all that is required. 15 & 16 Vict. c. 76, s. 206. *Ante,* 337; *see the form, Appendix, No.* 122.

Revival of Judgment.]—When a judgment in ejectment is more than six years old, it generally requires to be revived by *scire facias* before any execution can regularly issue under it. *Ante,* 338. This, however, is sometimes unnecessary. *Ante,* 338.

Executions—how issued, tested and indorsed.]—As the action is completed by the judgment, execution may issue by a different attorney without any order to change the attorney. *Topping* v. *Johnson,* 2 Bos. & P. 257.

By Reg. Prac. H. T. 1853, No. 71, "no writ of execution shall be issued till the judgment paper, postea or inquisition, as the case may be, has been seen by the proper officer; nor shall any writ of execution be issued without a præcipe being filed with the proper officer."

72. "Every writ of execution shall bear date on the day on which the same shall be issued, and shall be tested in the name of the Lord Chief Justice or of the Lord Chief Baron of the court from which the same shall issue, or in case of a vacancy of such office, then in the name of the senior puisne judge of the said court, and may be made returnable on a day certain in term." It may also be made returnable immediately after execution thereof. *Doe* d. *Hudson* v. *Roe,* 18 Q. B. 806; *see the forms of Execution, as prescribed by the Practice Rules of H. T.* 1853, *Schedule, Nos.* 24, 25; *post, Appendix, Nos.* 270—278.

73. "Every writ of execution shall be indorsed with the name and place of abode, or office of business of the attorney actually suing out the same; and in case such attorney shall not be an attorney of the court in which the same is sued out, then also with the name and place of abode or office of business of the attorney of such court in whose name such writ shall be taken out; and when the attorney actually suing out any writ shall sue out the same as agent for an attorney in the country, the name and place of abode of such attorney in the country shall also be indorsed upon the said writ; and in case no attorney shall be so employed to issue the writ, then it shall be indorsed with a memorandum expressing that the same has been sued out by the plaintiff or defendant in person, as the case may be, mentioning the city, town or parish, and also the name of the hamlet, street and number of the house of such plaintiff's or defendant's residence, if any such there be."

76. "Every writ of execution shall be indorsed with a direction to the sheriff, or other officer or person to whom the writ is directed, to levy the money really due and payable and sought to be recovered under the judgment, stating the amount, and also to levy interest

thereon, if sought to be recovered, at the rate of four pounds per centum per annum, from the time when the judgment was entered up, or if it was entered up before the 1st of October, 1838, then from that day; provided that, in cases where there is an agreement between the parties that more than four per cent. interest shall be secured by the judgment, then the indorsement may be accordingly to levy the amount of interest so agreed."

In every writ of execution, the names of *all* the defendants against whom the judgment has been obtained must be mentioned. The body or front part of the writ must *in all material points agree with the judgment.* 1 Chit. Arch. 554 (9th ed.). A writ of *habere facias possessionem* must agree with the verdict and judgment in the names of the parties; *Doe* d. *Taggart* v. *Sarah Butcher*, 3 M. & S. 557; and in the description of the property recovered: thus, if the verdict and judgment be for five-eighths of a cottage, it would be improper for the writ to issue for the whole cottage, and for the sheriff to deliver possession of the whole; *Roe* d. *Saul* v. *Dawson*, 3 Wils. 49; *Farr* v. *Denn*, 1 Burr. 366; nor, under a writ properly framed, should the sheriff set out and deliver five-eighths by metes and bounds. *Molineux* v. *Fulgam*, Palm. 289. *Post*, 346.

Where a *feme sole* defendant marries after verdict or after judgment, a writ of possession may issue against her in her maiden name. *Doe* d. *Taggart* v. *Butcher*, 3 M. & S. 557. But a *fi. fa.* against her for the costs would be inoperative. To obtain them, the judgment must first be revived as against the husband and wife. *S. C.* A married woman, when a co-plaintiff with her husband, is liable to be taken in execution for the defendant's costs, after a nonsuit or verdict for the defendant, and judgment thereupon. *Newton* v. *Rowe*, 9 Q. B. 948. But she may sometimes be discharged out of such custody upon proof that she has no separate property. *Larkin* v. *Marshall*, 4 Exch. 804; *Edwards* v. *Martyn*, 17 Q. B. 693.

It would be improper to issue, or at all events to execute, concurrent writs of *fi. fa.* and *ca. sa.* against several defendants for the costs. *Hodgkinson* v. *Whalley*, 1 Dowl. 298. Whenever any partial levy has been made under a *fi. fa.*, such levy must be recited in any subsequent execution, which must issue only for *the residue.* *Chapman* v. *Bowlby*, 8 M. & W. 249; 1 Dowl. N. S. 83. The manner of issuing and executing a *fi. fa.* or *ca. sa.* for costs is fully stated in 1 Chit. Arch. 591—626, and 637—652 (9th ed.).

Habere facias Possessionem.]—It is generally unadvisable to take possession of the property recovered by ejectment without suing out and executing a writ of *habere facias possessionem.* It has even been doubted whether it is lawful so to do. *Doe* d. *Stevens* v. *Lord*, 7 A. & E. 610; 2 N. & P. 604; 6 Dowl. 256; Watson's Sheriff, 317. It seems, however, that where possession is so taken (without any writ), the plaintiff enters by virtue of his title, and not under the judgment, which shall not put him in a worse condition than he was in before. *Badger* v. *Floid*, 12 Mod. 398; Holt, 199; *Withers* v. *Harris*, 2 Ld. Ray. 806, 808. In a recent action of trespass for mesne profits, it was held, that whether a writ of possession issues or not is immaterial: if possession be taken under the judgment, that is sufficient. "In the one case, the tenant is turned out; in the other, he goes out: he acquiesces in the judgment." *Wilkinson* v. *Kerby*, 15 C. B. 430; *id.*

440, Jervis, C. J.; and see *per* Parke, B., in *Barnett* v. *Earl of Guildford,* 11 Exch. 32; Run. Eject. 424; 2 Siderfin, 156; Co. Lit. 34 b; Roscoe on Real Actions, 341; Watson's Sheriff, 347. Where the defendant attorns to the plaintiff after judgment, or lets him into possession without any writ of possession, that is sufficient. *Calvart* v. *Horsfall,* 4 Esp. 167; *see form of Memorandum of Attornment, Appendix, No.* 269. It is frequently advisable to avoid executing a writ of possession, in order to save the sheriff's poundage, which is sometimes heavy. *Post,* 349.

When the plaintiff's title or right of possession expires after the service of the writ in ejectment and before the trial, the plaintiff is entitled to a verdict according to the fact, that he was entitled to possession at the time of bringing the action and serving the writ; and to a judgment for his costs of suit. 15 & 16 Vict. c. 76, s. 181; *ante,* 289. But he is not entitled to a writ of possession. So where the title has expired after verdict, and before execution issued, the court or a judge will, on a summary application, set aside an *habere facias possessionem,* but not the verdict or judgment. *Doe* d. *Butt* v. *Rous,* 1 E. & B. 419; *Doe* d. *Morgan* v. *Bluck,* 3 Camp. 447.

How executed.]—On the delivery of the writ to the sheriff, he makes out his warrant thereon. *See the forms, Appendix, Nos.* 279, 280, 281. It must be executed within a reasonable time, otherwise the sheriff will be liable to an action for the delay, and any consequential damage. *Mason* v. *Puynter,* 1 Q. B. 974; 1 Gale & D. 381; Watson's Sheriff, 317. It seems that, prior to the 15 & 16 Vict. c. 76, the sheriff might have demanded an indemnity before executing the writ. Gilb. Eject. 110; Ad. Eject. 301; Watson's Sheriff, 318. But this was seldom required: and now, as the plaintiff is a real person, it seems that the sheriff cannot lawfully refuse to execute the writ until he receives an indemnity. But the plaintiff, or some person duly authorized by him, must come and receive possession: Dalton's Sheriff, 257; Watson's Sheriff, 322: and he must, at his peril, point out to the sheriff the property recovered, and whereof possession is to be given under the writ: *per* Lord Mansfield, C. J., in *Cottingham* v. *King,* 1 Burr. 629; *Connor* v. *West,* 5 Burr. 2673; *Doe* d. *Drapers' Company* v. *Wilson,* 2 Stark. R. 477, Abbott, C. J.; Watson's Sheriff, 319: otherwise the sheriff may make a return that he was always ready and willing to execute the writ, but no person came to point out the lands. *Floyd* v. *Bethell,* Roll. Abr. Retorn (H.); Dalton's Sheriff, 256, 257; Watson's Sheriff, 322, 346; *see the form, Appendix, No.* 282.

If necessary, the officer may break open any outer or inner door, to enable him to execute the writ. *Semayne's case,* 5 Co. R. 91 b (2nd Resolution); 1 Smith, L. C. 39, 40; Dalton's Sheriff, 256; Watson's Sheriff, 75, 318. He may also raise the *posse comitatus.* Dalton's Sheriff, chap. 95; Watson's Sheriff, 318, 322. But he should not do this unless resistance be first shown. 2 Inst. 454; Watson's Sheriff, 73.

The sheriff should remove the several tenants in possession and their respective families and servants, and also their goods, from each messuage and each parcel of land, and deliver possession thereof to the plaintiff, or his attorney or agent. 1 Roll. Abr. Execution (H.), 2; Watson's Sheriff, 318. But if several tenements or parcels of land be in the possession of one defendant, it seems that a delivery of any one of them in the name of the whole is sufficient in law, if the plaintiff be therewith satisfied. *Floyd* v. *Bethell*, 1 Roll. R. 420, *per* Haughton, J.; Watson's Sheriff, 318; Ad. Eject. 301; Dalton's Sheriff, 256; 10 Vin. Abr. 539. If the *habere facias possessionem* be only *partly* executed, then upon a return to that effect made by the sheriff, an *alias habere facias possessionem* may issue for the residue. 2 Chit. Arch. 981 (9th ed.).

It seems that the claimant is entitled to *all the fixtures* annexed to the land at the time the writ is executed, because while so annexed they constitute part of the land. *Minshull* v. *Lloyd*, 2 M. & W. 450; *Weeton* v. *Woodcock*, 7 M. & W. 14; *Roffey* v. *Henderson*, 17 Q. B. 574. The tenant is entitled to remove them only *during his term*, or within a reasonable time after the expiration thereof, if he were tenant for life or at will. Amos and Ferard on Fixtures, 94, 107 (2nd ed.); *Heap* v. *Barton*, 12 C. B. 274. A defendant, who has *confessed* an ejectment, cannot afterwards remove any fixtures. *Fitzherbert* v. *Shaw*, 1 H. Blac. 258; *Heap* v. *Barton*, *supra*. The defendant in an ejectment is considered as a trespasser, and not as a tenant, from the day on which possession is claimed in the writ of ejectment. *Ante*, 82. Consequently he has no right to remove any fixtures *after that day*, his term having expired or been duly determined, and such reasonable time as he may have been entitled to as above mentioned (if any) having elapsed.

The plaintiff is entitled to the crops growing on the land when the *habere facias possessionem* is executed, notwithstanding they may have been previously seized by the sheriff under a *fieri facias* at the suit of a third person. *Hodgson* v. *Gascoigne*, 5 B. & A. 88. So with respect to crops severed after the day on which possession was claimed in the writ of ejectment. *Doe* d. *Upton* v. *Witherwick*, 3 Bing. 11; 10 Moore, 267. The sheriff has no right, on executing a writ of possession, to allow a year's rent under 8 Ann. c. 14, that statute contemplating an existing tenancy. *Hodgson* v. *Gascoigne, supra.*

A. having taken possession of land belonging to B., dug chalk from the soil, and converted it into lime. B. recovered judgment in ejectment against A., and upon execution of the writ of possession turned A.'s servants off the premises, refusing at the same time to allow them to remove the lime remaining on the premises. Upon trover for the lime: held, that these facts did not necessarily amount to a conversion. *Thoroughgood* v. *Robinson*, 14 Law J., N. S., Q. B., 87. But *semble*, that by the change of the chalk into lime the property in it vested in A. *Id., per* Lord Denman, C. J.

The mode of executing the writ of possession when the claimant recovers the entirety of any land, &c., is different from what it is when he recovers an *undivided portion* only. In the one case it is the duty of the sheriff to put the plaintiff in possession of the land, &c., by turning out all persons there; but in the other case, the duty of the sheriff is not to turn out the persons in possession, but only to put the plaintiff into possession of the particular portion to which he is entitled. *Per* Parke, B., in *Doe* d. *Hellyer* v. *King*, 6 Exch. 793, citing 2 Tidd's Prac. 1246; *Roe* d. *Saul* v. *Dawson*, 3 Wils. 49. Where five undivided eighth parts or shares are recovered, the sheriff should not set out and deliver five-eighths by metes and bounds. *Molineux* v. *Fulgam*, Palm. 289.

If there be any public highway, or private way, or other easement, over the land, the sheriff may deliver possession of the land, subject and without prejudice to such way or easement. *Goodtitle* d. *Chester* v. *Alker*, 1 Burr. 133, 137, 145. If the defendant have an easement upon the land recovered, the sheriff should deliver possession in such manner as not unnecessarily to interfere with such easement; otherwise relief may be obtained upon application to the court, or to a judge at chambers. *Doe* d. *The Queen and Finch* v. *Archbishop of York*, 14 Q. B. 81, 109.

If the sheriff deliver to the plaintiff more or other property than was actually recovered by the judgment, the court, or a judge at chambers, will, upon a summary application, supported by proper affidavits, order the plaintiff to make restitution of the excess. *Roe* d. *Saul* v. *Dawson*, 3 Wils. 49, cited 6 Exch. 794; Watson's Sheriff, 319. But the sheriff should not be ordered to cause such restitution to be made. *Doe* d. *Williams* v. *Williams*, 2 A. & E. 381; 4 N. & M. 259. An order to restore possession cannot be made upon any third person in possession, not being a party to the suit; it must mention *who* is to restore the possession; otherwise it cannot be enforced by attachment. *Doe* d. *Lewis* v. *Ellis*, 9 Dowl. 944.

Upon an *habere facias possessionem* the execution is not complete until the sheriff, or his bailiff, has delivered possession to the plaintiff and is gone. *Kingsdale* v. *Mann*, 6 Mod. 27; 1 Salk. 321; *Anon.*, 6 Mod. 115, *per* Holt, C. J.; *Molineux* v. *Fulgam*, Palm. 289; Watson's Sheriff, 318. If the sheriff give possession of part only, and make a return to that effect, the plaintiff may have an *alias habere facias possessionem* for the residue. *Devereux* v. *Underhill*, 2 Keb. 245; 2 Chit. Arch. 981 (9th ed.).

As a general rule, when once the sheriff has executed a writ of *habere facias possessionem*, and put the plaintiff into full and peaceable possession, no new writ can issue, whether the sheriff has or has not made any return to the writ. *Doe* d. *Pate* v. *Roe*, 1 Taunt. 55. But where the execution of the writ is, in effect, defeated by the defendant's misconduct, the writ may sometimes be considered as not having been executed. Thus, if the defendant re-enter and forcibly eject the plaintiff, immediately after possession has been delivered to him by the sheriff, and before any return has been made to the writ, the sheriff may again deliver possession to the plaintiff under and by virtue of the writ; *Molineux* v. *Fulgam*, Palm. 289; Watson's Sheriff, 318; or, under such circumstances, the court will order a new writ of possession to issue. *Pierson* v. *Tavernor*, 1 Roll. R. 353; *Kingsdale* v. *Mann*, 6 Mod. 27; 1 Salk. 321; *Devereux* v. *Underhill*, 2 Keb. 245; *Doe* d. *Pitcher* v. *Roe*, 9 Dowl. 971. The court will also grant an attachment against the defendant for his contempt in disturbing the execution of the writ. *Kingsdale* v. *Mann*, *supra*; *Style's case*, 2 Brownlow, 216; *Gallop's case*, *Id.* 253; *Upton and Well's case*, Leon. 145; or, instead of an attachment, will order him to pay the costs of and incident to the application for the new writ. *Doe* d. *Pitcher* v. *Roe*, 9 Dowl. 971. In a recent case, where a *few days* had elapsed after possession was delivered by the sheriff, and before it was forcibly retaken by the defendant, and the writ had not been returned, the court granted a rule *nisi* for a fresh writ of possession, or for the defendant to restore possession of the premises to the plaintiff; *Doe* d. *Lloyd* v. *Roe*, 2 Dowl. N. S. 407; with costs. *Doe* d. *Pitcher* v. *Roe*, 9 Dowl. 971. In an old case, where possession was delivered by the sheriff about 9 a.m., and towards 6 p.m. the plaintiff was forcibly turned out of possession, the court doubted whether, after so many hours distance, it could be looked . upon as a disturbance of execution. But they granted a rule nisi for an attachment. *Kingsdale* v. *Mann*, 6 Mod. 27. In an *ejectione firmæ* by *Upton* against *Wells*, judgment was given for the plaintiff, and upon the *habere facias possessionem* the sheriff returned, that in the execution of the said writ he took the plaintiff with him, and came to the house, recovered and removed thereout a woman and two children, which were all the persons which, upon diligent search, he could find in the said house, and delivered to the plaintiff peaceable possession to his thinking, and afterwards departed ; and immediately after three other persons, which were secretly lodged in the said house, expulsed the plaintiff again ; upon notice of which he returned again to the said house to put the plaintiff in full possession, but the others did resist him, so as without peril of his life, and of them that were with him in company, he could not do it. And upon this return the court awarded a new writ of execution, for that the same was no execution of the first writ, and also awarded an attachment against the parties. *Upton and Wells' case*, Leon. 145.

When a stranger forcibly turns the plaintiff out of possession after a writ of possession fully executed the plaintiff is put to another action, or to an indictment for a forcible entry. *Fortune* v. *Johnson*, Styles, 318, 408 ; *Doe* d. *Thompson* v. *Mirehouse*, 2 Dowl. 200. For the stranger may have a good title to possession, which is not affected by the judgment or execution. Bac. Abr. Eject. (G.) 3 ; Watson's Sheriff, 321. Upon an application for a fresh writ of possession it is indispensably necessary to connect the defendant with the dispossession of the plaintiff after the execution of the first writ. *Doe* d. *Thompson* v. *Mirehouse*, 2 Dowl. 200, Taunton, J.

Sheriff's return to Writ of Possession.]—A writ of *habere facias possessionem* may be returned by the sheriff if the plaintiff so require. *See the forms, Appendix, Nos.* 282—285. It is optional with the plaintiff to have it returned or not ; and, generally, it is unnecessary to have any return made. *Molineux* v. *Fulgam*, Palm. 289 ; *Devereux* v. *Underhill*, 2 Keb. 245 ; Watson's Sheriff, 321. But the plaintiff cannot, by omitting to call upon the sheriff to make his return to the writ, retain the right to sue out a new *habere facias possessionem* for a long period after possession has been delivered to him. *Doe* d. *Pate* v. *Roe*, 1 Taunt. 55. "If it could, the plaintiff, by omitting to call on the sheriff to make his return to the writ, might retain the right of suing out a new *habere facias possessionem* as a remedy for any trespass which the same tenant might commit within twenty years next after the date of the judgment." *Id. per cur.* Sometimes the award of the writ and the sheriff's return are entered on the roll. *See the form, Appendix, No.* 286. After a return has been made, stating that the sheriff has delivered possession to the plaintiff, no new writ of possession can issue. *Molineux* v. *Fulgam, supra ; Kingsdale* v. *Mann*, 6 Mod. 27 ; 1 Salk. 321.

Where, immediately after a writ of possession had been executed and returned, the defendant re-entered and ousted the plaintiff, an attachment was awarded upon affidavit; and it seems that if the writ had not been returned a new writ would have been awarded. *Gallop's case,* 2 Brownl. 253. But where the defendant entered and ousted the plaintiff a fortnight after the sheriff had put him in possession under a writ of *habere facias possessionem,* which writ had been returned by the sheriff, but not filed : held, that the plaintiff was not entitled to a new writ of possession, but was put to a fresh action. *Style's case,* 2 Brownl. 216; and see *Goodright* v. *Hart,* 2 Stra. 830.

Sheriff's Poundage.]—Upon executing a writ of possession the sheriff is entitled to certain fees: also to a poundage of 12*d.* in every 20*s.* of the yearly value of the property delivered under the writ. But if such yearly value exceed 100*l.* he is entitled only to 5*l.*, and 6*d.* in every 20*s.* of the yearly value beyond 100*l.* 3 Geo. 1, c. 15, s. 16; 2 Chit. Arch. 981 (9th ed.).

Writ of Restitution.]—If, after a writ of *habere facias possessionem* has been executed, the judgment be reversed for error, or set aside for irregularity, the court may award a writ of restitution. 2 Lil. Prac. Reg. 472, 474; *Doe* d. *Stratford* v. *Shail,* 2 Dowl. & L. 161. *See the forms,* 2 Lil. Entr. 635, *post, Appendix, No.* 290; Tidd's App. 587, 690 (8th ed.). Or, in the latter case, the court may order the claimant to restore the possession ; *Doe* d. *Stevens* v. *Lord,* 7 A. & E. 610; 2 N. & P. 605; 6 Dowl. 256; and in case of disobedience may award an attachment. *Anon.,* 2 Salk. 588; *Corbett* d. *Clymer* v. *Nicholls,* 2 Low. M. & P. 87. If the claimant abscond, so that an attachment is unavailing, the court may award a writ of restitution. *Goodright* d. *Russell* v. *Noright,* Barnes' Notes, 178 ; *Whittington* d. *Whittington* v. *Hards,* 20 Law J., N. S., Q. B., 406 ; 15 Jur. 771. So where the claimant refuses or fails to restore possession when ordered to do so, after the judgment has been reversed or set aside. *Doe* d. *Stratford* v. *Shail,* 2 Dowl. & L. 161.

CHAPTER XXXII.

SUGGESTIONS OF DEATHS, ETC.

—

—

THE death of all or any of the claimants, or of all or any of the defendants, before verdict, or before final judgment and execution, would of course more or less affect the action, and create difficulties which it was proper and necessary to provide against. Accordingly, the stat. 15 & 16 Vict. c. 76, contains a series of enactments for that purpose, ss. 190 to 199.

By sect. 190, "the death of a claimant or defendant shall not cause the action to abate, but it may be continued as hereinafter mentioned."

By sect. 191, "in case the right of the deceased claimant *shall survive to another claimant*, a suggestion may be made of the death, which suggestion shall not be traversable, but shall only be subject to be set aside if untrue, and the action may proceed at the suit of the surviving claimant; and if such a suggestion shall be made before the trial, then the claimant shall have a verdict and recover such judgment as aforesaid, upon its appearing that he was entitled to bring the action either separately or jointly with the deceased claimant."

A suggestion may be made under this section, either before or after verdict. *See the form, Appendix, No.* 292. It may be made without any leave of the court or a judge, and need not be verified by affidavit. It should be drawn by the claimant's attorney, and (if necessary) settled by counsel or a special pleader. Then a fair copy should be made on draft paper, and delivered to the defendant's attorney or agent. If it be untrue, an affidavit to that effect should be made by or on behalf of the defendant. *See the form, Appendix, No.* 293. And thereupon a summons should be taken out to set aside the suggestion with costs. *See forms of Summons and Order, Appendix, Nos.* 294, 295. If no such order be obtained, the suggestion, if made before the trial, should be entered on the record of nisi prius and subsequent proceedings: if made after trial, it should be entered on the judgment roll prior to the entry of the final judgment. In either case, the name of the court and cause should be omitted in such entry.

By sect. 192, "in case of the death *before trial* of one of several claimants, *whose right does not survive to another or others of the claimants*, where the legal representative of the deceased claimant shall not become a party to the suit in the manner hereinafter mentioned [s. 194, *post*, 352], a suggestion may be made of the death, which suggestion shall not be traversable, but shall only be subject to be set aside if untrue, and the action may proceed at the suit of the surviving claimant for such share of the property as he is entitled to, and costs."

A suggestion under this section can be made only *before trial. See the form, Appendix, No.* 296. It seems unnecessary to mention *in the suggestion* the special circumstances mentioned in the commencement of this section. The suggestion is to be made "of the death." If the special circumstances do not exist, the suggestion may be set aside as irregular: so if the suggestion be untrue. The mode of proceeding under this section is similar to that under sect. 191. *Ante,* 350.

By sect. 193, "in case of a *verdict for two or more claimants, if one of such claimants die before execution executed,* the other claimant may, whether the legal right to the property shall survive or not, suggest the death in manner aforesaid, and proceed to judgment and execution for recovery of possession of the entirety of the property and the costs; but nothing herein contained shall affect the right of the legal representative of the deceased claimant, or the liability of the surviving claimant to such legal representative, and the entry and possession of such surviving claimant under such execution shall be considered as an entry and possession on behalf of such legal representative in respect of the share of the property to which he shall be entitled as such representative, and the court may direct possession to be delivered accordingly."

A suggestion under this section can be made only *after verdict. See the form, Appendix, No.* 297. The mode of proceeding is similar to that under sect. 191, after trial. *Ante,* 350. The suggestion, when entered on the roll, will warrant a judgment and execution for the surviving claimants in their own names for the whole of the property recovered by the verdict. *See form of Judgment, Appendix, No.* 298.

After possession has been obtained under such judgment and execution, the "legal representative" of the deceased claimant may (if necessary), by a summary application, supported by a proper affidavit, obtain a rule or order for possession of his share of the property. (*Supra.*) The affidavit must show all the proceedings in the ejectment, including the suggestion as entered on the roll; also the applicant's title to a specific part or share of the property recovered, as the legal representative of the deceased claimant, with respect to such share; also any application for possession of such part made to the surviving claimant or his attorney, and the refusal or neglect to comply with such application. If the party claim as a legatee of leaseholds, the assent of the executors to the bequest should be stated in the affidavit; and the rule nisi should give *them* an opportunity of showing cause against the application.

By sect. 194, " In case of the *death of a sole claimant, or, before trial, of one of several claimants, whose right does not survive to another or others of the claimants,* the legal representative of such claimant may, *by leave of the court or a judge,* enter a suggestion of the death, and that he is such legal representative, and the action shall thereupon proceed; and if such suggestion be made before the trial, the truth of the suggestion shall be tried thereat, together with the title of the deceased claimant, and such judgment shall follow upon the verdict in favour of or against the person making such suggestion, as hereinbefore provided, with reference to a judgment for or against such claimant; and in case such suggestion in the case of a sole claimant be made after trial and before execution executed by delivery of possession thereupon, and such suggestion be denied by the defendant within eight days after notice thereof, or such further time as the court or a judge may allow, then such suggestion shall be tried; and if, upon the trial thereof, a verdict shall pass for the person making such suggestion, he shall be entitled to such judgment as aforesaid for the recovery of possession, and for the costs of and occasioned by such suggestion; and in case of a verdict for the defendant, such defendant shall be entitled to such judgment as aforesaid for costs."

Before this act, the death of a sole lessor of the plaintiff did not abate the action, which might be continued in the name of the nominal plaintiff, John Doe. But security for costs would be ordered. *Doe* d. *Earl of Egremont* v. *Stephens,* 2 Dowl. & L. 993. And if the lessor were only tenant for life, the possession of the property could not be recovered in that action, but only damages and costs. *Thrustout* d. *Turner* v. *Grey,* 2 Stra. 1056; and see *Doe* d. *Cozens* v. *Cozens,* 1 Q. B. 426; 9 Dowl. 1040; 2 Wms. Saund. 72, note (*n*).

A suggestion under this section can be made only by the "legal representative" of the deceased claimant, *i. e.,* by the person legally entitled to the property, as heir, executor, administrator, devisee or otherwise. It may be made before or after trial. *See the form, Appendix, Nos.* 302, 303. It cannot be made without previous leave of the court or a judge; to obtain which, a proper affidavit must be made, showing the proceedings in the action, the death of the claimant, and the applicant's title as legal representative of the deceased claimant with respect to the property in question. *See the form, Appendix, No.* 299. Upon such affidavit an application may be made to the court or a judge for leave to enter the suggestion: only a rule nisi or summons will be granted in the first instance. *See the forms, Appendix, Nos.* 300, 301. It must be served and afterwards heard and disposed of in the usual manner. When the order or rule absolute has been obtained, the suggestion may be prepared and delivered (*as ante,* 350), with a copy of the rule or order annexed.

If the suggestion be made before the trial, the truth of it will be tried thereat, together with the title of the deceased claimant. (*Supra.*) No traverse is necessary in such case. If the jury find the suggestion to be untrue, or that the deceased claimant was not entitled to possession, as alleged in the writ, it seems that the defendant is entitled to costs, and the party making the suggestion is not entitled to any costs. Gray on Costs, 198.

If the suggestion be made after the trial, it may be denied by the defendant *within eight days* after notice thereof, or such further time as the court or a judge may allow. *Ante*, 352. If the suggestion be not traversed within the time allowed, it will be considered as admitted, and the substituted plaintiff may thereupon proceed to sign judgment and sue out execution in his own name.

The traverse should be prepared by the defendant's attorney, and (if necessary) settled by counsel or a pleader. *See the form, Appendix, No.* 304. It should be indorsed with a notice requiring the plaintiff to reply within four days, otherwise judgment. If necessary, the plaintiff may obtain further time to reply upon a judge's summons and order. Within the time allowed the plaintiff must either demur or join issue upon the traverse, and afterwards proceed to a hearing or trial, as in other cases. The costs will abide the result. *Ante*, 352.

By sect. 195, " in case of the death before or after judgment of one of several defendants in ejectment, *who defend jointly*, a suggestion may be made of the death, which suggestion shall not be traversable, but only be subject to be set aside if untrue, and the action may proceed against the surviving defendant to judgment and execution."

According to the previous law, if one of several defendants died after issue joined, and before trial, his death might be suggested on the roll. *Far* v. *Denn*, 1 Burr. 363; 8 & 9 Will. 3, c. 11, s. 7. But if the lessor proceeded to trial, without entering a suggestion of the death, and obtained a verdict against all the defendants, it was erroneous; because there could be no verdict or judgment against a person not in being; Gilb. Eject. 98; Ad. Eject. 291. In ejectment against husband and wife, where the husband died after verdict, his death might be suggested, and thereupon the plaintiffs were entitled to judgment and execution against the wife. *Rigley* v. *Lee*, Cro. Jac. 356; *Lee* v. *Rewkeley*, 1 Roll. 14.

A suggestion may be made under this section either before or after judgment. *See the form, Appendix, No.* 305. The mode of proceeding on it, and to set it aside if untrue, is the same as under sect. 191. *Ante*, 350. If no order be obtained to set it aside, the subsequent proceedings will be against the surviving defendants only.

By sect. 196, " in case of the death of a *sole defendant, or of all the defendants* in ejectment, *before trial*, a suggestion may be made of the death, which suggestion shall not be traversable, but only be subject to set aside if untrue; and the claimants shall be entitled to judgment for recovery of possession of the property, unless some other person shall appear and defend within the time to be appointed for that purpose by the order of the court or a judge, to be made upon the application of the claimants; and it shall be lawful for the court or a judge, upon such suggestion being made, and upon such application as aforesaid, to order that the claimants shall be at liberty to sign judgment within such time as the court or judge may think fit, unless the person then in possession by himself or his tenant, or the legal representative of the deceased defendant, shall within such time appear and defend the action; and such order may be served in the same manner as the writ; and in case such person shall appear and defend the same, proceedings may be taken against such new defendant as if he had originally appeared and defended the action; and if no appearance be entered and defence made, then the claimant shall be at liberty to sign judgment pursuant to the order."

A suggestion under this section can be made only *before trial. See the form, Appendix, No.* 306. It is not clear to whom the suggestion should be delivered; whether to the attorney or agent for the late defendant, or to his legal representative, or to the tenant in possession, or whether it should be stuck up in the master's office. After the suggestion has been properly delivered an application may be made to the court or a judge for a rule or order that the claimants shall be at liberty to sign judgment within a time to be fixed by the court or judge, unless the person then in possession by himself or his tenant, or the legal representative of the deceased defendant, shall within such time appear and defend the action. *See forms of Rule and Order, Appendix, Nos.* 308, 309. The application for such rule or order should be supported by a proper affidavit showing the proceedings in the ejectment, the death of the defendant (or of all the defendants), and who is his legal representative, and who is or are in possession of the property claimed; also the suggestion, &c. *See the form, Appendix, No.* 307.

The rule or order may be served in the same manner as a writ in ejectment. Sect. 196; *ante*, Chap. X. It is, in fact, a sort of substitute for a new writ; and the advantage of it is, that the previous costs of the action are not wasted; besides which, the action will be deemed to have been commenced when the writ issued, whereas a fresh action might in some cases be too late.

If no appearance be entered within the time allowed by the rule or order, the claimant may sign judgment pursuant to the rule or order. Sect. 196. But he must file an affidavit of personal service of the rule or order, or obtain a further order of a judge for leave to proceed as if the rule or order had been personally served. *Ante,* 98.

The person named in the rule or order may enter an appearance in like manner as any other defendant named in a writ. *Ante,* 122. After which the plaintiff will not be permitted to discontinue his action without payment of *all* the costs of the cause; at least this is so in personal actions under sect. 138. *Benge* v. *Swaine, Administratrix, &c.,* 15 C. B. 784.

By sect. 197, "in case of the *death of a sole defendant, or of all the defendants* in ejectment *after verdict,* the claimants shall nevertheless be entitled to judgment as if no such death had taken place; and to proceed by execution for recovery of possession *without suggestion or revivor;* and to proceed for the recovery of the costs, in like manner as upon any other judgment for money against the legal representatives of the deceased defendant or defendants."

According to the previous law, when a sole defendant died after the commencement of the assizes and before verdict, or after verdict and before judgment, it did not abate the suit; nor could his death be alleged for error, provided the judgment was entered within two terms after the verdict. 17 Car. 2, c. 8.

In cases falling within this section the claimants may sign judgment in the same form and manner as if the defendant or defendants were alive, viz. for the recovery of the property according to the verdict, "with £.—— for costs." *See the form, Appendix, No.* 265. They may also, without any suggestion or revivor, sue out and execute a writ of *habere facias possessionem* in the usual manner. *See the form, Appendix, No.* 270. But to enforce the payment of the costs (if necessary), they must obtain leave to enter a suggestion against the executors or administrators of the defendant, and enter it accordingly, or sue out a writ of revivor pursuant to 15 & 16 Vict. c. 76, ss. 129, 130, 131. The necessary forms are given in those sections.

By sect. 198, "in case of the death before trial of one of several defendants in ejectment, who defends separately for a portion of the property *for which the other defendant or defendants do not defend,* the same proceedings may be taken as to such portion as in the case of the death of a sole defendant, *or* the claimants may proceed against the surviving defendants in respect of the portion of the property for which they defend."

It seems that in cases falling within this section the claimants must *elect* to proceed either for that portion of the property for which the deceased defendant defended separately; or against the surviving defendants for the residue of the property.

In the former case the proceedings will be similar to those under sect. 196. *Ante,* 354 ; *see form of Suggestion, Appendix, No.* 310. But it is difficult to say whether the plaintiff is liable to the other defendants for their costs of suit : he may be perfectly willing to proceed against them for the residue of the property claimed, but unable to do so, because of the manner in which this clause is worded.

If the claimant elect to proceed against the surviving defendants for the residue of the property, he should enter a suggestion of the death in the same manner as under sect. 191. *Ante,* 350.

By sect. 199, "in case of the death before trial of one of several defendants in ejectment, who defends separately in respect of property *for which surviving defendants also defend,* it shall be lawful for the court or a judge, at any time before the trial, to allow the person at the time of the death in possession of the property, or the legal representative of the deceased defendant, to appear and defend on such terms as may appear reasonable and just, upon the application of such person or representative ; and if no such application be made or leave granted, the claimant, suggesting the death in manner aforesaid, may proceed against the surviving defendant or defendants to judgment and execution."

An application under this section must be supported by a proper affidavit, showing that the party applying is entitled to make such application. *See the form, Appendix, Nos.* 312, 313. Thereupon a rule nisi or summons may be obtained. *See the forms, Appendix, Nos.* 314, 316. It must be served and heard and disposed of in the usual manner. *See forms of Order and Rule Absolute, Appendix, Nos.* 315, 317. The court or judge may impose "such terms as may appear reasonable and just." Sect. 199. Upon a rule or order being obtained the party should enter an appearance (*ante,* 122) ; and, if necessary, give notice to defend for part only (*ante,* 128), pursuant to the rule or order. Such appearance and notice must be entered on the record of nisi prius and subsequent proceedings in the usual manner. *Appendix, No.* 318.

If no such application be made, or leave granted, the claimant should suggest the defendant's death in like manner as under sect. 195 ; *ante,* 353 ; *see the form, Appendix, No.* 305 ; and proceed against the surviving defendant or defendants to judgment and execution. Sect. 199.

By the Common Law Procedure Act, 1854 (17 & 18 Vict. c. 125), s. 92, "where an action would, but for the provisions of ' The Common

Law Procedure Act, 1852,' have abated by reason of the death of either party, and·in which the proceedings may be revived and continued under that act, the defendant or person against whom the action may be so continued may *apply by summons* to compel the plaintiff, or person entitled to proceed with the action in the room of the plaintiff, to proceed according to the provisions of the said act within such time as the judge shall order ; and in default of such proceeding the defendant or other person against whom the action may be so continued as aforesaid shall be entitled to enter a suggestion of such default, and of the representative character of the person by or against whom the action may be proceeded with, as the case may be, and to have judgment for the costs of the action and suggestion against the plaintiff, or against the person entitled to proceed in his room, as the case may be, and in the latter case to be levied of the goods of the testator or intestate."

An application under this section must be made to a judge at chambers—not to the court. *See form of Summons, Appendix, Nos.* 319, 323. An affidavit in support of such application will generally be necessary, except when the facts are not disputed, and the party called on to show cause appears before the judge. Such affidavit must show all the facts necessary to bring the case within this section. It may easily be framed with reference to forms in Appendix, Nos. 299, 307.

Upon the hearing of the application the judge will *fix the time* within which the suggestion is to be made, and also within what time the claimant or his representative shall proceed to trial. *See form of Order, Appendix, No.* 320. A copy should be served on the opposite party or his attorney in the usual manner.

Within the time limited by the order the claimant or surviving claimant, or representative of the deceased claimant (as the case may be) should make a suggestion. *See the forms, Appendix, Nos.* 302, 303. In case of any default, the defendants may thereupon deliver a suggestion of such default. *See the forms, Appendix, Nos.* 321, 325. After which (without obtaining any further order) they may sign judgment, *see the forms, Appendix, Nos.* 322, 326, and proceed to tax their costs.

CHAPTER XXXIII.

DISCONTINUANCE OF ACTION, AND CONFESSION OF ACTION.

Discontinuance of Action.]—By 15 & 16 Vict. c. 76, s. 200, "the claimant in ejectment shall be at liberty *at any time* to discontinue the action as to one or more of the defendants by giving to the defendant or his attorney a notice headed in the court and cause, and signed by the claimant or his attorney, stating that he discontinues such action [*see the form, Appendix, No.* 327]; and thereupon the defendant, to whom such notice is given, shall be entitled to and may forthwith sign judgment for costs in the form contained in the Schedule (A) to this act annexed, marked No. 18, or to the like effect." *Form, Appendix, No.* 328.

Before the above enactment the claimant might have entered a *nolle prosequi* as against one of several defendants, who defended jointly, and have proceeded to trial as against the others; and such *nolle prosequi* might have been entered and recorded at nisi prius. *Gree* v. *Rolle and Newell,* 1 Ld. Raym. 716.

In personal actions a rule to discontinue is a proceeding in a cause, and may be set aside if obtained during a stay of proceedings. *Murray* v. *Silver,* 1 C. B. 638; 3 Dowl. & L. 26.

By sect. 201, "in case one of several claimants shall be desirous to discontinue, he may apply to the court or a judge to have his name struck out of the proceedings, and an order may be made thereupon upon such terms as to the court or judge may seem fit, and the action shall thereupon proceed at the suit of the other claimants."

A *sole* claimant may discontinue as a matter of course. *Supra.* But *one of several* claimants cannot do so without leave of the court or a judge. The reason for this is obvious. The legal estate may be vested in such claimant as a mere trustee for the others who may be entitled to use his name, and may have offered him before action an indemnity as to costs; whereas he may be colluding with the defendants to defeat the action contrary to substantial justice and equity. This of course the court or a judge would not permit to be done. *Ante,* 94.

The application should be supported by a proper affidavit showing under what circumstances and for what reason the applicant wishes to have his name struck out of the proceedings; and whether his name was used with or without his consent; and in the latter case whether any and what indemnity was offered to him before the commencement of the action; and if so, why he refused it, and would not consent to his name being used (or as the case may be). *See the form, Appendix, No.* 329.

Upon such affidavit a summons or rule nisi may be obtained. *See the form, Appendix, No.* 330. It should be served not only on the plaintiff's attorney, but also upon the defendants who have appeared, or their respective attorneys. It may be met by counter affidavits, showing the right of the other claimants to use the applicant's name as their trustee or otherwise; and (if the fact be so) that an indemnity against costs was offered before the commencement of the action.

Upon hearing the application the court or judge will make such rule or order as to them or him "may seem fit." *Ante,* 357; *see form of Order, Appendix, No.* 331. Frequently an order for an indemnity against the costs of the action will be sufficient. *Doe* d. *Vine* v. *Figgins,* 3 Taunt. 440; *Doe* d. *Prosser* v. *King,* 2 Dowl. 580; *Spicer* v. *Todd,* 2 Cr. & Jer. 165; *see forms of Order and Bond of Indemnity, Appendix, Nos.* 332, 333. The costs of the application should generally be granted to the applicant if his name has been used without his consent, unless an indemnity against costs was offered to him before action; but not when he has improperly refused to permit his name to be used.

If an order be made to strike out the applicant's name, it must be struck out accordingly, and the action shall thereupon proceed at the suit of the other claimants. *Ante,* 357. If their title be such that they cannot maintain the action, they (being then the sole claimants) may *discontinue it* pursuant to sect. 200. *Ante,* 357. And afterwards resort to a court of equity, or adopt such other proceedings as they may be advised, or deem expedient.

Discontinuance by not proceeding to Trial.]—This has been already considered. *Ante,* 186.

Confession of Action.]—By 15 & 16 Vict. c. 76, s. 203, "a sole defendant or all the defendants in ejectment shall be at liberty to confess the action, as to the whole or part of the property, by giving to such claimant a notice headed in the court and cause, and signed by the defendant or defendants, such signature to be attested by his or their attorney [*form, Appendix, No.* 334]; and thereupon the claimant shall be entitled to and may forthwith sign judgment, and issue execution for the recovery of possession and costs in the form contained in the Schedule (A) to this act annexed, marked No. 20, or to the like effect." *Form, Appendix, No.* 335.

After confessing the action, the defendant cannot lawfully remove any buildings or tenant's fixtures annexed to the premises. *Fitzherbert* v. *Shaw,* 1 H. Black. 258; *Heap* v. *Barton,* 12 C. B. 274.

By sect. 204, "in case one of several defendants in ejectment, who defends separately for a portion of the property *for which the other defendant or defendants do not defend* shall be desirous of confessing the claimant's title to such portion, he may give a like notice to the claimant [*form, Appendix, No. 336*]; and thereupon the claimant shall be entitled to and may forthwith sign judgment and issue execution for the recovery of possession of such portion of the property, and for the costs occasioned by the defence relating to the same [*form, Appendix, No. 337*]; and the action may proceed as to the residue."

By sect. 205, "in case one of several defendants in ejectment, who defends separately in respect of property *for which other defendants also defend*, shall be desirous of confessing the claimant's title, he may give a like notice thereof [*form, Appendix, No. 338*]; and thereupon the claimant shall be entitled to and may sign judgment against such defendant for the costs occasioned by his defence [*form, Appendix, No. 339*], and may proceed in the action against the other defendants to judgment and execution."

Warrant of Attorney.]—Formerly a warrant of attorney might have been given to appear to an ejectment and confess it or suffer judgment by default, whereupon judgment might have been entered up. *Doe* d. *Kingston* v. *Kingston*, 1 Dowl. N. S. 263; *Doe* d. *Beaumont* v. *Beaumont*, 2 *Id.* 972. But that seems impracticable in the new form of proceeding. 2 Chit. Arch. 990 (9th ed.).

CHAPTER XXXIV.

PROCEEDINGS IN ERROR.

---

1. *Error in Law.*]—By 15 & 16 Vict. c. 76, s. 208, "error may be brought in like manner as in other actions upon any judgment in ejectment, *after a special verdict* found by the jury, or a *bill of exceptions*, or *by consent after a special case stated;* but, except in the case of such consent as aforesaid, execution shall not be thereby stayed, unless the plaintiff in error shall, within four clear days after lodging the memorandum alleging error, or after the signing of the judgment, whichever shall last happen, or before execution executed, be bound unto the claimant, who shall have recovered judgment in such action of ejectment, in *double the yearly value* of the property, and *double the costs* recovered by the judgment, with condition, that if the judgment shall be affirmed by the court of error, or the proceedings in error be discontinued by the plaintiff therein, then the plaintiff in error shall pay such costs, damages, and sum or sums of money as shall be awarded upon or after such judgment affirmed or discontinuance; and it shall be lawful for the court wherein execution ought to be granted upon such affirmation or discontinuance, upon the application of the claimant, to issue a writ to inquire as well of the mesne profits as of the damage by any waste committed after the first judgment in ejectment, which writ may be tested on the day on which it shall issue, and be returnable immediately after the execution thereof; and upon the return thereof judgment shall be given, and execution awarded, for such mesne profits and damages, and also for costs of suit."

This section is in substance a re-enactment of the 16 & 17 Car. 2, c. 8, ss. 3, 4, whereby it was enacted, that no execution should be stayed by writ of error upon any judgment after verdict in ejectment, unless the plaintiff in error became bound in a reasonable sum to pay the plaintiff in ejectment all such costs, damages and sums of money as should be awarded to such plaintiff, upon judgment being affirmed, or on a nonsuit, or discontinuance had; and that in case of affirmance, discontinuance or nonsuit, the court might issue a writ to inquire, as well of the mesne profits, as of the damages of any waste committed after the first judgment; and upon the return thereof give judgment and award execution for the same, and also for costs of suit.

R

The sum in which the recognizance was taken under that statute was "double the yearly value and double the costs." Reg. H. T. 2 Will. 4, No. 27 (now repealed). The clerk of the errors usually ascertained the yearly value by the yearly rent. *Doe* d. *Webb* v. *Goundry*, 7 Taunt. 427. The plaintiff in error was not required to find any bail, but only to enter into his own recognizance. *S. C.* No notice of the intention to enter into such recognizance, nor of its having been filed, was necessary : it was the duty of the defendant in error to search for the recognizance before suing out execution. *S. C.* If the plaintiff in error could not enter into such recognizance, being an infant or married woman, or abroad, bail in error might be put in and justified, in lieu of such recognizance. *Keene* d. *Lord Byron* v. *Deardon*, 8 East, 298. Where bail were so put in, they might be examined as to their sufficiency, but the plaintiff in error could not. *S. C.* If the plaintiff, after obtaining a verdict in ejectment, sued out a writ of *habere facias possessionem*, without waiting to tax his costs, the defendant's writ of error would not operate as a supersedeas, because the amount to be inserted in the recognizance could not be ascertained. *Doe* d. *Messiter* v. *Dyneley*, 4 Taunt. 289. The remedy in such case was by a writ of restitution after the reversal of the judgment. Notwithstanding the proceedings in error, the lessor of the plaintiff might exercise his legal right of entry and take possession of the property, although he could not sue out a writ of execution. *Badger* v. *Floyd*, 12 Mod. 398; Holt, 199; *Withers* v. *Harris*, 2 Ld. Ray. 806, 808 ; *Ante*, 344 ; but see *Doe* d. *Stevens* v. *Lord*, 7 A. & E. 610; 2 N. & P. 604; 6 Dowl. 256. Bail in error were not chargeable with mesne profits, in an action upon their recognizance, unless the amount had been ascertained before action against them, by a writ of inquiry pursuant to the statute. *Doe* v. *Reynolds*, 1 M. & S. 247.

Most of the above decisions are applicable to sect. 208 (*ante*, 361), which has evidently been framed with reference to the 16 & 17 Car. 2, c. 8, ss. 3, 4.

We now proceed to consider fully the mode of proceeding in error pursuant to sect. 208.

In what Cases.]—Error can be brought, under the 15 & 16 Vict. c. 76, s. 208, only after a special verdict, a bill of exceptions, or "by consent after a special case stated." But by 17 & 18 Vict. c. 125, s. 32, "error may be brought upon a judgment upon a special case, in the same manner as upon a judgment upon a special verdict, *unless the parties agree to the contrary*." *Ante*, 326. Such agreement (if made) is usually incorporated into the special case. *See the forms, Appendix, Nos.* 148, 251. A demurrer to evidence seems to have been overlooked : it had long fallen into disuse.

"In no case shall error be brought for any error on a judgment with respect to costs, but the error (if any) in that respect may be amended by the court in which such judgment may have been given, on the application of either party." Reg. Pl. H. T. 1853, No. 27.

Mode of Proceeding.]—The 15 & 16 Vict. c. 76, s. 148, abolishes writs of error, and enacts that "the proceeding to error shall be *a step in the cause*," and shall be taken in manner therein mentioned. *Post*, 363. Consequently, the name of the court and the title of the cause is not reversed when the defendant proceeds in error, as was the case when the proceedings were commenced by writ, and in effect constituted a fresh action by the plaintiff in error against the defendant in error for the reversal of the judgment in the original action.

Quashing Proceedings in Error.]—"Courts of error shall have power to quash the proceedings in error in all cases in which error does not lie, or where they are taken against good faith, or in any case in which proceedings in error might heretofore have been quashed by such courts; and such courts shall in all respects have such jurisdiction over the proceedings as over the proceedings in error commenced by writ of error." 15 & 16 Vict. c. 76, s. 156; 1 Chit. Arch. 511 (9th ed.); *Hughes* v. *Lumley*, 4 E. & B. 358.

It seems that, before this enactment, a court of error could not quash the writ of error, but only the *allowance* of it. *Holmes* v. *Newlands*, 2 Dowl. N. S. 716.

Limitation of Time to proceed in Error.]—Proceedings in error must generally be commenced within six years after judgment signed or entered of record: 15 & 16 Vict. c. 76, s. 146: but if the party entitled to bring error is, "at the time of such title accrued," an infant, *feme covert, non compos mentis*, or beyond the seas, error may be brought within six years after such disability ceases. Sect. 147.

Memorandum of Error in Law.]—No writ of error is necessary: sect. 148: but "either party alleging error in law may deliver to one of the masters of the court a memorandum in writing in the form contained in the Schedule (A.) to this act annexed, marked No. 10, or to the like effect, entitled in the court and cause, and signed by the party or his attorney, alleging that there is error in law in the record and proceedings [*see the form, Appendix, No.* 340]; whereupon the master shall file such memorandum, and deliver to the party lodging the same a note of the receipt thereof; and a copy of such note, together with a statement of the grounds of error intended to be argued, may be served on the opposite party or his attorney." Sect. 149; *see the form, Appendix, No.* 341. Sometimes it may not be expedient to serve the copy note immediately after it has been obtained, because the roll must be made up and the suggestion of error entered thereon within ten days after such service. Sect. 153; *post*, 365.

"Proceedings in error *in law* shall be deemed a supersedeas of execution from the time of the service of a copy of such note, together with a statement of the grounds of error intended to be argued, *until default in putting in bail*, or an affirmance of the judgment, or discontinuance of the proceedings in error, or until the proceedings in error shall be otherwise disposed of without a reversal of the judgment: provided always, that if the grounds of error shall appear to be frivolous, the court or a judge, upon summons, may order execution to issue." Sect. 150.

Recognizance in lieu of Bail in Error.]—In other actions than ejectment, bail in error must be put in, pursuant to 15 & 16 Vict. c. 76, s. 151, when the defendant (not the plaintiff) brings error. *James* v. *Cochrane*, 9 Exch. 552. But in ejectment, it is sufficient for the plaintiff in error to enter into *his own recognizance*, pursuant to sect.

208. *Ante*, 361; *Doe* d. *Webb* v. *Goundry*, 7 Taunt. 427; *see the form, Appendix, No.* 347. The reason for the difference probably is, that the defendant cannot make away with the land. Where error is brought "*by consent* after a special case stated," no recognizance whatever is necessary; but if brought after a special case, pursuant to 17 & 18 Vict. c. 125, s. 32, a recognizance must be entered into, in order to render the proceedings in error a stay of execution.

Of course there can be no "default in putting in bail," within the meaning of sect. 150, except in those cases wherein bail in error is required: those words do not apply to actions of ejectment. Nevertheless a recognizance must be entered into by the plaintiff in error, pursuant to sect. 208, otherwise the proceedings in error will not operate as a stay of execution, unless brought "by consent, after a special case stated." *Ante*, 361. No recognizance is necessary where the plaintiff in error was also the claimant in the court below. *Duvergier* v. *Fellowes*, 7 Bing. 463; 5 Moo. & P. 403; 1 Dowl. 224; *Freeman* v. *Garden*, 1 Dowl. & Ry. 184; *James* v. *Cochrane*, 9 Exch. 552. No recognizance is necessary in any case, except for the purpose of making the proceedings in error a *stay of execution."* By entering into a recognizance, the plaintiff in error sometimes renders himself liable to pay costs of the defendant in error, to which otherwise he would not be subject. *Post*, 369. On the other hand, it is generally of importance to prevent the execution of a writ of possession, &c., pending the proceedings in error.

The recognizance must be entered into before a judge at chambers, and not before a commissioner for taking special bail in the country. This must frequently be very inconvenient, and ought to be remedied. The recognizance was formerly prepared by the clerk of the errors, but that office has been abolished, and the duties are performed by the masters of the court. 7 Will. 4 & 1 Vict. c. 30. The master ascertains the proper amount to be inserted in the recognizance by inquiries as to the amount of the rent reserved; *ante*, 362; *Doe* d. *Webb* v. *Goundry*, 7 Taunt. 427; and the costs allowed on taxation; *Doe* d. *Messiter* v. *Dyneley*, 4 Taunt. 289; *see form of Recognizance, Appendix, No.* 347. No bail in error are necessary: *Doe* d. *Webb* v. *Goundry*, 7 Taunt. 427: but only the recognizance of the plaintiff in error, who cannot be examined as to his sufficiency. *Keene* d. *Lord Byron* v. *Deardon*, 8 East, 298. The recognizance must be entered into "within four clear days after lodging the memorandum alleging error, or after the signing of the judgment, whichever shall last happen, or before execution executed." *Ante*, 361. Four clear days mean both days exclusive. *Rex* v. *Justices of Herefordshire*, 3 B. & A. 581; *Reg.* v. *Justices of Middlesex*, 3 Dowl. & L. 109. It is unnecessary to give any notice to the defendant in error of the intention to enter into such recognizance. *Doe* d. *Webb* v. *Goundry*, 7 Taunt. 427. The master attends to see it properly taken, and afterwards files it: no notice of it having been filed is necessary: it is the duty of the plaintiff in the ejectment to search for the recognizance before issuing a writ of possession. *S. C.*

Order for Execution, the Grounds of Error appearing frivolous.] — If the grounds of error intended to be argued (as stated in the notice) appear to be frivolous, the court, or a judge upon summons, may order execution to issue. 15 & 16 Vict. c. 76, s. 150; *ante*, 363; *see forms of Summons and Order, Appendix, Nos.* 348, 349; *Rules Nisi and Absolute, Id., Nos.* 350, 351.

Suggestion of Error.]—By 15 & 16 Vict. c. 76, s. 152, "the assignment of and joinder in error in law shall not be necessary or used, and, instead thereof, a suggestion to the effect that error is alleged by the one party and denied by the other, may be entered on the judgment roll in the form contained in schedule (A) to this act annexed, marked No. 11, or to the like effect [*see the form, Appendix, No.* 352]: provided that, in case the defendant in error intends to rely upon the proceeding in error being barred by lapse of time, or by release of error, or other like matter of fact, he may give four days written notice to the plaintiff in error to assign error as heretofore, instead of entering the suggestion; and he shall, within eight days, plead thereto the bar by lapse of time, or release of error, or other like matter of fact, and thereupon such proceedings may be had as heretofore." *For the forms of such Notice, Assignment of Errors and Plea in Bar, &c., see Appendix, Nos.* 354—359.

Entry on Roll.]—By 15 & 16 Vict. c. 76, s. 153, "the roll shall be made up, and the suggestion last aforesaid entered by the plaintiff in error within ten days after the service of the note of the receipt of the memorandum alleging error, or within such other time as the court or a judge may order; and in default thereof, or of assignment of error in cases where an assignment is required, the defendant in error, his executors or administrators, shall be at liberty to sign judgment of non pros."

Within the time limited by this section, the proceedings in the court below, to final judgment inclusive, must be entered on the judgment roll in that court, to which must be added the suggestion of error. *See form of Suggestion, Appendix, No.* 352.

The judgment below is usually entered on the roll by the successful party or his attorney, and he may generally delay doing so as long as he pleases. *Ante,* 337. But when proceedings in error are brought he should forthwith enter up the judgment, otherwise he may be compelled to do so upon application to the court or a judge. *Taylor* v. *Nesfield,* 4 E. & B. 462. And a reasonable time will be allowed the plaintiff in error to enter the suggestion of error after the roll is so carried in.

If the proceeding in error be founded on a bill of exceptions, the plaintiff in error should take care to obtain the judge's admission of his seal, and to have the bill of exceptions annexed to the record within the time above mentioned. *Ante,* 314—316.

Error by one or more of several Defendants.]—By 15 & 16 Vict. c. 76, s. 154, "in case error be brought upon a judgment given against several persons, and one or some only shall proceed in error, the memorandum alleging error and the note of the receipt of such memorandum shall state the names of the persons by whom the proceedings are taken; and in case the other persons, against whom judgment has been given, decline to join in the proceedings in error, the same may be continued, and the suggestion last aforesaid entered, stating the persons by whom the proceedings are brought, without any summons and severance, or if such other persons elect to join, then the suggestion shall state them to be, and they shall be deemed as plaintiffs in error, although not mentioned as such in the previous proceedings." *For the form of Memorandum in Error under this Section, and Note of Receipt thereof, see Appendix, No.* 342.

The other defendants may be required by notice in writing to elect to join or to decline to join in the proceedings in error. *See the form, Appendix, No.* 343. Thereupon such other defendants may by notice in writing elect to join or decline to join in such proceeding. *See the form, Appendix, No.* 346. If the defendants refuse or neglect to make such election, a summons may be taken out to compel them to do so before a judge. *See forms of Summons and Order, Appendix, Nos.* 344, 345. If they elect to join, the suggestion of error on the roll and all subsequent proceedings should include their names as plaintiffs in error, in the same manner as if they had originally joined in the proceedings in error. Sect. 154; *ante,* 365.

Setting down Proceedings in Error for Argument.]—"After the suggestion of error in law alleged and denied as prescribed by the Common Law Procedure Act, 1852, is entered, *either party* may set down the case for argument, and forthwith give notice in writing to the opposite party [*Form, Appendix, No.* 353], and proceed to the argument thereof as on a demurrer, *without any rule or motion for a concilium.*" Reg. Prac. H. T. 1853, No. 67. Under this rule a cause may be entered for argument in the Exchequer Chamber, at any sitting in error in term *or vacation,* four days before the sitting day. *The South Eastern Railway Company v. The South Western Railway Company,* 8 Exch. 367 ; 22 Law J., N. S., Exch., 72.

The record remains in the court below for all purposes until the master takes it into the court of error on the day appointed for the hearing of the case. *Wilkinson v. Sharland,* 11 Exch. 33. The court in banc may amend the record after final judgment and error brought. *S. C.*

Error Books.]—"Four clear days before the day appointed for argument, the plaintiff in error shall deliver copies of the judgment roll of the court below to the judges of the Queen's Bench on error from the Common Pleas or Exchequer, and to the judges of the Common Pleas on error from the Queen's Bench, and the defendant in error shall deliver copies thereof to the other judges of the Court of Exchequer Chamber before whom the case is to be heard; and in default by either party, the other party may, *on the following day,* deliver such books as ought to have been delivered by the party making default, and the party making default shall not be heard until he shall have paid for such copies, or deposited with the master a sufficient sum to pay for such copies." Reg. Prac. H. T. 1853, No. 68.

This rule requires the error books to be delivered four clear days before the day actually appointed for argument, and not four days before the second day of term, when the judges meet to appoint the days for argument. *Parr v. Jewell,* 16 C. B. 684.

In case of default by either party to deliver copies of the error book, the other should, "on the following day," deliver such copies for the party in default. *Sandall v. Bennett,* 2 A. & E. 204; *Hooper v. Woolmer,* 10 C. B. 370; *Dorsett v. Aspdin,* 11 C. B. 651; *Wilton v.*

Scarlett, 1 Dowl. & L. 810; *Scott* v. *Robson*, 2 Cr. M. & R. 29. If either party has neglected to deliver copies, and the other has not delivered them for him, before the case comes on for argument, the case will not be heard. *Sheddon* v. *Butt*, 11 C. B. 27; *Allan* v. *Waterhouse*, 1 Dowl. & L. 787. It will be struck out of the paper, and must afterwards be re-entered.

How heard and determined.]—By 15 & 16 Vict. c. 76, s. 155, " upon such suggestion of error alleged and denied being entered, the cause may be set down for argument in the court of error in the manner heretofore used : and the judgment roll shall, without any writ or return, be brought by the master into the court of error in the Exchequer Chamber, before the justices, or justices and barons, as the case may be, of the other two superior courts of common law, on the day of its sitting, at such time as the judges shall appoint, either in term or in vacation; or if the proceedings in error be before the High Court of Parliament, then before the High Court of Parliament, before or at the time of its sitting; and the court of error shall and may thereupon review the proceedings, and give judgment as they shall be advised thereon; and such proceedings and judgment, as altered or affirmed, shall be entered on the original record; and such further proceedings as may be necessary thereon shall be awarded by the court in which the original judgment was given."

The record remains in the court below until the master takes it into the court of error on the day appointed for the hearing of the case. *Wilkinson* v. *Sharland*, 11 Exch. 33.

Each party should, a reasonable time before the day appointed for argument, furnish his counsel with a copy on brief paper of the error book, including the points or grounds of errors, together with a few "observations" referring to the cases and authorities. Only one counsel will be heard on each side, but it is not unusual to employ another "to take notes," and make suggestions, &c. Either the junior may argue and the senior take notes, or *vice versâ*, as may be deemed most expedient. Sometimes a consultation is advisable in important cases.

On the argument, the counsel for the plaintiff in error is heard first; then the counsel for the defendant in error; and afterwards the counsel for the plaintiff in reply. 1 Chit. Arch. 532 (9th ed.).

The court of error will make every possible intendment in favour of the verdict and judgment, and will, if necessary, be astute in reconciling apparent inconsistencies. *Morres, Bart.* v. *Barry*, 2 Stra. 1180; 1 Wils. 1, *S. C.*; *Fisher* v. *Hughes*, 2 Stra. 908; *Worral* v. *Bent, Id.*, 835; *Rowe* v. *Power* d. *Boyce* (in error), 2 B. & P. New R. 2, 35; *Sleabourne* v. *Bengo*, 1 Ld. Raym. 561; Ad. Eject. 287.

A verdict cures almost any defect in setting out a title, though it cannot cure a defective title. *Small* d. *Baker* v. *Cole*, 2 Burr. 1159; and see *Doe* d. *Parsons* v. *Heather*, 8 M. & W. 158; 1 Dowl. N. S. 64; 1 Wms. Saund. 228, n. (1); 1 Smith's L. C. 333.

If it appear to the court of error that the grounds of error relied on may and ought to be cured by an amendment of the record in the court below, they will sometimes adjourn the hearing to enable such an application to be made. *Richardson* v. *Mellish*, 1 Cl. & Fin. 224; *Gregory* v. *The Duke of Brunswick*, 2 H. L. Cas. 415.

Immediately after the conclusion of the argument, the judges usually consult together and proceed to deliver judgment; but in difficult cases they sometimes take time to consider, and their judgment is afterwards written out by one of them, and settled or approved of by the others before they come into court to deliver it. If, however, they happen to disagree, each prepares and reads his own judgment, and according to the opinion of the majority the judgment is affirmed or reversed. If the court of error be equally divided, the judgment below will be affirmed. *Wright* v. *Doe* d. *Tatham*, 7 A. & E. 313, 408; *Deighton* v. *Greevil*, cited 1 Stra. 381; *Thornby* v. *Fleetwood*, 1 Stra. 379—383. In a very recent case which stood for judgment in the Exchequer Chamber, the Lord Chief Baron stated that the judges who had heard the argument were equally divided in opinion; and there must therefore be another argument when the court was differently constituted. *Young* v. *Billiter*, 24 April, 1855. This course is much more satisfactory than affirming the judgment under such circumstances.

By 15 & 16 Vict. c. 76, s. 157, "courts of error shall in all cases have power to give such judgment and award such process, as the court from which error is brought ought to have done, without regard to the party alleging error."

Formerly the court of error could only reverse an erroneous judgment, and give a proper judgment *in favour* of the plaintiff in error. *Gregory* v. *The Duke of Brunswick*, 3 C. B. 481, 495. But they could not give a proper judgment *against* him. *Pollitt* v. *Forrest*, 11 Q. B. 949, 967—973. In the latter case they could only reverse the erroneous judgment.

"Courts of error may award a repleader, or direct a *trial de novo*." Reg. Pl. H. T. 1853, No. 24.

The judgment as altered or affirmed shall be entered on the original record. *Ante*, 367; *see the forms, Appendix, Nos.* 360, 361. Such further proceedings as may be necessary thereon shall be awarded by the court below. *Ante*, 367.

Error in Parliament.]—Upon a judgment in ejectment of the Exchequer Chamber, error may be brought in the High Court of Parliament. *Ante*, 367; *Wright* v. *Doe* d. *Tatham*, 4 Bing. N. C. 489; Tidd's Appendix, 576. No second proceeding in error can be brought in the Exchequer Chamber, even upon another point not there decided. *Holmes* v. *Newlands*, 2 Dowl. N. S. 716.

Mesne Profits and Waste pending Error.]—If the judgment be affirmed, or the proceedings in error discontinued, an application may be made to the court below, or to a judge at chambers, for leave to issue a writ of inquiry as to the mesne profits and damage by waste pursuant to 15 & 16 Vict. c. 76, s. 208. *Ante*, 361; *see the forms, Appendix, Nos.* 362—369. Such writ is executed in like manner as a writ of inquiry of damages in a personal action. *See form of Inquisition thereon, Appendix, No.* 368. "Upon the return thereof judgment shall be given and execution awarded for such mesne profits and damages, and also for the costs of suit." *Ante*, 361; *see form of such Judgment, Appendix, No.* 369.

The bail in error (if any) are not liable for mesne profits or damage by waste (in an action on their recognizance) until after the amount has been ascertained by a writ of inquiry, &c., as above mentioned. *Doe* v. *Reynolds*, 1 M. & S. 247.

Costs in Error.]—By 15 & 16 Vict. c. 76, s. 148, "the proceeding to error shall be a step in the cause." By Reg. Prac. H. T. 1853, No. 69, "the costs of proceedings in error shall be taxed and allowed as costs in the cause." By Reg. Pl. H. T. 1853, No. 25, "the costs of proceedings in error shall be taxed and allowed as costs in the cause, and no double costs in error shall be allowed to either party."

The above enactment and rules merely regulate the mode of taxation, but do not alter the previous law as to the right to recover costs in error. Therefore no costs in error are recoverable, except where they might have been recovered before the above act. *Fisher* v. *Bridges,* 4 E. & B. 666. Thus, where the plaintiff in error succeeds, he is not entitled to his costs of proceeding in error. *Wyvil* v. *Stapleton,* 1 Stra. 617; *Fisher* v. *Bridges, supra.* But the court of error may award him such costs as the court below ought to have given him, viz. of the proceedings in that court. *Wyvil* v. *Stapleton,* 1 Stra. 617; *Adams* v. *Meredew,* 3 You. & Jer. 419; *Evans* v. *Collins,* 2 Dowl. & L. 989. The costs of a bill of exceptions are costs in error, and not costs in the court below. *Gardner* v. *Baillie,* 1 Bos. & P. 32; *Doe* d. *Harvey* v. *Francis,* 4 M. & W. 331; 7 Dowl. 193. The costs of a special verdict should be awarded to a successful plaintiff in error, because they form part of the costs below. *Gildart* v. *Gladstone,* 12 East, 668. So where there has been a verdict subject to a special case. Where the plaintiff in error succeeds *as to part,* no costs in error should be awarded to either party. *Bourne* v. *Gatcliffe,* 7 Man. & Gr. 852, 867; 11 Cl. & Fin. 45, *S. C.*

When the judgment below is affirmed in error, the defendant in error is generally entitled to costs *for the delay* occasioned by the proceedings in error. 3 Hen. 7, c. 10 (enforced by 19 Hen. 7, c. 20); Gray on Costs, 397; 1 Chit. Arch. 535 (9th ed.). But where there has been no such delay *unavoidably* occasioned by the proceedings in error, as where no recognizance was entered into, or bail in error put in, whereby the proceedings in error did not operate as a stay of proceedings, the defendant in error is not entitled to his costs in error. *Newlands* v. *Holmes,* 4 Q. B. 858; *Sutherland* v. *Wills,* 5 Exch. 980; *Wright* v. *Fairfield,* 2 B. & Adol. 959; 1 Chit. Arch. 535 (9th ed.). There may, however, be costs in error for the delay, even when no costs were recoverable in the original suit. *Ferguson* v. *Rawlinson, qui tam,* 2 Stra. 1084; 3 Burr. 1511.

Formerly, when a judgment after verdict was affirmed in error, the defendant in error was entitled to double costs. 13 Car. 2, st. 2, c. 2, s. 10; *Francis* v. *Doe* d. *Harvey,* 5 M. & W. 273; 7 Dowl. 523; *Shepherd* v. *Mackreth,* 2 H. Black. 284. But now, "no double costs in error shall be allowed to either party." Reg. Pl. H. T. 1853, No. 25.

Interest.]—By Reg. Pl. H. T. 1853, No. 26, "on error from one of the superior courts such court shall have power to allow interest *for such time as execution has been delayed* by the proceedings in error, for the delaying thereof; and the master, on taxing costs, may compute such interest without any rule of court or order of a judge for that purpose."

The 3 & 4 Will. 4, c. 42, s. 30, whereby courts of error are authorized to award interest for such time as execution has been delayed by the proceedings in error, applies only to judgments " in any action *personal ;*" not to ejectments.

Where the proceedings in error have not occasioned *any unavoidable delay* in suing out execution (no recognizance having been entered into, or bail in error put in) the master should not allow any interest. *Ante,* 369. Where interest is allowed, it should be calculated " for such time as execution has been delayed," at the rate of 4*l.* per cent. per annum. *Levy v. Langridge,* 4 M. & W. 337 ; 7 Dowl. 27. Either party may produce affidavits before the master to prove or disprove the delay, &c.

Restitution.]—If the judgment be reversed in error after a writ of possession has been executed, the defendant may sue out a writ of restitution. 2 Chit. Arch. 982 (9th ed.) ; *see the form,* 2 *Lil. Entr.* 635, *post, Appendix, No.* 370. But to obtain restitution of any costs levied, a *scire facias quare restitutionem non* must first issue, and afterwards a writ of restitution with a *fi. fa.* or *ca. sa. See the forms, Chitty's Forms,* 272, 273 (7th ed.). A *scire* appears unnecessary where the money has not only been levied, but actually paid over to the plaintiff. 1 Chit. Arch. 537 (9th ed.).

2. *Error in Fact.*]— By 15 & 16 Vict. c. 76, s. 158, " either party alleging error in fact may deliver to one of the masters of the court a memorandum in writing, in the form contained in the schedule (A.) to this act annexed, marked No. 12, or to the like effect, entitled in the court and cause, and signed by the party or his attorney, alleging that there is error in fact in the proceedings [*see the form, Appendix, No.* 371], together with an affidavit of the matter of fact in which the alleged error consists ; whereupon the master shall file such memorandum and affidavit, and deliver to the party lodging the same a note of the receipt thereof [*see the form, Appendix, No.* 372]; and a copy of such note and affidavit may be served on the opposite party or his attorney ; and such service shall have the same effect, and the same proceedings may be had thereafter as heretofore had after the service of the rule for allowance of a writ of error in fact."

" Within eight days after the filing with the master of the memorandum of error in fact, required by the Common Law Procedure Act, 1852, the plaintiff in error shall *assign* error [*see the form, Appendix, No.* 373]; and in default in error, his executors or administrators, shall be entitled to sign judgment of *non pros.*" Reg. Prac. H. T. 1853, No. 64 ; *see form of Judgment, Appendix, No.* 375 (*a*).

" No rule to plead to assignment of error in fact, or any other pleadings in error, shall be necessary, but either party may give to the opposite party a notice to answer such pleading within four days, otherwise judgment ; which notice may be delivered separately, or indorsed on the pleading." Reg. Prac. H. T. 1853, No. 65; *see form of Notice, Appendix, No.* 374.

The defendant in error must plead to the assignment of error within four days after notice, or obtain a judge's order for further time in the usual manner. *See form of Plea, Appendix, No.* 375. If the plaintiff merely reply *in nullo est erratum,* he will thereby admit the facts as alleged in the assignment of error, and the question will be, whether the facts so admitted constitute error. *Banks v. Newton,* 4 Dowl. & L. 638, note (*h*); 11 Q. B. 344.

" Notice of trial, and all other proceedings thereon, shall be the same as in issues joined in an ordinary action." `Reg. Prac. H. T. 1853, No. 66.

Discontinuance of Proceedings in Error.]—By 15 & 16 Vict. c. 76, s. 159, " the plaintiff in error, whether in fact or law, shall be at liberty to discontinue his proceedings by giving to the defendant in error a notice headed in the court and cause, and signed by the plaintiff in error or his attorney, stating that he discontinues such proceedings [*see the form, Appendix, No.* 376]; and thereupon the defendant in error may sign judgment for the costs of, and occasioned by, the proceedings in error [*see the form, Appendix, No.* 377], and may proceed upon the judgment on which the error was brought."

Confession of Error and Reversal of Judgment by Consent.]—By 15 & 16 Vict. c. 76, s. 160, " the defendant in error, whether in fact or law, shall be at liberty to confess error, and consent to the reversal of the judgment, by giving to the plaintiff in error a notice, headed in the court and cause, and signed by the defendant in error or his attorney, stating that he confesses the error, and consents to the reversal of the judgment [*see the form, Appendix, No.* 378]; and thereupon the plaintiff in error shall be entitled to and may forthwith sign a judgment of reversal." *See the form, Appendix, No.* 379.

Suggestion of Deaths.]—By 15 & 16 Vict. c. 76, s. 161, " the death of a plaintiff in error after service of the note of the receipt of the memorandum alleging error, with a statement of the grounds of error, shall not cause the proceedings to abate, but they may be continued as hereinafter mentioned."

Sect. 162, " in case of the death of one of several plaintiffs in error, a suggestion may be made of the death, which suggestion shall not be traversable, but shall only be subject to be set aside if untrue, and the proceedings may be thereupon continued at the suit of and against the surviving plaintiff in error, as if he were the sole plaintiff."

A suggestion under this section may be made by either party. It should be prepared by his attorney, and, if necessary, settled by counsel or a pleader; *see the form, Appendix, No.* 380; it should then be engrossed and delivered to the attorney or agent of the opposite party, and afterwards entered on the roll.

If untrue it may be set aside upon application to the court or a judge founded upon affidavit. *See forms of Affidavit, Summons and Order, Appendix, Nos.* 381, 382, 383.

Sect. 163, " in case of the death of a sole plaintiff or of several plaintiffs in error, the legal representative of such plaintiff or of the surviving plaintiff may, by leave of the court or a judge, enter a suggestion of the death, and that he is such legal representative, which suggestion shall not be traversable, but shall only be subject to be set aside if untrue, and the proceedings may thereupon be continued at the suit of and against such legal representative as the plaintiff in error; and if no such suggestion shall be made, the defendant in error may proceed to an affirmance of the judgment according to the practice of the court, or take such other proceedings thereupon as he may be entitled to."

A suggestion under this section can be entered only by the " legal representative" of the plaintiff or surviving plaintiff, with leave of the court or a judge; *see the form, Appendix, No.* 387; such leave may be obtained upon a proper affidavit of the facts. *See forms of Affidavit, Summons and Order, Appendix, Nos.* 384, 385, 386. A copy of the rule or order should be delivered with the suggestion.

Sect. 164, "the death of a defendant in error shall not cause the proceedings to abate, but they may be continued as hereinafter mentioned."

Sect. 165, "in case of the death of one of several defendants in error, a suggestion may be made of the death, which suggestion shall not be traversable, but only be subject to be set aside if untrue, and the proceedings may be continued against the surviving defendant."

The proceedings under this section are the same, *mutatis mutandis* as those under sect. 162 (*ante*, 371). *See form of the Suggestion, Appendix, No.* 388.

Sect. 166, "in case of the death of a sole defendant or of all the defendants in error, the plaintiff in error may proceed upon giving ten days' notice of the proceedings in error, and of his intention to continue the same, to the representatives of the deceased defendants; or if no such notice can be given, then, by leave of the court or a judge, upon giving such notice to the parties interested as he or they may direct."

Care must be taken to give the notice to the proper persons, *i.e.*, the legal representatives of the defendant, or of *all* the defendants. *See the form, Appendix, No.* 389. If for any special reason such notice cannot be given, then, upon an affidavit of the facts, showing who is or are beneficially interested in the property in question (supposing the defendant to have had any title), leave of the court or a judge may be obtained, upon an *ex parte* application, to give the notice to such parties as the court or judge may direct. A copy of the rule or order should accompany the notice.

Marriage of Female Plaintiff or Defendant in Error.]—By 15 & 16 Vict. c. 76, s. 167, "the marriage of a woman plaintiff or defendant in error shall not abate the proceedings in error, but the same may be continued in like manner as hereinbefore provided with reference to the continuance of an action after marriage."

This refers to sect. 141, which is as follows:—

" The marriage of a woman plaintiff or defendant shall not cause the action to abate, but the action may, notwithstanding, be proceeded with to judgment; and such judgment may be executed against the wife alone, or, by suggestion or writ of revivor pursuant to this act, judgment may be obtained against the husband and wife, and execution issue thereon; and in case of a judgment for the wife, execution may be issued thereupon by the authority of the husband, without any writ of revivor or suggestion; and if in any such action the wife shall sue or defend by attorney appointed by her when sole, such attorney shall have authority to continue the action or defence, unless such authority be countermanded by the husband, and the attorney changed according to the practice of the court."

CHAPTER XXXV.

MISCELLANEOUS MATTERS.

Jurisdiction of the Superior Courts and Judges in Ejectment generally.]—By 15 & 16 Vict. c. 76, s. 221, " the several courts and the judges thereof respectively shall and may exercise over the proceedings the like jurisdiction as heretofore exercised in the action of ejectment, so as to ensure a trial of the title, and of actual ouster, when necessary, only, and for all other purposes for which such jurisdiction may at present be exercised ; and the provisions of all statutes not inconsistent with the provisions of this act, and which may be applicable to the altered mode of proceeding, shall remain in force and be applied thereto."

The jurisdiction of the courts and judges under the above act is generally of a *legal nature.* They have no power (except in certain cases hereinafter mentioned) to stay proceedings in an ejectment *on equitable grounds;* nor can a defence on equitable grounds be pleaded. *Neave* v. *Avery*, 16 C. B. 328. The remedy (if any) is in a court of equity, which may grant a perpetual injunction against an ejectment upon such terms and conditions as it may think just and reasonable. *Shine* v. *Gough*, 1 Ball & Beatty (Irish R.), 436, 447 ; *Powell* v. *Thomas*, 6 Hare, 300. If a trustee, in violation of his duty, bring an ejectment against his *cestui que trust*, the latter can obtain relief against such action only in a court of equity by a bill or claim for an injunction, &c. *Balls* v. *Strutt*, 1 Hare, 146 ; *Denton* v. *Denton*, 7 Beav. 388 ; 8 Jur. 388 ; *Pugh* v. *Vaughan*, 12 Beav. 517 ; Hill on Trustees, 308 ; Lewin on Trusts, 482. A lease from a *cestui que trust* cannot be set up against the trustee, in any case, without the aid of a court of equity. *Baker* v. *Mellish*, 10 Ves. 554 ; *ante*, 73. A person who has the legal estate must prevail in a court of law ; and it makes no difference in this respect whether the plaintiff be a trustee for the defendant or not. *Ante*, 288. On the other hand, a defendant in ejectment cannot be prevented by the court or a judge from setting up an outstanding term or estate as a defence, although he does not claim or pretend to derive any right or title under or by virtue of such term or estate. *Ante,* 288, 298. But, if necessary, a court of equity will, in a proper case, restrain the defendant from setting up such outstanding term or estate, and so in effect compel the defendant to submit to a fair trial on the merits. Mitford (Lord Redesdale), Eq. Pl. 134, 135; *Pulteney* v. *Warren,* 6 Ves. 89; *Bond* v. *Hopkins,* 1 Sch. & Lef. (Irish R.), 430; *Crow* v. *Tyrrell,* 3 Madd. 181; *Leigh* v. *Leigh,* 1 Simon, 349; *Brackenbury* v. *Brackenbury,* 2 Jac. & Walk. 391; *Houghton* v. *Reynolds,* 2 Hare, 264; *Baker* v. *Harwood,* 7 Simon, 373; *Stansbury* v. *Arkwright,* 6 Simon, 481; 2 Daniell, Ch. Prac. 1525 (2nd ed.); 3 Chit. Eq. Index, 2270 (3rd ed.). But the bill must be filed, and the suit brought to a hearing, before the commencement of the ejectment. *Beer* v. *Ward,* Jacob, R. 194. The injunction will not be granted on motion. *Barney* v. *Luckett,* 1 Sim. & Stu. 419; *Ringer* v. *Blake,* 3 You. & Col. 591; 3 Jur. 1026. A court of equity never refuses to remove temporary bars to enable parties to try their rights, unless there be fraud imputable to the plaintiff, or the defendant is a purchaser for valuable consideration without notice. *Blennerhassett* v. *Day,* 2 Ball & Beatty (Irish R.), 137. Sometimes the obstacle created by an outstanding term may be avoided or overcome in a less expensive and more effectual manner than by resorting to a court of equity, viz. by using the name of the trustee of the term as a co-plaintiff, with his consent, if that can be obtained; otherwise without his consent, upon offering to him an indemnity against all costs. *Ante,* 75, 288. In other cases the defendant may sometimes be estopped at law from setting up the outstanding term as a defence. *Ante,* 213, 214, 288. Sometimes the term may be presumed to have been surrendered, or is extinguished by 8 & 9 Vict. c. 112. *Ante,* 227.

In some cases the common law courts and judges exercise a sort of equitable jurisdiction in actions of ejectment similar to what they possessed before the Common Law Procedure Act, 1852, which jurisdiction is expressly saved to them by sect. 221. *Ante,* 373. Thus, if a second ejectment be brought founded on the *same title,* they will stay the proceedings in such action until the costs of the prior ejectment are paid. *Ante,* 77—81. And after a prior unsuccessful ejectment for the *same premises,* they may stay the proceedings in a subsequent ejectment, until the plaintiff gives security for the payment of the defendant's costs. *Ante,* 81. In an action by a landlord against a tenant for a forfeiture occasioned by nonpayment of rent, the court or a judge may before trial stay the proceedings upon payment of the arrears of rent and costs. 15 & 16 Vict. c. 76, s. 212; *post,* Chap. XXXIX. s. 2. But no such relief will be granted where the forfeiture relied on is for not repairing, not insuring, or the like. The courts have no jurisdiction to stay the proceedings in an ejectment for not repairing, notwithstanding the repairs were all done before the commencement of the action. *Doe* d. *Mayhew* v. *Asby,* 10 A. & E. 71; 2 P. & D. 302. Even a court of equity will not relieve against a forfeiture for not repairing, not insuring, or the like: *Hill* v. *Barclay,* 18 Ves. 56; *Reynolds* v. *Pitt,* 19 Ves. 134; *Gregory* v. *Wilson,* 9 Hare, 683; *Green* v. *Bridges,* 4 Simon, 96, cited 6 Q. B. 961; *post,* Chap. XXXIX.: but only for *nonpayment of money, i. e.* rent, or rates and taxes. In an ejectment by a mortgagee against the mortgagor, &c.,

the court or a judge may stay the proceedings upon equitable terms, viz., payment of the principal money and interest due on the mortgage, with all costs incurred by the plaintiff both at law and in equity. 15 & 16 Vict. c. 76, ss. 219, 220; *post,* Chap. XLIV.

Rule on third Persons to pay Costs.]—Both before and since the Common Law Procedure Act, 1852, the court has exercised a summary jurisdiction in ejectment to compel parties not named in the record, but who really defended the action, to pay the plaintiff's costs. *Doe* d. *Masters* v. *Gray,* 10 B. & C. 110; *Hutchinson* v. *Greenwood,* 4 E. & B. 324; *Anstey* v. *Edwards,* 16 C. B. 212. No such jurisdiction is exercised in other forms of action. *Hayward* v. *Giffard,* 4 M. & W. 194; 6 Dowl. 699.

Lien for Costs.]—An attorney or solicitor has no lien on real property recovered in an action of ejectment for his costs. *Shaw* v. *Neale,* 25 Law Times R. 112, Romilly, M. R. He may have a general lien on his client's title deeds deposited with him for the purposes of the action, but not on any deeds entrusted to him otherwise than in his professional capacity. *Stevenson* v. *Blakelock,* 1 M. & S. 535. A client cannot give to his attorney or solicitor a lien on deeds of a higher nature than the interest which the client has in the deeds, so as to prejudice any third person interested in them. *Pelly* v. *Watkin,* 21 Law J., N. S., Chanc., 105.

Leave of the Court of Chancery to bring Ejectment, when necessary.]—If a receiver appointed by the Court of Chancery be in possession of the land claimed, an ejectment cannot be brought to recover it without first obtaining leave of that court. *Angel* v. *Smith,* 9 Ves. 335. But if the action be commenced before the claimant has any notice or knowledge of the appointment of a receiver, he need not make any such application until he is ready to execute his *habere facias possessionem. Townsend* v. *Somervile,* 1 Hogan (Irish R.), 99.

Discharge from Custody after Twelve Months' Imprisonment.]— By 48 Geo. 3, c. 123, s. 1, all prisoners in execution for *any debt or damages* not exceeding 20*l.* (exclusive of costs) shall be entitled to their discharge after having been in prison thereupon for the space of twelve calendar months.

This enactment has been held to extend to defendants in ejectment. *Doe* v. ——, 1 Dowl. 69; *Doe* d. *Daffey* v. *Sinclair,* 3 Bing. N. C. 778; 4 Scott, 477; 5 Dowl. 615; *Doe* d. *Symons* v. *Price,* 2 Dowl. & L. 752. The reason for this appears to have been, that the 1*s.* nominal damages formerly awarded in an ejectment brought the case *within the words* of the statute. *Doe* d. *Threlfall* v. *Ward,* 2 M. & W. 65; 5 Dowl. 290. But as no damages whatever are now recoverable in ejectment (except as between landlord and tenant), it is not clear that the above enactment now applies. *Doe* v. *Reynolds,* 10 B. & C. 481. But see 15 & 16 Vict. c. 76, s. 221. *Ante,* 373.

The plaintiff in an ejectment, who has lain in prison for twelve successive calendar months under an execution on a rule for the payment of costs not exceeding 20*l.,* may apply for his discharge under the above act. *Doe* d. *Smith* v. *Roe,* 6 Dowl. & L. 544; *Stead* v. *Anderson,* 9 C. B. 274. So it seems that a plaintiff in execution for the costs of a nonsuit under 20*l.* may be so discharged. *Bradley* v. *Webb*, 7 Dowl. 588; *Roylance* v. *Hewling*, 3 Man. & Gr. 282. But see *Tinmouth* v. *Taylor*, 10 B. & C. 114.

A notice of the intention to apply under the above act may be served before the expiration of the twelve months. *See the form*, Chit. Forms, 677 (7th ed.). It must be served ten clear days before the day therein mentioned. *Bolton* v. *Allen*, 1 Dowl. N. S. 309; *Burley* v. *Warrall*, 1 Dowl. & L. 145. The service must be on the plaintiff himself, not on his attorney. *Bolton* v. *Allen, supra; Johnson* v. *Routledge*, 5 Dowl. 579. If there be several plaintiffs, as they must have a joint interest, service upon any one of them is sufficient. *Bolton* v. *Allen, supra; Doe* d. *Smith* v. *Raynton*, 7 Dowl. 671; *Doe* d. *Daffey* v. *Sinclair*, 8 Bing. N. C. 778; 4 Scott, 477; 5 Dowl. 715; *Doe* d. *Threllford* v. *Ward*, 5 Dowl. 290. A proper affidavit must be made in support of the application. *See the form*, Chit. Forms, 678 (7th ed.). The rule is *absolute* in the first instance, if due notice has been given of the application. Cases *supra.*

PART THE THIRD.

PROCEEDINGS IN EJECTMENT BY AND AGAINST PARTICULAR PERSONS.

———◆———

CHAPTER XXXVI.

SPECIAL PROCEEDINGS BY LANDLORD AGAINST TENANT, ACCORDING TO THE STATUTE.

————

General Observations on 15 & 16 *Vict. c.* 76, *ss.* 213—218.]—The Common Law Procedure Act, 1852, contains several important enactments for the benefit of landlords in actions of ejectment at their suit. Sects. 213—217. But in no case is a landlord bound to avail himself of either of them. He is always at liberty to proceed in the ordinary manner like any other person. Sect. 218 expressly provides, that "nothing herein contained shall be construed to prejudice or affect any other right of action or remedy which landlords may possess in any of the cases hereinbefore provided for, otherwise than hereinbefore expressly enacted." It is, however, generally advisable for a landlord to avail himself of these enactments, when practicable, for they secure to him great and manifest advantages: *ex. gr.,* where a tenant under a lease or agreement in writing for a term certain holds over after the term has expired, and refuses to deliver up possession after a lawful demand in writing made pursuant to sect. 213, and the landlord thereupon brings ejectment, the tenant may be compelled to find *sureties for payment of the costs and damages* which shall be recovered in the action, before he will be permitted to defend it. So also, where a tenant from year to year, under a lease or agreement in writing, refuses to deliver up possession after his tenancy has been determined by a regular notice to quit, and also after a lawful demand of possession has been made in writing, pursuant to sect. 213. Again, by sect. 214, the landlord is enabled to recover the *mesne profits,* calculated from the day of the expiration or determination of the tenant's interest, down to the time of the verdict, or to any preceding day to be specially mentioned in the verdict; and the amount so recovered will form part of the damages for which security may have been given, pursuant to sect. 213. This renders a subsequent action of trespass for mesne profits unnecessary, and prevents delay, trouble and expense, besides (in some cases) securing to the landlord the amount recovered. Again, by sect. 215, where security has been obtained pursuant to sect. 213, and the claimant obtains the verdict, unless it appear to the judge that the finding of the jury was contrary to the evidence, or that the damages given were excessive, " such judge shall not, except by consent, make any order to stay judgment or execution, except on condition that within four days from the day of the trial the defendant shall actually find security" in manner therein mentioned; which security will effectually prevent him from doing any waste or damage, and from improperly selling or carrying off any of the standing crops, hay, straw or manure, after the verdict and before execution shall be finally made. Besides which, sect. 217 enables a landlord whose right of entry first accrues *in or after Hilary or Trinity Term* (which often happens) to proceed to trial *at the ensuing assizes,* which otherwise he might be unable to do in many cases.

We now proceed to consider each of the above-mentioned enactments fully.

1. *Where the Tenant wrongfully holds over.*]—By 15 & 16 Vict. c. 76, s. 213, "where the term or interest of any tenant now or hereafter holding under a *lease or agreement in writing* any lands, tenements or hereditaments for any *term or number of years certain,* or *from year to year,* shall have *expired,* or been *determined* either by the landlord or tenant by regular notice to quit, and such tenant, or any one holding or claiming by or under him, shall *refuse to deliver up possession accordingly, after lawful demand in writing* made and signed by the landlord or his agent [*see the form, Appendix, No.* 6], and *served personally* upon or *left at the dwelling-house or usual place of abode* of such tenant or person, and the landlord shall thereupon proceed by action of ejectment for the recovery of possession, it shall be lawful for him, at the foot of the writ in ejectment, to address a notice to such tenant or person, requiring him to find such bail, if ordered by the court or a judge, and for such purposes as are hereinafter next specified [*see the form, Appendix, No.* 16]; and upon the appearance of the party, on an affidavit of service of the writ and notice [*see the form, Appendix, No.* 42], it shall be lawful for the landlord producing the lease or agreement, or some counterpart or duplicate thereof, and proving the execution of the same by affidavit, and upon affidavit that the premises have been actually enjoyed under such lease or agreement, and that the interest of the tenant has expired or been determined by regular notice to quit, as the case may be, and that possession has been lawfully demanded in manner aforesaid [*see form of such Affidavit, Appendix, No.* 42], to move the court or apply by summons to a judge at chambers for a rule or summons for such tenant or person to show cause within a time to be fixed by the court or judge on a consideration of the situation of the premises, why such tenant or person should not enter into a recognizance by himself and two sufficient sureties in a reasonable sum, conditioned to pay the costs and damages which shall be recovered by the claimants in the action [*see forms of Rule Nisi and Summons, Appendix, Nos.* 43, 45]; and it shall be lawful for the court or judge, upon cause shown, or upon affidavit of the service of the rule or summons [*see the forms, Appendix, Nos.* 23, 26, 27], in case no cause shall be shown, to make the same absolute in the whole or in part, and to order such tenant or person, within a time to be fixed, upon a consideration of all the circumstances, to find such bail, with such conditions and in such manner as shall be specified in the said rule or summons, or such part of the same so made

absolute [*see form of such Rule or Order, Appendix, Nos.* 44, 46]: and in case the party shall neglect or refuse so to do, and shall lay no ground to induce the court or judge to enlarge the time for obeying the same, then the lessor or landlord filing an affidavit that such rule or order has been made and served, and not complied with [*see the form, Appendix, No.* 56], shall be at liberty to sign judgment for recovery of possession and costs of suit in the form contained in the Schedule (A.) to this act annexed, marked No. 21, or to the like effect." *See the form, Appendix, No.* 57.

This section is in substance a re-enactment of the 1 Geo. 4, c. 87, s. 1, with variations, the principle of which are—1. That the application may be made to a judge *at chambers.* 2. That the landlord may proceed under this section without the risk of being liable to pay *double costs.*

It seems that one of several tenants in common may proceed under the above section to recover his undivided share; and that in such case it will be no objection that the notice to quit and the demand of possession applied to the whole of the demised premises. *Doe* d. *Morgan* v. *Rotherham,* 3 Dowl. 690. A tenant in common may, however, give notice to quit the whole of the premises held under him, viz., his undivided part or share. *Cutting* v. *Derby,* 2 W. Blac. 1075; *see the form, Appendix, No.* 2.

Sect. 213 applies not only as between the landlord and his immediate tenant, but also as between the landlord and "any one holding or claiming by or under" the tenant, who has refused to deliver up possession after a lawful demand in writing. But it does not apply where the person in possession claims to hold the premises under a distinct title then vested in him, *ex. gr.,* as heir at law; and makes (in opposition to the application) an affidavit showing such title. *Doe* d. *Sanders* v. *Roe,* 1 Dowl. 4.

There must be a lease or agreement *in writing :* therefore a tenancy from year to year, without any writing, is not within the act. *Doe* d. *Earl Bradford* v. *Roe,* 5 B. & A. 770. So it would seem that where there has been a lease or agreement in writing for a term which has expired, after which a fresh tenancy from year to year has been created by oral agreement, or by payment and acceptance of rent or otherwise, without writing, and such new tenancy has been duly determined by a proper notice to quit, this section does not apply. *Doe* d. *Thomas* v. *Field,* 2 Dowl. 542. But where a tenant occupied under a written agreement for a lease for eight years (which lease was never executed), and the tenant held over after the expiration of the eight years, and the landlord thereupon gave him a notice to quit, but no subsequent rent had been paid: held, that the tenant was not to be treated as a tenant from year to year, but that there was a holding under an agreement for a lease within the 1 Geo. 4, c. 87. *Doe* d. *Anglesey* v. *Roe,* 2 D. & R. 565. In this case the notice to quit was not of itself sufficient to create a new tenancy from year to year. A notice desiring the tenant to quit the premises "which you hold under me, your term therein having long since expired," does not recognize a subsisting tenancy from year to year, subsequent to the term, but is a mere demand of possession. *Doe* d. *Godsall* v. *Inglis,* 3 Taunt. 54. If a tenancy from year to year has been created by a written agreement, the fact that a supplemental agreement is entered into, whereby the landlord agrees that the tenant shall continue tenant so long as the landlord shall continue the vicar of A., does not make the tenancy uncertain so as to preclude the landlord from requiring the tenant to enter into a recognizance. *Doe* d. *Newstead* v. *Roe*, 10 Jur. 925; 1 Saund. & Cole, 86, Wightman, J.

Where the tenant relies on a new tenancy not in writing as an answer to the application, his affidavit should show with precision the new term, and when and how it was created, &c. *Roe* d. *Durrant* v. *Doe*, 6 Bing. 574.

The tenancy must have been *for a term or number of years certain, or from year to year.* A tenancy for "three months certain," under a lease or agreement in writing, is sufficient. *Doe* d. *Phillips* v. *Roe*, 5 B. & A. 766; 1 D. & R. 433. But a tenancy "from quarter to quarter, determinable at the end of any quarter upon three months' notice," is not a tenancy for a "term certain," within the meaning of the act. *Doe* d. *Carter* v. *Roe*, 10 M. & W. 670; 2 Dowl. N. S. 449. So a tenancy for years determinable on lives is not within the act. *Doe* d. *Pemberton* v. *Roe*, 7 B. & C. 2. A tenancy under a lease "for one year certain, and so on from year to year," is a tenancy for two years at least, but determinable at the end of the second or any subsequent year by a proper notice to quit. *Doe* d. *Chadborn* v. *Green*, 9 A. & E. 658; 1 P. & D. 454. Such a tenancy appears to be within the act. Where a tenant held under a written agreement for a lease for eight years, which was never granted, and after the expiration of the eight years possession was demanded in writing: held, that security might be required under 1 Geo. 4, c. 87. *Doe* d. *Marquis of Anglesey* v. *Roe*, 2 D. & R. 565. But a lease for fourteen years, determinable by either party at the end of the first seven years, upon six months' notice, which was given by the tenant, is not within the act. *Doe* d. *Cardigan* v. *Roe*, 1 D. & R. 540.

The tenancy, if for a term or number of years certain, must have *expired by effluxion of time ;* or if from year to year, it must have been *determined by a regular notice to quit.* *Doe* d. *Tindal* v. *Roe*, 2 B. & Adol. 922; 1 Dowl. 143; *Doe* d. *Platter* v. *Bell*, 8 Jur. 1100, Patteson, J. The statute does not apply to a lease for fourteen years, determinable by either party at the end of the first seven years, and which has accordingly been determined by notice from the tenant; *Doe* d. *Cardigan* v. *Roe*, 1 D. & R. 540; nor where the landlord claims under a proviso for re-entry for non-performance of covenants; *Doe* d. *Cundey* v. *Sharpley*, 15 M. & W. 558; nor where the term has been surrendered; *Doe* d. *Tindal* v. *Roe, supra ;* nor where the tenant or his assignee claims to hold over after the expiration of the lease or agreement under a different title, *ex. gr.* as heir at law. *Doe* d. *Sanders* v. *Roe*, 1 Dowl. 4; or under a fresh tenancy from year to year created without any writing, whether such new tenancy has or has not been duly determined by a regular notice to quit. *Ante*, 380.

We have already fully considered the law with respect to "notices to quit," *ante*, Chap. III. pp. 29—57.

There must have been a *lawful demand in writing of possession*, made and signed by the landlord or his agent. *See the form, Appendix, No.* 6. Such demand is sufficient notwithstanding it goes on to say, "in default whereof I shall forthwith proceed by ejectment." *Doe* d. *Marquis of Anglesey* v. *Roe*, 2 D. & R. 565. But it is better to omit such words, and everything beyond the mere demand of possession.

It seems that the demand of possession may be served before the expiration of the term (to quit at the proper time), and that the usual notice to quit is sufficient. *Wilkinson* v. *Colley*, 5 Burr. 2694, 2698; *Cutting* v. *Derby*, 2 W. Black. 1075; *Hirst* v. *Horn*, 6 M. & W. 393. It must be "served personally upon, or left at the dwelling-house or usual place of abode" of the tenant or "person holding or claiming by or under him;" and, if possible, an *express refusal* to deliver up possession according to the notice should be obtained from the tenant, or other person in actual possession, at the time the demand is served. If the tenant or other person in possession happen to be not at home, further application should be subsequently made, in such manner as will be sufficient to satisfy the court or a judge that the tenant or other person has *refused* to deliver up possession. A tenant may, by his conduct, in effect refuse to deliver up possession, whilst professing by words his readiness and willingness to do so. This only increases the difficulty of proof.

Service on a clerk or warehouseman of the tenant, &c., at his place of business, where he does not reside or sleep, seems insufficient, it not being his dwelling-house or usual place of abode within the meaning of the act. See *Maybury* v. *Mudie*, 5 C. B. 283; 5 Dowl. & L. 360; *Russell* v. *Knowles*, 7 Man. & Gr. 1001; 8 Scott, N. R. 716; 2 Dowl. & L. 595, *S. C.*; *Thomas* v. *Thomas*, 2 Moo. & Sc. 730; *Allen* v. *Greensill*, 4 C. B. 100; *Ex parte Rice Jones*, 1 Low. M. & P. 357, 363; *Reg.* v. *Hammond*, 21 Law J., N. S., Q. B., 153. Where the demand of possession was put under the door of the tenant's house, his wife being therein, but refusing to open the door, and the tenant himself had absconded to America; held sufficient for a rule nisi. *Doe* d. *Selgood* v. *Roe*, 1 Harr. W. & W. 206.

A *sufficient refusal to deliver up possession*, after a lawful demand in writing, having been obtained, the landlord may proceed by action of ejectment for the recovery of possession, and at the foot of the writ in ejectment "address a notice to such tenant or person requiring him to find such bail, if ordered by the court or a judge, and for such purposes as are" specified in sect. 213. *Ante*, 379. And by the form, No. 21, in the schedule to the act, such notice may be as follows:—

"Take notice, that you will be required, if ordered by the court or a judge, to give bail by yourself and two sufficient sureties, conditioned to pay the costs and damages which shall be recovered in this action." *See Appendix, No.* 16.

In other respects the writ is in the common form, and must be served in the usual manner. *Ante*, Chap. X.

If the tenant or other person in possession do not appear, final judgment may be signed and execution issued in the usual manner. *Ante*, 131.

Upon an appearance being entered, an affidavit or affidavits should be made showing all the necessary facts to bring the case within sect. 213. *See the form, Appendix, No.* 42. It is not essentially necessary that the landlord join in any such affidavit. In most cases this may easily be avoided. His bailiff, steward, attorney or agent can generally prove the holding under the lease or agreement, and the notice to quit, demand of possession, &c.

It is desirable to avoid *annexing* the counterpart or duplicate lease or agreement to any affidavit, because, if annexed, it must be *filed with the affidavit*, whereas it may be wanted at the trial; and the landlord may also wish to retain it in his own possession as one of his title deeds. But the lease or agreement, or some counterpart or duplicate thereof, must be *produced* to the court or judge when the application is made, and the execution thereof must be proved by affidavit. *Doe* d. *Foucan* v. *Roe*, 2 Low. M. & P. 322. The marginal note of this case incorrectly says that the lease or agreement must be *annexed;* but the case itself does not so decide; and it has been held sufficient to verify the document in manner above suggested, getting it marked as an exhibit by the commissioner. *Doe* d. *Platter* v. *Bell*, 8 Jur. 1100, Patteson, J. It will be observed that in the Appendix, No. 42, the lease or agreement is not annexed to the affidavit. If the application be made to the court the rule nisi should be drawn up on reading (*inter alia*) the original lease or agreement, or counterpart or duplicate produced, as well as the affidavits and writings annexed. But upon application to a judge at chambers the summons does not mention the documents upon which the application is founded.

If there be an *attesting* witness to the original lease or agreement, or counterpart or duplicate, it is not essentially necessary that upon an application of this nature the execution of the deed or writing should be proved by such witness, especially since the 17 & 18 Vict. c. 125, s. 26. It is sufficient to establish a *primâ facie* case in support of the application, and therefore any person competent to prove the defendant's signature may make the necessary affidavit. *Doe* d. *Gowland* v. *Roe*, 6 Dowl. 35; *Doe* d. *Morgan* v. *Rotherham*, 3 Dowl. 690. But if the attesting witness be an attorney, and *refuse* to make an affidavit to prove the execution by the defendant of the deed or writing, the court, upon a summary application, will compel him to do so, and to pay the costs of the application. *Doe* d. *Avery* v. *Roe*, 6 Dowl. 518. If the attesting witness (whether an attorney or not), refuse to make an affidavit, a summons and order may be obtained for his examination before a judge or master pursuant to 17 & 18 Vict. c. 125, s. 48.

It seems that the counterpart or duplicate lease or agreement must be *duly stamped before* the application is made for the summons or rule nisi, and that it is not sufficient to move on a copy or on an instrument stamped after the rule nisi and before cause shown. *Doe* d. *Caulfield* v. *Roe*, 3 Bing. N. C. 329; 5 Dowl. 365; *Doe* d. *Holder* v. *Rushworth*, 4 M. & W. 74. The stamp acts enact that no instrument in writing liable to duty "shall be pleaded or given in evidence in any court, or admitted in any court to be *good, useful or available* in law or equity," until the instrument has been stamped with a lawful stamp. 5 W. & M. c. 21, s. 11; 55 Geo. 3, c. 184, s. 8; 13 & 14 Vict. c. 97, s. 2. But in *Doe* d. *Phillips* v. *Roe*, 5 B. & A. 766; 1 D. & R. 433, it was held that the lease or agreement need not be stamped before the rule is granted, it being time enough any time before the trial of the ejectment. This case must not be relied on since the more recent authorities above mentioned.

It is very important that the affidavits be *complete and sufficient in all respects*, to establish a *primâ facie* case within the statute; because, as a general rule, they cannot afterwards be amended, or any defect supplied by further affidavits; nor can a fresh application to the court be made upon new affidavits; unless leave for that purpose be given when the application is discharged. *Rex* v. *Bowditch*, 2 Chit. R. 278; *Reg.* v. *Inhabitants of Barton*, 9 Dowl. 1021; *Surridge* v. *Ellis*, 7 C. B. 1007; *Tilt* v. *Dickson*, 4 C. B. 744; *Joynes* v. *Collinson*, 13 M. & W.

558, 560, note (*b*). But see *Dodgson* v. *Scott*, 2 Exch. 457 ; 6 Dowl. & L. 27 ; *Pocock* v. *Pickering*, 18 Q. B. 789.

Under the 1 Geo. 4, c. 87, s. 1, the application could have been made only to the court in term time ; but under the 15 & 16 Vict. c. 76, s. 213, the landlord may " move the court, or apply by summons to a judge at chambers, for a rule or summons for such tenant or person to show cause," &c. *See forms of Rule Nisi and Summons, Appendix, Nos.* 43, 45.

Upon the application for the rule nisi or summons the court or judge, on a consideration of the situation of the premises, will *fix a time* for the tenant or person in possession to show cause, &c. ; but the amount of the " reasonable sum" for which the recognizance is to be entered into, or the time within which the recognizance is to be entered into, need not be mentioned in the rule nisi or summons. The court or judge will fix the *sum* and *time* "upon a consideration of all the circumstances," when the application is disposed of. *Doe* d. *Marquis of Anglesey* v. *Brown*, 2 D. & R. 688. A sum equal to *one year's value* of the premises, *with a reasonable sum for costs* (about 40*l.*) is usually required. *Doe* d. *Sampson* v. *Roe*, 6 Moore, 54 ; *Doe* d. *Levi* v. *Roe*, 6 C. B. 272. The amount will not be increased by reason of any dilapidations, or of any damage done to the business by shutting up the premises, or the like. *Doe* d. *Marks* v. *Roe*, 6 Dowl. & Low. 87 ; *Doe* d. *Levi* v. *Roe, supra.*

The rule nisi or summons having been obtained (*see the forms, Appendix, Nos.* 43, 45), must be served upon the tenant or person in possession in the usual manner, and an affidavit of such service should be made. *See the forms, Appendix, Nos.* 23, 26, 27.

Upon showing cause, the tenant, or other person mentioned in the rule or summons, may raise (*inter alia*) any or either of the following objections to the application. But if the objections relied on do not clearly appear on the face of the plaintiff's affidavits, an affidavit or affidavits should be made by or on behalf of the tenant, &c., clearly proving the facts upon which the objection is founded. *Roe* d. *Durrant* v. *Moore*, 6 Bing. 574. The tenant, &c. may show as cause :—1. That the lease or agreement was not *in writing* (*ante*, 380). 2. That it was not duly stamped when the rule nisi or summons was obtained (*ante*, 383). 3. That the execution of it by the defendant is not proved (*ante*, 383). 4. That the lease or agreement was not for a term certain, which has expired by effluxion of time (*ante*, 381). 5. That the tenancy from year to year under which the defendant last held the premises was created without any writing, or was a fresh tenancy created orally, or by the payment and acceptance of rent subsequent to the expiration or determination of the tenancy under the written lease or agreement mentioned in the plaintiff's affidavits (*ante*, 380). But in such case the affidavits in opposition should clearly show the creation of the new term or tenancy, and for what period, and at what rent, &c. *Roe* d. *Durrant* v. *Moore*, 6 Bing. 574. 6. That the tenancy from year to year has not been determined by a *regular* notice to quit (*ante*, 381). But in such case the affidavits in opposition should clearly show what notice to quit (if any) was given, and in what respect it was defective or insufficient ; or that no notice whatever was served either on the tenant, &c., or at his house, and that no such notice has ever come to the possession *or knowledge* of the tenant, &c. See the cases in which an application has been made to set aside proceedings in a personal action, no writ of summons having been served on the defendant. *Emerson* v. *Brown*, 7 Man. & Gr. 476; *Morris* v. *Coles*, 2 Dowl. 79; *Phillips* v. *Ensell*, 2 Dowl. 684; 1 Cr., Mee. & Ros. 374; 4 Tyr. 814, *S. C.* 7. That there has been no lawful demand of possession made pursuant to the statute (*ante*, 381, 382); but unless the defect clearly appear on the face of the plaintiff's affidavits, it should be shown by the affidavits in opposition in the same manner as the want of due notice to quit (*ante*, 384). 8. That there has been no sufficient refusal to deliver up possession (*ante*, 382). 9. That the tenant, &c. is entitled to retain possession under some *distinct title*, *ex. gr.*, as heir at law. *Doe* d. *Sanders* v. *Roe*, 1 Dowl. 4. But in such cases the title of the tenant, &c. should be clearly shown in such a manner as to satisfy the court or judge that the party *bonâ fide* has a title, not inconsistent with his holding during the term under the lease or agreement. The court or judge may permit the new matter to be answered by further affidavits. 17 & 18 Vict. c. 125, s. 45. 10. That the plaintiff's affidavits are materially defective on some or one of the above points. 11. That one of the plaintiff's affidavits is defective in form or otherwise objectionable (*see the Practice Rules of H. T.* 1853, *Nos.* 138—148, *Appendix, No.* 19, *notes*); and that without such affidavit there are not sufficient materials before the court or judge to support the application. Objections of this nature are usually taken in the first instance.

If the rule be made absolute, or the order granted, draw it up (*see the forms, Appendix, Nos.* 44, 46), serve a copy on the tenant or his attorney in the usual manner. An affidavit of service need not be prepared until it is wanted. *See the forms, Appendix, Nos.* 26, 27.

Bail, when so ordered, must be put in for the tenant in like manner as in a personal action. 1 Chit. Arch. 768 (9th ed.); *see form of Recognizance, Appendix, No.* 48). If taken before a commissioner in the country, there must be an affidavit of caption. *See the form, Appendix, No.* 49. The recognizance and affidavit must be filed with one of the masters. 15 & 16 Vict. c. 76, s. 216 (*post*, 389). Notice thereof must be given forthwith. *See the form, Appendix, No.* 51.

By Reg. Prac. H. T. 1853, No. 91, "notice of more bail than two shall be deemed irregular, unless by order of the court or a judge."

92. "The bail of whom notice shall be given shall not be changed without leave of the court or a judge."

93. "No person or persons shall be permitted to justify himself or themselves as good and sufficient bail for any defendant or defendants, if such person or persons shall have been indemnified for so doing by the attorney or attorneys concerned for any such defendant or defendants."

94. "If any person put in as bail to the action, except for the purpose of rendering only, be a practising attorney, or clerk to a practising attorney, or a sheriff's officer, bailiff or person concerned in the execution of process, the plaintiff may treat the bail as a nullity, and sue upon the bail-bond as soon as the time for putting in bail has expired, unless good bail be duly put in in the meantime."

95. "In the case of country bail, the bail-piece shall be transmitted and filed within eight days."

96. "A defendant may justify bail at the same time at which they are put in, upon giving four days' notice for that purpose, before eleven o'clock in the morning, and exclusive of Sunday. If the plaintiff is

S

desirous of time to inquire after the bail, and shall give one day's notice thereof as aforesaid to the defendant, his attorney or agent, as the case may be, before the time appointed for justification, stating therein what further time is required, such time not to exceed three days, then (unless the court or a judge shall otherwise order) the time for putting in and justifying bail shall be postponed accordingly, and all proceedings shall be stayed in the meantime."

97. "Every notice of bail shall, in addition to the descriptions of the bail, mention the street or place, and number (if any), where each of the bail resides, and all the streets or places, and numbers (if any), in which each of them has been resident at any time within the last six months, and whether he is a housekeeper or freeholder."

98. "If the notice of bail shall be accompanied by an affidavit of each of the bail, according to the following form [*Appendix, No.* 50], and if the plaintiff afterwards except to such bail, he shall, if such bail are allowed, pay the costs of justification; and if such bail are rejected, the defendant shall pay the costs of opposition, unless the court or a judge thereof shall otherwise order."

99. "If the plaintiff shall not give one day's notice of exception to the bail by whom such affidavit shall have been made, the recognizance of such bail may be taken out of court without other justification than such affidavit."

100. "Where notice of bail shall not be accompanied by such affidavit, and in bail in error, the plaintiff may except thereto within twenty days next after the putting in of such bail, and notice thereof given in writing to the plaintiff or his attorney; or where special bail is put in before any commissioner, the plaintiff may except thereto within twenty days next after the bail-piece is transmitted, and notice thereof given as aforesaid; and no exception to bail shall be admitted after the time hereinbefore limited." *See form of Notice of Exception, Appendix, No.* 52.

101. "Affidavits of justification shall be deemed insufficient unless they state that each person justifying is worth double the amount sworn to over and above what will pay his just debts, and over and above every other sum for which he is then bail, except when the sum sworn to exceeds 1,000*l.*, when it shall be sufficient for the bail to justify in 1,000*l.* beyond the sum sworn to." *See the form of Affidavit, Appendix, No.* 50.

102. "It shall be sufficient in all cases if notice of justification of bail be given two days before the time of justification." *See form of Notice, Appendix, No.* 53.

103. "In all cases bail, either to the action or in error, shall be justified, when required, within four days after exception, before a judge at chambers, both in term and vacation."

If for any reason (other than the gross neglect of the defendant or his attorney) sufficient bail be not put in, or do not justify in due time, an application should be made to the court or a judge (founded upon a proper affidavit) to enlarge the time for obeying the rule or order until a specified period. *See form of Summons, Appendix, No.* 47. But if the sureties be rejected for insufficiency, or do not appear to justify, such application should then be made orally, and in such case the rule or order for enlarging the time (if granted) will be absolute in the first instance.

After the time, or the enlarged time (if any), allowed for obeying the rule or order has elapsed, "the lessor or landlord filing an affidavit that such rule or order has been made and served, and not complied with [*see the form, Appendix, No.* 56], shall be at liberty to sign judgment for recovery of possession and costs of suit in the form contained in schedule (A) to this act annexed, marked No. 21, or to the like effect." Sect. 213; *see Appendix, No.* 57.

If the recognizance be filed and completed in due time, the plaintiff should make up the issue and proceed to trial in the usual manner. He should take care to be prepared to prove at the trial (*inter alia*) the service of notice of trial, and the amount of mesne profits to which he is entitled. *Infra.* If a verdict be found for the plaintiff, the judge will not order a stay of judgment or execution (to allow of an application for a new trial), except on condition that within four days from the day of the trial the defendant shall actually find security by a recognizance, with two sureties, not to commit waste, &c. (sect. 215; *post,* 388), unless it appear to the judge that the verdict was contrary to the evidence, or the damages given were excessive (*post,* 388); nor will execution be stayed by proceedings in error without a recognizance pursuant to sect. 208. *Ante,* 363; *Roe* d. *Durrant* v. *Moore,* 7 Bing. 124; 4 Moo. & P. 761; 1 Dowl. 203.

2. Verdict for mesne Profits.]—By 15 & 16 Vict. c. 76, s. 214, "whenever it shall appear on the trial of any ejectment, at the suit of a *landlord against a tenant,* that such tenant or his attorney hath been *served with due notice of trial,* the judge before whom such cause shall come on to be tried shall, whether the defendant shall appear upon such trial or not, permit the claimant on the trial, *after proof of his right to recover possession* of the whole or any part of the premises mentioned in the writ in ejectment, to go into *evidence of the mesne profits thereof* which shall or might have accrued from the day of the expiration or determination of the tenant's interest in the same, down to the time of the verdict given in the cause, or to some preceding day to be specially mentioned therein; and the jury on the trial finding for the claimant shall in such case give their verdict upon the whole matter, both as to the recovery of the whole or any part of the premises, and also as to the amount of the damages to be paid for such mesne profits [*see the form of Postea, Appendix, No.* 245 a]; and in such case the landlord shall have judgment within the time hereinbefore provided, not only for the recovery of possession and costs, but also for the mesne profits found by the jury [*see the form, Appendix, No.* 264]: provided always, that nothing hereinbefore contained shall be construed to bar any such landlord from bringing any action for the mesne profits which shall accrue from the verdict, or the day so specified therein, down to the day of the delivery of possession of the premises recovered in the ejectment."

This section is in substance a re-enactment of 1 Geo. 4, c. 87, s. 2. It applies to all actions of ejectment *as between landlord and tenant,* and is not confined to those cases in which security has been given pursuant to sect. 213 (*ante,* 379). Therefore its position between sects. 213 and 215 is somewhat inaccurate.

Mesne profits may be recovered under sect. 214, although the writ and issue do not contain any claim in respect of them. *Smith* v. *Tett,* 9 Exch. 307.

To enable the landlord to recover a verdict and judgment *for mesne profits* under this section, it must appear at the trial : 1. That the plaintiff was landlord, and the defendant tenant of the premises sought to be recovered, or some part thereof. 2. That the plaintiff has the right to recover possession of the whole or part of the premises mentioned in the writ of ejectment. 3. That the tenant or his attorney has been served with due notice of trial. But if the tenant appear at the trial, proof of due service of the notice of trial is unnecessary. *Doe* d. *Thompson* v. *Hodgson*, 2 Moo. & Rob. 283 ; 12 A. & E. 135 ; 4 P. & D. 142, *S. C.* Such appearance of itself amounts to sufficient proof that due notice of trial has been given. 4. Evidence of the mesne profits must be given, as in an action for mesne profits. See *post*, Chap. LXVIII. No notice of the plaintiff's intention to claim mesne profits need be mentioned in the writ or issue, or in any other manner before the trial. *Smith* v. *Tett*, 9 Exch. 307.

It is *optional* with the landlord to proceed under this section, or in the usual manner, and afterwards to bring an action of trespass for mesne profits : *post*, Chap. LXVIII. : or for double value or double rent : *post*, Chap. LXIX. : but it is to be observed, that where security has been given pursuant to sect. 213 (*ante*, 379), such security is conditioned "to pay the costs *and damages* which shall be recovered by the claimants in the action," and this will, of course, include all damages in respect of mesne profits, which may be recovered pursuant to this section, but not mesne profits, or double value, or double rent, to be recovered in any subsequent action.

3. *No stay of Judgment or Execution without a Recognizance not to commit Waste, &c.*]—By 15 & 16 Vict. c. 76, s. 215, " in all cases *in which such security shall have been given as aforesaid* [sect. 213, *ante*, 379], if upon the trial a verdict shall pass for the claimant, *unless* it shall appear to the judge before whom the same shall have been had, that the finding of the jury was contrary to the evidence, or that the damages given were excessive, such judge shall not, *except by consent*, make any order to stay judgment or execution, *except on condition that within four days* from the day of the trial, the defendant shall actually find security, by the recognizance of himself and two sufficient sureties, in such reasonable sum as the judge shall direct, conditioned not to commit any waste, or act in the nature of waste, or other wilful damage, and not to sell or carry off any standing crops, hay, straw or manure produced or made (if any) upon the premises, and which may happen to be thereupon, from the day on which the verdict shall have been given to the day on which execution shall finally be made upon the judgment, or the same be set aside, as the case may be : provided always, that the recognizance last above mentioned shall immediately stand discharged and be of no effect, in case proceedings in error shall be brought upon such judgment, and the plaintiff in error shall become bound in the manner hereinbefore provided." Sect. 208, *ante*, 361.

This section is very similar in substance to the 1 Geo. 4, c. 87, s. 3. It applies only where security has been given pursuant to sect. 213 (*ante*, 379). If the claimant obtain the verdict, judgment may be signed and execution issue for the recovery of possession of the property, or such part thereof as the jury shall find the claimant entitled to, and for costs, on the fifth day in term after the verdict, if the cause be tried in term time in London or Middlesex ; or within fourteen days after the verdict, if the cause be tried in vacation, whether in town or at the assizes (sect. 185, *ante*, 336); unless the judge order judgment or execution to be stayed until the fifth day of the next term, to give the defendant an opportunity to move for new trial, &c. No such order is to be made in cases falling within sect. 215, *except on condition* that within four days from the day of the trial the defendant shall actually find security, &c. *Ante*, 388; *see the form of such Order, Appendix, No.* 240. But an order to stay judgment or execution *without any such condition* may be made in the following cases: 1. Where it appears to the judge that the finding of the jury was contrary to the evidence. 2. Where it appears to the judge that the damages given were excessive. 3. By consent. *See the form of Order, Appendix, No.* 239.

The order, whether made with or without the above-mentioned "condition," should be drawn up and served forthwith. And the defendant should take care to enter into and file a proper recognizance (pursuant to sect. 216, *infra*) within four days after the verdict, *exclusive* of the day of trial. Reg. Prac. H. T. 1853, No. 174; *see form, Appendix, No.* 241. It seems that notice of such recognizance should be forthwith given, and the sureties may be compelled to justify in like manner as where a tenant is ordered to find bail before being permitted to defend. *See the forms, Appendix, Nos.* 50—55.

By 15 & 16 Vict. c. 76, s. 216, "all recognizances and securities entered into *as last aforesaid* [*ante*, 388], may and shall be taken respectively *in such manner, and by and before such persons* as are provided and authorized in respect of recognizances of bail upon actions and suits depending in the court in which any such action of ejectment shall have been commenced; and the officer of the same court with whom recognizances of bail are filed shall file such recognizances and securities, for which respectively the sum of two shillings and sixpence, and no more, shall be paid; but no action or other proceeding shall be commenced upon any such recognizance or security after the expiration of six months from the time when possession of the premises, or any part thereof, shall actually have been delivered to the landlord."

4. *Where Landlord's Right of Entry accrues in or after Hilary or Trinity Term.*]—By 15 & 16 Vict. c. 76, s. 217, "in all actions of ejectment hereafter to be brought in any of her Majesty's Courts at Westminster, *by any landlord against his tenant*, or against any person claiming through or under such tenant, for the recovery of any lands or hereditaments in any county, except London or Middlesex, where the tenancy shall expire, or the right of entry into or upon such lands or hereditaments shall accrue to such landlord, *in or after Hilary or Trinity Terms respectively*, it shall be lawful for the claimant in any such action, at any time *within ten days after such tenancy shall expire, or right of entry accrue* as aforesaid, *to serve* a writ in ejectment, in the form contained in the Schedule (A) to this act annexed, marked No. 13, except that it shall command the persons to whom it is directed *to appear within ten days* after service thereof in the court in which such action may be brought [*see the form, Appendix, No.* 17]; and the like proceedings shall be thereupon had as hereinbefore provided, save that it shall be sufficient to give *at least six clear days' notice of trial* to the defendant before the commission day of the assizes at which such ejectment is intended to be tried; and any de-

fendant in such action may, at any time *before* the trial thereof, apply to a judge by summons to stay or set aside the proceedings, or to postpone the trial until the next assizes [*see form of Summons, Appendix, No.* 19] ; and it shall be lawful for the judge, in his discretion, to make such order in the said cause as to him shall seem expedient."

This section is in substance a re-enactment of the 11 Geo. 4 & 1 Will. 4, c. 70, s. 36. It only applies to ejectments by landlords against their tenants, or persons claiming through or under them, for lands or hereditaments situate elsewhere than in London or Middlesex (*Doe* d. *Norris* v. *Roe*, 1 Dowl. 547); and where the right of entry first accrued in or after *Hilary* or *Trinity* Term. *Doe* v. *Roe*, 2 Cr. & Jer. 123; 1 Dowl. 304; *Doe* d. *Somerville* v. *Roe*, 4 Moo. & Sc. 747. The object of the enactment is to enable landlords to proceed to trial at the ensuing assizes, and to prevent tenants, or persons claiming through or under them, from wrongfully holding over until the second assizes, before which time (except for this enactment) the action could not be brought to trial, in many cases.

This section applies, not only where the tenancy has *expired*, or been duly *determined* by a notice to quit, but also to cases where a right of entry has first accrued under a *proviso for re-entry* for nonperformance of any covenant or agreement, on some day in or after Hilary or Trinity Term. *Doe* d. *Antrobus* v. *Jepson*, 3 B. & Adol. 402; *Doe* d. *Rankin* v. *Brindley*, 4 B. & Adol. 84.

An ejectment for nonpayment of half a year's rent due at *Christmas*, founded on a proviso for re-entry on nonpayment of rent for twenty-one days after it becomes due, would require the aid of this section, to enable the landlord to proceed to trial at the Spring Assizes (see also 15 & 16 Vict. c. 76, s. 210), except perhaps where the particular assizes occur late on the circuit, and the plaintiff loses no time. In such a case the right of entry would not accrue until the 16th January, the 15th being the last day to save the forfeiture.

The writ of ejectment under this section is in the usual form, except that it commands the persons to whom it is directed to appear within *ten* days (instead of *sixteen* days) after service thereof. *See Appendix, No.* 17. The claimant should only "claim to be entitled" to possession, without saying "on and since the —— day of ——, A.D. ——." Or if those words be used, care must be taken not to allege a title before the first day of the term, nor more than ten days before the writ can be *served*.

The writ must not only be *issued*, but also *served* within ten days after the tenancy expired, or the right of entry first accrued, otherwise the writ, or the service thereof (as the case may be), will be *irregular*. *Doe* d. *Rankin* v. *Brindley*, 4 B. & Adol. 84 ; 2 N. & M. 1. But the application must, as in other cases of irregularity, be made promptly. Reg. Prac. H. T. 1853, Nos. 135, 136 ; *see form of Summons, Appendix, No.* 18. The application should be supported by an affidavit, showing specially *when* the tenancy expired or the right of entry accrued, and when the writ was issued, and the copy served. Such copy should be annexed to the affidavit, and the irregularity relied on should be made to appear clearly. It cannot be objected at nisi prius that the action has not been commenced within ten days after the right of entry accrued, this being merely matter of irregularity. *Doe* d. *Rankin* v. *Brindley, supra*.

In case of nonappearance by the defendant within *ten* days (exclusive of the day of service, but inclusive of the last day, Reg. Prac. H. T. 1853, No. 174), the claimant may sign judgment and issue execution in the usual manner. *Ante,* 131.

If the defendant appear, the proceedings to trial are the same as in other cases (*ante,* 134, *et seq.*), except that "at least six clear days' notice of trial" must be given, *i.e., exclusive* both of the day of the notice and of the commission day. *Rex* v. *Justices of Herefordshire,* 3 B. & A. 581 ; *Zouch* v. *Empsey,* 4 B. & A. 522 ; *Re Prangley,* 4 A. & E. 781 ; 6 N. & M. 421 ; *Reg.* v. *Justices of Shropshire,* 8 A. & E. 173 ; 3 N. & P. 286 ; *Mitchell* v. *Forster,* 12 A. & E. 472 ; 4 P. & D. 150 ; 9 Dowl. 527 ; *Rex* v. *Justices of Middlesex,* 3 Dowl. & L. 109. The want of sufficient, or indeed of any, notice of trial will be waived if the defendant appear at the trial, and take his chance of the verdict. *Doe* d. *Antrobus* v. *Jepson,* 3 B. & Adol. 402. It is not necessary to prove at the trial that notice of trial has been given (*S. C.*), unless the claimant seeks to recover mesne profits. *Ante,* 388.

The defendant may at any time *before* the trial apply to a judge by summons to stay or set aside the proceedings, or to postpone the trial until the next assizes (*see form of Summons, Appendix, No.* 18); and upon any such application " it shall be lawful for the judge, in his discretion, to make such order in the said cause as to him shall seem expedient." Of course any application of the above nature should be supported by affidavit, showing the special circumstances; and the plaintiff may answer such affidavit, and may request the judge, if the application be not rejected or dismissed, to impose such terms upon the defendant as will prevent him from obtaining any undue advantage, or the plaintiff from suffering any unfair prejudice by the delay, &c.

CHAPTER XXXVII.

GENERALLY speaking, when a tenant for years under a lease or agreement *in writing* holds over after the expiration of his term, the best mode of proceeding against him is, first to make a *demand in writing* of possession, pursuant to 15 & 16 Vict. c. 76, s. 213 (*ante*, 379), and to *obtain his refusal* to deliver up possession (*ante*, 382), and afterwards to proceed by ejectment in the form and manner pointed out by that section; whereby he may be compelled to find sureties to pay the costs and damages to be recovered in the action, before he will be permitted to defend it. *Ante*, 378.

But it is optional with the landlord to avail himself of the above mode of proceeding, or to bring an ejectment in the ordinary manner. *Ante*, 378. In the latter case it is not necessary to prove any demand of possession, or refusal to deliver up possession, before action. 2 Arch. N. P. 392. But the special advantages given by the statute will be lost.

If a new tenancy from year to year has been created subsequently to the expiration of the lease, by the payment and acceptance of rent due at a later period, or by any other equivalent act, such tenancy must be determined by a regular notice to quit before an ejectment can be maintained. *Doe d. Hollingsworth* v. *Stennett*, 2 Esp. 717, Lord Kenyon, C. J.; *Bishop* v. *Howard*, 2 B. & C. 100; 3 D. & R. 293; *Doe* d. *Thompson* v. *Amey*, 12 A. & E. 476; 4 P. & D. 177; *Doe* d. *Lord* v. *Crago*, 6 C. B. 90; *ante*, 34. In such case the landlord cannot proceed according to sect. 213, the new tenancy not being under a lease or agreement *in writing*. *Ante*, 380; see *Doe d. Lansdell* v. *Gower*, 17 Q. B. 589.

A lease to A. and his assigns, habendum for his life, and for the lives of B. and C., is but one estate of freehold, to continue during three lives, and the survivor of them. *Rosse's case*, 5 Co. R. 13 a; Moore, 398; *Ross* v. *Aldwick*, Cro. Eliz. 491; *Bowles* v. *Poore*, Cro. Jac. 282; 1 Bulst. 135. A lease to M. and her heirs during the lives of T. E., M. E. and her son, A.'s granddaughter (then unborn), and the life of the survivor of them, determines on the deaths of T. E. and M. E. *Doe* d. *Pemberton* v. *Edwards*, 1 M. & W. 553; Tyr. & Gr. 1006. A lease for

ninety-nine years of A., B. and C., or the survivor of them, so long
live, does not create a freehold, but operates as a demise for a term
equal to the life of the survivor. *Earl of Derby* v. *Taylor,* 1 East,
502; *Doe* d. *Lord* v. *Crago,* 6 C. B. 90. A lease for sixty years, if
A. & B. so long live, is determined by the death of either A. or B.;
but if a lease be made for the lives of A. and B., the freehold is not determined by the death of one of them. *Hughes and Crowther's case,*
13 Co. R. 66. A lease to E. C. for ninety-nine years, if she should so
long live, with remainder over in the event of her death during the
said *term,* operates as a lease for ninety-nine years. *Wright* d. *Plowden* v. *Cartwright,* 1 Burr. 282; but see *contra, Green* v. *Edwards,*
Cro. Eliz. 216. A lease to A. during the minority of I. G., who is
then of the age of ten years, operates as a lease for eleven years, if
I. G. so long live. *Bishop of Bath's case,* 6 Co. R. 35; *Boraston's
case,* 3 Co. R. 19; *Say* v. *Smith,* Plow. 273, West, J. So a gift by
will to A. during the minority of B. is a bequest for a term of years
determinable upon the death of B. under age. It is not a freehold.
Whittombe v. *Lamb,* 12 M. & W. 813.

If a tenant for life grant a lease for ninety-nine years (not in pursuance of a power), it will cease on his death, and the remainderman
may then enter or maintain ejectment: but if the latter has since
received rent, or otherwise recognized the tenancy, the lease will not
be thereby established for the residue of the term thereby expressed to
be granted, but a new tenancy from year to year will be created, which
may be determined at the end of any year of the term mentioned in the
lease, upon the usual notice to quit being given. *Potter* v. *Archer,* 1
Bos. & P. 531; *Doe* d. *Simpson* v. *Butcher,* 1 Doug. 50; *Roe* d. *Jordan* v. *Ward,* 1 H. Blac. 97; *Doe* d. *Martin* v. *Watts,* 7 T. R. 83;
Doe d. *Collins* v. *Weller, Id.* 478; *Doe* d. *Tucker* v. *Morse,* 1 B. &
Adol. 365. If a tenant by the curtesy make a lease for years, reserving rent, the lease is so absolutely determined by his death, that no
acceptance of rent by the heir can make it good. *Miller* v. *Main-
waring,* Cro. Car. 397. But a new implied tenancy from year to year
may be thereby created. *Cases supra.*

Evidence for Plaintiff.]—The plaintiff must prove—
1. The lease or agreement in writing (if any) under which the
defendant held: *Fenn* d. *Thomas* v. *Griffith,* 6 Bing. 533; *Doe* v.
Harvey, 8 Bing. 241: this must be admitted in the cause (*ante,* 150),
or proved in the usual manner. *Ante,* 294. It must also be duly
stamped; 13 & 14 Vict. c. 97, Sched. Part I., tit. "Lease;" 17 & 18
Vict. c. 83; *Doe* d. *Estwick* v. *Way,* 1 T. R. 735; *Doe* d. *Walker* v.
Groves, 15 East, 244; *Doe* d. *Philip* v. *Benjamin,* 9 A. & E. 644; 1
P. & D. 440, 444. The duty is payable upon the consideration *as expressed,* not upon that actually paid. *Doe* d. *Kettle* v. *Lewis,* 10 B.
& C. 673. A duplicate lease executed by both parties must either be
stamped as a lease, or with a five shilling stamp, and also a *denoting*
stamp. 13 & 14 Vict. c. 97, Sched. Part I., tit. "Duplicate or Counterpart." But a counterpart lease, not executed by the lessor, does not
require a denoting stamp. 16 & 17 Vict. c. 59, s. 2. A counterpart
is sufficient even as against an assignee of the lease, without any notice to produce the lease. *Roe* d. *West* v. *Davies,* 7 East, 363; *Hughes*
v. *Clarke,* 10 C. B. 905. Where the subject matter of an agreement
is a limited interest, worth less than 20*l.,* in a thing worth more than

20*l.*, the agreement does not require a stamp. *Doe* d. *Morgan* v. *Amos*, 2 Man. & R. 180. An instrument purporting to be a lease for more than three years, which is not under seal, and consequently void as a lease, may be given in evidence to prove a tenancy from year to year (coupled with proof of payment of part of the rent expressed to be reserved), without being stamped as a lease. *Richardson* v. *Gifford*, 1 A. & E. 52; 3 N. & M. 325. A lessee who executes the counterpart of a lease, or any person claiming under him, cannot dispute its admissibility in evidence, or impeach its validity on the ground of the original lease not being properly stamped. *Paul* v. *Meek*, 2 You. & Jer. 116. Where there is an instrument by which it appears that one party is to give immediate possession and the other to take it, that is a lease, unless it can be collected *from the instrument itself* that it is an agreement only for a lease to be afterwards made. *Per* Lawrence, J., in *Morgan* d. *Dowding* v. *Bissell*, 3 Taunt. 65, cited by Jervis, C. J., in *Stratton* v. *Pettit*, 16 C. B. 420, 435; *ante*, 222. The 8 & 9 Vict. c. 106, s. 3, enacts, that a lease required by law (29 Car. 2, c. 3, s. 3) to be in writing shall be void at law, unless made by deed: nevertheless an instrument in writing (not under seal) purporting to be a lease for five years, and containing *words of present demise*, will amount to a lease void by the statute, rather than to a mere agreement for a lease, if it can be collected from the words used in the instrument itself that the parties *intended a lease*, and not a mere agreement. *Stratton* v. *Pettit*, 16 C. B. 420; *ante*, 223. If the lease or agreement were not in writing, the tenancy must be proved by parol evidence. Ros. Ev. 444; 2 Phil. Ev. 221. The evidence must show on which quarter day or other day in the year the term began and ended. *Doe* d. *Bingham* v. *Cartwright*, 3 B. & A. 326. An unstamped memorandum of the terms of letting, made at the time, and which was then read over to the parties and verbally assented to by them, and signed by the witness (but not by either of the parties), may be used by the witness to refresh his memory. *Lord Bolton* v. *Tomlin*, 5 A. & E. 856; 1 N. & P. 247; *Doe* d. *Brougham* v. *Cartwright*, 3 B. & A. 326; *Trewhitt* v. *Lambert*, 10 A. & E. 470; *Rex* v. *The Inhabitants of Wranch*, 2 A. & E. 514. So may any other memorandum made by the witness himself at or immediately after the letting, and whilst the facts were fresh in his memory. *Trewhitt* v. *Lambert, supra*. Where a proposal was made in writing by A. to let a piece of land to B. on certain terms contained in a written agreement between B. and C., and A. *afterwards agreed by parol* that B. should have the land upon the terms proposed: held, that the original proposal in writing was receivable in evidence without a stamp. *Drant* v. *Browne*, 3 B. & C. 665; 5 D. & R. 582; and see *Edgar* v. *Blick*, 1 Stark. R. 464; *Vaughton* v. *Brine*, 1 Man. & Gr. 359; 1 Scott, N. R. 258; *Vollans* v. *Fletcher*, 1 Exch. 20. A draft agreement for a lease, indorsed "We approve of the within draft," and signed by the parties or their attorney, does not require any stamp. *Doe* d. *Lambourne* v. *Pedgriph*, 4 C. & P. 312, Lord Tenterden, C. J. But where a parol agreement was made between A. and B. that the former should let, and the latter take, certain premises upon the terms and conditions contained in a lease of the same premises previously granted by A. and C.: held, in an action by A. against B. for rent and non-repair, that the lease could not be read in evidence unless duly stamped. *Turner* v. *Power*, 7 B. & C. 625. The terms and conditions of a lease in writing, whether under seal or not, may be proved by the oral admission of the defendant, without producing the lease, such admission constituting as against him primary evidence of the contents. *Howard* v. *Smith,* 3 Man. & Gr. 254; 3 Scott, N. R. 574; *ante,* 170.

2. That the lessee had possession of the premises sought to be recovered, or some part thereof, under or by virtue of the lease or agreement in writing, or the verbal letting (as the case may be). *Encroachments* made by the tenant during the term are generally presumed to have been added to the demised premises, and to *form part thereof* for the benefit of the tenant during the term, and afterwards for the landlord. *Ante,* 247; *Doe d. Lewis* v. *Rees,* 6 C. & P. 610, Parke, B.; *Doe d. Lloyd* v. *Jones,* 15 M. & W. 580; *Andrews* v. *Hailes,* 2 E. & B. 349; *Doe* d. *Croft* v. *Tidbury,* 14 C. B. 304. They may be recovered together with and as part of the demised premises; or if all the premises originally demised have been delivered up to the landlord, they may be recovered separately. *Andrews* v. *Hailes, supra.* And they may be so recovered at any time within the period limited for the recovery of the demised premises, *i. e.,* within twenty years after the expiration of the term. *Doe d. Croft* v. *Tidbury, supra.*

3. If the defendant be not the lessee, it must be proved that he came into possession *under or after* the lessee. *Humphrey* v. *Damion,* Cro. Jac. 300; *ante,* 224.

4. If the claimant be not the lessor, his title to the reversion must be deduced from the lessor, and proved in the usual manner. But if it be shown that the defendant has paid him some of the rent reserved by the lease, or submitted to a distress by him for such rent, and so in effect admitted his title, that will be sufficient. *Ante,* 219, 229.

5. It must appear that the term expired, or ceased, or became forfeited, *before* the commencement of the ejectment. *Wright* d. *Plowden* v. *Cartwright,* 1 Burr. 282; *Doe* d. *Patrick* v. *Duke of Beaufort,* 6 Exch. 498; *ante,* 288. All leases for years determinable on lives may determine not only by the deaths of the parties named, or by effluxion of time, but also by surrender or forfeiture. *Dormer* v. *Parkhouse,* 7 Mod. 371. If the lease were for lives, it must be shown by proper legal evidence that all the *cestui que vies* died before the commencement of the ejectment. *Doe* d. *Lord Arundell* v. *Fowler,* 14 Q. B. 700; *Doe* d. *France* v. *Andrews,* 15 Q. B. 756; *Doe* d. *Pritchard* v. *Dodd,* 5 B. & Adol. 689. But if a lease be granted for the lives of A. and B. and of an *unborn* third person, it will operate only as a lease for the lives of A. and B. *Doe* d. *Pemberton* v. *Edwards,* 1 M. & W. 553; Tyr. & Gr. 1006. A lease for lives may contain a power to add lives. *Doe* d. *Hardwicke* v. *Hardwicke,* 10 East, 549. A lease for sixty years, if A. and B. so long live, is determined by the death of either A. or B.; but if a lease be made for the lives of A. and B., the freehold is not determined by the death of one of them. *Hughes and Crowther's case,* 13 Co. R. 66; *Brudnell's case,* 5 Co. R. 9 a; *Ross's case, Id.* 12 a; Cro. Eliz. 491; Moore, 398; *Utty Dale's case,* Cro. Eliz. 182. A demise by A. to B. for the term of *his* natural life, may enure as a demise either for the life of A. or B., according to circumstances. But if the habendum be to B., his executors, administrators and assigns, a presumption is created in favour of a demise for the life of A.: such presumption is confirmed by a covenant by A. with B. for quiet enjoyment during the life of A.: such a covenant *per se* would amount to a demise. *Doe* d. *Pritchard* v. *Dodd,* 1 N. & M.

838; 5 B. & Adol. 689. Livery of seisin on a lease for lives is now unnecessary. 8 & 9 Vict. c. 106, s. 2.

6. It must appear that the action was commenced within the time allowed by the Statute of Limitations, 3 & 4 Will. 4, c. 27, ss. 5, 9. *Ante,* 11, 15; *Doe* d. *Croft* v. *Tidbury,* 14 C. B. 304.

7. If the claimant seek to recover mesne profits to the day of trial, or to any previous day, he must also prove that the defendant or his attorney has been served with due notice of trial. But if the defendant appear at the trial, such notice need not be proved. *Doe* d. *Thompson* v. *Hodgson,* 12 A. & E. 135; 4 P. & D. 142. No notice of the plaintiff's intention to claim mesne profits need be mentioned in the writ or issue, or in any other manner before the trial. *Smith* v. *Tett,* 9 Exch. 307. The amount which the claimant is entitled to recover for mesne profits must be shown, as in an action for mesne profits. *Post,* Chap. LXVIII.; and see *ante,* 292.

Evidence and Points for Defendant.]—The defendant may contend that the evidence for the plaintiff is insufficient upon some material point. *Ante,* 393—396. He may also produce contradictory evidence. He may object that the lease or agreement on which the plaintiff relies is not duly stamped. *Ante,* 393; *Doe* d. *Walker* v. *Groves,* 15 East, 244. He may also prove that subsequent to the expiration of the lease a new tenancy from year to year has been created by the payment and acceptance of rent due at a later period. *Ante,* 392. Such proof will defeat the action, unless the plaintiff produce evidence in reply, showing that the new tenancy was duly determined before action by a regular notice to quit, or by a disclaimer, surrender, or otherwise.

As a general rule a tenant is estopped from disputing his landlord's title, but he may show that it has *ceased subsequently to the demise.* We have fully considered the cases on this point. *Ante,* 213—222.

Sometimes a prior term may be shown to be undetermined by an attempted surrender on the granting of a new lease by a tenant for life who is since dead; although the original lease has been cancelled. *Roe* d. *Earl of Berkeley* v. *Archbishop of York,* 6 East, 86; 2 Smith, 167; *Davison* d. *Bromley* v. *Stanley,* 4 Burr. 240; *Doe* d. *Earl of Egremont* v. *Courtenay,* 11 Q. B. 702.

CHAPTER XXXVIII.

LANDLORD AGAINST TENANT FOR YEARS—AFTER DETERMINATION
OF THE TERM BY A SPECIAL NOTICE.

Proviso for Determination of Term.]—Leases are sometimes made for a term of years determinable at an earlier period by notice, &c., *ex. gr.* for twenty-one years, determinable at the end of the first seven or fourteen years by either party (or by the lessee), upon giving [twelve] calendar months' previous notice, &c.

The form of a proviso for determining a lease as above mentioned varies in almost every case. It may be as follows:

" Provided always, and it is hereby agreed and declared, that it shall and may be lawful to and for the said [*lessor*], his heirs and assigns, *or* executors, administrators and assigns, or the said [*lessee*], his executors, administrators and assigns, at the expiration of the first [seven *or* fourteen] years of the said term of [twenty-one] years, on giving notice in writing of such purpose and intent to the other of them, his heirs, executors, administrators or assigns (as the case may be), at least [twelve] calendar months before the expiration of such [seven *or* fourteen] years, to determine and make void these presents and the said term hereby granted, anything hereinbefore contained to the contrary notwithstanding ; without prejudice nevertheless to any claim or right of action accrued under or by virtue of these presents before or on the day when the same shall be determined as aforesaid."

Sometimes a proviso of this nature is framed much more unfavorably for the lessee, viz. by making it a *condition precedent* on his part not only to give the above notice, but also duly to pay all the rent, and perform all and singular the covenants on his part to the termination of the notice ; the consequence of which is, that in case of any breach of covenant the lessee is unable to determine the lease at the end of the first seven or fourteen years, in pursuance of the proviso ; his power to do so being conditional only, and the condition not being performed. *Friar* v. *Grey* (in error), 5 Exch. 584, 597 ; *S. C.*, 4 H. L. Cas. 565 ; *Friar* v. *Grey*, 15 Q. B. 891 ; *Porter* v. *Shepherd*, 6 T. R. 665. Such conditions should be objected to in the first instance, and before the lease is executed. But it would not be unreasonable to provide that the lessee (in addition to giving notice) should give up or quit possession, and also pay all rent and arrears of rent to the end of the period mentioned in the notice.

Where power is given to a party to determine a lease on giving a notice *in writing*, he cannot determine it by giving a parol notice. *Legg* d. *Scott* v. *Benion*, Willes, 43.

The notice may be in the following form, or to the like effect, viz. : —

" In pursuance of the proviso or power in this behalf contained in an indenture of lease, dated the —— day of ——, 18—, and made or expressed to be made between [" us," *or as the case may be*], I do hereby give you notice that it is my intention to determine and make void the said lease, and the term of [twenty-one] years thereby granted, at the end of the first [seven *or* fourteen] years of the said term. As witness my hand, this —— day of ——, 18—.''

See another form, Appendix, No. 4.

The notice must end with the first seven or fourteen years (as the case may be), according to the terms of the proviso, and not at any other time. *Cadby* v. *Martinez*, 11 A. & E. 720; 3 P. & D. 386.

The notice must be to quit *all* the demised premises, and not part only. But if the words used may comprise all the premises (as, *Town Barton, &c.*), the court will so construe them *ut res magis valeat quam pereat. Doe* d. *Rodd* v. *Archer*, 14 East, 245, 248. The landlord may, however, reserve to himself the right to determine the lease by notice as to all or *any part* of the land which he may want for building purposes; and, after the stipulated notice has been given, if possession be refused he may maintain ejectment. *Doe* d. *Wilson* v. *Abel*, 2 M. & S. 541.

If a lease be granted "for seven, fourteen or twenty-one years," the lessee only has the option of determining it at the end of the first seven or fourteen years. *Dann* v. *Spurrier*, 3 Bos. & Pul. 399, 442; *Doe* d. *Webb* v. *Dixon*, 9 East, 15.

Demise for twenty-one years; but if either party should die before the end of the said term, then the heirs, executors, &c. of the person so dying should give twelve months' notice to quit, &c. : held, that the lease could only be determined by twelve months' notice given by the representatives of the party dying before the end of the term; and, consequently, that such notice given by the lessor to the representatives of the lessee (who died during the term) did not determine the lease. *Legg* d. *Scott* v. *Benion*, Willes, 43.

Where a lease for twenty-one years contained a proviso that in case either the landlord or tenant, or their respective heirs, executors or administrators, wished to determine it at the end of the first fourteen years, and should give six months' notice in writing *under his or their respective hands*, the term should cease : held, that a notice to quit signed by *two only* of three executors of the lessor, to whom he had bequeathed the freehold as joint tenants, was not good under the proviso, although such notice purported to be given on behalf of all the executors — the proviso requiring the notice to be given " under the respective hands" of all of them. *Right* d. *Fisher* v. *Cuthell*, 5 East, 491; 2 Smith, 83; recognized and distinguished in *Doe* d. *Aslin* v. *Summersett*, 1 B. & Adol. 135, 141.

A proviso in a lease for twenty-one years, that if either of the parties shall be desirous to determine it in seven or fourteen years, it shall be lawful for either of them, *his executors or administrators*, so to do, upon twelve months' notice to the other of them, his heirs, executors or administrators, extends by reasonable intendment to the *devisee* of the lessor, he being entitled to the rent and reversion. *Roe* d. *Bamford* v. *Hayley*, 12 East, 464.

Lease of lands by indenture for twenty-one years, with proviso that it should be determinable by lessee or lessor at the end of the first seven or fourteen years, and memorandum, endorsed six years after the execution of the lease, " of its being agreed between the parties previously to the execution that the lessor shall not dispossess, nor cause the lessee to be dispossessed, of the said estate, but to have it for the term of twenty-one years from this present time, which memorandum was signed by the parties and stamped with a lease stamp, but *not sealed*: held, that the lessor might, notwithstanding such memorandum, determine the lease at the end of the first fourteen years; for that the memorandum did not operate as a new lease and a surrender of the first lease. *Goodright* d. *Nicholls* v. *Mark*, 4 M. & S. 30. Probably in such a case redress might be obtained in a court of equity.

When a lease has been determined by notice pursuant to a proviso in that behalf, and the landlord brings ejectment, he cannot compel the tenant to find sureties to pay the costs and damages pursuant to 15 & 16 Vict. c. 76, s. 213. *Doe* d. *Cardigan* v. *Roe*, 1 Dowl. & Ry. 540; and *Doe* d. *Cundey* v. *Sharpley*, 15 M. & W. 558; *ante*, 381.

Evidence for Plaintiff.]—The plaintiff must prove :—

1. The lease or agreement. This, or a counterpart or duplicate, must be produced, duly stamped, and must be admitted in the cause (*ante*, 150), or proved in the usual manner. *Ante*, 294, 393.

2. That the lessee held the premises sought to be recovered, or some part thereof, under or by virtue of such lease or agreement. If the defendant be not the lessee, it must be proved that he came into possession under or after the lessee. *Humphry* v. *Damion*, Cro. Jac. 300; *ante*, 224.

3. If the plaintiff be not the lessor, his derivative title from the lessor must be proved in the usual manner. But it will be sufficient to show that the defendant has paid to the claimant some part of the rent reserved by the lease, or submitted to a distress by the claimant for such rent. *Ante*, 219, 229.

4. The service of a sufficient notice to determine the lease : and it must appear that the term determined in pursuance of such notice before the day on which possession is claimed in the writ. *Ante*, 288.

5. If the claimant seek to recover the mesne profits to the day of trial, or to any previous day, he must also prove that the defendant or his attorney has been served with due notice of trial. But if the defendant appear at the trial such notice need not be proved. *Doe* d. *Thompson* v. *Hodgson*, 12 A. & E. 135; 4 P. & D. 142. No notice of the plaintiff's intention to claim mesne profits need be mentioned in the writ or issue, or in any other manner before the trial. *Smith* v. *Tett*, 9 Exch. 307. The amount which the claimant is entitled to recover for mesne profits must be proved as in an action for mesne profits. *Post*, Chap. LXVIII.; and see *ante*, 292.

Evidence and Points for Defendant.]—The defendant may contend that the evidence for the plaintiff is insufficient upon some material point. *Supra*. He may also produce contradictory evidence. But he is estopped from disputing his landlord's title to demise, although he may show by evidence that it has since expired, or been legally determined or parted with by way of mortgage, sale, or otherwise. *Ante*, 213—222.

CHAPTER XXXIX.

LANDLORD AGAINST TENANT—FOR A FORFEITURE.

---

1. *Conditions and Provisoes for Re-entry generally.*]—Leases for
years or for life usually contain divers covenants, and also a condition
or proviso for re-entry on breach of any of the covenants, or on breach
of some particular covenant or covenants. Sometimes the condition or
proviso extends to other acts or events than breaches of covenant, *ex.
gr.*, if the lessee shall become a bankrupt or an insolvent debtor. *Roe*
d. *Hunter* v. *Galliers*, 2 T. R. 133; *Doe* d. *Williams* v. *Davies*, 6 C.
& P. 614; *Doe* d. *Bridgman* v. *David*, 1 Cr. M. & R. 405; 5 Tyr.
125; *Doe* d. *Gatehouse* v. *Rees*, 4 Bing. N. C. 384; 6 Scott, 161;
Doe d. *Griffith* v. *Pritchard*, 5 B. & Adol. 765; 2 N. & M. 489;
Doe d. *Lloyd* v. *Ingleby*, 15 M. & W. 465. Or if the term shall be
taken in execution upon any judgment against him; *Davis* v. *Eyton*,
7 Bing. 154; 4 Moo. & P. 820; and such last-mentioned proviso will
prevail even against an extent at the suit of the crown. *Rex* v. *Topping*, M'Clel. & You. 544.

Sometimes the term itself is *limited conditionally, ex. gr.*, for ninety-
nine years, if the lessee, or some other person or persons therein named
shall so long live; *Hughes and Crowther's case*, 13 Co. R. 66; *Brudnell's case*, 5 Co. R. 9 a; or for a certain number of years, provided
the lessee shall so long continue to occupy the premises personally; in
which case it will cease and determine whenever he parts with the
possession, even by compulsion of law. *Doe* d. *Lockwood* v. *Clarke*,
8 East, 185. A lease of a house was made to a widow for forty years
sub conditione quod si tamdiu vixerit sola et inhabitaverit, and she died
in the house, unmarried, within the term: held, that these words made
a condition, and not a conditional limitation, and therefore that the
condition having been performed till her death, the term should go to
her executor. *Hardy* v. *Seyer*, Cro. Eliz. 414. A lease for twenty-
one years, if the lessee continue so long in the service of the lessor, is
not determined by the death of the lessor. *Wrenford* v. *Gyles*, Cro.
Eliz. 643; Noy, 70. Where it was "stipulated and *conditioned*" that
the lessee should not assign, transfer or underlet any part of the lands
and premises otherwise than to his wife, child or children, but there
was no express proviso for re-entry: held, that upon the breach of this
condition, the lessor might maintain an ejectment. *Doe* d. *Henniker*
v. *Watt*, 8 B. & C. 308, 316; 1 M. & R. 694; *Simpson* v. *Titterell*,
Cro. Eliz. 242; *Marsh* v. *Curteys*, Cro. Eliz. 528; Bac. Abr. Condition O. A proviso that the lessee shall pay 120*l.* per annum creates
both a covenant and a condition, for breach of which an ejectment
may be maintained without any express power of re-entry. *Harrington* v. *Wise*, Cro. Eliz. 486, cited 8 B. & C. 316. So with respect to
a proviso and covenant that the lessee shall not fell or cut any wood
but for necessary browse. *Earl of Pembroke* v. *Sir H. Berkeley*, Cro.
Eliz. 384, 560. A proviso that a lessee shall not alien his term without

the lessor's consent is a condition, and devising it is a breach. *Knight* v. *Mory*, Cro. Eliz. 60. Indeed it seems that every proviso amounts to a condition subsequent. *Doe* d. *Wilson* v. *Phillips*, 2 Bing. 13; 9 Moore, 46. A proviso in a lease with no penalty annexed is a condition; but if a penalty be annexed it is a covenant. *Simpson* v. *Tetterell*, Cro. Eliz. 242. If a lessee covenant that he will not do a certain act, on pain of forfeiture, it is a condition to defeat the estate. *Whitchcot* v. *Fox*, Cro. Jac. 398; *Thomas* v. *Ward*, Cro. Eliz. 202; 1 Leon. 245, S. C.

A mere breach of covenant, not fortified by a proviso for re-entry applicable to such covenant, will not enable the lessor to enter or maintain ejectment during the term, but only an action for damages. Lit. s. 325; *Doe* d. *Wilson* v. *Phillips*, 2 Bing. 13; 9 Moore, 46; *Doe* d. *Rudd* v. *Golding*, 6 Moore, 231; *Doe* d. *Rains* v. *Kneller*, 4 C. & P. 3; *Doe* d. *Dark* v. *Bowditch*, 8 Q. B. 973.

Where there is a proviso for re-entry the lessor may, immediately upon a forfeiture happening, enter and take actual possession; *Davis* v. *Burrell and Lane*, 10 C. B. 821; *Davis* v. *Eyton*, 7 Bing. 154; 4 Moo. & P. 820; or he may maintain ejectment without any previous entry for the forfeiture; *Goodright* d. *Hare* v. *Cator*, 2 Doug. 477; cited 4 C. B. 198; *Doe* d. *Wilson* v. *Abel*, 2 M. & S. 541; or he may demise the property to a new tenant, and the entry of such tenant will be equivalent to an entry by the lessor for the forfeiture; *Doe* d. *Griffith* v. *Pritchard*, 5 B. & Adol. 765; 2 N. & M. 489; but nothing of the sort can lawfully be done after the forfeiture (not being a continuing forfeiture) has been waived. *S. C.*; *Arnsby* v. *Woodward*, 6 B. & C. 519; 9 D. & R. 536. Upon a lawful entry being made for a condition broken or other forfeiture, the lessor is *in* of his previous estate, and the lease becomes void. *Simonds* v. *Lawnd*, Cro. Eliz. 239. But the lawfulness of the entry may be tried in a subsequent ejectment. *Doe* d. *Hutchins* v. *Lewis*, 1 Burr. 614, 619; 2 Ld. Ken. 320; *ante*, 77. No forfeiture will accrue for not doing that which could not lawfully be done by reason of an act of parliament made subsequently to the lease. *Doe* d. *Marquis of Anglesey* v. *The Churchwardens and Overseers of Rugeley*, 6 Q. B. 107.

How created.]—A condition or proviso for re-entry may be contained either in a lease or an agreement for a lease. If a tenant hold under an agreement for a lease (not amounting to an actual demise), which agreement specifies the covenants and conditions to be inserted in the lease, with a proviso for re-entry on breach of any covenants, an ejectment may be maintained against him for any breach, although no lease has ever been executed. *Doe* d. *Oldershaw* v. *Breach*, 6 Esp. 106, Macdonald, C. B.; *Doe* d. *Lloyd* v. *Powell*, 5 B. & C. 308, 312; *Doe* d. *Henniker* v. *Watt*, 8 B. & C. 308; 1 M. & R. 694; *Doe* d. *Nash* v. *Birch*, 1 M. & W. 402; Tyr. & Gr. 769; *Doe* d. *Thompson* v. *Amey*, 12 A. & E. 476; 4 P. & D. 177. The reason is that by entry and payment of rent under the agreement, a tenancy from year to year is created, subject to the terms and conditions of the intended lease, so far as the same can possibly apply to a tenancy from year to year. *Doe* v. *Amey*, *supra*; *Doe* d. *Davenish* v. *Moffatt*, 15 Q. B. 257.

A demise for any term not exceeding three years from the making thereof may be made subject to any special terms and conditions,

without any writing (*ante*, 222); and an unstamped memorandum of
such demise, stating the terms and conditions, which was read to the
parties, and verbally assented to by them, and signed by the witness
(but not by either of the parties), may be used to refresh the memory
of the witness to prove the demise. *Lord Bolton* v. *Tomlin*, 5 A. & E.
856.

To whom reserved.]—A right of entry cannot effectually be reserved
to a stranger to the legal estate, although he joins in the demise, and
has some equitable or beneficial estate or interest in the property. *Doe*
d. *Barber* v. *Lawrence*, 4 Taunt. 23; Lit. s. 347; Co. Lit. 214 b.
Thus, where by lease a mortgagee demised, and the executrix of the
mortgagor demised and confirmed, and a power of re-entry for breach
of covenants was reserved *to them, or either of them*: held, that the
deed operated as a demise by the mortgagee, and a confirmation by the
executrix; and that the proviso for re-entry enured only to the mortgagee, and not to both. *Doe* d. *Barney* v. *Adams*, 2 Cro. & Jer.
232; 2 Tyr. 289; and see *Moore* v. *Earl of Plymouth*, 3 B. & A. 66.
So, where trustees and *cestui que trust* join in a lease, reserving rent
to the *cestui que trust*, with a proviso for re-entry on nonpayment,
such power will enure only to the trustees; *Doe* d. *Barker* v. *Goldsmith*, 2 Cro. & Jer. 674; 2 Tyr. 710; so, where tenant for life and the
reversioner in fee join in a demise. *Treport's case*, 6 Co. R. 15.　But
if in any of the above cases the title of the parties does not appear by
recital or otherwise on the face of the deed, the tenant will be estopped
by the lease from denying that the lessors were joint tenants, or had
power to demise jointly. *Cases supra*.　No such estoppel arises where
the real title appears by recital or otherwise on the face of the deed.
Hermitage v. *Tomkins*, 1 Ld. Raym. 729; *Pargeter* v. *Harris*, 7 Q.
B. 708; *Right* d. *Jefferys* v. *Bucknall*, 2 B. & Adol. 278; *Doe* d.
North v. *Webber*, 3 Bing. N. C. 922, 925; *Greenaway* v. *Hart*, 14 C.
B. 349.

A., being possessed of a term of years, demised his whole interest to
B., subject to a right of re-entry on breach of a condition: held, that
A. might enter for the condition broken, although he had no reversion.
Doe d. *Freeman* v. *Bateman*, 2 B. & A. 168; and see *Baker* v. *Gostling*, 3 Bing. N. C. 85; 4 Moo. & Sc. 539; 5 Scott, 58.　Where
lessees made an underlease containing a proviso for re-entry by themselves, their executors, administrators and assigns, and by the superior
landlord, his heirs and assigns, on breach of any covenant: held, that
upon such breach the lessees alone (without the superior landlord)
might maintain ejectment. *Doe* d. *Bedford* v. *White*, 4 Bing. 276.
If a person, seised in fee, settle his estate on himself for life, with remainders to other persons, reserving a leasing power, which he afterwards exercises, reserving rent to himself, his heirs and assigns, those
in remainder shall have the benefit of the rent and covenants, and of
any proviso for re-entry contained in the lease.　So also, when a person, seised in fee, settles his estates on A. for life, with remainders, and
gives him a leasing power, which he exercises, reserving rent *during
the term* to himself, his *heirs and assigns*, the remainderman shall
have the benefit of the rent and covenants, and of any proviso for re-
entry contained in the lease. *Greenaway* v. *Hart*, 14 C. B. 340, 354;
Isherwood v. *Oldknow*, 3 M. & S. 382.　The reason is that the lease

takes effect out of the estate of the party creating the power, and much in the same manner as if it had been inserted in the settlement.

By whom enforced.]—The lessor may re-enter, or maintain ejectment, for a forfeiture (*ante*, 403), but not after he has parted with his reversion, absolutely or by way of mortgage ; *Fenn* d. *Matthews* v. *Smart*, 12 East, 443 ; *Doe* d. *Marriott* v. *Edwards*, 5 B. & Adol. 1065 ; *Doe* d. *Prior* v. *Ongley*, 10 C. B. 25 ; nor after his reversion has been merged and extinguished. *Webb* v. *Russell*, 3 T. R. 393, 402 ; *Thre'r* v. *Barton*, Moore, 94 ; *Dumpor's case*, 4 Co. R. 120 b. But where a person, being possessed of property for a term of years, demised for a term equal to his whole estate, subject to a proviso for re-entry on breach of any covenant : held, that on such breach he might maintain ejectment for the forfeiture ; *Doe* d. *Freeman* v. *Bateman*, 2 B. & A. 168 ; although he could not have distrained for rent, not having any reversion. *Parminter* v. *Webber*, 8 Taunt. 593 ; *Preece* v. *Corrie*, 5 Bing. 24 ; 2 Moo. & Pay. 57. A right to a particular estate may be forfeited, and he in remainder, though he has but a right, may take advantage of it. *Buckler's case*, 2 Co. R. 55 a ; Cro. Eliz. 450, 585 ; Moore, 423 ; 2 And. 29, *S. C.*

A power of re-entry reserved to the lessor, but not mentioning his heirs, or his executors or administrators, will not extend to them. *Hassell* d. *Hodgson* v. *Gowthwaite*, Willes, 500 ; *Doe* d. *Gregson* v. *Harrison*, 2 T. R. 425. If "assigns" be mentioned, but not heirs or executors, it seems that the assigns can take advantage of the condition only during the lessor's life, but not afterwards. Co. Lit. 215 b, note (1).

By the common law an assignee of the reversion could not take advantage of a proviso for re-entry ; Lit. s. 347 ; Ad. Eject. 53 ; for to prevent maintenance the law did not allow of an assignment of a right of entry or re-entry. Co. Lit. 214. But by 8 & 9 Vict. c. 106, s. 6, "a right of entry, whether immediate or future, and whether vested or contingent, into or upon any tenements or hereditaments in England, of any tenure, may be disposed of by deed." It has, however, been decided, that a right of entry for a condition broken is not assignable under this statute, which "does not relate to a right to re-possess or re-enter for a condition broken, but only to an original right where there has been a disseisin, or where the party has a right to recover lands, and his right of entry and nothing but that remains." *Hunt* v. *Bishop*, 8 Exch. 675, 680 ; 9 Exch. 635, *S. C.*

By 32 Hen. 8, c. 34, intituled "An Act concerning Grantees of Reversions, to take advantage of the Conditions to be performed by the Lessees," grantees or assignees of reversions, their heirs, executors, successors and assigns, "shall and may have and enjoy like advantages against the lessees, their executors, administrators and assigns, *by entry for non-payment of the rent, or for doing of waste, or other forfeiture,*" as the lessors or grantors themselves, or their heirs or successors, should or might have had and enjoyed.

The words "or other forfeiture," although general, do not extend to every breach of condition, "but only of such conditions as either are incident to the reversion, as rent, or for the benefit of the estate, as for not doing of waste, for keeping the houses in reparations, for making of fences, scouring of ditches, for preserving of woods, or such like, and not for the payment of any sum in gross, delivery of corn, wood, or the like." Co. Lit. 215 b (12th Resolution); Ad. Eject. 54 ; Shep. Touch. 176; 1 Smith, L. C. 28. In other words, any "other forfeiture" must be *ejusdem generis* with those particularly mentioned in the statute. The breach of a condition not to assign without licence is collateral, and not within the statute. *Lucas* v. *How*, Sir T. Raym. 250 ; *Collins* v. *Silley*, Styles, 265 ; *Pennant's case*, 3 Co. R. 64 ; Ad. Eject. 56. Where a tenant forfeits his estate by becoming insolvent, or by being attainted of felony, it seems that such forfeiture is not one whereof an assignee of the reversion may take advantage by the statute. *Doe* d. *Griffith* v. *Pritchard*, 5 B. & Adol. 765 ; 2 N. & M. 489.

An assignee of *part of the reversion, ex. gr.* for years, or life, in *all* the lands demised, is an assignee within this statute, and may take advantage of a condition broken in his time. Co. Lit. 215 a ; *Attoc* v. *Hemmings*, 2 Bulst. 281 ; *Kidwelly* v. *Brand*, Plow. 72 ; 1 Smith, L. C. 28 ; *Isherwood* v. *Oldknow*, 3 M. & S. 382 ; *Wright* v. *Burroughes*, 3 C. B. 685 ; 4 Dowl. & L. 438. But an assignee of the reversion in *part of the lands* is not ; for the condition being entire cannot be apportioned by the act of the parties, but shall rather be destroyed. Co. Lit. 215 a (4th and 5th Resolution) ; *Id.* 215 b, note (1), 19th ed. ; Ad. Eject. 56 ; *Dumpor's case*, 4 Co. R. 119 ; 1 Smith, L. C. 15, 18 ; *Knight's case*, 5 Co. R. 54 b (2nd and 3rd Resolutions) ; 1 And. 173 ; 3 Leon. 124 ; Moore, 199, *S. C.* Covenant will lie by assignee of the reversion of part of the demised premises against lessee for not repairing that part. *Twynam* v. *Pickard*, 2 B. & A. 105. The distinction is between a condition and a covenant. 1 Smith, L. C. 28.

Where a power of re-entry is reserved to the lessor, his heirs and assigns, in a lease granted by a tenant for life *in pursuance of a power*, the reversioner for the time being entitled to the estate under the deed or will creating the power is entitled to the benefit of the rent and covenants, and of the proviso for re-entry. *Greenaway* v. *Hart*, 14 C. B. 340, 354 ; *Isherwood* v. *Oldknow*, 3 M. & S. 382 ; *Rogers* v. *Humphrey*, 4 A. & E. 299 ; 1 Smith, L. C. 28. Where a power of re-entry for breach of covenants is reserved, and the reversion descends to coparceners, it seems that one or more of them cannot, without the other or others, maintain ejectment for a forfeiture, the condition or proviso for re-entry not being divisible. *Doe* d. *Rutzen* v. *Lewis*, 5 A. & E. 277. Where directors of a company granted a lease with a power of re-entry, and afterwards the company was incorporated by an act of parliament, which (amongst other things) enacted, "that all contracts, &c., theretofore entered into with the directors of the company should be as valid and effectual to all intents and purposes as if the company had been incorporated when the same contracts, &c., were entered into, and as if the same had been entered into with the said incorporated company :" held, that the incorporated company might support ejectment on the clause of re-entry. *Doe* d. *London Dock Company* v. *Knebell*, 2 Moo. & Rob. 66, Lord Denman, C. J. A lord entitled by escheat is not an assignee of the reversion within the meaning of this statute ; Co. Lit. 215 a ; nor is an assignee of a reversion by estoppel only ; *Awder* v. *Nokes*, Moore, 419 ; nor a person entitled to a subsequent estate into which the immediate reversion has merged. *Thre'r* v. *Barton*, Moore, 94 ; *Chaworth* v. *Phillips*, Moore, 876 ; *Webb* v. *Russell*, 3 T. R. 393, 401. Where this statute speaketh of leases it doth not extend to gifts in tail. Co. Lit. 215 a. But copyholds are within its intention and equity. *Glover* v. *Cope*, Carthew, 205 ; 3 Lev. 326 ; Skin. 305, *S. C.* ; *Whitton* v. *Peacock*, 3 Myl. & K. 325. The act only extends to reversions on demises *by deed*. *Standen* v. *Christmas*, 10 Q. B. 135 ; *Brydges* v. *Lewis*, 3 Q. B. 603 ; 2 Gale & D. 763.

How construed.]—"In the construction of covenants of this sort they are neither entitled to favour or disfavour, whether they are to create a forfeiture or to continue an estate ; but we are to put the fair construction upon them according to the apparent intention of the contracting parties." *Per* Lord Ellenborough, C. J., in *Goodtitle* d. *Luxmore* v. *Saville*, 16 East, 95. "I do not think provisoes of this sort are to be construed with the strictness of conditions at common law. These are matters of contract between the parties, and should, in my opinion, be construed as other contracts. The parties agree to a tenancy on certain terms, and there is no hardship in binding them to those terms. In my view of cases of this sort the provisoes ought to be construed according to the fair and obvious construction, without favour to either side." *Per* Lord Tenterden, C. J., in *Doe* d. *Davis* v. *Elsam*, Moo. & Mal. 191. See also *Doe* d. *Pitt* v. *Shewin*, 3 Camp. 134 ; *Doe* d. *Antrobus* v. *Jepson*, 3 B. & Adol. 402, 403 ; *Doe* d. *Baker* v. *Jones*, 2 Car. & K. 743.

On the other hand, there are many authorities to the effect that conditions and provisoes for re-entry *ought to be construed strictly.* "The general rule is, that a clause of re-entry be construed strictly." *Per* Lord Tenterden, C. J., in *Doe* d. *Palk* v. *Marchetti*, 1 B. & Adol. 720 ; Co. Lit. 219 b ; Vin. Abr. Condition (E r) ; 2 Arch. N. P. 407 ; *Doe* d. *Marquis of Anglesey* v. *The Churchwardens and Overseers of Rugeley*, 6 Q. B. 107 ; *Doe* d. *Lloyd* v. *Ingleby*, 15 M. & W. 465 ; *Id.* 469, Platt, B. Thus a proviso for re-entry in case of the breach of any covenant "hereinafter" contained, will not extend to covenants inserted *before* the proviso, although there is no subsequent covenant on the part of the lessee. *Doe* d. *Spencer* v. *Godwin*, 4 M. & S. 265. So a proviso for re-entry if the lessee "shall do, or cause to be done, any act, matter or thing contrary to and in breach of any of the covenants," has been held not to apply to a breach of the covenant to repair ; the omission to repair not being *an act done* within the meaning of the proviso. *Doe* d. *Sir W. Abdy* v. *Stevens*, 3 B. & Adol. 299. So a proviso for re-entry if the tenant "make default in performance of any of the clauses by the space of thirty days after notice," has been held not to apply to a breach of a covenant not to allow alterations in the premises, or permit new buildings to be made upon them without permission ; but only to things to be done in pursuance of notice, within thirty days after such notice. Therefore, where an undertenant had erected a portico contrary to the covenant, and notice was given to him to remove it, and to replace the premises in their former state, which he neglected to do for thirty days : held, that no forfeiture was incurred. *Doe* d. *Palk, Bart.* v. *Marchetti*, 1 B. & Adol. 715 ; see also *Doe* d. *Dalton* v. *Jones*, 4 B. & Adol. 126 ; 1 N. & M. 6.

Void or voidable.]—Where the proviso is, that on breach of any of the covenants, the lease "shall cease, determine and be *utterly void*, to all intents and purposes whatsoever," such words will be construed to

mean *void at the election of the lessor*. *Roberts* v. *Davey*, 4 B. &
Adol. 667 ; 1 Smith, L. C. 19. The lessee will not be allowed to take
advantage of his own wrongful act or omission, and to say that thereby
the lease has become void. *Rede* v. *Farr*, 6 M. & S. 121 ; *Doe* d.
Bryan v. *Bancks*, 4 B. & A. 401 ; *Arnsby* v. *Woodward*, 6 B. & C.
519 ; 9 D. & R. 536 ; *Roberts* v. *Davey*, 4 B. & Adol. 664 ; *Doe* d.
Nash v. *Birch*, 1 M. & W. 402 ; Tyr. & Gr. 769 ; *Reid* v. *Parsons*,
2 Chit. R. 247.   The lessor must do some act evidencing his intention
to enter for the forfeiture and determine the lease : *Roberts* v. *Davey*,
4 B. & Adol. 664 ; *Arnsby* v. *Woodward*, 6 B. & C. 519 ; 9 D. & R.
536 ; *Fenn* d. *Matthews* v. *Smart*, 12 East, 444, 451 : and the lease
will be *avoided from that time only* ; but previous arrears of rent may
be sued for, although upon re-entry the lessor is to have the premises
again " as if the said indenture had never been made." *Hartshorne*
v. *Watson*, 4 Bing. N. C. 178 ; *Load* v. *Green*, 15 M. & W. 216, 223 ;
Selby v. *Browne*, 7 Q. B. 620 ; and see *Franklin* v. *Carter*, 1 C. B.
750 ; 3 Dowl. & L. 213 ; *Johns* v. *Whitley*, 3 Wils. 127. The lessor
cannot avoid the lease after he has parted with the reversion. *Fenn* d.
Matthews v. *Smart*, 12 East, 444, 451 ; *Doe* d. *Marriott* v. *Edwards*,
5 B. & Adol. 1065 ; *Doe* d. *Prior* v. *Ongley*, 10 C. B. 25. Nor can
the grantee of the reversion avoid the lease for a forfeiture committed
before the reversion was conveyed to him. *Fenn* d. *Matthews* v.
Smart, *supra*. But by 8 & 9 Vict. c. 106, s. 6, " a right of entry,
whether immediate or future, and whether vested or contingent, into
or upon any tenements or hereditaments in England, of any tenure,
may be disposed of by deed." *Hunt* v. *Bishop*, 8 Exch. 675, 680 ;
ante, 405. The lessor may enter and take actual possession at any
time after the forfeiture has accrued, and before he has waived such
forfeiture ; *Davis* v. *Burrell and Lane*, 10 C. B. 821 ; but not afterwards. *Arnsby* v. *Woodward*, 6 B. & C. 519 ; 9 D. & R. 536. The
bringing of an ejectment for the forfeiture is equivalent to an entry,
and amounts to an election to determine the term from the day on which
the plaintiff claims to be entitled to possession, so as to prevent the
recovery of any *subsequent rent*. *Jones* v. *Carter*, 15 M. & W. 718 ;
Franklin v. *Carter*, 1 C. B. 750 ; 3 Dowl. & L. 213 ; *ante*, 82 ; but
see *Long* v. *Bilke*, 1 Man. & Gr. 87. No act or intimation of election
on the part of the plaintiff to avoid the lease is necessary *before* bringing
the action ; *Hyde* v. *Watts*, 12 M. & W. 254 ; 1 Dowl. & L. 479 ;
1 Smith, L. C. 20 ; unless, indeed, the lease be for a life or lives. Co.
Lit. 218 ; 2 Rep. 53 a ; 1 Wms. Saund. 287 d (n.) ; 4 Tyr. 625. But
no such election will avail, nor can an entry or ejectment be supported,
after the lessor has waived the forfeiture by the acceptance of subsequent rent, or otherwise ; *Doe* d. *Gatehouse* v. *Rees*, 4 Bing. N. C.
384 ; Lit. s. 131 ; Co. Lit. 211 b ; *infra* ; provided he then knew
of the forfeiture, but not otherwise. *Doe* d. *Gregson* v. *Harrison*, 2
T. R. 425 ; *Goodright* d. *Walter* v. *Davids*, 2 Cowp. 803 ; *Duppa* v.
Mayo, 1 Wms. Saund. 288 a, b, note (16) ; *Pennant's case*, 3 Co. R.
64 b.

Waiver of Forfeiture.]—If the lessor, or other person legally entitled to the reversion, knowing that a forfeiture has been incurred by
the breach of any covenant or condition, does any act whereby he acknowledges the continuance of the tenancy at a later period, he thereby
waives such forfeiture, and precludes himself from taking advantage

of it. Thus if he distrain for, or accept payment of, rent which accrued due *after* the forfeiture. *Marsh* v. *Curteys,* Cro. Eliz. 528 ; *Harvie* v. *Oswel,* Cro. Eliz. 572 ; .Co. Lit. 211 b ; *Pennant's case,* 3 Co. R. 64 b ; *Doe* d. *Gatehouse* v. *Rees,* 4 Bing. N. C. 384 ; 6 Scott, 161 ; *Goodright* d. *Walter* v. *Davids,* 2 Cowp. 803 ; *Fryett* d. *Harris* v. *Jefferys,* 1 Esp. 393 ; *Fox* v. *Swan,* Styles, 482 ; *Doe* d. *Griffith* v. *Pritchard,* 5 B. & Adol. 765 ; 2 N. & M. 489 ; and see *Goodright* d. *Charter* v. *Cordwent,* 6 T. R. 219 ; *Zouch* d. *Ward* v. *Willingale,* 1 H. Blac. 311. A mere demand of subsequent rent, which is not complied with, or even a distress for subsequent rent which is not submitted to, but replevied by the tenant, will not be sufficient to waive the forfeiture. *Blyth* v. *Dennett,* 13 C. B. 178 ; and see *Doe* d. *Nash* v. *Birch,* 1 M. & W. 402 ; Tyr. & Gr. 769. The receipt of rent due *prior* to the forfeiture is no waiver ; *Marsh* v. *Curteys,* Cro. Eliz. 528, *per cur.;* but if such receipt describe the lessee as the *then* tenant of the demised premises, that may amount to sufficient evidence of a waiver. *Green's case,* Cro. Eliz. 3, cited 1 M. & W. 406, Parke, B. Unless, indeed, the incidental circumstances appearing in evidence negative the presumed waiver. *Doe* d. *Digby* v. *Steel,* 3 Camp. 117 ; *Williams* v. *Humphreys,* 2 East, 237 ; *Doe* d. *Godsell* v. *Inglis,* 3 Taunt. 54 ; *Messenger* v. *Armstrong,* 1 T. R. 53. No waiver of any forfeiture will be implied, unless it appear that the lessor or reversioner had notice or knowledge of the breach of covenant or condition at the time of the supposed waiver. *Pennant's case,* 3 Co. R. 63 b ; *Duppa* v. *Mayo,* 1 Wms. Saund. 288 a, b, note 16 ; *Harvie* v. *Oswel,* Cro. Eliz. 553, 572 ; *Goodright* d. *Walter* v. *Davids,* 2 Cowp. 803 ; *Doe* d. *Gregson* v. *Harrison,* 2 T. R. 425. A lessor is not bound to take advantage of the first or any other breach of which he has notice or knowledge (except, perhaps, a condition not to *assign* without licence ; *Lloyd* v. *Crispe,* 5 Taunt. 249 ; 1 Smith, L. C. 20) ; and therefore his waiver thereof will not preclude him from maintaining an ejectment for any subsequent breach of the same covenant or condition. *Doe* d. *Boscawen* v. *Bliss,* 4 Taunt. 735 ; *Doe* d. *Sheppard* v. *Allen,* 3 Taunt. 78 ; *Doe* d. *Bryan* v. *Bancks,* 4 B. & A. 401. If the covenant be of a continuing nature, so that a breach thereof occurs from day to day so long as it remains unperformed, the waiver of any forfeiture up to a certain day will afford no defence to an ejectment for a subsequent or continued breach. Thus, where the covenant is to keep the demised premises in repair during the term ; *Doe* d. *Baker* v. *Jones,* 5 Exch. 498 ; *Fryett* d. *Harris* v. *Jefferys,* 1 Esp. 393 ; or to keep them insured in a certain manner from loss or damage by fire during the term ; *Doe* d. *Muston* v. *Gladwin,* 6 Q. B. 953, 956 ; *Penniall* v. *Harborne,* 11 Q. B. 368, 374, note (*b*) ; *Hyde* v. *Watts,* 12 M. & W. 254 ; 1 Dowl. & L. 479 ; *Doe* d. *Flower* v. *Peck,* 1 B. & Adol. 428 ; or not to use certain rooms in a particular manner. *Doe* d. *Ambler* v. *Woodbridge,* 9 B. & C. 376 ; 4 Man. & R. 302. Acceptance of rent, which becomes due pending a notice to repair, is no waiver of a subsequent forfeiture occasioned by non-compliance with such notice. *Doe* d. *Rankin* v. *Brindley,* 4 B. & Adol. 84 ; and see *Doe* d. *Baker* v. *Jones,* 5 Exch. 498, 505. Indeed it would seem that acceptance of rent due after the expiration of the notice will not bar an ejectment, if the premises subsequently continue unrepaired. *Fryett* d. *Harris* v. *Jefferys,* 1 Esp. 393, Lord Kenyon, C. J. But, *semble,* it would waive any forfeiture created by non-compliance with the notice within the time

T

therein mentioned. Ad. Eject. 152. Acceptance of rent after the commencement of an ejectment for a forfeiture is no waiver of such forfeiture. *Doe* d. *Morecroft* v. *Meux*, 1 C. & P. 346, Abbott, C. J.

Some positive act of waiver, as the receipt of rent, is necessary to preclude an ejectment for a forfeiture ; merely lying bye and witnessing the breach of covenant for six years does not amount to a waiver of the forfeiture. *Doe* d. *Sheppard* v. *Allen*, 3 Taunt. 78 ; *ante*, 409. But a lessor will not be permitted to take advantage of a forfeiture against a person who has purchased the lease *under his advice*, after the supposed forfeiture, unless the purchaser be guilty of some subsequent default. *Doe* d. *Sore* v. *Eykins*, 1 C. & P. 154 ; 1 Ry. & Moo. 29 ; and see *Pickard* v. *Sears*, 6 A. & E. 469 ; 2 N. & P. 488 ; *Gregg* v. *Wells*, 10 A. & E. 90 ; 2 P. & D. 296 ; *Freeman* v. *Cooke*, 2 Exch. 663 ; 6 Dowl. & L. 187 ; *Howard* v. *Hudson*, 2 E. & B. 1.

Particulars of Breaches.]—In ejectment for a forfeiture, a particular of the breaches on which the plaintiff relies may be obtained in the usual manner. *Ante*, 120.

Inspection of Lease.]—In ejectment for a forfeiture an inspection and copy of the lease may be obtained, by either party, under the circumstances mentioned *ante*, 120, 200.

Relief in Equity against Forfeiture.]—A court of equity will relieve against a forfeiture by non-payment of rent, but not in respect of any other act or omission, as for not repairing, not insuring, or the like. *Hill* v. *Barclay*, 18 Ves. 63 ; *Reynolds* v. *Pitt*, 19 Ves. 134 ; *Ex parte Vaughan*, 1 Turn. & Russ. 435 ; *Green* v. *Bridges*, 4 Simon, 100 ; *Harris* v. *Bryant*, 4 Russ. 91 ; *Gregory* v. *Wilson*, 9 Hare, 683, Wigram, V. C. ; 1 Smith, L. C. 21. A court of law has no jurisdiction to stay ejectment for a forfeiture. *Doe* d. *Mayhew* v. *Asby*, 10 A. & E. 71 ; 2 P. & D. 302 ; except under 15 & 16 Vict. c. 76, s. 216, in ejectment for non-payment of rent. The Court of Common Pleas refused to stay the proceedings in an ejectment for a forfeiture upon the ground that another action of ejectment was pending in the Queen's Bench between the same parties to recover the same premises upon a forfeiture, which it appeared was antecedent to, and entirely distinct from, that which formed the subject of the suit in the Common Pleas. *Doe* d. *Henry* v. *Gustard*, 4 Man. & Gr. 987 ; 5 Scott, N. R. 818 ; 2 Dowl. N. S. 615.

Emblements.]—Where a lessor avoids a lease under a condition or proviso for re-entry on breach of a covenant, the lessee is not entitled to emblements. *Davis* v. *Eyton*, 7 Bing. 154 ; 4 Moo. & P. 820 ; *Bulwer* v. *Bulwer*, 2 B. & C. 471, Abbott, C. J. But if the lessor omit to avail himself of the forfeiture, the tenant is entitled to the emblements. *Johns* v. *Whitley*, 3 Wils. 127.

Tenants' fixtures affixed to the freehold can be disannexed only during the continuance of the term, and therefore, as it seems, not after the term has been determined by a lawful entry for a forfeiture. *Weeton* v. *Woodcock*, 7 M. & W. 14 ; *ante*, 346.

2. For Non-payment of Rent—at Common Law.]—The usual remedy for the recovery of rent is by a distress, or by an action on the contract to recover the rent thereby reserved; *ante*, 287; or (where there is no lease or agreement *under seal*, and the tenant has entered) by an action for use and occupation. 11 Geo. 2, c. 19, s. 14; 6 A. & E. 839, note; *Hall* v. *Burgess*, 5 B. & C. 333; 8 D. & R. 67; *Smith* v. *Eldridge*, 15 C. B. 236; *Alford* v. *Vickery*, Car. & M. 280. But no ejectment can be maintained for nonpayment of rent, unless there be some *express condition or proviso* in the lease or agreement giving the landlord a right to re-enter and determine the lease or tenancy for such nonpayment. Lit. Sec. 325, 327; *Doe* d. *Rudd* v. *Golding*, 6 Moore, 231; *Doe* d. *Rains* v. *Kneller*, 4 C. & P. 3; *Brewer* d. *Lord Onslow* v. *Eaton*, 3 Doug. 230; cited 6 T. R. 220; *Doe* d. *Dixon* v. *Roe*, 7 C. B. 134; *Hill* v. *Kempshall*, *Id.* 975; Ad. Eject. 118; 2 Chit. Arch. 997 (9th ed.); or a right to enter and hold the premises, *quousque*, &c., *i. e.*, until the arrears be satisfied. Lit. s. 327; *Junott* v. *Cowley*, 1 Saund. 112 c; 1 Lev. 170; Sir T. Ray. 135, 158; 1 Sid. 223, 261, 344, *S. C.*; *Doe* d. *Biass* v. *Horsley*, 1 A. & E. 766; 3 N. & M. 567; *Doe* d. *Chawner* v. *Boulter*, 6 A. & E. 675, 682; 1 N. & P. 650; *Doe* d. *Darke* v. *Bowditch*, 8 Q. B. 973. If any such proviso allow a specified number of days for payment of the rent after it becomes due, no forfeiture can accrue by nonpayment until such time has elapsed. Plow. 172 a; *Doe* d. *Dixon* v. *Roe*, 7 C. B. 134. Where land is demised subject to a condition for re-entry on default in payment of the rent, the right of re-entry does not accrue until the rent has been duly demanded and default made. *Hill* v. *Kempshall*, 7 C. B. 975. A condition of re-entry, if rent be in arrear for a certain space of time after being demanded, and no distress on the premises, is not broken if no demand be made within the time, though the goods are removed from the premises before the time for making the demand ultimately expires. *Worcester* v. *Glover*, Cro. Eliz. 63.

The usual form of proviso is that given in " An Act to facilitate the granting of certain Leases" (8 & 9 Vict. c. 124), Sched. 2, Col. 2, Form 11, which is as follows:—

" Provided always, and it is expressly agreed, that if the rent hereby reserved, or any part thereof, shall be unpaid for fifteen (*a*) days after any of the days on which the same ought to have been paid (*although no formal demand shall have been made thereof*), or in case of the breach or nonperformance of any of the covenants and agreements herein contained on the part of the said lessee, his executors, administrators and assigns, then and in either of such cases it shall be lawful for the said lessor [his " heirs and assigns," *or* " executors, administrators and assigns"] at any time thereafter, into and upon the said demised premises, or any part thereof in the name of the whole, to re-enter, and the same to have again, repossess and enjoy, as of his or their former estate, anything *hereinbefore* (*b*) contained to the contrary notwithstanding."

It is to be observed that the above form uses the words, " although no formal demand shall have been made thereof." Such words, or any others to the like effect, are sufficient in law to dispense with the

---

(*a*) Twenty-one days or thirty days are more usual than fifteen days.
(*b*) The form in the act erroneously says " *hereinafter*," but the mistake does not appear so serious as in *Doe* d. *Spencer* v. *Godwin*, 4 M. & S. 265 (*ante*, 407).

necessity for a formal demand of the rent according to the strict rules of the common law. *Doe* d. *Harris* v. *Masters*, 2 B. & C. 490; 4 D. & R. 45; *Goodright* d. *Hare* v. *Cator*, 2 Doug. 477, 486; *Dormer's case*, 5 Co. R. 40 b; Pop. 22; Jenk. Cent. 257, *S. C.*; *Umphery* v. *Damyon*, 1 Bulst. 181.

Where less than half a year's rent is in arrear, *or* there is a sufficient distress on the demised premises to countervail *all* the arrears due; *Cross* v. *Jordan*, 8 Exch. 149; 17 Jur. 93; *Doe* d. *Forster* v. *Wandlass*, 7 T. R. 117; *and* there are no express words (as above) rendering a formal demand of the rent unnecessary, the landlord, or his heir, &c. (being the person entitled to the rent and reversion), must *duly make a formal demand of the rent according to the strict rules of the common law*, before any ejectment can be maintained for nonpayment of rent. *Molineux* v. *Molineux*, Cro. Jac. 144; *Doe* d. *Forster* v. *Wandlass*, 7 T. R. 117; Ad. Eject. 121; 1 Wms. Saund. 286 b, note (16), 6th ed.; Lush, Prac. 785; 2 Chit. Arch. 995 (9th ed.). Such rules are as follow :—

1. A demand of the rent must be made either by the landlord, &c., in person, or by an agent duly authorized on his behalf. Ad. Eject. 121. A power of attorney is usually given to the agent. *See the form, Appendix, No.* 10. The agent need not produce such power at the time of making the demand, unless the tenant then requires to see it: it is sufficient to inform the tenant that he holds such an authority. *Roe* d. *West* v. *Davies*, 7 East, 363; 1 Wms. Saund. 286 b, note (*k*). But he should be prepared to produce the original, and to deliver a copy thereof to the tenant, if required. If the tenant pay the money, he is not entitled to keep the power of attorney. *Pridmore* v. *Harrison*, 1 Car. & K. 613. Perhaps a mere receipt for the rent, signed by the landlord and duly stamped, would be sufficient, especially if the person making the demand be the known servant of the landlord; Plow. 70; or his steward or agent who usually receives his rents. But there is no reported decision to this effect; and therefore the safest course is for the landlord to go in person, or to execute a power of attorney. To obtain an attachment for nonpayment of money pursuant to a rule of court, the power of attorney, together with an affidavit verifying its execution, must be produced, and copies thereof respectively left with the party at the time the rule is served and the demand made. *Jackson* v. *Clarke*, M'Clel. 72; 13 Price, 208; *Laugher* v. *Laugher*, 1 Cr. & Jer. 368; 1 Tyr. 352; 1 Dowl. 284; *Price* v. *Duggan*, 4 Man. & Gr. 225; 4 Scott, N. R. 734; 1 Dowl. N. S. 709. But such strictness is unnecessary in other cases. *Roe* d. *West* v. *Davies, supra.*

2. The demand must be made *on the very last day* on which the rent can be paid to save the forfeiture. Plow. 70; *Smith and Bustard's case*, 1 Leon. 141; Co. Lit. 202 a; 1 Wms. Saund. 287 (6th ed.); Ad. Eject. 121; *Doe* d. *Forster* v. *Wandlass*, 7 T. R. 117. Therefore, if the proviso for re-entry be in case of nonpayment of the rent, or any part thereof, for *thirty days* after it becomes due, the demand must be made on the thirtieth day *after* the rent became due (exclusive of the day on which the rent became due; *Smith and Bustard's case*, 1 Leon. 141); and not on any other day before or afterwards. *Cases supra*; *Doe* d. *Dixon* v. *Roe*, 7 C. B. 134. But payment or tender by the tenant or his agent to the landlord or his agent on any day before the last day to save the forfeiture, is sufficient. *Cropp* v. *Hambleton*,

Cro. Eliz. 48; Moore, 223, *S. C.*; *Thompson* v. *Field,* Cro. Jac. 499
(2nd point); *Goodright* d. *Stevenson* v. *Noright,* 2 W. Blac. 746.
Payment before the day is a good performance of a condition to pay at
the day. *Burgaine* v. *Spurling,* Cro. Car. 283. If the proviso allow
no extra time for payment of the rent, the demand must be made on
the very day the rent becomes due. Co. Lit. 202 a, note (3); *Umphery*
v. *Damyon,* 1 Bulstr. 181.

3. The demand must be made not only on the proper day, but also
at a proper hour of the day, *i. e. a convenient time before and at sunset.* Co. Lit. 202 a; Plow. 172 a; *Maund's case,* 8 Co. R. 28;
Fabian and Windsor's case, 1 Leon. 305; *S. C., nom. Fabian* v. *Winston,* Cro. Eliz. 209; *Thompson* v. *Field,* Cro. Jac. 499; 1 Wms. Saund.
287 (6th ed.). Any time before sunset is sufficient, provided the demand be actually or constructively continued until sunset. There must
be a sufficient time to allow the money to be paid and counted before
sunset. *Cases supra.* Whether the demand commenced a quarter or
half an hour before sunset is immaterial, provided it be continued until
sunset. *Fabyan* v. *Rewmston,* Anderson, R. 252 (Case 262). But if
a demand be made shortly before sunset, and is not continued, actually
or constructively, until sunset, but the party goes away before that
time, it will not be deemed sufficient. *Wood and Chivers' case,* 4
Leon. 179. The court will not take judicial notice of the time of sunset on a particular day : that must be proved by evidence. *Collier* v.
Nokes, 2 Car. & K. 1012. A demand made on the proper day at one
o'clock is clearly bad. *Doe* d. *Wheeldon* v. *Paul,* 3 C. & P. 613,
Lord Tenterden, C. J. Yet a tender by the tenant or his agent at any
time before or after sunset would be sufficient to save the forfeiture.
Plow. 172 a; Co. Litt. 202 a; *Cropp* v. *Hambleton,* Cro. Eliz. 48. Rent
is *due* in the morning of the day appointed for payment, but is not *in
arrear* till the next day. *Dibble* v. *Bowater,* 2 E. & B. 564.

4. The demand must be made *at the proper place.* Therefore, if the
lease or agreement specify the place at which the rent is to be paid, the
demand must be made there, and not elsewhere. *Borough's case,* 4
Co. R. 73 (1st Resolution); *Buskin* v. *Edmunds,* Cro. Eliz. 415;
Moore, 408; Co. Lit. 202 a; 1 Wms. Saund. 287 (6th ed.); Ad. Eject.
121. But if no place be so appointed, the demand must be made upon
the land, and at the most notorious place of it ; and therefore, if there
be a dwelling-house upon the land, the demand must be made at the
front door of it ; but it is not necessary to enter the house, although
the door be open. Co. Lit. 201 b; 1 Wms. Saund. 287 (6th ed.); Ad.
Eject. 121. If the premises consist of a wood only, the demand must
be made at the gate of the wood, or at some highway leading through
the wood, or other most notorious place. And if one place be as notorious as another, the lessor hath election to demand it at which he
will. Co. Lit. 202 a. Such demand must be actually made, although
there be no person present on behalf of the tenant to answer it; *Kidwelly* v. *Brand,* Plow. 70 a, 70 b; Co. Lit. 201 b; 1 Wms. Saund. 287
(6th ed.); or it may be made on an undertenant. *Doe* d. *Brook* v.
Brydges, 2 D. & R. 29.

A tender by the tenant or his agent, to the landlord or his agent,
may be made at any place on or off the demised premises ; and if good
in other respects, it will be sufficient to save the forfeiture. Co. Lit.
202 a; *Id.* note (3); Ad. Eject. 121. Where a lessee covenants to pay
rent at the time and in the manner reserved by the lease, no place of

payment being named, it is no defence to an action *upon the covenant*
that the lessee was upon the land demised on the day the rent became
due, just before and at sunset, and was then and there ready to pay
the lessor, who was not there ready to receive it.　*Haldane* v. *Johnson*, 8 Exch. 689; 22 Law J., N. S., Exch. 264.　In such case it is
the duty of the lessee to find out the lessor, wherever he may happen
to be, *intra quatuor maria*, and to tender the rent to him personally.
S. C., Shep. Touch. 378.

　5. The demand must be made *of the precise sum* then payable, and
not one penny more or less.　*Fabian and Windsor's case*, 1 Leon. 305;
S. C., nom. Fabian v. *Winston*, Cro. Eliz. 209; 1 Wms. Saund. 287
(6th ed.); Ad. Eject. 121 (4th ed.); 2 Arch. N. P. 412.　If the rent
be payable quarterly, and more than one quarter is due, only the last
quarter's rent should be demanded, and not the previous arrears, otherwise the demand will be altogether bad; *Scot* v. *Scot*, Cro. Eliz. 73;
Thomkins v. *Pincent*, 7 Mod. 97; 1 Salk. 141; *Doe* d. *Wheeldon* v.
Paul, 3 C. & P. 613, Lord Tenterden, C. J.; Ad. Eject. 121, note (*b*);
because it is only in respect of the last quarter's rent that the forfeiture
(if any) will accrue, the previous arrears not having been duly demanded on the proper day for that purpose.

　The reason for all this nicety and exactness is, that the law leans
against forfeitures; and it is unreasonable that a valuable term should
be forfeited for nonpayment on the precise day of a small amount of
rent; especially when there is a sufficient distress on the demised premises to satisfy all the arrears of rent.

　Supposing such a demand to have been duly made, or to have been
dispensed with by some express stipulation in the lease or agreement
(*ante*, 411), the landlord may, on the day next after the last day to save
the forfeiture, or at any subsequent period (provided he has not waived
the forfeiture, *ante*, 408), maintain an action of ejectment, without
first making any *actual entry* on the demised premises, for the purpose
of determining the lease or tenancy on account of the forfeiture.
1 Wms. Saund. 287 a (6th ed.); *Id.* 287 d; *Goodright* d. *Hare* v.
Cator, 2 Doug. 477; cited 4 C. B. 198; *Hyde* v. *Watts*, 12 M. & W.
254; 1 Dowl. & L. 479; *Jones* v. *Carter*, 15 M. & W. 718.　But the
proceedings in such action may be stayed at any time *before the trial*,
upon payment of the arrears of rent, with costs to be taxed, upon a
summary application to the court or a judge: *post*, 421; *see form of
Summons and Order, Appendix, Nos.* 81, 82: or relief against the
forfeiture may be obtained in equity before or after the trial, and before or after execution executed; even more than six calendar months
after the latter period; and indeed, until from the great lapse of time
or other special circumstances, it has become unreasonable to grant
such relief.　Comyn, L. & T. 493; 1 Wms. Saund. 287 c; *Bowser* v.
Colby, 1 Hare, 109.　An equitable mortgagee of the tenant may file a
bill in equity to redeem, &c., after judgment and execution in an ejectment against the tenant.　*Gerahty* v. *Malone*, 1 H. L. Cas. 81.

　By Statute.]—The 4 Geo. 2, c. 28, A.D. 1731, after reciting (sect. 2)
that, " whereas great inconveniences do frequently happen to lessors
and landlords in cases of re-entry for nonpayment of rent by reason
of the many niceties that attend the re-entries at common law; and
forasmuch as when a legal re-entry is made, the landlord or lessor must
be at the expense, charge and delay of recovering in ejectment before he

can obtain the actual possession of the demised premises; and it often happens that after such a re-entry made, the lessee or his assignee, upon one or more bills filed in a court of equity, not only holds out the lessor or landlord, by an injunction, from recovering the possession, but likewise pending the said suit, do run much more in arrear, without giving any security for the rents due when the said re-entry was made, or which shall or do afterwards incur:" for remedy thereof proceeds to make certain enactments (ss. 2, 3, 4), which are re-enacted with a few immaterial variations, and in effect superseded, by 15 & 16 Vict. c. 76, ss. 210, 211, 212, which we now proceed to consider fully.

By 15 & 16 Vict. c. 76, s. 210, " in all cases *between landlord and tenant,* as often as it shall happen that *one half-year's rent* shall be in arrear, and the landlord or lessor, to whom the same is due, hath *right by law to re-enter* for the nonpayment thereof, such landlord or lessor shall and may, *without any formal demand or re-entry,* serve a writ in ejectment for the recovery of the demised premises; or in case the same cannot be legally served, or no tenant be in actual possession of the premises, then such landlord or lessor may affix a copy thereof upon the door of any demised messuage; or in case such action in ejectment shall not be for the recovery of any messuage, then upon some notorious place of the lands, tenements or hereditaments comprised in such writ in ejectment; and such affixing shall be deemed legal service thereof, which service or affixing such writ in ejectment *shall stand in the place and stead of a demand and re-entry;* and in case of judgment against the defendant for non-appearance, if it shall be made to appear to the court where the said action is depending, by affidavit, or be proved upon the trial, in case the defendant appears, that *half a year's rent was due* before the said writ was served, and that *no sufficient distress was to be found* on the demised premises, *countervailing the arrears then due,* and that the lessor had *power to re-enter,* then and in every such case the lessor shall recover judgment and execution, in the same manner as if the rent in arrear had been legally demanded, and a re-entry made; and in case the lessee or his assigns, or other person claiming or deriving under the said lease, shall permit and suffer judgment to be had and recovered on such trial in ejectment, and execution to be executed thereon, without paying the rent and arrears, together with full costs, and without proceeding for relief in equity within six months after such execution executed, then and in such case the said lessee, his assignee, and all other persons claiming and deriving under the said lease, shall be barred and foreclosed from all relief or remedy in law or equity, other than by bringing error for reversal of such judgment, in case the same shall be erroneous; and the said landlord or lessor shall *from thenceforth hold the said demised premises discharged from such lease;* and if on such ejectment a verdict shall pass for the defendant, or the claimant shall be nonsuited therein, then and in every such case such defendant shall have and recover his costs: provided that nothing herein contained shall extend to bar the right of any mortgagee of such lease, or any part thereof, who shall not be in possession, so as such mortgagee shall and do, within six months after such judgment obtained and execution executed, pay all rent in arrear, and all costs and damages sustained by such lessor or person entitled to the remainder or reversion as aforesaid, and perform all the covenants and agreements which, on the part and behalf of the first lessee, are and ought to be performed."

This section is similar to 4 Geo. 2, c. 28, s. 2, except that it omits the preamble (*ante*, 414). It applies only where the following circumstances concur, *viz.*:—

1. The ejectment must be "between landlord and tenant." But the assignee of a lessee, whether by way of mortgage or otherwise, is a "tenant" within the meaning of the enactment. *Doe* d. *Whitfield* v. *Roe*, 3 Taunt. 402; *Williams* v. *Bosanquet*, 1 Brod. & Bing. 238; 3 Moore, 500. So is a mere underlessee, because he is a "person claiming or deriving under the lease." *Doe* d. *Wyatt* v. *Byron*, 1 C. B. 623; 3 Dowl. & L. 31.

2. One half-year's rent at the least must be in arrear. Ad. Ejec. 122; *Hill* v. *Kempshall*, 7 C. B. 975.

3. "No sufficient distress *to be found* on the demised premises countervailing the arrears due;" *Doe* d. *Forster* v. *Wandlass*, 7 T. R. 117; *i.e., all* the arrears, and not merely half a year's rent, where more is due. *Cross* v. *Jordan*, 8 Exch. 149, overruling *Doe* d. *Powell* v. *Roe*, 9 Dowl. 548. But a strict search must be made on the demised premises after the last day for saving the forfeiture, and before the writ issues (or at all events before the writ is served, *Doe* d. *Dixon* v. *Roe*, 7 C. B. 134), to ascertain that there is no sufficient distress on any part of the demised premises; *Rees* d. *Powell* v. *King*, Forrest. R. 19; *S. C.*, cited 2 Brod. & Bing. 514; *Doe* d. *Forrest* v. *Wandlass*, 7 T. R. 117; *Doe* d. *Smelt* v. *Fuchan*, 15 East, 286; 1 Wms. Saund. 287 b, note (*p*), 6th ed.; unless, indeed, the tenant prevents an entry to distrain by locking the outer doors, &c., for in such case no sufficient distress can be "found," *i.e.,* "got at." *Doe* d. *Chippendale* v. *Dyson*, 1 Moo. & Mal. 77, Lord Tenterden, C. J.; *Doe* d. *Cox* v. *Roe*, 5 Dowl. & L. 272. Goods are not to be found on the demised premises, within the meaning of the act, unless they are so visibly there that a broker going to distrain would, using reasonable diligence, find them, so as to be able to distrain them. *Doe* d. *Haverson* v. *Franks*, 2 Car. & K. 678, Erle, J. If a distress be found on the demised premises sufficient to satisfy so much of the rent as would reduce the arrears to less than one half-year's rent, and it is wished to bring ejectment, *no distress should be taken;* but clear proof should be obtained as to the insufficiency of the distress to satisfy *all* the arrears. *Doe* d. *Haverson* v. *Franks*, 2 Car. & K. 678. A distress for rent, under which part was recovered, will not prevent an ejectment for the residue, provided such residue amount to half a year's rent or more, and there be no sufficient distress on the premises to satisfy such residue. *Brewer* d. *Lord Onslow* v. *Eaton*, 3 Doug. 230, cited 6 T. R. 220; *Doe* d. *Taylor* v. *Johnson*, 1 Stark. R. 411; and see *Ex parte Filton*, 1 B. & A. 369; 2 Chit. Arch. 997, 998 (9th ed.).

4. The landlord or lessor to whom the arrears are due must have "right by law to re-enter for nonpayment thereof." *Brewer* d. *Lord Onslow* v. *Eaton*, 3 Doug. 230, cited 6 T. R. 220. He can have no such right except by virtue of some condition or proviso for re-entry contained in the lease or agreement (*ante*, 411). 2 Chit. Arch. 997, note (*t*) (9th ed.). The right to re-enter must be a right to enter *and determine the lease* for nonpayment of the rent, and not merely a right to enter and hold the premises until the arrears are paid; otherwise this section will not apply. *Doe* d. *Darke* v. *Bowditch*, 8 Q. B. 973. Although perhaps an ejectment may be maintained to recover posses-

sion of the premises *quousque*, &c., by virtue of the common law (*ante*, 411). The twenty-one days, or other specified period mentioned in the proviso, must have elapsed before any forfeiture can accrue for nonpayment of the rent. *Doe* d. *Dixon* v. *Roe*, 7 C. B. 134. But if the proviso contain the words "being lawfully demanded," no demand will be necessary, if it be proved that half a year's rent was due before action brought, and no sufficient distress to be found on the demised premises. *Doe* d. *Scholefield* v. *Alexander*, 2 M. & S. 525 ; *Doe* d. *Earl of Shrewsbury* v. *Wilson*, 5 B. & A. 364 (4th point); *Id.* 384, 394 ; 1 Wms. Saund. 287 a, note (*o*) (6th ed.). Service of the writ of ejectment under the above circumstances is sufficient "without any formal demand or re-entry." The statute makes such service a substitute for, and equivalent to, a formal demand of the rent according to the strict rules of the common law (*ante*, 415). *Hassell* d. *Hodgson* v. *Gowthwaite*, Willes, 500, 507, note (*b*). And the right of re-entry by virtue of the statute must be taken to have accrued on the day when the forfeiture would have accrued at common law, if a demand of payment had been duly made, and not when the writ of ejectment was served. *Doe* d. *Lawrence* v. *Shawcross*, 3 B. & C. 752 ; 5 D. & R. 711.

If the tenant do not appear to the writ in due time, judgment may be signed for want of appearance on filing a judge's order (*ante*, 131). The affidavit for such order should show not only a sufficient service or affixing of the copy writ in ejectment, pursuant to sect. 210 (*ante*, 415), but also the other facts necessary to be "made to appear to the court" by that section, *viz.*, that before and at the time of the service of the writ the claimant was landlord and the defendant tenant of the premises sought to be recovered ; that half a year's rent, or more, was due before the writ was served, and that no sufficient distress was to be found on the demised premises countervailing the arrears then due, and that the lessor had power to re-enter. *See the form, Appendix, No.* 40. The claimant need not join in the affidavit ; his receiver or agent, with or without other persons, may be able to depose to all the necessary facts. *Doe* d. *Charles* v. *Roe*, 2 Dowl. 752 ; *Anon.*, 3 Moo. & Sc. 751. The affidavit must be *positive* as to the absence of a sufficient distress ; mere *belief* on that point will not be sufficient; *Doe* v. *Roe*, 2 Dowl. 413 ; *Doe* d. *Hicks* v. *Roe*, 1 Dowl. & L. 180 ; but if the affidavit clearly show that the tenant kept the premises locked up, so as to prevent all access to them for the purpose of making a distress, that will do, because it shows that there was no sufficient distress " to be found" on the premises, within the meaning of the statute. *Doe* d. *Cox* v. *Roe*, 5 Dowl. & L. 272 ; *Doe* d. *Haverson* v. *Franks*, 2 Car. & K. 678 ; *ante*, 416.

The affidavit should be laid before a judge at his chambers, indorsed with a memorandum, " For an order for leave to sign judgment, pursuant to 15 & 16 Vict. c. 76, s. 210." Such order will be made *ex parte* if the judge be satisfied with the affidavit. *See form of Order, Appendix, No.* 41. The affidavit will of course be filed at the judge's chambers. The order, together with a copy of the writ in ejectment, must be filed with the master at the time the judgment is signed. The judgment may be in the ordinary form for want of appearance. *Appendix, No.* 123. No suggestion of the facts stated in the affidavit appears to be necessary. *Doe* d. *Hitchins* v. *Lewis*, 1 Burr. 614 ; 2 Ld. Ken. 320, *S. C.* But it will be proper and advisable to write in the margin of the judgment, opposite the words "Therefore it is considered, &c.," the words "Judgment signed on the —— day of ——, 18——, pursuant to 15 & 16 Vict. c. 76, s. 210, by order of Mr. Justice ——, dated the —— day of ——, 18——." Unless a special affidavit be made as above suggested, the judgment will not operate in the special manner mentioned in sect. 210 (*ante*, 415); nor will the tenant, &c. be thereby barred from maintaining a cross action of ejectment against the landlord, &c., founded on a title derived under the lease, and commenced more than six calendar months after execution executed. *Doe* d. *Hitchins* v. *Lewis*, 1 Burr. 614; 2 Ld. Ken. 320, S. C.

Stay of Proceedings.]—At any time before execution executed in case of judgment by default, or at any time before trial, where the defendant appears (but not after the trial (*post*, 421)), the defendant may apply to the court or a judge to stay all further proceedings in the ejectment, upon payment of the arrears of rent, with costs to be taxed (15 & 16 Vict. c. 76, s. 212; *post*, 421); unless, indeed, there are other grounds of forfeiture beside the nonpayment of rent. *Goodtitle* v. *Holdfast*, 2 Stra. 900; *Doe* d. *Lambert* v. *Roe*, 3 Dowl. 557; *Doe* d. *Mayhew* v. *Asby*, 10 A. & E. 71; 2 P. & D. 302; *see forms of Summons and Order, Appendix, Nos.* 81, 82. A party obtaining such an order need not proceed on it unless he think fit: he cannot be compelled to do so. *Doe* d. *Harcourt* v. *Roe*, 4 Taunt. 883. He may abandon it even after the arrears of rent have been ascertained and the costs taxed. *Pugh* v. *Kerr*, 6 M. & W. 17; 8 Dowl. 218. The rent should be calculated only to the last rent day, and not to the day of computing; *Doe* d. *Harcourt* v. *Roe*, 4 Taunt. 883; and the costs should be taxed as between party and party. *Doe* d. *Capps* v. *Capps*, 3 Bing. N. C. 768.

Evidence for Plaintiff.—1. *When the Defendant does not appear at the Trial.*]—In case the defendant does not appear at the trial the claimant will be entitled to a verdict *for the property* sought to be recovered, without any proof of his title, &c. *Ante*, 280, 281. According to the former practice, and the stat. 4 Geo. 2, c. 28, s. 2, he would have been nonsuited for want of such appearance, and entitled thereupon to sign judgment against the casual ejector; *Turner* v. *Barnaby*, 1 Salk. 259; but not against the defendant in the ejectment. *Doe* d. *The Trustees of The Bedford Charity* v. *Payne*, 7 Q. B. 287. Upon such judgment the court would have allowed execution to issue as of course, and that notwithstanding the defendant had mortgaged the property, and taken the benefit of the Act for Relief of Insolvent Debtors, and inserted the arrears of rent in his schedule. *Doe* d. *Marquis of Westminster* v. *Suffield*, 5 Dowl. 660. The costs of the action would have been recovered under the consent rule. *Turner* v. *Barnaby*, 1 Salk. 259.

To recover a verdict for mesne profits in the defendant's absence, the usual proofs must be given. *Ante*, 292. And it would seem that for the purpose of making the judgment operate specially pursuant to sect. 210, the like proof must be given, as where the defendant appears at the trial. *Post*, 419. For although sect. 210 requires such proof at the trial "in case the defendant appears," (*ante*, 415,) the context shows this to mean "appears *to the writ or action.*" If such proof be not given at the trial, whether the defendant appears there or not, the judgment will operate merely as at common law, and will be no bar to a subsequent action by the tenant, his executors, administrators or assigns, to recover back the property for the remainder of the term granted by the lease, and to try in such action the question whether the term was or was not forfeited and duly determined for non-payment of the rent. *Doe* d. *Hutchins* v. *Lewis*, 1 Burr. 614, 619 ; 2 Ld. Ken. 320, *S. C.*

2. *When the Defendant appears at the Trial.*]—If the defendant appear at the trial the plaintiff must prove :—

1. The lease or agreement. *Ante*, 393. If there be no lease or agreement in writing the terms of the tenancy must be proved by parol evidence, which must show (*inter alia*) an express stipulation for a right to re-enter and determine the tenancy for non-payment of rent. An unstamped memorandum of the terms made at the time of letting, and which was then read over to the parties and verbally assented to by them, and signed by the witness (but not by either of the parties), may be used by the witness to refresh his memory and to enable him to prove the exact terms of the tenancy. *Lord Bolton* v. *Tomlin*, 5 A. & E. 856 ; *ante*, 394. If the plaintiff be not the lessor, his title to the reversion must be deduced from the lessor to the plaintiff, and proved in the usual manner. *Davy* v. *Matthew*, Cro. Eliz. 649. Also that the defendant had notice of the assignment to the plaintiff before or at the time when the rent was demanded or the forfeiture accrued. *Fraunce's case*, 8 Co. R. 89 b ; 2 Brownl. 277 ; *Hengen* v. *Payn*, Cro. Jac. 476 ; *ante*, 224.

2. That the lessee had possession of the premises sought to be recovered, or some part thereof, under or by virtue of the lease or agreement, or the verbal letting. And if the defendant be not the lessee it must be proved that he came into possession *under or after* the lessee. *Ante*, 224.

3. That half a year's rent or more was due and in arrear, and that the last day for saving the forfeiture for non-payment thereof had elapsed before the commencement of the action ; or, at all events, before the writ was served. *Ante*, 415. There must be some evidence of *non-payment*. *Doe* d. *Chandless* v. *Robson*, 2 C. & P. 245, Abbott, C. J. ; and see *Doe* d. *Bridger* v. *Whitehead*, 8 A. & E. 571 ; 3 N. & P. 557 (for not insuring). The receiver or agent of the landlord, who has been in the habit of receiving rent on his behalf, is competent to prove the non-payment. *Doe* d. *Charles* v. *Roe*, 3 Moo. & Sc. 751 ; 2 Dowl. 752. A variance between the amount of rent proved to be due, and the amount demanded by the plaintiff in the particulars of breaches, is not material. *Tenny* v. *Moody*, 3 Bing. 3 ; 10 Moo. 252 ; 1 Wms. Saund. 287 b, note (*q*).

It seems unnecessary to prove the *service of the writ* of ejectment, because that must have been served on or after its date. But if the rent became due, or the forfeiture accrued, or the search for the distress were made after the writ issued, and before the service thereof, such service must be proved ; 1 Wms. Saund. 287 b, note (*q*), 6th ed. ; and in other cases it will be prudent to prove it until there be a decision that it is unnecessary. Under the 4 Geo. 2, c. 28, s. 2, it was necessary to prove the date and fact of the service of the declaration in ejectment, because *that* was the commencement of the action, and it might have taken place months before the term of the declaration as entered on the record. *Doe* d. *Gooch* v. *Knowles*, 1 Dowl. & L. 198, 202.

4. That a proper search was made, but no sufficient distress found on the demised premises, or any part thereof, countervailing the arrears then due. *Ante*, 416.

5. That the claimant had power to re-enter and avoid the lease or tenancy for nonpayment of the rent. *Ante*, 411. This will appear by the lease or agreement, in writing or otherwise, as proved under the first head of proof above mentioned.

6. If the plaintiff seek to recover mesne profits the usual proofs in that behalf must be given. *Ante*, 292.

Evidence and Points for Defendant.]—If the defendant appear at the trial he may contend :—1. That the plaintiff's evidence on some or one of the above points is insufficient. He may also produce contradictory evidence. 2. Payment or satisfaction, before action, of all the rent, except less than one half year's rent. 3. That there was a sufficient distress on the demised premises, or some part thereof, sufficient to countervail all the arrears due (*ante*, 416), and that such distress might have been found with reasonable diligence. *Doe* d. *Haverson* v. *Franks*, 2 Car. & Kir. 678, Erle, J. But such proof will not avail if a strict demand of the rent, according to the rules of the common law (*ante*, 412), be proved. 4. Any waiver of the forfeiture by acceptance of subsequent rent or otherwise. *Ante*, 408.

Judgment and Execution.]—If the claimant obtain the verdict he will be entitled to sign judgment and issue execution at the expiration of fourteen days after the verdict, or on the fifth day in term after the verdict, *which shall first happen ; ante*, 336 ; or sooner, upon obtaining an order for speedy judgment and execution from the judge who tried the cause. *Ante*, 336. And the defendant must, *within six calendar months after execution executed*, either pay the rent and arrears, together with full costs, to the claimant, if he will accept the same without being compelled to do so, or he must, within the same period, proceed for relief in equity ; *ante*, 415 ; in which latter case sect. 211 will be applicable. *Infra*. In default of such payment or suit within the time above mentioned, no relief against the forfeiture can afterwards be obtained, either in equity or at law, except by proceedings in error to reverse the judgment, if erroneous. *Ante*, 415. A subsequent ejectment by the tenant against his landlord, to try whether the term granted by the lease was or was not forfeited and duly determined, cannot be supported. *Doe* d. *Hutchins* v. *Lewis*, 1 Burr. 614, 619 ; 2 Ld. Ken. 320, *S. C.* The landlord then holds the premises "discharged from such lease," pursuant to the statute. *Ante*, 415.

A summary application to stay all further proceedings in the ejectment, upon payment of all arrears of rent with costs, cannot be made *after trial. Post*, 421.

Relief in Equity.]—By 15 & 16 Vict. c. 76, s. 211, "in case the said lessee, his assignee, or other person claiming any right, title or interest, in law or equity, of, in, or to the said lease, shall, within the time aforesaid (*ante*, 415), proceed for relief in any court of equity, such person shall not have or continue any injunction against the proceedings at law on such ejectment unless he does or shall, within forty days next after a full and perfect answer shall be made by the claimant in such ejectment, bring into court, and lodge with the proper officer, such sum and sums of money as the lessor or landlord shall in his answer swear to be due and in arrear over and above all just allowances, and also the costs taxed in the said suit, there to remain till the hearing of the cause, or to be paid out to the lessor or landlord on good security, subject to the decree of the court; and in case such proceedings for relief in equity shall be taken within the time aforesaid, and *after execution is executed,* the lessor or landlord shall be accountable only for so much and no more as he shall really and *bonâ fide,* without fraud, deceit or wilful neglect, make of the demised premises from the time of his entering into the actual possession thereof; and if what shall be so made by the lessor or landlord happen to be less than the rent reserved on the said lease, then the said lessee or his assignee, before he shall be restored to his possession, shall pay such lessor or landlord what the money so by him made fell short of the reserved rent for the time such lessor or landlord held the said lands."

This section is similar to 4 Geo. 2, c. 28, s. 3. It would seem that a bill (not a claim) must be filed, because an *answer* is to be put in by the claimant. It may be filed at any time before the expiration of six calendar months after execution executed; *ante,* 415; but not afterwards; unless, indeed, the judgment was obtained pursuant to the common law, and not by virtue of sect. 210. *Ante,* 414.

If the bill do not pray an injunction against the proceedings at law, and the landlord has obtained possession of the demised premises, it is not necessary for the plaintiff in equity to pay into court, within forty days after answer, the arrears of rent, &c. *Bowser* v. *Colby,* 1 Hare, 109; 11 Law J., N. S., Ch. 132.

Relief cannot be obtained in equity against a forfeiture for nonpayment of rent and for other breaches of covenant contained in the lease. *Wadman* v. *Calcraft,* 10 Ves. 67; *Davis* v. *West,* 12 Ves. 475; *Bowser* v. *Colby,* 1 Hare, 109, 134. As for not repairing; *Hill* v. *Barclay,* 18 Ves. 56; or not insuring. *Green* v. *Bridges,* 4 Sim. 96; cited 6 Q. B. 961; *ante,* 410.

Stay of Proceedings before the Trial.]—By 15 & 16 Vict. c. 76, s. 212, "if the tenant or his assignee do or shall at any time *before the trial* in such ejectment pay or tender to the lessor or landlord, his executors or administrators, or his or their attorney in that cause, or pay into the court where the same cause is depending, all the rent and arrears, together with the costs, then and in such case, all further proceedings on the said ejectment shall cease and be discontinued; and if such lessee, his executors, administrators or assigns, shall, upon such proceedings as aforesaid, be relieved in equity, he and they shall have, hold and enjoy the demised lands, according to the lease thereof made, without any new lease."

This section is similar to 4 Geo. 2, c. 28, s. 4. A summary application, pursuant to this section, must be made "before the trial," even where the ejectment is not founded on sect. 210, but on the common law. *Doe* d. *West* v. *Davis,* 7 East, 363; *Doe* d. *Harris* v. *Masters,* 2 B. & C. 490; 4 D. & R. 45. Before or after the trial relief may be obtained in equity pursuant to sects. 210, 211. *Ante,* 415, 420. But it is more usual *before* the trial to apply to the court in term time, or to a judge in vacation. 2 Sellon, Prac. 127; Ad. Eject. 127; and see *Smeeton* v. *Collier*, 1 Exch. 457; 5 Dowl. & L. 184; *see forms of Summons and Order, Appendix, Nos.* 81, 82. Such application may be made by the "tenant or his assignee." This includes a mortgagee. *Doe* d. *Whitfield* v. *Roe*, 3 Taunt. 402; *Williams* v. *Bosanquet*, 1 Bro. & Bing. 238; 3 J. B. Moore, 500. Even a *sub-lessee* is within this section, which is as extensive as sect. 211. *Ante*, 420; *Doe* d. *Wyatt* v. *Byron*, 1 C. B. 623; 3 Dowl. & L. 31.

In ejectment by a landlord, the tenant moved to stay proceedings upon payment of rent-arrear and costs. On a rule to show cause it was insisted for the plaintiff that the case was not within the act, for that it was not an ejectment [for nonpayment of rent only] founded singly on the act, but that it was brought likewise on a clause of re-entry in the lease for not repairing, and the lease was produced in court: however, the rule was made absolute, *with liberty for the plaintiff to proceed upon any other title.* *Pure* d. *Withers* v. *Sturdy*, Bull. N. P. 97. The objection would have been a good one after judgment by default and execution executed; or after trial. *Ante*, 418.

Where the lessors of the plaintiff were both devisees and executors, and in each capacity rent was due to them, the defendant moved to stay proceedings on payment of the rent due to the lessors of the plaintiff as devisees, they not being entitled to bring ejectment as executors: there appeared to be a mutual debt to the defendant by simple contract, and the defendant offered to go into the whole account, taking in both demands, as devisees and executors, having just allowances, which the lessors of the plaintiff refused: whereupon the court made the rule absolute to stay proceedings on payment of the rent due to the lessors as devisees and costs. *Duckworth* d. *Tubley* v. *Tunstall*, Barnes' Notes, 184.

3. *For not Repairing.*] — Leases of houses, &c., usually contain a covenant to repair and keep in repair the demised premises during the term; also another covenant to repair specific defects, within three calendar months next after written notice thereof; also other covenants: after which follows a proviso for re-entry on breach of any covenant. *See the forms,* 8 & 9 *Vict. c.* 124, *Sched.* 2; *ante*, 411.

Unless there be a proviso for re-entry applicable to the covenants to repair, &c., a breach of such covenants will not be sufficient to support an ejectment, but only an action for damages. *Ante*, 403. Only nominal damages could be recovered *during the term.* *Marriott* v. *Cotton*, 2 Car. & K. 553. On the other hand, if there be such a proviso, the lessor or his assigns may maintain ejectment for the whole of the demised premises, if any part thereof be out of repair, at any time during the term, and that without giving any previous notice to the lessee, or his assigns or undertenant, to repair. *Doe* d. *Hills* v. *Morris*, 11 Law J., N. S., Exch., 313. So where a lessee covenants to pay rates and taxes, no demand is necessary to constitute a breach, so as to entitle the lessor to avail himself of the proviso for re-entry. *Davis* v. *Burrell*, 10 C. B. 821.

Where a lease contained a general covenant to repair and keep in repair the demised premises during the term; and also another covenant to repair specific defects within three months after notice thereof; and a proviso for re-entry on breach of any covenant; and the landlord gave the tenant a notice requiring him *forthwith* to put all the demised premises into repair, agreeable to the covenant in that behalf: held, that such notice would not prevent an ejectment being brought within three months afterwards, for breach of the general covenant to repair. *Roe* d. *Goatley* v. *Paine*, 2 Camp. 520, Lord Ellenborough, C. J. But in a similar case, where the landlord gave the tenant *notice to repair within three months* then next: held, that such notice amounted to a waiver of any forfeiture during the three months for breach of the general covenant to repair, and that no ejectment could be maintained until after the expiration of that period. *Doe* d. *Morecraft* v. *Meux*, 4 B. & C. 606; 7 D. & R. 98. Where a lease contained à general covenant to repair, &c., with a proviso for re-entry *in case of nonrepair for three months after notice*, or on breach of any other covenant: held, that no ejectment could be maintained for nonrepair until after the expiration of a three months' notice. *Doe* d. *Rankin* v. *Brindley*, 4 B. & Adol. 84; 1 N. & M. 1. Any such notice must be given to the lessee or his assigns, and not to a mere underlessee. *Swetman* v. *Cush*, Cro. Jac. 8; Moore, 680. Where an ejectment was prematurely brought, after a notice of the above nature, and a juror withdrawn by consent, upon the defendant's undertaking to put the premises in repair before the following Midsummer: held, that on breach of such undertaking a second ejectment might be maintained, founded on the original notice, which had not been waived, but only the time for compliance therewith extended. *Doe* v. *Brindley, supra;* and see *Fryett* d. *Harris* v. *Jefferys*, 1 Esp. 393. A lease from A. to B. contained a general covenant to repair; also a covenant to repair specific defects within two months after notice thereof, in failure whereof A. might re-enter and do such repairs at B.'s expense, with power to distrain for the amount as for rent in arrear; also a proviso for re-entry on breach of any covenant: held, that a notice by A. to B. to do certain repairs, in default whereof A. would do them, and charge B. with the expense, pursuant to the lease, amounted to a waiver of any forfeiture for breach of the general covenant to repair committed prior to the expiration of the notice; and that after the expiration of such notice, although A. might enter and do the repairs at B.'s expense, yet he could not maintain ejectment for any previous breach of the general covenant to repair. *Doe* d. *Rutzen* v. *Lewis*, 5 A. & E. 277; and see *Doe* d. *Pittman* v. *Sutton*, 9 C. & P. 706.

A covenant to repair and keep in repair the demised premises " and all such buildings, *improvements and additions* as should be made thereupon" by the lessee during his term, with a proviso for re-entry on breach of that covenant, is not broken, nor the term forfeited, by the lessee having altered the windows on the ground-floor into shop windows, and stopped up a doorway, and made a new one in a different place in the internal part of the house: because the covenant is only against *nonrepair*, and it is to be implied from the terms of the lease that additions and improvements were to be made. *Doe* d. *Dalton* v. *Jones*, 4 B. & Adol. 126; 1 N. & M. 6.

A covenant for a landlord to be allowed to come into a house to see the state of its repair, " at convenient times," is not broken by his not being allowed to go into some of the rooms, if the tenant has had no previous notice of his coming. *Doe* v. *Wetherell* v. *Bird*, 6 C. & P. 195, Lord Denman, C. J.

A covenant *forthwith* to put premises into repair must receive a reasonable construction, and is not limited to any specific time: therefore it is for the jury to say upon the evidence whether the defendant has done what he reasonably ought in performance of it. *Doe* d. *Pittman* v. *Sutton*, 9 C. & P. 706, Lord Denman, C. J.

If a tenant covenant to repair and keep in repair the demised premises during the term, he must rebuild them, if burnt down by accident, negligence or otherwise. *Bullock* v. *Dommitt*, 2 Chit. R. 608 ; 6 T. R. 650 ; 2 Wms. Saund. 422. He must also pay his rent in the same manner as if no fire had happened. *Belfour* v. *Weston*, 1 T. R. 310 ; *Baker* v. *Holtzapffell*, 4 Taunt. 45 ; *Holtzapffell* v. *Baker*, 18 Ves. 115 ; *Izon* v. *Gorton*, 5 Bing. N. C. 501 ; *Parker* v. *Gibbins*, 1 Q. B. 421 ; *Leeds* v. *Cheetham*, 1 Sim. 146.

A lessee who has covenanted to repair and keep in repair certain premises during a term, must have them in repair *at all times during the term*; and if they are at any time out of repair he is guilty of a breach of covenant. *Luxmore* v. *Robson*, 1 B. & A. 584, Lord Ellenborough, C. J. But only nominal damages can be recovered in an action commenced before the expiration of the term. *Marriott* v. *Cotton*, 2 Car. & K. 553. The non-repair is, however, a *continuing* breach of covenant for which an ejectment may be maintained upon the proviso for re-entry. *Doe* d. *Baker* v. *Jones*, 5 Exch. 498 ; *Doe* d. *Hemmings* v. *Durnford*, 2 Cr. & Jer. 667. The breaking a doorway through a wall of the demised house into an adjoining house, although done with the intention of reinstating it before the end of the term is a *continuing* breach of the covenant to repair and keep in repair during the term. *Doe* d. *Vickery* v. *Jackson*, 2 Stark. R. 293. So a covenant to repair and keep in repair all walls, &c. during the term, is broken if the lessee pull down a wall, which divides the court yard at the front of the house from another yard at the side of the house, although done with the intention to restore it before the end of the term. *Doe* d. *Wetherell* v. *Bird*, 6 C. & P. 195, Lord Denman, C. J.

A general covenant to repair is satisfied by the lessee keeping the premises in *substantial repair*: a literal performance of the covenant is not to be required. *Harris* v. *Jones*, 1 Moo. & Rob. 173, Tindal, C. J. And where a lessee covenants to keep *old* premises in repair he is not liable for such dilapidations as result from the natural operation of time and the elements. *Gutteridge* v. *Munyard*, 1 Moo. & Rob. 334, Tindal, C. J. And with a view to determine the relative sufficiency of repair the jury may inquire whether the house was new or old at the time of the demise. *Stanley* v. *Towgood*, 3 Bing. N. C. 4 ; 3 Scott, 313. And what was its *then* state of repair and condition *generally*. *Burdett*, Bart., v. *Withers*, 7 A. & E. 136. But not in detail. *Mantz* v. *Goring*, 4 Bing. N. C. 451 ; *S. C.*, nom. *Young* v. *Mantz*, 6 Scott, 277 ; *Belcher* v. *M'Intosh*, 8 C. & P. 720 ; 2 Moo. & Rob. 186. A covenant *to keep* old premises in repair, and to leave them in repair at the end of the term, means that the lessee will if necessary *put them into repair*; for otherwise they cannot be kept or left in repair pursuant to the covenant. *Payne* v. *Haine*, 16 M. & W. 541. Their age, and class, and general condition must be taken into consideration, but not particular defects or wants of repair at the time the term commenced. *S. C.* "It is now perfectly well settled that a general covenant to repair must be construed to have reference to the condition of the premises at the time when the covenant begins to operate." *Per* Parke, B., in *Walker* v. *Hatton,* 10 M. & W. 258. Under a covenant that the tenant "should and would substantially repair, uphold and maintain" a house, he is bound to keep up the inside painting. *Monk* v. *Noyes,* 1 C. & P. 265. The breaking a doorway through a wall of the demised house into an adjoining house, and keeping it open for a long space of time, amounts to breach of covenant to repair. *Doe* d. *Vickery* v. *Jackson,* 2 Stark. R. 293. An *omission* to repair is not a breach of a proviso that if the lessee shall " do or cause to be done any act " in breach of any of the covenants; although the lease contains a covenant to repair and keep in repair. *Doe* d. *Abdy* v. *Stephens,* 3 B. & Adol. 299. A private dwelling-house was demised for forty years by lease, containing a covenant to repair and keep in repair the premises, and all such buildings, *improvements and additions* as should be made thereupon by the lessee during the term ; with a proviso for re-entry on breach of any covenant. The lessee changed the lower windows into shop windows, and stopped up a door-way, making a new one in a different place, in the internal partition of the house: held, that no forfeiture was incurred, the lessee's covenant being only *against non-repair,* and it being implied, by the terms of the lease, that additions and improvements were to be made. *Doe* d. *Dalton* v. *Jones,* 4 B. & Adol. 126 ; 1 N. & M. 6.

Where the tenant undertakes to do repairs to the "satisfaction of the surveyor of the lessor," and the jury find that the repairs done *ought* to have satisfied such surveyor, ejectment for a forfeiture cannot be maintained. *Doe* d. *Baker* v. *Jones,* 2 Car. & K. 743, Pollock, C. B.; and see *Parson* v. *Sexton,* 4 C. B. 899, 909; *Moore* v. *Wolsey,* 4 E. & B. 243, 252, 256.

Waiver of Forfeiture.]—By distraining for, or accepting payment of rent which accrues due *after* a forfeiture for breach of covenant to repair, the landlord waives the forfeiture *to that time ; Fryett* d. *Harris* v. *Jefferys,* 1 Esp. 393, Lord Kenyon, C. J.; provided he then knew of the non-repair, but not otherwise, *Pennant's case,* 3 Co. R. 63 b; *Duppa* v. *Mayo,* 1 Wms. Saund. 288 a, 288 b, note (16); *Doe* d. *Gregson* v. *Harrison,* 2 T. R. 425 ; *Goodright* d. *Walter* v. *Davids,* Cowp. 803. But such distress or payment will not operate as a waiver of the *subsequent continuing breach* by non-repair. *Fryett* d. *Harris* v. *Jefferys, supra ; Doe* d. *Hemmings* v. *Durnford,* 2 Cr. & Jer. 667; *Doe* d. *Baker* v. *Jones,* 5 Exch. 498 ; *post,* 430. Accept-ance of rent which becomes due pending a notice to repair, is no waiver of a subsequent forfeiture occasioned by non-compliance with such notice. *Doe* d. *Rankin* v. *Brindley,* 4 B. & Adol. 84. Acceptance of rent after the commencement of an ejectment is no waiver of the for-feiture for which such action was brought. *Doe* d. *Morecraft* v. *Meux,* 1 C. & P. 346, Abbott, C. J.

No stay of Ejectment for Non-repair.]—A court of law has no jurisdiction to stay an ejectment for breach of covenant to repair, &c., although it clearly appears that such repairs were all done *before* ejectment brought. *Doe* d. *Mayhew* v. *Asby,* 10 A. & E. 71; 2 P. & D. 302. Nor can any relief be obtained in equity. *Hill* v. *Barclay,* 18 Ves. 56; *Gregory* v. *Wilson,* 9 Hare, 683, Wigram, V. C.

Evidence for Plaintiff.]—To maintain ejectment for a forfeiture for non-repair, the plaintiff must prove:—

1. The lease or duplicate or counterpart thereof containing the covenant to repair, and the proviso for re-entry. This must be duly stamped and admitted in the cause (*ante*, 150), or proved in the usual manner. *Ante*, 294, 393. If the plaintiff be not the lessor, the title to the reversion must be deduced from the lessor to the plaintiff, and proved iu the usual manner. *Davy* v. *Matthew*, Cro. Eliz. 649. And it must appear that the forfeiture accrued *after* the plaintiff became assignee. *Hunt* v. *Bishop*, 8 Exch. 675, 680; 9 Exch. 635, *S. C.* Where a lease is made in pursuance of a power, covenants and provisoes with or in favour of the lessor, *his heirs and assigns,* will enure for the benefit of a reversioner afterwards entitled to the estate under the deed or will creating the power. *Greenaway* v. *Hart*, 14 C. B. 340; *Isherwood* v. *Oldknow*, 3 M. & S. 382. But no right of re-entry can be reserved to a mere stranger. *Doe* d. *Barker* v. *Goldsmith*, 2 C. & J. 674; *ante*, 404. Or (in an underlease) to the superior landlord. *Doe* d. *Bedford* v. *White*, 4 Bing. 276.

2. That the lessee had possession of the premises sought to be recovered, or some part thereof, under or by virtue of such lease. If the defendant be not the lessee, it must be proved that he came into possession under or *after* the lessee. *Ante*, 215, 224; *Humphrey* v. *Damion*, Cro. Jac. 300. In *Doe* d. *Hemmings* v. *Durnford*, 2 Cro. & Jer. 667, it was erroneously supposed to be necessary to prove an *assignment* to the defendant. But an underlessee can have no better title than the lessee.

3. The notice to repair (if any). Such notice must be shown to have been served on the tenant, not on his under-lessee. *Swetman* v. *Cush*, Cro. Jac. 8.

4. The defects and wants of repair. *Ante*, 424. These should be proved in detail by surveyors, architects, builders or other competent persons, who have examined the premises. It is not necessary to show that the premises were out of repair on the precise day on which possession is claimed in the writ; if proved to be out of repair a short time previously, that is sufficient to throw upon the defendant the onus of proof that they were afterwards put into repair before the day mentioned in the writ. *Doe* d. *Hemmings* v. *Durnford*, 2 Cro. & Jer. 667.

5. Performance by the plaintiff of any condition precedent, *ex. gr.* the finding of rough timber, stones or other materials: *Thomas* v. *Cadwallader*, Willes, 496: repairs to be done by the plaintiff in the first instance: *Neale* v. *Ratcliffe*, 15 Q. B. 916; *Slater* v. *Stone*, Cro. Jac. 645: the appointment of a surveyor, "under whose direction, and to whose satisfaction," the repairs, &c. were to have been done: *Hunt* v. *Bishop*, 8 Exch. 675: and the like.

Evidence and Points for Defendant.]—The defendant may contend, 1. That the evidence for the plaintiff on some or one of the above points is insufficient. He may also produce contradictory evidence. 2. That the proviso for re-entry does not apply to an *omission* to repair, that not being "an act done" contrary to the proviso (if the proviso be so worded). *Doe* d. *Sir W. Abdy* v. *Stevens*, 3 B. & Adol. 299. 3. The non-performance by the plaintiff of a condition precedent, *ex.gr.* the appointment of a surveyor, under whose direction the repairs were to have been done. *Hunt* v. *Bishop*, 8 Exch. 675 ; 9 Exch. 635, *S. C.; Hunt* v. *Remnant*, 23 Law J., N. S., Exch. 135. 4. That the premises have been duly and sufficiently repaired and kept in repair pursuant to the covenant. *Ante*, 423—425. This can seldom, if ever, be established without calling witnesses on behalf of the defendant. It will not be sufficient to prove that all the necessary repairs were done before ejectment brought, if it appear that any of the premises were out of repair at any time during the term, contrary to the covenant, and that such forfeiture has not been waived. *Doe* d. *Mayhew* v. *Asby*, 10 A. & E. 71 ; 2 P. & D. 302 ; *Doe* d. *Baker* v. *Jones*, 5 Exch. 498. 5. That the plaintiff has waived any forfeiture for breach of the *general* covenant to repair, &c. by a notice to repair within three months. *Ante*, 423. Or by distraining for, or accepting payment of rent which became *due after the forfeiture*, with notice or knowledge of such forfeiture. *Ante*, 425. But this point will not avail if there has been any *subsequent continued* breach. *Ante*, 425.

4. *For Waste.*]—Where a lease contains a proviso for re-entry, "if the lessee, his executors, administrators or assigns, shall commit or permit any manner of waste in or upon the demised premises to the value of 10*s.*," *only such waste as produces an injury to the reversion* will be deemed to fall within the proviso ; and it will be a question for the jury whether *such waste to the value of* 10*s.* has been committed, taking into consideration all the circumstances proved before them. *Doe* d. *Earl of Darlington* v. *Bond*, 5 B. & C. 855 ; 8 D. & R. 738. "Upon the whole there is no authority for saying that any act can be waste which is not injurious to the inheritance, either, first, by diminishing the value of the estate ; or, secondly, by increasing the burthen upon it ; or, thirdly, by impairing the evidence of title." *Per cur.* in *Doe* d. *Grubb* v. *The Earl of Burlington*, 5 B. & Adol. 507, 517 ; 2 N. & M. 534. If a copyholder pull down a barn without any intention of rebuilding it, but no damage is thereby done to the inheritance (and the jury so find), the lord cannot recover from him the premises as forfeited by the commission of waste. *S. C.* A power to grant leases "so as no clause or clauses be contained in any of the said leases giving power to any lessee to commit waste, or exempting him, her or them from punishment for committing the same," may be executed by a lease containing a stipulation that the lessee shall build a new dwelling-house, and may pull down an outhouse and use the materials for so building, unless it appear by evidence that the inheritance will be thereby prejudiced. *Doe* d. *Earl of Egremont* v. *Stephens*, 6 Q. B. 208, 227.

If trees be *excepted* out of a demise containing a proviso for re-entry in case the lessee should "commit any waste in or upon the said demised premises, or any part thereof," the cutting down of such trees is not waste within the meaning of the proviso, nor can an ejectment be supported on that ground. *Goodright* d. *Peters* v. *Vivian*, 8 East, 190 ; and see *Russell* v. *Gulwell*, Cro. Eliz. 657. An exception of trees, &c. generally excepts the soil on which they grow ; *Whilster* v. *Paslow*, Cro. Jac. 487 ; unless that be manifestly contrary to the intention of the parties. *Pincomb* v. *Thomas*, Cro. Jac. 524 ; *Legh* v. *Heald*, 1 B. & Adol. 622. A lease was granted of a farm and tenement, and the quarries of paving and tile-stone in and upon the premises, with liberty and power to open and work the quarries, subject to an annual rent for the premises, except the quarries, and to the payment of a royalty for the stone obtained. Out of this demise were reserved and excepted " all timber trees, trees likely to become timber, saplings, and all other wood and underwood which then were or should at any time thereafter be standing, growing and being on the premises, and all mines, minerals, &c. which should thereafter be opened and found," and the lease contained a covenant " not to commit any waste, spoil or destruction by cutting down, lopping or topping any timber-trees, or trees likely to become timber, saplings or any other wood or underwood," and a power of re-entry for nonpayment of rent, or if the lessee, &c. should *commit any waste, spoil or destruction by any of the ways or means aforesaid,* and should not perform and keep all and singular the covenants, &c. contained in the lease. The assignee of the term having cut down and grubbed up certain saplings, wood and underwood *for the necessary purpose of working a quarry on the demised premises :* held, that the effect of the covenant was that the tenant should not so cut any of the trees excepted, as that such cutting should amount to an *excess of the right which it was intended that he should exercise,* and therefore that cutting trees in a manner *necessary to a reasonable exercise of the power to get the stone* was no breach of the covenant. *Doe* d. *Rogers* v. *Price,* 8 C. B. 894; see also *Doe* d. *Dalton* v. *Jones,* 4 B. & Adol. 126; *ante,* 425.

A covenant in a lease to deliver up at the end of the term all the trees standing in an orchard at the time of the demise, " *reasonable use* and wear only excepted," is not broken by removing trees decayed and past bearing from a part of the orchard which was too crowded, for that must be considered as " reasonable use of the orchard and trees" within the meaning of the exception. *Doe* d. *Jones* v. *Crouch,* 2 Camp. 449, Lord Ellenborough, C. J.

A covenant not to remove or grub up trees is broken by removing trees from one part of the premises to another; and so by taking away trees and planting others in lieu thereof of equal or greater value, unless those removed were dead. *Doe* d. *Wetherell* v. *Bird,* 6 C. & P. 195, Lord Denman, C. J.

Where a beneficial long lease reserved to the lessee liberty to cut down and dispose of all timber, &c. (the value of which was included in the premium), subject to a proviso that *when and so often* as the lessee should intend, during the term, to cut down and sell timber, he should give notice of such intention to the lessor, who should have a right of pre-emption within one month after the notice. The lease contained a proviso for re-entry on breach of any covenant. Held, that a single notice given by the lessee of his intention to cut down and sell *all* the timber on the estate, and a refusal by the lessor to purchase it, was sufficient to entitle the lessee to cut down timber in *different seasons* according to his convenience, without giving a fresh notice from time to time, the lessee having *bonâ fide* intended to cut down all the timber when he gave the notice. *Goodtitle* d. *Luxmore* v. *Saville,* 16 East, 87.

A forfeiture by committing waste may be waived in like manner as any other forfeiture. *Ante,* 408, 425; *post,* 430.

Evidence for Plaintiff.]—To maintain ejectment upon a proviso for re-entry for the commission of waste, the evidence must be similar, *mutatis mutandis,* to that in an ejectment for non-repair. *Ante,* 426.

It must be proved that the waste has produced a damage to the inheritance. *Ante*, 427.

Evidence and Points for Defendant.]—The defendant may contend : 1. That the plaintiff's evidence is insufficient on some or one material point. He may also produce contradictory evidence. 2. That the acts proved do not amount to "waste" within the true intent and meaning of the proviso. 3. Any waiver of the forfeiture, with knowledge thereof. *Ante*, 408. 4. A licence from the plaintiff to do the acts creating the supposed forfeiture. *Doe* d. *Wood* v. *Morris*, 2 Taunt. 52.

5. *For not Insuring.*]—Leases of houses, &c. frequently contain a covenant on the part of the lessee, his executors, administrators and assigns, to insure, and keep insured, against loss or damage by fire, the demised premises, or some part thereof, during the term, either in the joint names of the lessor and lessee; *Doe* d. *Muston* v. *Gladwin*, 6 Q. B. 953; or in the name of the lessor; *Penniall* v. *Harborne*, 11 Q. B. 368; or in the name of the lessee; and sometimes it is further stipulated that if the tenant omit so to insure, the landlord may do it, and recover the amount paid, by distress or otherwise, as for rent in arrear.

Any such covenant must be fortified by a proviso for re-entry applicable thereto, otherwise a breach of it will not support an ejectment. *Ante*, 403.

A covenant and proviso of the above nature must be complied with *strictly*, otherwise the title of the lessee will be bad and unmarketable; *Peniall* v. *Harborne*, 11 Q. B. 368; *Wilson* v. *Wilson*, 14 C. B. 616; and the lessor or his assigns may maintain ejectment; *Doe* d. *Muston* v. *Gladwin*, 6 Q. B. 953; *Doe* d. *Bridger* v. *Whitehead*, 8 A. & E. 571; 3 N. & P. 557; and a court of equity will give no relief against the forfeiture. *Green* v. *Bridges*, 4 Sim. 96, cited 6 Q. B. 961; *Gregory* v. *Wilson*, 9 Hare, 683, Wigram, V. C. Thus, where the covenant was to insure, and continue insured " in the joint names" of the landlord and tenant, but the tenant insured in his own name only: held, that ejectment was maintainable by the landlord's assignee. *Doe* d. *Muston* v. *Gladwin*. *supra*. But it seems that if in such case the tenant had insured in the landlord's name only, that would have been sufficient, because the landlord could not thereby have sustained any prejudice. *Havens* v. *Middleton*, 17 Jur. 271, Wood, V. C. But a covenant to insure in the landlord's name would not be satisfied by an insurance in the joint names of the landlord and tenant. *Penniall* v. *Harborne*, 11 Q. B. 368.

Where a lessee covenanted that he, his executors, administrators and assigns, would insure the demised premises, and keep them insured during the term, and deposit the policy with the lessor, this was holden to mean, not that the lessee should effect any one policy, and keep that particular policy on foot, but that he, his executors, administrators or assigns, should, during the whole term, keep the premises insured by one policy or another; and that it would be a breach if the premises were uninsured at any one time during the term; and that it would be a continuing breach for any length of time they were uninsured. *Doe* d. *Flower* v. *Peck*, 1 B. & Adol. 428; and see *Hyde* v. *Watts*, 12 M. & W. 254; 1 Dowl. & L. 479, *S. C.; Penniall* v. *Harborne*, 11 Q. B.

368; *Doe* d. *Darlington* v. *Ulph*, 13 Q. B. 204. So, a covenant to repair, and keep in repair, during the term, is a continuing covenant, and broken from day to day so long as the premises are out of repair. *Doe* d. *Baker* v. *Jones*, 5 Exch. 498.

Where a lease, executed on the 12th January, 1847, in pursuance of a decree for a specific performance, contained a covenant "to insure, and keep insured, the premises, at all times during the term," but the lessee omitted to insure until the 18th February, 1847; and the jury expressly found that such insurance was made within a reasonable time in that behalf: nevertheless, the court held, as matter of law, that it was not, and that the lessor was entitled to maintain ejectment. *Doe* d. *Darlington* v. *Ulph*, 13 Q. B. 204.

A covenant to keep the demised premises "insured in 800*l.*, in some sufficient insurance office in London or Westminster," must be construed to mean, insured *against loss or damage by fire*, in some proper office for that purpose. *Doe* d. *Pitt* v. *Shewin*, 3 Camp. 134. If the premium be not duly paid on the proper day, or within the extra time allowed for that purpose by the policy, but at a later period, so that the premises were *not insured for several days*, although no fire happened during that period, the lessor is entitled to re-enter for a forfeiture pursuant to the proviso. *S. C.*

A covenant to insure, and keep insured, is satisfied by a policy containing a proviso, "that in case of the death of the assured, the policy may be continued to his legal representative, provided an indorsement be made on the policy to that effect within three months after his death;" and that, notwithstanding no such indorsement was in fact made until after the three months had elapsed. *Doe* d. *Pitt* v. *Laming*, 4 Camp. 73. Lord Ellenborough, C. J., doubted whether such a proviso would affect the liability of the office to the executor upon the policy, supposing no such indorsement to be made. *S. C.*

Where the landlord has *misled* the tenant by giving him only an imperfect abstract of the lease (keeping the lease itself in his own possession), and the tenant has insured the property according to such abstract, the landlord will not be able to support an ejectment for a forfeiture in not insuring according to the terms of the lease. *Doe* d. *Knight* v. *Rowe*, Ry. & Moo. 343; 2 C. & P. 246, Abbott, C. J. So, where the landlord has led the tenant to suppose that he (the landlord) has exercised his right of insuring and charging the tenant with the amount, it will be a question for the jury whether the landlord has not so misled the tenant as to preclude himself from insisting on a forfeiture. *Doe* d. *Pittman* v. *Sutton*, 9 C. & P. 706, Lord Denman, C. J.; and see *Doe* d. *Morecraft* v. *Meux*, 4 B. & C. 606; *Doe* d. *Rankin* v. *Brindley*, 4 B. & Adol. 84; *Doe* d. *Rutzen* v. *Lewis*, 5 A. & E. 277.

By distraining for, or accepting payment of rent, with knowledge that the premises have not been properly insured, the landlord waives the forfeiture to the time such rent became due, but not any breach by the subsequent non-insurance. *Doe* d. *Muston* v. *Gladwin*, 6 Q. B. 953, 956; *Penniall* v. *Harborne*, 11 Q. B. 368, 374, note (*b*); *Hyde* v. *Watts*, 12 M. & W. 254; 1 Dowl. & L. 479; *Doe* d. *Baker* v. *Jones*, 5 Exch. 498; *Doe* d. *Flower* v. *Peck*, 1 B. & Adol. 428; *Doe* d. *Ambler* v. *Woodbridge*, 9 B. & C. 376. There can be no waiver except with knowledge of the forfeiture. *Pennant's case*, 3 Co. R. 63 b; *Duppa* v. *Mayo*, 1 Wms. Saund. 288 a, 288 b, note (16); *Doe* d. *Gregson* v. *Harrison*, 2 T. R. 425. Acceptance of rent after the commencement of an ejectment for a forfeiture is no waiver of such forfeiture. *Doe* d. *Morecroft* v. *Meux*, 1 C. & P. 346, Abbott, C. J.

No relief can be obtained in equity against an ejectment for a forfeiture by not insuring. *Green* v. *Bridges*, 4 Sim. 96, cited 6 Q. B. 961; *ante*, 410.

Evidence for Plaintiff.]—To maintain ejectment for a forfeiture by not insuring, the plaintiff must prove:—

1. The lease or duplicate or counterpart containing the covenant to insure and proviso for re-entry. This must be duly stamped, and admitted in the cause (*ante*, 150), or proved in the usual manner (*ante*, 294, 393). If the plaintiff be not the lessor, the title to the reversion must be deduced from the lessor to the plaintiff, and proved in the usual manner. *Davy* v. *Matthew*, Cro. Eliz. 649. And it must appear that the forfeiture accrued after the plaintiff became assignee. *Hunt* v. *Bishop*, 8 Exch. 675, 680; 9 *Id.* 635, *S. C.; ante*, 405.

2. That the lessee had possession of the premises sought to be recovered, or some part thereof, under or by virtue of such lease. If the defendant be not the lessee, it must be proved that he came into possession *under or after* the lessee. *Ante*, 215, 224.

3. That the premises have not been insured pursuant to the covenant. In some cases it may be difficult to prove a negative, but it must be done. *Doe* d. *Bridger* v. *Whitehead*, 8 A. & E. 571; 3 N. & P. 557. If necessary, the defendant himself may be served with a *subpœna duces tecum* to produce his lease, and any policy or policies of insurance against loss or damage by fire which he may have effected; and he may also be called and examined as a witness on behalf of the plaintiff. 14 & 15 Vict. c. 99, s. 2; but see *Boyle* v. *Wiseman*, 10 Exch. 647; *ante*, 204, 206. If necessary, an *inspection* may be obtained of any policy which has been effected, but is supposed to be insufficient. *Id.* s. 6. A notice to produce the policy at the trial will merely let in secondary evidence of the contents, if it be not produced when called for. *Doe* d. *Bridger* v. *Whitehead*, 8 A. & E. 571; 3 N. & P. 557. If the covenant be to insure in a particular office, a clerk from that office, who has searched the proper books without finding any policy effected by the defendant, will be able to prove the breach; but if a policy has been effected, and the defendant has neglected to pay the premiums in due time, it will be prudent to have the book produced in which the payment would appear if it had been made. 2 Arch. N. P. 416. If the defendant has paid the premium, but after the expiration of the extra time allowed for that purpose by the policy, that should be clearly proved. *Doe* d. *Pitt* v. *Shewin*, 3 Camp. 134; *ante*, 430.

Evidence and Points for Defendant.]—The defendant may contend:—1. That the evidence for the plaintiff on some or one of the above points is insufficient. He may also produce contradictory evidence. 2. That the premises have been duly and properly insured pursuant to the covenant. 3. That the plaintiff has by his conduct misled the defendant, and so prevented him from effecting a proper insurance (*ante*, 430). 4. That the plaintiff has waived the forfeiture up to a certain day, with full knowledge thereof (*ante*, 430); and that ever since that day the premises have been insured strictly in pursuance of the covenant.

6. *For exercising any prohibited Trade or Business*.]—A covenant not to carry on, or suffer to be carried on, in or upon the demised premises, or any part thereof, any trade or business whatsoever, or any specified trades or businesses, must be fortified by a proviso for re-entry applicable to such covenant; otherwise the breach of it will not support an entry or ejectment, but only an action for damages (*ante*, 403). As to the necessity for such covenants and provisoes, see *Feret* v. *Hill*, 15 C. B. 207.

A covenant and proviso of the above nature ought to be construed fairly and reasonably, according to the true intent and meaning of the parties, and not with the strictness of conditions at common law. *Doe* d. *Davis* v. *Elsam*, 1 Moo. & Mal. 189, Lord Tenterden, C. J. "In the construction of covenants of this sort, they are neither entitled to favour or disfavour, whether they are to create a forfeiture or to continue an estate; but we are to put the fair construction upon them according to the apparent intention of the contracting parties." *Per* Lord Ellenborough, C. J., in *Goodtitle* d. *Luxmore* v. *Saville*, 16 East, 95. "The real object in all these cases is to prevent the lowering of the tenement in the scale of houses, by the exercise, whether wholly or partially, of those trades which, in the judgment of the lessor, are likely to [be a nuisance to the neighbourhood, or to] prevent tenants from afterwards taking the premises, and which by so doing may depreciate their value at a future period." *Per* Lord Ellenborough, C. J., in *Gaskell* v. *Spry*, 1 B. & A. 619. In construing a covenant of this nature, it is particularly worthy of consideration whether such a trade as that complained of was carried on at the time of the demise; also the situation of the premises. *Gutteridge* v. *Munyard*, 7 C. & P. 129. A lessor has the right to demise subject to such terms and conditions as he may think fit. *Cujus est dare ejus est disponere.* "The parties agree to a tenancy on certain terms, and there is no hardship in binding them to those terms." *Per* Lord Tenterden, C. J., in *Doe* d. *Davis* v. *Elsam*, 1 Moo. & Mal. 191.

A covenant not to permit or suffer on the demised premises "any trade or business whatsoever" is broken by an assignment to a schoolmaster, who uses the premises for the purposes of his school; for a school may be as much a nuisance and annoyance to the neighbourhood as almost any other trade or business. *Doe* d. *Bish* v. *Keeling*, 1 M. & S. 95. A covenant not to carry on "any public business" in a house, but that it should "be used solely as a private dwelling-house," is broken by using it as a day school and dancing academy, notwithstanding the next door neighbours made no complaints. *Wickenden* v. *Webster*, Q. B., 7th May, 1856. Keeping a lunatic asylum is not an offensive *trade*. *Doe* d. *Wetherell* v. *Bird*, 2 A. & E. 161; 4 N. & M. 285. A proviso for re-entry in case the lessee, his executors, administrators or assigns, shall carry on certain specified trades and businesses (not mentioning that of a publican or licensed victualler), "or any other trade or business that may be or grow or lead to be offensive, or any annoyance or disturbance to any of the tenants of the lessor," &c., is not broken by opening and using the premises as a public house, without proof of its being offensive or an annoyance or disturbance to some of the tenants, &c. *Jones* v. *Thorne*, 1 B. & C. 715; 3 D. & R. 152. Carrying on the business of a retail brewer is no breach of a covenant not to carry on the business of a common brewer or retailer of beer. *Simons* v. *Farren*, 1 Bing. N. C. 126; 1 Scott, 105; 4 Moo. & Sc. 672.

A covenant that the lessee shall not exercise the trade of a butcher upon the premises is broken by his selling there raw meat by retail, although no beasts were there slaughtered. *Doe* d. *Gaskell* v. *Spry*, 1 B. & A. 617. So a covenant not to carry on the business of a pork-butcher on the demised premises, nor to use them for the sale of pork, is broken by the exposure there of carcases of pigs for sale, although such carcases are cut up, and contracts for the sale thereof completed elsewhere in the neighbourhood. *Doe* d. *Davis* v. *Elsam*, 1 Moo. & Mal. 189, Lord Tenterden, C. J.

A covenant to use the demised premises as a workhouse, for the sole use, maintenance and support of the poor of R., and not to convert the building, or the land, or to employ the profits thereof, to any other use, intent or purpose whatsoever, is not broken by ceasing to use the building as a workhouse pursuant to 4 & 5 Will. 4, c. 76, and an order of the poor law commissioners (not using it for any *other* purpose), and letting the land at rack rent, and applying the rent in aid of the poor rates. *Doe* d. *Marquis of Anglesea* v. *The Churchwardens and Overseers of Rugeley*, 6 Q. B. 107. So a compulsory discontinuance of Gilbert's Act (22 Geo. 3, c. 83) will not amount to a breach of covenant " not of themselves to discontinue to adopt the provisions of the statute." *Doe* d. *Lord Grantley* v. *Butcher*, 6 Q. B. 115, note.

It would seem that a covenant not to carry on or suffer upon the demised premises during the term any specified trades or businesses, or any trade or business whatsoever, is a covenant of a *continuing nature*, and broken from day to day so long as the prohibited trade or business is carried on. *Doe* d. *Ambler* v. *Woodbridge*, 9 B. & C. 376. Therefore, although the breach of it may be waived up to a certain period, in the same manner as a covenant to repair (*ante*, 425), or to insure (*ante*, 430), yet such waiver will not excuse any subsequent or continued breach. *Doe* d. *Ambler* v. *Woodbridge*, *supra; ante*, 409. If a lessee or his assignee exercise a prohibited trade on the demised premises for six years, the landlord living next door all the time, and making no objection, that will not prevent him from afterwards maintaining eject-ment for the forfeiture: mere silence is not sufficient; some positive act of waiver, as a receipt of rent, is necessary. *Doe* d. *Sheppard* v. *Allen*, 3 Taunt. 78; and see *Doe* d. *Boscawen* v. *Bliss*, 4 Taunt. 735; *Doe* d. *Bryan* v. *Bancks*, 4 B. & A. 401.

No relief can be obtained in equity against an ejectment for a for-feiture by carrying on any prohibited trade or business. *Ante*, 410. It stands on the same footing in this respect as a covenant to repair: *Hill* v. *Barclay*, 18 Ves. 56: or to insure. *Green* v. *Bridges*, 4 Sim. 96, cited 6 Q. B. 961.

Evidence for Plaintiff.]—To maintain ejectment for a forfeiture by carrying on any prohibited trade or business, the plaintiff must prove:—

1. The lease or the duplicate or counterpart thereof, or the agree-ment or a duplicate thereof, containing the covenant or stipulation against the trade or business, and the proviso for re-entry. This must be duly stamped, and admitted in the cause (*ante*, 150); or proved in the usual manner. *Ante*, 294, 393. If the plaintiff be not the lessor, the title to the reversion must be deduced from the lessor to the plaintiff,

U

and proved in the usual manner. *Davy* v. *Matthew*, Cro. Eliz. 649.
And it must appear that the forfeiture accrued after the plaintiff became
assignee. *Hunt* v. *Bishop*, 8 Exch. 675, 680; 9 Exch. 635, *S. C.*;
ante, 405.

2. That the lessee had possession of the premises sought to be recovered, or some part thereof, under or by virtue of such lease or
agreement. If the defendant be not the lessee, it must be proved that
he came into possession *under or after* the lessee. *Ante*, 215; *Humphry* v. *Damion*, Cro. Jac. 300.

3. The carrying on or exercising of some trade or business of such
a nature and in such a manner as to amount to a violation of the covenant or proviso. *Ante*, 432, 433.

Evidence and Points for Defendant.]—The defendant may contend:—1. That the evidence for the plaintiff, on some or one of the
above points, is insufficient. He may also produce contradictory evidence. 2. That, upon the true construction of the covenant, it is not
broken by the acts proved. 3. Any waiver of the forfeiture with knowledge thereof (*ante*, 408); but this will not avail if there has been any
subsequent continuance of the breach. *Ante*, 409.

7. *For assigning or underletting without Licence.*]—A covenant
not to assign or underlet without previous licence of the lessor, &c.
must be fortified by a proviso for re-entry applicable to such covenant;
otherwise the breach of it will not support an ejectment, but only an
action for damages. *Ante*, 403; *Doe* d. *Spencer* v. *Godwin*, 4 M. & S.
265.

The form of a covenant and proviso of the above nature varies considerably; and therefore the exact words used in any particular instance must be carefully considered, in order to ascertain whether there
has been a sufficient breach to support an ejectment.

Sometimes there is no covenant not to assign or underlet, but only a
proviso or condition for re-entry in case the lessee, &c., shall assign or
underlet without licence. This will be sufficient to support an ejectment, upon proof of the necessary facts. *Ante*, 402.

A covenant not to *assign* without licence is broken upon the execution by the lessee (without licence) of any deed whereby he parts with
the demised premises *for the whole of the residue of his term;* although
such deed purports to be merely a lease or under-lease for an equal or
longer term, at a different rent, payable to himself, and contains other
and different covenants and stipulations than those in the original lease.
Hicks v. *Downing*, 1 Lord Raym. 99; *Wollaston* v. *Hakewill*, 3 Man.
& Gr. 297, 323; 3 Scott, N. R. 593; *Parmenter* v. *Webber*, 8 Taunt.
593; *Preece* v. *Corrie*, 5 Bing. 24; 2 Moo. & P. 57; *Palmer* v. *Edwards*, 1 Doug. 187, note; *Thorn* v. *Woolcombe*, 3 B. & Adol. 595,
per cur.; 5 Man. & Ry. 157—162; 4 Man. & Gr. 145, note. For
although such deed may for some purposes operate, as between the
parties thereto, as a lease or under-lease; *Doe* d. *Freeman* v. *Bateman*,
2 B. & A. 168; *Pollock* v. *Stacey*, 9 Q. B. 1033; but without giving
any right to distrain for the rent thereby reserved, the lessor having
no reversion; *Parmenter* v. *Webber*, and *Preece* v. *Corrie*, *supra;* yet,
as between the parties and the original lessor, it operates as an assignment. *Ante*, 223; *Wollaston* v. *Hakewill*, and other cases, *supra*.

But the deed must operate and take effect as a valid assignment until defeated under the proviso for re-entry contained in the original lease; otherwise it will not be sufficient to support an ejectment for a forfeiture by assigning without licence. Therefore a covenant not to assign, &c. without licence will not be broken by a deed purporting to assign all the lessee's property for the benefit of his creditors, which deed is duly avoided as an act of bankruptcy under a petition for adjudication, before ejectment brought for the supposed forfeiture. *Doe d. Lloyd* v. *Powell,* 5 B. & C. 308, 312; 8 D. & R. 35.

By 8 & 9 Vict. c. 106, s. 3, "an assignment of a chattel interest, not being copyhold, in any tenements or hereditaments," "shall be void at law unless made by deed." Therefore an instrument in writing not under seal cannot amount to an "assignment," so as to create a forfeiture by assigning without licence. *Ante,* 226. But other words may be used in the covenant and proviso which would apply to such an instrument. An agreement to assign for the residue of a term, not exceeding three years, with possession given, may amount to an underlease. *Pollock* v. *Stacey,* 9 Q. B. 1033; but see *Barrett* v. *Rolph,* 14 M. & W. 348; *Cottee* v. *Richardson,* 7 Exch. 143, 147, Parke, B.; *ante,* 223, 224.

A covenant not to "alien, assign, transfer and set over, *or otherwise part with,*" the lease of a public house, is not broken by depositing the lease with the brewers to cover advances by them. *Doe d. Pitt* v. *Laming,* Ry. & Moo. 36; *Doe* d. *Pitt* v. *Hogg,* 1 C. & P. 160; 4 D. & R. 226, S. C.; *Doe* d. *Goodbehere* v. *Bevan,* 3 M. & S. 353.

A covenant not to assign without licence does not extend to an underlease. *Kennersley* v. *Orpe,* 1 Doug. 55. A covenant not to "assign, transfer or set over, or otherwise do or put away this present indenture of demise, or the premises hereby demised, or any part thereof," without licence, is not broken by an underlease. *Crusoe* d. *Blencowe* v. *Bugby,* 3 Wils. 234; 2 W. Black. 766. But a covenant not to "assign *or otherwise part with* this indenture of lease, or the premises hereby demised, or any part thereof, for the whole *or any part of the term* hereby granted," without licence, will extend to an underlease. *Doe* d. *Holland* v. *Worsley,* 1 Camp. 20. So a covenant not to "*set, let,* or assign over the demised premises, or any part thereof," without licence, is broken by an underlease. *Doe* d. *Gregson* v. *Harrison,* 2 T. R. 425. A covenant not to underlet, without licence, will restrain an assignment. *Greenaway* v. *Adams,* 12 Ves. 395. But a covenant not to "underlet or assign, or otherwise part with the demised premises, *or any part thereof,*" without licence, is not broken by taking in a lodger. *Doe* d. *Pitt* v. *Laming,* 4 Camp. 77. "The covenant can only extend to such under-letting as a licence might be expected to be applied for, and who ever heard of a licence from a landlord to take in a lodger?" *Id.* 78, *per* Lord Ellenborough, C. J. Where, however, a lease contained a proviso for re-entry in case the lessee, his executors or administrators, should "demise, lease, grant or let the demised premises, or any part thereof, or convey, alien, assign or set over the indenture, or his estate or interest therein, or any part thereof, to any person or persons whomsoever, for all or any part of the said term," without licence, and the lessee (without licence) entered into an agreement of partnership with a third person, and thereby stipulated that he should have the *exclusive* use of certain parts of the premises, and the use of the residue jointly with the lessee, and accordingly let him into possession: held, that the lessor was entitled to re-enter. *Roe* d. *Dingley* v. *Sales,* 1 M. & S. 297. "It is a parting with the exclusive possession of some part of the demised premises; whether gratuitously or for rent reserved is very immaterial to the landlord, who meant to guard against having any other than the person in whom he confided as tenant let into possession without his consent." *Id.* 208, Lord Ellenborough, C. J.

A covenant not to assign, &c., framed in the usual manner, will not extend to an assignment by act and operation of law. Therefore a covenant not to "let, set, assign, transfer, make over, barter, exchange or otherwise part with" the lease, or the premises thereby demised, or any part thereof, without licence, will not be broken by a seizure and sale by the sheriff under an execution founded on a judgment against the tenant signed on a warrant of attorney; *Doe* d. *Mitchinson* v. *Carter,* 8 T. R. 57; unless it be proved that the warrant of attorney was given by the tenant for the express purpose of enabling his creditor to take the lease in execution under the judgment; in which case the whole transaction, taken together, will be construed to amount to an assignment. *Doe* d. *Mitchinson* v. *Carter,* 8 T. R. 300. If a lessee become bankrupt, and the term passes to the official and other assignees, that will not amount to a breach of covenant not to assign, &c., without licence. *Goring* v. *Warner,* 2 Eq. Cas. Abr. 100; 7 Vin. Abr. 85, pl. 9; *Doe* d. *Goodbehere* v. *Bevan,* 3 M. & S. 353, 360, 361. Unless, indeed, he were adjudicated a bankrupt *upon his own petition,* pursuant to 12 & 13 Vict. c. 106, s. 93, which might, perhaps, be construed to amount to a voluntary assignment on his part. *Infra.* Nor will a subsequent sale and assignment by the assignees, although the covenant and proviso is, that the lessee, his executors, administrators *or assigns,* shall not assign, &c., without licence. *Doe* d. *Goodbehere* v. *Bevan,* 3 M. & S. 353. *Doe* d. *Cheere* v. *Smith,* 5 Taunt. 795; 1 Marsh, 359; *Philpot* v. *Hoare,* 2 Atk. 219. The reason seems to be:—*first,* that such a covenant is construed to apply only to ordinary assignments by the party, and not to extraordinary ones by act and operation of law; *secondly,* that where the law compels the violation of a private stipulation it thereby in effect repeals it *pro tanto. Doe* d. *Cheere* v. *Smith,* 5 Taunt. 795; *Doe* d. *Marquis of Anglesea* v. *The Churchwardens and Overseers of Rugeley,* 6 Q. B. 107, 112, 114. Nevertheless, a proviso for re-entry in the event of the lessee becoming bankrupt, or taking the benefit of any act for the relief of insolvent debtors, is valid. *Roe* d. *Hunter* v. *Galliers,* 2 T. R. 133. A lease contained a proviso for re-entry if the lessee, "his executors or administrators, or either of them," should become bankrupt : held, that on the executor of the lessee becoming bankrupt, although the term would not pass to his assignees in bankruptcy, he having no beneficial interest therein, yet the lessor was entitled to recover in ejectment. *Doe* d. *Williams* v. *Davies,* 6 C. & P. 614, Parke, B.; and see *Doe* d. *Bridgman* v. *David,* 1 Cr. M. & R. 405; 5 Tyr. 125. A lease for twenty-one years, "if the lessee shall so long continue to inhabit and dwell on the premises, and not assign, &c." will cease on the lessee becoming bankrupt, and his assignees taking possession and selling the property. *Doe* d. *Lockwood* v. *Clarke,* 8 East, 185. In this case the continuance of the term was expressly made to depend upon the personal occupation by the lessee.

It seems that if a lessee take the benefit of any act for the relief of insolvent debtors *upon his own petition,* that is a voluntary act on his part, and amounts to a breach of covenant not to assign without licence.

Wetherall v. *Geering,* 12 Ves. 512; Ambl. 480, *S. C.; Shee* v. *Hale,* 13 Ves. 404; 4 Bac. Abr. "Lease" T. (p. 886, 7th ed.). But it would be otherwise where a vesting order is made upon the application of a creditor pursuant to 1 & 2 Vict. c. 110, s. 36. Such an order would appear to stand upon the same footing as a petition for adjudication in bankruptcy at the instance of a creditor. *Ante,* 436.

It seems not to be clearly settled whether a *devise or bequest* of the term to any person other than the lessee's executor amounts to a breach of a covenant or proviso not to assign without licence. For the affirmative may be cited, 4 Bac. Abr. Leases, T. (p. 886, 7th ed.); *Knight* v. *Mory,* Cro. Eliz. 60; *Berry* v. *Stanton,* Cro. Eliz. 330; Poph. 106, *S. C.*; 2 Eden, 377; *Dumper* v. *Syms,* Cro. Eliz. 815; *Parry* v. *Harbert,* Dy. 45 b; 4 Leon. 5, *S. C.; Anon.* 3 Leon. 67. For the negative may be cited, *Fox* v. *Swan,* Styles, 483; *Crusoe* v. *Blencowe,* 3 Wils. 237, *per cur.*; 2 W. Blac. 766, *S. C.; Doe* v. *Bevan,* 3 M. & S. 361, *per* Bayley, J. In *Crusoe* v. *Blencowe* (*supra*), the court drew a distinction between *assigning* a lease and *the doing or putting it away.* A covenant and proviso against assigning without licence, "except by will," will operate to prevent the executors of the lessee from selling and assigning the term for payment of debts. *Lloyd* v. *Crispe,* 5 Taunt. 249; and see *Thornhill* v. *King,* Cro. Eliz. 757.

A covenant and proviso that the lessee (not saying his executors, &c.) will not assign without licence, will not extend to an assignment by his executors or administrators. *Smallpiece* v. *Evans,* Anderson, 124. A covenant that the lessee, "his executors or administrators," will not assign, &c., without licence, does not bind his assigns. *Doe* d. *Cheere* v. *Smith,* 5 Taunt. 795; 1 Marsh. 359; *Paul* v. *Nurse,* 8 B. & C. 486; 2 M. & R. 525. But a covenant that the lessee, "his executors, administrators *or assigns,*" will not assign without licence, will bind them respectively. *Sir W. Moore's case,* Cro. Eliz. 26; *Dumpor's case,* 4 Co. R. 120; 1 Smith's L. C. 15; *S.C. nom. Dumper* v. *Syms,* Cro. Eliz. 815; *Roe* d. *Gregson* v. *Harrison,* 2 T. R. 425. On a covenant that neither the lessee nor his assigns shall alien without licence, *except to his wife,* he devises the term to his wife, who takes husband, and *they assign it;* this is a breach of covenant. *Thornhill* v. *King,* Cro. Eliz. 757; and see *Lloyd* v. *Crispe,* 5 Taunt. 249. On a condition to assign only to A., after the performance A. may assign to another. *Whitchcot* v. *Fox,* Cro. Jac. 398; and see *Lloyd* v. *Crispe,* 5 Taunt. 249; 1 Smith, L. C. 20.

A licence to assign, &c., is usually granted by deed. *See the form,* 7 Jarm. Byth. 498 (2nd ed.); *Id.* 55—65; 2 Platt on Leases, 813; 1 Hughes, Concise Prec. 248 (2nd ed.). A verbal licence, without any writing, will not affect a covenant and proviso not to assign, &c., without the previous licence and consent *in writing* of the lessor, &c. *Doe* d. *Gregson* v. *Harrison,* 2 T. R. 425; 1 Smith, L. C. 18. Generally speaking, a licence not under seal to violate any covenant in a deed, is inoperative, the maxim being, *Quodlibet in lege eodem modo dissolvitur quo ligatum est. West* v. *Blakeway,* 2 Man. & Gr. 729, 751, 752; 9 Dowl. 846, *S. C.; Cordwent* v. *Hunt,* 8 Taunt. 596; 2 B. Moo. 660, *S. C.* But a written or even verbal licence will be sufficient, if so expressed in the lease.

A licence to assign all or any part of the demised premises puts an end to any condition not to assign, &c., without licence. *Dumpor's case,* 4 Co. R. 119 b; 1 Smith, L. C. 15, 18; *S. C. nom. Dumper* v.

Syms, Cro. Eliz. 815; *Leeds* v. *Crompton,* cited 4 Co. R. 120; Dyer, 152, pl. 7; Co. Lit. 215 a; Ad. Eject. 148. The reason is, that a condition is entire, and cannot be apportioned by act of the parties, but only by act in law, or by act and wrong of the lessee. *Dumpor's case, supra.* It seems, however, that it may be expressly stipulated in the lease that any licence or consent to assign shall not extinguish the condition. 1 Stew. Conv. 406. The usual practice is to take a fresh covenant not to assign, &c., with a new proviso for re-entry on breach thereof, on consenting to an assignment.

A lessor who has a right of entry reserved on breach of a covenant not to *underlet,* does not, by waiving his re-entry on one under-letting, lose his right to re-enter on a subsequent underletting. His waiver of the first forfeiture is not equivalent to an actual licence. *Doe* d. *Boscawen* v. *Bliss,* 4 Taunt. 735; and see *Doe* d. *Sheppard* v. *Allen,* 3 Taunt. 78; *Doe* d. *Bryan* v. *Bancks,* 4 B. & A. 401; 1 Wms. Saund. 208, n. (*s*); 1 Smith, L. C. 20. But it seems to be otherwise where the forfeiture is occasioned by *assigning* without licence, and such forfeiture is waived, because the condition is then entirely gone. *Lloyd* v. *Crispe,* 5 Taunt. 249; 1 Smith, L. C. 20.

By distraining for or accepting payment of rent *due subsequently* to any breach of covenant by assigning or underletting without licence, the lessor waives the forfeiture, provided he knew of it at the time of such distress or payment, but not otherwise. *Pennant's case,* 3 Co. R. 63 b; *Whitchcot* v. *Fox,* Cro. Jac. 398; *Mulcarry* v. *Eyres,* Cro. Car. 511; *Goodright* d. *Walker* v. *Davids,* Cowp. 803; *Doe* d. *Gregson* v. *Harrison,* 2 T. R. 425; note (16) to *Duppa* v. *Mayo,* 1 Wms. Saund. 288 a, 288 b; 1 Smith, L. C. 18. A mere demand of subsequent rent, not complied with, or even a distress for subsequent rent, not submitted to, but replevied by the tenant, does not amount to a waiver of any previous forfeiture. *Blythe* v. *Dennett,* 13 C. B. 178. Acceptance of rent after the commencement of an ejectment for a forfeiture is no waiver of such forfeiture. *Doe* d. *Morecraft* v. *Meux,* 1 C. & P. 346, Abbott, C. J.

Evidence for Plaintiff.]—To maintain ejectment for a forfeiture for assigning or underletting without licence the plaintiff must prove—

1. The lease, or a counterpart or duplicate thereof, or the agreement or a duplicate thereof, containing the covenant or stipulation not to assign or underlet, &c., and the proviso for re-entry. This must be duly stamped and admitted in the cause (*ante,* 150), or proved in the usual manner. *Ante,* 294, 303. It seems that an assignee of the reversion cannot maintain ejectment for a forfeiture by assigning without licence, because that is a *collateral* condition not running with the land. *Lucas* v. *How,* Sir T. Ray, 250; *Collins* v. *Silley,* Stiles, 265; *Pennant's case,* 3 Co. R. 64; Ad. Eject. 56; *ante,* 406.

2. That the lessee had possession of the premises sought to be recovered, or some part thereof, under or by virtue of such lease or agreement. And if the defendant be not the lessee, it must be proved that he came into possession *under or after* the lessee. *Ante,* 215, 224.

3. The assignment or under-lease. The production of this should, if necessary, be compelled by a *subpœna duces tecum* (*ante,* 172), or by notice to produce. *Ante,* 155. If the defendant claim or derive title under the deed, and produce it in pursuance of the notice, the execution of it need not be proved. *Pearce* v. *Hooper,* 3 Taunt. 60; *Carr*

v. *Burdiss,* 1 Cr. M & R. 782; 5 Tyr. 309; *ante,* 165. But if produced under other circumstances, or the party producing it under *subpœna duces tecum* does not claim an estate or interest under the deed, the execution of it must be admitted or proved in the usual manner. *Ante,* 164. And it should appear to be on a sufficient stamp. *Baker* v. *Gostling,* 1 Bing. N. C. 246; *ante,* 164, 393. If not produced, the plaintiff should be prepared with evidence to satisfy the judge that the deed is in the possession or power of the defendant (*ante,* 167); and also with secondary evidence of the contents. *Ante,* 169. Or, instead of the above formal proof of an *assignment,* the plaintiff may establish a *primâ facie* case on this point, by showing that the defendant came into possession *under or after the lessee. Ante,* 224; *Doe* d. *Hemmings* v. *Durnford,* 2 Cr. & Jer. 667. But it is not generally advisable to rest upon a *primâ facie* case, where a more complete one can be proved, especially in an ejectment for a forfeiture. Where it was proved that the premises were in possession of a stranger, and that he declared they were demised to him by another stranger, this was holden not to be sufficient. *Doe* v. *Payne,* 1 Stark. 86, Lord Ellenborough, C. J.; and see *Cripps* v. *Blank,* 9 D. & R. 480.

4. Some evidence should perhaps be given that the assignment or under-lease was made without the licence of the lessor, &c.; for sometimes the plaintiff must prove a negative; *ex. gr.,* nonpayment of rent; *Doe* d. *Chandless* v. *Robson,* 2 C. & P. 245; or not insuring. *Doe* d. *Bridger* v. *Whitehead,* 8 A. & E. 571; 3 N. & P. 577. Slight evidence on this point would, however, be sufficient; because the licence (if any) should be proved by the defendant, as part of his case.

Evidence and Points for Defendant.]—The defendant may contend, 1. That the evidence for the plaintiff is insufficient on some material point. *Ante,* 438. He may also produce contradictory evidence. 2. That upon the true construction of the covenant and proviso the act complained of does not amount to a breach. *Doe* d. *Lloyd* v. *Powell,* 5 B. & C. 308, 312; *ante,* 434—438. 3. That the covenant or proviso had previously been determined by a licence to assign, &c. *Ante,* 437. 4. That the assignment or under-lease complained of was made in pursuance of a *sufficient* licence and authority in that behalf. But a verbal licence will not avail, if the lease or agreement require a licence in writing. *Doe* d. *Gregson* v. *Harrison,* 2 T. R. 425. And a licence in writing (not under seal) will be insufficient, if the lease or agreement require a licence under hand and seal, or "by deed." Generally speaking, a licence not under seal to violate any covenant in a deed is inoperative. *Ante,* 437. 5. That after the forfeiture accrued and the claimant *knew* of the assignment or under-lease he distrained for, or accepted payment of subsequent rent, or did some other act acknowledging the continuance of the tenancy at a period later than the supposed forfeiture, and thereby in effect waived the forfeiture. *Ante,* 408; *Goodright* d. *Walter* v. *Davids,* 2 Cowp. 803; *Roe* d. *Gregson* v. *Harrison,* 2 T. R. 425; *Marsh* v. *Curteys,* Cro. Eliz. 528; *Whitchcot* v. *Fox,* Cro. Jac. 398; *Mulcarry* v. *Eyres,* Cro. Car. 511.

8. *For impugning Lessor's Title.*]—If a lessee do any act *in a court of record,* whereby he disaffirms or impugns the title of his lessor, his term is thereby forfeited, by virtue of the common law. Bac. Abr. Lease, T. 2; *Doe* d. *Jeffries* v. *Whittick,* Gow. 195. But this can

seldom happen now that real actions and fines and recoveries are abolished. 3 & 4 Will. 4, c. 74. A disclaimer by *matter in pais* is not sufficient to create a forfeiture for a term of years. *Doe* d. *Graves* v. *Wells*, 10 A. & E. 427; 2 P. & D. 396; *Rees* d. *Powell* v. *King*, Forrest. R. 19; *Doe* d. *Dillon* v. *Parker, Knt.*, Gow. 180. But a disclaimer of title by a tenant from year to year will frequently render a notice to quit unnecessary. *Ante*, 40, 42. Formerly a feoffment by a tenant for years created a forfeiture of his term, because it operated to pass more than the tenant could lawfully grant, viz., the fee, or the freehold. Bac. Abr. Lease, T 2. But by 8 & 9 Vict. c. 106, s. 4, a feoffment made after the 1st day of October, 1845, shall not have any tortious operation.

Formerly a fine levied by a tenant for years created a forfeiture of his term; but only the reversioner for the time being could have taken advantage of such forfeiture. *Fenn* d. *Matthews* v. *Smart*, 12 East, 444.

A termor, after deserting the demised premises, delivered up the possession of them, with the lease, to a party who claimed by title adverse to that of the landlord, with intent to assist him in setting up that title, and not that he should hold *bonâ fide* under the lease: held, that the term was forfeited by the act of betraying the possession. *Doe* d. *Ellerbrock* v. *Flynn*, 4 Tyr. 619; 1 Cr. M. & R. 137; but see *Doe* d. *Graves* v. *Wells*, 10 A. & E. 427; 2 P. & D. 402; *ante*, 42.

CHAPTER XL.

LANDLORD AGAINST TENANT FROM YEAR TO YEAR.

Nature of the Tenancy.]—A tenant from year to year is one who holds under some express or implied demise for an indefinite term, which may be determined at the end of the first or any subsequent year of the tenancy, either by the landlord or by the tenant by a regular notice to quit. *Ante*, 29. If no such notice be given, the tenancy will continue from year to year for any number of years, until surrendered or extinguished by the Statute of Limitations, or the lessor's title ceases. *Ante*, 30. The death of either party will not determine it. *Maddon* d. *Baker* v. *White*, 2 T. R. 159 ; *Doe* d. *Shore* v. *Porter*, 3 T. R. 13 ; *Mackay* v. *Mackreth*, 4 Doug. 213 ; 15 Ves. 241 ; *Doe* d. *Hull* v. *Wood*, 14 M. & W. 682. Unless, indeed, the lessor be tenant for his own life only. *Doe* d. *Thomas* v. *Roberts*, 16 M. & W. 778. A tenancy from year to year cannot be determined so as to bar the interest of the tenant's creditors, unless there be either a legal notice to quit, or a surrender in writing. *Doe* d. *Read* v. *Ridout*, 5 Taunt. 519.

A tenancy from year to year is a term. *Per* Littledale, J., in *How* v. *Kennett*, 3 A. & E. 662. Each year of the tenancy, as it elapses, is considered as a prolongation of the original term, and may be so pleaded. *Legg* v. *Strudwick*, 2 Salk. 413 ; *Birch* v. *Wright*, 1 T. R. 380, Buller, J.; *Oxley* v. *James*, 13 M. & W. 209 ; 3 Man. & Gr. 510, note. Leases from year to year appear at first view to give several distinct estates, "In truth they give only one time of continuance. That time, however, may be confined to one year, or extended to several years, according to circumstances attending the tenancy in its progress. In the first place, the lease is for one year certain, and after the commencement of every year, or perhaps after the expiration of that part of the year in which a notice of determining the tenancy

U 5

may be given, it is a lease for the second year; and in consequence of the original agreement of the parties every year of the tenancy constitutes part of the lease, and eventually becomes parcel of the term; so that lease which in the first instance is only for one year certain, may in event be a term for one thousand years. Under this species of tenancy the law considers the lease with a view to the time which has elapsed as arising from an estate for all that time including the current year; and with a view to the time to come, as a lease from year to year. For as all the time for which the land may be held under a running lease is originally given, and in effect passes, by the same instrument or contract, the whole time is consolidated, and every year as it commences forms part of the term." 3 Prest. Conv. 76, 77. On the other hand, a tenancy from year to year may be considered as recommencing each year, and may be pleaded as having commenced on the first day of the current year, although the tenant entered several years previously. *Tomkins* v. *Lawrence*, 8 C. & P. 729.

A demise by a tenant from year to year to another, also to hold from year to year, is in legal operation a demise from year to year only during the continuance of the original demise to the intermediate landlord. *Pike* v. *Eyre*, 9 B. & C. 909; 4 M. & R. 661. A tenant from year to year, underletting from year to year, has a reversion which entitles him to distrain. *Curtis* v. *Wheeler*, Moo. & M. 493. A tenant from year to year may make a lease for twenty-one years, but such term will of course cease whenever the tenancy from year to year is legally determined. *Mackay* v. *Mackreth*, 4 Doug. 213. B. holding land of A. for a term of years, underlets parts to C. from year to year; at the expiration of the term B. agrees with A. to hold on from month to month; in the absence of any new agreement between B. and C. the tenancy from year to year continues. *Peirse* v. *Sharr*, 2 Man. & R. 418. A tenancy from year to year created by a tenant for life will determine on his death. *Doe* d. *Thomas* v. *Roberts*, 16 M. & W. 774. A tenant-at-will at a yearly rent is a tenant from year to year. *Pope* v. *Gurland*, 4 You. & Col. 394; 10 Law J., N. S., Exch. Eq. 13. But it seems there may be a demise *at will de anno in annum*; 9 C. B. 643, note (b); or at a yearly rent. *Doe* d. *Dixie* v. *Davies*, 7 Exch. 91, Parke, B.; *Walker* v. *Giles*, 6 C. B. 662; Co. Lit. 956.

How created.]—A tenancy from year to year may be created by express contract; or by a contract implied by law; the latter is most usual.

By express Contract.]—Where parties mutually agree for a tenancy "from year to year," and possession is taken, such tenancy is thereby created, and it may be determined at the end of the first or any subsequent year of the tenancy by a regular notice to quit. *Doe* d. *Clark* v. *Smaridge*, 7 Q. B. 957; *Doe* d. *Plumer* v. *Mainby*, 10 Q. B. 472. But where a tenancy is created "for one year certain, and so on from year to year," it enures as a tenancy for two years at the least, and cannot be determined at the end of the first year. *Doe* d. *Chadborn* v. *Green*, 9 A. & E. 658; 1 P. & D. 454; *Birch* v. *Wright*, 1 T. R. 380; *White* v. *Durley*, 1 T. R. 159; *Bellasis* v. *Burbrick*, 1 Salk. 413; *Legg* v. *Strudwick*, 2 Salk. 414; 11 Mod. 203; *Hompel* v. *Hicks*, 2 Salk. 413; Holt, 414, *S. C.*; *Stanfill* v. *Hicks*, 1 Lord Ray.

280. It may, however, be determined by due notice to quit at the end of the second or any subsequent year of the tenancy. *Cases supra.*

A tenancy "for twelve months certain and six months notice afterwards," may be determined by notice to quit at the end of the first year. *Thompson* v. *Maberley*, 2 Camp. 573. But a demise "not for one year only, but from year to year," constitutes a demise for two years at least, and cannot be determined by a notice to quit at the end of the first year. *Denn* d. *Jacklin* v. *Cartwright*, 4 East, 31. A demise for one year and six months certain, at a rent payable on the usual quarter days, may be determined upon notice at the end of the second year of the tenancy. *Doe* d. *Robinson* v. *Dobell*, 1 Q. B. 806 ; and see *Berrey* v. *Lindley*, 3 Man. & Gr. 498. A tenancy "from year to year so long as both parties please" is determinable at the end of the first as well as of any subsequent year, unless in creating such tenancy the parties use words showing that they contemplate a tenancy for two years at least. *Doe* d. *Clark* v. *Smaridge*, 7 Q. B. 957 ; *Doe* d. *Plumer* v. *Mainby*, 10 Q. B. 473.

A mere permission to occupy land, &c., constitutes a tenancy at will only ; and, in order to create a tenancy from year to year, there must be some circumstances to show an intention to do so, such as payment of rent quarterly, or for some other aliquot part of a year. *Doe* d. *Hull* v. *Wood*, 14 M. & W. 682; 15 Law J., N. S., Exch. 41. Where no particular term is agreed on, but it is stipulated that the tenant shall pay so much a year for the premises, that will be sufficient to create a tenancy from year to year. *Doe* d. *Warner* v. *Browne*, 8 East, 166, 167.

Where the amount of rent payable by a tenant from year to year is altered by mutual consent, that does not create a fresh tenancy from year to year upon the old terms, *as from that day.* *Doe* d. *Monck* v. *Geekie*, 1 Car. & K. 307; 5 Q. B. 841. A verbal alteration of the rent reserved under a lease or agreement in writing will have no operation. *Crowley* v. *Vitty*, 7 Exch. 319. If, after the expiration of a lease in writing, the tenant verbally agree to hold over at an increased rent, nothing more being expressed between the parties respecting the terms of the new tenancy, they will be taken to be the same as under the old lease, so far as they may be applicable to the new tenancy. *Digby* v. *Atkinson*, 4 Camp. 275 ; *Torriano* v. *Young*, 6 C. & P. 8, Taunton, J.

A demise "for a year," or "for one year certain," does not create a tenancy from year to year, nor require any notice to determine it at the end of the year. *Ante*, 36 ; *Cobb* v. *Stokes*, 8 East, 358, 361 ; *Johnstone* v. *Huddlestone*, 4 B. & C. 937, Bayley, J.; *Wilson* v. *Abbott*, 9 B. & C. 89.

By implied Contract.]—When a person is let into possession under an agreement for a future lease, *and pays part of the agreed rent*, he thereby becomes tenant from year to year upon the terms of such intended lease so far as they are applicable to a yearly tenancy. *Doe* d. *Thompson* v. *Amey*, 12 A. & E. 476 ; 4 P. & D. 177 ; *Doe* d. *Rigge* v. *Bell*, 5 T. R. 471 ; 2 Smith's L. C. 72, 75 ; *Richardson* v. *Giffard*, 1 A. & E. 52; *Manning* v. *Lovejoy*, Ry. & Moo. 355, Abbott, C. J.; *Braithwaite* v. *Hitchcock*, 10 M. & W. 494; 2 Dowl. N. S. 444. And he is entitled to the usual notice to quit ; but at the expiration of the term mentioned in such agreement, the implied tenancy from year to year will cease without any notice to quit. *Doe* d. *Tilt* v. *Stratton*, 4 Bing. 446 ; 1 Moo. & P. 183 ; *Doe* d. *Bramfield* v. *Smith*, 6 East, 580 ; *Berrey* v. *Lindley*, 3 Man. & Gr. 498 ; *Id.* 514, Maule, J. ; *Doe* d. *Davenish* v. *Moffait*, 15 Q. B. 257, 265 ; *Tress* v. *Savage*, 4 E. & B. 36. Actual payment of rent is not always essential, although that perhaps is the clearest proof. *Cox* v. *Bent*, 5 Bing. 185 ; 2 Moo. & P. 281 ; *Vincent* v. *Godson*, 24 Law J., Chanc., 122, Lord Cranworth, L. C. Where the payment of the rent is allowed to stand over by mutual consent, that is sufficient. *S. C.* Payment of rent does not of itself create a tenancy from year to year, but is *only evidence* from which a jury may find the fact. *Finley* v. *The Bristol and Exeter Railway Company*, 7 Exch. 415, Parke, B. ; *Id.* 420, Martin, B. ; *Jones* v. *Shears*, 4 A. & E. 832. Where payment of rent unexplained would ordinarily imply a yearly tenancy, it is open to the payer or receiver of such rent to prove the circumstances under which such payment was made, for the purpose of repelling such implication. *Doe* d. *Lord* v. *Crago*, 6 C. B. 90 ; 17 Law J., N. S., C. P. 263.

The same law holds where a person is let into possession under a *void* lease (*ex. gr.*, a lease required to be *in writing* by the Statute of Frauds, 29 Car. 2, c. 3, ss. 1, 2, and not made *by deed*, 8 & 9 Vict. c. 106, s. 3 ; *Tress* v. *Savage*, 4 E. & B. 36), and pays or promises to pay part of the rent thereby expressed to be reserved. A tenancy from year to year upon the terms of such lease, so far as they can possibly apply to a yearly tenancy, will be thereby created. 2 Smith, L. C., 74 ; *Richardson* v. *Giffard*, 1 A. & E. 52 ; 2 N. & M. 325 ; *Clayton* v. *Blakey*, 8 T. R. 3 ; *Lee* v. *Smith*, 9 Exch. 662 ; *Doe* d. *Pennington* v. *Taniere*, 11 Q. B. 998, 1013. And such tenancy will cease without any notice to quit at the end of the void term mentioned in the lease. *Tress* v. *Savage*, 4 E. & B. 36.

Where a tenant for a term of years holds over after the expiration of his lease, and *continues to pay rent as before, which the landlord accepts*, a new tenancy from year to year is thereby created upon the same terms and conditions as those contained in the original lease, so far as the same are applicable to a yearly tenancy. *Doe* d. *Hollingworth* v. *Stennett*, 2 Esp. 717, Lord Kenyon, C. J. ; *Bishop* v. *Howard*, 2 B. & C. 100 ; 3 D. & R. 293 ; *Doe* d. *Thompson* v. *Amey*, 12 A. & E. 476 ; 4 P. & D. 177 ; *Hyatt* v. *Griffiths*, 17 Q. B. 505. . But the landlord may show that he accepted the rent from time to time under a mistake, and upon the supposition that one of the lives for which the lease was granted continued in existence. *Doe* d. *Lord* v. *Crago*, 6 C. B. 90 ; 17 Law J., N. S., C. P. 263. Any such new tenancy (when implied) will be deemed to have commenced at the same time of the year as the original term, and notice to quit should be given accordingly. *Doe* d. *Castleton* v. *Samuel*, 5 Esp. 173, Lord Ellenborough, C. J. ; *Doe* d. *Spicer* v. *Lea*, 11 East, 312 ; *Roe* d. *Jordan* v. *Ward*, 1 H. Black. 96 ; *Doe* d. *Martin* v. *Watts*, 7 T. R. 83 ; *Doe* d. *Collins* v. *Weller*, 7 T. R. 478 ; *Doe* d. *Tucker* v. *Morse*, 1 B. & Adol. 365. It may be determined by notice at the end of the first or any subsequent year. *Doe* d. *Clarke* v. *Smaridge*, 7 Q. B. 957 ; *Doe* d. *Plumer* v. *Mainby*, 10 Q. B. 473. It will be subject to the custom of the county, so far as such custom is not excluded by the terms of the expired lease. *Hutton* v. *Warren*, 1 M. & W. 466 ; Tyr. & Gr. 646 ; *ante*, 249. After the determination by the landlord of an estate at will, the tenant remained in possession, and being one of the assessors for the land tax in the parish, signed an assessment in which he was named as the occupier of the farm, and the landlord as the proprietor: held that this was evidence against the tenant, from which the jury might infer that a new tenancy at will had been created between the parties. *Turner* v. *Doe* d. *Bennett* (in error), 9 M. & W. 643. When a tenant of glebe land remained in possession for eight months after the death of the incumbent: held, that after such a lapse of time it was to be inferred that the new incumbent had assented to the new continuance of the tenancy on the same terms as before, and that a notice to quit was necessary. *Doe* d. *Cates* v. *Somerville*, 6 B. & C. 126, 132.

If a remainderman accept money, or any thing else reserved as rent in a lease granted by the previous tenant for life, which became *void* on the death of such tenant for life, he does not thereby confirm and establish the lease for the residue of the term thereby expressed to be granted, but he creates a new implied tenancy from year to year as between him and the tenant, on the old terms, and the tenant is entitled to the usual notice to quit. *Doe* d. *Potter* v. *Archer*, 1 Bos. & Pul. 531; *Doe* d. *Simpson* v. *Butcher*, 1 Doug. 50; *Jenkins* d. *Yeates* v. *Church*, 2 Cowp. 482; *Doe* d. *Martin* v. *Watts*, 7 T. R. 83; 2 Esp. 501, S. C.; *Doe* d. *Tucker* v. *Morse*, 1 B. & Adol. 365; *Bell* v. *Nangle*, 2 Jebb & Symes (Irish R.), 259; *Howard* v. *Sherwood*, Alcock & Napier (Irish R.), 217. Unless, indeed, the rent received be so grossly inadequate with reference to the annual value of the property, that the jury ought to presume and find that no such new tenancy was intended to be created. *Doe* d. *Brune* v. *Prideaux*, 10 East, 158; *Denne* d. *Brune* v. *Rawlins*, 10 East, 261; and see *Doe* d. *Lord* v. *Crago*, 6 C. B. 90. Any such new tenancy will be deemed to have commenced from the same day of the year as the original term, and the notice to quit should be given accordingly. *Roe* d. *Jordan* v. *Ward*, 1 H. Black. 96; *Doe* d. *Collins* v. *Weller*, 7 T. R. 478.

If, whilst a tenant from year to year is in possession of lands under an agreement reserving a certain rent, he agrees with his landlord to pay an increased rent, this will not have the effect of then creating a new tenancy. *Doe* d. *Monck* v. *Geekie*, 5 Q. B. 841; 1 Car. & K. 307; *Clarke* v. *Moore*, 1 Jones & Lat. (Irish R.), 723; *Crowley* v. *Vitty*, 7 Exch. 319.

If a mortgagee induce or compel a *subsequent* tenant of the mortgagor to attorn to and pay him rent, that will not operate to confirm the lease for the whole term thereby granted, but will create between the mortgagee and the tenant a new tenancy from year to year. *Doe* d. *Hughes* v. *Bucknell*, 8 C. & P. 567, Patteson, J.; *Doe* d. *Prior* v. *Ongley*, 10 C. B. 25 (3rd point). And such new tenancy will be subject to the terms and conditions of the lease, so far as the same are applicable to a yearly tenancy. *Doe* d. *Thompson* v. *Amey*, 12 A. & E. 476; 4 P. & D. 177; *Doe* d. *Davenish* v. *Moffatt*, 15 Q. B. 257, 265.

A *cestui que trust* who enters into possession of land becomes at law tenant at will to the trustee. *Garrard* v. *Tuck*, 8 C. B. 232, 250; *Freeman* v. *Barnes*, 1 Ventr. 80; 1 Siderfin, 349, 458, S. C.

How determined.]—A tenancy from year to year is usually determined by a regular notice to quit. *Ante*, 29. It may also be determined by a surrender; *ante*, 224—226; or by the landlord's entry for a forfeiture by virtue of an express proviso or condition in the demise; *ante*, 403; or by the death of the landlord, he being tenant for his own life only; *Doe* d. *Thomas* v. *Roberts*, 16 M. & W. 778; or by a disclaimer of the landlord's title. *Ante*, 41. A mere agreement between the landlord and tenant for an increase of the rent does not affect the tenancy in other respects. *Doe* d. *Monk* v. *Geehie*, 1 Car. & K. 307; 5 Q. B. 841; *Crowley* v. *Vitty*, 7 Exch. 319; Ad. Eject. 106.

Mode of Proceeding by Ejectment.]—Before commencing an ejectment against a tenant from year to year it is most important to ascertain that such tenancy has been duly determined by a regular notice to quit; *ante*, 29; or by a disclaimer of the plaintiff's title; *ante*, 41; or by a surrender; *ante*, 224—226; or that the tenant has been guilty of some act of forfeiture which entitles the landlord to re-enter, and to put an end to the tenancy pursuant to some express proviso or condition to that effect contained in the demise. *Ante*, Chap. XXXIX.

If the demise were *in writing*, and the tenancy has been determined by a *regular notice to quit*, it is generally advisable to make a *formal demand of possession in writing*, and to obtain *a refusal to deliver up such possession*, before commencing the action, and afterwards to proceed according to the 15 & 16 Vict. c. 76, s. 213 (*ante*, 379), because in such case the tenant will not be permitted to appear and defend the action without finding bail to pay the costs and damages which shall be recovered. *Ante*, 378. But it is optional with the landlord *not* to avail himself of the above mode of proceeding, and to sue by ejectment in the ordinary manner. *Ante*, 378. In the latter case it is unnecessary to make any written demand of possession, or to obtain any refusal to deliver up possession, after the determination of the tenancy and before commencing the ejectment.

Evidence for Plaintiff.]—In ejectment against a tenant from year to year the plaintiff must prove:—

1. The tenancy. If the defendant held under any lease or agreement in writing, it must be produced, and either admitted in the cause (*ante*, 150), or proved in the usual manner; *ante*, 294, 393; and it must be properly stamped. *Ante*, 393. If there were no such writing the tenancy must be proved by parol evidence. *Ante*, 394. Proof of payment of rent by the defendant to the plaintiff, or his agent, and of a proper notice to quit, is sufficient to establish a *primâ facie* case. *Doe* d. *Coore* v. *Clare*, 2 T. R. 740; *Doe* d. *Marsack* v. *Read*, 12 East, 57; *Doe* d. *Wood* v. *Morris*, 12 East, 237; *Doe* d. *Pritchard* v. *Dodd*, 5 B. & Adol. 689; 1 N. & M. 838. Unless, indeed, the plaintiff's witness knows of some lease or agreement in writing, under which the defendant has occupied. *Trewhitt* v. *Lambert*, 10 A. & E. 470. Generally speaking it is material to show on which particular quarter day, or at what other time of the year, the tenancy *originally commenced*, because the validity of the notice to quit frequently depends upon this evidence. *Ante*, 48. If, upon notice to quit given to a tenant, he gives notice to his undertenant to quit at the same time, and upon the expiration of the notice he quits so much as is occupied by himself, but his undertenant refuses to quit, an ejectment may be maintained against him for so much as his undertenant has not given up. If he does not intend to defend such possession he should not appear to the ejectment. *Roe* v. *Wiggs*, 2 B. & P. New R. 330.

2. If the plaintiff be not the lessor, his title to the reversion must be deduced from the lessor and proved in the usual manner. *Ante,* 224. But if it be shown that the defendant has paid to the plaintiff some of the rent reserved, or that he has submitted to a distress by the plaintiff for such rent, that will be sufficient *primâ facie* evidence on this point. *Ante,* 211. A reversion of a tenancy from year to year cannot pass without deed. *Brawley* v. *Wade,* M'Clel. 664.

3. A sufficient notice to quit must be proved; *ante,* 29; *Doe* d. *Hall* v. *Benson,* 4 B. & A. 588; *Doe* d. *Peters* v. *Hopkinson,* 3 D. & R. 507; or a disclaimer of the plaintiff's title; *ante,* 41; or a sufficient surrender; *ante,* 224–226; or some act creating a forfeiture, and giving the claimant a right of re-entry in pursuance of a proviso to that effect contained in the lease or agreement. *Ante,* Chap. XXXIX.

4. If the claimant seek to recover mesne profits the usual evidence in that behalf must be given. *Ante,* 292.

Evidence and Points for Defendant.]—The defendant may contend that the evidence for the plaintiff is insufficient upon some material point. *Ante,* 446. He may also produce contradictory evidence. Most frequently the defence (if any) rests upon some objection to the notice to quit; *Doe* d. *Castleton* v. *Samuel,* 5 Esp. 173; or the want of such notice. *Tress* v. *Savage,* 4 E. & B. 36. We have considered this subject fully. *Ante,* 29. Generally speaking the defendant cannot dispute the title of his lessor; *ante,* 213; but he may show by evidence that it has since expired, or been legally determined, or parted with by way of mortgage, sale or otherwise. *Ante,* 217; *Harmer* v. *Bean,* 3 Car. & K. 307.

CHAPTER XLI.

LANDLORD AGAINST TENANT AT WILL.

Nature of the Tenancy.]—A tenancy at will is where lands or tenements are let by one man to another, to have and to hold at the will of the lessor, by force of which lease the lessee is in possession. In this case the lessee is called tenant at will, because he .hath no certain or sure estate, for the lessor may put him out at what time it pleaseth him. Lit. s. 68; 2 Bl. Com. 145. And in law it is holden at the will of both parties, although expressed to be at the will of the lessor only. Co. Lit. 55 a; 6 C. B. 672, note (*a*); Watk. Conv. 1, 2. So, where a person lets land to another without limiting any certain or determinate estate, a tenancy at will is thereby created. Com. Dig. Estates (H, 1). *Richardson* v. *Langridge*, 4 Taunt. 128. A mere permission to occupy land constitutes a tenancy at will only. *Doe* d. *Hull* v. *Wood*, 14 M. & W. 682; 15 Law J., N. S., Exch. 41. A tenant at will *at a yearly rent* is a tenant from year to year. *Pope* v. *Garland*, 4 You. & Col. 394; 10 Law J., N. S., Exch. Eq. 13; but see *Doe* d. *Dixie* v. *Davies*, 7 Exch. 91, Parke, B.; *Walker* v. *Giles*, 6 C. B. 662; Co. Lit. 556. Either party may at any time determine a tenancy at will (*post*, 452). But if the rent be reserved, payable quarterly, and the lessor determine the tenancy before the end of any quarter, he will thereby lose that quarter's rent. *Leighton* v. *Theed*, 1 Ld. Ray. 707; 2 Salk. 413; *Layton* v. *Field*, 3 Salk. 222. On the other hand, if the tenant determine the tenancy during any such quarter, he must pay his rent to the end of that quarter. *S. C.; Carpenter* v. *Collins*, Yelv. 73; Co. Lit. 56 a [note, 374]. Moreover, if the tenancy be determined by the lessor, the tenant is entitled to emblements; but it is otherwise where the tenancy is determined by the tenant. Lit. s. 68; Co. Lit. 55 b; *Oland* v. *Burdwick*, Cro. Eliz. 460; *Bulwer* v. *Bulwer*, 2 B. & A.

470, 471; Watk. Conv. 3, 4. If the tenancy be determined by the death of either party, the tenant, or his legal personal representative, is entitled to emblements. Co. Lit. 55 b; Watk. Conv. 3, note. After the determination of a tenancy at will, the tenant is entitled to enter and remove his goods. Lit. s. 69. But he is not entitled *de jure* to retain possession for that purpose. *Doe d. Nicholl* v. *M'Kaeg,* 10 B. & C. 721; 5 Man. & Ry. 620. A tenant at will is liable to an action of trespass for voluntary waste committed by him; Co. Lit. 57 a; but he is not liable merely as such tenant to an action for *permissive* waste. *Harnett* v. *Maitland,* 16 M. & W. 257; *Torriano* v. *Young,* 6 C. & P. 8; Lit. s. 71; Co. Lit. 57 a [note, 377]. A tenant at will has an *estate,* and a privity with his landlord, and is therefore capable of accepting a release in enlargement of his estate. Lit. s. 460; Shep. Touch. 321; 2 Pres. Conv. 284. But he cannot assign his estate, because he would thereby determine his will to hold. Co. Lit. 57 a; *Jones* v. *Clerk,* Hard. 47; *Disdale* v. *Iles,* 2 Lev. 88; Sir T. Ray, 224; 1 Ventr. 247, *S. C.; Birch* v. *Wright,* 1 T. R. 382; *Doe* v. *Abbott,* Winton Sum. Ass. 1838, Parke, B.; cited Ros. Ev. 447. Nor can he underlet, for the same reason. *Per* Ashhurst, J., in *Moss* v. *Gallimore,* 1 Doug. 279; 1 Smith's L. C. 314; *Shaw* v. *Barbor,* Cro. Eliz. 830; *Blunden* v. *Baugh,* Cro. Car. 302. A tenant at will cannot, as against the landlord to whom he is tenant, constitute another person tenant at will; but he may make a tenant at will as against himself; *per* Patteson, J., in *Doe* d. *Goody* v. *Carter,* 9 Q. B. 865; or even a lease for years. *Blunden* v. *Baugh,* Cro. Car. 302. An assignment or underlease will not operate to determine the tenancy at will until the landlord has notice or knowledge of it. *Pinhorn* v. *Souster,* 8 Exch. 763. The general rule is, that a tenancy at will is not assignable, because the transfer determines the tenancy; yet the rule is subject to the qualification that a tenant at will cannot determine his tenancy by transferring his interest to a third party, without notice to the landlord. *Per* Cresswell, J., in *Melling* v. *Leak,* 24 Law J., N. S., C. P. 187; 16 C. B. 669, citing *Pinhorn* v. *Souster, supra.* An assignment or underlease by a tenant at will does not amount to a *disseisin* of the landlord, except at his option. *Blunden* v. *Baugh,* Cro. Car. 302.

Tenancy at Will—how created.]—An estate at will is the lowest estate that can be created by any contract or agreement, express or implied. Watk. Conv. 1 (8th ed.). A tenancy at sufferance is of an inferior nature, but that can be created only by implication of law (*post,* Chap. XLII.). In order to constitute a tenancy at will, something must be done by the lessor. *Per* Tindal, C. J., in *Doe* d. *Stanway* v. *Rock,* 4 Man. & Gr. 34. A person who lives in a house rent free by the sufferance and permission of the owner is a tenant at will. *Rex* v. *Collett,* Russ. & Ry. C. C. 498; *Rex* v. *Jobling, Id.* 525. A mere permission to occupy constitutes a tenancy at will only; and in order to create a tenancy from year to year, there must be some circumstances to show an intention to do so, such as payment of rent quarterly, or for some other aliquot part of a year. *Doe* d. *Hull* v. *Wood,* 14 M. & W. 682; 15 Law J., N. S., Exch. 41 (*ante,* 443). Where a person lets lands to another, without limiting any certain or determinate estate, a tenancy at will is thereby created. Com. Dig. Estates (H, 1). So, where a person lets another into possession under a contract of sale, or an agreement for a future lease, a tenancy at will is thereby created, and such tenancy must be determined by entry, or by a demand of possession, or otherwise, before ejectment can be maintained against the person so let into possession (*ante*, 58). A tenancy at will may be created *by express words*, either orally or by any deed or writing. *Doe* d. *Bastow* v. *Cox*, 11 Q. B. 122; *Doe* d. *Davies* v. *Thomas*, 6 Exch. 854; *Doe* d. *Dixie* v. *Davies*, 7 Exch. 89; *Walker* v. *Giles*, 6 C. B. 662. If an agreement be made to let premises so long as both parties like, and reserving a compensation accruing *de die in diem*, and not referable to a year, or any aliquot part of a year, it does not create a holding from year to year, but a tenancy at will strictly so called; and though the tenant has expended money on the improvement of the premises, that does not give him a term to hold until he is indemnified. *Richardson* v. *Langridge*, 4 Taunt. 128. The reservation of a yearly rent is not inconsistent with a tenancy at will. *Per* Parke, B., in *Doe* d. *Dixie* v. *Davies*, 7 Exch. 91; citing Co. Lit. 556, and *Walker* v. *Giles*, 6 C. B. 662; but see *Pope* v. *Garland*, 4 You. & Col. 394 (*ante*, 448). Generally speaking, the courts will, if possible, construe a tenancy for an indefinite period as a tenancy from year to year, rather than as a tenancy at will, because of the many inconveniences incident to a tenancy at will; *Doe* d. *Warner* v. *Browne*, 8 East, 166, 167; especially if there has been any payment of an annual rent, by quarterly or other payments. *Clayton* v. *Blakey*, 8 T. R. 3; 2 Smith, L. C. 74. When a tenancy at will is *implied by law*, and a payment of rent is made, for a year, half-year or quarter, such tenancy thereupon becomes a tenancy from year to year, unless the contrary be expressly stipulated when the payment is received. 2 Smith, L. C. 75, 77. But where a tenancy at will is created by express contract, it will not be converted into a tenancy from year to year by the mere payment and acceptance of rent by quarterly or other payments. *Doe* d. *Bastow* v. *Cox*, 11 Q. B. 122.

A tenancy at will may also arise *by implication of law*, as well as by express words. Thus, if a person enter as tenant under a lease which is void, he thereby becomes tenant at will to the lessor. *De Medina* v. *Polson*, Holt, N. P. C. 47; *Goodtitle* d. *Galloway* v. *Herbert*, 4 T. R. 680; *Denn* d. *Warren* v. *Fearnside*, 1 Wils. 176. If an annual rent be expressed to be reserved, payable quarterly, half-yearly or otherwise, a new tenancy from year to year (in lieu of the previous implied tenancy at will) will arise upon the payment and acceptance of any part of such rent. *Doe* d. *Rigg* v. *Bell*, 5 T. R. 471; *Clayton* v. *Blakey*, 8 T. R. 3; 2 Smith, L. C. 74. The principle is that by entry under the void lease, coupled with payment of any of the rent therein mentioned, a new tenancy from year to year, upon the terms of such lease, so far as they are applicable to a yearly tenancy, is created; *West* v. *Fritche*, 3 Exch. 216; *Richardson* v. *Giffard*, 1 A. & E. 52; *Doe* d. *Davenish* v. *Moffatt*, 15 Q. B. 257; or rather such facts, taken together, *constitute evidence* for the jury of such new implied tenancy. *Jones* v. *Shears*, 4 A. & E. 832; *Finlay* v. *The Bristol and Exeter Railway Company*, 7 Exch. 415, Parke, B.; *Id.* 420, Martin, B.

Where a tenancy from year to year would work a forfeiture of the lessor's estate, such a tenancy will not be raised by construction or implication of law. *Fenny* d. *Eastham* v. *Child*, 2 M. & S. 255.

A demise for life without livery of seisin formerly created only an estate at will. Lit. s. 70 ; *Sharpe's case*, 6 Rep. 26 a ; Cro. Eliz. 482; Moore, 458, *S. C.;* and see *Doe* d. *Roberton* v. *Gardiner*, 12 C. B. 319. But by 8 & 9 Vict. c. 106, s. 2, all corporeal tenements and hereditaments, as regards the conveyance of the immediate freehold thereof, shall be deemed to lie in grant as well as in livery. A lease for life, or for a longer period than three years from the making thereof, must be made by deed, otherwise it will be void at law. *Id.* s. 3 (*ante*, 222).

Where a minister of a dissenting congregation, after his election, was placed in possession of a chapel-house and dwellinghouse by certain persons in whom the legal fee was vested, in trust to permit and suffer the chapel to be used for the purpose of religious worship : held, that he was a mere tenant at will to those persons, and that his interest was determinable instanter by a demand of possession, without any previous notice to quit. *Doe* d. *Jones* v. *Jones*, 10 B. & C. 718 ; 5 Man. & Ry. 616 ; *Doe* d. *Nicholl* v. *M'Kaeg*, 10 B. & C. 721 ; 5 Man. & Ry. 620.

If a party be *let into possession* of land under a contract for the sale of it, which is not afterwards completed, he is tenant at will to the vendor. *Ball* v. *Cullimore*, 2 Cr. M. & R. 120; 5 Tyr. 753; 1 Gale, 96 ; *Doe* d. *Tomes* v. *Chamberlaine*, 5 M. & W. 14 ; *Right* d. *Lewis* v. *Beard*, 13 East, 210; *Doe* d. *Gray* v. *Stanion*, 1 M. & W. 695, 700; *Doe* d. *Parker* v. *Boulton*, 6 M. & S. 148, 150; *Doe* d. *Milburn* v. *Edgar*, 2 Bing. N. C. 498 ; *Doe* d. *Stanway* v. *Rock*, 4 Man. & Gr. 30; Car. & M. 549. But if no rent be agreed on he will not be liable to an action for use and occupation in respect of his possession during the time the contract is pending. *Winterbottom* v. *Ingham*, 7 Q. B. 611. He will, however, be liable to such action if he continue in possession after the contract has been finally broken off. *Howard* v. *Shaw*, 8 M. & W. 118 ; *Boileau* v. *Rutlin*, 2 Exch. 655, 676.

Where A., being in the possession of land, agreed with the executors of H. to purchase it from them for the lives of W. & G., and it was stipulated that A. should be entitled to the possession from the date of the agreement, and that the executors should make a good title within twenty-one days, but the purchase went off upon objections to the title; whereupon the executors gave A. the usual notice to quit : held that, upon proof of the above facts, and in the absence of any evidence as to a right of possession in A., the executors of H. were entitled to recover against A. in ejectment. *Doe* d. *Bord* v. *Burton*, 16 Q. B. 807.

A party who occupied a house as tenant from year to year entered into an agreement with his landlord for the purchase of his estate therein for 100*l.* : held that, as there was an implied condition in the contract that the landlord should make out a good title, the agreement for the purchase did not operate as a surrender by operation of law of the tenancy from year to year. *Doe* d. *Gray* v. *Stanion*, 1 M. & W. 695; Tyr. & Gr. 1066 ; and see *Tarte* v. *Darby*, 15 M. & W. 601, 606.

When a person is let into possession pending a negociation for a lease, which afterwards goes off, he is tenant at will, and may be ejected after a demand of possession. *Doe* d. *Hollingworth* v. *Stennett*, 2 Esp. 716, 717 ; *Doe* d. *Lambourn* v. *Pedgriph*, 4 C. & P. 312.

No man can, by entering on the land of another claiming to hold it as his tenant at will, become such tenant, without the assent of the owner. 2 Pres. Conv. 312; Co. Lit. 55 a. He is a mere disseisor, and his words, that he claims to hold the land only as tenant at will to the owner, cannot qualify his wrong. Co. Lit. 271 a. In order to constitute a tenancy at will something must be done by the lessor. *Per* Tindal, C. J., in *Doe* d. *Stanway* v. *Rock*, 4 Man. & Gr. 34; Car. & M. 549.

How determined.]—A strict tenancy at will may be determined at any time by either party, subject to the consequences already mentioned. *Ante*, 448; *Leighton* v. *Theed*, 1 Ld. Raym. 707; 2 Salk. 413; *Layton* v. *Field*, 3 Salk. 222.

By the Landlord.—The usual notice to quit is unnecessary to determine an estate at will. *Doe* d. *Tomes* v. *Chamberlaine*, 5 M. & W. 14; *Doe* d. *Rogers* v. *Pullen*, 9 Bing. 749. A demand of possession, or anything equivalent, made on the land by the landlord or his agent, is sufficient. *Doe* d. *Bastow* v. *Cox*, 11 Q. B. 122; Co. Lit. 55 b. "Unless you pay what you owe me I shall take immediate measures to recover possession of the property," coupled with proof of non-payment: held sufficient to determine a tenancy at will. *Doe* d. *Price* v. *Price*, 9 Bing. 356; 2 Moo. & Sc. 464. A verbal demand made on the wife of an undertenant, on the land, has been held sufficient. *Roe* d. *Blair* v. *Street*, 2 A. & E. 329; 4 N. & M. 42. But by words spoken away from the ground the will is not determined until the lessee hath notice. Co. Lit. 55 b.

A written demand of possession may be in the form or to the effect following, viz. :—

"Mr. C. D. I do hereby demand possession of the [messuages, buildings, land and premises], with the appurtenances, situate at ——, in the parish of ——, in the county of ——, and now in your occupation. As witness my hand, this —— day of ——, 18—."

(Signed) A. B."

If made by an agent, it may be as follows:

"Mr. C. D. I, the undersigned, as the agent of and for A. B., of ——, Esq., and on his behalf, do hereby demand possession of &c.:" *ut supra.*

A mere entry by the landlord, or his authorized agent, to take possession, is sufficient, although the lessee be absent; Co. Lit. 55 b; *Doe* d. *Moore* v. *Lawder*, 1 Stark. R. 308. So if the landlord do any act upon the land for which, if not entitled to possession, he would be liable to an action of trespass. Co. Lit. 55 b, 57 b, 245 b, cited 9 Mee. & W. 646, *per cur.* As if he enter and cut down a tree, not excepted from the demise; Co. Lit. 55 b; or dig for stones or minerals not so excepted; *Doe* d. *Bennett* v. *Turner*, 7 M. & W. 226; *S. C.* in error, 9 M. & W. 643, 646; or put his beasts upon common appendant to a manor demised at will; Co. Lit. 55 b; or deliver livery of seisin upon a feoffment; *Ball* v. *Cullimore*, 2 Cr. M. & R. 120; 5 Tyr. 753; 1 Gale, 96; *Doe* d. *Hindmarch* v. *Oliver*, 1 Car. & K. 543; or make any conveyance or demise to take effect immediately, of which the tenant has notice or knowledge. *Disdale* v. *Isles*, 2 Lev. 88; *S. C. nom. Hinchman* v. *Isles*, 1 Vent. 247; *Doe* d. *Dixie* v. *Davies*, 7 Exch. 89. "Every conveyance of the reversion is inconsistent with the will to occupy under him, but the tenant is not to be treated as a trespasser until he has had notice of the determination of the will—not formal notice, but knowledge of it. As soon as he has that he must know that he is not to occupy. That is the effect of the passage in Co. Lit. 55 b; and also of *Disdale* v. *Isles." Per* Parke, B., in *Doe* d. *Davies* v. *Thomas*, 6 Exch. 857. When a party creates a tenancy at will, and afterwards becomes insolvent, the vesting order, with knowledge thereof by the tenant, is a determination of the tenancy; and if the tenant after such information continue in possession, he may be treated as a trespasser. *Doe* d. *Davies* v. *Thomas*, 6 Exch. 854.

A distress for rent will not put an end to a tenancy at will, notwithstanding the landlord impounds the distress upon the premises; *per* Martin, B., in *Doe* d. *Davies* v. *Thomas*, 6 Exch. 858; but it was formerly otherwise.

If a woman make a lease at will reserving a rent, and she taketh husband, this is no countermand of the lease at will, but the husband and wife shall have an action of debt for the rent. Co. Lit. 55 b; *Henstead's case*, 5 Co. R. 10. So if the husband and wife make a lease at will of the wife's land, reserving a rent, and the husband die, yet the lease continueth. *S. C.* In like manner if a lease be made by two to two others at will, and one of the lessors or one of the lessees die, the lease at will is not determined in either of those cases. Co. Lit. 55 b; *Henstead's case*, 5 Co. R. 10. A conveyance in fee made by a third person to the lessor does not determine the estate of his tenant at will. *Doe* d. *Goody* v. *Carter*, 9 Q. B. 863.

If a lessor at will die, or be outlawed, the estate of his tenant at will is thereby determined. 5 Co. R. 116; Co. Lit. 55 b, 57 a.

By the Tenant.—A tenant at will may determine the tenancy at any time by an express declaration or notice that he will not continue to hold the land any longer; *Doe* d. *Bastow* v. *Cox*, 11 Q. B. 122; but he must also waive the possession, otherwise his declaration or notice will not avail as against the landlord. Co. Lit. 55 b, 57 a.

A written notice may be in the form given in the Appendix, No. 3, or to that effect.

If the tenant assign over or underlet the land to another, that amounts to a determination of the estate at will. *Ante*, 449. But not until the landlord has notice or knowledge of such assignment or underlease. *Pinhorn* v. *Souster*, 8 Exch. 763; *Melling* v. *Leake*, 16 C. B. 652. So if the tenant at will die; *Doe* v. *Stanway* v. *Rock*, Car. & M. 549; or suffer himself to be outlawed; Co. Lit. 55 b, 57 a; 5 Co. R. 116; or be attainted of treason. *Denn* d. *Warren* v. *Fearnside*, 1 Wils. 176; or commit voluntary waste. *Countess of Shrewsbury's case*, 5 Co. R. 13 a; Cro. Eliz. 777, 784, *S. C.*; Co. Lit. 55 b.

Ejectment cannot be maintained against a tenant at will until after his estate has been determined, and the right to possession must be claimed in the writ of ejectment from some day *after* such determination. *Goodtitle* d. *Galloway* v. *Herbert*, 4 T. R. 680; *Doe* d. *Jacobs* v. *Phillips*, 10 Q. B. 130; *Right* d. *Lewis* v. *Beard*, 13 East, 210; 2 Arch. N. P. 391. But the writ might issue at a later hour on the same day the tenancy is determined. *Doe* d. *Nicholl* v. *M'Kaeg*, 10 B. & C. 721; 5 Man. & Ry. 620; and see *Doe* d. *Graves* v. *Wells*, 10 A. & E. 427; 2 P. & D. 396; *Doe* d. *Bennett* v. *Long*, 9 C. & P. 773, 775; *Roe* d. *Wrangham* v. *Hersey*, 3 Wils. 274.

The landlord of a tenant at will at an agreed rent may distrain or sue for the arrears. Lit. s. 72; *Doe* d. *Benson* v. *Frost*, 6 Exch. 858, note (*a*); *Pinhorn* v. *Souster*, 8 Exch. 137, 173.

Evidence for the Plaintiff.]—In ejectment against a tenant at will the plaintiff must prove :—

1. The tenancy at will. We have already considered how such a tenancy may be created. *Ante*, 449—452.

2. The determination of such tenancy. We have already considered how the tenancy may be determined. *Ante*, 452, 453. This must appear to have taken place before the day from which the right of possession is claimed in the writ of ejectment; *ante*, 453; and it must appear that the writ issued within the time allowed by the Statute of Limitations. *Ante*, 13; *Doe* d. *Baker* v. *Coombes*, 9 C. B. 714; *Doe* d. *Stanway* v. *Rock*, 4 Man. & Gr. 30.

3. If the plaintiff be not the lessor, he must prove his title to the reversion. *Doe* d. *Smith* v. *Galloway*, 5 B. & Adol. 43; 2 N. & M. 240; *ante*, 224.

4. If the plaintiff seek to recover mesne profits the usual evidence in that behalf must be produced. *Ante*, 292.

Evidence and Points for Defendant.]—The defendant may insist that the evidence for the plaintiff is insufficient upon some material point (*supra*), and he may produce contradictory evidence. He may also prove that a tenancy from year to year has been created between him and the plaintiff. *Ante*, 450. But he is, like any other tenant, estopped from denying his landlord's title to demise to him. *Ante*, 214.

If any new tenancy be proved the plaintiff may, by evidence in reply, show that such tenancy has been legally determined by notice to quit, disclaimer, surrender or otherwise. *Doe* d. *Bennett* v. *Long*, 9 C. & P. 773, 774; *ante*, 300.

CHAPTER XLII.

Nature of the Tenancy.]—A tenant at sufferance is one who entered under a lawful title, which has since expired, or been legally determined, but who, nevertheless, wrongfully continues in possession without the assent or dissent of the person next entitled. Watk. Conv. 23 (8th ed.); Co. Lit. 57 b, 270 b; 2 Black. Com. 150; 1 Steph. Com. 273; 2 Crabb, Real Prop. 437; 1 Cruise, Dig. tit. IX. c. 2. Thus, where a tenant for years, or his assignee, wrongfully holds over after the expiration of his term; *Butler* v. *Duckmanton*, Cro. Jac. 169; *Doe* d. *Patrick* v. *Duke of Beaufort*, 6 Exch. 498, 503; or a tenant from year to year, or his assignee, wrongfully holds over after his tenancy has been duly determined by a notice to quit given by either party; or by the death of his lessor, who was only a tenant for his own life; *Doe* d. *Thomas* v. *Roberts*, 16 M. & W. 780, Parke, B.; or a tenant *pur autre vie* wrongfully retains possession after the death of the *cestui que vie*; *Allen* v. *Hill*, Cro. Eliz. 238; 3 Leon. 153; or a tenant for life, subject to a condition, holds over after such estate is determined by a breach of the condition; *Allen* v. *Hill*, Cro. Eliz. 238; or a tenant at will wrongfully retains possession after the death of the lessor. Vin. Abr. Estate (Tenant at Sufferance, D. c.) When an estate at will is determined, by entry or otherwise, if the tenant afterwards remain in possession he becomes tenant at sufferance. *Doe* d. *Bennett* v. *Turner*, 7 M. & W. 226; *S. C.* in error, 9 M. & W. 643; *Doe* d. *Goody* v. *Carter*, 9 Q. B. 863. A mortgagor who remains in possession after executing a mortgage which contains no re-demise, becomes tenant at sufferance to the mortgagee. *Powseley* v. *Blackman*, Cro. Jac. 659; 2 Roll. R. 284; *S. C.* cited 2 Q. B. 154. So in any other case, where a term or estate having ceased, or been surrendered, or conveyed, the tenant continues to retain possession. Co. Lit. 576, note 383; *Pennington* v. *Morse*, Dyer, 62; *Doe* d. *Crisp* v. *Barber*, 2 T. R. 749; *Graham* v. *Peat*, 1 East, 244; 2 Crabb, Real Prop. 437. An undertenant who is in possession at the determination of the original lease, and is permitted by the reversioner to hold over, is *quasi* a tenant at sufferance. *Simpkin* v. *Ashhurst*, 1 Cr. M. & R. 261; 4 Tyrw. 781. There is a great diversity between a tenant at will and a tenant at sufferance; for tenant at will is always by right, and tenant at sufferance entereth by a lawful lease and holdeth over by wrong. Co. Lit. 57 b, cited 3 C. B. 229, note '*b*). A tenant at will is entitled to emblements unless he determines the tenancy. *Ante*, 448. But a tenant at sufferance is not entitled to emblements. Vin. Abr. Emblements, 79; and *per* Parke, B., in *Doe* d. *Bennett* v. *Turner*, 7 M. & W. 235. A tenancy at sufferance cannot originate by agreement of the parties, but only by implication of law. Watk. Conv. 24. For if there be any such agreement it must create an estate at will at the least, and more commonly a tenancy from year to year. *Ante*, 449.

An instrument in these terms, " I hereby certify that I remain in the house, No. 3, Swinton Street, belonging to W. G., on sufferance only, and agree to give him possession at any time he may require:" held, not to amount to an agreement *for a tenancy*, so as to require a stamp. *Barry* v. *Goodman*, 2 M. & W. 768.

The law implies a tenancy at sufferance by reason of the neglect or laches of the person next entitled, who omits to enter. Co. Lit. 270 b, note (1). But when a tenant of the crown wrongfully holds over he is deemed a mere intruder, and not a tenant at sufferance, because the law will not impute laches to the crown. Co. Lit. 57 b; 4 Hen. 6, 12; *Finch's case*, 2 Leon. 143.

Strictly speaking a tenant at sufferance has no estate, but only the possession, and that without the privity or consent of the real owner. 2 Pres. Conv. 302. Therefore he cannot accept a release in enlargement of his estate. *Butler* v. *Duckmanton*, Cro. Jac. 169; *Allen* v. *Hill*, Cro. Eliz. 238; Co. Lit. 270 b; 2 Pres. Conv. 284. Nor can he assign his estate, for he has no estate to assign, and "one tenant at sufferance cannot make another." *Per* Lord Ellenborough, C. J., in *Thunder* d. *Weaver* v. *Belcher*, 3 East, 449.

A tenant at sufferance having the actual possession may maintain trespass against a wrongdoer. *Graham* v. *Peat*, 1 East, 244; 3 Steph. Com. 497; 2 Roll. Abr. 551. It seems that he may even maintain trespass against the real owner, if *forcibly* ejected without any previous demand of possession. *Doe* d. *Harrison* v. *Murrell*, 8 C. & P. 134, Lord Abinger, C. B. But *semble*, the action should be for the assault and battery rather than trespass *quare clausum fregit;* because the instant the owner enters on any part of the land to take possession he becomes actually and legally possessed. *Randall* v. *Stevens*, 2 E. & B. 641; *Jones* v. *Chapman* (in error), 2 Exch. 803, 821, Maule, J.; *ante*, 68. A tenant at sufferance, not having any estate, or legal right to possession, cannot maintain ejectment even against a mere wrongdoer. *Doe* d. *Crisp* v. *Barber*, 2 T. R. 749; *Doe* d. *Harrison* v. *Murrell*, 8 C. & P. 134, Lord Abinger, C. B.

A tenant at sufferance may be sued for use and occupation; *Bayley* v. *Bradley*, 5 C. B. 396; *Hellier* v. *Sillcox*, 19 Law J., N. S., Q. B., 295; but he is not liable to a distress for rent, because he does not hold *at an agreed rent;* *Alford* v. *Vickery*, Car. & M. 280, Coleridge, J.;

Jenner v. *Clegg,* 1 Moo. & Rob. 213, Parke, J. ; nor to an action of *trespass, before entry by the owner,* because actual possession, and not merely a right of possession, is necessary to support that form of action. *Ante,* 287.

An ejectment may be maintained against a tenant at sufferance, without any previous entry, or notice to quit, or demand of possession. *Doe* d. *Leeson* v. *Sayer,* 3 Camp. 8. But, generally speaking, when a tenant for years under a lease or agreement in writing holds over after the expiration of his term, or a tenant from year to year, under a lease or agreement in writing, holds over after his tenancy has been determined by a regular notice to quit, the best mode of proceeding against him is first to make a *demand in writing* of possession, pursuant to 15 & 16 Vict. c. 76, s. 213 ; *ante,* 379 ; and to *obtain his refusal* to deliver up such possession (*ante,* 382), and afterwards to proceed by ejectment in the form and manner pointed out by that section, whereby he may be compelled to find sureties to pay the costs and damages to be recovered in the action before he will be permitted to defend it. *Ante,* 378.

Evidence for Plaintiff.]—In ejectment against a tenant at sufferance the plaintiff must prove :—

1. The previous lawful tenancy or possession of the defendant. If he held under any deed or writing it must be duly stamped and admitted in the cause (*ante,* 150), or proved in the usual manner. *Ante,* 294, 393.

2. It must be proved that the tenancy under such deed or writing has expired, or been determined by a notice to quit, or by a surrender, or in some other legal manner. *Ante,* 447.

3. That the plaintiff is the party entitled to actual possession next after the end or determination of the defendant's previous term or estate. *Doe* d. *Smith* v. *Galloway,* 5 B. & Adol. 43 ; 2 N. & M. 240. A title by estoppel is sufficient. Thus where the plaintiff claims as devisee of H., who let L. into possession, and either L., or any person claiming through or under him, or "as his landlord," defends the action. *Doe* d. *Willis* v. *Birchmore,* 9 A. & E. 662 ; 1 P. & D. 448.

4. If the plaintiff seek to recover mesne profits, the usual proofs in that behalf must be given. *Ante,* 292.

Evidence and Points for Defendant.]—The defendant may insist that the evidence for the plaintiff is insufficient upon some material point; *Supra;* and he may produce contradictory evidence. He may also prove that a new tenancy from year to year has been created between him and the plaintiff; *ante,* 444 ; or a new tenancy at will. *Doe* d. *Bennett* v. *Turner,* 7 M. & W. 226, 235 ; *Turner* v. *Doe* d. *Bennett* (in error), 9 M. & W. 643. In reply to which the plaintiff may prove that such tenancy was duly determined before action by a notice to quit, a disclaimer, a demand of possession, a surrender, or otherwise. *Ante,* 300 ; *Doe* d. *Bennett* v. *Long,* 9 C. & P. 773, 774.

CHAPTER XLIII.

TENANT AGAINST LANDLORD.

When maintainable.]—A tenant for years, or for any other definite term, or for a life or lives, or from year to year, is generally entitled to actual possession of the demised premises during the continuance of his term or tenancy : consequently such tenant, his executors, administrators or assigns, may maintain ejectment against his landlord or any other person claiming through or under him after the demise made, who wrongfully deprives him or them of such possession during the term or tenancy, whether by entry, ejectment or otherwise. *Feret* v. *Hill,* 15 C. B. 207; *Doe* d. *Pearson* v. *Ries,* 8 Bing. 178; 1 Moo. & Sc. 264; *Doe* d. *Courtail* v. *Thomas,* 9 B. & C. 288; 4 M. & R. 218; *Doe* d. *Hutchins* v. *Lewis,* 1 Burr. 614, 619; 2 Ld. Ken. 320, *S. C.* So a tenant for years may maintain ejectment against a stranger who turns him out of possession during the term; but in such action he must prove (*inter alia*) his landlord's title. If the lessor had only a contingent estate at the time of the demise, but afterwards acquired an estate in possession, the demise would operate at first by estoppel only, but when the estate fell into possession it would feed the estoppel, and enable the tenant to maintain ejectment. *Doe* v. *Christmas* v. *Oliver,* 5 Man. & R. 202; 2 Smith, L. C. 417. Upon the death of a lessee for years in bad circumstances, his brother (who *subsequently* took out letters of administration) gave up possession to the landlord, in consideration of the latter relinquishing his claim to the arrears of rent. The brother, after obtaining letters of administration, offered to pay the rent, and demanded back the possession for the remainder of the term, which the landlord refused : held, that ejectment by the administrator against the landlord was maintainable. *Doe* d. *Hornby* v. *Glenn,* 1 A. & E. 49; 3 N. & M. 837. Where a term was taken in execution and sold under a *fi. fa.*, but no bill of sale or assignment was made by the sheriff to the purchaser : held, that the term continued in the debtor, who might maintain ejectment against the purchaser. *Doe* d. *Hughes* v. *Jones,* 9 M. & W. 372; 1 Dowl. N. S. 352.

A lease for years by a copyholder made contrary to the custom of the manor, and without any licence, is valid, except as against the lord of the manor and his grantees, &c. The lessee may therefore during the term maintain ejectment against the lessor, &c. *Downingham's case,* Owen, 17; *Doe* d. *Tressida* v. *Tressida,* 1 Q. B. 416; *Doe* d. *Robinson* v. *Bousfield,* 6 Q. B. 492. The lord may waive the forfeiture thereby created. *S. C.* Instead of granting a lease without licence, the owner of a copyhold may covenant or agree to grant a lease upon certain specified terms and conditions, with licence of the lord, provided such licence can be procured ; and that until such licence shall be obtained, and a lease granted accordingly, the tenant shall hold from year to year, subject to the terms and conditions before specified. The tenant will, by virtue of such covenant or agreement, coupled with entry thereunder, have nearly all the benefits of a lease. *Price* v. *Birch*, 4 Man. & Gr. 1 ; 1 Dowl. N. S. 270. But his tenancy may be determined by a regular notice to quit. *Doe* d. *Nunn* v. *Lufkin*, 4 East, 221 ; *Lufkin* v. *Nunn*, 1 B. & P. New R. 163.

A lessee cannot *before entry* maintain trespass *quare clausum fregit*, because actual possession, and not merely the right of possession, is necessary to maintain that form of action. Co. Lit. 296 b ; Com. Dig. Trespass, B. 1, 2 ; *Wheeler* v. *Montifiore*, 2 Q. B. 133, 156 ; *Turner* v. *Cameron's Coalbrook Steam Coal Company*, 5 Exch. 932 ; and see *Lichfield* v. *Ready*, 5 Exch. 939 ; *Lowe* v. *Ross*, 5 Exch. 553. But a lessee may before entry maintain ejectment, because a mere *interesse termini*, or right of possession during the term, is sufficient to support that form of action. Shep. Touch. 269 ; Co. Lit. 46 b ; *Doe* d. *Parsley* v. *Day*, 2 Q. B. 156, *per cur.* ; *Ryan* v. *Clark*, 14 Q. B. 73 ; 7 Dowl. & L. 8 ; and see *Saffyn's case*, 5 Co. R. 124 b ; Lit. ss. 66, 289 ; *ante*, 287. "It is distinctly laid down in *Williams* v. *Bosanquet* (1 Brod. & B. 238), that entry is not necessary to the vesting of a term of years in the lessee : the interest and legal right of possession, where the term is to commence immediately, and not in future, vests in the lessee before entry ; and of course the right of possession in the lessor is gone, though, for the purpose of maintaining an action of trespass, the lessee must enter, since that action is founded on the actual possession." *Per cur.* in *Ryan* v. *Clark*, 14 Q. B. 73 ; 7 Dowl. & L. 8, *S. C.* As to the nature of an *interesse termini*, and how it may be released, surrendered, merged or assigned, see *Doe* d. *Rawlings* v. *Walker*, 5 B. & C. 111 ; 7 D. & R. 487. A lease to commence upon the expiration of a previous lease conveys only an *interesse termini* until the expiration of the previous lease, and does not amount to an assignment of the reversion expectant on such lease. *Smith* v. *Day*, 2 M. & W. 684.

Evidence for Plaintiff.]—In ejectment by a tenant, or any person claiming through or under him, against the landlord, or any person claiming through or under him, the plaintiff must prove :—

1. The lease or demise. *Ante*, 393. This must be duly stamped (if in writing) ; *Goodtitle* d. *Estwick* v. *Way*, 1 T. R. 735 ; and must be admitted in the cause (*ante*, 150), or proved in the usual manner. *Doe* d. *Courtail* v. *Thomas*, 9 B. & C. 288. The attesting witness need not be called, unless the lease be made in pursuance of a power requiring it to be executed in the presence of and attested by one witness or more. 17 & 18 Vict. c. 125, s. 26. *Ante*, 294.

2. The identity of the parties and of the demised premises with the land claimed, or some part thereof, must be shown so far as may be necessary. *Ante*, 240, 289.

3. If the plaintiff be not the lessee, he must prove his derivative title : but it is not always necessary to prove *all* the mesne assignments : upon proof of the original lease, and of some of the most recent assignments, including that to the plaintiff, and of possession

thereunder, the intermediate assignments will be presumed. *Earl* d. *Goodwin* v. *Baxter*, 2 W. Black. 1228; 3 Stark. Ev. 914 (3rd ed.); but see *Doe* d. *Woodhouse* v. *Powell*, 8 Q. B. 576.

4. If the defendant be not the lessor, it must be shown that he claims possession through or under the lessor subsequent to the demise: as in *Doe* d. *Courtail* v. *Thomas*, 9 B. & C. 288; *Doe* d. *Morgan* v. *Powell*, 7 Man. & Gr. 980; 8 Scott, N. R. 687: or at all events that he entered into possession after the commencement of the term granted to the plaintiff: otherwise the lessor's title and right to demise must be proved in the usual manner.

Evidence and Points for Defendant:—

1. The defendant may dispute or deny the alleged demise.

2. He may contend that the writing proved by the plaintiff does not amount to a lease, but only to an agreement for a lease. *Ante*, 222; *Doe* d. *Morgan* v. *Powell*, 7 Man. & Gr. 980; 8 Scott, N. R. 687; *Doe* d. *Jackson* v. *Ashburner*, 5 T. R. 163; *Goodtitle* d. *Estwick* v. *Way*, 1 T. R. 735. If, however, the plaintiff has entered *and paid rent* under such agreement, a new tenancy will be implied by law upon the terms of such intended lease, so far as they are applicable to a yearly tenancy. *Doe* d. *Rigge* v. *Bell*, 5 T. R. 471; *Richardson* v. *Gifford*, 1 A. & E. 52; *Doe* d. *Thompson* v. *Amey*, 12 A. & E. 476; 4 P. & D. 177; *Mann* v. *Lovejoy*, Ry. & Moo. 355.

3. That the alleged demise does not comprise the premises for which the defendant defends, but only other and different tenements. *Bartlett* v. *Wright*, Cro. Eliz. 299; and see *Doe* d. *Freeland* v. *Burt*, 1 T. R. 701; *Doe* d. *Smith* v. *Galloway*, 5 B. & Adol. 43; *ante*, 240.

4. That the demise was void, being for more than three years, and not made *by deed*. *Ante*, 222. But if any of the rent has been paid, the new implied tenancy thereby created must be shown to have been duly determined by a regular notice to quit, or in some other legal manner. *Doe* d. *Rigge* v. *Bell*, 5 T. R. 471; 2 Smith, L. C. 72; *Clayton* v. *Blakey*, 8 T. R. 3; 2 Smith, L. C. 74. Unless, indeed, the term mentioned in the void lease has expired. *Tress* v. *Savage*, 4 E. & B. 36. The lease of a rectory house, &c., under which the plaintiff claims, may be shown to have become void by nonresidence under 13 Eliz. c. 20, although the defendant be a mere stranger; *Doe* d. *Crisp* v. *Barber*, 2 T. R. 749; or the defendant be the lessor himself. *Frogmorton* d. *Fleming* v. *Scutt*, 2 East, 467. A lease granted by a guardian in socage may be shown to have become void, or voidable and avoided by the infant on his attaining fourteen years. *Roe* d. *Parry* v. *Hodgson*, 2 Wils. 129.

5. That the tenancy, if from year to year or for any other uncertain period, has been duly determined by a regular notice to quit. *Ante*, 29.

6. That the term has been surrendered by deed; 8 & 9 Vict. c. 106, s. 3; *ante*, 224; or by act and operation of law. *Ante*, 225. But a sufficient legal surrender must be shown. *Doe* d. *Hornby* v. *Glenn*, 1 A. & E. 49; 4 N. & M. 837.

7. That the lease contains a condition or proviso for re-entry on breach of any of the covenants therein contained; and that a breach of some or one of such covenants was in fact committed, and that by reason thereof the defendant entered and avoided the lease; *Davis* v. *Burrell*, 10 C. B. 821; or brought ejectment, under which possession was obtained. The evidence of the breach of covenant will be similar

to that in an ejectment for a forfeiture. *Ante*, 400. Where A. procured B. to grant him a lease of premises, by means of a false representation that he intended to carry on a certain lawful trade therein, but having obtained possession, A. converted the premises into a common brothel, whereupon B. forcibly expelled him: held, that A. might maintain ejectment, the fraudulent misrepresentation and the subsequent illegal use of the premises, not being sufficient in law to avoid the lease. *Feret* v. *Hill,* 15 C. B. 207.

8. That the term has been determined and avoided by an ejectment for nonpayment of rent, pursuant to 15 & 16 Vict. c. 76, ss. 210, 211, 212; *ante*, 415—422.

9. That the term has been determined and avoided by summary proceedings before justices, pursuant to 11 Geo. 2, c. 19, ss. 16, 17, as amended by 57 Geo. 3, c. 52, the plaintiff having deserted the premises. *Post*, Chap. LXXII.

10. That the plaintiff has *underlet* the premises for a term which has not expired. This constitutes a good *primâ facie* defence, without showing that the defendant claims on behalf or for the benefit of the underlessee. *Ante*, 287, 288. But the plaintiff may in reply show such underlease to have expired, or to have been duly determined by notice to quit, surrender or otherwise. *Ante*, 300.

11. If the plaintiff be not the original lessee, his derivative title may be disputed. But it will be no defence that at the time of the demise the defendant (being the lessor) really had no right or title to demise; and that he has since acquired a legal title to the property; for the lease would create a demise by estoppel, and the subsequent estate would feed such estoppel: *Doe* d. *Christmas* v. *Oliver,* 5 Man. & R. 202; *Sturgeon* v. *Wingfield*, 15 M. & W. 224; 2 Smith, L. C. 417; *ante*, 221: besides which, a lessor is estopped from denying his title or right to demise. *Ante*, 220.

CHAPTER XLIV.

BY A MORTGAGEE.

1. *Mortgagee* v. *Mortgagor—before Default.*]—A mortgagor who remains in possession after the execution of a mortgage, containing no proviso or stipulation amounting in law to a re-demise, is not considered as a tenant from year to year to the mortgagee, nor even as a tenant at will; he is at most a tenant at sufferance, and may be treated either as a tenant or as a trespasser at the election of the mortgagee, who may maintain ejectment against him without any previous notice to quit or demand of possession. *Doe* d. *Roby* v. *Maisey*, 8 B. & C. 767; 3 M. & R. 107; *Doe* d. *Fisher* v. *Giles*, 5 Bing. 421; 2 Moo. & P. 749; *Smartle* v. *Williams*, 1 Salk. 245; *Melling* v. *Leak*, 16 C. B. 667, Williams, J.; *Doe* d. *Parsley* v. *Day*, 2 Q. B. 147; 2 Gale & D. 757. But the mortgagor may be considered as tenant at sufferance to the mortgagee, to enable the latter to maintain an action on the case against a wrongdoer, for damage done to his reversionary interest. *Partridge* v. *Bere*, 5 B. & A. 604; 1 D. & R. 272; *Hitchman* v. *Walton*, 4 M. & W. 409; *Id.* 415, Parke, B.; *Doe* d. *Higginbotham* v. *Barton*, 11 A. & E. 314; 3 P. & D. 198, *per cur.*; *Tew* v. *Jones*, 13 M. & W. 14, Rolfe, B. And possession by the mortgagor will amount to constructive possession by the mortgagee as against other persons so long as any principal or interest is paid by the mortgagor. 7 Will. 4 & 1 Vict. c. 28; *ante*, 24; *Doe* d. *Smith* v. *Webber*, 1 A. & E. 119; *Doe* d. *Jones* v. *Williams*, 5 A. & E. 291; *Doe* d. *Palmer* v. *Eyre*, 17 Q. B. 366. But the mortgagee cannot before entry maintain *trespass* against the mortgagor, or against any other person, because actual possession, and not merely the right of possession, is necessary to support that form of action. *Wheeler* v. *Montifiore*, 2 Q. B. 133, 156;

Turner v. *Cameron's Coalbrook Steam Coal Company,* 5 Exch. 932; *Lichfield* v. *Ready, Id.* 939.

It seldom happens that an ejectment is brought by the mortgagee against the mortgagor *before any default* in payment of the principal or interest: nevertheless, it may sometimes be necessary or advisable. It should, however, be remembered that a mortgagee, who enters into possession or receipt of the rents, is liable in equity for rents which he might have received but for his wilful neglect or default: he is required to be diligent, in order to restore the estate to the mortgagor. But it is not the practice in equity to direct an account to be taken with charges for wilful default, unless upon a special case made for that purpose, except in the case of a mortgagee in possession. *Lord Kensington* v. *Bouverie,* 25 Law Times R. 169, Lords Js. A mortgagee in possession who opens and works mines will be charged with receipts, but disallowed his expenses. *Thorneycroft* v. *Crocket,* 16 Simon, 445. But where the mortgagee is specially authorized, in case of default, to enter and work the mines, with extensive powers, he will not only be allowed the expenses of so doing, but also interest thereon. *Norton* v. *Cooper,* 25 Law J., N. S., Chanc. 121, Lords Js.

If the mortgage deed contain no proviso or stipulation amounting in law to a re-demise, and the mortgagor remains in possession, an ejectment may be maintained against him before any default; because the mortgagee's estate and right of entry vests immediately upon the execution of the deed, whether the mortgage be in fee; *Doe* d. *Roylance* v. *Lightfoot,* 1 M. & W. 553; *Doe* d. *Parsley* v. *Day,* 2 Q. B. 147; 2 Gale & D. 757; or for a term of years. *Rogers* v. *Grazebrook,* 8 Q. B. 895; and see *Gale* v. *Burnell,* 7 Q. B. 850; *Doe* d. *Parsley* v. *Day, supra.* When a person takes an assignment of a lease by way of mortgage as a security for money lent, the whole interest passes to him, and he becomes liable to the rent and covenants, although he has never occupied or become possessed in fact. *Williams* v. *Bosanquet,* 1 Brod. & B. 238; 3 Moore, 500; *Stone* v. *Evans,* Peake, Add. Cas. 94; *Burton* v. *Barclay and Perkins,* 7 Bing. 745; 5 Moo. & P. 785 (last point). Where the mortgagor remains in possession, and the mortgagee distrains upon him for arrears of interest "as for rent," in pursuance of a power in that behalf in the mortgage deed, but there is no clause that the mortgagor shall continue to hold possession until default, the distress does not amount to such a recognition of the mortgagor as tenant to the mortgagee, as to disentitle the latter to maintain ejectment, without any notice to quit. *Doe* d. *Wilkinson* v. *Goodier,* 10 Q. B. 957; and see *Doe* d. *Garrod* v. *Olley,* 12 A. & E. 481; 4 P. & D. 275. The receipt of interest upon the mortgage up to a certain day does not amount to a recognition of the mortgagor's lawful possession to that time, so as to defeat an ejectment by the mortgagee claiming to be entitled to possession from a previous day. *Doe* d. *Rogers* v. *Cadwallader,* 2 B. & Adol. 473.

If there be any proviso or stipulation in the mortgage deed that the mortgagor shall have quiet possession of the property *for a certain time, ex.gr.* until default of payment on a particular day, and the deed is executed by the mortgagee, it will operate as a re-demise. *Wilkinson* v. *Hall,* 3 Bing. N. C. 504; 4 Scott, 301; *Doe* d. *Lyster* v. *Goldwin,* 2 Q. B. 141; 1 Gale & D. 463. And no ejectment can be maintained by the mortgagee until after default made. *S. C.* The usual proviso for quiet enjoyment by the mortgagor until default, is sufficient. So any other words amounting to an agreement that the mortgagor shall hold or retain possession for a *certain* time or period, amounts in law to a re-demise. *Drake* v. *Munday,* Cro. Car. 207; Bac. Abr. Lease, K.; Arch. L. & T. 19; Shep. Touch. 272. But if the period during which the mortgagor is to hold be uncertain, or be made to depend upon some future event, as the giving of a notice, &c., the agreement or stipulation will amount only to a covenant, and not to a re-demise. Shep. Touch. 272; *Doe* d. *Parsley* v. *Day,* 2 Q. B. 153, 155, *per cur.*; *Doe* d. *Roylance* v. *Lightfoot,* 8 M. & W. 564, Parke, B.; *Gale* v. *Burrell,* 7 Q. B. 850; *Bishop of Bath's case,* 6 Co. R. 6, 34 b.; Cro. Jac. 71, *S. C.* This point appears to have been overlooked in *Wilkinson* v. *Hall,* 3 Bing. N. C. 508; 4 Scott, 301; and in *Doe* d. *Lyster* v. *Goldwin,* 2 Q. B. 143; 1 Gale & D. 463. It seems, however, that a re-demise until default on a certain day may be made defeasible by notice at an earlier day. *Fenn* v. *Bittleston,* 7 Exch. 152; *Brierly* v. *Kendall,* 17 Q. B. 937. No extra stamp duty appears to be payable on a grant or mortgage containing a proviso for occupation by the grantor or mortgagor until default, &c. *Doe* d. *Cross* v. *Tidbury,* 14 C. B. 304 (2nd point). Mere negative words that until default the mortgagee shall not intermeddle with the possession, &c., amount only to a covenant, and not to a re-demise. *Powseley* v. *Blackman,* Cro. Jac. 659, cited 2 Q. B. 154; Shep. Touch. 272.

By deeds of lease and release, dated 7th and 8th September, 1819, lands were mortgaged in fee, subject to a proviso that if the mortgagor should well and truly pay the principal money and interest on the 25th day of March then next, the mortgagee, his heirs and assigns, should and would reconvey and reassure the mortgaged premises to the mortgagor, his heirs and assigns. There was also a covenant that it should be lawful for the mortgagee, his heirs and assigns, from time to time and at all times, *after default* should be made in the payment of the principal money and interest, contrary to the proviso aforesaid, peaceably and quietly to enter into, have, hold, occupy, possess and enjoy the said premises; and also a covenant by the mortgagor for further assurance in case of such default: but there was *no covenant or proviso that the mortgagor should remain in possession until default:* held, that the mortgagee had the right of possession under the mortgage from the time of its execution, and not merely from the 25th March, 1820, and therefore that an ejectment for the recovery of the premises brought by the heir at law of the mortgagee within twenty years of the latter, but not of the former date (no interest having been paid in the mean time), was too late. *Doe* d. *Roylance* v. *Lightfoot,* 8 M. & W. 553. So a mortgage for the residue of a term, to secure 500*l.* and interest on 6th March, 1841, with a power of sale after default and three months' notice, and a covenant for quiet enjoyment by the mortgagee, *after default,* gives him an immediate right (before any default) to enter and maintain ejectment. *Rogers* v. *Grazebrook,* 8 Q. B. 895. A mortgage by bill of sale of goods and chattels to secure 518*l.* to be paid on 1st January, 1845, or on any earlier day to be appointed by a ten days' notice, with a proviso that the mortgagor shall retain possession until default, does not operate as a re-demise, the term or period during which the mortgagor is to retain possession being uncertain, and therefore the mortgagee is legally entitled to recover immediate possession, subject to any remedy against him for breach of covenant. *Gale* v. *Burnell,* 7 Q. B. 850.

If the mortgage deed be *not executed by the mortgagee* (as frequently happens), it cannot amount to a re-demise. 1 Powell on Mortgages, 171 (5th ed.); *Doe* d. *Roylance* v. *Lightfoot,* 8 M. & W. 564; *Id.* 565, Parke, B. But if there be any proviso or stipulation in the deed which would operate as a re-demise if executed by the mortgagee, and the mortgagor continues to occupy, and *pays rent* according to the terms of the deed, a new tenancy from year to year upon the terms of the deed may be implied; and such tenancy will warrant a distress for the rent; *West* v. *Fritchie,* 3 Exch. 216; and will afford a defence to an ejectment by the mortgagee commenced before any determination of such tenancy.

When by the mortgage deed the mortgagor agrees to hold as tenant *at will* to the mortgagee, at a yearly rent, payable quarterly, such tenancy is a strict tenancy at will, and not from year to year; and it will be determined by an entry by the mortgagee to take possession, or by a demand of possession, or by an assignment of the mortgagee's estate, made with the concurrence of the mortgagor, or with notice thereof to him. *Doe* d. *Dixie* v. *Davies,* 7 Exch. 89; *Doe* d. *Baston* v. *Cox,* 11 Q. B. 122; *Pinhorn* v. *Souster,* 8 Exch. 138. So by any other act whereby a tenancy at will may be determined. *Doe* d. *Davies* v. *Thomas,* 6 Exch. 854; *ante,* 452. But a mere assignment by either party of his estate and interest, without any notice thereof to the other, is not sufficient. *Pinhorn* v. *Souster, supra.* Such tenancy must have been legally determined by entry, or demand of possession or otherwise, before the mortgagee can maintain ejectment against the mortgagor, no default having been made in payment of the money secured by the mortgage.

. After Default.]—A mortgagor who remains in possession after the execution of the mortgage, and makes default in payment of the money thereby secured on the appointed day, may at any time afterwards be ejected by the mortgagee without any previous notice to quit or demand of possession. *Doe* d. *Fisher* v. *Giles,* 5 Bing. 421; 2 Moo. & P. 749; *Doe* d. *Roby* v. *Maisey,* 8 B. & C. 767. The mortgagor after such default is at most tenant at sufferance to the mortgagee, and may be treated either as such tenant or as a trespasser at the election of the mortgagee. *S. C.; ante,* 462.

Where certain lands were mortgaged in fee, and other lands for a long term, to secure 550*l.* with interest on the 5th October then next; but if not then paid it should be lawful for the mortgagee, *after giving one month's notice,* to enter into possession, and demise or sell the property; and the mortgagee covenanted not to let or sell until default made after one month's notice: held, that after the 5th October the mortgagee might maintain ejectment against the mortgagor *without any notice,* there being no re-demise for any certain period after that day. *Doe* d. *Parsley* v. *Day,* 2 Q. B. 147; 2 Gale & D. 757. So where a mortgage in fee contained an attornment by the mortgagor to the mortgagee as his tenant at a quarterly rent, recoverable by distress or action, "for better securing the principal money and all interest and expenses, and in contemplation and part discharge thereof," with a power of immediate entry and sale by the mortgagee upon default of payment: held, that immediately after such default the mortgagee or his assignee might, in pursuance of the power, enter or maintain ejectment against the mortgagor's representative, without any notice to quit. *Doe* d. *Snell and Short* v. *Tom,* 4 Q. B. 615; 3 Gale & D. 637,

(1) See Brown v. H. Metropolitan Counties Life Assurance Soc: 1 SC. 4 El. 832. and Turner v. Barnes 2 B&S. 435

By a deed of covenant to surrender copyholds by way of mortgage to secure 850*l.* with interest on the 11th July, 1836, with a reservation of a yearly rent of 50*l.* payable half yearly and recoverable by distress; and a proviso that such reservation of rent should not prejudice the right of the mortgagee to enter and evict the mortgagor at any time after default. The mortgagee distrained for rent: held, that notwithstanding such reservation of rent and distress, the mortgagee (who had been admitted under a surrender made pursuant to the covenant) might, after default made, evict the mortgagor without any notice to quit. *Doe* d. *Garrod* v. *Olley*, 12 A. & E. 481; 4 P. & D. 275. Generally speaking, the exercise of a *collateral power* to distrain "as for rent" will not affect the mortgagee's right to enter or maintain ejectment without any notice to quit or demand of possession. *Doe* d. *Wilkinson* v. *Goodier*, 10 Q. B. 957.

A mortgagee of copyholds cannot maintain ejectment before admittance, for until then he has no legal estate, or legal right to possession. *Roe* d. *Jefferys* v. *Hicks*, 2 Wils. 13, 15; *post*, Chap. LXVII. s. 2. It is not sufficient for this purpose that the conditional surrender to him has been entered on the court rolls, although that is all that is usually done until it becomes necessary to bring ejectment, or to sell the property. But the admittance, when made, relates back to the time of the surrender, and will support an ejectment claiming title from any day subsequent to the surrender, although the action be commenced before the admittance. *Holdfast* d. *Woollams* v. *Clapham*, 1 T. R. 600; *Doe* d. *Bennington* v. *Hall*, 16 East, 208; *post*, Chap. LXVII. s. 2. A mortgage of copyholds by a common law conveyance, without any surrender or admittance, passes only an *equitable* estate, and will not enable the mortgagee to maintain ejectment against the mortgagor, or any person claiming through or under him; especially if it appear on the face of the deed, by the recitals, or otherwise, that the property is copyhold, and has not been enfranchised. *Doe* d. *North* v. *Webber*, 3 Bing. N. C. 922.

Ejectment cannot be maintained against a railway or other company by a mortgagee "of the *undertaking*, and of the rates, tolls and other sums arising under the act," for no land or building is conveyed by such mortgage. *Doe* d. *Myatt* v. *The St. Helen's and Runcorn Gap Railway Company*, 2 Q. B. 364; 2 Railw. C. 756. But it is otherwise where a mortgage is of toll houses or toll gates, which are subjects of demise known to the law, and in which a legal estate may pass. *Doe* d. *Banks* v. *Booth*, 2 Bos. & P. 219; *Doe* d. *Thompson* v. *Lediard*, 4 B. & Adol. 137. A prior mortgage cannot be used to defeat an ejectment by a subsequent mortgagee, for the company, trustees or commissioners (as the case may be) are estopped by their deed from setting up the fact of an earlier mortgage to defeat the legal estate of their mortgagee. *Doe* d. *Watton* v. *Penfold*, 3 Q. B. 757; *Doe* d. *Levy* v. *Horne*, Id. 757, 760. A second or subsequent mortgagee of a bridge, and of the tolls thereof, may maintain ejectment against the commissioners. *S. C.* A mortgagee of turnpike tolls, toll houses, &c., who brings ejectment pursuant to 3 Geo. 4, c. 126, s. 49, cannot be defeated by a subsequent ejectment brought by the defendant as a mortgagee, with judgment therein by default, and a writ of possession executed before the trial of the first ejectment. At all events the plaintiff is entitled to a verdict and judgment in such ejectment, although, perhaps, not to sue out and execute a writ of *habere facias possessionem. Doe* d. *Butt* v. *Rous,* 1 E. & B. 419. As to the remedy by action to recover the mortgage money and interest, see *Horton* v. *The Westminster Improvement Commissioners,* 7 Exch. 780; *Pontet* v. *The Basingstoke Canal Company,* 3 Bing. N. C. 433; 4 Scott, 182.

Assignees of the mortgagee have the same right of entry and eject-ment against the mortgagor and his tenants as the mortgagee himself would have had if no assignment had been made by him. *Thunder* d. *Weaver* v. *Belcher,* 3 East, 449. But a transferee of a mortgage of turnpike tolls, in the general form given by the 3 Geo. 4, c. 126, s. 81, has no title until such transfer has been produced and notified to the clerk or treasurer of the trustees, and entered in the proper book kept by such clerk or treasurer. *Doe* d. *Jones* v. *Jones,* 5 Exch. 16.

Stay of Proceedings upon Payment of Principal, Interest and Costs, &c.] – By 15 & 16 Vict. c. 76, s. 219, " where an action of eject-ment shall be brought by any mortgagee, his heirs, executors, admi-nistrators or assignees, for the recovery of the possession of any mort-gaged lands, tenements and hereditaments, and *no suit shall be then depending* in any of her majesty's courts of equity in that part of Great Britain called England, for or touching the foreclosing or redeeming of such mortgaged lands, tenements or hereditaments; if the person *having right to redeem* such mortgaged lands, tenements and heredita-ments, and *who shall appear and become defendant* in such action, shall, at any time pending such action, pay unto such mortgagee, or, in case of his refusal, shall bring into court where such action shall be depending all the principal monies and interest due on such mortgage, and also all such costs as have been expended in any suit at law or in equity upon such mortgage (such money for principal, interest and costs to be ascertained and computed by the court where such action is or shall be depending, or by the proper officer by such court to be appointed for that purpose), the monies so paid to such mortgagee, or brought into such court, shall be deemed and taken to be in full satis-faction and discharge of such mortgage, and the court shall and may discharge every such mortgagor or defendant of and from the same accordingly; and shall and may, by rule of the same court, compel such mortgagee, at the costs and charges of such mortgagor, to assign, surrender or reconvey such mortgaged land, tenements and heredita-ments, and such estate and interest as such mortgagee has therein, and deliver up all deeds, evidences and writings in his custody relating to the title of such mortgaged lands, tenements and hereditaments, unto such mortgagor who shall have paid or brought such monies into the court, his heirs, executors or administrators, or to such other person or persons as he or they shall for that purpose nominate or appoint."

By sect. 220, " nothing herein contained shall extend to any case where the person against whom the redemption is or shall be prayed shall (by writing under his hand, or the hand of his attorney, agent or solicitor, to be delivered before the money shall be brought into such court of law, to the attorney or solicitor for the other side) insist, either that the party praying a redemption has not a right to redeem, or that the premises are chargeable with other or different principal sums than what appear on the face of the mortgage, or shall be admitted on the other side; or to any case where the right of redemption to the mortgaged lands and premises in question in any cause or suit shall be controverted or questioned by or between different defendants in the same cause or suit; or shall be any prejudice to any subsequent mortgage or subsequent incumbrance, anything herein contained to the contrary thereof in anywise notwithstanding."

These two sections correspond, as nearly as possible, with the 7 Geo. 2, c. 20, ss. 1, 3, so far as such last-mentioned sections relate to actions of ejectment. But where an action is brought on a bond for payment of the money secured by the mortgage, or performance of the covenants therein contained, any application to compel the mortgagee to receive the amount of his principal, interest and costs, must still be made under 7 Geo. 2, c. 20, which extends also to actions of covenant. *Dixon* v. *Wigram*, 2 Cr. & Jer. 613; *Smeeton* v. *Collier*, 1 Exch. 457; 5 Dowl. & L. 184; *Filbee* v. *Hopkins*, 6 Dowl. & L. 264; *Sutton* v. *Rawlings*, 3 Exch. 407; 6 Dowl. & L. 673. Neither of the above enactments apply where the mortgagee has entered into possession and attempted to sell the property under a power of sale. *Sutton* v. *Rawlings*, *supra.* Indeed the ejectment must be brought "for the recovery of the possession of the mortgaged lands, tenements or hereditaments," to warrant an application under sect. 219. On the other hand, the court will not stay the proceedings on payment of principal, interest and costs, where the mortgagor has agreed to convey the equity of redemption to the mortgagee. *Goodtitle* d. *Taysum* v. *Pope*, 7 T. R. 185; *Infra.*

If any suit be depending in any court of equity in England "for or touching the foreclosing or redeeming" of the mortgage, an application to compel the mortgagee to receive his principal, interest and costs, should be made to that court. 7 Geo. 2, c. 20, s. 2; *Doe* d. *Harrison* v. *Louch*, 6 Dowl. & L. 276, *per* Coleridge, J.

The application under sect. 219 may be made either to the court in banc or to a judge at chambers. *Smeeton* v. *Collier*, 1 Exch. 457; 5 Dowl. & L. 184; *Felton* v. *Ash*, Barnes' Notes, 177; *Doe* d. *Tubb* v. *Roe*, 4 Taunt. 887; *Doe* d. *Capps* v. *Capps*, 3 Bing. N: C. 768. In such cases the judge acts as the deputy of the court.

The application cannot be made before the party having the right to redeem *has appeared, and become a defendant in the action*—this is a condition precedent. *Doe* d. *Hurst* v. *Clifton*, 4 A. & E. 814; 6 N. & M. 857; *Doe* d. *Tubb* v. *Roe*, 4 Taunt. 887; *Doe* d. *Cox* v. *Brown*, 6 Dowl. 471. Therefore, if the action be brought against the mortgagor's tenant in possession, the mortgagor must obtain leave to appear and defend as landlord. If he have omitted to do so before judgment has been signed for want of appearance by his tenant, he must make a special application to the court or a judge to set aside such judgment and let him in to defend as landlord, so that he may be in a condition to apply under sect. 219. *Doe* d. *Tubb* v. *Roe*, 4 Taunt. 887; *ante*, 115, 132.

The application under sect. 219 may be made at any time after appearance, and before final judgment; even after verdict. *Doe* d. *Hurst* v. *Clifton*, 4 A. & E. 814; 6 N. & M. 857. But not after final judgment. 2 Chit. Arch. 1007 (9th ed.); *Ames* v. *Lloyd*, 2 Ves. & B. 15.

The application can be made only by or on behalf of the mortgagor or other person for the time being "having right to redeem" the mortgaged property. *Goodtitle* d. *Fisher* v. *Bishop*, 1 You. & Jer. 344; *Skinner* v. *Stacey*, 1 Wils. 80; *Goodtitle* d. *Taysum* v. *Pope*, 7 T. R. 185; *Doe* d. *Harrison* v. *Louch*, 6 Dowl. & L. 270.

The application should be supported by a proper affidavit or affidavits. The material points to be attended to in drawing the affidavit are as follows: it must state the particulars of the mortgage, *ex. gr.* the date, parties, parcels, sum secured, the arrears due, &c. It must show that the plaintiff is mortgagee, or the heir, executor, administrator or assignee of the mortgagee, and that the action is brought for the recovery of the possession of the mortgaged property; and that the defendant is the mortgagor, or derives title through him (showing how) and has the right to redeem the mortgage, and that he has entered an appearance to the ejectment as tenant in possession, or as landlord of the tenant in possession. It should show to what extent the ejectment has proceeded, so that it may appear the action is still pending, and that final judgment by default, or otherwise, has not been obtained. It should state that no suit is depending in any of her majesty's courts of equity in that part of Great Britain called England for or touching the foreclosing or redeeming of the mortgaged property. It does not appear necessary to swear to any tender of the principal, interest and costs to the plaintiff, or any refusal on his part to accept thereof, because the amount to be tendered must be ascertained by the court, or by one of the masters, before a proper tender can be made. *Filbee* v. *Hopkins*, 6 D. & L. 268, Patteson, J. There seems, however, to have been some misapprehension on this point. It certainly is not the usual practice for the defendant to tender at his peril such sum as he considers due for principal, interest and costs, and to obtain a refusal of the sum tendered *before* making the application, and to state such tender and refusal in the affidavit. But this was done in *Doe* d. *Harrison* v. *Louch*, 6 Dowl. & L. 270.

The rule nisi or summons should follow the language of sect. 219 as closely as possible. *Goodright* d. *Tonkyn* v. *Moore*, Barnes' Notes, 176; *see the forms, Appendix, Nos.* 83, 85, 87; Tidd's Forms, 672 (8th ed.); Ad. Eject. 320.

In answer to the application, the plaintiff may show by affidavit or otherwise:—1. That there is some defect in the defendant's affidavits, either in the title or the jurat, or in the body thereof. *Doe* d. *Cox* v. *Brown*, 6 Dowl. 471; *Filbee* v. *Hopkins*, 6 Dowl. & L. 204, 266; *see post, Appendix, No.* 19, *notes.* 2. That there is some suit depending in chancery for or touching the foreclosing or redeeming of the mortgage. *Ante*, 467. 3. That the applicant has not appeared and made himself a defendant in the ejectment. *Ante*, 468. 4. That the action is not pending, final judgment having been obtained. *Ante*, 468. 5. That the applicant has no right to redeem the mortgage; *ante*, 468; and that a written notice insisting on that point has been served, pursuant to sect. 220. *Ante*, 467. But such notice must state the facts or reasons why the defendant has no right to redeem; otherwise it will be insufficient. *Doe* d. *Harrison* v. *Louch*, 6 Dowl. & L. 270; *see the form, Appendix, No.* 88. 6. That the premises are chargeable with other or different principal sums than what appear on the face of the mortgage; and that a written notice insisting on that point has been served, pursuant to sect. 220. *Ante*, 467. But such notice should state the nature and amount of the ulterior demand, "for if the sum claimed is admitted it is no longer an objection to the order being made; and the defendant must know the claim, otherwise he cannot admit it. Besides, we are to see that a real demand is set up, of a nature which cannot be determined in this summary method; for if the mere insisting on further charges were sufficient, the intention of the act would be wholly defeated." *Per* Macdonald, C. B., in *Goodtitle d. Leon* v. *Lansdown*, 3 Anstr. 937, 939. Therefore a notice merely stating that the premises are charged with other sums than those appearing on the face of the mortgage, or that the mortgagor has no right to redeem (not stating for what reason), is insufficient. *Doe* d. *Harrison* v. *Louch*, 6 Dowl. & L. 270. But a proper notice may be given after the summons or rule nisi has been obtained. *Filbee* v. *Hopkins*, 6 Dowl. & L. 264. A second mortgage to another person, with notice thereof, will not be sufficient to prevent the mortgagor from staying an ejectment by the first mortgagee and obtaining the deeds, upon payment of the principal, interest and costs due to him. *Dixon* v. *Wagram*, 2 Cr. & Jer. 613. A mortgagor or his assignee is entitled to relief under this act without payment of a bond debt due from him to the mortgagee, not charged upon the property. But the mortgagor's heir or executor would not be relieved without payment of both debts. *Archer* d. *Hankey* v. *Snapp*, Andrews, 341; 2 Stra. 1107, *S. C.; Bingham* d. *Lane* v. *Gregg*, Barnes' Notes, 182. Where bond debts are, by agreement or otherwise, charges or liens upon the mortgaged property, that may be shown as an answer to the application. *Felton* v. *Ash*, Barnes' Notes, 177. Where there are two or more mortgages from the same person, who has become bankrupt, the court will not compel the plaintiff to permit one of them to be redeemed by the assignees, without the other or others. *Roe* d. *Kaye* v. *Soley*, 2 W. Black. 726. If the plaintiff claim to be entitled to interest subsequent to the payment into court of his principal, interest and costs, and until the reconveyance be executed, he should apply for such interest at the time the summons or rule nisi is disposed of. *Jordan* v. *Chowns*, 8 Dowl. 709. The master ought not, under the usual rule or order, to allow the plaintiff any interest due *before* the mortgage, and not thereby secured; nor the expense of the mortgage deed; nor the expense of any assignments of the mortgage; *Doe* d. *Blagg* v. *Steel*, 1 Dowl. 359; nor the expense of any declaration of trust by the mortgagee to his *cestui que trust*, on whose behalf the loan was made. *Martin's case*, 5 Bing. 160; 2 Moo. & P. 240. 7. The plaintiff may show that the right of redemption is "controverted or questioned by or between different defendants in the same cause or suit." Sect. 220; *ante*, 467. But this can seldom, if ever, happen in an ejectment. This part of sect. 220 is copied, without due consideration, from 7 Geo. 2, c. 20, s. 3, which has reference to sect. 2. of that act. 8. The plaintiff may show that if the defendant be permitted to redeem upon payment of the principal, interest and costs due to the plaintiff, that will prejudice some subsequent mortgage or subsequent incumbrance. Sect. 220; *ante*, 467. But such prejudice may generally be obviated by an indorsement on one or more of the deeds, before the delivery thereof to the defendant. *Dixon* v. *Wagram*, 2 Cr. & Jer. 613.

Cause is shown in the usual manner, and the application may be dismissed with or without costs, at the discretion of the court or judge. *Filbee* v. *Hopkins*, 6 Dowl. & L. 269. If an order or rule absolute be granted, it should be drawn up and served by the defendant or his attorney in the usual manner. *See the forms, Appendix, Nos.* 84, 86. An appointment to proceed thereon should be forthwith obtained from one of the masters, and a copy served on the plaintiff, or his attorney or agent.

The master ought not to allow any interest due before the mortgage, and not thereby secured; nor the expense of the mortgage deed; nor the expense of any assignment of the mortgage. *Doe* d. *Blagg* v. *Steel*, 1 Dowl. 359: nor the expense of any declaration of trust by the mortgagee to his *cestui que trust*, on whose behalf the loan was made: *Martin's case*, 5 Bing. 160; 2 Moo. & P. 240: nor any interest beyond the time when the money will be paid to the plaintiff, or, in case of his refusal, into court. *Jordan* v. *Chowns*, 8 Dowl. 709. But he will allow the costs of any suit in chancery to foreclose or redeem the mortgage; and, if necessary, the taxing master of that court will tax and ascertain the amount of such costs, which taxation the common law master will adopt. The plaintiff's costs of the ejectment should be taxed as between party and party, and not as between attorney and client. *Doe* d. *Capps* v. *Capps*, 3 Bing. N. C. 768. The master should allow the plaintiff his costs of and incident to any reconveyance that may be necessary, and should also settle and approve of the draft of such reconveyance, in case the parties differ about the same, provided the rule or order so directs. If the master decide erroneously on any point, his decision may be reviewed by the court. *Doe* d. *Blagg* v. *Steel*, 1 Dowl. 359.

The amount ascertained by the master's report to be due for principal, interest and costs should be forthwith tendered to the plaintiff, together with a proper deed of reconveyance to be executed by him. If he refuse to accept the money and to execute the deed, the amount should be immediately paid into court. After which an application may be made to compel the plaintiff within a specified time to execute the reconveyance, and to deposit it and the other title deeds and writings in his possession with the master; and also to pay the costs of the application. *Jordan* v. *Chowns*, 8 Dowl. 709.

Evidence for Plaintiff.]—To maintain ejectment against the mortgagor, the mortgagee must prove :—

1. The mortgage. This must either be admitted in the cause (*ante*, 150), or proved in the usual manner. *Ante*, 294; *Doe* d. *Garnons* v. *Knight*, 5 B. & C. 671; 8 D. & R. 348. It must be duly stamped. 13 & 14 Vict. c. 97, Sched. part 1, tit. "Mortgage;" *Doe* d. *Merceron* v. *Bragg*, 8 A. & E. 620; 3 N. & P. 644; *Doe* d. *Bartley* v. *Gray*, 3 A. & E. 89; 4 N. & M. 719; *Doe* d. *Scruton* v. *Snaith*, 8 Bing. 146; 1 Moo. & Sc. 230; *Doe* d. *Jarman* v. *Larder*, 3 Bing. N. C. 92; 3 Scott, 407; *Wroughton* v. *Turtle*, 11 M. & W. 561; 1 Dowl. & L. 473; *Doe* d. *Bowman* v. *Lewis*, 13 M. & W. 241; *Doe* d. *Snell* v. *Jones*, 4 Q. B. 615; 3 Gale & D. 637; *Paddon* v. *Bartlett*, 2 A. & E. 9; 4 N. & M. 1; *Lawrance* v. *Boston*, 7 Exch. 28; *Morgan* v. *Pike*, 14 C. B. 473. Generally speaking, the recitals in a mortgage are sufficient evidence against the mortgagor of the matters thereby recited, and any deeds therein mentioned need not be produced, nor the mortgagor's title otherwise proved. *Doe* d. *Rogers* v. *Brook*, 3 A. & E. 513; *Doe* d. *Pember* v. *Wagstaff*, 7 C. & P. 477. So the recitals in an assignment of the mortgage are evidence of the mortgage itself as against the parties to the assignment, or their subsequent tenants or assigns. *Doe* d. *Brame* v. *Maple*, 3 Bing. N. C. 832; 5 Scott, 35.

2. If the plaintiff be an assignee of the mortgagee, the transfer or assignment to him must be admitted in the cause (*ante*, 150), or proved in the usual manner. *Ante*, 294; *Doe* d. *Dixie* v. *Davies*, 7 Exch. 89; *Smartle* v. *Williams*, 1 Salk. 245; *Saloway* v. *Strawbridge*, 24

Law J., N. S., Chan. 393, Wood, V. C.; *Doe* d. *Rogers* v. *Brooks,* 3 A. & E. 513. It must be duly stamped. 13 Vict. c. 94, Sched. part 1, tit. "Mortgage;" *Doe* d. *Brame* v. *Maple,* 3 Bing. N. S. 832; 5 Scott, 35; *Doe* d. *Barnes* v. *Rowe,* 4 Bing. N. C. 737; 6 Scott, 525; *Martin* v. *Baxter,* 5 Bing. 160; 2 Moo. & P. 240; *Brown* v. *Pegg,* 6 Q. B. 1; *Doe* d. *Snell* v. *Jones,* 4 Q. B. 615; 3 Gale & D. 637; *Doe* d. *Crawley* v. *Gutteridge,* 17 Law J., N. S., Q. B. 99; *Sellick* v. *Trevor,* 11 M. & W. 722; *Doe* d. *Gaisford* v. *Stone,* 3 C. B. 176, 177.

3. The identity of the property comprised in the mortgage with that sought to be recovered, or some part thereof: *ante,* 240, 289: but if the description in the writ be applicable to the property described in the deed, no further evidence of identity appears to be necessary. 2 Arch. N. P. 422.

4. If the mortgage contain any proviso or stipulation amounting to a *re-demise for a certain period, ex. gr.,* until default of payment on a particular day, it must appear that default has been made, or that the tenancy has otherwise ceased. *Ante,* 463. But this is unnecessary if the stipulation amount only to a covenant, and not to a re-demise, it being for an uncertain period, depending upon subsequent notice, &c. *Ante,* 464.

The defendant, being tenant in possession under a lease for fourteen years, assigned the lease by way of mortgage to the plaintiff, and then committed a forfeiture, for which the lessor brought ejectment. It was agreed at a meeting of all the parties that judgment should be signed in the ejectment, that the lessor should grant a new lease to the plaintiff, and that the plaintiff should grant an underlease to the defendant. The new lease was accordingly granted to the plaintiff, who then delivered the key to the defendant, saying, "Go on as usual; pay the money" (due on the mortgage), "and when you have done so you shall have an underlease:" held, that this did not constitute the defendant a tenant from year to year. *Doe* d. *Rogers* v. *Pullen,* 2 Bing. N. C. 749; 3 Scott, 271.

5. It must appear that the plaintiff's title is not barred by the Statute of Limitations. *Ante,* 24; *Doe* d. *Gallop* v. *Vowles,* 1 Moo. & Rob. 261; *Doe* d. *Roylance* v. *Lightfoot,* 8 M. & W. 553.

Evidence and Points for Defendant.]—The defendant may contend :—1. That the evidence for the plaintiff is not sufficient on some material point. *Ante,* 471. He may also produce contradictory evidence. 2. That the action was not commenced within the twenty years allowed by 3 & 4 Will. 4, c. 27; and that there has been no payment of principal or interest, or other acknowledgment of the mortgagee's title, within that time. 7 Will. 4 & 1 Vict. c. 28; *ante,* 24; *Doe* d. *Roylance* v. *Lightfoot,* 8 M. & W. 553; *Doe* d. *Gallop* v. *Vowles,* 1 Moo. & Rob. 261. 3. That there has been no default, and that the mortgage contains a re-demise until default, or for some other *certain* period which has not elapsed. *Ante,* 463. 4. That before action the plaintiff assigned all his estate and interest in the property to some third person, not being one of the claimants. But the defendant is estopped from proving that at the time of the mortgage some third person really was entitled to the property, and from whom he has since obtained a lease. *Doe* d. *Ogle* v. *Vickers,* 4 A. & E. 782; 5 N. & M. 437. So neither the mortgagor, nor any person claiming through or under him, or defending the ejectment for his benefit, can be permitted to prove a prior mortgage to a third person in order to defeat the subsequent mortgage to the claimant. *Ante*, 221 ; *Doe* d. *Hurst* v. *Clifton*, 4 A. & E. 813 ; *Doe* d. *Gaisford* v. *Stone*, 3 C. B. 176 ; *Lindsey* v. *Lindsey*, Bull. N. P. 110 ; and see *Doe* d. *Leeming* v. *Skirrow*, 7 A. & E. 157 ; 2 N. & P. 123. Even public commissioners, &c., are estopped from setting up a prior mortgage to defeat a subsequent mortgage executed by them. *Doe* d. *Walton* v. *Penfold*, 3 Q. B. 757 ; *Doe* d. *Levy* v. *Horne, Id.* 757, 760. But there will be no such estoppel if the second mortgage recite the first, or mention it as an existing incumbrance. Co. Lit. 352 b ; Vin. Abr. Estoppel, A 2 ; *Doe* d. *North* v. *Webber*, 3 Bing. N. C. 922, 925 ; *Right* d. *Jefferys* v. *Bucknell*, 2 B. & Adol. 278 ; *Pargeter* v. *Harris*, 7 Q. B. 708 ; *Hermitage* v. *Tomkins*, 1 Lord Raym. 729. The trustees of a public turnpike act, which empowers them to erect toll houses and mortgage *the tolls*, and which declares that there shall be no priority among the creditors, have no power to mortgage the toll houses or gates. If, in fact, they have made such a mortgage, and an ejectment is brought against them by the mortgagee, they are not estopped by their deed from insisting that the act gives them no such power. *Fairtitle* d. *Mytton* v. *Gilbert*, 2 T. R. 169. Where a subsequent mortgagee of toll houses, &c., recovers in ejectment, he will hold as a trustee for parties having prior charges thereon. *Doe* d. *Thompson* v. *Lediard*, 4 B. & Adol. 137 ; 1 N. & M. 683. A mortgage executed by A., B., C., D. and E., as trustees of a turnpike road, is not invalidated by showing that A., who had acted as a trustee for many years, had not been appointed under seal, as required by the local act. *Doe* d. *Baggaley* v. *Hares*, 4 B. & Adol. 435 ; 2 N. & M. 237. A mortgagor cannot show that the mortgage was void by reason of any fraud to which he was party or privy. *Doe* d. *Roberts* v. *Roberts*, 2 B. & A. 367. But he may prove that he was induced to execute the deed by fraud, covin and misrepresentation of the mortgagee, and others in collusion with him. *Doe* d. *Woodhead* v. *Fallows*, 2 Cro. & Jer. 481 ; 2 Tyr. 460.

2. *Mortgagee against Prior Tenants of the Mortgagor.*]—A mortgage of property held by tenants of the mortgagor under leases for years, or tenancies from year to year created before the mortgage, conveys to the mortgagee *only the reversion and its incidents.* The mortgagee does not thereby acquire any *right of possession* which the mortgagor did not previously possess. *Rogers* v. *Humphreys*, 4 A. & E. 299 ; *Id.* 313, Lord Denman, C. J. ; 5 N. & M. 511, *S. C.* The tenants, without any attornment, immediately become tenants to the mortgagee ; 4 Anne, c. 16, s. 9 ; *ante*, 229 ; but they may safely continue to pay their rents to the mortgagor until they receive notice from the mortgagee of the grant or assignment to him. *Id.* s. 10 ; *Cook* v. *Moylan*, 1 Exch. 67 ; 5 Dowl. & L. 101 ; *see the forms, Appendix, Nos.* 7, 8. Until such notice is given the mortgagor has implied authority from the mortgagee to collect, and also to distrain for, the rent which becomes due subsequent to the mortgage. *Trent* v. *Hunt*, 9 Exch. 14. And whatever rents the mortgagor is so permitted to receive he is entitled to retain for his own use, without being liable to account for them to the mortgagee, either at law or in equity. *Ex parte Wilson*, 2 Ves. & B. 252 ; *Trent* v. *Hunt, supra.* But the mortgagee may at any time give notice of

his mortgage to the tenants, and require them to pay him all the arrears then due and all subsequent rents ; *see the forms, Appendix, Nos.* 7, 8 ; and thereupon he will be entitled to distrain or sue for all such arrears, &c. *Moss* v. *Gallimore*, 1 Doug. 279 ; 1 Smith's L. C. 310 ; *Rogers* v. *Humphreys*, 4 A. & E. 299, 313 ; 5 N. & M. 511 ; and see *Pope* v. *Biggs*, 9 B. & C. 245 ; *Lloyd* v. *Davies*, 2 Exch. 103. He may give a tenant from year to year notice to quit, or sue him for use and occupation ; *Burrows* v. *Graden*, 1 Dowl. & L. 213, 218 ; *Rawson* v. *Eiche*, 7 A. & E. 451 ; 2 N. & P. 423 ; 2 Arch. N. P. 422 ; but it would seem that the mortgagor cannot give such notice otherwise than in the name and as agent of the mortgagee, with his authority. *Trent* v. *Hunt*, 9 Exch. 14. If a tenant for years be guilty of any act or omission whereby his term becomes void or voidable under a proviso or condition in his lease, the mortgagee (not the mortgagor) may maintain ejectment for the forfeiture ; *Doe* d. *Marriott* v. *Edwards*, 5 B. & Adol. 1065 ; *Doe* d. *Prior* v. *Ongley*, 10 C. B. 25 ; but so long as any term or tenancy created before the mortgage remains unexpired, and not determined by notice to quit, forfeiture, or otherwise, it will be a bar to any ejectment by the mortgagee for the premises to which such term or tenancy relates. *Doe* d. *Da Costa* v. *Wharton*, 8 T. R. 2. In Lord *Mansfield's* time a mortgagee was allowed to give the tenants notice that he did not intend to disturb their possession, and thereupon to maintain ejectment. *White* d. *Whatley* v. *Hawkins*, Bull. N. P. 96 ; *Roe* d. *Bristow* v. *Pegg*, 4 Doug. 309, 311. But this doctrine has long been exploded ; 4 Doug. 314, note (*e*) ; 1 Smith's L. C. 295, note (*a*) ; *Doe* d. *Da Costa* v. *Wharton*, 8 T. R. 2. The proper mode of proceeding is to give the tenant notice of the mortgage, and to distrain or sue for the rent when it becomes due. *Supra.*

Evidence for Plaintiff.]—The mortgagee must prove :—

1. The mortgage. This must be duly stamped and admitted in the cause (*ante*, 150), or proved in the usual manner. *Ante*, 294.

2. The lease or tenancy of the defendant. This must be proved in the same manner as in an action by a landlord against his tenant for a forfeiture. *Ante*, 319, 419.

3. That the defendant held the premises sought to be recovered, or some part thereof, under or by virtue of the lease or agreement. *Ante*, 240, 289. This may be proved by showing that he took possession thereof as tenant after the date of the lease or agreement ; or that he has paid part of the rent thereby reserved ; or by an admission of the defendant as to his tenancy or holding under the lease or agreement. Where A. mortgaged to B., and C. afterwards wrote a memorandum on the mortgage to the effect that he had purchased the equity of redemption and charged the same with a further sum : held, in ejectment by B., that both A. and C. were estopped from disputing B.'s title. *Doe* d. *Gaisford* v. *Stone*, 3 C. B. 176 ; 15 Law J., N. S., C. P. 234.

4. That the term granted by the lease to defendant expired or became forfeited by reason of some act or omission of the defendant before or on the date of the claimant's title as alleged in the writ. The evidence on this point must be the same as in an ejectment by a landlord against his tenant for a forfeiture. *Ante*, 400.

5. If the tenancy were from year to year it must be shown to have

been duly determined by a regular notice to quit. *Ante,* 29; *Doe* d. *Bowman* v. *Lewis,* 13 M. & W. 241; 2 Dowl. & L. 667.

Evidence and Points for Defendant.]—The defendant may contend:—1. That the evidence for the plaintiff is not sufficient on some material point. *Ante,* 474. He may also produce contradictory evidence, showing that his term has not expired or been determined by due notice to quit, or forfeited as alleged. He may also defend himself by showing that there had been a *prior mortgage,* and that he had received notice from the prior mortgagee to pay rent to him, and had paid it accordingly; because the defendant does not thereby deny that the mortgagor who gave him possession had title, but simply that the plaintiff has *not a good derivative title. Doe* d. *Higginbotham* v. *Barton,* 11 A. & E. 307; 3 P. & D. 194. So also a tenant who has been let into possession by the second mortgagee himself may show such prior mortgage and notice; for the tenant thereby admits that his lessor, with respect to the first mortgagee, was in substance mortgagor in possession, not then treated as a trespasser, and so had title to demise; and the tenant is at liberty to go on to show that his lessor has subsequently been treated as a trespasser by the first mortgagee, whereby his (the lessor's) title and the tenant's rightful possession under him have been determined. *S. C.*

3. *Mortgagee against Subsequent Tenants of the Mortgagor.*]—A mortgagee may recover in ejectment, without giving notice to quit, against a tenant who claims under a lease from the mortgagor granted after the mortgage without the privity of the mortgagee. *Keech* v. *Hall,* 1 Doug. 21; 1 Smith, L. C. 293, 295, notes; *Thunder* d. *Weaver* v. *Belcher,* 3 East, 449. The reason is, that a tenant who comes in under the mortgagor, after the mortgage, cannot be in a better condition than the mortgagor himself, who is no more than a tenant at sufferance, not entitled to any notice to quit; and one tenant at sufferance cannot make another. *Id.* 451, *per* Lord Ellenborough, C. J. *A fortiori* he cannot demise for a term of years which shall be valid as against the mortgagee. *Doe* d. *Hughes* v. *Bucknell,* 8 C. & P. 566, Patteson, J. It makes no difference that the tenant has subsequently expended money on improvements, and that the mortgagee has occasionally gone to look at such improvements, for that is not of itself evidence for a jury that he has accepted the lessee as his tenant. *Doe* d. *Parry* v. *Hughes,* 11 Jur. 698.

But if the mortgagee have done any act with the concurrence of the tenant in possession *whereby a new tenancy has been created between them,* he cannot, during the continuance of such tenancy, eject the tenant. Thus, if he have demanded from the tenant payment of his rent, and the tenant has submitted to such demand, whereby a new tenancy from year to year has been impliedly created. *Doe* d. *Hughes* v. *Bucknell,* 8 C. & P. 566; *Doe* d. *Higginbotham* v. *Barton,* 11 A. & E. 307; 3 P. & D. 194, 199; *Doe* d. *Bowman* v. *Lewis,* 13 M. & W. 241. If upon such demand being made the tenant does not dissent, but continues in possession, and subsequently offers to pay the rent, that amounts to evidence from which the jury may infer and find assent. *Brown* v. *Storey,* 1 Man. & Gr. 117, 126; and see *Roberts* v. *Hayward,* 3 C. & P. 432; *Doe* d. *Whitaker* v. *Hales,* 7 Bing. 322;

5 Moo. & P. 132. But as the relation of landlord and tenant cannot be created without the assent of both parties (being founded upon a contract between them, express or implied), the mortgagee cannot, by merely giving notice of his mortgage to the tenant, and requiring the rent to be paid to him (to which the tenant does not assent), entitle himself to distrain or sue for the rent; his only remedy is to bring ejectment. *Evans* v. *Elliott*, 9 A. & E. 342; 1 P. & D. 256; *Rogers* v. *Humphrys*, 4 A. & E. 299; 5 N. & M. 511; *Partington* v. *Woodcock*, 6 A. & E. 690; 5 N. & M. 672; *Doe* d. *Higginbotham* v. *Barton*, 11 A. & E. 307; 3 P. & D. 194; 1 Smith, L. C. 317. If by threatening to eject the tenant, or "to put the law in force" (which means the same thing), he can induce the tenant to pay him the arrears of rent, the tenant may plead such compulsory payment to an action or distress by the mortgagor for the same rent. *Waddilove* v. *Barnett*, 2 Bing. N. C. 538, 572; 2 Scott, 763; 4 Dowl. 347, *S. C.; Johnson* v. *Jones*, 9 A. & E. 809; 1 P. & D. 651. In replevin the plea should be *riens in arrere*. *Jones* v. *Morris*, 3 Exch. 742. The reason is, that such compulsory payment in respect of a debt due from the mortgagor, and from which he ought to have protected his tenant, is equivalent to a payment to the mortgagor himself, or to his agent having authority implied by law to receive the same on his behalf. *Id.* 747. But the rent must be actually paid by the tenant to the mortgagee before a plea of *riens in arrere*, or a special plea of payment, can be supported. *Wheeler* v. *Branscomb*, 5 Q. B. 373; 1 Dav. & M. 406; *Wilton* v. *Dunn*, 17 Q. B. 294; 21 Law J., N. S., Q. B. 60. And such payment must have been made in consequence of a threat of the above nature, otherwise it will not be deemed compulsory. *Whitmore* v. *Walker*, 2 Car. & K. 615 (2nd point), Patteson, J. A threat *to distrain* for the rent might not be deemed sufficient, because the mortgagee had no legal right to distrain. *Supra.* But a threat "to put the law in force" would be construed as a threat to eject. *Johnson* v. *Jones*, 9 A. & E. 809; 1 P. & D. 651. Moreover, the payment must have been made to a mortgagee or incumbrancer to whom the landlord was liable for some debt or incumbrance charged on the property; not to a third person claiming as purchaser under a conveyance from the landlord prior to the demise. *Boodle* v. *Campbell*, 7 Man. & Gr. 386; 8 Scott, N. R. 104; 2 Dowl. & L. 66.

If by a threat or otherwise the mortgagee prevail on a tenant of the mortgagor to attorn and pay his rent to him (the mortgagee), that will not operate to confirm the lease held by the tenant for the whole term of years thereby granted, but only to create a new tenancy from year to year as between the mortgagee and the tenant. *Doe* d. *Hughes* v. *Bucknell*, 8 C. & P. 567, Patteson, J.; *Doe* d. *Prior* v. *Ongley*, 10 C. B. 25 (3rd point). Such new tenancy will be subject to the terms and conditions of the lease previously held by the tenant, so far as the same are at all applicable to a yearly tenancy. *Doe* d. *Thompson* v. *Amey*, 12 A. & E. 476; 4 P. & D. 177; *Doe* d. *Davenish* v. *Moffatt*, 15 Q. B. 257, 265. But the payment of rent will not relate back to the date or service of the notice of the mortgage, &c., so as to make the new tenancy commence from that time. *Evans* v. *Elliott*, 9 A. & E. 342; 1 P. & D. 256. For the purpose of a notice to quit, the new tenancy will be deemed to have commenced from the same day in the year as the original term. *Doe* d. *Collins* v. *Weller*, 7 T. R. 478.

Where a tenant attorns expressly as from a previous specified day, at a fixed rent, a distress may be made for the rent calculated from that day. *Gladman* v. *Plumer*, 15 Law J., N. S., Q. B. 80.

When a new tenancy from year to year has been created as between the mortgagee and the tenant, the mortgagee is thenceforth the landlord, and may distrain or sue for the rent; *Rogers* v. *Humphreys*, 4 A. & E. 299; 5 N. & M. 511; *Brown* v. *Storey*, 1 Man. & Gr. 117, 126; 1 Scott, N. R. 9; or maintain an action for use and occupation. *Doe* d. *Lord Downe* v. *Thompson*, 9 Q. B. 1037. But he cannot maintain ejectment against the tenant until the new tenancy has been determined by notice to quit, surrender, forfeiture or otherwise (*ante*, 474). Afterwards he may. *Doe* d. *Lord Downe* v. *Thompson*, 9 Q. B. 1037.

The receipt of *interest* on a mortgage does not amount to a recognition by the mortgagee of the lawful possession of the mortgagor or his tenants up to the time when such interest became due, so as to preclude him from maintaining an ejectment, claiming a right of possession from a previous day. *Doe* d. *Rogers* v. *Cadwallader*, 2 B. & Adol. 473. Even a distress for interest "as for rent," in pursuance of a power in the mortgage deed, is not sufficient to bar an ejectment. *Doe* d. *Wilkinson* v. *Goodier*, 10 Q. B. 957; *Doe* d. *Garrod* v. *Olley*, 12 A. & E. 481; 4 P. & D. 275. But if the mortgagee or his attorney or agent apply to the tenant in possession *for his rent* to pay interest due on the mortgage, and obtain payment thereof under threat of a distress, and so *avails himself of the possession of the tenant*, he cannot maintain an ejectment, claiming possession from an earlier period. *Doe* d. *Whitaker* v. *Hales*, 7 Bing. 322; 5 Moo. & P. 132.

Where by a lease for years the mortgagee demised, and the executrix of the mortgagor demised and confirmed, and a power of re-entry for breaches of covenant was reserved *to them or either of them:* held, that it operated as the demise of the mortgagee, and the confirmation of the mortgagor's representative; that the re-entry for breach of covenant enured to revest the estate in the mortgagee only; and that a count in ejectment laying the demise *jointly in the two*, could not be supported. *Doe* d. *Barney* v. *Adams*, 2 Cr. & Jer. 232; 2 Tyr. 289. But the result would be different under 15 & 16 Vict. c. 76, s. 180. *Ante*, 285.

Evidence for Plaintiff.]—The mortgagee must prove :—

1. The mortgage. This must be duly stamped, and admitted in the cause (*ante*, 150), or proved in the usual manner. *Ante*, 294.

2. That the defendant came into possession of the premises sought to be recovered, or some part thereof, under the mortgagor, as his tenant or by his permission, after the execution of the mortgage. If the lease or agreement under which the defendant holds can be proved, so much the better. He should have notice to produce it at the trial, or he may be served with a *subpœna duces tecum*.

3. If any new tenancy as between the mortgagee and the defendant has been created subsequent to the mortgage by payment of rent or otherwise (*ante*, 475), it must be proved that such tenancy has been determined by notice to quit, disclaimer, surrender, forfeiture, or otherwise, before or on the day of the claimant's right to possession as alleged in the writ. *Ante*, 288.

4. If the claimant be an assignee of the mortgagee, the transfer to him must be proved. *Thunder* d. *Weaver* v. *Belcher*, 3 East, 450.

Evidence and Points for Defendant.]—1. The defendant may raise the same points as the mortgagor (*ante*, 472). 2. He may contend that the plaintiff's proofs are insufficient upon some material point (*ante*, 477), and he may produce contradictory evidence. 3. He may prove that a new tenancy has been created since the mortgage as between himself and the mortgagee, and may insist that such tenancy has not expired, or been determined by notice to quit, forfeiture or otherwise (*ante*, 475). 4. He is estopped in the same manner as the mortgagor from proving that, before and at the time of the execution of the mortgage, the legal title, or the right to possession, was and still is outstanding in some third person (*ante*, 221). The reason is that estoppels bind, not only parties to the deed, but also their privies in estate, *i. e.*, persons claiming through or under them. *Trevivan* v. *Lawrence*, 1 Salk. 276; *Taylor* v. *Needham*, 2 Taunt. 278; *Pargeter* v. *Harris*, 7 Q. B. 708, 723; *Doe* d. *Viscount Downe* v. *Thompson*, 9 Q. B. 1037.

4. *Mortgagee against Subsequent Mortgagee.*]—The first mortgagee, whether in fee or for a term of years, may maintain ejectment against any subsequent mortgagee who has *taken possession*, claiming under a second or subsequent mortgage from the same mortgagor, because the latter incumbrance passes only the equity of redemption, or the reversion. The fact that the subsequent incumbrancer obtained possession under an ejectment against the mortgagor who remained in possession after the first mortgage, makes no difference. 1 T. R. 756 (*Goodtitle* v. *Morgan*); and see *Doe* d. *Smith* v. *Webber*, 1 A. & E. 119; 3 N. & M. 746. But the subsequent incumbrancer may file a bill or claim in equity to redeem the prior mortgage, and for relief against the ejectment upon equitable terms; 2 Chit. Eq., Index, 1451 —1455 (3rd ed.); or he may apply to the court in which the ejectment is brought for relief, pursuant to 15 & 16 Vict. c. 76, s. 219 (*ante*, 467). A first mortgagee ought, without a judicial proceeding, to accept payment from a second mortgagee, and thereupon to convey to him the mortgaged estate, with or without the concurrence of the mortgagor. *Smith* v. *Green*, 1 Collyer, 555; but see *Ramsbottom* v. *Wallis*, 5 Law J., N. S., Chanc. 92.

The plaintiff must prove:—

1. The mortgage to himself. This must be duly stamped, and admitted in the cause (*ante*, 150), or proved in the usual manner. *Ante*, 294.

2. That the mortgagor was in actual possession before or at the time of such mortgage; or in receipt of the rents and profits, and that the tenancies to him have expired, or been duly determined by notices to quit, surrender or otherwise.

3. The subsequent mortgage to the defendant need not be proved; nevertheless, it is often advisable to do so: he should at all events have notice to produce it at the trial; and the claimant should be prepared with evidence to show *when* the defendant took possession: the exact day is not material, but it must appear to have been after the date and execution of the first mortgage. If the defendant be shown to have obtained possession through or under the mortgagor, that may estop him from denying the plaintiff's title to the same extent as the mortgagor himself would have been estopped. *Ante*, 221. If the defendant be not estopped, as above mentioned, he may prove any outstand-

ing term or estate created before the first mortgage, and under which possession has been had at any time within twenty years before the commencement of the action. *Ante*, 288, 228. Such evidence will render it necessary for the plaintiff to prove that such term or estate has been assigned, surrendered or conveyed to the mortgagor or to himself, or to one of the plaintiffs, or that the term has become *satisfied*, and has ceased and determined, pursuant to 8 & 9 Vict. c. 112. *Ante*, 227.

Prior to the last-mentioned act, it was decided that a second mortgagee, who had no notice of the first mortgage at the time of taking the security to himself, and who obtained the title deeds, and also took an assignment of a term to attend the inheritance created before the first mortgage, might use such term in support of an ejectment against the first mortgagee. *Goodtitle* d. *Norris* v. *Morgan*, 1 T. R. 755. He might also have used it in defence of an ejectment brought by the first mortgagee.

Any existing term or tenancy created by the first mortgagee (*ante*, 475) may be proved to defeat an ejectment at his suit; unless, indeed, his tenant be joined in the action as one of the plaintiffs.

In *Middlesex*, mortgages and other incumbrances have priority according to the times when they are registered: *Westbrook* v. *Blythe*, 3 E. & B. 737; *Hughes* v. *Lumley*, 4 E. & B. 274: so in Yorkshire.

5. *Mortgagee against Strangers.*]—To entitle a mortgagee to maintain ejectment against a third person, who was in possession before the mortgage otherwise than as the tenant or agent of the mortgagor, the evidence must be the same as in ordinary cases between strangers. It must show that at the time of the mortgage the mortgagor was legally entitled to actual possession of the property; or that he had the right to dispose of such possession in the events which have happened. *Doe* d. *Harris* v. *Saunder*, 5 A. & E. 664; 1 N. & P. 119. And the deed of mortgage must be admitted in the cause (*ante*, 150), or proved in the usual manner. *Ante*, 294.

A *primâ facie* case may be established by proof that the mortgagor was in actual possession, or in receipt of the rents and profits, on some day within twenty years before the commencement of the action; *ante*, 211; and that he afterwards executed a mortgage of the property to the plaintiff; *ante*, 231; and that the term of the tenant from whom the rents and profits were received has expired, or been duly determined by notice to quit, surrender or otherwise.

If the defendant obtained possession *after* the date and execution of the mortgage (not as tenant or agent of the mortgagor, or of the mortgagee), the proofs must be similar to those above mentioned. If the mortgagor remained in possession until the defendant obtained possession, evidence to that effect, coupled with proof of the mortgage, will establish a *primâ facie* case. *Doe* d. *Smith* v. *Webber*, 1 A. & E. 119 (last point). If the mortgagee had taken possession before the defendant entered, evidence to that effect, with proof of the mortgage, will establish a *primâ facie* case. But in either instance such case might be rebutted as above mentioned.

If it can be shown that the defendant, although not a tenant of the mortgagor, really defends for his benefit, he will be estopped from denying the mortgagee's title in the same manner as the mortgagor himself. *Doe* d. *Hurst* v. *Clifton*, 4 A. & E. 813.

Proof by the defendant that *after* the date and execution of the mortgage he recovered possession of the property against the mortgagor (who remained in possession), by ejectment or by arbitration between them, will not be sufficient to defeat the action. Indeed, such evidence would be inadmissible as against the mortgagee. *Doe d. Smith* v. *Webber,* 1 A. & E. 119. The defendant may prove a previous conveyance or mortgage to himself, duly executed by the mortgagor; *Doe* d. *Harris* v. *Saunder,* 5 A. & E. 664; 1 N. & P. 119; or that the mortgagor first acquired the legal estate after the mortgage to the plaintiff; and that the mortgagor afterwards conveyed such legal estate to the defendant, as a purchaser for value, without notice of the mortgage to the plaintiff. *Right* d. *Jefferys* v. *Bucknell,* 2 B. & Adol. 278; *Doe* d. *Oliver* v. *Powell,* 1 A. & E. 531; 3 N. & M. 616.

*CHAPTER XLV.

BY A MORTGAGOR.

1. *Mortgagor* v. *Mortgagee.*]—If the mortgage deed contain a redemise for a certain period (*ante*, 463), and be executed by the mortgagee (*ante*, 464), and the mortgagee enter and take possession during such demise, and before any default (*ante*, 465), an ejectment may be maintained against him by the mortgagor. But such a case very seldom, if ever, happens. The ejectment must be commenced and the *writ served* before the term has ceased by default or otherwise. 15 & 16 Vict. c. 76, s. 181. *Ante*, 289; *Doe* d. *Gardner* v. *Kennard*, 12 Q. B. 244.

If the principal and interest secured by the mortgage be paid punctually on the appointed day, and by the terms of the deed it is *to be void* on such payment, the mortgagor may afterwards maintain ejectment against the mortgagee, if he remain in possession. But if the money be not paid until after the appointed day, or if the deed provide for a reconveyance, there must be a reconveyance from the mortgagee to the mortgagor before the latter can maintain ejectment. If there be any difficulty in obtaining such reconveyance the remedy is in equity.

2. *Mortgagor* v. *Tenant.*]—A lessor cannot maintain ejectment for a forfeiture against a tenant for years after he has assigned his reversion by way of mortgage. *Doe* d. *Marriott* v. *Edwards*, 6 C. & P. 208; 5 B. & Adol. 1065. It makes no difference that the mortgagee has not given the tenant notice of the mortgage, pursuant to 4 A...ii. c. 16, s. 10, *S. C.* A landlord cannot, after executing ɛ .mortgage, give a previous tenant from year to year notice to quit, and thereupon maintain ejectment, unless, indeed, the mortgage contain a *redemise for a term certain*, which has not ceased. *Doe* d. *Lyster* v. *Goldwin*, 2 Q. B. 143; *Id.* 155.

With respect to leases and tenancies subsequent to the mortgage, the tenant would be estopped from denying his landlord's title: therefore he would not be permitted to defeat an ejectment by the lessor for a forfeiture by merely proving the prior mortgage. *Alchorne* v. *Gomme*, 2 Bing. 54; 9 Moo. 143; *Doe* d. *Leeming* v. *Skirrow*, 7 A. & E. 157. But he may prove such mortgage and notice thereof, and that the mortgagee threatened to eject him, and so compelled him to attorn before the writ was served: *Doe* d. *Higginbotham* v. *Barton and Warburton*, 11 A. & E. 307; 3 P. & D. 194: for such evidence'

Y

does not show that the plaintiff had no right to demise to the defendant, but only that his title was defeasible and has since been legally defeated. *Ante,* 217.

3. *Mortgagor* v. *Strangers.*]—The legal estate being in the mortgagee, an ejectment cannot be maintained in the name of the mortgagor, except, perhaps, under circumstances similar to those in which the action might be maintained against the mortgagee himself. *Ante,* 481. Even then the title must be proved as in ordinary cases.

CHAPTER XLVI.

BY HEIR AT LAW.

By 3 & 4 Will. 4, c. 106, intituled " An Act for the Amendment of the Law of Inheritance," it is enacted, as follows :—

Definition of Terms.]—Sect. 1. " That the words and expressions hereinafter mentioned, which in their ordinary signification have a more confined or a different meaning, shall in this act, except where the nature of the provision or the context of the act shall exclude such construction, be interpreted as follows; (that is to say,) the word ' *land*' shall extend to manors, advowsons, messuages and all other hereditaments, whether corporeal or incorporeal, and whether freehold or copyhold, or of any other tenure, and whether descendible according to the common law, or according to the custom of gavelkind or borough-English, or any other custom, and to money to be laid out in the purchase of land, and to chattels and other personal property transmissible to heirs; and also to any share of the same hereditaments and properties or any of them, and to any estate of inheritance, or estate for any life or lives, or other estate transmissible to heirs, and to any possibility, right or title of entry or action, and any other interest capable of being inherited, and whether the same estates, possibilities, rights, titles and interests or any of them shall be in possession, reversion, remainder or contingency ; and the words ' *the purchaser*' shall mean the person who last acquired the land otherwise than by descent, or than by any escheat partition or inclosure by the effect of which the land shall have become part of or descendible in the same manner as other land acquired by descent; and the word ' *descent*' shall mean the title to inherit land by reason of consanguinity, as well where the heir shall be an ancestor or collateral relation, as where he shall be a child or other issue; and the expression '*descendants*' of any ancestor shall extend to all persons who must trace their descent through such ancestor; and the expression '*the person last entitled*' to land shall extend to the last person who had a right thereto, whether he did or did not obtain the possession or the receipt of the rents and profits thereof; and the word '*assurance*' shall mean any deed or instrument (other than a will) by which any land shall be conveyed or transferred at law or in equity; and every word importing the singular number only shall extend and be applied to several persons or things as well as one person or thing; and every word importing the masculine gender only shall extend and be applied to a female as well as a male."

Root of Descent.]—Sect. 2 enacts, "that in every case descent shall be traced *from the purchaser;* and to the intent that the pedigree may never be carried further back than the circumstances of the case and the nature of the title shall require, the person last entitled to the land shall, for the purposes of this act, be considered to have been the purchaser thereof, unless it shall be proved that he inherited the same, in which case the person from whom he inherited the same shall be considered to have been the purchaser, unless it shall be proved that he inherited the same; and in like manner the last person from whom the land shall be proved to have been inherited shall in every case be considered to have been the purchaser, unless it shall be proved that he inherited the same."

According to the previous law, when a person inherited an estate from his mother, and died intestate, it would go to *his heirs ex parte maternâ: Goodtitle* d. *Castle* v. *White*, 2 B. & P. New R. 383; *Doe* d. *Northey* v. *Harvey*, Ry. & Moo. 297: unless he had, by some conveyance or assurance, broken the descent, in which case the estate would descend *ex parte paternâ. Doe* d. *Harman* v. *Morgan*, 7 T. R. 103; and see *Doe* d. *Crosthwaite* v. *Dixon*, 5 A. & E. 834; 1 N. & P. 255. Now the descent is to be traced *from the mother*, and not from the heir.

Where land descends to the son of an illegitimate father, who is proved to have been the purchaser thereof, and the son dies seised, intestate and without issue, such land does not devolve upon his heirs *ex parte maternâ. Doe* d. *Blackburn* v. *Blackburn*, 2 Moo. & Rob. 547, Parke B.; Sug. R. P. Stat. 268.

Devise to Heir—Limitation to Grantor.]—Sect. 3 enacts, "that when any land shall have been devised by any testator, who shall die after the 31st day of December, 1833, to the heir or to the person who shall be the heir of such testator, such heir shall be considered to have acquired the land as a devisee, and not by descent; and when any land shall have been limited, by any assurance executed after the said 31st day of December, 1833, to the person or to the heirs of the person who shall thereby have conveyed the same land, such person shall be considered to have acquired the same as a purchaser by virtue of such assurance, and shall not be considered to be entitled thereto as his former estate or part thereof."

For the previous law, see *Reading* v. *Rawsterne*, 2 Ld. Raym. 829; *Doe* d. *Harman* v. *Morgan*, 7 T. R. 103; *Doe* d. *Pratt* v. *Timins*, 1

B. & A. 530; *Doe* d. *Crosthwaite* v. *Dixon*, 5 A. & E. 834; 1 N. & P. 255; Sug. R. P. Stat. 270.

A devisee takes as a purchaser, and if he die before entry his heir may inherit. *Doe* d. *Parker* v. *Thomas*, 3 Man. & Gr. 815, 821; 4 Scott, N. R. 449. A devisee of a contingent remainder, which becomes vested on his birth, takes as a purchaser, and, notwithstanding his death under age, his heir may inherit. *Foster* v. *Hayes*, 4 E. & B. 717.

Limitation to Heirs as Purchasers.]—Sect. 4 enacts, "that when any person shall have acquired any land by purchase under a limitation to the heirs, or to the heirs of the body, of any of his ancestors, contained in an assurance executed after the said 31st day of December, 1833, or under a limitation to the heirs, or to the heirs of the body, of any of his ancestors, or under any limitation having the same effect, contained in a will of any testator who shall depart this life after the said 31st day of December, 1833, then and in any of such cases such land shall descend, and the descent thereof shall be traced as if the ancestor named in such limitation had been the purchaser of such land."

There was before this enactment a *quasi* descent in such cases; but now the ancestor is to be treated as the first purchaser, although he never had any interest in the land. Sug. R. P. Stat. 271.

Brothers and Sisters.]—Sect. 5 enacts, "that no brother or sister shall be considered to inherit immediately from his or her brother or sister, but every descent from a brother or sister shall be traced through the parent."

In consequence of this and the next enactment, a father takes as heir in preference to his eldest son. Formerly the eldest brother might, as heir, have recovered by ejectment in the father's lifetime. *Doe* d. *Fleming* v. *Fleming*, 4 Bing. 266; *ante*, 236.

Lineal Ancestors admitted.]—Sect. 6 enacts, "that every lineal ancestor shall be capable of being heir to any of his issue; and in every case where there shall be no issue of the purchaser, his nearest lineal ancestor shall be his heir in preference to any person who would have been entitled to inherit, either by tracing his descent through such lineal ancestor, or in consequence of there being no descendant of such lineal ancestor, so that the father shall be preferred to a brother or sister, and a more remote lineal ancestor to any of his issue, other than a nearer lineal ancestor or his issue."

For the previous law see Chief Baron Hale's argument in *Collingwood* v. *Pace*, 1 Ventr. 413; 1 Steph. Com. 390 (3rd ed.). The maxim was, *Hæreditas nunquam ascendit.* Broom, Max. 229; 2 Black. Com. 211; Lit. s. 3; Co. Lit. 11 b.

Male Line.]—Sect. 7 enacts and declares, "that none of the maternal ancestors of the person from whom the descent is to be traced, nor any of their descendants, shall be capable of inheriting until all his paternal ancestors and their descendants shall have failed; and also that no female paternal ancestor of such person, nor any of her descendants, shall be capable of inheriting until all his male paternal ancestors and their descendants shall have failed; and that no female maternal ancestor of such person, nor any of her descendants, shall be capable of inheriting until all his male maternal ancestors and their descendants shall have failed."

The maternal line can seldom be reached, except where the person last seised, or last entitled to the land, *inherited the same ex parte maternâ*, in which case he is not to be deemed "the purchaser," or the person from whom the descent is to be traced. *Ante*, 484. According to the previous law the descent was to be traced *from the heir, but ex parte maternâ. Goodtitle* d. *Castle* v. *White*, 2 B. & P. New R. 383. Now, when the mother or any maternal relation is ascertained to be "the purchaser," the descent must be traced *from her:*—1. In her descending line. 2. In her paternal line. 3. In her maternal line.

Mother of Paternal Ancestor.]—Sect. 8 enacts and declares, "that where there shall be a failure of male paternal ancestors of the person from whom the descent is to be traced, and their descendants, the mother of his more remote male paternal ancestor, or her descendants, shall be heir or heirs of such person, in preference to the mother of a less remote male paternal ancestor, or her descendants; and where there shall be a failure of male maternal ancestors of such person and their descendants, the mother of his more remote male maternal ancestor, and her descendants, shall be the heir or heirs of such person, in preference to the mother of a less remote male maternal ancestor, and her descendants."

This section settles a disputed point in accordance with Blackstone's well-known view. 2 Black. Com. 238; 1 Steph. Com. 396; Sug. R. P. Stat. 273; *Davies* v. *Lowndes*, 5 Bing. N. C. 169.

Admission of Half Blood.]—Sect. 9 enacts, "that any person related to the person from whom the descent is to be traced by the half blood shall be capable of being his heir; and the place in which any such relation by the half blood shall stand in the order of inheritance, so as to be entitled to inherit, shall be next after any relation in the same degree of the whole blood and his issue where the common ancestor shall be a male, and next after the common ancestor where such common ancestor shall be a female, so that the brother of the half blood on the part of the father shall inherit next after the sisters of the whole blood on the part of the father and their issue, and the brother of the half blood on the part of the mother shall inherit next after the mother."

As the law before stood, the half blood (like the lineal ancestor) were totally excluded, and the land would escheat rather than go to any of them. 1 Steph. Com. 401; 2 Black. Com. 232, 233; Broom, Max. 232.

Attainted Blood.]—Sect. 10 enacts, "that when the person from whom the descent of any land is to be traced shall have had any relation who, having been attainted, shall have *died before such descent* shall have taken place, then such attainder shall not prevent any person from inheriting such land who would have been capable of inheriting the same, by tracing his descent through such relation, if he had not been attainted, unless such land shall have escheated in consequence of such attainder before the 1st day of January, 1834." See *post*, Chap. LIX.

Commencement of Act.]—Sect. 11 enacts, "that this act shall not extend to any descent which shall take place on the death of any person who shall die before the said first day of January, 1834."

Limitations before 1st January, 1834.]—Sect. 12 enacts, "that where any assurance executed before the said first day of January, 1834, or the will of any person who shall die before the same first day of January, 1834, shall contain any limitation or gift to the heir or heirs of any person, under which the person or persons answering the description of heir shall be entitled to an estate by purchase, then the person or persons who would have answered such description of heir, if this act had not been made, shall become entitled by virtue of such limitation or gift, whether the person named as ancestor shall or shall not be living on or after the said first day of January, 1834."

Table of Descents.]—For a table of descents according to the above act, see 1 Steph. Com. 414 (3rd ed.); Shelf. R. P. Stat. 425 (4th ed.); and for a good form of pedigree in a particular case, see *Angell* v. *Angell,* 9 Q. B. 331; *Doe* d. *Daniel* v. *Woodroffe,* 2 H. L. Cas. 815; *Wills* v. *Palmer,* 5 Burr. 2625; *post,* 489.

Evidence for Plaintiff.]—In ejectment by an heir at law, or by any person claiming through or under him, the plaintiff is generally entitled to begin. *Ante,* 284. But if the defendant admit that the ancestor died seised, and that the plaintiff is his heir at law, and the defendant relies on a will of such ancestor, the validity of which is disputed by the plaintiff, the defendant is entitled to begin. *Doe* d. *Woollaston* v. *Barnes,* 1 Moo. & Rob. 386; *Doe* d. *Smith* v. *Smart, Id.* 476. When the plaintiff begins, he must prove—

1. The *seisin or title* of the person last entitled to the land. *Ante,* 211; *Doe* d. *Hallen* v. *Ironmonger,* 3 East, 533; *Doe* d. *Payne* v. *Plyer,* 14 Q. B. 512.

Formerly the maxim was *seisina facit stipitem;* and therefore the inheritance was to be traced from the person who last died actually seised of the freehold and inheritance. Co. Lit. 11 b; *Jenkins* d. *Harris* v. *Pritchard,* 2 Wils. 45; 2 Black. Com. 209; Broom, Max. 226. There was no rule better known in Westminster Hall than this, "that a man that claimeth as heir in fee simple to any man by descent must make himself heir to him that was last seised of the actual freehold and inheritance." *Per* Lord Alvanley, C. J., in *Doe* d. *Andrew* v. *Hutton,* 3 Bos. & P. 648, citing Co. Lit. 15 b. The person last seised was he who was last in possession by himself or his tenant, or had received rent, or exercised some act of ownership, as entry, &c. 2 Black. Com. 209. But a devisee in fee being considered as a purchaser had, without an actual entry, such a seisin of the premises devised as would have enabled his heir to take from him by descent. *Doe* d. *Parker* v. *Thomas,* 3 Man. & Gr. 815, 821; 4 Scott, N. R. 449; *Foster* v. *Hayes,* 4 E. & B. 717. So a remainderman or reversioner, who died before his estate fell into possession, was sufficiently seised to enable such estate to descend to his heir. *Per* Lord Alvanley, C. J., in *Doe* d. *Andrew* v. *Hutton,* 3 Bos. & P. 648, citing Hale's MSS. in the Notes to Hargrave & Butler's Co. Lit. 14; and see *Strong* d. *Cummin* v. *Cummin,* 2 Burr. 767. Now the descent is, in every case, to be traced from the purchaser, *i. e.* from the person *last entitled* to the land, whether he did or did not obtain the possession, or the receipt of the rents and profits thereof, unless it be proved that he inherited the same. *Ante*, 484. If therefore a "seisin" of the person last entitled cannot be proved (he never having obtained actual or constructive possession), his *title* must be proved by deed, will, or by evidence of his pedigree, &c.; *Roe* d. *Thorne* v. *Lord*, 2 W. Black. 1099; and if it thereby appear that he inherited the property (*ante*, 484), or took it under a limitation in a deed or will to the heirs or to the heirs of the body of any of his ancestors, the descent must be traced from such ancestor (*ante*, 485), notwithstanding such person "shall be considered to have acquired the land as a purchaser or devisee, and not by descent. *Ante*, 484.

It is most important to ascertain correctly who is "the purchaser," or other the person from whom the descent is to be traced pursuant to 3 & 4 Will. 4, c. 106, s. 2 (*ante*, 484), as explained by sect. 1 (*ante*, 483), or as specially mentioned in the particular cases provided for by ss. 3, 4, 5. *Ante*, 484, 485.

2. The *death of the ancestor* must be proved in the usual manner; *ante*, 239; for *nemo est hæres viventis*. Co. Lit. 8 a; *Id*. 22 b; Broom, Max. 223. Letters of administration are not *primâ facie* evidence of the death. *Ante*, 239.

It need not be proved that the ancestor died *intestate*, for that will be presumed in the absence of evidence to the contrary. Hubback, Ev. of Succession, 64. If he left a will, that may be proved by the defendant as part of his defence. *Doe* d. *Chillcott* v. *White*, 1 East, 33; *Doe* d. *Lewis* v. *Lewis*, 1 Car. & K. 122. And in reply the plaintiff may show that such will was afterwards revoked; *Doe* d. *Gosley* v. *Gosley*, 2 Moo. & Rob. 243; 9 C. & P. 46; *ante*, 300; or that it was void, as to the particular devise, under the Mortmain Act; *Doe* d. *Burdett* v. *Wrighte*, 2 B. & A. 710; or that all the estates limited by the will have expired; *Turnough* v. *Stock*, 11 Exch. 37; or he may raise any objection to the will in like manner as a defendant sued by a devisee. *Post*, Chap. XLVII.

3. The descent or pedigree of the heir. *Roe* d. *Thorne* v. *Lord*, 2 W. Black. 1099. *Hæres legitimus est quem nuptiæ demonstrant*. Co. Lit. 76; Broom, Max. 219. Such title is generally proved by examined copies of the registers of the marriages, baptisms and burials (or deaths) of the several persons mentioned in the pedigree, together with evidence of identity. Hearsay evidence of pedigree is admissible. *Ante*, 234. We have already considered the mode of proving a marriage (*ante*, 236), a birth or baptism (*ante*, 239), and a death. (*Ante*, 239.) Proof of a death is not *primâ facie* evidence that the party died *without issue*. The latter is a distinct fact, which must, when material, be proved by evidence of reputation or otherwise. *Richards* v. *Richards*, 15 East, 294, note (*a*); *ante*, 240.

In making a title by pedigree, evidence that a man has not been heard of for many years is sufficient *primâ facie* to prove him dead without issue. *Rowe* v. *Hasland*, 1 W. Black. 404. After a great lapse of time parties will be presumed to be dead without issue, in the absence of any evidence to the contrary. *Doe* d. *Oldham* v. *Wolley*, 8 B. & C. 22; 3 C. & P. 402; *Doe* d. *Banning* v. *Griffen*, 15 East, 293; *ante*, 240. In pedigree cases an old will, by which the testator purports to leave all his property to collateral relations or friends, is very strong evidence of his having died without children. *Hungate*

v. *Gascoigne*, 2 Phil. R. 25; 15 Law J., N. S., Chanc. 382. Members of a family named in a marriage settlement 100 years old, and not mentioned in subsequent wills, &c., may be presumed to be dead without issue. *Doe* d. *Oldham* v. *Wolley*, *supra*.

A sketch or outline of the pedigree should generally be prepared. See the forms in *Angell* v. *Angell*, 9 Q. B. 231; *Doe* d. *Daniel* v. *Woodroffe*, 2 H. L. Cas. 815; *Wills* v. *Palmer*, 5 Burr. 2625; *ante*, 487. It is frequently advisable to prepare the pedigree in two forms, viz., one for the use of the judge and jury, showing only the parties through whom the descent is actually traced; and another for the use of counsel, comprising the former, but adding the collateral relations who have died without issue. In framing a pedigree to prove a collateral descent, first ascertain which of the ancestors were brothers, or brother and sister, or sisters, *and place their father at the top*. The dates of the birth, marriage and death of each party should be mentioned, so far as may appear necessary.

In tracing the pedigree *up* from "the purchaser" to the common ancestor, *all* the brothers and sisters, and half brothers and sisters of the respective parties through whom the pedigree is traced, up to the grandchildren of the common ancestor inclusive, must be proved to be *dead without issue*. 2 Arch. N. P. 355; *Richards* v. *Richards*, 15 East, 294, note (*a*). But in tracing the descent *down* from the common ancestor to the claimant, only the respective parties through whom the descent is traced, and their respective senior brothers (if any), must be proved to be *dead without issue*. 2 Arch. N. P. 355.

If the descent be traced through a female who had sisters or a sister still alive, or dead leaving issue still living, the claimant can recover only the share or proportion to which his mother or other female ancestor, if living, would have been entitled. 2 Arch. N. P. 351, 355.

When only one particular link in the pedigree is disputed, much expense may sometimes be saved by admissions made in writing before the trial (*see the form, Appendix, No.* 190); but if no such admissions be made, it may be expected, that at the trial, that particular link of the pedigree will be attacked, with respect to which the evidence is most insufficient, although not the one really in dispute between the parties. There is, however, no mode of *compelling* such admissions, except as to the certificates of baptisms, marriages and burials, which the opposite party should be called on to inspect and admit in the usual manner. *Ante*, 150.

On the trial of an issue as to the legitimacy of a child born of a married woman, the evidence of husband or wife to prove *access* or *non-access* is inadmissible. *Wright* v. *Holdgate*, 3 Car. & K. 158, Cresswell, J.; *Rex* v. *The Inhabitants of Sourton*, 5 A. & E. 180, 190; *Goodright* d. *Stevens* v. *Moss*, 2 Cowp. 594. So neither of them will be permitted to prove facts showing opportunities or want of opportunities of access. *Cases supra.* And expressions of feeling by the wife towards the husband are inadmissible. *Wright* v. *Holdgate, supra.* A wife who has a child born within three months after her marriage may be asked generally how long she had been acquainted with her husband before the marriage: but if she answers "upwards of a year," no further question can be put to her tending to disprove such access between the parties as might have resulted in the birth of a child. *A.* v. *A.*, 25 Law J., N. S., Chanc. 136, note. When a married woman has a child, the presumption is in favour of its legitimacy. Formerly the presumption was, that if the husband continued within the four seas, and was alive at the child's birth, such child could not be a bastard. But now the law allows inquiry ; the rule, however, being that those who dispute the fact of the child's legitimacy are bound to make out the contrary. The illegitimacy of a child born of a married woman is established beyond all dispute by evidence of her living in adultery at the time when the child was begotten, and of her husband then residing in another part of the kingdom, so as to make access impossible. *Barony of Say and Sele,* 1 H. L. Cas. 507. If the jury are satisfied that intercourse took place between the husband and wife at such times as in the course of nature to account for the birth of the child, such child must be taken to be the husband's child, although during the same period other men may have had intercourse with the mother. *Wright* v. *Holdgate,* 3 Car. & K. 158, Cresswell, J.; *Morris* v. *Davis,* 5 Cl. & Fin. 163 ; *Reg.* v. *Mansfield,* 1 Q. B. 444 ; *Cope* v. *Cope,* 1 Moo. & Rob. 269. The presumption of law arising from the fact of husband and wife sleeping together is irresistible as to the legitimacy of the child of the wife, unless there is clear and satisfactory evidence that some physical incapacity existed. *Legge* v. *Edmonds,* 25 Law J., N. S., Chanc. 125.

4. If the claimant be not the heir, he must (in addition to the above) prove his own title derived from the heir, *ex. gr.* by deed, will, or otherwise. *Doe* d. *Kimber* v. *Cafe,* 7 Exch. 675.

5. It must appear that the claimant's title is not barred or extinguished by the Statute of Limitations. *Ante,* 4; *Doe* d. *Human* v. *Pettit,* 5 B. & A. 223 ; *Doe* d. *George* v. *Jesson,* 6 East, 80 ; 2 Smith, 236; *Nepean, Bart.* v. *Doe* d. *Knight* (in error), 2 M. & W. 894.

6. And that the claimant's title as heir, or otherwise, accrued *on or before* the day on which possession is claimed in the writ. *Roe* d. *Wrangham* v. *Hersey,* 3 Wils. 274 ; *ante,* 95, 288.

7. If the defendant occupied as a tenant of the plaintiff's ancestor, it must appear that such term has expired, or become forfeited, or otherwise determined ; or (in case of a tenancy from year to year) that due notice to quit has been given, unless, indeed, the defendant has *disclaimed* the plaintiff's title, and so disentitled himself to the usual notice to quit. *Doe* d. *Calvert* v. *Frowd,* 4 Bing. 560 ; 1 Moo. & P. 480 ; *ante,* 41.

Evidence and Points for Defendant.]—The defendant may contend : 1. That the evidence for the plaintiff is insufficient on some material point. *Ante,* 487. He may also produce contradictory evidence. 2. That the supposed "purchaser," through whom the plaintiff claims, *inherited* the property (*ante,* 484) ; or took it under a limitation in some deed or will to the heirs, or to the heirs of the body, of one of his ancestors, from whom the descent ought to be traced. *Ante,* 484. 3. That the immediate ancestor of the plaintiff, or the previous owner through whom the title is derived, did not die seised of, or entitled to, the property for an estate of inheritance. *Doe* d. *Hallen* v. *Ironmonger,* 3 East, 533 ; *Doe* d. *Payne* v. *Plyer,* 14 Q. B. 512. He may be shown to have conveyed it away by deed or settlement; Ros. Ev. 462 (7th ed.); *Doe* d. *Tucker* v. *Tucker,* Moo. & Mal. 536 ; *Doe* d. *Lees* v. *Ford,* 2 E. & B. 970 ; or disposed of it by will ; *Doe* d. *Chillcott* v. *White,* 1 East, 33 ; *Doe* d. *Smith* v. *Smart,*

1 Moo. & Rob. 476; *Doe* d. *Gosley* v. *Gosley*, 2 Moo. & Rob. 243; *Doe* d. *Lewis* v. *Lewis*, 1 Car. & K. 122; or demised it for a term or tenancy which has not expired, nor been determined by a regular notice to quit. *Maddon* d. *Baker* v. *White*, 2 T. R. 159. 4. The plaintiff, or some person through whom he claims, may be illegitimate: *Goodright* d. *Stevens* v. *Moss*, 2 Cowp. 591; *Doe* d. *Fleming* v. *Fleming*, 4 Bing. 266; 2 Arch. N. P. 370—373; Broom, Max. 220: or some material link in the chain of his pedigree may be defective, or not sufficiently proved. Proof of the existence of a nearer heir is sufficient to defeat the claimant; *Doe* d. *Johnson* v. *The Earl of Pembroke*, 11 East, 504; *Doe* d. *Warren* v. *Bray*, Moo. & Mal. 166; notwithstanding the defendant does not claim or pretend to defend on behalf of such nearer heir, nor to derive any right or title through or under him. *Doe* d. *Northey* v. *Harvey*, Ry. & Moo. 297; *ante*, 288. The defendant may prove that the land claimed is subject to the custom of gavelkind or borough-English, and so that the plaintiff is not entitled. Co. Lit. 175 b; 2 Black. Com. 83, 84; Broom, Max. 331, 417.

Proof that any deceased ancestor of the plaintiff was an alien, will not defeat an ejectment by a British subject (*post*, Chap. LIX.); nor proof that any deceased ancestor was attainted for felony (*post*, Chap. LVIII.); but on the death of a peer, leaving his eldest son and heir who had been attainted, the peerage does not vest in the son, nor on his death in the nearest male heir, but is forfeited as much as if he had been a peer at the time of his attainder. *Perth Peerage*, 2 H. L. Cas. 865.

CHAPTER XLVII.

BY DEVISEE OF FREEHOLDS.

---

7 *Will.* 4 & 1 *Vict. c.* 26.]—The laws respecting the execution, revocation and operation of wills, codicils, and testamentary dispositions by way of appointment or otherwise, respectively made, or re-executed or republished, or revived by any codicil on or after the *first day of January,* 1838, is contained in the above statute, as amended by 15 & 16 Vict. c. 24. For the previous law (which is still in force with respect to wills, &c., made before and not re-executed or revived after the 1st January, 1838, *post,* 494), reference may be made to the following authorities, viz.: 1. As to the execution and attestation of wills, Stat. 29 Car. 2, c. 3, s. 5; 2 Arch. N. P. 374; 1 Wms. Exors. 52 to 72 (3rd ed.); 11 Jarm. Byth. 50 to 71 (3rd ed.). 2. As to the revocation of wills: stat. 29 Car. 2, c. 3, s. 6; 2 Arch. N. P. 380, 383; 1 Wms. Exors. 93 to 147; 11 Jarm. Byth. 87 to 127; Ros. Ev. 464—466. 3. As to the republication of wills: 2 Arch. N. P. 386; 1 Wms. Exors. 148 to 160; 11 Jarm. Byth. 127 to 136.

By 7 Will. 4 & 1 Vict. c. 26, intituled "An Act for the Amendment of the Laws with respect to Wills," it is enacted (sect. 1, *the interpretation clause*), "That in this act the word '*will*' shall extend to a testament, and to a codicil, and to an appointment by will or by writing in the nature of a will in exercise of a power, &c. And the words '*real estate*' shall extend to manors, advowsons, messuages, lands, tithes, rents and hereditaments, whether freehold, customary freehold, tenant right, customary or copyhold, or of any other tenure, and whether corporeal, incorporeal or personal, and to any undivided share thereof, and to any estate, right or interest (other than a chattel interest) therein; and the words '*personal estate*' shall extend to leasehold estates and other chattels real, and also to monies, shares of Government and other funds, securities for money (not being real estates), debts, choses in action, rights, credits, goods, and all other property whatsoever which by law devolves upon the executor or administrator, and to any share or interest therein: And every word importing the singular number only shall extend and be applied to several persons or things as well as one person or thing; and every word importing the masculine gender only shall extend and be applied to a female as well as a male."

This act extends to wills made abroad by Englishmen residing there, but *domiciled here. The Countess De Zichy Ferraris and J. W. Croker* v. *Marquis of Hertford,* 3 Curt. 468; *Croker* v. *Marquis of Hertford* (on appeal), 4 Moore, P. C. C. 339. A will of personal estate must always be executed according to the law of the domicile; *ex. gr.,* according to the law of Portugal, if the testator be domiciled there. *Stanley* v. *Bernes,* 3 Hagg. 373. If by the law of the foreign country wherein the domicile is no will can be made (as in Turkey), any will of personal estate (wherever situate) will be inoperative: unless, indeed, there be some special treaty enabling British subjects domiciled there to make wills; and in such case the will must be executed and attested in like manner as a will made in England. *Maltass* v. *Maltass,* 3 Curt. 231; but see Story's Conflict of Laws, ss. 465—468. A

will of real estate, wherever made, must always be executed in conformity with the law of the country wherein the land is situate.
Story's Conflict of Laws, s. 474.

Repeal of prior Acts.]—Sect. 2 repeals the previous statutes and
enactments relating to wills, viz.: 32 Hen. 8, c. 1; 34 & 35 Hen. 8,
c. 5; 10 Car. 1, sess. 2, c. 2 (Irish); 29 Car. 2, c. 3, ss. 5, 6, 12, 19,
20, 21, 22; 7 Will. 3, c. 12 (Irish); 4 & 5 Anne, c. 16, s. 14; 6 Anne,
c. 10 (Irish); 14 Geo. 2, c. 20, s. 9; 25 Geo. 2, c. 6 (except as to the
colonies); 25 Geo. 2, c. 11 (Irish); and 55 Geo. 3, c. 192, "except so
far as the same acts or any of them respectively relate *to any wills or
estates pur autre vie, to which this act does not extend.*"
Wills made prior to the 1st January, 1838, and not since re-executed,
revived or republished, are excluded from the operation of this act by
sect. 34: *post,* 513: consequently they fall *within the exception* in
this section, and are regulated by the acts previously in force. *Vide
supra.*

General enabling Clause.]—Sect. 3 enacts, "that it shall be lawful
for every person to devise, bequeath or dispose of, by his will executed
in manner hereinafter required, all real estate and personal estate
which he shall be entitled to, either at law or in equity, at the time of
his death, and which, if not so devised, bequeathed or disposed of,
would devolve upon the heir at law or customary heir of him, or, if he
became entitled by descent, of his ancestor, or upon his executor or
administrator; and that the power hereby given shall extend to all
real estate of the nature of customary freehold or tenant right, or customary or copyhold, notwithstanding that the testator may not have
surrendered the same to the use of his will, or notwithstanding that,
being entitled as heir, devisee or otherwise, to be admitted thereto, he
shall not have been admitted thereto, or notwithstanding that the same,
in consequence of the want of a custom to devise or surrender to the
use of a will or otherwise, could not at law have been disposed of by
will if this act had not been made, or notwithstanding that the same,
in consequence of there being a custom that a will or a surrender to
the use of a will should continue in force for a limited time only, or
any other special custom, could not have been disposed of by will, according to the power contained in this act, if this act had not been made;
and also to estates *pur autre vie,* whether there shall or shall not be
any special occupant thereof, and whether the same shall be freehold,
customary freehold, tenant right, customary or copyhold, or of any
other tenure, and whether the same shall be a corporeal or an incorporeal hereditament, and also to all contingent, executory or other
future interests in any real or personal estate, whether the testator may
or may not be ascertained as the person or one of the persons in whom
the same respectively may become vested, and whether he may be
entitled thereto under the instrument by which the same respectively
were created, or under any disposition thereof by deed or will; and
also to all rights of entry for conditions broken and other rights of
entry, and also to such of the same estates, interests and rights respectively, and other real and personal estate as the testator may be entitled to at the time of his death, notwithstanding that he may become
entitled to the same subsequently to the execution of his will."

Copyholds.—Before this act no person (except a customary heir) could devise a copyhold estate to which he had not been *admitted* either actually or constructively. *Doe* d. *Vernon* v. *Vernon*, 7 East, 8; *Doe* d. *Tofield* v. *Tofield*, 11 East, 246; *Doe* d. *Winder* v. *Lawes*, 7 A. & E. 195, 211, 213; *Matthew* v. *Osborne*, 13 C. B. 919. But the admission of a particular tenant operated as an admission of the remainderman also, because the particular estate and remainder made together but one estate. *Auncelme* v. *Auncelme*, Cro. Jac. 31; *Doe* d. *Winder* v. *Lawes*, 7 A. & E. 195, 210; *Phyphers* v. *Eburn*, 3 Bing. N. C. 250. And the want of a surrender to the use of a will was cured by 55 Geo. 3, c. 192. *Doe* d. *Clarke* v. *Ludlam*, 7 Bing. 275; 5 Moo. & P. 48; *Doe* d. *Smith* v. *Bird*, 5 B. & Adol. 695; *Doe* d. *Winder* v. *Lawes*, 7 A. & E. 195, 208.

Rights of Entry after a disseisin of the freehold could not have been devised before this act. *Goodright* d. *Fowler* v. *Forrester*, 8 East, 552; *Doe* d. *Souter* v. *Hull*, 2 D. & R. 38; *Doe* d. *Cooper* v. *Finch*, 1 N. & P. 130; *Baker* v. *Hacking*, Cro. Car. 387; *Attorney-General* v. *Vigor*, 8 Ves. 256, 282. But rights of entry after a mere dispossession, without the seisin of the freehold being taken away, or if possession were merely withheld, might have been devised. *Culley* v. *Doe* d. *Taylerson* (in error), 11 A. & E. 1008, 1021; 3 P. & D. 539, 553—557.

Choses in Action.—A mere debt or chose in action cannot be bequeathed under this act so as to enable the legatee to sue for it in his own name. *Bishop* v. *Curtis*, 21 Law J., Q. B. 391; 17 Jur. 23.

Donationes mortis causâ are not abolished by this act. *Moore* v. *Darton*, 4 De Gex & S. 517; 20 Law J., N. S., Chanc. 626.

Fees on Copyholds.]—Sect. 4 provides for the fees and fines payable by devisees of customary and copyhold estates.

Entries on Court Rolls.]—Sect. 5 provides that wills or extracts from wills containing devises of customary freeholds or copyholds shall be entered on the court rolls, and that the devisee shall be liable to the same fines, &c., as the heir would have been in case of no such devise.

Estates pur autre Vie.]—Sect. 6 relates to estates *pur autre vie* which are to be assets by descent, or in the hands of the executors or administrators, as the case may be.

Infants.]—Sect. 7 enacts, "that no will made by any person under the age of twenty-one years shall be valid." As to the previous law, see 1 Wms. Exors. 13, 14 (3rd ed.); 11 Jarm. Byth. 23, 24 (3rd ed.).

Married Women.]—Sect. 8 provides and enacts, "that no will made by any married woman shall be valid, except such a will as might have been made by a married woman before the passing of this act." This section seems to make no alteration in the previous law: the object of it is to qualify and restrict sect. 3. *Ante*, 494. A married woman could not before this act, nor can she now, dispose of her real estate by will, even with the consent of her husband: *Doe* d. *Stevens* v. *Scott*, 4 Bing. 505; 1 Moo. & P. 317; *Price* v. *Parker*, 16 Simon,

198; 34 & 35 Hen. 8, c. 5, s. 14 (now repealed by sect. 2, but in effect re-enacted by this section); nor of her copyholds; *George* v. *Jew,* Ambler, 627; *Doe* d. *Nethercote* v. *Bastle,* 5 B. & A. 492; 1 D. & R. 81; nor of her personal property, except with his consent given at the time of probate; *Henley* v. *Philips,* 2 Atk. 49; *Anon.,* 11 Mod. 221; which consent (although previously promised) may then be refused. 1 Roper Husb. & W. 170 (2nd ed.); 1 Wms. Exors. 44 (3rd ed.). If the consent to probate be once given, it cannot afterwards be retracted. *Maas* v. *Sheffield,* 1 Robertson, 364. The assent gives validity to the will. *Ex parte Fane,* 16 Simon, 406.

A married woman may, without her husband's consent, dispose by will of property vested in her as executrix, and in which she has no beneficial interest; *Scammill* v. *Wilkinson,* 2 East, 552; 1 Roper Husb. & W. 188, 189 (2nd ed.); also of property given or settled, or agreed to be given or settled to her separate use. *Fettyplace* v. *Gorges,* 1 Ves. jun. 46; 3 Bro. C. C. 8, *S. C.*; 1 Wms. Exors. 48 (3rd ed.); but see *Doe* d. *Stevens* v. *Scott,* 4 Bing. 505; 1 Moo. & P. 317. It makes no difference in this respect whether such property is or is not vested in trustees on her behalf. 1 Wms. Exors. 48 (3rd ed.). But the *savings* made by a wife from her separate estate, upon her death belong to her husband in his marital right, and not to her executor or administrator. *Bird* v. *Peagrum,* 13 C. B. 639; *Molony* v. *Kennedy,* 10 Simon, 254; *Tugman* v. *Hopkins,* 4 Man. & Gr. 389; 5 Scott, N. R. 464; *Messenger* v. *Clarke,* 5 Exch. 388. A wife may without her husband's consent dispose by will of property in pursuance of an agreement made before marriage, or of an agreement made for good consideration after marriage. 1 Roper Husb. & W. 170; 2 Wms. Exors. 45 (3rd ed.). She may also by will *appoint* any property, whether real or personal, in pursuance of an express power in that behalf vested in her under any deed, will, &c. 1 Sug. Pow. c. 4, s. 1; 2 Roper Husb. & W. c. 19, s. 3; *Logan* v. *Bell,* 1 C. B. 872; *Doe* d. *Beech* v. *Nall,* 6 Exch. 102; *Doe* d. *Woodcock* v. *Barthrop,* 5 Taunt. 382; *Driver* d. *Berry* v. *Thompson,* 4 Taunt. 294; *Doe* d. *Collins* v. *Weller,* 7 T. R. 478. But any such appointment must be proved in the ecclesiastical court as a testamentary instrument before it can be recognized in any court of law or equity. *Stone* v. *Forsyth,* 2 Doug. 708; *Jenkin* v. *Whitehouse,* 1 Burr. 431; *Ross* v. *Ewer,* 3 Atk. 160; *Rich* v. *Cockell,* 9 Ves. 376; *Stevens* v. *Bagwell,* 15 Ves. 139; 1 Sug. Pow. 18 (7th ed.). The probate thereof will be expressly limited to the property comprised in the power. *Tucker* v. *Inman,* Car. & M. 82; 4 Man. & Gr. 1049. Probate of the will of a married woman, made in pursuance of a power, having been refused by the Prerogative Court, because the will was not upon the face of it executed according to the requisites of the power: held, on appeal, by the Judicial Committee of the Privy Council, reversing such sentence, that the will was entitled to probate, the ecclesiastical courts having no jurisdiction to inquire as to the due execution of the power, but simply to grant probate of the will as a testamentary instrument, leaving it to a court of equity to determine the question of the due execution of the power. *Barnes* v. *Vincent,* 5 Moore, P. C. C. 201. The jurisdiction to determine whether a married woman had power to make an appointment in the nature of a will belongs to the Queen's temporal courts. *Tucker* v. *Inman,* Car. & M. 82; 4 Man. & Gr. 1049. The due execution of the power may sometimes be questioned in an action of ejectment. *Doe* d. *Beech* v. *Nall,* 6 Exch. 102.

Execution and Attestation of Wills.]—Sect. 9 enacts, "that no will shall be valid unless it shall be in writing and executed in manner hereinafter mentioned (that is to say), it shall be signed *at the foot or end thereof* [but now see 15 & 16 Vict. c. 24, *post*, 513] by the testator, or by some other person in his presence and by his direction; and such signature shall be made or acknowledged by the testator in the presence of two or more witnesses present at the same time, and such witnesses shall attest and shall subscribe the will in the presence of the testator, but no form of attestation shall be necessary."

The words "at the foot or end thereof" have been repealed by the 15 & 16 Vict. c. 24, *post*, 513. It is therefore unnecessary to consider the numerous decisions upon those words: they are referred to in 3 Chit. Stat. 1575, note (*b*) (2nd ed.).

Two witnesses are necessary and sufficient in all cases. No person should act as attesting witness to whom, or to whose wife or husband, any beneficial devise or legacy, &c. is given by the will. Sect. 15; *post*, 502. The will must be signed by or for the testator *before* it is attested. *Re Olding*, 2 Curt. 865; *Cooper* v. *Bockett*, 3 Curt. 648.

The signature of the testator may be written by himself, or by any other person in his presence and by his direction. An infant, a married woman, a devisee or legatee named in the will, and even one of the attesting witnesses may sign for the testator. *Re Bailey*, 1 Curt. 914; *Smith* v. *Harris*, 1 Robertson, 262. The party so signing should write the testator's name, not his own; but a mistake on this point is not material, because if the testator adopt an incorrect signature, it will operate in the same manner as if written by himself as and for his own name. *Re Clark*, 2 Curt. 329. A married woman made her will under a power in the lifetime of her second husband; she signed the will, not with the name she then bore, but with the name of her first husband: held, a sufficient signature. *Re Goods of Susan Glover*, 11 Jur. 1022.

A signature *by a mark*, if duly attested, is sufficient, although the name of the testator does not appear; *Re Bryce*, 2 Curt. 325; *Re Field*, 3 Curt. 752; *Roberts* v. *Phillips*, 4 E. & B. 450, 461; and notwithstanding it be proved that the testator was able to sign his name. *Baker* v. *Dening*, 8 A. & E. 94; *Taylor* v. *Dening*, 3 N. & P. 228. So either of the attesting witnesses may subscribe by a mark. *Post*, 499. It is no objection that the signature or mark of the testator was made with the assistance of a third person, who guided his hand. *Wilson* v. *Bedard*, 12 Simon, 28; 10 L. J., N. S., Chanc. 305; *Harrison* v. *Elvin*, 3 Q. B. 117, 118; 2 Gale & D. 769.

A signature *for the testator* should be made in the presence of the attesting witnesses, otherwise they will not be able to prove that it was made "in his presence and by his direction." But it will be sufficient if the testator expressly acknowledge to the witnesses that the signature was made for him by A. B., in his presence and by his direction. *Ilott* v. *Genge*, 4 Moore, P. C. C. 265. Such acknowledgment should be specially stated in the memorandum of attestation, although no form of attestation is required by the statute.

A signature *by the testator* may be made either in the presence or absence of the attesting witnesses. But in the latter case it must be acknowledged by the testator in their presence. *Re Regan*, 1 Curt. 908; *Re Mary Harrison*, 2 Curt. 863. No particular form of acknowledgment is necessary; but where the testator shows his signature to the witnesses, and requests them to attest it, which they accordingly do, that is sufficient. *Re Warden*, 2 Curt. 334; *Gaze* v. *Gaze*, 3 Curt. 451; *Blake* v. *Knight*, 3 Curt. 547; *Keigwin* v. *Keigwin*, 3 Curt. 607; *Re Ashmore*, 3 Curt. 756; *Cooper* v. *Bockett*, 4 Moore, P. C. C. 419; 10 Jur. 931; *Mitchell* v. *Thomas*, 6 Moore, P. C. C. 137; *Re Summers*, 2 Robertson, 295. On the other hand, if the signature be not shown to the witnesses, but the testator merely produces the paper and requests them to attest it (especially if it does not appear that each of them saw the signature before attesting it), that is not sufficient. *Re Rawlins*, 2 Curt. 326; *Re Harrison*, 2 Curt. 863; *Ilott* v. *Genge*, 3 Curt. 160; *S. C.* on appeal, 4 Moore, P. C. C. 265; 1 Robertson, 14, note. An acknowledgment by the testator that the paper produced is his will, but not acknowledging *the signature* to it, is insufficient. *Hudson* v. *Parker*, 1 Robertson, 14; *The Countess De Zichy Ferraris* v. *Marquis of Hertford*, 3 Curt. 479. The acknowledgment must be made to the witnesses by the testator himself, not by any third person who saw him sign. *Moore* v. *King*, 3 Curt. 243.

The signature by or for the testator must be made or acknowledged (as the case may require) *before*, and not after, the attestation thereof by the witnesses. *Re Olding*, 2 Curt. 865; *Re Byrd*, 3 Curt. 117; *Cooper* v. *Bockett*, 3 Curt. 648.

The signature must be "made or acknowledged in the presence of two or more witnesses *present at the same time*." *Re Allen*, 2 Curt. 331; *Re Simmonds*, 3 Curt. 79; *Moore* v. *King*, 3 Curt. 243; *Casement* v. *Fulton*, 5 Moore, P. C. C. 130; *Countess De Zichy Ferraris* v. *Marquis of Hertford*, 3 Curt. 479. According to the previous law it was not necessary that the witnesses should attest in the presence of each other; or that the testator should declare the instrument he executed to be his will; or that the witnesses should attest every page, folio or sheet; or that they should know the contents; or that each folio, page or sheet should be particularly shown to them, but each sheet must have been in the room at the time of the attestation. *Bond* v. *Seawell*, 4 Burr. 1775, *per cur.*

The witnesses must be not only bodily but *mentally present*, and conscious of the act done which they are required to attest. *Hudson* v. *Parker*, 1 Robertson, 14. Where the will is executed and attested in the *same room*, that is generally sufficient in the absence of fraud, although the bed curtains, &c. prevented some of the witnesses from seeing the testator sign, or prevented the testator from seeing some of them sign the attestation. *Newton* v. *Clarke*, 2 Curt. 320; but see *Tribe* v. *Tribe*, 1 Robertson, 775. If the execution and attestation take place in *different rooms*, it must appear that the respective positions of the parties were such as to render it possible for each of them to see what the other was doing. *Doe* d. *Wright* v. *Manifold*, 1 M. & S. 294; *Re Ellis*, 2 Curt. 395; *Re Colman*, 3 Curt. 118. If that be *possible* the execution and attestation will be deemed sufficient in the absence of proof to the contrary. Bac. Abr. tit. Wills, D 1; *Shires* v. *Glascock*, 2 Salk. 688; Carthew, 81; *Casson* v. *Dade*, 1 Bro. C. C. 99; Dick, 586; *Davy* v. *Smith*, 3 Salk. 395; *Winchelsea* v. *Wauchope*, 3 Russ. 444; *Tidd* v. *The Earl of Winchelsea*, Moo. & Mal. 12; *otherwise not*; *Broderick* v. *Broderick*, 1 P. Wms. 239; *Doe* d. *Ecclestone* v. *Petty*, Carthew, 79; 1 Shower, 89. Where the attesting witnesses retired from the room where the testator had signed, and subscribed their names in an adjoining room, and the jury found that from one part of the testator's room a person by inclining himself forwards with his head out of the door might have seen the witnesses, but that the testator was not in such a situation in the room that he might by so inclining have seen them : held, that the will was not duly attested. *Doe* d. *Wright* v. *Manifold*, 1 M. & S. 294 ; *Re Colman*, 3 Curt. 118. In the case of a blind testatrix, it must appear that she was aware of the attestation, and might have seen it written by the witnesses had she not been blind. *Re Piercy*, 1 Robertson, 278. It need not appear that the will was read over to her in the presence of the attesting witnesses. *Longchamp* v. *Fish*, 2 Bos. & P. New R. 415 ; but see *Fincham* v. *Edwards*, 3 Curt. 63.

The witnesses must attest *and subscribe* the will in the presence of the testator, who must not only be bodily, but also *mentally present*. If he be then in a state of insensibility, the attestation will be insufficient. *Right* d. *Cater* v. *Price*, 1 Doug. 241 ; *Doe* d. *Walker* v. *Stephenson*, 3 Esp. 284 ; *Doe* d. *Stephenson* v. *Walker*, 4 Esp. 50. So if attested in his presence, but without his privity or knowledge. *Longford* v. *Eyre*, 1 P. Wms. 740. A signing by the witnesses in the same room where the testator lay in bed with the curtains closed, he being totally unable to draw them aside, was held not to be a signing "in his presence." *Tribe* v. *Tribe*, 1 Robertson, 775 ; but see *Newton* v. *Clarke*, 2 Curt. 320. Motion for probate of a will signed by the deceased in the presence of two witnesses, but subscribed by them in an adjoining room, communicating with folding doors, but in such a situation that the deceased could not see them, rejected. *Re Colman*, 3 Curt. 118 ; and see *Re Ellis*, 2 Curt. 395 ; *Doe* d. *Wright* v. *Manifold*, 1 M. & S. 294.

The witnesses must all attest and subscribe *on the same occasion*, and not on different days. *Re Allen*, 2 Curt. 331 ; *Re Simmonds*, 3 Curt. 79 ; *Moore* v. *King*, 3 Curt. 243 ; *Casement* v. *Fulton*, 5 Moore, P. C. C. 130 ; 3 Moore, Ind. App. 395, *S. C.* The act of attesting (which is an act of mental observation) is distinct from that of subscribing : the witnesses must do *both*. *Hudson* v. *Parker*, 1 Robertson, 14 ; *Re Cope*, 2 *Id.* 335 ; and see *Doe* d. *Spilsbury* v. *Burdett*, 6 Man. & Gr. 386 ; 10 Cl. & Fin. 340, *S. C.* ; *Hooley* v. *Jones*, 2 Ecc. & Mar. Cas. 59 ; *Playne* v. *Scriven*, 1 Robertson, 772. Neither of the witnesses can subscribe another's name for him ; *Re Mead*, 1 Ecc. & Mar. Cas. 456 ; *Re White*, 2 *Id.* 461 ; but one may help another by guiding his hand. *Harrison* v. *Elvin*, 3 Q. B. 117 ; 2 Gale & D. 769. Either of them may subscribe by a mark : *Doe* d. *Davies* v. *Davies*, 9 Q. B. 648 ; *Re Clark*, 2 Curt. 329 ; *Re Ashmore*, 3 Curt. 756 ; *Re Amiss*, 2 Robertson, 116 ; *Harrison* v. *Harrison*, 8 Ves. 185 ; *Addy* v. *Grix*, *Id.* 504 : or by initials. *Re Christian*, 2 Robertson, 110. But a signature *with a dry pen*, made over a previous signature of the witness, is not sufficient. It amounts merely to an acknowledgment, and not to a fresh subscription. *Playne* v. *Scriven*, 1 Robertson, 772.

No form of attestation is necessary ; not even so much as the word "witnesses." *Bryan* v. *White*, 2 Robertson, 315 ; *Roberts* v. *Phillips*, 4 E. & B. 450, 457. It is sufficient if the witnesses merely attest and subscribe their names. *Warren* v. *Postlethwaite*, 2 Collier, C. C. 108 ; 14 Law J., N. S., Chanc. 422. The word " witness A. B., C. D. and E. F." was sufficient before the statute to satisfy a power requiring the will to be attested by three credible witnesses. *Doe* d. *Spilsbury* v. *Burdett*, 4 A. & E. 1. But it is always advisable that the attestation clause should express on the face of it that all the requisites of the statute have been complied with; because otherwise probate will not be granted in the common form without proof of such requisites by affidavit of some or one of the attesting witnesses. *Burgoyne* v. *Showler*, 1 Robertson, 5; *Re Batten*, 2 *Id.* 124; *Gove* v. *Gawen*, 3 Curt. 151; *Pennant* v. *Kingscote*, 3 Curt. 642. Moreover, a purchaser of real estate would require proof of such requisites by a statutory declaration made pursuant to 5 & 6 Will. 4, c. 62. Besides which, if the witnesses by their attestation expressly certify that all the requisites of the statute were complied with, they could not afterwards so easily defeat the will by evidence to the contrary. 17 & 18 Vict. c. 125, s. 22; *Goodtitle* d. *Alexander* v. *Clayton*, 4 Burr. 224; *Gove* v. *Gawen*, 3 Curt. 151; *Cooper* v. *Bockett*, 3 Curt. 648. It would in many cases *aid their memory* long after they had forgotten what actually took place. If the attestation do not mention that *all* the requisites of the statute have been complied with, and the attesting witnesses are dead, evidence to that effect may be left to the jury to find a compliance with the statute. *Croft* v. *Pawlet*, 2 Stra. 1109; *Hands* v. *James*, 2 Comyn, R. 531; *Doe* d. *Davies* v. *Davies*, 9 Q. B. 648, 650.

The act does not say *where* the attestation is to be written. It may, therefore, be indorsed or written on any part of the paper. *Re Chamney*, 1 Robertson, 757. If the attesting witnesses subscribe at different parts, that may be sufficient. *Roberts* v. *Phillips*, 4 E. & B. 450, 460.

Where there are obliterations, interlineations or other alterations in a will, they should be respectively marked in the margin or on some other part of the will opposite or near to such alterations, with the signature or initials of the testator and of the attesting witnesses; or they should be mentioned in the attestation clause, or in some other memorandum duly signed and attested; sect. 21; *Re Martin*, 1 Robertson, 712; otherwise, in the absence of proof to the contrary, they will be presumed to have been made after the execution of the will. *Doe* d. *Shallcross* v. *Palmer*, 16 Q. B. 747; *Cooper* v. *Bockett*, 4 Moore, P. C. C. 419; 10 Jur. 931; *Burgoyne* v. *Showler*, 1 Robertson, 5; *Gove* v. *Gawen*, 3 Curt. 151; *Pennant* v. *Kingscote*, *Id.* 642; Edwards' Abr. Cases, Prerog. Court, 53.

Where a testator, who died in 1821, struck the name of one of his devisees out of his will, and interlined the names of two other persons above the erasure, but those alterations were not noticed in the attestation clause, nor was there anything to show, or from which it could be inferred, that they were made before the will was executed; the court held that they did not affect the devise. *Simmons* v. *Rudall*, 1 Simon, N. S. 115; and see *Locke* v. *James*, 11 M. & W. 901; *Winsor* v. *Pratt*, 2 Brod. & B. 650. Alterations not proved to have been made before the attestation will be rejected, and probate granted of the will as it stood before such alterations. *Birch* v. *Birch*, 1 Robertson, 675; *Re Martin*, *Id.* 712; *Soar* v. *Dolman*, 3 Curt. 121. If probate be granted with any alterations of the will appearing therein, that will be conclusive evidence (so far as personal estate is concerned) that such alterations were duly made and attested according to the statute; because otherwise they would have been rejected and *omitted* from the probate.

Execution of Testamentary Appointments.]—Sect. 10 enacts, "that no appointment made by will, in exercise of any power, shall be valid, unless the same be executed in manner hereinbefore required; and every will executed in manner hereinbefore required shall, so far as respects the execution and attestation thereof, be a valid execution of a power of appointment by will, notwithstanding it shall have been expressly required that a will made in exercise of such power should be executed with some additional or other form of execution or solemnity."

As to the previous law, see *Burdett* v. *Doe* d. *Spilsbury* (in error), 6 Man. & Gr. 386; 7 Scott, N. R. 85; 10 Cl. & Fin. 360, *S. C.*; *Vincent* v. *The Bishop of Sodor and Man*, 8 C. B. 905; 5 Exch. 683, *S. C.*; *Johns* v. *Dickinson*, 8 C. B. 934; *Waterman* v. *Smith*, 9 Simon, 629.

Wills of Soldiers and Seamen.]—Sect. 11 provides, "that any soldier being in actual military service, or any mariner or seaman being at sea, may dispose of his *personal* estate as he might have done before the making of this act."

This section extends to merchant seamen; *Morrell* v. *Morrell*, 1 Hagg. 51; also to a purser in the navy; *Re Hayes*, 2 Curt. 338; also to soldiers in the service of the East India Company, *Re Donaldson*, 2 Curt. 386; although minors; *Re Farquhar*, 4 Ecc. & Mar. Cas. 651; also to superior officers in the army or navy. *Earl of Euston* v. *Lord Henry Seymour*, 2 Curt. 339. But not when in barracks either at home or abroad; only to those on an expedition or voyage. *Drummond* v. *Parish*, 3 Curt. 522; *White* v. *Repton*, 3 Curt. 818; *Re Hill*, 1 Robertson, 276. A letter written by a mariner in "Margate Roads," unattested, containing dispositive words, admitted as his will under this section. *Re Milligan*, 2 Robertson, 108; 7 Ecc. & Mar. Cas. 271. The will of a seaman who went on shore while his vessel was in harbour at Buenos Ayres, and there died by an accident, was allowed to pass as that of a seaman "at sea," under this section. *In the Goods of Lay*, 2 Curt. 375. An informal codicil made by a seaman engaged with the enemy, and on board ship, but in a river beyond the flux and reflux of the tide, is valid under this section. *In the Goods of Austin*, 17 Jur. 284; 21·Law T. 65. A will duly made under this section remains operative, unless expressly revoked, although the testator lives in England several years after the date of the will. *In the Goods of Leese*, 17 Jur. 216; 21 Law T. 24.

Bequests of Wages, &c. by Seamen.]—Sect. 12 relates to bequests of wages, pay, prize money, bounty money and allowances, or other monies payable in respect of services in her Majesty's navy; which are to be regulated (as before) by stat. 11 Geo. 4 & 1 Will. 4, c. 20. 1 Wms. Exors. 289.

Publication.]—Sect. 13 enacts, "that every will executed in manner hereinbefore required, shall be valid without any other publication thereof."

For the previous law, see the cases referred to under sect. 10. *Supra*; *British Museum* v. *White*, 6 Bing. 310; 3 Moo. & P. 609; *Wright* v. *Wright*, 7 Bing. 457; 5 Moo. & P. 316.

Attesting Witness's Competency.]—Sect. 14 enacts, "that if any person who shall attest the execution of a will shall, at the time of the execution thereof, or at any time afterwards, be incompetent to be admitted a witness to prove the execution thereof, such will shall not on that account be invalid."

Formerly a will of real estate, attested by only three witnesses, one of whom was not a credible, *i. e.* an admissible witness, was void. *Hatfield* v. *Thorp*, 5 B. & A. 589; *Holdfast* d. *Anstey* v. *Dowsing*, 2 Stra. 1253; *S. C.* in error, 1 W. Black. 8. This was, however, remedied by 25 Geo. 2, c. 6. *Infra.*

Gifts to attesting Witnesses.]—Sect. 15 enacts, "that if any person shall attest the execution of any will to whom, or to whose wife or husband, any beneficial devise, legacy, estate, interest, gift or appointment, of or affecting any real or personal estate (other than and except charges and directions for the payment of any debt or debts), shall be *thereby* given or made, such devise, legacy, estate, interest, gift or appointment shall, so far only as concerns such person attesting the execution of such will, or the wife or husband of such person, or any person claiming under such person or wife or husband, be utterly null and void, and such person so attesting shall be admitted as a witness to prove the execution of such will, or to prove the validity or invalidity thereof, notwithstanding such devise, legacy, estate, interest, gift or appointment mentioned in such will."

This section is not affected by the act for improving the law of evidence, 6 & 7 Vict. c. 85.

A devise or legacy given to J. S., by a will duly attested, will not be affected by J. S. afterwards becoming an attesting witness to a codicil to that will. *Gurney* v. *Gurney*, 3 Drewry, 208, Kindersley, V. C.

Formerly any devise or legacy to an attesting witness (there being only three such witnesses) rendered the will invalid so far as it related to real estate, because it was not attested by three or more *credible* witnesses, pursuant to the Statute of Frauds (29 Car. 2, c. 3, s. 5). *Holdfast* d. *Anstey* v. *Dowsing*, 2 Stra. 1253; *S. C.* in error, 1 W. Black. 8; *Hatfield* v. *Thorp*, 5 B. & A. 589. But by 25 Geo. 2, c. 6, it was enacted, that the devise or legacy in favour of the attesting witness should be void, and he should be admitted to prove the will. After that act a devise *to the wife* of the attesting witness rendered the witness incompetent and the will void. *Hatfield* v. *Thorp*, 5 B. & A. 589; but sect. 15 of the present act is differently worded in this respect. A devise to an attesting witness was held void under the 25 Geo. 2, c. 6, although there were three other credible witnesses to the will. *Doe* d. *Taylor* v. *Mills*, 1 Moo. & Rob. 288. For other decisions under that act, see 3 Chit. Stat. 1562 (2nd ed.).

Creditor attesting Witness.]—Sect. 16 enacts, "that in case by any will any real or personal estate shall be charged with any debt or debts, and any creditor, or the wife or husband of any creditor whose debt is so charged, shall attest the execution of such will, such creditor, notwithstanding such charge, shall be admitted a witness to prove the execution of such will, or to prove the validity or invalidity thereof."

Executor attesting Witness.]—Sect. 17 enacts, "that no person shall, on account of his being an executor of a will, be incompetent to be admitted a witness to prove the execution of such will, or a witness to prove the validity or invalidity thereof."

Revocation by Marriage.]—Sect. 18 enacts, "that every will made by a man or woman shall be revoked by his or her marriage (except a will made in exercise of a power of appointment, when the real or personal estate thereby appointed would not, in default of such appointment, pass to his or her heir, customary heir, executor or administrator, or the person entitled as his or her next of kin under the Statute of Distributions)."

For the previous law, see 11 Jarm. Byth. 87 to 92 (3rd ed.); 2 Arch. N. P. 384; *Marston* v. *Roe* d. *Fox* (in error), 8 A. & E. 14.

No Revocation by Presumption.]—Sect. 19 enacts, "that no will shall be revoked by any presumption of an intention on the ground of an alteration in circumstances."

For the previous law, see *Johnston* v. *Johnston,* 1 Phil. Ecc. R. 447—498, and the authorities there cited; Ros. Ev. 465 (7th ed.). Marriage and the birth of a child operated as an absolute revocation. *Walker* v. *Walker,* 2 Curt. 854.

Revocation by subsequent Will or Codicil, or Destruction of Instrument.]—Sect. 20 enacts, "that no will or codicil, or any part thereof, shall be revoked otherwise than as aforesaid, or by another will or codicil executed in manner hereinbefore required, or by some writing declaring an intention to revoke the same, and executed in the manner in which a will is hereinbefore required to be executed, or by the *burning, tearing, or otherwise destroying* the same by the testator, or by some person in his presence and by his direction, *with the intention* of revoking the same."

A revocation by a subsequent codicil, whether by express words of revocation, or by a devise inconsistent with a former devise, operates so far only as is necessary to effectuate the intention of the testator. *Doe* d. *Evers* v. *Ward,* 18 Q. B. 197; 21 Law J., Q. B. 145; *Williams* v. *Evans,* 1 E. & B. 727; 22 Law J., Q. B. 241; *Darley* v. *Martin,* 13 C. B. 683; *Lloyd* v. *Davies,* 15 C. B. 76; *Doe* d. *Murch* v. *Marchant,* 6 Man. & Gr. 813; 7 Scott, N. R. 644; *Doe* d. *Hearle* v. *Hicks,* 1 Cl. & Fin. 20; 6 Bligh, N. S. 37; *Harwood* v. *Goodright,* Cowp. 87. A testamentary paper relating to real estate alone, commencing, "this is the last will and testament of me, relating to all my real estate whatsoever:" held totally to revoke a prior will. *Plenty* v. *West,* 16 Beav. 173; and see *Stoddart* v. *Grant,* 1 Macq..H. L. Cas. 163.

Where a will is executed in duplicate a subsequent codicil (duly executed and attested) which revokes or alters one part of the will, operates in like manner on the other part. *Doe* d. *Strickland* v. *Strickland,* 8 C. B. 724.

A will, or any devise or legacy therein contained, cannot be revoked or destroyed within the meaning of *this* section by merely cancelling it with a pen and ink, or by any obliterations or alterations. Those are provided for and kept quite distinct by the next section.

Any act of burning, tearing, or otherwise destroying the will, must be done *animo revocandi;* and it is a question of fact for the jury whether the testator had completed the intended act of revocation;

Doe d. *Perkes* v. *Perkes*, 3 B. & A. 489. If the burning or tearing be partial or incomplete, it may, nevertheless, operate as a revocation, if so intended. *Bibb* d. *Mole* v. *Thomas*, 2 W. Black. 1043; *Winsor* v. *Pratt*, 2 Brod. & B. 650. A testator, being angry with one of the devisees named in his will, began to tear it, with the intention of destroying it; and, having torn it into four pieces, was prevented from proceeding further, partly by the efforts of a by-stander, who seized his arms, and partly by the entreaties of the devisee. Upon this he became calm, and, having put by the several pieces, he expressed his satisfaction that no material part of the writing had been injured, and that it was no worse : held, that it was on these facts properly left to the jury to say whether he had completely finished all that he intended to do for the purpose of destroying the will; and the jury having found that he had not, the court refused to disturb the verdict, and supported the will. *Doe* d. *Perkes* v. *Perkes*, 3 B. & A. 489. Where the testator threw his will on the fire, with intent to destroy it, and the devisee therein named snatched it off before more was burnt than the corner, and afterwards promised the testator that she would burn it, and pretended to have done so : held, that the revocation was not complete. *Doe* d. *Reed* v. *Harris*, 6 A. & E. 209. But held, that it was revoked as to the copyholds, to which the statute did not apply. *Doe* d. *Reed* v. *Harris*, 8 A. & E. 1.

The statute makes this important distinction between the act of burning, tearing or otherwise destroying the substance of a will, and a mere obliteration of its contents, viz., it allows the former acts, though unattested and unseen by any witness, to have a revoking effect, if done *animo revocandi* : whereas an obliteration must generally be attested pursuant to sect. 21.

Obliterations, Interlineations and other Alterations.] — Sect. 21 enacts, " that no *obliteration, interlineation* or *other alteration*, made in any will *after the execution thereof*, ❡hall be valid or have any effect, except so far as the words or effect of the will before such alteration shall not be apparent, unless such alteration shall be executed in like manner as hereinbefore is required for the execution of the will; but the will, with such alteration as part thereof, shall be deemed to be duly executed if the signature of the testator and the subscription of the witnesses be made in the margin, or on some other part of the will opposite or near to such alteration, or at the foot or end of or opposite to a memorandum referring to such alteration, and written at the end or some other part of the will."

This section applies only to alterations made in a will *after the execution thereof*. *Keigwin* v. *Keigwin*, 3 Curt. 607; *Greville* v. *Tyler*, 7 Moo. P. C. C. 320. But alterations appearing in a will or codicil will be presumed to have been made after the execution thereof unless the contrary be proved; *Doe* d. *Shallcross* v. *Palmer*, 16 Q. B. 747; *Cooper* v. *Bockett*, 4 Moo. P. C. C. 419; 10 Jur. 931; *ante*, 500; whereas alterations in a deed will be presumed to have been made before the execution thereof, unless the contrary be proved. *Doe* d. *Tatum* v. *Catomore*, 16 Q. B. 745. In *Keigwin* v. *Keigwin*, 3 Curt. 607, alterations on the face of a duly-executed will were held, upon the circumstances, to have been made before the execution.

Where a blank was left in a will for the insertion of legacies, and some were inserted in black and others in red ink, with sundry alterations and interlineations, probate was granted of such parts of the will as were in black ink; those in red being rejected on the presumption of their being inserted after execution. *Birch* v. *Birch,* 1 Robertson, 675; and see *Re Martin, Id.* 712; *Soar* v. *Dolman,* 3 Curt. 121.

To render any alterations or obliterations operative as a revocation *pro tanto* of what was originally written in the will, they must have been made *animo revocandi,* and not merely for the purpose of substituting other sums, &c. Therefore probate will be decreed of the will in its original form if the alterations or obliterations be not made and attested according to the statute, and it is apparent that the testator intended only a substitution, and not a revocation of the bequests altered. *Brooke* v. *Kent,* 3 Moo. P. C. C. 334.

Unattested alterations, &c. do not affect the previous devise. *Simmons* v. *Rudall,* 1 Sim. N. S. 115; *Locke* v. *James,* 11 M. & W. 901; *Winsor* v. *Pratt,* 2 Brod. & B. 650. Probate will be granted of the will as *it originally stood. Re Martin,* 1 Robertson, 712; *Birch* v. *Birch, Id.* 675; *Soar* v. *Dolman,* 3 Curt. 121.

If certain passages in a will are obliterated so effectually as not to be distinguished on the face of the will, that amounts to a complete revocation of the obliterated parts. *Townley* v. *Watson,* 3 Curt. 761. But if the original words can be deciphered by engravers or other skilled persons with or without the aid of a strong magnifying glass, they will not be considered as revoked. *Cooper* v. *Bockett,* 4 Moo. P. C. C. 419; *Lushington* v. *Onslow,* 6 Ecc. & Mar. Cas. 183; 12 Jur. 465. In *Brook* v. *Kent,* 3 Moo. P. C. C. 334, the words were erased so as to be quite illegible, but the particular alterations were stated in an unattested memorandum written by the testator on the will. Probate decreed (on appeal) of the will as it originally stood.

A line drawn through any part of a will *with a pencil* is not an obliteration, but merely something deliberative. *Francis* v. *Grover,* 5 Hare, 39; and see *Re Bushant,* 13 Jur. 458; *Re Ravenscroft,* 18 Law J., Chanc. 501.

Revival of revoked Will.] — Sect. 22 enacts, "that no will or codicil, or any part thereof, which shall be in any manner revoked shall be *revived* otherwise than by the re-execution thereof, or by a codicil executed in manner hereinbefore required, and showing an intention to revive the same; and when any will or codicil which shall be partly revoked, and afterwards wholly revoked, shall be revived, such revival shall not extend to so much thereof as shall have been revoked before the revocation of the whole thereof, unless an intention to the contrary shall be shown."

A testatrix duly executed a will, and subsequently thereto two other wills, in both of which was contained a clause revoking all former wills; she afterwards destroyed the two latter wills: held, that the first will was not thereby revived; and that parol evidence is not admissible to show an intention to revive. *Major* v. *Williams,* 3 Curt. 432.

One entire part of a will *in duplicate* in the possession of a testator being undestroyed, but the other part in the possession of his solicitor having been destroyed by the testator on the execution of a subsequent will made in 1838, in terms revoking the prior will: held, to be revived by a codicil, made subsequently to the second will, though referring to the first will merely by date, and that such reference sufficiently showed the intent to revive as required by sect. 22. and that

Z

parol evidence was not admissible to establish a mistake in the date. *Payne* v. *Trappes*, 1 Robertson, 583.

A codicil, whereby a testator confirms his will, does not give validity to an unattested alteration in a devise of lands made after the execution of the will; nor to a testamentary paper purporting to be a devise of lands unattested and unannexed to the will, and not referred to by such codicil. *Utterton* v. *Robins*, 1 A. & E. 423 ; *Haynes* v. *Hill*, 1 Robertson, 795. A codicil duly executed and attested, referring to a prior codicil or will not duly executed and attested, may give effect to it, *Re Smith*, 2 Curt. 796 ; *Sheldon* v. *Sheldon*, 1 Robertson, 81.

Generally speaking, a codicil which amounts to a republication of a will, makes the will speak as from the date of the codicil, so as to operate on subsequently acquired property. *Doe* d. *York* v. *Walker*, 12 M. & W. 591 ; *Duffield* v. *Duffield*, 3 Bligh, N. S. 260 ; *Duffield* v. *Elwes*, 3 B. & C. 705 ; 5 D. & R. 764. But the rule that a codicil confirming a will makes the will for many purposes to have the date of the codicil, is subject to the limitation that the intention of the testator be not defeated thereby. *Doe* d. *Biddulph* v. *Hole*, 15 Q. B. 848 ; 20 Law J., N. S., Q. B. 57.

Revocation—Subsequent Conveyance.]—Sect. 23 enacts, " that no conveyance or other act made or done subsequently to the execution of a will of or relating to any real or personal estate therein comprised, except an act by which such will shall be revoked as aforesaid, shall prevent the operation of the will with respect to such estate or interest in such real or personal estate as the testator shall have power to dispose of by will at the time of his death."

For the previous law, see 2 Arch. N. P. 383 ; *Roe* d. *Noden* v. *Griffits*, 4 Burr. 1961 ; *Doe* d. *Dilnot* v. *Dilnot*, 2 Bos. & P. New R. 401 ; *Doe* d. *Lushington* v. *Bishop of Llandaff*, *Id.* 491, 502 ; *Goodtitle* d. *Holford* v. *Otway*, 7 T. R. 399 ; *Schroder* v. *Schroder*, 23 Law T. 286, Wood, V. C. ; *S. C.* (on appeal), 24 Law T. 245 ; *Walker* v. *Armstrong*, 25 Law J., N. S., Chanc. 402.

Where a testator, subsequent to the date of his will, contracted for the sale of an estate specifically devised by the will: held (since the above act) that such devise became inoperative ; and that the devisee was not entitled to the purchase-money ; which formed part of the testator's personal estate, and belonged to his personal representatives. *Farrar* v. *Earl of Winterton*, 5 Beav. 1. In such case it would make no difference that the purchaser had deposited the title deeds with the testator as a security for part of the purchase-money remaining unpaid. *Moor* v. *Raisbeck*, 12 Simon, 123 ; *Ex parte Hawkins*, 13 Simon, 569. The section applies to cases where testators, having devised their estates, make conveyances of them *merely modifying the ownership ;* not where the thing devised is gone. *S. C.*

From what Period Will speaks.]—Sect. 24 enacts, " that every will shall be construed, *with reference to the real and personal estate comprised in it,* to speak and take effect, as if it had been executed immediately before the death of the testator, unless a contrary intention shall appear by the will."

The effect of this section is to extend to real estate the same rule of construction as to the time from which the will is to be construed as speaking, which before the act was applicable to personal estate. *Cole*

v. *Scott*, 1 Mac. & Gor. 518; 1 Hall & Tw. 477; *O'Toole* v. *Browne*, 3 E. & B. 572. But it will not make valid a will which was invalid in its inception, *ex. gr.* a will made by a married woman who afterwards survives her husband: it merely gives a rule *for the construction* of a valid testamentary instrument. *Price* v. *Parker*, 16 Simon, 198. Such rule applies only "with reference to the real and personal estate" comprised in the will; not with reference to the persons who are to take as legatees, &c. Therefore, where a testator directed his trustees to invest 1,200*l.*, and pay the income thereof to his daughter *Mary Ann* "for her life, or until her marriage, and after her decease or marriage, which shall first happen," to certain grandchildren of the testator; and the daughter married after the date of the will, but before the death of the testator: held, that the gift over to the grandchildren took effect; for that the will was to be referred to what was in the testator's mind at the time, and the words to be applied to the circumstances as they then stood. *Bullock* v. *Bennett*, 24 Law J., N. S., Chanc. 512; 25 Law Times R. 230, Lords Js. overruling a decision of Wood, V. C.

If a testator sell any real or personal property *specifically* given by his will, and afterwards purchase other property of the like nature to which the description in the will is applicable, such last-mentioned property may pass by the specific devise or bequest, if not otherwise specifically disposed of by any codicil. Hayes & Jarm. on Wills, 32, 33.

A testator devised all his *freehold* estate at B., which he purchased of C., by a will dated before, and republished by a codicil after the Wills Act; but a small piece of land purchased with the estate by the testator of C., and always held and mixed with it, was leasehold. After making the codicil the testator purchased the fee of that small piece of land, and the leasehold interest was merged: held, that notwithstanding the 24th section of the Wills Act, that the codicil did not pass the after-acquired fee. *Emuss* v. *Smith*, 2 De Gex & Sm. 722, 736, K. Bruce, V. C.

To take a devise out of the general rule established by this section, it is not necessary that "a contrary intention" should be expressed in so many words, or in some way quite free from doubt; but that it is to be gathered by adopting in reference to the expressions used by the testator the ordinary rules of construction applicable to wills. *Cole* v. *Scott*, 1 Mac. & Gor. 518; 1 Hall & Tw. 477. Thus, in a will of real and personal estate bearing a date, the testator gave "all the estates of which I am *now* seised or possessed," and used the word "now" in other parts of the will, clearly alluding to the period at which he was making his will: held, that the testator had thereby indicated a contrary intention, so as to take the case out of the general rule, and that real estate acquired after the date of the will was not affected by it. *S. C.* But a devise of all the estates whereof *I am seised* will extend to after-acquired property. *Doe* d. *York* v. *Walker*, 12 M. & W. 591.

Lapsed and void Devises.]—Sect. 25 enacts, "that unless a contrary intention shall appear by the will, such real estate or interest therein as shall be comprised or intended to be comprised in any devise in such will contained, which shall fail or be void by reason of the death of the devisee in the lifetime of the testator, or by reason of such devise being contrary to law or otherwise incapable of taking effect, shall be included in the residuary devise (if any) contained in such will."

A residuary devise will include all real estate not otherwise *effectually* disposed of, unless a contrary intention shall appear by the will. No such intention is to be collected from the attempt to devise a particular estate in another direction. *Ante*, 507. As to the previous law, see *Doe* d. *Gill* v. *Pearson*, 6 East, 173; 2 Smith, 295.

General Devise — Copyholds and Leaseholds.] — Sect. 26 enacts, " that a devise of the land of the testator, or of the land of the testator in any place or in the occupation of any person mentioned in his will. or otherwise described in a general manner, and any other general devise which would describe a customary, copyhold or leasehold estate, if the testator had no freehold estate which could be described by it, shall be construed to include the customary, copyhold and leasehold estates of the testator, or his customary, copyhold and leasehold estates, or any of them, to which such description shall extend, as the case may be, as well as freehold estates, unless a contrary intention shall appear by the will."

For the previous law, see *Rose* v. *Bartlett*, Cro. Car. 292; *Thompson* v. *Lady Hawley*, 2 Bos. & P. 303; *Hobson* v. *Blackburn*, 1 Myl. & K. 571; *Parker* v. *Marchant*, 5 Man. & Gr. 498; 6 Scott, N. R. 485; *Wilson* v. *Eden*, 5 Exch. 752; 11 Beav. 237; *Wilson* v. *Eden*, 14 Q. B. 256; 16 Beav. 153; *Quennell* v. *Turner*, 13 Beav. 240; *Reeves* v. *Baker*, 18 Beav. 372; 1 Jarm. on Wills, 616; 2 Roper on Leg. 1488 (4th ed.).

After the 55 Geo. 3, c. 192. copyholds would pass by a general devise of real estate, although the testator had both freehold and copyhold lands, and had not made any surrender to the use of his will. *Doe* d. *Edmunds* v. *Llewellin*, 2 Cr. M. & R. 503; 1 Gale, 193; *Stokes* v. *Solomons*, 9 Hare, 75.

Since this act any devise of land, which, *if the testator had no freehold*, would before the act have extended to the testator's customary, copyhold or leasehold estates, will now be construed to extend to them respectively (whether the testator had freeholds or not), unless a contrary intention clearly appear by the will. *Wilson* v. *Eden*, 5 Exch. 752. In this case the Court of Exchequer, in pronouncing judgment, said,—" Mr. Humphrey argued, that such contrary intention does appear here, because there is an express gift of all the residue of the personal estate to the testator's brother, which, he contended, was inconsistent with a gift of the leaseholds, which are part of the personal estate, to the trustees for the purpose of the settlement. But this is a fallacy. If before the statute a testator having leaseholds, but no freehold in Durham, had given all his lands in Durham to A. B., and all his personal estates to C. D., there can be no doubt but that A. B. would have taken the leaseholds. The circumstances in such a case show that, under the words personal estate, the testator did not mean to include his leaseholds; and if such would have been the construction before the statute in a case where the testator had only leaseholds, so now the same construction is, by the express words of the statute, to prevail, even though the testator had freeholds as well as leaseholds. The gift of all my personal estate clearly means only my personal estate not otherwise disposed of; and when the statute has made the general devise a valid disposition of the leaseholds, it follows that these are not included in the general description of all my personal estates, or all the residue of my personal estate." "The only other circumstances relied on by Mr. Humphrey, as showing an intention to exclude the leaseholds, were the powers of jointuring and leasing. But we attribute no weight to this part of his argument. The powers would be available in equity, so as to affect the renewed leases from time to time, and the case finds as a fact that such renewals were always regularly made." *Id.* 767.

General Devise—Appointment.]—Sect. 27 enacts, "that a general devise of the real estate of the testator, or of the real estate of the testator in any place or in the occupation of any person mentioned in his will, or otherwise described in a general manner, shall be construed to include any real estate, or any real estate to which such description shall extend (as the case may be), which he may have *power to appoint* in any manner he may think proper, and shall operate as an execution of such power, unless a contrary intention shall appear by the will; and in like manner a bequest of the personal estate of the testator, or any bequest of personal property described in a general manner, shall be construed to include any personal estate, or any personal estate to which such description shall extend (as the case may be), which he shall have power to appoint in any manner he may think proper, and shall operate as an execution of such power, unless a contrary intention shall appear by the will."

For the previous law, see *Denn* d. *Nowell* v. *Roake* (in error), 6 Bing. 475; *Doe* d. *Caldecott* v. *Johnson*, 7 Man. & Gr. 1047; 8 Scott, N. R. 761; *Hughes* v. *Turner*, 3 Myl. & K. 666; *Easum* v. *Appleford*, 10 Simon, 274, affirmed on appeal, 5 Myl. & Cr. 56.

By virtue of this section, taken in conjunction with sect. 24, a will may operate as an execution of a *power created subsequently* to the date of the will. *Stillman* v. *Weedon*, 16 Simon, 26.

Fee Simple without Words of Limitation.]—Sect. 28 enacts, "that where any real estate shall be devised to any person *without any words of limitation*, such devise shall be construed to pass the fee simple, or other the whole estate or interest which the testator had power to dispose of by will in such real estate, unless a contrary intention shall appear by the will."

The previous cases may be divided into four classes, viz.: 1. Where the devisee was held to take an estate for life only. *Doe* d. *Liversage* v. *Vaughan*, 5 B. & A. 464, 471; 1 D. & R. 52; *Doe* d. *Winder* v. *Lawes*, 7 A. & E. 195, 206; 2 N. & P. 195; *Doe* d. *Sams* v. *Garlick*, 14 M. & W. 698; *Doe* d. *Burton* v. *White*, 1 Exch. 526; *S. C.* in error, 2 Exch. 797; *Doe* d. *Kimber* v. *Cafe*, 7 Exch. 675; *Harding* v. *Roberts*, 10 Exch. 819; *Baker* v. *Tucker*, 3 H. L. Cas. 106; 14 Jur. 771. 2. Where the devisee was held to take in fee. *Knight* v. *Selby*, 3 Man. & Gr. 92; 4 Scott, N. R. 409; *Doe* d. *Atkinson* v. *Fawcett*, 3 C. B. 274; *Doe* d. *Roberts* v. *Williams*, 1 Exch. 414; *Doe* d. *Potton* v. *Fricker*, 6 Exch. 540; *Burton* v. *White*, 7 Exch. 720; *Footner* v. *Cooper*, 2 Drewry, 7. 3. Where the devisee was held to take an estate tail. *Doe* d. *Harris* v. *Taylor*, 10 Q. B. 718; *Doe* d. *Cannon* v. *Rucastle*, 8 C. B. 876; *Rimington* v. *Cannon* (in error), 12 C. B. 18; *Voller* v. *Carter*, 4 E. & B. 173; *Harrison* v. *Harrison*, 7 Man. & Gr. 988; 8 Scott, N. R. 872. 4. Where the devisee was held not to take an estate tail, but only for life. *Green-*

wood v. *Rotherwell*, 5 Man. & Gr. 628; 6 Scott, N. R. 670; 6 Beav. 492, *S. C.*; *Slater* v. *Dangerfield*, 15 M. & W. 263; *Kershaw* v. *Kershaw*, 3 E. & B. 845.

Words importing Failure of Issue.]—Sect. 29 enacts, "that in any devise or bequest of real or personal estate, the words "die without issue," or "die without leaving issue," or "have no issue," or any other words which may import either a want or failure of issue of any person in his lifetime or at the time of his death, or an indefinite failure of his issue, shall be construed to mean a want or failure of issue in the lifetime or at the time of the death of such person, and not an indefinite failure of his issue, unless a contrary intention shall appear by the will, by reason of such person having a prior estate tail. or of a preceding gift, being, without any implication arising from such words, a limitation of an estate tail to such person or issue, or otherwise : provided that this act shall not extend to cases where such words as aforesaid import if no issue described in a preceding gift shall be born, or if there shall be no issue who shall live to attain the age, or otherwise answer the description required for obtaining a vested estate by a preceding gift to such issue."

For the previous law, see J. V. Prior's Treatise on the Construction of Limitations, in which the words "issue" and "child" occur, and on the 29th section of this act. *Doe* d. *Ellis* v. *Ellis*, 9 East, 382, 386; *Doe* d. *Cadogan* v. *Ewart*, 7 A. & E. 636, 665; *Doe* d. *Harris* v. *Taylor*, 10 Q. B. 718.

The effect of this section may be thus illustrated. Suppose a gift by will of real and personal estate to A., and if he shall die without issue, then to B. in fee. According to the previous law A. would have taken an estate tail in the land; *Doe* d. *Ellis* v. *Ellis*, 9 East, 382; and would have been *absolutely* entitled to the personal property, as that could not be entailed ; *Harvey* v. *Fowell*, 12 Jur. 241; *Donn* v. *Penny*, 19 Ves. 545; whereas under the new law A. would take the *fee* of the real estate, and the whole interest in the personal estate, but defeasible as to both by his dying without leaving issue *living at his death*, in which event B. would become entitled by way of executory devise or executory bequest, notwithstanding any act of A. Hayes & Jarman on Wills, 31.

In ascertaining whether the words "die without issue" in a will made subsequently to the 7 Will. 4 & 1 Vict. c. 26, mean an indefinite failure of issue, an intention is not to be inferred from the use of those very words. *Re O'Burne* a lunatic, 1 Jones & La Touche, 352. "If a gift is to a man in tail, and for want of issue over, then the contrary appears ; for the whole line of issue is provided for by the antecedent gift, and the words introducing the gift over must refer to the same interest, therefore in such a case the words 'for want of issue' mean an indefinite failure of issue. So, if upon the true construction of the will, without making use of any implication arising from the words introducing the gift over, the first taker takes an estate tail, the words will equally import an indefinite failure of issue." *Id.* 354, Sugden, L. C.; and see *Green* v. *Green*, 3 De Gex & Sm. 480.

Estate of Trustees.]—Sect. 30 enacts, "that where any real estate (other than or not being a presentation to a church) shall be devised to any trustee or executor, such devise shall be construed to pass the fee simple, or other the whole estate or interest which the testator had power to dispose of by will in such real estate, unless a definite term of years, absolute or determinable, or an estate of freehold, shall thereby be given to him expressly or by implication."

This section must be read with reference to sect. 31 ; *infra.*

According to the previous law a devise to trustees, though with words of inheritance, passed to them only so much of the legal estate as the purposes of their trust required ; after which the legal estate vested in the parties beneficially entitled to the property. *Barker* v. *Greenwood,* 4 M. & W. 429 ; *Adams* v. *Adams,* 6 Q. B. 860, 866 ; *Cooke* v. *Blake,* 1 Exch. 220 ; *Doe* d. *Kimber* v. *Cafe,* 7 Exch. 675 ; *Ward* v. *Burbury,* 18 Beav. 190 ; Ros. Ev. 438 (7th ed.). But this led to many difficult questions, *ex. gr.* whether the purposes of the particular trust really required the legal estate, and if so, for what period. *Cases supra ; Warter* v. *Warter,* 2 Brod. & B. 349 ; *Doe* d. *White* v. *Simpson,* 5 East, 162 ; *Right* d. *Phillips* v. *Smith,* 12 East, 455 ; *Warter* v. *Hutchinson,* 1 B. & C. 721 ; *Doe* d. *Gratrex* v. *Homfrey,* 6 A. & E. 206 ; 1 N. & P. 401 ; *Doe* d. *Gord* v. *Reeds,* 2 M. & W. 129, 138 ; *Doe* d. *Rees* v. *Williams, Id.* 749 ; *Doe* d. *Jones* v. *Harrison,* 13 Law J., N. S., Q. B. 97 ; *Doe* d. *Muller* v. *Claridge,* 6 C. B. 641 ; *Poad* v. *Watson,* 25 Law Times R. 142, Q. B. Such questions are now prevented by the above enactment. If the trustees hereafter take more of the legal estate than is really necessary for the performance of their duties, they will, after such performance, stand seised or possessed of the property upon trust for the parties beneficially entitled, and the latter will take equitable instead of legal estates, and may, when necessary, obtain a conveyance of the legal estate from the trustees. *Blagrave* v. *Blagrave,* 4 Exch. 550 ; *Rackham* v. *Siddall,* 1 Mac. & Gor. 607 ; 2 Hall & Tw. 244 ; *Brown* v. *Whiteway,* 8 Hare, 145 ; *Riley* v. *Garney,* 19 Law J., N. S., Chanc. 146.

A general devise to trustees will include trust estates wherein the testator had no beneficial estate or interest, provided the will do not create, with respect to such property, any trust inconsistent with the original trust. *Langford* v. *Auger,* 4 Hare, 313. *Aliter,* where any inconsistent trust or purpose is thereby declared. *Doe* d. *Roylance* v. *Lightfoot,* 8 M. & W. 553; *Doe* d. *Guest* v. *Bennett,* 6 Exch. 892 ; *Lindsell* v. *Thacker,* 12 Simon, 178. Where a testator devised all his real estates whatsoever and wheresoever to T., her heirs and assigns, *charged with* 50l. *to* J. W. : held, that estates of which the testator was a trustee did not pass by the devise. *Rackham* v. *Siddall,* 16 Simon, 297 ; 12 Jur. 640.

Sect. 31 enacts, " that where any real estate shall be devised to a trustee without any express limitation of the estate to be taken by such trustee, and the beneficial interest in such real estate, or in the surplus rents and profits thereof, shall not be given to any person for life, or such beneficial interest shall be given to any person for life, but the purposes of the trust may continue beyond the life of such person, such devise shall be construed to vest in such trustee the fee simple, or other the whole legal estate which the testator had power to dispose of by will in such real estate, and not an estate determinable when the purposes of the trust shall be satisfied."

See the notes to sect. 30; *supra.*

Lapse—Estate Tail.]—Sect. 32 enacts, "that where any person to whom any real estate shall be devised *for an estate tail, or an estate in quasi entail*, shall die in the lifetime of the testator leaving issue who would be inheritable under such entail, and any such issue shall be living at the time of the death of the testator, such devise shall not lapse, but shall take effect as if the death of such person had happened immediately after the death of the testator, unless a contrary intention shall appear by the will."

As to the previous law, see *Doe* d. *Turner* v. *Kett*, 4 T. R. 601.

Lapse—Children or Issue.]—Sect. 33 enacts, "that where any person *being a child or other issue* of the testator, to whom any real or personal estate shall be *devised* or *bequeathed* for any estate or interest, not determinable at or before the death of such person, shall die in the lifetime of the testator leaving issue, and any such issue of such person shall be living at the time of the death of the testator, such *devise or bequest* shall not lapse, but shall take effect as if the death of such person had happened immediately after the death of the testator, unless a contrary intention shall appear by the will."

This section does not apply to a testamentary *appointment* in pursuance of a power. *Griffiths* v. *Gale*, 12 Sim. 354 ; 13 Law J., N. S., Chanc. 286. Nor to a gift or devise to sons, daughters, children or grandchildren *as a class ;* because the share intended for any one who dies in the testator's lifetime does not lapse, but the persons constituting the class at the time of the testator's death take the whole. *Doe* d. *Stewart* v. *Sheffield*, 13 East, 526 ; *Viner* v. *Francis*, 2 Cox, 190 ; *Barber* v. *Barber*, 3 Myl. & Cr. 697 ; *Lee* v. *Ram*, 4 Hare, 250. In such cases, if the testator by a codicil revoke the gift as to one member of the class, the others take the whole. *Shaw* v. *M'Mahon*, 4 Dru. & War. 431 ; and see *Fullford* v. *Fullford*, 16 Beav. 565.

Where this section applies, the deceased devisee or legatee takes the property as though he had survived the testator, and it will pass by his will; his children or other issue do not take independently of him, as substituted devisees or legatees. *Johnson* v. *Johnson*, 3 Hare, 157, Wigram, V. C. A testator, by a will made before this act came into operation, bequeathed a share of his residuary estate to one of his sons, who was also thereby made one of his devisees in trust and executor of his estate. The son died after this act came into operation, leaving issue, and after his death the testator made a codicil to his will altering the bequests to another child, but in other respects confirming his will. It was held, that the gift to the son did not lapse, but that the same, so far as it was real estate, descended to the heir at law of the son, and, so far as it was personal estate, to his executrix under a will made before this act came into operation. *Winter* v. *Winter*, 5 Hare, 306 ; and see *Skinner* v. *Ogle*, 1 Robertson, 363 ; *Aaron* v. *Aaron*, 3 De Gex & Sm. 475. So where a testator by his will, made since this act, gave to his son a residuary share of his estate. The son died after the act came into operation, but before the date of the will, leaving children : it was held, under this section, that the will took effect, although, according to the law prior to the statute, there would have been no effectual devise or bequest. *Mower* v. *Orr*, 7 Hare, 473. A testator devised an estate to his son, J. W., in fee. J. W. died intestate before the testator : held, that the estate descended to J. W.'s son and heir. *Wisden* v. *Wisden*, 2 Smale & G. 396; 18 Jur. 1090. Devise and bequest to all the testator's children (without naming them); a subsequent codicil confirmed the gift as mentioned in his will "to his surviving children" (naming them all). One died in the testator's lifetime, leaving children, who survived the testator : held, that the survivorship had relation to the testator's death, and not to the date of the will, and that the representatives of the deceased child took nothing under this section. *Pullford* v. *Fullford,* 16 Beav. 565.

When Act operates.]—Sect. 34 enacts, " that this act shall not extend to any will made before the first day of January, 1838; and that every will re-executed, or republished, or revived by any codicil, shall, for the purposes of this act, be deemed to have been made at the time at which the same shall be so re-executed, republished or revived; and that this act shall not extend to any estate *pur autre vie* of any person who shall die before the first day of January, 1838."

Wills dated before the 1st day of January, 1838, may come within the act if re-executed, republished or revived by a codicil subsequently to the above date. *Brooke* v. *Kent,* 3 Moore's P. C. C. 334, 347; 1 Ecc. & Mar. Cas. 93, *S. C.* A codicil which recites the previous will, and *ratifies and confirms it,* does in effect *republish* the will within the meaning of this section. *Doe* d. *York* v. *Walker,* 12 M. & W. 591. A codicil attested by only two witnesses is sufficient to republish a will made before the above date, and to which three witnesses were necessary. *Andrews* v. *Turner,* 3 Q. B. 177. The effect of republication of the will by a codicil is the same as if the testator had at the date of the codicil made a will in the words of the will so republished. *Winter* v. *Winter,* 5 Hare, 306; *Wilson* v. *Eden,* 5 Exch. 752; 11 Beav. 237; *Skinner* v. *Ogle,* 1 Robertson, 363; *Aaron* v. *Aaron,* 3 De Gex & Sm. 475.

Where a testator duly executed a will in 1835, and, after the 1st January, 1838, cut therefrom his signature, it was held that, notwithstanding sect. 34, it was not the intention that wills executed before the 1st January, 1838, should be exempted from the provisions of the statute *with respect to any act done to such wills after that date;* and that the cutting off of the signature amounted to a revocation of the will under section 20. *Hobbs* v. *Knight,* 1 Curt. 768; and see *Longford* v. *Little,* 2 Jon. & Lat. (Irish R.), 633; *Clarke* v. *Scripps,* 16 Jur. 783.

Scotland.]—Sect. 35 enacts, " that this act shall not extend to Scotland."

The Wills Amendment Act, 1852.]—By 15 & 16 Vict. c. 24, s. 1, after reciting that, "where, by an act passed in the first year of the reign of her majesty Queen Victoria, intituled 'An Act for the Amendment of the Laws with respect to Wills,' it is enacted, that no will shall be valid unless it shall be signed at the foot or end thereof by the testator, or by some other person in his presence and by his direction;" "every will shall, so far only as regards the position of the signature of the testator, or of the person signing for him as aforesaid, be deemed to be valid within the said enactment, as explained by this act, if the signature shall be so placed at, or after, or following, or under, or beside, or opposite to, the end of the will, that it shall be apparent on the face of the will that the testator intended to give effect by such his signature to the writing signed as his will, and that no such will shall be affected by the circumstance that the signature shall not follow or be immediately after the foot or end of the will, or by the circumstance that a blank space shall intervene between the concluding word of the will and the signature, or by the circumstance that the signature shall be placed among the words of the testimonium clause, or of the clause of attestation, or shall follow, or be after, or under the clause of attestation, either with or without a blank space intervening, or shall follow, or be after, or under, or beside, the names, or one of the names, of the subscribing witnesses, or by the circumstance that the signature shall be on a side or page, or other portion of the paper or papers containing the will, whereon no clause or paragraph or disposing part of the will shall be written above the signature, or by the circumstance that there shall appear to be sufficient space on or at the bottom of the preceding side or page, or other portion of the same paper on which the will is written, to contain the signature; and the enumeration of the above circumstances shall not restrict the generality of the above enactment; but no signature under the said act or this act shall be operative to give effect to any disposition or direction which is underneath or which follows it, nor shall it give effect to any disposition or direction inserted after the signature shall be made."

Sect. 2. "The provisions of this act shall extend and be applied to every will already made, where administration or probate has not already been granted or ordered by a court of competent jurisdiction in consequence of the defective execution of such will, or where the property, not being within the jurisdiction of the ecclesiastical courts, has not been possessed or enjoyed by some person or persons claiming to be entitled thereto in consequence of the defective execution of such will, or the right thereto shall not have been decided to be in some other person or persons than the persons claiming under the will, by a court of competent jurisdiction, in consequence of the defective execution of such will."

Sect. 3. "The word 'will' shall, in the construction of this act, be interpreted in like manner as the same is directed to be interpreted under the provisions in this behalf contained in the said act of the first year of the reign of her majesty Queen Victoria." *Ante,* 493.

Sect. 4. "This act may be cited as 'The Wills Act Amendment Act, 1852.'"

Evidence for Plaintiff.]—In ejectment by a devisee of freeholds the plaintiff is always entitled to begin. *Doe* d. *Bather* v. *Brayne,* 5 C. B. 655; *ante,* 284. He must prove:—

1. The will. The original must be produced; Ros. Ev. 1, 104 (7th ed.); Bull. N. P. 246; *Doe* d. *Wild* v. *Ormerod,* 1 Moo. & Rob. 466. The probate is not even secondary evidence, although the will is shown to have been lost or destroyed. *Doe* d. *Ash* v. *Calvert,* 2 Camp. 389, Lord Ellenborough, C. J. In such case an *examined* copy should be proved; or some person who has read the original will should speak to the contents from his recollection. Ad. Eject. 247. Unless the will be *admitted* in the cause (*ante,* 150), it must be proved by some or one of the attesting witnesses; 17 & 18 Vict. c. 125, s. 26; *ante,* 294. The attesting witnesses, or some or one of them, must prove that the will was *duly executed and attested pursuant to the* 7 *Will.* 4 & 1 *Vict.* c. 26, *s.* 9 (*ante,* 497), *as amended by* 15 & 16 *Vict.* c. 24. (*Ante,* 513.)

We have already considered fully those enactments and the decisions thereon. *Ante,* 497 to 500, and 513. It is not necessary to prove that the will was actually read over to the testator before he executed it. *Mitchell* v. *Thomas,* 6 Moore, P. C. C. 137. In the absence of proof to the contrary, it will be presumed that the testator was cognizant of the contents. *Browning* v. *Budd,* 6 Moore, P. C. C. 430. The burthen of proof of the due execution and validity of the will of course lies upon the party claiming under it. *Paske* v. *Ollott,* 2 Phil. R. 323; *Barry* v. *Butlin,* 2 Moore, P. C. C. 480; *Browning* v. *Budd,* 6 Moore, P. C. C. 430. If any one of the attesting witnesses can prove that *all* the requisites of the statutes were duly complied with, it is unnecessary to call the other attesting witnesses. *Doe* d. *Stutsbury* v. *Smith,* 1 Esp. 391, Lord Kenyon, C. J.; Bull. N. P. 264; *Longford* v. *Eyre,* 1 P. Wms. 741; *Provis* v. *Reed,* 5 Bing. 435; *Wright* v. *Doe* d. *Tatham* (in error), 1 A. & E. 23, *per cur.* But on a feigned issue of *"devisavit vel non,"* directed by the Court of Chancery, it is generally necessary for a devisee claiming under the will to call all the attesting witnesses. *Bootle* v. *Blundell,* 19 Ves. 264; Cooper, 136, *S. C.*; *Bowman* v. *Bowman,* 2 Moo. & Rob. 501; *M'Gregor* v. *Topham,* 3 H. L. Cas. 132, 155; 2 Tayl. Ev. 1417 (2nd ed.). If, however, the devisee be the defendant, it is not necessary for him to call all the attesting witnesses. *Tatham* v. *Wright,* 2 Russ. & Myl. 1; Ros. Ev. 112 (8th ed.). If any attesting witness either cannot or will not prove that all the requisites of the statute were duly complied with, it will generally be necessary to call the other attesting witnesses (if living); Ad. Eject. 252. In *Dayrell* v. *Glascock,* Skinner, 413, one of the attesting witnesses would not swear to the facts he had attested. Holt, C. J., held that proof of his attestation was sufficient, for otherwise it would be in the power of a third person to defeat the will of the deceased by a *non mi ricordo;* and see *Doe* d. *Davies* v. *Davies,* 9 Q. B. 648; *Bennett and Field* v. *Sharp,* 25 Law Times R. 10. Positive affirmative evidence by the subscribing witnesses of the facts of a testator acknowledging his signature in their joint presence, and of their subscribing in conformity with the requisites of the law, is not absolutely essential to the validity of testamentary papers. When the inaccuracy and imperfect recollection of witnesses are established, the court (or a jury) may, upon the circumstances of the case, presume due execution. *Leech* v. *Bates,* 1 Robertson, 714; *Blake* v. *Knight,* 3 Curt. 547. Where two of the attesting witnesses were dead, and the third, who was a marksman, had no remembrance of having attested the will: held, that proof of the signatures of the two deceased witnesses, without proof of the signature of the testator, or of the marksman, was sufficient evidence *for the jury* of the due execution of the will. *Doe* d. *Davies* v. *Davies,* 9 Q. B. 648. Where both the attesting witnesses denied the due execution of the will, and there appeared no circumstances on which the court could found a presumption that the recollection of the witnesses was infirm on the subject, probate was refused. *Pennant* v. *Kingscote,* 3 Curt. 642. Where one of the attesting witnesses was dead, but his signature was proved, the second denied his signature, but was disbelieved by the jury on the trial of an issue, and the third proved his attestation, but had no memory as to the signature or publication by the testator: held, that the due execution of the will might be presumed. *Hitch* v. *Wells,* 10 Beav. 84. Where an attesting witness unexpectedly denies his handwriting, and the jury find against the will, a new trial will be granted upon affidavits of surprise, &c. *Goodtitle* d. *Alexander* v. *Clayton*, 4 Burr. 2224. Where all the three attesting witnesses swore that the will had not been duly executed according to the Statute of Frauds, the devisee, upon strong contradictory evidence, obtained the verdict. *Austin* v. *Willes*, Bull. N. P. 264 ; and see *Bennett and Field* v. *Sharp*, 25 Law Times, 10. Where the three subscribing witnesses to a will were called, and denied their hands, the court admitted the plaintiff to contradict that evidence, and he succeeded in supporting the will against such testimony. *Pike* v. *Badmering*, cited 2 Stra. 1096. So where all or any of the attesting witnesses deny the sanity or mental capacity of the testator. *Hudson's case*, Skinner, 79 ; *Lowe* v. *Joliffe*, 1 W. Black. 365. In this case the three attesting witnesses were afterwards convicted of perjury. *Rex* v. *Nireys and Galey*, Id. 416. " I have always thought that if any attention at all ought to be paid to the testimony of witnesses who deny they have attested, it ought to be the slightest possible. Perhaps the best way would be to disregard it altogether." *Per* Shadwell, V. C., in *Wilson* v. *Beddard*, 12 Simon, 34 ; cited with approbation by Lord Brougham in *M'Gregor* v. *Topham*, 3 H. L. Cas. 156.

Where all the attesting witnesses are dead, or insane, proof of their death or insanity, and of their signatures to the attestation, will be sufficient. *Croft* v. *Pawlet*, 2 Stra. 1109 ; *Bernett* v. *Taylor*, 9 Ves. 381. In such case the testator's signature need not be proved. *Doe* d. *Davies* v. *Davies*, 9 Q. B. 648. But if proved, the plaintiff's case may be thereby strengthened. Where the attestation of a will stated that it was "signed, sealed, published and declared by the testatrix as her last will and testament, in the presence of us," but it did not say that the witnesses attested in the presence of the testatrix : all of them were dead, and one of them was proved to have been an attorney of good character : held sufficient evidence for the jury that the will had been duly attested in the presence of the testatrix. *Hands* v. *James*, Comyn R. 531 ; and see *Croft* v. *Pawlet*, 2 Stra. 1109 ; *Doe* d. *Davies* v. *Davies*, 9 Q. B. 648, 650. Either party may call not only the attesting witnesses, but any other persons who happened to be present when the will was executed, and can state what then took place. *Doe* d. *Smale* v. *Allen*, 8 T. R. 147 ; *Roberts* v. *Phillips*, 4 E. & B. 450, 451. Where both the attesting witnesses stated that they did not remember seeing the testatrix sign, and one of them positively that the testatrix did not sign in his presence : held, that the attorney who prepared the will, and was present when it was executed, might prove that it was duly signed by the testatrix, in the presence of the attesting witnesses ; although he was an executor and beneficially interested under the will : upon his evidence probate was granted. *Bennett and Field* v. *Sharp*, 25 Law Times, 10.

By 17 & 18 Vict. c. 125, s. 27, "comparison of a disputed writing with any writing proved to the satisfaction of the judge to be genuine, shall be permitted to be made by witnesses ; and such writings, and the evidence of witnesses respecting the same, may be submitted to the court and jury as evidence of the genuineness, or otherwise, of the writing in dispute." *Ante*, 294.

A will more than thirty years old, if produced from the proper custody, proves itself. Its age is to be reckoned from its date, and not from the time of the testator's death. *Doe* d. *Oldham* v. *Woolley*, 8 B.

& C. 22; *Man* v. *Ricketts*, 7 Beav. 93. It is no objection to the will being *read* in evidence, that possession has not followed it, because until it is read the court cannot know how the will directs the possession to go. *Doe* d. *Lloyd* v. *Passingham*, 2 C. & P. 440, Burrough, J. The attesting witnesses need not be called, although shown to be alive, and capable of being produced. *Doe* d. *Oldham* v. *Woolley*, *supra*. If there be any rasures, interlineations or alterations, upon which the claimant relies, they should be explained by evidence showing when and by whom they were made. Gilb. Ev. 100, 101; *ante*, 504; *Cooper* v. *Bockett*, 4 Moore, P. C. C. 419; *Doe* d. *Shallcross* v. *Palmer*, 16 Q. B. 747.

Generally speaking, an ancient will should be *produced from the proper custody ; ex. gr.* from the ecclesiastical court in which it has been proved, or by some or one of the executors, or trustees or devisees. In this respect an ancient will stands on the same footing as an ancient grant : as to which the rule is, that ancient grants are not to be received in evidence, without proof of their execution, unless they can be accounted for as coming from the hands of some one connected with the estate to which they relate. If produced from the British Museum, or the Bodleian Library at Oxford, or any other public institution, that is not sufficient. *Swinnerton* v. *Marquis of Stafford*, 3 Taunt. 91.

If the *sanity* or *mental capacity* of the testator to make a will be called in question (*post*, 522), the plaintiff should produce all his evidence on that point in the first instance, or he should reserve the whole of it as " evidence in reply," and prove only the other necessary facts. He cannot be permitted to produce part of his evidence on the above point in the first instance, and the remainder of it as evidence in reply. *Ante*, 300, 301. As to what constitutes insanity or incapacity to make a will, see *post*, 522; *Waring* v. *Waring*, 6 Moore, P. C. C. 341. Moral insanity, or the perversion of the moral feelings, not accompanied with *insane delusion*, which is the legal test of insanity, is not sufficient to invalidate a will. *Frere* v. *Peacocke*, 1 Robertson, 442.

2. The death of the testator must be proved. *Doe* d. *Graham* v. *Penfold*, 8 C. & P. 536 ; *ante*, 239.

3. The seisin or title of the testator at the time of his death must be proved in like manner as if he were living and sought to recover the property. *Doe* d. *Lloyd* v. *Passingham*, 6 B. & C. 305; 9 D. & R. 416; *Doe* d. *Cross* v. *Cross*, 8 Q. B. 714. Proof that he was in actual possession, or in receipt of the rent, shortly before his death, is *primâ facie* evidence of a seisin in fee. *Ante*, 211. But it is not generally advisable to rely on mere *primâ facie* evidence of title, where better and more conclusive evidence can be produced. Proof of a title in the testator by estoppel is sufficient as against any person affected by such estoppel. *Doe* d. *Willis* v. *Birchmore*, 9 A. & E. 662; 1 P. & D. 448; *Doe* d. *Marlow* v. *Wiggins*, 4 Q. B. 367; 3 Gale & D. 504; *Doe* d. *Nicoll* v. *Bower*, 16 Q. B. 805. It is unnecessary to prove that the testator was *actually seised* of the property at the time of his death : if it be shown that he was *legally entitled* to it for an estate in fee simple, that is sufficient; because a right of entry may be devised; 7 Will. 4 & 1 Vict. c. 26, s. 3; *ante*, 494; and such right will pass by a devise of the land to which it relates. *Doe* d. *Souter* v. *Hull*, 2 D. & R. 38.

4. It must appear that the testator was in possession of the property or in receipt of the rent within twenty years before the commencement of the action; *Holloway* v. *Rakes*, cited 2 T. R. 55; or that for some other reason the right and title of the plaintiff claiming through him has not been extinguished by the Statute of Limitations. 3 & 4 Will. 4, c. 27; *ante*, 4; *Doe* d. *Cook* v. *Danvers*, 7 East, 299; 3 Smith, 291; and see *Doe* d. *Milner* v. *Brightwen*, 10 East, 583; *Doe* d. *Souter* v. *Hull*, 2 D. & R. 38.

5. If the testator had *demised* the property, and was merely in receipt of the rent, it must be shown that the tenancy has expired (*Doe* d. *Angell* v. *Angell*, 9 Q. B. 328), or has been determined by a regular notice to quit; *ante*, 29; *Doe* d. *Leicester* v. *Biggs*, 2 Taunt. 109; *Doe* d. *Collins* v. *Weller*, 7 T. R. 478; *Doe* d. *Rawlings* v. *Walker*, 5 B. & C. 111; 7 D. & R. 487; *Doe* d. *Wawn* v. *Horn*, 3 M. & W. 333; *Doe* d. *Nicoll* v. *Bower*, 16 Q. B. 805; or in some other legal manner; *ante*, 445, 446; because otherwise the plaintiff's remedy is by distress or action for the rent, &c., but not by ejectment. *Doe* d. *Wawn* v. *Horn*, 3 M. & W. 333; *Doe* d. *Da Costa* v. *Wharton*, 8 T. R. 2; *ante*, 66, 287. He may, however, show that there has been a covenant or condition broken after the testator's death, by reason whereof, and of a proviso for re-entry contained in the lease, he, as assignee of the reversion, is entitled to maintain ejectment. *Ante*, Chap. XXXIX.

6. In case there be any estates limited by the will prior to the devise to the plaintiff, the determination of such estates by death, forfeiture or otherwise, must be shown: Ros. Ev. 463; *Doe* d. *Norfolk* v. *Hawke*, 2 East, 481; *Doe* d. *Beck* v. *Heakin*, 6 A. & E. 495; *Doe* d. *Liversage* v. *Vaughan*, 5 B. & A. 464; 1 D. & R. 52: also of any estates arising out of them; *ex. gr.* a tenancy by the courtesy; *Doe* d. *Kenrick* v. *Lord Beauclerk*, 11 East, 657; or a jointure estate appointed pursuant to a power contained in the will. *Zouch* d. *Woolston* v. *Woolston*, 1 W. Black 281; 2 Burr. 1136; recognized in *Doe* d. *Milborne* v. *Milborne*, 2 T. R. 721, 725.

7. It must appear that upon the true construction of the will, and in the events which have since happened, the plaintiffs, or some or one of them, are or is *legally entitled to actual possession* of the property mentioned in the writ of ejectment, or some part thereof. *Doe* d. *Andrew* v. *Lainchbury*, 11 East, 290; *Doe* d. *Strong* v. *Goff*, *Id.* 668; *Right* d. *Phillips* v. *Smith*, 12 East, 455; *Doe* d. *Pilkington* v. *Spratt*, 5 B. & Adol. 731; 2 N. & M. 524; *Doe* d. *Gratrex* v. *Homfray*, 6 A. & E. 206; 1 N. & P. 401; *Doe* d. *Haw* v. *Earles*, 15 M. & W. 450; *Doe* d. *Knight* v. *Chaffer*, 16 M. & W. 656; *Doe* d. *Angell* v. *Angell*, 9 Q. B. 328; *Doe* d. *Bailey* v. *Sloggett*, 5 Exch. 107; *Doe* d. *Blakiston* v. *Haslewood*, 10 C. B. 544. A mere right to the rents and profits is not sufficient; *Doe* d. *Leicester* v. *Biggs*, 2 Taunt. 109; *Doe* d. *Da Costa* v. *Wharton*, 8 T. R. 2; *ante*, 66, 287; nor an equitable title; *Doe* d. *Leicester* v. *Biggs*, 2 Taunt. 109; *Doe* d. *Cadogan* v. *Ewart*, 7 A. & E. 636, 670; 3 N. & P. 197; nor a mere power of sale. *Doe* d. *Hampton* v. *Shotter*, 8 A. & E. 905; 1 P. & D. 124. In order to a correct construction of the will, reference should be had to such of the provisions of the statute 7 Will. 4 & 1 Vict. c. 26 as may be applicable: *ante*, 492: also to the last edition of Jarman on Wills (this is by far the best book on the subject); Wms. Exors. (5th ed.); 11 Jarm. Byth. 136—406 (3rd ed.).

8. The *identity* of the land claimed, or some part thereof with that devised, must be made to appear. *Doe* d. *Preedy* v. *Holtom,* 4 A. & E. 76 ; *Id.* 82, Coleridge, J. ; *Doe* d. *Hemming* v. *Willetts,* 7 C. B. 709 ; *Doe* d. *Renow* v. *Ashley,* 10 Q. B. 663 ; *Doe* d. *Bailey* v. *Sloggett,* 5 Exch. 107 ; *Ricketts* v. *Turquand,* 1 H. L. Cas. 473 ; *Doe* d. *Gore* v. *Langton,* 2 B. & Adol. 680 ; *Doe* d. *Ashforth* v. *Bower,* 3 B. & Adol. 453 ; *Doe* d. *Templeman* v. *Martin,* 4 B. & Adol. 771 ; *Richardson* v. *Watson, Id.* 787, 799 ; Broom's Max. 265. Whether parcel or not of the thing devised is always matter of evidence. *Per* Buller, J., in *Doe* d. *Freeland* v. *Burt,* 1 T. R. 704 ; *Goodtitle* d. *Radford* v. *Southern,* 1 M. & S. 299 ; *Doe* d. *Beach* v. *Earl of Jersey,* 3 B. & C. 870, 873 ; *ante,* 240, 289. But evidence is not admissible to show that the testator *intended* to comprise in the devise *other* property than that mentioned. *Miller* v. *Travers,* 8 Bing. 244 ; *Doe* d. *Oxenden* v. *Chichester,* 4 Dow. Parl. C. 65, cited 8 Bing. 254 ; *Doe* d. *Preedy* v. *Holtom,* 4 A. & E. 76 ; *Id.* 82, Coleridge, J. It seems that freehold may pass by a will giving the estate a local description and name, though it be mistakenly called leasehold, there being no other property answering to the name and description. *Denn* d. *Wilkins* v. *Kemeys,* 9 East, 366. Sometimes the local description is inaccurate. *Gauntlett* v. *Carter,* 17 Beav. 586 ; *Armstrong* v. *Buckland,* 18 Beav. 204 ; *Attwater* v. *Attwater,* 18 Beav. 330. Sometimes the occupation is inaccurately described as to part. *Doe* d. *Campton* v. *Carpenter,* 16 Q. B. 181 ; *Doe* d. *Hubbard* v. *Hubbard,* 15 Q. B. 227 ; *Nightingall* v. *Smith,* 1 Exch. 879 ; *Morrell* v. *Fisher,* 4 Exch. 591 ; *Doe* d. *Renow* v. *Ashley,* 10 Q. B. 663 ; *Doe* d. *Hemmings* v. *Willett,* 7 C. B. 709. Where the object of a testator's bounty or the subject of disposition (*i. e.* the *person* or *thing* intended) is described in terms which are applicable indifferently to more than one person or thing, evidence is admissible to prove which of the persons or things so described was intended by the testator. Wigram on Extrinsic Ev. 78 (2nd ed.). In no case is parol evidence admissible *to vary* the words of a deed or will, but only to explain their meaning, when there is any latent ambiguity. *Attorney-General* v. *Clapham,* 4 De Gex, Mac. & Gor. 591. In *Shore* v. *Wilson,* 9 Cl. & Fin. 355, and *Drummond* v. *Attorney-General,* 2 H. L. Cas. 837, parol evidence was received *only* to enable the court to understand and construe the deed, to show the real meaning of the words used. In expounding a will, the court is to ascertain, not what the testator *intended,* as contradistinguished from what *his words express,* but what is the meaning of the *words he has used.*" *Per* Parke, J., in *Doe* d. *Gwillim* v. *Gwillim,* 5 B. & Adol. 129 ; and see *Doe* d. *Templeman* v. *Martin,* 4 B. & Adol. 783 ; Wigram on Extrinsic Ev. 7 (2nd ed.).

9. The *identity* of the claimant with the person named in the will must appear by evidence or otherwise. *Mostyn* v. *Mostyn,* 5 H. L. Cas. 155. If there be any ambiguity on this point *patent* on the face of a will, it cannot be explained or aided by parol evidence. Wigram on Extrinsic Ev. 2, 65—75, 126 (2nd ed.). Thus where the devise is to " one of the sons of J. S. ;" *Strode* v. *Russel,* 2 Vern. 624 ; *Altham's case,* 8 Co. R. 155 ; Broom's Max. 261 ; or if the devisee's name be left in blank. *Hunt* v. *Hort,* 3 Bro. C. C. 311, cited 8 Bing. 254 ; *Baylis* v. *Attorney-General,* 2 Atk. 239 ; *Castleton* v. *Turner,* 3 Atk. 258 ; *Clayton* v. *Lord Nugent,* 13 M. & W. 200. But evidence was admitted to show who was meant by a bequest to "—— Price, the

son of —— ;" *Price* v. *Page,* 4 Ves. 680 ; because intimate friends
are in the habit of calling each other by their surnames only.
Per Rolfe, B., in *Clayton* v. *Lord Nugent,* 13 M. & W. 207. So
parol evidence is admissible of facts showing that a bequest to " Mrs.
G." meant Mrs. Gregg. *Abbott* v. *Massie,* 3 Ves. 148. " The Lord
Chancellor does not say in that case *what* evidence was to be received.
Probably the testator was in the habit of calling Mrs. Gregg
' Mrs. G.' " *Per* Rolfe, B., in *Clayton* v. *Lord Nugent,* 13 M. &
W. 204. Devises or bequests to A., B., C., D., &c., are void, and
parol evidence is not admissible to show what persons were intended
by those letters. *Clayton* v. *Lord Nugent,* 13 M. & W. 200.

If the ambiguity be not patent on the face of the will, but is created
by parol evidence of extrinsic circumstances, it is called a *latent* ambiguity; with respect to which the rule is, that, inasmuch as the
ambiguity is raised by extrinsic evidence, so it may be removed in the
same manner. *Ambiguitas verborum latens verificatione suppletur ;
nam quod ex facto oritur ambiguum verificatione facti tollitur.* Bac.
Max. Reg. 23 ; Broom's Max. 260, 263 ; Wigram on Extrinsic Ev.
59, 126 (2nd ed.) ; 2 Phil. Ev. 315 (9th ed.). Extrinsic evidence is
only admitted to assist in the construction of wills where the ambiguity
is created by matter *dehors* the will. *Bernasconi* v. *Atkinson,* 23
Law J., N. S., Chanc. 184 ; 17 Jur. 128. Where the object of a testator's bounty is described in terms which are applicable indifferently
to more than one person, evidence is admissible to prove which of the
persons so described was intended by the testator. Wigram on Extrinsic Ev. 78 (2nd ed.). Thus, if a man has two sons both baptized by the
name of *John,* and conceiving that the elder (who had been long absent) is dead, devises his land by his will in writing to his son John
generally, and in truth the elder is living ; in this case the younger
son may in pleading, or in evidence, allege the devise to him ; and if
it be denied, he may produce witnesses to prove his father's intent, that
he thought the other to be dead ; or that he, at the time of the will
made, named his son John the younger, and the writer left out the
addition ' the younger.' *Per cur.* in *Cheyney's case,* 5 Co. R. 68 ;
Counden v. *Clerke,* Hob. 32 ; *Altham's case,* 8 Co. R. 155. A devise
to " John Cluer of Calcot" may be shown by evidence to be intended
for the son, and not for the father, who died after the date of the will
and in the lifetime of the testatrix. *Jones* v. *Newman,* 1 W. Black.
60. A devise to " George Gord, the son of *Gord,*" may be explained
by evidence of the testator's declarations as to the person intended.
Doe d. *Gord* v. *Needs,* 2 M. & W. 129. A testatrix devised land to
John Allen, the grandson of her brother Thomas, his heirs and assigns,
charged with the payment of 100*l.* " to each and every the brothers
and sisters of the aforesaid John." At the time of making the will
there were two persons named John Allen, grandsons of Thomas
Allen, one of whom had several brothers and several sisters ; the other
had only one brother and one sister : held, that parol evidence of
declarations of the testatrix that she had left all her property to the
grandson who had only one brother and one sister were admissible to
show which grandson should take under the devise ; and that it was
no objection to such evidence that the declarations were subsequent to
the making of the will. *Doe* d. *Allen* v. *Allen,* 12 A. & E. 451 ; 4 P.
& D. 220. A testator devised land to his niece, Mary R., for life,
remainder to " her three daughters, Mary, *Elizabeth* and Ann," in fee

as tenants in common. At the date of the will Mary B. had two legitimate daughters, Mary and Ann, living, and one illegitimate, named Elizabeth : held, that extrinsic evidence was admissible to rebut the claim of Elizabeth, by showing that Mary B. formerly had a legitimate daughter named Elizabeth, who died some years before the date of the will ; and that the testator did not then know of her death, or of the birth of the illegitimate daughter : held also, in ejectment for the land by the illegitimate daughter, that letters purporting to have been written and sent, thirty years before, by the testator to his niece Mary B., and produced from the proper custody, were admissible against the plaintiff, without proof of the handwriting, to show the testator's apprehension of the state of Mary B.'s family. *Doe* d. *Elizabeth Thomas* v. *Beynon*, 12 A. & E. 431 ; 4 P. & D. 193. A testator devised lands to his son John H. for life ; and from his decrease to the testator's grandson *John H.*, *eldest son* of the said John H., for life ; and on his decease to the first son of the body of his said grandson John H. in tail male, with other remainders over. At the time of making the will the testator's son John H. had been twice married ; by his first wife he had one son *Simon*, by his second wife a son *John*, and other younger sons and daughters : held, that evidence of *the instructions given by the testator for his will, and of his declarations,* was not admissible to show which of these two grandsons was intended by the description of the will. *Doe* d. *Simon Hiscocks* v. *John Hiscocks*, 5 M. & W. 363. But the court did not decide that no evidence was admissible of *facts* from which a conclusion might be drawn whether the testator meant the eldest son Simon, or John, the eldest son of the second family. It is to be observed that the description was not correct as *to either* party, and could not be made so by any evidence whatever. And see *Mostyn* v. *Mostyn*, 5 H. L. Cas. 155. A devise to the second son of *Edward* Weld, of Lulworth, may be shown to mean the second son of *Joseph* Weld, of Lulworth (there being no Edward Weld). *Lord Camoys* v. *Blundell*, 1 H. L. Cas. 778 ; *Blundell* v. *Gladstone*, 1 Phil. R. 274 ; 11 Simon, 467. An error in the name or sex of the devisee will not render the devise invalid if it can be shown to apply to no other person than the claimant. *Ryall* v. *Hannam*, 10 Beav. 536 ; 16 Law J., N. S., Chanc. 491. A testator, by his will dated in November, 1845, devised an estate to "his dear wife Caroline." He had been twice married : in 1834 to Mary and in 1840 to Caroline ; they both survived him, and he lived with the latter up to the time of his death, in November, 1845 : held, that the words "dear wife" were not inapplicable to Caroline, and that she was entitled as devisee. *Doe* d. *Gains* v. *Rouse*, 5 C. B. 422 ; 17 Law J., N. S., C. P. 108 ; and see *Pratt* v. *Matthew*, 25 Law J., N. S., Chanc. 409. Evidence of conversations with the testator, after the execution of his will, is not admissible as proof of the *intention* of the testator, but is admissible to prove the testator's *knowledge of the state of the family* in whose favour a devise was made by the will. *Lord Camoys* v. *Blundell*, 1 H. L. Cas. 778.

10. If the plaintiff be not himself the devisee, he must prove the devisee's title (as *ante*, 514) ; and also his own derivative title from the devisee, *ex. gr.*, by deed ; *Denne* d. *Bowyer* v. *Judge*, 11 East, 288 ; *Doe* d. *Bruce* v. *Martyn*, 8 B. & C. 497 ; 2 Man. & R. 485 ; *Doe* d. *Pilkington* v. *Spratt*, 5 B. & Adol. 731 ; 2 N. & M. 524 ; or will, or descent, &c.

Evidence and Points for Defendant.]—The defendant may contend—

1. That the evidence for the plaintiff is insufficient on some material point. *Ante*, 514—521. He may also produce contradictory evidence.

2. That the will was not duly executed and attested according to the statute. *Ante*, 497. In support of this objection he may call any attesting witness not already examined on behalf of the plaintiff; Bull. N. P. 264; or any other person who happened to be present when the will was executed, and can speak to what then took place. *Doe* d. *Small* v. *Allen*, 8 T. R. 147; *Roberts* v. *Phillips*, 4 E. & B. 450, 451. But *declarations* of the testator tending to show that the will was not duly executed and attested, are inadmissible. *Provis* v. *Reed*, 5 Bing. 435.

3. That the will is a forgery. *Doe* d. *Stutsbury* v. *Smith*, 1 Esp. 391; 2 Arch. N. P. 388.

4. That the testator was induced to execute it by fraud. *Bransby* v. *Kerridge*, Bull. N. P 266; Swin. pt. 7, s. 3, pl. 1; 1 Wms. Exors. 38 (3rd ed.). Thus where the testator, at the time of executing the will, asked whether the contents were the same as a former will, and was answered in the affirmative, contrary to the fact. *Doe* d. *Small* v. *Allen*, 8 T. R. 147. So where one will was substituted for another without the testator's knowledge. *S. C.* Fraud and imposition upon weakness is a sufficient ground to set aside a will of real estate. *Lord Donegal's case*, 2 Ves. sen. 408; *Mountain* v. *Bennett*, 1 Cox, 335, 356. Imbecility produced by age or sickness, of which the devisee has taken advantage, is sufficient to avoid a will. Ros. Ev. 464; 1 Wms. Exors. 38, 40 (3rd ed.); *Mynn* v. *Robinson*, 2 Hagg. 179; *Marsh* v. *Tyrrell, Id.* 84; *Ingram* v. *Wyatt*, 1 Hagg. 94; *Trimlestown* v. *D'Alton*, 1 Dow. Parl. C., N. S. 85. Exaggeration of the conduct of a party benefited by a will towards the testatrix, though it induce her to revoke the will, and the bequest made in his favour, and to execute another will to his exclusion, is not such a fraud as to destroy free agency and render the will invalid: neither does such conduct amount to undue influence or importunity. *Browning* v. *Budd*, 6 Moore, P. C. C. 430.

5. That the testator, at the time of executing the will, was of *non sane memory*, *i. e.* not mentally competent to make a will. 2 Arch. N. P. 389; *Doe* d. *Stephenson* v. *Walker*, 4 Esp. 50. But a lunatic may make a will *during a lucid interval*. *Beverley's case*, 4 Co. Rep. 123 b; 11 Jarm. Byth. 25 (3rd ed.); *Re Watts*, 1 Curt. 594; *Rodd* v. *Lewis*, 2 Cas. temp. Lee, 176; *Hall* v. *Warren*, 9 Ves. 610; 1 Wms. Exors. 17 (3rd ed.). It is not enough that a testator, when he makes his will, has sufficient memory to answer familiar and usual questions; he ought to have a disposing memory, so as to be able to make a disposition of his lands with understanding and reason. *Marquis of Winchester's case*, 6 Co. R. 23 a; 4 Burn's Ecc. Law, 49; *Mountain* v. *Bennett*, 1 Cox, 356. The will itself may be evidence of a sound mind or lucid interval; and one made by a person while confined in an asylum, has been established by the reasonableness of its provisions. *M'Adam* v. *Walker*, 1 Dow. Parl. C. 178; *Cartwright* v. *Cartwright*, 1 Phil. 90. Where a will was executed on the 21st of January, containing a just and proper distribution of the testator's property, and on the 24th, only three days after, a codicil thereto was signed and executed, the effect of which would have been to leave the eldest son nearly destitute, the

will was held valid, and probate refused to the codicil, on the ground that the deceased was not *then* in the possession of a sound and disposing memory. *Brounker* v. *Brounker*, 2 Phillimore, 57. A will well executed shall not be set aside, or the testator considered *non compos*, on account of the dispositions therein being imprudent or unaccountable. *Burr* v. *Davall*, 8 Mod. 59. As to the criteria by which to test and ascertain whether natural or innate eccentricity has exceeded the bounds of legal testamentary capacity, see *Medway* v. *Croft*, 8 Curt. 671. If the defendant succeed in proving that the testator has been affected by habitual derangement, then it is for the plaintiff to show sanity and competency at the time when the will was executed. *Attorney-General* v. *Parnther*, 3 Bro. C. C. 441. Where the case is one of temporary delirium, arising from transient causes, as fever, &c., slight evidence of restored sanity will be sufficient. *Brogden* v. *Brown*, 2 Add. Ec. R. 445. Where the evidence is conflicting, the safest course is try the question by the evidence of collateral facts; as by the correspondence, acts done with relation to property, and the circumstances attending the preparation and execution of the will itself. *Tatham* v. *Wright*, 2 Russ. & Myl. 21, 22. The public and private acts and conduct of the testator shortly before and after the will was executed, may be sufficient to prove his sanity, even where all the attesting witnesses swear that he was utterly incompetent to make a will. *Hudson's case*, Skinner, 79; *Lowe* v. *Jolliffe*, 1 Wm. Black. 365. Letters written *to* the testator, but not shown to have been indorsed, or acted on, or answered by him, are not admissible evidence of his sanity. *Wright* v. *Doe* d. *Tatham* (in error), 4 Bing. N. C. 489.

6. That the testator at the time of executing the will was an infant. 7 Will. 4 & 1 Vict. c. 26, s. 7; *ante*, 495.

7. That the testatrix at the time of executing the will was a married woman. 7 Will. 4 & 1 Vict. c. 26, s. 8; *ante*, 495.

8. That the testator was not seised of or legally entitled to the property for an estate of inheritance in fee simple at the time of his death. *Ante*, 517. Some other person may be shown to have been so entitled, although the defendant do not prove any right of possession through or under him: or the testator may be shown to have had only a life estate: *Harding* v. *Roberts*, 10 Exch. 819: or that he was only a joint tenant with another person who survived him: Lit. s. 287; *Swift* v. *Roberts*, 1 W. Black. 476; 3 Burr. 1488; *Doe* d. *Culkin* v. *Tomkinson*, 2 M. & S. 166, 168: or that the testator by a deed of conveyance parted with the property before his death: *ante*, 506; *Doe* d. *Blayney* v. *Savage*, 1 Car. & K. 487: or that he demised for a term of years which has not expired: *Doe* d. *Collins* v. *Weller*, 7 T. R. 478; *Doe* d. *Rawlings* v. *Walker*, 5 B. & C. 111; 7 D. & R. 487: or from year to year, and that such tenancy has not been duly determined by a regular notice to quit. *Doe* d. *Wawn* v. *Horn*, 3 M. & W. 333; *Doe* d. *Leicester* v. *Biggs*, 2 Taunt. 109; *Doe* d. *Nicoll* v. *Bower*, 16 Q. B. 805.

9. That upon the true construction of the will the plaintiff is not legally entitled to actual possession of the property devised; *Doe* d. *Gallini* v. *Gallini*, 5 B. & Adol. 621, 643; *Doe* d. *Dean and Chapter of Westminster and others* v. *Freeman and wife*, 1 T. R. 389; he may be entitled only to the rents and profits; *Doe* d. *Leicester* v. *Biggs*, 2 Taunt. 109; or some other person may be entitled under the

will to a prior estate, not shown to have been determined. *Doe* d. *Beck* v. *Heakin*, 6 A. & E. 495; *Doe* d. *Norfolk* v. *Hawke*, 2 East, 481; *Doe* d. *Kenrick* v. *Lord Beauclerk*, 11 East, 657. The property in question may have been devised to another person in fee, and not to the plaintiff; *Doe* d. *Bailey* v. *Sloggett*, 5 Exch. 107; or the devise to the plaintiff may be *too remote*, and therefore void; *Goodman* v. *Goodright* (in error), 1 W. Black. 188; 2 Burr. 873; *Doe* d. *Cadogan* v. *Ewart*, 7 A. & E. 648; or the plaintiff may not have performed a condition precedent, whereof he had due notice; *Doe* d. *Taylor* v. *Crisp*, 8 A. & E. 779; 1 P. & D. 37; 7 Dowl. 584; or the plaintiff may be entitled under the will only to an *equitable* estate; the legal estate in fee, or for a less period, being vested in the trustees named in the will; *ante*, 511; *Doe* d. *Rees* v. *Williams*, 2 M. & W. 749, 757; *Doe* d. *Cadogan* v. *Ewart*, 7 A. & E. 636, 670; 3 N. & P. 197; or the plaintiff may be one of the attesting witnesses to the will, or the husband or wife of one of the attesting witnesses, and so the devise in his or her favour void. *Ante*, 502. If the plaintiff claim under a deed of appointment made under a power contained in the will, the defendant may contend that the appointment was not a due execution of the power, and therefore void. *Doe* d. *Milborne* v. *Milborne*, 2 T. R. 721; and see *Doe* d. *Hellings* v. *Bird*, 11 East, 49.

10. The defendant may prove that the will was *revoked* by the subsequent marriage of the testator or testatrix; *ante*, 503; or by a subsequent will or codicil duly executed and attested; *ante*, 503; or by the testator's burning, tearing or otherwise destroying the will on which the claimant relies; *ante*, 503; or by subsequent alterations duly executed and attested pursuant to the statute; *ante*, 504; or by a subsequent conveyance. *Ante*, 506. On the other hand, the claimant may show in reply (in some of the above cases) that the will was subsequently revived. *Ante*, 505.

11. That the claimant's right and title has been extinguished by the Statute of Limitations, 3 & 4 Will. 4, c. 27. *Ante*, 4; *Doe* d. *Roberton* v. *Gardiner*, 12 C. B. 319, 324.

12. Or that by reason of some act or event subsequent to the testator's death, and before action, the plaintiff has ceased to be legally entitled to actual possession of the property devised, *ex. gr.* he may have conveyed all his estate in the property to another person; *Roe* d. *Haldane and Urry* v. *Harvey*, 4 Burr. 2484; or he may have demised it to some third person, not being one of the plaintiffs, for a term which is still in force; *ante*, 30, 395; *Doe* d. *Wawn* v. *Horn*, 3 M. & W. 333; or he may, before entry, have *disclaimed* the estate devised. A devisee in fee may by deed disclaim the estate devised to him, and in such case the disclaimer relates back to the testator's death, and prevents the devise from ever operating. *Townson* v. *Ticknell*, 3 B. & A. 31; *Beghie* v. *Crook*, 2 Bing. N. C. 70; 2 Scott, 128; *Doe* d. *Chigney* v. *Harris*, 16 M. & W. 517; *Watson* v. *Pearson*, 2 Exch. 583; *Higgins* v. *Frankis*, 20 Law J., N. S., Chanc. 16. It seems that a disclaimer may be by parol. 1 C. B. 381, note (*d*); *Doe* d. *Chigney* v. *Harris*, *supra*. If, however, the devisee does not disclaim any estate in the land, but only of benefit under the will, at the same time asserting a title paramount, he may afterwards, on ascertaining that he has no such title, recover the lands as devisee. *Doe* d. *Smyth* v. *Smith*, 6 B. & C. 112. A trustee who has once acted or assented, will not afterwards be permitted to disclaim, or to refuse to permit his name to be

made use of in an action by *cestui que trust* upon an indemnity. *Orchard* v. *Coulstrong*, 6 Man. & Gr. 75. Any dealing with a trust estate will amount to an acceptance of the trust. *Talbot* v. *Earl Radnor*, 3 Myl. & K. 252 ; *Urch* v. *Walker*, 3 Myl. & Cr. 702. A verbal assent is sufficient. *Doe* d. *Chigney* v. *Harris*, 16 M. & W. 517. By accepting a devise of lands, a rent-charge issuing out of those and other lands will be extinguished. *Dennett* v. *Pass*, 1 Bing. N. C. 388.

Evidence in Reply.]—If the defendant attempt to impeach the will by showing that one of the attesting witnesses (who is dead) fraudulently obtained the signature of another attesting witness, after the testator's death, the plaintiff may in reply give evidence as to the respectability and character of the attesting witness whose conduct is impugned. *Provis* v. *Reed*, 5 Bing. 435 ; *Doe* d. *Stephenson* v. *Walker*, 4 Esp. 50. If a deed of conveyance from the testator be relied on by the defendant, the plaintiff may show that such deed was obtained by fraud and imposition on the testator. *Doe* d. *Blayney* v. *Savage*, 1 Car. & K. 487 ; for other cases, see *ante*, 300.

CHAPTER XLVIII.

BY DEVISEE OF COPYHOLDS.

Evidence for Plaintiff.]—In ejectment by a devisee of copyholds, the evidence for the plaintiff will be similar in most respects to that in an action by a devisee of freeholds. *Ante*, 514—521.

1. The original will must be produced. *Anon.*, 1 Ld. Raym. 735, Holt, C. J. The probate is not admissible. *Jervoise* v. *The Duke of Northumberland*, 1 Jac. & Walk. 570 ; *Archer* v. *Slater*, 11 Sim. 507. A recital, in the admittance, of the devise to the plaintiff, is not evidence, except as against the lord. *Anon.*, 1 Ld. Raym. 735 ; Bull. N. P. 108. The execution and attestation of the will pursuant to 7 Will. 4 & 1 Vict. c. 26, s. 9 (*ante*, 497), as amended by 15 & 16 Vict. c. 24 (*ante*, 513), must be proved in the usual manner (*ante*, 514), unless admitted in the cause. *Ante*, 150.

2. The seisin or title of the testator must be proved. *Denn* d. *Satterthwaite* v. *Satterthwaite*, 1 W. Black. 519 ; *Green* d. *Crew* v. *King*, 2 W. Black. 1211 ; *Doe* d. *Simpson* v. *Simpson*, 4 Bing. N. C. 333 ; 5 Scott, 770 ; *Doe* d. *Hickman* v. *Hickman*, 4 B. & Adol. 6 ; 1 N. & M. 780. This is generally done by showing his *admittance* as entered in the court rolls ; but other evidence of seisin or title will sometimes be sufficient. Ros. Ev. 467 (7th ed.) ; 2 Arch. N. P. 344 ; *ante*, 211. Formerly no person, could devise a copyhold estate to which he had not been *admitted* either actually or constructively. *Doe* d. *Vernon* v. *Vernon*, 7 East, 8 ; *Doe* d. *Tofield* v. *Tofield*, 11 East, 246 ; *Doe* d. *Winder* v. *Lawes*, 7 A. & E. 211, 213 ; *Matthew* v. *Osborne*, 13 C. B. 919. But the admission of a particular tenant operated as an admission of the remainderman also ; because the particular estate and the remainder made together but one estate. *Doe* d. *Winder* v. *Lawes*, 7 A. & E. 195, 210 ; *Phyphers* v. *Eburn*, 3 Bing. N. C. 250 ; *Auncelme* v. *Auncelme*, Cro. Jac. 31. And a customary heir might devise without admittance, and without payment of the fine due to the lord on the descent. *Doe* d. *Perry* v. *Wilson*, 5 A. & E. 321. Now copyhold estates may be devised "notwithstanding that the testator may not have surrendered the same to the use of his will, or notwithstanding that being entitled as heir, devisee, *or otherwise*, to be admitted thereto, he shall not have been admitted thereto." *Ante*, 494. An admittance may be had at a customary court baron of the manor which is attended by both freehold and copyhold tenants ; *Doe* d. *Evans* v. *Walker*, 15 Q. B. 28, 32 ; but not at a court baron attended by freehold tenants only. *S. C.* An admittance may be proved by the stamped copy signed by the steward ; Lit. s. 75 ; 1 Scriven, Cop. 590 ; Peake's Ev. 94. His handwriting should be proved, unless admitted in the cause ; *ante*, 150 ; or the document be more than thirty years old. *Dean and Chapter of Ely* v. *Stewart*, 2 Atk. 45 ; *Rowe* v. *Brenton*, 3 Man. & R. 296 ; 8 B. & C. 737. An admittance may be proved by the court rolls, without producing the stamped copy ; *Doe* d. *Bennington* v. *Hall*, 16 East, 208 ; *Doe* d.

Garrod v. *Olley,* 12 A. & E. 481 ; 4 P. & D. 275 ; or by an examined copy, stamped or unstamped. *Doe* d. *Cawthorn* v. *Mee,* 4 B. & Adol. 617 ; 1 N. & M. 424 ; *Doe* d. *Burrows* v. *Freeman,* 12 M. & W. 844 ; 1 Car. & K. 386. Where a surrender was made in 1774, and there was no record of it on the court rolls, the books of the manor containing an entry of the admission, which recited the surrender, were received as evidence of the surrender. *Rex* v. *Inhabitants of Thruscross,* 1 A. & E. 126 ; 3 N. & M. 284 ; and see *Doe* d. *Garrod* v. *Olley,* 12 A. & E. 481 ; 4 P. & D. 275. It has been held that a surrender and presentment may be proved by the draft of an entry produced from the muniments of the manor, and the parol testimony of the foreman of the homage jury who made the presentment. *Doe* d. *Priestley* v. *Calloway,* 6 B. & C. 484 ; 9 D. & R. 518 ; and see *Anon.,* 1 Ld. Raym. 735. If the original roll be put in, it may be shown to be incorrect by producing the minute of the steward or other evidence. 6 B. & C. 494 ; 1 Scriven, Cop. 253. The rolls are not records, and therefore any mistake in them may be corrected by parol evidence. *Towers* v. *Moor,* 2 Vern. 98 ; *Burgess* v. *Foster,* 1 Leon. 289 ; *Brend* v. *Brend,* Cas. temp. Finch. 254 ; *Kite and Queenton's case,* 4 Co. R. 25 ; Co. Copyh. s. 40 ; *Doe* d. *Priestley* v. *Calloway,* 6 B. & C. 494, 495.

3. The death of the testator should be proved. *Doe* d. *Graham* v. *Penfold,* 8 C. & P. 536 ; *ante,* 239.

4. The admittance of the plaintiff as devisee. *Jefferies' case,* 1 Ld. Ken. 110 ; *Rex* v. *Wilson,* 10 B. & C. 80, Lord Tenterden, C. J., cited 6 Q. B. 633 ; *Doe* d. *Evans* v. *Walker,* 15 Q. B. 28 ; 2 Arch. N. P. 345. The admittance of a tenant for life operates also as an admission of the remainderman ; *Doe* d. *Winder* v. *Lawes,* 7 A. & E. 195, 210 ; *Auncelme* v. *Auncelme,* Cro. Jac. 31 ; even where such remainder is contingent. *Phypers* v. *Eburn,* 3 Bing. N. C. 250. Therefore a devisee in remainder has only to prove the admittance of the tenant for life, and not any subsequent admission of himself. Ros. Ev. 467 (7th ed.). An admittance after the commencement of the action is sufficient ; because when made it *relates back* to the testator's death ; it may, therefore, be made at any time before the trial. *Holdfast* d. *Woollams* v. *Claphan,* 1 T. R. 600 ; *Doe* d. *Bennington* v. *Hall,* 16 East, 208 ; *Doe* d. *Nicholson* v. *Welford,* 4 P. & D. 79 (3rd point) ; *Rex* v. *Inhabitants of Thruscross,* 1 A. & E. 129, *per* Parke, J. Some evidence of the identity of the plaintiff with the devisee and person admitted should be produced. *Doe* d. *Hanson* v. *Smith,* 1 Camp. 197. But if the name be at all unusual very slight evidence on this point is generally sufficient. Ros. Ev. 97, 216. If the plaintiff be not the devisee he must prove the devisee's title, and his own surrender and admittance. *Doe* d. *Pilkington* v. *Spratt,* 5 B. & Adol. 731 ; 2 N. & M. 524 ; *Doe* d. *Evans* v. *Walker,* 15 Q. B. 28. As to the identity of the land claimed, see *ante,* 519.

The other evidence will be the same as in an action by a devisee of freeholds. *Ante,* 514 to 521. Any limitations prior to the devise to the plaintiff must be shown to have determined. *Doe* d. *Stevenson* v. *Glover,* 1 C. B. 448.

Evidence and Points for Defendant.]—The defendant may contend that the evidence for the plaintiff is insufficient on some material point. *Ante,* 526 to 527. He may also produce contradictory evidence. He may raise any other point, and take any other objection which may be made by a defendant sued by a devisee of freeholds. *Ante,* 522.

CHAPTER XLIX.

BY LEGATEE OF LEASEHOLDS.

Evidence for Plaintiff.]—In ejectment by a legatee of leaseholds the plaintiff must prove :—

1. The probate. The original will is not admissible. *Rex* v. *Barnes*, 1 Stark. R. 243 ; *Pinney* v. *Pinney*), 8 B. & C. 335 ; Phil. Ev. 543 (8th ed.) The seal of the ecclesiastical court on the probate proves itself. *Kempton* v. *Cross*, Rep. temp. Hardw. 108. The act book of the ecclesiastical court, containing an entry of the will having been proved, and of probate granted to the executors therein named, is admissible without accounting for the non-production of the probate. *Cox* v. *Allingham*, Jacob, 514 ; Bull. N. P. 246. The production of the original will, with the act of the ecclesiastical court ordering probate, is admissible and sufficient evidence, without accounting for the non-production of the probate. *Doe* d. *Bassett* v. *Mew*, 7 A. & E. 240 ; *Doe* d. *Edwards* v. *Gunning*, *Id.* 240 ; 2 N. & M. 260 ; *Denn* d. *Tarzwell* v. *Barnard*, 2 Cowp. 595. Where by the practice of an ecclesiastical court no book was kept, but grants of probate were recorded by a minute indorsed on, or entered at the foot of the original will and written by the officer of the court: held, that the production of the original will, with such minute upon it, was sufficient. *S. C.* ; *Gorton* v. *Dyson*, 1 Brod. & B. 219 ; *Waite* v. *Gale*, 2 Dowl. & L. 925. An examined copy or extract, or a certified copy or extract from such act book, made pursuant to 14 & 15 Vict. c. 99, s. 14, is admissible. *Dorrett* v. *Meux*, 15 C. B. 142. If the probate be lost an exemplification of it may be obtained from the ecclesiastical court, which will be admissible evidence ; *Shepherd* v. *Shorthose*, 1 Stra. 412 ; Bull. N. P. 246 ; or a certified copy made pursuant to 14 & 15 Vict. c. 99, s. 14. *Dorrett* v. *Meux*, 15 C. B. 142.

The probate must appear to have been sufficiently stamped to cover (*inter alia*) the improved value of the property sought to be recovered. *Doe* d. *Richards* v. *Evans*, 10 Q. B. 476 ; 16 Law J., N. S., Q. B. 305 ; *Jones* v. *Howells*, 2 Hare, 342 ; *Howard* v. *Prince*, 10 Beav. 312.

If the ecclesiastical court had no jurisdiction to grant probate of the particular will the probate is void. Ros. Ev. 616. Thus if probate be granted by a diocesan court where the testator had *bona notabilia* (goods of the value of 5*l.* or upwards), in more than one diocese in the same province. Bull. N. P. 24 ; *Prince's case*, 5 Co. R. 29 b ; Cro. Eliz. 718 ; 2 Anderson, 132 ; 3 Leon. 278, *S. C.* A prerogative probate is not void, but only voidable, where the testator had *bona notabilia* in one diocese only, or no *bona notabilia* in any diocese. *Prince's case, supra.* Such probate is valid until avoided by sentence of the proper ecclesiastical court. *Rex* v. *Loggen and Froome*, 1 Stra. 73.

A probate granted by a competent court is conclusive of the validity and contents of the will (including the appointment of executors), until it be repealed. *Sir R. Raine's case,* 1 Ld. Raym. 262; *Allen* v. *Dundas,* 3 T. R. 130; *Allan* v. *M'Pherson,* 1 H. L. Cas. 191; *Reg.* v. *Turner,* 2 Car. & K. 734, Erle, J. Therefore, in an ejectment for leaseholds the defendant cannot object that the will was forged; *S. C.; Noel* v. *Wells,* 1 Lev. 235, 236; and see *per* Pollock, C. B., in *Bancks* v. *Ollerton,* 10 Exch. 178; or that the testator was mentally incompetent to make a will; or that he did not duly execute it; for all such questions should be raised and decided in the ecclesiastical court before probate is granted, or upon an application to revoke the probate; *Noel* v. *Wells,* 1 Lev. 236; Bull. N. P. 247; Ros. Ev. 145 (7th ed.); or upon an appeal to the privy council. *Allan* v. *M'Pherson,* 1 H. L. Cas. 191. Where the will of a lunatic had been admitted to probate, the court, upon the petition of the executrix, ordered a fund in court belonging to the lunatic's estate to be transferred to trustees to be approved by the commissioner, to be held by them upon the trusts of the will, although such will was made after the time from which the testator had been found by inquisition to have been of unsound mind. *In re Garden,* 13 Law J., N. S., Chanc. 439. So the probate is conclusive evidence of the validity of any alterations appearing therein, because the ecclesiastical court will *omit* from the probate all such alterations, &c., as are not proved to have been duly made and attested. *Ante,* 505.

2. *The assent of the executors* must be proved; for until such assent the term does not vest in the legatee, but in the executors. 2 Wms. Exors. 1084 (3rd ed.); *Doe* d. *Maberley* v. *Maberley,* 6 C. & P. 126; *Attorney-General* v. *Potter,* 5 Beav. 164; 14 Law J., N. S., Chanc. 16; *Webster* v. *Johnston,* cited 17 C. B. 521. Where a term of years is bequeathed to an executor for his own use, it does not vest in him as legatee until he assents to it as executor; *Young* v. *Holmes,* 1 Stra. 70; *Doe* d. *Hayes* v. *Sturges,* 7 Taunt. 217; 2 Marsh, 505; Toller, 345; 2 Wms. Exors. 1091 (3rd ed.); but he may so assent, by conduct or otherwise, before or without obtaining probate. *Fenton, Administrator, &c.* v. *Clegg,* 9 Exch. 680; *Johnson* v. *Warwick,* 17 C. B. 516. Where a term of years is bequeathed to him absolutely, his entry may amount to an assent, but if it be bequeathed to him for life, something more than mere entry is necessary to constitute an assent. *Doe* d. *Hayes* v. *Sturges,* 7 Taunt. 217; 2 Marsh, 505. Where an executrix had a life estate in a chattel under a bequest, her taking possession of the chattel is no assent to a further bequest thereof in remainder. *Richards* v. *Brown,* 3 Bing. N. C. 493; 4 Scott, 262. A special assent appears to be necessary in such case. *Rose* v. *Bartlett,* Cro. Car. 292: but see *Trail* v. *Bull,* 1 Coll. C. C. 352. Generally speaking, an assent by an executor to a bequest to the first devisee operates as an assent to the remainder over. *Foley* v. *Burnell,* 4 Bro. P. C. 34. After the executor's assent the legatee may maintain or defend ejectment, even against the executor. *Doe* d. *Lord Saye and Sele* v. *Guy,* 3 East, 120; 4 Esp. 154, *S. C.; Johnson* v. *Warwick,* 17 C. B. 516; *Fenton* v. *Clegg,* 9 Exch. 680; *Doe* d. *Sturges* v. *Tatchell,* 3 B. & Adol. 675. The assent of an executor to a bequest is not a matter of law, but a question of fact for the jury. *Mason* v. *Farnell,* 12 M. & W. 674; 1 Dowl. & L. 576. The assent may be express or implied. The executor may not only in direct terms autho-

A A

rize the legatee to take possession of the property bequeathed to him, but his concurrence may be inferred either from indirect expressions or particular acts; and such constructive permission will be equally available. 2 Wms. Exors. 1087 (3rd ed.); *Doe* d. *Maberley* v. *Maberley*, 6 C. & P. 126; *Doe* d. *Sturges* v. *Tatchell*, 3 B. & Adol. 675; *Fenton* v. *Clegg*, 9 Exch. 680; *Johnson* v. *Warwick*, 17 C. B. 516. But an ambiguous expression ought not to be left to the jury as evidence of assent. *Doe* d. *Chidgey* v. *Harris*, 16 M. & W. 517; *Id.* 520, Alderson, B.; 1 Rop. Leg. 736 (3rd ed.). So with respect to ambiguous conduct. *Doe* d. *Hayes* v. *Sturges*, 7 Taunt. 217; 2 Marsh, 505. But slight evidence of assent, either by words or conduct, is frequently sufficient, the act of assent being lawful. The assent may be made subject to any lawful condition precedent, and will not operate as an assent until such condition be performed. Went. Off. Ex. 429 (14th ed.); 2 Wms. Exors. 1089 (3rd ed.). Where executors unconditionally assent to a bequest of leaseholds they are not entitled to be indemnified from the subsequent rent and covenants in the lease out of the testator's general estate. *Shadbolt* v. *Woodfall*, 2 Collyer, 30, K. Bruce, V. C. Generally speaking, a slight assent is sufficient, it being a rightful act. *Noel* v. *Robinson*, 1 Vern. 94; *Doe* d. *Maberley* v. *Maberley*, 6 C. & P. 126; 2 Wms. Exors. 1087 (3rd ed.). If a term of years or other chattel be bequeathed to A. for life, with remainder to B., and the executor assents to the interest of A., such assent will enure to vest that of B., and *e converso:* for the particular estate and the remainder constitute together but one estate. *Welcden* v. *Elkington*, Plow. 521; *Lampet's case*, 10 Co. Rep. 47 b; *Adams* v. *Pierce*, 3 P. Wms. 12; *Young* v. *Holmes*, 1 Stra. 70; *Foley* v. *Burnell*, 4 Bro. P. C. 34; *Trail* v. *Bull*, 1 Coll. C. C. 352; 2 Wms. Exors. 1088 (3rd ed.). An executor may assent to a bequest before probate. 1 Wms. Exors. 213; 2 *Id.* 1090; *Fenton* v. *Clegg*, 9 Exch. 680. The assent of any one of several executors is sufficient. 2 Wms. Exors. 757, 1090, 1096; and see *Doe* d. *Stace* v. *Wheeler*, 15 M. & W. 623. The assent of a married woman executrix, without the concurrence of her husband, is not binding. 2 Wms. Exors. 769, 1090. The assent, when given, relates back to the time of the testator's death. 2 Wms. Exors. 1091; *Saunder's case*, 5 Co. Rep. 12 b. Generally speaking, it cannot afterwards be retracted. 2 Wms. Exors. 1090; *Doe* d. *Lord Saye and Sele* v. *Guy*, 3 East, 120; *Foley* v. *Burnell*, 4 Bro. P. C. 34. An administrator cannot bind the intestate's estate by any assent to the application or disposal thereof before obtaining letters of administration, which do not relate back. *Morgan* v. *Thomas*, 8 Exch. 302.

3. The title of the testator must be proved; and it must appear that he had only a chattel and not a freehold interest in the premises; *Doe* d. *Digby* v. *Steel*, 3 Camp. 115, 116; because when a person dies in possession, the presumption is that he was seised in fee, in the absence of proof of title for a less estate. Ad. Eject. 255; *ante*, 239. Generally speaking, the lease under which the testator held, either as lessee or assignee, and the subsequent assignments (if any), must be put in and proved in the usual manner (*ante*, 294, 393), unless *admitted* in the cause. *Ante*, 150. In ejectment by an executor (or by a legatee after the executor's assent), it is sufficient *primâ facie* evidence that the testator had a chattel interest in the premises, to put in the defendant's answer to a bill in equity stating "he believed the testator was *possessed of the leasehold* premises in the bill mentioned." *Doe* d.

Digby v. *Steel*, 3 Camp. 115. It must appear that the testator was in possession of the property, or in receipt of the rent, for a term certain, or as tenant from year to year, within twenty years before the commencement of the action ; or that, for some other reason, the right and title of the plaintiff claiming through him has not been extinguished by the Statute of Limitations, 3 & 4 Will. 4, c. 27. *Ante*, 4. If the testator had underlet the property, and was merely in receipt of the rent, it must be shown that the underlease has expired or been determined by a regular notice to quit; *Doe* d. *Wawn* v. *Horn*, 3 M. & W. 333; *ante*, 29; or in some other legal manner; because otherwise the plaintiff's remedy is by distress or action for the rent, &c. reserved in the underlease, but not by ejectment. *Ante*, 287, 411. He may, however, show that there has been, after the testator's death, a breach of some covenant or condition contained in the underlease, by reason whereof, and of a proviso for re-entry therein contained, he, as assignee of the reversion, is entitled to maintain ejectment. *Ante*, Chap. XXXIX. It must also appear that the term to which the testator was entitled had not expired or been determined before the service of the writ in ejectment. *Ante*, 217, 289. If the property be bequeathed to any other person before the plaintiff, it must appear that such prior estate had ceased by death, forfeiture or otherwise, before the day on which possession is claimed in the writ. *Doe* d. *Norfolk* v. *Hawke*, 2 East, 481. It must appear that upon the true construction of the will, and in the events which have since happened (including the executor's assent), the plaintiffs, or some or one of them, are or is *legally entitled to actual possession* of the property mentioned in the writ of ejectment, or some part thereof. *Ante*, 66, 287. A mere right to the rents and profits is not sufficient; nor a merely equitable title. *Ante*, 66, 287. The *identity* of the property and of the plaintiff must be shown in like manner as in an ejectment by a devisee of freeholds. *Ante*, 519.

Evidence and Points for Defendant.]—The defendant may contend :—

1. That the evidence for the plaintiff is insufficient on some material point. *Ante*, 528. He may also produce contradictory evidence.

2. That the probate is void, having been granted by a court *which had no jurisdiction. Ante*, 528. In support of this objection the defendant may prove that the testator had *bonâ notabilia* in another diocese of the same province. *Ante*, 528. But it would seem that any objection of this sort should be taken, and supported by evidence, and the judge should decide upon it, *before the probate is read in evidence ;* because the objection is one of a preliminary nature, and in substance amounts to this : viz., that the probate produced is not legal evidence of the contents of the will. All preliminary questions of that nature should be so decided before the document is admitted in evidence. *Bartlett* v. *Smith*, 11 M. & W. 483 ; *Cleave* v. *Jones*, 7 Exch. 421 ; *Id.* 425, Parke, B.; *Painter* v. *Hill*, 2 Car. & K. 924.

3. That the probate is not sufficiently stamped. *Hunt* v. *Stevens*, 3 Taunt. 113, cited 4 M. & W. 193 ; *Carr* v. *Roberts*, 2 B. & Adol. 905 ; *Jones* v. *Howells*, 2 Hare, 342 ; *Howard* v. *Prince*, 10 Beav. 312. The stamp must be sufficient to cover (*inter alia*) the improved value for the time being of the property claimed. *Doe* d. *Richards* v. *Evans*, 10 Q. B. 476; *ante*, 528. But the probate may be stamped without

payment of the duty, upon security given for the amount, pursuant to 55 Geo. 3, c. 184, s. 49. *Doe* d. *Hanley* v. *Wood,* 2 B. & A. 724, 733; *Howard* v. *Prince,* 10 Beav. 312. This objection should be supported and disposed of in like manner as the previous one above mentioned. *Doe* d. *Fryer* v. *Coombs,* 3 Q. B. 687.

4. That no sufficient evidence of the executor's assent has been proved. *Ante,* 529.

5. That the testator's title has not been sufficiently proved. *Ante,* 530. Some third person may be shown to be legally entitled to actual possession of the property by virtue of some underlease from the testator, or otherwise. *Ante,* 531. It makes no difference that the defendant does not show any right or title under such third person, nor claim the possession on his behalf. *Doe* d. *Wawn* v. *Horn,* 3 M. & W. 333; *ante,* 287, 288.

6. That upon the true construction of the will, and in the events which have happened, the plaintiffs, or any or either of them, are not nor is entitled to actual possession of the property mentioned in the writ of ejectment, or any part thereof. A mere right to the rents and profits is not sufficient. Nor a merely equitable title. *Ante,* 66, 287. The identity of the property or of the plaintiff may be disputed or disproved. *Ante,* 519.

CHAPTER L.

BY EXECUTORS OR ADMINISTRATORS.

For what Property.]—Executors or administrators may recover by ejectment any land or tenements whereof their testator or intestate died possessed or entitled for a term of years. *Roe* d. *Bendall* v. *Summerset*, 2 W. Black. 692; 5 Burr. 2608; *Doe* d. *Stace* v. *Wheeler*, 15 M. & W. 623; or as tenant from year to year; *Doe* d. *Shore* v. *Porter*, 3 T. R. 13; *Doe* d. *Hull* v. *Wood*, 14 M. & W. 682; *Doe* v. *Bradbury*, 2 Dowl. & Ry. 706; provided the term still continues; *Doe* v. *Wood and Doe* v. *Bradbury, supra;* and there has been no assent by the executors, or any or either of them, to a bequest of the property to a legatee; *Doe* d. *Sturges* v. *Tatchell*, 3 B. & Adol. 675; *Johnson* v. *Warwick*, 17 C. B. 516; *ante*, 529; and the action is brought within the time limited by the 3 & 4 Will. 4, c. 27; *ante*, 4, 12.

An executor or administrator is in law an assignee. *Sir W. More's case*, Cro. Eliz. 26; *Tilney* v. *Norris*, 1 Ld. Raym. 553; 1 Salk. 309; *Buckworth* v. *Simpson*, 1 Cr. M. & R. 834; 5 Tyr. 344.

An executor or administrator is entitled to a freehold *pur autre vie* to which his testator or intestate was entitled, and whereof there is no special occupant; 29 Car. 2, c. 3, s. 12; *Doe* d. *Lewis* v. *Lewis*, 9 M. & W. 622; but not where the heir takes as special occupant. *Atkinson* v. *Baker*, 4 T. R. 229; *Carpenter* v. *Carpenter*, 3 E. & B. 918. An executor or administrator is not entitled to be admitted to copyholds held *pur autre vie*. *Zouch* d. *Forse* v. *Forse*, 7 East, 186; 3 Smith, 191.

The executor of a termor of copyholds must be *admitted* and pay a fine to the lord. *Earl of Bath* v. *Abney*, 1 Burr. 206. Where three persons are appointed executors and trustees of copyholds two of them may disclaim by deed, to the intent that the other may alone be admitted upon the trusts of the will; and in such case only a single fine will be payable. *Lord Wellesley* v. *Withers,* 4 E. & B. 750.

Probate.]—The title of an executor is derived from the will; not from the probate, which is merely *evidence* of the will. 1 Wms. Exors. 212 (3rd ed.); *Graysbrook* v. *Fox,* Plow. 281; *Smith* v. *Milles,* 1 T. R. 480, *per* Ashhurst, J. An executor may, therefore, claim the possession from a day prior to that on which the probate was granted. *Roe* d. *Bendall* v. *Summerset,* 2 W. Black. 692; 5 Burr. 2608; and see *Woolley, Executrix, &c.* v. *Clark,* 5 B. & A. 744; 1 D. & R. 409. It seems that the action may be commenced before any probate has been obtained, and that it is sufficient to procure probate just before the trial, or when further proceedings in the action are stayed by a rule of court or judge's order until the probate is produced. *Webb, Executor, &c.* v. *Adkins,* 14 C. B. 401; *Thompson* v. *Reynolds,* 3 C. & P. 123.

All the executors named in the will *may* join, although probate has been granted to some of them only. 2 Wms. Exors. 1467 (3rd ed.); *Creswick* v. *Woodhead,* 4 Man. & Gr. 811. On the other hand, it seems that as the whole term and estate is vested in each executor, any one or more of them (without the others) may recover in ejectment the whole of the property. *Doe* d. *Stace* v. *Wheeler,* 15 M. & W. 623; and see *Heath* v. *Chilton,* 12 M. & W. 632; *Pannell* v. *Finn,* Cro. Eliz. 347; Moore, 350; 1 Gould, 185, S. C.

If there be several executors they may all sue jointly by attorney, though some of them are infants under seventeen years of age. *Foxwist* v. *Tremain,* 2 Saund. 212; 1 Sid. 449; 1 Mod. 47, 172, 296.

Letters of Administration.]—An administrator derives his title from the letters of administration, and he cannot maintain an ejectment commenced before such letters have been granted. 1 Wms. Exors. 311 (3rd ed.); *Martin* v. *Fuller,* Comberb. 371; *Wankford* v. *Wankford,* 1 Salk. 301, Powys, J.; *Pratt* v. *Swaine,* 8 B. & C. 285; 2 Man. & Ry. 350; *Morgan* v. *Thomas,* 8 Exch. 302; *Fuller* v. *Mackay,* 2 E. & B. 573. But he may by his writ in ejectment claim possession from any day subsequent to the intestate's death, even before the letters of administration were granted. Selwyn's N. P. 716 (10th ed.); *Lessee of Patten* v. *Patten,* 1 Alcock & Napier (Irish), R. 493; *Barnett* v. *Earl of Guilford,* 11 Exch. 19, 32; and see *Rex* v. *Inhabitants of Horsely,* 8 East, 410; *Pratt* v. *Swaine,* 8 B. & C. 287, Bayley, J.; 2 Man. & R. 350, S. C.; *Tharpe* v. *Stallwood,* 5 Man. & Gr. 760; 1 Dowl. & L. 24; *Foster* v. *Bates,* 12 M. & W. 226; 1 Dowl. & L. 400. " In the case of an administration a man cannot sue out a writ as administrator until he has obtained his letters of administration, although, when he has obtained them, all tortious acts done to the deceased's property relate back to the time of his death, so as to enable the administrator to sue for them." *Per* Parke, B., in *Yorston* v. *Fether,* 14 M. & W. 854; *Welchman* v. *Sturgis,* 13 Q. B. 552. But it seems that he must enter before he can maintain *trespass. Barnett* v. *Earl of Guilford,* 11 Exch. 19, 32. The doctrine of relation by which the letters of administration are held to relate back to acts done between the death of the intestate and the taking out of the letters of administration, exists only in those cases where such relation operates *for the benefit* of the estate. *Morgan* v. *Thomas,* 8 Exch. 302.

No "cause of action" accrues to an administrator *as such*, until he has obtained letters of administration. *Cary* v. *Stephenson*, 2 Salk. 421; Carth. 335; Skin. 555; 4 Mod. 372, *S. C.*; *Murray* v. *East India Company*, 5 B. & A. 204; *Skeffington* v. *Whitehurst*, 3 You. & Col. 34. Detinue cannot be maintained by an administrator against a person who has had possession of the goods of the intestate, but has ceased to hold them prior to the grant of administration. *Crossfield* v. *Such*, 8 Exch. 825.

An administrator with the will annexed stands on the same footing as any other administrator. *Fuller* v. *Mackay*, 2 E. & B. 573; *Phillips* v. *Hartley*, 3 C. & P. 121, 123, Best, C. J.; *Fenton* v. *Clegg*, 9 Exch. 680; *Johnson* v. *Warwick*, 17 C. B. 516.

An administrator *de bonis non*, with the will annexed, cannot recover leasehold property bequeathed by the will, and to which bequest the executor has assented. *Doe* d. *Sturges* v. *Tatchell*, 3 B. & Adol. 675; *Fenton, Administrator, &c.* v. *Clegg*, 9 Exch. 680; *Johnson* v. *Warwick*, 17 C. B. 516.

Evidence for Plaintiffs.]—In ejectment by executors or administrators the plaintiffs must prove:—

1. The probate (*ante*, 528) or letters of administration. They must be sufficiently stamped. *Ante*, 528; *Doe* d. *Richards* v. *Evans*, 10 Q. B. 476; *Easton* v. *Carter*, 5 Exch. 8; 1 Low. M. & P. 222; *Jones* v. *Howells*, 2 Hare, 342; 12 Law J., N. S., Chanc. 365; *Christian* v. *Devereux*, 12 Simon, 264. If the probate or letters of administration be lost an exemplification thereof may be obtained; *Shepherd* v. *Shorthose*, 1 Stra. 412; Bull. N. P. 246; *Doe* d. *Edwards* v. *Gunning*, 2 N. & P. 260; 7 A. & E. 240; or a certified copy or extract made pursuant to 14 & 15 Vict. c. 99, s. 14. *Dorrett* v. *Meux*, 15 C. B. 142. The will itself, with minutes indorsed thereon of probate having been granted, is sufficient, upon proof that no other record is kept. *Doe* d. *Bassett* v. *Mew*, 7 A. & E. 240; 2 N. & P. 266, note.

2. The title of the testator or intestate. *Ante*, 530. It must appear that the testator or intestate was in possession of the property or in receipt of the rent for a term certain, or as tenant from year to year, within twenty years before the commencement of the action; or that for some other reason the right and title of the plaintiffs as his executors or administrators has not been extinguished by the Statute of Limitations, 3 & 4 Will. 4, c. 27; *ante*, 4, 12; and that the term to which the testator or intestate was entitled had not expired or been determined before the service of the writ. *Doe* d. *Hull* v. *Wood*, 14 M. & W. 682; *Doe* v. *Bradbury*, 2 Dowl. & Ry. 706; *ante*, 290.

If the testator or intestate had underlet the property, and was merely in receipt of the rent, it must be shown that the underlease has expired or been determined by a regular notice to quit; *Doe* d. *Wawn* v. *Horn*, 3 M. & W. 333; *ante*, 35, 288; or in some other legal manner; *Doe* d. *Mee* v. *Litherland*, 4 A. & E. 784; *ante*, 445; because otherwise the remedy of the executors or administrators is by distress or action for the rent, &c., reserved in the underlease, but not by ejectment. *Ante*, 66, 287.

They may, however, show that there has been a breach of covenant or condition contained in the underlease, by reason whereof, and of a proviso for re-entry therein contained, they, as assignees of the reversion, are entitled to maintain ejectment. *Doe* d. *Bedford* v. *White,* 4 Bing. 276 ; *ante,* Chap. XXXIX.

If the defendants be undertenants of the testator or intestate, proof of the underlease, &c., and that the defendants occupied by virtue thereof, and that the term thereby granted has expired or been duly determined by a regular notice to quit, will be sufficient evidence as against the defendants of the title of the testator or intestate ; and the defendants will be thereby estopped from denying such title. *Ante,* 213, 215. So if it be shown that the defendants obtained the possession through or under any such undertenant. *Ante,* 215.

If the testator have expressly bequeathed the property, or his term therein, to any third person, that will not defeat an ejectment by his executors or administrators, with the will annexed, unless it appear that they, or some or one of them, have or has assented to such bequest. *Ante,* 529.

Evidence and Points for Defendant.]—The defendant may contend :—1. That the evidence for the plaintiffs is insufficient on some material point. *Ante,* 535. He may also produce contradictory evidence. But a tenant cannot dispute his landlord's title, although he may show it to have ceased subsequently to the demise to him. *Ante,* 209, 213 —221. 2. That the probate or letters of administration is or are void (*ante,* 531), or not sufficiently stamped ; *Doe* d. *Richards* v. *Evans,* 10 Q. B. 476 ; *ante,* 531. 3. That the plaintiffs have assented to a bequest of the property to some third person, not being one of the claimants. *Ante,* 529. 4. That the testator or intestate granted an underlease to some other person, which has not expired or been duly determined by a notice to quit or otherwise. *Doe* d. *Wawn* v. *Horn,* 3 M. & W. 333 ; *ante,* 35, 288. 5. That the testator or intestate was not at the time of his death entitled to the property ; *Doe* d. *Roberts* v. *Polgrean,* 1 H. Black. 535; or was entitled to it for an estate of freehold not devised to the plaintiffs. *Doe* d. *Hampton* v. *Shotter,* 8 A. & E. 905 ; 1 P. & D. 124.

CHAPTER LI.

BY ASSIGNEES OF A BANKRUPT.

Statutes and Treatises.]—The Bankrupt Law Consolidation Act, 1849 (12 & 13 Vict. c. 106), as amended by 15 & 16 Vict. c. 77, 17 & 18 Vict. c. 119 and 18 & 19 Vict. c. 15, constitutes the present code in bankruptcy. The best treatises upon it are :—Shelford's B. L. (2nd ed.) ; Archbold's B. L., by Flather (11th ed.).

Leave for Assignees to sue or defend.]—The assignees of a bankrupt, "*with leave of the court* first obtained, upon application to such court, *but not otherwise*, may commence, prosecute or defend any action at law, or suit in equity, which the bankrupt might have commenced and prosecuted or defended ; and in such case the costs to which they may be put in respect of such suit or action shall be allowed out of the proceeds of the estate and effects of the bankrupt." 12 & 13

A A 5

Vict. c. 106, s. 153. They may also, after notice to creditors, with leave of the court, accept of compositions for debts, and submit differences or disputes to arbitration. *Id.*

It never was necessary for the assignees to obtain the consent of the creditors to enable them to commence an action at law. *Hussey* v. *Fidell,* 12 Mod. 324; *Spragg* v. *Bincks,* 4 Ves. 583. But under the present acts, if they bring or defend an ejectment or other action without first obtaining leave of the Court of Bankruptcy, they will probably, in the event of failure, be disallowed the costs of the action (on both sides). The court in which the action is brought will not stay the proceedings, at the instance of the defendant, on the ground that the action was commenced and is prosecuted without leave of the Court of Bankruptcy. *Doe* d. *Clarke* v. *Spencer,* 3 Bing. 203, 370; and see *Sutcliffe* v. *Brooke,* 14 M. & W. 855, 858; *Doe* d. *Morrison* v. *Glover,* 15 Q. B. 103; *Piercy* v. *Roberts,* 1 Myl. & K. 4; *Jones* v. *Yates,* 3 You. & Jer. 373; *Spooner* v. *Payne,* 2 De Gex & Sm. 439.

The court will not, at the instance of a defendant in ejectment, interfere against a plaintiff who uses the names of the assignees as co-plaintiffs without their permission, they having given up the property to the bankrupt, under whom the plaintiff claims. *Doe* d. *Vine* v. *Figgins,* 3 Taunt. 440. On the other hand, if the bankrupt consent to his name being used by his assignees, as a co-plaintiff with them, or if he consent to join with them in a reference of an action at their suit, he will thereby incur a *personal* liability to the opposite party. *In re Milnes and Robertson,* 15 C. B. 451; *Id.* 722.

The object of sect. 153 is to protect the bankrupt's estate from loss by unnecessary litigation and costs. Before leave of the court will be granted, the commissioner must be satisfied that the action can be *successfully* prosecuted or defended (as the case may be), and that the assignees are able to produce *sufficient evidence* to entitle them to the verdict.

Official Assignee.]—Forthwith, after adjudication, the court shall appoint an official assignee to act with the assignee or assignees to be chosen by the creditors. 12 & 13 Vict. c. 106, ss. 39, 102; Arch. B. L. 206 (11th ed.). "And all the personal estate and effects, and the *rents and profits* of the real estate, and the *proceeds of sale* of all the estate and effects, real and personal, of the bankrupt, shall in every case be possessed and received by such official assignee alone, save where it shall be otherwise directed by the court." Sect. 39. It is his duty to take and keep possession of it, even when the property becomes legally vested in himself and the creditors' assignees. *Hamber* v. *Hall,* 10 C. B. 780. "Until assignees shall be chosen by the creditors of the bankrupt, the official assignee shall, to all intents and purposes whatever, be *deemed to be sole assignee of the bankrupt's estate and effects.*" Sect. 40. On his death or removal the court may appoint another. Sect. 42. The official assignee is a necessary party, as one of the plaintiffs, in an action by the assignees of a bankrupt; but if omitted by mistake, the court or a judge will sometimes permit the writ to be amended by adding his name. *Baker* v. *Neave,* 1 Cr. & Mee. 112; 3 Tyr. 233; *Holland* v. *Phillips,* 10 A. & E. 149; 2 P. & D. 336. If his name be used by the trade assignees as a co-plaintiff without his consent, security for costs may sometimes be obtained. *Laws* v. *Bott,* 16 M. & W. 362; 4 Dowl. & L. 559; *Ex*

parte Turquand, 3 Mont. D. & D. 475; Shelf. B. L. 48 (2nd ed.);
ante, 357, 358.

Creditors' Assignees.]—The creditors' assignees are usually chosen
and appointed at the first public sitting, or at some adjournment thereof,
pursuant to 12 & 13 Vict. c. 106, s. 139; Shelf. B. L. 246 (2nd ed.);
Arch. B. L. 210 (11th ed.). Such parts of the real and personal property of the bankrupt as vest in the assignees pass to them by virtue
of their appointment, without any assignment or conveyance. Sects.
141, 142; Arch. B. L. 220 (11th ed.); Shelf. B. L. 252 (2nd ed.).
A right of entry will so pass; *Michell* v. *Hughes,* 6 Bing. 689; 4
Moore, 577; *Doe* d. *Shaw* v. *Steward,* 1 A. & E. 300; 3 N. & M.
372; and formerly the right to bring a real action. *Smith* v. *Coffin,*
2 H. Black. 445. As to other property, possibilities, &c., see *post,*
542. The official assignee and the creditors' assignees have a *joint*
title to the bankrupt's estate. *Man* v. *Ricketts,* 1 Phil. R. 617; 15
Law J., N. S., Chanc. 79. The estate of the assignees of a bankrupt
is a *special* estate, a creation of the statutes relating to bankrupts. It
has not all the incidents either of a common law joint tenancy, or of a
common law tenancy in common. 9 C. B. 641, note (*c*). The title
of the assignees to the bankrupt's *real* property does not relate back to
the act of bankruptcy; therefore they should not claim to be entitled
to possession on a day prior to their appointment. *Doe* d. *Esdaile* v.
Mitchell, 2 M. & S. 446; *Cary* v. *Crisp,* 1 Salk. 108; *Jervis* v.
Tayleur, 3 B. & A. 560, Bayley, J.; *Doe* d. *Danson* v. *Parke,* 4 A.
& E. 816; *Sidebottom* v. *Barrington,* 3 Beav. 524; Arch. B. L. 216
(11th ed.).

Personal Estate.]—By 12 & 13 Vict. c. 106, s. 141, "when any
person shall have been adjudged a bankrupt, all his personal estate
and effects, present and future, wheresoever the same may be found or
known, and all property which he may purchase, or which may revert,
descend, be devised or bequeathed or come to him, *before he shall have
obtained his certificate,* and all debts," &c., " shall become absolutely
vested in the assignees for the time being for the benefit of the creditors
of the bankrupt by virtue of their appointment," and his assignees
" shall have like remedy to recover the same *in their own names* as the
bankrupt himself might have had if he had not been adjudged bankrupt." The official assignee is a necessary party as one of the plaintiffs. *Ante,* 538.

Leaseholds.]—Terms for years belonging to the bankrupt, being
part of his personal estate, vest in his assignees by virtue of their
appointment; but as they may be of no value, the assignees may elect
to take, or decline to take, any particular lease or agreement for a
lease, and the property therein comprised, 12 & 13 Vict. c. 106, s. 145.
Arch. B. L. 233 (11th ed.); 1 Smith, L. C. 455; *Bourdillon* v. *Dalton,* 2 Esp. 233; *Turner* v. *Richardson,* 7 East, 335; *Copeland* v.
Stephens, 1 B. & A. 593; *Graham* v. *Allsop,* 3 Exch. 186. If they
enter to take possession as assignees, or do any equivalent act, that will
amount to an election to take the property, and they will thereupon
become liable to the rent and covenants, in like manner as other
assignees; Arch. B. L. 234 (11th ed.); *Hanson* v. *Stevenson,* 1 B. &
Adol. 303; *Thomas* v. *Pemberton,* 7 Taunt. 206; *Clarke* v. *Hume,*

Ry. & Moo. 207 ; *Welch* v. *Myers,* 4 Camp. 568 ; *Ansell* v. *Robson,* 2 Cr. & Jer. 610 ; *Wakefield* v. *Brown,* 9 Q. B. 209 ; *Magnay* v. *Edwards,* 13 C. B. 479 ; but not to an action for use and occupation prior to the time when they took possession. *Naish* v. *Tatlock,* 2 H. Black. 320 ; *Richardson* v. *Hall,* 1 Brod. & B. 50 ; see *contra, Gibson* v. *Courthorpe,* 1 D. & R. 205. They may at any time get rid of their liability by an assignment. *Odell* v. *Wake,* 3 Camp. 394 ; *Taylor* v. *Shum,* 1 Bos. & P. 21 ; *Paul* v. *Nurse,* 8 B. & C. 486 ; 2 Man. & R. 525. But not by a disclaimer ; *Clark* v. *Hume,* Ry. & Moo. 207 ; nor by delivering up the key to the landlord. *Ansell* v. *Robson,* 2 Cr. & Jer. 610 ; *Hanson* v. *Stevenson,* 1 B. & A. 303. Such assignment may lawfully be made to anybody who will accept it, even to a pauper or a beggar ; *Likeux* v. *Nash,* 2 Stra. 1221 ; *Taylor* v. *Shum,* 1 Bos. & P. 21 ; *Onslow* v. *Corrie,* 2 Madd. 330 ; *Wilkins* v. *Fry,* 2 Rose, 371 ; or to the bankrupt himself ; *Doe* d. *Cheere* v. *Smith,* 5 Taunt. 795. But leave of the Court of Bankruptcy should first be obtained.

If the assignees wilfully abstain from making any such election they may be compelled to elect by a motion or petition to the Court of Bankruptcy. 12 & 13 Vict. c. 106, s. 145 ; *Doe* d. *Cheere* v. *Smith,* 5 Taunt. 795. Formerly the court could not have given the lessor his costs of the application, either against the assignees or out of the bankrupt's estate ; *Ex parte Bright,* 2 Glyn & J. 79 ; *Ex parte Hapton,* 2 Mont. D. & D. 347 ; but now see sect. 249, which authorizes the court " to award costs in all matters before it." Wise's B. L. 160 ; Shelf. B. L. 278. If the assignees, upon being served with the order, will do no act to elect, the court will make a declaration that the assignees have declined to take the lease or agreement. *Ex parte Blandy,* 1 Deac. 286 ; Arch. B. L. 234 (11th ed.).

Until the assignees have made their election, the leasehold property remains vested in the bankrupt, and he is personally liable to the rent and covenants. *Copeland* v. *Stephens,* 1 B. & A. 593 ; *Turner* v. *Richardson,* 7 East, 335 ; *Auriol* v. *Mills,* 1 H. Black. 433 ; 4 T. R. 94 ; 1 Smith's L. C. 455. But if the assignees decline to take the property, or the benefit of the lease or agreement, the bankrupt may, within fourteen days after notice thereof, get rid of his liability by delivering up the lease or agreement to the person then entitled to the rent. 12 & 13 Vict. c. 106, s. 145. If there be no written lease or agreement it is sufficient to deliver up the key and possession of the premises. *Slack* v. *Sharp,* 8 A. & E. 366 ; 3 N. & P. 390 ; *Ex parte Hopton,* 2 Mont. D. & D. 347 ; but see *Ex parte Sutton,* 2 Rose, 86 ; *Maples,* App., *Pepper,* Resp., 18 C. B. 177. It seems, however, that section 145 is confined to cases between lessor and lessee, and their respective assigns, and not to extend to cases between a lessee and his assignee of the lease. *Manning* v. *Flight,* 3 B. & Adol. 211 ; *Taylor* v. *Young,* 3 B. & A. 521 ; *Young* v. *Taylor,* 8 Taunt. 315 ; 2 Moo. 326. An agreement to procure a lease to be granted by a third person to the bankrupt is an agreement within this section. *Ex parte Beneche,* 2 Mont. & A. 692 ; 3 *Id.* 697 ; 1 Deac. 186 ; 2 *Id.* 46, *S. C.* Where the lease had been deposited with a third person as a security for a debt, the court, on the petition of the lessor, ordered the assignees to elect. *Ex parte Clunes,* 1 Madd. 76 ; *Ex parte Banbury,* 7 Jur. 660 ; *Ex parte Vardy,* 3 Mont. D. & D. 340 ; *Ex parte Norton, Id.* 312.

So long as the property remains vested in the bankrupt, or in his assignees, or their assigns, the landlord may distrain for the rent, not exceeding one year's rent accrued prior to the day of the filing of the petition for adjudication of bankruptcy; 12 & 13 Vict. c. 106, s. 129; and all subsequent rent. Arch. B. L. 132 (11th ed.); Shelf. B. L. 216 (2nd ed.); *Briggs* v. *Sowry*, 8 M. & W. 729; *Newton* v. *Scott*, 9 M. & W. 434; 10 *Id.* 471; *Phillips* v. *Hervill*, 6 Q. B. 944; *Bagge*, App., *Mawby*, Resp., 8 Exch. 641. A landlord *must* distrain in order to enforce his claim for arrears against the assignees. *Gethin* v. *Wilks*, 2 Dowl. 189; Shelf. B. L. 216 (2nd ed.).

If a trader before his bankruptcy deposit a lease as a security for money, but no mortgage or assignment of it is made, the assignees may recover the property by ejectment, for the mere deposit confers no legal title. *Doe* d. *Maslin* v. *Roe*, 5 Esp. 105. But it does not follow that they can recover the deed. *Wood* v. *Grimwood*, 5 Man. & Ry. 551.

A term of years or right of entry vested in husband and wife in right of the wife, will upon the husband's bankruptcy pass to his assignees. *Michell* v. *Hughes*, 6 Bing. 689; 4 Moo. & P. 577. Even a reversionary term which *may* fall into possession during the coverture, and which is not vested in a trustee for the wife's separate use, will pass to the assignees. *Doe* d. *Shaw* v. *Steward*, 1 A. & E. 300; 3 N. & M. 372.

A term of years may lawfully be granted subject to a condition or proviso for re-entry in the event of the lessee, his executors, administrators or assigns, becoming bankrupt. *Roe* d. *Hunter* v. *Galliers*, 2 T. R. 133; *Hickinbotham* v. *Groves*, 2 C. & P. 492; *Doe* d. *Bridgman* v. *David*, 1 Cr. M. & R. 405; 5 Tyr. 125; *S. C.* nom. *Doe* d. *Williams* v. *Davies*, 6 C. & P. 614; *Weeton* v. *Woodcock*, 7 M. & W. 14; Shelf. B. L. 280 (2nd ed.). A term may be so limited as to cease on the lessee becoming bankrupt, or ceasing to occupy the property for his own benefit. *Doe* d. *Lockwood* v. *Clarke*, 8 East, 185; and see *Doe* d. *Shaw* v. *Steward*, 1 A. & E. 300; 3 N. & M. 372. In such cases the lessor may lawfully re-enter for the forfeiture on the bankruptcy of the lessee, or even of his executor; *Doe* v. *David, supra*; but not after the lessor has accepted *subsequent* rent, with full knowledge of the bankruptcy, and thereby waived the forfeiture. *Ante*, 408.

A lease contained a proviso for re-entry on assignment without licence. The lessee executed a general assignment of all his property for the benefit of his creditors. He was afterwards made bankrupt: held, that the assignees in bankruptcy were entitled to the lease, and that it was not forfeited by the general assignment, because that was an act of bankruptcy, and consequently void as against them. *Doe* d. *Lloyd* v. *Powell*, 5 B. & C. 308; 8 D. & R. 35.

Freeholds.]—By 12 & 13 Vict. c. 106, s. 142, "when any person shall have been adjudged a bankrupt, all lands, tenements and hereditaments, *except copy or customaryhold*, in England, Scotland, Ireland, or in any of the dominions, plantations or colonies belonging to her majesty, to which the bankrupt is entitled, and all interest to which such bankrupt is entitled in any of such lands, tenements or hereditaments, and of which he might, according to the laws of the several countries, dominions, plantations or colonies, have disposed, and all such lands, tenements and hereditaments as he shall purchase, or shall descend, be devised, revert to, or come to such bankrupt *before he shall have obtained his certificate,* and all deeds, papers and writings respecting the same, shall become *absolutely vested in the assignees* for the time being, for the benefit of the creditors of the bankrupt, *by virtue of their appointment, without any deed of conveyance* for that purpose; and as often as any such assignee or assignees shall die, or be lawfully removed or displaced, and a new assignee or assignees shall be duly appointed, such of the aforesaid real estate as shall remain unsold or unconveyed, shall by virtue of such appointment vest in the new assignee or assignees, either alone or jointly with the existing assignees, as the case may require, without any conveyance for that purpose."

Where a conveyance from the bankrupt would require to be registered or enrolled, the certificate of the appointment of his assignees in bankruptcy must be registered or enrolled (sect. 143) as in Middlesex, Yorkshire, and the Colonies.

The real estate of a bankrupt remains vested in him until the official assignee is appointed. The title of the assignees does not relate back to the act of bankruptcy, as in the case of personal estate. *Ante,* 539. An appointment executed by a bankrupt after the appointment of assignees is void as against them, and they may maintain ejectment against the appointee. *Doe* d. *Coleman* v. *Britain,* 2 B. & A. 93. A right of entry vested in husband and wife, in right of the wife, passes to the assignees of the husband if he become bankrupt. *Michell* v. *Hughes,* 6 Bing. 689; 4 Moo. & P. 577; *Doe* d. *Shaw* v. *Steward,* 1 A. & E. 300; 3 N. & M. 372. A contingent remainder or reversion of the bankrupt will pass to the assignees, notwithstanding the estate does not fall into possession until after he has obtained his certificate. *Higden* v. *Williamson,* 3 P. Wms. 132. But a mere possibility that the lands will come to the bankrupt as heir at law by descent, will not pass to the assignees, unless the property descends before he obtains his certificate. *Moth* v. *Frome,* Ambler, 394; *Carleton* v. *Leighton,* 3 Mer. 667; Arch. B. L. 222 (11th ed.); and see *Johnson* v. *Smiley,* 17 Beav. 223.

Copyholds and Customary Property.]—A bankrupt's copyhold and customary property does not vest in his assignees, being expressly excepted by sect. 142; *ante,* 541. But "the court shall have power to sell, and by deed indented and enrolled in the courts of the manor or manors whereof the lands respectively may be holden to convey for the benefit of the creditors, any copyhold or customaryhold lands, or any interest to which any bankrupt is entitled therein, and thereby to entitle or authorize any person or persons on behalf of the Court of Bankruptcy to surrender the same, for the purpose of any purchaser being admitted thereto." 12 & 13 Vict. c. 106, s. 209. The conveyance is to be made by bargain and sale direct from the commissioner to the vendee. *Ex parte Holland,* 4 Mad. 483; *Drury* v. *Mann,* 1 Atk. 86; see the form, Arch. B. L., Book II., 116 (11th ed.). The deed should authorize some person therein named to make a surrender to the vendee, and it must be entered on the court rolls. The vendee is to compound for the lord's fines, &c., and thereupon the lord is to "grant unto such vendee, upon request, the said copyhold or customary lands or tenements for such estate or interest as shall have been so conveyed to him as aforesaid, reserving the ancient rents, customs and services, and shall admit him tenant of the same." Sect. 210. Formerly the commissioners in bankruptcy assigned the bankrupt's copyholds to his assignees; *Crisp* v. *Pratt,* Cro. Car. 549; *Doe* d. *Johnson* v. *Liversedge,* 11 M. & W. 517; and this might have been done even after the bankrupt's death. *Doe* d. *Spencer* v. *Clark,* 5 B. & A. 458; 1 D. & R. 44. But it would seem that now only a purchaser from the court who has been admitted (not the bankrupt's assignees), can maintain ejectment for copyhold or customary land of the bankrupt. Before any such sale the bankrupt himself may maintain ejectment.

It is doubtful whether a copyhold tenant, who has become bankrupt, can be guilty of a forfeiture by disclaiming to be tenant of the manor, after a conveyance of his interest in the premises to a purchaser under the bankruptcy. *Clarke* v. *Arden,* 16 C. B. 227.

Mortgaged Property.]—By 12 & 13 Vict. c. 106, s. 149, " if any bankrupt shall have granted, conveyed, assured or pledged any real or personal estate, or deposited any deeds, such grant, conveyance, assurance, pledge or deposit being upon condition or power of redemption at a future day by payment of money or otherwise, the assignees may, *before* the time of the performance of such condition, make tender or payment of money, or other performance, according to such condition, as fully as the bankrupt might have done; and after such tender, payment or performance, such real or personal estate *may be sold* and disposed of for the benefit of the creditors."

This section enables the assignees of a bankrupt mortgagor to pay or tender the principal money and interest *before* the appointed day; which the bankrupt himself could not have done; but it does not authorize the assignees to make any such payment or tender *after* the appointed day. *Dunn* v. *Massey,* 6 A. & E. 479; 1 N. & P. 578.

It would seem that where a tender is made pursuant to this section, and the money refused, *the court* (not the assignees) may direct the mortgaged property to be sold for the benefit of the creditors. The 6 Geo. 4, c. 16, s. 70, authorized the assignees to sell and dispose of the property under such circumstances. But the above section is differently worded in this respect; and therefore it would seem that upon a tender being duly made, the legal estate does not vest in the assignees, nor can they maintain ejectment; but the power of sale given by sect. 149 must be executed by the assignees under the direction of the court, after which the purchaser may maintain ejectment against the mortgagee, or any person claiming through or under him.

There is an elaborate note on this section in Shelf. B. L. 286 (2nd ed.).

Property settled or conveyed by the Bankrupt without valuable Consideration.]—By 12 & 13 Vict. c. 106, s. 126, " if any bankrupt *being at the time insolvent,* shall (except upon the marriage of any of his children, or for some *valuable* consideration) have conveyed, assigned or transferred to any of his children, or to any other person, any hereditaments, &c., the court shall have power to order the same to be sold and disposed of for the benefit of the creditors under the bankruptcy; and every such sale shall be valid against the bankrupt,

and such children and persons, and against all persons claiming under
him."

It would seem, from the decisions under section 125 of the same
act, that the legal estate does not vest in the assignees; but there must
be an *order for sale, and a sale* and conveyance of the property, by
the assignees to a purchaser before the settlement or conveyance thereof
by the bankrupt can be defeated. *Heslop* v. *Baker*, 6 Exch. 740;
Quartermaine v. *Bittlestone*, 13 C. B. 133, 156; 14 *Id.* 155. And
that the order may be made *ex parte*. *Ex parte Heslop*, 1 De Gex,
Mac. & Gor. 479, Lords Js.; *Ex parte Barlow*, 2 *Id.* 921; *Quartermaine* v. *Bittlestone, supra*. But it is not conclusively binding on the
party prejudiced by it. *Graham* v. *Furber*, 14 C. B. 134; *Hamilton*
v. *Bell*, 10 Exch. 545.

A trader becomes "insolvent" when he is unable to make his payments as usual. *Bayley* v. *Schofield*, 1 M. & S. 353, Le Blanc, J.
It means a general inability to pay his debts, or to meet his engage-
ments. *Ex parte Pearse*, 2 Deac. & Chit. 464, Rose, J.; *Parker* v.
Gossage, 2 Cr. M. & R. 617; *Biddlecombe* v. *Bond*, 4 A. & E. 332;
Doe d. *Griffiths* v. *Pritchard*, 5 B. & Adol. 777, Taunton, J.; Shelf.
B. L. 210 (2nd ed.). It is not confined to cases where the party takes
the benefit of an Act for the Relief of Insolvent Debtors, unless the
context so requires. *Cases supra; In re Birmingham Act*, 3 Simon,
421. It does not follow that a trader is not insolvent because he may
ultimately have a surplus upon the winding up of his affairs. *Bayley*
v. *Schofield*, 1 M. & S. 353, Le Blanc, J.

As to what does or does not amount to a valuable consideration, see
Shelf. B. L. 211—213 (2nd ed.); *Walker* v. *Burrows*, 1 Atk. 94;
Smith v. *Keating*, 6 C. B. 148, 149.

*Property fraudulently disposed of by the Bankrupt before his
Bankruptcy, with Intent to defeat or delay his Creditors.*]—By 13
Eliz. c. 5 (made perpetual by 29 Eliz. c. 5), every feoffment, gift,
grant, alienation, bargain and conveyance of lands, tenements, hereditaments, goods and chattels, or of any of them, or of any lease, rent,
common or other profit out of the same, devised and contrived of
malice, fraud, covin, collusion or guile, to the end, purpose or *intent to
delay, hinder or defraud creditors and others* of their just and lawful
actions, suits, &c., shall be deemed and taken (only as against that
person or persons, his or their heirs, successors, executors, administrators *and assigns*, and every of them, whose actions, suits, &c. might
thereby be in anywise disturbed, hindered, delayed or defrauded) to be
clearly and utterly void, frustrate and of none effect; any pretence,
colour, feigned consideration, expressing of use, or other matter or
thing to the contrary notwithstanding. Sect. 2. Provided that this
act, or anything therein contained, shall not extend to any estate or
interest in lands, &c. which is or shall be upon *good consideration* and
bonâ fide lawfully conveyed or assured to any person or persons, or
bodies politic or corporate, not having at the time of such conveyance
or assurance to them made, any manner of notice or knowledge of such
covin, fraud or collusion as aforesaid; anything before mentioned to
the contrary hereof notwithstanding. Sect. 6.

For the decisions under this act, see 2 Chit. Stat. 163—171 (2nd
ed.); 1 Smith's L. C. 9 (notes to *Twine's case*); Roberts on Fraudulent Conveyances, 3; Bac. Abr. Fraud, (c).

The assignees of a bankrupt or of insolvent debtor represent his creditors, and therefore any conveyance, &c. which is fraudulent and void as against creditors, is fraudulent and void as against the assignees, and they may recover back the lands in ejectment. *Doe* d. *Grimsby* v. *Ball,* 11 M. & W. 531; *Graham* v. *Furber,* 14 C. B. 410; *Norcutt* v. *Dodd,* 5 Jur. 835; *Doe* d. *Read* v. *Ridout,* 5 Taunt. 519.

A conveyance which is fraudulent and void as against creditors, &c. may nevertheless be valid as between the parties; *Doe* d. *Roberts* v. *Roberts,* 2 B. & A. 367; *Robinson* v. *M'Donnel,* *Id.* 134; and also against any other person privy and consenting to it. *Steel* v. *Brown and Parry,* 1 Taunt. 381. The exception is when the conveyance is fraudulent and void on grounds of public policy. *Higgins* v. *Pitt,* 4 Exch. 312.

When it is attempted to invalidate a conveyance, &c. by showing it to fall within the provisions of this statute, a question arises for the jury, viz., whether the transaction was *bonâ fide,* and the deed really intended to operate as expressed; or whether it was fraudulent, and merely a contrivance to defeat or delay creditors, the real object being to protect the property for the benefit of the conveying party, or any of his family or relations. *Marshall* v. *Lamb,* 5 Q. B. 115; *Cook* v. *Rogers,* 7 Bing. 438; 5 Moo. & P. 353; *Groom* v. *Watts,* 4 Exch. 727. A deed may be fraudulent and void within the statute, although made for full valuable consideration, if there be a *secret trust* for the benefit of the grantor. *Twine's case,* 3 Co. R. 80; 1 Smith's L. C. 1.

A conveyance of *all,* or substantially all, a trader's property, in consideration of a past debt, amounts of itself to an act of bankruptcy, without any actual fraud, because it necessarily tends to defeat and delay the other creditors. *Graham* v. *Chapman,* 12 C. B. 85. It makes no difference in this respect that the conveyance is made for the benefit of all the trader's creditors. *Rothwell* v. *Timbrell,* 1 Dowl. N. S. 778; *Lackington* v. *Elliott,* 7 Man. & Gr. 538. But a *bonâ fide* sale or mortgage stands on a different footing. *Baxter* v. *Pritchard,* 1 A. & E. 456; *Rose* v. *Haycock,* *Id.* 460, note; *Lee* v. *Hart,* 10 Exch. 555. So where the deed does not comprise all or nearly all the trader's property; *Wedge* v. *Newlyn,* 4 B. & Adol. 831; *Chase* v. *Goble,* 2 Man. & Gr. 930; especially if the trader be then solvent. *Porter* v. *Walker,* 1 Man. & Gr. 688, Littledale, J.

Any fraudulent grant or conveyance by a trader of any of his lands or tenements, goods or chattels, does of itself amount to an act of bankruptcy. 12 & 13 Vict. c. 106, s. 67; Shelf. B. L. 89, 95.

Property sold and conveyed by the Bankrupt after the Act of Bankruptcy.]—By 12 & 13 Vict. c. 106, s. 133, "all conveyances by any bankrupt *bonâ fide* made and executed before the filing of the petition for adjudication of bankruptcy, and all contracts, dealings and transactions by and with any bankrupt really and *bonâ fide* made and entered into before the filing of such petition, shall be deemed to be valid, nowithstanding any prior act of bankruptcy by such bankrupt committed, provided the person so dealing with such bankrupt had not at the time of such conveyance, contract, dealing or transaction, notice of any prior act of bankruptcy by him committed: provided also, that nothing herein contained shall be deemed or taken to give validity to any conveyance or equitable mortgage made or given by any bankrupt by way of fraudulent preference of any creditor of such bankrupt."

For the decisions under this section, and the corresponding sections in previous acts (6 Geo. 4, c. 16, ss. 81, 82; 2 Vict. c. 11, s. 12; 2 & 3 Vict. c. 29), see 1 Chit. Stat. 246, note (*i*), (2nd ed.); Shelf. B. L. 222—238 (2nd ed.); Arch. B. L. 340 (11th ed.).

By 12 & 13 Vict. c. 106, s. 134, "no purchase from any bankrupt *bond fide* and for valuable consideration, where the purchaser *had notice* at the time of such purchase of an act of bankruptcy by such bankrupt committed, shall be impeached by reason thereof, unless a fiat or petition for adjudication of bankruptcy shall have been sued out or filed within twelve months after such act of bankruptcy." *Earl Granville* v. *Danvers*, 7 Simon, 121; Arch. B. L. 342 (11th ed.); Shelf. B. L. 238 (2nd ed.).

Property contracted for by the Bankrupt.]—By 12 & 13 Vict. c. 106, s. 146, "if any bankrupt shall have entered into any agreement for the purchase of any estate or interest in land, the vendor thereof, or any person claiming under him, if the assignees shall not (upon being thereto required) elect whether they will abide by and execute such agreement, or abandon the same, may apply to the court, and the court may thereupon order them to deliver up the agreement, and the possession of the premises to the vendor or person claiming under him, or make such other order thereon as such court shall think fit." *Ex parte Bridger*, 1 Deac. 581; *Ex parte Fletcher*, 1 Deac. & Chit. 356; Arch. B. L. 252 (11th ed.).

Trust Property.]—Real and personal estate vested in a bankrupt merely as trustee, or as an executor or administrator, and in which he has *no beneficial estate or interest*, does not pass to his assignees, but remains in the bankrupt. Arch. B. L. 325 (11th ed.); *Ex parte Gennys*, Mont. & M. 258; *Gardner* v. *Rowe*, 2 Sim. & Stu. 346; 5 Russ. 258.

The authority of the Court of Bankruptcy is confined to such real property of the bankrupt "which he shall have *in his own right* before he became bankrupt, as also all such interest in any such lands, tenements and hereditaments as such bankrupt *may lawfully depart withal*, and all his money," &c. 12 & 13 Vict. c. 106, s. 89. If the bankrupt have any beneficial estate or interest in a reversionary term devised to his wife, and not to a trustee for her separate use, it will pass to his assignees in bankruptcy. *Doe* d. *Shaw* v. *Steward*, 1 A. & E. 300; 3 N. & M. 372; *Bennet* v. *Davis*, 2 P. Wms. 316.

When a trustee becomes bankrupt, the Lord Chancellor may appoint a new trustee; 12 & 13 Vict. c. 106, s. 130; *Ex parte Smith*, 4 Deac. 214; Arch. B. L. 325 (11th ed.); 1 Chit. Stat. 246, note (*b*) (2nd ed.); or a receiver. *Ex parte Ellis*, 1 Atk. 101; *Langley* v. *Hawke*, 5 Madd. 46.

Property sold by the Assignees.]—The 12 & 13 Vict. c. 106, s. 131, enacts, "that no title to any real or personal estate sold under any bankruptcy shall be impeached by the bankrupt, or any person claiming under him, in respect of any defect in the fiat or petition for adjudication, or in any of the proceedings under the same, unless the bankrupt shall, *within the time allowed by this act* (*post*, 547), have commenced proceedings to dispute, dismiss or annul the fiat, petition or adjudication, and duly prosecuted the same."

The assignees of a bankrupt do not "claim under him" within the meaning of this section, but adversely to him by act and operation of law. *Gould* v. *Shoyer*, 6 Bing. 738; 4 Moo. & P. 635; *Earl Granville* v. *Danvers*, 7 Simon, 121.

A deed of conveyance from the assignees to a purchaser is liable to stamp duty, notwithstanding sect. 138. *Flather* v. *Stubbs*, 2 Q. B. 614.

Death or Removal of Assignees not to abate Suit—Suggestion.]— By 12 & 13 Vict. c. 106, s. 157, "whenever an assignee shall die or be removed, or a new assignee shall be chosen, no action at law or suit in equity shall be thereby abated; but the court in which any action or suit is depending may, upon the suggestion of such death or removal and new choice, allow the name of the surviving or new assignee to be substituted in the place of the former; and such action or suit shall be prosecuted in the name or names of the said surviving or new assignee or assignees, in the same manner as if he had originally commenced the same."

This section applies to the official assignee, as well as to the creditors' assignees. *Man* v. *Ricketts*, 7 Beav. 484; *S. C.* (on appeal), 1 Phil. R. 617; *Mendham* v. *Robinson*, 1 Myl. & K. 217; *Lloyd* v. *Waring*, 1 Coll. C. C. 536. But not to assignees when defendants. 1 Chit. Stat. 261, note (*d*) (2nd ed.); *Bainbridge* v. *Blair*, 1 You. 386; *Mendham* v. *Robinson*, 1 Myl. & K. 217. The rule for leave to enter a suggestion is absolute in the first instance. *Westall* v. *Sturges*, 4 Moo. & P. 217; *Bates* v. *Sturges*, 7 Bing. 585; 5 Moo. & P. 568.

Gazette, when Evidence of Bankruptcy, &c.]—The 12 & 13 Vict. c. 106, s. 233, enacts, "that if the bankrupt shall not (if he were within the United Kingdom at the date of the adjudication) within twenty-one days [now two calendar months: 17 & 18 Vict. c. 119, s. 24] after the advertisement of the bankruptcy in the London Gazette or (if he were in any other part of Europe at the date of the adjudication) within three months after such advertisement, or (if he were elsewhere at the date of the adjudication) within twelve months after such advertisement, have commenced an action, suit or other proceeding to dispute or annul the fiat, or the petition for adjudication, and shall not have prosecuted the same with due diligence and with effect, the Gazette containing such advertisement shall be *conclusive evidence* in all cases as against such bankrupt, and in all actions at law or suits in equity brought by the assignees for *any debt or demand* for which such bankrupt might have sustained any action or suit, had he not been adjudged bankrupt, that such person so adjudged bankrupt *became a bankrupt* before the date and suing forth of such fiat or before the date and filing of the petition for adjudication, and that such fiat was sued forth or such petition filed *on the day* on which the same is stated in the Gazette to bear date."

This section applies to all actions (including ejectment) which the bankrupt himself might have maintained if no bankruptcy had intervened, but not to those actions in which the bankruptcy is a material ingredient to the cause of action, as in cases of fraudulent preferences, and conveyances valid as against the bankrupt himself, but fraudulent and void as against his creditors and as against his assignees in bankruptcy, who represent the creditors. *Kitchener* v. *Power*, 3 A. & E. 232; 4 N. & M. 710; *Alsager* v. *Close*, 10 M. & W. 576; *Doe* d. *Johnson* v. *Liversedge*, 11 M. & W. 519; 2 Stark. Ev. 125, note; *Pennell* v. *Hume*, 5 July, 1855, Kindersley, V. C.; 1 Jur. N. S. 669. In the former class of cases it is immaterial to the defendant whether he be sued by the bankrupt or by his assignees; but in the latter he could not be sued at all, except for the bankruptcy. *Per* Patteson, J., in *Smith* v. *Woodward*, 4 C. & P. 542. For ascertaining whether or not the case is within the section, the criterion is whether the bankruptcy be only a formal step in the evidence, or whether it be so essentially a part of the ground of action that without proof of it no party could recover in respect of the alleged cause: and this is to be decided by the judge upon the opening of the evidence at the trial. *Kitchener* v. *Power*, 3 A. & E. 232; 4 N. & M. 710.

Section 233 applies, notwithstanding the claimants are not described in the writ as assignees of the estate and effects of the bankrupt. *Doe* d. *Johnson* v. *Liversedge*, 11 M. & W. 517. Also to actions commenced before the limited time within which the bankrupt might dispute the adjudication, but which do not come on for trial until after that time has elapsed. *Earith* v. *Schroder*, Moo. & Mal. 24. Also to actions partly founded on a notice to quit, or demand of possession, or other act done by the assignees subsequent to the bankruptcy, and which might have been done by the bankrupt had he not become bankrupt. *Alsager* v. *Close*, 10 M. & W. 576; *Kitchener* v. *Power*, 3 A. & E. 232; 4 N. & M. 710; *Smith* v. *Woodward*, 4 C. & P. 541.

The Isle of Man is not " within the United Kingdom," within the meaning of this section. *Davison* v. *Farmer*, 6 Exch. 242.

The Gazette, when admissible under this section, operates as *conclusive evidence* that the party *became a bankrupt, i. e.*, that he, being a trader, and owing a sufficient debt to the petitioning creditor, committed an act of bankruptcy: also that the petition for adjudication was duly filed *on the day* on which the same is stated in the Gazette to bear date. But it would seem that the adjudication of bankruptcy must be proved: also the several appointments of the official and creditors' assignees. These may be proved by the production of the original documents, or of sealed office copies. *Post*, 549.

Notice to dispute the Petitioning Creditor's Debt, the Trading and the Act of Bankruptcy.]—The 12 & 13 Vict. c. 106, s. 234, enacts, " that in any action, *other than* an action brought by the assignees for any debt or demand for which the bankrupt might have sustained an action had he not been adjudged bankrupt, and whether at the suit of or against the assignees, or against any person acting under the warrant of the court for anything done under such warrant, no proof shall be required, at the trial, of the petitioning creditor's debt, or of the trading or act of bankruptcy respectively, unless the other party in such action shall, if defendant *at or before pleading*, and if plaintiff, *before issue joined*, give notice in writing to such assignees or other person that he intends to dispute some and which of such matters [*see the form, Appendix, No.* 107]: and in case such notice shall have been given, if such assignees or other person shall prove the matter so disputed, or the other party admit the same, the judge before whom the cause shall be tried may (if he think fit) grant a certificate of such proof or admission; and such assignees or other person shall be entitled to the costs occasioned by such notice; and such costs shall, if such assignees or other person shall obtain a verdict, be added to the costs, and if the other party shall obtain a verdict, shall be deducted from the costs, which such other party would otherwise be entitled to receive from such assignees or other persons."

This section extends to actions of ejectment (*Doe* d. *Johnson* v. *Liversedge*, 11 M. & W. 517; *Doe* d. *Mawson* v. *Liston*, 4 Taunt. 471) other than and except those to which sect. 233 applies, and in which the Gazette is made conclusive evidence of the bankruptcy, &c. *Ante,* 547. As there are now no pleadings in ejectment, it would seem that the notice required to be given by defendants, pursuant to sect. 234, should be given before the appearance is entered, or on the same day, or at the latest when notice to defend for part only is served. *Pennell* v. *Hume*, 1 Jur., N. S. 669, Kindersley, V. C. The notice must specify which of the matters the defendant intends to dispute, viz., the petitioning creditor's debt, the trading and the act of bankruptcy. *See the form, Appendix, No.* 107. Whichever is not mentioned in the notice will be considered as admitted for all the purposes of the cause. *Porter* v. *Walker*, 1 Man. & Gr. 686; *Hernaman* v. *Barber*, 14 C. B. 583; 15 C. B. 774, *S. C.* A notice to dispute "the bankruptcy" is too general. *Trimley* v. *Uwins*, 6 B. & C. 537; 9 D. & R. 548. A notice that the party "was not duly declared a bankrupt," is not sufficient. *Moon* v. *Raphael*, 7 C. & P. 115.

Sealed Proceedings and Copies to be Evidence.]—The 12 & 13 Vict. c. 106, s. 236, enacts, "that any fiat, petition for adjudication of bankruptcy, adjudication of bankruptcy, petition for arrangement between a debtor and his creditors, assignment, appointment of assignees, certificate, deposition, or other proceeding, or order in bankruptcy, or under any such petition for arrangement, appearing to be sealed with the seal of the court, or any writing purporting to be a copy of any such document and purporting to be so sealed, shall at all times, and on behalf of all persons, and whether for the purposes of this act or otherwise, be admitted in all courts whatever as evidence of such documents respectively, and of such proceedings and orders having respectively taken place or been made, and be deemed respectively records of the court, without any further proof thereof, and no such document or copy shall be receivable in evidence unless the same appear to be so sealed, except where otherwise in this act specially provided." Proviso as to fiats and proceedings entered of record before 2 & 3 Will. 4, c. 114, and copies thereof.

Judicial Notice of Signatures and Seals.]—The 12 & 13 Vict. c. 106, s. 237, enacts "that all courts, judges, justices and persons judicially acting, and other officers, shall take judicial notice of the signature of any commissioner or registrar of the court, and of the seal of the court, subscribed or attached to any judicial or official proceeding or document to be made or signed under the provisions of this act:" *and see* 8 & 9 *Vict. c.* 113, *s.* 1; 14 & 15 *Vict. c.* 99, *ss.* 9, 10, 11; Shelf. B. L. 454.

Evidence of Declaration of Insolvency.]—The 12 & 13 Vict. c. 106, s. 238, enacts, "that a copy of a declaration of insolvency under this act [sect. 70], purporting to be certified by the Lord Chancellor's secretary of bankrupts or any of his clerks as a true copy, shall be received as evidence of such declaration having been filed."

By 17 & 18 Vict. c. 119, declarations of insolvency are to be filed with the registrar of the district, and copies thereof are to be received as evidence. Sects. 16—19.

The *date* of the filing must be proved, notwithstanding it is mentioned in a memorandum indorsed thereon. *Reg.* v. *Lands*, 25 Law J., N. S., M. C. 14.

Petition under Insolvent Debtors' Act in England or India, how proved.]—The 12 & 13 Vict. c. 106, s. 239, enacts, "that a copy of any petition filed in the Court for the Relief of Insolvent Debtors in England, or in any court for the relief of insolvent debtors at Calcutta, Madras or Bombay, or at the settlement of Prince of Wales Island, Singapore and Malacca, and of any vesting order, schedule, order of adjudication, and other orders and proceedings purporting to be signed by the officer in whose custody the same shall be, or his deputy, certifying the same to be a true copy of such petition, vesting order, schedule, order of adjudication or other order or proceedings, and appearing to be sealed with the seal of such court, shall at all times be *admitted under this act as sufficient evidence* of the same, and of such proceedings respectively having taken place, without any other proof whatever given of the same."

The *date* of the filing of the petition must be proved, notwithstanding it is mentioned in a memorandum indorsed thereon. *Reg.* v. *Lands*, 25 Law J., N. S., M. C. 14.

Advertisement in Gazette and Newspapers when Evidence.]—The 12 & 13 Vict. c. 106, s. 240, enacts, "that a copy of the *London Gazette*, and of any newspaper containing any such advertisement as is by this act directed or authorized to be made therein respectively, shall be evidence of any matter therein contained, and of which notice is by this act directed or authorized to be given by such advertisement; and all proceedings or notices required by this act to be inserted in the *London Gazette* shall be marked with the seal of the court from which such proceedings or notices shall be issued, and certified by one of the registrars of the said court."

Law of Evidence Act (6 & 7 Vict. c. 85), extended.]—By 12 & 13 Vict. c. 106, s. 241, "the provisions of an act passed in the parliament holden in the sixth and seventh years of the reign of her present majesty, intituled ' An Act for improving the Law of Evidence,' shall be applicable to any matter or proceeding in prosecution under the provisions of this act, and to any matter, question or inquiry arising in any court of law or equity out of or consequent upon any such matter or proceeding."

The 6 & 7 Vict. c. 85, referred to by the above enactment, has been altered by 15 & 16 Vict. c. 99, s. 1, and 16 & 17 Vict. c. 83, s. 4.

Depositions of deceased Witnesses and Copies to be Evidence.]—The 12 & 13 Vict. c. 106, s. 242, enacts, "that in the event of the death of any witness deposing to the petitioning creditor's debt, trading, or act of bankruptcy, under any bankruptcy heretofore or hereafter, or under any petition for arrangement, the deposition of any such deceased witness purporting to be sealed with the seal of the court, or a copy thereof purporting to be so sealed, shall *in all cases* be received as evidence of the matters therein respectively contained."

No deposition is admissible under this section until the death of the witness has been proved to the satisfaction of the judge (not the jury) before whom the action is tried.

If assignees in bankruptcy cause depositions to be enrolled, that does not make such depositions admissible as against them during the life of the witnesses. *Chambers* v. *Bernasconi*, 1 Cr. M. & R. 347. But depositions taken before the adjudication of bankruptcy, on behalf of the petitioning creditor, are afterwards admissible against him, although the witnesses be living. *Gardner* v. *Moult*, 10 A. & E. 464; 2 P. & D. 403; *Cole* v. *Hadley*, 11 A. & E. 807; 3 P. & D. 458.

Evidence for Plaintiffs.]—Before the commencement of an ejectment by the assignees of a bankrupt, leave of the Court of Bankruptcy should be obtained; *ante*, 537; but such leave need not be proved at the trial, and the want of it does not constitute any defence. *Ante*, 538.

It is frequently advisable to join the bankrupt as a co-plaintiff with the assignees; *Cary* v. *Crisp*, 1 Salk. 108; *Doe* d. *Danson* v. *Parke*, 4 A. & E. 816; *ante*, 285; especially when there is any danger of the bankruptcy being successfully disputed; or the property is copyhold or customaryhold, and has not been sold; *ante*, 542; *Doe* d. *Danson* v. *Parke*, 4 A. & E. 816; or trust property, wherein it is doubtful whether the bankrupt has any beneficial estate or interest, as to the whole or part. *Ante*, 546. But if he permit his name to be so used, he will thereby become personally liable to the defendants for any costs to be adjudged to them. *Ante*, 538.

The title of the assignees to the bankrupt's real property *does not relate back to the act of bankruptcy; ante*, 539; therefore they should not claim possession from a day prior to their appointment as assignees.

The Gazette is *conclusive evidence* of the trading, petitioning creditor's debt and act of bankruptcy, and of the petition for adjudication, provided the action be one which the bankrupt himself might have maintained had he not become bankrupt, and the time allowed to the bankrupt to dispute the bankruptcy has elapsed; *ante*, 547; but it seems that the adjudication of bankruptcy, and the several appointments of the plaintiffs as official and creditor's assignees, must be proved. *Ante*, 548. The production of the original documents, or of official sealed copies thereof, will be sufficient. *Ante*, 549.

If the action be brought to defeat a fraudulent preference, it will not be necessary to prove either the petitioning creditor's debt, the trading, or the act of bankruptcy, unless notice has been duly given to dispute them or some or one of them. *Ante*, 548. But whichever is so disputed must be proved in the usual manner. If any witness who proved them before the Court of Bankruptcy be shown to be dead, his depositions, or a sealed copy thereof, will be admissible. *Ante*, 550. But in actions wherein the assignee's title comes into question *incidentally*, the petitioning creditor's debt, the trading, and the act of bankruptcy, must all be proved in the usual manner. *Doe* d. *Mawson* v. *Liston*, 4 Taunt. 741; *Doe* d. *Barraud* v. *Lawrence*, 2 C. & P. 134; *Doe* d. *Sheldon* v. *Sheldon*, 3 A. & E. 265; 4 N. & M. 857; *Reg.* v. *Lands*, 25 Law J., N. S., M. C. 14. If the act of bank-

ruptcy consist of a declaration of insolvency, or of a petition to the
Court for Relief of Insolvent Debtors, it may be proved by a sealed
office copy. *Ante,* 549, 550. The *date of filing* should be proved notwithstanding it is mentioned in a memorandum indorsed thereon. *Reg.*
v. *Lands,* 25 Law J., N. S., M. C. 14.

Generally speaking, sealed copies of proceedings in bankruptcy are
admissible ; *ante,* 549 ; and judicial notice is taken of the signatures
and seals. *Ante,* 549. Sometimes advertisements are evidence of the
matters therein mentioned. *Ante,* 550. Where certain parts only of
a book containing proceedings in bankruptcy are put in by the assignees, the defendant or his counsel has no right to use other parts
without putting them in as his evidence. *Whitfield* v. *Aland,* 2 Car.
& K. 1015, Wilde, C. J. ; *ante,* 164.

If the action be one which might have been maintained by the bankrupt, had he not become bankrupt, the assignees must prove the bankrupt's title in like manner as he would have done; also their own
derivative title as assignees. *Ante,* 548. Proof that the defendant
held as a tenant of the bankrupt, or obtained possession of the property
from him, will show a title by estoppel ; *ante,* 209, 213 ; *Doe* d.
Biddell v. *Abrahams,* 1 Stark. R. 305 ; but in such case it must be
shown that the defendant's title has expired, or been duly determined
by notice to quit, demand of possession, surrender, forfeiture, or otherwise, as in an action by a landlord against his tenant. *Ante,* 392 to
457 ; *Doe* d. *Duncan* v. *Edwards,* 9 A. & E. 554 ; 1 P. & D. 408.
Mesne profits may sometimes be recovered upon proper evidence in
that behalf. *Ante,* 292.

If the action be brought to defeat a fraudulent preference, the
defendant must have due notice to produce the deed in question ; *ante,*
155 ; and the plaintiffs must be prepared with proof of such notice and
secondary evidence of the contents of the deed. *Ante,* 169. Also
with such further evidence as may be necessary to show that the deed
amounted to a " fraudulent preference" of a creditor of the bankrupt;
Arch. B. L. 54, 61 (11th ed.) ; Shelf. B. L. 211 (2nd ed.) ; also their
own derivative title as assignees. *Ante,* 548.

Generally speaking, a voluntary settlement or conveyance, without
valuable consideration, by the bankrupt before his bankruptcy, cannot
be disputed by the assignees in an ejectment at their suit ; but there
must be an order for sale, and a sale and conveyance to a purchaser ;
ante, 543 ; so also the assignees cannot maintain ejectment for copyholds or customary property of the bankrupt ; *ante,* 542 ; nor for
property vested in him as a trustee, or executor, or administrator, and
in which he has no beneficial estate or interest. *Ante,* 546.

Evidence and Points for the Defendant.]—The defendant cannot
dispute the petitioning creditor's debt, the trading, or the act of bankruptcy, unless he has given due notice of his intention so to do, at the
time of appearing to the action, or, at the latest, when notice to defend
for part only was served. *Ante,* 549. If, by any accident or oversight,
this was then omitted, he should obtain leave of the court or a judge to
withdraw his appearance and to appear *de novo,* with notice to dispute
such of the above matters as are intended to be disputed at the trial.
Poole v. *Bell,* 1 Stark. R. 328 ; *Willock* v. *Westmacott,* 2 Camp. 184;
Radmore v. *Gould,* Wightw. 80 ; 1 Rose, 123 ; *Gardner* v. *Slack,* 6
Moore, 489 ; *Lawrence* v. *Crowder,* 1 Moo. & P. 511. If, however,

the action is one which might have been maintained by the bankrupt had he not become bankrupt, and the time has elapsed within which the bankrupt might have disputed the bankruptcy, the Gazette will be *conclusive evidence* of the petitioning creditor's debt, the trading, the act of bankruptcy, and the petition for adjudication. *Ante,* 547.

The defendant may contend that the plaintiff's evidence is insufficient on some material point. *Ante,* 551. He may also produce contradictory evidence. He may prove that the property in question is copyhold or customary land, and, consequently, that the assignees have no right to maintain ejectment for it; *ante,* 542; or that it is trust property wherein the bankrupt has no beneficial estate or interest; *ante,* 546; or that the bankrupt before his bankruptcy executed a voluntary settlement or conveyance of the property; *ante,* 543; not being a fraudulent preference; *ante,* 544; *Crisp* v. *Pratt,* Cro. Car. 549; T. Jones, 487; or that the bankrupt, before his bankruptcy, demised the property to the defendant for a term or tenancy which has not expired or been determined by notice to quit, demand of possession, or otherwise; *ante,* 552; or that the bankrupt's title ceased on his bankruptcy. *Ante,* 541.

It will be no defence to prove that the action has been brought without leave of the Court of Bankruptcy; *ante,* 538; or that the bankrupt *after* his bankruptcy executed an appointment in favour of the defendant, or of any other person. *Doe* d. *Coleman* v. *Britain,* 2 B. & A. 93. Unless, indeed, the transaction is protected by sect. 133 (*ante,* 545), or sect. 134. *Ante,* 546.

CHAPTER LII.

BY A BANKRUPT.

A BANKRUPT will not be compelled to give security for costs in an ejectment commenced and prosecuted by him *for his own benefit*. *Doe d. Colnaghi* v. *Bläck*, 5 Scott, 714. But where he sues for the benefit of some third person, who does not join in the action as a co-plaintiff, such security will be ordered. *Perkins* v. *Adcock*, 14 M. & W. 808 ; 3 Dowl. & L. 270 ; *Goatley* v. *Emmott*, 15 C. B. 291. The court will not, at the instance of the defendant in an ejectment, interfere against a plaintiff who uses the names of the assignees as co-plaintiffs without their permission, they having given up the property to the bankrupt, and the plaintiff claiming under him. *Doe d. Vine* v. *Figgins*, 3 Taunt. 440. If a bankrupt join with his assignees as a co-plaintiff in an ejectment, he will thereby render himself personally liable to the defendants for their costs. *In re Milnes and Robertson*, 15 C. B. 451 ; *Id.* 722.

A bankrupt may dispute his bankruptcy by an action of ejectment : but such action must be commenced within two calendar months after the advertisement of the bankruptcy in the London Gazette, provided the bankrupt was in the United Kingdom at the date of the adjudication. 17 & 18 Vict. c. 119, s. 24. If elsewhere in Europe, within three calendar months. 12 & 13 Vict. c. 106, s. 233. If in any other part of the world, within twelve calendar months. *Id.* If no action, suit or other proceeding to dispute or annul the petition for adjudication be commenced within the time so limited, or shall not be prosecuted with due diligence and with effect, the Gazette containing such advertisement will be *conclusive evidence* against the bankrupt, that he *became a bankrupt* before the date and filing of the petition for adjudication, and that such petition was filed on the day on which the same is stated in the Gazette to bear date. Sect. 233 ; *ante*, 547.

Trust Property.]—Real estate and terms for years vested in a bankrupt as trustee, executor, administrator, or the like, and in which he has *no beneficial estate or interest*, do not pass to his assignees in bankruptcy, but remain vested in him. *Ante*, 546 ; *Dangerfield* v. *Thomas*, 9 A. & E. 292 ; 1 P. & D. 287 ; *D'Arnau* v. *Chesneau*, 13 M. & W. 796, 809 ; *Houghton* v. *Kœnig*, 18 C. B. 235. And in respect thereof he may maintain ejectment, in like manner as if he had never become bankrupt.

Leaseholds.]—Terms for years, leases, and agreements for leases, belonging to a bankrupt in his own right, remain vested in him, notwithstanding his bankruptcy, *until the assignees elect to take them*. *Ante*, 539. Until then he may maintain ejectment for the demised property in like manner as if he had not become bankrupt. If his title be defeated *after service of the writ* and before trial, he will nevertheless be entitled to a verdict and judgment for his costs. *Ante,* 289.

The copyholds of a bankrupt appear to remain vested in him, until sold to a purchaser pursuant to 12 & 13 Vict. c. 106, ss. 209, 210. *Ante,* 542. They are expressly excepted by sect. 142, and therefore do not vest in his assignees; consequently the bankrupt may maintain ejectment for them before any such sale. If his title be defeated *after service of the writ* and before trial, he will nevertheless be entitled to a verdict and judgment for his costs. *Ante,* 289.

Other Property.]—An uncertificated bankrupt may acquire property, and contract for the benefit of his assignees, and may sue in respect of such property or contract, unless they interfere. *Herbert* v. *Sayer,* 5 Q. B. 965; 2 Dowl. & L. 49, 63; *Jackson* v. *Burnham,* 8 Exch. 173. A bankrupt may, of course, sue for property to which he first becomes entitled after the allowance of his certificate.

CHAPTER LIII.

BY ASSIGNEES OF AN INSOLVENT DEBTOR.

The Statutes generally.]—The acts in force relating to insolvent debtors are the 1 & 2 Vict. c. 110; 2 & 3 Vict. c. 39; 5 & 6 Vict. c. 116; 7 & 8 Vict. c. 70; 7 & 8 Vict. c. 96; 8 & 9 Vict. c. 127; 10 & 11 Vict. c. 102. These are collected in 2 Chit. Stat. 581 to 643 (2nd ed.); also in Shelford on Insolvency, which is the best treatise on the subject.

Vesting Order.]—Upon a petition being presented by an insolvent debtor in custody, pursuant to 1 & 2 Vict. c. 110, s. 35, or by one of his detaining creditors, sect. 36, a vesting order may be made, sect. 37, whereby *all the real and personal estate and effects* of such prisoner (except wearing apparel, &c. not exceeding 20*l.*), and all his future estate and effects acquired in any manner before his final discharge, is vested in the provisional assignee of the court, without any conveyance or assignment. The vesting order has precisely the same effect as the assignment from the insolvent to the provisional assignee, for which it was substituted. *Woodland* v. *Fuller*, 11 A. & E. 859; 3 P. & D. 570; *Drury* v. *Houndsfield*, 11 A. & E. 101; 4 P. & D. 386; *Squire* v. *Huetson*, 1 Q. B. 308; 4 P. & D. 633; *Smith* v. *Wetherell*, 5 Dowl. & L. 278; *Sayer* v. *Dufaur*, id. 313; 11 Q. B. 325; *Doe* d. *Davies* v. *Thomas*, 6 Exch. 854. It does not pass any property wherein the insolvent has only a legal estate, but no equitable or beneficial estate or interest. *Garry* v. *Sharratt*, 10 B. & C. 716. It is valid as to property in Middlesex, without being registered, except as against purchasers for value without notice. *Lee* v. *Green*, 25 Law J., N. S., Chanc. 269.

A vesting order may be avoided by a petition for adjudication of bankruptcy, presented within two calendar months after the petition under the Insolvent Debtors' Act, sects. 39, 40. *Walker* v. *Edmondson*,

1 Low. M. & P. 772. But all acts done by the assignees before such avoidance will be good and valid. Sect. 44. So also it may become void by the insolvent's petition being *dismissed*. Sect. 37. But where the insolvent is discharged, without adjudication, by the consent or default of his detaining creditors, and his petition is *not dismissed*, there must be a re-vesting order pursuant to sect. 92, before any of the property will re-vest in the insolvent. *Kernot* v. *Pittis* (in error), 2 E. & B. 406, 421; *Tudway* v. *Jones*, 24 Law J., N. S., Chanc. 507, Wood, V. C. And it seems that such order will not be made whilst any of the creditors remain unsatisfied. *S. C.*

Appointment of Assignees.]—Assignees of an insolvent debtor are usually appointed by the court at the hearing: and upon their acceptance of such appointment being signified to the court, all the property of the insolvent previously vested in the provisional assignee passes to them by virtue of their appointment, without any conveyance or assignment. 1 & 2 Vict. c. 110, s. 45; *York* v. *Brown*, 10 M. & W. 78; *Willis* v. *Elliott*, 4 Bing. 332; 1 Moo. & P. 19. But a certified office copy of the vesting order and appointment must be registered, enrolled or recorded, where necessary, in like manner as a conveyance or assignment. Sect. 46.

Under the 5 & 6 Vict. c. 116, it is not essentially necessary that a creditors' assignee be appointed. *Lewis* v. *Harris*, 11 Q. B. 724. "In many cases of insolvency no creditors' assignee is ever chosen." *Id.* 730, *per cur.*; and see *Doe* d. *Davies* v. *Thomas*, 6 Exch. 854. An order vesting the insolvent's estate in his creditors' assignees may be made either before or after he has been discharged from custody. *Kitching* v. *Croft*, 12 A. & E. 586; 4 P. & D. 839.

Actions by the Assignees.]—The assignees of an insolvent debtor may maintain ejectment *in their own names* for property legally vested in them as such assignees. 1 & 2 Vict. c. 110, s. 51; *Doe* d. *Davies* v. *Thomas*, 6 Exch. 854. They may be described in the writ of ejectment as "assignees of the estate and effects of C. D. an insolvent debtor;" but this is unnecessary. No consent of creditors, or leave of the court, is necessary to enable them to maintain or defend an action at law. Sect. 51. But it is otherwise with respect to suits in equity, arbitrations, and compositions. Sect. 51. Before the appointment of any creditors' assignee, the provisional assignee may sue in his own name, "if the court shall so order." Sect. 42; *Doe* d. *Davies* v. *Thomas*, 6 Exch. 854. But the want of such order will constitute no defence to an action at his suit. *Doe* d. *Clarke* v. *Spencer*, 3 Bing. N. C. 370; *Spooner* v. *Payne*, 2 De Gex & Sm. 439; *ante*, 538. Upon the appointment of a creditors' assignee, and his acceptance thereof, the provisional assignee ceases to have any estate or interest; therefore he should not be joined as a co-plaintiff with the creditors' assignee.

Upon the death or removal of an assignee, the action shall not abate, but the court in which the action is brought may allow a suggestion to be made and the action to proceed in the names of the new assignees. Sect. 53. New assignees may be appointed whenever necessary. Sect. 65; *Cole* v. *Coles*, 6 Hare, 517.

Leaseholds.]—Formerly all leases and agreements for leases belonging to the insolvent vested absolutely in the provisional assignee without any option on his part to reject them. *Crofts* v. *Pick*, 1 Bing. 354; 8 Moo. 384; *Doe d. Clarke* v. *Spencer*, 3 Bing. 203; *Doe* d. *Palmer* v. *Andrews*, 2 C. & P. 593; 4 Bing. 348; 12 Moore, 601. Now the assignees have the like option to accept or reject a lease, or an agreement for a lease, as assignees in bankruptcy. 1 & 2 Vict. c. 110, s. 50; *ante,* 539. And they are entitled to a reasonable time to decide whether they will accept the lease or not. *Lindsay* v. *Limbert,* 2 C. & P. 526, Best, C. J.; 12 Moore, 209, *S. C.* If they accept it, they will of course be liable to the rent and covenants; so will their executors until fresh assignees are appointed. *Abercrombie* v. *Hickman,* 8 A. & E. 683. But such liability may be got rid of by an assignment. *Ante,* 540.

Copyholds and Customary Property.]—By 1 & 2 Vict. c. 110, s. 47, "in case such prisoner shall be entitled to any copyhold or customary estate, a certified copy of such vesting order as aforesaid, and a like certified copy of the appointment of such assignee or assignees as aforesaid, shall be entered on the court rolls of the manor of which such copyhold or customary estate shall be holden; and thereupon it shall be lawful for such assignee or assignees to surrender or convey such copyhold or customary estate to any purchaser or purchasers of the same from such assignee or assignees, as the said court shall direct; and the rents and profits thereof shall be in the meantime received by such assignee or assignees for the benefit of the creditors of such prisoner, without prejudice nevertheless to the lord or lords of the manor of which any such copyhold or customary estate shall be holden." This clause is merely directory; and therefore a sale by the assignees may be valid, notwithstanding the above directions have not been strictly complied with. *Doe d. Phillips* v. *Evans,* 1 Cr. & Mee. 450; 3 Tyr. 339; *Wright* v. *Maunder,* 4 Beav. 512; *Cole* v. *Coles,* 6 Hare, 517. The copyholds and customary property of an insolvent debtor vest in the provisional assignee by virtue of the vesting order (sect. 37), and in the creditors' assignee upon his accepting his appointment, (sect. 45), and before any entry of such vesting order or appointment upon the court rolls. *Doe* d. *Smith* v. *Glenfield,* 1 Bing. N. C. 729; 1 Scott, 699. Consequently the assignees of an insolvent debtor may maintain ejectment for copyhold or customary property of the insolvent: whereas it seems that assignees in bankruptcy cannot do so. *Ante,* 542.

Fraudulent Preferences.]—By 1 & 2 Vict. c. 110, s. 59, it is enacted, "that if any such prisoner shall, *before or after his imprisonment,* being in insolvent circumstances, *voluntarily* convey, assign, transfer, charge, deliver, or make over, any estate real or personal, security for money, bond, bill, note, money, property, goods or effects whatsoever, *to any creditor* or creditors, or to any person or persons in trust for, or to or for the use, benefit or advantage of any creditor or creditors, every such conveyance, assignment, transfer, charge, delivery, and making over, shall be deemed and is hereby declared to be fraudulent and void as against the provisional or other assignee or assignees of such prisoner appointed under this act: provided always, that no such conveyance, assignment, transfer, charge, delivery, or making over, shall be so deemed fraudulent and void, unless made *within three months* before the commencement of such imprisonment, *or* with the view or intention by the party so conveying, assigning, transferring, charging, delivering, or making over, of petitioning the said court for his discharge from custody under this act."

"This clause is taken without any substantial change from the 32nd section of the 7 Geo. 4, c. 57; and the cases decided on that section are equally applicable to the 1 & 2 Vict. c. 110, s. 59." *Per cur.* in *Thompson* v. *Jackson*, 3 Man. & Gr. 626.

The above section applies not only to assignments made voluntarily within three months before the commencement of the imprisonment, or during the continuance of such imprisonment, but extends to assignments made at any time, even a year previous to the imprisonment, if made *with the view or intention* of petitioning the court for the insolvent's discharge. *Becke* v. *Smith*, 2 M. & W. 191. If he does it, contemplating bankruptcy or insolvency, then, if insolvency intervenes, the insolvent's assignees are entitled to sue; if bankruptcy, the assignees in bankruptcy. *Ogden* v. *Stone*, 11 M. & W. 494; *Id.* 496, *per* Parke, B. If, amongst other results, the party contemplates insolvency, and makes the payment to defeat an equal distribution of his effects amongst his creditors, that is sufficient. *Id.* 496, *per* Alderson, B.; and see *Aldred* v. *Constable*, 4 Q. B. 674. The 7 & 8 Vict. c. 96, s. 19, for the "protection" of insolvent debtors, is differently worded in this respect. Under that act a voluntary conveyance made more than three months before the filing of the petition is valid, unless proof be given that *at the time* the conveyance or assignment, &c., he had the definite view or intention of petitioning the court for protection. *Thoyts* v. *Hobbs*, 9 Exch. 810.

An assignment made after the commencement of the imprisonment stands on the same footing as an assignment made within three months before the commencement of the imprisonment. *Binns* v. *Towsey*, 7 A. & E. 869; 3 N. & P. 88; *per cur.* in *Becke* v. *Smith*, 2 M. & W. 198. If it be made voluntarily, and without any pressure or new consideration, even for the benefit of all the creditors, it will be deemed fraudulent and void: *Binns* v. *Towsey, supra*; *Stuckey* v. *Drewe*, 2 Myl. & K. 190: otherwise if made by reason of any pressure or application on the part of a creditor or creditors, or for any new consideration. *Davies* v. *Acocks*, 2 Cr. M. & R. 461; 5 Tyr. 963; *Knight* v. *Ferguson*, 5 M. & W. 389; *Arnell* v. *Bean*, 6 Moo. & P. 151; 8 Bing. 91.

An assignment by an insolvent *within three months* before his imprisonment, in trust for creditors executing the deed, is void as against his assignees (under 1 & 2 Vict. c. 110, s. 57), if made without a new consideration and without pressure. *Thompson* v. *Jackson*, 3 Man. & Gr. 621; 4 Scott, N. R. 234. It makes no difference in this respect that the assignment is made for the benefit of *all* the creditors. *Jackson* v. *Thompson*, 2 Q. B. 887; 2 Gale & D. 598; *Binns* v. *Towsey*, 7 A. & E. 869; 3 N. & P. 88.

It is not necessary, in order to support a conveyance or transfer made by an insolvent trader to a creditor, to show that it was made in consequence of *pressure* on the part of the creditor: in order to invalidate it, it must appear to have *originated in the voluntary act* of the trader, and not in a *bond fide* application of the creditor. *Doe* d. *Roydell* v. *Gillett*, 2 Cr. M. & R. 579. "It is not necessary to show pressure: you must show that the conveyance originated in the voluntary act of the insolvent, whereas here it was *made in consequence of the creditor's asking for it.* That is the meaning of the term voluntary. Here the transfer originated in a demand for it. I should infer that it was a very clear case for the defendants." *Id.* 581, *per* Parke, B.; *Mogg* v. *Baker*, 4 M. & W. 348. Any application is sufficient, if the jury *find as a fact* that the assignment or payment, &c., was *made in consequence of such application,* and not for the mere purpose of defeating a creditor, or to defeat the acts relating to bankrupts or insolvent debtors. *Van Casteel* v. *Booker,* 2 Exch. 691, 698; *Cook* v. *Pritchard,* 5 Man. & Gr. 329; *Cook* v. *Rogers,* 7 Bing. 438; 5 Moo. & P. 353; *Mogg* v. *Baker,* 4 M. & W. 348. In *Thompson* v. *Jackson,* 3 Man. & Gr. 621 (where pressure is mentioned in the marginal note), the court said, "The only question is whether he made it voluntarily, that is, whether he made it *of his own proper motion, or on the suggestion of a creditor;*" and see *Mogg* v. *Baker,* 4 M. & W. 348; *Id.* 627. "We think the word 'voluntarily' is used in the statute to denote either an assignment made without such valuable consideration as is sufficient to induce a party acting really and *bonâ fide* under the influence of such consideration, or an assignment made in favour of a particular creditor *spontaneously* and without any pressure on his part to obtain it. If in any case a doubt arises as to the real value of the consideration, or as to the real motive of the debtor in making the assignment, such question must be decided by the jury, who will determine whether it is a *bonâ fide* transaction or a mere collusion to evade the statute." *Per cur.* in *Arnell* v. *Bean,* 8 Bing. 91; 6 Moo. & P. 151; *Wainwright* v. *Miles,* 3 Moo. & Sc. 211. It is for the assignees of the insolvent who seek to avoid the deed to make out that it was the voluntary act of the insolvent, and not the result of any pressure or application by the creditor. *Doe* d. *Lamb* v. *Gillett,* Tyr. & Gr. 114; 2 Cr. M. & R. 579.

An assignment made by an insolvent for the benefit of all his creditors, under the influence of pressure or for a new consideration, is valid as against his assignees under the act. *Davies* v. *Acocks,* 2 Cr. M. & R. 461; 5 Tyr. 963; *Knight* v. *Ferguson,* 5 M. & W. 389. Whether a release by the creditors contained in the deed of assignment for their benefit constitutes a sufficient new consideration, is not clear; but it would rather seem to be sufficient. *Id.* 392, 397, Parke, B.

Property fraudulently disposed of by the Insolvent with intent to defeat or delay his Creditors.]—The same law holds as in cases of bankruptcy. *Ante,* 544; *Doe* d. *Grimsby* v. *Ball,* 11 M. & W. 531; *Norcutt* v. *Dodd,* 1 Cr. & Phil. 10.

Evidence for the Plaintiffs.]—In ejectment by the assignees of an insolvent debtor, the plaintiffs must prove:—

1. The vesting order. *York* v. *Brown,* 10 M. & W. 78; 2 Dowl. N. S. 283. But they need not prove the petition for such order. *Delafield* v. *Freeman,* 6 Bing. 294; 3 Moo. & P. 704; *Doe* d. *Hemming* v. *Willetts,* 7 C. B. 709; *Houndsfield* v. *Drury,* 11 A. & E. 98. The vesting order itself, or a copy thereof on paper or parchment, *purporting to be signed* by the officer in whose custody the same shall be, or his deputy, certifying the same to be a true copy, *and purporting to be sealed* with the seal of the court, is sufficient "without any other proof whatever given of the same." 1 & 2 Vict. c. 110, s. 105;

Houndsfield v. *Drury*, 11 A. & E. 98. Or the vesting order may be proved by a copy made *on parchment*, and "purporting to have the certificate of the provisional assignee of the said court, or his deputy for that purpose, indorsed thereon, and to be sealed with the seal of the said court." Sect. 46; *Jackson* v. *Thompson*, 2 Q. B. 889; 2 Gale & D. 598. The seal of the court need not be proved. *Doe* d. *Duncan* v. *Edwards*, 9 A. & E. 554; 1 P. & D. 408; nor the signature of the officer or his deputy; nor the authority of the latter. *Jackson* v. *Thompson*, *supra*; *Houndsfield* v. *Drury*, 11 A. & E. 98.

An office copy of the insolvent's petition and schedule, and of the copy of causes annexed thereto (all duly certified and sealed), are not sufficient to prove that the insolvent was in *actual custody within the walls* of a prison at the time of his petition. *Hills* v. *Mitsom*, 8 Exch. 751. Certified copies of the schedule, &c. may be given in evidence under this act, not only by the insolvent and his assignees and creditors, but also by other persons. *Price* v. *Assheton*, 1 You. & Col. 441.

2. The appointment of the plaintiffs as assignees and their acceptance of such appointment. 1 & 2 Vict. c. 110, s. 45. This may be proved by a copy *on parchment*, signed and sealed pursuant to sect. 46. *Supra*. The assignee of an insolvent debtor, on his acceptance of the appointment, has vested in him all the estate of the insolvent *from the date of the vesting order*. *Yorke* v. *Brown*, 10 M. & W. 78; 2 Dowl. N. S. 283. The order appointing the plaintiffs to be assignees is only evidence of their appointment, but not of the time from which their title accrues; to prove *that*, the vesting order, or an office copy thereof signed and sealed, should be produced; *S. C.*; but an office copy (signed and sealed) of the order of adjudication, which recites the date of the vesting order, is sufficient evidence of such date. *S. C.* The property may be claimed from any day subsequent to the vesting order, *ex. gr.* during the time when there was only a provisional assignee; the appointment of the creditors' assignee relates back to the date of the vesting order. *S. C.*

3. If the action be one which the insolvent himself might have maintained if no vesting order had been made, the assignees must prove the insolvent's title in like manner as he would have done; also their own derivative title as assignees. *Ante*, 560. Proof that the defendant held as tenant of the insolvent, or obtained possession of the property from him, will show a title by estoppel; *ante*, 209, 213; but in such case it must be shown that the defendant's title has expired, or been determined by notice to quit, demand of possession, surrender, forfeiture, or otherwise, as in an action by a landlord against his tenant. *Ante*, Chap. XXXVII. to XLI.; *Doe* d. *Duncan* v. *Edwards*, 9 A. & E. 554; 1 P. & D. 408; *Doe* d. *Davies* v. *Thomas*, 6 Exch. 854. Mesne profits may sometimes be recovered, upon proper evidence in that behalf. *Ante*, 292.

If the action be brought to defeat a fraudulent preference, the defendant must have due notice to produce the deed in question; *ante*, 155; and the plaintiffs must be prepared with proof of such notice, and secondary evidence of the contents of the deed. *Ante*, 169. Also with such further evidence as may be necessary to prove that the deed amounted to a fraudulent preference; *ante*, 558; also their own derivative title as assignees.

Evidence and Points for the Defendant.]—The defendant may

contend that the plaintiffs' evidence is insufficient on some material point. *Ante*, 560. He may also produce contradictory evidence: he may prove that the insolvent debtor was an uncertificated bankrupt before and at the time when the vesting order was made; 1 & 2 Vict. c. 110, s. 40; *ante*, 556; or that within two calendar months next after the petition for such order, a petition for adjudication of bankruptcy was presented, and the insolvent duly adjudged a bankrupt; sect. 39; *ante*, 556; or that the insolvent's petition to the Court for Relief of Insolvent Debtors has been *dismissed*. Sect. 37; *ante*, 557. To prove the bankruptcy of the insolvent for the above purpose all the necessary requisites must be proved, viz., the petitioning creditor's debt, the trading, the act of bankruptcy, the petition for adjudication, the adjudication, the appointment of assignees, &c. *Ante*, 551. The defendant may prove a lease or tenancy in himself, or in any third person, created by the insolvent before the vesting order, and which has not since expired or been determined by notice to quit, or otherwise; *Doe* d. *Duncan* v. *Edwards*, 9 A. & E. 554; 1 P. & D. 408; *Doe* d. *Davies* v. *Thomas*, 6 Exch. 854; or that the insolvent was a mere trustee, executor or administrator, and had *no beneficial estate* or interest in the property sought to be recovered, and, consequently, that it did not pass to his assignees but remains vested in him. *Ante*, 556.

CHAPTER LIV.

BY AN INSOLVENT DEBTOR.

AN insolvent debtor may maintain ejectment for land vested in him for an estate in possession as trustee, executor, administrator, or the like, and in which he has no beneficial estate or interest. He stands on the same footing in this respect as a bankrupt. *Ante*, 546, 556.

When an insolvent debtor sues for the benefit of some third person who does not join in the action as a co-plaintiff, security for costs will be ordered: *Goatley* v. *Emmott*, 15 C. B. 291; but not where the insolvent sues for his own benefit. *Doe* d. *Colnaghi* v. *Blick*, 5 Scott, 714.

Formerly leases for years and agreements for leases vested in the provisional assignee, without any option on his part to take or reject them; *ante*, 557; and, therefore, a lessee whose property had been assigned to the provisional assignee could not afterwards eject his sub-tenant upon the expiration or determination of his tenancy, notwithstanding the provisional assignee had never entered, or otherwise consented to take the term, and no permanent assignee had been appointed. *Doe* d. *Palmer* v. *Andrews*, 2 C. & P. 593; 4 Bing. 348; 12 Moore, 601. But it would seem now to be otherwise, because, under the 1 & 2 Vict. c. 110, s. 50, the assignees of an insolvent debtor have the like option to accept or reject a lease or an agreement for a lease as assignees in bankruptcy. *Ante*, 558. Consequently, until they assent to take the term it will remain vested in the insolvent, and he may maintain ejectment where he might have done so if no vesting order had ever been made. If his title be defeated *after service of the writ*, and before trial, he will, nevertheless, be entitled to a verdict and judgment for his costs. *Ante*, 289.

An insolvent debtor has not such an interest in property assigned to or vested in his assignees, under the insolvent debtors acts, as will entitle him to enter into any litigation respecting it. *Rochfort* v. *Battersby*, 2 H. L. Cas. 388; but see *Marks* v. *Hamilton*, 7 Exch. 323. As to the effect of a vesting order, and when a revesting order is necessary, see *ante*, 556. An insolvent debtor may sue *in equity* without a revesting order where there is an admitted surplus of his estate. *Wearing* v. *Ellis*, 25 Law J., N. S., Chanc. 248.

An insolvent debtor may sue in respect of a cause of action which first accrued after the vesting order, and before his final discharge, unless his assignees interfere. *Jackson* v. *Burnham*, 8 Exch. 173; and see *Williams* v. *Chambers*, 10 Q. B. 337. He may, of course, sue for property which first vested in him after his final discharge under the act.

CHAPTER LV.

BY TENANT BY ELEGIT.

THE writ of elegit was given by the Statute of Westminster 2 (13 Edw. 1, c. 18), and the operation of it was extended by 1 & 2 Vict. c. 110, s. 11, which authorizes the sheriff, &c. " to make and deliver execution unto the party in that behalf suing of *all* such lands, tenements, rectories, tithes, rents and hereditaments, *including lands and hereditaments of copyhold and customary tenure,* as the person against whom execution is so sued, or any person in trust for him, shall have been seised or possessed of at the time of entering up the said judgment, or at any time afterwards, or over which such person shall at the time of entering up such judgment, or at any time afterwards, have any disposing power which he might, without the assent of any other person, exercise for his own benefit." *See Form of the Writ, Appendix, No.* 287. A writ of elegit cannot be sued out for part only of the sum recovered by a judgment, unless it shows on the face of it that the residue of the judgment has been satisfied or otherwise disposed of. *Sherwood* v. *Clark,* 15 M. & W. 764.

Before the 1 & 2 Vict. c. 110, only a moiety of the defendant's lands could be taken under an elegit; *Pullen* v. *Birkbeck,* 1 Lord Raym. 718; 1 Salk. 563; Carth. 453, *S. C.;* and only a moiety of the remaining moiety under a second elegit; and no copyholds could be taken. *Morris* v. *Jones,* 2 B. & C. 243; 3 D. & R. 263, 603.

A mortgagee is not a trustee for the mortgagor (subject to the mortgage) within the meaning of the above enactment. *The Mayor, Aldermen and Burgesses of Poole* v. *Whitt,* 15 M. & W. 571. If the property be legally vested in a trustee for the benefit of the judgment debtor, *and of any other person or persons,* it cannot be taken under an elegit. *Doe* d. *Hull* v. *Greenhill,* 4 B. & A. 684; *Harris* v. *Pugh,* 4 Bing. 335. If a trustee has conveyed away the lands before execution sued, though he was seised in trust for the defendant alone at the time of the judgment, the lands cannot be taken in execution. *Hunt* v. *Coles,* 1 Com. R. 226. The property of a municipal corporation acquired after the 5 & 6 Will. 4, c. 76, cannot be taken in execution under an elegit for a debt contracted before the act. *Arnold* v. *Ridge,* 13 C. B. 745; *Doe* d. *Parr* v. *Roe,* 1 Q. B. 700. "A man can never have a thing extended on an execution, unless he may grant or assign it." *Per* Shelley, J., Dyer, 7 b. Only impropriate rectories and tithes in lay hands can be taken in execution or charged in equity under this act. *Hawkins* v. *Gathercole,* 24 Law J., N. S., Chanc. 332.

The sheriff summons a jury to assist him in executing a writ of elegit; 2 Inst. 396; and they, after hearing the evidence produced before them, find of what lands, &c. the defendant, or any person in trust for him, was seised or possessed at the time the judgment was entered up, or at any time afterwards; and for what estate or interest, and the annual value. And the sheriff thereupon returns that he has on the day of taking the inquisition caused to be delivered to the plaintiff the said lands, &c., to hold according to the nature and tenure thereof to him and his assigns, according to the form of the statutes in such case made and provided, until the [debt and] damages in the writ mentioned, together with interest upon the same as therein mentioned, shall have been levied." *See Form of Inquisition and Return, Appendix, No.* 288.

Formerly it was necessary to set out with certainty the lands, &c. by metes and bounds; *Pullen* v. *Burbeak,* Carthew, 453, Holt, C. J.; *Fenny* d. *Masters* v. *Durrant,* 1 B. & A. 40; and also the county and parish or ville in which they lay. Dyer, 208. But since the 1 & 2 Vict. c. 110, s. 11, which authorizes all the lands, &c., instead of a moiety of them, to be taken in execution under an elegit, such certainty is not required; and any description of them, which would be sufficient for a deed of conveyance, will do. *Roberts* v. *Parry,* 13 M. & W. 356; 2 Dowl. & L. 430; *Sherwood* v. *Clark,* 15 M. & W. 764. Their annual value, and the debtor's estate or interest in them, must be stated as above mentioned. Moore, 8; Hutton, 16; Brownlow, 38. If the inquisition upon an elegit find a lease of one date when it is in fact of a different date, and the sheriff sell it according to their appraisement, and not generally, the sale is void. *Palmer* v. *Humphrey,* Cro. Eliz. 584.

The sheriff is only entitled to take twelve pence for every twenty shillings of the yearly value of the land extended for executing the writ. 3 Geo. 1, c. 15, s. 16; *Nash* v. *Allen,* 4 Q. B. 784; 1 Dav. & M. 16.

The writ and inquisition must be returned and filed; 2 Arch. N. P. 425; Dyer, 100 (in margin); 2 Inst. 396; *Garraway* v. *Harrington,* Cro. Jac. 569; *Stonehouse* v. *Ewen,* 2 Strange, 874; Chit. Forms, 309, 327 (7th ed.); and an entry thereof made on the judgment roll. *See the Form, Appendix, No.* 289.

The sheriff does not usually deliver actual possession under or by virtue of a writ of elegit. *Lowthal* v. *Tomkins,* 2 Eq. Ca. Abr. 380, recognized by Lord Kenyon, C. J., in *Taylor* v. *Cole,* 3 T. R. 295. But it seems that he may lawfully do so if the debtor himself be in occupation of the premises. *Per* Gibbs, C. J., in *Rogers* v. *Pitcher,* 6 Taunt. 206; *Chatfield* v. *Parker,* 8 B. & C. 543. In other cases he certainly cannot do so. *Per* Lord Kenyon, C. J., in *Taylor* v. *Cole,* 3 T. R. 295. The usual course is for the sheriff to make a return to the effect above mentioned, which return *when filed* operates in like manner as a conveyance for value by the debtor, with a constructive legal delivery of the lands, &c. mentioned in the inquisition. *Lowthal* v. *Tomkins,* 2 Eq. Ca. Abr. 380; *Taylor* v. *Cole,* 3 T. R. 295, Lord Kenyon, C. J. The party who sued out the writ then becomes "tenant by elegit," and stands in much the same position as if the person against whom the elegit issued had on the day when the judgment was entered up, or at any time afterwards when he first became seised or possessed of the lands, &c. executed a grant or assignment thereof for the amount of the judgment debt and interest to the tenant by elegit for a term or period equal to that mentioned in the inquisition. Whatever the debtor could not lawfully grant or assign cannot be extended under an elegit. Dyer, 76, Shelley, J. A municipal corporation cannot lawfully part with their real property acquired by them after the passing of the 5 & 6 Will. 4, c. 76, in satisfaction of a debt contracted by the old corporation before the passing of that act. Therefore such property cannot be extended under an elegit. *Arnold* v. *Ridge*, 13 C. B. 745; *Doe* d. *Purr* v. *Roe*, 1 Q. B. 700. Only impropriate rectories and tithes in lay hands can be taken in execution, or charged in equity under the 1 & 2 Vict. c. 110, s. 11. *Hawkins* v. *Gathercole*, 24 Law J., N. S., Chanc. 332.

A tenant by elegit does not before entry become actually possessed, so as to maintain trespass; nor is he before entry in possession by himself or his tenant, so as to be permitted to defend an ejectment by lessor against lessee for a forfeiture. *Croft* v. *Lumley*, 4 E. & B. 274, 614; *Thompson* v. *Tomkinson*, 11 Exch. 442.

If the debtor himself be in possession of the lands, &c., an ejectment may be maintained against him. 2 Arch. N. P. 424; *Doe* d. *Parr* v. *Roe*, 1 Q. B. 700; *Doe* d. *Roberts* v. *Parry*, 13 M. & W. 356; 2 Dowl. & L. 430. But the writ of inquisition must be previously filed. 2 Arch. N. P. 425; Dyer, 100 (in margin); 2 Inst. 396; *Stonehurst* v. *Ewen*, 2 Stra. 874. So if the lands, &c. be in the possession of any tenant of the debtor, whose tenancy commenced after the judgment was entered up. *Doe* d. *Putland* v. *Hilder*, 2 B. & A. 782; *Doe* d. *Evans* v. *Owen*, 2 Cr. & Jer. 71; 2 Tyr. 149. But if the tenancy commenced before the date of the judgment, the writ and inquisition will only operate as an assignment of the reversion; and no ejectment can be maintained against the tenant in possession until the expiration or determination of the tenancy. *Doe* d. *Da Costa* v. *Wharton*, 8 T. R. 2; Ad. Eject. 78. If, however, the tenant suffer judgment by default, the execution debtor will not be permitted to defend as landlord, and to avail himself of the tenancy to defeat the ejectment. *Doe* d. *Cheese* v. *Creed*, 2 Moo. & P. 648; 5 Bing. 327. The tenant by elegit may, without any attornment, distrain or sue for rent which becomes due after the filing of the writ and inquisition; *Lloyd* v. *Davies*, 2 Exch. 103; *Ramsbottom* v. *Buckhurst*, 2 M. & S. 565; provided the writ and inquisition be valid, but not otherwise. *Arnold* v. *Ridge*, 13 C. B. 745. Where rent became due after the delivery of a writ of elegit to the sheriff, and before the inquisition thereon: held, that the execution creditor was not entitled to the rent. *Sharp* v. *Key*, 8 M. & W. 379; 9 Dowl. 770. He may determine a previous tenancy from year to year by a regular notice to quit, after which he may maintain ejectment. 2 Arch. N. P. 424. If a tenant by elegit be *lawfully* evicted from the property, without any fraud or collusion on his part, before his debt, damages and costs have been fully satisfied, he may have a writ of *scire facias* pursuant to 32 Hen. 2, c. 5, and upon obtaining judgment thereon may sue out another elegit for the residue.

Where lands had been taken possession of under an elegit, the court ordered it to be referred to the master to take an account of the rents and profits received; and if upon inquiry it appeared that the debt had been satisfied, possession to be restored to the defendant. *Price* v. *Varney*, 3 B. & C. 733; 5 D. & R. 612.

A judgment creditor, in possession under an elegit of lands belonging to the debtor, instituted a suit in equity for the sale of the property: held, that such creditor was bound to account *as mortgagee in possession*. *Bull* v. *Faulkner*, 1 De Gex & S. 685; 17 Law J., N. S., Chanc. 23.

Notwithstanding the 1 & 2 Vict. c. 110, s. 13 (which gives to a judgment the effect of an equitable charge upon the land of the debtor), an equitable mortgagee retains his right *in equity* to enforce his security against the title of a creditor under a subsequent judgment, although the latter may have acquired the legal seizure and possession of the land under an elegit, without notice of the mortgage. *Whitworth* v. *Gaugain*, 1 Phil. C. C. 728; 15 Law J., N. S., Chanc. 433.

Evidence for Plaintiff.]—A tenant by elegit must give in evidence an office copy of the judgment roll, containing an entry of the award of the elegit and of the inquisition and sheriff's return. *Ramsbottom* v. *Buckhurst*, 2 M. & S. 565; 2 Arch. N. P. 425; Gilb. Ev. 9. Such copy must be admitted in the cause (*ante*, 150), or proved to have been examined with the roll. 2 Phil. Ev. 199 (10th ed.); Ros. Ev. 81 (7th ed.); *ante*, 252. Proof that the officer of the court read the roll whilst the witness examined the copy is sufficient. *Rolf* v. *Dart*, 2 Taunt. 52; *Reid* v. *Margison*, 1 Camp. 469. If the copy contain abbreviations not in the original, it will be rejected. *Reg.* v. *Christian*, Car. & M. 388. Formerly examined office copies of the elegit and inquisition were deemed necessary. Gilb. Ev. 9. But it was ruled otherwise in *Ramsbottom* v. *Buckhurst, supra.*

If the ejectment be brought against the judgment debtor and *other defendants*, it will be sufficient (after the formal proofs) to show that the judgment debtor was entitled to the property under a lease for lives at the time the judgment was obtained, or at any time afterwards, and thereupon the onus of proof will be thrown upon the other defendants to show their title. *Doe* d. *Evans* v. *Owen*, 2 Cr. & Jer. 71; 2 Tyr. 149.

If the defendant in the ejectment be not the debtor named in the elegit, it must be proved that he became tenant to the debtor, or obtained possession from him *after* the day when the judgment was entered up; *Doe* d. *Putland* v. *Hilder*, 2 B. & A. 782; or that the defendant's tenancy has since expired, or been determined by a regular notice to quit. *Doe* d. *Da Costa* v. *Wharton*, 8 T. R. 2; 2 Arch. N. P. 424; Ad. Eject. 78. But it is not necessary to prove the debtor's title, because that is already found by the inquisition, which is *primâ facie* evidence against any person claiming through or under him. 2 Arch. N. P. 425.

Evidence and Points for Defendant.]—The defendant may contend that the evidence of the claimant is insufficient in some material point; *supra;* and he may produce contradictory evidence. He may show that the debtor had no legal right to grant or assign the property, and consequently that the elegit was inoperative. Dyer, 7 b, *per* Shelley, J.; *Arnold* v. *Ridge*, 13 C. B. 745, 760; *Doe* d. *Parr* v. *Roe*, 1 Q. B. 700. If the property be vested in a trustee, the defendant may show that the trust was for the benefit of some other person or persons besides the judgment debtor, and not for him only. *Doe* d. *Hull* v. *Greenhill*, 4 B. & A. 684; *Harris* v. *Pugh*, 4 Bing. 335. The defendant may show that before the date of the judgment the debtor became bankrupt, and that the property vested in his assignees; but the validity of the proceedings may be disputed. *Doe* d. *Mawson* v. *Lister*, 4 Taunt. 741. He may show that the debtor, before the date of the judgment, conveyed the property to him the defendant, or to any third person by way of sale or mortgage; but the validity of such conveyance may be disputed. *Rogers* v. *Pitcher*, 6 Taunt. 202, 210, note; *The Mayor, &c. of Poole* v. *Whitt*, 15 M. & W. 571; *Westbrook* v. *Blythe*, 3 E. & B. 737; *Chatfield* v. *Parker*, 8 B. & C. 543. He may show that before the date of the judgment the debtor demised the property to the defendant, or to some third person, for a term which has not expired, or been duly determined by notice to quit, surrender or otherwise. *Doe* d. *Da Costa* v. *Wharton*, 8 T. R. 2; Ad. Eject. 78; *Doe* d. *Evans* v. *Owen*, 2 Cr. & Jer. 71; 2 Tyr. 149; *Doe* d. *Chatfield* v. *Parker*, 8 B. & C. 543; 2 Man. & R. 540. But if the tenant in possession suffer judgment by default, the judgment debtor, defending as his landlord, will not be allowed to raise such a defence. *Doe* d. *Cheese* v. *Creed*, 5 Bing. 327; 2 Moo. & Pay. 658. He may show that after the date of the judgment the debtor *appointed* the property to him under and by virtue of a power created before the date of the judgment. *Doe* d. *Wigan* v. *Jones*, 10 B. & C. 459; 5 D. & R. 563. He may object to the validity of the inquisition, on the ground that it does not show with sufficient certainty the particular lands, &c., or where they are situate (*ante*, 565), or their annual value, or the debtor's estate or interest therein. Moore, 8; Hutton, 16; Brownlow, 38. But he cannot object that the judgment against the debtor was irregularly obtained, or that it is erroneous, or that it was entered up by virtue of a warrant of attorney void for usury; *Hughes* v. *Lumley*, 4 E. & B. 274; or that it was not revived by *scire facias* or otherwise before the elegit was sued out. *Habberton* v. *Waterfield*, 4 Camp. 58. He may show that the whole judgment debt has been fully paid and satisfied by the judgment debtor. *Hughes* v. *Lumley*, 4 E. & B. 274; and see *Price* v. *Varney*, 3 B. & C. 733; 5 D. & R. 612.

CHAPTER LVI.

BY PURCHASER UNDER A FIERI FACIAS.

Evidence for Plaintiff.]—In ejectment by the purchaser under a *fieri facias* against the judgment debtor, the plaintiff must prove :—

1. The judgment, provided the claimant be the plaintiff in that action ; *Doe* d. *Bland* v. *Smith*, 2 Stark. R. 199 ; Holt, N. P. C. 589 ; but not otherwise. *Doe* d. *Batten* v. *Murless*, 6 M. & S. 110. In the latter case, the writ itself is sufficient evidence of the judgment as against the defendant, who might have applied to have it set aside or reversed if irregular or erroneous. *S. C.*

2. An office copy of the writ of *fieri facias*. This must either be admitted in the cause (*ante*, 150), or proved to have been examined with the original writ filed at the proper office. *Ante*, 253.

3. The assignment or bill of sale from the sheriff. Until such assignment be actually executed, the property remains in the debtor. *Doe* d. *Hughes* v. *Jones*, 9 M. & W. 372 ; 1 Dowl. N. S. 352 ; *Playfair* v. *Musgrove*, 14 M. & W. 239 ; 3 Dowl. & L. 72. But a sale of goods under a *fi. fa.* may be complete and effectual, without any deed of assignment or bill of sale. *Hernaman* v. *Bowker*, 11 Exch. 760 ; 25 Law J., N. S., Exch. 69. If the sheriff sell before the writ is returnable, he may execute the assignment after the return day. *Doe* d. *Stevens* v. *Donstan*, 1 B. & A. 230. Proof that the assignment was executed in the name of the sheriff, and sealed with his seal of office, by A. B., *acting as undersheriff*, is sufficient, without showing A. B.'s authority. It will be presumed that he had sufficient authority to do all things necessary to complete the execution. *Doe* d. *James* v. *Brawn*, 5 B. & A. 243, cited 8 Q. B. 1042, *per* Patteson, J. ; Ad. Eject. 256. The sale will be deemed valid and effectual to pass the property to the vendee, notwithstanding the *fieri facias* is afterwards set aside for irregularity. Dyer, 363, pl. 24 ; *Hoe's case*, 5 Co. R. 90 b ; *Manning's case*, 5 Co. R. 96 b, 143 ; Gilb. on Executions, 20 ; *Doe* d. *Emmett* v. *Thorn*, 1 M. & S. 425.

4. It must be shown that the execution debtor was possessed for a *term of years*, or as tenant from year to year, either as lessee or assignee. *Doe* d. *Batten* v. *Murless*, 6 M. & S. 110 ; *Doe* d. *Westmoreland* v. *Smith*, 1 Man. & Ry. 137. That he was *in possession* is not sufficient, because that merely shows a *primâ facie* seisin in fee, which cannot be taken in execution under a *fi. fa.* *Doe* d. *Batten* v. *Murless, supra.* So an equitable reversionary interest in a term cannot be seized and sold under a *fi. fa.* *Scott* v. *Scholey*, 8 East, 467 ; *Metcalfe* v. *Scholey*, 2 B. & P. New R. 461 ; *Burden* v. *Kennedy*, 3 Atk. 739 ; *Martindale* v. *Booth*, 3 B. & Adol. 498 ; and see *The Mayor, &c. of Poole* v. *Whitt*, 15 M. & W. 571. But a term of years may be taken and sold under a *fi. fa.* against the lessee or assignee, notwith-

standing he has underlet the property. It would, however, be improper for the sheriff to enter and turn the tenant out of possession. *R.* v. *Deane,* 2 Show. 85 ; Bac. Abr. Execution (C.) ; *Taylor* v. *Cole,* 3 T. R. 295 ; *Playfair* v. *Musgrove,* 14 M. & W. 239 ; 3 Dowl. & L. 72. If the sheriff, upon a *fieri facias,* take upon himself to recite the term which the defendant has, and misrecites it, and sells the same term, the sale is void ; but if he sells all the interest that the defendant has in the land, it is enough, notwithstanding the misrecital. *Palmer's case,* 4 Co. R. 74 a ; Moore, 542 ; Cro. Eliz. 601 ; *S. C.* The assignment of the sheriff will operate in like manner as an assignment of the reversion by the judgment debtor : and the purchaser may distrain for the subsequent rent when due without any attornment by the undertenant ; *Lloyd* v. *Davies,* 2 Exch. 103 ; but he cannot maintain ejectment against the undertenant, without showing that his tenancy has since expired, or been duly determined by notice to quit or otherwise. *Doe* d. *Da Costa* v. *Wharton,* 8 T. R. 2.

Evidence and Points for Defendant.]—The defendant may contend that the evidence for the claimant is insufficient on some material point: *ante,* 569 : and he may produce contradictory evidence. If the defendant be the judgment debtor, he may show that he held the property as tenant in fee, or for life, or for some other estate which could not legally be taken in execution under a *fi. fa.* against him. *Doe* d. *Batten* v. *Murless,* 6 M. & S. 110 ; *ante,* 569. If the defendant be an undertenant of the judgment debtor, he may show that his tenancy is still in force. *Supra.* Generally speaking, no objection can be taken to the regularity of the judgment, or of the writ, because the judgment debtor is the only person who may raise such an objection, and he must do so by an application to the court to set aside the judgment or writ for irregularity, or bring a writ of error. *Ante,* 569. But the execution of the writ, or the assignment from the sheriff, may be shown to be void. *Palmer's case, supra.*

CHAPTER LVII.

BY OWNER OF A RENT CHARGE.

THE grantee or devisee of a rent charge, with a *power of entry* and perception of profits when the rent charge is in arrear beyond a certain period, may after the lapse of such period enter into and hold possession of the land until the arrears are satisfied: or he may maintain ejectment. *Jemott* v. *Cowley*, 1 Saund. 112 c; 1 Lev. 170; 1 Sid. 223, 261, 334; Sir T. Ray. 135, 158, *S. C.; Havergill* v. *Hare*, Cro. Jac. 510. No previous demand of the arrears is necessary, *unless expressly required* by the deed or will. *Doe* d. *Biass* v. *Horsley*, 1 A. & E. 766; 3 N. & M. 567. But a previous demand, or even a previous distress for the arrears, must be made if the deed or will so require. *S. C.; Havergill* v. *Hare*, Cro. Jac. 510. When a demand is necessary, it must be duly made according to the strict rules of the common law; *i. e.* on the last day allowed for payment of the money, just before and at sunset, at the proper place, by the party entitled, or his duly authorized agent, of the precise sum then payable (not including any previous arrears). *Ante*, 412. It makes no difference in this respect that more than half a year's rent charge is in arrear, and no sufficient distress on the premises to satisfy the arrears, because the 15 & 16 Vict. c. 76, s. 210, does not apply to an ejectment to enforce a seizure *quousque*, &c., but only to ejectments for a forfeiture by nonpayment of rent. *Doe* d. *Darke* v. *Bowditch*, 8 Q. B. 973.

A lawful entry or ejectment will suspend any tenancy created subsequently to the deed or will under which the plaintiff claims: and if the tenant in possession attorn to the owner of the rent charge, he will thereby become his tenant from year to year, determinable upon payment of all the arrears of the rent charge; and such tenancy may be determined by a notice to quit, notwithstanding the tenant's original lease was for a long term of years, such term being suspended so long as any arrears remain unpaid. *Doe* d. *Chawner* v. *Boulter*, 6 A. & E. 675; 1 N. & P. 650.

An entry or ejectment by the owner of a rent charge is not in the nature of a seizure for a forfeiture, but only a seizure *quousque*, &c.; *i. e.*, until the arrears be satisfied with the costs and expenses of the seizure. *Doe* d. *Biass* v. *Horsley*, 1 A. & E. 766; 3 N. & M. 567; *Doe* d. *Darke* v. *Bowditch*, 8 Q. B. 973. When the arrears, &c. are satisfied, the right of possession ceases, and an ejectment may be maintained against the owner of the rent charge if he continue in possession: and that notwithstanding he may have expended large sums in necessary repairs, &c.: such expenditure will not give him a right, even in equity, to retain possession. *Hooper* v. *Cooke*, 25 Law Times R. 286, M. R.

If a rent charge be granted in fee, with a power to the grantee, his heirs *and assigns*, to enforce payment thereof by distress, or by entry and perception of rents and profits until, &c., such rent charge and power may be assigned, and the assignee may maintain ejectment in his own name. *Havergill* v. *Hare*, Cro. Jac. 510. If the entry be made in the lifetime of the grantee, who dies before the arrears are satisfied, the right of possession till such arrears be satisfied will pass, not to the heir, but to the executors of the grantee, who may maintain ejectment. *Doe* d. *Sugden* v. *Weaver*, 2 Car. & K. 754. Where a testator gave a rent charge to his widow during her widowhood, with power *to her* to enter for nonpayment of the rent, and to hold until the arrears were satisfied, and gave the rent charge, after the marriage or death of the widow, to B., his executors, administrators and assigns (without repeating the power to enter): held, that the executors of B., after the marriage of the widow and the death of B., could not maintain ejectment upon nonpayment of the rent charge. *Hassell* d. *Hodson* v. *Gowthwaite*, Willes, 500.

CHAPTER LVIII.

BY FELONS.

No forfeiture of land accrues upon a mere *conviction* of any felony, but only upon *attainder, i. e.* when judgment of death is pronounced. If the defendant be sentenced to transportation, that is not sufficient. *Rex* v. *Bridger,* 1 M. & W. 145; Tyr. & Gr. 437; 2 Inst. 55; 4 Bl. Com. 386. A copyhold of inheritance is not forfeited by a conviction of felony without attainder, unless there be a special custom in the manor. *Rex* v. *Willes,* 3 B. & A. 510; 1 Scriven, Cop. 440. With such a custom a forfeiture may accrue upon conviction; *Rex* v. *Lady Mildmay,* 5 B. & Adol. 254; 1 N. & M. 778; or even upon a presentment of the felony by the homage. *Borneford* v. *Packington,* 1 Leon. 1; *Gittins* v. *Cowper,* 2 Brownl. 217. An outlawry does not occasion any forfeiture, unless it be for a capital crime. Gilb. Ten. 242; 1 Scriven, Cop. 442 (4th ed.). If a copyholder be attainted of treason, his estate is forfeited to the lord of the manor; 2 Hawk. P. C. c. 49, s. 7; not to the crown, unless by express act of parliament. *Lord Cornwallis's case,* 2 Ventr. 39.

Ejectment may be maintained for freehold lands by a person attainted of felony, when there has been *no office found* on behalf of the crown. *Doe* d. *Griffith* v. *Pritchard,* 5 B. & Adol. 765; 2 N. & M. 489. The office found must be an *office of intitling* under the great seal, and not a mere office of information under the exchequer seal. *Page's case,* 5 Co. R. 52 a. If such office be found after the commencement of the ejectment, the plaintiff will be entitled to a verdict, finding that he was entitled at the time of bringing the action and serving the writ, and to a judgment for his costs of suit. 15 & 16 Vict. c. 76, s. 181; *ante,* 289. The principle is, that except as to the queen, who has an inchoate right capable of being perfected by office and seizure, the attainted party has a good right against all the world, and may grant in virtue of such right, though the title which he conveys is defeasible, being subject to the crown's paramount right. *Nichols* v. *Nichols,* Plow. 486; 2 Shep. Touch. 232; 2 Vin. Abr. Alien (A), pl. 18.

If a copyholder be attainted of treason or felony, his copyhold is immediately forfeited to the lord of the manor. 2 Hawk. P. C. c. 49, s. 7. The lord may thereupon enter, or maintain ejectment for the forfeiture; see *post,* Chap. LXVII., Sect. 1; *Lord Cornwallis's case,* 2 Ventr. 39; but until he does so, the copyhold remains in the tenant, notwithstanding his attainder. *Doe* d. *Evans* v. *Evans,* 5 B. & C. 584; 8 D. & R. 399. A mere conviction, without attainder, is not sufficient to create a forfeiture, *Rex* v. *Willes,* 3 B. & A. 510, unless there be a special custom. *Rex* v. *Lady Mildmay,* 5 B. & Adol. 254; 1 N. & M. 778; *supra.*

Where a copyholder was convicted of a capital felony, but pardoned upon condition of remaining two years in prison, and the lord did not enter or do any act towards seizing the copyhold: held, that at the expiration of the two years the copyholder might maintain an ejectment for the land against one who had ousted him, inasmuch as the pardon restored his competency (6 Geo. 4, c. 25, s. 1), and the estate would not vest in the lord without any act done by him. *Doe* d. *Evans* v. *Evans*, 5 B. & C. 584; 8 D. & R. 399.

After the death of a person attainted his descendants may inherit. 3 & 4 Will. 4, c. 106, s. 10; *ante*, 486. But on the death of a peer, leaving his eldest son and heir who had been attainted, the peerage does not vest in the son, nor on his death in the nearest heir male, but is forfeited as much as if he had been a peer at the time of his attainder. *Perth Peerage*, 2 H. L. Cas. 865.

It would seem that a tenant in tail who has committed murder, may afterwards, and before conviction, bar the entail, &c. *Stevens* d. *Costard* v. *Winning*, 2 Wils. 219; *Anon.*, 4 Leon. 84, pl. 177; Goldsb. 102, pl. 7, *S. C.*; Vin. Abr. Alien (A), pl. 18.

If a tenant *for life* be attainted of treason and dies, the remainderman may enter, because only the life estate is forfeited to the crown upon office found. If, however, the office erroneously find that the party attainted was seised in fee, it must be avoided by a traverse, or *amoveas manum*, before the remainderman can enter or maintain ejectment. *Linch* v. *Cook*, 2 Salk. 469.

Upon attainder all the *personal* property and rights of action of the offender vest in the crown without office found. *Bullock* v. *Dodds*, 2 B. & A. 258. Any assignment made just before the trial, without consideration or value, is fraudulent and void as against the crown. *Morewood* v. *Wilks*, 6 C. & P. 144; *Shaw* v. *Bran*, 1 Stark. R. 319. But a *bond fide* assignment made before the day of trial (even after the commission day), in consideration of a pre-existing debt or other good consideration, is valid. *Perkins* v. *Bradley*, 1 Hare, 219; *Whitaker* v. *Wisbey*, 12 C. B. 44.

A lease may contain a proviso for re-entry in the event (amongst other things) of the lessee being convicted of felony; but this is extremely unusual. It is not clear whether an attainder for felony will avoid a lease containing a proviso for re-entry if the lessee shall "become insolvent, or unable in circumstances to go on with the management of the farm." *Doe* d. *Griffith* v. *Pritchard*, 5 B. & Adol. 765; 2 N. & M. 489. At all events such a forfeiture may be waived: and it does not constitute a continuing forfeiture. *S. C.*

CHAPTER LIX.

BY ALIENS.

The Statutes and Treatises.]—The acts relating to aliens are collected in 1 Chit. Stat. 15—27 (2nd ed.). The principal act now in force is the 7 & 8 Vict. c. 66. For the law relating to aliens, denizens and persons naturalized, see Hansard on Aliens ; and the supplement ; Co. Lit. 2 b, 129 a ; 1 Bac. Abr. tit. " Aliens ;" 2 Vin. Abr. tit. " Aliens ;" 1 Com. Dig. tit. " Alien."

Who are Aliens.]—An alien is a foreigner, *i. e.* a person born out of the dominions *and legiance* of the king (*or* queen regnant) ; Co. Lit. 129 a, b. ; and not being the child of a natural-born subject of the united kingdom, either on the paternal (4 Geo. 2, c. 21), or maternal (7 & 8 Vict. c. 66, s. 3) side ; nor a grandchild whose *father* was the child of a natural-born subject. 13 Geo. 3, c. 21.

Persons born on the English seas are not aliens. Molloy, 370 ; 2 Vin. Abr. 262.

If an alien friend come into England when he is an infant, and always afterwards continues there, and is sworn to the king, yet he continues an alien. 14 Hen. 4, c. 20 ; 1 Roll. 195 ; 2 Vin. Abr. " Alien" (C) ; Com. Dig. " Alien" (A).

The children of aliens born within the united kingdom, or within any of the dominions of her majesty, are natural-born subjects, and not aliens. 1 Bac. Abr. tit. " Aliens" (A). But if aliens come as enemies into the realm, and possess themselves of a town or fort, and one of them has issue born here, this issue is an alien; for it is not *cœlum* or *solum* that makes a subject, but the being born within the allegiance and under the protection of the king. 7 Co. R. 18 a; 1 Bac. Abr. tit. "Aliens" (A).

The children of natural-born subjects of the united kingdom, *although born abroad*, are not aliens, but natural-born subjects. 25 Edw. 3, st. 2; 7 Anne, c. 5, s. 3, explained by 4 Geo. 2, c. 21; 7 & 8 Vict. c. 66, s. 3. It is sufficient if the father be a natural-born subject; 4 Geo. 2, c. 21; *Bacon* v. *Bacon*, Cro. Car. 601; *Wall's case*, 3 Knapp, P. C. C. 13; *Jephson* v. *Reira*, id. 130; *Fitch* v. *Weber*, 6 Hare, 51; or the mother. 7 & 8 Vict. c. 66, s. 3. But it is otherwise with respect to children born abroad, whose fathers have been attainted of high treason or felony; or whose fathers were, at the time of the birth of such children respectively, in the actual service of any foreign prince or state, then in enmity with the crown of England or Great Britain. 4 Geo. 2, c. 21, s. 2; *Fitch* v. *Weber*, 6 Hare, 51.

The grandchildren of any natural-born subject, although born abroad, are natural-born subjects, provided their *father* was a subject of the united kingdom. 13 Geo. 3, c. 21.

By the common law no person can make any title to land, or maintain ejectment, as the heir of an alien. *Doe* d. *Count Duroure*, 4 T. R. 300; *Doe* d. *Thomas* v. *Acklam*, 2 B. & C. 779; 4 D. & R. 394; *Doe* d. *Auchmuty* v. *Mulcaster*, 5 B. & C. 771; 8 D. & R. 593; *Doe* d. *Stansbury* v. *Arkwright*, 5 C. & P. 575. But by 11 & 12 Will. 3, c. 6, explained by 25 Geo. 2, c. 39, natural-born subjects may inherit as heirs of aliens, and make out their pedigrees through aliens, provided such subjects were in being and capable to take at the death of the person who last died seised of the land. See *post*, 579.

Denizens.]—A denizen is an alien born, who has obtained from the king (*or* queen regnant) letters of denization. Co. Lit. 129 a; *Calvin's case*, 7 Co. R. 6; Com. Dig. "Alien" (D 1). He may *afterwards* purchase or take *and hold* lands in fee simple, or for any less estate; and may dispose thereof by deed or will; and has heritable blood, so that upon his death intestate his lands of inheritance will descend to his issue born after the letters of denization, but not to those born before. Co. Lit. 8, 129 a; *Godfrey* v. *Dixon*, Cro. Jac. 539; Styles' R. 139, *S. C.*; Bac. Abr. "Aliens" (B); Com. Dig. "Alien" (D 2).

Persons naturalized.]—The principal difference between a denizen and a person naturalized is, that a denizen has heritable blood only from the time of obtaining the letters of denization, and his previous issue cannot inherit; *supra;* whereas the issue of a person naturalized, although born before such naturalization, may inherit in like manner as if the party naturalized had been born a subject of this realm. Co. Lit. 129 a; Com. Dig. Alien (B 2); 2 Vin. Abr. Alien (F.). But an act of naturalization will not relate back to a previous conveyance executed by the alien, so as to confirm the title of a purchaser. *Fish* v. *Klein*, 2 Meriv. 431.

Formerly an alien could not be *naturalized* except by act of parliament. Co. Lit. 129 a; *Godfrey* v. *Dixon*, Cro. Jac. 539, *per* Montague, C. J.; Heywood's County Elec. 253; Com. Dig. Alien (B 2). But now by 7 & 8 Vict. c. 66, aliens desirous of becoming naturalized may present a memorial to one of her majesty's principal secretaries of state (sect. 7) ; who may grant a certificate (sect. 8), which is to be enrolled in chancery (sect. 9), and the alien is to take an oath of allegiance, &c. Sect. 10.

Sect. 6 enacts, " that upon obtaining the certificate and taking the oath hereinafter prescribed, every alien now residing in, or who shall hereafter come to reside in any part of Great Britain or Ireland, with intent to settle therein, shall enjoy all the rights and capacities which a natural-born subject of the united kingdom can enjoy or transmit, except that such alien shall not be capable of becoming of her majesty's privy council, nor a member of either house of parliament, nor of enjoying such other rights and capacities, if any, as shall be specially excepted in and by the certificate to be granted in manner hereinafter mentioned."

Sect. 13 enacts, " that all persons who have been naturalized before the passing of this act, and who shall have resided in the united kingdom during five successive years, shall be deemed entitled to and shall enjoy all such rights and capacities of British subjects as may be conferred on aliens by the provisions of this act."

Sect. 14 provides, that the act shall not prejudice rights then existing.

Sect. 15 enacts, " that nothing herein contained shall be construed so as to take away or diminish any right, privilege or capacity, heretofore lawfully possessed by or belonging to aliens residing in Great Britain or Ireland, so far as relates to the possession or enjoyment of any real or personal property, but that all such rights shall continue to be enjoyed by such aliens in as full and ample a manner as such rights were enjoyed before the passing of this act."

Sect. 16 enacts, " that any woman married, or who shall be married to a natural-born subject, or person naturalized, shall be deemed and taken to be herself naturalized, and have all the rights and privileges of a natural-born subject."

This enactment is not merely declaratory, but alters the previous law. *The Count de Wall's case,* 6 Moore's P. C. C. 216 ; 12 Jur. 145, *S. C.; Calvin's case,* 7 Co. R. 25 a; Co. Lit. 31 b; *Reg.* v. *Manning,* 2 Car. & K. 887 ; 1 Den. C. C. 467.

The 13 Geo. 2, c. 7, 20 Geo. 2, c. 44, 2 Geo. 3, c. 25, 13 Geo. 3, c. 25, naturalize, on certain terms, foreign protestants and others, who settle, as therein mentioned, in any of his majesty's colonies in America.

Personal and Real Property of Aliens.]—By 7 & 8 Vict. c. 66, s. 4, it is enacted, " that from and after the passing of this act (6th August, 1844), every alien, being the subject of a friendly state, shall and may take and hold, by purchase, gift, bequest, representation or otherwise, every species of personal property, *except chattels real,* as fully and effectually, to all intents and purposes, and with the same rights, remedies, exemptions, privileges and capacities, as if he were a natural-born subject of the United Kingdom."

Sect. 5 enacts, " that every alien now residing in, or who shall hereafter come to reside in, any part of the United Kingdom, and being a subject of a friendly state, may by grant, lease, demise, assignment, bequest, representation or otherwise, *take and hold* any lands, houses, or other tenements, *for the purpose of residence or of occupation* by him or her, or his or her servants, or *for the purpose of any business, trade or manufacture,* for any term of years *not exceeding twenty-one years,* as fully and effectually, to all intents and purposes, and with the same rights, remedies, exemptions and privileges, except the right to vote at elections for members of parliament, as if he were a natural-born subject of the United Kingdom."

This section virtually repeals, *pro tanto,* the 32 Hen. 8, c. 16, s. 13, by which it was enacted, that all leases of any *dwelling-house or shop* within this realm, or any of the king's dominions, made to any stranger, artificer or handicraftsman, born out of the king's obeisance, not being denizen, shall be void and of none effect; and that no stranger, artificer or handicraftsman born out of the king's obeisance, not being denizen, shall take any lease of any dwelling house or shop within this realm, or in other the king's dominions, upon pain to lose and forfeit for every time doing contrary to this act one hundred shillings; and that no person shall grant or let to farm any dwelling-house or shop to any such stranger, artificer or handicraftsman, not being denizen, to the intent to dwell or inhabit the same, upon like pain of one hundred shillings." That enactment extended only to such messuages as were "dwelling-houses or shops," but not to other buildings comprised within the term "messuages," *ex. gr.* barns, stables, chapels, and the like. *Jevens* v. *Harridge and Uxor, Administrators of Levemere,* 1 Wms. Saund. 6. It applied not only to leases, but also to agreements for leases to aliens; *Lappierre* v. *M'Intosh,* 9 A. & E. 157 ; 1 P. & D. 629 ; or to third persons on behalf of aliens, made to evade the act. *Bailey* v. *Cathrey,* 1 Dowl. N. S. 456. But it did not extend to assignments to aliens of leases previously granted to natural-born subjects. *Wootton* v. *Steffenoni,* 12 M. & W. 129. And where an alien occupied land under a void lease or agreement, and, consequently only as tenant from year to year, he was liable to an action for use and occupation. *Pilkington* v. *Peach,* 2 Show. 135.

If an alien purchase or otherwise acquire land in fee simple, or for any less estate (except for a term not exceeding twenty-one years, as allowed by 7 & 8 Vict. c. 66, s. 5, *ante,* 577), the conveyance thereof will vest the estate in him *until office found, or until his death,* which shall first happen ; for he is *competent to take, although not to hold,* land. Co. Lit. 2 b ; Dyer, 283 b ; Com. Dig. "Alien" (C. 2) ; 2 Vin. Abr. "Alien" (A.) ; 2 Prest. Conv. 259 ; *Duplessis* v. *Attorney-General* (in error), 1 Bro. P. C. 415 (Toml. ed.) ; *Anon.,* 1 Leon. 47, Anderson, C. J. ; cited 1 Car. & K. 392, note. An alien cannot even *take* land by act of law, as by descent. Therefore if a woman possessed of a term of years marry an alien, such marriage is no gift in law to him of the term. *Theobalds* v. *Duffoy,* 9 Mod. 104. But it seems that an alien husband and his wife may be seised or possessed of land in right of the wife. *Doe* d. *Miller* v. *Rogers,* 1 Car. & K. 390. So he may take and hold land *in autre droit, ex. gr.,* as executor, administrator, or the like. *Caroon's case,* Cro. Car. 8 ; *post,* 580.

An office found on behalf of the crown must be an *office of entitling,* issued under the great seal, and not a mere office of information issued under the seal of the Exchequer. *Page's case,* 5 Co. R. 52 a ; 1 Car. & K. 391, note ; Hansard on Aliens, 123, note (*f*). Upon office found the estate of the alien becomes vested in the crown, and the title relates back to the time when the property first vested in the alien, so as to avoid any conveyance, mortgage, lease or other disposition made by him. *King* v. *Boys,* 3 Dyer, 283 b, pl. 31 ; 2 Pres. Conv. 247 ;

Burt. Comp. s. 192. In the meantime, *i. e.* until office found, the estate remains vested in the alien. Case LXI. 1 Leon. 47; Case CLXXV. 4 Leon. 82; Com. Dig. "Alien" (C. 4). But upon his death (without heirs, being natural-born subjects entitled to take under 11 & 12 Will. 3, c. 6, as explained by 25 Geo. 1, c. 39 (*infra*), the law casts the estate upon the crown, without any office found. *Willion* v. *Berkley*, Plow. 229; Finch, L. 232. In such case an office of information usually issues under the great seal, for the purpose of putting the estate in charge. 1 Car. & K. 392, note.

Natural-born Subjects may inherit as Heirs of Aliens.]—By 11 & 12 Will. 3, c. 6, intituled "An Act to enable his Majesty's Natural-born Subjects to inherit the Estate of their Ancestors, either lineal or collateral, notwithstanding their Father or Mother were Aliens," it is enacted as follows: — " Whereas divers persons born within the king's dominions are disabled to inherit and make their titles by descent from their ancestors by reason that their fathers or mothers, or some other ancestor (by whom they are to derive their descent), was an alien, and not born within the king's dominions; for remedy whereof be it enacted, that all and every person or persons, *being the king's natural-born subject or subjects,* within any of the king's realms or dominions, shall and may hereafter lawfully inherit and be inheritable as heir or heirs to any honours, manors, lands, tenements or hereditaments, and make their pedigrees and titles by descent from any of their ancestors, lineal or collateral, although the father and mother, or fathers or mothers, or other ancestor of such person or persons, by, from, through or under whom he or she, or they shall or may make or derive their title or pedigree, were or was, or is or are, or shall be born out of the king's allegiance, and out of his majesty's realms or dominions, as freely, fully and effectually, to all intents and purposes, as if such father or mother, or fathers or mothers, or other ancestor or ancestors, by, from, through or under whom he, she or they shall or may make or derive their title or pedigree, had been naturalized or natural-born subject or subjects within the king's dominions; any law or custom to the contrary notwithstanding."

The above act was explained by the 25 Geo. 2, c. 39, whereby it is declared, " that the said statute shall not extend, or be deemed, taken or construed to extend, to give any right or title to any person or persons to inherit as heir or heirs, or coheir or coheirs, to any person dying seised of any manors, lands, tenements or hereditaments in possession, reversion or remainder, by enabling any such person or persons to claim or derive his, her or their pedigree through any alien ancestor or ancestors, unless the person or persons so claiming or deriving his, her or their title, as heir or heirs, coheir or coheirs, was or were, or shall be *in being and capable to take* the same estate as heir or heirs, coheir or coheirs, by virtue of the said statute, *at the death of the person who shall so last die seised* of such manors, lands, tenements or hereditaments, and to whom he, she or they shall so claim to be heir or heirs, coheir or coheirs, by force of the said statute."

Sect. 2 provides, that in case the descent be cast upon the daughter of an alien, and he has subsequently a son born, or another daughter, the estate shall thereupon be divested in favour of such son, or so as to let in the subsequent daughter as a coparcener.

An office found in the alien's lifetime will prevent him from *dying seised* of the land, and consequently will prevent his issue (although natural-born subjects) from being entitled to take as heirs under the above statutes.

Actions by Aliens.]—An alien enemy cannot maintain any action, real or personal, until peace be restored. Co. Lit. 129 b; 1 Chit. Pl. 11 (7th ed.); Com. Dig. "Alien" (C. 5); *Alcinous* v. *Nigreu*, 4 E. & B. 217. But in personal actions the objection must be pleaded in abatement in due time. *Shepeler* v. *Durant*, 14 C. B. 582. And the plaintiff may reply the queen's licence and permission to reside here. 3 Chit. Pl. 427; *Alciator* v. *Smith*, 3 Camp. 245; *Boulton* v. *Dobree*, 2 Camp. 163; Co. Lit. 129 b (note 203); Com. Dig. "Alien" (C. 5).

An alien friend may maintain any *personal* action; Co. Lit. 129 b; *Pisani* v. *Lawson*, 6 Bing. N. C. 90; 8 Scott, 180; 8 Dowl. 57; although, if he reside abroad, security for costs may be ordered.

In Co. Lit. 129 b, it is said that an alien "cannot maintaine either reall or mixt actions." This is adopted in some other works of considerable authority. Gilb. Hist. of C. B. 166. There is, however, no reported case in which it has been decided that ejectment cannot be maintained by an alien, although there are several in which persons *claiming as heirs* have failed for want of title, on the ground that their ancestor was an alien, and consequently had no inheritable blood. Whether their ancestors were or were not aliens appears to have been the main question. *Doe* d. *Count Duroure* v. *Jones*, 4 T. R. 300; *Doe* d. *Thomas* v. *Acklam*, 2 B. & C. 779; 4 D. & R. 394; *Doe* d. *Auchmuty* v. *Mulcaster*, 5 B. & C. 771; 8 D. & R. 593; *Doe* d. *Stansbury* v. *Arkwright*, 5 C. & P. 575. Upon principle it would seem that so long as a sufficient estate remains vested in the alien, *i. e.* until office found (*ante*, 578), he may maintain ejectment. Formerly he might have suffered a recovery before office found, which would have been valid, except as *against* the crown. *Anon.*, 4 Leon. 84, pl. 177; Goldsb. 102, pl. 7, *S. C.*; Vin. Abr. "Alien" (A.), pl. 18. So a conveyance, mortgage or lease by an alien is valid, except as against the crown. 2 Prest. Conv. 247. Even an attainted felon may maintain ejectment until office found; *ante*, 573; and so it would seem that an alien may maintain ejectment until office found; *Doe* d. *Miller* v. *Rogers*, 1 Car. & K. 390; for until then the legal estate remains vested in him. *Ante*, 578; Hansard on Aliens, 133, 162. Such action would be liable to be defeated (except as to the costs) upon office found after the service of the writ and before the trial, upon due proof that the claimant is an alien, and of the office found, &c. But even then the alien would be entitled to a verdict finding that he was entitled at the time of bringing the action and serving the writ, and to a judgment for his costs of suit. 15 & 16 Vict. c. 76, s. 181; *ante*, 289. If the action be founded on a lease authorized by the 7 & 8 Vict. c. 66, s. 5 (*ante*, 577), it would not be prejudiced or defeated, even by an office found. An alien husband may join as a co-plaintiff with his wife in an ejectment to recover her lands. *Doe* d. *Miller* v. *Rogers*, 1 Car. & K. 390, Coleridge, J. So an alien may maintain ejectment *in autre droit*, *ex. gr.*, as executor, administrator, head of a corporation, or the like. *Caroon's case*, Cro. Car. 8; 2 Vin. Abr. "Alien" (A. 1, pl. 19); Co. Lit. 129 a, b.

CHAPTER LX.

BY OR AGAINST LUNATICS.

An ejectment must be brought in the name of the lunatic, and not of the committee of his estate; for the latter is but a bailiff, and has no estate or interest in the land. *Drury* v. *Fitch*, Hutt. 16; *Cocks* v. *Darson*, Hob. 215; *Knipe* v. *Palmer*, 2 Wils. 130.

By 16 & 17 Vict. c. 70, the committee of the estate of a lunatic may surrender a lease and accept a fresh one *in the name* and on behalf of the lunatic, under an order of the Lord Chancellor. Sect. 113. So he may execute conveyances, mortgages and other deeds and contracts, *in the name* and on behalf of the lunatic, as the Lord Chancellor shall order. Sects. 116—138. And "every surrender, lease, agreement, deed, conveyance, mortgage or other disposition granted, accepted, made or executed by virtue of this act, shall be as valid and legal to all intents and purposes as if the person in whose name or on whose behalf the same was granted, accepted, made or executed, had been of sound mind, and had granted, accepted, made or executed the same." Sect. 139.

In ejectment *against* a lunatic the writ should generally be served on the lunatic personally, as in ordinary cases. *Ante,* 100.

When a lunatic is entitled to be admitted tenant of copyhold land, the committee may offer himself to be admitted tenant in the name and on behalf of the lunatic, in default whereof the lord should proceed according to the 16 & 17 Vict. c. 70, ss. 108—112; or he may cause the land to be seised *quousque* in the usual manner; *Dimes* v. *The Grand Junction Canal Company,* 9 Q. B. 469, 514; but not for a forfeiture. 16 & 17 Vict. c. 70, s. 112.

CHAPTER LXI.

BY GUARDIANS.

A guardian in socage is where the *legal* estate in lands descends to an infant heir under the age of fourteen years. His next of blood, to whom the inheritance cannot possibly descend, is by the common law his guardian in socage. Lit. s. 123; Co. Lit. 87 b. Thus, if the land descend to the heir on the part of the father, then the mother (*Rex* v. *Inhabitants of Witby*, 2 M. & S. 504), or other next cousin on the part of the mother, shall have the wardship; and if the land descend to the heir on the part of the mother, then the father or next friend on the part of the father shall have the wardship of such lands or tenements; and when the heir cometh to the age of fourteen years complete, he may enter and oust the guardian in socage, and occupy the land himself if he will; and such guardian in socage shall not take any issues or profits of such lands or tenements to his own use, but only to the use and profit of the heir; and of this he shall render an account to the heir after he accomplishes the age of fourteen years. But such guardian upon his account shall have allowance of all his reasonable costs and expenses in all things, &c. Lit. ss. 123, 124; 52 Hen. 3, c. 17; 2 Chit. Stat. 569 (2nd ed.). An action of account lies against a stranger as guardian who enters and receives the profits. *Hughes* v. *Hanys*, Cro. Car. 229.

If the infant's title be merely *equitable*, no guardianship in socage arises. *Rex* v. *Inhabitants of Toddington*, 1 B. & A. 560.

A guardian in socage has the legal estate of the infant vested in him until the infant attains the age of fourteen years. In the meantime the guardian may maintain trespass or ejectment, or avow for *damage feasant*, or make admittance to copyhold, or demise in his own name, until the infant comes to the age of fourteen years. *Per cur.* in *Wade* v. *Baker and Cole*, 1 Lord Raym. 131; *Shopland* v. *Ryoler*, Cro. Jac. 55, 98. But no longer. *Roe* d. *Parry* v. *Hodgson*, 2 Wils. 129. He may maintain ejectment in his own name as guardian so long as the infant remains under the age of fourteen, but not afterwards. *Doe* d. *Rigge* v. *Bell*, 5 T. R. 471. In such action he must prove—1. The seisin in fee of the person from whom his ward claims. 2. The heirship of the ward. 3. That the ward is under the age of fourteen years. 4. That the plaintiff is the next of blood, to whom the inheritance cannot descend. 5. That the defendant's tenancy (if any) has expired, or been duly determined by a proper notice to quit, or otherwise. *Doe* d. *Rigge* v. *Bell*, 5 T. R. 471; *Maddon* d. *Baker* v. *White*, 2 T. R. 159.

A testamentary guardian is one appointed by the father of an infant pursuant to 12 Car. 2, c. 24, ss. 8, 9. 2 Chit. Stat. 570 (2nd ed.).

During his guardianship, which continues until the infant attains the age of twenty-one years, he has precisely the same authority and power over the infant's lands as a guardian in socage, "and may bring such action or actions in relation thereto as by law a guardian in common socage might do." Sect. 9. In ejectment by a testamentary guardian he must prove—1. The seisin in fee of the father, or other person through whom the infant claims. 2. The title of the infant by descent, devise or otherwise. 3. The due execution of the deed or will, which appoints the plaintiff to be guardian of the infant. The probate is not sufficient. 4. The minority of the ward. 5. That the defendant's tenancy (if any) has expired, or been duly determined by a proper notice to quit, or otherwise. *Doe* d. *Rigge* v. *Bell,* 5 T. R. 471.

The infant, when of age, may avoid any lease granted by the guardian during his minority. *Roe* d. *Parry* v. *Hodgson,* 2 Wils. 129.

Guardian by Nurture.]—A guardian for nurture has only the care of the person and education of the infant, and has nothing to do with his land as such guardian. *Ratcliffe's case,* 3 Co. R. 37; *Pigot* v. *Garnish,* Cro. Eliz. 734. Therefore he cannot maintain ejectment. Ad. Eject. 48.

CHAPTER LXII.

BY INFANTS.

An infant may maintain ejectment in his own name. *Doe* d. *Thomas* v. *Roberts,* 16 M. & W. 778. And it seems that he may do so, notwithstanding he is under the age of fourteen, and has a guardian in socage; or under the age of twenty-one, and has a testamentary guardian, appointed pursuant to 12 Car. 2, c. 24, ss. 8, 9; *Doe* d. *Halsworth* v. *Hancock,* Derby Sum. Ass. 1836, Park, J.; Ad. Eject. 49; or such guardian may maintain ejectment in his own name. *Ante,* 582. But an infant cannot, by entry or ejectment *during his infancy,* avoid a lease or conveyance made by him, apparently for his benefit at the time. *Zouch* d. *Abbott* v. *Parsons,* 3 Burr. 1794, 1808; 1 W. Black. 575, *S. C.; Maddon* d. *Baker* v. *White,* 2 T. R. 159; *Drury* v. *Drury,* 5 Bro. P. C. 570. If the infant heir of a deceased mortgagee reconvey the estate upon the balance of principal and interest being paid to the executors, he cannot afterwards during his infancy avoid such reconveyance. *Zouch* v. *Parsons, supra.* No person can *as agent* of an infant make a lease or tenancy from year to year, so as to bind the infant. *Doe* d. *Thomas* v. *Roberts,* 16 M. & W. 778.

A lease to an infant is not void, but voidable only; and if it be beneficial to him, he is liable to be sued for the rent reserved. *Kelsey's case,* Cro. Jac. 320. The surrender of an infant lessee by deed is void; but his surrender in law by the acceptance of a new lease is good, if such new lease increase his term or decrease his rent. *Lloyd* v. *Gregory,* Cro. Car. 501; Jones, 405, *S. C.* A tenancy from year to year cannot be created by the attorney or agent of and for an infant. *Doe* d. *Thomas* v. *Roberts,* 16 M. & W. 778. A tenancy from year to year created by the ancestor of an infant, and through whom he claims as heir, must be duly determined by a proper notice to quit before the infant can maintain ejectment. *Maddon* d. *Baker* v. *White,* 2 T. R. 159.

An infant should not sue in person or by attorney, but by his *prochein amy* or guardian. 2 Chit. Arch. 1166 (9th ed.). Such *prochein amy* or guardian, though liable to the defendant for the costs, is not a party to the suit, but simply a person appointed by the court to look after the interests of the infant, and manage the suit for him. *Sinclair* v. *Sinclair,* 13 M. & W. 640; *Melluish* v. *Collier,* 15 Q. B. 878. The infant's father is usually appointed, but the court or a judge will appoint some other person with the father's consent. *Claridge* v. *Crawford,* 1 D. & R. 13; *Watson* v. *Fraser,* 8 M. & W. 660; 9 Dowl. 741. If the father be in insolvent circumstances, some other person should be appointed. *Duckett* v. *Satchwell,* 12 M. & W. 779; 1 Dowl. & L.

980. If the infant be too young to sign a petition for the appointment of a *prochein amy*, his father may do so for him. *Eades* v. *Booth*, 8 Q. B. 718; 3 Dowl. & L. 770. Where several executors sue, and one of them is an infant, those of full age may appoint an attorney for themselves and the infant. *Rutland* v. *Rutland*, Cro. Eliz. 378; 2 Saund. 213, n.; 1 Roll. Abr. 288, pl. 3. If an infant sue alone without a *prochein amy* or guardian to answer costs, the court or a judge will, upon the application of the defendant, stay the proceedings until a *prochein amy* or guardian be appointed, or security given for costs. *Noke* v. *Windham*, 2 Stra. 694; *Throgmorton* d. *Miller* v. *Smith, Id.* 932; *Anon.*, 1 Wils. 130; *Doe* d. *Roberts* v. *Roberts*, 6 Dowl. 556. But a previous application should be made for such security to the plaintiff or his attorney; and if it be complied with, no subsequent application should be made to the court. *Anon.*, 1 Cowp. 128.

The evidence in an ejectment by or against an infant is the same as if he were of full age.

CHAPTER LXIII.

By 6 & 7 Will. 4, c. 32, intituled "An Act for the Regulation of Benefit Building Societies," such societies may be established for the purchase or erection of dwelling-houses, &c. in manner therein mentioned, with power to make "such proper and wholesome rules and regulations for the government and guidance of the same," as therein mentioned; sect. 1; and from time to time to alter and amend such rules as occasion shall require, or annul or repeal the same, and to make new rules in lieu thereof, under such restrictions as are in this act contained. Sect. 1. And it shall and may be lawful to and for any such society in and by the rules thereof to describe the form or forms of conveyance, mortgage, transfer, agreement, bond or other instrument which may be necessary for carrying the purposes of the said society into execution. Sect. 3.

Sect. 4 enacts, " that all the provisions of a certain act made and passed in the tenth year of the reign of his late Majesty King George the Fourth, intituled ' An Act to consolidate and amend the Laws relating to Friendly Societies,' and also the provisions of a certain other act made and passed in the fourth and fifth years of the reign of his present Majesty King William the Fourth, intituled ' An Act to amend an Act of the Tenth Year of his late Majesty King George the Fourth to consolidate and amend the Laws relating to Friendly Societies,' so far as the same or any part thereof may be applicable to the purpose of any benefit building society, and to the framing, certifying, enrolling and altering the rules thereof, shall extend and apply to such benefit building society and the rules thereof, in such and the same manner as if the provisions of the said acts had been herein expressly re-enacted."

The 18 & 19 Vict. c. 63, intituled "An Act to consolidate and amend the Law relating to Friendly Societies," repeals the whole of the 10 Geo. 4, c. 56, and the 4 & 5 Will. 4, c. 40 ; but it does not repeal the 6 & 7 Will. 4, c. 32, nor any of the enactments therein contained. Consequently sect. 4, which in effect *incorporates and re-enacts* those two acts, so far as they are applicable to benefit building societies, is not affected by their repeal. They now continue in force *as part of sect.* 4, so far as they are applicable to benefit building societies. *Verba relata inesse videntur.* See the 55 Geo. 3, c. 184 (The General Stamp Act), s. 8, and the decisions thereon. *The Attorney-General* v. *Brown,* 3 Exch. 662; *Gingell* v. *Purkins,* 4 Exch. 720, 724. Also the 43 Geo. 3, c. 59, s. 1 (relating to county bridges), and the decisions thereon. *Reg.* v. *The Inhabitants of Merionethshire,* 6 Q. B. 343; *Reg.* v. *The Inhabitants of Brecon,* 15 Q. B. 813.

By 6 & 7 Will. 4, c. 32, s. 5, the trustees named in any mortgage made on behalf of such societies, or the survivors or survivor of them, or the trustees for the time being, may indorse on any mortgage or further charge a receipt for the monies thereby secured, which shall operate as a reconveyance.

Sect. 8 enacts, "that no rules of any such society, or any copy thereof, nor any transfer of any share or shares in any such society, shall be subject or liable to or charged with any stamp duty or duties whatsoever." And by 10 Geo. 4, c. 56, s. 37, bonds and other securities, instruments and documents, taken by or relating to any benefit building society, are exempt from stamp duty. This includes mortgages to the society or their trustees. *Walker* v. *Giles,* 6 C. B. 662.

One of the rules of each benefit building society must specify " whether a reference of *every matter in dispute* between any such society, or any person acting under them, and any individual member thereof, or person claiming on account of any member, shall be made to such of his majesty's justices of the peace as may act in and for the county in which such society may be formed, or to arbitrators to be appointed in manner hereinafter directed." 10 Geo. 4, c. 56, s. 27. Two transcripts of the rules, signed by three members, and countersigned by the clerk or secretary, must be certified by the barrister appointed to certify the rules of savings banks; 4 & 5 Will. 4, c. 40, s. 4; or, since the 3rd July, 1846, by the registrar of friendly societies in England; 9 & 10 Vict. c. 27, s. 10; one copy of which is to be kept by such registrar, and the other by the society. The society is duly constituted and entitled to the usual privileges and advantages from the time when the certified rules are framed, and not from the date of the certificate. *Williams* v. *Hayward,* 25 Law J., N. S., Chanc. 289. Mortgages and other securities, rules, transfers, &c. made in pursuance of any of the above acts, are exempt from stamp duty. 10 Geo. 4, c. 56, s. 37 ; 6 & 7 Will. 4, c. 32, s. 8; *Walker* v. *Giles,* 6 C. B. 662; *Barnard* v. *Pilsworth, Id.,* 698, note; *Williams* v. *Hayward, supra.*

Generally speaking, all disputes between a building society, or its officers, and any individual member thereof, or person claiming on account of any member, must be referred to arbitration, or to justices, according to the rule of the society made pursuant to 10 Geo. 4, c. 56, s. 27. The jurisdiction of the superior courts at Westminster and of the county courts is ousted by such statutable rule. *Reeves* v. *White,* 17 Q. B. 995; 21 Law J., N. S., Q. B. 169; *Ex parte Payne,* 5 Dowl. & L. 679; *Crisp* v. *Bunbury,* 8 Bing. 394. But if the dispute be in respect of any claim or demand of the society against any member thereof, *not as a member,* but as a mortgagor, or in some other capacity, the arbitrators or justices (as the case may be) will have no jurisdiction, and may be restrained by prohibition from deciding the matter in dispute. *Reg.* v. *Trafford,* 4 E. & B. 122; *Grinham* v. *Card,* 7 Exch. 833. So where the administrator of a member of a friendly society claims the amount secured by a policy of assurance granted by the society. *Kelsall* v. *Tyler,* 25 Law J., N. S., Exch. 153. The remedy in such cases must be sought in the superior courts; *Cutbill* v. *Kingdom,* 1 Exch. 494; *Morrison* v. *Glover,* 4 Exch. 430, 444; *Doe* d. *Morrison* v. *Glover,* 15 Q. B. 103; or in the County Court; *Ex parte Payne,* 5 Dowl. & L. 679; or in the Court of Chancery. *Fleming* v. *Self,* 1 Kay, 518; 3 De Gex, Mac. & Gor. 997; *Mulloch* v. *Jenkins,* 21 Law J., N. S., Chanc. 65, M. R.; *Mosley* v. *Baker,* 6

Hare, 87; 1 Hall & Tw. 301; *Burbridge* v. *Cotton*, 21 Law J., N. S., Chanc. 201, Parker, V. C.

Ejectment may be maintained by the trustees for the time being of a benefit building society upon a mortgage of leaseholds, containing a covenant to pay the defendant's subscription and redemption monies, and *the rent reserved to the landlord*, with a power of entry and sale, &c. in case of any default. *Doe* d. *Morrison* v. *Glover*, 15 Q. B. 103. But it seems that an action of covenant could not be maintained on such a deed for nonpayment of the subscription and redemption monies. *Reeves* v. *White*, 17 Q. B. 995; 21 Law J., N. S., Q. B. 169. The mortgagor may file a bill in equity to redeem the mortgage. *Mosley* v. *Baker*, 6 Hare, 87; 1 Hall & Tw. 301; *Fleming* v. *Self*, 1 Kay, 518; 3 De Gex, Mac. & Gor. 997; *Reg.* v. *Trafford*, 4 E. & B. 122.

All the real and personal property of a benefit building society is "vested in the treasurer or trustee of such society *for the time being*, for the use and benefit of such society, and the respective members thereof," with full power to bring or defend any action or suit "touching or concerning the property, right or claim aforesaid of or belonging to or had by such society: provided such person shall have been thereunto duly authorized by the consent of the majority of members present at any meeting of the society or committee thereof; and such person so appointed shall and may in all cases concerning the property, right or claim aforesaid of such society, sue and be sued, plead and be impleaded in his or her *proper name, as treasurer or trustee of such society*, without other description;" and no such suit or action is to abate by the death or removal of the plaintiff, but the succeeding treasurer or trustee may continue it in the name of the original plaintiff. 10 Geo. 4, c. 56, s. 21; *Reg.* v. *Cain*, Car. & M. 309.

An ejectment on behalf of a benefit building society should be brought in the name or names of the treasurer or trustees *for the time being*, in whom the legal estate is vested; *Reg.* v. *Cain, supra;* and not in the names of the trustees to whom the mortgage was made. But the latter may join in the action as coplaintiffs, and their doing so may frequently prevent doubtful points being raised.

If an action be brought by the treasurer or trustees without the authority mentioned in the proviso contained in 10 Geo. 4, c. 56, s. 21, the defendant cannot avail himself of such want of authority as a defence to the action. *Doe* d. *Morrison* v. *Glover*, 15 Q. B. 103; and see *Doe* d. *Clarke* v. *Spencer*, 3 Bing. N. C. 203, 370; *Sutcliffe* v. *Brooke*, 14 M. & W. 855.

The rules of the society may be proved by the production from the proper custody of the book kept by the society containing a transcript of the rules certified by the registrar of friendly societies, pursuant to 9 & 10 Vict. c. 27; or by the barrister appointed to certify the rules of savings banks, pursuant to 10 Geo. 4, c. 56, and 4 & 5 Will. 4, c. 32; but if certified by the latter, it may be necessary to prove that they were enrolled at the sessions. This, however, is not clear. *Walker* v. *Giles*, 6 C. B. 662. Such evidence is clearly unnecessary when the rules have been certified by the registrar, pursuant to 9 & 10 Vict. c. 27; *Id.*, 685. Judicial notice will be taken of the registrar's or barrister's signature. 8 & 9 Vict. c. 113, s. 1.

When the rules of a benefit society are proved by an examined copy of the transcript filed with the clerk of the peace, the witness must prove that he examined the copy with *all* the rules. *Reg.* v. *Boynes*, 1 Car. & K. 65. The rules should be *read to him* while he examines the copy. *Ante*, 253. There must be no abbreviations in the copy which are not in the original. *Reg.* v. *Christian*, Car. & M. 388. The witness must be able to state in whose custody the original transcript was when he examined the copy, so that it may appear to have been *in the proper custody. Ante*, 253.

The plaintiffs, or some or one of them, must be proved to be the trustees or treasurer for the time being of the society. *Reg.* v. *Cain*, Car. & M. 309.

In other respects the evidence will be the same as in an ejectment by mortgagee *v.* mortgagor. *Ante*, Chap. XLIV.

Friendly Societies are now regulated by 18 & 19 Vict. c. 63. The rules and tables of any such society, and all alterations and amendments thereof, and all copies thereof or extracts therefrom, and all writings and documents relating to a friendly society, and *purporting to be signed by the registrar*, shall, in the absence of any evidence to the contrary, be received in all courts of law and equity and elsewhere, without proof of the signature thereto.

CHAPTER LXIV.

AGAINST RAILWAY AND OTHER COMPANIES.

Estates and Interests of every Party to be purchased by Agreement or otherwise.]—Railway and other companies incorporated by act of parliament, and requiring land for the purposes of their undertakings, should purchase *the respective estates and interests therein of every party,* pursuant to the provisions of their special act, and of The Lands Clauses Consolidation Act, 1845 (8 & 9 Vict. c. 18). If the company purchase land from a tenant for years only, his landlord may maintain ejectment against the company after the expiration of the term. *Doe*

d. *Patrick* v. *Duke of Beaufort*, 6 Exch. 498; *Rex* v. *The Stainforth and Keadby Canal Company*, 1 M. & S. 32. If they purchase from the reversioner or landlord only, the tenant's term or estate will not be thereby affected. *Doe* d. *Hutchinson* v. *The Manchester, Bury and Rossendale Railway Company*, 14 M. & W. 687, 689; *The Norwich Railway Company* v. *Wodehouse*, 11 Beav. 382. If they purchase from a copyholder only, the rights and interests of the lord will not be affected. *Dimes* v. *The Grand Junction Railway Company*, 9 Q. B. 469; and see *Same Company* v. *Dimes*, 15 Simon, 402; 2 Mac. & Gor. 285; 2 Hall & Tw. 92. If the land be mortgaged, but the mortgagor remains in possession, they cannot safely purchase from him only. *Ranken* v. *The East and West India Docks and Birmingham Junction Railway Company*, 12 Beav. 298; 19 Law J., N. S., Chanc. 153. If there be several tenants in common the estate and interest of each should be purchased. *Doe* d. *Wawn* v. *Horn and Others*, 3 M. & W. 333; 5 *Id.* 564.

The necessary purchases may be made "by agreement" with the owners, and with all persons having any estate or interest in such lands, or enabled by statute to sell and convey the same: 8 & 9 Vict. c. 18, ss. 6—15; *Collins* v. *The South Staffordshire Railway Company*, 7 Exch. 5: or they may be made "otherwise than by agreement," *i.e.* under the compulsory powers vested in them. Sects. 16—68; *Doe* d. *Payne* v. *The Bristol and Exeter Railway Company*, 6 M. & W. 320. Such powers must generally be exercised within three years after the passing of their special act, or within some other limited time: s. 123; *Brocklebank* v. *The Whitehaven Junction Railway Company*, 15 Simon, 632; *Williams* v. *The South Wales Railway Company*, 3 De Gex & Sm. 354: and after the whole of the capital of the company has been subscribed for. Sect. 16; *Doe* d. *Payne* v. *The Bristol and Exeter Railway Company*, 6 M. & W. 320.

Parties enabled to sell and convey.]—By 8 & 9 Vict. c. 18, s. 7, "it shall be lawful for all parties being seised, possessed of, or entitled to any such lands, or any estate or interest therein, to sell and convey or release the same to the promoters of the undertaking, and to enter into all necessary agreements for that purpose; and particularly it shall be lawful for all or any of the following parties so seised, possessed, or entitled as aforesaid, so to sell, convey or release; (that is to say,) all corporations, tenants in tail or for life, married women seised in their own right or entitled to dower, guardians, committees of lunatics and idiots, trustees or feoffees for charitable or other purposes, executors and administrators, and all parties for the time being entitled to the receipt of the rents and profits of any such lands in possession, or subject to any estate in dower, or to any lease for life, or for lives and years, or for years, or any less interest; and the power so to sell and convey or release as aforesaid may lawfully be exercised by all such parties, *other than* married women entitled to dower, or lessees for life, or for lives and years, or for years, or for any less interest, not only on behalf of themselves and their respective heirs, executors, administrators and successors, but also for and on behalf of every person entitled in reversion, remainder or expectancy after them, or in defeazance of the estates of such parties; and as to such married women, whether they be of full age or not, as if they were sole and of full age; and as to such guardians, on behalf of their wards; and as to such committees, on behalf of the lunatics and idiots of whom they are the committees respectively; and that to the same extent as such wives, wards, lunatics and idiots respectively, could have exercised the same power under the authority of this or the special act if they had respectively been under no disability; and as to such trustees, executors and administrators, on behalf of their cestui que trusts, whether infants, issue unborn, lunatics, femes covert, or other persons, and that to the same extent as such cestui que trusts respectively could have exercised the same powers under the authority of this and the special act if they had respectively been under no disability."

By sect. 8, the power to enfranchise copyholds, and "the power to release lands from any rent-charge or incumbrance, and to agree for the apportionment of any such rent-charge or incumbrance, shall extend to and may lawfully be exercised by every party hereinbefore authorized to sell and convey or release lands to the promoters of the undertaking."

Notice of Intention to take Land.]—By 8 & 9 Vict. c. 18, s. 18, "when the promoters of the undertaking shall require to purchase or take any of the lands which by this or the special act, or any act incorporated therewith, they are authorized to purchase or take, they shall give *notice thereof to all the parties interested* in such lands, or to the parties enabled by this act to sell and convey or release the same, or such of the said parties as shall, after diligent inquiry, be known to the promoters of the undertaking, and by such notice shall demand from such parties the particulars of their estate and interest in such lands, and of the claims made by them in respect thereof; and every such notice shall *state the particulars of the land so required*, and that the promoters of the undertaking are willing to treat for the purchase thereof, and as to the compensation to be made to all parties for the damage that may be sustained by them by reason of the execution of the works."

A notice when given pursuant to sect. 18 operates as a *binding contract* on the company to take the particular land therein described, at a price to be fixed by agreement, or by arbitration, or by a jury, or by justices, according to the statute, and the company cannot afterwards withdraw the notice, or rescind such contract, except by consent. *Doo* v. *The London and Croydon Railway Company*, 1 Railw. Cas. 257; 3 Jur. 258; *Salmon* v. *Randall*, 3 Myl. & Cr. 439; *Edinburgh, Perth and Dundee Railway Company* v. *Leven*, 1 Macqueen, H. L. Cas. 284; *Stone* v. *The Commercial Railway Company*, 4 Myl. & Cr. 124; 1 Railw. Cas. 400, 401; *Rex* v. *Hungerford Market Company*, 4 B. & Adol. 327; 1 N. & M. 112; *Rex* v. *The Commissioners of Market Street, Manchester*, 4 B. & Adol. 333, n.; *Tawney* v. *The Lynn and Ely Railway Company*, 4 Railw. Cas. 615; 16 Law J., N. S., Chanc. 282. The notice does not amount to an *actual taking* of the land therein mentioned, within the meaning of sect. 68, post, 595; but only to a contract to take. *Burtinshaw* v. *The Birmingham and Oxford Junction Railway Company*, 5 Exch. 475, 484; 6 Railw. Cas. 609. The company may be compelled by a mandamus to have the amount of the purchase or compensation money ascertained by arbitration, or by a jury, or by justices, according to the statute: *Reg.* v. *The Birmingham and Oxford Junction Railway Company*, 15 Q. B. 634; *Rex* v. *Hungerford Market Company*, 4 B. & Adol. 327; 1 N. & M. 112; *Reg.* v. *The Eastern Counties Railway Company*, 2 Q. B.

347; 1 Gale & D. 589; *Reg.* v. *The London and Greenwich Railway Company*, 3 Q. B. 166; *Reg.* v. *The Great Northern Railway Company*, 14 Q. B. 25; Arch. Crown Off. Prac. 257: provided there have been a sufficient demand and refusal. *Ex parte Senior, In re The South Yorkshire, Doncaster and Goole Railway Company*, 7 Dowl. & L. 86. An action of debt will afterwards lie to recover the amount so assessed, with costs: *Richardson* v. *The South-Eastern Railway Company*, 2 Low. M. & P. 409; 11 C. B. 154; *S. C.* (in error), 15 C. B. 810: or to recover the amount awarded by the arbitrator or umpire. *Gould* v. *The Staffordshire Potteries Waterworks Company*, 5 Exch. 214; 1 Low. M. & P. 264. But the company cannot be compelled to complete the purchase by a bill in equity for a specific performance of the contract created by the notice: the remedy provided by the statute must be pursued. *Hill* v. *The Great Northern Railway Company*, 24 Law J., N. S., Chanc. 212, Kindersley, V. C.; see *contra, Walker* v. *The Eastern Counties Railway Company*, 6 Hare, 594.

A notice to take certain land will not prevent the company from giving a second or subsequent notice to take *other* land. *Stamps* v. *The Birmingham and Stour Valley Railway Company*, 7 Hare, 251; 2 Phil. R. 673; 6 Railw. Cas. 123; 17 Law J., N. S., Chanc. 431; *Simpson* v. *The Lancaster and Carlisle Railway Company*, 15 Simon, 580; Shelf. Railw. 260 (3rd ed.).

" No party shall at any time be required to sell or convey to the promoters of the undertaking *a part only of any house or other building or manufactory*, if such party be willing and able to sell and convey the whole thereof." 8 & 9 Vict. c. 18, s. 92. If such party, upon being served with a notice to take part, give the promoters a counter notice to take the whole, the latter are thereupon absolved from the contract created by their notice, and *have the option* to take the whole or none. *Reg.* v. *The London and South-Western Railway Company*, 12 Q. B. 775; 5 Railw. Cas. 669; and see Shelf. Railw. 345 (3rd ed.); *Barker* v. *The North Staffordshire Railway Company*, 2 De Gex & Sm. 55; 5 Railw. Cas. 412.

Conveyances.]—The *legal* estate in any land agreed to be taken does not vest in the company until a conveyance thereof is executed pursuant to 8 & 9 Vict. c. 18, s. 81, or a deed poll pursuant to sects. 85 or 87. *Doe d. Robins* v. *The Warwick Canal Company*, 2 Bing. N. C. 483; 2 Scott, 7; *The Earl of Harborough* v. *Shardlow*, 7 M. & W. 87; *Dimes* v. *The Grand Junction Railway Company*, 9 Q. B. 469; *Patrick* v. *The Duke of Beaufort*, 6 Exch. 498; but see *Doe d. Payne* v. *The Bristol and Exeter Railway Company*, 6 M. & W. 320; *Bruce* v. *Willis*, 11 A. & E. 463; 3 P. & D. 220; *Doe d. Armitstead* v. *The North Staffordshire Railway Company*, 16 Q. B. 526; *Doe d. Hudson* v. *The Leeds and Bradford Railway Company, Id.* 796. A court of equity will not by injunction restrain the company from taking possession of land to which they are entitled, but of which they have not obtained any conveyance. *Williams* v. *The South Wales Railway Company*, 3 De Gex & Sm. 354.

Any conveyance duly made in pursuance of the act " shall operate to merge all terms of years attendant by express declaration, or by construction of law, on the estate or interest so thereby conveyed, and to bar and to destroy all such estates tail, and all other estates, rights, titles, remainders, reversions, limitations, trusts and interests what-soever of and in the lands comprised in such conveyances which shall have been purchased or compensated for by the consideration therein mentioned ; but although terms of years be thereby merged, they shall *in equity* afford the same protection as if they had been kept on foot, and assigned to a trustee for the promoters of the undertaking to attend the reversion and inheritance." 8 & 9 Vict. c. 18, s. 81.

A conveyance of copyholds must be inrolled. Sect. 95. As to the fines and fees thereupon payable to the lord and steward respectively, see *The Ecclesiastical Commissioners for England* v. *The London and South-Western Railway Company*, 14 C. B. 743 ; *Cooper* v. *The Norfolk Railway Company*, 3 Exch. 546 ; 6 Railw. Cas. 94, *S. C.* A conveyance from the copyholder only will not affect the rights or interests of the lord. *Dimes* v. *Grand Junction Railway Company*, 9 Q. B. 469 ; 5 Railw. Cas. 34 ; and see *Grand Junction Canal Company* v. *Dimes*, 15 Simon, 402 ; 2 Mac. & Gor. 285 ; 2 Hall & Tw. 92. The purchase of a long term of years will not bar or affect the reversion in fee. *Rex* v. *Stainforth and Keadby Canal Company*, 1 M. & S. 32 ; *Doe* d. *Patrick* v. *Duke of Beaufort*, 6 Exch. 498. On the other hand, the purchase of a reversion in fee will not affect or prejudice any previous term or other estate. *Doe* d. *Hutchinson* v. *The Manchester, Bury and Rossendale Railway Company*, 14 M. & W. 687, 689.

Where property of a married woman is taken and sold under the compulsory powers of an act, no inquiry as to whether any provision has been made in lieu of the interests given up need be made. *In re Foster*, 7 C. B. 120.

Entry on Lands.]—By 8 & 9 Vict. c. 18, s. 84, "the promoters of the undertaking shall not, except by consent of the owners and occu-piers, enter upon any lands which shall be required to be purchased or permanently used for the purposes and under the powers of this or the special act until they shall have either *paid to every party having any interest in such lands, or deposited in the Bank,* in manner herein mentioned, the purchase-money or compensation agreed or awarded to be paid *to such parties respectively for their respective interests therein:* provided always, that for the purpose merely of surveying and taking levels of such lands, and of probing or boring to ascertain the nature of the soil, and of setting out the line of the works, it shall be lawful for the promoters of the undertaking, after giving not less than three, nor more than fourteen days' notice to the owners or occupiers thereof, to enter upon such lands without previous consent, making compensation for the damage thereby occasioned to the owners or occupiers thereof."

The concluding proviso does not render it necessary for the com-pany to make compensation *before* commencing the works occasioning the damage. *Hutton* v. *The London and South-Western Railway Company*, 7 Hare, 259 ; 13 Jur. 486 ; *Lister* v. *Lobley*, 7 A. & E. 124 ; *Paddock* v. *Forrester*, 1 Dowl., N. S., 527 ; Shelf. Railw. 334 (3rd ed.) While the damage is *in progress bonâ fide*, the court will not award a madamus for compensation. *Ex parte Parkes*, 9 Dowl. 614.

Sect. 16 allows the company to enter *for temporary purposes*, to make accommodation works *necessary* or *convenient* for the purposes of the railway. *Sadd* v. *The Maldon, Witham and Braintree Rail-

way Company, 6 Exch. 143; *Beardmore* v. *The London and North-Western Railway Company*, 1 Mac. & Gord. 112. But they cannot enter and take land *for permanent purposes* without first making compensation. *Ramsden* v. *The Manchester, South Junction and Altrincham Railway Company*, 1 Exch. 723.

Sect. 85 allows the promoters to enter upon lands before any purchase thereof and without consent, upon making a deposit in the bank, and giving a bond by way of security as therein mentioned. This mode of proceeding was successfully adopted in *Doe* d. *Payne* v. *The Bristol and Exeter Railway Company*, 6 M. & W. 320. For the form of bond, see *Hosking* v. *Phillips*, 3 Exch. 168; 5 Railw. C. 560; 12 Jur. 1030; *Poynder* v. *The Great· Northern Railway Company*, 2 Phil. C. C. 330; 5 Railw. C. 196; 16 Sim. 3; *Barker* v. *The North Staffordshire Railway Company*, 2 De Gex & S. 55; 5 Railw. C. 412; *Willey* v. *The South-Eastern Railway Company*, 1 Mac. & Gor. 58; 1 Hall & Tw. 56; Shelf. Railw. 335 (3rd ed.). An entry under this section is not considered as an exercise of their compulsory powers. *Marquis of Salisbury* v. *The Great Northern Railway Company*, 21 Law J., N. S., Q. B. 185. The ascertaining the amount of compensation after lands have been entered upon and taken under this section, is no exercise of a compulsory power on the part of the company. *Doe* d. *Armitstead* v. *North Staffordshire Railway Company*, 16 Q. B. 526; 20 Law J., N. S., Q. B. 249; 15 Jur. 944. Where a railway company have complied with the provisions of this section, and have entered upon the land within the prescribed period for exercising their compulsory powers, their continuance in possession after the prescribed period, without having the compensation assessed and the land conveyed to them, is not unlawful, and an ejectment cannot be maintained against them under such circumstances. *S. C.* The 68th section applies to lands entered upon and used pursuant to this section; and the landowner is in such case bound to initiate proceedings for settling the compensation. *S. C.; Doe* d. *Hudson* v. *The Leeds and Bradford Railway Company*, 16 Q. B. 796. He should give notice of the particulars and amount of his claim, and cannot file a bill in equity for an injunction. *Adams* v. *The London and Blackwall Railway Company*, 2 Mac. & Gor. 118; 19 Law J., N. S., Chanc. 557.

Compensation for Lands taken or injuriously affected.]—By 8 & 9 Vict. c. 18, s. 68, "if any party shall be entitled to any compensation in respect of any lands, or of any interest therein, which shall *have been taken* for or injuriously affected by the execution of the works, and for which the promoters of the undertaking *shall not have made satisfaction* under the provisions of this or the special act, or any act incorporated therewith, and if the compensation claimed in such case shall exceed the sum of fifty pounds, such party may have the same settled either by arbitration or by the verdict of a jury, as he shall think fit; and if such party desire to have the same settled by arbitration, it shall be lawful for him to give notice in writing to the promoters of the undertaking of such his desire, stating in such notice the nature of the interest in such lands in respect of which he claims compensation, and the amount of the compensation so claimed therein; and unless the promoters of the undertaking be willing to pay the amount of compensation so claimed, and shall enter into a written agreement for that purpose within twenty-one days after the receipt of any such notice from any party so entitled, the same shall be settled by arbitration in the manner herein provided; or if the party so entitled as aforesaid desire to have such question of compensation settled by jury, it shall be lawful for him to give notice in writing of such his desire (a) to the promoters of the undertaking, stating such particulars as aforesaid, and unless the promoters of the undertaking be willing to pay the amount of compensation so claimed, and enter into a written agreement for that purpose, they shall, within twenty-one days after the receipt of such notice, issue their warrant to the sheriff to summon a jury for settling the same in the manner herein provided, and in default thereof they shall be liable to pay to the party so entitled as aforesaid the amount of compensation so claimed, and the same may be recovered by him, with costs, by action in any of the superior courts."

To bring a case within this section, the company must have taken *actual possession* of the land; a mere notice of their intention to take amounts merely to a contract to take (*ante*, 592), but not to an actual taking; *Burkenshaw* v. *The Birmingham and Oxford Junction Railway Company*, 5 Exch. 475; 6 Railw. Cas. 609; or the land must have been injuriously affected by *something done* by the company under or by virtue of their act. *Glover* v. *The North Staffordshire Railway Company*, 16 Q. B. 912; 20 Law J., N. S., Q. B. 376; 15 Jur. 673; *Bland* v. *Crowley*, 6 Exch. 532; Shelf. Railw. 243, 303 (3rd ed.). For any thing done which is not authorized by their act, the party injured may maintain an action of trespass; *Scales* v. *Pickering*,, 1 Moo. & P. 195; 4 Bing. 448; *Ramsden* v. *The Manchester, South Junction and Altrincham Railway Company*, 1 Exch. 723; or case (according to the nature of the injury). *Wilks* v. *The Hungerford Market Company*, 2 Bing. N. C. 281; *Wiggins* v. *Boddington*, 3 C. & P. 544; *Jones* v. *Bird*, 5 B. & A. 837; *Turner* v. *The Sheffield and Rotherham Railway Company*, 10 M. & W. 425; *Pilgrim* v. *The Southampton and Dorchester Railway Company*, 7 C. B. 205; *Worsley* v. *The South Devon Railway Company*, 20 Law J., N. S., Q. B. 254; *Lawrence* v. *The Great Northern Railway Company, Id.* 293; *Abraham* v. *The Great Northern Railway Company, Id.* 322.

A party entitled to any estate or interest in land whereof the company have *taken possession* pursuant to their acts, should serve them with a notice of the particulars and amount of his claim: he should not file a bill in equity. *Adams* v. *The London and Blackwall Railway Company*, 2 Mac. & Gor. 118; 19 Law J., N. S., Chanc. 557.

If the company dispute the claimant's title to *any* compensation, and they have entered into possession of the land, they should take care to issue their warrant to the sheriff within twenty-one days after receipt of the claimant's notice, otherwise they will be liable to pay him the *whole amount as claimed*, with costs. *Glover* v. *The North Staffordshire Railway Company*, 16 Q. B. 912; *Burkenshaw* v. *The Birmingham and Oxford Junction Railway Company*, 5 Exch. 475; 6 Railw. Cas. 609.

(a) If he desire to have a *special* jury, that should be mentioned in the notice. *Railstone* v. *The York, Newcastle and Berwick Railway Company*, 15 Q. B. 404, 412.

The warrant should mention all those facts which are necessary to give the sheriff and jury jurisdiction to inquire as to the value of the land taken, or of the claimant's interest therein; but it need not state other preliminary facts as to which the sheriff and jury cannot inquire. *Ostler* v. *Cooke,* 13 Q. B. 143; *Reg.* v. *Justices of Worcestershire,* 3 E. & B. 477; *Doe* d. *Payne* v. *The Bristol and Exeter Railway Company,* 6 M. & W. 320.

The jury may find that the claimant has sustained *no damage whatever; Reg.* v. *The Lancaster and Preston Junction Railway Company,* 6 Q. B. 759; *Bradby* v. *The Southampton Local Board of Health,* 4 E. & B. 1014; but they have no power to inquire whether the party has any title to what he claims: they must assess the damages upon the principle that he is so entitled, otherwise their verdict and the judgment thereon may be brought up before the Queen's Bench upon a certiorari and quashed, as having been made without jurisdiction. *Reg.* v. *The London and North-Western Railway Company,* 3 E. & B. 443. So the jury or an arbitrator cannot determine whether the company are excused from the obligation to pay by any collateral matter, such as whether an agreement between the promoters and the claimant, whereby the promoters undertook to build a good and substantial wall, has been broken, or whether the breach of such agreement was the cause of the land being injuriously affected. *In re Byles and the Ipswich Dock Commissioners,* 11 Exch. 464; 25 Law J., N. S., Exch. 53; and see *Reg.* v. *The Metropolitan Commissioners of Sewers,* 1 E. & B. 694; *In re Bradby and The Local Board of Health for Southampton,* 4 E. & B. 1014. The claimant's title may be disputed in the subsequent action to recover the amount of the compensation assessed. *Cases supra.* For the form of declaration and pleas in such action, see *Glover* v. *The North Staffordshire Railway Company,* 16 Q. B. 912; *Railstone* v. *The York, Newcastle and Berwick Railway Company,* 15 Q. B. 404; *Richardson* v. *The South-Eastern Railway Company,* 11 C. B. 154; 2 Low. M. & P. 409; *S. C.* (in error), 15 C. B. 810.

Interests omitted to be purchased.]—By 8 & 9 Vict. c. 18, s. 124, "if at any time after the promoters of the undertaking shall have entered upon any lands which, under the provisions of this or the special act, or any act incorporated therewith, they were authorized to purchase, and which shall be permanently required for the purposes of the special act, any party shall appear to be entitled to any estate, right or interest in, or charge affecting such lands which the promoters of the undertaking shall *through mistake or inadvertence* have failed or omitted duly to purchase or to pay compensation for, then, whether the period allowed for the purchase of lands shall have expired or not, the promoters of the undertaking shall remain in the undisturbed possession of such lands, provided, within six months after notice of such estate, right, interest or charge, in case the same shall not be disputed by the promoters of the undertaking, or in case the same shall be disputed, then within six months after the right thereto shall have been finally established by law in favour of the party claiming the same, the promoters of the undertaking shall purchase or pay compensation for the same, and shall also pay to such party, or to any other party who may establish a right thereto, full compensation for the mesne profits or interest which would have accrued to such parties respectively in respect thereof, during the interval between the entry of the promoters of the undertaking thereon and the time of the payment of such purchase money or compensation by the promoters of the undertaking, so far as such mesne profits or interest may be recoverable in law or equity ; and such purchase money or compensation shall be agreed on or awarded and paid in like manner as according to the provisions of this act the same respectively would have been agreed on or awarded and paid in case the promoters of the undertaking had purchased such estate, right, interest or charge before their entering upon such land, or as near thereto as circumstances will admit."

This section applies to any land, estate or interest which the company have failed or omitted duly to purchase, *through mistake or inadvertence ;* as where they purchase the land from the wrong person, or by some oversight altogether omit to purchase any particular estate or interest. The company may proceed under this section to take and purchase the land within six months after judgment has been obtained against them in an ejectment; and a court of equity will not restrain them from so doing. *Hyde* v. *The Corporation of Manchester*, 5 De Gex & S. 249; 16 Jur. 189; 12 C. B. 474 ; *Webster* v. *The South-Eastern Railway Company*, 1 Simon, N. S., 272; 6 Railw. Cas. 698; 20 Law J., N. S., Chanc. 194.

By sect. 125, " In estimating the compensation to be given for any such last-mentioned lands, or any estate or interest in the same, or for any mesne profits thereof, the jury, or arbitrators, or justices, as the case may be, shall assess the same according to what they shall find to have been the value of such lands, estate or interest, and profits, at the time such lands were entered upon by the promoters of the undertaking, and without regard to any improvements or works made in the said lands by the promoters of the undertaking, and as though the works had not been constructed."

By sect. 126, " In addition to the said purchase money, compensation or satisfaction, and before the promoters of the undertaking shall become absolutely entitled to any such estate, interest or charge, or to have the same merged or extinguished for their benefit, they shall, when the right to any such estate, interest or charge shall have been disputed by the company, and determined in favour of the party claiming the same, pay the *full costs and expenses of any proceedings at law or in equity* for the determination or recovery of the same to the parties with whom any such litigation in respect thereof shall have taken place ; and such costs and expenses shall, in case the same shall be disputed, be settled by the proper officer of the court in which such litigation took place."

Full costs and expenses under this section mean as between attorney or solicitor and client. *Doe* d. *Hyde* v. *The Mayor, &c. of Manchester*, 12 C. B. 474.

Evidence for Plaintiff.]—In ejectment against a railway or other company for land, &c., taken by them for the purposes of their act, the plaintiff must prove *a legal right to actual possession* of the land claimed, or some part thereof, in like manner as in ordinary cases ; *ante*, 287 ; and it must appear that such title is not barred by the Statute of Limitations. *Ante*, 4.

Where the plaintiff relies upon the fact that the whole capital of the company had not been subscribed before they took his land, and consequently that they had no right to exercise their compulsory powers, the onus of proving such fact lies on him. *Doe* d. *Payne* v. *The Bristol and Exeter Railway Company*, 6 M. & W. 320, 340.

In the following cases the claimants have successfully maintained ejectment against railway companies. *Doe* d. *Patrick* v. *The Duke of Beaufort*, 6 Exch. 498; *Doe* d. *Hutchinson* v. *The Manchester, Bury and Rossendale Railway Company*, 2 Car. & K. 162; 14 M. & W. 687; *Hyde* v. *The Mayor, &c. of Manchester*, 12 C. B. 474; *Doe* d. *Robins* v. *The Warwick Canal Company*, 2 Bing. N. C. 483; 2 Scott, 7; *Dimes* v. *The Grand Junction Canal Company*, 9 Q. B. 469. But in other cases the actions have been unsuccessful. *Doe* d. *Payne* v. *The Bristol and Exeter Railway Company*, 6 M. & W. 320; *Doe* d. *Armitstead* v. *The North Staffordshire Railway Company*, 16 Q. B. 526; *Doe* d. *Hudson* v. *The Leeds and Bradford Railway Company*, *Id.* 796; *Doe* d. *Wawn* v. *Horn*, 3 M. & W. 333; but see 5 M. & W. 564.

Ejectment will not lie against a railway company by a mortgagee "of the undertaking, and of the rates, tolls and other sums arising under the act," for no land or building is conveyed by such mortgage. *Doe* d. *Myatt* v. *The St. Helens and Runcorn Gap Company*, 2 Q. B. 364; 1 Gale & D. 663; 2 Railw. Cas. 756. But it is otherwise where the mortgage is of toll-houses, toll-gates, &c. *Doe* d. *Banks* v. *Booth*, 2 Bos. & P. 219; *Doe* d. *Thompson* v. *Lediard*, 4 B. & Adol. 137; *Doe* d. *Watton* v. *Penfold*, 3 Q. B. 757; *Doe* d. *Levy* v. *Horne*, *Id.* 760, 766; *Horton* v. *The Westminster Improvement Commissioners*, 7 Exch. 780.

If a legal title to *actual possession* cannot be proved, but only a legal remainder or reversion, or an equitable estate or interest, the claimant should not proceed by ejectment, but should claim compensation, and proceed against the company in due time, pursuant to 8 & 9 Vict. c. 18, s. 68 (*ante*, 595). Even where a legal title to actual possession can be proved, it is generally more advisable to claim compensation under that section, than to proceed by ejectment; *Jubb* v. *The Hull Dock Company*, 9 Q. B. 443; unless the claimant has been guilty of unnecessary delay. *Rex* v. *The Stainforth and Keadby Canal Company*, 1 M. & S. 32; *Rex* v. *The Cockermouth Inclosure Commissioners*, 1 B. & Adol. 378. If the company failed or omitted to purchase the plaintiff's estate or interest *otherwise than by mistake or inadvertence* (*ante*, 597), an ejectment may be preferable; or if the company have *wilfully* entered, contrary to the provisions of the act, and the claimant was the party then in possession, he may maintain an action for penalties. 8 & 9 Vict. c. 18, s. 89; *Hutchinson* v. *The Manchester, Bury and Rossendale Railway Company*, 15 M. & W. 314.

Where a railway company agreed with the landlord for part of a farm, and afterwards by a mistake he, on the same day, conveyed the part to the company, and granted a lease of the whole to a tenant, and a question arose whether the landlord or the company should make compensation to the tenant, but the company took possession, and the tenant brought ejectment: held, that the company could maintain a suit to stay the ejectment and ascertain the rights, and an inquiry was directed. *Norwich Railway Company* v. *Wodehouse*, 11 Beav. 382.

We have already considered in what manner a writ in ejectment is to be served upon a railway or other company. *Ante*, 108.

Evidence and Points for Defendants.]—The company may contend that the plaintiff's evidence is insufficient on some material point. They may also produce contradictory evidence. They may prove an outstanding term, or a tenancy from year to year vested in any third person; *Doe* d. *Wawn* v. *Horn*, 3 M. & W. 333 ; or a conveyance to the company of the plaintiff's estate and interest, made either by the plaintiff himself or by some other person enabled by statute to sell and convey the same on his behalf (*ante*, 591) ; or a deed poll executed by the company pursuant to 8 & 9 Vict. c. 18, s. 85, or s. 87. They may prove, that, although no conveyance has been actually executed, yet such proceedings have taken place under their act that they are entitled to withhold possession from the claimant; and that his only remedy is to obtain compensation pursuant to the statute. *Doe* d. *Armitstead* v. *The North Staffordshire Railway Company*, 16 Q. B. 526 ; *Doe* d. *Hudson* v. *The Leeds and Bradford Railway Company*, *Id.* 796 ; *Doe* d. *Payne* v. *The Bristol and Exeter Railway Company*, 6 M. & W. 320. They may prove any legal estate *prior* to that of the claimant, vested in them or in any other person, whether they derive title through or under such other person or not: but to obtain the protection of a term of years, which has become merged by the conveyance to them, they must go into a court of equity. *Ante*, 594.

If the facts be such that no defence can be established at law, nor relief obtained in equity, the company, having *through mistake or inadvertence* failed or omitted duly to purchase, or to pay compensation for, the plaintiff's estate or interest, pursuant to the statute, they should within six months after the verdict, or at the latest within six months after final judgment, take all necessary steps and proceedings to purchase, and actually purchase, the plaintiff's estate or interest, pursuant to sects. 124—126. *Ante*, 597.

CHAPTER LXV.

BY A RECTOR.

In ejectment by a rector to recover possession of his rectory, or of the parsonage house, glebe or tithes, the plaintiff must prove.—

1. That he has been *presented, admitted, instituted and inducted :* Gilb. Ev. 228; *Dr. Hasker's case,* Comb. 202; *Snow* d. *Crawley* v. *Phillips,* 1 Sid. 220; *Doe* d. *Watson* v. *Fletcher,* 8 B. & C. 25: but he need not show a title in his patron, for institution and induction, although upon the presentation of a stranger, are sufficient to put the rightful patron to his *quare impedit.* Bull. N. P. 105.

Where the institution purports to be made "on the cession" of the previous incumbent (who is still living, and from whom the defendant obtained possession), that is sufficient *primâ facie* evidence of such cession having been duly made, it having been acted on. *Doe* d. *Kerby* v. *Carter,* Ry. & Moo. 237, Littledale, J. Where the plaintiff was presented by the crown on the ground that the defendant had obtained his appointment by simony, and the plaintiff was instituted and inducted on such presentation, and managed, notwithstanding impediments, *to read himself in* so as to comply with the statute 13 & 14 Car. 2, c. 6, s. 1 : held, that ejectment was maintainable, notwithstanding the objection that the church being full, the defendant could only be removed by *quare impedit. Doe* d. *Watson* v. *Fletcher,* 8 B. & C. 25 ; and see *Snow* d. *Crawley* v. *Phillips,* 1 Sid. 220. But, generally speaking, when the plaintiff has been for some time in undisputed possession as rector, he need not prove that he subscribed and read the thirty-nine articles, and administered the sacraments within the respective times prescribed by the statute 13 Eliz. c. 12, s. 3, for, in the absence of proof to the contrary, it shall be presumed that he acted lawfully rather than otherwise. *Powell* v. *Milburn,* 3 Wils. 355, 366; 2 W. Black. 851; *Monke* v. *Butler,* 1 Roll. R. 83. In an ejectment tried before Lord Chief Justice Wilmot at Salisbury, a prebendary sought to recover a house built upon his prebendal site ; the prebendary was called upon to prove the several requisites before mentioned; the chief justice said, "these shall be presumed upon sound principles of law." Cited 3 Wils. 366. After long possession of a benefice with cure of souls (*ex. gr.* fifteen years), it will be presumed that a rector was inducted, and duly read the thirty-nine articles. *Chapman* v. *Beard,* 3 Anstr. 942. Proof by several of his parishioners that they *generally* attended the plaintiff's church during divine service for two months next after his first appointment, and never heard him read the thirty-nine articles, is not sufficient to rebut the above presumption. *S. C.* It is not necessary to prove that before and at the time of his presentation the claimant was in holy orders; *Dr. Hasker's case,* Comb. 202 ; and per Holt, J., "if he is *laicus* the presentation is not void,

D D

only voidable, that he was entitled to possession having established his temporal title to the thing, and his religious or political title shall be presumed." *S. C.*, cited 3 Wilson, 367.

Presentation may be made orally or by writing. Co. Lit. 120 a. Formerly it could not be proved by the person making the presentation, although he were only the grantee of the avoidance, because of his supposed interest. Bull. N. P. 105; but now see 6 & 7 Vict. c. 85.

Institution may be proved by the letters testimonial of institution; or by the official entry in the public register of the diocese. Ad. Eject. 257. A bishop's register of presentations and institutions is kept for the use of all persons claiming title to livings in his diocese, and they have a legal right to inspect them. *Rex* v. *Bishop of Ely*, 8 B. & C. 112; *S. C.* nom. *Finch* v. *Bishop of Ely*, 2 Man. & Ry. 127.

Induction may be proved either by some person present at the ceremony, or by the indorsement on the mandate of the ordinary to induct, or by the return of the mandate, if any has been made. Ad. Eject. 257. Upon proof of possession of the benefice for a long period, *ex. gr.* fifteen years, induction and the due reading of the thirty-nine articles will be presumed. *Chapman* v. *Beard*, 3 Anstr. 942.

Proof of payment by the defendant as a parishioner, to the plaintiff as rector, of tithes in respect of lands situate in the parish, is *primâ facie* evidence of the plaintiff's title as against the defendant. *Chapman* v. *Beard, supra*. But an ejectment for a parsonage and glebe will not be supported by showing that the plaintiff entered and took the tithes belonging thereto, because the tithes and the rectory are not the same. *Hems* v. *Stroud*, Latch, 61.

If the defendant can be shown to have been a tenant *of the plaintiff* in respect of the property sought to be recovered, and that such tenancy has expired, or been duly determined by notice to quit or otherwise, that will be sufficient, without further proof of the plaintiff's title. *Ante*, 229, 231. A tenant of glebe land who has *paid rent* to the incumbent will not be permitted to prove a simoniacal presentation of the plaintiff in order to avoid his title. *Cooke, clerk* v. *Loxley*, 5 T. R. 4. In such cases the defendant is estopped from disputing the plaintiff's title. *Ante*, 213.

A lease of a rectory house, &c. by a rector becomes void by 13 Eliz. c. 20, by his non-residence for eighty days, of which a stranger, or the rector himself, may take advantage, and there is no distinction in this respect between a demise by deed or by parol. *Doe* d. *Crisp* v. *Barber*, 2 T. R. 749; *Frogmorton* d. *Fleming* v. *Scott*, 2 East, 467. A rector's lessee holding under a lease which has become void by the rector's non-residence cannot maintain ejectment, even against a stranger who enters without any title whatever; *Doe* d. *Crisp* v. *Borber, supra;* but he may maintain trespass. *Graham* v. *Peat*, 1 East, 244.

Upon the death of an incumbent leases and tenancies from year to year created by him become void as against his successor. *Doe* d. *Kerby* v. *Carter*, Ry. & Moo. 237, Littledale, J.; *Doe* d. *Tennyson* v. *Lord Yarmouth*, 1 Bing. 24; 7 Moore, 258. A lease by the incumbent of a benefice, in whatever terms it is framed, operates in law as a demise so long only as he continues incumbent, for he could not pass a greater interest. *Wheeler* v. *Heydon*, Cro. Jac. 328; Bulst. 83; Brownl. 135, *S. C.*; *Price* v. *Williams*, Tyr. & Gr. 197; 1 M. & W. 6. But if the successor receive rent from the tenants, or even suffer them to remain in undisturbed possession for eight or nine months, a new tenancy from year to year as between him and them will be implied ; and such tenancy must be duly determined by notice to quit or otherwise before he can maintain ejectment. *Doe* d. *Cates* v. *Somerville,* 6 B. & C. 126 ; 9 D. & R. 100. But the lease itself is not thereby confirmed for the whole term therein expressed to be granted. The perpetual curate of a curacy augmented by the governors of Queen Anne's bounty, made a lease for years of mines, &c., which was confirmed by the ordinary and immediate patron, but was not confirmed by the patron paramount. The successor of the perpetual curate accepted the rent reserved, for five years, and inspected the mines under the powers contained in the lease : held, that the lease was *void* at common law for want of confirmation by the patron paramount, and therefore was not set up by the acceptance of rent by the lessor's successor in the curacy. *Doe* d. *Bramwall* v. *Collinge,* 7 C. B. 939 ; 18 Law J., N. S., C. B. 305.

If a lease be made by a rector in pursuance of a power conferred by act of parliament or otherwise, and an entire rent reserved, and any part of the premises could not be legally demised, the whole demise is void as against his successor. *Doe* d. *Griffiths* v. *Lloyd,* 3 Esp. 78 ; and see *Neale* v. *Mackenzie,* 1 M. & W. 747. But if the reversion expectant, on the determination of *such* a lease, be sold pursuant to the Land Tax Redemption Acts, the sale cannot be avoided by a subsequent rector. *Doe* d. *Strikland* v. *Woodward,* 1 Exch. 273 ; 17 Law J., N. S., Exch. 1.

2. That the property sought to be recovered, or some part thereof, forms part of the property belonging to the rectory. An entry of the receipt of ecclesiastical dues in the books of a deceased rector is evidence for his successor, on the ground of an absence of all interest to mis-state the fact in the rector making such entry, which could not possibly be evidence for himself. *Per cur.* in *Roe* d. *Brune* v. *Rawlings,* 7 East, 290 ; *Anon.,* Bunbury, 46, 180.

3. It must appear that the claimant or some of his predecessors have been in possession or receipt of rents within the time allowed by the Statute of Limitations, 3 & 4 Will. 4, c. 27, s. 29. *Ante,* 25. This should generally be proved by showing the actual possession and enjoyment thereof, or the receipt of the rents and profits thereof, as rector, by the claimant or by some of his predecessors.

Evidence and Points for Defendant.]—The defendant may contend that the plaintiff's evidence is insufficient in some material point. *Ante,* 601. He may also produce contradictory evidence. He may show that the plaintiff's appointment was obtained by simony, and was consequently void. *Snow* d. *Crawley* v. *Phillips,* 1 Sid. 220 ; *Doe* d. *Watson* v. *Fletcher,* 8 B. & C. 25. But a tenant of glebe land, who has *paid rent* to the incumbent, is estopped from proving that his title was void for simony. *Cooke, clerk,* v. *Loxley,* 5 T. R. 4. If the plaintiff be a *lessee* of the rector, the defendant may show (*inter alia*) that the plaintiff's lease has become void under 13 Eliz. c. 20, by reason of the rector's non-residence for eighty days. *Doe* d. *Crisp* v. *Barber,* 2 T. R. 749. If the defendant obtained possession as tenant to a previous incumbent, he is not thereby estopped from denying the title of the plaintiff as the new incumbent. He may also prove a new tenancy from year to year, as between the plaintiff and himself, created by payment of rent, or otherwise, since the death of the previous incumbent. *Doe* d. *Cates* v. *Somerville*, 6 B. & C. 126. But in the absence of proof of a new tenancy express or implied the incumbent of a living may maintain ejectment against parties in possession of the glebe lands, though the current year of a tenancy from year to year, created by his predecessor, is unexpired. *Doe* d. *Kerby* v. *Carter*, Ry. & Moo. 237, Littledale, J.

The vicar of a parish cannot recover the school house by ejectment, although it may have been built on what is evidently part of the churchyard, if it appear that the house was built on the site of a very old school house, the site of which might have been granted before the disabling statutes ; but if part of a house is built on ground taken from the churchyard recently, the vicar may recover that part. *Doe* d. *Coyle* v. *Cole*, 6 C. & P. 359.

Where a vicar brings ejectment claiming in right of his vicarage, a letter written by a former vicar is admissible in evidence for the defendant ; and a witness for the plaintiff may be asked as to what is inscribed on a tablet fixed up in the church. *S. C.*

Although a preacher at an endowed meeting house has such an interest in the office and its emoluments as will entitle him to a mandamus, if disturbed in the use of the pulpit, he has not such a legal interest in the endowment as will entitle him to retain possession *against the trustees* of such endowment. *Doe* d. *Evans* v. *Jones*, 5 Man. & Ry. 753. The minister of a dissenting chapel is generally only a tenant at will to the trustees, and his interest may be determined by a demand of possession, without any notice to quit. *Doe* d. *Jones* v. *Jones*, 10 B. & C. 718 ; 5 Man. & Ry. 616 ; *Doe* d. *Nicholl* v. *M'Kaeg*, 10 B. & C. 721 ; 5 Man. & Ry. 620 ; *ante*, 451.

CHAPTER LXVI.

BY CHURCHWARDENS AND OVERSEERS.

———

By 59 Geo. 3, c. 12, s. 17, it is enacted, "that all buildings, lands and hereditaments, which shall be purchased, hired or taken on lease by the churchwardens and overseers of the poor of any parish, by the authority and for any of the purposes of this act, shall be conveyed, demised and assured to the churchwardens and overseers of the poor of every such parish respectively, and their successors, in trust for the parish; and such *churchwardens and overseers* of the poor, and their successors, shall and may and they are hereby empowered to accept, take and hold, *in the nature of a body corporate,* for and on behalf of the parish, all such buildings, lands and hereditaments, *and also all other buildings, lands and hereditaments belonging to such parish;* and all actions, suits, indictments and other proceedings for or in relation to any such buildings, land or hereditaments, or the rent thereof, or for or in relation to any other buildings, lands or hereditaments belonging to such parish, or the rent thereof, and in all actions and proceedings upon or in relation to any bond to be given for the faithful execution of the office of an assistant overseer, it shall be sufficient *to name* the churchwardens and overseers of the poor for the time being, *describing them as the churchwardens and overseers of the poor* of the parish for which they shall act, and naming such parish; and no action or suit, indictment or other proceeding shall cease, abate, or be discontinued, quashed, defeated or impeded by the death of the churchwardens and overseers named in such proceedings, or the deaths or death of any of them, or by their removal or the removal of any of them from, or the expiration of, their respective offices."

Before the above act the reversion of parish property demised by churchwardens and overseers did not vest in their successors without an assignment, and consequently there was often considerable difficulty in recovering the rent reserved, or the possession of the property. *Doe* d. *Grundy* v. *Clarke,* 14 East, 488; *Phillips* v. *Pearce,* 5 B. & C. 433; 8 D. & R. 53. On the other hand, demises of parish property made by the churchwardens and overseers before the passing of the act passed no estate for the term thereby expressed to be granted, and the lessees might be treated as mere tenants from year to year, and ejected after due notice to quit. *Doe* d. *Higgs* v. *Terry,* 4 A. & E. 274; 5 N. & M. 556; *Doe* d. *Hobbs* v. *Cockell,* 4 A. & E. 478; 6 N. & M. 179. The main object of the enactment was to remedy inconveniences of the above nature.

The above enactment does not extend to copyholds; *Doe* d. *Bailey* v. *Foster,* 3 C. B. 215; *In re Paddington Charities,* 8 Simon, 629; nor to freeholds vested in *known* trustees: *The Churchwardens and Overseers of St. Nicholas, Deptford,* v. *Sketchley,* 8 Q. B. 394, over-ruling *Rumball* v. *Munt, Id.* 382: but it does apply where the heir of the last surviving trustee is unknown, and it is doubtful in whom the legal estate is vested. *Doe* d. *Jackson* v. *Hiley*, 10 B. & C. 885; 5 Man. & R. 706; explained in *Allason* v. *Stark*, 1 P. & D. 183, 192; 9 A. & E. 255, *S. C.*

It has been held that a demise for ninety-nine years *to a committee*, of a house and premises, for the purpose of converting them into a poor house for the use of the parish, vests in the churchwardens and overseers of the parish by virtue of the statute. *Alderman* v. *Neate*, 4 M. & W. 704. But a demise to churchwardens and overseers *jointly with other persons*, *ex. gr.*, the surveyors of the highways, is not within the statute. *Uthwatt* v. *Elkins*, 13 M. & W. 772.

Lands devised upon special trusts *for other than parish purposes* are not within the statute. *Allason* v. *Stark*, 9 A. & E. 255; 1 P. & D. 183. Therefore where lands are devised for the relief of the most poor and needy people of good life and conversation of a parish, and for putting out poor boys apprentices, they do not constitute parish property, nor vest in the churchwardens and overseers of the parish. *Allason* v. *Stark*, *supra*; and see *Cankell* v. *The Windsor Union*, 4 Bing. N. C. 348; 5 Scott, 716. But the statute vests in the churchwardens and overseers of the parish all the buildings, lands and hereditaments *belonging to the parish*, not merely where the rents and profits are applicable to the relief of the poor, but where they are applicable to those purposes for which church rates are levied. *Doe* d. *Jackson* v. *Hiley*, 10 B. & C. 885; 5 M. & R. 706.

Property to which the above enactment applies vests in the churchwardens and overseers of the poor as a *quasi corporation;* but they are not made a complete body corporate. They are merely empowered " to accept, take and hold in the nature of a body corporate." They may therefore accept a demise without using any common seal ; and a demise made to them by their names of office (without mentioning their Christian or surnames) is sufficient. *Smith* v. *Adkins*, 8 M. & W. 362; 1 Dowl. N. S. 129. There must, however, be officers of *both* sorts before parish property will vest in any of them. Therefore where two overseers were appointed, one of whom was afterwards appointed (by custom) sole churchwarden: held, that the act did not vest parish property in them. *Woodcock* v. *Gibson*, 4 B. & C. 462; *Id.* 464, Bayley, J.; and see *Rex* v. *All Saints, Derby*, 13 East, 143. A demise of parish property by the churchwardens only is inoperative. *Phillips* v. *Pearce*, 5 B. & C. 433; 8 D. & R. 43. So a demise by one of the overseers is insufficient. *Doe* d. *Landsdell* v. *Gower*, 17 Q. B. 589. But it would seem that a lease not under seal, for less than three years, may be made in the names and on behalf of the churchwardens and overseers by any one of them, with the authority and consent of the others. *S. C.*

Although a parish forms part of a union under 4 & 5 Will. 4, c. 76, the parish land is not divested out of the churchwardens and overseers so as to disable them from bringing ejectment, either by sect. 21 of that act, or by the 5 & 6 Will. 4, c. 69, s. 3. *Doe* d. *Norton* v. *Webster*, 12 A. & E. 442; 4 P. & D. 270. " There is no transfer of the estate, but a mere power to sell." *Id.* 273, Patteson, J.; *Worg* v. *Relf*, 20 Law J., N. S., M. C. 125.

Before commencing an ejectment to recover parish property, churchwardens and overseers, or their legal advisers, should consider fully the various preliminary points mentioned in Chapter VIII. (*ante,* 72), particularly whether it be not practicable to obtain possession by entry (*ante*, 67); *Wildbor* v. *Rainforth*, 8 B. & C. 4; 2 Man. & Ry. 85; and whether it would not be more advisable to proceed by way of summary application to a magistrate pursuant to 59 Geo. 3, c. 12, ss. 24, 25, or 5 & 6 Will. 4, c. 69, s. 5 (*post*, Chapter LXXIII.), or by an action of trespass. *Matson* v. *Cook*, 4 Bing. N. C. 392; 6 Scott, 179; *ante*, 73.

In ejectment by churchwardens and overseers to recover parish property, they must be *named* in the writ, and also *described* as churchwardens and overseers of the parish. *Doe* d. *Churchwardens and Overseers of Llandesilio* v. *Roe*, 4 Dowl. 222; *Ward* v. *Clarke*, 12 M. & W. 747; 1 Dowl. & L. 1027. Thus, "A. B. and C. D., churchwardens of the parish of ——, in the county of ——, and E. F. and G. H., overseers of the said parish." *Doe* d. *Norton* v. *Webster*, 4 P. & D. 270; 12 A. & E. 442. Or thus: "A. B., C. D., E. F. and G. H., churchwardens and overseers of the parish of ——, in the county of ——." *Doe* d. *Bowley* v. *Barnes*, 8 Q. B. 1037.

Evidence for Plaintiffs.]—In ejectment by churchwardens and overseers the plaintiffs must prove:—

1. That the property sought to be recovered "belongs to the parish." *Ante*, 605. Proof that it was conveyed or demised to the plaintiffs or their predecessors in office for parish purposes; *ante*, 606; or that it has been used for many years as a residence for paupers, or as a workhouse, or for other parish purposes, will be sufficient.

2. That the plaintiffs were the churchwardens and overseers of the parish on the day mentioned in the writ. Evidence that before and at that time, and afterwards, they acted as such churchwardens and overseers is *primâ facie* sufficient. *Doe* d. *Bowley* v. *Barnes*, 8 Q. B. 1037; 15 Law J., N. S., Q. B. 293. Or their election and appointment may be proved.

3. It must appear that the plaintiffs' title is not barred by the Statute of Limitations. *Doe* d. *Landsdell* v. *Gower*, 17 Q. B. 589; *Doe* d. *Robinson* v. *Hinde*, 2 Moo. & Rob. 441; *Doe* d. *Edney* v. *Benham and Billett*, 7 Q. B. 976.

4. That the defendant's title (if any) has been duly determined by a proper notice to quit, or by a demand of possession, as the case may require. *Doe* d. *Higgs* v. *Terry*, 4 A. & E. 274; 5 N. & M. 556; *Doe* d. *Hobbs* v. *Cockell*, 4 A. & E. 478; 6 N. & M. 179; *ante*, 43. Generally speaking it will be necessary to show when and under what circumstances the defendant originally obtained possession of the property; but proof of payment of rent by him to the churchwardens and overseers of the parish will be sufficient *primâ facie* evidence of their title as against him. *Ante*, 231.

Evidence and Points for Defendant.]—The defendant may contend that the plaintiffs' evidence is insufficient upon some material point. *Supra*. He may also produce contradictory evidence. He may prove a defect in the plaintiffs' election or appointment, and so show that they are not the lawful churchwardens and overseers. *Ante*, 606. He may show that the property in question is not parish property; *ante*, 605; that it is vested in *known* trustees for special purposes; *ante*, 605; that the plaintiffs' title as churchwardens and overseers is barred by the Statute of Limitations. *Doe* d. *Lansdell* v. *Gower*, 17

Q. B. 589; *Doe* d. *Robinson* v. *Hinde*, 2 Moo. & Rob. 441; that the defendant was tenant from year to year, by payment of an annual rent, or otherwise, and that such tenancy has not been duly determined by a regular notice to quit; *ante*, 29, 43, 441; or if the defendant were merely a tenant at will, he may show that such tenancy was not determined on or before the day mentioned in the writ by a demand of possession, entry or otherwise. *Ante*, 58, 448, 453. He may show that any third person (not being one of the claimants) is legally entitled to actual possession of the land, notwithstanding he does not pretend to hold for or under such third person. *Ante*, 287, 288. But if a tenancy to the plaintiffs, or their predecessors in office, be proved, the defendant will be thereby estopped from denying their title to demise the property to him. *Ante*, 209, 213.

CHAPTER LXVII.

FOR COPYHOLDS.

1. BY THE LORD.—*For the whole Manor.*]—A manor is a large track of land originally granted by the king to some baron or other person

of rank, who afterwards gave parts of it to his immediate followers, to be holden of him, subject to suits and services ; and retained the residue for his own use. The parts so retained were called the lord's demesnes, and the unenclosed and uncultivated parts thereof were called the lord's waste. This must have happened before the Statute of *Quia Emptores* (18 Edw. 1, stat. 1), because no manor can have been legally created subsequently. *Sir Moyle Finch's case,* 6 Co. R. 63 a ; *Morris* v. *Smith,* Cro. Eliz. 38 ; Owen, 108. Even a copyhold estate cannot be created within the time of legal memory ; *Roe* d. *Newman* v. *Newman,* 2 Wils. 125 ; *Revell* v. *Jodrell,* 2 T. R. 415 ; and if the lord of a manor *convey* a customary estate to a tenant he cannot reserve to himself the ancient services ; for the tenant, by reason of the Statute *Quia Emptores,* must then hold of the superior lord. *Bradshaw* v. *Lawson,* 4 T. R. 443 ; *Doe* d. *Reay* v. *Huntington,* 4 East, 271. Lands once severed from a manor can never become part of the manor again, except by reputation. *Rex* v. *Duchess of Buccleugh,* 6 Mod. 151 ; 3 Dyer, 270, pl. 28 ; *Lee* v. *Brown,* 2 Mod. 69.

A manor may contain several smaller manors in which courts are held for the ease of the tenants, but in law they shall all be taken as one manor. *Green* v. *Proude,* 1 Mod. 117 ; *Sir H. Nevill's case,* 11 Co. R. 17 a ; Cro. Jac. 327 ; 5 Bulst. 135, *S. C.*

A manor always consists of demesnes and services, *i. e.* of the freeholds reserved by the lord for his own use (including the waste), and of the copyholds belonging to his tenants, and in respect whereof the services are rendered. Whenever the demesnes are severed from the copyholds, or the services become extinct, then the manor itself is destroyed. *Sir Moyle Finch's case,* 6 Co. R. 63, 64. So if the number of suitors (*i. e.* copyholders) be reduced to less than two, the manor itself is lost. Perk. s. 670 ; Co. Cop. s. 31 ; *Bradshaw* v. *Lawson,* 4 T. R. 443 ; *Gay* v. *Kay,* Cro. Eliz. 662 (but now see 4 & 5 Vict. c. 35, s. 86). After a manor has been so destroyed or lost it may continue to exist as a " reputed manor," and will pass in a conveyance by the word " manor." *Thinne* v. *Thinne,* 1 Sid. 190 ; 1 Lev. 28 ; *Sir Moyle Finch's case, supra ; Mallett* v. *Mallett,* Cro. Eliz. 524 ; *Id.* 707 ; *Curzon* v. *Lomax,* 5 Esp. 60 ; *Soane* v. *Ireland,* 10 East, 259.

Where a legal manor has once existed, declarations of persons deceased as to its boundary are still admissible in evidence, though the manor has ceased to exist otherwise than by reputation. *Doe* d. *Sir William Molesworth, Bart.* v. *Sleeman,* 9 Q. B. 298.

Where the boundaries of an actual or reputed manor are disputed, they may be proved to include a particular parcel of land, by showing acts of ownership over it : *ante,* 231, 246 ; *Curzon* v. *Lomax,* 5 Esp. 60 ; *Doe* d. *Barrett* v. *Kemp,* 7 Bing. 332 ; 5 Moo. & P. 173, *S. C.,* in error, 2 Bing. N. C. 102 ; 2 Scott, 9 : or by admissions and declarations of the occupier for the time being : *ante,* 231, 232 : or by the entries of a deceased steward, charging himself with rents received in respect of the property in question. *Doe* d. *Earl of Ashburnham* v. *Michael,* 17 Q. B. 276 ; *ante,* 234. The lord of a manor, *legally entitled thereto for an estate in possession,* may recover it by an ejectment. *Hems* v. *Stroud,* Latch, 61 ; *Doe* d. *Watson* v. *Fletcher,* 8 B. & C. 25 ; 2 Man. & R. 104. A reputed manor may be described in the writ as a " manor." *Soane* v. *Ireland,* 10 East, 259 ; and evidence of title to a reputed manor will support the action. *Curzon* v. *Lomax,* 5

Esp. 60; *Steel* v. *Prickett,* 2 Stark. R. 463, 471; *Doe* d. *Sir W. Molesworth, Bart.* v. *Sleeman,* 9 Q. B. 298.

The evidence will be similar to that in an action for freeholds. The lord is in fact the freeholder, subject of course to the rights of his copyhold tenants. *Barnett* v. *Earl of Guilford,* 11 Exch. 19. "In the eye of the law the tenants of the manor are only *quà* tenants at will to the lord. The lord is seised in fee of the whole." *Per* Lord Kenyon, C. J., in *Roe* d. *Hale* v. *Wegg,* 6 T. R. 710. There can be no general occupancy of a copyhold, because the freehold is always in the lord. *Zouch* d. *Forse* v. *Forse,* 7 East, 186; 3 Smith, 191. A copyholder in fee is only the owner of a particular estate. *Pyster* v. *Hembury,* Cro. Jac. 103; 4 Mod. 346, cited 1 Ld. Ray. 131; *Barnett* v. *Earl of Guilford, supra.* A *primâ facie* case of seisin in fee may be proved in the usual manner (*ante,* 211), or the deed or will under which the lord derives his title may be produced and proved, as in other cases. *Doe* d. *Gibbons, Bart.* v. *Pott,* 2 Doug. 710; *Roe* d. *Hale* v. *Wegg,* 6 T. R. 708. The existence of the manor may be proved by showing the holding of courts, the appointment of game-keepers and the like, even without producing the court rolls or other documentary evidence. *Doe* d. *Beck* v. *Heakin,* 6 A. & E. 495; 2 N. & P. 660. It seems that *reputation* alone is admissible to prove the existence of a manor, without any proof of the actual exercise of any manorial right. *Steel* v. *Prickett,* 2 Stark. R. 463, 471. But it is generally unadvisable to rely on such evidence, where better can be produced.

For Part of the Demesnes or Wastes.]—The lord of a manor may recover by ejectment *any part of the demesnes or wastes* legally vested in him for an estate in possession, and upon which any person has wrongfully intruded. *Curzon* v. *Lomax,* 5 Esp. 60; *Doe* d. *Earl of Dunraven* v. *Williams,* 7 C. & P. 332; *Doe* d. *Dearden* v. *Maden,* 4 B. & Adol. 880; 1 N. & M. 533; *Doe* d. *Padwick* v. *Wittcomb,* 6 Exch. 601; *Doe* d. *Baker* v. *Coombes,* 9 C. B. 714; *Doe* d. *Earl of Ashburnham* v. *Michael,* 17 Q. B. 276. But where an inclosure has been made from the waste for a long period (twelve or thirteen years), and seen by the steward from time to time without objection, a jury may infer a licence from the lord; and such licence must be determined by notice or otherwise before an ejectment can be supported. *Doe* d. *Foley* v. *Wilson,* 11 East, 56; *Doe* d. *Earl of Dunraven* v. *Williams,* 7 C. & P. 332. Where the lord and his servants entered and broke down several parts of the fences only three days before the ejectment: held a sufficient revocation of any implied licence. *Doe* d. *Beck* v. *Heakin,* 6. A. & E. 495; 2 N. & P. 660. But such acts would not be sufficient to prevent the operation of the Statute of Limitations. 3 & 4 Will. 4, c. 27, s. 10; *Doe* d. *Baker* v. *Coombes,* 9 C. B. 714. *Primâ facie* the lord of the manor is entitled to all waste lands within the manor, and it is not essential that the lord should show acts of ownership of such lands; and evidence that the public have been used to throw rubbish on waste land is rather evidence that it belongs to the lord than to any private individual. *Doe* v. *Earl of Dunraven* v. *Williams,* 7 C. & P. 332.

Strips of waste land lying between a highway and enclosed lands within a manor, do not *primâ facie* belong to the lord of the manor, but to the owners of the enclosed lands, whether they be freeholders, copyholders or leaseholders. *Doe* d. *Pring* v. *Pearsey*, 7 B. & C. 304; 9 D. & R. 908; *Hollis* v. *Goldfinch*, 1 B. & C. 205; 2 D. & R. 316; *Steele* v. *Prickett*, 2 Stark. R. 463; *Grose* v. *West*, 7 Taunt. 39; *ante*, 243. Therefore, when the lord seeks to recover them by eject-ment, he must prove not only his title to the manor, but also acts of ownership over the property claimed, or over other strips of land of a like nature within the manor. *Doe* d. *Barrett* v. *Kemp*, 7 Bing. 332; 5 Moo. & P. 173; *S. C.* in error, 2 Bing. N. C. 102; 2 Scott, 9; *Tyrwhitt* v. *Wynne*, 2 B. & A. 554; *Grose* v. *West*, 7 Taunt. 39; Anon. Lofft, 358; *ante*, 244.

In actions of trespass against the lord of a manor, in which the question is, whether the *locus in quo* be part of the plaintiff's estate or waste of the manor, a perambulation of such manor by the lord, in-cluding the land in question, is evidence, as showing an assertion of ownership by the lord, though it be not proved that any person on behalf of the plaintiff was present at the perambulation, or knew of it. *Woolway* v. *Roe*, 1 A. & E. 114; 3 N. & M. 849.

Sandpits or gravel-pits in the waste may be copyhold tenements, distinct from the waste, and demisable by custom. *Doe* d. *Church-wardens of Croydon* v. *Cook*, 5 Esp. 221; and see *Wilson* v. *Page*, 4 Esp. 71; *Bateson* v. *Green*, 5 T. R. 411. In ejectment by the lord of a manor for mines situate within the manor, proof of possession of the manor is not sufficient as against a defendant who has been in pos-session of the mines for more than twenty years; for the manor and mines may be distinct inheritances. *Rich* d. *Lord Cutten* v. *Johnson*, 2 Stra. 1142; and see *Micklethwait* v. *Winter*, 6 Exch. 644. In copyhold lands, although the property in mines be in the lord, the possession of them is in the tenant: *Lewis* v. *Branthwaite*, 2 B. & A. 437; *Bourne* v. *Taylor*, 10 East, 189: so with respect to timber. *Whitehurst* v. *Holsworthy*, 4 M. & S. 340.

Lands formed by alluvion, that is, by gradual and imperceptible deposit on the shore of the sea, belong to the lord of the manor, and not to the king *jure coronæ*. *Rex* v. *Lord Yarborough*, 2 Bligh, N. S. 147; 1 Dow. & Cl. 178. As to the seashore between high and low water mark, see *Attorney-General* v. *Chambers*, 23 Law J., N. S., Chanc. 662; *Lowe* v. *Govill*, 3 B. & Adol. 863. Acts of owner-ship exercised by the lord of a manor upon the seashore adjoining, between high and low water mark, such as the exclusive taking of sand, stones and seaweed, may be called in aid to show that the shore is parcel of the manor, although an ancient grant under which the manor was held, professing to grant wreck of the sea, &c., did not grant *littus maris*. *Calmady* v. *Rowe*, 6 C. B. 861; *Duke of Beau-fort* v. *The Mayor of Swansea*, 3 Exch. 413.

For Copyholds forfeited.]—When a copyholder commits an act by which he forfeits his lands, he who is lord *at the time* of the forfeiture committed may enter or maintain an ejectment by reason of the for-feiture: *Clarke* v. *Arden*, 16 C. B. 227: but this right is confined to the lord for the time being: *Lady Montague's case*, Cro. Jac. 301; 1 Bulstr. 190, *S. C.*; *Keen* v. *Kirby*, 1 Mod. 19; *Eastcourt* v. *Weeks*, 1 Salk. 186: unless the act of forfeiture destroy the estate (as a fine, or feoffment with livery used to do), and then the heir of the lord in whose time it was committed may take advantage of it. *Doe* d. *Tar-rant* v. *Hellier*, 3 T. R. 162; 1 Watk. Cop. 344. Where, however, a copyholder, holding of a manor belonging to a bishopric, committed a forfeiture by felling timber during the vacancy of the see, the succeeding bishop was allowed to maintain an ejectment against him. *Read* v. *Allen,* Bull. N. P. 107. Where a manor is vested in two or more sisters as coparceners, and a forfeiture is committed, unless they jointly take advantage of it, the survivor cannot do so. *Eastcourt* v. *Weeks,* 1 Salk. 186; *Anon.* 1 Freem. 516.

The lord may enter for waste committed by a copyholder for life, though there be an intermediate estate in remainder between the estate of the copyholder for life and the lord's reversion. *Doe* d. *Folkes* v. *Clements,* 2 M. & S. 68; *Smarky* v. *Penhallow,* 2 Ld. Raym. 1000; 6 Mod. 13; *Head* v. *Taylor,* 12 Mod. 123; Holt, 161.

A lessee for years of a manor, being *dominus pro tempore,* may take advantage of a forfeiture committed by a copyholder: 1 Roll. Abr. 509; 2 Saund. 422: so may the grantee of the lord, or the lessee of such grantee. *East* v. *Harding,* Cro. Eliz. 498; Moor, 392, *S. C.* But no such lessee or grantee can take advantage of any forfeiture committed before the creation of his estate. *Penn* v. *Merivall,* Owen, 63; Latch, 227; Palm. 416.

A seizure *quousque* to compel admittance stands on a different footing to a seizure for a forfeiture. The latter can be made only by the lord for the time being. *Ante,* 612. But the heir or devisee of a lord may seize *quousque* to compel admittance after default made in the time of his ancestor or testator, and due proclamations made at three successive courts. *Doe* d. *Bover* v. *Trueman,* 1 B. & Adol. 736.

No forfeiture can arise from the act of any person other than the copyhold tenant or the husband of a female copyholder. Therefore, if if a stranger, or a disseisor, or a guardian, or a *cestui que trust,* commit waste, the copyholder shall not forfeit his land. Co. Cop. s. 59, tr. 137, 138; 4 Leon. 241; *Clifton's case,* 4 Co. R. 27 a. So if a surrenderee commit felony, and is attainted before admittance. *Roe* d. *Jefferys* v. *Hicks,* 2 Wils. 13; 1 Ld. Ken. 110, *S. C.* But if a surrenderor be attainted of felony before admittance of the surrenderee, the lord may take advantage of the forfeiture. *Rex* v. *Lady Mildmay,* 5 B. & Adol. 254; 1 N. & M. 778. If a tenant for life commit a forfeiture, it will neither prejudice nor benefit the remainderman, but the lord shall have the land during such tenant's life. *Rastall* v. *Turner,* Cro. Eliz. 598; *Baspole* v. *Long,* Cro. Eliz. 879; Noy, 42, *S. C.; Head* v. *Taylor,* 12 Mod. 123; Holt, 161; *Margaret Podger's case,* 9 Co. R. 107. If a husband, seised of a copyhold in right of his wife, make a lease not warranted by the custom, it is a forfeiture of the estate during the life of the husband only. *Saverne* v. *Smith,* Cro. Car. 7; 2 Roll. R. 344, 361, 372; *Hedd* v. *Chalener,* Cro. Eliz. 149. If the husband of a feme copyholder for life commit waste, it is a forfeiture of his estate. *Clifton's case,* 4 Co. R. 27 a. If a tenant in tail commit a forfeiture, it will affect his issue in tail. Co. Cop. ss. 59 to 138. The forfeiture of one joint tenant will not affect the other's part. *Id.* If the lessee of a copyholder commit waste, his term will be forfeited to the lord, but not the reversion of the copyholder. Kitchen, 246. If a copyholder demise with licence of the lord, and afterwards commits a forfeiture, it will not prejudice the lease. *Clarke* v. *Arden,* 16 C. B. 227. So where the copyholder surrenders his estate after having made a demise for years with or without licence of the lord. *Doe* d. *Beaden* v. *Pyke,* 5 M. & S. 146.

Any act which creates a forfeiture of part of a copyhold tenement creates a forfeiture of the whole; but several distinct tenements will not be forfeited by any act which applies to only one of them; *Taverner's case,* 4 Co. R. 27; Cro. Eliz. 353; 3 Leon. 109, *S. C.;* although all be held by one copy, yet several *habendums* or *tenendums* will make distinct tenements. *S. C.;* Gilb. Ten. 246.

A forfeiture of a copyholder may be waived by the lord. *Doe* d. *Tarrant* v. *Hellier,* 3 T. R. 162; *Anon.,* Freem. 516, cited 1 B. & Adol. 744. Any act of the lord whereby the tenant is recognized as a copyholder after the forfeiture accrued, operates as a waiver of the forfeiture, *ex. gr.,* acceptance of subsequent rent or services. *Garrard* v. *Lister,* 1 Keb. 15; Co. Cop. s. 61, tr. 140; *Bacon* v. *Thurley,* Toth. 107; *Hamlen* v. *Hamlen,* 1 Bulstr. 189; *Eastcourt* v. *Weeks,* 1 Salk. 186; Freem. 517, *S. C.* An amerciament made on the tenant, whether levied or not. 1 Brownl. 149; *Braunche's case,* 1 Leon. 104; 1 Freem. 517. A presentment of the death of the copyholder who committed the forfeiture, and the entry thereof on the court rolls. *Doe* d. *Tarrant* v. *Hellier,* 3 T. R. 162, 171. The admission of his heir: *Clerk* v. *Wentworth,* Toth. 107: or of his surrenderee, Kitch. 177. " Not only the admission of the copyholder or his heir, but any recognition on the part of the lord, would preclude him from taking advantage of a forfeiture." *Per* Lord Kenyon, C. J., in *Doe* d. *Tarrant* v. *Hellier,* 3 T. R. 171. But the forfeiture must be known to the lord at the time of the supposed waiver. Co. Cop. s. 61, tr. 140; Gilb. Ten. 247; *Matthews* v. *Whetton,* Cro. Car. 233; Jones, 249. The lord will be presumed to have notice of nonattendance at court, nonpayment of rent, and the like; *Lord Cornwallis' case,* 2 Ventr. 39; but not of an attainder of the copyholder for treason or felony. *S. C.*

Generally speaking a presentation by the homage of the forfeiture is not necessary to entitle the lord to avail himself of it; such presentment being merely in the nature of notice to the lord of the forfeiture. *East* v. *Harding,* Cro. Eliz. 499; Owen, 63; Moore, 392, *S. C.; Lord Cornwallis's case,* 2 Ventr. 38; Gilb. Ten. 246; 1 Watk. Cop. 346; *In re Winton,* Bull. N. P. 107. It is, however, generally safer and more advisable to get the forfeiture presented; and if there be a custom for it, such custom must be pursued. Gilb. Ten. 246; and see Co. Cop. s. 58. tr. 135; Crabb. on Real Prop. s. 893.

The lord or his steward may enter and seize for a forfeiture: *Benson* v. *Strode,* 2 Show. 152; *Trotter* v. *Blake,* 2 Mod. 230: or the lord may bring an ejectment: *Lord Cornwallis's case,* 2 Ventr. 38; *Barnett* v. *Earl of Guilford,* 11 Exch. 21, 22: or he may demise the property as forfeited, and thereupon his lessee may enter or bring ejectment. *Milfax* v. *Baker,* 1 Lev. 26; 2 Danvers, 192.

An entry or ejectment for a forfeiture must be made or commenced within twenty years next after the forfeiture accrued; *ante,* 11; *Whitton* v. *Peacock,* 3 Myl. & Keen. 325; *Doe* d. *Tarrant* v. *Hellier,* 3 T. R. 162, 172; and not after any waiver of the forfeiture. *Supra.*

Forfeiture by Attainder for Treason or Felony.]—If a copyholder be *attainted* of any treason or felony, he generally forfeits his estate to the lord of the manor ; but no such forfeiture accrues before attainder (*i. e.* sentence of death recorded), without a special custom. *Rex* v. *Willes,* 3 B. & A. 510. By custom the forfeiture may accrue upon conviction : *Rex* v. *Lady Mildmay,* 5 B. & Adol. 254; 1 N. & M. 778: or even upon a presentment of the felony by the homage. *Borne-*

ford and Packington's case, 1 Leon. 1; *Gittins* v. *Cowper*, 2 Brownl. 217. Where a copyholder was convicted of a capital felony, but pardoned upon condition of remaining two years in prison, and the lord did not do any act towards seizing the copyhold: held, that at the expiration of the two years the copyholder might maintain an ejectment for the land against one who had ousted him. *Doe* d. *Evans* v. *Evans*, 5 B. & C. 584; 8 D. & R. 399. An outlawry does not occasion any forfeiture, unless it be for a capital crime. Gilb. Ten. 242; 1 Scriven, Cop. 442 (4th ed.). If a copyholder be attainted of treason, his estate is forfeited to the lord of the manor; not to the queen, unless by express act of parliament. *Lord Cornwallis's case*, 2 Ventr. 39.

The attainder of a surrenderee *before admittance* does not create any forfeiture. *Ante*, 613.

Forfeiture by a Lease without Licence.]—A lease for more than one year by a copyholder, where there is no custom or licence to warrant it, is a forfeiture of the copyhold; *East* v. *Harding*, Cro. Eliz. 498; Owen, 63; Moore, 392, *S. C.; Jackman* v. *Hoddesden*, Cro. Eliz. 351; *Richards* v. *Sely*, 2 Mod. 79; *Lady Montague's case*, Cro. Jac. 301; *Lutterel* v. *Weston*, *Id.*, 308; *Matthews* v. *Whetton*, Cro. Car. 233; Jones, 249, *S. C.*; and the lord may thereupon grant it, without a seizure; *Page* v. *Smith*, 3 Salk. 100; *Milfax* v. *Baker*, 1 Lev. 27; *Peters* v. *Mills*, Bull. N. P. 107; and without the forfeiture being presented by the homage: *East* v. *Harding*, *supra:* or he may enter, or maintain ejectment. But a subsequent reversioner cannot take advantage of such forfeiture. *Lady Montague's case*, Cro. Jac. 301; *Margaret Podger's case*, 9 Co. R. 104 a; 1 Brownl. 181; 2 *Id.*, 134, 153. Nor can the lord or his grantee maintain ejectment during the lease after accepting a surrender of the copyholder's estate; *Doe* d. *Beaden* v. *Pyke*, 5 M. & S. 146; provided he then knew of the lease. *Matthews* v. *Whetton*, Cro. Car. 233; T. Jones, 249, *S. C.* If a licence to demise has been obtained, the lease must strictly pursue it, otherwise it will be void; *Jackson* v. *Neal*, Cro. Eliz. 395; *Haddon* v. *Arrowsmith*, *Id.*, 461; Poph. 105; but a licence to demise for twenty-one years will warrant a lease for three years. *Goodwin* v. *Longhurst*, Cro. Eliz. 535; and see *Isherwood* v. *Oldknow*, 3 M. & S. 382, 392. A lease for three years without any limitation, under a licence to lease for five years if A. so long live, is good. *Worledge* v. *Benbury*, Cro. Jac. 436. Instead of granting a lease without licence, the owner of a copyhold may covenant to grant a lease upon certain terms and conditions, *with the licence of the lord* of the manor, provided such licence can be procured; and that until such licence shall be obtained, and a lease granted accordingly, the tenant shall hold from year to year, subject to the terms and conditions before specified. The tenant will, on entry by virtue of such deed, have nearly all the benefits of a lease, and no forfeiture will accrue; *Price* v. *Birch*, 4 Man. & Gr. 1; 1 Dowl. N. S. 720; *Lenthall* v. *Thomas*, 2 Keb. 267; *Pistor* v. *Cater*, 9 M. & W. 315; but his tenancy may be determined at the end of any year of the term, by the usual notice to quit. *Doe* d. *Nunn* v. *Lufkin*, 4 East, 221; 1 Smith, 90; *Lufkin* v. *Nunn*, 1 B. & P. New R. 163. A lease by a copyholder for one year, with a covenant to renew yearly for ten years, is not a forfeiture. *Lady Montague's case*, Cro. Jac. 301. A lease for three years, warranted by the custom, contained a covenant to renew it every three years, *toties quoties* for twenty-one years : held, that this was a lease for only three years, after the expiration of which, no fresh lease having been granted, the lessor might maintain ejectment. *Fenny* d. *Eastham* v. *Child*, 2 M. & S. 255.

If a husband seised of a copyhold in right of his wife make a lease not warranted by the custom, it is a forfeiture of the estate during the life of the husband only. *Laverne* v. *Smith*, Cro. Car. 7 ; 2 Roll. R. 344, 361, 372 ; *Hedd* v. *Chelener*, Cro. Eliz. 149. A lease for more than one year, made contrary to the custom of the manor, and without licence, is valid as between the parties and their respective assigns. *Post*, 627.

A lease granted by a copyhold tenant, under a licence of the lord, is not affected by a forfeiture of the tenant's estate, such licence operating as a confirmation by the lord ; and consequently, pending the term created thereby, the lord cannot maintain ejectment for the land. *Clarke* v. *Arden*, 16 C. B. 227. And it is competent to a purchaser of the tenant's interest in the copyhold tenement, who comes in and defends as landlord, and who is in receipt of the rents, to set up the lease as a bar to the lord's claim. *S. C.*

Forfeiture by Waste.]—If a copyholder be guilty of voluntary or permissive waste, he thereby forfeits his copyhold. 1 Inst. 63 ; 1 Crabb on Real Prop., s. 877. Thus, if he cut down trees for repairs, and does not repair within a reasonable time, it is a forfeiture. *East* v. *Harding*, Cro. Eliz. 498 ; Moor, 392. It is a question for the jury whether the trees cut down were wanted, and *bonâ fide* intended for the purpose of repairs. *Doe* d. *Foley* v. *Wilson*, 11 East, 56. If he employ them for the repair of other tenements, it will be a forfeiture ; *Nash* v. *Earl of Derby*, 2 Vern. 537 ; but not if he has cut more than is immediately wanted, and keep what is not wanted for future repairs, because he may not know precisely how much is necessary. *East* v. *Harding, supra.* A custom that a copyholder *for life* may cut down and sell timber trees at pleasure is unreasonable and void, but perhaps such a custom may be good for a copyholder of inheritance. *Rockey* v. *Huggens*, Cro. Car. 220 ; *Denn* d. *Joddrell* v. *Johnson*, 10 East, 266. Where a copyholder may take trees for reparation, the loppings and tops belong to him, and he may sell them to help to defray the charges. *Sanford* v. *Stevens*, 3 Bulstr. 282. But he may not top timber trees, and make them pollards ; *Reachy* v. *The Duke of Somerset*, 1 Stra. 447 ; nor grub up hedges ; nor destroy boundaries or landmarks ; 1 Roll. Abr. 508 ; *Paston* v. *Mann*, Hetley, 8 ; Lit. R. 267, 268 ; nor open mines or quarries without the lord's licence or a special custom. Gilb. Ten. 327 ; *Rowe* v. *Brenton*, 8 B. & C. 737 ; 3 Man. & Ry. 133. Any act of the above nature operates as a forfeiture, of which the lord for the time being may avail himself by entry or ejectment. *Rockey* v. *Huggins*, Cro. Car. 220.

If a copyholder pull down a barn, without any intention of rebuilding, the lord cannot recover the place from him on the ground of a forfeiture, if the jury find that the premises are not damaged. *Doe* d. *Grubb* v. *Earl of Burlington*, 5 B. & Adol. 507 ; 2 N. & M. 534.

The lord may enter or maintain ejectment for a forfeiture occasioned by waste committed by a copyholder for life, though there be an intermediate estate in remainder between the estate of the copyholder for life and the lord's reversion, for were it otherwise the tenant for life and remainderman, by combining together, might strip the inheritance of all the timber. *Doe* d. *Folkes* v. *Clements*, 2 M. & S. 68. The estate for life is forfeited to the lord, and when the tenant for life dies the remainderman will be entitled to possession. *Ante*, 613.

Forfeiture for Refusal of Rent or Services.]—If a copyholder *refuse* his rent or services, it is a forfeiture; 1 Roll. Abr. 506; Dyer, 211 b, *in marg.*; *Clarke* v. *Arden*, 16 C. B. 227; but mere non-payment of rent is insufficient. Moor, 622; Lit. R. 268. There must be a demand and refusal. Co. Cop. s. 162. Silence, or an insufficient excuse, may amount to a refusal. If a copyholder be to pay rent at a certain day, and the lord of the manor comes upon the land at the last instant of the day, and demands his rent, and there be none to pay it, it is a forfeiture of the estate. *Crisp* v. *Fryer*, Cro. Eliz. 505; Noy, 58; Moore, 350, *S. C.*; Co. Cop. s. 163. So may the non-performance of a promise to pay on a subsequent day. *Grey* v. *Ulisses*, Lach, 122.

The refusal to pay on demand a *reasonable fine* due to the lord creates a forfeiture; 1 Roll. Abr. 507; *Jackman* v. *Hoddesdon*, Cro. Eliz. 351; *Hobart's case*, 4 Co. R. 27 b; Cro Eliz. 779; Moore, 622, *S. C.*; *Doe* d. *Twining* v. *Muscott*, 12 M. & W. 832; but not if the fine be unreasonable, or it be doubtful whether the fine is justly payable; *Barnes* v. *Corke*, 3 Lev. 309; Co. Entr. 64; *Clarke* v. *Arden*, 16 C. B. 227; or upon what principle it ought to be calculated. *Trotter* v. *Blake*, 2 Mod. 230. It lies on the copyholder to show that the fine is unreasonable. *Denny* v. *Leman*, Hob. 135; *Doe* d. *Twining* v. *Muscott*, 12 M. & W. 832, 842.

The question whether a fine be reasonable, or the refusal to pay it a forfeiture, may be tried in an action of debt or assumpsit to recover the fine. *Wilson* v. *Hoare*, 2 B. & Adol. 350; *Grant* v. *Astle*, 2 Doug. 731, note (4). No fine is payable until *after* admittance. *Lord Wellesley* v. *Withers*, 4 E. & B. 750. The non-payment of an unreasonable fine, where the custom is uncertain, is no forfeiture of a copyhold. *Hobart's case*, 4 Co. R. 27 b; Cro. Eliz. 779; Moor, 622; *Willowe's case*, 13 Co. R. 1; *Trotter* v. *Blake*, 2 Mod. 230. But where the fine is arbitrary, and does not exceed two years' improved rent or value, it will be presumed to be reasonable in the absence of proof to the contrary. *Doe* d. *Twining* v. *Muscott*, 12 M. & W. 832, 842.

If a copyholder, being duly summoned to do suit and service in the lord's court, and having no lawful excuse, refuse to come, it is a forfeiture. *Taverner and Cromwell's case*, 3 Leon. 108; 1 Roll's Abr. 506; 3 Bulstr. 80, 268; *Fryer* v. *Crisp*, Cro. Eliz. 505; Noy. 68, *S. C.* So if he refuse to be sworn upon the homage; or, when sworn, refuse to present according to his oath. Moor, 350; Kitch, 180. So if he disclaim being tenant to the lord; Kitch. 248; but not if he come into court and renounce his copy. 1 Roll. Abr. 107.

Generally speaking, the refusal must be wilful and absolute. Therefore a legal excuse will prevent a forfeiture, *ex. gr.*, illness, or great weakness, or the duties of some important office calling him elsewhere; Co. Cop. 159; or a *subpœna ad testificandum*. So if he be in debt and afraid of being arrested. *Id.* If the copyholder, upon being requested by the lord to come and do his services, answer that, "if they are due, he will do them, but it shall be tried at law first whether they are due," this is no forfeiture, the refusal not being absolute and wilful. *Barnham* v. *Higgens*, Latch, 14; *Id.* 133; and see 1 Roll. R. 429; 3 Bulstr. 80, 268. So if the copyholder say, "if it be a court, I appear; if not, I do not appear," this is not a sufficient refusal to create a forfeiture. *Parker* v. *Cook*, Styles, 241. Unless, indeed, there be no controversy about the legality of the court, and the copyholder so acts as a shift or evasion. *Id.*, Bac. Abr. Copyhold (L 1).

Evidence for Plaintiff in Ejectment for a Forfeiture.]—In an ejectment by the lord of a manor for a forfeiture, he must prove :—

1. His own title to the manor *at the time* of the forfeiture. *Ante,* 612. This may be proved as *ante,* 611. If it be shown that the defendant has been *admitted by the plaintiff* and done fealty to him, that will be sufficient to establish a title by estoppel. *Doe* d. *Nepean* v. *Budden,* 5 B. & A. 626. A title to the manor which first became vested in the plaintiff after the forfeiture is not sufficient. *Ante,* 612.

2. That the property in question is a copyhold tenement of the manor. This will appear by the court rolls, with some evidence of identity, if necessary.

3. The admission of the defendant, or of the person whose act occasioned the forfeiture. *Ante,* 613.

4. The act whereby the forfeiture was created. *Ante,* 614 to 617. The evidence on this point should be as strong and clear as possible. *Hamlen* v. *Hamlen,* 1 Bulstr. 190; *Doe* d. *Foley* v. *Wilson,* 11 East, 56.

5. If the forfeiture has been presented by the homage, the entry thereof on the court rolls should be proved. But such presentment is not absolutely necessary (*ante,* 614), except where there is a custom requiring it. *Ante,* 614.

6. If any warrant of seizure for the forfeiture has been made and executed, that may as well be proved unless there be some special reason to the contrary. *Doe* d. *Tarrant* v. *Hellier,* 3 T. R. 162; *Dimes* v. *The Grand Junction Canal Company,* 9 Q. B. 469. But a written warrant appears to be unnecessary; *Trotter* v. *Blake,* 2 Mod. 229, cited 9 Q. B. 517; and the bringing an ejectment for the forfeiture is sufficient without any previous seizure.

7. If the defendant be a tenant of the copyholder it is unnecessary to prove any determination of such tenancy by notice to quit, or otherwise. The defendant's term must fail with the estate out of which it is derived; unless, indeed, the demise was made with the licence of the lord. *Clarke* v. *Arden,* 16 C. B. 227, 252. Were it otherwise, an entry or ejectment for a forfeiture would frequently be defeated.

Evidence and Points for Defendant.]—The defendant may contend that the plaintiff's evidence is insufficient in some material point. *Supra.* He may also produce contradictory evidence. But in an ejectment by the lord for a forfeiture, the copyhold tenant who has been admitted and done fealty to the plaintiff cannot dispute his title to the manor, nor will he be permitted to prove that the legal estate was at the time of such admittance outstanding in a trustee for the plaintiff; and the widow of such tenant, claiming under him in respect of her freebench, is estopped in like manner. *Doe* d. *Nepean* v. *Budden,* 5 B. & A. 626; 1 D. & R. 243.

The defendant may prove a licence from the lord to do the act relied on as a forfeiture, or facts from which such a licence may be implied and found by a jury; *Doe* d. *Foley* v. *Wilson*, 11 East, 56; or a waiver of the forfeiture (*ante*, 614), with notice or knowledge of the forfeiture before or at the time of such waiver. *Ante*, 614.

The defendant may prove that the lands claimed have been enfranchised by the plaintiff, or by some previous lord of the manor; or facts from which such an enfranchisement may be inferred: upon proper evidence an enfranchisement may be presumed, even against the crown. *Roe* d. *Johnson* v. *Ireland*, 11 East, 280.

If it appear that the lord's right of entry for the forfeiture accrued more than twenty years before action, that is a good defence. *Doe* d. *Tarrant* v. *Hellier*, 3 T. R. 162, 172; *Whitton* v. *Peacock*, 3 Myl. & K. 325.

After a Seizure quousque.]—The lord is entitled always to have a tenant on the court rolls in respect of each copyhold tenement. When a tenant dies his death is usually presented by the homage and entered on the court rolls. 1 Scriven, Cop. 285 (4th ed.); 2 *Id.* 1149, 1150. But it is now sufficient if the death of the tenant be recorded by the lord or steward at a court held without the presence of homagers, and, consequently, without any presentment of the fact. 4 & 5 Vict. c. 35, ss. 86, 89; 1 Scriven, Cop. 287, note (*a*). When a tenant in fee dies the lord may give express notice to his customary heir to come in and be admitted; or he may cause three proclamations to be made, at three consecutive courts for such heir to come in and be admitted. *Doe* d. *Bover* v. *Trueman*, 1 B. & Adol. 736. The proclamations may be in general terms for any person to come in and make title, &c.; and the presentment of default may also be general, though the person next in remainder be known. *Doe* d. *Whitbread* v. *Jenney*, 5 East, 522; 2 Smith, 116. Each proclamation, and the non-appearance of the heir on each occasion, should be entered on the court rolls; or the proclamations may be made pursuant to 4 & 5 Vict. c. 35, s. 86. After the third proclamation the lord or his steward may enter and seize *quousque*, provided the heir do not tender himself for admission at either of the courts. *Doe* d. *Earl of Carlisle* v. *Towns*, 2 B. & Adol. 585; *Roe* d. *Ashton* v. *Hutton*, 2 Wils. 162; *Doe* d. *Twining* v. *Muscott*, 12 M. & W. 832. The lord may seize *quousque* in virtue of a right which accrued to the preceding lord, on default of the heirs coming in to be admitted; and that although he be the devisee, and not the heir of the preceding lord. *Doe* d. *Bover* v. *Trueman*, 1 B. & Adol. 736.

But the lord or his heir cannot seize for an *absolute forfeiture*, *pro defectu tenentis*, unless there be a special custom in that behalf. *Lord Salisbury's case*, 1 Lev. 63; *Doe* d. *Tarrant* v. *Hellier*, 3 T. R. 162; *Doe* d. *Bover* v. *Trueman*, 1 B. & Adol. 748, *per cur.* Such special custom will not bind an infant heir; *Rex* v. *Dilliston*, 1 Salk. 386; 3 Mod. 221; 1 Show. 31, 83; Comb. 118; Carth. 41, *S. C.*; nor a feme covert; *Doe* d. *Tarrant* v. *Hellier*, 3 T. R. 162; *Doe* d. *Twining* v. *Muscott*, 12 M. & W. 832; nor a lunatic; nor a person beyond seas, when the proclamations were made. *Whitton* v. *Williams*, Cro. Jac. 101 (2nd point); *Underhill* v. *Kelsey*, Cro. Jac. 226; *Lechford's case*, 8 Co. R. 99. In such cases the lord should proceed according to the 11 Geo. 4 & 1 Will. 4, c. 65, s. 9; *Doe* d. *Twining* v. *Muscott*, 12 M. & W. 832; or (in lunacy cases) the 16 & 17 Vict. c. 70, ss. 108—112; or he may seize *quousque*. *Dimes* v. *The Grand Junction Canal*

Company, 9 Q. B. 469, 514 ; *Doe* d. *Twining* v. *Muscott*, 12 M. & W. 832. Upon a seizure *quousque* a written warrant is usually made to the bailiff; but this is not absolutely necessary, a verbal authority is sufficient. *Trotter* v. *Blake*, 2 Mod. 229, cited 9 Q. B. 517. If the warrant be to seize absolutely as for a forfeiture, instead of to seize *quousque*, it may be shown by evidence that only a seizure *quousque* was actually made, and the jury may so find. *Dimes* v. *The Grand Junction Canal Company*, 9 Q. B. 469, 517. But an absolute seizure for a forfeiture cannot afterwards be set up by the lord as a seizure *quousque*. *Doe* d. *Tarrant* v. *Hellier*, 3 T. R. 162. Although the lord proceeds in the first instance on his right to enter and seize *quousque pro defectu tenentis*, if that be answered, he may nevertheless recover on a right of entry and seizure *quousque* the fine be satisfied. *Doe* d. *Twining* v. *Muscott*, 12 M. & W. 832. A seizure *quousque* makes no difference in the right of the heir. The lord seizes *only till the tenant comes in;* that seizure does not give him any adverse title. *Per* Coleridge, J., in *Le Keux* v. *Harrison*, 6 Q. B. 637. "It is clear on principle, that if proclamation is made, and the land seized till the heir comes in, and the heir afterwards does come, the lord cannot answer his claim by saying that parties who have not appeared are entitled." *Per* Lord Denman, C. J., in *Doe* v. *Le Keux* v. *Harrison*, 6 Q. B. 636. After a seizure *quousque* the heir may tender himself to be admitted at the lord's court, and if then refused admittance by the lord or his steward, he may maintain ejectment. *Doe* d. *Burrell* v. *Bellamy*, 2 M. & S. 87. It will be no defence to such action for the lord to prove that the claimant's ancestor devised the property to a third person, who has never claimed to be admitted. *Doe* d. *Le Keux* v. *Harrison*, 6 Q. B. 631.

If any one of several persons entitled as devisees to be admitted, comes and prays to be admitted, the lord cannot afterwards seize *quousque* ; *Roe* d. *Ashton* v. *Hutton*, 2 Wils. 162; except, perhaps, to enforce the payment of a reasonable fine, payable upon admittance. *Doe* d. *Twining* v. *Muscott*, 12 M. & W. 832.

Generally speaking, the admittance of a tenant for life under a surrender or will operates as an admission of the remainderman or reversioner. *Post*, 626. But where by custom a remainderman is bound to be admitted, and to pay a fine on such admittance, the lord may make the usual proclamations at three consecutive courts, requiring him by name, or requiring generally "any person entitled" to come in and be admitted; and in case of default may seize *quousque*, and afterwards enforce such seizure by an ejectment. *Doe* d. *Whitbread* v. *Jenney*, 5 East, 522.

Evidence for Plaintiff.]—In an ejectment by the lord of a manor to enforce a seizure *quousque*, he must prove :—

1. His own title to the manor. This may be proved as *ante*, 611. A title by estoppel would be sufficient. *Doe* d. *Nepean* v. *Budden*, 5 B. & A. 626 ; 1 D. & R. 243. If his title first accrued after the seizure *quousque* he must prove the title of his predecessor, and his own derivative title as heir, devisee, grantee or lessee. *Doe* d. *Bover* v. *Trueman*, 1 B. & Adol. 736.

2. That the property in question is a copyhold tenement of the manor. This will appear by the court rolls, with some evidence of identity, if necessary. *Doe* d. *Twining* v. *Muscott*, 12 M. & W. 832.

3. The admission of the deceased copyhold tenant. This may be proved by the court rolls, or by examined copies thereof. *Post*, 624 to 626.

4. The death of such copyhold tenant. This must be proved in the usual manner. *Ante*, 239.

5. The presentment by the homage of such death.

6. The three proclamations made pursuant to 4 & 5 Vict. c. 35, s. 86, or at three consecutive courts, for the heir of the deceased tenant to come in and be admitted. *Doe* d. *Bover* v. *Trueman*, 1 B. & Adol. 736; *Dimes* v. *The Grand Junction Canal Company*, 9 Q. B. 469, 517.

7. That the heir did not come in and offer himself to be admitted at either of those courts. *Doe* d. *Earl of Carlisle* v. *Towns*, 2 B. & Adol. 585; *Roe* d. *Ashton* v. *Hutton*, 2 Wils. 162.

8. The warrant of seizure *quousque*, and the execution thereof. *Doe* d. *Bover* v. *Trueman*, 1 B. & Adol. 736. If the warrant be incorrect, viz., for an absolute forfeiture instead of a seizure *quousque*, parol evidence is admissible to show that only a seizure *quousque* was actually made; *Dimes* v. *The Grand Junction Canal Company*, 9 Q. B. 469, 517; but proof of an absolute seizure for a forfeiture will not do without evidence of a special custom. *Doe* d. *Tarrant* v. *Hellier*, 3 T. R. 162.

A seizure *quousque* for nonpayment of a reasonable fine payable on admittance may support this action, notwithstanding the lord relies in the first instance on a seizure *quousque pro defectu tenentis*. *Doe* d. *Twining* v. *Muscott*, 12 M. & W. 832.

Evidence and Points for Defendant.]—The defendant may contend that the plaintiff's evidence is insufficient on some material point. *Ante*, 620 to 621. He may also produce contradictory evidence. He may show that one of the parties entitled to be admitted tendered himself in court when one of the proclamations was made, and that the lord or his steward then refused to admit him without the others. *Roe* d. *Ashton* v. *Hutton*, 2 Wils. 162. He may also show that after the seizure *quousque*, and before the commencement of the action, he tendered and offered himself at the lord's court for admission; and that he was either then admitted, or refused admission, by the lord or his steward. *Doe* d. *Burrell* v. *Bellamy*, 2 M. & S. 87; *Doe* d. *Le Keux* v. *Harrison*, 6 Q. B. 631.

2. BY SURRENDEREE.]—Copyholds pass by surrender and admittance, which together constitute one assurance. *Selwyn* v. *Selwyn*, 2 Burr. 1131; 4 *Id.*, 1962; 5 *Id.*, 2786, 2787; *Roe* d. *Jefferys* v. *Hicks*, 2 Wils. 13, 15. The admission is required for the protection and security of the lord, and is in the nature of an assent by him to the surrender. *Roe* d. *Cosh* v. *Lovelass*, 2 B. & A. 456, Abbott, C. J. But the surrender is the material part of the conveyance. The admission thereon is mere form. *Per* Lord Mansfield, C. J., in *Roe* d. *Noden* v. *Griffits*, 4 Burr. 1961; and see 5 Burr. 2786. In making admittances the lord is only an instrument, and the surrenderee when admitted is *in by the surrenderor*, and paramount the charges and incumbrances of the lord. *Tavernor's case*, 4 Co. R. 27 a; Cro. Eliz. 353; 3 Leon. 107, *S. C.* Any inaccuracy in the admittance is generally immaterial. "The form of admission, whatever it may be, enures according to the

title." *Per cur.* in *Doe* d. *Winder* v. *Lawes*, 7 A. & E. 210; *Id.*, 214;
2 N. & P. 195; *Westwick* v. *Wyer*, 4 Co. R. 28 a; Co. Cop. 110;
Doe d. *Milner* v. *Brightwen*, 10 East, 583; *Right* d. *Dean and Chapter of Wells* v. *Bawden*, 3 East, 260, 267. An admission in pursuance
of a surrender not being a voluntary act, it is immaterial whether the
lord had or had not at the time of such admission a good title to the
manor. *Doe* d. *Burgess* v. *Thompson*, 5 A. & E. 532; 1 N. & P. 215.
If the lord be an infant, his admission of a copyholder upon a surrender is binding. *Per* Lord Mansfield, C. J., in *Zouch* d. *Abbott* v.
Parsons, 3 Burr. 1801. So the acts of one who is a steward *de facto*,
although not *de jure*, are good. *Parker* v. *Kett*, 1 Lord Raym. 658;
1 Salk. 95; 12 Mod. 467.

A copyhold cannot be surrendered at a day to come. *Leigh* v.
Brace, 5 Mod. 267. A surrender, with admittance thereon, operates
to pass only such estate, if any, as the surrenderor then has. *Goodtitle*
d. *Faulkner* v. *Morse*, 3 T. R. 365; *Doe* d. *Ibbott* v. *Cowling*, 6 T. R.
63; *Doe* d. *Blacksell* v. *Tomkins*, 11 East, 185; *Doe* d. *Tofield* v.
Tofield, 11 East, 246; *Matthew* v. *Osborne*, 13 C. B. 919; 2 Arch.
N. P. 343. "In order to pass an estate by surrender, the estate must
pass into the hands of the lord, through which it must be taken. A
fine differs from the case of a surrender, for that will be good against
the heir by estoppel, although it passes no estate at all; but if a surrender be not good, there will be no estoppel, and no estate can pass
into the hands of the lord." *Per* Lord Hardwicke, L. C., in *Taylor* v.
Philips, 1 Ves. 230; cited 3 T. R. 371. If the heir apparent of a copyholder in fee make a surrender in the lifetime of his ancestor, and survive him, the heir of the person making such surrender will not be
thereby estopped from recovering by ejectment against the surrenderee.
Goodtitle d. *Faulkner* v. *Morse*, 3 T. R. 365; and see *Doe* d. *Ibbott*
v. *Cowling*, 6 T. R. 63. Devisees of *contingent* remainders in a copyhold, not being in the seisin, cannot make a surrender of their interest;
nor will a surrender made by them operate by estoppel to bind them
or their heirs. *Doe* d. *Blacksell* v. *Tomkins*, 11 East, 185; *Doe* d.
Baverstock v. *Rolfe*, 8 A. & E. 650; 3 N. & P. 648. A surrender to
husband and wife, and the survivor, and after the death of the survivor
to the right heirs of both, "vests an immediate fee simple in the husband and wife by entireties, and the husband cannot alien or devise
any part of it; but on his death the whole survives to his wife."
Green d. *Crew* v. *King*, 2 W. Black. 1211; *Doe* d. *Dormer* v. *Wilson*,
4 B. & C. 303. A surrender by a married woman without the concurrence of her husband is void. *Stevens* v. *Tyrrell*, 2 Wils. 1. So if
she be not examined separately from her husband by the steward or
other person taking the surrender, according to the custom of the
manor. *Smithson* v. *Cage*, Cro. Jac. 526; *Burdet's case*, Cro. Eliz.
48; *Burgess* v. *Foster*, 1 Leon. 289.

Until admittance the legal estate does not vest in the surrenderee,
but remains in the surrenderor and his heirs. *Fisher* v. *Wigg*, 1 P.
Wms. 17; *Berry* v. *Greene*, Cro. Eliz. 349; *Browne* v. *Dyer*, 11 Mod.
73; *Doe* d. *Shewen* v. *Wroot*, 5 East, 132; 1 Smith, 363; *Roe* d.
Cosh v. *Loveless*, 2 B. & A. 456; *Rex* v. *Wilson*, 10 B. & C. 80, Lord
Tenterden, C. J.; *Watson* v. *Waltham*, 2 A. & E. 485; 4 N. & P.
537; *Matthew* v. *Osborne*, 13 C. B. 919.

A surrenderee before admittance has neither *jus in re* nor *jus ad rem*,
i. e. neither a right of possession, nor a right of property. *Phillibrown*

v. *Ryland*, 8 Mod. 352. He cannot enter or maintain ejectment, though the lord refuse admittance without just cause. *Berry* v. *Greene*, Cro. Eliz. 349. His remedy is by mandamus, or bill in equity, to compel admittance. 4 Burr. 1961; Watk. Cop. 72 (4th ed.); *Id.*, 131. If the lord refuse to admit the surrenderee on account of a disagreement as to the fine to be paid, the court will by mandamus compel him; because the right to a fine cannot arise until *after* admittance. *Rex* v. *The Lord and Steward of the Manor of Hendon*, 2 T. R. 484; *Reg.* v. *Lord Wellesley*, 2 E. & B. 924; *Lord Wellesley* v. *Withers*, 4 E. & B. 750. When the surrenderee is admitted, the admittance *relates back to the time of the surrender* for all purposes whatever, except as against the lord. *Benson* v. *Scott*, 1 Salk. 185; 3 Lev. 385; *Burgaine* v. *Spurling*, Cro. Car. 283; *Doe* d. *Wheeler* v. *Gibbons*, 7 C. & P. 161. Therefore an ejectment commenced after a surrender and before admittance may be supported by an admittance at any time before the trial. *Holdfast* d. *Woollams* v. *Clapham*, 1 T. R. 600; *Doe* d. *Bennington* v. *Hall*, 16 East, 208; *Doe* d. *Nicholson* v. *Welford*, 12 A. & E. 61; 4 P. & D. 77 (3rd point). An admittance under a conditional surrender by way of mortgage will relate back to the date of such surrender, so as to defeat a subsequent surrender to a purchaser or mortgagee, notwithstanding the latter first obtains admittance. *Doe* d. *Wheeler* v. *Gibbons*, 7 C. & P. 161, Park, J.; *Burgaine* v. *Spurling*, Cro. Car. 283. The principle is, that "as between surrenderor and surrenderee the latter cannot be prejudiced by any act done by the former subsequent to the surrender, but is entitled to be admitted to the estate free from all mesne incumbrances." *Per cur.* in *Rex* v. *Lady Mildmay*, 5 B. & Adol. 279.

If the surrenderor die before admittance, his widow shall not be entitled to dower or freebench, because the surrenderee on admittance has a prior title by relation to the surrender. *Benson* v. *Scott*, 1 Salk. 185; 3 Lev. 385. The heir of a surrenderee, who was never admitted, cannot after admittance recover against the widow of the surrenderee, because the admittance relates back to the surrender, and enures for her benefit in respect of her freebench. *Vaughan* d. *Atkins* v. *Atkins*, 5 Burr. 2765, 2787.

Before the act for the amendment of the laws with respect to wills (7 Will. 4 & 1 Vict. c. 26) a surrenderee of copyholds who had not been admitted could not effectually devise the property so as to pass the legal estate. *Doe* d. *Tofield* v. *Tofield*, 11 East, 246; *Matthew* v. *Osborne*, 13 C. B. 919. So a devisee could not before admittance devise the legal estate. *Doe* d. *Vernon* v. *Vernon*, 7 East, 8. But now by sect. 3 of the above act the power of devising thereby given shall extend to all copyholds, &c., "notwithstanding that the testator may not have surrendered the same to the use of his will, or notwithstanding that, being entitled as heir, devisee *or otherwise, to be admitted thereto*, he shall not have been admitted thereto." *Ante*, 494.

The customary heir of a deceased copyholder in fee has the legal estate vested in him *before admittance*, except as against the lord. *Doe* d. *Taylor* v. *Crisp*, 6 A. & E. 779; 1 P. & D. 37; *Doe* d. *Hinton* v. *Rolfe*, 3 N. & P. 648; *Rex* v. *Bennett*, 2 T. R. 197; *Joyner* v. *Lambert*, Cro. Jac. 36. But the lord may compel him to come in and be admitted, by three proclamations made at three consecutive courts, and by a subsequent seizure *quousque*. *Lord Salisbury's case*, 1 Lev. 63; *Doe* d. *Bover* v. *Trueman*, 1 B. & Adol. 736; *Dimes* v. *The Grand*

Junction Canal Company, 9 Q. B. 469, 511. After which he must either be admitted or tender and offer himself to be admitted before he will be in a condition to maintain ejectment against the lord. *Doe* d. *Burrell* v. *Bellamy,* 2 M. & S. 87; *Doe* d. *Le Keux* v. *Harrison,* 6 Q. B. 631.

Evidence for Plaintiff.]—In ejectment for copyholds by a surrenderee the claimant must prove:—

1. The seisin or title of the surrenderor previous to the surrender. *Ante,* 622. This may be proved *primâ facie* in like manner as when the property is freehold. *Ante,* 211.

Where a *primâ facie* title is relied on, it is unnecessary to prove that the surrenderor was ever *admitted,* for that might go on *ad infinitum.* The defendant may be left to prove that the surrenderor, or one of the previous persons through whom the title is derived, was never admitted.

But it is not generally advisable to rely on a *primâ facie* case where evidence of a more conclusive nature can be produced. Therefore the *admittance* of the surrenderor in pursuance of a surrender or some other legal title, and his subsequent possession of the property, or receipt of the rents within twenty years next before action, should generally be proved.

How far it may be expedient, on behalf of the claimant, to carry back the proof of the title, or to endeavour to throw such proof on the defendant, must of course depend upon the nature of the title, and of the point or question (if any) intended to be raised.

2. The surrender to the plaintiff, and his admittance thereon, must be proved. Both are necessary, as they together constitute one assurance (*ante,* 621), and the surrender does not pass the legal estate until admittance. *Ante,* 622. But an admittance after action brought and just before the trial is sufficient, because it relates back to the date of the surrender for all purposes, except as against the lord. *Ante,* 623. The surrender and admittance may be proved by the stamped copy of the admission purporting to be made in pursuance of the surrender, and signed by the steward. Lit. s. 75; 1 Scriven Cop. 590; Peake's Ev. 94. His handwriting should be proved unless the document be admitted in the cause (*ante,* 150), or be proved to have been obtained from the steward, or to have been produced to and admitted by him; *Doe* d. *Burrows* v. *Freeman,* 1 Car. & Kir. 386, Coleridge, J.; or the document be more than thirty years old. *Dean and Chapter of Ely* v. *Stewart,* 2 Atk. 45; *Rowe* v. *Brenton,* 3 Man. & Ry. 296; 8 B. & C. 737. Entries in a steward's book about thirty years old, and coming from the proper custody, are admissible in evidence without proving the handwriting of the steward. *Wynne* v. *Tyrwhitt,* 4 B. & A. 376.

A surrender out of court, presented and inrolled afterwards, and the admission thereon, may be proved by an *examined copy* of the court roll, without producing the original surrender, or the stamped copy of the admission. *Doe* d. *Cawthorn* v. *Mee,* 4 B. & Adol. 617; 1 N. & M. 424; *Rowe* v. *Brenton,* 3 Man. & R. 303; 8 B. & C. 737. An examined copy of court rolls is admissible in evidence to prove a surrender, without being stamped, the provision in the General Stamp Act as to copies of court rolls applying only to such copies as are given out and signed by the steward. *Doe* d. *Burrows* v. *Freeman,* 1 Car. & K.

386; 12 M. & W. 844. To prove an examined copy it is sufficient for the witness to swear that he examined the copy, whilst another person read the original; *Reid* v. *Margison*, 1 Camp. 469; *ante*, 253; but the copy should contain no abbreviations which are not in the original, otherwise it will be rejected. *Reg.* v. *Christian*, Car. & M. 388.

The surrender and admittance may be proved by the original entries on the court rolls, without the production of any stamped copy. *Doe* d. *Bennington* v. *Hall*, 16 East, 208. The court rolls, containing a presentment of an admittance upon a surrender out of court, are primary evidence of the surrender, as between surrenderor and surrenderee, without producing the original surrender, or inquiring into the sufficiency of the stamp upon it. *Doe* d. *Garrod* v. *Otley*, 12 A. & E. 481; 4 P. & D. 275. They are also admissible as against a stranger to prove the surrender and admittance. *Doe* d. *Bennington* v. *Hall*, 16 East, 208. The original roll may, however, be shown to be incorrect, by production of the minute of the steward and other evidence. 1 Scriven, Cop. 253; *Doe* d. *Priestley* v. *Calloway*, 6 B. & C. 494, 495. The rolls are not records, and therefore any mistake in them may be corrected by parol evidence. *S. C.; Towers* v. *Moor*, 2 Vern. 98; *Burgen* v. *Foster*, 1 Leon. 289; *Brend* v. *Brend*, Cas. temp. Finch, 254; *Kite and Queinton's case*, 4 Co. R. 25; Co. Cop. s. 40. An entry in the record book of a manor of an admittance to a copyhold, reciting a surrender of the same copyhold to the use of a will, is admissible evidence of the surrender, the steward not being able to find the surrender itself on the roll or elsewhere, and the surrenders being irregularly kept in the manor, although all the other surrenders were either preserved or recorded on the roll. *Rex* v. *The Inhabitants of Thruscross*, 1 A. & E. 126; 3 N. & M. 284. A surrender and presentment may be proved by the draft of an entry produced from the muniments of the manor, and the parol evidence of the foreman of the homage who made the presentment. *Doe* d. *Priestley* v. *Calloway*, 6 B. & C. 484; 9 D. & R. 518.

Evidence of the *identity* of the plaintiffs with the persons named in the surrender, and admitted thereon, must be produced. *Doe* d. *Hanson* v. *Smith*, 1 Camp. 196.

It is unnecessary to prove the lord's title. An admission in pursuance of a surrender not being a voluntary act, the lord's title is immaterial. *Doe* d. *Burgess* v. *Thompson*, 5 A. & E. 532; 1 N. & P. 215; *ante*, 622.

The steward of a manor may be appointed by deed or by parol. *Down's case*, 4 Co. R. 29 b; Cro. Eliz. 323; *Lady Holcroft's case*, 4 Co. R. 30 b. He may take surrenders out of the manor, and a custom to the contrary is void; but he could not before 4 & 5 Vict. c. 35, s. 88, *admit* a person out of the manor. *Tukely* v. *Hawkins*, 1 Ld. Ray. 76; *Clifton* v. *Molineux*, 4 Co. R. 27 a; *Dudfield* v. *Andrews*, 1 Salk. 184; *Doe* d. *Leach* v. *Whittaker*, 5 B. & Adol. 409; 3 N. & M. 225 (2nd and 4th points). The steward appointed by parol may take a surrender and examine a feme covert out of court. *Smithson* v. *Cage*, Cro. Jac. 526. The steward may authorize a man to take a surrender out of court, and so may his deputy. A deputy may do whatever his principal might have done, except make a deputy; and he cannot be appointed with less power. But a deputation to do a particular act will make a man servant *pro hâc vice*. A deputy may act in his own name. The acts of one who is a steward *de facto*,

E E

though not *de jure,* are good. *Parker* v. *Kett,* 1 Ld. Ray. 658; 1 Salk. 95; 12 Mod. 467. A surrender may be taken not only by the steward or his deputy, but also by any other person authorized by the custom of the manor to take surrenders. Thus where a surrender was taken by S., who stated that he held the office of clerk of the castle of the manor, by patent from the lord, that there was a custom for him to take surrenders, that the steward also took them, and that he (S.) had a concurrent jurisdiction with the steward; but the patent contained no authority to that effect: held evidence for the jury that S. was entitled by custom to take the surrender. *Doe* d. *Stillwell* v. *Millersh,* 5 A. & E. 540; 1 N. & P. 30. It is a good custom that a feme covert copyholder may surrender to two tenants of the manor out of court. *Erish* v. *Rivers,* Cro. Eliz. 717. By special custom she may be separately examined before two customary tenants. *Driver* d. *Berry* v. *Thompson,* 4 Taunt. 294.

The lord of a manor, or his steward, or the deputy of such steward, may admit at any time or place, either within or out of such manor, and without holding a court for such manor, any person entitled to be admitted. 4 & 5 Vict. c. 35, s. 88.

The admittance of a tenant for life operates as an admission of the remainderman claiming under the same surrender or will; but not so as to bar the lord of his fine. Co. Cop. 41, 56; *Brown's case,* 4 Co. R. 22 b; *Warsopp* v. *Abell,* 5 Mod. 306; *Gyppen* v. *Bunney,* Cro. Eliz. 504; Moore, 465; *Auncelme* v. *Auncelme,* Cro. Jac. 31; *Doe* d. *Whitbread* v. *Jenney,* 5 East, 522; *Pyphers* v. *Eburn,* 3 Bing. N. C. 250; *Church* v. *Mundy,* 12 Ves. 426, 431; *Doe* d. *Baverstock* v. *Rolfe,* 8 A. & E. 650; 3 N. & P. 648. Therefore where a surrender is made to the use of A. for life, with remainder to B. in fee, and A. is admitted; upon his death B. may maintain ejectment without any further admittance. *Baspool* v. *Long,* Cro. Eliz. 879; Noy, 42, S. C.; *Auncelme* v. *Auncelme,* Cro. Jac. 31; *Doe* d. *Whitbread* v. *Jenney,* 5 East, 522; *Doe* d. *Baverstock* v. *Rolfe,* 8 A. & E. 650; 3 N. & P. 648; 2 Arch. N. P. 343. "The authorities are numerous and clear to show that the admission of the particular tenant is the admission of the remainderman also; and the principle on which that has been laid down applies equally to the reversioner, namely, that the particular estate and the remainder make but one estate." *Per cur.* in *Doe* d. *Winder* v. *Lawes,* 7 A. & E. 210; 2 N. & P. 195, S. C.

By the general rule of copyhold law a surrender out of court must be presented at the next court; but by custom it may be presented at the second or third court. Comyn's Dig. Copyhold, tit. Presentment; *Moor* v. *Moore,* 2 Ves .sen. 601; Co. Cop. 88; Gilbert's Ten. 280. Whether a custom to present at an indefinite period would be good, seems doubtful. *Doe* d. *Priestley* v. *Calloway,* 9 D. & R. 518; 6 B. & C. 484, 493, Lord Tenterden, C. J. A custom that if the surrenderee of a copyhold do not take it up at the next court he shall be barred, is good; but the nonclaim of a tenant for life shall not bar him in remainder. *Baspool* v. *Long,* Cro. Eliz. 879; Noy, 42, *S. C.* Where, by the custom of a manor, it is provided that every surrenderee ought to come within three years after the surrender has been presented, and take up the same, and pay his fine, the omission to come does not avoid the estate—it only applies as between the lord and the tenant, and not as between third parties, so as to avoid an admittance at a later period. *Doe* d. *Warwick* v. *Coombes,* 14 Law J., N. S., Q. B. 37.

A conveyance of copyholds by grant or other common law assurance, without a surrender to the lord, will not pass the legal estate, nor enable the grantee to maintain ejectment, even as against the widow of the grantor. *Doe* d. *North* v. *Webber*, 3 Bing. N. C. 922. Unless, indeed, the deed affects merely the possession, as a lease or licence. *Infra.*

Evidence and Points for Defendant.]—The defendant may contend that the plaintiff's evidence is insufficient on some material point. *Ante*, 624 to 626. He may also produce contradictory evidence. He may show a *title to possession* in himself or some third person (not being one of the plaintiffs) under a demise: *infra:* or under a contract for purchase which has not been determined by a demand of possession. *Doe* d. *Newby* v. *Jackson*, 1 B. & C. 448 ; 2 D. & R. 514 ; *ante*, 58. He may prove a subsequent surrender to himself as a *bond fide* purchaser for value, and his admittance thereon ; and that the prior surrender to the plaintiff was void under the 27 Eliz. c. 4, as against the defendant. *Doe* d. *Tunstill* v. *Bottriell*, 5 B. & Adol. 131 ; 2 N. & M. 64. He may show that the surrender to the plaintiff is void under the Mortmain Act, 9 Geo. 2, c. 36. *Doe* d. *Howson* v. *Waterton*, 3 B. & A. 149. Or that the plaintiff's title is barred by the Statute of Limitations. *Ante*, 4. Thus where copyholds were granted to A. for the lives of herself and B., and in reversion to C. for other lives ; A. died, having devised to B., who entered and kept possession for more than twenty years ; on his death C. brought ejectment : held, that the action was barred by the Statute of Limitations, for that C.'s right of possession accrued on the death of A., inasmuch as there cannot be a general occupant of copyhold land. *Doe* d. *Foster* v. *Scott*, 4 B. & C. 706 ; 7 D. & R. 190.

3. BY LESSEE OF A COPYHOLDER.]—A copyholder cannot make a lease of his copyhold tenement even for a year or less, except by custom ; and such a lease may by custom be void against his heir in the event of his death during the term. *Turner* v. *Hodges*, Hetley, 126 ; Lit. Rep. 233. In most manors a copyholder may demise for one year or less without any licence of the lord. 1 Scriven, 457. By special custom he may demise for three, seven, fourteen or twenty-one years, without any such licence. *Id.* 457. If a copyholder make a lease for more than one year, contrary to the custom of the manor, and without the licence of the lord, he thereby forfeits his copyhold. *Ante*, 615. But such lease, although void against the lord for the time being and his grantees, is valid as between the parties themselves and their respective assigns ; so that the lessee may maintain ejectment upon it as against the lessor or any other person, except the lord of the manor and his assigns. *Downingham's case*, Owen, 17 ; *Doe* d. *Tressider* v. *Tressider*, 1 Q. B. 416 ; *Doe* d. *Robinson* v. *Bousfield*, 1 Car. & K. 558 ; 6 Q. B. 492 ; 1 Crabb, Real Prop. 701.

A lease from a copyholder, with or without the licence of the lord, cannot be defeated by a subsequent surrender to the lord, and a regrant by him to another person. *Doe* d. *Beadon* v. *Pyke*, 5 M. & S. 146. A lease granted by a copyhold tenant under a licence of the lord is not affected by a subsequent forfeiture of the tenant's estate, such licence operating as a confirmation by the lord. *Clarke* v. *Arden*, 16 C. B. 227.

The evidence will be the same as in an ejectment by a tenant against his landlord for freeholds demised. *Ante*, 458. The lessor's title must, if necessary, be proved, as in an action by a surrenderee; *ante*, 624; or devisee; *ante*, 526; or heir; *post*, 629. But no admittance of the lessee by the lord need be proved; "For mere possession, admittance is not necessary." *Per* Lord Denman, C. J., in *Watson* v. *Waltham*, 2 A. & E. 491; 4 N. & M. 587, *S. C.*

A copyholder licensing his lessee to commit waste on condition of his doing a subsequent act to diminish the damage thereby occasioned, cannot eject him for a forfeiture incurred by his committing the waste without performing the subsequent act. *Doe* d. *Wood* v. *Morris*, 2 Taunt. 52.

4. BY A DEVISEE.]—See *ante*, 526.

5. BY CUSTOMARY HEIR.]—The customary heir of a deceased copyholder in fee may maintain ejectment *without admittance*, except as against the lord. *Doe* d. *Taylor* v. *Crisp*, 6 A. & E. 778; 1 P. & D. 37; *Doe* d. *Hinton* v. *Rolfe*, 3 N. & P. 648; *Rex* v. *Bennett*, 2 T. R. 197; *Barnett* v. *Earl of Guilford*, 11 Exch. 19; 1 Scriv. Cop. 290 (4th ed.); 1 Watk. Cop. 244. Such right is not limited to an ejectment commenced before the first proclamation for the heir to come in and be admitted. *Per cur.* in *Doe* d. *Bover* v. *Trueman*, 1 B. & Adol. 747. But in an ejectment against the lord, after a seizure *quousque*, the heir must prove either an admittance, or that he tendered and offered himself for admittance, and was refused by the lord or his steward, either in or out of court. *Doe* d. *Burrell* v. *Bellamy*, 2 M. & S. 87; *Doe* d. *Le Keux* v. *Harrison*, 6 Q. B. 631; *Austen* v. *Osborn*, Comyn, R. 245; *Barnett* v. *Earl of Guilford*, 11 Exch. 19. Sometimes an admittance is necessary to enable the heir to recover in ejectment even against a stranger; as where the copyhold was held for the joint lives of the ancestor and the lord, with a tenant right of renewal, binding the lord to admit the customary heir of the copyholder. *Doe* d. *Hamilton* v. *Clift*, 12 A. & E. 566; 4 P. & D. 579; *Doe* d. *Dand* v. *Thompson*, 13 Q. B. 670. But in ordinary cases the admittance of a copyholder in fee operates as an admittance of him *and his heirs;* in like manner as the admittance of the surrenderee or devisee of a particular estate operates as an admittance of the remainderman claiming under the same surrender or will. *Ante*, 626. The heir of a copyholder may surrender a reversion descended to him, before admittance; and if it be to one for life, remainder in fee, the admittance of tenant for life admits him in remainder. *Colchin* v. *Colchin*, Cro. Eliz. 662. A customary heir may devise without admittance, and without payment of the lord's fine; and he might have done so, even before the Wills Act (7 Will. 4 & 1 Vict. c. 26). *Right* d. *Taylor* v. *Banks*, 3 B. & Adol. 664; *Doe* d. *Perry* v. *Wilson*, 5 A. & E. 321.

An ejectment may be maintained by the customary heir of A., who was customary heir of B., a deceased copyholder in fee, although neither A. nor the claimant was ever admitted. *Doe* d. *Winder* v. *Lawes*, 7 A. & E. 195; 2 N. & P. 195. A copyhold is devised by A. to B. for life, remainder to C. in fee; B. is admitted and dies; C. has *before entry* a descendible estate; and upon the death of C. his customary heir, and not the customary heir of A., is entitled to the copyhold. *Doe* d. *Parker* v. *Thomas*, 3 Man. & Gr. 815, 821; 4 Scott, N. R. 419; and see *Foster* v. *Hayes*, 4 E. & B. 717.

A customary heir cannot maintain *trespass* without entry; but after entry there is a relation back to the actual title as against a wrongdoer, and he may maintain an action for trespasses committed prior to his entry. *Barnett* v. *Earl of Guilford*, 11 Exch. 19.

The lord may be compelled by a mandamus to admit the customary heir of a deceased copyholder in fee. *Rex* v. *The Brewers' Company*, 3 B. & C. 172; 4 D. & R. 492 (overruling *Rex* v. *Rennett*, 2 T. R. 197). Even where the lord disputes the claimant's legitimacy, and claims the land by escheat. *Reg.* v. *Dendy*, 1 E. & B. 829; 1 Bail C. C. 117. Where a copyholder devised his copyhold tenement, but the devisee disclaimed: held, that the heir was entitled to a mandamus to admit him. *Rex* v. *Wilson*, 10 B. & C. 80. So where the devisee did not come in, or claim to be admitted. *Doe* d. *Le Keux* v. *Harrison*, 6 Q. B. 631. Upon an application of this nature any dispute as to the amount of the fine payable to the lord will not be gone into, because no right to the fine can arise until *after* admittance. *Rex* v. *The Lord and Steward of the Manor of Hendon*, 2 T. R. 484; *Reg.* v. *Lord Wellesley*, 2 E. & B. 924; and see *Lord Wellesley* v. *Withers*, 4 E. & B. 750; *Graham* v. *Sime*, 1 East, 632. It seems however, that coparceners are entitled to be admitted to copyhold tenements *as one heir*, and upon the payment of one set of fees. *Rex* v. *The Lord and Steward of the Manor of Bonsall*, 3 B. & C. 173. Where an estate is devised to three persons as trustees and executors, two of them may disclaim, to the intent that the other may be admitted alone, and in such case only a single fine will be payable. *Lord Wellesley* v. *Withers*, 4 E. & B. 750.

Evidence for Plaintiff.]—In ejectment for copyholds by the heir, the claimant must prove:—

1. The seisin in fee of his ancestor. *Doe* d. *Player* v. *Nicholls*, 1 B. & C. 336; 2 D. & R. 480. This must be proved in like manner as in an action by a surrenderee (*ante*, 624), or devisee (*ante*, 526), according to the nature of the title.

2. His own title as heir. This must be proved in like manner as in ejectment for freeholds (*ante*, 487); but the plaintiff must show himself to be the *customary* heir, and, if necessary, the custom of the manor must be proved. *Doe* d. *Goodwin* v. *Spray*, 1 T. R. 466; *Doe* d. *Beebee* v. *Parker*, 5 T. R. 26; *Doe* d. *Foster* v. *Sisson*, 12 East, 62; *Reeve* v. *Malster*, Cro. Car. 410; *Doe* d. *Aistrop* v. *Aistrop*, 2 W. Blac. 1228; *Doe* d. *Milner* v. *Brightwen*, 10 East, 538. In the absence of proof to the contrary, the heir at law will be presumed to be the customary heir. A custom that lands shall descend to the youngest son shall not extend to the youngest brother. *Bayley* v. *Stevens*, Cro. Jac. 198. A custom that lands shall descend to the eldest sister, where there is neither a son nor a daughter, does not extend to an eldest niece. *Doe* d. *Goodwin* v. *Spray*, 1 T. R. 466. A customary of a manor, appearing to be of great antiquity, and delivered down with the court rolls from steward to steward, although not signed by any person, is good evidence to prove the course of descent within the manor. *Doe* d. *Goodwin* v. *Spray*, 1 T. R. 466. An entry on the court rolls stating the mode of descent is admissible, though no instances of any persons having taken according to it be proved. *Doe* d. *Beebee* v. *Parker*, 5 T. R. 26. A single admittance to a copyhold

is evidence to prove the custom of a manor for lands to descend to the youngest nephew. *Doe* d. *Mason* v. *Mason*, 3 Wils. 63.

3. It is not necessary to prove that the claimant has been *admitted* as heir (*ante*, 628), unless the defendant be lord of the manor (*ante*, 628), or the claimant's ancestor held only for the joint lives of himself and the lord, with a right of renewal. *Doe* d. *Hamilton* v. *Clift*, 12 A. & E. 566; 4 P. & D. 579; *Doe* d. *Dand* v. *Thompson*, 13 Q. B. 670.

4. If the defendant were a tenant of the claimant's ancestor, such tenancy must be shown to have expired, or to have been determined by notice to quit or otherwise, in like manner as in an action for freeholds. *Ante*, 490.

5. Lastly, it must appear that the claimant or his ancestor has been in possession or receipt of the rents within twenty years; *Doe* d. *Linsey* v. *Edwards*, 5 A. & E. 95; or that some other person was within that period in possession as tenant by the courtesy, or for some other estate which has ceased. *Doe* d. *Milner* v. *Brightwen*, 10 East, 583; and see *Doe* d. *Cook* v. *Davers*, 7 East, 299; 3 Smith, 291; *Doe* d. *Dormer* v. *Wilson*, 4 B. & A. 303.

Evidence and Points for Defendant.]—The defendant may contend that the plaintiff's evidence is insufficient on some material point. *Ante*, 629. He may also produce contradictory evidence. He may show that the claimant's ancestor held only for the joint lives of himself and the lord, and that the claimant has never been admitted. *Doe* d. *Dand* v. *Thompson*, 13 Q. B. 670. But, generally speaking, it is no defence that the claimant has not been admitted as heir (*ante*, 628), unless the defendant be the lord of the manor. *Ante*, 628. Whether the defendant be the lord or not, it will be no defence to prove that the claimant's ancestor devised the property to a third person who has never claimed to be admitted. *Doe* d. *Le Keux* v. *Harrison*, 6 Q. B. 631. But proof of a valid devise, with admittance thereon, will defeat the action. *Doe* d. *Parker* v. *Thomas*, 4 Scott, N. S. 449; 11 Law J., N. S., C. P. 124. So proof of a surrender by the claimant's ancestor with admittance thereon before or after his death, and even subsequently to the commencement of the action, will establish a good defence, because the admittance always relates back to the date of the surrender. *Ante*, 623. So proof of a lease granted by the late tenant to the defendant, or to any third person, will defeat the action, unless it appear that such lease has expired or been duly determined by notice to quit or otherwise.

A lease by a copyholder for more than a year, contrary to the custom and without the licence of the lord, is valid as between the parties and their respective representatives. *Ante*, 627. The defendant may prove that by the custom of the manor the widow of the claimant's ancestor is entitled to all the property for her life for her freebench (*infra*) and her marriage, and that she is still living, and has been admitted.

6. By a Widow for her Freebench.]—Where there is a custom in a manor that the widow shall enjoy during her widowhood the whole or part of the customary lands whereof her husband died seised, as of freebench, she may, after admittance, or after challenging her right

and praying to be admitted, maintain an ejectment, even against the lord; because it is an excrescence which, by the custom and the law, grows out of the estate. Ad. Eject. 48; Co. Cop. s. 4; *Goodwin* v. *Longhurst*, Cro. Eliz. 535; *Doe* d. *Burrell* v. *Bellamy*, 3 M. & S. 87. But the husband must die *legally seised; Right* d. *Dean and Chapter of Wells* v. *Bawdon*, 3 East, 260; *Parker* v. *Bleeke*, Cro. Car. 568; unless there be a special custom to the contrary. *Riddell* v. *Jenner*, 10 Bing. 29; 3 Moo. & Sc. 673. A lease for years by a copyholder with the licence of the lord, where the widow by custom would be entitled to her freebench if the copyholder had died seised, defeats the widow of her freebench. *Salisbury* d. *Cook* v. *Hard*, 2 Cowp. 481; *Fareley's case*, Cro. Jac. 36.

If the widow's claim be in the nature of dower, an ejectment will not lie before assignment; Ad. Eject. 48; *Jurdan* v. *Stone*, Hutt. 18; *Howard* v. *Bartlett*, Hob. 181; *Doe* d. *Nutt* v. *Nutt*, 2 C. & P. 430; but she must levy a plaint, in the nature of a writ of dower, in the lord's court. *Chapman* v. *Sharpe*, 2 Show. 184. A wife is not dowable of a copyhold without a special custom. *Shaw's case*, 4 Co. R. 30 b; Moore, 410; Cro. Eliz. 426, *S. C.* A custom that a wife shall have all her husband's copyhold lands in fee, as her freebench for life, in preference to his children, is good. *Boraston* v. *Hay*, Cro. Eliz. 415.

Sometimes by custom a widow is entitled to her freebench only so long as she continues a widow and chaste; and ejectment may be maintained against her, as for a forfeiture, on proof of her incontinence. *Doe* d. *Ashew* v. *Ashew*, 10 East, 520. The widow of a tenant in tail of copyhold is entitled to her freebench though there is no custom as to the freebench of widows of tenants in tail, but only as to the freebench of widows of tenants in fee. *Norfolk* v. *Sanders*, 3 Doug. 303.

In some cases a widow may be compelled by a bill in equity *to elect* between her dower and freebench, and the benefits given her by her husband's will devising the estate. *Lowes* v. *Lowes*, 5 Hare, 501; 15 Law J., N. S., Chanc. 369; *Grayson* v. *Deakin*, 3 De Gex & S. 298; 18 Law J., N. S., Chanc. 114; *Taylor* v. *Taylor*, 1 You. & Coll. 727; *Raynard* v. *Spence*, 4 Beav. 103. Sometimes not. *Holditch* v. *Holditch*, 2 You. & Coll. 18; *Smith* v. *Lyne, Id.*, 345; *Farmer* v. *Elworthy*, 4 Beav. 487.

7. BY GRANTEE.]—Copyholds pass by a surrender and admittance, and not by a grant or other common law assurance. *Loveday* v. *Winter*, 5 Mod. 245; 1 Com. 40; 1 Salk. 186; 1 Wms. Saund. 277 b. The grantee of a copyhold estate in fee, claiming under a grant or release executed by a copyholder, has only an equitable estate, and cannot maintain ejectment even against the widow of the grantor. *Doe* d. *North* v. *Webber*, 3 Bing. N. C. 922; 5 Scott, 189. But if the deed merely affect *the possession* (as a lease or licence) it may create a legal estate. *Ante*, 627. "For mere possession, admittance is not necessary." *Per* Lord Denman, C. J., in *Watson* v. *Waltham*, 2 A. & E. 491; 4 N. & M. 537, *S. C.* A release may be made by a copyholder to any person who has *been admitted*, although erroneously; but not to a mere disseisor. *Kite and Queinton's case*, 4 Co. R. 25 a; *Whitton* v. *Williams*, Cro. Jac. 101; *Doe* d. *Milner (Bart.)* v. *Brightwen*, 10 East, 583, 595. A release by a copyholder to the lord's grantee of

the freehold is an extinguishment of the copy. *Anon.*, Cro. Eliz. 21.
After a surrender upon condition and admittance thereon, the condition
may be released by deed. *Hull* v. *Shar-Brook*, Cro. Jac. 36.

Voluntary grants of copyhold by the lord can be made only according to the custom of the manor. *Rex* v. *Inhabitants of Welby*, 2 M.
& S. 504. Where there is no custom for that purpose, the lord of a
manor cannot make a new grant of a copyhold. *Rex* v. *Inhabitants
of Hornchurch*, 2 B. & A. 189. A custom enabling the lord to grant
in fee, warrants a grant to a man and the heirs of his body, or for life,
or for years. *Gravenor's case*, 4 Co. R. 23 a; Poph. 33, 35; *Stanton*
v. *Barnes*, Cro. Eliz. 373, cited 2 Lord Raym. 1001, Holt, C. J.
Where grants have been made by copy for life, a grant *durante vidui-
tate* is good; but not *vice versâ*. *Down's case*, 4 Co. R. 29 b; Cro.
Eliz. 323, *S. C.* Under a custom to grant copyholds to two or three
for their lives and the life of the survivor, to hold separately in succession, and *non aliter*, the lord may grant to one and his assigns, to
hold for the lives of three persons and the life of the survivor, notwithstanding he may be entitled by the custom of the manor to a heriot on
the death of every such person successively dying seised. *Smartle* v.
Penhallow, 2 Lord Raym. 994; 6 Mod. 63; 1 Salk. 188; 3 Salk. 181,
S. C. The grant by a lord of a manor of copyhold lands to his wife
immediately is void. *Firebrass* d. *Symes* v. *Pennant*, 2 Wils. 254.

The lord of a manor, in making grants of copyhold tenements, cannot alter the ancient rent. If he attempt to do so the grant will be
void as against his successor. *Doe* d. *Rayner* v. *Strickland*, 2 Q. B.
792; 2 Gale & D. 278.

When a copyhold tenement escheats, or become forfeited to the
lord, he may grant it by copy to any other person in fee, or for any
less estate, according to the custom of the manor; and thereupon such
person may be admitted, and will be a copyholder. *Badger* v. *Ford*,
3 B. & A. 153. The grantee of a reversion in a copyhold by direct
grant from the lord, may, upon the death of the previous tenant for
life, maintain an ejectment *without admittance;* because such a grant
in effect includes an admittance, so far as any is necessary. *Roe* d.
Cash v. *Loveless*, 2 B. & A. 453. An admittance is in the nature of
an assent by the lord to a surrender made by his copyhold tenant. It
applies only to those cases where a surrender is first necessary. *Id.*,
458.

If there be a custom within a manor for the lord to grant parcels of
the waste by copy of court roll, the premises granted in the above
mode may be described as copyhold premises, though the date of
the first grant of them be modern. *Lord Northwick* v. *Stanway*, 3
Bos. & P. 346. An estate granted by copy, &c., omitting the words
"at the will of the lord," shall be intended to be a customary freehold. *Hughs* v. *Harrys*, Cro. Car. 229. A confirmation to a tenant
of his customary estate, free from all rents and services except one
penny yearly, and suit of court, &c., will extinguish the copyhold,
and create a customary freehold. *Doe* d. *Reay* v. *Huntingdon*, 4
East, 271; and see *Bradshaw* v. *Lawson*, 4 T. R. 443.

A person who has been admitted as *administrator de bonis non* to
the grantee of a copyhold *pur autre vie*, having no title in such character, cannot recover in ejectment by virtue of such admission as upon
a new and substantive grant of the lord. *Zouch* d. *Forse* v. *Forse*, 7

East, 186; 3 Smith, 191. But in ordinary cases an admittance will operate, and may be so pleaded, as a grant from the lord. *Pyster* v. *Hemling*, Cro. Jac. 103; 4 Mod. 346, cited 1 Lord Raym. 131, marg.

Voluntary grants by lords by defeasible title are not binding on the rightful owners; *secus*, as to admittances. *Chudleigh's case*, 1 Co. R. 120 a; Poph. 70; 1 And. 309, *S. C.*; *Clerke's case*, 4 Co. R. 23 b; *Rous and Aster's case*, 4 Co. R. 24 a; Moo. 236; 2 Leon. 45; Owen, 27, *S. C.* Where the custom of a manor is *quod dominus pro tempore* may demise in possession or reversion, the grant of a tenant in dower shall bind the heir, though the reversion does not fall into possession during the estate of her who made the grant. *Gay* v. *Kay*, Cro. Eliz. 661.

PART THE FOURTH.

ACTIONS OF TRESPASS FOR MESNE PROFITS: FOR DOUBLE
VALUE AND DOUBLE RENT: FOR RECOVERY OF TENEMENTS
IN THE COUNTY COURTS: SUMMARY PROCEEDINGS BEFORE
JUSTICES FOR THE RECOVERY OF SMALL TENEMENTS, DE-
SERTED PREMISES, OR PARISH PROPERTY: FORCIBLE ENTRY
AND DETAINER.

CHAPTER LXVIII.

TRESPASS FOR MESNE PROFITS, &c.

In an action of ejectment no damages are recoverable, except as between landlord and tenant, and then only at the option of the landlord,

pursuant to 15 & 16 Vict. c. 76, s. 214; *ante*, 292, 387; nor can any costs be recovered where judgment is obtained for want of an appearance. *Ante*, 131. The remedy provided by law by way of supplement to the action of ejectment, is an action of *trespass for mesne profits*, &c. Such action will lie equally after a judgment by default as after a verdict in the ejectment. *Aslin* v. *Parker*, 2 Burr. 665; 1 Smith, L. C. 264; and *per* Lord Mansfield, C. J. " There is no distinction between a judgment in ejectment upon a verdict, and a judgment by default. In the first case the right of the plaintiff is tried and determined against the defendant; in the last case it is confessed. An action for the mesne profits is consequential to the recovery in ejectment. It may be brought by the lessor of the plaintiff in his own name, or in the name of the nominal lessee; and in either shape it is equally his action. The tenant is concluded by the judgment, and cannot controvert the title, consequently he cannot controvert the plaintiff's possession, because his possession is part of his title; for the plaintiff, to entitle himself to recover in an ejectment, must show a possessory right not barred by the Statute of Limitations. This possession, like all others, only concludes the parties as to the *subject matter* of it. Therefore, *beyond* the time laid in the demise, it proves nothing at all, because, beyond that time, the plaintiff has alleged no title, nor could be put to prove any. As to the *length of time the tenant has occupied*, the judgment proves nothing; nor as to the *value*. And therefore it was proved in this case (and must be in all) *how long* the defendant enjoyed the premises, and what the value was: and it appeared that the time of such occupation by the defendant was within the time laid in the demise." *S. C.* " From the time of *Aslin* v. *Parker*, 2 Burr. 665, down to *Doe* v. *Wright*, 10 A. & E. 763; 2 N. & P. 672, it has always been held that a judgment by default in an action of ejectment, followed by a writ of possession, even though not pleaded, is evidence of the title and possession of the plaintiff, as against the tenant in possession, from the day of the demise in the declaration: and on the authority of the last-mentioned case, it is now well settled, that, if properly pleaded, it is an estoppel." *Per* Jervis, C. J., in *Wilkinson* v. *Kirby*, 15 C. B. 443.

In an action for mesne profits, &c., the plaintiff may recover a compensation in damages for the use and occupation of the premises recovered in the ejectment during the period they were actually or constructively occupied by the defendant: *Doe* v. *Harlow*, 12 A. & E. 40; *Doe* v. *Challis*, 17 Q. B. 166: also such further damages as the jury may think fit to give to the plaintiff for his trouble, &c., under the special circumstances proved before them. *Goodtitle* v. *Tombs*, 3 Wils. 121, Gould, J.; 1 Smith, L. C. 269. Also compensation for any damage done to the premises by the defendants during their occupation, and any other special damage to which the plaintiff may be legally entitled in respect of the trespasses; provided such damage be specially stated in the declaration and sufficiently proved, but not otherwise. *Dunn* v. *Large*, 3 Doug. 335, cited by Cresswell, J., in *Doe* d. *Marks* v. *Roe*, 3 Dowl. & L. 88. Also the costs of and incident to the previous action of ejectment. *Doe* v. *Huddart*, 2 Cr. M. & R. 316; 5 Tyr. 846; 4 Dowl. 437, *S. C.*; 1 Smith, L. C. 264.

By issuing and serving a writ in ejectment, the claimant elects to treat the defendants *as trespassers* on and from the day mentioned in the writ; and he cannot afterwards sue them *as tenants* for rent, or for use and occupation, subsequent to that day. *Birch* v. *Wright*, 1

T. R. 378; *Jones* v. *Carter*, 15 M. & W. 718; *Francklin* v. *Carter*, 1 C. B. 750; 3 D. & L. 213. The only remedy for the subsequent occupation, &c., is by an action of trespass for mesne profits. *Birch* v. *Wright*, 1 T. R. 378, 387. But after a landlord has recovered in ejectment against his tenant he may maintain debt upon the stat. 4 Geo. 2, c. 28, for *double the yearly value* of the premises during the time the tenant held over after the expiration of the landlord's notice to quit; for such double value is given by way of penalty, and not as rent. *Soulsby* v. *Neving*, 9 East, 310. An action of debt for *double rent* under 11 Geo. 2, c. 19, s. 18, where the tenant holds over after the expiration of a notice to quit given by himself, seems to stand upon a different footing in this respect, and not to be maintainable after an ejectment, because in such action the defendant is sued *as a tenant for rent.* *S. C.*; *Doe* d. *Cheney* v. *Batten*, Cowp. 245; *Timmins* v. *Rowlinson*, 3 Burr. 1603; Ad. Eject. 115, 334, note (*c*); 1 Chit. Pl. 216 (7th ed.).

The action for mesne profits may be brought pending proceedings in error upon the ejectment, and the court will not stay the proceedings in such action until the proceedings in error are determined, for the plaintiff's remedy should not be put in peril by the contingency of the deaths of parties, or of witnesses, or other accidents which may occur during the delay. *Donford* v. *Ellys*, 12 Mod. 138. In a recent case, a judgment in ejectment was pleaded in reply by way of estoppel, to which the defendant rejoined, that a writ of error was pending in parliament on such judgment: held, on demurrer, that the rejoinder was bad. *Doe* v. *Wright*, 10 A. & E. 763; 2 P. & D. 672.

In what Court.]—An action for mesne profits, &c., not exceeding 50*l.*, may be brought in the county court. But if the amount recoverable exceed 5*l.*, and in other cases falling within the 9 & 10 Vict. c. 95, s. 128, the action may be brought in one of the superior courts. The writ of summons should be in the common form, and should not be specially indorsed, pursuant to 15 & 16 Vict. c. 76, s. 25, the action being in trespass, and not for a debt or liquidated demand within the meaning of that section.

By whom.]—Generally speaking, the action should be brought by *all* the claimants in the ejectment in whose favour the judgment was obtained. *Chamier and Plestow* v. *Clingo and Willett*, 5 M. & S. 64; *S. C. nom. Chamier* v. *Llingon*, 2 Chit. R. 410. But to recover mesne profits in respect of any occupation, &c., *prior* to the day on which possession was claimed in the writ of ejectment, it must be shown that the plaintiffs were during such period *jointly entitled* to the tenements, &c., and in actual or constructive possession thereof, until the committing of the trespasses complained of. The evidence must be such as would support an ordinary action of trespass *quare clausum fregit*, complaining of an expulsion; as to which see Ros. Ev. 512 (7th ed.). The judgment in ejectment will not be any evidence of the plaintiff's title *prior* to the day on which possession was claimed in the writ of ejectment: *Aslin* v. *Parker*, 2 Burr. 665, 668; 1 Smith, L. C. 264, 267; *ante*, 635: and the defendants will not be estopped from pleading to the claim for such *previous* mesne profits, any plea which would be a good defence to an action of trespass for an expulsion, &c. *Doe* v. *Wellsman*, 2 Exch. 368; 6 D. & L. 179.

A tenant in common, who has recovered in ejectment against his co-tenant, may maintain an action of trespass for mesne profits, &c., without proof of an actual ouster. *Goodtitle* v. *Tombs*, 3 Wils. 118.

The customary heir of a copyhold tenement cannot maintain trespass without entry; but after entry there is a *relation back to the actual title*, as against a wrongdoer, and he may maintain an action for trespasses committed prior to his entry. *Barnett* v. *The Earl of Guilford*, 11 Exch. 19. So an administrator may, after entry, recover for trespasses to leasehold property committed prior to the grant of the letters of administration. *Id.* 19, 32; *ante*, 534.

Against whom.] — Generally speaking, an action of trespass for mesne profits, &c., should be brought against all, or some or one of the persons against whom judgment was obtained in the ejectment for want of appearance, or after verdict, or by confession or otherwise. *Aslin* v. *Parker*, 2 Burr. 665; 1 Smith, L. C. 264; *Wilkinson* v. *Kirby*, 15 C. B. 430. It may include any person let in to defend the ejectment "as landlord," and against whom a verdict and judgment has been obtained. *Doe* v. *Challis*, 17 Q. B. 166; *Doe* v. *Harlow*, 12 A. & E. 40. It may also include any person under whom the tenants in possession held as his tenants during the action of ejectment, and to whom notice of the ejectment was duly given, pursuant to 15 & 16 Vict. c. 76, s. 209. *Ante*, 115. But such notice and also the tenancy must be sufficiently proved, otherwise the judgment in ejectment will not be admissible in evidence against such person. *Hunter* v. *Britts*, 3 Camp. 455; *Doe* v. *Harvey*, 8 Bing. 239; *Matthews* v. *Osborne*, 13 C. B. 919. It may also include any person who as landlord or otherwise *caused or procured* the tenants in possession to defend the ejectment, or to withhold possession of the premises from the claimants on demand made by them. *Doe* v. *Harlow*, 12 A. & E. 40; *Doe* v. *Challis*, 17 Q. B. 166; *Id.* 168, Patteson, J.; and see *Barnett* v. *The Earl of Guilford*, 11 Exch. 22.

But although the several persons above mentioned *may* be included in an action of trespass for mesne profits, &c., it by no means follows that they *should* be so included. In many cases it would be more advisable to bring distinct actions; because in a joint action *only one and the same sum* can be recovered as damages against all or any of the defendants, and not several and distinct damages against them respectively: the declaration must allege the trespasses to have been committed by them jointly, and no separate damages can be found against any one or more without acquitting the rest. *Hill* v. *Goodchild* (in error), 5 Burr. 2790; *Mitchell* v. *Milbank*, 6 T. R. 199; *Eliot* v. *Allen*, 1 C. B. 18, 30; *Smith* v. *Pritchard*, 8 C. B. 587, 589; *Clark* v. *Newsam and Edwards*, 1 Exch. 131, 140. It is, therefore, inexpedient to include as a defendant in a joint action any person who is not liable for *all* the damages, &c. *Gregory* v. *Cotterell*, 1 E. & B. 360, 371; *Rodney* v. *Strode*, Carth. 19; 3 Mod. 101; *Johns* v. *Dodsworth*, Cro. Car. 192.

An action of trespass for mesne profits may be maintained against any person who, as undertenant or otherwise, has occupied the premises *after* the judgment in ejectment. *Doe* v. *Whitcombe*, 8 Bing. 46; *Doe* v. *Harvey*, 8 Bing. 239. But as against him no damages can be recovered in respect of the costs of the ejectment, or of the mesne profits, &c., prior to his own occupation; *Girdlestone* v. *Por-*

ter, Woodf. L. & T. 419 (7th ed.); Ad. Eject. 337; and, therefore, he should not be joined with other defendants who are liable to such costs and previous mesne profits.

Formerly an action of trespass for mesne profits, &c., could not have been maintained against executors or administrators for trespasses committed or mesne profits received in the lifetime of the testator or intestate; the maxim being *actio personalis moritur cum personâ.* 1 Chit. Pl. 218 (7th ed.). But by 3 & 4 Will. 4, c. 42, s. 2, an action of trespass, &c., "may be maintained against the executors or administrators of any person deceased, for any wrong committed by him in his lifetime to another, in respect of his property, real or personal, so as such injury shall have been committed within six calendar months before such person's death, and so as such action shall be brought within six calendar months after such executors or administrators shall have taken upon themselves the administration of the estate and effects of such person; and the damages to be recovered in such action shall be payable in like order of administration as the simple contract debts of such persons." 1 Smith, L. C. 269.

The Declaration.]—The proceedings in an action of trespass for mesne profits, &c., are the same as in an ordinary action of trespass. *For the form of declaration, see Appendix, No.* 390, *and the notes.* If the plaintiff seek to recover any special damage for injuries done to the property by waste, spoil, &c., it must be specially stated in the declaration. *See the form, Appendix, No.* 391. If the premises (an inn, &c.) have been shut up, and the custom thereby destroyed, that must be specially stated in the declaration, otherwise no damages can be recovered on that account. *Dunn* v. *Large*, 3 Doug. 335, cited by Cresswell, J., in *Doe* d. *Marks* v. *Roe*, 3 Dowl. & L. 88. The venue is local, and must be laid in the county where the lands lie. 1 Chit. Pl. 216 (7th ed.). As to the mode of laying the venue in Lancashire or Warwickshire, see *ante*, 135. The premises should be described by their names or abuttals, or otherwise, as in an ordinary action of trespass *quare clausum fregit.* Reg. Pl. H. T. 1853, No. 18; *see Appendix, No.* 390, *note* (*b*). The time when the defendants broke and entered the lands, &c., need not be mentioned, nor the length of time during which they kept the plaintiff ousted therefrom; *Ive* v. *Scott*, 9 Dowl. 993; *Higgins* v. *Highfield*, 13 East, 407; 15 & 16 Vict. c. 76, s. 49; all that is now only matter of evidence. Any special damage must be expressly stated in the declaration as above mentioned, also the costs of the ejectment. If any of such costs have not been actually paid by the plaintiff, care must be taken to state that the plaintiff has "necessarily incurred and become liable to pay" them; not that he has actually paid them. *Richardson* v. *Chasen*, 10 Q. B. 756; *Jones* v. *Lewis*, 9 Dowl. 143; *Adams* v. *Dansey*, 6 Bing. 507. The damages claimed at the end of the declaration should be sufficient to cover the utmost amount of all the mesne profits and other damages to which the plaintiff is or may be entitled, together with the costs of the ejectment. There is no harm in claiming too much, but in no case can the plaintiff recover more than he has claimed. *Tomlinson* v. *Blacksmith*, 7 T. R. 132; *Tebbs* v. *Barron*, 4 Man. & Gr. 844; *Watkins* v. *Morgan*, 6 C. & P. 661.

Pleas.]—The defendant may plead any plea which would be a good

defence to an action of trespass for an expulsion, &c. ; except so far as
he may be estopped from so pleading by the judgment in the ejectment,
and subject to such estoppel being replied. Thus he may plead :—
1. Not guilty. 2. The Statute of Limitations. 3. Leave and licence.
4. That the tenements were not the plaintiff's ; *see Appendix, No.* 392 ;
or he may plead :—1. As to the trespasses, &c., on and after the day
on which possession was claimed in the writ of ejectment, payment of
a sufficient sum of money into court. 2. As to the residue of the
declaration not guilty. 3. As to such residue the Statute of Limitations. 4. As to such residue leave and licence. 5. As to such residue
that the tenements were not plaintiff's. 6. As to such residue *liberum
tenementum. See the forms, Appendix, No.* 393. But if the defendant plead to the whole declaration *liberum tenementum,* or a traverse
of the plaintiff's property, the plaintiff may reply by way of estoppel
to so much of the plea as attempts to put in issue the plaintiff's right
of possession on the day mentioned in the writ of ejectment, and from
thence until and on the day on which possession was obtained. *Wilkinson* v. *Kirby,* 15 C. B. 430 ; *infra.* The defendant may plead a
release, or accord and satisfaction, or any other good defence to the
action. 2 Arch. N. P. 434 ; *Chatfield* v. *Parker,* 8 B. & C. 543 ; *see
Appendix, Nos.* 394, 395. But a discharge of the defendant under
any act for the relief of insolvent debtors, or by bankruptcy and certificate, constitutes no defence. *Goodtitle* v. *North,* 2 Doug. 584 ;
Lloyd v. *Peell,* 3 B. & A. 407 ; *Moggridge* v. *Davis,* 1 Wightwick,
16 ; 1 Rose, 120, *S. C.* So a set-off cannot be pleaded, the action
being for a tort, and not for a debt or liquidated demand. Ad. Eject.
341. The defendant may, however, obtain credit by way of reduction
of damages for any ground rent or rent charge to which the premises,
and the plaintiff as the owner thereof were legally liable, and which has
been actually paid by the defendant. *Doe* v. *Hare,* 4 Tyr. 29 ; 2 Cr.
& Mee. 145. In a case where the defendant had a cross-claim against
the plaintiff for money expended on the premises, a court of equity
granted an injunction to restrain the proceedings at law because of the
absence of the right of set-off in this action. *Earl Cawdor* v. *Lewis,*
1 You. & Col. 427. Perhaps in a case of this nature the set-off may
be pleaded by way of equitable defence, *pro tanto,* pursuant to 17 & 18
Vict. c. 125, s. 83.

Replications, &c.]—The plaintiff may generally reply to the defendant's plea or pleas by " joining issue" thereon. *See the form, Appendix, No.* 396. This will operate as a traverse of all the material
allegations in the plea or pleas, and also as a joinder of issue thereon.
15 & 16 Vict. c. 76, s. 79. But in some cases a mere traverse is not
sufficient ; a new assignment may be necessary. *Glover* v. *Dixon,* 9
Exch. 158 ; Ros. Ev. 523 (7th ed.). So if the defendant plead that
the tenements were not the plaintiff's as alleged, or *liberum tenementum,* or that A. B. was seized in fee, and demised to the defendant for
a term which has not elapsed, it will be material to consider whether the
plaintiff should "join issue" upon it, or reply the judgment in ejectment by way of estoppel. *Wilkinson* v. *Kirby,* 15 C. B. 430. If he
"join issue" upon the plea, the estoppel will be thereby waived, and
the question whether the plaintiff really was entitled to the possession
will be one for the jury, the judgment in ejectment being evidence, but
not conclusive evidence, for the plaintiff. *Vooght* v. *Winch,* 2 B. & A.

662; *Doe* v. *Huddart*, 2 Cr. M. & R. 316; 5 Tyr. 846; 4 Dowl. 437; *Matthews* v. *Osborne*, 13 C. B. 919; *Lord Feversham* v. *Emerson*, 11 Exch. 385; *ante*, 250. In *Dimes* v. *The Grand Junction Canal Company*, 9 Q. B. 469, the plaintiff omitted to reply the estoppel, and the whole question of his title was fully gone into, and, after a special verdict, judgment was given against him in the Queen's Bench; but such judgment was reversed in the Exchequer Chamber. When the plaintiff replies by way of estoppel the replication should be confined to so much of the plea as applies to the day on and from which possession was claimed in the writ to the day when possession was obtained under the judgment. *Doe* v. *Wellsman*, 2 Exch. 368; 6 D. & L. 179; *Wilkinson* v. *Kirby*, 15 C. B. 430. *See the form, Appendix, No.* 397. If the defendant who so pleads was not a defendant in the action of ejectment, the replication by way of estoppel should show (*inter alia*) that he was the landlord of one of the tenants in possession, and had due notice of the ejectment pursuant to 15 & 16 Vict. c. 76, s. 209 (*ante*, 115), and an opportunity of defending the action if he had thought fit. *Hunter* v. *Britts*, 3 Camp. 455; *Matthews* v. *Osborne*, 13 C. B. 919; *see the form, Appendix, No.* 398. A judgment in ejectment obtained by default may be pleaded as an estoppel, in the same manner as a judgment after verdict. *Wilkinson* v. *Kirby*, 15 C. B. 430; *Aslin* v. *Parker*, 2 Burr. 665; 1 Smith's L. C. 264; *ante*, 635; *see the form, Appendix, No.* 399.

The defendant may rejoin to a plea of estoppel by "joining issue" upon it. *See the form, Appendix, No.* 400. This will put in issue all the material facts alleged; or he may demur to it. *Bather* v. *Brayne*, 7 C. B. 815; *Wilkinson* v. *Kirby*, 15 C. B. 430; *see the form, Appendix, No.* 401. But it is not sufficient in law to rejoin that error is pending on the judgment in ejectment, and that no possession has ever been had or taken under or by virtue of such judgment. *Doe* v. *Wright*, 10 A. & E. 763; 2 P. & D. 762.

Evidence.]—The evidence for the plaintiff must of course depend upon the nature of the pleas pleaded; also upon the fact whether the plaintiff seeks to recover mesne profits from a day prior to that on which possession was claimed in the writ of ejectment, or only from that day until possession was obtained under the judgment; also upon the number of defendants, especially if any of them were not defendants in the ejectment.

"In actions for trespass to land, the plea of not guilty shall operate as a denial that the defendant committed the trespass alleged in the place mentioned, but not as a denial of the plaintiff's possession, or right of possession of that place, which, if intended to be denied, must be traversed specially." Reg. Pl. H. T. 1853, No. 19.

It is generally necessary for the plaintiff to prove —1. His own title. 2. The defendant's possession for the period in respect whereof mesne profits, &c. are claimed. 3. The annual value of the premises, or rather the value of the possession during the defendant's wrongful occupation. 4. The special damage (if any). 5. The costs of the ejectment.

1. *Plaintiff's Title.*—An office copy of the judgment roll in the action of ejectment should be produced. It must either be admitted by all the defendants in the usual manner (*ante*, 150), or be proved to

have been examined with the original judgment roll. *Ante*, 253. The words must not be abbreviated. *Reg.* v. *Christian*, Car. & M. 388. The judgment in ejectment when so proved is strong *primâ facie* evidence of the plaintiff's title and right of possession on the day mentioned in the writ of ejectment, and from thence until possession was obtained under the judgment. *Doe* v. *Huddart*, 2 Cr. M. & R. 316; 5 Tyr. 846; 4 Dowl. 437; *Aslin* v. *Parker*, 2 Burr. 665; 1 Smith's L. C. 264. But it is not conclusive, except when replied by way of estoppel. *Vooght* v. *Winch*, 2 B. & A. 662; *Doe* v. *Huddart, supra; Matthew* v. *Osborne*, 13 C. B. 919; *Dimes* v. *The Grand Junction Canal Company*, 9 Q. B. 469, 483. It is not admissible in evidence, except as against the defendants in the ejectment and their privies in estate. *Outram* v. *Morewood*, 3 East, 346; *Decosta* v. *Atkins*, Bull. N. P. 87; *ante*, 250. A judgment in ejectment against the wife cannot be given in evidence in an action against the husband and wife for mesne profits. *Denn* v. *White and wife*, 7 T. R. 112. A judgment against B. is no evidence against C., unless it be proved that B. was tenant of C.; and if the tenancy were under a lease or agreement in writing, that must be proved in the usual manner, and not by parol evidence. *Doe* v. *Harvey*, 8 Bing. 239; *ante*, 393. It must also be shown that C. had due notice of the ejectment pursuant to 15 & 16 Vict. c. 76, s. 209 (*ante*, 115), and the opportunity of defending the ejectment, if he had thought fit to do so. *Hunter* v. *Britts*, 3 Camp. 455; *Matthew* v. *Osborne*, 13 C. B. 919. Proof of a promise by C. to pay the rent and costs will be evidence for the jury, from which they may infer and find that he had due notice of the ejectment. *Hunter* v. *Britts, supra.* Upon the same principle, proof of a promise by the indorser of a bill or note, after it became due, to pay the amount is evidence for the jury that the defendant had due notice of the presentment for payment and dishonour of the bill or note, because otherwise it is not to be supposed that he would have made any such promise. *Croxon* v. *Worthen*, 5 M. & W. 5; *Campbell* v. *Webster*, 2 C. B. 258; *Lundie* v. *Robinson*, 7 East, 232. A judgment in ejectment against C., who defended as landlord of B., is evidence against B. *Doe* v. *Whitcombe*, 8 Bing. 46; *Doe* v. *Harlow*, 12 A. & E. 42, note (*d*). But the tenancy of B. must be proved by legal evidence; and if any lease or agreement in writing exists, it must be proved in the usual manner; *Doe* v. *Harvey*, 8 Bing. 239; *ante*, 393; and perhaps the service of the writ of ejectment on him should also be proved.

If the plaintiff seek to recover mesne profits from a day *prior* to the day on which possession was claimed in the ejectment, he must prove his prior title, and that he was in actual or constructive possession at the time of the trespasses. *Barnett* v. *The Earl of Guilford*, 11 Exch. 19. The judgment in ejectment is no evidence of such prior title. *Aslin* v. *Parker*, 2 Burr. 665; 1 Smith's L. C. 264; *ante*, 635; Ad. Eject. 342. "It appears to be the established practice in these actions, where the plaintiff seeks to recover profits anterior to the day of the demise from the tenant in possession, or at any date from an occupier not the tenant in possession, that the plaintiff may recover them, if he proves his title to the possession at the time the profits were so taken, and also the execution of the writ of possession, or actual possession taken; for taking actual possession has the same effect as the execution of an *habere facias possessionem*." *Per* Parke, B., in *Barnett* v. *Earl of Guilford*, 11 Exch. 32, who refers to the note of

Serjeant Manning in *Butcher* v. *Butcher*, 1 Man. & R. 221; 7 B. & C. 332; 2 Stark. Ev. 453 (3rd ed.). In trespass a mere right to possession, without any actual or constructive possession, is not sufficient. *Ante*, 287; Ros. Ev. 512 (7th ed.); Ad. Eject. 342. But an actual entry relates back to the prior title as against a wrongdoer. *Barnett* v. *Earl of Guilford*, 11 Exch. 19.

2. *Defendant's Occupation.*—The judgment in ejectment is no evidence that the defendant was in actual occupation of the premises, or that he withheld them from the claimant; *Doe d. James* v. *Stanton*, 2 B. & A. 373, Bayley, J.; except perhaps from the day on which the writ in ejectment was served (such service being proved or admitted), and the day on which judgment was obtained; the defendant having appeared and defended the action. *Dodwell* v. *Gibbs, Gent. one, &c.*, 2 C. & P. 615, Garrow, B.; *Doe* v. *Challis*, 17 Q. B. 166. If a servant or other person not claiming any right or title be served with a writ in ejectment, he should not appear, but suffer judgment by default; otherwise he will be personally liable, and the fact of his being only a servant will not furnish any defence. *Doe d. Cuff* v. *Stradling*, 2 Stark. R. 187; *Doe* d. *James* v. *Stanton*, 2 B. & A. 371. A judgment by default is therefore no evidence in a subsequent action for mesne profits of the defendant ever having been in possession. *Id.* 373, *per* Bayley, J. The plaintiff must prove that the defendants were actually or constructively in the occupation of the premises, and withheld the same from him. *Doe* v. *Harlow*, 12 A. & E. 40; *Doe* v. *Challis*, 17 Q. B. 166. Also the time of such occupation, &c.; otherwise he will be entitled to recover only nominal damages, besides the costs of the ejectment. *Ive* v. *Scott*, 9 Dowl. 993.

If the writ of possession have been returned and filed, it is usual and proper to prove an admitted or examined office copy of it. But if it be shown that after the judgment in ejectment, the plaintiff was *let into possession by the defendant* without any writ of possession being executed, that is sufficient. *Calvart* v. *Horsfall*, 4 Esp. 167, Lord Ellenborough, C. J. Whether a writ of possession issues or not is immaterial. " In the one case the tenant is turned out; in the other, he goes out; he acquiesces in the judgment." *Per* Jervis, C. J., in *Wilkinson* v. *Kirby*, 15 C. B. 440. " Taking actual possession has the same effect as the execution of an *habere facias possessionem.*" *Per* Parke, B., in *Barnett* v. *Earl of Guilford*, 11 Exch. 32. But see *Doe* d. *Stevens* v. *Lord*, 7 A. & E. 610; 2 N. & P. 604; 6 Dowl. 256; *ante*, 344.

3. *Value of Mesne Profits.*—The annual value of the premises, or the value of the possession during the time they were wrongfully occupied by the defendants, must be proved; otherwise the plaintiff will be entitled to recover only nominal damages in respect thereof. *Ive* v. *Scott*, 9 Dowl. 993. The judgment in ejectment proves nothing as to the value. *Aslin* v. *Parker*, 2 Burr. 665, 668; 1 Smith's L. C. 264; *ante*, 635. The jury are not confined to the mere rent, but may take into consideration the special circumstances. *Goodtitle* v. *Tombs*, 3 Wils. 121; *post*, 643.

4. *Special Damage.*—Any special damage alleged in the declaration must be sufficiently proved; otherwise nothing can be recovered in respect of it. *Post*, 644; Ad. Eject. 346.

5. Costs of Ejectment.—The amount of the costs of the ejectment must be proved; otherwise nothing can be recovered in respect of such costs. Generally speaking, it is necessary to prove the judgment in ejectment for the purpose of recovering the costs of that action, even where it may not be necessary to prove it, in order to show the plaintiff's title, there being no plea putting such title in issue. *Ante*, 640. We have already considered in what cases and against whom the judgment in ejectment is admissible in evidence. *Ante*, 641. If the costs have been taxed, the judgment will prove the amount, and no further or extra costs can be recovered. *Post*, 644. If they have not been taxed, the judgment in ejectment being for want of an appearance, the amount must be proved as in an action upon an attorney's bill, and it should be shown that the charges are reasonable as between attorney and client. *Doe* v. *Huddart*, 2 Cr. M. & R. 316; 5 Tyr. 846; 4 Dowl. 437. The plaintiff may recover by way of damages costs incurred by him in a court of error in reversing an erroneous judgment in ejectment obtained against him by the defendant. *Nowell* v. *Roarke*, 7 B. & C. 404; 1 M. & R. 170; and see *Foxhall* v. *Barnett*, 2 E. & B. 928.

Damages.]—In trespass for mesne profits the plaintiff may recover the value of the possession of the land, &c., calculated as in an action for use and occupation, during the period he has been *actually kept out of possession thereof by the defendant. Ante*, 635. But the jury are not confined to the mere rent; they may take into consideration the plaintiff's trouble, &c., occasioned by the defendant's conduct. *Goodtitle* v. *Tombs*, 3 Wils. 121. "I have known four times the value of the mesne profits given by a jury in this sort of action of trespass; if it were not to be so, sometimes complete justice could not be done to the party injured." *Id.* 121, *per* Gould, J. "Damages are not confined to the mere rent of the premises, but the jury may give more if they please." *Id.* 121, *per* Wilmot, C. J.

Unless the annual value of the premises, and the time the plaintiff has been kept out of possession of them by the defendant, be proved, the plaintiff will be only entitled to nominal damages, beyond the costs of the ejectment. *Ive* v. *Scott*, 9 Dowl. 993.

A defendant is liable only for the mesne profits, &c. during the time that he or his tenants, agents or servants have kept the plaintiff out of possession. *Girdlestone* v. *Parker*, Woodf. L. & T. 419 (7th ed.); Ros. Ev. 535 (7th ed.). He is not liable during the period his under-tenant has wrongfully held over, without his consent and against his will, for under such circumstances the action should be against the undertenant. *Burne* v. *Richardson*, 4 Taunt. 720. But if the defendant have put another person in possession as his tenant or otherwise, and *requested him to stay on*, or to hold possession, or the like, he is liable as a trespasser by such other person, upon the principle *qui facit per alium facit per se. Doe* v. *Harlow*, 12 A. & E. 42; *Doe* v. *Challis*, 17 Q. B. 166.

More than six years' mesne profits may be recovered unless the defendant has pleaded the Statute of Limitations. Ad. Eject. 345; *Id.* 339.

If the plaintiff seek to recover mesne profits from a day anterior to that on which possession was claimed in the writ of ejectment, he must

ıs title. The judgment in the ejectment is no evidence
title. *Ante,* 635.

ıge" cannot be recovered unless properly stated in the
sufficiently proved. *Dunn* v. *Large,* 3 Doug. 335,
ll, J., in *Doe* d. *Marks* v. *Roe,* 6 Dowl. & L. 88.

the mesne profits and other damages (if any) to which
· be entitled, he may recover the costs of the previous
ıt, provided they be specially stated in the declaration,
ə. *Ante,* 638. If such costs have been taxed he is
·ecover the amount as taxed, but nothing in respect of
f the difference between costs as between party and
as between attorney and client. *Doe* v. *Hare,* 2 Dowl.
·ax v. *Filliter,* 11 M. & W. 80; 2 Dowl. & L. 186;
ı, 7 Moore, 471. If, however, the costs have not been
ı having been obtained for want of an appearance,
·ecover the costs of the ejectment as between attorney
ot merely such amount as would be allowed on taxa-
party and party. *Doe* v. *Davis,* 1 Esp. 358, Lord
Doe v. *Huddart,* 2 Cr. M. & R. 316; 5 Tyr. 846; 4
ı.; *Grace* v. *Morgan,* 2 Bing. N. C. 534; 2 Scott,
ə the plaintiff has incurred costs in error in reversing
ı jectment obtained by the defendant, he may recover
ch costs as part of his damages. *Nowell* v. *Roarke,* 7
M. & R. 170; and see *Foxhall* v. *Barnett,* 2 E. & B.

defendants are sued the plaintiff can recover only such
or some of them are jointly liable to. He cannot re-
mages against the several defendants either jointly or
ly one sum against all or some of them, the rest being
mages against one only, the others being acquitted.

may prove in reduction of damages that he has paid
, to which the premises and the plaintiff as the owner
le. *Ante,* 639.

costs in this action follow the event as in an action of
ıusum fregit. If the plaintiff recover a verdict for 5*l.*
ior court, he must obtain a certificate under 13 & 14
; or an order under 15 & 16 Vict. c. 54, s. 4, to entitle
'the verdict be for less than 40*s.* he must *also* obtain a
3 & 4 Vict. c. 24, s. 2. If the verdict be for the de-
ılaintiff be nonsuited, then the defendant is entitled to
c. 3.

CE

I. *Double Value.*]—By 4 (
case any tenant or tenants fı
person or persons who are oı
tenements or hereditaments,
such tenant or tenants, shal
or hereditaments, after the
after demand made, and nc
possession thereof, by his or
persons to whom the remain
or hereditaments shall belon
lawfully authorized, then aı
holding over, shall, *for and*
hold over, or keep the persc
the said lands, tenements an
person or persons so kept oı
trators or assigns, *at the rat*
tenements and hereditament
are detained, to be recovere(
by action of debt, whereun
obliged to give special bail
penalty there shall be no rel

When a tenant holds over
landlord, the penalty is doub
rent, which might not in (
Soulsby v. *Neving,* 9 East, 3
After recovering the posse
the landlord may maintain
tenant held over after the ex
sion was obtained in the eje
The action for double valu
remedy which the landlord
but is cumulative. The two
ejectment is in order to get p
held; the action of debt for
the landlord for the wrong.'
Of course no previous actio
landlord to recover double vı
ın ejectment, but is more beı
2 W. Black. 1077. One teı
for the double value of his m
An action for double valu
ın the county court; and thɛ

CHAPTER LXIX.

ACTIONS FOR DOUBLE VALUE AND DOUBLE RENT.

I. *Double Value.*]—By 4 Geo. 2, c. 28, s. 1, it is enacted, "that in case any tenant or tenants for any term of *life, lives or years,* or other person or persons who are or shall come into possession of any lands, tenements or hereditaments, by, from or under, or by collusion with such tenant or tenants, shall *wilfully* hold over any lands, tenements or hereditaments, after the determination of such term or terms, and after demand made, and notice *in writing* given, for delivering the possession thereof, by his or their landlords or lessors, or the person or persons to whom the remainder or reversion of such lands, tenements or hereditaments shall belong, his or their agent or agents *thereunto lawfully authorized,* then and in such case such person or persons so holding over, shall, *for and during the time, he, she and they shall so hold over,* or keep the person or persons entitled out of possession of the said lands, tenements and hereditaments, as aforesaid, pay to the person or persons so kept out of possession, their executors, administrators or assigns, *at the rate of double the yearly value* of the lands, tenements and hereditaments so detained, for so long time as the same are detained, to be recovered in any of his majesty's courts of record, by action of debt, whereunto the defendant or defendants shall be obliged to give special bail; against the recovering of which said *penalty* there shall be no relief in equity."

When a tenant holds over after demand and notice in writing *by the landlord,* the penalty is double the yearly *value;* not double the yearly rent, which might not in some cases be an adequate satisfaction. *Soulsby* v. *Neving,* 9 East, 313, Lord Ellenborough, C. J.

After recovering the possession of demised premises by an ejectment, the landlord may maintain debt for double value for the time the tenant held over after the expiration of the notice to quit until possession was obtained in the ejectment. *Soulsby* v. *Neving,* 9 East, 310. The action for double value " has no reference to any antecedent remedy which the landlord had to recover possession by ejectment, but is cumulative. The two actions are brought *diverso intuitu;* the ejectment is in order to get possession of the premises wrongfully withheld; the action of debt for the double value is in order to indemnify the landlord for the wrong." *Id.* 314, *per* Lord Ellenborough, C. J. Of course no previous action of ejectment is *necessary* to entitle the landlord to recover double value. The action " stands in the place of an ejectment, but is more beneficial and effectual." *Cutting* v. *Derby,* 2 W. Black. 1077. One tenant in common may maintain an action for the double value of his moiety. *S. C.*

An action for double value, not exceeding 50*l.,* may be maintained in the county court; and the defendant cannot oust the jurisdiction by alleging title to the premises in himself, if it be proved that he has admitted himself to have been tenant to the plaintiff at the times when the rent accrued, and from which the holding over commenced. *Wickham* v. *Lee*, 12 Q. B. 521 ; 18 Law J., Q. B. 21.

In *Wilkinson* v. *Colley*, 5 Burr. 2698, the court held this to be a remedial law, the penalty being given to the party aggrieved. But in *Lloyd* v. *Rosbee*, 2 Camp. 454, Lord Ellenborough said, "this is a penal statute, and is to be construed strictly." So in *Robinson* v. *Learoyd*, 7 M. & W. 54, Parke, B., said that the statute is penal, and is to be construed strictly. An action may be penal as against the defendant, although brought by the party grieved. *Earl Spencer* v. *Swannell*, 3 M. & W. 154, 162 ; 6 Dowl. 326 ; *Fife* v. *Bousfield*, 6 Q. B. 100 ; 2 D. & L. 481. The stat. 11 Geo. 2, c. 9, s. 3 (respecting fraudulent removals to avoid distresses for rent) is remedial as well as penal. *Brooke* v. *Noakes*, 8 B. & C. 537 ; *Id.* 541, *per* Bayley, J.

The act does not extend to weekly tenancies. *Lloyd* v. *Rosbee*, 2 Camp. 453 ; *Sullivan* v. *Bishop*, 2 C. & P. 359 ; whether a tenancy from quarter to quarter is within the act appears doubtful. It would rather seem not, if the statute be construed strictly. *S. C.* ; *Wilkinson* v. *Hall*, 3 Bing. N. C. 508 ; 4 Scott, 301. One tenant in common may maintain an action for the double value of his money. *Cutting* v. *Derby*, 2 W. Black. 1077.

The tenant must *wilfully* hold over, *i. e.*, contumaciously and not merely by mistake, under a fair and reasonable claim of title. *Wright* v. *Smith*, 5 Esp. 203 ; *Soulsby* v. *Neving*, 9 East, 313, Lord Ellenborough, C. J. Whether his claim to hold over be *bonâ fide* or a mere pretence, is a question for the jury; a claim to hold over by virtue of a custom of the country which does not apply to the demised premises, will not protect the tenant from liability to double value. *Hirst* v. *Horn*, 6 M. & W. 393. Where one of several tenants wilfully holds over, without the assent of his co-tenants, the latter will not be liable. *Draper* v. *Crofts*, 15 M. & W. 166 ; and see *Christy* v. *Tancred*, 9 M. & W. 438 ; *Tancred* v. *Christy* (in error), 12 M. & W. 316, 323. Where husband and wife hold over after notice given to the wife, before her marriage, the husband may be sued alone for double value. *Lake* v. *Smith*, 1 B. & P., New R. 174.

There must be a "demand made, and notice *in writing* given." *Ante*, 645. The usual notice to quit given to a tenant from year to year is sufficient, and no further demand upon or after the expiration of the tenancy is necessary. *Wilkinson* v. *Colley*, 5 Burr. 2694, 2698 ; *Cutting* v. *Derby*, 2 W. Black. 1075 ; *Hirst* v. *Horn*, 6 M. & W. 393. But the notice must amount to a valid and binding notice to quit. *Johnson* v. *Huddleston*, 4 B. & C. 922 ; 7 D. & R. 411. If it require the tenant to quit on the wrong day, or on the correct day at twelve o'clock *at noon*, that is not sufficient. *Page* v. *More*, 15 Q. B. 684. A notice requiring the tenant to quit on the proper day "or I shall insist on double rent" (instead of double value) is sufficient, and does not give the tenant the option of holding over. *Doe* d. *Matthews* v. *Jackson*, 1 Doug. 175 ; *Doe* d. *Lyster* v. *Goldwin*, 2 Q. B. 143 ; and see *Page* v. *More*, *supra*. A notice to quit lands on a given day, "or at such time as your holding shall expire next after the expiration of half a year from the receipt of this notice" is sufficient in an action for double value. *Hirst* v. *Horn*, 6 M. & W. 393.

The notice must be signed by the landlord or his agent " thereunto lawfully authorized." A receiver or agent authorized to let, and to sue or distrain for rent, has sufficient authority to give the notice. *Poole* v. *Warren*, 8 A. & E. 582; 3 N. & P. 693. So a receiver in chancery, with the usual powers, may give the notice in his own name. *Wilkinson* v. *Colley*, 5 Burr. 2694; and see *Trent* v *Hunt*, 9 Exch. 14.

A second notice to quit or pay double rent, given after the usual notice to quit, is no waiver of the first notice, unless so intended. *Messenger* v. *Armstrong*, 1 T. R. 53.

Where a demise is for a *certain time*, no notice to quit is necessary at or before the end of the term to put an end to the tenancy (*ante*, 36); but a demand of possession and notice in writing pursuant to the statute, are necessary to entitle the landlord to double value. *See the form, Appendix, No. 5.* Such demand may be made at any reasonable distance of time after the expiration of the term, provided the landlord have done no act in the meantime to acknowledge the continuance of the tenancy; and he will thereupon be entitled to double value as from the time of such demand, and not from the expiration of the tenancy. *Cobb* v. *Stokes*, 8 East, 358. If the rent were before reserved quarterly, and such demand be made in the middle of a quarter, the landlord cannot recover any rent or compensation for use and occupation for the antecedent fraction of such quarter. *S. C.* The notice and demand may, however, be served before the expiration of the term, requiring the tenant to deliver up possession on the expiration of his term; *Wilkinson* v. *Colley*, 5 Burr. 2694; *Cutting* v. *Derby*, 2 W. Black. 1075; and in such case the double value should be calculated from the expiration of the term, for so long as the tenant holds over.

Tenants in common cannot sue jointly for double value for holding over, unless there has been a joint demise; *Wilkinson and another* v. *Hall*, 1 Bing. N. C. 713; 1 Scott, 675; but each may sue separately. *Wilkinson* v. *Hall*, 3 Bing. N. C. 508; 4 Scott, 301; *Cutting* v. *Derby*, 2 W. Black. 1075. An action for double value cannot be maintained by husband *and wife*, where the tenant holds over the wife's land after the expiration of a term therein granted by the husband alone. *Harcourt and Wife* v. *Wyman*, 3 Exch. 817; and see *Wallis* v. *Harrison*, 5 M. & W. 142; 7 Dowl. 395. The administratrix of an executor cannot sue for the double value of lands demised by the testator, and held over by the defendant; but must obtain letters of administration *de bonis non*, even though the tenant has attorned to her. *Tingrey* v. *Brown*, 1 Bos. & P. 310.

The declaration must correctly state the nature of the plaintiff's title, and of the defendant's tenancy; a tenancy from quarter to quarter (if sufficient) must not be stated as a tenancy " for a term of years, from year and year." *Wilkinson* v. *Hall*, 3 Bing. N. C. 508; 4 Scott, 301. A tenancy of the wife's lands, under a demise from the husband alone, must not be stated as a tenancy under the husband and wife. *Harcourt and Wife* v. *Wyman*, 3 Exch. 817. *See Forms of Declarations, Appendix, Nos.* 404, 405; 2 Chit. Pl. 342 (7th ed.).

The venue is transitory; for although the action is of a penal nature, it is brought by the party grieved. *Fife* v. *Bousfield*, 6 Q. B. 100; 2 D. & L. 481; *Blanché* v. *Hooper*, 6 Q. B. 877, note (*b*).

The action being of a penal nature (*ante*, 646), the defendant may plead to a declaration or count for double value, *nil debet*, or not guilty, "by statute 21 Jac. 1, c. 4, s. 4, Public General Act." *Earl Spencer* v. *Swannell,* 3 M. & W. 154; 6 Dowl. 326; *Harcourt* v. *Wyman,* 3 Exch. 819; *see the form, Appendix, No.* 60. But it is not unusual for the defendant to traverse specially the principal allegations in the declaration: *ex. gr.,* the alleged tenancy of the defendant; the plaintiff's title to the reversion; the alleged notice and demand; the due determination of the tenancy, and the like. *Page* v. *More,* 15 Q. B. 684; *Wilkinson* v. *Hall,* 3 Bing. N. C. 508; 4 Scott, 301. So the defendant may plead specially that he held over the tenements under a fair claim of title to hold the same, and not contumaciously. *Poole* v. *Warren,* 8 A. & E. 582; *ante,* 646. But whenever a defendant may plead the general issue "by statute," any defence whatever may be given in evidence under that plea; *Maund* v. *The Monmouthshire Canal Company,* 1 Car. & M. 606, Cresswell, J.; except perhaps a defence founded on a local or personal act passed prior to the 5 & 6 Vict. c. 97.

If the jury find that the holding over was not wilful and contumacious, but *bonâ fide* under a supposed title and fair claim of right, they should find for the defendant. *Ante,* 646. So, if any other material allegation in the declaration be not sufficiently proved. *Page* v. *More,* 15 Q. B. 684; *Harcourt and Wife* v. *Wyman,* 3 Exch. 817; *Wilkinson* v. *Hall,* 3 Bing. N. C. 508; 4 Scott, 301.

If the jury find for the plaintiff, the amount of damages should be calculated "at the rate of double the yearly value of the lands, tenements and hereditaments so detained." *Ante,* 645. "The value of the soil itself, and everything which, by having been attached to it, becomes part of the soil, is no doubt to be estimated for this purpose, as well as that of all easements, rights and appurtenances thereto belonging or enjoyed therewith; and that value is what an occupier would give, and the landlord would otherwise have received for the use of the freehold and everything connected with it, during the time that the possession is withheld. But where a compensation is paid jointly for the use of the tenement and its appurtenances, *and for something else,* as, for instance, for the landlord's performance of a contract to do something which would be beneficial to the occupier, the compensation so paid, though an entire sum, is not entirely for the value of the occupation, though by the contract of the parties the portion applicable to each is not ascertained. If by the contract of the parties a separate sum was fixed as a compensation for each subject, there would be no difficulty in the case; and the omission to make that apportionment, in truth, makes no other difference than that it renders it less easy to ascertain the value of each part." *Per cur.* in *Robinson* v. *Learoyd,* 7 M. & W. 48, 53. Therefore where the plaintiff, being the owner of a woollen mill and steam engine, let to the defendant a room in the mill, together with a supply of power from the steam engine by means of a revolving shaft in the room: held, in an action for double value, that in estimating the damages the value of the power supplied could not be included. *S. C.*

The damages should be calculated for so long time as the premises are detained (*ante,* 645), *i. e.,* from the time when the notice to quit expired, or the demand of possession was served after the end of a term certain; *Cobb* v. *Stokes,* 8 East, 358; *ante,* 647; until the defendant quits possession. *Booth* v. *Macfarlane,* 1 B. & Adol. 904. It makes no difference in this respect that the possession was recovered by an ejectment. *Soulsby* v. *Neving,* 9 East, 310; *ante,* 645.

II. Double Rent.]—By 11 Geo. 2, c. 19, s. 18, it is enacted' "that from and after the said 24th day of June, 1738, in case any tenant or tenants shall give notice of his, her or their intention to quit the premises by him, her or them holden, at a time mentioned in such notice, and shall not accordingly deliver up the possession thereof at the time in such notice contained, that then the said tenant or tenants, his, her or their executors or administrators, shall from thenceforward pay to the landlord or landlords, lessor or lessors, *double the rent* or sum which he, she or they should otherwise have paid, to be levied, sued for and recovered at the same time and in the same manner as the single rent or sum before the giving such notice could be levied, sued for or recovered; and such double rent or sum shall continue to be paid during all the time such tenant or tenants shall continue in possession as aforesaid."

When the tenant gives notice to quit, the probability is that he holds at rack-rent; and if he hold over after the expiration of his own notice, he is liable to pay *double rent*; whereas, when he holds over after the expiration of a notice duly given by the landlord, he must pay *double value. Ante,* 645.

Double rent may be distrained for. *Humberstone* v. *Dubois,* 10 M. & W. 765; 2 Dowl. N. S. 506; *Timmins* v. *Rowlinson,* 3 Burr. 1603; *Johnson* v. *Huddlestone,* 4 B. & C. 922; 7 D. & R. 411. It has been decided that a landlord has no right to distrain for double rent upon a *weekly* tenant, who holds over after a notice to quit given by the tenant. *Sullivan* v. *Bishop,* 2 C. & P. 359, Best, C. J. But this appears to be a mistake. Bullen on Distress, 116, note (5); 2 Chit. Pl. 344, note (*v*) (7th ed.).

The statute applies to all tenancies determinable by notice to quit, whether created by lease under seal, or by lease in writing, or by an oral demise; and the tenant's notice to quit need not be in writing. *Timmins* v. *Rowlinson,* 3 Burr. 1603; 1 W. Blac. 533. But the statute applies only where the tenant has the power of determining his tenancy by a notice to quit, and where he has actually given a *valid* notice, sufficient to determine the tenancy. *Johnson* v. *Huddlestone,* 4 B. & C. 922; 7 D. & R. 411. A notice to quit on the wrong day, or on the right day at twelve o'clock *at noon,* is insufficient. *Page* v. *More,* 15 Q. B. 684. A notice that the tenant will quit as soon as he can get another situation is not sufficient, although it appear that he has got another situation. *Farrance* v. *Elkington,* 2 Camp. 591. A tenant who, after giving notice to quit, holds over for a year, and pays double rent to that time, may then quit, without giving any fresh notice. *Booth* v. *Macfarlane,* 1 B. & Adol. 904. "The words of the statute are very clear. 'Such double rent shall continue to be paid during all the time such tenant shall continue in possession as aforesaid.'" *Id.* 906, *per* Lord Tenterden, C. J. By accepting the single rent the landlord may waive his right to double rent, without waiving the notice to quit, or his right to maintain ejectment. It depends, however, upon the *intention* with which the money was received. *Doe* d. *Cheney* v. *Batten,* Cowp. 243.

It would seem that double rent cannot be recovered after an ejectment, except for that period which elapsed after the determination of the notice and before the day on which possession is claimed in the writ of ejectment, because the landlord cannot blow hot and cold, and treat the defendant both as a trespasser and as a tenant, during the same

F F

period. Single rent could not be recovered for the holding subsequent to the date mentioned in the writ in ejectment. *Birch* v. *Wright*, 1 T. R. 378; 2 Smith, L. C. 378; *Bridges* v. *Smith*, 5 Bing. 410; 2 Moo. & P. 740; *Jones* v. *Carter*, 15 M. & W. 718; *Francklin* v. *Carter*, 1 C. B. 750; 3 D. & L. 213. Double rent is to be "levied, sued for and recovered at the same time and in the same manner as the single rent." *Ante*, 649. The distinction is between double rent and double value. *Soulsby* v. *Neving*, 9 East, 310; *ante*, 645.

In a declaration for double rent, the nature of the defendant's tenancy, and of the plaintiff's title to the reversion, must be correctly described, in like manner as in an action for double value. *Ante*, 647; *Harcourt* v. *Wyman*, 3 Exch. 817; and see *Humberstone* v. *Dubois*, 10 M. & W. 765; 2 Dowl. N. S. 506. *For form of declaration for double rent, see Appendix, Nos.* 406, 407; 2 Chit. Pl. 344 (7th ed.). A second count for single rent or for use and occupation should be added. *Thoroton* v. *Whitehead*, 1 M. & W. 14; 4 Dowl. 747.

The venue is transitory (*ante*, 647), and the defendant may plead to a declaration or count for double rent, *nil debet* by statute. *Ante*, 647.

The jury may find for so much as the tenant appears to have overheld, without reference to the sum demanded, so that it be not more than that sum. *Anon.*, Lofft. 275. The single rent should be calculated from the time of the determination of the tenancy during all the time the defendant has held over, in like manner as if the tenancy had continued; and then the amount should be doubled. If the rent were reserved quarterly or otherwise, the double rent must be calculated as above mentioned to the proper quarter-day. Probably single rent for any fractional part of a quarter to the time of the defendant's quitting possession may be recovered under a count for use and occupation. It seems that the double rent ceases whenever the tenant quits possession. *Booth* v. *Macfarlane*, 1 B. & Adol. 904; *ante*, 649. And that where one of several joint tenants holds over, without the assent of his co-tenants, after the expiration of notice to quit given by or on behalf of all of them, the co-tenants are not liable to double rent. *Ante*, 646. Nor can double rent be recovered after an ejectment from the day on which possession was claimed in the writ. *Ante*, 649.

CHAPTER LXX. ,

ACTIONS FOR THE RECOVERY OF SMALL TENEMENTS IN THE COUNTY COURTS.

Repeal of the County Courts Act, 9 & 10 Vict. c. 95, as to Actions for Possession of Small Tenements, after Term ended or determined.]—By 19 & 20 Vict. c. 108, intituled "An Act to amend the Acts relating to the County Courts," the whole of sections 122, 123, 126 and 127 of the County Courts Act, 9 & 10 Vict. c. 95, are repealed, except as to acts done under them.   Sect. 2.

Previous Acts and Amended Act to be construed as one Act.]—By 19 & 20 Vict. c. 108, s. 3, this act and the 9 & 10 Vict. c. 95 ; 12 & 13 Vict. c. 101 ; 13 & 14 Vict. c. 61, and 15 & 16 Vict. c. 54, " shall be read and construed as one act, as if the several provisions in the said recited acts contained, not inconsistent with the provisions of this act, were repeated and re-enacted in this act."

Time and Mode of Proceedings to be regulated by Rules of Practice.]—By 19 & 20 Vict. c. 108, s. 5, " where the time within which, or where the mode in which, any proceeding should be taken in the county court is not prescribed, either in this act or in any act relating to the county courts, such time and mode shall be appointed by the *rules of practice, orders and forms* to be made as hereinafter provided."   Vide sect. 32.

Actions for Recovery of Small Tenements by Landlords after Term expired, or determined by Notice to quit.]—By 19 & 20 Vict. c. 108, s. 50, " when the term and interest of the tenant of any corporeal hereditament, *where neither the value of the premises nor the rent* payable in respect thereof shall have *exceeded* 50*l. by the year*, and upon which *no fine or premium* shall have been paid, *shall have expired, or shall have been determined* either by the landlord or the tenant *by a legal notice to quit*, and such tenant, or any person holding or claiming by, through or under him, *shall neglect or refuse to deliver up possession accordingly*, the landlord may enter a plaint, at his option, either against such tenant or against such person so neglecting or refusing, *in the county court of the district in which the premises lie* for the recovery of the same, and thereupon a summons shall issue to such tenant or such person so neglecting or refusing ; and if the defendant shall not, at the time named in the summons, show good cause to the contrary, then, *on proof of his still neglecting or refusing* to deliver up possession of the premises, *and of the yearly value and rent* of the premises, *and of the holding, and of the expiration or other determination of the tenancy, with the time and manner thereof, and of the title of the plaintiff* if such title has accrued since the letting of the premises, *and of the service of the summons* if the defendant shall not appear thereto, the judge may order that possession of the premises mentioned in the plaint be given by the defendant to the plaintiff, either forthwith or on or before such day as the judge shall think fit to name ; and if such order be not obeyed, the registrar, whether such order can be proved to have been served or not, shall at the instance of the plaintiff issue a warrant authorizing and requiring the high bailiff of the court to give possession of such premises to the plaintiff."
By sect. 51, " in any such plaint against a tenant as in the last preceding section is specified, the plaintiff may add a claim *for rent or mesne profits, or both*, down to the day appointed for the hearing, or to any preceding day named in the plaint, *so as the same shall not*

exceed 50*l.*, and any misdescription in the nature of such claim may be amended at the trial."

Mode of Proceeding.]—The time and mode of proceeding under sections 50 and 51 will be regulated by certain rules of practice, orders and forms, to be made pursuant to sect. 5. *Ante*, 652; *for the forms see Appendix, No.* 408 *et seq.*

The following may be stated as a concise outline of the practice, subject to any alterations to be made by the rules, &c. above mentioned.

The action must be commenced by a plaint entered in the county court of the district wherein the tenements are situate; *see the form, Appendix, No.* 408; and thereupon a summons shall issue. *See the form, Appendix, No.* 409. This must be served pursuant to sect. 54. *Post*, 662. The decision of the judge as to the sufficiency of the service is conclusive. *Robinson* v. *Lenaghan*, 2 Exch. 333. Either party may require a jury to be summoned to try the action. 9 & 10 Vict. c. 95, s. 70. Where no jury is summoned the judge decides all questions of law and fact. *Id. s.* 69. Either party may obtain at the registrar's office a summons for witnesses, with or without a clause requiring the production of deeds, papers and writings, and in any such summons any number of names may be inserted. *Id. s.* 85; *see form of Summons, Appendix, No.* 414. Witnesses may be summoned without leave of the court, either in the home or foreign district. The bailiff will serve the witnesses. 9 & 10 Vict. c. 95, s. 85. It is sufficient if the summons be served a reasonable time before the actual hearing. When the summons is served, the reasonable expenses of coming to, staying at, and returning from the place of trial must be paid or tendered to the witness in like manner as upon a *subpœna. Ante*, 176. The scale of allowance per day to witnesses in the county court is as follows:—

	s.	*d.*
Gentlemen, merchants, bankers and professional men	7	6
Tradesmen, auctioneers, accountants, clerks and yeomen	5	0
Journeymen, labourers, and the like	2	0
Travelling expenses, per mile, one way	0	6

In case of disobedience to a summons the witness may be fined 10*l.* 9 & 10 Vict. c. 95, ss. 86, 87. If a witness happen to be present at the trial he cannot refuse to give evidence, although he has not been summoned. *Id. s.* 86. Either party may summon and examine the other party or his wife as a witness.

Either party may give the other a *notice to produce*, in like manner as in a superior court. *Ante*, 155; *see form in Appendix, No.* 413.

Either party may give the other a *notice to admit*, in like manner as in a superior court. *Ante*, 150; *see form in Appendix, No.* 412.

Either party may obtain an *inspection of documents* in the possession or power of the opposite party, and *in which he has an interest*, in like manner as in a superior court. *Ante*, 200.

If the plaintiff be desirous of not proceeding in the cause he may give notice thereof to the registrar, and to the defendant, by prepaid post letter; and after the receipt of such notice the defendant will not be entitled to any further costs than those incurred up to the receipt of such notice, unless the judge shall otherwise order.

The hearing of the cause may be adjourned by consent or otherwise, pursuant to the rule of court in that behalf, and upon the terms therein mentioned.

Either party may appear at the hearing, or at any adjournment thereof, in person, or by his counsel or attorney. 15 & 16 Vict. c. 54, s. 10. No previous notice of his intention to employ a barrister or attorney to act as his advocate at the hearing is necessary. But the attorney employed must sign the roll or book kept by the clerk of the court for that purpose, if he have not previously done so.

When the cause is called on, if neither party appear, it will be struck out by the direction of the judge; and in such case no hearing fee will be payable. If the defendant appear, but the plaintiff does not, the judge may in his discretion award to the defendant costs, in the same manner and to the same extent as to counsel, attorney, witnesses and other matters, as if the cause had been tried; but no hearing fee shall be charged. If when the cause is called on the plaintiff do not pay the hearing fee on being required to do so, he shall be deemed not to have appeared. If the plaintiff appear, but the defendant does not, the due service of the summons, pursuant to sect. 54 (*post*, 662), must be proved in the first instance by the bailiff of the court. The decision of the judge as to the sufficiency of the service is conclusive. *Robinson* v. *Lenaghan*, 2 Exch. 333.

Evidence for Plaintiff.]—The plaintiff must prove:—

1. That the ordinary relation of landlord and tenant of the property claimed has existed between the plaintiff and the defendant; or between the plaintiff and some other person, by, through or under whom the defendant holds or claims. *Ante*, 652; *Jones* v. *Owen*, 5 Dowl. & L. 669; *Banks* v. *Rebbeck*, 2 Low. M. & P. 452. The evidence on this point will be similar to that in an ejectment by a landlord against a tenant for years after the term has expired; *ante*, 393; or in an ejectment by a landlord against a tenant from year to year after the term has been determined by a notice to quit. *Ante*, 446. It is not necessary to show that the plaintiff was the original lessor; it is sufficient to prove when the term expired or was determined he was the *immediate reversioner* of the tenements; or if such reversion then belonged to several persons, as joint tenants, coparceners, or tenants in common, that the plaintiff was one of the persons so entitled. 9 & 10 Vict. c. 95, s. 142. But if the title of the plaintiff accrued since the letting of the premises, such title must be deduced from the landlord and proved in the usual manner. Under the 9 & 10 Vict. c. 95, where the plaintiff claimed as mortgagee, and the defendant under a demise from the mortgagor *subsequent* to the mortgage, and the defendant had never attorned to the plaintiff or consented to hold under him: held, that the statute did not apply, and consequently that the county court had no jurisdiction. *Jones* v. *Owen*, 5 Dowl. & L. 669. So where the defendant had been let into possession under an agreement to purchase, one of the terms of which was that he should pay 8s. a-week rent, to be afterwards deducted from the purchase-money, and it appeared that he had paid sums which together with the set-off equalled the amount of the purchase-money: held, that the ordinary relation of landlord and tenant did not exist between the parties, and therefore that the county court had no jurisdiction. *Banks* v. *Rebbeck*, 2 Low. M. & P. 452.

The defendant must be proved to be either the tenant to whom the demise was made, or a person "holding or claiming by, through or under him." *Ante,* 652. Any person who obtains the possession from the tenant directly or indirectly, either as an assignee or under-tenant, or by fraud and collusion with the tenant is within the statute, and estopped from denying the landlord's title. *Ante,* 215. Proof that the defendant came into possession after the original tenant entered, and during the continuance of the demise, is *primâ facie* evidence that he obtained possession as assignee of the term. *Ante,* 224. Any proof by the defendant to the contrary will probably show that he is a person holding or claiming by, through or under the tenant within the meaning of the statute.

There must be no real dispute or question between the parties as to the right or title of the plaintiff, or of the defendant, to the tenements; otherwise the county court will have no jurisdiction; 9 & 10 Vict. c. 95, s. 58; unless by the written consent of both parties, signed by them or their attorneys. 19 & 20 Vict. c. 108, s. 25. But without any such consent it is the duty of the judge to ascertain that such a question legally may, and actually does, exist between the parties. *Lilley* v. *Harvey,* 5 Dowl. & L. 648; *Fearon* v. *Norvall, Id.* 439; *Marwood* v. *Waters,* 13 C. B. 820. Generally speaking, a tenant cannot dispute his landlord's title. *Ante,* 213. And where, and so far as, that rule is applicable, no such dispute or question can legally arise between the parties (*a*). In some cases, however, a tenant may prove that since the demise his landlord's title has ceased, or been duly determined, or assigned over to some third person who has made a fresh demise or conveyance to the defendant; *ante,* 217; or, if the plaintiff be not the original lessor, or the person from whom the defendant obtained possession of the demised premises, the latter may prove that he paid rent to the plaintiff, or submitted to a distress made by him for rent, by mistake and in ignorance of the real facts; and that the plaintiff really has no title. *Ante,* 218. In such cases, upon proof of facts of the above nature, the county court would have no jurisdiction to proceed further. 9 & 10 Vict. c. 95, s. 58; *Marwood* v. *Waters,* 13 C. B. 820. But it is the duty of the judge to inquire into the facts and to hear the evidence, so far as is necessary to ascertain that a real question as to the title legally may and actually does exist between the parties; and that it is not a mere pretence raised by the defendant for the sole purpose of ousting the jurisdiction of the county court. If it appear that no such question can legally be raised by the defendant, or that no such question does actually exist, and that the objection is a mere pretence of the defendant for the purpose above mentioned, the judge should overrule the objection and proceed to hear and determine the action. *Fearon* v. *Norvall,* 5 Dowl. & L. 439; *Lilley* v. *Harvey, Id.* 648; *Owen* v. *Pearce, Id.* 654, note (*e*). If he decide erroneously upon the above point, the defendant may appeal to one of the superior courts at Westminster; *post,* 663; *Mountnoy* v. *Collier,*

(*a*) *Barbour* v. *Barlow,* 8th July, 1856, *per* Bramwell, B., at chambers. In this case the defendant had obtained an order *ex parte* for a prohibition, upon an affidavit stating that the title to land was in question. The plaintiff applied to rescind such order upon an affidavit, showing that the defendant had occupied as tenant of the plaintiff, and *had paid him rent,* and that the term had been duly determined by notice to quit. The learned judge rescinded the previous order.

1 E. & B. 630; or a prohibition may be applied for, either to one of the superior courts, or to a judge of one of those courts, either in term time or vacation; 13 & 14 Vict. c. 61, s. 22; 19 & 20 Vict. c. 108, ss. 40, 41, 42; *Jones* v. *Owen*, 5 Dowl. & L. 669; *Marwood* v. *Waters*, 13 C. B. 820; *Re Chew* v. *Holroyd*, 8 Exch. 249; formerly, if such court or judge directed the applicant to declare in prohibition, pursuant to 1 Will. 4, c. 21, the question of jurisdiction became one of pleading and evidence. *Thompson* v. *Ingham*, 2 Low. M. & P. 216. But now, " when an application shall be made to a superior court or a judge thereof for a writ of prohibition to be addressed to a judge of a county court, the matter shall be finally disposed of by rule or order, and no declaration or further proceedings in prohibition shall be allowed." 19 & 20 Vict. c. 108, s. 42.

2. That "neither the value of the premises nor the rent payable in respect thereof" has exceeded 50*l.* by the year. *Ante*, 652. Under the 9 & 10 Vict. c. 95, s. 122, if the rent reserved were under 50*l.* per annum, and no fine paid, the court had jurisdiction, notwithstanding the annual value of the premises had increased, by buildings or otherwise, to a much greater amount than 50*l.* *In re Earl of Hurrington* v. *Ramsay*, 8 Exch. 879; 2 E. & B. 669; *Fearon* v. *Norvall*, 5 Dowl. & L. 445; but see *Crowley* v. *Vitty*, 7 Exch. 319. Now neither the rent nor the annual value may exceed 50*l.*, and this must be proved at the trial, whether the defendant appear or not.

3. That " no fine or premium" was paid for the lease. *Ante*, 652.

4. That the term or tenancy has *expired* or *been determined* either by the landlord or the tenant by a legal notice to quit. *Ante*, 652. The statute expressly requires proof at the trial of the holding, and of the expiration or other determination of the tenancy, *with the time and manner thereof*, whether the defendant appear or not. We have fully considered the law as to notices to quit. *Ante*, 29. When the landlord seeks to recover the premises by reason of a forfeiture committed by the tenant, and a condition or proviso of re-entry, the action must be brought in one of the superior courts; *Doe* d. *Cundey* v. *Sharpley*, 15 M. & W. 558; *ante*, 381; except in cases within sect. 52. *Post*, 659.

5. That the defendant has neglected or refused, and still neglects or refuses to deliver up possession of the premises. For the purpose of showing this, a demand of possession should be made, and, if possible, a refusal obtained in like manner as under the 15 & 16 Vict. c. 76, s. 213; *ante*, 382. The act requires " proof of his *still neglecting* or refusing to deliver up possession of the premises." *Ante*, 652. But proof that he retains possession of them after a demand made, as above mentioned, will be *primâ facie* evidence that he still refuses, or at all events *neglects*, to deliver up the possession.

6. If the defendant do not appear at the trial, the service of the summons must be proved. *Ante*, 652. As to the mode of service, *vide* sect. 54. *Post*, 662. The judge's decision as to the sufficiency of the service is conclusive. *Robinson* v. *Lenaghan*, 2 Exch. 333.

7. If the plaintiff seek to recover rent or mesne profits pursuant to sect. 51 (*ante*, 652), he must prove *the amount* in like manner as in an action of ejectment. *Ante*, 292, 307, 643. But the other evidence as to the tenancy, &c. will generally be sufficient to prove the amount or value of the mesne profits.

Evidence and Points for Defendant.]—The defendant may contend that the plaintiff's evidence is insufficient on some material point. *Ante*, 654. He may also produce contradictory evidence, so far as he is not estopped from so doing by the relation of landlord and tenant. *Ante*, 213. He may show that the ordinary relation of landlord and tenant never existed as between him and the plaintiff, or as between any persons under whom they respectively claim. *Jones* v. *Owen*, 5 Dowl. & L. 669; *Banks* v. *Rebbeck*, 2 Low. M. & P. 452; *ante*, 654. But, generally speaking, if the defendant's tenancy to the plaintiff be sufficiently proved, or if it appear that the defendant obtained possession through or under the plaintiff or his tenant, the defendant will not be permitted to dispute the plaintiff's title. He is not legally entitled to do so, but is estopped; *ante*, 213; and where that is the case, no dispute or question as to the title can arise, so as to exclude the jurisdiction of the county court. *Barbour* v. *Barlow*, *ante*, 655, *note*. Sometimes, however, he may show that since the demise the plaintiff's title has expired or ceased, or been determined, or assigned to some person from whom the defendant has obtained a fresh demise or conveyance; *ante*, 217; or that the defendant has a title to the premises not inconsistent with his tenancy to the plaintiff during the term. When anything of this sort is proved, and a *bonâ fide* question as to title sufficiently appears, the judge should abstain from deciding in favour of either party for want of jurisdiction. 9 & 10 Vict. c. 95, s. 58. The question is not whether the defendant has a good title to the possession, but whether there is a *bonâ fide* question or dispute as to the title which may legally exist between the parties. *Sewell* v. *Jones*, 1 Low. M. & P. 525. If it appear to the judge that the defendant's objection is one which he is not legally entitled to make (he being estopped as above mentioned), or that it is not a real and *bonâ fide* question, but a mere pretence raised for the sole purpose of excluding the jurisdiction of the county court, the judge should overrule it, and proceed to hear and decide the action on the merits. *Lilley* v. *Harvey*, 5 Dowl. & L. 648; *Owen* v. *Pearce*, *Id.* 654, note (*c*). If he decide erroneously upon the point of jurisdiction, an application may be made to one of the superior courts for a writ of prohibition; *Cases, supra; Jones* v. *Owen*, 5 Dowl. & L. 669; and see *Bunbury* v. *Fuller*, 9 Exch. 140; or such application may be made to a judge at chambers either in term time or vacation. 13 & 14 Vict. c. 61, s. 22. Formerly, if the court or judge directed the applicant to declare in prohibition, pursuant to 1 Will. 4, c. 21, the question of jurisdiction then became one of pleading and evidence. *Thompson* v. *Ingham*, 1 Low. M. & P. 216. But now see 19 & 20 Vict. c. 108, s. 42. *Ante*, 656.

Verdict and Judgment.]—If the cause be tried by a jury, the judge submits to them any disputed question of fact, and sums up the evidence in the same manner as in an action tried before a jury in one of the superior courts; and when their verdict is given, judgment is thereupon pronounced for the plaintiff, or for the defendant (according to the verdict), with costs.

If the cause be tried without a jury (as is usually the case), the judge decides all questions both of law and fact, and gives a verdict and judgment at the same time, stating the reasons for his decision, if it appear to him necessary or expedient so to do.

The judge may direct the plaintiff to be *nonsuited* in any case where the evidence is insufficient to entitle him to a verdict. 9 & 10 Vict. c. 95, s. 89. But if the cause be tried by a jury, the plaintiff may object to be nonsuited, and elect to take his chance of the verdict. *Stancliffe,* App., *Clarke,* Resp., 7 Exch. 439; *ante,* 304. On the other hand, the plaintiff may at any time before the verdict is pronounced by the jury, or by the judge (as the case may be), elect to. be nonsuited, so as to avoid a verdict and judgment against him. *Robinson* v. *Lawrence,* 7 Exch. 123; 2 Low. M. & P. 673; *Outhwaite* v. *Hudson,* 7 Exch. 380.

If a verdict and judgment be found for the plaintiff, the judge will "order that possession of the premises mentioned in the plaint be *given by the defendant to the plaintiff,* either forthwith, or on or before such a day as the judge shall think fit to name." *Ante,* 652; *see form in Appendix, No.* 415.

The successful party is entitled to his costs. The judge in each case directs what number of witnesses are to be allowed on taxation of costs, and their allowance for attendance will be according to the scale mentioned *ante,* 653, unless otherwise ordered, but will in no case exceed the allowances therein mentioned. The costs of witnesses, whether they have been examined or not, may in the discretion of the judge be allowed, although they have not been summoned. The costs of proving any document, whether printed or written, will not be allowed for without a special order of the judge, unless the opposite party has had due notice to admit it; but if he has neglected or refused to comply with such notice, and the judge think it reasonable that the admission should have been made, the party refusing shall bear the expense of proving such document, whatever may be the event of the cause. The expense of employing a barrister or attorney by either party will not be allowed on taxation of costs, unless by order of the judge. 9 & 10 Vict. c. 95, s. 91; 13 & 14 Vict. c. 61, s. 6. But the allowance of costs for such barrister or attorney shall not be affected by the want of notice to the opposite party of the intention to employ a barrister or attorney.

All costs between party and party shall be taxed by the clerk of the court, but his taxation may be reviewed by the judge upon the application of either party; and it shall not be necessary that the costs shall be taxed in court, or during the sitting of the court at which judgment is given.

A *new trial* may be moved for *on the day of hearing, if both parties are present,* or at the first court held next after the expiration of twelve clear days from such day of hearing, provided certain notices be given, but not at any subsequent court, unless by leave of the judge, and on such terms as he shall think fit. It is not competent to a county court judge, when he has once heard and disposed of an application for a new trial, to re-hear the case at a subsequent court. He may be restrained from so doing by prohibition. *The Great Northern Railway Company* v. *Mossop,* 17 C. B. 130; 25 Law J., N. S., C. P. 22.

If the yearly rent or value of the premises exceed 20*l.,* the unsuccessful party may appeal pursuant to sect. 68. *Post,* 663.

If the order for delivery of possession made at the hearing (*supra*) be not obeyed, the registrar, whether such order can be proved to be served or not, shall at the instance of the plaintiff issue a warrant, authorizing and requiring the high bailiff of the court to give possession of such premises to the plaintiff. *Ante,* 652 ; *see the form, Appendix, No.* 417. As to the effect and operation of such warrant, and the protection thereby afforded to the high bailiff, &c., see *post,* 662. The plaintiff is also protected from any action of *trespass,* notwithstanding any irregularity or informality in the proceedings. *Post,* 662.

Actions for Recovery of Small Tenements by Landlords for Nonpayment of Rent.]—By 19 & 20 Vict. c. 108, s. 52, " when the rent of any corporeal hereditament, *where neither the value of the premises nor the rent* payable in respect thereof exceeds 50*l.* by the year, *shall for one half year be in arrear,* and the landlord shall have *right by law to re-enter* for the non-payment thereof, he may, *without any formal demand or re-entry,* enter a plaint *in the county court of the district in which the premises lie* for the recovery of the premises; and thereupon a summons shall issue to the tenant, *the service whereof shall stand in lieu of a demand and re-entry,* and if the tenant shall, five clear days before the return day of such summons, pay into court all the rent in arrear and the costs, the said action shall cease, but if he shall not make such payment, and shall not at the time named in the summons show good cause why the premises should not be recovered, then, *on proof of the yearly value and rent* of the premises, *and of the fact that one half-year's rent was in arrear* before the plaint was entered, *and that no sufficient distress was then to be found* on the premises to countervail *such arrear, and of the landlord's power to re-enter, and of the rent being still in arrear, and of the title of the plaintiff,* if such title has accrued since the letting of the premises, *and of the service of the summons* if the defendant shall not appear thereto, the judge may order that possession of the premises mentioned in the plaint be given by the defendant to the plaintiff on or before such day, not being less than four weeks from the day of hearing, as the judge shall think fit to name, unless within that period all the rent in arrear and the costs be paid into court; and if such order be not obeyed, and such rent and costs be not so paid, the registrar shall, whether such order can be proved to have been served or not, at the instance of the plaintiff, issue a warrant, authorizing and requiring the high bailiff of the court to give possession of such premises to the plaintiff, and the plaintiff *shall from the time of the execution of such warrant hold the premises discharged of the tenancy,* and the defendant, and all persons claiming by, through or under him, shall, so long as the order of the court remains unreversed, be barred from all relief in equity or otherwise."

Before this enactment the county court had no jurisdiction where possession was claimed by reason of a forfeiture and a right to re-enter during the term for non-payment of rent, but only where the term had ended, or been determined by a regular notice to quit.

This section is very similar in substance and effect to the 15 & 16 Vict. c. 76, s. 210; *ante,* 415; but it is restricted and confined to small cases, *i. e.* where neither the annual value, nor the rent, exceeds 50*l. Supra; and see ante,* 656. Any fine or premium paid for the lease will not deprive the county court of jurisdiction under this section, as it would under section 50. *Ante,* 652.

Mode of Proceeding.]—The mode of proceeding under this section is similar (*mutatis mutandis*) to that under sections 50 and 51. *Ante*, 653.

Before entering his plaint, the plaintiff should clearly ascertain:—
1. That he has "a right by law to re-enter for the non-payment" of the half-year's rent in arrear. *Ante*, 659. He can have no such right except by virtue of some condition or proviso for re-entry contained in the lease or agreement (whether by deed, writing or oral agreement, express or implied), under which the defendant holds; *ante*, 403, 416; nor until the time or period (if any) thereby allowed to save the forfeiture has elapsed. *Doe* d. *Dixon* v. *Roe*, 7 C. B. 134; *ante*, 417.
2. That there is no sufficient distress to be found on the premises to countervail *such arrear*. As to the mode of proving this, see *ante*, 416. The distress need not be sufficient to countervail "all the arrears," if more than one half-year's rent be due: but it is otherwise under 15 & 16 Vict. c. 76, s. 210, which is differently worded in this respect. *Ante*, 415, 416.

Evidence for Plaintiff.]—At the hearing the plaintiff must prove:—
1. The tenancy. This must be proved in like manner as in an ejectment by a landlord against a tenant. *Ante*, 393, 419. If necessary, the defendant must be served with a notice to produce the lease or agreement, and the plaintiff must be prepared with secondary evidence of the contents, in like manner as in a superior court. *Ante*, 155.
2. That neither the rent nor the value of the premises exceeds 50*l.* by the year. *Ante*, 659.
3. That one half-year's rent was in arrear before the plaint was entered. As to proof of *non-payment*, see *ante*, 419.
4. That before and at the time when the plaint was entered, the landlord had power to re-enter for non-payment of the said half-year's rent. This will appear by the lease or agreement under which the defendant holds, or by the parol evidence of the tenancy including the express condition or proviso for re-entry for non-payment of rent. *Ante*, 403, 416. It must appear that the number of days (if any) allowed by such condition or proviso for payment of the rent to save the forfeiture elapsed before the plaint was entered. *Doe* d. *Dixon* v. *Roe*, 7 C. B. 134; *ante*, 417.
5. If the plaintiff be not the lessor, his title must be deduced from the lessor, and proved in the usual manner. *Ante*, 224, 419.
6. If the defendant do not appear the service of the summons must be proved. *Ante*, 659. This is usually done in the first instance, and before any other evidence is given. No such proof is necessary when the defendant appears.

Evidence and Points for Defendant.]—The defendant may contend that the plaintiff's evidence is insufficient on some material point. *Supra.* He may also produce contradictory evidence. He may show that the annual value of the premises exceeds 50*l.*, although the rent be less. He may prove payment of the rent claimed, or any part thereof. He may show that there was a sufficient distress to be found on the premises with reasonable diligence. *Ante*, 416. He may contend that the landlord had no right to re-enter for non-payment of the half-year's rent, the lease or agreement containing no condition or proviso to that effect; *ante*, 411, 416; or that the number of days allowed oy any such condition or proviso had not elapsed before the plaint was entered. *Doe* d. *Dixon* v. *Roe*, 7 C. B. 134 ; *ante*, 417. If the plaintiff be not the lessor the defendant may dispute the plaintiff's title as deduced from the lessor ; but if the defendant obtained possession of the premises from the plaintiff he cannot dispute or deny his right to demise, because a tenant cannot dispute his landlord's title. *Ante*, 213. He may, however, prove that *since the demise* the plaintiff has parted with his reversion by sale, mortgage or otherwise, or that it has since expired, or been determined in some legal manner. *Ante*, 217.

Verdict and Judgment.]—If the verdict be for the plaintiff the judge may " order that possession of the premises mentioned in the plaint be given by the defendant to the plaintiff on or before such day not being less than four weeks from the day of hearing, as the judge shall think fit to name, unless within that period all the rent in arrear and the costs be paid into court." *Ante*, 659 ; *see form of Order, Appendix, No.* 415.

The judge directs in each case what number of witnesses are to be allowed, and also as to the expense of employing a barrister or attorney by either party, and as to the expense of proving documents, in like manner as in an action for recovery of tenements after the term has expired or been determined. *Ante*, 658.

The unsuccessful party may move for a new trial, or appeal, in like manner as in an action for recovery of tenements after the term has expired or been determined. *Ante*, 658 ; *post*, 663.

The defendant may put an end to all further proceedings by paying into court the arrears of rent and costs, within the time in that behalf allowed by the order made on the hearing. *Supra*.

If such order be not obeyed, and such rent and costs be not so paid, the registrar shall, whether such order can be proved to have been served or not, at the instance of the plaintiff, issue a warrant, authorizing and requiring the high bailiff of the court to give possession of such premises to the plaintiff. *Ante*, 659 ; *see the form, Appendix, No.* 417. As to the effect and operation of such warrant, and the protection thereby afforded to the high bailiff, &c., see *post*, 662. The plaintiff is also protected from any action of *trespass*, notwithstanding any irregularity or informality in the proceedings. *Post*, 662. Moreover " the plaintiff shall from the time of the execution of such warrant hold the premises *discharged of the tenancy*, and the defendant, and all persons claiming by, through or under him, shall, so long as the order of the court remains unreversed, be barred from all relief in equity or otherwise." *Ante*, 659. To avoid this the defendant should pay the arrears of rent and costs into court pursuant to the order made at the hearing.

Sub-Tenant served with Summons to recover Possession must forthwith give Notice thereof to his immediate Landlord, who may come in and defend.]—By 19 & 20 Vict. c. 108, s. 53, "where any summons for the recovery of a tenement as is hereinbefore specified shall be served on or come to the knowledge of any sub-tenant of the plaintiff's immediate tenant, such sub-tenant being an occupier of the whole or of a part of the premises sought to be recovered, he shall *forthwith give notice thereof to his immediate landlord, under penalty of forfeiting three years' rack rent* of the premises held by such sub-tenant to such landlord, to be recovered by such landlord by action *in the court from which summons shall have issued ;* and such landlord on the receipt of such notice, if not originally a defendant, may be added or substituted as a defendant to defend possession of the premises in question."

This enactment is similar in substance and effect to the 15 & 16 Vict. c. 76, s. 209, which is fully treated of, *ante,* 115—118.

The time and mode in which the tenant's immediate landlord may be added or substituted pursuant to the above section will be prescribed by the rules, orders and forms to be made pursuant to sect. 5. *Ante,* 652.

Service of Summons.]—By 19 & 20 Vict. c. 108, s. 54, "a summons for the recovery of a tenement may be served like other summonses to appear to plaints in county courts ; and if the defendant cannot be found, and his place of dwelling shall either not be known, or admission thereto cannot be obtained for serving any such summons, a copy of the summons shall be posted on some conspicuous part of the premises sought to be recovered, and such posting shall be deemed good service on the defendant."

Warrant for Possession.]—By 19 & 20 Vict. c. 108, s. 55, "any warrant to a high bailiff to give possession of a tenement shall justify the bailiff named therein in entering upon the premises named therein, with such assistants as he shall deem necessary, and in giving possession accordingly, but no entry upon any such warrant shall be made except between the hours of nine in the morning and four in the afternoon."

By sect. 56, "every such warrant shall, on whatever day it may be issued, bear date on the day next after the last day named by the judge in his order for the delivery of possession of the premises in question, and shall continue in force for three months from such date and no longer, but no order for delivery of possession need be drawn up or served."

Amendments.]—By 19 & 20 Vict. c. 108, s. 57, "the judge of a county court may at all times amend all defects and errors in any proceeding in such court, whether there is anything in writing to amend by or not, and whether the defect or error be that of the party applying to amend or not ; and all such amendments may be made with or without costs, and upon such terms as to the judge may seem fit ; and all such amendments as may be necessary for the purpose of determining in the existing suit the real question in controversy between the parties shall be so made, if duly applied for."

Consequences of Irregularities and Informalities.]—By 19 & 20 Vict. c. 108, s. 60, "no officer of a county court in executing any warrant of a county court, and *no person at whose instance* any such warrant shall be executed, shall be deemed a trespasser by reason of any irregularity or informality in any proceeding on the validity of which such warrant depends, or in the form of such warrant, or in the mode of executing it, but the party aggrieved may bring an action for any special damage which he may sustain by reason of such irregularity or informality against the party guilty thereof, and in such action he shall recover no costs, unless the damages awarded shall exceed *forty shillings.*"

The 9 & 10 Vict. c. 95, ss. 124, 125, containing provisions of a similar nature, are not repealed by 19 & 20 Vict. c. 108, s. 2.

Appeal.]—By 19 & 20 Vict. c. 108, s. 68, "an appeal from the decision of a county court, *on the same grounds* and *subject to the same conditions* as are provided by the fourteenth section of the act of the thirteenth and fourteenth years of the reign of her present majesty, chapter sixty-one, shall be allowed in all actions of replevin where the amount of rent or damage exceeds 20*l.*, *and in all actions for the recovery of tenements where the yearly rent or value of the premises exceeds* 20*l.*, and in proceedings in interpleader where the money claimed, or the value of the goods or chattels claimed, or of the proceeds thereof exceeds 20*l.*, and in all actions and proceedings where the sum claimed exceeds 20*l.*"

The 14th section of 13 & 14 Vict. c. 61 (referred to in the above enactment) is as follows:—" And be it enacted, that if either party in any cause of the amount to which jurisdiction is given to the county courts by this act shall be dissatisfied with the determination or direction of the said court *in point of law, or upon the admission or rejection of any evidence,* such party may appeal from the same to any of the superior courts of common law at Westminster, two or more of the puisne judges whereof shall sit out of term as a court of appeal for that purpose, provided that such party shall, *within ten days* after such determination or direction, *give notice* of such appeal to the other party, or his attorney, and *also give security,* to be approved by the clerk of the court [now called the registrar, 19 & 20 Vict. c. 108, s. 8], for the costs of the appeal, whatever may be the event of the appeal, and for the amount of the judgment, if he be the defendant and the appeal be dismissed: provided nevertheless, that such security, so far as regards the amount of the judgment, shall not be required in any case where the judge of the county court shall have ordered the party appealing to pay the amount of such judgment into the hands of the clerk of the county court [now called the registrar] in which such action shall have been tried, and the same shall have been paid accordingly ; and the said court of appeal may either order a new trial on such terms as it thinks fit, or may order judgment to be entered for either party, as the case may be, and may make such order with respect to the costs of the said appeal, as such court may think proper ; and such orders shall be final."

The 15th section of 13 & 14 Vict. c. 61, enacts, "that such appeal shall be in the form of a case agreed on by both parties, or their attorneys, and if they cannot agree, the judge of the county court, upon being applied to by them or their attorneys, shall settle the case and sign it ; and such case shall be transmitted by the appellant to the rule department of the masters' office of the court in which the appeal is to be brought."

This section applies to appeals under 19 & 20 Vict. c. 108, s. 69 ; *vide* sect. 3, *ante,* 652.

By section 69 of 19 & 20 Vict. c. 108, "no appeal shall lie from the decision of a county court, if before such decision is pronounced both parties shall agree, in writing signed by themselves or their attorneys or agents, that the decision of the judge shall be final, and no such agreement shall require a stamp."

By sect. 70, " where by this act, or any act relating to the county courts, a party is required to give security, such security shall be at the cost of the party giving it, and in the form of a bond, with sureties, to the other party or intended party in the action or proceeding : provided always, that the court in which any action on the bond shall be brought may by rule or order give such relief to the obligors as may be just, and such rule or order shall have the effect of a defeasance of such bond."

By sect. 71, " where by this act, or any act relating to the county courts, a party is required to give security, he may in lieu thereof deposit with the registrar, if the security is required to be given in a county court, or with a master of the superior court, if the security is required to be given in such court, a sum equal in amount to the sum for which he would be required to give security, together with a memorandum, to be approved of by such registrar or master, and to be signed by such party, his attorney or agent, setting forth the conditions on which such money is deposited, and the registrar or master shall give to the party paying a written acknowledgment of such payment; and the judge of the county court, when the money shall have been deposited in such court, or a judge of the superior court, when the money shall have been deposited in a superior court, may, on the same evidence as would be required to enforce or avoid such bond as in the last preceding section is mentioned, order such sum so deposited to be paid out to such party or parties as to him shall seem just."

Lancashire and Durham.]—By 19 & 20 Vict. c. 108, s. 86, "all the provisions of this act applicable to superior courts and judges thereof shall apply to the Court of Common Pleas at Lancaster and Court of Pleas at Durham, and the judges thereof respectively, being judges of one of the common law courts at Westminster, and all the said provisions applicable to masters of superior courts shall apply to the respective prothonotaries of the Court of Common Pleas at Lancaster and Court of Pleas at Durham, and their respective deputies, acting in the execution of the duties of such officers : provided that any writs of *certiorari* to be issued by the orders of such courts, or of a judge thereof, shall be issued out of the chanceries of the counties palatine of Lancaster and Durham respectively, and shall be made returnable in the said Court of Common Pleas at Lancaster and Court of Pleas at Durham respectively, in the same manner as other writs of *certiorari* of such counties palatine respectively."

Fees payable.]—The 19 & 20 Vict. c. 108, schedule (C), authorizes certain fees to be taken in the county courts in actions for the recovery of tenements, and in other actions, viz. :—

For every plaint—ten pence in the pound.

For every hearing—two shillings in the pound. An additional hearing fee shall be taken for every new trial. No fee shall be payable for hearing any application for a new trial, or to set aside proceedings, &c.

For every jury—five shillings shall be paid to the registrar by the party demanding the jury, on such demand, for the use of the jurors.

For issuing every warrant against the body or goods—eighteen pence in the pound on the amount for which such warrant shall issue.

For issuing every warrant to deliver possession of tenements—eighteen pence in the pound.

In plaints for the recovery of tenements when the term has expired or been determined by notice, all poundage, except as aforesaid [*i. e.* except where otherwise specified in this schedule] shall be estimated on the amount of the weekly, monthly or yearly rent of the tenement, as such tenement shall have been let by the week or by the month, or for any longer period; and if no rent shall have been reserved, then on the amount of the half-yearly value of the tenement, to be fixed by the registrar.

If in any plaint for the recovery of tenements a claim be made for rent or mesne profits, an additional poundage shall be paid on the amount of such claim.

In plaints for the recovery of tenements for nonpayment of rent, all poundage, except as aforesaid [*i. e.* except where otherwise specified in this schedule], shall be estimated on the amount of the half-yearly rent of the tenement.

In every case where the poundage would, but for this rule, be estimated on an amount exceeding 20*l.*, it shall be estimated at 20*l.* only.

In every case where the poundage cannot be estimated by any rule in this schedule, it shall be estimated on 20*l.*

All fractions of a pound, for the purpose of calculating poundage, shall be treated as an entire pound.

Where the plaintiff recovers less than the amount of his claim, so as to reduce the scale of costs, he shall pay the difference, unless the reduction shall be caused by a set-off.

No increase of fees shall be made by reason of there being more than one plaintiff or defendant.

No other fees shall be taken on any account.

The schedule allows certain fees to the high bailiff, brokers and appraisers on the seizure, appraisement and sale of goods.

(666)

CHAPTER LXXI.

RECOVERY BEFORE JUSTICES OF SMALL TENEMENTS.

By 1 & 2 Vict. c. 74, intituled "An Act to facilitate the Recovery of Possession of Tenements after due Determination of the Tenancy," after reciting that "whereas it is expedient to provide for the more speedy and effectual recovery of the possession of premises *unlawfully held over after the determination of the tenancy,*" it is enacted (sect. 1), " that from and after the passing of this act, when and so soon as the term or interest of the tenant of any house, land or other corporeal hereditaments held by him *at will, or for any term not exceeding seven years,* either without being liable to the payment of any rent, or at a rent *not exceeding the rent of* 20*l. a year,* and upon which *no fine* shall have been reserved or made payable, shall have *ended, or shall have been duly determined by a legal notice to quit or otherwise;* and such tenant, or (if such tenant do not actually occupy the premises, or only occupy a part thereof) any person by whom the same or any part thereof shall be then actually occupied, shall neglect or refuse to quit and deliver up possession of the premises, or of such part thereof respectively, it shall be lawful for the landlord of the said premises or his agent to cause the person so neglecting or refusing to quit and deliver up possession to be served (in the manner hereinafter mentioned) with a written notice in the form set forth in the schedule to this act [*see Appendix, No.* 418], signed by the said landlord or his agent, of his intention to proceed to recover possession under the authority and according to the mode prescribed in this act; and if the tenant or occupier shall not thereupon appear at the time and place appointed, and show to the satisfaction of the justices hereinafter mentioned reasonable cause why possession should not be given under the provisions of this act, and shall still neglect or refuse to deliver up possession of the premises, or of such part thereof of which he is then in possession, to the said landlord or his agent, it shall be lawful for such landlord or agent to give to such justices proof of the holding, and of the end or other determination of the tenancy, with the time or manner thereof; and where the title of the landlord has accrued since the letting of the premises, the right by which he claims the possession; and upon proof of service of the notice, and of the neglect or refusal of the tenant or occupier as the case may be, it shall be lawful for the justices acting for the district, division or place within which the said premises or any part thereof shall be situate, in petty sessions assembled, or any two of them, to issue a warrant [*Form, Appendix, No.* 420] under their hands and seals to the constables and peace officers of the district, division or place within which the said premises or any part thereof shall be situate, commanding them within a period therein named, *not less than twenty-one nor more than thirty clear days* from the date of such warrant, to enter (by force if needful) into the premises and give possession of the same to such landlord or agent: provided always, that entry upon any such warrant shall not be made on a Sunday, Good Friday or Christmas Day, or at any time except between the hours of nine in the morning and four in the afternoon: provided also, that nothing herein contained shall be deemed to protect any person on whose application and to whom any such warrant shall be granted from any action which may be brought against him by any such tenant or occupier for or in respect of such entry and taking possession, where such person had not at the time of granting the same *lawful right to the possession* of the same premises: provided also, that nothing herein contained shall affect any rights to which any person may be entitled as outgoing tenant by the custom of the country or otherwise."

Sect. 2 enacts, "that such notice of application intended to be made under this act may be served either personally or by leaving the same with some person being in and apparently residing at the place of abode of the person so holding over as aforesaid; and that the person serving the same shall read over the same to the person served, or with whom the same shall be left as aforesaid, and explain the purport and intent thereof: provided that if the person so holding over cannot be found, and the place of abode of such person shall either not be known or admission thereto cannot be obtained for serving such summons, the posting up of the said summons on some conspicuous part of the premises so held over shall be deemed to be good service upon such person."

Sect. 3 enacts, "that in every case in which the person to whom any such warrant shall be granted had not at the time of granting the same lawful right to the possession of the premises, the obtaining of any such warrant as aforesaid shall be deemed a trespass by him against the tenant or occupier of the premises, although no entry shall be made by virtue of the warrant; and in case any such tenant or occupier will become bound with two sureties as hereinafter provided, to be approved of by the said justices, in such sum as to them shall seem reasonable, regard being had to the value of the premises and to the probable costs of an action, to sue the person to whom such warrant was granted, with effect and without delay, and to pay all the costs of the proceeding in such action, in case a verdict shall pass for the defendant, or the plaintiff shall discontinue or not prosecute his action, or become nonsuit therein, execution of the warrant shall be delayed until judgment shall have been given in such action of trespass ; and if upon the trial of such action of trespass a verdict shall pass for the plaintiff, such verdict and judgment thereupon shall supersede the warrant so granted, and the plaintiff shall be entitled to *double costs* in the said action of trespass," [now to a full and reasonable indemnity as to all costs, charges and expenses incurred in and about the action, in lieu of double costs. 5 & 6 Vict. c. 97, s. 2.]

Sect. 4 enacts, " that every such bond as hereinbefore mentioned shall be made to the said landlord or his agent at the costs of such landlord or agent, and shall be approved of and signed by the said justices; and if the bond so taken be forfeited, or if upon the trial of the action, for securing the trial of which such bond was given, the judge by whom it shall be tried shall not indorse *upon the record in court* that the condition of the bond hath been fulfilled, the party to whom the bond shall have been so made may bring an action, and recover thereon : provided always, that the court where such action as last aforesaid shall be brought may, by a rule of court, give such relief to the parties upon such bond as may be agreeable to justice, and such rule shall have the nature and effect of a defeazance to such bond."

Sect. 5 enacts, " that it shall not be lawful to bring any action or prosecution against the said justices by whom such warrant as aforesaid shall have been issued, or against any constable or peace officer by whom such warrant may be executed, for issuing such warrant or executing the same respectively, by reason that the person on whose application the same shall be granted had not lawful right to the possession of the premises."

Sect. 6 enacts, " that where the landlord at the time of applying for such warrant as aforesaid had lawful right to the possession of the premises, or the part thereof so held over as aforesaid, neither the said landlord nor his agent, nor any other person acting in his behalf, shall be deemed to be a trespasser by reason merely of any irregularity or informality in the mode of proceeding for obtaining possession under the authority of this act, but the party aggrieved may, if he think fit, bring an action in the case for such irregularity or informality, in which the damage alleged to be sustained thereby shall be specially laid, and may recover full satisfaction for such special damage, with costs of suit: provided that if the special damage so laid be not proved, the defendant shall be entitled to a verdict, and that if proved, but assessed by the jury at any sum not exceeding five shillings, the plaintiff shall recover no more costs than damages, unless the judge before whom the trial shall have been held shall certify upon the back of the record that in his opinion full costs ought to be allowed."

Sect. 7 enacts, " that in construing this act the word ' premises' shall be taken to signify lands, houses or other corporeal hereditaments; and that the word ' person' shall be taken to comprehend a body politic, corporate or collegiate, as well as an individual; and that every word importing the singular number shall, where necessary to give full effect to the enactments herein contained, be deemed to extend and be applied to several persons or things as well as one person or thing; and that every word importing the masculine gender shall where necessary extend and be applied to a female as well as a male; and that the term 'landlord' shall be understood as signifying the person entitled to the immediate reversion of the premises, or if the property be held in joint tenancy, coparcenary or tenancy in common, shall be understood as signifying any one of the persons entitled to such reversion; and that the word 'agent' shall be taken to signify any person usually employed by the landlord in the letting of the premises, or in the collection of the rents thereof, or specially authorized to act in the particular matter by writing under the hand of such landlord."

Sect. 8 enacts, "that this act shall not extend to Scotland or Ireland."

In what Cases.]—The act of 1 & 2 Vict. c. 74, was not repealed by the County Courts Act, 9 & 10 Vict. c. 95, which contained very similar provisions (sects. 122—127); nor is it repealed by the County Courts Amendment Act, 19 & 20 Vict. c. 108, s. 50. The remedy under the 1 & 2 Vict. c. 74, is more summary and less expensive than under the County Court Acts. Moreover, the justices have jurisdiction in some cases wherein the county court has no jurisdiction : *ex. gr.* where there exists a *bond fide* dispute or question as to the title; or where the term has been determined by entry *for a forfeiture* other than for non-payment of rent. Besides which, the *agent* of the landlord may do what is necessary on his behalf before the justices, without employing any attorney or counsel. Sometimes also, for other reasons, two justices may be considered by the landlord or his agent a preferable tribunal to the county court. Formerly no costs could be awarded by the justices to either party; but now see 11 & 12 Vict. c. 43, s. 18.

The following circumstances must concur to authorize proceedings under this act, viz. :—1. The premises must have been *demised* under some lease or agreement, express or implied, either at will, or for a term *not exceeding seven years* (there is no such limit in the County Court Acts). 2. The rent reserved, if any, must not have exceeded 20*l. per annum* (the county courts have jurisdiction where neither the value of the premises nor the rent exceeds 50*l.* by the year. (*Ante,* 652.) 3. The demise must have been made without any fine or premium. 4. The term or tenancy must have *ended* or have been *duly determined by a legal notice to quit, or otherwise.* A determination of the term by entry for a forfeiture, pursuant to a condition or proviso for re-entry, seems sufficient, by reason of the words " or otherwise," which are not contained in the County Courts Act. *Ante,* 652. 5. The tenant, or some person claiming through or under him, as assignee, undertenant, or otherwise, must have neglected or refused to deliver up possession of the demised premises, or of some part thereof, after the end or determination of the term. If an undertenant or assignee wrongfully retain possession of any part of the demised premises after the end or determination of the term, any proceedings under this act should be adopted against him, and not against the original lessee. 6. Only the " landlord" or his " agent" can proceed under this act. Therefore the ordinary relation of landlord and tenant must have existed between the parties at the end or determination of the demise. *Jones* v. *Owen*, 5 Dowl. & L. 669; *Banks* v. *Rebbeck*, 2 Low. M. & P. 452. But the landlord need not be the original lessor; if he derive a good title to the reversion from such lessor, *ex. gr.* as his assignee, heir, executor, devisee, or otherwise, that is sufficient. The act says expressly " that the term ' landlord' shall be understood as signifying the person *entitled to the immediate reversion* of the premises; or if the property be held in joint-tenancy, coparcenary, or tenancy in common, shall be understood as signifying any one of the persons entitled to such reversion; and that the word ' agent' shall be taken to signify any person usually employed by the landlord in the letting of the premises, or in the collection of the rents thereof, or specially authorized to act in the particular matter by writing under the hand of such landlord." Sect. 7; *ante*, 669.

The act provides that nothing therein contained shall affect any rights to which any person may be entitled as *outgoing tenant by the custom of the country or otherwise.* Sect. 1; *ante*, 667. As to the custom of the country, see *ante*, 249.

Mode of proceeding.]—The first step is to give a notice pursuant to sect. 1; *ante*, 666; *see the form, Appendix, No.* 418. Before this notice is given it should be ascertained on what day (not sooner than seven *clear* days after service of the notice, both days exclusive), and at what hour and place, it will be convenient for the justices to hear the application. If the notice be signed by the agent, he must have sufficient authority, pursuant to sect. 7. *Ante*, 669. The notice must be served pursuant to sect. 2. *Ante*, 667.

The complaint must then be lodged. *See the form, Appendix, No.* 419. If necessary, a summons to compel the attendance of any witness or witnesses may be obtained pursuant to 11 & 12 Vict. c. 43, s. 7. The form of such summons is given in the schedule to that act (G. 1).

At the time and place appointed by the notice the landlord or his agent must attend with his witnesses and documentary evidence—and he must then (whether the tenant appear or not) give to the justices " proof of the holding and of the end or other determination of the tenancy, with the time or manner thereof; and where the title of the landlord has accrued since the letting of the premises, the right by which he claims the possession." Sect. 1; *ante*, 667. The evidence on these points should be the same as in an action in the county court. *Ante*, 654—656. He must also prove the due service of the notice pursuant to sect. 2 (*ante*, 667), unless, indeed, the tenant appear at the hearing; in which case such proof would appear to be unnecessary. *Doe* d. *Thompson* v. *Hodgson*, 12 A. & E. 135; 4 P. & D. 142. The neglect or refusal of the tenant or occupier to deliver up possession must be shown; *ante*, 667; but this will sufficiently appear if the tenant *retain possession* of the demised premises or any part thereof after the end or determination of the term; and especially after the service of the notice.

The defendant may appear either in person or by counsel or attorney on his behalf. 11 & 12 Vict. c. 43, s. 12. He may contend that some or one of the concurring circumstances before mentioned (*ante*, 669) do not exist; or that the complainant's proofs are insufficient on some material point; *ante*, 670; but he cannot defeat the proceeding, or deprive the justices of jurisdiction, merely by showing or proving the existence of some *bona fide* dispute or question as to the title. The justices may, if they think fit, hear and determine any such dispute or question, however doubtful or difficult it may be. But it is otherwise in the county court, because of sect. 58 of the 9 & 10 Vict. c. 95. If the justices in the exercise of their discretion decline to adjudicate upon a difficult point or question as to the title, it seems that the Court of Queen's Bench will not compel them to do so by a mandamus, but will leave the party to his ordinary remedy by ejectment. *Ex parte Fulder*, 8 Dowl. 535; *Ex parte William Davy*, 2 Dowl. N. S. 24. Formerly no costs could be awarded by the justices to either party, but now see 11 & 12 Vict. c. 43, s. 18.

If the claimant's proofs be sufficient, the justices may issue a warrant pursuant to *sect.* 1. *Ante*, 667; *see the form, Appendix, No.* 420. The warrant must be directed to the constables and peace officers of the district, division or place, within which the premises or some part thereof are or is situate, or to some or one of them, and not to any other person. *Jones* v. *Chapman*, 14 M. & W. 124; 2 Dowl. & L. 907. Under this warrant possession will be delivered to the landlord or his agent at the time therein mentioned.

But the tenant may obtain a further order of the justices to stay the execution of the warrant of possession upon entering into a bond with two sureties pursuant to sect. 4. *Ante*, 668; *see the form of such bond, Appendix, No.* 421. The act says that such bond shall be made "at the costs of such landlord or agent." Sect. 4; *ante*, 668. A similar mistake was made in the County Courts Act, 9 & 10 Vict. c. 95, s. 127; but now see 19 & 20 Vict. c. 108, s. 70, *ante*, 664.

The obtaining a warrant of possession under this act amounts to a constructive act of trespass by the landlord, against the tenant or occupier, for which the latter may maintain an action of trespass *quare clausum fregit*, although no entry shall have been made by virtue of the warrant, provided the landlord had not at the time of the suing out of such warrant lawful right to the possession of the premises. Sect. 3; *ante*, 667; *Darlington* v. *Pritchard*, 4 Man. & Gr. 783; 5 Scott, N. R. 610; 2 Dowl. N. S. 664. But if at the time of applying for the warrant he had such right of possession, neither the landlord nor his agent, nor any other person acting on his behalf, shall be deemed to be a trespasser by reason merely of any irregularity or informality in the mode of proceeding for obtaining possession under the authority of the act. Sect. 6; *ante*, 668. The only remedy in such case is by a special action for the damage actually occasioned by such irregularity or informality. Sect. 6; *ante*, 668.

It has never been decided whether a tenant, who has been turned out of possession under a warrant obtained under this act, may afterwards maintain ejectment against the landlord to recover back the possession of the demised premises. But as he may afterwards maintain trespass *quare clausum fregit*, if the landlord had no right to the possession (*Jones* v. *Chapman*, 14 M. & W. 124; 2 Dowl. & L. 907), there seems no sufficient reason why he should not also maintain ejectment. A proceeding under this act is very much in the nature of a summary ejectment, and, therefore, ought not finally to conclude the right or title.

No action or prosecution can be maintained against the justices or constables for issuing or executing the warrant, even where the person on whose application the warrant was granted had not lawful right to the possession of the premises ; sect. 5 ; *ante*, 668 ; provided the warrant was directed to and executed by the proper constables of the district, &c. *Jones* v. *Chapman,* 14 M. & W. 124; 2 Dowl. & L. 907. The only remedy in such case is against the party who obtained the warrant. It seems doubtful whether sect. 5 extends to third persons who assist the constable in executing the warrant. *Darlington* v. *Pritchard,* 4 Man. & Gr. 783, 794 ; 5 Scott, N. R. 610; 2 Dowl. N. S. 664; but see *Jones* v. *Chapman, supra.*

CHAPTER LXXII.

RECOVERY BEFORE JUSTICES OF DESERTED PREMISES.

By 11 Geo. 2, c. 19, s. 16, after reciting that "whereas landlords are often great sufferers by tenants running away in arrear, and not only suffering the demised premises to lie uncultivated without any distress thereon, whereby their landlords or lessors might be satisfied for the rent-arrear, but also refusing to deliver up the possession of the demised premises, whereby the landlords are put to the expense and delay of recovering in ejectment," it is enacted, "that from and after the said twenty-fourth day of June, 1738, if any tenant holding any lands, tenements or hereditaments *at a rack rent*, or where the rent reserved shall be *full three-fourths of the yearly value* of the demised premises, who shall be in arrear for one year's rent [now half a year's rent; 57 Geo. 3, c. 52, *post*, 674], shall *desert* the demised premises,

G G

and leave the same uncultivated or unoccupied, *so as no sufficient distress can be had to countervail the arrears of rent*, it shall and may be lawful to and for two or more justices of the peace of the county, riding, division or place (having no interest in the demised premises), *at the request* of the lessor or landlord, lessors or landlords, or his, her or their bailiff or receiver, to go upon and view the same, and to affix, or cause to be affixed, on the most notorious part of the premises, notice in writing what day (at the distance of fourteen days at the least) they will return to take a second view thereof; and if upon such second view, the tenant, or some person on his or her behalf, shall not *appear and pay the rent in arrear*, or there shall not be sufficient distress upon the premises, then the said justices may put the landlord or landlords, lessor or lessors, into the possession of the said demised premises, and the lease thereof to such tenant, *as to any demise therein contained only, shall from thenceforth become void.*"

Sect. 17 provides, " that such proceedings of the said justices shall be examinable in a summary way by the next justice or justices of assize of the respective counties in which such lands or premises lie; and if they lie in the city of London, or county of Middlesex, by judges of the Courts of King's Bench or Common Pleas; and if in the counties palatine of Chester, Lancaster or Durham, then before the judges thereof; and if in Wales, then before the Court of Grand Sessions [abolished by 1 Will. 4, c. 70] respectively, who are hereby respectively empowered *to order restitution to be made to such tenant, together with his or her expenses and costs*, to be paid by the lessor or landlord, lessors or landlords, if they shall see cause for the same; and in case they shall affirm the act of the said justices, to award costs not exceeding five pounds for the frivolous appeal."

By 57 Geo. 3, c. 52, after reciting the 11 Geo. 2, c. 19, s. 16 (*ante*, 673), " and whereas it is expedient for the due protection of the interest of landlords, that so much of the said act as requires a tenant to be in arrear for one year's rent should be altered, and that the provisions of the said act should be *extended to tenancies where no right of entry in case of non-payment is reserved to the landlord*," it is enacted, " that the provisions, powers and remedies by the said recited act given to lessors and landlords in case of any tenant deserting the demised premises, and leaving the same uncultivated or unoccupied, so as no sufficient distress can be had to countervail the arrears of rent shall be extended to the case of tenants holding any lands, tenements or hereditaments at a rack rent, or where the rent reserved shall be full three-fourths of the yearly value of the demised premises, and who shall be in arrear for *one half year's rent* (instead of one year as in the said recited act is provided and enacted), and who shall hold such lands and tenements or hereditaments under any demise or agreement, either written or verbal, and *although no right or power of re-entry be reserved or given* to the landlord in case of non-payment of rent, who shall be *in arrear for one-half year's rent, instead of for one year* as in the said recited act is provided and enacted."

Before this act it was doubtful whether a right of entry for non-payment of rent was not necessary under 11 Geo. 2, c. 19, s. 16; but since the 57 Geo. 3, c. 52, such right of entry is clearly unnecessary. *Edwards* v. *Hodges*, 15 C. B. 477.

Metropolitan Police District.]—With respect to deserted premises situate within the limits of the Metropolitan Police District, it is enacted by 3 & 4 Vict. c. 84, s. 13, "that after the passing of this act none of the police magistrates within the Metropolitan Police District shall be required to go upon any deserted lands, tenements or hereditaments for the purpose of viewing the same, or affixing any notices thereon, or of putting the landlord or landlords, lessor or lessors into the possession thereof, under the provisions of an act passed in the eleventh year of the reign of King *George* the Second, intituled ' *An Act for more effectual securing the Payment of Rents, and preventing Frauds by Tenants,*' or of an act passed in the fifty-seventh year of the reign of King *George* the Third, for altering the last-recited act, but that in every case within the Metropolitan Police District, in which by the said acts, or either of them, two justices are authorized to put the landlord or lessor into possession of such deserted premises, it shall be lawful for one of the police magistrates, upon the request of the lessor or landlord, or his or her bailiff or receiver, made in open court, and upon proof given to the satisfaction of such magistrate of the arrear of rent, and desertion of the premises by the tenant as aforesaid, to issue his warrant directed to one of the constables of the Metropolitan Police Force, requiring him to go upon and view the premises, and to affix thereon the like notices as under the said acts or either of them are required to be affixed by two justices of the peace; and upon the return of the warrant, and upon proof being given to the satisfaction of the magistrate, before whom the warrant shall be returned, that it has been duly executed, and that neither the tenant or any person on his or her behalf has appeared and paid the rent in arrear, and that there is not sufficient distress upon the premises, it shall be lawful for such magistrate to issue his warrant to a constable of the Metropolitan Police Force, requiring him to put the landlord or lessor into the possession of the premises; and every constable to whom any such warrant shall be directed shall duly execute and return the same, subject to the provisions contained in an act passed in the last session of parliament, intituled ' *An Act for further Improving the Police in and near the Metropolis*' [2 & 3 Vict. c. 47], as to the execution of warrants directed to constables of the Metropolitan Police Force; and upon the execution of such second warrant the lease of the premises to such tenant, as to any demise therein contained only, shall thenceforth be void."

For the Forms of Proceedings under this Act, see Appendix, Nos. 425 to 431, and 440 to 442.

City of London.]—By 11 & 12 Vict. c. 43, s. 34, "it shall be lawful for the lord mayor of the city of London, or for any alderman of the said city, for the time being, sitting at the Mansion House or Guildhall justice rooms in the said city, to do alone any act, at either of the said justice rooms, which by any law now in force, or by any law not containing an express enactment to the contrary hereafter to be made, is or shall be directed to be done by more than one justice." This applies to proceedings in the city of London under the before-mentioned acts. *Edwards* v. *Hodges*, 24 Law Times R. 114. But although such mayor or alderman sitting as aforesaid has all the power of two justices, yet he has not the power of a metropolitan police magistrate acting under 3 & 4 Vict. c. 84, s. 13 (*supra*), and therefore he cannot send a constable to view the premises, and to affix the notice, &c.,

but must proceed in like manner as two or more justices.   *Edwards* v. *Hodges*, 15 C. B. 477 ; 24 Law Times R. 237.

Stipendiary Magistrates.]—A stipendiary magistrate in any city, town, liberty, borough or place (other than the city of London, or the Metropolitan Police District), should proceed in like manner as two or more justices.   11 & 12 Vict. c. 43, s. 33.

Cases within the above Statutes.]—The foregoing statutes do not contain any exception with respect to leases made in consideration of any fine or premium.   Therefore any such fine or premium is immaterial, except so far as it tends to show that the rent reserved is not a rack rent, or not full three-fourths of the yearly value of the demised premises.   The statutes apply to all demises, whether written or verbal, however long may be the term, and however large may be the amount of rent reserved.   In *Ex parte Pilton*, 1 B. & A. 369, the term was twelve years, and the rent 300*l.* a year, besides 525*l.* paid for fixtures. It matters not that the lease or agreement contains no condition or proviso for re-entry for non-payment of rent ; 57 Geo. 3, c. 52 ; *ante*, 674 ; *Edwards* v. *Hodges*, 24 Law Times, 114, 237 ; 15 C. B. 437 ; and therefore this mode of proceeding may sometimes be adopted where no action of ejectment could be supported ; *ante*, 403 ; besides which, when possession is obtained under these acts the term granted by the lease becomes void ; *ante*, 674 ; but the following circumstances must concur : viz. :—1. The rent reserved must be a rack rent, or full three-fourths of the yearly value of the demised premises ; 2. One half a year's rent at the least must be in arrear ; and 3., The premises must have been *deserted*, and left uncultivated or unoccupied, so as no sufficient distress can be had to countervail the arrears of rent.   If more than half a year's rent be in arrear, and there is a sufficient distress on the premises to countervail half a year's rent, but not all the arrears, the best plan is for the landlord to distrain and sell, and afterwards, if the unsatisfied rent be equal to half a year's rent or more, to apply to the justices.   *Ex parte Pilton*, 1 B. & A. 369 ; and see *Brewer* d. *Lord Onslow* v. *Eaton*, Ad. Eject. 132, note (*e*) ; *Doe* d. *Taylor* v. *Johnson*, 1 Stark. R. 411.   It seems, however, that the justices have jurisdiction where there appears to be a sufficient distress on the premises to satisfy half a year's rent, but not sufficient to satisfy all the arrears.   *Cross* v. *Jordan*, 8 Exch. 149 ; 17 Jur. 93, overruling *Doe* d. *Powell* v. *Roe*, 9 Dowl. 548 ; *Doe* d. *Forster* v. *Wandlass*, 7 T. R. 117.   [These cases were decided under the 4 Geo. 2, c. 28, s. 2, which was re-enacted by 15 & 16 Vict. c. 76, s. 210 ; *ante*, 415.] If the premises are shut up and locked in such a manner that no sufficient distress *can be had, i. e.,* got at, to countervail the arrears of rent, it seems that the justices may properly exercise their jurisdiction under these acts.   *Vide* 4 Geo. 2, c. 28, s. 2, and 15 Vict. c. 76, s. 210, where the words are no sufficient distress *to be found.   Doe* d. *Chippendale* v. *Dyson*, 1 Moo. & Mal. 77 ; *Doe* d. *Cox* v. *Roe*, 5 Dowl. & L. 272 ; *Doe* d. *Haverson* v. *Franks*, 2 Car. & K. 678 ; *ante*, 415, 416.

It is not necessary that any information or complaint should be made *on oath* in order to justify the interference of magistrates under the acts of 11 Geo. 2, c. 19, s. 17, and 57 Geo. 3, c. 52.   *Basten* v. *Carew*, 3 B. & C. 649 ; 5 D. & R. 558 ; and see 11 & 12 Vict. c. 43,

s. 10. A mere complaint or *request* by the landlord, or his bailiff or receiver, to the proper justices, is sufficient. *Basten* v. *Carew, supra.* No *proof* of the preliminary facts appears to be necessary to give the justices jurisdiction to act. *S. C.;* 11 & 12 Vict. c. 43, ss. 1, 10. But upon an application to a metropolitan police magistrate proof must be made to his satisfaction of the arrear of rent, and desertion of the premises by the tenant. 3 & 4 Vict. c. 84, s. 13 ; *ante,* 675. Before other justices the usual course is to prefer a printed or written information and complaint. *See the form, Appendix, No.* 422. But an oral complaint and request without any writing appears to be sufficient. 11 & 12 Vict. c. 43, s. 8.

Upon being so requested, two or more justices of the peace of the county, riding, division or place (having no interest in the premises) are to go upon and view the premises. *Ante,* 674. "The justices are upon their own view to determine whether the premises are deserted or not." *Per* Abbott, C. J., in *Basten* v. *Carew,* 3 B. & C. 654. As to what does or does not amount to a desertion, see *post,* 678. Also whether the premises have been left uncultivated or unoccupied so as no sufficient distress can be had to countervail the arrears of rent. *Ante,* 674. Also whether the rent reserved is a rack rent, or full three-fourths of the yearly value of the demised premises. *Ante,* 673. Upon these points they may, if they think fit, receive the evidence or statements of any broker, surveyor or other competent person, or of the landlord, or his bailiff or receiver : but they ought to form their own judgment or conclusion. The statutes of 11 Geo. 2, c. 19, s. 16, and 57 Geo. 3, c. 52, do not require any proof as to the amount of the rent reserved, or of the arrears due ; and therefore the justices may act upon what is stated to them on those points in the information or complaint. But if the landlord, or his bailiff or receiver, wilfully misstate the amount of the rent reserved, or of the arrears, and so induce the justices to act where they ought not, an action on the case may be maintained against him. *Per* Bayley, J., in *Basten* v. *Carew,* 3 B. & C. 655. Upon an application to a metropolitan police magistrate proof must be made to his satisfaction of the arrears of rent and desertion of the premises. 3 & 4 Vict. c. 84, s. 13, *ante,* 675. But the other statutes do not require this. If the justices entertain doubts on any material point, and therefore refuse to proceed, the Court of Queen's Bench will not compel them to do so by a mandamus. *Ex parte Fulder,* 8 Dowl. 535 ; and see *Ex parte Wm. Davy,* 2 Dowl. N. S. 24. If the justices decide erroneously and *corruptly* in favour of the landlord, they may be punished by a criminal information. *Basten* v. *Carew,* 3 B. & C. 655, Bayley, J.; Cole on Criminal Informations, 25. But in ordinary cases where they decide erroneously, the remedy is by an appeal pursuant to sect. 17 (*ante,* 674), and not by action against the justices, constables or landlord, &c. *Basten* v. *Carew,* 3 B. & C. 649 ; 5 D. & R. 558. Such an action cannot be maintained even after the decision of the justices has been reversed on appeal. *Ashcroft* v. *Bourne,* 3 B. & Adol. 684. The principle is that where a magistrate has *jurisdiction over the subject matter,* trespass will not lie, even after the conviction has been quashed. *Haylock* v. *Sparke,* 1 E. & B. 471 ; *Barton* v. *Bricknell,* 13 Q. B. 393 ; *Ratt* v. *Parkinson,* 20 Law J., M. C. 208 ; 11 & 12 Vict. c. 44, s. 1. And he has jurisdiction over the subject matter, if the facts *as stated in the information* are sufficient in law to give him jurisdiction. It makes no difference in this respect whether the facts so stated are true or false.   *Brittain* v. *Kinniard,* 1 Brod. & B. 432, 442; *Cave* v. *Mountain,* 1 Man. & Gr. 257; *Reg.* v. *Bolton,* 1 Q. B. 66, 72—76; 4 P. & D. 679; *Reg.* v. *Justices of Buckinghamshire,* 3 Q. B. 807.

If the justices on their view find that the premises are deserted, and have been left uncultivated or unoccupied, so as no sufficient distress can be had (*ante,* 677), they should affix or cause to be affixed on the most notorious part of the premises, notice in writing, what day (at the distance of fourteen days at the least, *i. e.* fourteen *clear* days), they will return to take a second view thereof.   *See the form, Appendix, No.* 423.

Upon the day appointed in the notice the justices should take a second view of the premises; and if upon such second view the tenant, or some person on his or her behalf, shall not *appear and pay the rent in arrear,* or there shall not be a sufficient distress upon the premises, then the said justices may put the landlord into possession.   *Ante,* 674.

If the tenant or any person on his behalf appear on the second occasion, *but does not pay the rent in arrear,* such appearance amounts to nothing, provided there be no sufficient distress upon the premises. *Ex parte Pilton,* 1 B. & A. 369; *Id.* 372, *per* Lord Ellenborough, C. J.

Where a tenant ceased to reside on the premises for several months, and left them without any furniture or other property therein sufficient to answer the arrears of rent, but the landlord knew where the tenant was to be found, and a servant of the tenant was occasionally on the premises to show them to any person who might wish to see them, and such servant happened to be on the premises when the justices first came, and two persons were painting the premises for the tenant when the justices came the second time : held, on motion to the Court of King's Bench by way of appeal pursuant to sect. 17, that the justices were right in deciding that the premises had been *deserted* within the meaning of the act.   *Ex parte Pilton,* 1 B. & A. 369; and *per* Lord Ellenborough, C. J., " when the justices went on the first occasion, they found, it is true, a person on the premises; but he was not there for the purpose of taking care of the premises; he did not sleep there, and he does not even state in his affidavit that he ever was there except when the justices came.   The possession, as by him, is therefore obviously *colourable.*   As to the two persons being there the second time the justices came, it is wholly immaterial; for it is not pretended that there was any one there who appeared and *paid the rent* in arrear, as is required by the statute.   There is therefore no objection in substance to the proceeding of the magistrates."   *Id.* 372. On the other hand, in a case where the wife and children of the tenant remained on the premises, but there was no furniture in the house, except three or four chairs, which were stated by the wife to belong to a neighbour : held, on appeal (reversing the decision of the justices), that the premises had not been *deserted* within the meaning of the act. *Ashcroft* v. *Bourne,* 3 B. & Adol. 684.

After having put the landlord into possession, the justices should make a record of what they have done, in which should be stated all the circumstances necessary to give them jurisdiction, and to show that they have pursued the directions of the statute.   *See the form, Appendix, No.* 424.   Such record will be conclusive as to the facts therein stated, and will protect the justices, and also the constables and landlord from any action of trespass *quare clausum fregit* at the suit of the tenants. *Basten* v. *Carew*, 3 B. & C. 649; 5 D. & R. 558; *Ashcroft* v. *Bourne*, 3 B. & Adol. 684; and see *Haylock* v. *Sparke*, 1 E. & B. 471. It will also prevent the tenant from maintaining a subsequent ejectment to recover back possession of the premises, because when the justices put the landlord into possession of the demised premises, "the lease thereof to such tenant, as to any demise therein contained only, shall from thenceforth become void." 11 Geo. 2, c. 19, s. 16; *ante*, 674. But the tenant continues liable for the arrears of rent, and previous breaches of covenant to repair, &c. When the term ceases, so does all liability in respect of *subsequent* breaches of covenant to pay rent and repair, &c. *during the term.* *Hartshorne* v. *Watson*, 4 Bing. N. C. 178; *Franklin* v. *Carter*, 1 C. B. 750; 3 Dowl. & L. 213; *Johnson* v. *Gibson*, 1 E. & B. 415; *Selby* v. *Browne*, 7 Q. B. 620; and see *Pitman* v. *Woodbury*, 3 Exch. 4; *Swatman* v. *Ambler*, 8 Exch. 72.

The tenant may appeal against the proceedings of the justices, pursuant to 11 Geo. 2, c. 19, s. 17. *Ante*, 674. The appeal is by a summary application to the next justices of assize for the county in which the premises lie; or if they lie in London or Middlesex, to the judges of the Queen's Bench or Common Pleas (not the Exchequer). *Ante*, 674. Such justices of assize, &c. act as individuals, and not as a court, on the hearing of the appeal; and therefore any order they make should be signed by themselves, and not by the associate or any other officer of the court. *The Queen* v. *Sewell*, 8 Q. B. 161. No previous notice of the intended appeal seems to be necessary. But if such notice be given to the landlord, and also to each of the justices whose acts are complained of, perhaps the justices of assize will think fit to make an order of restitution, &c. *absolute* in the first instance, especially if the landlord appear. The assizes in some counties are so short that there would not be sufficient time for an order nisi to be made and served, and cause to be afterwards shown against it during the assizes. It is therefore generally advisable to give a notice to the landlord and also to each of the justices of the peace. *See the form, Appendix, No.* 432. An affidavit of the service of such notice should be made. *See the form, Appendix, No.* 433. Other affidavits must also be made showing the facts upon which the tenant relies in support of his appeal. The affidavits should not be entitled in any court or matter, and should be sworn before a justice of the peace, and not before a commissioner for taking affidavits in the Court of Queen's Bench or Common Pleas. Generally speaking, if no notice has been given, an order to show cause, &c. will be made in the first instance. *See the forms, Appendix, Nos.* 434, 438. But the justices of assize may, if they think fit, make an order absolute in the first instance, if due notice of the application be proved. If an order to show cause be made, it should be signed by the judges, and not by their associate. *Reg.* v. *Sewell*, 8 Q. B. 161. A copy of it should be served on the landlord, and also on the justices of the peace therein mentioned. An affidavit of such service should be made. *See the form, Appendix, No.* 435.

Cause is shown by affidavit and otherwise, as on an ordinary motion. *Ex parte Pilton*, 1 B. & A. 369. If the appeal be allowed, full costs may be given; and the amount thereof should be mentioned in the order. Upon the latter point, see *Reg.* v. *Clark*, 5 Q. B. 887; *The London and North-Western Railway Company* v.

Quick, 5 Dowl. & L. 685; *The Wilts, Somerset and Weymouth Railway Company* v. *Fooks,* 3 Exch. 728. But see *Gould* v. *The Staffordshire Potteries Waterworks Company,* 5 Exch. 214; 1 Low. M. & P. 264; *Reg.* v. *Inhabitants of Eardisland,* 3 E. & B. 960. Such costs may and ought to be allowed in proper cases, notwithstanding the landlord appears and shows cause against the application in the first instance. *Rennie* v. *Beresford,* 15 M. & W. 84; 3 Dowl. & L. 469. If the appeal be dismissed as frivolous, not more than 5*l.* can be awarded for costs. Sect. 17; *ante,* 674; *see form of Order of Dismissal, Appendix, No.* 437. If an order be made for restitution, &c., it should be signed by the justices, and not by any officer of the court. *Reg.* v. *Sewell,* 8 Q. B. 161; *see the forms, Appendix, Nos.* 436, 439. It should direct *the sheriff* of the county in which the premises lie to cause restitution of possession to be made to the tenant; otherwise there may be considerable difficulty in enforcing it. *Reg.* v. *Trail,* 12 A. & E. 761; 4 P. & D. 325. The Court of Queen's Bench will not by mandamus compel the justices to restore possession. *S. C.* But if the order be valid, an indictment will lie for wilfully disobeying it. *Reg.* v. *Sewell,* 8 Q. B. 161.

If the appeal be successful, and possession be restored, the tenant cannot afterwards maintain an action of trespass *quare clausum fregit* against the justices, constables, or landlord, &c. *Ashcroft* v. *Bourne,* 3 B. & Adol. 684; *Basten* v. *Carew,* 3 B. & C. 649; 5 D. & R. 558; *ante,* 677. But the term granted by the lease will revive, or rather the avoidance thereof will be superseded.

CHAPTER LXXIII.

RECOVERY BEFORE JUSTICES OF PARISH HOUSES OR LAND.

BY 59 Geo. 3, c. 12, s. 24, reciting, "and whereas difficulties have frequently arisen, and considerable expenses have sometimes been incurred by reason of the refusal of persons who have been permitted to occupy, or who have intruded themselves into parish or town-houses, or other tenements or dwellings built or provided for the habitation of the poor, or otherwise belonging to such parishes, to deliver up the possession of such houses, tenements or dwellings, when thereto required ; and it is expedient to provide a remedy for the same ;" it is enacted, " that if any person *who shall have been permitted to occupy* any parish or town house, or any other tenement or dwelling belonging to or provided by or at the charge of any parish, for the habitation of the poor thereof, *or who shall have unlawfully intruded himself* or herself into any such house, tenement or dwelling, or into any house, tenement or hereditament belonging to such parish, shall *refuse or neglect* to quit the same, and deliver up the possession thereof to the churchwardens and overseers of the poor of any such parish, within one month after notice and demand in writing for that purpose, signed by such churchwardens and overseers, or the major part of them, shall have been delivered to the person in possession, or in his or her absence affixed on some notorious part of the premises, it shall be lawful for any two of his majesty's justices of the peace, upon complaint to them (a) made by one or more of the churchwardens and overseers of the poor of the parish in which any such house, tenement or dwelling shall be situated, to issue their summons to the person against whom such complaint shall be made, to appear before such justices at a time and place to be appointed by them, and to cause such summons to be delivered to the party against whom the complaint shall be made, or in his or her absence to be affixed on the premises seven days at the least before the time appointed for hearing such complaint; and such justices are hereby empowered and required, upon the appearance of the defendant or upon proof on oath that such summons hath been delivered or affixed as is hereby directed, to proceed to hear and determine the matter of such complaint, and if they shall find and adjudge

(a) By 3 Geo. 4, c. 23, s. 2, any one justice may receive the information and issue the summons.

the same to be true, then by warrant under their hands and seals to cause possession of the premises in question to be delivered to the churchwardens and overseers of the poor of the parish, or to some of them."

Sect. 25 enacts, " that if any person to whom any land appropriated, purchased or taken under the authority of this act, for the employment of the poor of any parish, or to whom any other lands belonging to such parish, or to the churchwardens and overseers thereof, or to either of them, *shall have been let for his or her own occupation*, shall refuse to quit and to deliver up the possession thereof to the churchwardens and overseers of the poor of such parish, *at the expiration of the term* for which the same shall have been demised or let to him or her, or if any person or persons shall *unlawfully enter upon, or take or hold possession* of any such land, or any other land or hereditaments belonging to such parish, or to the churchwardens or overseers, or to either of them, it shall be lawful for such churchwardens and overseers of the poor, or any of them, *after such notice and demand of possession* as is by this act directed in the case of parish houses, to exhibit a complaint against the person or persons in possession of such land, before two (a) of his majesty's justices of the peace, who are hereby authorized and required to proceed thereon, and to hear and determine the matter thereof, and if they shall find and adjudge the same to be true, to cause possession of such land to be delivered to the churchwardens and overseers of the poor, or some of them, in such and the like course and manner as are by this act directed with regard to parish houses."

By 5 & 6 Will. 4, c. 69, s. 5, it is enacted, " that the powers and authorities given by the said act of the fifty-ninth of King George the Third, and by the said act of the second year of the present reign to justices of the peace to cause possession of parish houses, and lands and portions of land to be delivered to the churchwardens and overseers of the poor, and any other auxiliary powers or provisions in the said acts or other acts contained in relation thereto, shall extend to and shall be exercised by such justices in respect of any houses and lands and portions of land which are or may be *vested in or under the management or control of the guardians* of the poor of any union or parish, in the same manner as if the names of those officers had been inserted in the said acts instead of the names of the churchwardens and overseers of the poor."

Decisions.]—Although a parish forms part of a union under 4 & 5 Will. 4, c. 76, the legal estate in houses and land belonging to such parish remains vested in the churchwardens and overseers, and is not by sect. 21 of that act, or by the 5 & 6 Will. 4, c. 69, s. 5, transferred from them to the guardians of the union. *Doe* d. *Norton* v. *Webster*, 12 A. & E. 442; 4 P. & D. 270; *Worge* v. *Relf*, 20 Law J., M. C., 125. But if such property, although not "vested" in the guardians, be "under their management or control," it would seem clear that summary proceedings might be adopted by the guardians pursuant to the statute.

In all cases to which the provisions of the above acts respectively apply, it is optional with the parish officers to proceed in a summary

---

(a) By 3 Geo. 4, c. 23, s. 2, any one justice may receive the information and issue the summons.

way, pursuant to the statute, or by entry, or by ejectment in the usual manner. *Wildbor* v. *Rainforth*, 2 Man. & Ry. 85; 8 B. & C. 4. "The statute was not intended to take away a right which the owner of property had at common law to enter and take possession, if it could be done peaceably, but to provide an expeditious mode whereby parish officers might obtain possession where it was obstinately withheld, and that they might not do that which had before been sometimes done, viz., might not turn occupiers out *vi et armis*, which led to further expense and litigation." *Id.* 6, *per* Lord Tenterden, C. J.

"The provisions of the statute are equally applicable whether the party has *wrongfully intruded* himself into the premises, or has been *suffered* by the parish officers to occupy them." *Per* Bayley, J., in *Wildbor* v. *Rainforth*, 8 B. & C. 4; 2 Man. & Ry. 85. If the property has been *let to him as a tenant*, and the term has expired, the case falls within sect. 25, and not within sect. 24. *Reg.* v. *Justices of Middlesex*, 7 Dowl. 767; but see *Reg.* v. *Bolton*, 1 Q. B. 66; 4 P. & D. 679. A person who is merely allowed to occupy parish property as a pauper is not a tenant. *Per* Lord Tenterden, C. J., in *Wildbor* v. *Rainforth*, 8 B. & C. 6. He is no more a tenant than a lunatic confined in an asylum is a tenant of his cell. *Martin* v. *Goble*, 1 Camp. 320; 4 Burn's J. 393, note (*a*) (29th ed.).

The principal differences between sections 24 and 25 seem to be— 1. That section 24 applies to parish or town *houses and other buildings*; whereas section 25 relates to parish *land*. 2. Section 24 applies to any house or building which a pauper "shall have been permitted to occupy," or into which any person (whether a pauper or not) "shall have unlawfully intruded himself or herself;" but not where the party has occupied as a tenant at an agreed rent. *Supra*. Whereas section 25 applies where the land has been let to any poor person *for his or her own occupation*, and the term has expired; or where the party has unlawfully entered upon or taken or held possession of any such land. 3. In either case there must be a month's notice in writing, and demand of possession signed and delivered pursuant to the statute, and a refusal or neglect to give up possession during such month.

It would seem that a tenancy from year to year is a *term* within the meaning of section 25; and that when it ceases by reason of a notice to quit duly given, it *expires* within the meaning of the words " at the expiration of the term," contained in that section.

Mode of Proceeding.]—The first step is to give a month's notice and demand of possession. *See the forms, Appendix, Nos.* 443, 444. It must be signed by all the churchwardens and overseers, " or the major part of them." *Ante*, 681. It must be delivered to the person in possession, or in his or her absence affixed on some notorious part of the premises: usually the front door. Generally speaking, notices do not require personal service; but the delivery thereof, to the wife or other member of the family, or to the servant of the party, at his place of abode is sufficient. *Ante*, 53. A *lunar* month's notice is sufficient. *Lacon* v. *Hooper*, 6 T. R. 224. Such notice may expire at any part of the year, without reference to the time when the party was first permitted to occupy (sect. 24; *ante*, 681), or the expiration of the term. Sect. 25; *ante*, 682. Upon or after the expiration of the month mentioned in the notice, the parish officers, or some or one of them, should attempt to take possession, in order that it may clearly appear that the party "*refused or neglected*" to quit and deliver up possession. *Ante,* 681. Immediately after such refusal or neglect an information and complaint may be made by one or more of the churchwardens and overseers (*ante,* 681), or guardians (*ante,* 682), as the case may require. *See the form, Appendix, No.* 445. Such complaint may be made to any two of her Majesty's justices of the peace for the county, &c. in which the premises are situate. By 3 Geo. 4, c. 23, s. 2, any one justice may receive the information and issue the summons. The information and complaint need not be made upon oath. *Basten* v. *Carew,* 3 B. & C. 649; 5 D. & R. 558; *ante,* 681. The truth of it is to be ascertained on the return of the summons, &c., when the defendant may appear and dispute the facts. The summons must be directed to the person against whom the complaint is made, and must require him to appear before the justices at a particular time and place. *See the form, Appendix, No.* 446. It is usually served by the constable of the parish wherein the premises are situate, but the justices may direct any other person to serve it. It must be delivered to the defendant personally, or in his or her absence affixed on the premises, seven days at the least before the time appointed for hearing the complaint. *Ante,* 681. The seven days must be reckoned exclusively both of the day of service and of the day appointed for the hearing. *Reg.* v. *Justices of Shropshire,* 8 A. & E. 173; 3 N. & P. 286; *Mitchell* v. *Foster,* 12 A. & E. 472; 4 P. & D. 150; 9 Dowl. 527. At the appointed time and place both parties should appear with their respective witnesses; and the justices will proceed to hear and determine the matter of the complaint in the usual manner. But if the defendant do not appear, proof on oath must be given in the first instance that the summons was duly delivered or affixed pursuant to the statute. *Ante,* 681. The complainant or his witnesses must then prove on oath, in the usual manner, all the material facts, as alleged in the information. The defendant may dispute or disprove any of such facts, and he may urge any matter to show that the case is not within the statute. If the complaint be not established by evidence to the satisfaction of the justices they may dismiss it with or without costs. 11 & 12 Vict. c. 43, s. 18. If they find and adjudge the matter of the complaint to be true, they may thereupon immediately issue a warrant under their hands and seals, directing the chief and petty constables to cause possession of the premises in question to be delivered to the churchwardens and overseers of the poor, or to some of them. *See the form, Appendix, No.* 447. Some or one of the constables to whom such warrant is directed will execute it in like manner as a sheriff's officer executes a warrant on a writ of *habere facias possessionem. Ante,* 345. The constable should make a return on the warrant stating what he has done. *See the form, Appendix, No.* 448. And if wished a record of the whole proceedings may be made in like manner as under the statutes relating to deserted premises; *ante,* 678; but this is very seldom, if ever, done.

As the statute gives no appeal the decision of the justices cannot be questioned, except indirectly by a subsequent action of ejectment; unless, indeed, the information be substantially defective, and shows upon the face of it, without the aid of extrinsic evidence, that the justices had no jurisdiction.

CHAPTER LXXIV.

FORCIBLE ENTRY AND DETAINER.

1. *At Common Law.*]—It seems that at common law a man disseised of any lands or tenements might lawfully retake possession by force. 1 Hawk. P. C. c. 64, s. 1; *Anon.*, 3 Salk. 169; Co. Lit. 257 a, note, 199; 3 Bac. Abr. 711 (7th ed.); 13 Vin. Abr. 379. But this is not clear. *Rex* v. *Wilson*, 8 T. R. 364, *per* Lord Kenyon, C. J. Probably the rule was that such force might be used as did not occasion an *actual* breach of the public peace. The owner of a house may, under a plea of *liberum tenementum* to an action of trespass, justify entering it with a strong hand and pulling it down, whilst the plaintiff (an intruder) and his family were actually in it. *Burling* v. *Read*, 11 Q. B. 904. But a commoner cannot justify doing so to abate a nuisance. *Perry* v. *Fitzhowe*, 8 Q. B. 757.

An indictment will lie at common law for a forcible entry with strong hand, or with multitude of persons, in a violent and tumultuous manner, in breach of the public peace. *Rex* v. *Blake*, 3 Burr. 1732, *per* Wilmot, J.; *Rex* v. *Bathurst*, Sayer, 225. Such indictment may be preferred either at the assizes, or at the quarter sessions. *See the form, Appendix, No.* 451. But it is more usual, and generally more expedient to proceed at the quarter sessions under the statutes, because restitution of possession may be awarded under an indictment pursuant to the statute, but not under an indictment at common law. Besides which it seems that the evidence of a forcible entry under an indictment at common law must be stronger than is necessary to support an indictment under the statutes, and must show at the least such an amount of force as constitutes an actual breach of the public peace. *Rex* v. *Wilson,* 8 T. R. 357; *Rex* v. *Blake,* 3 Burr. 1731.

An indictment will not lie for a mere trespass *vi et armis,* and an unlawful expulsion from land, that being only a private injury, and the subject of a civil action. *Rex* v. *Blake and fifteen others,* 3 Burr. 1731; *Rex* v. *Storr, Id.* 1699; *Rex* v. *Atkins, Id.* 1706. An indictment for a forcible entry must allege some force and violence, or show some riot, or breach of the peace. The usual words *vi et armis* without *manu forti,* are insufficient; *Warner and Collins' case,* Cro. Eliz. 461; but if the indictment charge that the defendants unlawfully and *with strong hand* entered and expelled the prosecutor or disseised him, that is sufficient. *Rex* v. *Wilson and eleven others,* 8 T. R. 357; *Andrews* v. *Lord Cromwell,* Cro. Jac. 31. Such an indictment cannot be supported by evidence of a mere trespass; but there must be proof of such force, or at the least such show of force, as was calculated to prevent any resistance. *Rex* v. *Smyth,* 5 C. & P. 201; 1 Moo. & Rob. 156.

2. *By Statute.*]—By 5 Rich. 2, stat. 1, c. 8, "the king enjoineth that none from henceforth make entry into any lands and tenements, but in case where entry is given by the law, and in such case *not with strong hand, nor with multitudes of people, but only in lawful, peaceable and easy manner.* And if any man from henceforth do the contrary, and thereof be duly convict, he shall be punished by imprisonment of his body, and thereof ransomed at the king's will."

By 15 Rich. 2, c. 2, "for confirming and amending former statutes respecting riots and forcible entries," — "also it is accorded and assented, that the statutes and ordinances, made and not repealed, concerning those *who make entries with strong hand* into lands and tenements, or other possessions whatsoever, *and hold themselves therein with force,* and also concerning those who make insurrections, or great ridings, riots, routs or assemblies, in disturbance of the peace, or of the common law, or in affray of the people, shall be holden and kept, and fully executed; *adding thereto,* that at all times that such forcible entries shall be made, and complaint thereof cometh to the justices of peace, or to any of them, that such justices or justice take sufficient power of the county, and go to the place where such force is made; and if he or they find any that hold such place forcibly, after such entry made, they shall be taken and put into the next gaol, there to abide convict by the record of such justices or justice, until they have made fine and ransom to the king: and that all people of the county, as well the sheriff as other, shall be attendant upon the same justices to go and assist the same justices, to arrest such offenders, upon pain of imprisonment, and to make fine to the king: and in the same manner it shall be done concerning those who make such forcible entries in benefices or offices of holy church."

By 4 Hen. 4, c. 8, intituled "A special assize shall be maintainable against a disseisor with force," the lord chancellor may in his discretion grant a special assize to try any forcible entry, under which the defendant, if convicted, "shall have one year's imprisonment, and yield to the party grieved his double damages."

By 8 Hen. 6, c. 9, intituled "The duty of justices of peace when land is entered upon or detained with force," after reciting at length the 15 Rich. 2, c. 2 (*supra*), "and for that the said statute doth not extend to entries in tenements in peaceable manner and after holden with force, nor if the persons which enter with force into lands and tenements be removed and avoided before the coming of the said justices or justice as before, nor any pain ordained if the sheriff do not obey the commandments and precepts of the said justices, for executing the said ordinance, many wrongful and forcible entries be daily made into lands and tenements by such as have no right," it is ordained, " that the said statute, and all other statutes of such entries or alienations made in times past shall be holden and duly executed ; *adding thereto,* that if from henceforth any doth make *any forcible entry* in lands and tenements, or other possessions, *or them do hold forcibly after complaint thereof* made within the same county where such entry is made, to the justices of peace, or to one of them, by the party grieved, that the justices or justice *so warned,* within a convenient time shall cause, or one of them shall cause the said statute duly to be executed, and that at the costs of the party so grieved."

Sect. 3. "And moreover, though that such persons making such entry *be present,* or else *departed before the coming of the said justices or justice,* nevertheless the same justices or justice in some good town next to the tenements so entered, or in some other convenient place according to their discretion, shall have, or either of them shall have *authority and power to inquire* by people of the same county, as well of them that *make such forcible entries* into lands and tenements, as of them *which hold the same with force ;* and if it be found before any of them that any doth contrary to this statute, then the said justices or justice shall cause the said lands and tenements *so entered or holden as afore to be reseised,* and shall put the party so put out *in full possession* of the same lands and tenements *so as aforesaid entered or holden.*"

Sect. 4 authorizes the justices or justice to issue a warrant or precept to the sheriff of the county to summon a jury to inquire of any forcible entry. *See the form, Appendix, No.* 456. It also renders the sheriff liable to a penalty of 20*l.* for every default on his part.

Sect. 5 provides how such penalty shall be recovered with costs and expenses.

Sect. 6. "And moreover, if any person be put out or *disseised* of any lands or tenements in *forcible manner,* or *put out peaceably, and after holden out with strong hand ;* or after such entry any feoffment or discontinuance in anywise thereof be made to defraud, and take away the right of the possessor ; that the party grieved in this behalf shall have assize of *novel disseisin* [abolished by 3 & 4 Will. 4, c. 27, s. 36], or a *writ of trespass against such disseisor ;* and if the party grieved recover by assize, or by *action of trespass,* and it be found by verdict, or in other manner by due form in the law that the party defendant *entered with force* into the lands and tenements, *or them after his entry did hold with force,* that the plaintiff shall recover his *treble damages* against the defendant ; and moreover, that he make fine and ransom to the king ; and that mayors, justices or justice of peace, sheriffs, and bailiffs of cities, towns and boroughs having franchise, shall have in the said cities, towns and boroughs *like power to remove such entries, and in other the articles aforesaid, arising within the same,* as the justices of peace and sheriffs in counties and countries aforesaid have."

Sect. 7. " Provided always, that they which keep their possessions with force in any lands and tenements whereof they or their ancestors, or they whose estates they have in such lands and tenements, *have continued their possessions in the same by three years or more,* be not endangered by force of this statute."

By 31 Eliz. c. 11, after reciting as " one very good proviso or clause" the 7th section of 8 Hen. 6, c. 9 (*ante,* 687), it is enacted, "that no restitution upon any *indictment* of forcible entry, or holding with force, be made to any person or persons, if the person or persons so indicted hath had the occupation, or hath been in quiet possession, by the space of *three whole years together next before* the day of such indictment so found, and his, her or their estate or estates therein *not ended or determined,* which the party indicted shall and may allege for stay of restitution, and restitution to stay until that be tried, if the other will deny or traverse the same; and if the same allegation be tried against the same person or persons so indicted, then the same person or persons so indicted to pay such costs and damages to the other party as shall be assessed by the judges or justices before whom the same shall be tried; the same costs and damages to be recovered and levied as is usual for costs and damages contained in judgments upon other actions."

By 21 Jac. 1, c. 15, intituled " An Act to enable Judges and Justices of the Peace to give Restitution of Possession in certain Cases," it is enacted, " that such judges, justices or justice of the peace, as by reason of any act or acts of parliament now in force are authorized and enabled upon inquiry to give restitution of possession unto tenants of any estate of freehold of their lands or tenements, which shall be entered upon with force, or from them withholden by force, shall by reason of this present act have the like and the same authority and ability from henceforth (upon indictment of such forcible entries, or forcible withholdings before them duly found) *to give like restitution of possession unto tenants for terms of years, tenants by copy of court roll,* guardians by knight service, tenants by elegit, statute merchant and staple, of lands or tenements by them so holden, which shall be *entered upon by force, or holden from them by force.*"

3. *What amounts to a Forcible Entry.*]—An entry into any land or tenement made " with strong hand, or with multitude of people," in order to take or obtain possession (whether with or without title), is a forcible entry within the meaning of the statutes, although no actual breach of the public peace takes place. If the entry be made with force and violence, or with menaces of personal violence, or with offensive weapons, or with multitude of people, or with other show of force calculated to create terror or alarm, or to intimidate and to prevent any resistance, it is a forcible entry within the meaning of the statutes. Co. Lit. 257 b; 6 Com. Dig. tit. " Forcible Entry" (A 2); 1 Hawk. P. C. c. 64, ss. 20, 21.

In general it seemeth clear that to denominate an entry forcible within the meaning of the statutes, it ought to be accompanied with some circumstances of *actual violence or terror ;* and therefore that an entry which hath no other force than such as implied by law in every trespass whatsoever, is not within these statutes. 1 Hawk. P. C. c. 64, ss. 25—28; *Rex* v. *Smith,* 5 C. & P. 201; 1 Moo. & Rob. 156; and see *Rex* v. *Blake,* 3 Burr. 1731; *Rex* v. *Wilson,* 8 T. R. 357.

To constitute a forcible entry or a forcible detainer, it is not necessary that any one should be assaulted, but only that the entry or detainer should be with such number of persons and show of force as is calculated to deter the rightful owner from sending the persons away and resuming his own possession. *Milner* v. *Maclean*, 2 C. & P. 17, Abbott, C. J.; *Baron Snigge* v. *Shirton*, Cro. Jac. 199. A single person may be guilty of a forcible entry. 1 Hawk. P. C. c. 64, s. 29; Co. Lit. 257 a, b; Lamb, Eiren. 134. A multitude of people is generally understood to mean ten or more; but there is no definite rule on this point : · it is left a good deal to the judgment and discretion of the justices. Co. Lit. 257 a; 6 Com. Dig. tit. " Forcible Entry" (A 2).

· If several come in company, where their entry is *not lawful*, and all of them, saving one, enter in a peaceable manner, and that one only use force, it is a forcible entry in them all, because they come in company to do an unlawful act; and therefore the act of one is the act of them all, and he is presumed to be only the instrument of the rest. But otherwise it is where one had a right of entry; for there they only come to do a lawful act, and· therefore it is the force of him only that used it. 3 Bac. Abr. 717 (7th ed.); Dalton's J. 303.

If two come to make a forcible entry, and one breaks open the door of the house, and two or three hours· after the other enters peaceably without a weapon, the door being open, yet it is a forcible entry by him. *Beade* v. *Orme*, Noy. 136; 13 Vin. Abr. 380. All those who accompany a man when he makes a forcible entry shall be adjudged to enter with him within the intent of these laws, whether they actually come upon the lands or not. 1 Hawk. P. C. c. 64, s. 22. But he who barely agrees·to a forcible entry previously made to his use, without his knowledge or privity, shall not be adjudged to make an entry within these statutes, because he no way concurred in or promoted the force. *Id.* s. 24; 3 Bac. Abr. 718 (7th ed.); 13 Vin. Abr. 380.

A joint tenant or tenant in common may offend against the purport of these statutes, either by forcibly ejecting or forcibly holding out his companion ; for though the entry of such a tenant be lawful *per my et per tout*, so that he cannot in any case be punished in an action of trespass at the common law, yet the lawfulness of his entry no way excuses the violence, or lessens the injury done to his companion; and consequently an indictment of forcible entry into a moiety of a manor, &c. is good. 3 Bac. Abr. 719 (7th ed.); 1 Hawk. P. C. c. 64, s. 33; Fitz. N. B. 249 (D); 13 Vin. Abr. 381, pl. 14.

If a person *legally entitled* to the possession of any messuage or land can *manage to enter peaceably* (as is generally the case) he may afterwards proceed to turn out the previous tenant, and his family and servants, and his and their goods and chattels, in the manner before mentioned (*ante*, 69), without being thereby guilty of a forcible entry; Crompton's J., 162, 163; and his *entry being lawful* he may afterwards defend his possession by force, without being guilty of a forcible detainer within the meaning of any of the statutes. *Rex* v. *Oakley*, 4 B. & Adol. 307; 1 N. & M. 58; *Rex* v. *Wilson*, 3 A. & E. 817; 5 N. & M. 164; *post*, 690. On the other hand, if the previous tenant merely refuse to go out of possession when requested so to do, and vexatiously continue therein, in spite of the owner, that does not of itself amount to a forcible detainer. 1 Hawk. P. C. c. 64, s. 30; 1 Russ. on Crimes, 311. But it does amount to a new unlawful entry, for which he is liable to an action of trespass. *Butcher* v. *Butcher*, 7 B. & C. 399; 1 Man. & Ry. 220; *Hey* v. *Moorhouse*, 6 Bing. N. C. 52 ; 8 Scott, 156. Upon such refusal the owner or his agent may gently lay hands on him and attempt to turn him out; and if the tenant then forcibly and violently resist being turned out, and manages with strong hand (with or without the assistance of his family and servants) to withhold and retain possession, he will thereby be guilty of a forcible detainer within the meaning of the statutes, and for which he may be indicted, or summarily convicted. Hawk. P. C. c. 64, ss. 23, 34; *per* Parke, J., in *Rex* v. *Oakley*, 4 B. & Adol. 312.

In some of the books it is said that if one *enter peaceably*, and when he is come in, useth violence, this is a forcible entry. Lamb, Eiren. 134, cited 13 Vin. Abr. 380. But this, it seems, should be understood where the party has no legal title or right of entry; in which case his subsequent misconduct will be considered as part of his *unlawful* entry.

A forcible entry may be resisted by force, without any previous request to desist. *Polkinghorn* v. *Wright*, 8 Q. B. 197. "There is a manifest distinction between endeavouring to turn a man out of a house or close into which he has previously entered quietly, and resisting a forcible attempt to enter. In the first case a request is necessary; in the latter not. This distinction was expressly taken in *Green* v. *Goddard*, 2 Salk. 641, and *Weaver* v. *Bush*, 8 T. R. 78." *Per cur.* in *Polkinghorn* v. *Wright*, 8 Q. B. 206.

4. *What amounts to a Forcible Detainer.*] — Forcible detainer is where a man *enters unlawfully*, but in a *peaceable* manner, and afterwards *detains possession by force*. 6 Com. Dig. tit. "Forcible Entry" (B 1); Fitz. N. B. 248 (C), (D); 13 Vin. Abr. 381. The same circumstances which will make an entry forcible (*ante*, 688) will also make a detainer forcible. 1 Hawk. P. C. c. 64, s. 30; 1 Russ. on Crimes, 310; 3 Bac. Abr. 718 (7th ed.). From whence it seems to follow that whoever keeps in his house an unusual number of people or unusual weapons for the purpose of defending his possession, or threatens to do some bodily hurt to the former possessor or his agent, if he dare return, is guilty of a forcible detainer; although no attempt be made to re-enter. *Baron Snigge* v. *Shirton*, Cro. Jac. 199; Lamb, Eiren. 136, 137; 1 Hawk. P. C. c. 64, s. 30; 1 Russ. on Crimes, 310. But the entry must have been *unlawful*, otherwise there cannot be a forcible detainer within the meaning of the statutes. *Rex* v. *Oakley*, 4 B. & Adol. 307; 1 N. & M. 58. In a conviction for a forcible detainer there must be an adjudication of unlawful entry. *Rex* v. *Wilson*, 3 A. & E. 817; 5 N. & M. 164. A conviction merely stating *an entry* and forcible detainer is insufficient. *Rex* v. *Oakley*, *supra*. A forcible entry (even with title) is an unlawful entry, which will render a subsequent forcible detainer unlawful. On the other hand, " a person who has a right of possession may *enter peaceably*, and being in possession may retain it, and plead that it is his soil and freehold." *Per* Lord Kenyon, C. J., in *Taylor* v. *Cole*, 3 T. R. 295.

A tenant for years, or at will, who forcibly detains possession from the reversioner, or his agent, after the term has ended, or the will determined, is guilty of a forcible detainer within the meaning of the statute, because the moment the reversioner, by himself or his agent, enters to take possession, he becomes lawfully seised or possessed (*ante*, 67, 68), and the tenant then becomes a trespasser. His subsequent continuance in possession amounts in judgment and construction of law to a *new unlawful entry*; and if after that he detains the possession with a strong hand, &c., he is guilty of a forcible detainer, for which he may be indicted or convicted in a summary manner. Hawk. P. C. c. 64, ss. 34, 23, 53; *per* Parke, J., in *Rex* v. *Oakley,* 4 B. & Adol. 312.

But a man will not be guilty of the offence of a forcible detainer for merely refusing to go out of a house, and continuing therein in despite of another: 1 Hawk. P. C. c. 64, s. 30; 1 Russ. on Crimes, 311: so that is not a forcible detainer if a lessee at will, after the determination of the will, denies possession to the lessor when he demands it, or shuts the door against the lessor when he would enter. Com. Dig. tit. "Forcible Detainer," B 2; 1 Russ. on Crimes, 311. Mere words, or acts of the above nature, are not sufficient: there must be more force and violence, or show of force and intimidation, to constitute a forcible detainer. But if the lessor or his agent, having peaceably entered to take possession, civilly request the tenant to depart, and on his refusal or neglect attempts to turn him out, whereupon the tenant violently resists, and manages with strong hand forcibly to retain possession, that will amount to a forcible detainer within the meaning of the statutes. *Ante,* 689, 690.

5. *Action of Trespass under* 8 *Hen.* 6, *c.* 9, *s.* 6.]—An action of trespass under this act for a forcible entry or detainer can be maintained only *against a disseisor,* and consequently only by a freeholder, as no other person can be "disseised." *Cole* v. *Eagle,* 8 B. & C. 409; 13 Vin. Abr. 383; Fitz. N. B. 248 (E); *see form of Declaration, Appendix, No.* 449. In such action restitution of possession cannot be awarded; 13 Vin. Abr. 387, pl. 5; but the plaintiff may recover *treble damages,* as well for the mesne occupation as for the first entry; Co. Lit. 257 b; *Milner* v. *Maclean,* 2 C. & P. 17; together with full costs, charges and expenses pursuant to 5 & 6 Vict. c. 97, s. 2, in lieu of treble costs to which he was previously entitled; 2 Inst. 289; Co. Lit. 257 b; *Milner* v. *Maclean,* 2 C. & P. 17; *Id.* 19, note (c); unless, indeed, the declaration contain other counts, and general damages are assessed, in which case the plaintiff can recover only single damages, with the usual costs as between party and party.

To an action of the above nature the defendant may plead not guilty "by statute 21 Jac. 1, c. 4, s. 4, Public General Act." *See the form, Appendix, No.* 450. Under such plea he may dispute or disprove the plaintiff's title, &c.; *Ross* v. *Clifton,* 11 A. & E. 631; 1 Gale & D. 72; 9 Dowl. 1033; *Maund* v. *The Monmouthshire Canal Company,* Car. & M. 606; or he may plead not guilty, and *liberum tenementum. Davison* v. *Wilson,* 11 Q. B. 890; *see forms of several Pleas, Appendix, Nos.* 392—395. To a plea of *liberum tenementum* the plaintiff cannot reply or new assign that the entry was with force and violence, and with strong hand, or with multitude of persons, for that does not show the defendant to be liable to a civil action, but only to an indictment. *Meriton* v. *Coombes,* 1 Low. M. & P. 510; *Davison* v. *Wilson,* 11 Q. B. 890; *Burling* v. *Read, Id.* 904; 1 Hawk. P. C. c. 64, s. 3; Co. Lit. 257 a, note 199.

6. *Indictment under the Statutes.*]—Instead of an action of trespass for treble damages, and full costs, charges and expenses, but upon which no restitution of possession can be obtained (*supra*), the party grieved may prefer an indictment under the statute (*ante,* 686—688) for a forcible entry or detainer, at the general quarter sessions of the peace.

See the form, Appendix, No. 452. Upon such indictment being found there by the grand jury, and before the defendant has been convicted, a writ of restitution may be awarded if the court think fit. 3 Bac. Abr., Forcible Entry (F); *see the form, Appendix, No.* 453. But it is entirely in the discretion of the court to grant or refuse such writ. *Reg.* v. *Harland,* 2 Moo. & Rob. 141; 8 A. & E. 826; 1 P. & D. 93, *S. C.*

An indictment or inquisition *under the statute* for a forcible entry or forcible detainer must state what estate the prosecutor had in the property, so that restitution may be made; otherwise it is bad in substance. *Rex* v. *Dorney,* 12 Mod. 417; 1 Salk. 260; *Rex* v. *Griffith,* 3 Salk. 169; *Rex* v. *Blake,* 3 Burr. 1732, Wilmot, J.; *Rex* v. *Wilson,* 8 T. R. 360, Lord Kenyon, C. J.; *Reg.* v. *Bowser,* 8 Dowl. 128; *Rex* v. *Wanhope,* Sayer, 142; *Rex* v. *Bathurst, Id.* 225. But it is sufficient to allege that the prosecutor was "seised," without describing more particularly for what estate. *Rex* v. *Hoare,* 6 M. & S. 266; *Ellis' case,* Cro. Jac. 634. If he had only a term of years then the entry must be laid into the freehold of A. in the possession of B., and the restitution must be accordingly. *Reg.* v. *Griffith,* 3 Salk. 169; 13 Vin. Abr. 389, pl. 2, 4.

No indictment can warrant an award of restitution unless it find that the wrongdoer both ousted the party grieved, and also continueth his possession at the time of the finding of the indictment, for it is a repugnancy to award restitution of possession to one who never was in possession, and it is in vain to award it to one who doth not appear to have lost it. 1 Hawk. P. C. c. 64, s. 41.

An indictment on 8 Hen. 6, c. 9, for a forcible entry *vi et armis,* not saying *manu forti,* is bad. *Warner and Collins' case,* Cro. Eliz. 461. But the allegation of a disseisin *manu forti* is sufficient, without any expulsion being stated. *Andrews* v. *Lord Cromwell,* Cro. Jac. 31.

It has been said that if the indictment be not before the justices *at sessions* restitution of the property cannot be granted; for though justices of oyer and terminer, or general gaol delivery, may inquire of forcible entries, and fine the parties, yet they cannot award a writ of restitution. 1 Hawk. P. C. c. 64, s. 51; 3 Bac. Abr. 723 (7th ed.). But this seems questionable. 1 Russ. on Crimes, 314, note (a); *Reg.* v. *Harland,* 8 A. & E. 826; 1 P. & D. 93; 2 Moo. & Rob. 141; 13 Vin. Abr. 384, pl. 7; Jenk. 197, pl. 6. At all events if the indictment be preferred at the sessions, and removed by certiorari into the Queen's Bench, that court may award restitution. *Rex* v. *Marrow,* Cas. temp. Hardw. 174; 1 Hawk. P. C. c. 64, s. 51; Dalton, c. 44, p. 98; 3 Bac. Abr. 723.

7. *Summary Proceedings before Justices on View.*]—When complaint is made to a justice of peace of a forcible entry and detainer, or of an unlawful entry and forcible detainer (which complaint may be made orally, and without oath), the justice should go to the house or other place mentioned, and there upon his own view ascertain whether the place is *holden by force* against the former possessor or not. If he be satisfied that it is, then he should summon the offender to appear before him forthwith to answer the charge; and whether the defendant appear or not, the justice must examine witnesses to ascertain the nature of the defendant's entry; *i. e.,* whether it were forcible, or peaceable but unlawful. For if it were lawful and peaceable, the

subsequent detainer by force is no offence. *Rex* v. *Wilson*, 3 A. & E. 817; 5 N. & M. 164; *Rex* v. *Oakley*, 4 B. & Adol. 307; 1 N. & M. 58. If the entry were peaceable, and there appear to be a *bond fide* dispute as to the title, the justice may with propriety decline to proceed any further, and the Court of Queen's Bench will not compel him to do so. *Ex parte William Davy*, 2 Dowl. N. S. 24; and see *Ex parte Fulder*, 8 Dowl. 535. If he be satisfied that the entry was forcible, or that it was unlawful and the detainer forcible, he should make a record of the force, &c., and issue his warrant for the apprehension and commitment of the offenders. 13 Vin. Abr. 384; *see the forms*, 1 Arch. *Justice*, 355, 356.

A single justice may make a record of such a forcible holding, and such record is not traversable, because the justice of peace, in making thereof, acts not as a minister, but as a judge. 1 Hawk. P. C. c. 64, s. 8. The same justice may assess the fine for this offence, either before the time of conviction or after: *Leighton's case*, 1 Salk. 353: but it is said that such justice of peace hath no power to commit the offender to gaol, unless he do it immediately upon the fact, or unless the offender shall afterwards refuse to find sureties for his good behaviour. 1 Hawk. P. C. c. 64, s. 8. A conviction for a forcible entry was quashed because no fine was set. *Rex* v. *Elwell*, 2 Ld. Raym. 1514; 2 Stra. 794. So where a fine was set, but there was no adjudication that the defendant should be committed until the fine was paid. *Rex* v. *Hood*, Sayer, 176.

Justices of the peace upon their view of a force *cannot meddle with the possession* without an inquisition and the verdict of a jury. 1 Hawk. P. C. c. 64, s. 50. If they *find force*, they are, upon the view, to remove it and commit the offender, but not to award restitution without inquisition. All they can do is to remove the force, and commit them that use it, and to make a record thereof; 13 Vin. Abr. 384, pl. 9, 10; and then to adjourn the matter and issue a precept to the sheriff to summon a jury, &c.

8. *Inquisition and Restitution.*]—Upon complaint of a forcible entry and detainer, or of an unlawful entry and forcible detainer, made to a justice by the party grieved, the justice may issue a precept directed to the sheriff of the county, commanding him to summon and return a jury to inquire into the matter. 8 Hen. 6, c. 9, s. 3; *ante*, 687; *see the form, Appendix, No.* 456. He should also summon the defendants to appear before the jury to answer the charge. 1 Hawk. P. C. c. 64, s. 60; 3 Bac. Abr. 724 (7th ed.); 13 Vin. Abr. 390, pl. 4; *see form of Summons, Appendix, No.* 455. At the day and place appointed, the justice, jury, and the complainant and his witnesses, should attend. The defendants may also attend with their witnesses. The jury are then sworn. *See form of Oath, Appendix, No.* 457. The facts may be opened by the counsel or attorney for the complainant, or by the party himself, in the usual manner. But any such introductory statement may be omitted. The evidence on behalf of the complainant is then produced. It should show either a forcible entry and detainer, or a peaceable but unlawful entry and a forcible detainer. *Rex* v. *Wilson*, 3 A. & E. 817; 5 N. & M. 164; *Rex* v. *Oakley*, 4 B. & Adol. 307; 1 N. & M. 58; 1 Hawk. P. C. c. 64, s. 59. Formerly the party dispossessed was not a competent witness to prove the offence.

Rex v. *Beavan*, Ry. & Moo. 242; *Rex* v. *Williams*, 9 B. & C. 549; but now see 6 & 7 Vict. c. 85; 14 & 15 Vict. c. 99, ss. 1, 2; 16 & 17 Vict. c. 83, s. 4. If a forcible entry be proved, the defendant cannot impeach the complainant's title. *Rex* v. *Williams, supra.* But it will be sufficient for the defendant to allege for stay of restitution that he or his ancestor has been in possession of the property for three years or more, and that his estate therein is not ended or determined. 8 Hen. 6, c. 9, s. 7; *ante,* 687; 31 Eliz. c. 11; *ante,* 688; *Baron Snigge* v. *Shirton,* Cro. Jac. 199; 3 Bac. Abr. Forcible Entry (G.); 13 Vin. Abr. Forcible Entry (G.). The complainant may deny or traverse such allegation; and if it be found against the defendant he shall pay such costs and damages to the other party as shall be assessed by the justices. *Ante,* 688; *Rex* v. *Goodenough,* 2 Ld. Raym. 1036. The *amount* of such costs and damages must be assessed by the justices. And see 11 & 12 Vict. c. 43, s. 18.

If the jury find the offence proved, an inquisition should be drawn up and sealed by them and the justice. *See the form, Appendix, No.* 458. It is kept by the justice, unless removed into the Queen's Bench by certiorari.

If an inquisition of forcible entry be removed into the Queen's Bench by certiorari, there can be no restitution if the defendant either traverse the force (*Reg.* v. *Winter,* 2 Salk. 587), or plead three years' quiet possession before the force. *Rex* v. *Harris,* 1 Salk. 260. But if he so plead, and it is found against him, he must pay costs; *ante,* 688; *Reg.* v. *Goodenough,* 2 Ld. Raym. 1036; and a writ of restitution may issue after the verdict and judgment thereon.

Upon the inquisition being found, the justice will immediately put the complainant into peaceable possession of the property, if the defendants will quietly suffer him so to do: and the justice will then make an indorsement on the inquisition of such possession having been delivered. *See the form, Appendix, No.* 459. But if the defendants will not quietly permit the justice to put the complainant in possession, the justice should issue his warrant directed to the sheriff of the county, commanding him to put the complainant into possession. *See the form, Appendix, No.* 460. In executing this warrant, the sheriff may use such force as may be necessary: 15 Rich. 2, c. 2; *ante,* 686; 1 Hawk. P. C. c. 64, s. 52: and he may break open outer doors, if necessary, after having first demanded admission. Dalton's J., c. 44. The justice should indorse on the inquisition a memorandum of his warrant, and what has been done under it. *See the form, Appendix, No.* 461.

In cities, towns and boroughs having franchise, the mayors, justices, sheriffs and bailiffs, have like power as justices elsewhere to remove forcible entries, &c. 8 Hen. 6, c. 9, s. 6; *ante,* 687; *Reg.* v. *Layton,* 1 Salk. 353.

9. *Supersedeas of Restitution.*]—The same justices by whom a restitution is awarded, or *any one* or more of them, may afterwards supersede the precept for restitution before it is executed, upon the indictment or inquisition appearing to them or him to be insufficient. But it seems to be agreed that no other justices or other court whatsoever have such power, except the Queen's Bench. 1 Hawk. P. C. c. 64, s. 61. However, it is certain that a certiorari from the Queen's Bench is a supersedeas to such restitution. *Id.* s. 63. The justices of that court may

even set aside a restitution after it has been executed, upon the indictment or inquisition being removed before them by certiorari, and
quashed for insufficiency. *Id.* s. 63. So where the defendant, after
removal of the indictment into the Queen's Bench, traverses the force
and obtains a verdict. *Id.* s. 63. So where it sufficiently appears that
the justices of the peace have been irregular in their proceedings, as by
refusing to try a traverse of the force tendered by the defendant. *Id.*
s. 63; *Reg.* v. *Winter*, 2 Salk. 587. But it is always in the discretion of the court to grant or refuse restitution in such cases. 1 Hawk.
P. C. c. 64, ss. 65, 66.

Where an indictment or inquisition of forcible entry or detainer, on
which restitution has been had, is quashed, re-restitution shall be
awarded; *Ford's case*, Cro. Jac. 151; unless an outstanding term be
shown. *Rex* v. *Toslin*, 2 Salk. 587.

APPENDIX.

FORMS IN EJECTMENT, ETC.

1. *Notice to quit, given by the Landlord or his Agent* (ante, 47).

To Mr. C. D.

Sir,—I hereby [*if given by an agent, say "as agent for* Mr. A. B., your landlord, and on his behalf"] give you notice to quit and deliver up possession of the [house *or* farm, land] and premises, with the appurtenances, situate [at ——, *or* in the parish of ——,] in the county of ——, which you hold of [me *or* him] as tenant thereof, on the [twenty-fifth] day of [March] next (*a*), [or at the expiration of the year of your tenancy which shall expire next after the end of one-half year from the service of this notice]. Dated the —— day of —— 18—.

Yours, &c.

A. B. [*or* E. F. of ——, agent for A. B.]

N.B.—*If it be wished to make the notice primâ facie evidence as to the time when the tenancy commenced, omit the concluding words,* "*or at the expiration,*" *&c. and serve the notice on the tenant* personally, *and either read it to him or get him to read it in your presence.* (Ante, 50.) *By way of precaution against any damage arising from the omission of the above words, a second notice, including them, may be served in due time by another witness.*

---

2. *Notice to quit given by a Tenant in Common* (ante, 48).

To Mr. C. D.

Sir,—I hereby give you notice of my intention to determine the tenancy under which you now hold of me [one undivided third part or share, *as the case may be*] of and in the [messuage *or* farm, land] and premises, with the appurtenances, situate at ——, in the county of ——, and require you to quit the same on the —— day of —— next [or at the expiration of the year of your tenancy which shall expire next after the end of one half year from the service of this notice(*b*)]. Dated the —— day of ——, 18—.

Yours, &c.

A. B.

---

3. *Notice to quit given by the Tenant or his Agent* (ante, 47).

To A. B., Esq.

Sir,—I hereby [*if given by an agent, say "as agent for* Mr. C. D., your tenant, and on his behalf"] give you notice that it is [my *or* his] intention to quit and deliver up possession of the [house *or* farm, land] and premises, with the appurtenances, situate [at —— *or* in the parish of ——],

---

(*a*) Insert the proper day. See *ante*, 48.
(*b*) See note to No. 1, *supra*.

H H

in the county of ——, now held by [me *or* him] as your tenant thereof, on the [twenty-fifth] day of [March next(*c*)]. Dated the —— day of ——, 18—.

Yours, &c.

C. D. [*or* G. H. of ——, agent for C. D.]

---

4. *Notice to determine a Lease for twenty-one Years, at the End of the first seven or fourteen Years, pursuant to a Proviso or Power therein contained (ante,* 398).

To Mr. C. D.

Sir,—In pursuance of the proviso or power in that behalf contained in an indenture of lease, dated the —— day of ——, 18—, made or expressed to be made between [*as the case may be*], I the undersigned [being the assignee of the immediate reversion of and in the tenements, with the appurtenances, demised by the said lease] do hereby give you notice that it is my intention to avoid the said lease, and to put an end to the term thereby granted, at the end of the first [seven *or* fourteen, *or as the case may be*] years of the said term. Dated the —— day of ——, 18—.

Yours, &c.

A. B.

N.B.—*For another form, see ante,* 398.

---

5. *Demand of Possession at the End of a Term of Years, otherwise double Value (ante,* 647).

To Mr. C. D.

Sir,—I do hereby [as agent for and on behalf of your landlord A. B., Esq.] demand and require you to quit and deliver up the possession of [*describe the premises shortly*] with the appurtenances, situate [at ——, *or* in the parish of ——,] in the county of ——, forthwith, [*or if the term have not expired, say* on the expiration of your term therein, which will expire on or about the —— day of —— next [*or* instant]]: And take notice that if you hold over the said premises after [the service hereof *or* after expiration of this notice] you will be liable to pay double value for the said premises, pursuant to the statute in such case made and provided. Dated this day of —— 18—.

Yours, &c.

A. B. of —— [*or* E. F. of ——, agent for A. B., Esq., of ——.]

N.B.—*If the tenant hold only from year to year, the usual notice to quit is sufficient* (ante, 646). *The above notice may be served before or after the expiration of the term* (ante, 647). *But no unnecessary delay should take place.* Cobb *v.* Stokes, 8 East, 358.

---

6. *Demand of possession pursuant to* 15 & 16 *Vict. c.* 76, *s.* 213 (*ante,* 379).

To Mr. C. D.

Sir,—I do hereby, [*if given by an agent, say* " as the agent of and for A. B., Esq., your landlord, and on his behalf,"] according to the form of the statute in such case made and provided, demand of and require you forthwith to quit and deliver up possession of [the messuage, land and premises *or* the farm and premises, *or as the case may be*], with the appurtenances situate and being [at —— *or* in the parish of ——,] in the county of ——, and which were held by you under a [lease *or* agreement] in writing, bearing date the —— day of ——, 18—, [for the term of —— years, which

---

(*c*) The words, " or at the expiration of the year of [my *or* his] tenancy which shall expire next after the end of one half year from the service of this notice," may be added, if wished; but they are unusual in a notice given by a tenant, because he generally knows at what time of the year his tenancy commenced.

expired on or about the —— day of —— last, *or* as tenant from year to year, which tenancy was determined by [me *or* the said A. B. *or* you, *as the case may be,*] on the —— day of —— last, by a regular notice to quit before then duly given]. Dated this —— day of —— 18—.

Yours, &c.

A. B. [*or* E. F. of ——, agent for the said A. B.]

N.B.—*This demand may be addressed to the tenant "or any one holding or claiming by or under him," and may be "served personally upon or left at the dwelling-house or usual place of abode of such tenant or person,"* 15 & 16 *Vict.* c. 76, s. 213 (ante, 379). *And if possible an express refusal to deliver up possession pursuant to the notice should be obtained* (ante, 382).

---

7. *Notice of Mortgage by the Mortgagee to the Mortgagor's Tenant* (*ante*, 473).

To Mr.——.

Sir,—Take notice, that by an indenture dated the —— day of ——, 18—, and made or expressed to be made between [*as the case may be*], the [messuage or dwelling-house and land, *or as the case may be*], with the appurtenances, situate and being [at ——, *or* in the parish of ——,] in the county of ——, now in your possession (together with other hereditaments) were conveyed and assured unto and to the use of me the said ——, my heirs and assigns [*or* executors, administrators and assigns, for a term of —— years from the —— day of ——, 18—], for securing the sum of £——, with interest for the same at the rate of £—— per cent. per annum [at a day now past, *or* on the —— day of —— next]. And you are hereby required to pay to me all rent and arrears of rent now due and payable, and hereafter to become due and payable from you in respect of the said premises in your possession: And in case of any default I shall distrain or sue for the said rent, or bring an action of ejectment to recover possession of the said [messuage *or* dwelling-house and land], with the appurtenances, in your possession, or otherwise put the law in force, as I may be advised. Dated this —— day of ——, 18—.

Yours, &c.

——, of ——.

---

8. *The like, by Mortgagee's Attorney* (*ante*, 473).

To Mr. ——.

Sir,—Take notice, that by an indenture dated the —— day of —— 18—, and made or expressed to be made between [*as the case may be*], the [farm and lands, *or as the case may be*], with the appurtenances, situate [at ——, *or* in the parish of ——], in the county of ——, now in your possession (together with other hereditaments) were conveyed and assured unto the said C. D. [*the Mortgagee*], his heirs and assigns, [*or* his executors, administrators and assigns, for a term of —— years from the —— day of ——, 18—], for securing the sum of £——, with interest for the same at the rate of £—— per cent. per annum [at a day now past, *or* on the —— day of —— next]: Now I do hereby, as the attorney of and for the said C. D., and on his behalf, give you notice of the said indenture, and require you to pay to the said C. D. all rent and arrears of rent now due and payable, and hereafter to become due and payable, from you in respect of the said premises in your possession: And take notice, that, in case of any default, the said C. D. will distrain or sue for the said rent, or bring an action of ejectment to recover possession of the said [farm and lands], with the appurtenances, in your possession, or otherwise put the law in force, as he may be advised. Dated this —— day of ——, 18—.

Yours, &c.

G. H. of ——, attorney for the said C. D.

H H 2

9. *Acknowledgment of Title to Bar the Statute of Limitation (ante, 18).*

I, C. D., of ——, do hereby admit and declare that I am now in possession of [*or* in receipt of the rents and profits of] all that messuage, &c., *describe the property so as to identify it,* with the appurtenances, situate [at ——, *or* in the parish of ——,] in the county of ——, by the sufferance and permission of A. B., of ——, Esq., and subject to the title of the said A. B., under whom I now hold the same. Dated this —— day of ——, 18—.

To A. B., Esq.   C. D.

N.B.—*No stamp is necessary;* Barry *v.* Goodman, 2 M. & W. 768; *nor on a memorandum of attornment* (ante, 230).

———

10. *Letter of Attorney to demand Rent and Arrears (ante, 412).*

Know all men by these presents, that I, A. B., of ——, [Esquire], Have made, ordained, authorized, constituted and appointed, and by these presents Do make, ordain, authorize, constitute and appoint, E. F., of ——, gentleman, my true and lawful attorney, for me, and in my name, and to my use, to ask, demand and receive of and from C. D., of ——, the sum of £—— for [one quarter's] rent of [a messuage *or* farm, land] and premises, with the appurtenances, situate at ——, *or* in the parish of ——, in the county of ——, now held by him as my tenant, and which will become due on the —— day of ——[instant *or* next]: Also (separately) all arrears of rent now due and owing to me from the said C. D., in respect of the said premises; and on payment of the said monies respectively, good and sufficient receipts, acquittances, releases or other sufficient discharges, for the monies received, and for so much of the said rent in respect whereof the same shall be paid or received, for me and in my name, to make and sign, or to make, sign, seal and deliver (as may be necessary), and to do all other lawful acts and things whatsoever concerning the premises, as fully in every respect as I myself might or could do if I were personally present, Hereby ratifying and confirming and allowing all and whatsoever my said attorney shall in my name lawfully do in and about the premises by virtue of these presents. In witness whereof I have hereunto set my hand and seal this —— day of ——, A.D. 18—.

Signed, sealed and delivered in the presence of   A. B. (L.S.)
         I. K., of ——.

———

11. *Retainer of an Attorney to bring and prosecute an Ejectment (ante, 75).*

To Mr. E. F.

Sir,—I [*or* We] do hereby retain and employ you as [my *or* our] attorney, to bring and prosecute an action of ejectment in one of the superior courts of law at Westminster in [my name, *or* our names], either alone or jointly with any other name or names (as may appear necessary or expedient), for the recovery of the possession of [*describe the property concisely*], with the appurtenances, situate [at ——, *or* in the parish of ——], in the county of ——, now in the possession of C. D., his under-tenants or assigns. Dated the —— day of ——, 18—.

Signatures.

———

12. *Retainer by the Defendant (indorsed on Copy Writ).*

Mr. G. H.—I hereby retain you as my attorney to appear and defend the within action on my behalf.

Date   *Signature of defendant.*

———

13. *The like—another Form (not indorsed on Copy Writ).*
In the [Q. B., C. P. *or* Exch.]
      Between A. B. and [another *or* others]............ Plaintiffs,
              and
        C. D. and [another *or* others]............ Defendants.

I [*or* We] hereby retain you as [my *or* our] attorney to defend this action of ejectment on [my *or* our] behalf. Dated the ―― day of ―― 18―.
    To Mr. G. H.   *Signatures.*   •

---

14. *Precipe for a Writ of Ejectment (ante, 97).*

――shire (*d*). Writ in ejectment for [*names of claimants*] against [*names of defendants* (*e*)].
  Date.   E. F. of ――, agent for G. H. of ――.

---

15. *Writ of Ejectment (ƒ) (ante, 83).*

Victoria, by the grace of God of the United Kingdom of Great Britain and Ireland Queen, Defender of the Faith, To [*names of all the tenants in possession* (*g*)], and all persons (*h*) entitled to defend the possession of [*describe the property with reasonable certainty* (*i*)] in the parish of ―― in the county of ――, to the possession whereof [*names of all the claimants* (*k*)], some or one of them (*l*), claim [*or* claims] to be entitled [*or* to have been on and since the ―― day of ――, in the year of our Lord one thousand eight hundred and ―― entitled, or to be entitled (*m*)], and to eject all other persons

---

(*d*) The county in which the lands lie. In ejectment, the venue is local. *Ante*, 135.

(*e*) The property claimed need not be mentioned in the precipe, nor the day from which possession is claimed.

(*ƒ*) For the outline form of the writ as given in 15 & 16 Vict. c. 76, Schedule A., No. 13., see *ante*, 82.

(*g*) For directions who should or should not be made defendants, and how they should be named, see *ante*, 75, 83. It is sometimes advisable to bring two or more actions, when the parcels and tenants are numerous. *Ante*, 76, 83.

(*h*) These words refer to landlords, to whom the tenants in possession ought to give immediate notice when the writ is served (*ante*, 115); also to any other persons *not known* to the claimant to be in possession of any part of the property, but who may wish to appear and defend the action with leave of the Court or a Judge (*ante*, 124).

(*i*) For full directions how to describe the property, see *ante*, 85, 92. Although it must be described "with reasonable certainty," the description need not be such as to identify it, or to enable it to be distinguished from other property (*ante*, 86); and the abuttals or boundaries should never be mentioned, unless for some special object or purpose.

(*k*) For directions who should be named as claimants, see *ante*, 74, 93. The character in which the claimants sue, *ex gr.*, as executors, administrators, assignees, heir, &c., never need be stated. But churchwardens and overseers who sue *as such* should be so described in the writ. *Ante*, 94, 607.

(*l*) When there is only one claimant, strike out or omit the words "some or one of them." When there are only two claimants, strike out or omit the word "some." But any mistake on this point is not material.

(*m*) The plaintiffs usually claim only "to be entitled," *i.e.*, on the day when the writ issues; but it is sometimes important to claim from a previous day, with a view to the subsequent action for mesne profits, &c. (*ante*, 94, 641). Where that is done, it seems advisable generally to add the

therefrom : These are to will and command you, or such of you as deny the alleged title, within sixteen (n) days after service hereof, to appear in our Court of [Queens Bench, *or* Common Pleas, *or* Exchequer, *as the case may be*], at Westminster, to defend the said property, or such part thereof as you may be advised; in default whereof judgment may be signed, and you turned out of possession. Witness [*name of Chief Justice, or Chief Baron, or, in case of a vacancy, name of Senior Puisne Judge of the Court*] at Westminster, the [*day on which the writ issues*] —— day of ——, in the year of our Lord one thousand eight hundred and ——, [*or*, in the —— year of our reign.]

(*Indorsement.*)

This writ was issued by E. F. of —— [agent for J. K., of ——], attorney for the said claimants [*or* claimant.]

Or,

This writ was issued in person by A. B., who resides at [*mention the city, town or parish, and also the name of the hamlet, street and number of the house of the claimant's residence, if any such there be.*]

If there be more than one claimant say, " And by C. D. who resides at" [*describe his residence as above:*] " And by E. F. who resides at" [*describe his residence in like manner.*]

N.B.—*The date when the writ issues need not be indorsed, nor any memorandum of the service of the writ.*

---

16. *Writ in Ejectment, with a Notice to find Bail, pursuant to* 15 & 16 *Vict. c.* 76, *s.* 213 (*ante*, 379).

Form of writ and indorsements, as *ante*, No. 15 ; at the foot of the writ add the following notice :—

In the [Q. B., C. P. *or* Exch.]

Between A. B., plaintiff, and C. D., defendant.

Take notice that you will be required, if ordered by the court or a judge, to give bail by yourself and two sufficient sureties, conditioned to pay the costs and damages which shall be recovered in this action.

Yours, &c.

G. H. [attorney *or* agent for the said claimant.]

To Mr. C. D., the above-named defendant.

N. B.—*The body of this notice is given by* 15 & 16 *Vict. c.* 76, *Schedule A., No.* 21. *It does not clearly appear to be necessary to entitle it in the cause, or to direct it to the defendant, or to subscribe it with the name of the plaintiff, or his attorney or agent. But it will be prudent to do so until it be decided to be unnecessary.* Doe d. Beard v. Roe, 1 M. & W. 360 ; Chitty's Forms, 557 (7th Ed.)

---

words " or to be entitled," as in the text (*supra*). This appears to have been done without objection in *Scott* v. *Reynall* (26 Law Times R. 256—Q. B.; *ante*, 96). But it is not clear that the writ may be so framed *in the alternative*. *Ante*, 96. If the writ be so framed and judgment be signed for want of an appearance, the judgment will not operate as an estoppel to prevent the defendants in a subsequent action of trespass for mesne profits from denying the plaintiffs' title prior to the date of the writ in ejectment. *Scott* v. *Reynall, supra.* But a verdict in ejectment finds that the claimant " on the —— day of ——, A.D. 18—, was and still is entitled to the possession," &c., as alleged in the writ. And the words " or to be entitled," if added as above suggested, may sometimes save the claimants from a nonsuit. *Ante*, 95, 288.

(n) When the writ issues pursuant to sect. 217 of The Common Law Procedure Act, 1852 (*ante*, 389), the defendants should be commanded to appear within *ten* days instead of *sixteen* days (*post*, No. 17).

17. *Writ in Ejectment pursuant to 15 & 16 Vict. c. 76, s. 217 (ante, 389).*

Same as ante, No. 15, *except that it should command the defendants to appear " within ten days" instead of sixteen days.*

An affidavit of service of this writ may be in the ordinary form : for if the writ be improperly issued in this form, it may be set aside as irregular. In Chitty's Forms, 565 (7th Ed.), a special form of affidavit is given : but this would seem to be unnecessary for the reasons above mentioned. The affidavits should however show a proper service made within ten days next after the date and issuing of the writ.

———

18. *Summons to stay or set aside Proceedings under 15 & 16 Vict. c. 76, s. 217, or to postpone the Trial until the next Assizes (ante, 391).*

Usual commencement (post, No. 22), Why the proceedings in this action should not be set aside or stayed, or the trial postponed until the next [spring *or* summer] assizes for the county of ——, pursuant to the 217th section of the Common Law Procedure Act, 1852. Dated the —— day of ——, 18—. *Judge's signature.*

———

N.B.—*If any irregularity be relied on, it should be specially mentioned in the summons. It seems that an application of the above nature may be made where there is no irregularity in the plaintiff's proceedings, but so much expedition may operate unjustly. Upon such application " it shall be lawful for the judge, in his discretion, to make such order in the said cause as to him shall seem expedient"* (ante, 390).

———

19. *Affidavit (General Form) by one Deponent.*

In the [Q. B., C. P. *or* Exch. (o)].
　　　　Between [*names of all the claimants* (p)], plaintiffs,
　　　　　　　　　　and
　　　　　　　[*names of all the defendants* (q)], defendants.

I (r), A. B., of [*state deponent's true place of abode and addition* (s),] ——,

(o) In the Exchequer it is unnecessary to say, " In the Exchequer *of Pleas."　Salmon* v. *Rollin,* 7 Dowl. 852.

" An affidavit sworn before a judge of any of the courts shall be received in the court to which such judge belongs, though not entitled of that court, but not in any other court unless *entitled of the court* in which it is to be used." Reg. Prac. H. T. 1853, No. 144.

It seems that the affidavit may be entitled with the name of the proper court *after* it has been sworn before a commissioner of such court. *Perse* v. *Browning,* 1 M. & W. 362; *White* v. *Irving,* 2 M. & W. 127; 5 Dowl. 289. But the propriety of doing this may be doubted.

(p) The names of all the plaintiffs must be stated, as in the writ. They must not be abbreviated thus :—A. B. *and another,* or A. B. *and others.　Doe* d. *Prynne* v. *Roe,* 8 Dowl. 340; *Doe* d. *Cousins* v. *Roe,* 4 M. & W. 68; 7 Dowl. 53. A mere transposition of the names is immaterial. *Doe* d. *Montgomery* v. *Roe,* 1 Dowl. & L. 695. The omission of an *e* mute is immaterial. *Gray* v. *Coombs,* 10 C. B. 72. The name of any plaintiff whose death has been suggested pursuant to 15 & 16 Vict. c. 76, ss. 191, 192 or 193, should be omitted; or if inserted, the words " (since deceased)" should be added : except perhaps in an affidavit to set aside the suggestion as untrue. The name of any plaintiff substituted or added pursuant to sect. 194 should be inserted.

(q) The names of all the defendants *as stated in the writ* should be inserted, whether they have appeared to the writ or not : also the name of any landlord or other person who may have been admitted to defend pur-in the county of ——, Esquire, [the above-named plaintiff, *or* defendant, *or* one of the above-named plaintiffs *or* defendants," *or* " I, N. M., clerk to

---

suant to 15 & 16 Vict. c. 76, s. 172. The name of any deceased defendant whose death has been suggested pursuant to s. 195 or 198, should be omitted; or if inserted the words " (since deceased)" should be added : except perhaps in an affidavit to set aside the suggestion as untrue. The name of any defendant substituted or added pursuant to s. 196 or 199 should be inserted.

The names of the defendants for the time being should not be abbreviated thus,—C. D. *and another,* or C. D. *and others. Doe d. Prynne* v. *Roe,* 8 Dowl. 340 ; *Doe* d. *Cousins* v. *Roe,* 4 M. & W. 68 ; 7 Dowl. 53. If any defendant be named in the writ by initials, or by any contraction of his christian name, or in any other respect misnamed in the writ, the affidavit should *in its title* name him in the same incorrect manner. *Sims* v. *Prosser,* 15 M. & W. 151 ; 3 D. & L. 491 ; *Reg.* v. *Sheriff of Surrey,* in a cause of *Smith* v. *Neely,* 8 Dowl. 510. But, if he have appeared by his correct name, adding sued as ——, any subsequent affidavit may name him correctly. *Lomax* v. *Kilpin,* 16 M. & W. 94 ; 4 D. & L. 295. But the words " sued as———" should not be added. *Baldwin* v. *Bauerman,* 12 C. B. 152 ; *Shrimpton* v. *Carter,* 3 Dowl. 648 ; *Tagg* v. *Simmonds,* 4 Dowl. & L. 582.

(*r*) By Reg. Mich. Vac. 1854, No. 2, " Every affidavit to be hereafter used in any cause or civil proceeding in any of the said Superior Courts of Common Law shall be *drawn up in the first person,* and shall be *divided into paragraphs,* and every paragraph shall be *numbered consecutively,* and, as nearly as may be, shall be *confined to a distinct portion of the subject.* No costs shall be allowed for any affidavit or part of an affidavit substantially departing from this rule. This rule not to be in force till the first day of Easter Term next," [1855.]

(*s*) " The *addition* and *true place of abode* of every person making an affidavit shall be inserted therein." Reg. Prac., H. T. 1853, No. 138. An omission to comply with this rule renders the affidavit irregular, but not a nullity. *Seymour* v. *Maddox,* 1 Low. M. & P. 543. If the affidavit be made by a party to the cause, it is sufficient to describe him as A. B., of &c. [*state his true place of abode*], " the above-named plaintiff," *or* " one of the defendants above named," without any other *addition. Shirer* v. *Walker,* 2 Man. & Gr. 917 ; 3 Scott, N. R., 239 ; 9 Dowl. 667 ; *Angel* v. *Ihler,* 5 M. & W. 163 ; Jerv. N. R. 59, note ; *Brooks* v. *Farlar,* 3 Bing. N. C. 291 ; 3 Scott, 654 ; 5 Dowl. 361. But his true place of abode must be stated. *Collins* v. *Goodyer,* 2 B. & C. 563. The addition of " agent of the plaintiff in this cause" is sufficient. *Luxford* v. *Groomborough,* 2 Dowl. N. S. 332 ; *Matthewson* v. *Baistow,* 3 D. & L. 327. " A. B., of No. 21, Tokenhouse-yard in the city of London, clerk to C. D., of the same place " (not stating C. D.'s addition), is sufficient. *Cooper* v. *Folkes,* 1 Man. & Gr. 942 ; 2 Scott, N. R. 200 ; 9 Dowl. 46. " Late clerk to &c." is a sufficient addition. *Simpson* v. *Drummond,* 2 Dowl. 473. " Managing clerk to A. B., of " &c., is sufficient ; but " *acting as* managing clerk to A. B., of &c. the plaintiff's attorney," is not sufficient. *Graves* v. *Browning,* 6 A. & E. 805. " M. B., clerk, S. N., of " &c. [*not saying* " of " *or* " to " S. N., of &c.], is insufficient. *Shakespear* v. *Willan,* 19 Law J., N. S., Exch. 184. " Articled clerk," not saying to whom, or in what profession, is insufficient. *Reg.* v. *Reeve,* 4 Q. B. 211 ; 3 Gale & D. 560. " Assessor " is insufficient. *Natham* v. *Cohen,* 3 Dowl. 370 ; 1 Harr. & Wool. 107.

The affidavit should state the " true place of abode " of each deponent. This seems necessary even when the affidavit is made by a party to the cause. *Collins* v. *Goodyer,* 2 B. & C. 563. Strictly speaking, the place of abode of any person is where he resides and sleeps ; not his place of business elsewhere. *Reg.* v. *Hammond,* 21 Law J., N. S., Q. B. 153. But, in an affidavit it is sufficient to state the deponent's place of business, where he is generally

E. F., of ——, gentleman, the attorney in this cause for the above-named plaintiffs *or defendants, or defendant* ——, *as the case may be*], make oath and say,

1. That (*t*) [*here state the facts, or some distinct portion of the subject, clearly and concisely, and in the first person* (*r*)].

2. That (*t*), &c. [*ut supra.*]

Sworn (*u*) at ——, in the [county] of ——, on the ——⎱ [*signature of*
    day of ——, 18—. ⎰ *deponent*].
            Before me (*x*), E. F., a commissioner, &c. (*y*).

Or,

Sworn at my chambers, in Rolls Garden, Chancery Lane, ⎱
    the —— day of ——, 18—. ⎰
            Before me [*judge's or baron's signature*].

Or,

Sworn at the [Queens Bench *or* Common Pleas, *or* Ex-⎱
    chequer] Judges' Chambers in Rolls Garden, Chancery ⎰
    Lane, on the —— day of ——, 18—.
            Before me (*x*), O. P., a commissioner, &c. (*y*).

Or,

Sworn in Court at Westminster Hall, on the —— day of ⎱
    ——, 18—. ⎰
                      By the Court.

For other forms of jurats, see Chit. Forms, 860 (7th ed.)

N.B.—*If the deponent be a marksman or evidently illiterate, see post,* 706, 707. *If there be several deponents, their names must be mentioned in the jurat.* See the next form.

---

to be found during the day. *Haslope* v. *Thorne,* 1 M. & S. 103; *Alexander* v. *Milton,* 2 Cr. & Jer. 424; 1 Dowl. 570. In an affidavit by an attorney's clerk, it is unnecessary for him to state his own residence if he state that of his master. *Strike* v. *Blanchard,* 5 Dowl. 216; *Alexander* v. *Milton, suprà.* But an affidavit describing the deponent as "T. H. S., clerk to E. J., Esq., Barrister at Law, and Assessor of the Court of Passage of the Borough of Liverpool," is insufficient. It does not state the place of abode of either party. *Winch* v. *Williams,* 12 C. B. 416; 21 Law J., N. S., C. P. 216. "H. B., clerk to the above-named defendant," is insufficient for the same reason. *Elton* v. *Martindale,* 5 Dowl. & L. 248. "A. B., clerk to C. D., the defendant's attorney," is not sufficient. *Daniels* v. *May,* 5 Dowl. 83. The residence of an attorney's clerk need not be given in an affidavit made by him jointly with his master, in which the residence of the latter is stated. *Bottomley* v. *Belchamber,* 4 Dowl. 26. "C. F. C., of &c., attorney to the above-named defendant, and *R. M., his clerk*," is sufficient. *S. C.*

If the affidavit state the deponent's place of residence *with reasonable certainty*, that is sufficient, without stating the number of the house, or the name of the street, &c., or the name of the parish or township. Thus, "of Lawrence Pountney, in the city of London," *Miller* v. *Miller,* 2 Scott, 117; "of Kennington, in the county of Surrey," *Wilton* v. *Chambers,* 1 Harr. & Wool. 116; "of Ely, in the county of Cambridge," *Hunt's Bail,* 4 Dowl. 272; 1 Harr. & Wool. 520; "of Bath, in the county of Somerset, Esq.;" *Coppin* v. *Potter,* 10 Bing. 443; 4 Moo. & Sc. 272; 2 Dowl. 785; "of the city of London, merchant," *Vaissier* v. *Alderson,* 3 M. & S. 166, have respectively been held sufficient. So, where the deponent described himself as, "late of Tyrone, in the county of Tyrone in Ireland, but now of Dublin Castle;" *Stewart* v. *Gaveran,* 1 Harr. & Wool. 699: "late in the Compter Prison of Giltspur Street, in the city of London," is sufficient, the deponent having been only recently discharged, and continuing to sleep there, and having no other place of abode. *Sedley* v. *White,* 11 East, 528. But, gene-

rally speaking, "late of &c." without stating any present address, is insufficient. *S. C.* A foreigner, who has come to England only for a temporary
purpose, may describe himself as of his foreign domicile, and need not state
his address here. *Bouhet* v. *Kittoe*, 3 East, 154. If the deponent be a prisoner in the custody of the sheriff or of the keeper of the Queen's Prison, he
may be so described in an affidavit. *Jervis* v. *Jones*, 4 Dowl. 610 ; *Sharpe* v.
Johnson, 4 Dowl. 324 ; 2 Scott, 405 ; 2 Bing. N. C. 246.

(*t*) See *ante*, note (*r*). If the affidavit be made by several, it will generally be necessary to commence each paragraph thus " I, the said A. B.
say," *or* "We the said A. B., C. D. and E. F. severally say" (*see the next
form*). But it is not necessary to commence each paragraph with the word
" That." It is generally omitted in chancery affidavits. Its insertion frequently gives a stiffness and formality which may as well be avoided.

(*u*) *The Jurat.*—By Reg. Prac. H. T. 1853, No. 139, " In every affidavit
made by two or more deponents, the names of the several persons making
such affidavit shall be written in the jurat."

It seems insufficient to say sworn by " both the deponents." *Houlden* v.
Fasson, 6 Bing. 236 ; 3 Moo. & P. 559. The jurat should mention the
name of each deponent; *Lackington* v. *Atherton*, 6 Scott, N. R. 240 ; 5
Man. & Gr. 292, note ; 2 Dowl. N. S. 904 ; and should state that they were
severally sworn. *Pardoe* v. *Territt*, 6 Scott, N. R. 273 ; 5 Man. & G. 291 ;
2 Dowl. N. S. 903. If there be two deponents and two distinct jurats, the
name of a deponent must be mentioned in each jurat. *Cobbett* v. *Oldfield*,
16 M. & W. 469 ; 4 D. & L. 492.

The *time* of swearing the affidavit must be stated in the jurat ; 2 Chit.
Arch. 1453 (9th ed.); *Blackwell* v. *Allen*, 7 M. & W. 146; *The Duke of Bruns-
wick* v. *Slowman*, 8 C. B. 617 : 7 D. & L. 251; *The Duke of Brunswick* v.
Harmer, 1 Low. M. & P. 505 ; *In re Lloyd*, 15 Q. B. 682 ; 1 Low. M. & P.
545 ; also the *place* and *county ; Cass* v. *Cass*, 1 D. & L. 698; *Thomas* v.
Stannaway, 2 D. & L. 111 ; 2 Chit. Arch. 1453.

The date mentioned in the jurat may be referred to for the purpose of
supplying a date in the body of the affidavit when necessary. *Craig* v. *Lloyd*,
3 Exch. 232 ; *Holmes* v. *The London and South Western Railway Company*,
13 Q. B. 87 ; but see *Abrahams* v. *Davison*, 6 C. B. 622.

Interlineations and Erasures.—" No affidavit shall be read or made use of in
any matter depending in court *in the jurat* of which there shall be any interlineation or erasure." Reg. Prac. H. T. 1853, No. 140.

This rule applies to affidavits sworn in India. *Re Page*, 5 Dowl. & L.
475 ; *Re Fagan*, 5 C. B. 436 ; or in Canada, *Re Millard*, 5 C. B. 753 ; 6
Dowl. & L. 86 ; or in Australia. *Re Tierney*, 15 C. B. 761.

A rasure is not necessarily an erasure ; the former is sometimes made to
remove excrescences or grease spots. *Re Millard, supra.* A line drawn
through two words in a jurat, leaving them perfectly legible, vitiates the
affidavit. *Williams* v. *Clough*, 1 A. & E. 376. If the date be struck out and
another inserted, the affidavit cannot be read. *Chambers* v. *Barnard*, 9 Dowl.
557 ; 1 Harr. & Wool. 670 ; so if any interlineation be made. *Re Tierney*, 15
C. B. 761. But if the words " a commissioner, &c." be struck out, and an
addition made to the jurat, that is not an erasure or interlineation within
the rule, the words struck out forming no part of the jurat. *Dawson* v. *Wills*,
10 M. & W. 662 ; 2 Dowl. N. S. 465. If the words "before me" are
struck out, and the words " By the court" subscribed, that is no objection.
Austin v. *Grange*, 4 Dowl. 576. If any mistake be made in the jurat, the
proper course is to strike it out and write a fresh one. 2 Chit. Arch. 1455
(9th ed.)

Any interlineation or erasure in the *body* of the affidavit should be marked
with the initials of the judge's clerk or commissioner if at all material. *Re
Worthington*, 5 C. B. 511. But immaterial alterations need not be so marked.
Re Imeson and Horner, 8 Dowl. 651. ˙

Illiterate Deponents.—" Where any affidavit is sworn before any judge, or any commissioner, by any person who, from his or her signature, appears to be illiterate, the judge's clerk or commissioner taking such affidavit shall certify or state in the jurat that the affidavit was read in his presence to the party making the same, and that such party seemed perfectly to understand the same, and also that the said party wrote his or her mark or signature in the presence of the judge's clerk or commissioner taking the said affidavit." Reg. Prac. H. T. 1853, No. 141.

The form of the jurat may be as follows :—

"Sworn by the above-named deponent A. B., at ——, in the county of ——, on the —— day of ——, 18—, the affidavit having first been read in my presence to the said A. B., who seemed perfectly to understand the same, and wrote his [mark *or* signature] in my presence. Before me,

"——, a commissioner, &c."

Where a deponent signs by *a mark*, the jurat must be framed in accordance with the above rule. *Wilson* v. *Blakey*, 9 Dowl. 352. The rule extends to an affidavit sworn in court. *Haynes* v. *Powell*, 3 Dowl. 599. If the affidavit be sworn before a commissioner, the jurat must express that the affidavit was read *in his presence* to the deponent. But it need not be read to the deponent by the commissioner himself; although formerly otherwise. *Rex* v. *The Sheriff of Middlesex*, in *Disney* v. *Anthony*, 4 Dowl. 765.

(*z*) An affidavit sworn before a commissioner, omitting in the jurat the words "before me," is bad. *Graham* v. *Ingleby*, 1 Exch. 651 ; 5 Dowl. & L. 737 ; *Reg.* v. *The Inhabitants of Bloxham*, 5 Q. B. 528 ; 2 Dowl. & L. 168 ; *Reg.* v. *The Inhabitants of Norbury*, 5 Q. B. 534, note. If sworn before a judge at his chambers, the words "before me" may be omitted. *Empey* v. *King*, 13 M. & W. 519 ; 2 Dowl. & L. 375 ; so if sworn in court. *Thorne* v. *Jackson*, 3 C. B. 661 ; 4 Dowl. & L. 478.

Before whom not to be sworn.—"No affidavit of the *service of process* shall be deemed sufficient if sworn before the plaintiff's own attorney or his clerk." Reg. Prac. H. T. 1853, No. 142.

"Where an agent in town, or an attorney in the country, is the attorney *on the record*, an affidavit sworn before the attorney in the country shall not be received; and an affidavit sworn before an attorney's clerk shall not be received in cases where it would not be receivable if sworn before the attorney himself; but this rule shall not extend to affidavits to hold to bail." *Ib.*, No. 143.

Independently of the above rule, it seems that the court will reject an affidavit sworn before the attorney of the party on whose behalf the application is made, even where there is no record. *In re Gray*, 1 Bail C. C. 93 ; 21 Law J., N. S., Q. B. 380. But see *Doe* d. *Grant* v. *Roe*, 5 Dowl. 409.

(*y*) "A commissioner, &c.," is sufficient where the affidavit is entitled in the proper court. *Kennett and Avon Canal Company* v. *Jones*, 7 T. R. 451 ; *Burdekin* v. *Potter*, 9 M. & W. 13 ; 1 Dowl. N. S. 134 ; *Munden* v. *Duke of Brunswick*, 4 C. B. 321 ; 4 Dowl. & L. 807 ; but the "&c." should not be omitted ; *Hill* v. *Royston*, 7 Jur. 930. "By commission" is sufficient. *Hopkins* v. *Pledger*, 1 Dowl. & L. 119 ; *Fairbrass* v. *Pettit*, 12 M. & W. 453 ; 1 Dowl. & L. 622.

The Chief Justice's clerk's list of commissioners is conclusive evidence as to whether a particular person is a commissioner of the English court for taking affidavits in Scotland or Ireland, pursuant to 3 & 4 Will. 4, c. 42, s. 42. *Sharpe* v. *Johnson*, 4 Dowl. 314 ; 2 Bing N. C. 246 ; 2 Scott, 405, *S. C.*

Exhibits.—A commissioner before whom an affidavit is sworn ought to certify that any exhibit annexed (or produced) is the document referred to in the affidavit. In *Re Allison*, 10 Exch. 561. The certificate should be written on some convenient part of the exhibit; the form may be as follows :—

"This is the [paper writing] marked [A] referred to in the affidavit of [*name of deponent*] sworn before me on this —— day of ——, 18—.

(Signed) ——, a Commissioner, &c.

20. Affidavit (General Form) by two or more Deponents (a).
Title of court and cause as ante, No. 19.

We, A. B. of [*state deponent's true place of abode and addition*] ——, in the county of ——, Esq., [the above named plaintiff or defendant, *or* one of the above-named plaintiffs *or* defendants, *as the case may be*]; E. F., clerk to G. H., of ——, the attorney in this cause for the above-named ——; and J. K. of ——, *broker*, severally make oath and say [as follows :]

1. [I, the said A. B. say] That [*here state some distinct portion of the subject, clearly and concisely, and in the first person.*]
2. [We the said E. F. and J. K., severally say] That, &c., *ut supra.*
3. [I, the said J. K. say] That, &c., *ut supra.*
4. [We, the said A. B., E. F. and J. K., severally say] That, &c., *ut supra.*

The above-named deponents A. B., E. F.
and J. K. (*b*) were severally sworn at
——, in the [county] of ——, on the
—— day of ——, 18—,
                  Signatures of the
                  deponents.

Before me,
             ——, a commissioner, &c.

For other forms of jurat, see ante, 705, *but mention the names of the deponents in the jurat,* ut supra.

---

21. Solemn Affirmation, in lieu of an Affidavit.
Title of court and cause, as ante, No. 19.

I, A. B., of ——, in the county of ——, [grocer], do solemnly, sincerely and truly affirm and declare, that the taking of any oath is according to my religious belief unlawful : And I do also solemnly, sincerely and truly affirm and declare,—

1. That [&c.]
                      (Signed)   A. B.

Solemnly affirmed at ——, in the [county]
of ——, on the —— day of ——, 18—,
                Before me,
           O. P., a commissioner, &c.

N.B. *A solemn affirmation in lieu of an oath should not be permitted unless the judge or commissioner be " satisfied of the sincerity" of the objection to be sworn from conscientious motives.* 17 & 18 Vict. c. 125, s. 20 (*ante*, 292).

---

22. Judge's Summons (Outline of).

B. [and another,
or others,]
         v.
D. [and another,
or others.]
             Let the [plaintiffs' *or* defendants'] attorney or agent attend me at my chambers in Rolls' Garden, [tomorrow, *or* on —— day next], at —— of the clock in the ——noon, to show cause why [*here state the subject matter, as the case may require.*]

Dated the —— day of ——, 18—.

                         Judge's signature.

N.B.—*If to be attended by counsel, add a memorandum thus :—*" The [plaintiff *or* defendant, *or* defendant C. D., *as the case may be*], will attend by counsel." 2 Chit. Arch. 1501 (9th ed.).

" The costs of attending by counsel, or special pleader before a judge at

---

(*a*) See notes to No. 19.
(*b*) See rule No. 139, and the other rules, *ante*, 706.

chambers, shall in no case be allowed, as between party and party, unless the judge shall certify for such allowance." Directions to the Masters, H. T., 1853, No. 6.

The summons must be served before seven o'clock, P.M., on any day except Saturday, and before two o'clock, P.M., on that day. Reg. E. T. 1856, *ante*, 147.

In Term time, summonses are usually made returnable at three o'clock in the afternoon : in vacation at eleven o'clock in the forenoon. But they may be made returnable at ten o'clock at Westminster. *Blake* v. *Warren*, 6 M. & W. 151; 8 Dowl. 173; 2 Chit. Arch. 1502. A summons is no stay of proceedings *until returnable; Calze* v. *Lord Lyttelton*, 2 W. Blac. 954; when returnable it operates as a stay of proceedings, if so expressed, or if its nature be such as to render a stay of further proceedings necessary; 2 Chit. Arch. 1502 (9th ed.); *Morris* v. *Hunt*, 2 B. & A. 355; *Wells* v. *Secret*, 2 Dowl. 447; *Byles* v. *Walker*, 5 Dowl. 232; *Spenceley* v. *Shouls*, Id. 562; *Beazley* v. *Bailey*, 16 M. & W. 58; 4 D. & L. 271; but not otherwise, *Phillips* v. *Birch*, 4 Man. & Gr. 403; 2 Dowl. N. S. 97. If then adjourned by consent, or by direction of the judge, it stays all further proceedings until finally disposed of. *Sarjent* v. *Brown*, 2 Dowl. N. S. 985; 2 Chit. Arch. 1503, 1505 (9th ed.) If unsuccessful, the applicant has the remainder of the day on which the application is refused, to take the next step. *Mengens* v. *Perry*, 15 M. & W. 537; *Evans* v. *Senior*, 4 Exch. 818; 1 Low. M. & P. 170; 2 Chit. Arch. 1492, 1506 (9th ed.)

If the facts upon which the application is founded be not disputed (as is frequently the case at chambers), they need not be proved by affidavit, but the judge will act upon the uncontradicted statements of each party, or of his attorney or agent. *Power* v. *Jones*, 6 Exch. 121; *Doe* d. *Childs* v. *Roe*, 1 E. & B. 279. And in such case if a subsequent application be made to the court to set aside the judge's order, the facts stated before the judge, and upon which his order was made, must be brought before the court by affidavit. *Doe* d. *Beard* v. *Roe*, 1 M. & W. 360; *Doe* d. *Child* v. *Roe*, 1 E. & B. 279. But either party may require before the judge, that the facts upon which the application is founded or opposed shall be proved by affidavit. And in such case the judge will generally adjourn the hearing of the summons until a particular day, to enable the parties to obtain such affidavits as appear to be necessary.

---

23. *Affidavit of Service of Summons, and Attendance thereon.*
Title of court and cause, as ante, No. 19.

I, M. N., clerk to ——, of ——, gent., the [attorney *or* agent] in this action for the [plaintiff *or* defendant, *or* defendant C. D., *as the case may be*], make oath and say,—

1. I did, on the —— day of —— [instant *or* last] [personally] serve Mr. ——, the [attorney *or* agent] in this action for the ——, with a true copy of the summons hereunto annexed. [*If the service were not personal, omit the word* " personally," *and say* " by delivering such copy to and leaving the same with [a clerk, *or* female servant *or* man servant, *as the case may be*] of the said ——, at his chambers *or* dwelling-house, situate ——.

2. I did, on the —— day of —— instant, duly attend the said summons from [eleven] of the clock till [half-past eleven] of the clock in the [fore]noon of that day, at the chambers of [the Lord Chief Justice of this Honourable Court, *or* Lord Chief Baron of this Honourable Court, *or* at the Queen's Bench *or* Common Pleas, *or* Exchequer Judge's Chambers, in Rolls Gardens, Chancery Lane. But the [plaintiff's *or* defendant's] attor-

ney or agent did nôt attend the said summons, nor did any person attend the same on his behalf, to my knowledge or belief.

Sworn, &c. (*ante*, 705.)

---

24. *Judge's Order (Outline of).*

B. [and another } Upon [reading the several affidavits of —— and ——,
   or others]   and the paper writings thereto respectively annexed,
   v.   and upon] hearing the attornies or agents on both
D. [and another sides, [*or* for, &c., *or* counsel on both sides, *or* coun-
   or others.]   sel for the ——, and the attorney or agent for the
——, *or as the case may be: if made by consent say,* " and by consent,"] I do order that [*here state the subject-matter of the order, as the case may require. If counsel allowed, say,* " counsel allowed."] Dated the —— day of ——, 18—.

                                      [*Judge's signature.*]

N.B.—*A Judge's order is generally as effectual as a rule of court, except for the purposes of an attachment.* 2 Chit. Arch. 1507 (9th ed.) *But in many cases a summons and order will not be granted* during term time, *on the ground that the application is of such a nature that it should be made to the court.* 2 Chit. Arch. 1499 (9th ed.) *A judge at chambers acts as the deputy or representative of the court; and his power (especially in vacation) is nearly as extensive as that of the court.* Smeeton *v.* Collier, 1 Exch. 457; 5 Dowl. & L. 184; Ross *v.* Gandell, 7 C. B. 766.

The party in whose favour an order is made has generally the option of drawing it up, or abandoning it. M'Dougall *v.* Nicholls, 3 A. & E. 813; 5 N. & M. 366; Solly *v.* Richardson, 6 Dowl. 774; 2 Chit. Arch. 1507 (9th ed.) *He has a sort of* locus pœnitentiæ *until the order be drawn up and served, or otherwise acted on;* 4 Mee. & W. 67; Parke, B.; *but not afterwards.* Griffin *v.* Dickinson, 7 Dowl. 860; Geraud *v.* Austin, 1 Dowl. N. S. 703.

Generally speaking, an erroneous order made by a judge at chambers may be set aside upon application to the court, 2 Chit. Arch. 1509 (9th ed.), *provided the order be not made* " by consent," Hall *v.* West, 1 Dowl. & L. 412; Leach *v.* Swallow, 8 Dowl. 199, 201; Firth *v.* Harris, Id. 437, *and the application be made within a reasonable time;* i. e. *before the end of the term next after the date and making of the order;* Meredith *v.* Gittens, 21 Law J., N. S., Q. B. 273; Orchard *v.* Moxey, Id., Exchequer, 79, n.; Collins *v.* Johnson, 16 C. B. 588, 1608; *and the applicant have not, by accepting costs or other benefit under the order, precluded himself from moving to set it aside.* Pearce *v.* Chaplin, 9 Q. B. 802; Tinkler *v.* Hilder, 4 Exch. 187; 7 Dowl. & L. 61; King *v.* Simmonds, 2 Dowl. & L. 786; 7 Q. B. 293, n. *The affidavits (if any) upon which the order was made must be brought before the court upon the application to set aside the order. So must any facts stated* orally *before the judge by either party, and upon which the judge acted.* Doe d. Beard *v.* Roe, 1 M. & W. 360; Doe d. Child *v.* Roe, 1 E. & B. 279. *New or additional facts may also be proved by affidavit.* Gibbons *v.* Spalding, 11 M. & W. 173; Sanderson *v.* Proctor, 10 Exch. 189; Peterson *v.* Davis, 6 C. B. 235; 6 Dowl. & L. 79; Pike *v.* Davis, 6 M. & W. 546; 8 Dowl. 387: *but see* Hawkins *v.* Akrill; 1 Low. M. & P. 242; Alexander *v.* Porter, 1 Dowl. N. S. 299.

An application is sometimes made to the judge at chambers to rescind his own order: such application will be deemed an election *to appeal to the judge himself, instead of to the court; consequently no further application to the court will be permitted.* Thompson *v.* Becke, 4 Q. B. 759; 1 Dav. & M. 49; 2 Dowl. & L. 786. *But see* Grandin *v.* Maddams, 6 Dowl. & L. 241; Re Stretton, 14 M. & W. 806; 3 Dowl. & L. 278; Peterson *v.* Davis, 6 C. B. 235; 6 Dowl. & L. 79.

---

25. *Rule Nisi (Outline of).*

In the [Q. B., C. P. *or* Exch.]

[Mon]day, the —— day of ——, 18—.

B. [and another] ⎱ Upon reading the affidavit of ——, and the paper
v. ⎰ writing thereto annexed, and the several affidavits of
D. [and others.] —— and —— ; and upon hearing Mr. ——, of counsel for —— : It is ordered, that the [plaintiffs *or* defendants, *or as the case may be*] do on —— day, the —— day of —— [instant *or* next], show cause why [*here state the subject-matter of the rule ; in some cases, the grounds upon which the rule nisi is granted must be shortly stated therein,* 17 & 18 *Vict. c.* 125, *s.* 33: [And that in the meantime all further proceedings be stayed (*c*):] Upon notice of this rule to be given to the said ——, or his attorney, [*or their respective attorneys*], in the meantime.

By the Court.

---

26. *Affidavit of Service of a Rule Nisi.*
Title of court and cause, as ante, No. 19.

I, A. B., clerk to C. D. of ——, gent., the [attorney *or* agent] in this action for the ——, make oath and say,

1. I did on the —— day of —— [instant *or* last] [personally] serve Mr. ——, the [attorney *or* agent] in this action for the ——, with a true copy of the rule hereunto annexed ; *if the service were not personal omit the word "personally" and say,* " by delivering such a copy to, and leaving the same with, a [clerk *or* female servant] of the said Mr. ——, at his [chambers *or* dwelling-house], situate, &c.

Sworn, &c. (*ante,* 705.)

N.B.—*The affidavit need not state that the original rule was produced and shown at the time of service.* Doe *d.* Wright *v.* Roe, 6 M. & S. 230, note (*c*); *except in cases of attachment, when the service must be personal.*

---

27. *The like in another Form, not annexing the Rule Nisi.*
Commence as ante, No. 26.

I did on the —— day of —— [instant *or* last] [personally] serve Mr. ——, the [attorney *or* agent] in this action for the [above-named plaintiffs *or* defendants —— —— *as the case may be*] with a true copy of a rule of this honourable court made in this cause on the —— day of —— [instant *or* last], (another true copy of which said rule is hereunto annexed marked A). *If the service were not personal omit the word "* personally," *and say* " by delivering such first-mentioned copy to and leaving the same with a [clerk *or* female servant] of the said ——, Mr. ——, at his [chambers *or* dwelling-house] situate ——."

Sworn, &c. (*ante,* 705.)

N.B.—*The affidavit need not state that the original rule was produced and shown at the time of service* (Doe *d.* Wright *v.* Roe, 6 M. & S. 230, note)(*c*); *except in cases of attachment, when the service must be personal.*

(*c*) By Reg. Prac. H. T. 1853, No. 160, " Rules to show cause shall be no stay of proceedings unless two days' notice of the motion shall have been served on the opposite party, except in the cases of rules for new trials, or to enter a verdict or nonsuit, notice in arrest of judgment, or for judgment *non obstante veredicto,* to set aside an award, or an annuity deed, or to enter a suggestion, or by the special direction of the court."

28. *Rule absolute (Outline of).*

In the [Q. B., C. P. *or* Exch.]

　　　　　　　　　　　　[Thurs]day, the —— day of —— 18—.

B. [and another] ⎫　Upon reading the several affidavits of —— and
　　　　v.　　　⎬　—— and the affidavit of ——, and the paper writing
D. [and others].　⎭　thereto annexed; and upon hearing counsel [on both
sides, *or as the case may be*]: It is ordered, that [*here state the order according
to the decision of the court*].

　　　　　　　　Mr. —— for the plaintiffs.
　　　　　　　　Mr. —— for the defendants.
　　　　　　　　　　　　　　　By the Court.

———

29. *Affidavit of personal Service of the Writ* (*ante*, 99, 111).
Commence as ante, Nos. 19, 20, *or* 21.

1. That the paper writing hereunto annexed, marked (A), is a true copy of
the writ of ejectment issued in this action out of and under the seal of this
honourable court, and of the indorsement on the said writ before the service
thereof as hereinafter mentioned.

2. I did, on the —— day of —— [instant *or* last] *personally* serve the
above named C. D., tenant in possession of [part of] the property in the
said writ mentioned, with a true copy of the said writ and of the said
indorsement thereon (*d*).

Sworn, &c. (*ante*, 705.)

———

30. *Affidavit of Service of the Writ on Tenant's Wife* (*ante*, 101, 112).
Commence as ante, Nos. 19, 20 *or* 21.

1. That the paper writing hereunto annexed, marked (A), is a true copy of
the writ of ejectment issued in this action out of and under the seal of this
honourable court, and of the indorsement on the said writ before the service
thereof as hereinafter mentioned.

2. I did on the —— day of —— [instant *or* last] serve the above
named C. D., tenant in possession of [part of] the property in the said
writ mentioned, with a true copy of the said writ, and of the said indorsement thereon,* by delivering such true copy to and leaving the same with
[Mary D. (*e*)], the wife of the said C. D., at his [dwelling-house *or* place of
residence *or* place of business] situate on and being part of the property in
the said writ mentioned, [*if situate elsewhere, say* situate at —— in the
county of ——, and at the time of such service the said C. D. and the said
Mary(*e*) D. were living together as man and wife] (*d*).

Sworn, &c. (*ante*, 705.)

———

31. *Affidavit of Service of the Writ on Tenant's Servant, or some Member of his
Family* (*ante*, 102, 113).
Same as ante, No. 30, *to the* *.

By delivering such true copy to and leaving the same with the [son *or*
daughter, *or* female servant *or* man servant, *as the case may be*] of the said

———

(*d*) It seems unnecessary to add, "And at the same time I explained to
the said C. D. the intent and meaning of such service" (*ante*, 100). But
such words can do no harm if the explanation were really made.

Let the paper annexed be marked as an exhibit in the usual manner.

(*e*) If wife's christian name be unknown call her "Mrs. D."

C. D. at the dwelling-house [*or* place of residence] of the said C. D. situate on and being part of the property in the said writ mentioned (*g*).

3. On the —— day of —— [instant *or* last] I again called at the said dwelling-house [*or* place of residence] of the said C. D. when the said [*son, &c. as the case may be*] informed me that he had delivered to the said C. D. the said copy writ so served as aforesaid (*h*), which information I verily believe to be true.

Or instead of the above, say—

3. On the —— day of —— [instant *or* last] I saw the said C. D. when he mentioned that he had received the said copy writ so served as aforesaid.

Sworn, &c. (*ante*, 705.)

———

32. *Affidavit of Service of Writ on the Tenant's Attorney, Agent or Bailiff* (*ante*, 104, 113).

Same as ante, No. 30, to the *.

By delivering such copy to and leaving the same with G. H., the [attorney *or* agent *or* bailiff] of the said C. D. on the property in the said writ mentioned, the said C. D. and his family then being absent therefrom.

3. *Here state facts showing specially the authority of G. H. to accept service of the copy writ. It will not be sufficient that G. H. said he had such authority, because such statement may have been false and made collusively ; but facts must be stated showing that G. H. really had such authority, or from which that may reasonably be inferred.*

4. *If another copy of the writ, &c. were affixed on the outer door state the fact. See next form.*

Sworn, &c. (*ante* 705.)

———

33. *Affidavit of Service of Writ, where the Tenant is abroad, or has absconded, or evades Service* (*ante*, 105, 113).

Same as ante, No. 30, to the *.

By affixing such copy on the [front outer door of the principal messuage, *or on some other conspicuous part, describing it*] of the [said part of the] property in the said writ mentioned, no person being then in or upon the [said part of the] said property, or any part thereof, to the best of my knowledge and belief.

3. *Here state specially the facts, showing that C. D. is abroad or has absconded or keeps out of the way to evade service of the writ.* See Chit. Forms, 53 (7th ed.) *If any such facts are stated upon information, the affidavit should mention by whom it was given, and the deponent should pledge his belief of its truth.*

4. For the reasons and under the circumstances above stated, I verily believe that the said C. D. [is abroad, *or* has absconded to avoid his creditors, *or* keeps out of the way to avoid being served with the writ in this action.]

Sworn, &c. (*ante*, 705.)

If any other service has been made on the attorney, agent or bailiff of C. D., state it, as in No. 32.

———

(*g*) See note to No. 29.

(*h*) Or state whatever was said, tending to show that the copy writ reached the hands of C. D. and deponent's belief of the truth. If the party served can be induced to join in the affidavit so much the better (*ante*, 113).

———

34. *Affidavit of Service of Writ on one of several Joint Tenants* (*ante*, 108, 113).

Commence as ante, Nos. 19, 20 *or* 21.

1. That the paper writing hereunto annexed, marked (A) is a true copy of the writ of ejectment issued in this action out of and under the seal of this honourable court, and of the indorsement on the said writ before the service thereof as hereinafter mentioned.

2. I did on the —— day of —— [instant *or* last] serve the above-named C. D., E. F. and G. H., tenants in possession of [part of] the property in the said writ mentioned with a true copy of the said writ, and of the said indorsement thereon, by delivering such copy to and leaving the same with the said [E. F.] on the said [part of the said] property (*i*).

3. At the time of the said service, the said C. D., E. F. and G. H. were in possession of the said [part of the said] property as joint tenants thereof and not otherwise [*add, if the fact*, and they carried on therein their trade and business of —— in co-partnership together, under the name, style or firm of [C. D. and Company.]

Sworn, &c. (*ante* 705.)

----

35. *Affidavit of Service of Writ on one of several Executors* (*ante*, 108).

Same as ante, No. 34, but instead of Clause 3, say—

3. Before the said service the said C. D., E. F. and G. H. had entered into possession of the said [part of the said] property, as executors of the last will and testament of O. P. deceased, and at the time of the said service they the said C. D., E. F. and G. H. were possessed of the said [part of the said] property jointly as such executors as aforesaid, and not otherwise.

Sworn, &c. (*ante*, 705.)

----

36. *Affidavit of Service of Writ pursuant to the Companies Clauses Consolidation Act,* 1845 (*ante*, 108, 113).

Commence as ante, Nos. 19, 20 *or* 21.

1. That the paper writing hereunto annexed, marked (A), is a true copy of the writ of ejectment issued in this action out of and under the seal of this honourable court, and of the indorsement on the said writ before the service thereof as hereinafter mentioned.

2. On the —— day of —— [last *or* instant] I served the [*name of the company*], tenants in possession of the property in the said writ mentioned, with a true copy of the said writ, and of the said indorsement thereon, by leaving such copy with one of their clerks at their principal office, situate [&c.], *or* by transmitting such copy through the post in an envelope, directed to the said company at their principal office [*or* at one of their principal offices], situate [&c.] That such direction was in the following words [*copy it verbatim*] ; and the postage was prepaid by a proper stamp or stamps affixed on the said envelope ; *or say*, " by delivering the same personally to the secretary of the said company," *or say*, "by delivering the same personally to M. N., Esq., one of the directors of the said company (the said company not then having any secretary)."

Take care to show a service in strict compliance with the act relating to the company (*ante*, 113).

Sworn, &c. (*ante*, 705.)

N.B.—*On submitting this affidavit to the judge draw his attention to the particular act and section pursuant to which the service was made.*

(*i*) See the note to No. 29.

37. *Affidavit of Service of the Writ in Ejectment in a Case of vacant Possession*
(ante, 110).

Commence as ante, Nos. 19, 20 *or* 21.

1. That the paper writing hereunto annexed, marked (A), is a true copy of the writ of ejectment issued in this action out of and under the seal of this honourable court, and of the indorsement on the said writ before the service thereof as hereinafter mentioned.

2. On the —— day of —— [instant *or* last], I posted a copy of the said writ, and of the said indorsement thereon, upon the front door of the principal dwelling-house on the land in the said writ mentioned [*or on some other conspicuous part of the property, according to the fact*].

3. At the time of such service the said premises in the said writ mentioned were vacant and deserted by the above-named C. D., who lately was in possession and occupation of the same as tenant thereof [to the above-named plaintiff]; but no person (except myself) was in or upon the said premises, or any part thereof, at the time I posted the said copy writ as aforesaid, to the best of my knowledge and belief: And the said C. D. had before then removed himself and his family, and his goods and chattels, from the said premises, and had utterly deserted and abandoned the possession of the said premises, and no person was then in possession of the said premises or any part thereof, to the best of my knowledge and belief.

4. *Here state specially any other facts tending to corroborate the above, ex. gr. information from neighbours, tax collectors and others, adding deponent's belief that such information is true.*

5. *If ejectment brought for non-payment of rent, show arrears due, and no sufficient distress, as in Form No.* 40. *If for non-repair, non-cultivation or other breach of covenant, state the lease and the particular covenant, and the proviso for re-entry, and the facts necessary to show a breach of covenant, and a right to re-enter for such breach.*

Sworn, &c. (*ante,* 705.)

---

38. *Judge's Order for Leave to serve the Writ in a particular manner, and in case of Non-appearance to sign Judgment (ante, 98, 114).*

Commence as ante, No. 24.

I do order that the plaintiffs be at liberty to serve the defendant [C. D.] with the writ of ejectment issued in this action in manner following, viz., by affixing or posting a copy of the said writ, together with this order, or a duplicate hereof, on [*describe some conspicuous part of the property*]; and by delivering another copy of the said writ, together with a copy of this order, or of a duplicate hereof, to ——, at —— [*describe the person and place with reasonable certainty*]: And in case the said C. D. shall not appear in this action within [sixteen] days next after such service as aforesaid, I do order that the plaintiffs be at liberty to sign judgment in this action against the said C. D. for want of appearance or defence by him, on filing with the master an affidavit of such service, together with a copy of the said writ. Dated the —— day of ——, 18—.

Judge's signature.

N.B.—*A rule of court to the above effect may easily be framed.*

---

39. *Judge's Order for Leave to sign Judgment for Want of Appearance or Defence (ante,* 98, 114).

B. [and another] ⎫ Upon reading the affidavit of ——, and the paper
    v.   ⎬ writing thereto annexed, I do order that the plain-
D. [and others]. ⎭ tiffs be at liberty to sign judgment in this action of ejectment against the defendant C. D., for want of appearance or defence by him. Dated the —— day of ——, 18—.

[*Judge's signature.*]

40. *Affidavit for Order or Rule for Leave to sign Judgment pursuant to Sect.* 210 *of the Common Law Procedure Act,* 1852 (*ante,* 417).

Commence as ante, Nos. 19, 20 *or* 21. *Then state service of the writ, as* ante, *Nos.* 29, 30, 31 *or* 37.

3. I, the said ——, say, that the said C. D. hath not appeared in this action, and that the time for such appearance has elapsed.

4. I, the said ——, say, that I am and for many [*or* several, *or* two *or* three] years now last past, have been the [steward *or* agent, and] receiver of rents of the above-named plaintiff [*omit this, if the plaintiff himself joins in the affidavit*].

5. I, the said ——, say, that before and at the time when the said writ was served as aforesaid, there was due to [me *or* to the said A. B.], as landlord of the said [messuage, land and] premises, for the recovery of the possession of which this action is brought, from the said C. D., who then was the tenant thereof, the sum of [£50] for half a year's rent of the same, which became due on the —— day of ——, A.D. 18—, *or say,* "at Lady Day last," *or as the case may be,* [and also the further sum of £200 for previous arrears of rent of the same premises, then and still remaining unpaid, making together the sum of £250], under and by virtue of [an indenture of lease *or* a lease in writing, dated the —— day of ——, A.D. 18—, and made between [me *or* the said A. B.], of the one part, and the said C. D., of the other part. And that [I *or* the said A. B.], before and at the time of the service of the said writ as aforesaid, had power to re-enter the said [messuage, land] and premises for nonpayment of [the said rent so in arrear as aforesaid *or* for nonpayment of the said half-year's rent which so as aforesaid became due on the —— day of ——, 18—, *or* at Lady Day last, *or as the case may be.* And also for non-payment of the said previous rent so in arrear as aforesaid, and for nonpayment of every or any part thereof respectively], under and by virtue of the said lease, and a condition or proviso for re-entry in that behalf contained in the said lease.]

6. I, the said ——, say, that I did on the —— day of —— last [*some day very shortly before the writ in ejectment issued, or at all events before it was served*] carefully inspect and examine the [messuage, land] and premises sought to be recovered in this action for the purpose of ascertaining whether there was to be found in or upon the said [messuage, land] and premises, or any part thereof respectively, a sufficient distress to countervail the arrears of rent due to the said plaintiff as aforesaid, or any part thereof. And I say, that there was not on the said —— day of —— last, nor at the time of the commencement of this action, nor when the said writ was served as aforesaid, in or upon the said [messuage, land] and premises, or any part thereof respectively, a sufficient distress to countervail the said arrears of rent due to the said plaintiff as aforesaid [*add, if the fact,* nor a sufficient distress to countervail the said rent or sum of £50, which so as aforesaid became due from the said defendant to the said plaintiff, for the half year ending on the said —— day of —— 18—, *or* on Lady-day last, *or as the case may be*].

Sworn by, &c. (*ante,* 708).

N.B.—*The above affidavit should be laid before a judge at his chambers, indorsed in the usual manner and with a memorandum as follows :* "For an order for leave to sign judgment pursuant to 15 & 16 Vict. c. 76, s. 210." *An ordinary judgment for want of appearance has not the same effect as a judgment under this section* (*ante,* 418).

———

41. *Order for Leave to sign Judgment pursuant to* 15 & 16 *Vict. c.* 76, *s.* 210 (*ante,* 417).

B. ⎰Upon reading the affidavit of —— and others, and the paper writing
v. ⎱ thereto annexed, I do order that the plaintiff be at liberty to sign
D. ⎰ judgment in this action pursuant to the 210th section of the Common Law Procedure Act, 1852. Dated the —— day of —— 18—.

As to the form of judgment, see ante, 417, 418.   *Judge's signature.*

42. Affidavit (k) to compel a Tenant to give Security, pursuant to 15 & 16 Vict. c. 76, s. 213 (ante, 379, 382).

Commence as ante, Nos. 19, 20 *or* 21.

1. [I, the said A. B. say], that by a [lease *or* agreement in writing, bearing date the —— day of ——], in the year 18—, and made between [me] the said A. B., of the one part, and the defendant C. D., of the other part; [I], the said A. B., did [demise *or* agree to let] to the said C. D. [a certain dwelling-house and premises *or* a certain farm, lands and premises, *or as the case may be*], with the appurtenances, situate and being [No. —— in —— street], in the parish of ——, in the county of —— (being the tenements and premises, with the appurtenances, for the recovery whereof this action of ejectment is brought), To hold the same to the said C. D. [his executors, administrators and assigns], from the —— day of ——, in the year 18—, for the term of —— years, *or* from year to year, *or* for one year certain, and so on from year to year, *according to the fact*], at the rent and subject to the terms and conditions in the said [lease *or* agreement] mentioned.

2. [I, the said A. B., say], that the [parchment *or* paper] writing now produced to me, marked [A], is [the lease *or* agreement, *or* a counterpart *or* duplicate of the said lease *or* agreement, *as the case may be*] so made as aforesaid.

3. [I, the said ——, say], that I was present and did see (*l*) the defendant C. D. [sign, seal and deliver as his act and deed, *or* sign] the [lease *or* agreement, *or* counterpart, *or* duplicate, marked A, now produced to me, and that the name C. D., subscribed thereto] as a party executing the same, is of the proper handwriting of the said C. D. And the name ——, set and subscribed [thereto *or* to the memorandum of attestation indorsed thereon], as the attesting witness, is of the proper handwriting of me the said ——.

4. We, the said —— and ——, severally, say, that the [tenements] and premises sought to be recovered in this action have been actually enjoyed by the defendant C. D. under the above-mentioned [lease *or* agreement]. And that the term and interest of the said C. D. in the said premises [expired by effluxion of time, *or* were determined by a regular notice to quit], on the —— day of —— last.

5. I, the said ——, say, that after the said term and interest of the defendant C. D. in the said premises [had so expired *or* had been so determined] as aforesaid, that is to say, on the —— day of ——, in the year 18—, I, the said ——, did [personally] serve the said C. D. with a demand in writing, made and signed by [the said A.B., *or* by ——, the agent of and for the said A. B.], requiring the said C. D. forthwith to quit and deliver up possession of the aforesaid premises to the said A. B. [*if the demand were not served* "personally," *omit that word and say*, by leaving such demand at the dwelling-house *or* usual place of abode of the said C. D., situate and being No. —— in —— street, in the parish of ——, in the county of ——, with the [wife *or* son, daughter *or* female servant, *as the case may be*] of the said C. D.] And that the paper writing hereunto annexed, marked (B), is a [duplicate *or* a true copy] of the said demand in writing so served as aforesaid.

6. I, the said ——, say, that [*here show a "refusal" by C. D. to deliver up possession, ex gr.,* at the time when the said demand of possession was so served upon the said C. D. as aforesaid, he the said C. D., after reading the said demand, said that he would not deliver up possession of the property

---

(*k*) This affidavit may, if wished, be separated into two or three distinct affidavits. Vide s. 213, *ante*, 382.

(*l*) The attesting witness need not join in the affidavit. 2 Chit. Arch. 1003, 9th Ed.; Chit. Forms, 558. As to the mode of proof in that case, see *ante*, 383.

until Michaelmas next. [*This part of the affidavit must of course vary in each particular case. If the notice were not served personally, a subsequent application to C. D. should be shown, and an express refusal to deliver up possession, or facts tantamount to such refusal, should be sworn to. Ante,* 382; Chit. Forms, 559.

7. I, the said ——, say, that after such demand and refusal as aforesaid, that is to say, on the —— day of ——, in the year 18—, this action was commenced by a writ in ejectment, duly issued out of and under the seal of this honourable court, with a notice at the foot of the said writ, as follows [*copy notice*].

8. I, the said ——, say, that the paper writing hereunto annexed, marked (C), is a true copy of the said writ and of the said notice, and of the indorsements made on the said writ before the service thereof, as hereinafter mentioned.

9. I, the said ——, say, that I did on the —— day of —— [instant *or* last] [personally] serve the defendant C. D. with a true copy of the said writ, and of the said notice at the foot of the said writ, and of the said indorsements on the said writ. [*If the service were not made "personally," omit that word, and say,* by leaving the same with the wife, *or* son, *or* daughter, *or* female servant of the said C. D. at his dwelling-house *or* usual place of abode, situate and being at No. ——, in —— street, in the parish of ——, in the county of ——].

10. I, the said ——, say, that on the —— day of —— [instant *or* last], the said C. D. appeared to the said writ [by G. H., his attorney, *or* in his proper person, *as the case may be*].

Sworn by, &c. (*ante,* 708).

N.B.—*Let the lease or agreement produced to the deponents be marked as an exhibit. It is not absolutely necessary that the landlord join in the above affidavit. His steward, bailiff, attorney, or agent, may be able to swear to the facts. The above form may be easily altered in such case. For other similar forms, see* Chit. Forms, 558, 559 (7th Ed.).

---

43. *Rule Nisi for Bail* (*ante,* 379, 384).
Commence as ante, No. 25.

Why the defendant should not, within a time to be fixed by the court upon a consideration of all the circumstances, enter into a recognizance by himself and two sufficient sureties in a reasonable sum, conditioned to pay the costs and damages which shall be recovered in this action by the claimant, pursuant to the 213th section of the Common Law Procedure Act, 1852, upon notice of this rule to be given to the defendant or his attorney in the mean time.

By the Court.

N.B.—*The above rule should be made returnable at a time to be fixed by the court on a consideration of the situation of the premises.* 15 & 16 Vict. c. 76, s. 213 (*ante,* 384).

---

44. *Rule absolute for Bail* (*ante,* 385).
Commence as ante, No. 28.

It is ordered that the defendant do within the space of —— days from this day enter into a recognizance by himself and two sufficient sureties in the sum of £—— (*m*), conditioned to pay the costs and damages which shall be recovered in this action by the claimants, pursuant to the 213th section of the Common Law Procedure Act, 1852.

Mr. —— for the plaintiff.
Mr. —— for the defendant.
By the Court.

(*m*) *Ante,* 384.

45. *Summons for Bail to pay the Costs and Damages* (*ante*, 379, 384).

Commence as ante, No. 22.

Why the defendant should not, within a time to be fixed by me upon a consideration of all the circumstances, enter into a recognizance by himself and two sufficient sureties in such sum as I shall think reasonable in that behalf, conditioned to pay the costs and damages which shall be recovered in this action by the claimants, pursuant to the 213th section of the Common Law Procedure Act, 1852. Dated the —— day of ——, 18—.

Judge's signature.

N.B.—*The above summons should be made returnable at a time to be fixed by the judge on a consideration of the situation of the premises.* 15 & 16 Vict. c. 76, s. 213 (ante, 384).

---

46. *Order thereon.*

Commence as ante, No. 24.

I do order that the defendant do within —— days from this day enter into a recognizance by himself and two sufficient sureties in the sum of £——(*n*), conditioned to pay the costs and damages which shall be recovered in this action by the claimant, pursuant to the 213th section of the Common Law Procedure Act, 1852. Dated the —— day of ——, 18—.

Judge's signature.

---

47. *Summons to enlarge the Time for putting in Bail* (*ante*, 386).

Commence as ante, No. 22.

Why the time for the defendant to put in bail, pursuant to the [rule of court *or* the order of Mr. Justice (*or* Baron) ——,] made in this action, on the —— day of ——, 18—, should not be enlarged until the —— day of —— next, inclusive. Dated the —— day of ——, 18—.

Judge's signature.

N.B.—*The order will follow the language of the summons.*

---

48. *Recognizance of Bail* (*ante*, 385).

In the [Q. B., C. P., *or* Exch.]

    The —— day of —— A. D. 18—.

——
to wit. } A. B. against C. D.

Ejectment for the recovery of [*as in the writ*], with the appurtenances, in the parish of —— in the county of ——.

The sureties are—

    M. N. of —— in the county of —— [grocer],

        and

    O. P. of —— in the county of —— [esq.]

Recognizance of the above-named defendant } and his sureties, in £——.

By rule of Court [*or* by order of the Hon. Mr. Justice (*or* Baron) ——,] dated the —— day of ——, 18—.

        G. H., of ——,

           Defendant's attorney.

Taken and acknowledged conditionally, this } —— day of ——, 18—.

        Before me,

        Judge's signature.   (*See over.*)

(*n*) *Ante*, 384.

Acknowledgment of the above Recognizance.

You do jointly and severally acknowledge to owe to the above-named
A. B. the sum of £ ——, on condition that you, C. D., shall pay the costs
and damages (if any) which shall be recovered by the said A. B. in this
action. Are you content?

N.B.—*To save trouble each of the bail may make an affidavit of justification,
pursuant to* Reg. Prac. H. T. 1853, No. 98. *See the Form, post, No. 50.*

49. *Affidavit of taking of Bail before a Commissioner (ante, 385).*
Title of court and cause, as ante, No. 19.

I, R. S., of —— in the county of ——, [gent.], make oath and say,—
1. That the recognizance of bail or bail piece hereunto annexed was duly
taken and acknowledged by the above-named defendant C. D. and by M. N.,
of ——, and O. P., of ——, the bail therein named, before —— , gentleman,
the commissioner, who took same in my presence, on the —— day of ——,
18—, [*or* instant, *or* last past].

Sworn, &c. (*ante*, 705.)

50. *Affidavit of Justification of Bail (ante, 386).*
Title of court and cause, as ante, No. 19.

I, N. M., [of ——, grocer,] one of the bail for the above-named defendant, make oath and say,—
1. That I am a [housekeeper *or* freeholder, *as the case may be*], residing
at —— [*describing particularly the street or place, and number, if any.*]
2. That I am worth property to the amount of £—— [*the amount required
by the practice of the courts*] over and above what will pay all my just debts,
[*if bail in any other action, add,* and every other sum for which I am now
bail.]
3. That I am not bail for any defendant except in this action, [*or, if bail
in any other action or actions, add,* except for C. D., at the suit of E. F., in the
court of ——, in the sum of £——; for G. H., at the suit of I. K., in the
court of ——, in the sum of £——; *specifying the several actions, with the
courts in which they are brought, and the sums in which the deponent is bail.*]
4. That my property, to the amount of the said sum of £——, [*if bail in
any other action or actions, here add,* and of all other sums for which I am now
bail as aforesaid,] consists of [*here specify the nature and value of the property
in respect of which the bail purposes to justify, as follows :* stock in trade in my
business of ——, carried on by me at ——, of the value of £—— ; of good
book debts owing to me to the amount of £—— ; of furniture in my house,
at ——, of the value of £——; of a [freehold *or* leasehold] farm of the
value of £—— situate at ——, occupied by——; *or of other property, par-
ticularizing each description of property with the value thereof*].
5. That I have for the last six months resided at ——, [*describing the
place or places of such residence.*]

Sworn, &c. (*ante*, 705.)

N.B.—*The above form is prescribed by the Practice Rule of* H. T. 1853, No.
98, *altered to the first person, pursuant to* Reg. Mic. Vac. 1854.

51. *Notice of filing Recognizance of Bail, &c. (ante, 385).*
Title of court and cause, as ante, No. 19.

Take notice, that the recognizance entered into by the defendant and his
sureties pursuant to the [rule of court *or* order of the honourable Mr.
Justice (*or* Baron) ——], made in this cause on the —— day of ——, 18—,
was this day filed with the honourable Mr. Justice [*or* Baron] ——, at his
chambers, in Rolls Garden, Chancery Lane ; and that the names and additions

of the said sureties are M. N., of ——, in the county of ——, [grocer,] and
O. P., of ——, in the county of ——, [Esq.,] and that the said M. N. is a
[housekeeper *or* freeholder], and has, during the last six months, resided at
[*mention all the streets or places, and numbers (if any) in which M. N. has
been resident at any time within the last six months*], and that the said O. P.
is a [freeholder *or* housekeeper], and has, during the last six months,
resided at [*mention all the streets or places and numbers (if any) in which O.P.
has been resident at any time within the last six months*]. [And that each of
them, the said M. N. and O. P., has made an affidavit of justification, which
said affidavits accompany this notice, and copies whereof are herewith left.]
Dated the —— day of ——, 18—.　　　　　　　Yours, &c.
　　　　　　　　　　　　　　　G. H. of ——, defendant's attorney.
　To Mr. E. F. the plaintiff's attorney [*or* agent].

　N.B.—*The original affidavits of the bail should be produced, and copies left
with the notice ; or the original affidavits should be left with the notice and
copies kept.*

---

52. *Notice of Exception to Bail* (*ante*, 386).
　In the [Q. B., C. P., *or* Exch.]
　　A. B. *v.* C. D.
　I have excepted to the sureties put in for the defendant in this action,
and require them to justify on oath as sufficient sureties for the said
defendant. Dated the —— day of ——, 18—.
　　　　　　　　　　　　　E. F. of ——, plaintiff's attorney.
　To Mr. G. H. the defendant's attorney [*or* agent].

　N.B.—*The exception must be entered in the book kept at the judge's chambers before the above notice is given.*

---

53. *Notice of Justification of Bail* (*ante*, 386).
　　Title of court and cause, as ante, No. 19.
　Take notice that M. N. of ——, in the county of ——, [grocer,] and
O. P., of ——, in the county of ——, [Esq.,] the sureties already put in for
the defendant in this action, and of whom you have before had notice, will
on —— day next, being the —— day of —— inst., justify themselves in open
court, Westminster Hall, in the county of Middlesex, [*or* before the honourable Mr. Justice (*or* Baron) ——, or such other judge as shall be then
sitting at chambers in Rolls Gardens, Chancery Lane,] as good and sufficient
sureties for the said defendant. Dated the —— day of ——, 18—.
　　　　　　　　　　　　　　　　Yours, &c.
　　　　　　　　　　　　　G. H. of ——, defendant's attorney.
　To Mr. E. F. the plaintiff's attorney [*or* agent].

---

54. *Rule for Allowance of Bail* (*ante*, 386).
　　Commence as ante, No. 28.
　It is ordered that the sureties put in for the defendant in this action, who
have this day justified themselves in court, be allowed, and the recognizance
filed (*a*).
　　　　　　　　　Mr. —— for the plaintiff.
　　　　　　　　　Mr. —— for the defendant.
　　　　　　　　　　　　　　By the Court.

(*a*) If costs of justification ordered pursuant to the practice rule of H. T.
1853, No. 98, say, "And it is ordered that the plaintiff do pay to the
defendant, or his attorney, the costs of justification of the said sureties, to
be taxed by the master."

55. *Order for the Allowance of Bail (ante, 386).*

B. ⎱ Upon reading the affidavit of ——, and the paper writing thereto
v. ⎰ annexed, I do order that the sureties put in for the defendant in this
D. ⎰ action, who have this day justified themselves before me at my
chambers in Rolls Gardens, Chancery Lane, be allowed, and the recognizance filed. [*If costs of justification ordered pursuant to Reg. Prac. H. T.
1853, No. 98, say,* " And I order that the plaintiff do pay to the defendant
or his attorney the costs of justification of the said sureties, to be taxed by
the master.] Dated the —— day of ——, 18—.

Judge's signature.

56. *Affidavit of Service of Rule or Order for Bail, and of Noncompliance there-with (ante, 387).*

Commence as ante, Nos. 19, 20, or 21.

1. That the rule [*or order*] hereunto annexed, marked (A), was duly made
in this action, as it purports to have been.

2. I did on the —— day of —— [instant *or* last] [personally] serve the
defendant [*or* Mr. ——, the attorney in this action for the defendant] with a
true copy of the said [rule *or* order]. [*If the service were not personal, omit the
word " personally," and state the service according to the fact. See ante,
No. 26.*]

3. [*Here state any order made to enlarge the time for putting in bail.*]

4. That the defendant has not complied with the said rule [*or* order], and
no bail has yet been put in pursuant to the said rule [*or* order].

Sworn, &c. (*ante,* 705).

N. B.—*In lieu of paragraph 1, it may be stated,* that on the [*date of rule*]
—— day of ——, A. D. 18—, a rule was made in this action, whereby [*state
effect of rule*], and a true copy of which rule is hereunto annexed marked (A).

57. *Judgment for Want of Bail (ante, 387).*

In the [Q. B., C. P. *or* Exch.]

The [*date of writ*] —— day of ——, A.D. 18—.

Venue (*a*), ⎱ On the day and year above written, a writ of our lady the
to wit. ⎰ Queen issued forth of this court, with a notice thereunder
written; the tenor of which writ and notice follows in these words (that is
to say),

Victoria, by the grace of God [*here copy the writ and notice; which latter
may be as follows:*]

" Take notice, that you will be required, if ordered by the court or a
judge, to give bail by yourself and two sufficient sureties, conditioned to
pay the costs and damages which shall be recovered in this action."

And [C. D.] has appeared by ——, his attorney, [*or* in person,] to the
said writ, and has been ordered to give bail, pursuant to the statute, and has
failed so to do: therefore it is considered that the said [*here insert name
of landlord*] do recover possession of the [land *or* tenements] in the said writ
mentioned, with the appurtenances, together with £ —— for costs of suit.

N.B.—*This form is given in the Schedule to 15 & 16 Vict. c. 76, No. 21.
In the margin, opposite the words* " Therefore it is considered," &c., *write a
memorandum, thus:* " Judgment signed on the —— day of ——, 18—."

(*a*) The venue is local (*ante,* 135).

58. *Notice from Tenant to Landlord, or his Bailiff or Receiver, of a Writ in Ejectment (ante, 116).*

Address and date (as in a Letter).

[Dear] Sir,

Enclosed I send you, as [the bailiff *or* receiver of A. B., Esq.] my landlord, copy of a writ in ejectment, served upon me for the recovery of the possession of the [messuage, *or* farm, land] and premises, situate at ——, *or* in the parish of ——, in the county of ——, held by me as your tenant, [*or* as tenant of the said A. B.]

I am [&c.]

To ——. C. D.

N.B.—*Almost any form will do. Keep a copy of the writ, and of the above notice, with a memorandum indorsed, stating when and how sent or delivered.*

---

59. *Declaration by a Landlord against his Tenant, for a Penalty of Three Years' improved or Rack-rent, for not forthwith giving Notice of a Writ of Ejectment, pursuant to 15 & 16 Vict. c. 76, s. 209, (ante, 117).*

In the [Q. B., C. P. *or* Exch.]

The —— day of ——, A.D. 18—.

Venue } A. B. by E. F. his attorney, [*or* in person, *as the case may* to wit. } *be*,] sues C. D. For that the defendant, and one G. H. and one J. K., at the respective times hereinafter mentioned, were tenants to the plaintiff of certain lands and tenements of the plaintiff, with the appurtenances, situate in the parish of ——, in the county of ——, and there held the same, and were in the possession thereof, as such tenants thereof to the plaintiff as aforesaid : And whilst the defendant and the said G. H. and J. K. were such tenants, and so in possession as aforesaid, to wit, on [*teste of writ in ejectment*] the —— day of ——, in the year of Lord 18—, one L. M. [one N. O. and one P. Q.] caused to be issued out of the court of our Lady the Queen, before [the Queen herself, *or* her Justices of the Bench, *or* the Barons of her Exchequer,] at Westminster, in the county of Middlesex, according to the provisions of " The Common Law Procedure Act, 1852," and the course and practice of the said Court, a certain writ in ejectment for the recovery of the possession of the said lands and tenements, with the appurtenances, so held by and in the possession of the defendant, and of the said G. H. and J. K., as tenants thereof to the plaintiff as aforesaid : And afterwards, whilst the defendant and the said G. H. and J. K. were such tenants, and so in possession as aforesaid, and whilst the said writ in ejectment was in full force, to wit, on the —— day of ——, in the year of our Lord 18—, the said writ was served and made known to the defendant, according to the provisions of the " Common Law Procedure Act, 1852," and the course and practice of the said court in that behalf, and the said writ then came to the knowledge of the defendant: Yet the defendant did not forthwith give notice of the said writ in ejectment to the plaintiff, nor to any bailiff or receiver of the plaintiff, but neglected so to do, contrary to the form of the statute in such case made and provided : By reason whereof the defendant forfeited and became liable to pay to the plaintiff the sum of £——, being the value of three years' [improved *or* rack] rent of the said lands and tenements, with the appurtenances, so held by and in the possession of the defendant, and of the said G. H. and J. K., as tenants thereof to the plaintiff as aforesaid ; and thereby an action hath accrued to the plaintiff to demand and have of and from the defendant the said sum of £——, yet the defendant hath not paid to the plaintiff the said sum of £——, or any part thereof.

And the plaintiff claims £—— [*the amount of the penalty*].

---

60. *Plea of the General Issue " by Statute," to the foregoing Declaration,* (*ante,* 117).

In the [Q. B., C. P. *or* Exch.]

The —— day of ——, A. D. 18—.

D. ats. B. By statute 21 Jac. 1, c. 4, s. 4. Public General Act.	The defendant by ——, his attorney [*or* in person], says [That he is not guilty, *or* That he does not owe to the plaintiff the said sum of £——, or any part thereof].

N.B.—*The marginal note must not be omitted. Reg. Pl. H. T.* 1853, *No.* 21 (*ante,* 117).

———

61. *Demand on Plaintiff's Attorney whether the Writ was issued by him or with his Authority or Privity* (*ante,* 118).

Title of court and cause, as ante, No. 19.

On behalf of the above-named [defendants *or* defendant C. D. *as the case may be*], and in pursuance of The Common Law Procedure Act, 1852, I do hereby demand and require you forthwith to declare to me whether the writ of ejectment issued in this action, and whereon your name is indorsed as the attorney for the above-named plaintiffs, has been issued by you, or with your authority or privity. Dated the —— day of ——, 18—.

Yours, &c., G. H. of ——, attorney [*or* agent] for the above-named [defendants *or* defendant C. D.]

To Mr. E. F.

———

62. *Declaration that it was or was not* (*ante,* 119).

In the [Q. B., C. P. *or* Exch.]

B. [and another] *v.* D. [and others.]

I do hereby declare that the writ of ejectment issued in this action [was *or* was not, *as the case may be*] issued by me or with my authority or privity. Dated the —— day of ——, 18—.

To Mr. G. H., the defendant's attorney [*or* agent].	Yours, &c., E. F., of ——.

———

63. *Summons thereon to stay all further Proceedings* (*ante,* 119).

Commence as ante, No. 22.

Why all further proceedings in this action should not be stayed pursuant to The Common Law Procedure Act, 1852, sect. 169; Mr. E. F., whose name is indorsed on the writ in ejectment as the plaintiff's attorney, having declared that such writ has not been issued by him or with his authority or privity. Dated the —— day of ——, 18—.

Judge's signature.

N.B.—*If taken out on behalf of some or one of the defendants, the other defendants, their attorneys or agents, should also be called on to show cause, &c.*

———

64. *Order thereon* (*ante,* 119).

Commence as ante, No. 24.

I do order that all further proceedings in this action be stayed pursuant to The Common Law Procedure Act, 1852, sect. 169; Mr. E. F., whose name is indorsed on the writ in ejectment as the plaintiff's attorney, having declared that such writ has not been issued by him, or with his authority or privity. Dated the —— day of ——, 18—.

Judge's signature.

65. *Summons for Particulars of Plaintiff's Address, &c. (ante, 119).*
Commence as ante, No. 22.

Why Mr. E. F., the plaintiff's attorney, should not within a time to be fixed and allowed on the hearing of this application, declare in writing to Mr. G. H., the defendant's attorney in this action, the profession, occupation or quality and place of abode of [the plaintiff *or* of each of the plaintiffs], pursuant to The Common Law Procedure Act, 1852, sect. 169, on pain of being guilty of a contempt of court: [And why all further proceedings in this action should not be stayed in the meantime.] Dated the —— day of ——, 18—.

Judge's signature.

---

66. *Order thereon (ante, 119).*
Commence as ante, No. 24.

I do order that Mr. E. F., the plaintiff's attorney, do within —— days declare in writing to Mr. G. H., the defendant's attorney in this action, the profession, occupation or quality, and place of abode, of [the plaintiff *or* each of the plaintiffs], pursuant to The Common Law Procedure Act, 1852, sect. 169, on pain of being guilty of a contempt of court: [And that all further proceedings in this action be stayed in the meantime.] Dated the —— day of ——, 18—.

Judge's signature.

---

67. *Particulars of the Plaintiff's Address &c. (ante, 119).*
Title of court and cause as ante, No. 19.

The following particulars are delivered pursuant to the order of [Mr. Justice —— *or* Mr. Baron ——], dated the —— day of ——, 18—.

The plaintiff [A. B. is, *state his profession, occupation or quality*] and his place of abode is at [*describe his residence with convenient certainty*, ex. gr. No. 10, Green Street, Grosvenor Square, in the county of Middlesex, *or mention the name of the house and the parish, town, ville, &c., as the case may be.*]

Repeat the above as to the other plaintiffs, mutatis mutandis.
Dated the —— day of ——, 18—.

To Mr. G. H., the attorney [*or* agent] for the [defendants *or* for the defendant C. D. *as the case may be*].	Yours, &c. E. F., of ——, Attorney [*or* agent] for the above-named plaintiffs.

68. *Affidavit for better Particulars of the Property claimed (ante, 119).*
Commence as ante, Nos. 19, 20 or 21.

1. That on the —— day of —— [instant *or* last] I was served with the copy writ in ejectment hereunto annexed, marked (A).

2. That before and at the time of the said service of the said copy writ I was and still am in the possession [by myself *or* by —— and —— my tenants] of [*describe the property so as to identify it, or at all events with reasonable certainty*].

3. That I do not know, and cannot tell from the said copy writ, whether this action is brought to recover the whole of the said property of which I am so in possession as aforesaid, or only of some and what part thereof.

Sworn, &c. (*ante*, 705.)

---

69. *Summons for better Particulars of the Property claimed (ante, 119).*
Commence as ante, No. 22.

Why the plaintiffs should not deliver to the defendant's attorney or agent particulars in writing of the property claimed ; such property not being described in the writ with reasonable certainty : And why all further proceedings in this action should not be stayed in the meantime. Dated the —— day of ——, 18—.

Judge's signature.

---

70. *Order thereon.*
Commence as ante, No. 24.

I do order that the plaintiffs do deliver to the defendant's attorney or agent particulars in writing of the property claimed, [such property not being described in the writ with reasonable certainty] : And that all further proceedings in this action be stayed in the meantime. Dated the —— day of ——, 18—.

Judge's signature.

---

71. *Particulars of the Property claimed* (*ante,* 119).
Title of court and cause, as ante, No. 19.

This ejectment is brought to recover [*describe the property with more certainty than in the writ, so as to inform the defendant what is really claimed, but no abuttals or boundaries need be stated*], with the appurtenances, situate in the parish of ——, in the county of ——. The above particulars are delivered pursuant to the order of Mr. [Justice *or* Baron] ——, dated the —— day of ——, 18—. Dated the —— day of ——, 18—.

Yours, &c.

To Mr. G. H., the [defendant's]   E. F., of ——, plaintiff's attorney
attorney [*or* agent].   [*or* agent.]

---

72. *Summons for Particulars of Breaches* (*ante,* 120).
Commence as ante, No. 22.

Why the plaintiffs should not deliver to the defendant's attorney or agent particulars of the breaches of covenant for which this action is brought, and why all further proceedings in this action should not be stayed in the mean time. Dated the —— day of ——, 18—.

Judge's signature.

---

73. *Order thereon.*
Commence as ante, No. 24.

I do order that the plaintiffs deliver to the defendant's attorney or agent particulars of the breaches of covenant for which this action is brought, and that all further proceedings in this action be stayed in the meantime. Dated the —— day of ——, 18—.

Judge's signature.

---

74. *Particulars of Breaches* (*ante,* 120).
Title of court and cause, as ante, No. 19.

The following are the particulars of the breaches of covenant for which this action is brought, delivered pursuant to the order of Mr. [Justice *or* Baron] ——, dated the —— day of ——, 18—.

This action is founded on an indenture of lease, dated the —— day of ——, 18—, made or expressed to be made between [the above-named A. B.] of the one part, and [the above-named C. D.] of the other part, containing divers covenants and conditions, and a proviso or power of re-entry for non-payment of rent, or nonperformance of covenants as therein mentioned.

The breaches of covenant on which the plaintiff will rely are as follows :—

1. Nonpayment of £——, being [—— quarters' rent] due on the —— day of ——, 18—.

2. Nonperformance of the covenant to insure and keep insured [&c. *describe the breach concisely with reference to the language of the covenant, and show when, or in what respect, the covenant was not duly performed.*]

3. For not repairing, [&c. *describe the breach concisely with reference to the language of the covenant ; and add, or annex and refer to, a detailed statement of the dilapidations and want of repairs, &c.*]

4. [*State any other breaches in like manner, and with reference to the words of the covenant.*]

Dated the —— day of ——, 18—.

Yours, &c.

To Mr. G. H., the [defendant's] } . E. F., of ——, plaintiff's attorney
attorney [*or* agent]. } [*or* agent].

───────

75. *Summons to stay Proceedings until Costs of a previous Ejectment, &c. paid* (*ante,* 80).

Commence as ante, No. 22.

" Why all further proceedings in this action should not be stayed until the sum of £——, being the amount of the taxed costs in a former action of ejectment brought in the Court of [Q. B., C. P., *or* Exch.] by —— against ——, for recovery of [the same premises, *or* part of the same premises, *or* the same premises and other land and premises held under the same title, *or* other land and premises held under the same title, *as the case may be,*] together with interest on the said sum at the rate of four pounds per centum per annum from the [*date of judgment in previous ejectment*] —— day of ——, in the year of our Lord 18—, on which day the judgment in the said action was entered up (*a*), are paid. Dated the —— day of ——, 18—.

Judge's signature.

───────

76. *Order thereon.*

Commence as ante, No. 24.

I do order that all further proceedings in this action be stayed until [*follow the language of the summons, No.* 75]. Dated the —— day of ——, 18—.

─────

Judge's signature.

───────

77. *Rule Nisi, to stay Proceedings until the Costs of a previous Ejectment, &c. paid* (*ante,* 80).

Commence as ante, No. 25.

Why all further proceedings in this action should not be stayed until [*as in Form No.* 75 *to the end, but omitting the date and signature ; then go on thus*], upon notice of this rule to be given to the plaintiff or his attorney in the meantime. By the Court.

─────────────────────────────────────

(*a*) If costs of action for mesne profits, &c. remain unpaid, here say :—
" And also the sum of £ ——, being the amount of the taxed costs in an action of trespass for mesne profits consequent upon the above-mentioned ejectment, brought in the [said] Court of [Q. B., C. P. *or* Exch.] by the said —— against the said ——, together with interest on the said last-mentioned sum, at the rate of four pounds per centum per annum from the [*date of judgment*] —— day of ——, in the year of our Lord 18—, on which day the judgment in the said last-mentioned action was entered up, are respectively paid. Dated the —— day of ——, 18—.

Judge's signature."

78. *Rule Absolute.*

Commence as ante, No. 28.

It is ordered, that all further proceedings in this action be stayed until [*as in the Rule Nisi, but omitting the concluding sentence*].

Mr. —— for the plaintiffs.
Mr. —— for the defendants.
By the Court.

———

79. *Summons to stay Proceedings till Security be given for Defendant's Costs* (*ante,* 81, 121).

Commence as ante, No. 22.

Why the plaintiff should not give to the defendant [*or* the defendant C. D.] such security for the payment of the said defendant's costs as one of the masters shall approve of : and why all further proceedings in this cause should not be stayed until such security be given pursuant to the 93rd section of The Common Law Procedure Act, 1854. Dated the —— day of ——, 18—.

Judge's signature.

———

80. *Order thereon.*

Commence as ante, No. 24.

I do order, that the plaintiff give to the defendant [*or* defendant C. D.] such security for the payment of the said defendant's costs as one of the masters shall approve of : and that all further proceedings in this cause be stayed until such security be given pursuant to the 93rd section of The Common Law Procedure Act, 1854. Dated the —— day of ——, 18—.

Judge's signature.

———

81. *Summons to stay Proceedings upon Payment of Rent and Arrears, with Costs* (*ante,* 418).

Commence as ante, No. 22.

Why it should not be referred to one of the masters to compute the rent and arrears of rent due from the defendant to the plaintiff, and to tax the plaintiff's costs of this action ; and why, upon the defendant paying to the plaintiff, or to Mr. ——, his attorney in this action, or in case either of them shall refuse to accept the same, paying into court what the master shall find due, and allow for the said rent and arrears and costs, all further proceedings in this action should not be stayed. Dated the —— day of ——, 18—.

Judge's signature.

———

82. *Order thereon.*

Commence as ante, No. 24.

I do order, that it be referred to one of the masters to compute the rent and arrears of rent due from the defendant to the plaintiff, and to tax the plaintiff's costs of this action ; and that, upon the defendant paying to the plaintiff, or to Mr. E. F., his attorney in this action, or, in case either of them shall refuse to accept the same, paying into court what the master shall find due and allow for the said rent and arrears and costs, all further proceedings in this action [as to the nonpayment of rent] be stayed, [with liberty for the plaintiff to proceed on any title other than for nonpayment of rent].

Dated the —— day of ——, 18—.

Judge's signature.

N.B.—*The words within brackets will be added by the judge, if the plaintiff claim for any other forfeiture ; but they need not be inserted in the summons. Sometimes a rule is obtained. See the Forms,* Chit. Forms, 555, 556. (*Both of these appear to be inaccurate.*)

83. *Summons for Leave for Mortgagor to bring Principal, Interest and Costs into Court (ante, 469).*

Commence as ante, No. 22.

Why, upon the defendant's bringing into court in this action all the principal monies and interest due to the plaintiff on his mortgage upon the premises for which this action is brought; and also all such costs as have been expended in any suit or suits at law or in equity upon such mortgage, including the costs of this action (such money for principal, interest and costs to be ascertained and computed and taxed by one of the masters), the money so brought into court should not be deemed and taken to be in full satisfaction and discharge of such mortgage, and the defendant be discharged of and from the same accordingly; and why, upon the said money being so brought into court, the plaintiff should not, at the costs and charges of the defendant, assign, surrender or reconvey the mortgaged premises and such estate and interest as the plaintiff has therein unto the defendant and his [heirs *or* executors or administrators], or to such other person or persons as he or they shall for that purpose nominate or appoint; such assignment, surrender or reconveyance to be settled by one of the masters in case the parties differ about the same, and the amount of such last-mentioned costs and charges to be ascertained by one of the masters in case the parties differ about the same; and why, upon the said money being so brought into court and the said last-mentioned costs and charges paid or tendered to the plaintiff or his attorney, the plaintiff should not deliver up all deeds, evidences and writings in his custody or power relating to the title to the said mortgaged premises unto the defendant or his [heirs *or* executors or administrators], or to such other person or persons as he or they shall for that purpose nominate or appoint; and why, upon the said money being so brought into court, all further proceedings in this action (except for the purposes aforesaid) should not be stayed.

Dated the —— day of ——, 18—.

Judge's signature.

---

84. *Order thereon.*

Commence as ante, No. 24.

I do order, that upon the defendant's bringing into court in this action all the principal monies and interest due to the plaintiff on his mortgage upon the premises for which this action is brought; and also all such costs as have been expended in any suit or suits at law or in equity upon such mortgage, including the costs of this action (such money for principal, interest and costs to be ascertained and computed and taxed by one of the masters), the money so brought into court shall be deemed and taken to be in full satisfaction and discharge of such mortgage, and the defendant be discharged of and from the same accordingly; and I further order that, upon the said money being so brought into court, the plaintiff do, at the costs and charges of the defendant, assign, surrender or reconvey the mortgaged premises, and such estate and interest as the plaintiff has therein, unto the defendant and his [heirs *or* executors or administrators], or to such other person or persons as he or they shall for that purpose nominate or appoint; such assignment, surrender or reconveyance to be settled by one of the masters in case the parties differ about the same, and the amount of such last-mentioned costs and charges to be ascertained by one of the masters in case the parties differ about the same; and I do further order that upon the said money being so brought into court, and the said last-mentioned costs and charges paid or tendered to the plaintiff or his attorney, the plaintiff do deliver up all deeds, evidences and writings in his custody or power relating to the title to the said mortgaged premises, unto the defendant or his [heirs *or* executors or administrators], or to such other person or persons as he or they shall for that purpose nominate or appoint; and I do further order that, upon the said money being so brought into court, all further proceedings in this action (except for the purposes aforesaid) be stayed.

Dated the —— day of ——, 18—.

Judge's signature.

---

85. *Rule Nisi for Leave for Mortgagor to bring Principal, Interest and Costs into Court (ante, 469).*
Commence as ante No. 25.

Why upon the defendant's bringing into court [*as in a summons, ante, No. 83, omitting the date*], upon notice of this rule to be given to the plaintiff or his attorney in the meantime.

By the Court.

---

86. *Rule Absolute.*
Commence as ante, No. 28.

It is ordered [*as in the rule nisi, mutatis mutandis*].

Mr. —— for the plaintiff.
Mr. —— for the defendant.
By the Court.

---

87. *Rule Nisi to stay Proceedings in Ejectment on a Mortgage on Payment of Principal, Interest and Costs, Reconveyance to be executed and Deeds delivered up (ante, 469).*
Commence as ante, No. 25.

Why it should not be referred to one of the masters to ascertain what is due for principal and interest on the mortgage to the plaintiffs, dated the —— day of ——, 18 —, in the affidavit of —— mentioned, and also to tax the plaintiffs their costs in this action: And why the plaintiffs should not accept the amount of such principal, interest and costs so ascertained to be due in discharge of such mortgage, and execute an assignment or reconveyance to the defendant, or as the master shall direct; such assignment or reconveyance to be settled by the master in case the parties differ about the same: And why the plaintiffs should not deliver up all deeds, evidences and writings in [their or either of their] possession relating to the premises comprised in such mortgage; or why, in case of [their *or* either of their] refusal so to do, the said principal, interest and costs should not be paid into court, to abide the further order of the said court, and be deemed and taken to be in full satisfaction of the said mortgage, and why all further proceedings in this cause should not be stayed: And that in the meantime proceedings be stayed, upon notice of this rule to be given to the plaintiff or his attorney in the meantime.

By the Court.

---

88. *Note in Writing controverting the Right to redeem, &c. (ante, 469).*
Title of court and cause as ante, No. 19.

I, the undersigned [as the attorney *or* agent of the plaintiff] do hereby insist that the defendant has not a right to redeem the mortgaged premises sought to be recovered in this action, because [*here state the reason why he is not so entitled*] *or,* do hereby insist that the mortgaged premises sought to be recovered in this action are chargeable with other and different principal sums than what appear on the face of the mortgage dated the —— day of ——, 18—, (that is to say) with the sum of £—— [*here specify the sums so chargeable, and the time of the advance, and short particulars of the deed, me-*

morandum or writing (if any) creating the further charge.]
day of ——, 18—.

To the above-named defendant
and to Mr. G. H. his attorney
[*or* agent].

A. B., the plaintiff [*or* ь.
attorney *•or* agent of the ав—
named plaintiff].

---

89. *Affidavit for Leave to appear and defend (ante, 124).*
Commence as ante, Nos. 19, 20 or 21.

1. That this is an action of ejectment brought for the recovery of the possession of [*describe the property as in the writ*], in the parish of ——, in the county of ——.

2. That I am in possession [by myself, *or* by the above-named C. D., as my tenant] of [the land and premises, *or describe the part*, being part of the land and premises] sought to be recovered in this action.

Sworn, &c. (*ante*, 705.)

---

90. *Order for Leave to appear and defend, pursuant to Section 172 (ante, 124).*
Commence as ante, No. 24.

B.
v.
D.

I do order that the said O. P. be at liberty to appear in this action [*if as landlord, say* as landlord of C. D., named in the writ], and to defend for [all or any part of the property claimed, *or for* —— *describe the part*, being part of the property claimed]. Dated the —— day of ——, 18—.

Judge's signature.

---

91. *Summons for a Landlord to be at liberty to appear and defend after Judgment has been regularly signed against his Tenant for Want of Appearance (ante, 115, 132).*
Commence as ante, 22.

Why O. P. [*name of landlord*] should not be at liberty forthwith to appear in this action as landlord of the defendant C. D., and to defend for [all or any part of the property claimed, *or for* —— *describe the part*, being part of the property claimed]: And why all further proceedings in this action against the said C. D. should not be stayed until after judgment shall have been obtained in this action against the said O. P. Dated the —— day of ——, 18—.

Judge's signature.

N. B.—*A special affidavit must be made in support of this application, combining the Forms Nos. 89 and 128, with such variations as the circumstances may render necessary. The order will follow the language of the summons, adding such terms and conditions as the judge may think reasonable. See post, No. 130.*

---

92. *Appearance by Attorney of one or more Defendants named in the Writ (ante, 126).*

A. B. [and another,
or others,]
against
C. D. [I. K., L. M.
and others.]

G. H., attorney for C. D. [I. K. and L. M.], appears for [him *or* them].

Entered the —— day of ——, 18—.

93. *Appearance in Person of a Defendant named in the Writ (ante, 126).*

A. B. [and another, or others,] against C. D. [and another, or others.] } The defendant C. D. appears in person. The address of the defendant C. D. is at [No. —, —— Street, Grosvenor Square, in the county of Middlesex, *or as the case may be*].

Entered the —— day of ——, 18—.

N. B.—*The defendant's address for service within three miles of the General Post Office, London, must also be entered in the address book kept at the master's office.* Reg. Prac. H. T. 1853, No. 166 (ante, 126).

---

94. *Appearance by Attorney of a Landlord not named in the Writ (ante, 127).*

A. B. [and another, or others,] against C. D., E. F. and G. H. } N. M., attorney for O. P., appears for him as landlord of the said [C. D., E. F. and G. H., *or as the case may be*].

Entered the —— day of ——, 18—.

By order of Mr. [Justice *or* Baron] ——, dated the —— day of ——, 18—.

---

95. *Appearance in Person by a Landlord not named in the Writ (ante, 127).*

A. B. [and another, or others,] against C. D., E. F. and G. H. } O. P. appears in person as landlord of [the said C. D., *or* of the defendants]. The address of the said O. P. is at [No. —, —— Street, London, *or as the case may be*].

Entered the —— day of ——, 18—.

By order of Mr. [Justice *or* Baron] ——, dated the —— day of ——, 18—, [*or* By rule of court, dated the —— day of ——, 18—].

N. B.—*The landlord's address for service within three miles of the General Post Office, London, must also be entered in the address book kept at the master's office.* Reg. Prac. H. T. 1852, No. 166 (ante, 126).

---

96. *Appearance of a Person not named in the Writ, as a Tenant in Possession (ante, 126).*

Same as ante, Nos. 94 *and* 95, *but omitting the words* "As landlord of," *&c.*

---

97. *Notice of Appearance entered for a Defendant or Defendants named in the Writ (ante, 127, 128).*

Title of court and cause as ante, No. 19.

Take notice, that I have entered an appearance in this action for the defendant C. D. [*or* for all the defendants, *as the case may be* (q).] Dated the —— day of ——, 18—.

Yours, &c.

To Mr. E. F. the plaintiff's attorney [*or* agent]. } G. H. of ——, attorney [*or* agent] for the defendant C. D. [*or* for the defendants].

(q) A notice to defend for part only may be added thus:—"And take notice that the said C. D. hereby limits his defence to [*describe the part with reasonable certainty*], with the appurtenances, situate in the parish of ——, in the county of ——, [now in the possession of the said C. D. and] being a part only of the property mentioned in the writ. Dated," &c.: or such notice may be given subsequently in due time. *Post, Nos.* 101, 102.

98. *Notice of Appearance by the Attorney of a Landlord or other Person not named in the Writ (ante,* 127, 128).

Title of court and cause as ante, No. 19.

Take notice, that I have entered an appearance in this action for O. P. [as landlord of the defendants, *or* of the defendant C. D. *as the case may be*] by leave of the Hon. Mr. [Justice *or* Baron] ——(r). Dated the —— day of ——, 18—.

<table>
<tr><td></td><td>Yours, &c.</td></tr>
<tr><td>To Mr. ——, the plaintiff's }
attorney [*or* agent].</td><td>G. H. of ——, attorney for the
said O. P.</td></tr>
</table>

---

99. *Notice of such Appearance in Person (ante,* 127, 128).

Title of court and cause as ante, No. 19.

Take notice, that I, the undersigned O. P., have entered an appearance in this action [as landlord of the defendants *or* of the defendant C. D., *as the case may be, or omit these words where O. P. appears as a tenant in possession*] by leave of the Hon. Mr. [Justice *or* Baron] ——(s). Dated the —— day of ——, 18—.

<table>
<tr><td></td><td>Yours, &c.</td></tr>
<tr><td></td><td>O. P.</td></tr>
<tr><td>To Mr. E. F. plaintiff's }
attorney [*or* agent].</td><td>*Address as entered in the appearance and
address book.*</td></tr>
</table>

---

100. *Notice by an Attorney that he is authorized to act as the Attorney for a Defendant who has appeared in Person (ante,* 127).

Title of court and cause as ante, No. 19.

Take notice, that I am authorized to act in this cause as attorney for the defendant [C. D.] Dated the —— day of ——, 18—.

<table>
<tr><td></td><td>Yours, &c.</td></tr>
<tr><td>To Mr. E. F. the plaintiff's }
attorney [*or* agent].</td><td>G. H. of ——, attorney
for the said [C. D.]</td></tr>
</table>

N. B.—*A like notice (mutatis mutandis) may be given on behalf of the plaintiff* (ante, 97, 127).

---

101. *Notice to defend for Part only (ante,* 128).

Title of court and cause as ante, No. 19.

Take notice, that the defendant [*or* the defendant C. D. *if there be other defendants*], having appeared in this action, hereby limits his defence to [*describe the part with reasonable certainty (see the next Form, post,* 734)], with the appurtenances, situate in the parish of ——, in the county of ——, and [now in the possession of the said defendant], being a part only of the property mentioned in the writ. Dated this —— day of ——, 18—.

<table>
<tr><td></td><td>Yours, &c.</td></tr>
<tr><td>To Mr. E. F. the plaintiff's }
attorney [*or* agent].</td><td>G. H. of ——, attorney [*or* agent]
for the defendant [C. D.]</td></tr>
</table>

(r) A notice to defend for part only may be added (as *ante, No.* 97) or given subsequently in due time. See *post, No.* 103.

(s) A notice to defend for part only may be added thus:—" And take notice that I hereby limit my defence to [*describe the part with reasonable certainty*], with the appurtenances, situate in the parish of ——, in the county of ——, [and now in the possession of the said C. D. *or* in my possession, and] being a part only of the property mentioned in the writ. Dated, &c.:" or such notice may be given subsequently in due time.

102. *Notice to defend for divers Parts* (*ante*, 128).

Title of court and cause as ante, No. 19.

Take notice, that the defendant [*or* the defendant C. D. *if there be other defendants*], having appeared in this action, hereby limits his defence to [*here describe the parts with reasonable certainty*, ex. gr.], **First,** all that messuage or tenement, blacksmith's shop, beast-house, barn, garden and six closes or pieces of land to the same belonging, in the occupation of the defendant [*or* defendant C. D.], containing together thirteen acres and thirteen perches or thereabouts (formerly estimated to contain thirteen acres), situate in the parish of —— in the county of ——, being part of a farm or estate known as *Porthgwin*, and being part of the property mentioned in the writ. *Secondly,* four other closes or pieces of land, containing together eight acres and eighteen perches, or thereabouts, of arable, meadow and pasture, in the occupation of the defendant [*or* defendant C. D.] (not being part of the said farm or estate known as *Porthgwin*, but other and distinct property), situate in the parish of —— in the county of ——, and being other part of the property mentioned in the writ. *Thirdly,* a cottage, garden and land, containing one rood and twenty-six perches, or thereabouts, in the occupation of the defendant, situate in the parish of —— in the county of ——, and being other part of the property mentioned in the writ. Dated this —— day of ——, 18—.

Yours, &c.

To Mr. E. F. the plaintiff's } attorney [*or* agent].

G. H. of ——,
Defendant's agent.

———

103. *Notice to defend for Part only, by a Landlord or other Person not named in the Writ* (*ante*, 128).

Title of court and cause as ante, No. 19.

Take notice, that O. P. has appeared in this action [as landlord of the defendant C. D. *or as the case may be*], by leave of the Hon. Mr. [Justice *or* Baron] ——, and that the said O. P. hereby limits his defence to [*describe the part with reasonable certainty*], with the appurtenances, situate in the parish of —— in the county of ——, and now in the possession of the said [C. D. *or* O. P.], being a part only of the property mentioned in the writ. Dated this —— day of ——, 18—.

Yours, &c.

To Mr. E. F. the plaintiff's } attorney [*or* agent].

N. M. of ——, attorney for
the above-named O. P.

———

104. *Notice by a Defendant that he defends as a Joint Tenant, or Tenant in Common or Coparcener with the Claimant of all the Property claimed* (*ante*, 130).

Title of court and cause as ante, No. 19.

Take notice, that the defendant [C. D.] has appeared in this action, and defends as a [joint tenant *or* tenant in common *or* coparcener] with the plaintiff, and admits the right of the plaintiff to an undivided share of the property mentioned in the writ, that is to say, to one equal undivided moiety [*or* third, fourth, fifth, &c. part] thereof, but the defendant denies any actual ouster of the plaintiff from the said property ; [and take notice that the said defendant has filed an affidavit in pursuance of the 188th section of the Common Law Procedure Act, 1852]. Dated the —— day of ——, 18—.

Yours, &c.

To Mr. E. F. the plaintiff's } attorney [*or* agent].

G. H. of ——,
Defendant's attorney.

105. *The like, for part only (ante,* 130).

Title of court and cause as ante, No. 19.

Take notice, that the defendant [C. D.] has appeared in this action, and that he hereby limits his defence to [*describe the part with reasonable certainty*], with the appurtenances, situate in the parish of —— in the county of ——, being a part only of the prcperty mentioned in the writ. And that the defendant [C. D.] defends for such part as a [joint tenant, *or* tenant in common, *or* coparcener] with the plaintiff, and admits the right of the plaintiff to an undivided share of the said part of the said property, that is to say, to one equal undivided moiety [*or* third, fourth, fifth, &c. part] thereof, but the said defendant [C. D.] denies any actual ouster of the plaintiff from the said part of the said property above described; and take notice that the defendant [C. D.] has filed an affidavit in pursuance of the 188th section of the Common Law Procedure Act, 1852. Dated the —— day of ——, 18—.

Yours, &c.

To Mr. ——, the plaintiff's } 　　G. H. of ——, attorney for the
attorney [*or* agent]. 　　　　　　defendant [C. D.]

---

106. *Affidavit by a Joint Tenant, Tenant in Common or Coparcener, denying Ouster, &c. (ante,* 130).

Commence as ante, No. 19.

1. I am a [joint tenant, *or* tenant in common, *or* coparcener, *as the case may be*] with the plaintiff [*or* with A. B. one of the plaintiffs] of the property mentioned in the writ in this action [*or* of, *describe the part correctly*, with the appurtenances, situate in the parish of ——, in the county of ——, being part of the property mentioned in the writ in this action].

2. I am legally entitled as such [joint tenant, tenant in common, *or* coparcener] as aforesaid to [*state deponent's part or share, ex. gr.* one equal undivided moiety, *or* third, fourth, fifth, &c. part, *as the case may be*] of the said property in the said writ mentioned [*or* of the said part of the said property above described].

3. I have not ousted the plaintiff from the said property in the said writ mentioned [*or* from the said part of the said property above described].

Sworn, &c. (*ante,* 705.)

N.B.—*This affidavit is to be filed at the master's office at the time of appearance, or within four days after* (ante, 131).

---

107. *Notice to dispute the Petitioning Creditor's Debt, Trading and Act of Bankruptcy, or some or one of them (ante,* 548).

Title of court and cause, as ante, No. 19.

Take notice, that it is the intention of the defendant [*or* of the defendant C. D. *if there be more than one defendant*], on the trial of this action, to dispute the [petitioning creditor's debt, the trading and the act of bankruptcy, *or specify which of them is intended to be disputed*]. Dated the —— day of ——, 18—.

Yours, &c.

To the above-named plaintiffs, } 　G. H. of ——, attorney [*or* agent] for
and to Mr. ——, their attor- } 　　the defendant [C. D.]
ney [*or* agent]. }

N.B.—*This notice must be served on the day of the appearance, with the notice thereof; or at the latest, with the notice to defend for part only* (ante, 549).

108. *Summons for better Particulars of the Property defended* (ante, 129).
Commence as ante, No. 22.

Why the defendants [*or* the defendant C. D.] should not, within [three] days, deliver to the plaintiff's attorney or agent better particulars of the property for which they defend [*or* he defends], such property not being described with reasonable certainty in the notice to defend for part, dated the —— day of ——, 18—. And why, in default of such particulars being so delivered, the said notice should not be set aside as irregular. Dated the —— day of ——, 18—.

Judge's signature.

---

109. *Order thereon.*
Commence as ante, No. 24.

I do order that the defendants [*or* defendant C. D.] do, within [three] days, deliver to the plaintiff's attorney or agent better particulars of the property for which they defend [*or* he defends], such property not being described with reasonable certainty in the notice to defend for part, dated the —— day of ——, 18—. And I order that, in default of such particulars being so delivered, the said notice be set aside as irregular. Dated the —— day of ——, 18—.

Judge's signature.

---

110. *Summons to set aside an Appearance with Costs, the Defendant's Address being illusory and fictitious* (ante, 126).
Commence as ante, 22.

Why the appearance in this action, entered by the defendant C. D. in person, should not be set aside for irregularity, with costs, to be taxed by one of the masters, and to be paid by the said C. D. to the plaintiff or his attorney, on the ground that the address of the said C. D. given in the said appearance [and entered in the master's book] is illusory and fictitious: and why the plaintiff should not be permitted to proceed in this action by sticking up the proceedings herein in the master's office without further service. Dated the —— day of ——, 18—.

Judge's signature.

---

111. *Order thereon.*
Commence as ante, 24.

I do order that the appearance in this action, entered by the defendant C. D. in person, be set aside for irregularity, with costs, to be taxed by one of the masters, and to be paid by the said C. D. to the plaintiff or his attorney, on the ground that the address of the said C. D. given in the said appearance [and entered in the master's book] is illusory and fictitious: and I do order that the plaintiff be at liberty to proceed in this action by sticking up the proceedings herein in the master's office, without further service. Dated the —— day of ——, 18—.

Judge's signature.

---

112. *Summons to confine an Appearance and Defence to Part of the Property claimed* (ante, 129).
Commence as ante, No. 22.

Why the appearance and defence of the said C. D. should not be confined to [*describe the property in the possession of C. D. and his tenants correctly, as in the affidavit*], with the appurtenances, situate in the parish of ——, in the county of ——, being part of the property mentioned in the writ, the said C. D. not being in possession, by himself or his tenants, of the residue of the property mentioned in the said writ and thereby claimed, or of any part of such residue. Dated the —— day of ——, 18—.

Judge's signature.

113. *Affidavit in support of such Application (ante,* 129).

Commence as ante, Nos. 19, 20 *or* 21.

1. That the paper writing hereunto annexed, marked (A), is a true copy of the writ in ejectment issued in this action, and of the indorsements thereon.

2. On the —— day of —— [instant *or* last], the above-named defendant C. D. entered an appearance in this action [in person *or* by —— his attorney], and that no notice has been served (*t*) by or on behalf of the said C. D. limiting his defence in this action to a part only of the property mentioned in the said writ, and the time for giving any such notice has elapsed.

3. That, at the time of the commencement of this action, the said C. D. was and still is in possession, by himself and his tenants, of a part only of the property mentioned in the said writ, (that is to say,) [*describe the part with reasonable certainty, as in a notice to defend for part*], with the appurtenances, situate in the parish of ——, in the county of ——. And that the said C. D., at the time of the commencement of this action, was not, nor is he, by himself or any of his tenants, in possession of the residue of the property mentioned in the said writ, and thereby claimed, or of any part of such residue.

Sworn by, &c. (*ante,* 708.)

N.B.—*The plaintiff himself need not join in the affidavit, if his attorney, agent or bailiff can swear to the necessary facts.*

———

114. *Order thereon.*

Commence as ante, No. 24.

I do order that the appearance and defence of the defendant C. D. be confined to [*follow the language of the Summons, No.* 112, *to the end*]. Dated the —— day of ——, 18—.

Judge's signature.

———

115. *Summons to confine an Appearance and Defence to Part of the Property described in Defendant's Notice, the Plaintiffs not claiming the Residue thereof (ante,* 130).

Commence as ante, No. 22.

Why the appearance and defence of the said C. D. should not be confined to [*describe the property in the possession of C. D. and his tenants correctly, as in the affidavit*], with the appurtenances, situate in the parish of ——, in the county of ——, being part of the property mentioned in the writ, the said C. D. not being in possession by himself or his tenants of the residue of the property mentioned in the said writ and thereby claimed, or of any part of such residue; and the plaintiffs not claiming to recover in this action the possession of the residue of the property described in the notice of the said C. D., dated the —— day of ——, 18—, signed by [E. S. as the attorney for] the said C. D., nor any part of such residue, but other and different property only. Dated the —— day of ——, 18—.

Judge's signature.

———

116. *Affidavit in Support of such Application (ante,* 130).

Commence as ante, No. 113, *to the entry of appearance inclusive, then go on thus :—*

3. I, the said ——, say, that on the —— day of —— [instant *or* last] a notice was duly served on behalf of the said C. D. on [me] as the plaintiff's

———

(*t*) Where the plaintiff sues in person, the affidavit must show that no notice has been filed in the master's office. Sect. 174 (*ante,* 123).

attorney in this action [a true copy whereof is hereunto annexed, marked Y, *or* in the words and figures following (that is to say) : *set out verbatim the notice to defend for part only*].

4. I, the said —— say, that at the time of the commencement of this action [*as in No.* 113, *pl.* 3, *to the end, then go on thus*] :—

5. I, the said —— say, that the said notice of the —— day of —— 18—, describes and includes not only the said part of the property in the said writ mentioned, which is so in the possession of the said C. D. [by himself and his tenants] as aforesaid, but also other and different property not mentioned in the said writ nor thereby claimed, and which is not sought to be recovered in this action.

Sworn by, &c. (*ante,* 708).

————

117. *Order thereon.*

Commence as ante, No. 24.

I do order that the appearance and defence of the defendant C. D. be confined to [*follow the language of the summons, No.* 115, *to the end*]. Dated the —— day of ——, 18—.

Judge's signature.

————

118. *Summons to rescind a previous Order (allowing a third Person not named in the Writ to appear and defend for Part), and also the Appearance entered in pursuance thereof, the Plaintiffs not claiming any of the Property so defended, but other and different Property only (ante,* 129).

Commence as ante, No. 22.

Why [my] order, dated the —— day of ——, 18—, should not be rescinded, and the appearance of the said O. P. in pursuance thereof struck out, the plaintiffs not claiming to recover in this action the possession of any part of the property for which the said O. P. defends this action as described in his notice, dated the —— day of —— 18—, signed by [E. S. as the attorney for] the said O. P., but other and different property only : And the said O. P. not being in possession by himself or his tenants of any part of the property mentioned in the writ of ejectment in this action and thereby claimed. Dated the —— day of ——, 18—.

Judge's signature.

————

119. *Order thereon.*

Commence as ante, No. 24.

I do order that my order dated the —— day of —— be rescinded, and that the appearance of the said O. P. in pursuance thereof be struck out, the plaintiffs not claiming [*follow the language of the summons to the end.*]

————

120. *Summons to amend a previous Order, and to confine the Appearance and Defence to Part of the Property described in Defendant's Notice, the Plaintiffs not claiming the Residue thereof (ante,* 129).

Commence as ante, No. 22.

Why [my] order, dated the —— day of ——, 18—, and the appearance and defence of the said O. P. in pursuance thereof, should not be amended and confined to [*describe the property in the possession of O. P. and his tenants correctly as in the affidavit*], with the appurtenances, situate in the parish of ——, in the county of ——, being part of the property mentioned in the writ, the said O. P. not being in possession by himself or his tenants of the residue of the property mentioned in the said writ, and thereby claimed, or any part of such residue, and the plaintiffs not claiming to recover in this action the possession of the residue of the property described in the notice of the said O. P., dated the —— day of ——, 18—, signed by [E. S. as the attorney for] the said O. P., nor any part of such residue, but other and different property only.　Dated the —— day of ——, 18—.

Judge's signature.

---

121. *Order thereon.*

Commence as ante, No. 24.

I do order that my order, dated &c. and the appearance and defence of the said O. P. in pursuance thereof, be amended and confined to [*follow the language of the summons to the end*].　Dated the —— day of ——, 18—.

Judge's signature.

---

122. *Incipitur of a Judgment* (*ante,* 337).

At the top of the judgment paper describe concisely the nature of the Judgment, ex. gr.

Judgment in ejectment for want of appearance against ——.

Judgment in ejectment upon a verdict against ——.

Judgment in ejectment by confession against —— (*or as the case may be*).

In the [Q. B., C. P. *or* Exch.]

The [*date of writ*] —— day of ——, A.D. 18—.

Venue (*u*),　On the day and year above written, a writ of our lady the
to wit.　Queen issued forth of this court, in these words (that is to say),

Victoria, by the grace of God [*here copy the writ to the words* "and to eject all other persons therefrom," *inclusive.*]

N.B.—*The remainder of the entry may be made when necessary for the purpose of evidence, or of proceedings in error, or the like.*

---

123. *Judgment where no Defendant appears* (*ante,* 123, 131).

In the [Q. B., C. P. *or* Exch.]

The [*date of writ*] —— day of ——, A.D. 18—.

Venue (*x*),　On the day and year above written, a writ of our lady the
to wit.　Queen issued forth of this court, in these words (that is to say),

Victoria, by the grace of God [*here copy the writ*]; and no appearance has been entered or defence made to the said writ : Therefore it is considered (*y*), that the said [*here insert the names of the persons in whom title is alleged in the writ*] do recover possession of the [land *or* tenements *or* property *or* premises] in the said writ mentioned, with the appurtenances.

N.B.—*The above form is given by 15 & 16 Vict. c. 76, s. 177, Schedule A., No. 14. At the time of signing the judgment it is sufficient to enter on the roll, and on a sheet of draft paper, a mere incipitur of the judgment : as ante, No. 122. But as the judgment is so short it is generally better to enter it at length in the first instance.*

(*u*) The venue is local, and must be laid in the county, &c. where the lands lie, *ante,* 135.　In Lancashire it should be laid thus :—" Lancashire, northern division, to wit," *or* " Lancashire, southern division, to wit," according as the lands lie.　*Thompson v. Hornby,* 9 Q. B. 978.　Formerly Warwickshire was divided, but now see 17 & 18 Vict. c. 35 (*ante,* 135).

(*x*) The venue is local, *ante,* 135.

(*y*) In the margin, opposite the words " Therefore it is considered, &c.," write a memorandum thus—" Judgment signed on the [*date*] —— day of —— 18—."

124. *Judgment for Non-appearance as to Part, and Issue as to the Residue (ante, 123, 131, 135; see post, No. 125).*

The [*date of the writ*] —— day of ——, A.D. 18—.

In the [Q. B., C. P. *or* Exch.]

Venue (z), ⎰ On the day and year above written, a writ of our lady the
to wit.   ⎱ Queen issued forth of this court, in these words (that is to
say),

Victoria, by the grace of God [*here copy the writ*]; and C. D. has, on the
—— day of ——, A.D. 18—, appeared by ——, his attorney [*or in person*],
to the said writ, and has defended for a part of the land [*or tenements, or
premises or property*], in the writ mentioned; that is to say, [*here state the
part*]; and no appearance has been entered or defence made to the said
writ, except as to the said part: Therefore it is considered (a) that the said
A. B. [*the claimant*] do recover possession of the land [*or tenements or
premises or property*] in the said writ mentioned, except the said part, with
the appurtenances, and that he have execution thereof forthwith; and as to
the rest, let a jury come, &c.

N.B. *This form is given by 15 & 16 Vict. c. 76, s. 177, Sched. A., No. 15;
see note to No. 123.*

———

125. *Judgment for Want of Appearance as against some of the Defendants, and
Issue as to the others (ante, 131, 134).*

In the [Q. B., C. P. *or* Exch.]

The [*date of the writ*] —— day of ——, A.D. 18—.

Venue (b), ⎰ On the day and year above written, a writ of our lady the
to wit.   ⎱ Queen issued forth of this court, in these words (that is
to say),

Victoria, by the grace of God [*here copy the writ*]; and no appearance
has been entered or defence made to the said writ by the said [*names of defendants who have not appeared*]: Therefore it is considered that (c) the said
[*names of claimants*], do recover possession of the [land *or* tenements *or*
property *or* premises] in the said writ mentioned, with the appurtenances,
as against the said [*names of defendants who have not appeared*]: And [*names
of defendants who have appeared*] have [*or* has] on the —— day of ——,
A.D. 18—, appeared by ——, [their *or* his] attorney [*or in person*], to the
said writ, and defended for the whole (d) of the [land *or* tenements *or* property *or* premises] therein mentioned: Therefore let a jury come, &c.

———

126. *The like—another Form (ante, 131, 134).*

*Commence as ante, No. 125, to the end of the copy writ inclusive; then proceed
thus :*

And C. D. has, on the —— day of ——, A.D. 18—, appeared by ——,
his attorney [*or in person*], to the said writ, and defended for the whole of
the [land *or* tenements *or* property *or* premises] therein mentioned, and no
appearance has been entered or defence made to the said writ by the said
[*names of defendants who have not appeared*], wherefore the said A. B. ought
to recover against the said [*names of defendants who have not appeared*] possession of the [land *or* tenements *or* property *or* premises] in the said writ
mentioned; but because it is convenient that there should be but one
award of execution in this behalf, therefore let all further proceedings

———

(z) The venue is local, *ante*, 135.
(a) Make a marginal note of the date, as *ante*, 739, note (y).
(b) The venue is local, *ante*, 135.
(c) See the next two Forms.
(d) If for part only, see No. 124.

against the said [*names of defendants who have not appeared*] be stayed until the trial and determination of the issue herein between the said A. B. and the said C. D.: And to try that issue let a jury come, &c.

N.B. *This form is given in Chitty's Forms, 546 (7th ed.).*

---

127. *Judgment for Want of Appearance against the Defendant named in the Writ, and Issue against his Landlords (some being Infants), as to the whole of the Property (ante, 131, 135).*

Same as ante, No. 125, to the end of the judgment by default for want of appearance, then proceed thus:

And E. K. an infant, under the age of twenty-one years, by R. K., admitted by the court here as guardian of the said E. K., to defend for her: And A. T. an infant, under the age of twenty-one years, by J. J., admitted by the court here as guardian of the said A. T. to defend for him: And J. B. and Ann his wife and E. T., by G. H., their attorney, have on the [*day of appearance*] —— day of ——, A.D. 18—, by leave of [the Hon. Sir George Bramwell, Knight, one of the Barons of this court, *or as the case may be, post,* Nos. 135, 136], appeared to the said writ, and defended as landlords [*and landladies*] of the said [*name of the tenant in possession named in the writ*], for the whole of the [land *or* tenements *or* property *or* premises] therein mentioned: Therefore let a jury come, &c.

See No. 135, post.

---

128. *Affidavit to set aside on Terms a regular Judgment entered for Want of Appearance (ante, 132).*

Commence as ante, Nos. 19, 20 or 21.

1. That the paper writing hereunto annexed, marked (A), is, as I believe, a copy of the writ of ejectment issued in this action.

2. That upon the —— day of —— [last *or* instant], the said copy writ was served upon me [personally, *or describe the mode of service according to the fact*].

3. That [*here state the special facts showing why and under what circumstances the defendant did not appear in due time to the writ, and whether it was by mere mistake, inadvertence or otherwise. The form must of course vary in each case, and it may sometimes be material that some other person or persons should corroborate the defendant on this part of his affidavit.*]

4. That on the —— day of —— [instant *or* last] judgment was signed in this action [against me *or* the said C. D.], for want of an appearance.

5. That no execution hath yet issued on the said judgment, as I have been informed, by the [clerk of the plaintiff's attorney *or* agent, *or as the case may be*] and verily believe.

Or,

5. That on the —— day of —— [instant *or* last] possession of the property claimed [*or* of ——, *describe the part*, being part of the said property claimed] was delivered to the plaintiff by a bailiff or officer of the sheriff of ——, under and by virtue of a warrant granted by the said sheriff upon a writ of habere facias possessionem issued in this action, and [I *or* the said C. D.] was then turned out of possession of the said [part of the said] property, under and by virtue of the said last-mentioned writ.

6. That I am advised and verily believe that I have a good defence to this action as to [the whole *or* the said part] of the said property claimed, upon the merits. [*Sometimes it may be advisable to describe shortly the nature of the defence upon the merits, concluding thus:* "That for the reasons and under the circumstances aforesaid, I am advised," *&c. ut supra.*]

Sworn &c. (*ante,* 705.)

129. *Summons thereon (ante, 132).*
Commence as ante, No. 22.

Why the judgment signed in this action against the defendant [*or* the defendant C. D., *as the case may be*] for want of appearance, [and all subsequent proceedings thereon,] should not be set aside, and the said [defendant *or* C. D.] be allowed forthwith to appear and defend this action for all the property claimed, [*or for* ——, *describe the part*, being part of the property claimed,] upon such terms as shall appear to me just and reasonable. [*If an* habere facias possessionem *has been executed*, say, " And why the plaintiff should not restore and re-deliver to the said defendant the possession of the said [part of the said] property." Dated the —— day of ——, 18—.

Judge's signature.

130. *Order thereon.*
Commence as ante, No. 24.

I do order that the judgment signed in this action against the defendant [*or* the defendant C. D., *as the case may be*] for want of appearance, [and all subsequent proceedings thereon,] be set aside, and the said [defendant *or* C. D.] be allowed forthwith to appear and defend this action for [all the property claimed, *or for* ——, *describe the part*, being part of the property claimed:] And I order that the said [defendant *or* C. D.] deliver notice of his intention to defend for part only, on the same day on which he appears, and not afterwards; and that he do accept short notice of trial (if necessary) for the next assizes to be holden in and for the county of ——: And I do order that the said [defendant *or* C. D.] do pay to the plaintiffs their costs of the said judgment, and of and incident to this application, to be taxed by one of the masters: And I do order that the plaintiffs restore and re-deliver to the said [defendant *or* C. D.] the possession of the said [above-mentioned part of the said] property. Counsel allowed. Dated the —— day of ——, 18—.

Judge's signature.

N.B.—*The terms of the order will of course vary according to the discretion of the judge.*

131. *Issue where there is a Defence as to the whole (ante, 134).*

In the [Q. B., C. P. *or* Exch.]

The [*date of writ*] —— day of ——, A. D. 18—.

Venue (*e*), } On the day and year above written, a writ of our lady the to wit. } Queen issued forth of this court, in these words (that is to say),

Victoria by the grace of God [*here copy the writ*] ; and C. D. has, on the —— day of ——, A.D. 18—, appeared by ——, his attorney [*or* in person], to the said writ, and defended for the whole of the land [*or* tenements, *or* property, *or* premises] therein mentioned : Therefore let a jury come, &c.

N.B.—*This form is given by* 15 & 16 *Vict. c.* 76, *s.* 178, *Sched.* (*A.*), *No.* 16, *except that* " land " *only is therein mentioned.*

(*e*) The venue is local, *ante*, 135.

132. *Issue where there is a Defence as to Part only (ante, 134).*

In the [Q. B., C. P. or Exch.]

The [*date of writ*] —— day of ——, A.D. 18—.

Venue (*f*), } On the day and year above written, a writ of our lady the
to wit. } Queen issued forth of this court in these words (that is to
say),

Victoria, by the grace of God [*here copy the writ*]; and C. D. has on the
—— day of ——, A.D. 18—, appeared by ——, his attorney, [*or in person*]
to the said writ, and has defended for a part of the land [*or tenements, or
premises, or* property] in the said writ mentioned; that is to say [*here state
the part*]; and no appearance has been entered or defence made to the said
writ, except as to the said part: Therefore it is considered (*g*) that the said
A. B. [*the claimant*] do recover possession of the land [*or tenements, or
premises, or* property] in the said writ mentioned, except the said part, with
the appurtenances, and that he have execution thereof forthwith; and as to
the rest, let a jury come, &c.

N.B.—*This form is given by 15 & 16 Vict. c. 76, s. 177, Sched. (A.), No. 15,
except that the word* "land" *only is therein mentioned; see the notes to No.* 123,
ante. For other forms see ante, Nos. 125, 126, 127 ; *post, Nos.* 133 *to* 138.

———

133. *Issue where there are Defences by several Defendants as to different Parts
(ante, 134).*

In the [Q. B., C. P. or Exch.]

The [*date of writ*] —— day of ——, A.D. 18—.

Venue (*h*), } On the day and year above written, a writ of our lady the
to wit. } Queen issued forth of this court in these words (that is to
say,)

Victoria by the grace of God [*here copy the writ*]; and C. D. has on the
—— day of ——, A.D. 18—, appeared by ——, his attorney [*or in person*],
to the said writ, and has defended for a part of the land [*or tenements or
premises, or* property] in the said writ mentioned; that is to say [*here state
the part*]: And G. H., I. K. and L. M. have on the —— day of ——, A.D.
18—, appeared by ——, their attorney [*or in person*], to the said writ, and
have defended for other parts, being the residue of the land [*or tenements,
or premises, or* property] in the said writ mentioned; that is to say [*here
state the part*]: Therefore let a jury come, &c.

N.B.—*See note to No.* 123. *If there be no defence as to part, see ante, No.*
124.

———

134. *Issue as against some of the Defendants who defend for the whole, and
the Claimants abandon all further Proceedings against other Defendants
named in the Writ, but who have not been served (ante,* 135).

Same as ante, No. 131, *to the end.*

After the words "Therefore let a jury come, &c.," *proceed thus :*—And the
said [*names of defendants who have not been served and have not appeared*] not
having been served with the said writ, and not having appeared or made any
defence to the same, the said [*claimants*] abandon all further proceedings
herein against [them *or* him.]

N.B.—*This form is given in* Chit. Forms, 547, 7th edit. *See post, Nos.*
143, 144.

———————————————————

(*f*) The venue is local, *ante,* 135.

(*g*) In the margin opposite the words "Therefore it is considered," &c.,
write a memorandum thus: "Judgment signed on the [*date*] —— day of
——, 18—."

(*h*) The venue is local, *ante,* 135.

185. *Issue where there is a Defence as to the whole by the Defendants as Tenants, and also by their Landlord (ante, 127, 135).*

In the [Q. B., C. P. *or* Exch.]

The [*date of writ*] —— day of ——, A.D. 18—.

Venue (*i*), } On the day and year above written, a writ of our lady the
to wit. } Queen issued forth of this court, in these words (that is to
say),

Victoria, by the grace of God [*here copy the writ*] ; and C. D., I. K. and
L. M. have on the —— day of ——, in the year aforesaid [*or* in the year of
our Lord 18—], appeared by ——, their attorney [*or* in person] to the said
writ, and defended for the whole of the [land, *or* tenements, *or* premises, *or*
property] therein mentioned: And O. P. has also on the —— day of ——,
A.D. 18—, by leave of the Hon. Sir ——, knight [one of the judges *or* barons
of this court, *or* one of her Majesty's justices of her Court of Queen's Bench
or Common Pleas, *or* one of the barons of her Majesty's Exchequer, *as the
case may be*], appeared by ——, his attorney [*or* in person], to the said writ,
and defended as landlord of the said C. D., I. K. and L. M. for the whole
of the [land, *or* tenements, *or* premises, *or* property] therein mentioned:
Therefore let a jury come, &c.

See ante, No. 127.

———

186. *Issue where the Landlord appears, but the Defendants named in the Writ
do not appear (ante, 127, 135).*

Same as No. 125 *to the end of the judgment by default for want of appearance ;
then proceed thus :—*

And O. P. has on the —— day of ——, A.D. 18—, by leave of the Hon.
Sir ——, Knight, [one of the Judges *or* Barons of this Court, *or* one of her
Majesty's Justices of her Court of Queen's Bench, *or* Common Pleas, *or* one
of the Barons of her Majesty's Exchequer, *as the case may be*] appeared by
——, his attorney [*or* in person], to the said writ, and defended as landlord
of the said [*defendants named in the writ, or some of them, as the case may be*],
for the whole (*k*) of the [land *or* tenements, *or* premises *or* property] therein
mentioned : Therefore let a jury come, &c.

———

187. *Issue where the Defendant defends for the whole as a Joint Tenant, Tenant
in Common, or Coparcener (ante, 130, 135).*

In the [Q. B., C. P. *or* Exch.]

The [*date of writ*] —— day of ——, A.D. 18—.

Venue (*i*), } On the day and year above written, a writ of our lady the
to wit. } Queen issued forth of this court, in these words (that is to
say),

Victoria, by the grace of God [*here copy the writ*] ; and C. D. has on the
—— day of ——, A.D. 18—, appeared by —— , his attorney [*or* in person],
to the said writ, and defended for the whole of the property therein mentioned, as a [joint tenant, *or* tenant in common, *or* coparcener] with the
said [A. B.], and has admitted the right of the said A. B. to an undivided
share of the said property, (that is to say) to one equal undivided [moiety
or third, fourth, fifth, &c. part] thereof: But the said C. D. has denied any
actual ouster of the said A. B. from the said property : Therefore let a jury
come, &c.

———

(*i*) The venue is local, *ante*, 135.
(*k*) If for part only, see *ante*, Nos. 124, 126. When some of the landlords are infants and defend by guardian, see *ante*, No. 127.

138. *Issue where one of the Defendants defends for Part as a Joint Tenant, or Tenant in Common, or Coparcener [and where another Defendant defends in the ordinary manner for other Part], with Judgment for Want of Appearance as to the Residue (ante, 135, 138).*

In the [Q. B., C. P. *or* Exch.]

The [*date of writ*] —— day of ——, A.D. 18—.

Venue (m), } On the day and year above written, a writ of our lady the Queen
to wit. { issued forth of this court, in these words (that is to say),

Victoria, by the grace of God [*here copy the writ*]: and C. D. has on the —— day of ——, A.D. 18—, appeared by —— his attorney [*or* in person] to the said writ, and has defended for a part of the land [*or* tenements, *or* premises *or* property] in the said writ mentioned (that is to say), [*here state the part*] as a [joint tenant *or* tenant in common, *or* coparcener] with the said A. B.; and has admitted the right of the said A. B. to an undivided share of the said part, (that is to say) to one equal undivided [moiety *or* third, fourth, fifth, &c. part] thereof: But the said C. D. has denied any actual ouster of the said A. B. from the said part of the said land [*or* • tenements, *or* premises *or* property]: And E. F. has on the —— day of ——, A.D. 18—, appeared by —— his attorney [*or* in person], and has defended for a part of the land [*or* tenements, *or* premises *or* property] in the said writ mentioned, (that is to say) [*here state the part*]: And no appearance has been entered or defence made to the said writ, except as to the said parts: Therefore it is considered (*n*) that the said A. B. do recover possession of the said land [*or* tenements, *or* premises *or* property] in the said writ mentioned, except the said parts, with the appurtenances, and that he have execution thereof forthwith: And as to the rest, let a jury come, &c.

---

139. *Summons to set aside an Issue for Irregularity, with Costs, the Defendant's Notice to defend for Part only [or as a Joint Tenant, Tenant in Common or Coparcener] not having been entered in the Issue (ante, 135).*

Commence as ante, No. 22.

Why the issue delivered in this action should not be set aside for irregularity, with costs to be taxed by one of the masters, and paid by the plaintiff to the defendant [C. D.] or his attorney, the notice of the said [C. D.] to defend [for part only, *or* as a joint tenant *or* tenant in common, *or* coparcener with the plaintiff] not having been entered or stated in the said issue according to The Common Law Procedure Act, 1852. Dated the —— day of ——, 18—.

Judge's signature.

---

140. *Order thereon.*

Commence as ante, No. 24.

I do order that the issue delivered in this action be set aside for irregularity, with costs [*follow the language of the summons to the end*]. Dated the —— day of ——, 18 –.

Judge's signature.

---

141. *Summons for Leave to amend the Issue, without Prejudice to the Notice of Trial (ante, 134).*

Commence as ante, No. 22.

Why the plaintiffs should not be at liberty to amend the issue upon payment of [3s. 4d.] costs, without prejudice to the notice of trial. Dated the —— day of ——, 18 –.

Judge's signature.

(*m*) The venue is local, *ante*, 135.
(*n*) Opposite the words "Therefore it is considered, &c.," write "Judgment signed on the —— day of ——, 18—."

K K

142. *Order thereon.*

Commence as ante, No. 24.

I do order that the plaintiffs be at liberty to amend the issue upon payment of [3*s.* 4*d.*] costs, without prejudice to the notice of trial.   Dated the —— day of ——, 18—.

Judge's signature.

143. *Affidavit for Order to amend Writ by striking out Names of some of the Defendants who have not been served (ante, 135).*

Commence as ante, Nos. 19, 20 or 21.

1. That this action of ejectment was commenced on the —— day of ——, A.D. 18—, by a writ then issued out of and under the seal of this honorable court, a true copy whereof is hereunto annexed, marked (A).

2. That [I. K. and L. M.], two of the defendants named in the said writ, have not, nor hath either of them, been served with the said writ or any copy thereof, either personally or otherwise [except in a manner which has been held insufficient by the honorable Mr. Justice (*or* Baron) —— upon an application for an order for leave to sign judgment in this action as against the said I. K. and L. M. (*or as the case may be*)].

3. The said [I. K. and L. M.] have not, nor hath either of them, entered any appearance to this action.

4. The defendants [C. D., E. F. and G. H.] have appeared to this action by Mr. ——, their attorney *or* by their respective attornies.

5. That [*here state any notice to defend for part only; or that no such notice has been given, and that the time for giving any such notice has expired*].

6. The plaintiffs are desirous of proceeding with this action as against the said defendants [C. D., E. F. and G. H.] only; and for that purpose to amend their said writ, by striking out the names of the said [I. K. and L. M.]

Sworn, &c. (*ante,* 705.)

N.B.—*Annex copy writ, marked (A).   See note to No.* 144, *infra.*

144. *Order thereon (ante,* 135).

B. [and another] ⎫ Upon reading the affidavit of ——, and upon hearing
     v.   ⎬ Mr. ——, the plaintiffs' attorney, I do order that the
D. [and others]. ⎭ plaintiffs be at liberty to amend the writ of ejectment issued in this action, by striking out the names of the defendants [I. K. and L. M.], who have not been served therewith and have not appeared.   And I order that the plaintiffs do forthwith serve the other defendants or their respective attornies or agents [*or* the defendant C. D. or his attorney or agent] with a copy of this order, and of the said writ as amended.   Dated the —— day of ——, 18—.

Judge's signature.

For another mode of disposing of the defendants who have not been served with the writ, see ante, 134, *and Form No.* 134.

145. *Order of Reference before Trial, with Special Clauses (ante,* 320).

B. [and another] ⎫ Upon hearing the attornies or agents on both sides, and
     v.   ⎬ by consent, I do order that this action of ejectment be
D. [and others]. ⎭ referred to the award, order, arbitrament, final end and determination of —— Esq., barrister at law, who shall make and publish his award in writing of and concerning the matter referred, ready to be delivered to the said parties in difference, or such of them as shall require the same, or to either of them, or, if they or either of them shall be dead before the making of the said award, to their respective personal representatives who shall require the same, on or before the first day of [Michaelmas] term now next: And, by the like consent, I do further order, that the said arbitrator, in case he shall not be able to make his award in the premises

by the time hereinbefore limited for that purpose, shall and may be at liberty, either with or without the consent of the said parties if he shall think fit, by writing under his hand, to enlarge the time for making his said award, so that it shall not be extended beyond the first day of [Hilary] term now next: And, by the like consent, I do further order, that the said parties shall in all things abide by, perform, fulfil and keep such award so to be made as aforesaid, and that the costs of the said action, and also the costs of [the reference and award, shall [abide the event of the said award, *or* shall be in the discretion of the said arbitrator, who shall award and direct by whom and to whom the same respectively shall be paid] : And, by the like consent, I do further order, that the said arbitrator shall be at liberty (if he shall think fit) to examine the said parties to this suit, and their respective witnesses, upon oath or affirmation: And that the said parties do and shall, if necessary, produce before the said arbitrator all books, deeds, papers and writings, in their or either of their custody, possession or power, touching or relating to the matter referred; and that each party do, upon the said reference, admit all deeds, grants, assignments, documents, letters and copies of letters, and all other muniments of title, notices and copies thereof, and all probates of wills, in evidence, as if they were the originals; and do admit in evidence all copies of surrenders or admissions, and other entries on court-rolls, on plain paper or parchment, unstamped or other- wise; and all certificates of baptism, marriage and burial, and all extracts from baptismal, marriage, or burial books or registers, without proof or pro- duction of the books from whence the said extracts are or purport to be taken, saving all just exceptions to the admissibility of all such documents, as evidence in this cause: And, by the like consent, I do further order, that the said arbitrator shall have power, on the application of either party, either before, at or after the said reference, to cause any amendment to be made in the record and proceedings in this action; and that, notwithstand- ing this order, either party shall be at liberty to apply to a judge of this court to make any such amendment, or as to any admissions to be made on the said reference, and in case of refusal, as to the costs of proof, but that neither party shall be compelled so to apply: And, by the like consent, I do further order, that the said arbitrator shall, in the event of his finding in favour of the plaintiffs, have power to order immediate possession to be given of the land and premises in question in this action to the plaintiffs or either of them [and also how, and in what manner, such possession shall be given, and if not given, how it shall be taken, and who shall be at the ex- pense thereof] : And, by the like consent, I do further order, that if any application be made to her majesty's Court of [Queen's Bench] for the purpose of setting aside the said award, it shall be lawful for the said court to refer the matter back to the said arbitrator, who shall in that case have power to make a new award in the premises, or to amend the award by him first made, within such time as by the said court shall be ordered and directed in that behalf, and he shall have the same powers under the said reference from the court as are contained in the present order of reference; and that such new or amended award shall be binding upon the said parties as an award to be made under this order: And, by the like consent, I fur- ther order, that neither party shall bring or prosecute any action or suit at law or in equity against the said arbitrator, or bring any proceeding in error, or prefer any bill in equity against each other, of and concerning the matter so as aforesaid referred; and that, if either party shall, by affected delay or otherwise, wilfully prevent the said arbitrator from making an award, he shall pay such costs to the other as the said arbitrator, or the said Court of [Queen's Bench], shall think reasonable and just: And, by the like consent, I do further order, that this order shall and may, at the instance of either party, be made a rule of her majesty's Court of [Queen's Bench], if such court shall so please. Dated the —— day of ——, 18—.

Judge's signature.

KK 2

146. *Summons for Special Case before Trial* (*ante,* 138).
Commence as ante, No. 22.

Why a special case should not be stated in this action pursuant to the 179th section of the Common Law Procedure Act, 1852. Dated the —— day of ——, 18—.

Judge's signature.

------

147. *Order thereon.*
Commence as ante, No. 24.

And by consent, I do order that a special case be stated in this action pursuant to the 179th section of the Common Law Procedure Act, 1852. Dated the —— day of ——, 18—.

Judge's signature.

------

148. *Special Case before Trial* (*ante,* 138).
Title of court and cause as ante, No. 19.

This action of ejectment was commenced on the —— day of ——, A.D. 18—, by a writ of our lady the Queen issued forth of this court in these words :

Victoria, by the grace of God [*here copy the writ, and state the appearances and notices* (*if any*) *as in the issue*].

The following case is stated for the opinion of the court, by consent of the parties, and by order of the Honorable Mr. Justice [*or* Baron] ——, dated the —— day of ——, 18—, pursuant to the 179th section of the Common Law Procedure Act, 1852.

CASE.
Here state concisely all the material facts.

The court is to be at liberty to draw any inferences or find any facts which in the opinion of the court or jury ought to have drawn or found; [also to amend the writ, and any of the subsequent proceedings, as the court may think fit].

[No proceedings in error shall be brought by either party upon the judgment of the court upon this case (*o*).]

The question for the opinion of the court is whether [*here state the question*].

If the court shall be of opinion that [*here state the plaintiffs' point*], then judgment shall be entered for the plaintiffs by confession for the whole of the [land *or* tenements, *or* premises *or* property] claimed in the writ [without costs, *or* with costs to be taxed], immediately after the decision of the case or otherwise, as the court may think fit].

If the court shall be of opinion that [*here state the defendants' point*], then a [nolle prosequi *or* judgment by confession for the defendants without costs *or* with costs to be taxed], shall be entered immediately after the decision of the case or otherwise, as the court may think fit.

Counsel's signature " for the plaintiffs."
Counsel's signature " for the defendants."

------

149. *Special Cases before Trial* (*other Forms*), *ante,* 138.

Whether a devise to plaintiff of all the testator's *effects* included a remainder in fee. *Doe* d. *Haw* v. *Earles,* 15 M. & W. 450 ; and see *Doe* d. *Evans* v. *Walker,* 15 Q. B. 28.

Whether under a will S. J. took an estate tail, or an estate in fee simple

------

(*o*) Vide 17 & 18 Vict. c. 125, s. 32 (*ante,* 326).

with an executory devise over in certain events. *Doe* d. *Johnson* v. *Johnson,* 8 Exch. 81.

As to the true construction of a will and codicil taken together or separately, whether M. D. took an absolute interest in certain leaseholds, or subject to an executory bequest over in favour of the children of the testator's son. *Darley* v. *Martin,* 13 C. B. 684; and see *Cole* v. *Goble, id.* 445.

Whether upon the construction of a will, and in the events that had happened, the plaintiffs were entitled to parts of certain lands as tenants in common in fee. *Greenwood* v. *Sutcliffe,* 14 C. B. 226.

What estate the trustees under a will took under a devise to them without words of inheritance. *Doe* d. *Kimber* v. *Cafe,* 7 Exch. 675; now see 1 Vict. c. 26, ss. 30, 31 (*ante,* 511).

Whether J. P. took a fee under a marriage settlement, or a will (without words of inheritance). *Doe* d. *Pottow* v. *Fricker,* 6 Exch. 510; and see *Doe* d. *Burton* v. *White,* 1 Exch. 526; *S. C. in error,* 2 Exch. 797; *Burton* v. *White,* 7 Exch. 720.

Whether the limitations in a marriage settlement were too remote. *Doe* d. *Lees* v. *Ford,* 2 E. & B. 970.

Whether upon the facts as stated, plaintiff or defendant entitled to the property. *Westbrook* v. *Blythe,* 3 E. & B. 737; and see *Hughes* v. *Lumley,* 4 E. & B. 274.

For other forms, see *post,* No. 252.

---

150. *Notice of Special Case being set down for Argument* (*ante,* 138).

Title of court and cause as ante, No. 19.

Take notice that [I *or* we] have this day set down the special case in this action for argument on —— day, the —— day of ——, [instant *or* next]. Dated the —— day of ——, 18—.

Yours, &c.

To Mr. ——, the defendant's }
  [*or* plaintiff's] attorney. } ——————,
  plaintiff's [*or* defendant's] attorney.

---

151. *Final Judgment after a Special Case* (*ante,* 139).

In the [Q. B., C. P. *or* Exch.]
  On the [*date of writ*] —— day of ——, A.D. 18—.

Venue, } On the day and year above written, a writ of our lady the Queen to wit. } issued forth of this court in these words (that is to say),

Victoria, by the grace of God [*here copy the writ*]; and C. D. has, on the —— day of ——, appeared by ——, his attorney, to the said writ, and defended for the whole of the [land *or* tenements, or premises *or* property] therein mentioned [*or state appearances and notices* (*if any*) *to defend for part only, as in an issue*].

Afterwards on the [*date of judge's order for special case*] —— day of ——, A.D. 18—, by consent of the parties, and by leave of [the Honorable Sir ——, Knight, one of the judges *or* barons of this court (*or as the case may be*)], a special case is stated in this action according to the provisions of The Common Law Procedure Act, 1852, and the previous practice of this court, as follows:—

Copy the Special Case.

Afterwards on the [*day of entering final judgment*] —— day of ——, A.D. 18—, come here the parties aforesaid, and the court is of opinion that [*state the opinion of the court on the question or questions stated in the case, in the affirmative or negative, as the case may be*]: Therefore it is considered [*here state the judgment according to the rule, which should agree with the terms of the special case, ex. gr.*]: That the said A. B. do recover possession of the said [land *or* tenements, *or* premises *or* property] in the said writ mentioned, with the appurtenances, and £—— for his costs of suit. *Or that*

the said C. D. be acquitted, and that he recover against the said A. B.
£—— for his costs of defence.

N.B. *On signing the judgment a mere incipitur may be entered as ante*, No. 122.

In the margin of the judgment, opposite the words "Therefore it is considered, &c.," *write* "Judgment signed on the [*date of signing judgment*] —— day of ——, 18—."

If by the terms of the special case a "*nolle prosequi*" *or* "*judgment by confession*" *is to be entered, introduce it just before the words* "Therefore," *&c. as follows*:—" And hereupon the said A. B., in pursuance of the terms of the said special case, says, that he will not further prosecute his action against the said C. D.: Therefore" [*as above*] *or* "And hereupon the said C. D., in pursuance of the terms of the said special case, confesses the said action of the said A. B.: Therefore" [*as above*].

---

152. *Retainer to Counsel at the Assizes* (ante, 140).

Venue.—Spring [*or* Summer] assizes, 18—.

B. *v.* D.

Retainer for the [claimant *or* defendant].

Mr. ——

E. F. of ——,

    Agent for G. H. of ——.   [*Date*].

One gua.

---

153. *Retainer to Counsel in London or Middlesex* (ante, 140).

In the [Q. B., C. P. *or* Exch.]

B. *v.* D.

[London *or* Middlesex.] Retainer for the [claimant *or* defendant].

Mr. ——

E. F. of ——,

    Agent for G. H. of ——.   [*Date*].

One gua.

---

154. *Summons to change the Place of Trial* (ante, 142).

Commence as ante, No. 22.

Why the trial of this action should not take place in the county of ——, instead of the county of ——, wherein the venue is laid (*p*). Dated the —— day of ——, 18—.

Judge's signature.

---

155. *Order thereon.*

Commence as ante, No. 24.

I do order that the trial of this action take place in the county of ——, instead of the county of ——, wherein the venue is laid. Dated the —— day of ——, 18—.

Judge's signature.

---

156. *Suggestion of the above Order* (ante, 142).

In the [Q. B., C. P. *or* Exch.]

B. [and another] ⎱ And now on the [*date when pleaded* (*q*)] —— day of
    v.　　　　 ⎰ ——, A.D. 18—, it is suggested, and manifestly appears
D. [and others]. ⎰ to the court here, that by an order of the Honorable Mr.
[Justice *or* Baron] ——, made in this action on the [*date of order*] ——

(*p*) It is unnecessary to mention the suggestion to be entered on the record, for that may be made by either party as of course when the order is obtained.

(*q*) The suggestion being a mere entry on the record, and not a pleading, need not be entitled with the date when pleaded. *Barnett* v. *Earl of Guilford*, 11 Exch. 23, note; see *post*, No. 292, note.

day of ——, 18—, it was ordered, that the trial of this action should take place in the county of——, instead of the county of ——, wherein the venue is laid. Therefore let a jury of the said county of —— come &c.

---

157. *Consent to a Trial before the Court, or a Judge without a Jury (ante, 143).*

Title of court and cause as ante, No. 19.

We the undersigned do hereby consent to leave the decision of the matters in question in this cause to the court, pursuant to the first section of the Common Law Procedure Act, 1854, if the court or a judge shall think fit to allow such trial. Dated this —— day of ——, 18—.

> E. F., of ——,
> Attorney for the plaintiffs.
> G. H. of ——,
> Attorney for the defendants.

N.B.—*This consent must be signed by all the parties or their attornies* (ante, 143).

---

158. *Affidavit verifying the Signature to such Consent (ante, 143).*

Commence as ante, Nos. 19, 20 *or* 21.

1. I was present on the —— day of —— [instant *or* last], and did see E. F., the attorney in this action for the above-named plaintiffs, sign the paper writing hereunto annexed, marked (A), and I say that the signature "E. F." appearing subscribed to the said paper writing is of the proper handwriting of the said E. F.

2. I was present on the —— day of —— [instant *or* last], and did see G. H., the attorney in this action for all the above-named defendants, sign the said paper writing; and I say that the signature "G. H." appearing subscribed to the said paper writing is of the proper handwriting of the said G. H.

Sworn, &c. (*ante*, 705.)

---

159. *Summons for Trial by the Court, or a Judge without a Jury (ante, 143).*

Commence as ante, No. 22.

Why the matters in question in this cause should not be tried by the court pursuant to the first section of the Common Law Procedure Act, 1854.

Dated the —— day of ——, 18—.

> *Judge's signature.*

---

160. *Order thereon.*

Commence as ante, No. 24.

And by consent, I do order that the matters in question in this cause be tried by the court pursuant to the first section of the Common Law Procedure Act, 1854. Dated the —— day of ——, 18—.

> *Judge's signature.*

---

161. *Issue to be tried before a Judge without a Jury (ante, 143).*

Commence as ante, Nos. 131 *to* 138 :

Omitting the words "Therefore let a jury come, &c.," *or* "and as to the rest let a jury come, &c.," *instead of which proceed thus :—*

And the parties aforesaid, having by consent in writing duly signed left the decision of the said matters in question to the court, it was on the —— day of ——, A.D. 18— [*date of rule or order for allowance of trial*], by a rule of this court [*or* by an order of the Hon. Sir ——, knight, one of her majesty's justices of her Court of Queen's Bench [*or* Common Pleas, *or* one of the barons of her majesty's Court of Exchequer, *as the case may be*], ordered that such trial should be allowed: Therefore let the same be had accordingly.

---

162. *Subpœna to testify before a Judge (ante*, 143).

Same as post, Nos. 192, 193:

Omitting the words "by a jury."

---

163. *Nisi prius Record in such case (ante*, 143).

This is a mere copy on parchment of the issue, *ante*, No. 161.

---

164. *Postea at the Assizes upon a Trial without a Jury (ante*, 143).

Afterwards on the [*commission day of the assizes*] —— day of ——, 18—, at ——, in the county [*or* city] of ——, at the assizes there holden in and for the said county [*or* city] before [Sir ——, knight, one of her majesty's justices of her Court of Queen's Bench *or* Common Pleas, *or* one of the barons of her majesty's Court of Exchequer, *as the case may be, if before a chief justice or chief baron, state his name and title as in an ordinary postea, post, Nos.* 242—244], come the parties within mentioned, by their respective attornies within mentioned [*or* in their proper persons, *as the case may be*], for the trial of the said matters in question: And the said judge [*or* baron, *or* chief justice, *or* chief baron, *as the case may be*] decides that A. B. [*the claimant*] within mentioned, on the —— day of ——, A.D. 18—, was and still is entitled to possession of the [land *or* tenements] within mentioned (*r*), as in the writ alleged (*s*): Therefore, &c.

---

165. *Postea in London or Middlesex upon a Trial without a Jury (ante*, 143).

Afterwards on the [*first day of the sittings, or the day of the trial*] —— day of ——, 18—, at [the Guildhall of the city of London, *or* Westminster Hall in the county of Middlesex], before [Sir ——, knight, one of her majesty's justices of her Court of Queen's Bench *or* Common Pleas, *or* one of the barons of her majesty Court of Exchequer, *as the case may be; or if tried before the chief justice or chief baron, state the fact, as in the prescribed form of postea on a trial before a jury (post, Nos.* 242—244): *if tried before two judges, state the names of both, and of the court of which they are judges*], come the parties within mentioned, by their respective attornies within mentioned [*or* in their proper persons, *as the case may be*], for the trial of the said matters in question: And the said [judge, *or* baron, *or* chief justice, *or* chief baron, *as the case may be*] decides that [*here proceed as in No.* 164 *to the end*]: Therefore, &c.

(*r*) If for part only say, "was and still is entitled to possession of [*describe the part*], being part of the [land *or* tenements] within mentioned, as in the said writ alleged (*s*). And the said [judge, *or* baron, *or* chief justice, *or* chief baron] decides that the said A. B. on the said —— day of ——, 18—, was not nor is entitled to possession of the residue of the said [land *or* tenements] or any part thereof: Therefore, &c."

(*s*) If mesne profits be assessed say, "and the said [judge, *or* baron, *or* chief justice, *or* chief baron] assesses the damages to be paid by the said C. D. to the said A. B. for the mesne profits of the said [land *or* tenements, *or* part of the said land *or* tenements], from the day of the [expiration *or* determination] of the said C. D.'s interest in the same, down to the —— day of ——, 18—, over and above his costs of suit, to £——. [*Here state the decision as to the residue, if any, ut supra* (*r*)]: Therefore, &c."

166. *Judgment thereon for the Plaintiff (ante, 143).*

Copy the issue and then proceed thus :—

Afterwards on the [*day of signing final judgment*] —— day of ——, 18—, come the parties aforesaid by their respective attornies aforesaid [*or* in their proper persons, *as the case may be*], and [Sir ——, knight, one of her majesty's justices of her Court of Queen's Bench *or* Common Pleas, *or* one of the barons of her majesty's Exchequer, *as the case may be ; or if tried before the chief justice or chief baron, state the fact as in the prescribed form of postea in a trial before a jury (post, Nos. 242—244) : if tried before two judges state the names of both, and of the court of which they are judges*], by whom the said matters in question were tried, hath [*or* have] sent hither his [*or* their] record had before him [*or* them] in these words: Afterwards [*copy the postea*]: Therefore it is considered that the said A. B. do recover possession of the said land [*or* tenements] in the said writ mentioned, with the appurtenances, and that he have execution thereof forthwith. And it is further considered that the said A. B. do recover against the said C. D. [*if mesne profits assessed, say,* the said monies by the said judge, *or* baron, *or* chief justice, *or* chief baron, *as the case may be,* so assessed, and] £—— for his costs of suit.

*In the margin, opposite the words "*Therefore it is considered, &c.,*" write "*Judgment signed on the —— day of ——, 18—.*"*

---

167. *Execution thereon (ante, 143).*

The same as in ordinary cases, *post,* Nos. 270 to 278.

---

168. *Notice of Trial at the Assizes (indorsed on the Issue), (ante, 146).*

To Mr. G. H., the defendant's attorney [*or* agent].

Take notice of trial in this cause for the next assizes, to be holden at [*name of assize town*] in and for the county of ——. Dated the —— day of ——, 18—.

             Yours, &c.

                E. F., of ——,

                    Plaintiff's attorney [*or* agent].

---

169. *The like, delivered separately (ante, 146).*

Title of court and cause as ante, No. 19.

Take notice of trial in this cause for the next assizes, to be holden at [*name of assize town*] in and for the county of ——. Dated the —— day of ——, 18—.

             Yours, &c.

To Mr. G. H., the defendant's attorney [*or* agent].   E. F., of ——, plaintiff's attorney [*or* agent].

---

170. *Notice of Trial in London or Middlesex (ante, 146).*

Under the short title of the cause indorsed on the issue (t), say—

Take notice of trial in this cause for the [first, second *or* third] sittings within the present —— term [*or* for the first sittings *or* the adjourned sittings after the present —— term], to be holden at [the Guildhall in and for the city of London, *or* at Westminster Hall in and for the county of Middlesex]. Dated the —— day of ——, 18—.

             Yours, &c.

To Mr. G. H., the defendant's attorney [*or* agent].   E. F., of ——, plaintiff's attorney [*or* agent].

(t) If delivered separately, to be entitled with the name of the court and cause, as *ante,* No. 19.

171. *Notice of Trial by Continuance (ante, 148).*
Title of court and cause as ante, No. 19.

I hereby continue the notice of trial given you in this cause to the next sitting in [*or* to the first sitting after] this present —— term. Dated the —— day of ——, 18—.

Yours, &c.

To Mr. G. H., the defendant's }   E. F., of ——, plaintiff's attorney
attorney [*or* agent].   [*or* agent].

---

172. *Notice of Countermand (ante, 148).*
Title of court and cause as ante, No. 19.

I hereby countermand the notice of trial given you in this cause. Dated the —— day of ——, 18—.

Yours, &c.

To Mr. G. H., the defendant's }   E. F., of ——, plaintiff's attorney
attorney [*or* agent].   [*or* agent].

---

173. *Affidavit for Costs of the Day for not Proceeding to Trial (ante,* 149).
Commence as ante, Nos. 19, 20 *or* 21.

1. That this is an action of ejectment, and on the —— day of —— last, notice of trial was given in this action on behalf of the plaintiffs [*or* plaintiff], for the last assizes holden at ——, in and for the county of —— [*or as the case may be*].

2. The above-named plaintiffs [*or* plaintiff] did not proceed to the trial of this action at the said [assizes], nor countermand the said notice of trial in due time, according to the rules and practice of this honourable court.

Sworn, &c. (*ante,* 705.)

N.B.—*It is unnecessary to swear to costs of the day having been incurred, for that is matter for the master.*

---

174. *Rule thereon (Q. B. or C. P.), ante,* 149.

In the [Q. B. *or* C. P.]

——day, the —— day of ——, 18—.

B. [and another] }   Upon reading the affidavit of ——, it is ordered, that
    v.   the attornies of both parties shall attend the master, and
D. [and others.] } he shall examine the matter and tax the [defendants their] costs, for that the [plaintiffs have] not proceeded to trial pursuant to [their] notice; which costs, when taxed, shall be paid by the plaintiffs to the defendants, if it shall appear to the master that costs ought to be allowed.

Upon the motion of Mr. ——.

By the Court.

---

175. *The like in Exch. (ante,* 149).

In the Exchequer.

——day, the —— day of ——, 18—.

B. [and another] }   Upon the motion of Mr. ——, counsel for the defend-
    v.   ants, and upon reading the affidavit of ——, it is ordered,
D. [and others.] } that the plaintiffs do pay to the defendants their costs, to be taxed by one of the masters, for that the plaintiffs did not proceed to the trial of this cause at the last assizes for the county of ——, pursuant to notice; unless cause be shown to the contrary, on ——day, the —— day of —— [instant *or* next].

By the Court.

176. *Notice to Plaintiff to proceed to Trial, pursuant to 15 & 16 Vict. c. 76, s. 202 (ante, 136).*

Title of court and cause as ante, No. 19.

Take notice, that the defendants [*or* the above-named defendant C. D., *as the case may be*] hereby require [*or* requires] the [plaintiff *or* plaintiffs] to proceed to the trial of this action at the assizes to be held in and for the county of —— [*or* at the sittings to be held at Westminster, in and for the county of Middlesex, *or* at Guildhall, in and for the city of London, *as the case may be*] next after the expiration of twenty days from the service of this notice. Dated the —— day of ——, 18—.

Yours, &c.
G. H., of ——,

To Mr. E. F., the plaintiff's attorney [*or* agent].　　Attorney [*or* agent] for the defendants [*or* for the defendant C. D.]

---

177. *Summons to set aside the above Notice, with Costs for Irregularity (ante, 137).*

Commence as ante, No. 22.

Why the notice to proceed to trial, dated the —— day of ——, 18—, should not be set aside for irregularity, the same having been given prematurely and contrary to the provisions of the Common Law Procedure Act, 1852; and why the [defendants *or* the defendant C. D.] should not pay to the plaintiffs, or their attorney, the costs of this application, to be taxed by one of the masters. Dated the —— day of ——, 18—.

Judge's signature.

---

178. *Order thereon.*

Commence as ante, No. 24.

I do order that the notice to proceed to trial, dated the —— day of ——, 18—, be set aside for irregularity, with costs to be taxed by one of the masters and paid by the [defendants *or* the defendant C. D.] to the plaintiffs or their attorney. Dated the —— day of ——, 18—.

Judge's signature.

---

179. *Summons to extend the Time for Proceeding to Trial (ante, 137).*

Commence as ante, No. 22.

Why the time for proceeding to the trial of this action should not be extended [to the fifth *or* last day of next —— term, *or* until the —— day of —— next]. Dated the —— day of ——, 18—.

Judge's signature.

---

180. *Order thereon.*

Commence as ante, No. 24.

I do order that the time for proceeding to the trial of this action be extended to [*specify the time as above*]. Dated the —— day of ——, 18—.

Judge's signature.

---

181. *Judgment against Plaintiff for not Proceeding to Trial pursuant to Notice* (*ante*, 136).

In the [Q. B., C. P. *or* Exch.]

On the [*date of writ*] —— day of ——, A.D. 18——.

Venue, ⎫ On the day and year above written, a writ of our lady the
to wit. ⎬ Queen issued forth of this court in these words (that is to
say),

Victoria by the grace of God [*here copy the writ*]; and C. D. has on the —— day of ——, A.D. 18——, appeared by —— his attorney [*or* in person] to the said writ, and A. B. has failed to proceed to trial, although duly required so to do: Therefore it is considered that the said C. D. be acquitted, and that he recover against the said A. B. £—— for his costs of defence.

N.B.—*In the margin write, opposite the words* "Therefore," &c., "Judgment signed on the —— day of ——, 18——."

---

182. *Notice to produce* (*ante*, 159).

Title of court and cause, as ante, No. 19.

Take notice, that you are hereby required to produce to the court [and jury] on the trial of this cause [*describe the documents shortly as directed*, *ante*, 159; *or as in a subpœna duces tecum*, post, No. 194]: And all other deeds, books, papers and writings whatsoever relating to or containing any entry relating to the matters in question in this cause. Dated the —— day of ——, 18——.

Yours, &c.

To the above-named defendants ⎫ ——, of ——,
[*or* plaintiffs], and to Mr. ——, ⎬ Plaintiff's [*or* defendant's] attorney
their attorney [*or* agent]. ⎭ [*or* agent].

---

183. *Affidavit of Service of Notice to produce* (*ante*, 163).

Commence as ante, No. 19.

1. I did on the —— day of —— [instant *or* last] [personally] serve E. F. the attorney in this cause for the above-named [defendants *or* plaintiffs] with a notice, of which a true copy is hereunto annexed, marked (A). *If the service were not personal omit the word* personally, *and say,*—" By delivering such notice to, and leaving the same with, a [clerk *or* female servant] of the said E. F. at his [office *or* dwelling-house], situate and being at [No. ——, —— street, in the city of London," *as the case may be*].

Sworn, &c. (*ante*, 705.)

N.B.—*The affidavit need not mention the notice to admit.*

---

184. *Notice to admit* (*ante*, 151).

In the [Q. B., C. P., *or* Exch.]

A. B. *v.* C. D.

Take notice, that the [plaintiff *or* defendant] in this cause proposes to adduce in evidence the several documents hereunder specified, and that the same may be inspected by the [defendant *or* plaintiff], his attorney or agent. at ——, on ——, between the hours of ——; and the [defendant *or* plaintiff] is hereby required, within forty-eight hours from the last-mentioned hour, to admit that such of the said documents as are specified to be originals were respectively written, signed or executed as they purport respectively to have been; that such as are specified as copies are true copies, and such documents as are stated to have been served, sent or delivered, were so served, sent or delivered respectively, saving all just exceptions to the admissibility of such documents as evidence in this cause. Dated, &c.

To E. F., attorney [*or* agent] }   G. H., attorney [*or* agent] for [plain-
for [defendant *or* plaintiff].   }   tiff *or* defendant].

[Here describe the documents, the manner of doing which may be as follows]:—

ORIGINALS.

Description of the Documents.	Date.
Deed of covenant between A. B. and C. D., first part, and E. F., second part	1st January, 1848.
Indenture of lease from A. B. to C. D.	1st February, 1848.
Indenture of release between A. B., C. D., first part, &c.	2nd February, 1848.
Letter—defendant to plaintiff....................	1st March, 1848.
Policy of insurance on goods by ship Isabella, on voyage from Oporto to London	3rd December, 1847.
Memorandum of agreement between C. D., captain of the said ship, and E. F.	1st January, 1848.
Bill of exchange for 100*l.*, at three months, drawn by A. B. on and accepted by C. D., endorsed by E. F. and G. H.	1st May, 1849.

COPIES.

Description of Documents.	Dates.	Original or Duplicate served, sent or delivered, when, how and by whom.
Register of baptism of A. B., in the parish of X.	1st January, 1808.	
Letter—plaintiff to defendant	1st February, 1848.	Sent by general post, 2nd February, 1848.
Notice to produce papers	1st March, 1848.	Served 2nd March, 1848, on defend-ant's attorney, by E. F., of ——.
Record of a judgment of the Court of Queen's Bench in an action J. S. *v.* J. N.	Trinity Term, 10th Vict.	
Letters-patent of King Charles II. in the Rolls' Chapel.	1st January, 1680.	

---

185. *Summons for further Time to make Admissions (ante,* 152).

Commence as ante, No. 22.

Why the [defendant *or* plaintiff] should not have —— days further time to make the admissions mentioned in the notice to admit, dated the —— day of ——, 18—, and signed by ——, the [plaintiff's *or* defendant's] attorney. Dated the —— day of ——, 18—.

Judge's signature.

186. *Order thereon.*

Commence as ante, No. 24.

I do order that the [defendant *or* plaintiff] have —— days further time to make the admissions mentioned in the notice to admit, dated the —— day of ——, 18—, and signed by ——, the [plaintiff's *or* defendant's] attorney. Dated the —— day of ——, 18—.

Judge's signature.

187. *Admission of Documents in pursuance of Notice (ante, 152).*

In the [Q. B., C. P. *or* Exch.]

B. [and another]   } I [*or* we] do hereby make the admissions required
v.   } in the within-written notice [so far as the same relates
D. [and others.]   } to the several documents therein numbered or marked respectively 1, 3, 5, 6, &c., *as the case may be :* And I *or* we do hereby refuse to make the admissions required by the within-written notice, so far as the same relates to the several documents therein numbered or marked respectively 2, 4, &c., *as the case may be*]. Dated the —— day of ——, 18—,

E. F., of ——,
Attorney for the [plaintiff *or* defendant].

N.B.—*To be indorsed on the notice to admit, or a copy.*

188. *Affidavit of Signature to Admissions (ante, 153).*

Commence as ante, No. 19.

1. I was present on the —— day of —— [instant *or* last], and did see E. F., the attorney in this cause for the above-named [plaintiffs *or* defendants, *or* defendant C. D., *as the case may be*], sign the admissions hereunto annexed, marked (A) ; and that the signature " E. F." subscribed to the said admissions is of the proper handwriting of the said E. F.

Sworn &c. (*ante*, 705.)

189. *Affidavit of Signature to Admissions (another Form), ante, 153.*

Commence as ante, No. 19.

1. That the admissions hereunto annexed, marked (A), are signed by E. F., the attorney in this cause for the above-named [plaintiffs *or* defendants, *or* defendant C. D., *as the case may be*]: And that the signature "E. F." subscribed to the said admissions is of the proper handwriting of the said E. F.

2. I know and am well acquainted with the handwriting of the said E. F., and I have frequently seen him write and sign his name.

Sworn, &c. (*ante*, 705.)

190. *Mutual Admissions of Documents and Copies, and of Facts not in Dispute (to save Expense of Proof), (ante, 489).*

Title of court and cause as ante, No. 19.

We the undersigned, for the purpose of saving unnecessary expense in the proof of certain undisputed facts on the trial of this cause, do hereby consent and agree to admit on the trial of this cause that the several documents hereunder specified, and numbered respectively 1, 2, 3, 4, were respectively written, signed or executed as they purport respectively to have been ; saving all just exceptions to the admissibility of all such documents as evidence in this cause. We also consent and agree to admit on the trial of this cause the several copies and extracts of documents hereunder specified and numbered respectively 5, 6, 7, 8; and that the same respectively are true and correct copies or extracts of and from the original documents as they purport to be, and that such original documents respectively were duly executed by the parties thereto respectively; and that such copies and extracts respectively shall or may be used as primary evidence, and not merely as secondary evidence of the contents of the said original documents respectively, and that no proof of the said original documents respectively shall be required, nor any evidence to account for the nonproduction thereof, saving all just exceptions to the said copies and extracts respectively which would apply to the originals if produced and duly proved in the usual manner as evidence in this cause. We also consent and agree to admit on the trial of this cause, That [*here state any facts mutually agreed on*].

List of the Documents above mentioned and referred to.

Description of Documents.	Date.
1. Indenture of Lease from A. B. to C. D. .. .. [*Describe each document as in the Notice to admit, ante, 757.*]	1st January, 18—.

Dated the —— day of ——, 18—.

E. F., attorney for the plaintiffs,
G. H., attorney for the defendants.

191. *Judge's Certificate that Refusal to admit was reasonable* (ante, 154).
In the [Q. B., C. P. or Exch.]
B. [and another] ⎫ I do hereby certify that the [defendant's *or* plaintiff's]
  v.   ⎬ refusal to admit [the document marked —— in the
D. [and others.] ⎭ within *or* above written notice] was reasonable. Dated the —— day of ——, 18—.

Judge's signature.

N.B.—*To be written "at the trial" on or under the notice to admit; or a certificate to the like effect may be written on separate paper, describing the notice to admit by its date or otherwise.*

192. *Subpœna to testify at the Assizes* (ante, 173).
Victoria, by the grace of God of the United Kingdom of Great Britain and Ireland Queen, Defender of the Faith: To [*names of witnesses not exceeding four*], greeting: We command you, that, laying aside all and singular business and excuses, you and every of you be and appear in your proper persons before our justices assigned to take the assizes in and for the *county* of ——, at [*name of assize town*] in the said *county*, on [*the commission day of the assizes*] the —— day of —— next, by [nine] of the clock in the forenoon of the same day, to testify all and singular those things which you or either of you know in a certain cause now depending in our court [before us *in* Q. B., *or in* C. P. before our justices, *or in Exch.* before the barons of our Exchequer] at Westminster, between A. B., plaintiff, and C. D., defendant, in an action of ejectment on the part of the [plaintiff *or* defendant] and on that day to be tried [by a jury of the country (*x*)], and so from day to day until the said cause be tried; and this you or any of you

(*x*) Omit these words if the trial is to be had without a jury.

shall by no means omit under the penalty upon each of you of one hundred pounds. Witness [*in Q. B.*, John Lord Campbell; *in C. P.*, Sir John Jervis, knight; *in Exch.*, Sir Frederick Pollock, knight,] at Westminster, the [*some day in term time*] —— day of ——, in the year of our Lord 18—.

N.B.—*To be indorsed with the attorney's name or firm, address and date of issuing.*

---

193. *Subpœna to testify in London or Middlesex (ante, 173).*
Form as ante, No. 192.

Except that instead of saying before our justices, &c., say in Q. B. before our right trusty and well beloved John Lord Campbell, our chief justice, assigned to hold pleas in our court before us; *or in C. P.* before Sir John Jervis, knight, our chief justice of the bench at Westminster; *or in Exch.* before Sir Frederick Pollock, knight, lord chief baron of our Court of Exchequer at Westminster], at [the Guildhall of the city of London, *or* Westminster Hall in the county of Middlesex], on [*the first day of the particular sitting*] ——day, the —— day of —— [next *or* instant], by [ten] of the clock in the forenoon of the same day, to testify, [*&c., as in No.* 192].

---

194. *Subpœna duces tecum (ante, 186).*

Victoria, by the grace of God of the United Kingdom of Great Britain and Ireland Queen, Defender of the Faith: To [*names of witnesses not exceeding four*], greeting: We command you, that laying aside all and singular business and excuses, you and every of you be and appear in your proper persons before [*as in Form No.* 192 *or* 193, *as the case may be, to the words "to* testify," *&c., then proceed as follows*], to testify all and singular those things which you or either of you know in a certain cause now depending in our court [before us, *or in C. P.* before our justices, *or in Exch.* before the barons of our Exchequer,] at Westminster, between A. B., C. D. and E. F., plaintiffs, and G. H., I. K. and L. M., defendants, in an action of ejectment on the part of the [plaintiffs *or* defendants], and on that day to be tried [by a jury of the country (*y*)], and so from day to day until the said cause be tried: And that you bring with you and produce at the time and place aforesaid [*here shortly describe the documents required, ex. gr.* A deed dated —— purporting to be "a lease," *or* "a duplicate lease," *or* "a counterpart lease," from —— to ——. A deed dated ——, purporting to be "an assignment," *or* "a conveyance," from —— to ——. A deed dated ——, expressed to be made between A. B. of the first part; C. D. of the second part; E. F. of the third part; and G. H. of the 4th part. A paper writing, dated ——, purporting to be "an agreement," *or* "a memorandum of agreement," between I. K. and L. M. A paper writing, dated ——, purporting to be a receipt "for rent," *or* "for the sum of £——," signed by ——. All receipts for rent given by or on behalf of ——, to ——. A paper writing, dated ——, purporting to be "a notice to quit," *or* "a demand of possession," signed by —— and addressed to ——. A paper writing, dated ——, purporting to be a letter or note from —— to ——. All other letters and notes purporting to be written by—— to ——. *Describe in like manner any other known documents with convenient certainty:* Together with all drafts, copies and extracts of and from the above-mentioned documents respectively; and all other deeds, agreements, receipts, notices, letters, books, papers and writings, touching or relating to the above-named [plaintiffs or either of them], or to the above-named [defendants or either of them], or to any land, tenement matter or thing in question in the above action]: And this you or any of

---

(*y*) Omit these words if the trial is to be had without a jury.

you shall by no means omit under the penalty upon each of you of one hundred pounds.

Witness [*as ante, No.* 192].

N.B.—*The duces tecum clause is frequently introduced immediately before the words* "to testify," *&c., which reads awkwardly. The above form seems preferable, but either will do.*

----

195. *Affidavit for a Rule or Order for a Subpœna to be served in Scotland or Ireland* (*ante,* 198).

Commence as ante, Nos. 19, 20 *or* 21.

1. That the paper writing hereunto annexed, marked (A), is a true copy of the issue joined in this action.

2. That I. K., who is at present residing at —— in that part of the United Kingdom of Great Britain and Ireland called [Scotland *or* Ireland], is a material and necessary witness for the [plaintiff *or* defendant, *or* defendant C. D., *as the case may be*] on the trial of this cause.

3. That [*here state specially such facts as will make it appear to the court or a judge that* "*it is proper to compel the personal attendance*" *of the witness on the trial of the action. His knowledge of material facts touching the matters in question, and the circumstances under which he acquired such knowledge, should be stated. If the witness have in his possession any material documents, describe them and their short contents or nature, in such a manner as to show them to be material to the matters in question in the action*].

4. That the personal attendance of the said I. K. on the trial of this cause is required only for the purpose of this cause as a witness on behalf of the [plaintiff *or* defendant], and not for any other object or purpose whatsoever.

Sworn, &c. (*ante,* 705.)

N. B.—*In term time the application should be made to the court, but in vacation to a judge at chambers. In the latter case the affidavit should be indorsed in the usual manner, and with a memorandum as follows*—

"For an order for a writ of [subpœna ad testificandum *or* subpœna duces tecum] in the special form, for service within the United Kingdom pursuant to 17 & 18 Vict. c. 34."

----

196. *Order for such a Subpœna* (*ante,* 198).

Commence as ante, No. 24.

I do order that a writ of [subpœna ad testificandum *or* subpœna duces tecum] shall issue in this action in the special form, pursuant to 17 & 18 Vict. c. 34, commanding [*name of the witness*] to attend the trial of this action wherever he shall be within the United Kingdom, as a witness on the part of the [plaintiffs *or* defendants] [and *to* bring with him and produce on that occasion—*describe the documents shortly as in a subpœna, ante, No.* 194].

Dated the —— day of —— 18—. 　　　　　*Judge's signature.*

----

197. *Subpœna ad testificandum to be served in Scotland or Ireland* (*ante,* 198).

Victoria, by the grace of God of the United Kingdom of Great Britain and Ireland Queen, Defender of the Faith : To [*name of witness*], greeting : We command you, *wherever you shall be within our United Kingdom,* that laying aside all and singular business and excuses, you be and appear in your proper person before [*remainder as ante, No.* 192 *or* 193, *omitting the words* " or either of you," " or any of you," " upon each of you."]

"This writ is issued pursuant to 17 & 18 Vict. c. 34, by the special order of [the court, *or* Mr. Justice *or* Baron ——], dated the —— day of ——, 18—."

Indorsement as ante, No. 192.

198. *Subpœna duces tecum to be served in Scotland or Ireland (ante, 198).*

Victoria, by the grace of God of the United Kingdom of Great Britain and Ireland Queen, Defender of the Faith: To [*name of witness*], greeting: We command you, *wherever you shall be within our United Kingdom,* that laying aside all and singular business and excuses, you be and appear in your proper person before [*remainder as ante, No. 194, omitting the words,* "or either of you," "or any of you," "upon each of you."]

"This writ is issued pursuant to 17 & 18 Vict. c. 34, by the special order of [the court, *or* Mr. Justice *or* Baron ——], dated the —— day of ——, 18——."

Indorsement as ante, No. 192.

———

199. *Affidavit for Habeas Corpus and Testificandum (ante, 198).*
Commence as ante, No. 19.

1. That notice of trial has been given in this action for the next assizes to be holden at ——, in and for the county of —— [*or* that this cause has been set down for trial at the —— sitting in the present —— Term to be holden at Westminster Hall, in and for the county of Middlesex, *or* at the Guildhall, in and for the city of London].

2. That E. F., now a prisoner for debt in the county gaol of ——shire, [*or* in custody of the keeper of the Queen's Prison,] is and will be a material witness for me at the trial of this action.

3. I am advised and verily believe that I cannot safely proceed to the trial of this action without the testimony of the said E. F.

4. That the said E. F. is ready and willing to attend as a witness at the trial of this action.

Sworn, &c. (*ante*, 705.)

N.B.—*The affidavit may be made by the plaintiff's attorney or agent, if preferred.*

———

200. *Habeas Corpus to testify (ante, 199).*

Victoria, by the grace of God of the United Kingdom of Great Britain and Ireland Queen, Defender of the Faith, to [the sheriff of ——, *or* the keeper of the Queen's Prison, *or as the case may be*], greeting: We command you that you have the body of E. F. detained in our prison under your custody, as it is said, under safe and secure conduct before [*as in a subpœna, ante, Nos.* 192 *or* 193] on the —— day of —— next, by [ten] of the clock in the forenoon of the same day, then and there to testify the truth according to his knowledge in a certain cause now depending in our court before [us, *or in C. P.* before our justices of the bench at Westminster, *or in Exch.* before the barons of our Exchequer at Westminster]: and then and there to be tried between A. B. plaintiff and C. D. defendant, in an action of ejectment on the part of the said A. B. [*or* C. D.]: And immediately after the said E. F. shall then and there have given his testimony before our said [Justices, *or* Chief Justice, *or* Chief Baron, *as the case may be*], that you return him the said E. F. to our said prison under safe and secure conduct, and have there this writ. Witness [*name of Chief Justice or Chief Baron*], at Westminster, the —— day of ——, in the —— year of our reign.

To be indorsed with the attorney's name and place of business. The judge's signature on the back must be obtained (ante, 199).

———

201. *Precipe for Habeas Corpus ad Testificandum (ante, 199).*

Venue, { Habeas corpus to testify between A. B. plaintiff and C. D. de-
to wit. { fendant, on the part of the [plaintiff *or* defendant].

Attorney's name and address and date.

---

202. *Affidavit in support of Application for a Discovery of Documents (ante, 202).*
Commence as ante, No. 19.

I, [*name*] of ——, the above-named plaintiff, [*or* one of the above-named
plaintiffs *or* defendants, *as the case may be*], make oath and say,—

1. This action of ejectment was commenced on or about the —— day
of ——, 18—, and is brought for the recovery of the possession of [*as in
the writ*].

2. That [*state appearances and notices (if any) to defend for part as in an
issue ; also any subsequent proceedings in the cause*].

3. That divers deeds and documents respectively relating to the title of
the property sought to be recovered in this action or some part thereof (z),
are now, as I verily believe, in the possession or power of the [plaintiffs *or*
defendants, *or* plaintiff —— *or* defendant ——, *as the case may be*].

4. I am entitled to the production of the said deeds and documents
respectively, for the purpose of discovery or otherwise, on the following
grounds, viz. : [*here state the grounds ; show that the party in possession holds
them partly on his own account, and partly as a trustee for and on behalf of the
deponent, or as the case may be : this part of the affidavit must vary in each case
according to the facts*].

Sworn, &c. (*ante,* 705).

---

203. *Summons for Discovery of Documents (ante, 202).*
Commence as ante, No. 22.

Why the [plaintiffs, *or* the plaintiff A. B., *or* the defendants, *or* the defendant C. D., *as the case may be*] should not, within —— days, answer on
affidavit, stating what documents relating to the property in question in this
cause or any part thereof [they have in their, *or* he has in his] possession
or power : and what [they know *or* he knows] as to the custody any documents relating to the said property or any part thereof are in : And whether [they object *or* he objects], (and if so on what grounds) to the production of such of them as are in [their *or* his] possession or power. Dated
the —— day of ——, 18—.

Judge's signature.

---

204. *Order thereon.*
Commence as ante, No. 24.

I do order that the [plaintiffs *or* plaintiff A. B., *or* defendants *or* defendant
C. D., *as the case may be*] do, within —— days, answer on affidavit, stating
what documents relating to the property in question in this cause, or any
part thereof [they have in their *or* he has in his] possession or power : and
what [they know *or* he knows] as to the custody any documents relating
to the said property or any part thereof are in : And whether [they object
or he objects] (and if so on what grounds) to the production of such of
them as are in [their *or* his] possession or power. Dated the —— day of
——, 18—.

Judge's signature.

(z) It will be better, if possible, to describe more particularly the deeds
and documents, and to state shortly their dates, parties, nature and effect,
in such manner as to show the deponent's interest therein. See Chit. Forms,
133, note (a).

205. *Summons for Leave to inspect and take Copies or Extracts of Documents* (*ante*, 202).

Commence as ante, No. 22.

Why the [plaintiff *or* defendant, *or* defendant C. D., *as the case may be*], and his attorney or agent, should not be at liberty to inspect and take copies of, and extracts from, the following documents, viz.: *describe the documents. If application by defendant, add*—" and why in the meantime all further proceedings herein should not be stayed." Dated the —— day of ——, 18—.

Judge's signature.

206. *Order thereon.*

Commence as ante, No. 24.

I do order that the defendant or his attorney shall be at liberty to inspect the lease dated ——, 18 –, and to take a copy thereof, and make extracts therefrom: And that in the meantime all further proceedings be stayed. Dated the —— day of ——, 18—.

Judge's signature.

N.B.—*This was the form of order made in* Doe d. Child v. Roe, 1 E. & B. 280. *See the next form.*

207. *The like, more special.*

Commence as ante, No. 24.

I do order that the [plaintiff *or* defendant, *or* defendant C. D., *as the case may be*], and his attorney or agent, shall be at liberty to inspect [and take copies of, and extracts from] the following documents, viz.: [*describe the documents*]. And I do order that the [defendants *or* defendant C. D., *or* the plaintiffs, *as the case may be*] do produce the said documents for inspection as aforesaid at [the office of Mr. ——, the defendant's *or* plaintiff's attorney or agent, situate at ——, in the county of ——], on [the —— day of —— instant], between the hours of —— of the clock in the forenoon, and —— of the clock in the afternoon of the same day. And I do order that the [defendants *or* defendant C. D., *or* the plaintiffs, *as the case may be*] do forthwith, and before such inspection as aforesaid, make and deliver to the said Mr. —— a copy of each of the following documents, viz. [*describe them*]; and also such copies or extracts as the said Mr. —— shall require of the following documents, viz. [*describe them*]. And I do order that the [plaintiff *or* defendant, *or* defendant C. D., *as the case may be*] do pay to the said Mr. —— the costs of such inspection as aforesaid, and also for the said copies and extracts respectively [at stationers' prices]. And I do order that until such copies and extracts be made and delivered, and such inspection granted as aforesaid, all further proceedings herein be stayed [*omit this if the application be made by the plaintiff*]. Dated the —— day of ——, 18—.

Judge's signature.

N.B.—*The order will of course vary according to the judge's discretion in each case.*

208. *Summons for Leave to deliver Interrogatories for the Examination of the Opposite Party (ante, 204).*

Commence as ante, No. 22.

Why the [plaintiff *or* defendant] should not be at liberty [within —— days] to deliver to the [defendant *or* plaintiff], or his attorney, interrogatories in writing. And why the [defendant *or* plaintiff] should not within ten days answer the questions in writing by affidavit. Dated the —— day of ——, 18—.

Judge's signature.

N.B.—*The above is taken from the printed form used at the judges' chambers, but the next form seems preferable.*

---

209. *The like (another Form).*
Commence as ante, No. 22.

Why the [plaintiffs, *or* the defendants, *or* the defendant C. D., *as the case may be*] should not be at liberty (*a*) within [one week] to deliver to the [defendants, *or* the defendant C. D., *or* the plaintiffs, *or* the plaintiff A. B., *as the case may be*], or [their *or* his] attorney, interrogatories in writing upon certain matters as to which discovery is sought, and to require the said ——, within ten days, to answer the questions in writing by affidavit, to be sworn and filed in the ordinary way, pursuant to the 51st section of the Common Law Procedure Act, 1854. Dated the —— day of ——, 18—.

Judge's signature.

---

210. *Order thereon.*
Commence as ante, No. 24.

I do order that the [plaintiffs *or* defendants, *or* defendant C. D., *as the case may be*] be at liberty within [one week] to deliver to the [defendants, *or* the defendant C. D., *or* the plaintiffs, *or* the plaintiff A. B., *as the case may be*], or [their *or* his] attorney, interrogatories in writing upon certain matters as to which discovery is sought, and to require the said ——, within ten days, to answer the questions in writing by affidavit, to be sworn and filed in the ordinary way, pursuant to the 51st section of the Common Law Procedure Act, 1854. Dated the —— day of ——, 18—.

Judge's signature.

---

211. *Affidavit of Plaintiff and his Attorney, or Agent, in support of Application for Leave to deliver Interrogatories (ante,* 204).
Commence as ante, No. 20.

We, A. B., of ——, the above-named plaintiff, [*or* one of the above-named plaintiffs,] and E. F., of ——, gentleman, the attorney [*or* agent] in this cause for the plaintiff [*or* plaintiffs], severally make oath and say,—

1. This action of ejectment was commenced on the —— day of ——, 18—, by a writ then issued to recover possession of [*as in the writ*].

2. That [*here state appearances and notices (if any) to defend for part, as in an issue*].

3. That no issue has yet been delivered in this cause [*or* that issue in this cause was delivered on the —— day of ——, 18—, but no notice of trial has yet been given].

4. That interrogatories in writing have been prepared [and settled by counsel] on behalf of the plaintiff [*or* plaintiffs] for the examination of the defendants [*or* of the defendant C. D., *as the case may be*] in this action upon divers matters as to which discovery is sought, and upon which matters the said —— would be liable to be called and examined as [witnesses *or* a witness] in this cause on behalf of the plaintiff [*or* plaintiffs].

(*a*) In other actions say, " with the declaration," *or* " with his plea or pleas :" but in ejectment some time should be mentioned, *ante,* 202.

5. We believe that the plaintiff [*or* plaintiffs] will derive material benefit in this cause from the discovery which he seeks [*or* they seek] as aforesaid, and that he has [*or* they have] a good cause of action upon the merits.

The above-named A. B. and E. F. were }   A. B.
severally sworn, &c. (*ante*, 708.) }   E. F.

N.B.—*Where it happens, from unavoidable circumstances, that the plaintiff cannot join in the affidavit, the circumstances by which he is prevented from joining therein should be specially stated.* 17 & 18 Vict. c. 125, s. 52 (*ante*, 203).

---

212. *Affidavit of Defendant and his Attorney, or Agent, in support of Application for Leave to exhibit Interrogatories* (*ante*, 204).

Commence as ante, No. 20.

We, C. D., of ——, the above-named defendant, [*or* one of the above-named defendants,] and G. H., of——, gentleman, the attorney [*or* agent] in this cause for the defendant [*or* defendants, *or* defendant C. D., *as the case may be*], severally make oath and say,—

1. This action of ejectment was commenced on or about the —— day of ——, 18—, by a writ then issued to recover possession of [*as in the writ*].

2. That [*here state appearances and notices (if any) to defend for part, as in an issue*].

3. That no issue has yet been delivered in this cause [*or* that issue in this cause was delivered on the —— day of ——, 18—, but no notice of trial has yet been given].

4. That interrogatories in writing have been prepared [and settled by counsel] on behalf of the defendant [*or* defendants, *or* defendant C. D., *as the case may be*] for the examination of the plaintiffs [*or* of the plaintiff A B., *as the case may be*] in this action upon divers matters as to which discovery is sought, and upon which matters the said —— would be liable to be called and examined as [witnesses *or* a witness] in this cause on behalf of the defendants.

5. We believe that the defendants [*or* the defendant C. D. *as the case may be*] will derive material benefit in this cause from the discovery which [they seek *or* he seeks] as aforesaid, and that [they have *or* he has] a good defence to this action upon the merits.

6. That the discovery sought as aforesaid is not sought for the purpose of delay.

The above-named C. D. and G. H. were }
severally sworn, &c. (*ante*, 708.) }

See note, ante, No. 211.

---

213. *Interrogatories for Examination of Defendants* (*ante*, 203).

In the [Q. B., C. P. *or* Exch.]

Between [*names of claimants*] ——, plaintiffs.
and
[*names of defendants*] ——, defendants.

Interrogatories for the examination of the defendants [*or* defendant C. D., *as the case may be*], delivered by and on behalf of the plaintiffs, with leave of [the Hon. Sir ——, Knight, one of the Judges (*or* Barons) of this court, *or* of her Majesty's Court of Q. B. *or* C. P., *or* one of the Barons of her Majesty's Exch., *as the case may be*,] pursuant to his order dated the —— day of ——, 18—, and The Common Law Procedure Act, 1854.

1. [*Here state the various questions : divide them into distinct interrogatories, as may be convenient, and number them* 1, 2, 3, 4, &c. (*See the Forms of forty-*

five Interrogatories in Chester *v.* Wortley, 18 C. B. 239.) *If possible, frame each question so as to elicit a full discovery, without the possibility of evasion, otherwise than by an insufficient answer.*]

(*Indorsement.*)

In the [Q. B., C. P. *or* Exch.]

B. [and another], }
      v.   } Interrogatories.
D. [and others.] }

To Mr. ——, the defendant's attorney [*or* attorney
    for the defendant C. D.]

The defendants are [*or* the defendant C. D. is] hereby required, within ten days, to answer the within interrogatories or questions in writing, by affidavit, to be sworn and filed in the ordinary way, pursuant to the provisions of The Common Law Procedure Act, 1854. Dated this —— day of ——, 18—.

            E. F. of ——, [plaintiff's attorney].

---

214. *Interrogatories for the Examination of the Plaintiffs (ante,* 203).

In the [Q. B., C. P. *or* Exch.]

    Between [*names of claimants*] ——, plaintiffs.
           and
    [*names of defendants*] ——, defendants.

Interrogatories for the examination of the [plaintiffs *or* plaintiff A. B., *as the case may be*], delivered by and on behalf of the [defendants, *or* defendant C. D., *as the case may be*], with leave of the Hon. Sir ——, Knight, one of the Judges (*or* Barons) of this court, *or* of her Majesty's Court of ——, pursuant to his order dated the —— day of ——, 18—, and The Common Law Procedure Act, 1854.

1. [*Here state the various questions : divide them into distinct interrogatories, as may be convenient, and number them* 1, 2, 3 *and* 4, *&c. If possible, frame each question so as to elicit a full discovery, without the possibility of evasion, otherwise than by an insufficient answer. The following were used in* Flitcroft *v.* Fletcher, 11 Exch. 543 (*ante,* 204), *viz.*] :—

1. In what character, or in what right, do you, and each of you, claim to be entitled to the possession of the premises claimed by you in this action?

2. Do you, or any of you, claim to be entitled to the same, as heir at law of H. F., deceased?

3. If so, do you allege that you, or any of you, are his heir at law, and through what links do you trace such heirship?

4. Do you, or any of you, claim to be entitled as grantees from or trustees for any person or persons claiming to be heir at law of the said H. F.?

5. If so, who is or are the person or persons whose grantees or trustees you, or any of you, claim to be? and how do you allege that such person or persons is or are the heir at law of the said H. F.? and through what links do you trace such heirship?

6. Have you, or any of you, any right to or interest in the said premises except as aforesaid ; and if so, what is the nature of such right or interest?

(*Indorsement.*)

In the [Q. B., C. P. *or* Exch.]

B. [and another] }
      v.   } Interrogatories.
D. [and others]. }

    To Mr. ——, the plaintiff's attorney.

The plaintiffs are [*or* the plaintiff A. B. is] hereby required, within ten days, to answer the within interrogatories or questions in writing, by affidavit to be sworn and filed in the ordinary way pursuant to the provisions of The Common Law Procedure Act, 1854. Dated this —— day of ——, 18—.

G. H., of ——,
Attorney for the defendants [*or* for the defendant C. D., *as the case may be*].

---

215. *Summons for further Time to answer Interrogatories (ante, 205).*
Commence as ante, No. 22.

Why the [defendants, *or* defendant C. D., *or* the plaintiffs, *or* the plaintiff A. B., *as the case may be*] should not have [a month's] further time to answer the interrogatories delivered in this cause. Dated the —— day of ——, 18—.

Judge's signature.

---

216. *Order thereon.*
Commence as ante, No. 24.

I do order that the [defendants, *or* defendant C. D. *or* the plaintiffs, *or* the plaintiff A. B., *as the case may be*] have —— days further time to answer the interrogatories delivered in this cause [*add any terms or conditions the judge may think reasonable*]. Dated the —— day of ——, 18—.

Judge's signature.

---

217. *Affidavit in answer to Interrogatories (ante, 205).*
Title of court and cause as ante, No. 19.

I, A. B. [*or* C. D.] of —— [gent.], the above-named [plaintiff *or* defendant], in answer to the several interrogatories delivered in this action by and on behalf of the above-named [defendant *or* plaintiff], make oath and say as follows :—

1. In answer to the first of the said interrogatories, I say, That [*as the case may be*].
2. To the second of the said interrogatories, I say, That [&c.]
3. To the third of the said interrogatories, I say, That [&c.]
[*In like manner answer fully each interrogatory, or show some excuse for not doing so, ante, 205.*]
Sworn, &c. (*ante, 705.*)

N.B.—*The affidavit should answer fully each interrogatory, or should show just cause for any omission. It should be divided into separate paragraphs, numbered 1, 2, 3, 4, &c., corresponding with the interrogatories. It should generally be settled by counsel, and, if possible, should be framed so as not to prejudice the party interrogated. It should be sworn and filed with one of the masters within the ten days allowed, or further time should be obtained upon application to a judge at chambers.*

---

218. *Summons for Oral Examination, &c. after insufficient Answer to Interrogatories (ante, 206).*
Commence as ante, No. 22.

Why [the plaintiffs, *or* the plaintiff A. B., *or* the defendants, *or* the defendant C. D., *as the case may be*] should not be orally examined before [me *or* before J. W., Esq., one of the masters] upon the points mentioned in the paper writing hereunto annexed, his answer to the interrogatories delivered in this action by and on behalf of —— being insufficient on such points :

And why the said —— should not attend before [me *or* the said master] for the purpose of being orally examined as aforesaid, at such time and place, or times and places, as [I *or* the said master] shall by note in writing under [my *or* his] hand from time to time appoint for that purpose: And why the said —— should not produce before [me *or* the said master], at the time and place, or times and places, to be so appointed as aforesaid [*describe shortly any documents or writings required*] : And why I should not impose such terms as to such examination, and the costs of this application and of the proceedings thereon and otherwise, as to me shall seem just, pursuant to the 53rd section of The Common Law Procedure Act, 1854. Dated the —— day of ——, 18—. *Judge's signature.*

This summons will be attended }
   by counsel for the ——.   }

---

219. *Points to be annexed to such Summons (ante, 206).*

Points.

1. That the [plaintiffs *or* defendants, *or* defendant C. D., *as the case may be*, have not *or*] has not sufficiently answered the —— interrogatory [*or* that part of the —— interrogatory which inquires ——, *as the case may be*].

2. That the said —— has not, &c. [*as above, as to each interrogatory not sufficiently answered.*]

N.B.—*These points should be prepared or carefully settled by counsel.* Ante, 206.

---

220. *Order for Oral Examination, &c. (ante, 206).*

Commence as ante, No. 24.

I do order that the [plaintiffs, *or* plaintiff A. B., *or* defendants, *or* defendant C. D., *as the case may be*] be orally examined before [me, *or* before J. W., Esq., one of the masters,] upon the points mentioned in the paper hereunto annexed, his answer to the interrogatories delivered in this action by and on behalf of —— being insufficient in such points : And I order that the said —— do attend before [me *or* the said master] for the purpose of being orally examined as aforesaid, at such time and place, or times and places, as [I *or* the said master] shall by note in writing under [my *or* his] hand, from time to time appoint for that purpose : And that the said —— produce before [me *or* the said master], at the time and place, times and places, to be so appointed as aforesaid [*describe shortly the documents or writings*] : And I order that [*here state such terms as to the examination and the costs of the application, and of the proceedings thereon and otherwise, as to the judge may seem just*]. Dated the —— day of ——, 18—.

Judge's signature.

N.B.—*The costs may be reserved (by express words) until after the examination has been had, and may then be directed to be costs in the cause, or costs of the* [*plaintiffs or defendants*] *in the cause; or to be taxed and paid by the party in fault, as to the judge may appear just.*

---

221. *Record of Nisi Prius (ante, 272).*

This is merely a copy (on parchment of the prescribed size) of the issue, &c. See ante, Nos. 131—138.

If any defendant defend for part only, or as a landlord, or as a joint tenant, tenant in common or coparcener, that will appear by the issue, and consequently on the nisi prius record.

The particulars of the claim and defence, if any, or copies thereof, shall be annexed to the record by the claimants. 15 & 16 Vict. c. 76, s. 180.

L L

222. *Notice for Special Jury by Plaintiff or Defendant in a Country Cause* (*ante*, 260).

Title of court and cause as ante, No. 19.

Take notice, that it is the intention of the [plaintiffs *or* defendants] to have this cause tried by a special jury. Dated the —— day of——, 18—.

Yours, &c.

To the above-named [defendants *or* plaintiffs], and to Mr. ——, their attorney [*or* agent]. }   [*name and address*], [plaintiffs' *or* defendants'] attorney [*or* agent].

---

223. *Notice to Sheriff that the Cause is to be tried by a Special Jury* (*ante*, 264).

Title of court and cause as ante, No. 19.

Take notice, that this cause is to be tried by a special jury of the county [*or* city] of ——. Dated the —— day of ——, 18—.

Yours, &c.

To the sheriff of ——, and his undersheriff. }   [*name and address*] [plaintiff's *or* defendant's] attorney [*or* agent].

---

224. *Affidavit for Rule for a Special Jury in London or Middlesex on behalf of the Defendant* (*ante*, 261).

Commence as ante, Nos. 19, 20 *or* 21.

1. That this is an action of ejectment for [land and premises], in the parish of —— [in the city of London, *or* in the county of Middlesex].

2. That issue has been joined in this action, and notice of trial given for the [first] sitting to be holden [at the Guildhall in and for the city of London, *or* at Westminster Hall in and for the county of Middlesex] : And that the first day of such sitting is ——day, the —— day of —— [instant *or* next (*a*)].

Or, if no notice of trial has been given, say

2. That issue has been joined in this action, and the venue laid in [London *or* Middlesex] ; but no notice of trial has been given in this action. Sworn, &c. (*ante*, 705.)

---

225. *Rule for a Special Jury in London or Middlesex* (*ante*, 261).

Commence as ante, No. 232, *post.*

It is ordered that at the expense of the [plaintiff *or* defendant] forty-eight special jurors shall be nominated out of the jurors' book and special jurors' list for the [city of London *or* county of Middlesex] qualified to serve on special juries for the said [city *or* county], and be reduced before [the secondaries of the said city, *or* the undersheriff of the said county], of whom twelve shall be struck out by each party, and the remaining twenty-four jurors shall be placed on a panel for the trial of the said cause, pursuant to the stat. 6 Geo. 4, c. 50, and The Common Law Procedure Act, 1852 : And that the [sheriffs of the said city, *or* sheriff of the said county] do cause the said twenty-four jurors to be summoned to attend at the said trial : and that they do attend accordingly. On the motion of Mr. ——, for the [plaintiff *or* defendant].

By the Court.

(*a*) The application for the rule must be made more than six days before this day. *Ante*, 261.

226. *Summons for Leave to nominate and strike a Special Jury according to the old Practice (ante, 260).*

Commence as ante, No. 22.

Why a special jury of the county of —— should not be nominated and struck at the expense of the [plaintiff *or* defendant] for the trial of this cause, pursuant to the practice before and at the time of the passing of The Common Law Procedure Act, 1852. Dated the —— day of ——, 18—.

Judge's signature.

---

227. *Order thereon.*

Commence as ante, No. 24.

I do order that a special jury of the county of —— be nominated and struck at the expense of the [plaintiff *or* defendant] for the trial of this cause, pursuant to the practice before and at the time of the passing of The Common Law Procedure Act, 1852. Dated the —— day of ——, 18—.

Judge's signature.

N.B.—*For forms of rule nisi and rule absolute for the above purpose, see* Chit. Forms, 198, 199 (7th ed.)

---

228. *Certificate for Costs of Special Jury (ante, 264).*

I do hereby certify that the within action was a proper cause to be tried by a special jury. Dated the —— day of ——, 18—.

Judge's signature.

N.B.—*To be indorsed upon the back of the Nisi Prius record immediately after the verdict* (ante, 264).

---

229. *Challenge to the Array (ante, 268).*

B. ⎫ And now at this day, to wit, on the [*commission day, or first day of the*
v. ⎬ *sitting*] —— day of ——, 18—, come as well the plaintiff as the de-
D. ⎭ fendant, by their respective attornies aforesaid; and the jurors of the jury impannelled also come; and hereupon the [defendant *or* plaintiff] challengeth the array of the said panel, because he saith, That [*here state with certainty and precision the matter of challenge, see ante*, 268]: And this he is ready to verify, wherefore he prayeth judgment, and that the said panel may be quashed.

---

230. *Affidavit for a View (ante, 270).*

Commence as ante, No. 19.

1. That this is an action of ejectment for the recovery of the possession of [*as in the writ*]: And on behalf of the [plaintiff *or* defendant] it is considered expedient that a view be had by some of the jury in the usual manner of the property in question.

2. That the place at which the view is to be made is at ——, in the parish of ——, in the county of ——: And that the office of the undersheriff of the said county of —— is situate at ——, in the said county: And that the distance of the said place at which the said view is to be made from the said office of the said undersheriff is about —— miles [and one-half *or* one quarter of another mile], and [does not *or* does] exceed five miles.

Sworn, &c. (ante, 705.)

or N.B.—*The exact distance is not material; the main point is whether it does does not exceed five miles.*

L L 2

231. *Præcipe for Rule or Order for a View (ante, 270).*

In the [Q. B., C. P. *or* Exch.]

Venue, ⎱   Rule *or* order for a view in ejectment between A. B., plaintiff,
to wit. ⎰ and C. D., defendant, to be had on ——day, the —— day of
——, 18—, at —— o'clock in the [fore] noon.
Name of plaintiff's shower,
    M. N.
Name of defendant's shower,
    O. P.

[*Name and address.*]
[plaintiff's *or* defendant's attorney.]
[*Date.*]

232. *Rule for a View (ante, 270).*

In the [Q. B., C. P. *or* Exch.]

                      —— day, the —— day of ——, 18—.

B. ⎱   Upon reading the affidavit of ——, it is ordered that the sheriff of
v. ⎰ ——, according to the statute in that case made and provided, shall
D. ⎰ have [six or more of the jury, *or*, *if a special jury*, *say*, six or more of
the first twelve of the jury] summoned and impannelled to try the [matters
in question (*b*)] between the said parties, or as many more of them as he shall
think fit, to take a view of the place in question on ——, the —— day of ——
next, at —— of the clock in the ——noon of the same day [which said
jurors shall meet at the house of J. S., known by the name or sign of ——,
at ——, in the said county, and may then and there be refreshed at the
equal charges of the said parties]: And that M. N., on the part of the
plaintiff, and O. P., on the part of the defendant, shall show the place in
question to those jurors, but that no evidence shall be given on either side
at the time of taking the said view: And the sheriff of —— shall return the
names of such of the said jurors as shall view the said place to the Associate
in the Court of [Q. B., C. P. *or* Exch.] for the purpose of their being called as
jurymen upon the trial of this cause: And it is further ordered that the
[plaintiff *or* defendant], his attorney or agent, shall deposit in the hands of
the undersheriff of the said county the sum of £ —— (*c*) for payment of the
expenses of the same view, pursuant to the statute of the sixth year of king
George the Fourth, chap. 30, sect. 23, and the general rule made in Hilary
Term, 1853, No. 49: And if such sum shall be more than sufficient to pay
the expenses of the said view, the surplus shall be forthwith returned to the
[plaintiff's *or* defendant's] attorney: And if such sum shall not be sufficient
to pay such expenses, the deficiency shall be forthwith paid by the said
[plaintiff's *or* defendant's] attorney to the said undersheriff; the [plaintiff
or defendant] hereby consenting that in case no view shall be had, or if a
view shall be had by any of the said jurors, whether they shall happen to be
any of the first twelve jurors or not, yet the said trial shall proceed, and no
objection shall be made on account thereof.

Side bar.   By the Court.

(*b*) This seems a more proper expression than "issue" or "issues" in
an action of ejectment.

(*c*) *Ante,* 270.

233. *Summons for Inspection of the Property by the Party and his Witnesses, or by the Jury (ante, 208).*

Commence as ante, No. 22.

Why the plaintiff [and his witnesses] should not be at liberty to inspect the property in question in this action [or why the jury before whom this action is to be tried should not inspect the property in question], situate at ——, in the county of ——. Dated the —— day of ——, 18—.

Judge's signature.

---

234. *Order thereon.*

Commence as ante, No. 24.

I do order that the plaintiff [and his witnesses] be at liberty to inspect the property in question in this action on ——, the —— day of —— [instant *or* next], between the hours of —— of the clock in the forenoon and —— of the clock in the afternoon. [*Add such terms as to costs or otherwise as the judge may think fit. If an inspection by the jury be ordered, say,*] I order that six or more of the jury before whom this action is to be tried do inspect the property in question, situate at ——, in the county of ——. [*Add such terms and directions as to costs and otherwise as may appear proper to the judge. See form of Rule for a View, ante, No. 232.*] Dated the —— day of ——, 18—.

Judge's signature.

---

235. *Ne Recipiatur (ante, 273).*

In the [Q. B., C. P. *or* Exch.]

A. B. [and another] *v.* C. D. [and others.]

Do not receive or enter for trial the record of Nisi Prius in this action, the proper time for entering it having elapsed.

Yours, &c.,

G. H., of ——,

To the Associate. Defendant's attorney [*or* agent].

[*Date and hour.*]

---

236. *Note of Exceptions at the Trial (ante, 313).*

In the [Q. B., C. P. *or* Exch.]

A. B. *v.* C. D.

Exception by [defendant *or* plaintiff.]

That [*describe the document shortly*] is not admissible evidence on behalf of the [plaintiff *or* defendant], and ought not to be received or left to the jury.

That [*describe the document shortly*] is admissible evidence on behalf of the [plaintiff *or* defendant], and ought to be received and left to the jury.

That E. F. is admissible as a witness on behalf of the [plaintiff *or* defendant], and that his evidence ought to be received and left to the jury.

That G. H. is inadmissible as a witness on behalf of the [plaintiff *or* defendant], and that his evidence ought not to be received or left to the jury.

That the proposed evidence of I. K. on behalf of the [plaintiff *or* defendant] is inadmissible, and ought not to be received or left to the jury.

That the evidence for the plaintiff is not sufficient to call for an answer or explanation by evidence on the part of the defendant, and that upon such evidence the jury ought to be directed to find a verdict for the defendant. (*See Bill of Exceptions, post, No. 237.*)

That the evidence for the defendant is such as conclusively to entitle him to a verdict, and the jury ought to be directed to find a verdict for the defendant.

That the judge ought not to direct the jury that [*here state the direction objected to.*] (*See Bill of Exceptions*, No. 238, *post.*)

That the judge ought to direct the jury that [*here state the point contended for*], and the judge ought not to direct the jury that [*here state the direction objected to*].

That the judge ought himself to decide, as matter of law, that [*state the point contended for*], and he ought not to leave it to the jury to decide it as a question or matter of fact.

N.B.—*The above are merely examples on points of most frequent occurrence.*

---

237. *Bill of Exceptions by Defendant, where Plaintiff's Evidence held to be sufficient for the Jury* (*ante*, 314).

Copy the record of Nisi Prius verbatim ; then proceed thus :

Afterwards, on the [*commission day of the assizes*] —— day of ——, A.D. 18—, at ——, in the county [*or city*] of ——, before [*names and titles of the judges of assize, as in a postea*, No. 243], justices of our said lady the Queen, assigned to take the assizes in and for the said county [*or city*], the said matters in question between the said parties came on to be tried by a jury of the said county [*or city*] of ——, for that purpose duly impannelled : at which day came there as well the said A. B. as the said C. D., by their respective attornies aforesaid : and the jurors of the jury aforesaid impannelled to try the said matters in question being called, also came, and were then and there in due manner drawn by ballot, approved and sworn to try the said matters in question : • and upon the said trial of the said matters in question the counsel learned in the law for the said A. B., to maintain and prove the said matters in question on his part, gave in evidence that [*here set out the evidence on the part of the plaintiff; then proceed as follows*] : whereupon the said counsel for the said A. B. did then and there insist before the said justices, on behalf of the said A. B., that the several matters so produced and given in evidence on the part of the said A. B. were sufficient, and ought to be admitted and allowed as sufficient evidence, unless the same should be explained or answered by evidence on behalf of the said C. D., to entitle the said A. B. to a verdict, and prayed the said justices to direct the jury to that effect : but the counsel learned in the law for the said C. D. did not offer any evidence on his behalf, but did then and there insist before the said justices, that the said several matters did not require any explanation or answer by evidence, and were not sufficient, nor ought to be admitted or allowed to entitle the said A. B. to a verdict; and that, upon the evidence so given by the said A. B., the said C. D. was entitled to a verdict, and prayed the said justices so to direct the jury : but the said justices did then and there declare and deliver their opinion to the jury aforesaid, that the said several matters so produced and given in evidence on the part of the said A. B. were sufficient, and ought to be admitted and allowed to entitle the said A. B. to a verdict [and that, *here state any other special direction to the jury upon the matters in question* (*if any*); (*see Tidd's Appendix*, 327-8, 8th ed.)], and with that direction left the same to the jury : whereupon the counsel for the said C. D. did then and there, and before the giving of the verdict hereinafter mentioned, on behalf of the said C. D., except to the aforesaid opinion and direction of the said justices, and insisted that the said matters were not sufficient to entitle the said A. B. to a verdict, and did not require any explanation or answer by evidence on the part of the said C. D.: and the said jury then and there gave their verdict that the said A. B., on the —— day of ——, A.D. 18— [*the day mentioned in the writ*], was, and at the time of the giving of their said verdict still was, entitled to the possession of the [land *or* tenements] in the said writ mentioned, as in the said writ alleged : and inas-

much as the several matters so produced and given in evidence on the part
of the said A. B., and the said objections taken by the said counsel for the
said C. D., and the said opinion and direction of the said justices, do not
appear by the record of the verdict aforesaid, the said counsel for the said
C. D. did then and there, and before the giving of the said verdict, propose
their aforesaid exception to the said opinion and direction of the said justices, and requested the said Sir ——, Knight, so being one of the said
justices, to put his seal [*or say*, requested them or one of them to put their
or his seals or seal] to this bill of exceptions containing the several matters so produced and given in evidence on the part of the said A. B. as
aforesaid, and the said opinion and direction of the said justices thereon,
according to the form of the statute in such case made and provided ; and
thereupon the said Sir ——, Knight, as one of the said justices, in pursuance of such request, and of the statute in such case made and provided,
did put his seal to this bill of exceptions on the said [*commission day*] ——
day of ——, in the year of our Lord 18—.

Judge's signature. (L.S.)

---

238. *Bill of Exceptions by Defendant, where, notwithstanding Defendant's
Evidence, the Judge directed the Jury to find a Verdict for the Plaintiff*
(*ante*, 314).

Commence as ante, No. 237, *to the* *.

And upon the said trial of the said matters in question, the counsel
learned in the law for the said A. B., to maintain and prove the said matters
in question on his part, gave in evidence that [*here set out the evidence on the
part of the plaintiff ; and afterwards, in like manner, the evidence for the
defendant ; then proceed as follows*] :—Whereupon the said counsel for the
said C. D. did then and there insist before the said justices, on behalf of
the said C. D., that the several matters so produced and given in evidence
on the part of the said C. D. as aforesaid were sufficient, and ought to be
admitted and allowed as decisive evidence to entitle the said C. D. to a
verdict; and the said counsel for the said C. D. did then and there pray
the said justices to admit and allow the said matters so produced and given
in evidence for the said C. D. to be conclusive evidence in favour of the
said C. D. to entitle him to a verdict : But to this the counsel learned in
the law of the said A. B. did then and there object and insist before the
said justices that the same were not sufficient, nor ought to be admitted or
allowed, to entitle the said C. D. to a verdict: And the said justices did
then and there declare and deliver their opinion to the jury aforesaid, that
the said several matters so produced and given in evidence on the part of
the said C. D. were not sufficient to entitle the said C. D. to a verdict ; and
with that direction left the same to the jury: whereupon the said counsel
for the said C. D. did then and there, and before the giving of the verdict
hereinafter mentioned, on behalf of the said C. D., except to the aforesaid
opinion and direction of the said justices, and insisted on the said several
matters as entitling the said C. D. to a verdict upon the said matters in
question : And the said jury then and there gave their verdict, that the said
A. B., on the —— day of ——, A.D. 18— [*the day mentioned in the writ*] was,
and at the time of the giving of their said verdict still was, entitled to the
possession of the [land *or* tenements] in the said writ mentioned, as in the
said writ alleged : And inasmuch as the said several matters so produced and
given in evidence on the part of the said C. D., and by his counsel aforesaid
objected and insisted on as entitling him to a verdict on the said matters in
question, and the said opinion and direction of the said justices do not
appear by the record of the verdict aforesaid, the said counsel for the said
C. D. did then and there, and before the giving of the said verdict, propose
their aforesaid exception to the said opinion and direction of the said

justices, and requested the said Sir ——, Knight, so being one of the said justices, to put his seal [*or say,* requested them or one of them to put their or his seals or seal] to this bill of exceptions, containing the several matters so produced and given in evidence on the part of the said C. D. as aforesaid, and the said opinion and direction of the said justices thereon, according to the form of the statute in such case made and provided : and thereupon the said Sir ——, Knight, as one of the said justices, at the request of the said counsel for the said C. D., did put his seal to this bill of exceptions pursuant to the statute in such case made and provided on the said [*commission day*] —— day of ——, in the year of our Lord 18—.

Judge's signature (L.S.)

---

239. *Order to stay Judgment or Execution by Landlord against* ***Tenant, without*** *any Recognizance not to commit Waste, &c. (ante, 389).*

B. ⎰   Upon hearing counsel [*or* the attornies] on both sides, [and by
v. ⎱   consent, *or* upon the application of Mr. ——, of counsel for the
D. ⎰ defendant,] I do order that judgment on the verdict in this action be stayed until the fifth day of next —— term, unconditionally, it appearing to me [that the finding of the jury was contrary to the evidence ; *or* that the damages given were excessive, *as the case may be*]. Dated the —— day of ——, 18—.

Judge's signature.

N.B.—*Omit the words* "by consent," *or* "it appearing," *&c. One or the other appears necessary, but not both.*

---

240. *Order to stay Judgment or Execution by a Landlord, on* ***condition that the*** *Tenant, together with two Sureties, enter into a Recognizance* ***not to*** *commit Waste, &c. (ante, 389).*

B. ⎰   Upon application of Mr. ——, of counsel for the defendant, I
v. ⎱   do order that judgment on the verdict in this action be stayed
D. ⎰ [*or,* that execution in this action be stayed] until the fifth day of next —— term ; on condition that within four days from this day (being the day of the trial) the defendant shall actually find security, by the recognizance of himself and two sufficient sureties, in the sum of £—— (*d*), conditioned not to commit any waste, or act in the nature of waste, or other wilful damage, and not to sell or carry off any standing crops, hay, straw or manure produced or made (if any) upon the premises, and which may happen to be thereupon from the day on which the said verdict was given to the day on which execution shall finally be made upon the judgment, or the same be set aside, as the case may be. Dated the —— day of ——, 18—.

Judge's signature.

---

241. *Recognizance of Defendant and his two Sureties not to commit Waste, &c.* (*ante,* 389).

Form of Recognizance as ante, No. 48.

Acknowledgment thereof.—You do jointly and severally acknowledge to owe to the above-named A. B. the sum of £ —— : on condition that you, C. D., do not commit any waste, or act in the nature of waste, or other wilful damage, or sell or carry off any standing crops, hay, straw or manure

---

(*d*) "Such reasonable sum as the judge shall direct" (*ante,* 388).

produced or made (if any) upon the premises in question in this action, and which may happen to be thereupon from the day on which the verdict in this action was given to the day on which execution shall finally be made upon the judgment in this action, or the same be set aside, as the case may be. ——, Are you content?

N.B.—*The affidavits of bail, and notice of recognizance, &c. will be the same as ante, Nos. 49—55,* mutatis mutandis.

---

242. *Postea (ante, 334).*

Afterwards, on the —— day of ——, A.D. 18—, before —— and ——, justices of our lady the Queen, assigned to take the assizes in and for the within county, come the parties within mentioned ; and a jury of the said county being sworn to try the matters in question between the said parties, upon their oath say, that A. B. [*the claimant*] within mentioned, on the —— day of ——, A.D. 18—, was and still is entitled to the possession of the land within mentioned, as in the writ alleged : Therefore, &c.

This form is No. 17 in the Schedule to 15 & 16 *Vict. c.* 76. (*For other forms of postea, see Nos.* 243—250.)

---

243. *Postea at the Assizes (ante, 306, 334).*

Afterwards, on the [*commission day of the assizes*] —— day of ——, A.D. 18—, at ——, in the county [*or* city] of ——, before [*names and titles of the Judges of Assize, ex. gr.,* the Right Hon. John Lord Campbell, her Majesty's Chief Justice of her Court of Queen's Bench ; *or* the Right Hon. Sir John Jervis, Knight, her Majesty's Chief Justice of her Court of Common Pleas; *or* the Right Hon. Sir Frederick Pollock, Knight, Chief Baron of her Majesty's Court of Exchequer; *or* Sir ——, Knight, one of her Majesty's Justices of her Court of Queen's Bench *or* Common Pleas ; and Sir ——, Knight, one of the Barons of her Majesty's Court of Exchequer], justices of our lady the Queen, assigned to take the assizes in and for the within county [*or* city and county *or* town and county, *as the case may be*], come the parties within mentioned, by their respective attornies within mentioned [*or* in their proper persons, *as the case may be*] : And a jury of the said county [*or* city and county *or* town and county, *as the case may be*], being sworn to try the matters in question between the said parties, upon their oath say [*here state the finding according to the fact, ex gr.,* That [A. B.] within mentioned, on the [*day named in the writ of ejectment*] —— day of ——, A.D. 18—, was and still is entitled to the possession of the [land *or* tenements, *or* premises, *or* property] within mentioned, as in the said writ alleged(*e*): *or* That [A. B., J. K. and L. M., *names of plaintiffs entitled*] within mentioned on the [*day named in the writ*] —— day of ——, A.D. 18—, were and still are entitled to the possession of [*describe the part recovered ; if the part be an undivided part or share, describe it as ante,* 87], with the appurtenances, situate and being in the parish of ——, in the county of ——, being part of the [land *or* tenements, *or* premises, *or* property] within mentioned, as in the said writ alleged(*e*): and the jurors aforesaid, upon their oath aforesaid, further say, that [*names of all the claimants*] within mentioned, or any or either of them, were not nor was on the said —— day of ——, A.D. 18—, entitled to the possession of the residue of the [land *or* tenements, *or* premises, *or* property] within mentioned, or any part thereof, as in the said writ alleged.] Therefore, &c.

(*e*) Where mesne profits are assessed, see the next form.

244. *Postea in London or Middlesex, with Mesne Profits assessed* (*ante,* 292, 334, 387).

Afterwards, on the [*first day of the particular sitting*] —— day of ——, A.D. 18—, at [the Guildhall of the city of London *or* at Westminster Hall in the county of Middlesex, *as the case may be*], before [*name and title of the chief or other judge as ante, No.* 243], come the parties within mentioned by their respective attornies within mentioned [*or* in their proper persons, *as the case may be*] : And a jury of the said [city *or* county] being sworn to try the matters in question between the said parties, upon their oath say, That [*here state the finding of the jury according to the fact ; see ante, No.* 243. *If mesne profits were assessed, say,* And the jurors aforesaid, upon their oath aforesaid, assess the damages to be paid by the said C. D. to the said A. B. for the mesne profits of the said [*land or tenements, or part of the said land or tenements*] from the day of the [*expiration or determination*] of the said C. D.'s interest in the same, down to the —— day of ——, A.D. 18—, over and above his costs of suit, to £——. *Here state the finding as to the residue of the land* (*if any*) *as ante, No.* 243.] Therefore, &c.

----

245. *Postea for Landlord, with Damages assessed for Mesne Profits* (*ante,* 292, 334, 387).

Commence as ante, No. 243 *or* 244, *to the finding as to the title of the claimant inclusive, then proceed thus :*

And it appearing in evidence to the jurors aforesaid, that this action was brought by and at the suit of the said A. B., as landlord of the said [*land or tenements*], with the appurtenances, against the said C. D. as his tenant thereof, under a lease [*or* agreement] in writing [for a term of years which expired on the —— day of ——, A.D. 18—, *or* from year to year, which tenancy was determined on the —— day of ——, A.D. 18—, by a regular notice to quit:] And that the said attorney in this action of and for the said C. D. hath been served with due notice of trial in this action : The jury aforesaid, upon their oath aforesaid, in pursuance of the statute in such case made and provided, find and assess the damages of the said A. B. for the mesne profits of the said [*land or tenements*], with the appurtenances, from the said —— day of ——, A.D. 18—, being the day of the [*expiration or determination*] of the said C. D.'s interest in the said [*land or tenements*], with the appurtenances, down to the time of giving their verdict in this action [*or* down to the —— day of ——, A.D. 18—, when the said C. D. quitted and delivered up the possession of the said [*land or tenements*] with the appurtenances, to the said A. B.] at the sum of £——, over and above his costs of suit. Therefore, &c.

N.B.—*This form is taken from Tidd's Appendix,* 677 (*with variations*)*: but it does not appear necessary for the jury to find expressly all the facts necessary to entitle them to assess the mesne profits.* Chit. Forms, 563, 7th ed. (*ante,* No. 244).

245a. *Postea where Plaintiff's Title expired after the Writ was served* (*ante,* 290, 334).

Commence as ante, No. 243 *or* 244.

Upon their oath say, that A. B. [*the claimant*] within mentioned, on the [*day named in the writ*] —— day of ——, A.D. 18—, and from thence until and at the bringing of this action and the service of the writ within mentioned, was entitled to the possession of the [land] within mentioned, as in the said writ alleged: but that the said title of the said A. B. expired after such service and before this day ; and the said A. B. is not now entitled to the possession of the said [land] or any part thereof: Therefore, &c.

246. *Postea on a Nonsuit (ante, 304, 334).*

Afterwards, on the [*commission day of the assizes, or first day of the sittings*] —— day of ——, A.D. 18—, at [*as ante, No.* 243 *or* 244], before [*as ante, No.* 243 *or* 244], come the within-named [*defendants' names*], by their attorney within mentioned [*or* in person]; and a jury of the said [*county or* city] being sworn to try the matters in question between the parties within mentioned, the said A. B. [*the claimant*], although solemnly called, comes not, nor does he further prosecute his suit in this behalf against the said [*defendants' names*] : Therefore, &c.

---

247. *The like where Plaintiff nonsuited after Evidence given (ante, 304, 334).*

Commence as ante, No. 243 *or* 244, *to the words* "upon their oath say," *but omit those words, and proceed thus :*

After evidence being given to them, thereupon withdrew from the bar here to consider of the verdict to be by them given upon the premises ; and after they had considered thereof, and agreed among themselves, they returned to the bar here to give their verdict in this behalf: Whereupon the said A. B. [*the claimant*], being solemnly called, comes not, nor does he further prosecute his suit in this behalf against the said [*defendants' names*] : Therefore, &c.

---

248. *Postea on a Verdict for Defendant (ante, 306, 334).*

Commence as ante, No. 243 *or* 244, *to the words* "upon their oath say," *inclusive, then proceed thus :*

That [*names of all the claimants*] within mentioned or any or either of them were not, nor was [*if only one claimant say* "was not"] on the said —— day of ——, A.D. 18—, entitled to the possession of the said [land *or* tenements, *or* premises, *or* property] within mentioned, or any part thereof, as in the said writ alleged : Therefore, &c.

---

249. *Special Verdict (ante, 326).*

Commence as ante, No. 243 *or* 244, *to the words* "upon their oath say, That," *after which state the facts specially according to the evidence on both sides and the directions, ante,* 327 ; *conclude thus :*

But whether or not upon the whole matter aforesaid, by the jurors aforesaid in form aforesaid found, the said A. B. [*the claimant*] within mentioned on the [*day named in the writ of ejectment*] —— day of ——, A.D. 18—, was and still is entitled to the possession of the [land *or* tenements] within mentioned, as in the said writ alleged, the jurors aforesaid are altogether ignorant: And thereupon they pray the advice of the court of our said lady the Queen before [*in Q. B.* the Queen herself ; *in C. P.* her justices at Westminster ; *in Exch.* the barons of her Exchequer at Westminster]: And if upon the whole matter aforesaid it shall seem to the said court that the said A. B. was and still is so entitled as aforesaid, then the jurors aforesaid upon their oath aforesaid say, That the said A. B., on the —— day of ——, A.D. 18—, was and still is entitled to the possession of the [land *or* tenements] within mentioned as in the said writ alleged : But if upon the whole matter aforesaid it shall seem to the said court that the said A. B. was not nor is so entitled as aforesaid, then the jurors aforesaid, upon their oath aforesaid, say, That the said A. B., on the —— day of ——, 18—, was not nor is entitled to the possession of the [land *or* tenements] within mentioned as in the said writ alleged.

[*Final judgment thereon, post, Nos.* 266, 267. *For other forms of special verdicts, see post, No.* 250.]

250. *Special Verdicts (other Forms), ante, 326.*

Verdict for defendant as to part, and special verdict as to the residue. *Allen* v. *Rivington,* 2 Saund. 108 a.

As to the true construction of a will. *Doe* d. *Cannon* v. *Rucastle,* 8 C. B. 876.

Whether the first son of A. took an estate tail, or only an estate for life, under a will. *Kershaw* v. *Kershaw,* 3 E. & B. 845.

Whether G. W. took a fee under a will containing the word "estate," not in the devise itself, but in a subsequent part of the will. *Doe* d. *Burton* v. *White,* 1 Exch. 526 ; *S. C. in error,* 2 Exch. 797 ; and see *Burton* v. *White,* 7 Exch. 720 ; *Doe* d. *Potter* v. *Fricker,* 6 Exch. 510.

Whether under a residuary devise to N. W. " and her children who have issue, share and share alike," such of N. W.'s children as had no issue at the time of the testator's death took any interest. *Doe* d. *Burton* v. *White, supra.*

For other Forms, see ante, No. 149, post, No. 252.

---

251. *Special Case after Verdict (ante, 323).*
Title of court and cause as ante, No. 19.

This action of ejectment was commenced on the —— day of ——, A.D. 18—, by a writ of our lady the Queen issued forth of this court, in these words :

Victoria, by the grace of God [*here copy the writ, and the remainder of the record of Nisi Prius*].

The cause came on to be tried before the [Right] Honourable [Lord Chief Justice or Lord Chief Baron ——, *or* Mr. Justice *or* Baron ——,] at the [spring *or* summer] assizes, 18—, held at ——, in and for the county of ——, [*or* at the —— sittings in London *or* Middlesex, in *or* after —— Term, 18—] when a verdict was found for the plaintiffs [*or for some or one of them, as the case may be*] for [the whole of the land and premises claimed, *or* for, *describe the part recovered,* being part of the land and premises claimed, and for the defendants as to the residue], subject to the opinion of this court upon the following

CASE.

[*Here state concisely all the material facts proved and admitted at the trial in such a manner as fairly to raise the real question.*]

The court is to be at liberty to draw any inferences, or find any facts, which, in the opinion of the court, a jury ought to have drawn or found.

[*Also to amend the writ and any of the subsequent proceedings as the court may think fit.*]

[No proceedings in error shall be brought by either party upon the judgment of the court upon this case (*f*).]

The question for the opinion of the court is, whether [*here state the question*].

If the court shall be of opinion that [*here state the plaintiffs' point*], then the verdict entered for the [plaintiffs] shall stand [*if necessary, say* for the whole or such part of the land and premises as the court shall think they, or any or either of them, are or is entitled to recover, and the verdict shall be entered for the residue (if any) for the defendants].

If the court shall be of opinion that [*here state the defendants' point*], then the verdict entered for the [plaintiffs] shall be set aside, and instead thereof [a verdict shall be entered for the defendants, *or* a nonsuit shall be entered].

Counsel's signature " for the plaintiffs."
Counsel's signature " for the defendants."

(*f*) See 17 & 18 Vict. c. 125, s. 32, *ante,* 326.

252. *Special Case after Verdict (other Forms), ante,* 323.

Special case stating a will and various deeds under which the plaintiff and defendant respectively claimed. Each party to be allowed to refer to any of the deeds, instruments and probates of the wills which relate to the matter of this case. Memorials and inrolments of all such of the beforementioned deeds and instruments respectively, as by law were required to be registered or inrolled, were duly registered and inrolled. Question, whether the verdict should be entered for the plaintiff or for the defendant. *Doe* d. *Agar* v. *Brown,* 2 E. & B. 331.

Whether the plaintiff, as appointee under a settlement, was entitled to recover, the defendant being a purchaser for value from the settlor without notice of the settlement, and having ,obtained an assignment of two outstanding satisfied mortgage terms to a trustee on his behalf. Held, that such terms afforded a good defence. *Cottrell* v. *Hughes,* 15 C. B. 532. [N.B.—This case sets out divers settlements, mortgages, conveyances, executed and acknowledged by married women, and an appointment. Question, whether the plaintiff was entitled to recover in this action. If the court shall be of that opinion, the verdict for the plaintiff is to stand, but if the court shall be of a contrary opinion, the verdict is to be entered for the defendant.]

Whether the plaintiff was entitled to all or any part of certain settled property as heir of the settlor, who died entitled to the ultimate reversion in fee, but not in actual seisin or possession. Held, that she was not. *Jenkins* d. *Harris and wife* v. *Prichard,* 2 Wills. 45 [*but now see* 3 & 4 *Will. IV. c.* 106, *s.* 1, *ante,* 483].

Ejectment for copyholds by customary heir of testator against the father of a devisee in fee who *died before entry.* Liberty to turn the case into a special verdict. Will and pedigree annexed to form part of the case. *Parker* v. *Thomas,* 3 Man. & Gr. 815.

Whether the will of a married woman was a due execution of a power reserved to her in her marriage settlement. *Doe* d. *Beech* v. *Nall,* 6 Exch. 102.

Whether the plaintiff took a contingent remainder under a will, and if so, whether such remainder was defeated by a subsequent deed executed and acknowledged by a married woman. Judgment for defendants on the second point. *Bancks* v. *Ollerton,* 10 Exch. 168.

Whether certain evidence objected to by the claimants at the trial was admissible: Also, whether if it was admissible the claimants, under the circumstances stated, were entitled to recover: Also, whether if it, or any part of it, was not admissible, the claimants, under the above circumstances, were entitled to recover. *Doe* d. *Hamilton* v. *Clift,* 12 A. & E. 566; 4 P. & D. 579; and see *Doe* d. *Dand* v. *Thompson,* 13 Q. B. 670.

Whether plaintiff barred by the Statute of Limitations: Held not, he having received rents and profits within twenty years. *Doe* d. *Robertson* v. *Gardiner,* 12 C. B. 319, 324.

For other Forms, see ante, Nos. 149, 250.

---

253. *Rule Nisi to set aside a Verdict or Nonsuit, and instead thereof to enter a Verdict for the other Party or a Nonsuit (pursuant to leave reserved), or for a New Trial (ante,* 321).

In the [Q. B. *or* Exch.]

———day, the —— day of ——, 18—.

B. [and another] ⎱ It is ordered that the [defendant *or* plaintiff], upon
    v.   ⎰ notice of this rule to be given to his attorney, shall upon
D. [and others.] —— next show cause why the [verdict *or* nonsuit] obtained in this cause should not be set aside, and [instead thereof a verdict entered for the defendant *or* plaintiff, *or* a nonsuit entered, *or*] a new trial

granted between the parties, on the following grounds :—*Here state concisely the grounds upon which the rule nisi is granted*, ex. gr. :

1. For the erroneous rejection of [*describe the document shortly*] as evidence for the ——.

2. For the erroneous admission of [*describe the document shortly*] as evidence for the ——.

3. For the erroneous rejection of the evidence of O. P., on behalf of the ——.

4. For the erroneous admission of the evidence of Q. R., on behalf of the ——.

5. For misdirection, the judge having [*here state concisely the nature of the alleged misdirection.*]

6. For an erroneous nonsuit, notwithstanding the plaintiff appeared by his counsel when called at the trial, and objected to be nonsuited (*ante*, 304).

7. That the verdict was against the weight of evidence.

8. That the verdict was contrary to the evidence, and to the direction of the judge, and perverse.

And in the meantime all proceedings be stayed. Upon the motion of Mr. ——.

By the Court.

---

254. *The like in C. P.* (*ante*, 321).

In the Common Pleas.

——day, the —— day of ——, 18—.

A. *v.* B. } Upon reading the record of nisi prius between the said [and others.] } parties, it is ordered that the plaintiff, upon notice of this rule to be given to him or his attorney, shall show cause to this court on [Friday] next why the verdict found for him on the trial of this cause at the [sitting after last term, holden at Guildhall in and for the city of London] should not be set aside, and instead thereof a verdict entered for the defendants on the ground that [*here state concisely all the grounds upon which the rule was granted*, ante, No. 253]: And in the meantime, and until this court shall otherwise order, let the postea remain in the hands of the associate, and the entry of final judgment on the said verdict be stayed.

By the Court.

On the motion of Mr. —— for the defendants.

255. *Rule absolute* (*ante*, 321).

Commence as ante, No. 28.

It is ordered that the verdict obtained in this action be set aside, and [a nonsuit entered, *or* and a verdict entered for the defendants, *or* a new trial had between the parties] on the following grounds :—

1. *Here state concisely the grounds upon which the rule is made absolute.*

            Mr. —— for the plaintiffs.

            Mr. —— for the defendants.

By the Court.

---

256. *Notice of Appeal to the Exchequer Chamber against the Refusal of a Rule Nisi to enter a Verdict or a Nonsuit on a Point reserved* (*ante*, 322).

Title of court and cause as ante, No. 19.

Take notice, that the defendants will appeal to the Court of Exchequer Chamber pursuant to the provisions of The Common Law Procedure Act, 1854, against the decision of this honourable court, on the —— day of —— [instant *or* last], whereby an application made on behalf of the defendants for a rule calling on the plaintiffs to show cause why the verdict obtained in this cause should not be set aside and a nonsuit entered [*or* a verdict entered for the defendants upon the point reserved at the trial] was refused. Dated this —— day of ——, 18—.

Yours, &c.

To Mr. E. F., the plaintiffs' attorney, and }   G. H., of ——,
to the Masters of this Honourable Court. }   Defendants' attorney.

See another Form, Chit. Forms, 824 (7th edit.)

---

257. *Notice of Appeal when Rule Nisi discharged (ante, 322).*

Title of court and cause as ante, No. 19.

Take notice, that the defendants will appeal to the Court of Exchequer Chamber pursuant to the provisions of The Common Law Procedure Act, 1854, against a rule of this honourable court made in this cause on the —— day of —— [instant *or* last], whereby a previous rule made in this cause on the —— day of —— last was discharged. Dated this —— day of ——, 18—.

Yours, &c.

To Mr. E. F., the plaintiffs' attorney, and }   G. H., of ——,
to the Masters of this Honourable Court. }   Defendants' attorney.

---

258. *Notice of Appeal when Rule made absolute (ante, 322).*

Title of court and cause as ante, No. 19.

Take notice, that the plaintiffs will appeal to the Court of Exchequer Chamber pursuant to the provisions of The Common Law Procedure Act, 1854, against a rule of this court made in this cause on the —— day of —— [instant *or* last], whereby it was ordered that [&c.] Dated this —— day of ——, 18—.

Yours, &c.

To Mr. G. H., the defendants' attorney, and }   E. F., of ——,
to the Masters of this Honourable Court. }   Plaintiffs' attorney.

---

259. *Special Case on Appeal when Rule Nisi refused (ante, 322).*

In the Exchequer Chamber.

Between [*names of claimants*], plaintiffs,
and
[*names of defendants*], defendants.

Appeal by the defendants.

The following case is stated pursuant to the 39th section of The Common Law Procedure Act, 1854, by way of appeal by the defendants from a decision of her Majesty's Court of [Q. B., C. P. *or* Exch.], made on the —— day of ——, A.D. 18—, whereby an application made on behalf of the defendants for a rule calling on the plaintiffs to show cause why the verdict obtained in this cause should not be set aside, and instead thereof [a nonsuit entered, *or* a verdict entered for the defendants pursuant to leave reserved at the trial] upon the following grounds, viz. [*state them*], was refused.

This action was commenced on the —— day of ——, A.D. 18—, by a writ of our lady the Queen, issued forth out of her Majesty's Court of [Q. B., C. P. *or* Exch.] at Westminster, in these words :—

Victoria, by the grace of God [*here copy the writ, and the remainder of the record of nisi prius*].

The cause came on to be tried before the [Right] Hon. [Lord Chief Justice *or* Lord Chief Baron ——, *or* the Hon. Mr. Justice (*or* Baron) ——] at the [spring *or* summer] assizes, 18—, held at ——, in and for the county of —— [*or* at the —— sitting in London *or* Middlesex, in *or* after —— term, 18—,] when the following facts were proved. *Here set forth*

" *so much of the evidence and the ruling or judgment objected to as may be neces-*
sary to raise the question for the decision of the Court of Appeal " (17 & 18
Vict. c. 125, *s.* 139). *The facts should be stated much in the same manner as
in a bill of exceptions, or special case after verdict, or as in a special verdict. The
leave given at the trial to move upon the point reserved must of course be stated ;
also the verdict : then proceed thus :—*

Within the time in that behalf allowed by the rules and practice of the
said court, viz., on the —— day of ——, A.D. 18—, the defendants by their
counsel applied to the said court of [Q. B., C. P. *or* Exch.], in pursuance of
the leave so reserved at the said trial as aforesaid, for a rule calling on the
plaintiffs to show cause why the said verdict obtained in this cause should
not be set aside and [a nonsuit entered, *or* a verdict entered for the defend-
ants] on the following grounds [*or* upon the following (amongst other)
grounds], viz. *State shortly the grounds relied on as in a rule nisi.*

The said Court of [Q. B., C. P. *or* Exch.] decided against the said application, and refused to grant any rule to show cause.

The defendants appeal from the said decision pursuant to the provisions
of The Common Law Procedure Act, 1854. Due notice of such appeal has
been given pursuant to the said act.

> The question for the opinion of the Court of Appeal is, whether
> the said Court of [Q. B., C. P. *or* Exch.] ought to have granted
> a rule to show cause in pursuance of the said application upon
> the grounds above mentioned, or any or either of them. If
> yea, a rule to show cause to be granted according to the judg-
> ment of the Court of Appeal, and to be afterwards argued and
> disposed of in that court, pursuant to the provisions of The
> Common Law Procedure Act, 1854.
>
> Counsel's *signature* " for the plaintiffs."
> Counsel's *signature* " for the defendants."

See another Form, Chit. Forms, 825 (*7th edit.*)

———

260. *Special Case on Appeal when Rule Nisi discharged* (*ante,* 322).

In the Exchequer Chamber.

> Between [*names of claimants*], plaintiffs,
>   and
> [*names of defendants*], defendants.

Appeal by the defendants.

The following case is stated pursuant to the 39th section of The Common
Law Procedure Act, 1854, by way of appeal by the defendants from a rule
of her Majesty's Court of [Q. B., C. P. *or* Exch.] made in these words.
[*Copy the rule appealed against, verbatim*].

The previous rule so discharged was in these words : —[*Copy the rule nisi*].

This action was commenced [*here proceed as ante, No.* 259, *to the verdict
inclusive*].

Within the time in that behalf allowed by the rules and practice of the
said court, viz., on the [*date of rule nisi*] —— day of ——, A.D. 18—, the ·
defendants, in pursuance of the said leave so reserved at the said trial as
aforesaid, applied for and obtained the rule to show cause, dated the ——
day of ——, 18—, a copy whereof is hereinbefore set forth.

Afterwards on the —— day of ——, A.D. 18—, the said Court of [Q. B.,
C. P. *or* Exch.] discharged the said rule to show cause by another rule,
dated on the day and year last aforesaid, a copy whereof is hereinbefore set
forth.

The defendants appeal from the said last-mentioned decision and rule,
pursuant to the provisions of The Common Law Procedure Act, 1854. Due
notice of such appeal has been given pursuant to the said act.

> The question for the opinion of the Court of Appeal is, whether
> the said rule of the —— day of ——, 18—, [*the rule nisi*]

ought to have been discharged, or ought to have been made absolute upon all or any of the grounds therein stated. The Court of Appeal to make such rule upon this appeal as it shall think fit, and to proceed thereon pursuant to the provisions of The Common Law Procedure Act, 1853.

Counsel's signature "for the plaintiffs."
Counsel's signature "for the defendants."

See another Form, Chit. Forms, 825 (7th edit.)

---

261. *Special Case on Appeal when Rule made absolute (ante,* 322).

In the Exchequer Chamber.

Between [*names of claimants*], plaintiffs,
and
[*names of defendants*], defendants.

Appeal by the plaintiffs.

The following case is stated pursuant to the 39th section of The Common Law Procedure Act, 1854, by way of appeal by the plaintiffs from a rule of her Majesty's Court of [Q. B., C. P. *or* Exch.] made in these words :—[*Copy the rule absolute*].

This action was commenced [*here proceed as ante, No.* 259, *to the verdict inclusive*].

Within the time in that behalf allowed by the rules and practice of the said court, viz., on the [*date of rule nisi*] —— day of ——, A.D. 18—, the defendants in pursuance of the said leave so reserved at the said trial as aforesaid applied for and obtained a rule in the following words :—[*Copy the rule nisi*].

Afterwards, on the —— day of ——, A.D. 18—, the court made the said rule absolute by another rule dated on the day and year last aforesaid, a copy whereof is hereinbefore set forth.

The plaintiffs appeal from the said last-mentioned decision and rule, pursuant to the provisions of The Common Law Procedure Act, 1854. Due notice of such appeal has been given pursuant to the said act.

The question for the opinion of the Court of Appeal is, whether the said rule of the —— day of ——, 18—, [*the rule absolute*] ought to have been made upon all or any of the grounds therein stated, or whether the said previous rule to show cause, dated the —— day of ——, 18—, ought to have been discharged. The Court of Appeal to make such rule upon this appeal as it shall think fit, and to proceed thereon pursuant to the provisions of The Common Law Procedure Act, 1854.

Counsel's signature "for the plaintiffs."
Counsel's signature "for the defendants."

See another Form, Chit. Forms, 825 (7th edit.)

261a. *Judgment of Exchequer Chamber on an Appeal (ante,* 322).

Copy the case for the appeal as stated by the parties, and then proceed thus :—

Afterwards on —— [*the day of judgment of Court of Appeal*] in the Court of Exchequer Chamber of our lady the Queen, before the justices of the Common Bench of our lady the Queen and the barons of her Exchequer, [*or, if the appeal be from the Common Pleas, say,* before the justices of our lady the Queen assigned to hold pleas in the court of our lady the Queen before the Queen herself and the barons of her Exchequer ; *or, if the appeal be from the Exchequer, say,* before the justices of our lady the Queen assigned to hold pleas in the court of our lady the Queen before the Queen herself and the justices of the Common Bench of our said lady the Queen], come the parties aforesaid by their respective attornies aforesaid ; and the said Court of Appeal decide that, &c. [*state the decision of the court upon the questions raised by the case on appeal*]: And it is considered by the said Court of

Appeal that the plaintiff do recover against the defendant (g) £—— for his costs which the plaintiff hath sustained and expended in the said appeal, and that the plaintiff have execution thereof.

This form is given by Reg. Mich. Vac. 1854, *Sched. No.* 21.

---

262. *Final Judgment after Verdict for the Claimants for all the Property (ante,* 337).

After the entry of the issue and postea, as ante, Nos. 131—138, *and* 242—245, *omitting the words* " Therefore &c.," *proceed thus :—*

Therefore it is considered that the said A. B. do recover against the said C. D. possession of the [land *or* tenements, *or* premises, *or* property] in the said writ mentioned, with the appurtenances, and £ —— for his costs of suit.

In the margin, opposite the words "Therefore it is considered," *write,* " Judgment signed on the —— day of ——, 18—." *At the time of signing the judgment a mere incipitur may be entered, as ante, No.* 122.

---

263. *Final Judgment after Verdict for all or some of the Claimants as to Part of the Land, and for Defendant as to the Residue (ante,* 337).

After the entry of the issue and postea, as ante, Nos. 131—138, *and* 242—245, *omitting the words* " Therefore &c.," *proceed thus :—*

Therefore it is considered that the said [*names of claimants who obtained the verdict*] do recover against the said —— possession of the said —— [*describe the part recovered as in the verdict*], with the appurtenances, being part of the said [land *or* tenements, *or* premises, *or* property] in the said writ mentioned, and to the possession whereof they have been found entitled as aforesaid, and £—— for [their] costs of suit as to the said part : And it is further considered that the said [*defendants' names*] be acquitted as to the residue of the said [land *or* tenements, *or* premises, *or* property] in the said writ mentioned, and go thereof without day, &c. : And that they recover against the said [*names of all the claimants*] £—— for their costs of defence as to the said residue.

See note to No. 262.

---

264. *Final Judgment after a Verdict for a Landlord, with Mesne Profits assessed (ante,* 337).

After the entry of the issue and postea, as ante, Nos. 131—138, *and* 242—245, *omitting the words* " Therefore &c.," *proceed thus :—*

Therefore it is considered that the said A. B. do recover against the said C. D. possession of the [land *or* tenements, *or* property] in the said writ mentioned, with the appurtenances : And also the said sum of £ —— so found and assessed as aforesaid as the damages of the said A. B. for the said mesne profits of the said [land *or* tenements, *or* premises, *or* property], which have accrued as aforesaid : And also £—— for the said A. B.'s costs of suit. *See note to No.* 262.

---

265. *Final Judgment after a Nonsuit or a Verdict for Defendants (ante,* 337).

After the entry of the issue and postea, as ante, Nos. 131—138, *and* 246—248, *omitting the words* " Therefore &c.," *proceed thus :—*

Therefore it is considered that the said A. B. take nothing by his said writ : And that the said C. D. do go without day, &c. : And that the said C. D. do recover against the said A. B. £—— for his costs of defence.

See note to No. 262.

(g) " The Court of Appeal shall give such judgment as ought to have been given in the court below." 17 & 18 Vict. c. 125, s. 41, *ante,* 322 ; see *post,* Nos. 262—268.

266. Final Judgment for Plaintiff after a Special Verdict (ante, 329, 337).

After the entry of the issue, as ante, Nos. 131—138, and the postea as ante, No. 249, proceed thus :—

Afterwards on the [*day of signing judgment on the special verdict*] —— day of ——, A.D. 18—, [*in Q. B.* before our said lady the Queen, *in C. P.* before the justices of our said lady the Queen, *in Exch.* before the barons of the Exchequer of our said lady the Queen] at Westminster, come as well the said A. B. as the said C. D. by their respective attornies aforesaid : And hereupon all and singular the premises being seen, and by the said court here fully understood, and mature deliberation being thereupon had, it appears to the said court here that the said A. B., on the —— day of ——, A.D. 18—, was and still is entitled to the possession of the [land *or* tenements, *or* premises, *or* property] above mentioned as in the said writ alleged : Therefore it is considered that the said A. B. do recover against the said C. D. possession of the [land *or* tenements, *or* premises, *or* property] in the said writ mentioned, with the appurtenances, and £—— for his costs of suit.

See note to No. 262.

———

267. Final Judgment for Defendant after a Special Verdict (ante, 329, 337).

Commence as ante, No. 266, to the words " mature deliberation being thereupon had*" inclusive, then proceed thus :—*

It appears to the said court here that the said A. B., on the —— day of ——, A.D. 18—, was not nor is entitled to the possession of the [land *or* tenements, *or* premises, *or* property] above mentioned, or any part thereof, as in the said writ alleged : Therefore it is considered that the said A. B. take nothing by his said writ ; and that the said C. D. do go thereof without day, &c. : And that the said C. D. do recover against the said A. B. £—— for his costs of defence.

See note to No. 262.

———

268. Final Judgment after a Verdict subject to a Special Case (ante, 325, 337).

After the entry of the issue as ante, Nos. 131—138, and the postea as ante, Nos. 242—244, omitting the words "Therefore &c.," proceed thus :—

And the said verdict was so given by the consent of both parties, subject to a special case, as follows :—[*Copy the special case*].

Afterwards on the [*day of signing final judgment*] —— day of ——, A.D. 18—, come here the parties aforesaid, and the court is of opinion that [*here state the opinion of the court on the question or questions stated in the case, in the affirmative or negative, as the case may be*] : Therefore it is considered that the said A. B. do recover against the said C. D. possession of the said [land *or* tenements, *or* premises, *or* property] in the said writ mentioned, with the appurtenances, and £—— for his costs of suit—*Or*, therefore it is considered that the said verdict be set aside, and instead thereof [a nonsuit entered *or* a verdict entered for the defendant, *as the case may be*], pursuant to the terms of the said special case ; and that the said C. D. be acquitted, and that he recover against the said A. B. £—— for his costs of defence.

See the notes to Nos. 151 and 262. If the parties specially agree that no error shall be brought on the judgment, the postea and judgment may be in the usual form without any mention of the special case.

———

269. *Memorandum of Attornment after a Judgment in Ejectment (ante, 230, 345).*

Title of court and cause, as ante, No. 19.

Whereas the above-named A. B. lately recovered judgment in this action of ejectment for [*describe the property as in the writ or judgment*], with the appurtenances, situate in the parish of ——, in the county of —— : Now we, the undersigned, being respectively tenants [and undertenants] in possession of divers parts of the property so recovered as aforesaid, do hereby severally attorn and become tenants to the said A. B., his heirs [or executors, administrators] and assigns, of and for such part and parts of the said property as is or are now in our respective possession for the term and terms, and subject to the rent and rents, and to the several stipulations and conditions under which we respectively now hold the said part and parts of the said property so in our respective possession as aforesaid : And we have this day each paid one shilling to [Mr. E. F. as the agent of and for] the said A. B., on account and in part of our respective rent and rents. As witness our hands this —— day of ——, 18—.

Signatures.

N.B.—*The above document not creating any fresh tenancy, or new terms, but being a mere attornment, and nothing more, does not require any stamp.* Doe *d.* Linsey *v.* Edwards, 5 A. & E. 95, 102 ; Doe *d.* Wright *v.* Smith, 8 A. & E. 255 ; 3 N. & P. 335 (*ante*, 230).

---

270. *Writ of Habere Facias Possessionem (without a Fi. Fa. or Ca. Sa. for the costs), (ante, 342).*

Victoria, by the grace of God of the United Kingdom of Great Britain and Ireland Queen, Defender of the Faith, to the sheriff of ——, greeting : Whereas A. B., lately in our Court of [Queen's Bench, *or* Common Pleas, *or* Exchequer of Pleas, *as the case may be*], at Westminster, by the judgment of the same court recovered possession of —— [*here describe the property as in the writ of ejectment ; or if part only of the land has been recovered, describe such part as in the judgment*], with the appurtenances, in your bailiwick, in an action of ejectment at the suit of the said A. B. against C. D. : Therefore we command you that you omit not, by reason of any liberty of your county, but that you enter the same (*h*), and without delay you cause the said A. B. to have possession of the said [land and premises], with the appurtenances : And in what manner you have executed this our writ make appear [to us, *or in C. P.* to our justices, *or in Exch.* to the barons of our Exchequer, *as the case may be*], at Westminster, immediately upon the execution hereof, and have you there then this writ. Witness [*name of Chief Justice or Chief Baron*] ——, at Westminster, the [*day the writ issues*] —— day of ——, in the year of our Lord 18—.

To be indorsed with the name and address of the attorney and agent, pursuant to Reg. Prac. H. T. 1853, *No.* 73 (*ante*, 343).

---

271. *Writ of Habere Facias and Fi. Fa. for Costs (ante,* 342).

Victoria, by the grace of God of the United Kingdom of Great Britain and Ireland Queen, Defender of the Faith, to the sheriff of ——, greeting : Whereas A. B., lately in our Court of [Queen's Bench, *or* Common Pleas, *or* Exchequer of Pleas, *as the case may be*], at Westminster, recovered possession of [*here describe the property as in the writ of ejectment ; or if part only of the land has been recovered, describe such part as in the judgment*], with the

---

(*h*) A *non omittas* clause may be inserted in writs sued out of Q. B. or C. P., as well as in the Exch.

appurtenances, in your bailiwick, in an action of ejectment at the suit of the said A. B. against C. D. : Therefore we command you, that [*in Exchequer say*, you omit not, by reason of any liberty in your county, but that you enter the same, and] without delay you cause the said A. B. to have possession of the said [land and premises], with the appurtenances ; and we also command you that [*if in Exchequer say*, you omit not by reason of any liberty of your county, but that you enter the same, and that] of the goods and chattels of the said C. D. in your bailiwick you cause to be made £——, which the said A. B. lately, in our said court, recovered against the said C. D. for the said A. B.'s costs of the said suit, whereof the said C. D. is convicted ; together with interest upon the said sum, at the rate of four pounds per centum per annum, from the —— day of ——, in the year of our Lord 18—, on which day the judgment aforesaid was entered up, and have that money and interest aforesaid in our said court immediately after the execution hereof, to be rendered to the said A. B., and that you do all things as by the statute passed in the second year of our reign you are authorized and required to do in that behalf: And in what manner you shall have executed this our writ make appear [*in Q. B. to us, or in C. P. before our justices, or in Exch.* before the barons of our Exchequer, *as the case may be*], at Westminster, immediately after the execution hereof; and have you there then this writ. Witness [*&c. as in No.* 270].

See notes to No. 270. *Also indorse the amount to be levied, pursuant to Reg. Prac. H. T.* 1853. *No.* 76 (*ante,* 343), *thus :* " Levy £——, with interest thereon, at the rate of four pounds per centum per annum, from the [*date of judgment*] —— day of ——, 18— ; besides —— for this writ and the warrant thereon. Also sheriff's poundage, officers' fees, and all other legal incidental expenses."

---

272. *Writ of Habere Facias and Ca. Sa. for Costs* (*ante,* 342).

Victoria, by the grace of God of the United Kingdom of Great Britain and Ireland Queen, Defender of the Faith, to the sheriff of ——, greeting: Whereas A. B., lately in our Court of [Queen's Bench, *or* Common Pleas, *or* Exchequer of Pleas, *as the case may be*], at Westminster, recovered possession of [*here describe the property as in the writ of ejectment ; or if part only of the land has been recovered, describe such part as in the judgment*], with the appurtenances, in your bailiwick, in an action of ejectment at the suit of the said A. B. against C. D. : Therefore we command you that [*in Exch. say*, you omit not, by reason of any liberty in your county, but that you enter the same, and] without delay you cause the said A. B. to have possession of the said [land and premises], with the appurtenances: And we also command you that you [*in Exch. say*, omit not, by reason of any liberty in your county, but that you enter the same, and] take the said C. D., if he shall be found in your bailiwick, and him safely keep, so that you may have his body [before us, *or in C. P.* before our justices, *or in Exch.* before the barons of our Exchequer, *as the case may be*], at Westminster, immediately after the execution hereof, to satisfy the said A. B. £——, which the said A. B. lately in our said court recovered against the said C. D. for the said A. B.'s costs of the said suit, whereof the said C. D. is convicted ; together with interest upon the said sum, at the rate of four pounds per centum per annum, from the —— day of ——, A.D. 18—, on which day the judgment aforesaid was entered up ; and have you there then this writ. Witness [*&c. as in No.* 270].

See notes to Nos. 270, 271.

---

273. *Writ of Habere Facias and Fi. Fa. for Mesne Profits and Costs*
(*ante,* 342).

Same as ante, No. 271, *to the words* " cause to be made £——" *inclusive ;
then proceed thus :—*

Which the said A. B. lately in our said court, in the said action, recovered
against the said C. D. for the damages of the said A. B. for certain mesne
profits of the said [land and premises], whereof the said C. D. is convicted :
and also £——, which the said A. B. lately in our said court recovered
against the said C. D. for the said A. B.'s costs of the said suit, whereof the
said C. D. is convicted : together with the interest upon the said sums, at
the rate of four pounds per centum per annum, from the —— day of ——,
A.D. 18—, on which day the judgment aforesaid was entered up ; and have
such monies and interest as aforesaid in our said court immediately [&c.
remainder as in No. 271].

See notes to Nos. 270, 271.

---

274. *Writ of Habere Facias and Ca. Sa. for Mesne Profits and Costs* (*ante,* 342).
Same as ante, No. 272, *to the words* " to satisfy the said A. B. £——"
inclusive ; then proceed thus :—

Which the said A. B. lately in our said court, in the said action, recovered
against the said C. D. for the damages of the said A. B., for certain mesne profits
of the said [land and premises], whereof the said C. D. is convicted : and
also £——, which the said A. B. lately in our said court recovered against
the said C. D. for the said A. B.'s costs of the said suit, whereof the said
C. D. is convicted : together with interest upon the said sums, at the rate
[&c. remainder as in No. 272].

See notes to Nos. 270, 271.

---

275. *Writ of Fi. Fa. for Plaintiff's Costs* (*ante,* 342).

Victoria, by the grace of God of the United Kingdom of Great Britain
and Ireland Queen, Defender of the Faith, to the sheriff of ——, greeting :
We command you, that [*if in Exch. say,* you omit not, by reason of any
liberty of your county, but that you enter the same and] of the goods and
chattels of C. D. in your bailiwick you cause to be made £——, which
A. B. lately in our Court of [Queen's Bench, *or* Common Pleas, *or* Exchequer
of Pleas, *as the case may be*] recovered against him, for the said A. B.'s
costs of suit in an action of ejectment brought by the said A. B. against the
said C. D. in that court, whereof the said C. D. is convicted : together with
interest upon the said sum, at the rate of four pounds per centum per
annum, from the —— day of ——, in the year of our Lord ——, on which
day the judgment aforesaid was entered up, and have that money, with such
interest as aforesaid [before us, *or in C. P.* before our justices, *or in Exch.*
before the barons of our Exchequer, *as the case may be*], at Westminster,
immediately after the execution hereof, to be rendered to the said A. B. ;
and that you do all things as by the statute passed in the second year of
our reign you are authorized and required to do in that behalf : And in
what manner you shall have executed this our writ make appear to [us, *or
in C. P.* to our justices, *or in Exch.* to the barons of our Exchequer, *as the
case may be*], at Westminster, immediately after the execution hereof, and
have you there then this writ. Witness [&c. *as in No.* 270].

See notes to Nos. 270, 271.

276. *Writ of Ca. Sa. for Plaintiff's Costs (ante, 342).*

Victoria, by the grace of God of the United Kingdom of Great Britain and Ireland Queen, Defender of the Faith, to the sheriff of ——, greeting: We command you, that you [*in Exch. say,* omit not by reason of any liberty in your county, but that you enter the same, and] take C. D., if he shall be found in your bailiwick, and him safely keep, so that you may have his body [before us, *or in C. P.* before our justices, *or in Exch.* before the barons of our Exchequer, *as the case may be*], at Westminster, immediately after the execution hereof, to satisfy A. B. £——, which the said A. B. lately in our Court of [Queen's Bench, *or* Common Pleas, *or* Exchequer of Pleas, *as the case may be*], recovered against him for the said A. B.'s costs of suit in an action of ejectment brought by the said A. B. against the said C. D. in that court, whereof the said C. D. is convicted; together with interest upon the said sum, at the rate of four pounds per centum per annum, from the —— day of——, in the year of our Lord ——, on which day the judgment aforesaid was entered up; and have you there then this writ. Witness [*&c. as in No.* 270].

See notes to Nos. 270, 271.

---

277. *Writ of Fi. Fa. for Defendant's Costs (ante, 342).*
Commence as ante, No. 275.

Of the goods and chattels of A. B., in your bailiwick, you cause to be made £——, which C. D., lately in our Court of [Queen's Bench, *or* Common Pleas, *or* Exchequer of Pleas, *as the case may be*], recovered against him for the said C. D.'s costs of defence in an action of ejectment brought by the said A. B. against the said C. D. in that court, whereof the said A. B. is convicted; together with interest [*&c. as in No.* 275, *to the end; only reversing the names*].

---

278. *Writ of Ca. Sa. for Defendant's Costs (ante, 342).*
Same as No. 276, *only reversing the names, and saying "* costs of defence*" instead of "* costs of suit.*"*

---

279. *Sheriff's Warrant on Habere Facias (ante, 345).*

[*Cheshire*] } I. K., Esq., sheriff of the county aforesaid, to I. S., my bailiff,
to wit. } greeting: By virtue of her Majesty's writ of habere facias possessionem to me directed and delivered, I command you that you deliver to A. B. [*the claimant*] possession of [*describe the property as in the writ*], with the appurtenances, in my bailiwick, and forthwith certify the same to me. Given under the seal of my office this —— day of——, 18—.

(L.S.) By the sheriff.

---

280. *Sheriff's Warrant on Habere Facias and Fi. Fa. for Costs (ante, 345).*

[*Cumberland*] } I. K., Esq., sheriff of the county aforesaid, to I. S. and T. R.,
to wit. } my bailiffs, greeting: By virtue of her Majesty's writ of habere facias possessionem and fi. fa., to me directed and delivered, I command you, and each of you, jointly and severally, that you, or one of you, deliver to A. B. possession of [*describe the property as in the writ*], with the appurtenances, in my bailiwick, and forthwith certify the same to me: Also, that of the goods and chattels of C. D., in my bailiwick, you, or one of you, cause to be made £—— [together with interest upon the said sum, at the rate of four pounds per centum per annum, from the —— day of

——, in the year of our Lord 18—, on which day the judgment in the said writ mentioned was entered up], so that I may have that money [and interest] before [our lady the Queen, *or in C. P.* before the justices of our lady the Queen, *or in Exch.* before the barons of her Majesty's Exchequer], at Westminster, immediately, as required by the said writ : And that you do all such things, &c. : And in what manner you shall have executed this warrant certify to me immediately after the execution thereof. Given under the seal of my office, this —— day of ——, 18—.

(L.S.)   **By the sheriff.**

Levy £—— besides [*as indorsed on the writ*].

---

281. *Sheriff's Warrant on Habere Facias and Ca. Sa., for Costs* (*ante*, 345).

[*Durham*] }   I. K., Esq., sheriff of the county aforesaid, to I. S. and T. R., to wit. } my bailiffs, greeting : By virtue of her Majesty's writ of habere facias possessionem and ca. sa. to me directed and delivered, I command you and each of you, jointly and severally, that you, or one of you, deliver to A. B. possession of [*describe the property, as in the writ*], with the appurtenances, in my bailiwick, and forthwith certify the same to me : Also, that you [omit not, by reason of any liberty in my county, but that you enter the same, and] take C. D. wheresoever he shall be found in my bailiwick, and him safely keep, so that I may have his body before [our lady the Queen, *or in C. P.* before the justices of our lady the Queen, *or in Exch.* before the barons of her Majesty's Exchequer], at Westminster, immediately, as required by the said writ : And in what manner you shall have executed the said warrant certify to me immediately after the execution thereof. Given under the seal of my office, this —— day of ——, 18—.

(L.S.)   **By the sheriff.**

Levy £—— besides [*as indorsed on the writ*].

---

282. *Sheriff's Return, that no Person came to point out the Land* (*ante*, 86, 345, 348).

I certify [*in Q. B.* our lady the Queen, *or in C. P.* the justices within mentioned, *or in Exch.* the barons within mentioned] that this writ was delivered to me on the —— day of ——, A.D. 18—, since which time I have always been ready and willing to execute the same, as within I am commanded : but neither the within-named A. B., nor any person on his behalf, ever came to show me the [land *or* tenements] within mentioned, or any part thereof, or to receive possession of the same, or any part thereof, from me.

The answer of
——, Esq., sheriff.

---

283. *Sheriff's Return to Habere Facias, of Possession delivered* (*ante*, 348).

By virtue of this writ to me directed, on the —— day of ——, in the year 18—, I delivered to the within-named A. B. possession of the within-mentioned [land *or* tenements] and premises, with the appurtenances, as within I am commanded.

——, Esq., sheriff.

---

284. *Sheriff's Return to a Writ of Habere Facias and Fi. Fa. for Costs, of the due Execution thereof* (*ante*, 348).

Commence as ante, No. 283, to the signature, which omit ; then proceed thus :
I further certify and return, that the within-named C. D. hath not any

goods or chattels in my bailiwick whereof I can cause to be made the costs [and interest] within mentioned, or any part thereof, as within I am commanded. *Or say*, I further certify and return, that I have caused to be made of the goods and chattels of the within-named C. D. the costs [and interest] within mentioned, which I have ready at the time and place within mentioned, to be rendered to the said A. B., as within I am commanded.

——, Esq., sheriff.

For other forms of returns to a fi. fa., see Watson's Sheriff, 479.

---

285. *Sheriff's Return to a Writ of Habere Facias and Ca. Sa. for Costs, of the due Execution thereof (ante, 348).*

Commence as ante, No. 283, *to the signature, which omit ; then proceed thus :*

I further certify and return, that the within-named C. D. is not found in my bailiwick : *or say*, I further certify and return, that I have taken the within-named C. D., whose body I have ready to satisfy the said A. B. the costs [and interest] within mentioned, as within I am commanded.

——, Esq., sheriff.

For other forms of returns to a ca. sa., see Watson's Sheriff, 473.

---

286. *Entry on Roll of Award of Writ of Possession, with the Sheriff's Return (ante, 348).*

Afterwards, to wit, on the [*teste of writ of possession*] —— day of ——, A.D. 18—, the said A. B. comes into court here, and prays the writ of our lady the Queen to be directed to the sheriff of ——, commanding him that [he omit not by reason of any liberty in his county, but that he enter the same, and] without delay he cause the said A. B. to have possession of the said [land *or* tenements] and premises, with the appurtenances, and it is granted to him, returnable immediately upon the execution thereof. Afterwards, on the [*date of sheriff's return*] —— day of ——, A.D. 18—, the said sheriff, to wit, I. K., Esq., sheriff of the said county, returns to the said court here, that by virtue of the said writ to him directed, he did on the —— day of ——, A.D. 18—, cause possession of the said [land *or* tenements] and premises, with the appurtenances, to be delivered to the said A. B., as by the said writ he was commanded.

---

287. *Writ of Elegit on a Judgment for the Plaintiff in a Personal Action (ante, 564).*

Victoria, by the grace of God of the United Kingdom of Great Britain and Ireland Queen, Defender of the Faith, to the sheriff of ——, greeting : Whereas A. B. lately in our Court of [Queen's Bench, *or* Common Pleas, *or* Exchequer of Pleas, *as the case may be*], by the judgment of the same court, recovered against C. D. £——, [*the amount of all the monies recovered by the judgment*,] whereof the said C. D. is convicted : and afterwards the said A. B. came into our said court, and, according to the form of the statutes in such case made and provided, chose to be delivered to him all the goods and chattels of the said C. D. in your bailiwick, except his oxen and beasts of the plough, and also all such lands, tenements, rectories, tithes, rents and hereditaments, including lands and hereditaments of copyhold or customary tenure, in your bailiwick, as the said C. D., or any person in trust for him, was seised or possessed of on the —— day of ——, in the year of our Lord —— (i), on which day the judgment aforesaid was entered up, or at any time afterwards, or over which the said C. D. on that day, or at any time afterwards, had any disposing power which he might, without the assent of any other person, exercise for his own benefit, to hold

---

(i) The day on which the judgment was entered up.

to him the said goods and chattels as his proper goods and chattels, and
hold the said lands, tenements, rectories, tithes, rents and hereditame
respectively, according to the nature and tenure thereof, to him and
assigns, according to the form of the said statutes, until the said su
together with interest thereon at the rate of four pounds per centum
annum from the —— day of ——, in the year of your Lord —— (*k*), sl
have been levied : Therefore we command you that [*if sued out of the Co
of Exchequer say*, Therefore we command you that you omit not, by rea
of any liberty of your county, but that you enter the same, and] with
delay you cause to be delivered to the said A. B., by a reasonable price a
extent, all the goods and chattels of the said C. D. in your bailiwick, exc
his oxen and beasts of the plough, and also all such lands, tenemer
rectories, tithes, rents and hereditaments, including lands and hereditame
of copyhold or customary tenure, in your bailiwick, as the said C. D. or a
person in trust for him, was seised or possessed of on the said —— day
—— (*l*), or at any time afterwards, or over which the said C. D. on t
day, or at any time afterwards, had any disposing power, which he mig
without the assent of any other person, exercise for his own benefit, to h
the said goods and chattels to the said A. B. as his proper goods and chatt
and also to hold the said lands, tenements, rectories, tithes, rents and he
ditaments respectively, according to the nature and tenure thereof, to h
and to his assigns, until the said £—— , together with interest as aforesa
shall have been levied : And in what manner you shall have executed t
our writ make appear to [us, *or in C. P.* to our justices, *or in Exch.* to
barons of our Exchequer, *as the case may be*], at Westminster, immediat
after the execution hereof, under your seal and the seals of those by wh
oath you shall make the said extent and appraisement, and have you th
then this writ. Witness, ——, at Westminster, the —— day of ——, in
year of our Lord ——.

N.B.—*To be indorsed with the name and address of the attorney, &c., as
other cases* (*ante*, 342).

The Practice Rules of H. T., 1853, *also give the form of writs of elegi*
other cases, viz. :—

No. 10. Writ of elegit on a rule for payment of money.

No. 11. Writ of elegit on a rule for payment of money and costs.

No. 12. Writ of elegit on a judgment of an inferior court removed i
one of the superior courts.

No. 13. Writ of elegit on a rule or order for payment of money made
an inferior court, and removed into one of the superior courts.

No. 14. Writ of elegit on a rule or order for payment of money
costs made in an inferior court, and removed into one of
superior courts.

The above forms may be seen in 13 C. B. 60—71 ; 1 E. & B. xl.—x
See also Chitty's Forms, 324—333, 7th ed.

288. *Inquisition thereon and Return to the Writ* (*ante*, 565).

Venue, } An inquisition indented taken at ——, in the county of ——
to wit. } the —— day of ——, in the year of our Lord 18—, before me
S., Esq., sheriff of the said county, by virtue of her Majesty's writ to
directed in this behalf, and to this inquisition annexed, by the oat
[*names of twelve jurors who concur in the finding*], twelve honest and la
men of the county aforesaid, who being sworn and charged upon their

---

(*k*) The day on which the judgment was entered up, or in case the ji
ment was entered up prior to the 1st of October, 1838, say, " from the
day of October, in the year of our Lord 1838."

(*l*) The day in which the judgment was entered up.

say, that C. D., named in the writ hereunto annexed, on the day of the taking of this inquisition [had no goods or chattels in my bailiwick, to the knowledge of the said jurors, *or* was possessed in his own right of the goods and chattels following, that is to say, *here describe the goods,* of the price of £—— as of his own proper goods and chattels, which said goods and chattels I the said sheriff have caused to be delivered to the said A. B. [*the plaintiff*], to hold the said goods and chattels in part satisfaction of his [debt] damages and interest in the said writ mentioned, as by the said writ I am commanded]: And the jurors aforesaid upon their oath aforesaid do further say, that the said C. D. on the [*date of final judgment*] —— day of ——, in the year of our Lord 18— (on which day the judgment in the said writ mentioned was obtained), was seised in his demesne as of fee of and in all [*describe the property as in a conveyance*], situate, lying and being in the parish of ——, in the county aforesaid, now in the tenure and occupation of O. P., and being of the clear yearly value of £—— in all issues beyond reprises: And of and in [*describe any other property, and its situation and value in like manner*]: And also of and in one undivided moiety (the whole into two equal moieties to be divided) of and in one messuage or dwelling-house and —— acres of [arable, meadow *or* pasture land, *as the case may be*], with the appurtenances, situate, lying and being in the parish of ——, in the said county, now in the tenure or occupation of Q. R. [*the abuttals may be here stated, but this is not necessary, ante,* 565], the said moiety being of the clear yearly value of £—— in all issues beyond reprises: And also of and in one undivided [third] part (the whole into *three* equal parts to be divided) of and in [*describe the property as in a conveyance, and its situation and value as above*]: which said lands and tenements [firstly and secondly above described, and which said *moiety* of the said lands and tenements thirdly above described, and which said [third] part of the said lands and tenements fourthly above described, *as the case may be*], I the said sheriff, on the day of the taking of this inquisition, have caused to be delivered to the said A. B. by a reasonable price and extent, to hold as his freehold to him and his assigns according to the force of the statute in such case made and provided, until [the residue (m) of] the [debt] damages and interest in the said writ mentioned shall be thereof levied, as by the said writ I am commanded. [(m) And the jurors aforesaid upon their oath aforesaid do further say, that the said C. D., on the day of the taking of this inquisition aforesaid, had no other or more goods or chattels in my bailiwick to the knowledge of the said jurors]: And the jurors aforesaid upon their oath aforesaid do further say, that neither the said C. D., nor any person or persons in trust for him, had on the [*date of judgment*] —— day of ——, in the year of our Lord 18— (on which day the judgment in the said writ mentioned was obtained), or at any time afterwards, any other or more lands or tenements in my bailiwick, to the knowledge of the said jurors. *In witness* whereof as well I, the said sheriff, as the jurors aforesaid, have severally set our respective seals to this inquisition, on the day and year and at the place aforesaid.

Seals of sheriff and twelve jurymen.

Indorse on the writ of elegit a return, as follows :—

The execution of the within writ appears in the inquisition hereunto annexed.

The answer of
S. S., Esq., sheriff.

(m) Omit these words where there were no goods or chattels delivered in part satisfaction, &c.

---

289. *Entry on the Roll of Award of Elegit, and of Return of Inquisition there[*
(ante, 565).

After the entry of the final judgment proceed thus :

Afterwards, to wit, on the [*teste of elegit*] —— day of ——, A.D. 18—
comes here the said A. B. [by his attorney aforesaid *or* in person], an[
according to the form of the statute in such case made and provided, choos[
to be delivered to him all the goods and chattels of the said C. D., except h
oxen and beasts of the plough, and also all such lands, tenements, rectorie
tithes, rents and hereditaments, including lands and hereditaments of cop[
hold or customary tenure, in the county of ——, as the said C. D., or an
person in trust for him, was seised or possessed of on the [*date of judgmen[*
—— day of ——, A.D. 18—, on which day the judgment aforesaid was en
tered up, or at any time afterwards, or over which the said C. D., on the da
and year last aforesaid, or at any time afterwards, had any disposing pow[
which he might, without the assent of any other person, exercise for his ow
benefit ; to hold to him the said goods and chattels as his proper goods an
chattels, and to hold the said lands, tenements, rectories, tithes, rents an
hereditaments respectively, according to the nature and tenure thereof, [
him and his assigns, according to the form of the said statutes, until the sai
£——, together with interest thereon at the rate of £4 per centum p[
annum from the [*date of judgment*] —— day of ——, A.D. 18—, shall hav
been levied : And the said A. B. prays the writ of our said lady the Quee
thereupon, to be directed to the sheriff of ——, and it is granted to him, &[
returnable here immediately after the execution thereof, &c.

Afterwards, to wit, on the [*day when sheriff's return filed*] —— day [
——, A.D. 18—, comes here the said A. B. [by his attorney aforesaid *or* i
person] : And the sheriff, to wit, S. S., Esq., sheriff of the county aforesai[
now here returns the writ afterwards to him in form aforesaid directed, i
all things served and executed, together with a certain inquisition to th
said writ annexed, taken before the said sheriff in the premises by virtue [
the said writ ; which said inquisition follows in these words, that is to sa[
An inquisition [*copy it verbatim*].

For an award of several writs of elegit into different counties, see Chi[
Forms, 329.

---

290. *Writ of Restitution after Judgment by Default set aside for Irregularit[*
(ante, 349).

Victoria, by the grace of God of the United Kingdom of Great Britai[
and Ireland Queen, Defender of the Faith, to the sheriff of ——, greeting
Whereas A. B., lately in our Court of [Q. B., C. P. *or* Exch. of Pleas, *as th*
case may be], by the judgment of the same court, recovered possession of ——
[*here describe the property as in the judgment*], with the appurtenances, in you
bailiwick : And whereas we afterwards, to wit, on the [*teste of writ of haber[*
facias possessionem] —— day of ——, A.D. 18—, by our writ commanded yo[
[*if in Exch.* say, to omit not by reason of any liberty in your county, but t[
enter the same and] without delay to cause the said A. B. to have posses
sion of the said [land and premises], with the appurtenances ; and in wha
manner you should have executed that our writ you should make appear t[
[us, *or in C. P.* to our justices, *or in Exch.* to the barons of our Exchequer, a[
the case may be], at Westminster, immediately upon the execution of our sai[
writ, and that you should have there then that writ : And because since th[
issuing of our said writ it hath appeared [to us, *or in C. P.* to our justices[
or in Exch. to the barons of our Exchequer], at Westminster, that the sai[
judgment obtained by the said A. B. as aforesaid was irregularly obtained, and
such judgment has since been set aside and vacated in and by our said cour[
for irregularity : And because our said writ thereupon issued improvidentl[
and unjustly : Therefore we command you that if possession of the sai[

[land and premises], with the appurtenances, hath, by virtue of our said writ, been given or delivered to the said A. B., then that without delay you cause restitution of the said [land and premises], with the appurtenances, to be made to the said C. D. [*or* to I. K., the landlord and owner of the said land and premises, with the appurtenances, at whose instance the judgment aforesaid hath been set aside by our said court for irregularity as aforesaid]; and that whatever has been done by virtue of our said writ, you deem altogether void and of no effect, as you will answer the contrary at your peril: And in what manner you shall have executed this our writ make appear to [us, *or in C. P.* to our justices, *or in Exch.* to the barons of our Exchequer], at Westminster, on the —— day of ——next, and have there then this writ. Witness ——, at Westminster, the —— day of ——, in the year of our Lord 18— [*or* in the —— year of our reign.]

(Indorsement.)

This writ was issued by G. H., of —— [agent for N.M. of ——], attorney, for the within-named C. D. [*or* I. K].

By rule of court dated the —— day of ——, 18—.

See post, No. 370.

---

291. *Writ of Habere facias Possessionem on a Rule to deliver Possession of Land pursuant to an Award* (*ante*, 222, 320).

Victoria, by the grace of God of the United Kingdom of Great Britain and Ireland Queen, Defender of the Faith, to the sheriff of ——, greeting: We command you that you omit not by reason of any liberty of your county, but that you enter the same, and without delay you cause A. B. to have possession of —— [*here describe the lands and tenements as in the rule for the delivery of possession*], and which lands and tenements by a rule of our Court of Queen's Bench, [*or* Common Pleas, *or* Exchequer of Pleas,] dated the —— day of ——, 18—, made pursuant to the sixteenth section of The Common Law Procedure Act, 1854, E. F. (*the party named in the rule*) was ordered to deliver possession to the said A. B.: And in what manner you have executed this our writ make appear to us [*or in C. P.* to our justices, *or in Exch.* to the barons of our Exchequer], at Westminster, immediately after the execution hereof, and have you there then this writ. Witness ——, at Westminster, the —— day of ——, in the year of our Lord ——.

This form is prescribed by the Rules of Mich. Vac., 1854, *Sched. No.* 17. *It must be issued, tested and indorsed in the usual manner* (*ante*, 343).

---

292. *Suggestion before or after Trial of the Death of one of the Claimants, whose Right survives* (*ante*, 350).

In the [Q. B., C. P. *or* Exch.]

B. [and others]	And now on the [*day when pleaded*(n)] —— day of
v.	——, in the year of our Lord 18—, it is suggested and
D. [and another.]	manifestly appears to the court here*, that after the

---

(n) In *Barnett* v. *The Earl of Guilford*, 11 Exch. 23 (note), the court said that the rule of court which required pleadings to be dated on the day on which they were delivered did not apply to a suggestion, which was a mere entry on the record. It is to be observed, that the entry commences by stating the day when the suggestion is made; a further statement of such date in the heading or title is superfluous, and should be omitted, but it will do no harm.

The name of the court and the short title of the cause should be omitted in the entry on the roll.

issuing of the writ in this action [or after the trial of this action, *as the case may be*] and before this day, the said [*deceased claimant*] died: Therefore let no further proceedings be had in this action at the suit of the said [*deceased claimant*]; and let this action proceed at the suit of the said [*surviving claimants*] according to the form of the statute in such case made and provided.

---

293. *Affidavit of a Suggestion being untrue (ante, 351).*
Commence as ante, Nos. 19, 20, *or* 21.

1. That on or about the —— day of —— [instant *or* last] a suggestion was delivered in this action, in the words following:—[*Copy it verbatim*].

2. That the said suggestion is untrue in that part of it which states that [*state untrue part, ex. gr.*] after the issuing of the writ in this action, *or after* the trial of this action, the said A. B. died: And I say that in truth and in fact [*here state facts showing the suggestion to be untrue, ex. gr.*] the said A. B. is now alive, and I saw and conversed with him on the —— day of —— instant at ——, *or* the said A. B. died on or about the —— day of ——, in the year of our Lord 18——, and before the —— day of ——, in the year of our Lord 18——, when the writ in this action issued, *or* when the trial of this action took place.

3. That the said A. B. was buried in the parish of ——, in the county of ——, on or about the —— day of ——, 18——, and that the paper writing hereto annexed, marked (A), is a certificate of the burial of the said A. B., which I lately examined with the original entry in the register book of burials kept in and for the said parish, and the said certificate contains a true copy of such entry.

Sworn, &c. (*ante*, 705.)

N.B.—*Clause* 3 *is not essential, but it may tend to strengthen and confirm Clause* 2.

---

294. *Summons to set aside a Suggestion as untrue with Costs (ante, 351).*
Commence as ante, No. 22.

Why the suggestion made in this action on [*date of suggestion*] the —— day of ——, 18——, should not be set aside as untrue, with costs to be taxed, and paid by —— to ——, or to Mr. E. F., his attorney. Dated the —— day of ——, 18——.

Judge's signature.

---

295. *Order thereon.*
Commence as ante, No. 24.

I do order that the suggestion made in this action on the —— day of ——, 18——, be set aside as untrue, with costs to be taxed, and paid by —— to ——, or to Mr. E. F., his attorney. Dated the —— day of ——, 18——.

Judge's signature.

---

296. *Suggestion before Trial of the Death of one of the Claimants, whose Right does not survive (ante,* 351).
Commence as ante, No. 292, *to the* *, *then proceed thus :—*

That after the issuing of the writ in this action, and before this day, the said [*deceased claimant*] died: Therefore let no further proceedings be had in this action at the suit of the said [*deceased claimant*]: And let this action proceed at the suit of the said [*surviving claimants*] for such share of the property claimed as [they are, *or* he is] entitled to, and costs, according to the form of the statute in such case made and provided.

297. *Suggestion after Verdict of the Death of one of the Claimants (ante, 351).*

Commence as ante, No. 292, to the *, then proceed thus :—

That after the trial and verdict in this action, and before this day, the said [*deceased claimant*] died : Therefore let no further proceedings be had in this action at the suit of the said [*deceased claimant*] : And let this action proceed at the suit of the said [*surviving claimants*] according to the form of the statute in such case made and provided.

---

298. *Final Judgment after the above Suggestion (ante, 351).*

Enter an incipitur on paper as ante, No. 122. Afterwards (when necessary) enter on the roll the verdict and postea ; then the suggestion, as ante, No. 297, omitting the name of the court and of the cause, then proceed thus :—

And now on the [*day of signing final judgment*] —— day of ——, A.D. 18—, the said [*surviving claimants*] pray judgment : Therefore it is considered that the said [*surviving claimants*] do recover possession of the [*land or tenements, or premises, or property*] in the said writ mentioned, with the appurtenances, and £—— for costs.

In the margin, opposite the words, " Therefore it is considered, &c.," *write* " Judgment signed on the —— day of ——, 18—." *If the verdict were for part only for the claimants, and as to the residue for the defendants, the judgment must be entered accordingly. See ante, No. 263.*

---

299. *Affidavit for Leave to enter a Suggestion by the legal Representative of a deceased Claimant (ante, 352).*

Commence as ante, Nos. 19, 20 or 21.

1. That this action was commenced on or about the —— day of ——, in the year 18—, by a writ issued forth out of this court in the words following :—Victoria, &c. [*copy the writ verbatim*].

2. That [*state appearance and subsequent proceedings if any*].

3. That after the issuing of the said writ, and on or about the —— day of ——, in the year 18—, the said A. B. died.

4. That the property claimed in the said writ is of freehold tenure, and that the said A. B., before and at the time of his death, was or claimed to be seised thereof, or entitled thereto, in fee simple.

5. That the said A. B. died intestate, and that I the said —— am the [*eldest son and*] heir at law of the said A. B. deceased, and as such heir I am the legal representative of the said A. B. as to the said property claimed in the said writ ; *or say,* that the said A. B. duly made his last will and testament in writing, bearing date the —— day of ——, in the year 18—, and executed and attested according to law, and thereby he gave and devised to me the property claimed in the said writ (amongst other hereditaments) in manner following (that is to say) [*copy the devise verbatim, omitting the trusts, if long, but instead thereof saying* "upon certain trusts in the said will particularly mentioned :"] And I say that I am as such devisee as aforesaid, the legal representative of the said A. B. deceased, as to the said property claimed in the said writ.

Sworn, &c. (*ante,* 705.)

N.B.—*If the party claim as executor, state the probate. If as legatee, state the probate and the assent of the executor, and alter paragraph 4 by stating the property to be leasehold, and* "that A. B. before and at the time of his death was or claimed to be possessed thereof, or entitled thereto for a term of years, whereof about —— years are now unexpired."

300. *Summons for Leave to enter a Suggestion by the legal Representative of a deceased Claimant (ante, 352).*

B. [and others] ⎱ 　Let the defendants, their attorney or agent [and the
　　　v.　　 ⎰ claimants, E. F., G. H., &c., *names of the surviving claim-*
D. [and another.] ⎰ *ants*, their attorney or agent], attend me at my chambers,
in Rolls Garden, Chancery Lane, on —— next, at —— of the clock in the
——noon, to show cause why B. B., of ——, should not be at liberty to
make a suggestion of the death of the claimant [A. B.], and that he the
said B. B. is the legal representative of the said A. B. deceased, pursuant to
the 194th section of The Common Law Procedure Act, 1852. Dated the
—— day of ——, 18—.

　　　　　　　　　　　　　　　　　　　　　Judge's signature.

301. *Rule Nisi for Leave to enter a Suggestion by the legal Representative of a deceased Claimant (ante, 352).*

In the [Q. B., C. P. or Exch.]

　　　　　　　　　　——day, the —— day of ——, A.D. 18—.
B. [and others] ⎱ 　Upon reading the affidavit of [B. B. and the paper
　　　v.　　 ⎰ writing thereto annexed], and upon hearing Mr. ——, of
D. [and another.] ⎰ ——, counsel for the said B. B., it is ordered, that the
claimants [*names of the surviving claimants*] and also the defendants do, on
—— day the —— day of —— [instant *or* next], show cause why the said
B. B. should not be at liberty to make a suggestion of the death of the
claimant [A. B.]: And that he the said B. B. is the legal representative of
the said A. B. deceased, pursuant to the 194th section of The Common Law
Procedure Act, 1852: upon notice of this rule to be given to the said [*surviving claimants*], and the defendants or their respective attornies in the
meantime.

　　　　　　　　　　　　　　　　　　　　　By the Court.

302. *Suggestion of the Death of a Sole Claimant, by his legal Representative ante, 352).*

In the [Q. B., C. P. *or* Exch.]

　A. B. —— ⎱ 　And now on the [*day when pleaded*(*o*)] —— day of
　　　v.　　 ⎰ ——, A.D. 18—, comes here B. B., by ——, his attorney
C. D. [and another ⎰ [*or* in person], and the said A. B. comes not ; and here-
　or others.] ⎰ upon the said B. B., by leave of [the court here, *or*
the (*p*) Hon. Sir ——, knight, one of the justices *or* barons of this court,
or one of her Majesty's justices of her Court of Queen's Bench, *or* Common
Pleas, *or* one of the barons of her Majesty's Court of Exchequer, *as the case
may be*], suggests and gives the court here to understand and be informed,
that after the [issuing of the writ in this action, *or* after the trial in this
action] and before this day the said A. B. died : And that the said B. B. is
the heir at law of the said A. B., deceased, *or* heir of the said A. B. deceased according to the custom of the manor of ——, in the county of
——, whereof the property in the said writ mentioned is parcel, *or* executor
of the last will and testament of the said A. B., deceased, *or* administrator
of the goods and chattels, rights and credits, which were of the said A. B.,
deceased, at the time of his death, who died intestate, *or* the devisee *or*
legatee, named in the last will and testament of the said A. B., deceased, of
the property in the said writ mentioned : And that the said B. B. as such
[heir, executor, administrator, devisee *or* legatee, *as the case may be*], is the

---

(*o*) See note to No. 292.
(*p*) If a privy councillor, say, "The *Right* Honorable."

legal representative of the said A. B., deceased, as to the property in the said writ mentioned : Therefore let no further proceedings be had in this action at the suit of the said A. B., and let this action proceed at the suit of the said B. B., according to the form of the statute in such case made and provided.

It seems sufficient to suggest the death of A. B., and that the said B. B. is the legal representative of the said A. B., deceased, without showing how he is such representative. Chit. Forms, 547, note (*b*), 7th edit.

---

303. *Suggestion before Trial of the Death of one of several Claimants, whose Right does not survive to his legal Representative* (*ante*, 352).

In the [Q. B., C. P. *or* Exch.]

A. B. [and others] ⎱ And now on the [*date when pleaded* (*q*)] —— day
v. ⎰ of ——, A.D. 18—, come here the said [*names of the*
C. D. [and another]. ⎰*surviving claimants*] by ——, their attorney [*or* in person], and also B. B., by ——, his attorney [*or* in person] : And the said [*deceased claimant*] comes not: And hereupon the said B. B. by leave of [the court here, *or* of the (*r*) Hon. Sir ——, knight, one of the justices *or* barons of this court, *or as the case may be ; see No.* 302], according to the form of the statute in such case made and provided, gives the court here to understand and be informed, that after the issuing of the writ in this action, and before this day, the said [*deceased claimant*] died: And that the said B. B. is the [heir at law of the said deceased, *or* the executor *or* administrator &c., *as in No.* 302: And that the said B. B. as such heir *or* executor, &c., *as the case may be*, is the] legal representative of the said [*deceased claimant*] as to the property [*or* as to his part or share of the property] in the said writ mentioned : Therefore let no further proceedings be had in this action at the suit of the said [*deceased claimant*]: And let this action proceed at the suit of the said [*surviving claimants*] and of the said B. B., according to the form of the statute in such case made and provided.

---

304. *Traverse by Defendants of the above Suggestion* (*ante*, 353).

In the [Q. B., C. P. *or* Exch.]

On the [*day when pleaded*] —— day of ——, A.D. 18—.
B. [and another] ⎱ And the defendants, by —— their attorney [*or* in
v. ⎰ person], say that the said suggestion of the said B. B. is
D. [and others]. ⎰not true in substance and in fact: And the said B. B. joins issue hereon.

N.B.—*Any material allegation in the suggestion may be selected and traversed in the usual form.*

---

305. *Suggestion of the Death of one of several Defendants, who defend jointly* (*ante*, 353).

In the [Q. B., C. P. *or* Exch.]

B. [and another] ⎱ And now, on the [*date when pleaded* (*q*)], —— day of
v. ⎰ ——, A.D. 18—, it is suggested and manifestly appears
D. [and others]. ⎰ to the court here, that after the issuing of the writ in this action [*or* after the judgment obtained in this action], and before this day, the said [*deceased defendant*] died; and the said [*surviving defendants*] survived him : Therefore let no further proceedings be had in this action against the said [*deceased defendant*]: And let this action proceed

---

(*q*) See note to No. 292.
(*r*) See note (*p*).

against the said [*surviving defendants*] according to the form of the statute in such case made and provided.

---

306. *Suggestion before Trial of the Death of a sole Defendant, or of all the Defendants (ante, 354).*

In the [Q. B., C. P. *or* Exch.]

B. [and others] } And now, on the [*date when pleaded*(*z*)] —— day of
  v.   } ——, A.D. 18—, it is suggested and manifestly appears
  D.   } to the court here, that after the issuing of the writ in this action, and before this day, the defendant [*or* the defendants respectively] died: Therefore let the plaintiffs be at liberty to proceed according to the form of the statute in such case made and provided.

---

307. *Affidavit for a Rule or Order for leave to sign Judgment after a Suggestion of the Defendant's Death, unless, &c. (ante, 354).*

Commence as ante, Nos. 19, 20 *or* 21.

1. That this action was commenced on or about the —— day of ——, in the year 18—, by a writ issued forth out of this court in the words following:—Victoria, &c. [*copy the writ verbatim*].

2. That [*state appearance and subsequent proceedings, exclusive of the suggestion of defendant's death*].

3. That after the issuing of the said writ, and on or about the —— day of ——, in the year 18—, the above-named defendant C. D. died [*if more than one defendant, state in like manner the death of each*].

4. That on the —— day of ——, in the year 18—, I, the said ——, delivered [*personally*] to Mr. ——, who was and acted as the attorney [*or* agent] in this action for the said C. D. in his lifetime, a suggestion in writing in the words following [*copy the suggestion verbatim*]. [*If not delivered "personally," omit that word and say,*—By delivering such suggestion to and leaving the same with a clerk of the said Mr. ——, at his office, situate, &c., *as the case may be*].

5. That on the —— day of ——, in the year 18—, I stuck up a copy of the above suggestion in the office of the masters of this honourable court, situate [*&c. ante,* 126, *note* (*a*)], in the place where notices are usually affixed.

6. That the property mentioned in the said writ is freehold of inheritance, and the said C. D. died intestate; and that G. H., of ——, is the [eldest son and heir at law of the said C. D.,] deceased, and as such heir the said G. H. now is the legal representative of the said C. D., deceased.

Or,

6. That the property mentioned in the said writ is freehold of inheritance, and the said C. D. duly made his last will and testament in writing, bearing date the —— day of ——, in the year 18—, and executed and attested according to law: and thereby, &c. gave and devised (amongst other things) as follows—[*copy the devise to G. H. verbatim, omitting the trusts if long, but instead thereof saying,* "Upon certain trusts in the said will particularly mentioned."] And I say that the said G. H., as such devisee as aforesaid, now is the legal representative of the said C. D., deceased.

If the property be leasehold, then, instead of the above, say,—

6. That the property mentioned in the said writ is leasehold, and held for a term of years not yet expired; and the said C. D. died intestate: and letters of administration of the goods and chattels, rights and credits, which were of the said C. D. at the time of his death, were granted to G. H., of &c., on or about the —— day of ——, in the year 18—, by the [Prerogative

---

(*z*) See note to No. 292.

or Consistory] Court of the [Archbishop *or* Bishop] of ——: And the said G. H., as such administrator, now is the legal representative of the said C. D., deceased.

Or say,—

6. That the property mentioned in the said writ is leasehold, and held for a term of years not yet expired: And the said C. D. duly made his last will and testament in writing, bearing date the —— day of ——, in the year 18—, and thereof appointed by G. H., of &c., sole executor [who duly proved the same in the [Prerogative *or* Consistory] Court of the [Archbishop *or* Bishop] of ——, on or about the —— day of ——, in the year 18—]: And the said G. H., as such executor as aforesaid, now is the legal representative of the said C. D., deceased.

7. That E. F., of ——, now is in possession by himself [*or* his tenant I. K.] of the property mentioned in the said writ.

Sworn, &c. (*ante,* 705).

———

308. *Rule for Leave to sign such Judgment, unless, &c.* (*ante,* 354).

In the [Q. B., C. P. *or* Exch.]

——day, the —— day of ——, A.D. 18—.

B. [and others]   Upon reading the affidavit of —— [and the paper
    v.   writing thereto annexed], and upon hearing Mr. —— of
    D.   counsel for the claimants: It is ordered, that the claimants shall be at liberty to sign judgment [*within such time as the court shall think fit; ex. gr.*]: after the expiration of *sixteen* days from the service of a copy of the writ in this action, and of this rule on E. F., who is now in possession by himself or his tenant of the property claimed, and on G. H., the legal representative of the defendant C. D. deceased: unless within the said *sixteen* days the said E. F. and G. H., or such of them as deny the alleged title of the claimants, shall appear and defend this action according to the 196th section of The Common Law Procedure Act, 1852: Provided that such judgment shall be signed within [sixty days] next after the date of this rule, and not afterwards (*a*).

By the Court.

———

309. *Order for Leave to sign such Judgment, unless, &c.* (*ante,* 354).

B. [and others]   Upon reading the affidavit of ——, and the paper
    v.   writing thereto annexed, and upon hearing the claim-
    D.   ants' attorney or agent, I do order that the claimants shall be at liberty to sign judgment [after the expiration of *sixteen* days] from the service of a copy of the writ in this action, and of this order, on E. F., who is now in possession, by himself or his tenant, of the property claimed, and on G. H., the legal representative of the defendant C. D., deceased: unless within the said *sixteen* days the said E. F. and G. H., or such of them as deny the alleged title of the claimants, shall appear and defend the action, according to the 196th section of The Common Law Procedure Act, 1852: Provided (*a*) that such judgment shall be signed within [sixty days] next after the date of this order, and not afterwards (*a*). Dated the —— day of——, 18—.

Judge's signature.

———

(*a*) Sect. 196 requires the court, or judge, to fix a time *within which* judgment shall be signed (*ante,* 353).

———

310. *Suggestion before Trial of the Death of one of several Defendants who defended separately for a Portion of the Property for which the other Defendant or Defendants do not defend (ante, 355).*

Commence as ante, No. 305, to the word " Therefore," then go on thus :

Therefore let the plaintiffs be at liberty to proceed according to the form of the statute in such case made and provided for that portion of the property for which the said [*deceased defendant*] defended this action: And let no further proceedings be had in this action against the said [*surviving defendants*] in respect of the portion of the property for which they defend.

Or, instead of the above, say,—

Therefore let no further proceedings be had in this action against the said [*deceased defendant*], or for that portion of the property for which he defended : And let this action proceed against the said [*surviving defendants*] for that portion of the property for which they defend, according to the form of the statute in such case made and provided.

---

311. *Suggestion before Trial of the Death of one of several Defendants who defended separately in respect of Property for which surviving Defendants also defend (ante, 355).*

Form as ante, No. 305.

---

312. *Affidavit for Leave to appear and defend as the legal Representative of a deceased Defendant (ante, 355).*

Form as ante, No. 299, mutatis mutandis. If any suggestion of the defendant's death has been made, state it ; conclude thus :

That I am desirous of being allowed to appear and defend this action for the said property for which the said A. B. defended as aforesaid, upon such terms as may appear reasonable and just, pursuant to the statute in such case made and provided.

Sworn, &c. (*ante,* 705).

---

313. *The like by " the Person in Possession" of the Property at the Time of the Defendant's Death (ante, 355).*

Commence as ante, No. 299, pl. 1, 2, 3.

4. That at the time of the death of the said A. B., I was, and still am, in actual possession of the property for which the said A. B. defended as aforesaid ; and I am desirous of being allowed to appear and defend this action for the said property upon such terms as may appear reasonable and just, pursuant to the statute in such case made and provided.

Sworn, &c. (*ante,* 705.)

---

314. *Summons for Leave to the legal Representative of a deceased Defendant, or to the Person in Possession at the Time of his Death, to appear and defend (ante, 355).*

B. [and others]
    v.
D. [and another or others].

Let the plaintiffs, their attorney or agent, and also the defendants, I. K., L. M., &c., [*names of the surviving defendants*], their attorney or agent, attend me at my chambers, in Rolls Garden, Chancery Lane, to-morrow [*or on ——* day next] at —— of the clock in the ——noon, to show cause why D. D., as the legal representative of the defendant C. D., deceased, [*or as the person at the time of the death of the defendant C. D., deceased, in possession of [part of] the property claimed, and for which the said C. D. defended,] should not be allowed to appear and defend this action for the said [part of the said] property on such terms as upon the hearing of this application may appear reasonable and just, pursuant to the 199th section of The Common Law Procedure Act, 1852. Dated the —— day of ——, 18—.

Judge's signature.

---

315. *Order thereon.*
Commence as ante, No. 24.

. I do order that the said D. D., as the legal representative of the said C. D., deceased, [*or* as the person at the time of the death of the said C. D., in possession of [part of] the property claimed, and for which the said C. D. defended,] be allowed to appear and defend this action for the said [part of the said] property pursuant to the 199th section of The Common Law Procedure Act, 1852, on the following terms and conditions:—The said D. D. shall enter such appearance within —— days now next [and shall give notice that he intends to defend for the said part of the said property within —— days next after such appearance] : And the claimants shall thereupon be at liberty to deliver an [amended] issue, stating therein the death of the said C. D., and the said appearance [and notice] of the said D. D. [*here add any other terms that may appear reasonable and just*]: And I do order that the costs of all parties of and incident to this application be costs in the cause: Provided always, that if the said D. D. shall not enter such appearance [and give such notice] within the time in that behalf above limited, I do hereby order that the said application of the said D. D. be, and the same is hereby discharged, with costs to be taxed, and paid by the said D. D. to the claimants, or to Mr. —— their attorney. [And I certify for the allowance of counsel on this application.] Dated the —— day of ——, 18—.

Judge's signature.

---

316. *Rule to show Cause why the legal Representative of a deceased Defendant, or the Person in Possession at the Time of his Death, should not be allowed to appear and defend (ante,* 355).

In the [Q. B., C. P. *or* Exch.]

——day, the —— day of ——, A.D. 18—.

B. [and others] ⎱ Upon reading the affidavit of D. D., [and the paper
     v.   ⎰ writing thereto annexed,] and upon hearing Mr. ——,
D. [and another ⎱ of counsel for the said D. D.: It is ordered, that the
  or others]. ⎰ plaintiffs, and also the defendants, I. K., L. M., &c. [*names of the surviving defendants*], do on —— day, the —— day of ——, [instant *or* next], show cause why the said D. D., as the legal representative of the defendant C. D., deceased, [*or* as the person at the time of the death of the defendant C. D., deceased, in possession of [part of] the property claimed, and for which the said C. D. defended,] should not be allowed to appear and defend this action for the said [part of the said] property, on such terms as upon the hearing of this application may appear reasonable and just, pursuant to the 199th section of The Common Law Procedure Act, 1852; upon notice of this rule to be given to the said plaintiffs and the said [*names of the surviving defendants*] or their respective attornies in the meantime.

By the Court.

317. *Rule Absolute.*

In the [Q. B., C. P. *or* Exch.]

——day, the —— day of ——, A.D. 18—.

B. [and others] ⎞ Upon reading the rule made in this cause on the ——
      v. ⎟ day of —— [instant *or* last], and the affidavits of ——
D. [and another ⎨ and the paper writings thereto respectively annexed, and
 or others]. ⎠ upon hearing Mr. —— of counsel for D. D., and Mr.
—— of counsel for the claimants, and Mr. —— of counsel for the defendants, *or as the case may be,* it is ordered that the said D. D., as the legal
representative of the said C. D., deceased, [*or* as the person at the time of
the death of the said C. D., deceased, in possession of [part of] the property claimed, and for which the said C. D. defended,] be allowed to appear
and defend this action for the said [part of the said] property pursuant to
the 199th section of The Common Law Procedure Act, 1852, on the following terms and conditions: The said D. D. shall enter such appearance
within —— days now next [and shall give notice that he intends to defend
for the said part of the said property within —— days next after such
appearance]: And the claimants shall thereupon be at liberty to deliver an
[amended] issue, stating therein the death of the said C. D., and the said
appearance [and notice] of the said D. D. [*here add any other terms that may
appear reasonable and just*]: And it is ordered that the costs of all
parties of and incident to this application, be costs in the cause: Provided
always, that if the said D. D. shall not enter such appearance [and give such
notice] within the time in that behalf above limited, it is ordered that the
said application of the said D. D. be and the same is hereby discharged
with costs, to be taxed and paid by the said D. D. to the claimants, or to
Mr. ——, their attorney.

By the Court.

---

318. *Issue after an Appearance [and Notice to defend for Part] by the legal
Representative of a deceased Defendant, or by the Person in Possession
at the Time of his Death (ante, 355).*

*Copy the issue as originally delivered, then enter a suggestion of the defendant's
death, see Nos. 305 and 306, then proceed thus:—*

Afterwards, on the —— day of ——, A.D. 18—, D. D., as the legal
representative of the said C. D. deceased, [*or* as the person in possession of
the said [part of the] property claimed at the time of the death of the said
C. D.,] by leave of the [court here, *or* of the Hon. Sir ——, knight, one of
the judges of this court, *or as the case may be*], appeared by ——, his
attorney, to the said writ, and defended for the whole of the land (*c*) therein
mentioned [*or* for, *describe the part,* being part of the land (*c*) in the said
writ mentioned]: Therefore let a jury come, &c.

---

319. *Summons (under 17 & 18 Vict. c. 125, s. 92) to compel a surviving
Claimant to make a Suggestion of the Death of a deceased Claimant
(ante, 356).*

B. [and another] ⎞ Let A. B., the surviving claimant, his attorney or
      v. ⎨ agent, attend me at my chambers in Rolls Gardens,
D. [and others]. ⎠ Chancery Lane, to-morrow, *or* on —— day next, at
—— of the clock in the ——noon, to show cause why the said A. B. should
not make a suggestion of the death of ——, the deceased claimant, and

---

(*c*) The word " tenements," *or* " premises," *or* " property," may be used
instead of the word " land."

proceed thereon [to trial] according to the provisions of The Common Law Procedure Act, 1852, within such time as I shall order on the hearing of this application, and why, in default of any such proceeding, the defendants should not be at liberty to enter a suggestion and proceed thereon pursuant to the 92nd section of The Common Law Procedure Act, 1854. Dated the —— day of —— , 18—. *Judge's signature.*

N.B.—*The affidavit in support of this application will of course vary according to the facts. It must be framed in like manner, mutatis mutandis, as ante, No. 299. The affidavit should state all things necessary to bring the case within 17 & 18 Vict. c. 125, s. 92 (ante, 355). An affidavit is generally unnecessary at chambers, where the facts are not disputed. See note to No. 22.*

320. *Order thereon.*
Commence as ante, No. 24.

I do order that A. B., the surviving claimant [*or* the said A. B.], do within the next —— days make a suggestion of the death of ——, the deceased claimant, and do before the next —— term proceed thereon [to trial] according to the provisions of The Common Law Procedure Act, 1852 : And that in default of any such proceeding the defendants shall be at liberty to enter a suggestion and proceed thereon pursuant to the 92nd section of The Common Law Procedure Act, 1854. Dated the —— day of ——, 18—. *Judge's signature.*

321. *Suggestion of Default after the above Order (ante,* 856).
In the [Q. B., C. P. *or* Exch.]

B. [and another] ⎰ And now, on the [*date when pleaded (d)*] —— day of
v. ⎱ ——, A.D. 18—, it is suggested by the defendants and
D. [and others]. manifestly appears to the court here, that after the issuing of the writ in this action the said [*name of deceased claimant*] died and the said A. B. survived him : And after such death the defendants applied by a judge's summons, pursuant to The Common Law Procedure Act, 1854, to compel the said A. B., as such surviving claimant, to proceed in this action according to the provisions of The Common Law Procedure Act, 1852, within such time as the judge should order : And that upon the hearing of such application the Hon. Sir ——, Knight, one of the [Judges *or* Barons] of this court [*or* one of her Majesty's Justices of her Court of Queen's Bench *or* Common Pleas, *or* one of the Barons of her Majesty's Exchequer, *as the case may be*], duly made an order in this action as follows [*copy the order verbatim (see ante, No.* 320)] : And it is further suggested by the defendants and manifestly appears to the court here, that the said A. B. did not [make a suggestion of the death of the said *deceased claimant, or* proceed to trial, *as the case may be*], within the time in that behalf ordered as aforesaid, but therein failed and made default : Therefore, &c.

See the next Form.

322. *Judgment upon the above Suggestion (ante,* 356).
In the [Q. B., C. P. *or* Exch.]
On the [*date of writ in ejectment*], A.D. 18—.
Venue, ⎰ On the day and year above written, a writ of our lady the
to wit. ⎱ Queen issued forth of this court in these words :—
Victoria, by the grace of God [*here copy the writ; then state any appearance and subsequent proceedings in the usual form*].
On the [*date of suggestion*] —— day of ——, A.D. 18—.
And now [*copy the suggestion as ante, No.* 321, *to the end; conclude thus :—*

(*d*) See note to No. 292.

Therefore it is considered that the said [*names of defendants*] be acquitted And that they recover against the said A. B. £—— for their costs of defence.

In the margin, opposite the words " Therefore it is considered, &c.," *write* " Judgment signed on the —— day of ——, 18—." *At the time of signing the judgment a mere incipitur may be entered. See the Form No.* 122.

---

323. *Summons under* 17 & 18 *Vict. c.* 125, *s.* 92, *to compel the legal Representative of a deceased Claimant to make a Suggestion of the Death, &c.* (*ante,* 356).

B. ——⎫ Let E. F., the legal representative of A. B., the de-
v.   ⎬ ceased claimant, his attorney or agent, attend me at my
D. [and others].⎭ chambers in Rolls Garden, Chancery Lane, to-morrow, or on —— day next, at —— of the clock in the —— noon, to show cause why the said E. F. should not make a suggestion of the death of the said A. B. deceased, and that he the said E. F. is such legal representative, and proceed thereon [to trial] according to the provisions of The Common Law Procedure Act, 1852, within such time as I shall order on the hearing of this application: And why, in default of any such proceeding, the defendants should not be at liberty to enter a suggestion and proceed thereon pursuant to the 92nd section of The Common Law Procedure Act, 1854. Dated the —— day of ——, 18—. *Judge's signature.*

See the note to No. 319.

---

324. *Order thereon.*

Commence as ante, No. 24.

I do order that E. F., the legal representative of A. B., the deceased claimant, [*or* the said E. F.,] do within the next —— days make a suggestion of the death of the said A. B. deceased, and that he the said E. F. is such legal representative, and do before the next —— term proceed thereon [to trial] according to the provisions of The Common Law Procedure Act, 1852: And that in default of any such proceeding the defendants be at liberty to enter a suggestion and proceed thereon pursuant to the 92nd section of The Common Law Procedure Act, 1854. Dated the —— day of ——, 18—.

Judge's signature.

---

325. *Suggestion of Default after the above Order* (*ante,* 356).

In the [Q. B., C. P. *or* Exch.]

B. ——⎫ And now, on the [*date when pleaded* (*e*)] —— day of
v.   ⎬ ——, in the year of our Lord 18—, it is suggested by
D. [and others].⎭ the defendants, and manifestly appears to the court here, that after the issuing of the writ in this action the said A. B. died: And that E. F. is the [executor of the last will and testament of the said A. B. deceased, *or* the administrator, heir, &c., *as the case may be ; see ante, No.* 302: and that the said E. F. as such [executor] (*f*) is the] legal representative of the said A. B., deceased, as to the property in the said writ mentioned: And that after the death of the said A. B. the defendants applied by a judge's summons pursuant to The Common Law Procedure Act, 1854, to compel the said E. F., as such legal representative of the said A. B., deceased, to make a suggestion of the death of the said A. B.,

---

(*e*) See note to No. 292.
(*f*) See note at the end of No. 302.

deceased, and that he, the said E. F., is such legal representative as aforesaid, and to proceed thereon according to the provisions of The Common Law Procedure Act, 1852, within such time as the judge should order: And that upon the hearing of such application the Hon. Sir ——, Knight, one of the [Judges *or* Barons] of this court, [*or* one of her Majesty's Justices of her Court of Queen's Bench *or* Common Pleas, *or* one of the Barons of her Majesty's Exchequer, *as the case may be*,] duly made an order in this action as follows [*copy the order verbatim; see ante, No.* 324]: And it is further suggested by the defendants, and manifestly appears to the court, that the said E. F. did not [make any such suggestion as in the said order directed, *or* proceed to trial, *as the case may be*], within the time in that behalf ordered as aforesaid, but therein failed and made default: Therefore, &c.

See the next Form.

326. *Judgment upon the above Suggestion (ante,* 356).

Same as ante, No. 322, *to the word* "Therefore;" *conclude thus :—*
Therefore it is considered that the said [*names of defendants*] be acquitted: And that they recover against the said E. F. as [executor] as aforesaid, £—— for their costs of defence, to be levied of the goods and chattels which were of the said A. B., deceased, at the time of his death, in the hands of the said E. F. as [executor] as aforesaid, to be administered.

See the note to No. 322.

327. *Notice of Discontinuance (ante,* 357).

Title of court and cause as ante, No. 19.

Take notice, that the plaintiff hereby discontinues this action [*if only as to some or one of the defendants say,* "as to the defendant ——."] Dated this —— day of ——, 18—.

Yours, &c.

| To the above-named defendants [*or* defendant ——, *as the case may be*], and to Mr. G. H., their [*or* his] attorney [*or* agent]. | A. B., the plaintiff in person, *or* E. F., the plaintiff's attorney. *Address.* |

328. *Judgment on Discontinuance (ante,* 357).

In the [Q. B., C. P. *or* Exch.]

On the [*date of writ*] —— day of ——, A.D. 18—.
Venue, On the day and year above written, a writ of our lady the
to wit. Queen issued forth of this court in these words (that is to say), Victoria, by the grace of God [*here copy the writ*]: and C. D. has, on the —— day of ——, appeared by —— his attorney [*or* in person] to the said writ, and A. B. has discontinued the action: Therefore it is considered that the said C. D. be acquitted, and that he recover against the said A. B. £—— for his costs of defence.

N.B.—*In the margin, opposite the words,* "Therefore it is considered," &c. *write* "Judgment signed on the [*date*] —— day of ——, 18—."

329. *Affidavit of one of the Claimants in support of Application to have his Name struck out of the Writ, &c. (ante,* 358).

Title of court and cause as ante, No. 19.

I, A. B., of ——, in the county of —— [gentleman], one of the persons named in the writ of ejectment issued in this cause, as one of the claimants or plaintiffs make oath and say,—
1. That I have seen the copy of the above-mentioned writ, which I have been informed and verily believe was served on the above-named C. D., and

a copy whereof is hereunto annexed, marked (A); *or,* that the copy writ of ejectment hereunto annexed, marked (A) was, as I have been informed and verily believe, served upon the above-named C. D., as one of the defendants in this action.

2. That I never authorized Mr ——, who appears by the indorsement on the said copy of the said writ to be the attorney for the [plaintiffs *or* claimants] in this action, or Messrs. ——, his agents, or either of them, or any or either of the above-named plaintiffs, or any other person or persons whomsoever, to make use of my name as one of the claimants or plaintiffs in this action, or for the recovery of possession of the property claimed in the said writ or any part thereof: And that my name has been inserted in the said writ as one of the claimants or plaintiffs entirely without my consent or authority [*add, if the fact,* and against my will. *If any application for leave to use the deponent's name has been made and refused, here state the facts specially*].

3. That the above-named C. D. is in possession of [part of] the property claimed in the said writ, as my tenant, and I am desirous that he should continue such tenant, *or as the case may be* (*g*).

Sworn, &c. (*ante,* 705.)

---

330. *Summons to strike out of the Writ, &c., the Name of one of the Claimants* (*ante,* 358).

B. [and others]   } Let the claimants [*names of other claimants*], their
    v.   } attorney or agent, and also the defendants, their at-
D. [and another.] } torney or agent, attend me at my chambers, in Rolls Garden, on —— next, at —— of the clock in the ——noon, to show cause why the name of the claimant A. B. should not be struck out of the writ of ejectment and all subsequent proceedings in this action, pursuant to the 201st section of The Common Law Procedure Act, 1852: [And why the said claimants [*repeat names of other claimants*], or Mr. E. F. their attorney, should not pay to the said A. B., or to Mr. I. K. his attorney, his costs of nd incident to this application, to be taxed by one of the masters].

Dated this —— day of ——, 18—.

Judge's signature.

---

331. *Order thereon* (*ante,* 358).
Commence as ante, No. 24.

I do order that the name of the claimant A. B. be struck out of the writ of ejectment and all subsequent proceedings in this action pursuant to the 201st section of The Common Law Procedure Act, 1852 [*here insert such terms as to the judge may seem fit*]: And I order that [the claimants [*names of the other claimants*], or Mr. E. F., the attorney for the claimants in this action,] do pay to the said A. B., or to Mr. I. K. his attorney, his costs of and incident to this application (including therein any costs which shall have been paid by the said A. B. as hereinafter ordered), to be taxed by one of the masters: And I order that the said A. B. do pay to the defendants or to Mr. L. M., their attorney, their costs of and incident to this application, to be taxed by one of the masters, [counsel allowed]. Dated the —— day of ——, 18—.

Judge's signature.

N.B.—*The terms of the order will of course vary according to the circumstances and the discretion of the judge. The defendants should not appear on the application merely to ask for costs; see the next two forms.*

(*g*) This last clause is not essential; any other good reason may be substituted.

332. *Order for Indemnity to a Claimant against Costs* (ante, 358).

Commence as ante, No. 24.

I do order that all further proceedings in this action by the claimants be stayed until the claimants [*state names of the other claimants*] shall have given to the claimant A. B. such security against the costs of this action on both sides as one of the masters shall approve of: [And I do order that the claimants [*repeat names of the other claimants*] do pay to the said A. B. his costs of and incident to this application, and of such security to be given as aforesaid, to be taxed by the master (counsel allowed)]. Dated this —— day of ——, 18—.

Judge's signature.

333. *Bond of Indemnity to a Claimant against Costs* (ante, 358).

KNOW ALL MEN BY THESE PRESENTS, that we B. B., of ——, Esq., I. K., of ——, tailor, and L. M., of ——, farmer, are held and firmly bound to A. B., of ——, gent., in the sum of £——, to be paid to the said A. B., or his certain attorney, executors, administrators or assigns, for which payment to be well and truly made we bind ourselves jointly and severally, and our and each of our heirs, executors and administrators, firmly by these presents, sealed with our seals. Dated this —— day of ——, A.D. 18—.

WHEREAS an action of ejectment has been commenced and is now pending in her Majesty's Court of [Q. B., C. P. *or* Exch.] at Westminster, in the names of the said A. B. and the above bounden B. B. as the claimants or plaintiffs against C. D. as the tenant or defendant, for the recovery of the possession of [*describe the property as in the writ*]: And by an order of the Hon. Mr. [Justice *or* Baron] ——, dated the —— day of ——, 18—, and made in the said action upon the application of the said A. B., it was ordered that all further proceedings in the said action by the claimants should be stayed until the claimant B. B. should have given to the said A. B. such security against the costs of the said action (on both sides) as one of the masters should approve of: *And whereas* the said B. B., and the above bounden I. K. and L. M. as sureties for the said B. B., have agreed to give such indemnity by entering into the above-written bond or obligation with the condition hereunder written, and the said indemnity hath been approved of by ——, Esq., one of the said masters:

NOW THE CONDITION of the above-written bond or obligation is such that if the above bounden B. B., I. K. and L. M., or some or one of them, or the heirs, executors or administrators of them, or of some or one of them, do and shall save harmless and keep indemnified the said A. B., his heirs, executors, administrators and assigns, and his and their lands and tenements, goods and chattels, of, from and against all costs in the said action (on both sides respectively), and all judgments, rules, orders, executions, attachments, actions, suits, claims and demands whatsoever, touching or relating to any such costs, or any part thereof respectively, and from all losses, claims, costs, charges and expenses, which he or they respectively may bear or incur by reason of the nonpayment of any such costs as aforesaid, then the above-written bond or obligation to be void, else to remain in full force and virtue.

Signed, sealed and delivered by the above-named } B. B. (L.S.)
    B. B., I. K. and L. M. in the presence of   } I. K. (L.S.)
                                          L. M. (L.S.)

                     O. P., of ——.

N.B.—*The master's approval should be obtained before the bond is executed; and he will fix the amount of the penalty.*

334. *Confession by all the Defendants or by a sole Defendant, as to all or Part of the Property claimed (ante, 358).*

Title of court and cause as ante, No. 19.

Take notice that [we *or* I] do hereby confess this action as to the whole of the property claimed [*or* as to (*describe the part*) being part of the property claimed]. Dated this —— day of ——, 18—.

To the above-named plaintiffs, and to }
 Mr. E. F., their attorney [*or* agent]. }
       Signatures of all the
       defendants.

Signed by the above-named defendants in my presence; and I hereby declare that I am the attorney in this action for the said defendants, and that I subscribe as such attorney.

               O. P., of ——.

---

335. *Judgment by Confession (ante, 358).*

In the [Q. B., C. P. *or* Exch.]

    On the [*date of writ*] —— day of ——, A.D. 18—.

Venue, } On the day and year above written, a writ of our lady the Queen
to wit. } issued forth of this court in these words (that is to say),

Victoria, by the grace of God [*here copy the writ*] : and C. D. has, on the —— day of ——, A.D. 18—, appeared by —— his attorney [*or* in person] to the said writ; and the said C. D. has confessed the said action [*or* has confessed the said action as to part of the said [land *or* tenements, *or* property, *or* premises], that is to say, [*here state the part*] : Therefore it is considered that the said A. B. do recover possession of the [land *or* tenements, *or* property, *or* premises] in the said writ mentioned [*or* of the said part of the said land *or* tenements, *or* property, *or* premises in the said writ mentioned], with the appurtenances, and £—— for costs.

In the margin, opposite the words "Therefore it is considered, &c.," *write* "Judgment signed on the —— day of ——, 18—."

---

336. *Confession by one of several Defendants who defends separately for Part (ante, 359).*

Title of court and cause as ante, No. 19.

Take notice, that I do hereby confess this action as to [*describe the part*], being part of the property claimed, and for which the other defendants do not defend. Dated this —— day of ——, 18—.

To the above-named plaintiffs, and to }
 Mr. ——, their attorney [*or* agent]. }   C. D.

Signed by the above-named defendant C. D. in my presence; and I hereby declare that I am the attorney in this action for the said defendant C. D., and that I subscribe as such attorney.

               O. P., of ——.

---

337. *Judgment by Confession as to one of several Defendants (ante, 359).*

In the [Q. B., C. P. *or* Exch.]

    On the [*date of writ*] —— day of ——, A.D. 18—.

Venue, } On the day and year above written, a writ of our lady the Queen
to wit. } issued forth of this court in these words (that is to say),

Victoria, by the grace of God [*here copy the writ*] : and C. D. has, on the —— day of ——, A.D. 18—, appeared by —— his attorney [*or* in person] to the said writ, and has defended for a part of the land in the said writ mentioned (that is to say), [*here state the part*] : and I. K. and L. M. have, on the —— day of ——, A.D. 18—, appeared by —— their attorney [*or* in person] to the said writ, and have defended for other part of the land in the said writ mentioned (that is to say), [*here state the part*] : and N. M. and O. P. have, on the —— day of ——, A.D. 18—, appeared by —— their attorney [*or* in person] to the said writ, and have defended for other part of the land in the said writ mentioned (that is to say), [*here state the part*] being the remainder of the land in the said writ mentioned : And the said C. D. has confessed the said action as to the said part of the said land defended by him as aforesaid (that is to say) [*here state the part as above*] : Therefore it is considered that the said [*names of claimants*] do recover against the said C. D. possession of the said last-mentioned part of the said land, with the appurtenances, and also £—— for their costs, occasioned by the defence of the said C. D. relating to the same ; and as to the rest, let a jury come, &c.

N.B.— *In each instance where the word* "land" *occurs, the word* "tenements," *or* "property," *or* "premises" (*as may appear most appropriate*), *may be used ; see note to No.* 335).

-----

338. *Confession by one of several Defendants as to all or Part of the Property claimed, and for which other Defendants also defend* (*ante,* 359).
Form as ante, No. 334.

-----

339. *Judgment thereon for Costs, and Issue as against the other Defendants* (*ante,* 359).

Form as ante, No. 337 (*mutatis mutandis*), *to the word* "Therefore ;" *conclude thus :—*

Therefore it is considered that the said [*names of claimants*] do recover against the said C. D. possession of [the said land, *or* the said part of the said land], with the appurtenances, and also £—— for their costs, occasioned by his defence ; and as to the other defendants let a jury come, &c.

See note to No. 335.

-----

340. *Memorandum of Error in Law* (*ante,* 363).
In the [Q. B., C. P. or Exch.]
The [*day of lodging note of error*] —— day of ——, in the year of our Lord 18—.
A. B. and C. D.
The plaintiff [*or* defendant] says that there is error in law in the record and proceedings in this action ; and the defendant [*or* plaintiff] says that there is no error therein.
(Signed)   A. B. plaintiff,
[*or* C. D., defendant],
[*or* E. F., attorney for plaintiff *or* defendant].
N.B.—*This is the Form No.* 10 *in the Schedule to* 15 & 16 *Vict. c.* 76.

-----

341. *Master's Note of the Receipt of Memorandum of Error.*
In the [Q. B., C. P. or Exch.]
       A. B. ——, plaintiff,
       and
       C. D. ——, defendant.
I have this day received a memorandum in writing, in the form hereunder written, alleging that there is error in law in the record and proceedings in this action ; and I have filed such memorandum.
       A. D. Croft, Master.
       Date.

Here copy verbatim the memorandum of error in law, ante, No. 340. *The grounds of error intended to be argued should be written after the copy memorandum of error, thus :*

The grounds of error intended to be argued, are—
       1. That [*here state concisely some ground of error*].
       2. That [*here state any other ground, and so on*].
Dated the —— day of ——, 18—.

                          Yours, &c.

To Mr. E. F., the attorney [*or agent*] }   G. H., of ——, attorney for the
for the above-named A. B.   }   above-named C. D.

---

342. *Memorandum of Error in Law by some or one of several Defendants*
(*ante*, 366).

In the [Q. B., C. P. *or* Exch.]
           The [*day of lodging note of error*] —— day of ——,
                 in the year of our Lord 18—.

A. B. and C. D. and others [*or* another].

The defendants [C. D., E. F. and G. H.] say that there is **error in law in**
the record and proceedings in this action; and the plaintiff **says that there**
is no error therein.

       (Signed)   M. N., attorney **for defendants**
                          [C. D., E. F. and G. H.]

For the master's note and grounds of error, see No. 341.

---

343. *Notice to other Defendants of Proceeding in Error, and Request to them to*
elect to join, or to decline to join therein (*ante*, 366).

Title of court and cause as ante, No. 19.

Take notice, that the above-named defendants [C. D., E. F. and G. H.]
have commenced proceedings in error on the judgment in this action; and
that the paper writing hereunto annexed is a copy of the **master's note** of
the receipt of the memorandum of error lodged by the said **defendants, with**
a statement of the grounds of error intended to be argued: **And the above-**
named defendants [I. K. and L. M.] are hereby required **forthwith to elect**
to join, or to decline to join, with the said [C. D., E. F. **and G. H.**] in the
said proceedings in error as plaintiffs therein, pursuant to the **154th section**
of The Common Law Procedure Act, 1852; otherwise an **application will**
be made to the court or a judge in that behalf. Dated **the —— day of**
——, 18—.

                         Yours, &c.

To the above-named defendants }   M. N., of ——, attor**ney for the said**
I. K. and L. M., and to Mr.   }   [C. D., E. F. and G. H.]
O. P., their attorney.   }

*Annex copy master's note and grounds of error as delivered **to the opposite***
party.

---

344. *Summons for the other Defendants to elect to join, or to decline to join, as*
Plaintiffs in the Proceedings in Error (*ante*, 366).

B. [and another] }   Let the defendants [I. K. and L. M.], **or their attorney**
     v.   }   [*or* agent], attend me at my chambers in **Rolls Garden**
D. [and others.] } [to-morrow *or* on —— next] at —— of **the clock in the**
—— noon, to show cause why the said defendants [I. K. and **L. M.**] **should**
not forthwith elect to join or not to join with the defendants [**C. D., E. F. and**
G. H.] as plaintiffs in the proceedings in error in this **action; and why**
in default of such election within twenty-four hours after service of **the order**
to be made on this application the said [I. K. and L. M.] should **not be con-**
sidered as declining to join in such proceedings, and the **defendants [C. D.,**
E. F. and G. H.] be at liberty to continue the said proceedings **in error, and**
to enter a suggestion of error in their own names, without any **summons and**

severance, pursuant to the 154th section of The Common Law Procedure Act, 1852. Dated the —— day of ——, 18—.

Judge's signature.

N.B.—*It does not seem necessary to serve the claimants with this summons, or to call upon them to show cause, &c.*

---

345. *Order thereon (ante, 366).*

Commence as ante, No. 24.

B. [and another]⎱   I do order that the defendants [I. K. and L. M.] do
       v. ⎰ forthwith [*or* within —— hours now next] elect to join
D. [and others.] ⎰ or not to join with the defendants [C. D., E. F. and G. H.] as plaintiffs in the proceedings in error in this action ; and in default of such election within [twenty-four hours after service of this order] I do order that the said [I. K. and L. M.] shall be considered as declining to join in such proceedings, and the defendants [C. D., E. F. and G. H.] be at liberty to continue the said proceedings in error, and to enter a suggestion of error in their own names, without any summons and severance, pursuant to the 154th section of The Common Law Procedure Act, 1852. Dated the —— day of ——, 18—.

Judge's signature.

N.B.—*A copy of this order should be served upon the claimants' attorney, with a notice that the defendants [I. K. and L. M.] have or have not elected to join as plaintiffs in error in pursuance of the order.*

---

346. *Notice by the other Defendants that they elect to join (or decline to join) as Plaintiffs in the Proceedings in Error (ante, 366).*

Title of court and cause as ante, No. 19.

The defendants [I. K. and L. M.] hereby elect to join [*or* decline to join] with the defendants [C. D., E. F. and G. H.] as plaintiffs in the proceedings in error in this action. Dated the —— day of ——, 18—.

Yours, &c.

To the above-named defendants ⎱   O. P., of ——, attorney for the said
[C. D., E. F. and G. H.], and to ⎰   [I. K. and L. M.]
Mr. M. N., their attorney. ⎰

---

347. *Recognizance of the Plaintiff in Error (ante, 364).*

In the [Q B., C. P. *or* Exch.]

The —— day of ——, in the year of our Lord 18—.

Venue. ⎱
to wit. ⎰   A. B. *v.* C. D.

Error from the [Q. B., C. P. *or* Exch. of Pleas] to the Exch. Chamber, on a judgment in ejectment for the recovery of [*as in the judgment*], with the appurtenances, in the parish of ——, in the county of ——.

Recognizance of the above-named C. D. in £—— (h).

G. H., of ——, defendant's attorney.

Taken and acknowledged this ——⎱
   day of ——, 18—, before me, ⎰

Judge's signature.

You do acknowledge to owe to the above-named A. B. the sum of £——, on condition that if the judgment in this action shall be affirmed by the Court of Exchequer Chamber, or the proceedings in error be discontinued by you, then you the said C. D. shall pay such costs, damages and sum or sums of money as shall be awarded upon or after such judgment affirmed or discontinued. Are you content?

(h) Ante, 364.

348. *Summons for Leave to issue Execution, the grounds of Error appearing to be frivolous* (*ante*, 365).

Commence as ante, No. 22.

Why the plaintiffs should not be at liberty to issue execution upon the judgment obtained in this cause, the grounds of error intended to be argued and of which notice has been given, appearing to be frivolous. Dated the —— day of ——, 18—.

Judge's signature.

349. *Order thereon.*

Commence as ante, No. 24.

I do order that the plaintiffs be at liberty to issue execution upon the judgment obtained in this cause, the grounds of error intended to be argued, and of which notice has been given, appearing to be frivolous. Dated the —— day of ——, 18—.

Judge's signature.

350. *Rule Nisi for Leave to issue Execution, the grounds of Error appearing to be frivolous* (*ante*, 365).

Commence as ante, No. 25.

Show cause why the plaintiff should not be at liberty to issue execution upon the judgment obtained in this cause, the grounds of error intended to be argued, and of which notice has been given, appearing to be frivolous.

Upon notice of this rule to be given to the defendants or their attorney in the meantime.

By the Court.

351. *Rule Absolute.*

Commence as ante, No. 28.

It is ordered that the plaintiffs be at liberty to issue execution upon the judgment obtained in this cause, the grounds of error intended to be argued, and of which notice has been given, appearing to be frivolous.

Mr. —— for the plaintiff.
Mr. —— for the defendant.

By the Court.

352. *Suggestion of Error on the Roll* (*ante*, 365).

The —— day of ——, in the year of our Lord 18—.

[*The day of making the entry on the roll.*]

The plaintiff [*or* defendant] says that there is error in the above record and proceedings; and the defendant [*or* plaintiff] says there is no error therein.

N.B.—*This form is No.* 11 *in the Schedule to* 15 & 16 *Vict. c.* 76.

353. *Notice of Proceedings in Error being set down for Argument* (*ante*, 366).

In the [Q. B., C. P. *or* Exch.]

A. B. and C. D.

Take notice, that [I *or* we] have this day set down the proceedings in error in this cause for argument in the Exchequer Chamber, on the —— day of —— [instant *or* next]. Dated the —— day of ——, 18—.

Yours, &c.

To Mr. ——, the [defendant's *or* ⎰ E. F., attorney for the plaintiff [*or* G. H., plaintiff's] attorney [*or* agent]. ⎱ attorney for the defendant.]

354. *Notice to Plaintiff in Error to assign Error, instead of entering a Suggestion (ante, 365).*

In the Exchequer Chamber.

A. B. and C. D.

Take notice, that the above-named A. B. intends to rely upon the proceeding in error being barred by [lapse of time, *or* by release, *or other like matter of fact*] : And the above-named C. D. is hereby required within four days to assign error according to the practice before The Common Law Procedure Act, 1852, instead of entering a suggestion pursuant to that act. Dated this —— day of ——, 18—.

Yours, &c.

To Mr. G. H., attorney for }   E. F., of ——,
  the said C. D.   }   Attorney for the said A. B.

355. *Judgment of Non Pros. for not assigning Error pursuant to Notice (ante, 365).*

Enter an incipitur on paper as ante, No. 122, with a heading or title, as above: then sign judgment of non pros. Afterwards, when necessary, enter on the judgment roll in the court below (after the entry of the final judgment) as follows :—

Afterwards, on the [*day of lodging the note of error*] —— day of ——, A.D. 18—, the said C. D. delivered to one of the masters of the court here a memorandum in writing in the form required by and according to the statute in that case made and provided, alleging that there was error in law in the record and proceedings aforesaid : Afterwards on the [*date of notice to assign errors*] —— day of ——, A.D. 18—, the said A. B. gave notice in writing to the said C. D., that he the said A. B. intended to rely upon the proceeding in error being barred by [lapse of time, *or* by release, *as in the notice*] and thereby required the said C. D., within four days, to assign error according to the practice before The Common Law Procedure Act, 1852, instead of entering a suggestion pursuant to that act: yet the said C. D. did not within four days after the service of such notice assign any error or errors in the record and proceedings aforesaid, but therein failed and made default : Therefore on the —— day of ——, A.D. 18—, it was considered by [*on error from Q. B. say*, the justices of the Common Bench of our said lady the Queen and the barons of her Exchequer; *on error from C. P. say*, the justices of our lady the Queen assigned to hold pleas in the court of our said lady the Queen before the Queen herself, and the barons of her Exchequer ; *on error from Exch. say*, the justices of our lady the Queen assigned to hold pleas in the court of our said lady the Queen, before the Queen herself and the justices of the Common Bench of our said lady the Queen] in the Exchequer Chamber at Westminster, that the said C. D. take nothing by his said proceedings in error ; and that the said A. B. go thereof without day, &c. : [And it was further considered by the said justices [and barons] in the said Exchequer Chamber that the said A. B. recover against the said C. D. £—— for his damages and costs by him sustained and expended by reason of the delay of execution of the judgment aforesaid, on pretence of prosecuting the said proceedings in errror, and that the said A. B. have execution thereof, &c. (*i*)].

(*i*) Omit this where no costs in error recoverable, *ante*, 369.

N N

356. *Assignment of Errors, pursuant to Notice (ante,* 365).

In the Exchequer Chamber.

On the [*day of assigning errors*] —— day of ——, A.D. 18—.

B. } The said C. D., by G. H. his attorney, says that in the record and
v. } proceedings aforesaid, [and also in the matters recited and contained
D. } in the said bill of exceptions, and also in giving the verdict aforesaid,]
and also in giving the judgment aforesaid, there is manifest error in this, to
wit, that the matters stated in the said [bill of exceptions, *or* special verdict,
or special case] are not sufficient in law to entitle the said A. B. to possession
of the said [*describe the property recovered as in the writ or judgment*] on the
said [*the day mentioned in the writ of ejectment*] —— day of ——, A.D. 18—,
and to eject all other persons therefrom : There is also error in this, to wit,
that the [chief justice] before whom, &c., at and upon the trial of the said
matters in question did [*here state the point or points as in the bill of exceptions ;
see Tidd's App.* 548] : There is also error in this, to wit, that by the record
aforesaid it appears that the verdict aforesaid [*if for part only, say as to the
said—describe the part recovered*] was given for the said A. B., whereas by the
law of the land the verdict [as to the said part] ought to have been given for
the said C. D. : There is also error in this, to wit, that by the record aforesaid
it appears that the judgment aforesaid, in form aforesaid given, was given for
the said A. B. against the said C. D. [as to, *describe the part recovered*],
whereas by the law of the land judgment ought to have been given [as to
the said part] for the said C. D. against the said A. B. : And the said C. D.
prays that the judgment aforesaid [as to the said part] for the errors aforesaid, and others in the record and proceedings aforesaid, may be reversed,
annulled and altogether held for nothing, and that he may be restored to all
things which he hath lost by occasion of the judgment aforesaid, &c.

For other forms see Tidd's Appendix, 547, *&c.*

———

357. *Plea in Bar to Assignment of Error in Law (ante,* 365).

In the Exchequer Chamber.

On the [*day when pleaded*] —— day of ——, A.D. 18—.

B. } The said A. B., by E. F. his attorney, says that [*here state the matter
v. } of fact relied on, ex. gr.* "that the said proceedings in error were first
D. } commenced and the memorandum in error delivered to one of the
masters of the court here more than six years after the said judgment was
signed and entered of record, and not at any time within six years next
after the said judgment was signed or entered of record ;" *or state a release
of errors as in Tidd's App.* 554, 555, *or other like matter of fact. No formal
conclusion or prayer of judgment appears to be necessary*].

———

358. *Replication thereto (ante,* 365).

In the Exchequer Chamber.

On the [*day when pleaded*] —— day of ——, A.D. 18—.

B. } The said C. D. says that the said alleged release is not his deed [*or
v. } that on the —— day of ——, A.D. 18—, when the said judgment was
D. } signed and entered of record [he *or* she] the said C. D. was an infant
within the age of twenty-one years, *or* a feme covert and the wife of one
D. D., since deceased, *or* a lunatic and of unsound mind, *or* beyond the
seas : And that within six years next after [he *or* she] the said C. D. became
and was of full age, *or* discovert, *or* of sound mind, *or* returned from beyond
the seas, *as the case may be,* [he *or* she] the said C. D. commenced the said
proceedings in error and delivered the said memorandum in error to one of
the masters of the court here, and is now prosecuting the same with effect,
pursuant to the provisions of the statute in such case made and provided.
No formal conclusion or prayer of judgment appears to be necessary.

359. Rejoinder (ante, 365).

In the Exchequer Chamber.

On the [*day when pleaded*] —— day of ——, A.D. 18—.

B. ⎫
v. ⎬ And the said A. B. joins issue upon the replication of the said C. D.
D. ⎭

N. B.—*In the issue or paper book, add* "Therefore let a jury come, &c."

------

*360. Entry of Judgment of Affirmance by the Exchequer Chamber (ante,
368).*

After the entry of the judgment on the roll in the action, proceed thus :—

Afterwards, on the [*day of lodging the note of error*] —— of ——, A.D.
18—, the said [C. D. *or* A. B.] delivered to one of the masters of the
court here a memorandum in writing in the form required by and according
to the statute in that case made and provided, alleging that there was error
in law in the record and proceedings aforesaid : And afterwards on [*the day
of making the entry of the suggestion on the roll*] the —— day of ——, A.D.
18—, the said [A. B. *or* C. D.] said that there was no error therein: And
thereupon afterwards on [*the day of giving judgment in the Exchequer Chamber*]
the —— day of ——, A.D. 18—, in the Exchequer Chamber of our lady the
Queen [*on error from Q. B. say*, before the justices of the Common Bench
of our said lady the Queen and the barons of her Exchequer ; *on error from
the C. P. say*, before the justices of our said lady the Queen assigned to hold
pleas in the court of our said lady the Queen before the Queen herself, and
the barons of her Exchequer ; *on error from the Exch. say*, before the justices of our lady the Queen assigned to hold pleas in the court of our lady
the Queen before the Queen herself, and the justices of the Common Bench
of our said lady the Queen], came as well the said A. B. as the said C. D. by
their respective attornies aforesaid :● And it appeared to the said Court of
Error in the Exchequer Chamber that there was no error in the record and
proceedings aforesaid, or in giving the judgment aforesaid : Therefore it was
considered by the said Court of Error that the judgment aforesaid be in all
things affirmed and stand in full force and effect, the said causes above for
error suggested [*or* assigned] in anywise notwithstanding : [And it was
further considered by the same court that the said A. B. recover against the
said C. D. £—— for his damages and costs by him sustained and expended
by reason of the delay of execution of the judgment aforesaid, on pretence
of the prosecution of the said proceedings in error, and that the said A. B.
have execution thereof (*k*)]: And thereupon the record and proceedings
aforesaid, with the judgment aforesaid so affirmed by the said Court of
Error as aforesaid, and the said judgment of the said Court of Error, were
by the said master duly brought back into the said court here, in order that
the said court here might award such further proceedings as might be necessary upon the record aforesaid, and upon the said judgment and proceedings so affirmed as aforesaid, according to the form of the statute in such
case made and provided.

------

361. Entry of Judgment of Reversal by the Exchequer Chamber (ante, 368).

Commence as ante, No. 360, to the ●, then proceed thus :—

And it appeared to the said Court of Error that there was manifest error
in the record and proceedings aforesaid, and in giving the judgment aforesaid : Therefore it was considered by the said Court of Error that the judgment aforesaid for the errors aforesaid be reversed, annulled and alto-

------

(*k*) Omit this where no costs in error are recoverable, *ante*, 369.

gether holden for nought; and that the said C. D. be restored to all things which he hath lost by occasion of the said judgment &c.: [And it was further considered by the said Court of Error that the matters in question between the parties aforesaid be again tried by a jury (*l*)]: And thereupon the record and proceedings aforesaid, with the judgment aforesaid so reversed by the said Court of Error as aforesaid, and the said judgment of the said Court of Error, were by the said master duly brought back into the said court here, in order that the said court here might award such further proceedings as might be necessary upon the record aforesaid, and upon the said judgment and proceedings so affirmed as aforesaid, according to the form of the statute in such case made and provided.

---

362. *Summons for Leave to Issue a Writ of Inquiry as to Mesne Profits, &c. after Judgment affirmed in Error, or Proceedings in Error discontinued (ante, 368).*

Commence as ante, No. 22.

Why the plaintiff should not be at liberty to issue a writ to inquire as well of the mesne profits as of the damage by any waste committed after the judgment obtained in this action on the —— day of ——, 18—, pursuant to the 208th section of The Common Law Procedure Act, 1852, the said judgment having been affirmed in error [*or* the proceedings in error on the said judgment having been discontinued]. Dated the —— day of——, 18—.

Judge's signature.

---

363. *Order thereon.*

Commence as ante, No. 24.

I do order that the plaintiff be at liberty [*follow the language of the Summons*]. Dated the —— day of ——, 18—.

Judge's signature.

---

364. *Rule Nisi for Leave to Issue a Writ of Inquiry as to Mesne Profits, &c. after Judgment affirmed in Error, or Proceedings in Error discontinued (ante, 368).*

Commence as ante, No. 25.

Upon reading the judgment roll in this action [and the affidavit of —— and the paper writing thereto annexed (*if any*)], and upon hearing Mr. ——, of counsel for the claimant, it is ordered that the defendant [*or* defendants, *as the case may be*] do on ——day the —— day of —— [instant *or* next] show cause why the plaintiff should not be at liberty to issue a writ to inquire as well of the mesne profits as of the damage by any waste committed after the judgment obtained in this action on the —— day of ——, A.D. 18—, pursuant to the 208th section of the Common Law Procedure Act, 1852, the said judgment having been affirmed in error, [*or* the proceedings in error having been discontinued.]

Upon notice of this rule to be given to the defendant [*or* defendants], or his [*or* their] attorney, in the meantime.

By the Court.

(*l*) Omit this if a trial de novo be not ordered.

365. *Rule Absolute (ante, 368).*

Commence as ante, No. 28.

It is ordered that the plaintiff be at liberty to issue a writ to inquire [*follow the language of the rule nisi, omitting the words* "Upon notice," &c.].

Mr. —— for the plaintiff.
Mr. —— for the defendant.

By the Court.

---

366. *Writ of Inquiry as to Mesne Profits, &c. after Judgment affirmed in Error (ante, 368).*

Victoria, by the grace of God of the United Kingdom of Great Britain and Ireland Queen, Defender of the Faith, to the sheriff of [*the county where the lands lie*] ——, greeting : Whereas on the [*teste of writ in ejectment*] —— day of ——, A.D. 18—, A. B. sued and prosecuted out of our court [*in Q. B.* before us, *in C. P.* before our justices, *in Exch.* before the barons of our Exchequer], at Westminster, our writ in ejectment in these words (that is to say), Victoria, by the grace of God [*here copy the writ*] : And such proceedings were thereupon had in our said court before [us, *or* our justices, *or* the barons of our Exchequer, *as the case may be*], at Westminster aforesaid ; that it was on the [*date of final judgment*] —— day of ——, A.D. 18—, considered by the same court, that the said A. B. should recover possession of the [land *or* tenements] in the said writ mentioned, with the appurtenances, and £—— for costs of suit : And afterwards on the [*day of lodging note of error*] —— day of ——, A.D. 18—, the said C. D. delivered to one of the masters of our said court before [us, *or* our justices, *or* the barons of our Exchequer, *as the case may be*] a memorandum in writing in the form required by and according to the statute in that case made and provided, alleging that there was error in law in the record and proceedings aforesaid :* And such proceedings were thereupon had that afterwards on the [*date of judgment in Exchequer Chamber*] —— day of ——, A.D. 18—, it was considered by [*in error from Q. B. say*, our justices of the Common Bench and the barons of our Exchequer ; *in error from C. P. say*, by our justices assigned to hold pleas in our court before us, and the barons of our Exchequer ; *in error from Exch. say*, by our justices assigned to hold pleas in our court before us, and our justices of the Common Bench] in our Court of Exchequer Chamber at Westminster, that the judgment aforesaid in form aforesaid given should be in all things affirmed and stand in full force and effect, the causes of error [suggested *or* assigned, *as the case may be*], and alleged by the said C. D. in anywise notwithstanding : And thereupon the said judgment in. error was entered upon the original record in our said court before [us *or* our justices of the Common Bench *or* the barons of our Exchequer, *as the case may be*], at Westminster, pursuant to the provisions of The Common Law Procedure Act, 1852 : And afterwards, to wit, on the [*date of rule or order for writ of inquiry*] —— day of ——, A.D. 18—, the said A. B. applied to our said court before [us *or* our justices of the Common Bench, *or* the barons of our Exchequer, *as the case may be*], at Westminster, for our writ to inquire as well of the mesne profits as of the damage by any waste committed after the said judgment obtained in the said action on the [*date of original judgment*] —— day of ——, A.D. 18—, pursuant to the 208th section of The Common Law Procedure Act, 1852, and it was granted to him accordingly : Therefore, according to the form of the said act, we command you, that by the oath of twelve good and lawful men of your bailiwick, you diligently inquire as well of the mesne profits as of the damage by any waste committed after the [*date of first judgment*] —— day of ——, A.D. 18—, on which day the said first judgment in ejectment was entered up : And the inquisition which you shall thereupon take, make known to [us, *or in C. P.* to our justices, *or in*

Exch. to the barons of our Exchequer], at Westminster, immediately after the execution hereof, under your seal and the seals of those by whose oath you shall take that inquisition; and have you then there this writ. Witness ——, at Westminster, the [*day of issuing*] —— day of ——, A.D. 18—.
By rule of court, dated the —— day of
——, 18—.

Or,

By order of Mr. justice [*or* baron] ——,
dated the —— day of ——, 18—.

Indorsement.

E. F., of ——, [agent for I. K., of ——,]
attorney for the within-named A. B.

---

367. *Writ of Inquiry as to Mesne Profits, &c. after Proceedings in Error discontinued (ante, 368).*

Victoria, &c. *as ante, No.* 366, *to the* * : And such proceedings were thereupon had that afterwards, on the [*date of notice of discontinuance*] —— day of —— A.D. 18—, the said C. D. discontinued his proceedings in error by giving to the said A. B. a notice headed in the court and cause and signed by [G. H., the attorney of] the said C. D., stating that he thereby discontinued such proceedings: And thereupon on the [*date of judgment in Exchequer Chamber*] it was considered by our [justices, &c. *as in No.* 366], in our Court of Exchequer Chamber at Westminster, that the said C. D. should take nothing by his said proceedings in error, and that the said A. B. should go thereof without day, &c.: And that the said A. B. should recover against the said C. D. £—— for his costs of and occasioned by the said proceedings in error: Afterwards, to wit, on the [*date of rule or order for writ of inquiry*] —— day of ——, A.D. 18—, the said A. B. applied to our said court, &c. [*remainder as ante, No.* 366].

---

368. *Inquisition on Writ of Inquiry as to Mesne Profits, &c. (ante, 368).*

—— } An inquisition indented, taken at the house of ——, called or
to wit. } known by the name or sign of ——, at ——, in the said county of ——, on the —— day of ——, A.D. 18—, before ——, Esq., sheriff of the county aforesaid, by virtue of a writ of our lady Queen Victoria to the said sheriff directed and to this inquisition annexed, to inquire of certain matters in the said writ specified, by the oath of [*names of twelve jurors*], honest and lawful men of the said county, who upon their oath say, that the mesne profits of the said [land *or* tenements], with the appurtenances, in the said writ mentioned, from the [*date of first judgment in ejectment*] —— day of ——, A.D. 18—, down to the [*date of the writ of inquiry*] —— day of ——, A.D. ——, amount to the sum of £—— : And that the damage by waste committed on the said [land *or* tenements], with the appurtenances, during the period last aforesaid, amounts to the sum of £——. In witness whereof as well I, the said sheriff, as the said jurors, have set our seals to this inquisition, the day and year first above written.

Sheriff's seal.
Seals of twelve jurors.

(*Indorsement on the writ.*)
The execution of this writ appears in the inquisition hereunto annexed.
The answer of
——, Esq., sheriff.

---

369. *Judgment thereon* (*ante,* 368).

On signing judgment enter a mere incipitur on paper, as ante, No. 122; *after-*
wards (*when necessary*) *enter on the judgment roll* (*after the entry of the*
judgment in error, (*ante, No.* 360), *as follows :—*

Afterwards, on the [*date of rule or order for writ of inquiry*] —— day of
——, A.D. 18—, in the said court here comes the said A. B., by his attorney
aforesaid, and prays the writ of our said lady the Queen to be directed to
the sheriff of ——, commanding him that by the oath of twelve good and
lawful men of his bailiwick he diligently inquire as well of the mesne
profits as of the damage by any waste committed after the said judgment
obtained in the said action on the [*date of original judgment*] —— day of
——, A.D. 18—, pursuant to the 208th section of The Common Law Procedure Act, 1852, and it is granted to him, &c.: And thereupon the said
sheriff is commanded that by the oath of twelve good and lawful men of his
bailiwick he diligently inquire as well of the mesne profits as of the damage
by any waste committed after the [*date of original judgment*] —— day of
——, A.D. 18—, on which day the said first judgment was entered up :
And that he send the inquisition, which he shall thereupon take to [our
said lady the Queen, *or in C. P.* to the said justices, *or in Exch.* to the said
barons], at Westminster, immediately after the execution of the said writ,
under his seal, and the seals of those by whose oath he shall take that
inquisition, together with the said writ : Afterwards, on the [*day of signing*
judgment for mesne profits, &c.] —— day of ——, A.D. 18—, before [our
said lady the Queen, *or in C. P.* before the justices of our said lady the
Queen of the Bench, *or in Exch.* before the barons of our Exchequer of our
said lady the Queen], at Westminster aforesaid, comes the said A. B. by his
attorney aforesaid, and the sheriff, to wit, O. P. Esq., sheriff of the said
county of ——, now here returns a certain inquisition indented, taken
before him at [the house of ——, called or known by the name or sign of
——, at ——, in the said county of —— [*as in the inquisition*], on the ——
day of ——, A.D. 18—, by the oath of twelve good and lawful men of his
bailiwick] ; by which it is found [*as in the inquisition*] that the mesne
profits of the said [land *or* tenements], with the appurtenances, so recovered
by the said A. B. as aforesaid, from the [*date of first judgment in ejectment*]
—— day of ——, A.D. 18—, down to the —— day of ——, A.D. 18— [*as in*
the inquisition], amount to the sum of £—— : And that the damage by
waste committed on the said [land *or* tenements], with the appurtenances,
during the period last aforesaid, amounts to the sum of £—— : Therefore
it is considered that the said A. B. recover against the said C. D. the said
sums of £—— and £—— by the said inquisition above found : And also
£—— for costs of suit, according to the form of the statute in such case
made and provided : Which said sums, in the whole, amount to £——.

In the margin, opposite the words " Therefore it is considered, &c.," *write*
" Judgment signed on the —— day of ——, 18—."

———————

370. *Writ of Restitution after Judgment reversed in Error* (*ante,* 370).
Commence as ante, No. 290, *to the* *.

And because, since the issuing of our said writ, the judgment aforesaid
hath been reversed by [*on error from Q. B. say,* our justices of the Common
Bench and the barons of our Exchequer; *on error from C. P. say,* our justices
assigned to hold pleas in our court before us and the barons of our Exchequer; *on error from Exch. say,* our justices assigned to hold pleas in our
court before us and our justices of the Common Bench] in our Court of
Exchequer Chamber at Westminster, for certain errors therein ; and
because our said writ thereupon issued improvidently and unjustly : Therefore we command you [*as in No.* 290].

371. *Memorandum of Error in Fact (ante, 370).*

In the [Q. B., C. P. or Exch.]

The —— day of ——, in the year of our Lord 18—.

[*The day of lodging note of error.*]

A. B. and C. D., in error.

The plaintiff [*or* defendant] says, that there is error in fact in the record and proceedings in this action, in the particulars specified in the affidavit hereunto annexed.

(Signed)   A. B., plaintiff,

[*or* C. D., defendant,]

[*or* E. F., attorney for plaintiff *or* defendant].

N.B.—*This is the Form No.* 12 *in the Schedule to* 15 & 16 *Vict. c.* 76; *annex affidavit in the usual form, ante, Nos.* 19, 20 *or* 21, *stating the error in fact intended to be relied on, ex. gr.,* That on the —— day of ——, A.D. 18 —, the defendant appeared in this action by —— his attorney : And the defendant, at the time of the said appearance, and also on the —— day of ——, A.D. 18—, (on which day the judgment in this action was entered up,) was under the age of twenty-one years, in which case the defendant ought to have been admitted to appear in this court to defend this action by his guardian and not by his attorney, *or as the case may be.*

---

372. *Master's Note of the Receipt of Memorandum and Affidavit (ante, 370).*

In the [Q. B., C. P. or Exch.]

A. B., ——, plaintiff,

and

C. D., ——, defendant.

I have this day received a memorandum in writing, and an affidavit thereunto annexed, in the forms hereunder written, stating that there is error in fact in the record and proceedings in this action in the particulars specified in the said affidavit : And I have filed such memorandum and affidavit.

A. D. Croft, master.

Date.

Here copy verbatim the memorandum and affidavit.

A copy of the above must be served on the attorney or agent for the opposite party; no grounds of error need be stated in any other manner.

---

373. *Assignment of Error in Fact (ante, 370).*

In the [Q. B., C. P. or Exch.]

On the [*day of assigning error*] —— day of ——, A.D. 18—.

B. ⎫ The defendant [in person *or* by —— his attorney] says, that in the

v. ⎬ record and proceedings aforesaid, and also in giving the judgment

D. ⎭ aforesaid, there is manifest error in this, to wit, that he, the defendant, appeared in the suit aforesaid by —— his attorney : nevertheless the said defendant, at the time of his said appearance, and also at the time of giving the judgment aforesaid, was an infant under the age of twenty-one years, in which case the said defendant ought to have been admitted to appear in the court aforesaid to defend the suit aforesaid by his guardian, and not by his attorney : Therefore in that there is manifest error, and the said defendant prays that the judgment aforesaid, for the error aforesaid, may be revoked, annulled and altogether held for nothing, and that he may be restored to all things which he hath lost by occasion of the judgment aforesaid, &c.

For an assignment of " coverture" see Tidd's Appendix, 544.

374. Notice to plead to Assignment of Error (ante, 370).

The plaintiff is to plead hereto within four days, otherwise judgment. Dated, &c.

N.B.—*To be indorsed on assignment of error, or to be delivered separately: in which latter case it must be entitled in the court and cause.*

---

375. Plea to Assignment of Error in Fact (ante, 370).

In the [Q. B., C. P. *or* Exch.]

On the [*day when pleaded*] —— day of ——, A.D. 18—.

B. ⎫   The plaintiff [in person *or* by E. F. his attorney] says, that the
v. ⎬   defendant at the time of his said appearance, and also at the time of
D. ⎭   giving the judgment aforesaid, was of the full age of twenty-one years : [Therefore let a jury come, &c.].

N.B.—*If the plaintiff reply in nullo est erratum, he thereby admits the facts as alleged in the assignment of error, and the question is whether such facts constitute error.* Banks *v.* Newton, 4 Dowl. & L. 638, note (*h*); 11 Q. B. 344.

---

375 a. Judgment of Non Pros for not Assigning Error in Fact (ante, 370).

Enter an incipitur on paper as ante, No. 122, with a heading or title as above; then sign judgment of non pros: afterwards (when necessary) enter on the judgment roll in the court below (after the entry of the final judgment) as follows :—

Afterwards, on the [*day of lodging note of error and affidavit*] —— day of ——, A.D. 18—, the said C. D. delivered to one of the masters of the court here a memorandum in writing and an affidavit thereunto annexed in the form required by and according to the statute in that case made and provided, alleging that there was error in fact in the record and proceedings aforesaid in the particulars specified in the said affidavit : But the said C. D. did not within eight days after the filing with the said master of the said memorandum of error in fact assign error according to the practice of the said court here and the rule of court in that behalf, but therein failed and made default : Therefore on the —— day of ——, A.D. 18—, it is considered by the court here that the said C. D. take nothing by his said proceedings in error, and that the said A. B. do go thereof without day, &c. [*If costs in error recoverable (ante, 369), say—*"And it is further considered by the court here that the said A. B. recover against the said C. D. £—— for his damages and costs by him sustained and expended by reason of the delay of execution of the judgment aforesaid, on pretence of prosecuting the said proceedings in error, and that the said A. B. have execution thereof, &c."]

---

376. Notice of Discontinuance of Proceedings in Error (ante, 371).

Title of court and cause as ante, No. 354.

Take notice, that the above-named C. D. hereby discontinues his proceedings in error in this cause. Dated the —— day of ——, 18—.

Yours, &c.

C. D., plaintiff in error,
or
G. H., of ——,
attorney for the said C. D.

To the above-named A. B., and
to Mr. E. F., his attorney
[*or* agent].

377. Judgment on Discontinuance of Proceedings in Error (ante, 371).

Enter an incipitur on paper as ante, No. 122, *with a heading or title as above, adding " costs £ ——;" then sign judgment: afterwards, when necessary, enter on the judgment roll in the court below (after the entry of the final judgment) as follows :—*

Afterwards, on the [*day of lodging note of error*] —— day of ——, A.D. 18—, the said C. D. delivered to one of the masters of the court here a memorandum in writing in the form required by and according to the statute in that case made and provided, alleging that there was error in law, in the record and proceedings aforesaid : Afterwards, on the [*date of notice of discontinuance*] —— day of ——, A.D. 18—, the said C. D. discontinued his proceedings in error by giving to the said A. B. a notice headed in the court and cause, and signed by [G. H. the attorney of] the said C. D., stating that he thereby discontinued such proceedings: Therefore on the —— day of ——, A.D. 18—, it was considered by [the justices, &c. *as in No.* 355] in the Exchequer Chamber at Westminster, that the said C. D. take nothing by his said proceedings in error, and that the said A. B. do go thereof without day, &c. : And that the said A. B. recover against the said C. D. £—— for his costs of and occasioned by the said proceedings in error.

---

378. Confession of Error and Consent to Reversal of Judgment (ante, 371).
Title of court and cause as ante, No. 354.

Take notice, that the above-named A. B. hereby confesses the error suggested [*or* assigned] by the said C. D., and consents to the reversal of the judgment in this cause. Dated the —— day of ——, 18—.

Yours, &c.

To the above-named C. D., and   A. B., defendant in error,
to Mr. G. H., his attorney   *or*
[*or* agent].   E. F., attorney for the said A. B.

---

379. Judgment of Reversal on Confession of Error in Law (ante, 371).

Enter an incipitur on paper as ante, No. 122, *with a heading or title as above ; then sign judgment. Afterwards, when necessary, enter on the judgment roll in the court below (after the entry of the final judgment) as follows :—*

Afterwards, on the [*day of lodging note of error*] —— day of ——, A.D. 18—, the said C. D. delivered to one of the masters of the court here a memorandum in writing in the form required by and according to the statute in that case made and provided, alleging that there was error in law in the record and proceedings aforesaid : Afterwards, on the [*date of confession of error*] —— day of ——, A.D. ——, the said A. B. confessed the said error and consented to the reversal of the above judgment, by giving to the said C. D. a notice headed in the court and cause and signed by [E. F. the attorney of] the said A. B., stating that he thereby confessed the error [suggested *or* assigned, *as the case may be*], by the said C. D., and consented to the reversal of the said judgment : Therefore, on the —— day of ——, A.D. 18—, it was considered by [the justices, &c. *as in No.* 355] in the Exchequer Chamber at Westminster, that the judgment aforesaid, for the error aforesaid, be reversed, annulled and altogether held for nothing, and that the said C. D. be restored to all things which he hath lost by occasion of the said judgment, &c.

---

380. *Suggestion of the Death of one of several Plaintiffs in Error (ante, 371).*

In the Exchequer Chamber.

B. [and another] ⎱ And now, on the [*date when pleaded* (n)] —— day of
    v. ⎰ ——, A.D. 18—, it is suggested and manifestly ap-
D. [and others.] peers to [*in error from the Q. B. say,* the justices of
our lady the Queen of the Bench, and the barons of the Exchequer of our
said lady the Queen; *in error from the C. P. say,* the justices of our lady the
Queen before the Queen herself, and the barons of the Exchequer of our
said lady the Queen; *in error from the Exch. say,* the justices of our said lady
the Queen before the Queen herself and the justices of our said lady the
Queen of the Bench] in the Exchequer Chamber at Westminster:* That
after the commencement of the proceedings in error in this action, and
before this day, the said [*name of deceased plaintiff in error*] died: Therefore
let the said proceedings in error be continued at the suit of and against the
said [*names of surviving plaintiffs in error*] as if [they *or* he] were the sole
[plaintiffs *or* plaintiff] in error, according to the form of the statute in such
case made and provided.

---

381. *Affidavit of untruth of Suggestion (ante, 371).*

Same as ante, No. 293, mutatis mutandis.

---

382. *Summons to set aside Suggestion as Untrue (ante, 371).*

Same as ante, No. 294, mutatis mutandis.

---

383. *Order thereon (ante, 371).*

Same as ante, No. 295, mutatis mutandis.

---

384. *Affidavit for Leave to enter a Suggestion of the Death of a sole Plaintiff in Error by his legal Representative (ante, 372).*

In the Exchequer Chamber.

A. B. and C. D.

Commence as ante, Nos. 19, 20 *or* 21—1. That the paper writing hereunto
annexed marked (A) is a true copy of the issue delivered in this action.

2. That the cause was tried before Lord Chief Justice ——, *or* the Lord
Chief Baron, *or* Mr. Justice (*or* Baron) ——, at the [spring *or* summer]
assizes for the county of ——, held at ——, in the said county, when [the
defendant tendered a bill of exceptions, which was afterwards duly sealed
by the said lord chief justice, *or* lord chief baron, *or* justice *or* baron, *as
the case may be*], and a verdict was found for the plaintiff for the property
claimed in the said writ, *or* for [*describe the part*] being part of the property
claimed in the said writ, and as to the residue of the said property for the
defendant; *or say,* when the jury found a special verdict, *or* a verdict for the
plaintiff subject to a special case.

3. On the —— day of ——, A.D. 18—, final judgment was signed in the
said action for the [plaintiff].

4. [*State proceedings in error according to the facts.*]

5. After the commencement of the said proceedings in error, and on or
about the —— day of ——, A.D. 18—, the said C. D. died.

6. The said property so recovered against the said C. D. as aforesaid
[*or* so claimed in the said writ] is of freehold tenure, and the said C. D.
was at the time of his death seised thereof or entitled thereto in fee simple,
[*or as the case may be; remainder of affidavit as in No.* 299, *mutatis
mutandis*].

Sworn, &c. (*ante,* 705).

(n) See note to No. 292.

385. *Summons for Leave to enter a Suggestion by the legal Representative of a Sole Plaintiff in Error deceased (ante, 372).*

Commence as ante, No. 22.

B. } Why D. D., of ——, should not be at liberty to make a suggestion
v. } of the death of C. D., the plaintiff in error, and that he the said
D. } D. D. is the legal representative of the said C. D., deceased, pursuant to the 163rd section of The Common Law Procedure Act, 1852. Dated the —— day of ——, 18—.

Judge's signature.

386. *Order thereon (ante, 372).*

Commence as ante, No. 24.

I do order that D. D., of ——, be at liberty [within —— days] to make a suggestion of the death of C. D., the plaintiff in error, and that he the said D. D. is the legal representative of the said C. D., deceased, pursuant to the 163rd section of The Common Law Procedure Act, 1852. Dated the —— day of ——, 18—.

Judge's signature.

387. *Suggestion of the Death of a Sole Plaintiff in Error, by his legal Representative (ante, 372).*

In the Exchequer Chamber.

A. B. } And now, on the [*day when pleaded(o)*] —— day of ——, in
v. } the year of our Lord 18—, before the [*justices, &c. in No.* 380], in
C. D. } the Exchequer Chamber at Westminster, comes D. D. by ——
his attorney [*or* in person], and by leave of the Hon. Sir ——, knight, [one of the justices of our said lady the Queen before the Queen herself, *or* one of the justices of our said lady the Queen of the Bench, *or* one of the barons of the Exchequer of our said lady the Queen, *as the case may be*], suggests and gives the said justices [and barons] to understand and be informed that after the commencement of the proceedings in error in this action, and before this day, the said C. D. died: And that the said D. D. is the [heir, &c., *as the case may be, as in No.* 302]: And that the said D. D. as such [heir, &c.] is the legal representative of the said C. D., deceased, as to the said property so recovered against the said C. D. as aforesaid: Therefore let the said proceedings in error be continued at the suit of and against the said D. D. as the plaintiff in error, according to the form of the statute in such case made and provided.

388. *Suggestion of the Death of one of several Defendants in Error (ante, 372).*

Same as ante, No. 380, *to the* *.

That after the commencement of the proceedings in error in this action, and before this day, the said [*name of deceased defendant in error*] died: Therefore let the said proceedings in error be continued against the said [*names of surviving defendants in error*] according to the form of the statute in such case made and provided.

(*o*) See note to No. 292.

389. *Notice to Representatives of deceased Defendant in Error of the intention of Plaintiff in Error to proceed (ante, 372).*

Title of court and cause as ante, No. 354.

Take notice, that on the [*day of lodging note of error*] —— day of ——, A.D. 18—, the above-named C. D. commenced proceedings in error in this action, and then lodged with one of the masters of the court of [Q. B., C. P. or Exch.] a memorandum in writing of error in law, pursuant to the provisions of The Common Law Procedure Act, 1852, and that the paper writing hereunto annexed, marked (A), is a copy of the said master's note of the receipt of the said memorandum of error, with a statement of the grounds of error intended to be argued [*here state shortly any subsequent proceedings in error according to the facts*]: And take notice, that it is the intention of the above-named C. D. (being the plaintiff in error) to continue the said proceedings in error after the expiration of ten days from the service of this notice, pursuant to the 166th section of The Common Law Procedure Act, 1852. Dated the —— day of ——, 18—.

Yours, &c.

To —— and ——, the representatives } G. H. of ——, attorney for the
of the above-named A. B. } above-named C. D.

N.B.—*To be served on the heir, executors, administrators or devisees of the deceased claimant, being his legal representatives as to the property in question, according as the same is freehold, leasehold or copyhold.*

---

390. *Declaration in Trespass for Mesne Profits and Costs (ante, 638). See the next Form.*

In the [Q. B., C. P. or Exch.]

The [*date when pleaded*] —— day of ——, A.D. 18—.

Venue (p), } A. B. by E. F. his attorney [*or in person, as the case may be*] to wit. } sues C. D., for that the defendant broke and entered certain tenements of the plaintiff (that is to say) [*describe them as in the ejectment, or by names or abuttals as in an ordinary action of trespass (q)*], situate and being in the parish of ——, in the county of ——, and ejected, expelled, put out and removed the plaintiff from his possession and occupation thereof and kept him so ejected and expelled for a long time (r), and during that time took and received to the use of the defendant the issues and profits of the said tenements, with the appurtenances,* whereby the plaintiff during all

---

(*p*) The venue is local; 1 Chit. Pl. 216 (7th edit.) If the county be divided, the venue should be laid in the proper division of the county in which the lands lie, thus :—"Lancashire, northern division, to wit ;" *or* "Lancashire, southern division, to wit ;" *Thompson* v. *Hornby*, 9 Q. B. 978. Warwickshire is not now divided, 17 & 18 Vict. c. 35 (*ante*, 135).

(*q*) By the pleading rules of H. T. 1853, No. 18, " In actions for trespass to land, the close or place in which, &c. must be designated in the declaration by *name*, or *abuttals*, or *other description ;* in failure whereof the plaintiff may be ordered to amend with costs, or give such particulars as the court or a judge may think reasonable." As to *naming* a close see *Brownlow* v. *Tomlinson*, 1 Man. & G. 484 ; 8 Dowl. 827 ; *Curling* v. *Mills,* 6 Man. & Gr. 173 ; *Howell* v. *Thomas*, 7 C. & P. 342. Where the close or place in which, &c. is described in the declaration by abuttals, it is sufficient to mention *some* of them ; *North* v. *Ingammells*, 9 M. & W. 249 ; 1 Dowl. N. S. 151. But abutting *towards*, &c. is incorrect, because that does not exclude any intervening land ; *Lempriere* v. *Humphreys*, 3 A. & E. 181 ; 4 N. & M. 638 ; 1 Harr. & Woll. 171, *S.C.*

(*r*) This is sufficient without saying for how long. *Higgins* v. *Highfield*, 13 East, 407 ; *Ive* v. *Scott*, 9 Dowl. 993 ; 15 & 16 Vict. c. 76, s. 49.

the time aforesaid not only lost the issues and profits of the said tenements, with the appurtenances, but was deprived of the use of the same tenements with the appurtenances [and also of the opportunity and means of cultivating the same (*s*)], and was forced and obliged to and did bring and prosecute a certain action of ejectment for the recovery of the possession of the said tenements, with the appurtenances ; and was also forced and obliged to and did necessarily pay and expend divers sums of money, and also necessarily incur and became liable to pay divers other sums of money, in and about the recovering of the possession of the said tenements, with the appurtenances: And the plaintiff claims £——(*t*).

391. *Declaration in Trespass for Mesne Profits and Costs, stating Special Damage (ante, 638).*

Commence as ante, No. 390, *to the* *, *then proceed thus :—*

And during that time ploughed up, turned up and subverted the earth and soil of the said closes, and cut down divers timber and other trees growing and being on the said closes [*here state any other act of trespass, as in an action of trespass quare clausum fregit,* 3 *Chit. Pl.* 660—664, 7*th edit.*]: And during that time caused and procured great waste, spoil, damage, deterioration and injury to the said [messuages, buildings and land], and excessively and irregularly cropped and damaged the said land, and used the said tenements, with the appurtenances, in an unhusbandlike, untenantlike and improper manner, whereby the plaintiff, during all the time aforesaid, not only lost the issues and profits of the said tenements, with the appurtenances, but was deprived of the use and means of cultivating the same [and was hindered and prevented from carrying on his trade and business of a —— in and upon the said tenements, as he might and otherwise would have done]; and whereby the said tenements, with the appurtenances, and the plaintiff's estate and interest therein, have been and are greatly injured and deteriorated in value ; and whereby the plaintiff was forced and obliged to, and did bring and prosecute a certain action of ejectment for the recovery of the possession of the said tenements, with the appurtenances, and was also forced and obliged to and did necessarily pay and expend divers sums of money, and also necessarily incur and became liable to pay divers other sums of money in and about the recovering of the possession of the said tenements, with the appurtenances: And the plaintiff claims £—— (*t*).

See the notes to No. 390.

392. *Pleas in Trespass for Mesne Profits (ante, 639).*

    1. *Not Guilty.*
    2. *The Statute of Limitations.*
    3. *Leave and Licence.*
    4. *That the Tenements were not Plaintiff's.*

In the [Q. B., C. P. *or* Exch.]

    The [*date when pleaded*] —— day of ——, A.D. 18—.

D. ⎰
ats. ⎱ 1. The defendant by G. H., his attorney [*or in person*] says that
B. ⎰ he is not guilty.

2. And for a further plea the defendant says, that he was not guilty within six years before this suit.

(*s*) Omit these words if totally inapplicable.

(*t*) Claim enough to cover all the arrears of rent or mesne profits, and all other damages which the jury may give (*ante,* 643), including the costs of the ejectment. There is no harm in claiming too much, but the plaintiff can in no case recover more than he has claimed ; *Tomlinson* v. *Blacksmith,* 7 T. R. 132; *Tebbs* v. *Barron,* 4 Man. & Gr. 844; *Watkins* v. *Morgan,* 6 C. & P. 661.

3. And for a further plea the defendant says, that he did what is complained of by the plaintiff's leave.

4. And for a further plea the defendant says, that the said [tenements] respectively were not the plaintiff's as alleged.

N.B.—*The above pleas or any of them may be pleaded together, as of course, without leave of the court or a judge.* 15 & 16 *Vict. c.* 76, *s.* 84.

<hr>

393. *Pleas in Trespass for Mesne Profits, &c.* (*ante*, 639).

1. *As to the Trespasses, &c., on and after a specified Day—Payment into Court.*
2. *As to the Residue of the Declaration—Not Guilty.*
3. *As to ditto—The Statute of Limitations.*
4. *As to ditto—Leave and Licence.*
5. *As to ditto—That the Tenements were not Plaintiff's.*
6. *As to ditto—Liberum tenementum.*

In the [Q. B., C. P. *or* Exch.]

The [*date when pleaded*] —— day of ——, A.D. 18—.

D. } 1. The defendant by G. H., his attorney [*or* in person] as to the
ats. } alleged trespasses and causes of action on and after the —— day of
B. } ——, in the year of our Lord 18— (*u*), brings into court the sum of
£——, and says that the said sum is enough to satisfy the claim of the plaintiff in respect of the matter herein pleaded to.

2. And for a further plea as to the residue of the declaration the defendant says, that he is not guilty.

3. And for a further plea as to the said residue the defendant says, that he was not guilty within six years before this suit.

4. And for a further plea as to the said residue the defendant says, that he did what is complained of in the said residue of the declaration by the plaintiff's leave.

5. And for a further plea as to the said residue the defendant says, that at the respective terms when, &c. in the said residue of the declaration mentioned the said [tenements] respectively were not the plaintiff's as alleged.

6. And for a further plea as to the said residue the defendant says, that at the respective times, when, &c. in the said residue of the declaration mentioned the said [tenements] respectively were the closes, soil and freehold of the defendant [I. S.]: Whereupon the defendant [I. S., in his own right, and the defendant T. R., as the servant of the said I. S., and by his command], committed the trespasses in the said residue of the declaration complained of.

N.B.—*An order for leave to plead the above pleas is necessary.*

<hr>

394. *Plea of Justification* (*to an Action of Trespass for Mesne Profits, &c.*) *as incoming Tenant of one H. H., and by virtue of a special Stipulation between him and the Plaintiff* (*ante*, 639).

7. And for a further plea the defendant says, that before and at the time of the alleged trespasses, the plaintiff had become and was tenant from year to year to one H. H., of a certain farm and lands upon, amongst others, the terms that, when notice should have been given by either party to determine the said tenancy, the next incoming or succeeding tenant of the said farm and lands should be at liberty, on and after the 11th day of October next preceding the end or determination of the said tenancy, to enter upon such part of the said farm and lands as, according to the course of husbandry,

<hr>

(*u*) The day on which the right to possession is claimed and recovered in the ejectment.

then came and was in turn for being sown with wheat, in order to plough, and cultivate, and prepare the same for being sown, and to sow the same with wheat, and to cultivate the same land when sown, the plaintiff being afterwards allowed, by his said landlord, a half-year's rent and taxes for the said part of the said land so entered upon : And the defendant further says, that the said H. H., before the 11th day of October, A.D. 1853, gave notice to the plaintiff to quit the said farm and lands, and to determine the said tenancy on the 6th day of April, in the year of our Lord 1854, the then current year of the said tenancy, ending on the day and year last aforesaid ; and the defendant, before the committing of the alleged trespasses, had agreed with the said H. H. to become and be, and the defendant, in fact was, at the time of the committing of the alleged trespasses, the next incoming or succeeding tenant of the said farm and lands, within the true intent and meaning of the stipulation in that behalf aforesaid : And the defendant further says, that the said closes in the declaration mentioned were and are part of the said farm and lands, and that on the said 11th day of October, A.D. 1853, the said closes were and thence continued to be, until and at the time of the committing of the said trespasses in the declaration mentioned, such part of the said farm and lands as, according to the said course of husbandry, came and was in turn for being sown with wheat : And the said H. H. hath always been ready and willing to allow the plaintiff a half-year's rent and taxes for the said closes, according to the aforesaid stipulation in that behalf; of all which premises respectively the plaintiff always had notice and well knew : And the defendant further says, that after the said 11th day of October, A.D. 1853, he the defendant as such next incoming or succeeding tenant of the said farm and lands with the authority of the said H. H., and in pursuance of the stipulation in that behalf aforesaid, entered into the said closes, and ploughed, and cultivated, and prepared the same for being sown, and did sow the same with wheat, and cultivated the same closes when so sown, as it was lawful for him to do for the cause aforesaid, which are the supposed trespasses in the declaration mentioned.

N.B.—*To this plea the plaintiff replied by way of estoppel—see the Form, post, No. 399,—to which the defendant demurred on the ground that the plea " does not deny the title or possession of the plaintiff, and the matters contained in it are not inconsistent with the recovery in the ejectment."*

395. *Other Pleas in Trespass for Mesne Profits, &c.*

8. *Release.*   9. *Accord and Satisfaction* (ante, 639).

8. And for a further plea the defendant says, that, after the accruing of the causes of action in the declaration mentioned, and before this suit, the plaintiff, by deed, released the defendant therefrom.

9. And for a further plea the defendant says, that, after the accruing of the causes of action in the declaration mentioned, and before this suit, the defendant paid to the plaintiff, who then accepted and received of and from the defendant, the sum of £ ——, in full satisfaction and discharge of the said causes of action.

396. *Replication " joining Issue" to Pleas in an Action of Trespass for Mesne Profits* (ante, 639).

In the [Q. B., C. P. *or* Exch.]
The [*date when pleaded*] —— day of ——, A.D. 18—.

B.
v.   } The plaintiff joins issue upon the defendant's [first, second, third,
D.   &c.] pleas.

N.B.—*Sometimes it is necessary for the plaintiff to new assign, or to reply by way of estoppel* (ante, 639).

397. *Replication by way of Estoppel, as to Part of a Plea denying Plaintiff's Title in an Action of Trespass for Mesne Profits* (ante, 640).

In the [Q. B., C. P. *or* Exch.]

The [*date when pleaded*] —— day of ——, A.D. 18—.

B. ⎱
v. ⎰ 1. The plaintiff joins issue upon the defendant's [first, second, and
D. ⎰ third] pleas.

2. And the plaintiff, as to so much of the [fourth] plea as alleges that [the said tenements respectively were not the plaintiff's, *or* that the said tenements respectively were the closes, soil and freehold of the defendant, *follow the language of the plea*] on the [*day on which possession was claimed in the ejectment*] —— day of ——, in the year of our Lord 18—, and from that day until and on the [*date of judgment (x) in the ejectment*] —— day of ——, in the year of our Lord 18—, the plaintiff says that the defendant ought not to be admitted to plead so much of the said plea as aforesaid, because the plaintiff says, That on the [*teste of writ in ejectment*] —— day of ——, in the year of our Lord 18—, he the said A. B. caused to be issued out of the court of our lady the Queen, before [the Queen herself *or* her justices of the Bench, *or* the barons of her Exchequer] at Westminster, in the county of Middlesex, according to the provisions of The Common Law Procedure Act, 1852, and the course and practice of the said court, a certain writ in ejectment, the tenor whereof was and is as follows: Victoria [&c. *copy the writ verbatim*], which said writ before and at the time of the issuing thereof, as aforesaid, was indorsed with [the name and abode of the attorney issuing the same, *or* the name and residence of the said A. B.] according to the provisions of the said act, and the course and practice of the said court; and that afterwards, and whilst the said writ was in full force, the same was served upon the said C. D. therein named, who duly appeared to the said writ, and defended the said action for [the whole of the property in the said writ mentioned]: And such proceedings were thereupon had in the said action, that afterwards, on the [*commission day of the assizes*] —— day of ——, in the year of our Lord 18—, before —— and —— justices of our lady the Queen, assigned to take the assizes in and for the county of ——, came the said A. B. and the said C. D., and also a jury of the county aforesaid; and the said jury being sworn to try the matters in question between the said parties, upon their oath said, That the said A. B., on the —— day of ——, in the year of our Lord 18—, was, and still was on the said [*commission day*] —— day of ——, in the year of our Lord 18—, entitled to possession of, [*describe the property recovered, as in the postea*], as in the said writ of ejectment alleged, [and that the said A. B. was not entitled to the residue of the tenements in the said writ mentioned, or any part thereof, as in the said writ alleged]; and afterwards, on the [*date of final judgment in the ejectment*] —— day of ——, in the year of our Lord 18—, it was considered by the court of our said lady the Queen before [the Queen herself *or* her justices, *or* the barons of her Exchequer] at Westminster, that the said A. B. should recover possession of [*describe the part recovered as in the judgment*], being part of the tenements in the said writ mentioned, and £—— for costs: And it was further considered that the said C. D. should be acquitted as to the residue of the tenements in the said writ mentioned, and that he should recover against the said A. B. £—— for his costs of defence as to the said residue; as by the record and proceedings aforesaid now remaining in the said court of our said lady the Queen before [the Queen

---

(x) Perhaps this may be made to extend to the day when possession was delivered by the sheriff under the *habere facias possessionem*, but if so, the plea must go on to show the issuing and execution of such writ (see *post*, No. 399).

herself *or* her justices, *or* the barons of her Exchequer] at Westminster, fully appear,* which said judgment is still in full force ; and the plaintiff says that the now plaintiff, and the said A. B., in the record and proceedings aforesaid mentioned, are one and the same person, and not other or different persons : And that the now defendant C. D., and the said C. D. in the record and pro- ceedings aforesaid mentioned, are one and the same person, and not other or different persons ; and that the [closes and tenements] in which, &c., in the declaration mentioned, at the several times in the said declaration, and hereinbefore respectively mentioned, were and are [part and parcel of] the said tenements whereof the now plaintiff recovered the possession by the said verdict and judgment as aforesaid, and not other or different tenements ; wherefore the plaintiff prays judgment, if the defendant ought to be admitted to plead so much of the said [fourth] plea, as in the introductory part of this replication is mentioned.

♦3. And as to the residue of the said [fourth] plea, the plaintiff joins issue thereon.

---

398. *The like where Defendant was the Landlord, and had Notice of the Writ in Ejectment, but did not appear to defend " as Landlord," but his Tenant defended (ante,* 640).

Commence as ante, No. 397, *to the* ***, *after which proceed thus :—*
" Which said judgment is still in full force, and the plaintiff further says, that before and at the time when the said C. D. was served with the said writ in ejectment as aforesaid, he the said C. D. held and occupied the said tene- ments, with the appurtenances, so recovered by the said A. B. by the said verdict and judgment as aforesaid, as tenant thereof to the now defendant: And that the said C. D. forthwith, after being served with the said writ in ejectment as aforesaid, gave notice thereof to the now defendant, according to the form of the statute in such case made and provided : And that the now defendant could and might, if he had thought fit, have applied to the said court of our said lady the Queen before [the Queen herself *or* her justices *or* the barons of her Exchequer] at Westminster, or to a judge of one of the superior courts of law at Westminster, according to the form of the statute in such case made and provided, for leave to appear and defend the said action of ejectment as landlord of the said C. D. for the said tenements, with the appurtenances, so in the possession and occupation of the said C. D. as tenant thereof to the now defendant as aforesaid ; but the defendant wholly neglected and omitted so to do : And the said C. D. afterwards appeared to the said action, and such proceedings were thereupon had in the said action, as hereinbefore in that behalf mentioned : And the plaintiff says, that the now plaintiff and the said A. B., in the record and proceedings aforesaid mentioned, are one and the same person, and not other or different persons ; and that the [closes and tenements] in which, &c., in the declara- tion mentioned, at the several times in the said declaration, and hereinbefore respectively mentioned, were and are [part and parcel of] the said tene- ments whereof the now plaintiff recovered the possession by the said verdict and judgment aforesaid, and not other or different tenements ; wherefore the plaintiff prays judgment, if the defendant ought to be admitted to plead so much of the said [fourth] plea, as in the introductory part of this repli- cation is mentioned.

3. And as to the residue of the said [fourth] plea, the plaintiff joins issue thereon.

399. *Replication by way of Estoppel to the whole Plea, showing a Judgment obtained in Ejectment by Default and Writ of Possession executed (ante, 640).*

In the [Q. B., C. P. *or* Exch.]

The [*date when pleaded*] —— day of ——, A.D. 18—.

B. ⎫
v. ⎬ 1. The plaintiff joins issue upon the defendant's [first, third and
D. ⎭ fourth] pleas.

2. And as to the defendant's [second] plea the plaintiff says, that the defendant ought not to be admitted to plead that plea, because the plaintiff says, That on the [*teste of writ in ejectment*] —— day of ——, A.D. 18—, he the said A. B. caused to be issued out of the court of our lady the Queen, before [the Queen herself *or* her justices of the Bench, *or* the barons of her Exchequer], at Westminster, in the county of Middlesex, according to the provisions of The Common Law Procedure Act, 1852, and the course and practice of the said court, a certain writ in ejectment, the tenor whereof was and is as follows:—Victoria [&c. *copy the writ verbatim*], which said writ, before and at the time of the issuing thereof as aforesaid, was indorsed with [the name and abode of the attorney issuing the same, *or* the name and residence of the said A. B.] according to the provisions of the said act, and the course and practice of the said court; and the plaintiff says that the said [closes] in which, &c., in the declaration mentioned, at the several times in the said declaration and hereinbefore respectively mentioned, were and are [part and parcel of] the said [tenements] in the said writ mentioned, and not other or different [tenements]: And that the said A. B., in the said writ mentioned, was and is the now plaintiff A. B., and not another or different person; and that the said C. D., in the said writ mentioned, was and is the now defendant C. D., and not another or different person; and that the said C. D., at the time of the issuing of the said writ, and of the service thereof as hereinafter mentioned, was the tenant in possession of the said [closes], in which, &c., in the declaration mentioned, being, and which then were and are [part and parcel of] the said [tenements] in the said writ mentioned; and the plaintiff says that afterwards, and whilst the said writ was in full force, the said C. D. was served with and had due notice of the said writ, according to the course and practice of the said court; and that no appearance was entered or defence made to the said writ, and that no defence was made in or to the action commenced by the said writ: And the plaintiff says that afterwards, and whilst the said action of ejectment was pending in the said court, such proceedings were thereupon had in the said action, that, before the commencement of this suit, the plaintiff, by the consideration and judgment of the said court of our said lady the Queen, before [the Queen herself *or* her justices, *or* the barons of her Exchequer], at Westminster, recovered possession of the said [tenements], with the appurtenances, in the said writ mentioned, as by the record and proceedings thereof, still remaining in the said last-mentioned court, more fully and at large appears; which said judgment is still in full force: And the plaintiff further says, that after the said judgment was recovered as aforesaid, and whilst the same was in force, to wit, on the [*teste of writ of habere facias possessionem*] —— day of ——, A.D. 18—, the plaintiff for having and obtaining execution of and upon the said judgment, sued and prosecuted out of the said court of our lady the Queen, before [the Queen herself *or* her justices, *or* the barons of her Exchequer], at Westminster aforesaid, according to the course and practice of the said court, a certain writ of our said lady the Queen, called a writ of *habere facias possessionem* in ejectment, directed to the sheriff of ——, by which last-mentioned writ our said lady the Queen commanded the said sheriff that [he should omit not by reason of any liberty of his county, but that he should enter the same, and (*omit these words if not in the writ*)] without delay he should cause the said A. B. to have possession of the

said [land and premises, *or as the case may be*], with the appurtenances : And that in what manner the said sheriff should have executed that writ, he should make appear to [our said lady the Queen *or* to the justices of our said lady the Queen, *or* to the barons of the Exchequer of our said lady the Queen], at Westminster, immediately upon the execution of that writ, and that the said sheriff should have there then that writ, which said last-mentioned writ afterwards and whilst it was in full force was delivered to W. W., Esq., who then and from thence until, and at and after the execution of the said writ, was sheriff of the said county of ——, to be executed in due form of law : By virtue of which last-mentioned writ, the said **W. W.** so being sheriff of the said county of —— as aforesaid, afterwards, to wit, on the —— day of ——, in the year last aforesaid, did cause the plaintiff to have possession of the said [land and premises], with the appurtenances, in the said last-mentioned writ mentioned, being the said [closes] in which, &c., in the declaration mentioned, according to the exigency of the said last-mentioned writ ; and afterwards and before the commencement of this suit, returned to [our said lady the Queen *or* to the justices of our said lady the Queen, *or* to the barons of the Exchequer of our said lady the Queen], at Westminster, upon the said last-mentioned writ, that by virtue of that writ to him directed, he on the —— day of ——, A.D. 18—, caused the plaintiff to have possession of the said [land and premises], with the appurtenances, as by the said last-mentioned writ he was commanded ; as by the said last-mentioned writ, and the said return thereof, still remaining of record in the said last-mentioned court, fully appears : Wherefore the plaintiff prays judgment if the defendant ought to be admitted against the said recovery, record and proceedings, to plead the said [second] plea to the said declaration.

N.B.—*In the case from which this precedent was prepared, the defendant demurred on the ground, " That the replication to the second plea does not show that the trespasses in the declaration were after the issuing of the writ in ejectment, and that the plaintiff is seeking to recover the mesne profits only from the time of the issuing of the writ, and that the defendant is not estopped from denying the possession or title of the plaintiff before that time."*

400. *Rejoinder by Defendant to a Replication by way of an Estoppel, in an Action of Trespass for Mesne Profits* (*ante,* 640).

In the [Q. B., C. P. *or* Exch].
　　　　　　　　The [*date when pleaded*] —— day of ——, A.D. 18—.

D. ats. } The defendant joins issue upon the plaintiff's replication, by way of estoppel, to part of the [fourth] plea.

Or the defendant may select and traverse any material allegation or allegations.

401. *Demurrer by Defendant to a Replication by way of Estoppel, in an Action of Trespass for Mesne Profits* (*ante,* 640).

In the [Q. B., C. P. *or* Exch].
　　　　　　　　The [*date when pleaded*] —— day of ——, A.D. 18—.

D. ats. B . } The defendant says, that the plaintiff's replication, by way of estoppel, to part of the [fourth] plea is bad in substance.

N.B.—*In the margin, some substantial matter of law* intended to be argued *must be stated.* 15 & 16 *Vict. c.* 76, *s.* 89, *ex gr.*: "The matter of law intended to be argued on behalf of the defendant is, that the facts, as alleged in the replication, are not sufficient in law to estop the defendant. [That the replication is too extensive, and being bad in part, it is bad altogether]." *Doe* v. *Wellsman,* 2 Exch. 368 ; 6 Dowl. & L. 179.

402. *Plea in Trespass for an Assault and Battery, &c., justifying in Defence of Possession of a Messuage, &c. (ante, 69).*

And for a —— plea [to the said —— count, *or* as to the assaulting, beating, shaking, pushing, dragging and ill-treating the plaintiff, in the said —— count mentioned, *or* except as to the alleged wounding in the declaration mentioned (*y*)], the defendants say, "That the defendant C. D. before, and at the said time when, &c. was *lawfully possessed* (*z*) of a certain dwelling-house and premises, with the appurtenances, situate and being at ——, in the county of —— : And the said C. D. being so possessed thereof, the plaintiff, just before the said time when, &c. was unlawfully in the said dwelling-house and premises, and with force and arms stayed and continued therein, making a noise and disturbance, without the leave or licence and against the will of the said C. D.; and during all that time greatly disturbed and disquieted the said C. D. in the peaceable and quiet possession and enjoyment of his said dwelling-house and premises: And thereupon the said C. D. then requested the plaintiff to go and depart from and out of the said dwelling-house and premises, and to cease his said disturbance, which the plaintiff then refused to do: And thereupon the said C. D. in his own right, and the said other defendants as the servants of the said C. D. and by his command, at the said time when, &c. in defence of the said possession of the said C. D. of the said dwelling-house and premises, gently laid hands upon the plaintiff in order to remove, and did [gently endeavour to] remove (*a*), the plaintiff from and out of the said dwelling-house and premises, as they lawfully might for the cause aforesaid: [And thereupon (*a*), the plaintiff, with strong hand, forcibly resisted the said endeavour of the defendants, and endeavoured forcibly to stay and continue in the said dwelling-house and premises without the leave or licence and against the will of the said C. D.: Whereupon the said C. D. in his own right, and the said other defendants as the servants of the said C. D. and by his command, at the said time when, &c., in order to preserve the possession of the said C. D. of the said dwelling-house and premises, did then and there resist and oppose the said forcible and unlawful conduct of the plaintiff, and then gently removed him from and out of the said dwelling-house and premises, and in so doing did necessarily and unavoidably a little assault, beat, shake, push, drag and ill-treat (*b*) the plaintiff, as they lawfully might for the cause aforesaid:] And so the defendants in fact say, that the damage and injury in the said [—— count of the] declara-

---

(*y*) If *all* the alleged trespasses can be justified, it is not necessary to specify, or to except any of them in the introductory part of the plea. If a *wounding* be charged that should be excepted, or special matter of justification introduced into the plea. *Moriarty v. Brooks*, 6 C. & P. 684; *Oakes and Wife v. Wood*, 2 M. & W. 791. A plea of *molliter manus imposuit*, in the usual form, will not justify repeated blows and several times knocking the plaintiff down. *Gregory v. Hill*, 8 T. R. 299. A forcible entry may be forcibly resisted without any previous request to depart, &c.; 3 Chit. Pl. 325; *Green v. Goddard*, 2 Salk. 641; *Tullay v. Reed*, 1 C. & P. 6, Park, J.; *Polkinhorn v. Wright*, 8 Q. B. 197. A forcible entry will justify an assault and beating with a stick. *Weaver v. Bush*, 8 T. R. 78.

(*z*) *Liberum tenementum* will not be sufficient to justify an assault, but a lawful possession must be alleged. *Roberts v. Tayler*, 1 C. B. 117; 3 D. & L. 1. The moment a person legally entitled to possession enters peaceably to take possession, he thereby becomes lawfully possessed (*ante*, 68).

(*a*) Omit these words and those in the subsequent brackets, if contrary to the fact, or unnecessary to justify the acts complained of.

(*b*) These words must agree with the declaration, or the introductory part of the plea.

tion mentioned, which then happened to the plaintiff, was occasioned by the defendant's said defence of the said C. D.'s possession of the said dwelling-house and premises against the plaintiff, [and in so as aforesaid resisting and opposing the said forcible and unlawful conduct of the plaintiff], which are the supposed trespasses [in the introductory part of this plea mentioned, and] whereof the plaintiff hath above complained against the defendants.
See pleas in Hayling *v.* Okey, 8 *Exch.* 531.

---

403. *Justification in Trespass of an Expulsion, &c. by one Defendant as Tenant from Year to Year, and by the others as his Servants (ante,* 69).

And for a further plea [to the said —— count, or as to—*enumerate the trespasses intended to be justified ; if the plea applies to the whole declaration say only,* " And for a further plea"] the defendants say, that before any of the said times when, &c. E. C. was seised in his demesne as of fee of and in the said [dwelling-house *or* close] in the [declaration *or* —— count] mentioned, and in which, &c. with the appurtenances ; and being so thereof seised, he the said E. C., before any of the said times when, &c. demised the said [dwelling-house *or* close] in which, &c., with the appurtenances, to the defendant C. D., To have and to hold the same to him the said C. D. thenceforth for a certain term, to wit, from year to year, for so long time as the said E. C. and the defendant C. D. should respectively please : By virtue of which demise the said C. D. afterwards, and before any of the said times when, &c. entered into the said [dwelling-house *or* close] in which, &c. with the appurtenances, and became and was possessed thereof according to the said demise, and afterwards ceased to have the actual possession thereof : And the defendants further say, that afterwards, in order to regain possession of the said [dwelling-house *or* close] in which, &c. (the said last-mentioned demise, and the tenancy thereby created being still subsisting), the defendant C. D., and the other defendants, as his servants, and by his command, broke and entered the said [dwelling-house *or* close] in which, &c., and remained therein for a certain space of time, as they lawfully might for the cause aforesaid, which are the supposed trespasses in the [declaration *or* —— count, *or* in the introductory part of this plea] mentioned.

N.B.—*Generally the expulsion is considered as mere matter of aggravation, before a new assignment ; and therefore it is sufficient in the first instance to justify the breaking and entering.* Taylor *v.* Cole, 3 T. R. 292 ; *S. C. in error,* 1 H. Blac. 561 ; Harvey *v.* Brydges, 14 M. & W. 437 ; 3 D. & L. 55 ; *S. C. in error,* 1 Exch. 261. *If the entry be alleged in the declaration to have been made* "with strong hand, &c.," *that is primâ facie mere aggravation.* Davison *v.* Wilson, 11 Q. B. 890.

---

404. *Declaration for Double Value under* 4 Geo. 2, c. 28, s. 1, *for holding over after the Determination of a Yearly Tenancy by Notice to quit (ante,* 647).

In the [Q. B., C. P. *or* Exch].

     The [*date when pleaded*] —— day of ——, A.D. 18—.

Venue (c), }   A. B., by E. F. his attorney [*or* in person, *as the case may*
 to wit. } *be*], sues C. D. ; for that the defendant before and at the time of the giving of the notice and making the demand as hereinafter mentioned, and from thence until and upon the [*day when tenancy determined*] —— day of ——, A.D. 18—, held and enjoyed certain tenements, with the appurtenances, as tenant thereof to the plaintiff from year to year, for so long time as the

---

(c) The venue is transitory (*ante,* 647).

plaintiff and defendant should respectively please, the reversion of the said tenements, with the appurtenances, during all that time belonging to the plaintiff: And thereupon, whilst the defendant so held and enjoyed the said tenements, with the appurtenances, as tenant thereof to the plaintiff as aforesaid, and whilst the said reversion so belonged to the plaintiff, to wit, on the [*date of notice to quit*] —— day of ——, A.D. 18—, the plaintiff gave a notice in writing to the defendant, and thereby then demanded and required the defendant to quit and deliver up the possession of the said tenements, with the appurtenances, to the plaintiff on the said [*day when tenancy determined*] —— day of ——, A.D. 18—, on which day the term, estate and interest of the defendant in the said tenements, with the appurtenances, determined: Nevertheless, the defendant, not regarding the statute in such case made and provided, did not nor would, on the determination of the said tenancy as aforesaid, deliver the possession of the said tenements, with the appurtenances, to the plaintiff, according to the said notice so given, and the said demand so made as aforesaid, but wholly neglected and refused so to do, and wilfully held over the said tenements, with the appurtenances, after the determination of the said term and tenancy, and after the said notice so given, and the said demand so made as aforesaid, for a long space of time; during which time the defendant did keep the plaintiff out of possession of the said tenements, with the appurtenances (he the plaintiff, during all that time, being entitled to the possession thereof), contrary to the form of the statute in such case made and provided: And the plaintiff avers that the said tenements, with the appurtenances, during the said time of holding over the same, and keeping the plaintiff out of the possession thereof as aforesaid, were of great yearly value, to wit, of the yearly value of [£100]: And by reason of the premises, and by force of the statute in such case made and provided, the defendant became liable to pay to the plaintiff a large sum of money, to wit [£80], being at the rate of double the yearly value of the said tenements, with the appurtenances, for so long a time as the same were so detained as aforesaid, yet the defendant hath not paid the same or any part thereof (*d*): And the plaintiff claims [£100].

————

405. *Declaration for Double Value under* 4 *Geo.* 2, *c.* 28, *s.* 1, *for holding over after the Expiration of a Term of Years, and a written Notice and Demand of Possession* (*ante,* 647).

In the [Q. B., C. P. *or* Exch.]
          The [*date when pleaded*] —— day of ——, A.D. 18—.
Venue (*e*), } A. B., by E. F. his attorney [*or* in person, *as the case may*
     to wit. { *be*], sues C. D.; For that the defendant for a long time held and enjoyed certain tenements, with the appurtenances, as tenant thereof to the plaintiff, to wit, for a certain term of years which ended on the —— day of ——, A.D. 18—; the reversion of the said tenements, with the appurtenances, during all that time belonging to the plaintiff: And [upon *or* after] the expiration and determination of the said term and whilst the defendant continued in possession of the said tenements, with the appurtenances, and whilst the plaintiff was so as aforesaid entitled to the possession thereof, to wit, on the [*date of written demand of possession*] —— day of ——, A.D. 18—, the plaintiff, by a certain notice in writing then made and signed by [him *or* by one G. H. his agent in that behalf thereunto lawfully authorized] and delivered to the defendant, demanded and required the defendant to deliver the possession of the said tenements, with the

————

(*d*) A count for use and occupation, or a count in trespass for mesne profits, &c., or any other count, may be added, as may appear necessary or expedient.

(*e*) The venue is transitory (*ante,* 647).

appurtenances, to the plaintiff: Nevertheless the defendant, not regarding the statute in such case made and provided, did not nor would on the expiration and determination of the said term, and upon such demand being made and notice given as aforesaid, deliver the possession of the said tenements, with the appurtenances, to the plaintiff, according to the said demand so made and the said notice so given as aforesaid, but wholly neglected and refused so to do, and wilfully held over the said tenements, with the appurtenances, after the expiration and determination of the said term, and after the said demand so made and the said notice so given as aforesaid, for a long space of time, during which time the defendant did keep the plaintiff out of possession [*remainder as in No.* 404].

---

406. *Declaration for Double Rent, under* 11 *Geo.* 2, *c.* 19, *s.* 18 (*ante,* 650).

In the [Q. B., C. P. *or* Exch.]

The [*date when pleaded*] —— day of ——, A.D. 18—.

Venue (*f*), } A. B., by E. F. his attorney [*or in person, as the case may*
  to wit. } *be*], sues C. D.; For that the defendant, before and at the time of the giving of the notice hereinafter mentioned, held and enjoyed certain tenements, with the appurtenances, as tenant thereof to the plaintiff from year to year, for so long time as the plaintiff and defendant should respectively please, at and under the yearly rent of £——, payable [quarterly, to wit, on &c. *state days of payment*], the reversion of the said tenements, with the appurtenances, during all that time belonging to the plaintiff: And thereupon, whilst the defendant so held and enjoyed the said tenements, with the appurtenances, as tenant thereof to the plaintiff as aforesaid, and whilst the said reversion so belonged to the plaintiff, to wit, on the [*date of notice to quit*] —— day of——, A.D. 18—, the defendant gave notice to the plaintiff of his, the defendant's, intention to quit the said tenements, with the appurtenances, on the [*day when tenancy ended pursuant to the notice*] —— day of ——, A.D. 18—, on which last-mentioned day the term, estate and interest of the defendant in the said tenements, with the appurtenances, determined pursuant to the said notice: Nevertheless the defendant, not regarding the statute in such case made and provided, did not nor would, according to the said notice, deliver up the possession of the said tenements, with the appurtenances, to the plaintiff at the time in the said notice contained, to wit, on the said [*date when tenancy ended as mentioned in the notice*] —— day of ——, A.D. 18—, but wholly neglected and refused so to do, and wrongfully and injuriously held over, and kept and withheld the possession of the said tenements, with the appurtenances, from the plaintiff for a long space of time, (he, the plaintiff, during all that time being entitled to the possession thereof,) contrary to the form of the statute in such case made and provided: By reason whereof and by force of the said statute the defendant became liable to pay to the plaintiff a large sum of money, to wit, £——, being at the rate of double the rent or sum which the defendant would have been liable to pay to the plaintiff for and in respect of the said tenements, with the appurtenances, if no such notice had been given by the defendant as aforesaid: And which said last-mentioned sum of money hath arisen and accrued due and payable to the plaintiff after the expiration of the said notice, and during the said time when the defendant so wrongfully continued in and kept possession of the said tenements, with the appurtenances, as aforesaid (*g*): And the plaintiff claims £——.

(*f*) The venue is transitory (*ante,* 650).

(*g*) A count for single rent, or for use and occupation, or trespass for mesne profits, or any other counts, may be added as may appear necessary or expedient.

407. *Indebitatus Count for Double Rent (ante,* 650).

For [money payable by the defendant to the plaintiff for] double rent of a [messuage *or* farm] and premises of the plaintiff, held by the defendant as tenant thereof to the plaintiff, for one year's rent, [*or* one-half of a year's rent *or* one quarter of a year's rent,] which accrued after the expiration of a regular notice to quit, duly given by the defendant to the plaintiff, that the defendant would quit the said [messuage *or* farm] and premises.

See Chit. Forms, 80 (7th *edit.*)

---

408 *to* **417.** *Forms of Proceedings in the County Courts in Actions for Possession, &c.*

These will be found annexed to the county courts rules and regulations to be made pursuant to 19 & 20 Vict. c. 108 [*now in preparation,* 1*st October,* 1856].

---

418. *Notice* (*h*) *of Owner's intention to apply to Justices to recover Possession of small Tenements, under* 1 *&* 2 *Vict.* c. 74 (*ante,* 666, 670).

I, ——, [owner *or* agent to ——, the owner, *as the case may be*], do hereby give you notice, That unless peaceable possession of the tenement [*shortly describing it*] situate at ——, which was held of [me, *or* of the said ——, *as the case may be*], under a tenancy [from year to year, *or as the case may be*], which [expired *or* was determined by notice to quit from the said —— *or otherwise, as the case may be*], on the —— day of ——, and which tenement is now held over and detained from the said ——, be given to ——, the [*owner or agent*], on or before the expiration of seven clear days from the service of this notice, I, ——, shall, on —— next, the —— day of ——, at —— of the clock of the same day, at ——, apply to her majesty's justices of the peace acting for the district of —— [*being the district, division or place in which the said tenement, or any part thereof, is situate*] in petty sessions assembled, to issue their warrant directing the constables of the said district to enter and take possession of the said tenement, and to eject any person therefrom. Dated this ——.

(Signed)   ——

To Mr. ——.   [owner *or* agent].

---

419. *Complaint before Two Justices pursuant to* 1 *&* 2 *Vict.* c. 74 (*ante,* 670).

The complaint of ——, [owner *or* agent, *&c. as the case may be,*] made before us, two of her Majesty's justices of the peace acting for the district of ——, in petty sessions assembled, who saith that the said —— did let to —— a tenement consisting of —— for ——, under the rent of ——, and that the said tenancy [expired *or* was determined by notice to quit, given by the said ——, *as the case may be*], on the —— day of —— : And that on the —— day of —— the said —— did serve on —— [*the tenant over-holding*] a notice in writing of his intention to apply to recover possession of the said tenement (a duplicate of which notice is hereto annexed) by giving [*&c. describing the mode in which the service was effected*] ∴ and that notwithstanding the said notice the said —— [refused *or* neglected] to deliver up possession of the said tenement, and still retains the same.

(Signed)   ——.

Taken the —— day of —— ⎰
Before us, ⎱
(Signed)   ——
——.

[See over.]

(*h*) This and the next two Forms are given in the schedule to the act of 1 & 2 Vict. c. 74, and therefore should be adhered to as closely as possible.

O O

A duplicate of the notice of intention to apply is to be annexed to this complaint.

———

420. *Warrant to Peace Officers to take and give Possession pursuant to 1 & 2 Vict. c. 74 (ante, 667, 671).*

Whereas [*set forth the complaint*] we, two of her Majesty's justices of the peace, in petty sessions assembled, acting for the —— of ——, do authorize and command you, on any day within —— days from the date hereof, [except on Sunday, Christmas Day and Good Friday, *to be added, if necessary,*] between the hours of nine in the forenoon and four in the afternoon, to enter (by force, if needful) and with or without the aid of ——, [*the owner or agent, as the case may be*], or any other person or persons whom you may think requisite to call to your assistance, into and upon the said tenement, and to eject thereout any person, and of the said tenement full and peaceable possession to deliver to the said —— [*the owner or agent*]. Given under our hands and seals this —— day of ——.

To ——, and all other constables and peace ⎰　　　　　—— (L.s.)
officers acting for the [district] of ——. ⎱　　　　　—— (L.s.)

N.B.—*The warrant must be directed to the constables and peace officers of the district, division or place within which the premises or some part thereof are or is situate, or to some or one of them, and not to any other person.* Jones *v.* Chapman, 14 M. & W. 124; 2 Dowl. & L. 907; 2 Exch. 803.

———

421. *Bond to stay Warrant of Possession under 1 & 2 Vict. c. 74 (ante, 671).*

Know all men by these presents that we [*names, addresses and additions of tenant and two sureties*] are jointly and severally held and firmly bound to [*landlord or his agent*] of —— [Esq.], in the sum of £—— of lawful British money to be paid to the said ——, or to his certain attorney, executors, administrators or assigns, For which payment to be well and truly made we bind ourselves and each and every of us in the whole, and the heirs, executors and administrators of us, and each and every of us, jointly and severally, firmly by these presents. Sealed with our seals. Dated this —— day of ——, 18—.

Whereas the above-named —— did on the [*date of warrant*] —— day of ——, 18—, obtain a warrant under the hands and seals of J. P. and Q. R., two of her Majesty's justices of the peace, in petty session assembled, acting in and for the [district of ——, in the county of ——], dated on that day and directed to —— and all other constables and peace officers acting for the [district of ——] aforesaid, authorizing and commanding them respectively on any day within —— days from the date of the said warrant, [except on Sunday, *&c. as in the warrant,*] between the hours of nine in the forenoon and four in the afternoon, to enter (by force, if needful), and with or without the aid of ——, the [*owner or agent, as in the warrant*], or any other person or persons whom they respectively might think requisite to call to their assistance, into and upon a certain tenement [*describing it shortly as in the notice or warrant*] situate at ——, and to eject thereout any person ; and of the said tenement full and peaceable possession to deliver to the said —— : And which said warrant was issued under and by virtue of an act passed in a session of parliament holden in the first and second years of the reign of Queen Victoria, intituled "An Act to facilitate the Recovery of Possession of Tenements after due Determination of the Tenancy :"

Now the condition of the above-written obligation is such, that if the said [*tenant*] do and shall, according to the statute in such case made and provided, sue the said [*obligee*] in an action of trespass, with effect and without delay, and do and shall pay all the costs of the proceedings in such action, in case a verdict shall pass thereon for the said [*obligee*] [or any or either of them, *if more than one*], or the said [*tenant*] shall discontinue or not prosecute his said action, or become nonsuit therein, then this present obligation shall be void, otherwise to remain in full force and virtue.

Signed, sealed and delivered by the ⎫ —— (L.S.)
   above-named ——, in the pre- ⎬ —— (L.S.)
   sence of ——. ⎭ —— (L.S.)

We approve of the above bond.

(Signed)   J. P. ⎫
           Q. R. ⎬ Justices.

---

422. *Information and Request to Justices to view deserted Premises* (*ante,* 677).

—— ⎱ The information and request of [I. K. as the bailiff *or* receiver
to wit. ⎰ of] A. B. of —— [gentleman], taken and made this —— day of
——, in the year of our Lord 18—, before us [J. P. and Q. R., Esquires],
two of her Majesty's justices of the peace for the [*here state the county,
riding, division or place, as the case may be*] :

Who saith, that C. D., late of —— [labourer], is tenant to the said A. B. of [a certain messuage or dwelling-house, lands, tenements and premises, *or as the case may be*], with the appurtenances, situate at ——, within the said [county, riding, division *or* place, *as the case may be*], under a demise thereof by the said A. B. unto the said C. D. [for —— years, *or* as tenant from year to year], at the yearly rent of £——, payable [quarterly on the —— day of ——, the —— day of ——, the —— day of ——, and the —— day of ——, during the said term, *or as the case may be*] : And that such rent is [a rack rent, *or* full three-fourths of the yearly value of the said demised premises] : And that the said C. D. is now in arrear £—— for [more than (*i*)] one-half year's rent of the said premises : And that the said C. D. hath deserted the said premises, and left the same [uncultivated and] unoccupied, so as no sufficient distress can be had to countervail the said arrears of rent : And the said [I. K. as the bailiff *or* receiver of the said] A. B. thereupon requests us the said justices (neither of us having any interest in the said demised premises) to go upon and view the same, and to take such proceedings thereupon in that behalf, according to the statutes in such case made and provided, that the said A. B. may be put into possession of the said premises in pursuance of the said statutes.

Taken before us, the justices aforesaid, at ——, on the day and year first above mentioned.

J. P.
Q. R.

---

423. *Notice to be affixed on deserted Premises* (*ante,* 678).

To C. D., late of —— [labourer].

Take notice, that [I. K. as the bailiff *or* receiver of] A. B. of —— [gentleman], hath this day stated unto us J. P. and Q. R., two of her Majesty's justices of the peace for [the county of ——, *or* the riding, division *or* place, &c., *as the case may be*] ; That you C. D. are tenant to the said A. B. of [*recite information and request to the words* " Taken," *&c., which omit*] : And we as such justices aforesaid (neither of us having any interest in the said demised premises) in pursuance of the said request of the said [I. K. as the bailiff *or* receiver of the said] A. B. and of the statutes in such case made and provided, have now come upon the said demised premises, and have viewed the same, and we find the same to be deserted and left [uncultivated and unoccupied, *or* unoccupied] so as no sufficient distress

---

(*i*) One half-a-year's rent in arrear is sufficient.

can be had to countervail the said arrears of rent: And we find that the said yearly rent of £—— is [a rack rent, *or* full three-fourths of the yearly value of the said demised premises]: And we now hereby give you notice, that we the said justices will return to the said demised premises on [*not sooner than fourteen days exclusive of the days of the first and second view*] the —— day of ——, 18—, to take a second view thereof: And if on such second view you the said C. D., or some person on your behalf, do not then appear here, and pay the rent so in arrear as aforesaid, and if there shall not then be sufficient distress upon the said premises to countervail the said arrears of rent, we shall then put the said A. B. into possession of the said demised premises, according to the form of the statutes in such case made and provided. As witness our hands this —— day of ——, 18—.

J. P.
Q. R.

---

424. *Record of Proceedings of Justices (ante, 678)*.

—— ⎱
to wit. ⎰ Be it remembered, that on the —— day of ——, A.D. 18—, at ——, in the said [county], [I. K. as the bailiff *or* receiver of] A. B., of —— [gentleman], came before us J. P. and Q. R., Esquires, two of the justices of our lady the Queen assigned to keep the peace in the said [county, riding, division *or* place, *as the case may be*], and also to hear and determine divers felonies, trespasses and other misdemeanors in the said [county *or* riding &c.] committed; and informed us that C. D., late of ——, [labourer] then was tenant to the said A. B. of [*recite information and request in the past tense, to the words* "Taken," *&c., which omit*]; which complaint and request of the said [I. K. as the bailiff *or* receiver of the said] A. B. by us the aforesaid justices being heard, we the said justices (neither of us having any interest in the said demised premises) did in pursuance of the said request, and of the statutes in such case made and provided, on the said —— day of ——, in the year aforesaid, personally go upon the said demised premises and viewed the same, and then and there upon such view found that the said premises had been and then were deserted and left [uncultivated and unoccupied, *or* unoccupied], so as no sufficient distress could be had to countervail the said arrears of rent; and we then and there also found the said yearly rent of £—— to be [a rack rent, *or* full three-fourths of the yearly value of the said demised premises]: And thereupon we did then and there [affix *or* cause to be affixed] on the outer door of the principal messuage on the said demised premises, such outer door being the most notorious part of the said demised premises, a notice in writing under our hands of the said information and request of the said [I. K. as the bailiff *or* receiver of rents of the said] A. B.: And that in pursuance thereof, and of the statutes in such case made and provided, we the said justices (neither of us having any interest in the said demised premises) had then come upon the said demised premises and had then viewed the same; and that we found the same to be deserted and left [uncultivated and unoccupied, *or* unoccupied] so as no sufficient distress could be had to countervail the said arrears of rent; and that we found the said yearly rent of £—— to be [a rack rent, *or* full three-fourths of the yearly value of the said demised premises]; and that we the said justices would return to the said demised premises on the —— day of ——, in the year aforesaid, to take a second view thereof, and that if on such second view the said C. D. or some person on his behalf did not then appear there, and pay the rent so in arrear as aforesaid, and if there should not then be sufficient distress upon the said premises to countervail the said arrears of rent, we should then put the said A. B. into possession of the said demised premises according to the form of the statutes in such case made and provided: And afterwards on the said —— day of ——, in the year aforesaid (being the day in that behalf ap-

pointed in and by the said notice as aforesaid), we the said justices, in pursuance of the said notice, and of the statutes in such case made and provided, did return to the said demised premises and take a second view thereof: And the said C. D. did not, nor did any person on his behalf, then appear and pay the said rent in arrear, and there was then no sufficient distress upon the said premises to countervail the said arrears of rent : Therefore we the said justices (neither of us having any interest in the said demised premises) did then and there put the said A. B. into possession of the said demised premises in pursuance of the statutes in such case made and provided. In witness whereof we the said justices have hereunto set our hands and seals at —— aforesaid, on the —— day of ——, A.D. 18—.

J. P. (L.S.)
Q. R. (L.S.)

---

425. *Information and Request to a Metropolitan Police Magistrate (ante,* 675).

Metropolitan ⎱ The information and request of [I. K. as the bailiff *or* Police District, ⎰ receiver of] A. B., of —— [gentleman], taken and made to wit. ⎰this —— day of ——, A.D. 18—, before me, M. N., Esq., one of her Majesty's justices of the peace for the metropolitan police district, sitting at the police court at —— within the said district, in open court upon the oath of the said [I. K. *or* A. B.], who saith that C. D., late of —— [labourer], is tenant to the said A. B. of [a certain messuage, dwelling-house, lands, tenements and premises, *or as the case may be*], with the appurtenances, situate at ——, in the said county of [Middlesex], and within the said metropolitan police district, under a demise thereof by the said A. B. unto the said C. D. [for —— years, *or* as tenant from year to year] at the yearly rent of £——, payable [quarterly on the —— day of ——, the —— day of ——, the —— day of ——, and the —— day of ——, during the said term, *or as the case may be*]: And that such rent is [a rack rent, *or* full three-fourths of the yearly value of the said demised premises]: And that the said C. D. is now in arrear £—— for [more than (*j*)] one half-year's rent of the said premises, and that the said C. D. hath deserted the said premises and left the same [uncultivated and] unoccupied, so as no sufficient distress can be had to countervail the said arrears of rent: And the said [I. K. as the bailiff *or* receiver of the said] A. B. thereupon requests me the said M. N. (I, the said M. N., having no interest in the said demised premises) to issue my warrant directed to one of the constables of the metropolitan police force, according to the form of the statutes in such case made and provided ; and proof on oath is now given in open court to my satisfaction of the said arrear of rent, and of the said desertion of the said demised premises by the said C. D. as aforesaid, and of the several other matters aforesaid.

Taken before me in open court, at the police court aforesaid, on the —— day of ——, 18—.

M. N.

---

426. *Warrant to Metropolitan Police Constable to view and affix Notice (ante,* 675).

To W. T., one of the constables of the metropolitan police force.

Whereas information and request hath this day been laid before me, M. N., Esq., one of her Majesty's justices of the peace for the metropolitan police district, sitting at the police court at ——, within the said district, in open court by [I. K. as the bailiff *or* receiver of] A. B., of —— [gentleman], stating that C. D., late of ——, is tenant to the said A. B. of [recite infor-

---

(*j*) Half-a-year's rent in arrear is sufficient, 674.

mation to the words "Taken," &c., *which omit*] : Now I the said justice (having no interest in the said demised premises) do hereby direct and require you the said constable to go upon and view the said demised premises and to affix upon the most notorious part thereof a notice in writing, according to the form of the statutes in such case made and provided; and also to return to the said demised premises on the day in that behalf appointed in and by the said notice to take a second view of the said demised premises pursuant to the said statutes. But you are not to deliver possession of the said demised premises to the said A. B., without a further warrant in that behalf.

Given under my hand and seal this —— day of ——, A.D. 18—, at the police court aforesaid.

M. N. (L.S.)

---

427. *Notice to be affixed by the Metropolitan Police* **Constable** (*ante*, 675).

To C. D., late of —— [labourer].

Take notice, that in pursuance of a warrant under the hand and seal of M. N., Esq., one of her Majesty's justices of the peace for the metropolitan police district, bearing date the —— day of ——, A.D. 18—, and made upon the information and request of [I. K. as the bailiff *or* receiver of] A. B. of —— [gentleman], and in pursuance of the statutes in such case made and provided, I the undersigned W. T., being one of the constables of the metropolitan police force, have now come upon and viewed [a certain messuage *or* dwelling-house, lands, tenements and premises, *as in the warrant*], with the appurtenances, situate at ——, in the county of [Middlesex], and within the metropolitan police district, late in your occupation as tenant thereof to the said A. B., but which you have deserted and left [uncultivated and] unoccupied, so as no sufficient distress can be had to countervail the sum of £—— now due and in arrear for the rent thereof for [more than] one half a year : And take notice, that I the said W. T. will return to the said demised premises on the —— day of ——, 18—, to take a second view thereof; and that if on such second view you the said C. D., or some person on your behalf, do not then appear here and pay the rent so in arrear as aforesaid, and if there shall not then be a sufficient distress upon the said demised premises to countervail the said arrears of rent, a further warrant may issue to put the said A. B. into the possession of the said premises, according to the form of the statutes in such case made and provided. As witness my hand this —— day of ——, 18—.

W. T.

---

428. *Return of Metropolitan Police Constable to the* **Warrant** (*ante*, 675).

By virtue of the [above *or* within] warrant, I did on the —— day of ——, 18—, go upon and view the demised premises therein mentioned, and did then affix on [the outer door of the principal messuage on the said demised premises], being the most notorious part of the said premises, a notice in writing according to the form of the statutes in such case made and provided (a duplicate of which notice is hereunto annexed, marked (O)) : And I did afterwards return to the said demised premises on the —— day of ——, 18—, being the day in that behalf appointed in and by the said notice to take, and did then take, a second view of the said demised premises, as by the said warrant I am commanded, but the said C. D. or any person on his behalf did not then appear and pay the said arrears of rent.

The answer of
W. T.,
Police constable.
Date.

(*Duplicate notice to be annexed.*)

429. *Warrant of Possession to Metropolitan Police Constable (ante,* 675).

To W. T., one of the constables of the metropolitan police force. Whereas information and request was on the —— day of ——, A.D. 18—, laid before me, M. N., Esq., one of her Majesty's justices of the peace for the metropolitan police district, then sitting at the police court at ——, within the said district, in open court, by [I. K. as the bailiff *or* receiver of] A. B. of —— [gentleman], stating upon oath that C. D., late of ——, then was tenant to the said A. B. of [*recite information in the past tense to the words* " Taken," *&c., which omit*]: And whereas I the said justice (having no interest in the said demised premises) did on the said —— day of ——, 18—, in pursuance of such request, and of the statutes in such case made and provided, issue my warrant under my hand and seal, bearing date the day and year last aforesaid and directed to you the said W. T., being one of the constables of the metropolitan police force, and did thereby direct and require you the said constable to go upon and view the said demised premises, and to affix upon the most notorious part thereof a notice in writing according to the form of the statutes in such case made and provided; and also to return to the said demised premises on the day in that behalf appointed in and by the said notice to take a second view of the said demised premises pursuant to the said statutes: And whereas you the said constable did [this day *or* on the —— day of —— in the year aforesaid] make a return to me of the due execution of the said warrant, stating that by virtue of the said warrant you did on the —— day of ——, 18—, go upon and view the said demised premises, and that you did then affix on [the outer door of the principal messuage on the said demised premises], being the most notorious part of the said demised premises, a notice in writing according to the form of the statutes in such case made and provided (a duplicate of which notice was annexed to the said return): And that you did afterwards return to the said demised premises on the —— day of ——, 18—, being the day in that behalf appointed in and by the said notice to take, and did then take a second view of the said demised premises as by the said warrant you were commanded, but that the said C. D. or any person on his behalf did not then appear and pay the said arrears of rent: And whereas proof on oath has this day been given in open court in the police court aforesaid, before me the said justice, and to my satisfaction, that the said warrant has been duly executed, and that neither the said C. D. nor any person on his behalf has appeared and paid the said rent in arrear; and that there is not sufficient distress upon the said demised premises to countervail the said arrears of rent: Now I the said M. N. (having no interest in the said demised premises) do hereby direct and require you the said constable forthwith to put the said A. B. into the possession of the said demised premises in pursuance of the statutes in such case made and provided.

Given under my hand and seal this —— day of ——, A.D. 18—, at the police court aforesaid.

M. N. (L.S.)

─────────

430. *Return of Metropolitan Police Constable to the Warrant of Possession (ante,* 675).

By virtue of the [above *or* within] warrant, I did, on the —— day of ——, in the year of our Lord 18—, put the said A. B. into possession of the demised premises in the said warrant mentioned, in pursuance of the statutes in such case made and provided.

The answer of
W. T.,
Police constable.
Date.

─────────

431. *Record of Proceedings of a Metropolitan Police Magistrate, under 3 & 4 Vict. c. 84, s. 13 (ante, 675).*

Metropolitan ⎫ Be it remembered, that on the —— day of ——,
Police District, ⎬ A.D. 18—, [I. K. as the bailiff *or* receiver of] A. B. of
   to wit. ⎭ ——, [gentleman,] came before me, M. N., Esq., one of
the justices of our lady the Queen, assigned to keep the peace in the said
metropolitan police district, and also to hear and determine divers felonies,
trespasses and other misdemeanors in the said district committed, I the
said justice then sitting at the police court at ——, within the said district,
and then and there in open court, upon his oath, informed me that C. D.,
late of ——, [labourer,] then was tenant to the said A. B. of [*recite information and request in the past tense, to the words* "Taken," &c., *which omit*] : which
complaint and request of the said [I. K. as the bailiff *or* receiver of the said]
A. B. being heard, I, the said justice (having no interest in the said
demised premises), did on the said —— day of ——, 18—, in pursuance of
such request and of the statutes in such case made and provided, issue my
warrant under my hand and seal, bearing date the day and year last aforesaid, and directed to W. T., then being one of the constables of the metropolitan police force; and I the said justice did in and by the said warrant direct
and require the said constable to go upon and view the said demised premises, and to affix upon the most notorious part thereof a notice in writing,
according to the form of the statutes in such case made and provided, and
also to return to the said demised premises on the day in that behalf
appointed in and by the said notice, to take a second view of the said
demised premises, pursuant to the said statutes : And afterwards, on the
—— day of ——, in the year aforesaid, the said constable made a return to
me, the said justice, of the due execution of the said warrant by him, stating
that by virtue of the said warrant he did, on the —— day of ——, 18—, go upon
and view the said demised premises, and that he did then affix on [the outer
door of the principal messuage on the said demised premises], being the
most notorious part of the said demised premises, a notice in writing, according to the form of the statutes in such case made and provided (a duplicate of which notice was annexed to the said return), and that he did afterwards return to the said demised premises on the —— day of ——, 18—,
being the day in that behalf appointed in and by the said notice to take,
and did then take a second view of the said demised premises as by the said
warrant he was commanded ; but that the said C. D., or any person on his
behalf, did not then appear and pay the said arrears of rent : And afterwards,
on the —— day of ——, in the year aforesaid, proof on oath was given
before me, the said justice, in open court at the police court aforesaid, and
to my satisfaction, that the said warrant had been duly executed, and that
neither the said C. D. nor any person in his behalf had appeared and paid
the said rent in arrear, and that there was not then sufficient distress upon
the said demised premises to countervail the said arrears of rent; whereupon I, the said justice (having no interest in the said demised premises),
did, on the said —— day of ——, in the year aforesaid, in pursuance of the
statutes in such case made and provided, issue my warrant under my
hand and seal, bearing date the day and year last aforesaid, and directed to
the said W. T., then being one of the constables of the said metropolitan
police force, and did thereby direct and require the said constable forthwith
to put the said A. B. into the possession of the said demised premises, in
pursuance of the statutes in such case made and provided : And afterwards,
on the —— day of ——, in the year aforesaid, the said constable made a
return to me, the said justice, that by virtue of the said warrant, he the said
constable did, on the —— day of ——, in the year of our Lord 18—, put
the said A. B. into possession of the said demised premises, in pursuance of
the statutes in such case made and provided : *In witness* whereof, I, the said

justice, have hereunto set my hand and seal at the police court aforesaid, on the —— day of ——, A.D. 18—.

M. N. (L.s.)

---

432. *Notice of intended Application to the Justices of Assize, for an Order of Restitution, &c. (ante, 679).*

Take notice, that on the first day of the next assizes, to be holden at ——, in and for the county of ——, or so soon after as counsel can be heard, an application will be made to her Majesty's justices assigned to take the assizes in and for the said county, on behalf of C. D., late of ——, [labourer,] pursuant to the statutes 11 Geo. 2, c. 19, s. 17, and 59 Geo. 3, c. 52, for an order, that the proceedings of J. P. and Q. R., Esqrs., two of her Majesty's justices of the peace for the [county, riding, &c.] of ——, under and by virtue whereof A. B., on the —— day of —— [last *or* instant], obtained possession of [a certain messuage *or* dwelling-house, lands, tenements and premises, *or as the case may be*], with the appurtenances, situate at ——, in the said [county *or* riding, &c.] of ——, lately in the occupation of the said C. D., may be reversed or set aside; and that the said A. B. forthwith make restitution to the said C. D. of the possession of the said premises, with the appurtenances; and that the sheriff of the said county of —— cause such restitution to be made; and that the said A. B. pay to the said C. D. his costs and expenses of and incident to the said application. Dated this —— day of ——, 18—.

Yours, &c.

To Mr. A. B. and also to   C. D. [*or* E. F. of ——,
J. P. & Q. R., Esqrs.   Attorney for the said C. D.]

---

433. *Affidavit of Service of such Notice (ante, 679).*

I, G. H., clerk to E. F. of ——, attorney at law, make oath and say:—

1. That I did, on the —— day of —— instant, [personally] serve A. B., the person named in the notice hereunto annexed, marked (O), with a duplicate copy of the said notice, signed by C. D. therein named, [*if the service were not personal, omit the word* "personally," *and say*,] By delivering the said duplicate copy to, and leaving the same with the [wife, *or* son, *or* daughter, *or* man servant, *or* female servant, *as the case may be*] of the said A. B. at his dwelling-house, situate at ——, in the county of ——, [*repeat this as to each magistrate*].

Sworn at ——, in the county of ——, on
     the —— day of ——, 18—, before me,   G. H.
              M. N.
     A justice of the peace for the county of ——.

---

434. *Order Nisi upon an Appeal made to the Justices of Assize (ante, 679).*

Ex parte   Upon the application of C. D., made in pursuance of the
   C. D.   statutes 11 Geo. 2, c. 19, s. 17, and 57 Geo. 3, c. 52, and upon hearing Mr. ——, of counsel for the said C. D., and upon reading the affidavit of the said C. D. [*or* the several affidavits of ——, and ——, and the paper writings thereunto respectively annexed], we the undersigned, being her Majesty's justices assigned to take the present assizes in and for the [county] of ——, do hereby order that A. B. and also J. P. & Q. R., Esqrs., two of her Majesty's justices of the peace for the [county *or* riding, &c.] of ——, upon notice hereof to be given to them respectively, do appear before us at ——, in the said [county] of ——, on the —— day of —— [instant

or next], and show cause why the proceedings of the said **J. P.** and **Q. R.,** as such justices as aforesaid, under and by virtue whereof the said **A. B.,** on the —— day of —— last, obtained possession of [a certain messuage *or* dwelling-house, lands, tenements and premises, *or as the case may be*], with the appurtenances, situate at ——, in the [county *or* riding, &c.] of ——, lately in the occupation of the said **C. D.,** should not be reversed or set aside : And why the said **A. B.** should not forthwith make restitution to the said **C. D.** of the possession of the said premises, with the appurtenances : And why the sheriff of the said [county] of —— should not cause such restitution to be made : And why the said **A. B.** should not pay to the said **C. D.** his costs and expenses of and incident to this application.

Signatures of the Judges (*k*).

---

435. *Affidavit of Service of Order Nisi* (*ante*, 679).

I, **G. H.,** clerk to **E. F.,** of ——, attorney at law, make oath and say :—

1. That I did, on the —— day of —— instant, [personally] serve **A. B.,** the person named in a certain order, a true copy whereof is hereunto annexed, marked (O), with a true copy of the said order: [*If the service were not personal, omit the word "*personally,*" and say,*] By delivering the said last-mentioned copy to, and leaving the same with the [wife, *or* son, *or* daughter, *or* man servant, *or* female servant, *as the case may be*,] of the said **A. B.,** at his dwelling-house, situate at ——, in the county of ——, [*repeat this as to each magistrate, numbering each paragraph*].

Sworn, &c. (*ante*, 849).

G. H.

---

436. *Order Absolute* (*ante*, 680).

Ex parte ⎰ Upon the application of **C. D.,** made in pursuance of the
C. D. ⎱ statutes 11 Geo. 2, c. 19, s. 17, and 57 Geo. 3, c. 52, and upon hearing counsel for the said **C. D.,** and also for **A. B.,** and upon reading the several affidavits of —— and —— [and the paper writings thereto respectively annexed], We, the undersigned, being her Majesty's justices assigned to take the present assizes in and for the [county] of ——, do hereby order that the proceedings of **J. P.** and **Q. R.,** Esqrs., two of her Majesty's justices of the peace for the [county *or* riding, &c.] of ——, under and by virtue whereof the said **A. B.,** on the —— day of —— last, obtained possession of [a certain messuage *or* dwelling-house, lands, tenements and premises, *or as the case may be*], with the appurtenances, situate at —— in the said [county *or* riding, &c.] of ——, lately in the occupation of the said **C. D.,** be and the same are hereby reversed and set aside : And we further order that the said **A. B.** do forthwith make restitution to the said **C. D.** of the possession of the said premises, with the appurtenances : And we further order that the sheriff of the said [county] of —— do cause such restitution to be made : And we further order that the said **A. B.** do pay to the said **C. D.** the sum of £ —— for his costs and expenses of and incident to the said application. Dated this —— day of ——, 18—.

Signatures of the Judges (*k*).

(*k*) Not of the associate (*ante*, 679, 680).

437. *Order dismissing the Appeal with Costs (ante, 680).*

Ex parte } Upon the application of C. D., made in pursuance of the
C. D. { statutes 11 Geo. 2, c. 19, s. 17, and 57 Geo. 3, c. 52, and upon
hearing counsel for the said C. D., and also for A. B., and upon reading the
several affidavits of —— and ——, [and the paper writings thereto respectively annexed], We, the undersigned, being her Majesty's justices assigned
to take the present assizes in and for the [county] of ——, do hereby order
that the proceedings of J. P. and Q. R., Esqrs., two of her Majesty's
justices of the peace for the [county or riding, &c.] of ——, under and by
virtue whereof the said A. B., on the —— day of —— last, obtained
possession of [a certain messuage or dwelling-house, lands, tenements and
premises, *or as the case may be*], with the appurtenances, situate at —— in
the said [county or riding, &c.] of ——, lately in the occupation of the
said C. D., be and the same are hereby affirmed : And we further order that
the said C. D. do pay to the said A. B. the sum of £—— (m) for his costs
of the said application, the same being a frivolous appeal within the meaning
of the said statutes. Dated the —— day of ——, 18—.

Signatures of the Judges (n).

438. *Order Nisi upon an Application to the Court of Q. B. or C. P. pursuant to
11 Geo. 2, c. 19, s. 17, and 57 Geo. 3, c. 52 (ante, 679).*

In the [Q. B. or C. P.]

——day, the —— day of ——, A.D. 18—.

Ex parte } Upon the application of C. D., made in pursuance of the
C. D. { statutes 11 Geo. 2, c. 19, s. 17, and 57 Geo. 3, c. 52, and upon
reading the affidavit of the said C. D. [or, the several affidavits of —— and
——, and the paper writings thereunto respectively annexed], It is ordered,
that A. B., and also J. P. and Q. R., Esqrs., two of her Majesty's justices
of the peace for the [county or riding, &c.] of ——, upon notice hereof to
be given to them respectively, do appear before the judges of this court at
Westminster Hall, in the county of Middlesex, on the —— day of ——
[instant or next], and show cause why the proceedings of the said justices,
under and by virtue whereof the said A. B., on the —— day of —— last,
obtained possession of [a certain messuage or dwelling-house, lands, tenements and premises, *or as the case may be*], with the appurtenances, situate
at ——, in the county of Middlesex [or in the city of London], lately in the
occupation of the said C. D., should not be reversed or set aside, and why
the said A. B. should not forthwith make restitution to the said C. D. of the
possession of the said premises, with the appurtenances : And why the
sheriff of the said [county of Middlesex or the sheriffs of the said city of
London] should not cause such restitution to be made : And why the said
A. B. should not pay to the said C. D. his costs and expenses of and incident to this application.

Upon the motion of Mr. ——.

Signatures of the Judges (n).

439. *Order Absolute (ante, 680).*

In the [Q. B. or C. P.]

——day, the —— day of ——, A.D. 18—.

Ex parte } Upon the application of C. D., made in pursuance of the
C. D. { statutes 11 Geo. 2, c. 19, s. 17, and 57 Geo. 3, c. 52, and upon
hearing counsel for the said C. D., and also for A. B., and upon reading the

---

(m) Not exceeding £5 (ante, 680).
(n) Not of the associate (ante, 679, 680).

[order made in this matter on the —— day of ——, instant *or* last and] **the** several affidavits of —— and —— [and the paper writings thereto respectively annexed], We the undersigned justices of her Majesty's **Court of** [Queen's Bench *or* Common Pleas], at Westminster, do hereby **order that** the proceedings of J. P. and Q. R., Esquires, two of her Majesty's **justices** of the peace for the [county of Middlesex *or* city of London], **under and by** virtue whereof the said A. B., on the —— day of —— last, obtained possession of [a certain messuage *or* dwelling-house, lands, tenements **and** premises, *or as the case may be*], with the appurtenances, situate at ——, **in the** said [county of Middlesex *or* city of London], lately in the **occupation of** the said C. D., be and the same are hereby reversed and set aside : **And we** further order that the said A. B. do forthwith make restitution **to the said** C. D. of the possession of the said premises, with the appurtenances: **And** we further order that the [sheriff of the county of Middlesex, *or* **sheriffs of** the city of London] do cause such restitution to be made : And **we further** order that the said A. B. do pay to the said C. D. the sum of £ —— **for his** costs and expenses of and incident to this application.

Mr. —— for the said C. D.

Mr. —— for the said A. B.

Signatures of the Judges (p).

---

440. *Order Nisi to reverse Proceedings of a Metropolitan Police* **Magistrate** (*ante*, 675).

In the [Q. B. *or* C. P.]

—— day, the —— day of ——, A.D. 18—.

Ex parte) Upon the application of C. D., made in pursuance of **the**
  C. D.) statutes 11 Geo. 2, c. 19, s. 17, 57 Geo. 3, c. 52, and 3 & 4 **Vict.** c. 84, s. 13, and upon reading the affidavit of the said C. D. [*or* the **several** affidavits of —— and ——, and the paper writings thereunto **respectively** annexed], It is ordered, that A. B. and also M. N., Esq., one of the **magistrates** for the metropolitan police district, upon notice hereof to **be given to** them respectively do appear [&c. *as ante, No.* 438, *substituting* **the words** " police magistrate" *for* "justices"].

---

441. *Order Absolute* (*ante*, 675).

In the [Q. B. *or* C. P.]

—— day, the —— day of ——, A.D. 18—.

Ex parte) Upon the application of C. D., made in pursuance of **the**
  C. D.) statutes 11 Geo. 2, c. 19, s. 17, 57 Geo. 3, c. 52, and 3 & 4 Vict. c. 84, s. 13, and upon hearing counsel for the said C. D., **and also for** A. B., and upon reading [&c., *as ante, No.* 439].

---

442. *Order dismissing the Appeal with Costs* (*ante*, 675).

In the [Q. B. *or* C. P.]

—— day, the —— day of ——, A.D. 18—.

Ex parte) Upon the application of C. D., made in pursuance **of the**
  C. D.) statutes 11 Geo. 2, c. 19. s. 17, 57 Geo. 3, c. 52, **and 3 & 4** Vict. c. 84, s. 13, and upon hearing counsel for the said C. D., **and also for** A. B., and upon reading the several affidavits of —— and —— [**and the** paper writings thereto respectively annexed], We the undersigned **justices of** her Majesty's Court of [Queen's Bench *or* Common Pleas], at **Westminster,** do hereby order that the proceedings of M. N., Esq., one of **the police** magistrates acting at ——, within the metropolitan police district, **under and** by virtue whereof [*remainder as ante, No.* 437].

Signatures of the Judges (p).

(p) Not of the associate or master, (*ante*, 679, 680).

443. *Notice to quit a Parish or Town House, pursuant to 59 Geo. 3, c. 12, s. 24* (*ante,* 683).

To I. K. of ——.

Pursuant to the statute passed in the 59th year of the reign of King George the Third, intituled " An Act to amend the Laws for the Relief of the Poor," we hereby give you notice to quit the [parish *or* town house *or* tenement, *or* dwelling, *describe it correctly*], belonging to [*or* provided by, *or* at the charge of] the parish of ——, in the county of ——, for the habitation of the poor thereof, situate in the said parish of —— [*or as the case may be*], and which you have been permitted to occupy, [*or* into which you have unlawfully intruded yourself], and to deliver up the possession thereof to the said churchwardens and overseers of the poor of the said parish of ——, within one month after this notice and demand in writing for that purpose. Dated this —— day of ——, 18—.

A. B. }	Churchwardens of the
C. D. }	above parish.
E. F. }	Overseers of the poor
G. H. }	of the said parish.

N.B.—*To be signed by the churchwardens and overseers, or the major part of them, and addressed and delivered to the person in possession, or, in his or her absence, affixed on some notorious part of the premises* (ante, 681, 683). *A duplicate or examined copy should be kept for proof of service.*

---

444. *Notice to quit Parish Land, pursuant to 59 Geo. 3, c. 12, s. 25* (*ante,* 683).

To I. K. of ——.

Pursuant to the statute passed in the 59th year of the reign of King George the Third, intituled " An Act to amend the Laws for the Relief of the Poor," we hereby give you notice to quit all that piece of parish land, containing [*twenty-five perches*], little more or less, situate in the parish of ——, in the county of ——, being land [appropriated *or* purchased, *or* taken] under the authority of the above-mentioned act, for the employment of the poor of the [said] parish of ——, [*or say,* being land belonging to the said parish of ——, *or* being land belonging to the churchwardens and overseers of the poor of the said parish of ——, *as the case may be,*] and which land was heretofore let to you, for your own occupation, for a term which has expired, [*or say,* and into which land you have unlawfully entered upon and taken possession, *or* of which land you unlawfully hold possession], and to deliver up possession thereof to the churchwardens and overseers of the poor of the said parish of ——, within one month after this notice, and demand in writing for that purpose.

A. B. }	Churchwardens of the
C. D. }	above parish.
E. F. }	Overseers of the poor
G. H. }	of the said parish.

See note to No. 443.

Nos. 445 *to* 448 *are framed with reference to No.* 443, *but may easily be altered so as to agree with the above notice ; so where the proceedings are by the guardians of any union or parish, and not by the churchwardens or overseers.*

---

445. *Information before Justices, pursuant to 59 Geo. 3, c. 12, ss. 24, 25* (*ante,* 684).

County of } The information and complaint of ——, [one] of the
—— } [churchwardens *or* overseers of the poor] of the parish of

——, in the said county, taken and made(r) this —— day of ——, in the year of our Lord 18—, before [me, J. P., Esq., one(s), *or* us, J. P. and Q. R., Esqrs., two] of her Majesty's justices of the peace in and for the said county, who saith that I. K., a poor person residing in the parish of ——, in the said county, [having been permitted to occupy, *or* having unlawfully intruded himself into] a [parish *or* town house, *or* tenement, *or* dwelling, *as the case may be*, belonging to *or* having been provided by, *or* at the charge of the said parish of ——, for the habitation of the poor thereof, situate in the said parish of ——, *or as the case may be*], has [refused *or* neglected] to quit the same and deliver up the possession thereof to the churchwardens and overseers of the poor of the said parish of ——, within one month after notice, and demand in writing for that purpose, signed by [the major part of] the churchwardens and overseers of the poor of the said parish, and [delivered to him, the said I. K., personally, *or* in the absence of the said I. K. affixed on the front door, *or some notorious part, describing it*, of the said house, *or* tenement, *or* dwelling, *as the case may be*, being a notorious part of the said premises]: The said complainant, therefore, prays such redress in the premises as to law does appertain.

Taken before me [*or* us] the justice [*or* justices] aforesaid, at ——, in the said county, on the day and year first above mentioned.

J. P.

[Q. R.]

——

446. *Summons thereon (ante, 684).*

County of ⎬ To I. K., of ——, [labourer]: Whereas ——, [one] of —— ⎭ the [churchwardens *or* overseers of the poor] of the parish of ——, in the said county, has this day preferred an information and complaint against you, the said I. K., before [me, J. P., Esq., one, *or* us, J. P. and Q. R., Esqrs., two] of her Majesty's justices of the peace, in and for the said county: For that you, the said I. K., being a poor person residing in the parish of ——, in the said county, and [having been permitted to occupy, *or* having unlawfully intruded yourself into] a [parish *or* town house, tenement *or* dwelling, *describe it as in the information*, belonging to *or* having been provided by *or* at the charge of the said parish of ——, for the habitation of the poor thereof, situate in the said parish of ——, *or as the case may be*], have [refused *or* neglected] to quit the same and deliver up the possession thereof to the churchwardens and overseers of the poor of the said parish of ——, within one month after notice and demand in writing for that purpose, signed by [the major part of] the churchwardens and overseers of the poor of the said parish, and [delivered to you the said I. K. personally, *or* in the absence of you, the said I. K., affixed on the front door of the said house, *or* tenement, *or* dwelling, *as in the information*, being a notorious part of the said premises].

These are therefore to command you, in her Majesty's name, to be and appear on the —— day of —— [instant *or* next], at —— o'clock in the —— noon, at ——, in the said county, before [me *or* us], or such justices of the peace for the said county as may then be there, to answer the said complaint, and to be further dealt with according to law. Given under [my hand and

——

(r) The information and complaint need not be made *on oath* (*Baston v. Carew*, 3 B. & C. 649 ; *ante*, 684), nor signed by the complainant.

(s) By 3 Geo. 4, c. 23, s. 2, one justice is competent to receive the information and issue the summons.

seal *or* our hands and seals], this —— day of ——, A.D. 18—, at ——, in the county aforesaid.

J. P. (L.S.)

[Q. R.] (L.S.)

N.B.—*This summons must be delivered to I. K. personally, or, in his absence, affixed on the premises seven days at least, i. e., seven clear days, before the time appointed for the hearing* (ante, 681, 684). *A duplicate or examined copy should be kept for proof of service.*

---

447. *Warrant for Delivery of Possession* (ante, 684).

County of } To the chief constable of the hundred of ——, to the —— } petty constables of the parish of ——, in the said hundred and county, and to each and every of them:

Whereas ——, [one] of the [churchwardens *or* overseers of the poor] of the parish of ——, in the said county, did on the —— day of —— last, prefer an information and complaint against I. K., before [me, J. P., Esq., one, *or* us, J. P. & Q. R., Esqrs. two] of her Majesty's justices of the peace in and for the said county: For that the said I. K., being a poor person residing in the parish of ——, in the said county, and [having been permitted to occupy *or* having unlawfully intruded himself into] a [parish *or* town house *or* tenement, *or* dwelling, *describe it as in the information*, belonging to *or* provided by, *or* at the charge of the said parish of ——, for the habitation of the poor thereof, situate in the said parish of ——, *or as the case may be*], had [refused *or* neglected] to quit the same and deliver up the possession thereof to the churchwardens and overseers of the poor of the said parish of —— within one month after notice and demand in writing for that purpose, signed by [the major part of] the churchwardens and overseers of the poor of the said parish, and [delivered to him, the said I. K. personally, *or* in the absence of him, the said I. K. affixed on the front door of the said house, *as in the information*, being a notorious part of the said premises]: And whereas, upon the appearance of the said I. K. (*t*) this day before us, in pursuance of a summons for that purpose, we the said justices have proceeded to hear and determine the matter of the said complaint: And we have found and adjudged, and do find and adjudge the same to be true: *We* do therefore charge and command you, that you without delay go to and cause possession of the premises in question to be delivered to the churchwardens and overseers of the poor of the said parish of ——, or to some of them, pursuant to the statute in such case made and provided: Herein fail not. Given under our hands and seals at ——, in the said county of ——, on the —— day of ——, A.D. 18—.

J. P. (L.S.)

[Q. R.] (L.S.)

(*t*) If I. K. did not appear, omit the statement of his appearance, and in lieu thereof say: "And whereas, on the —— day of —— last, a summons was duly issued under the hand of me the said J. P., as such justice as aforesaid [*or* under the hands of us, the said J. P. and Q. R. as such justices as aforesaid], requiring the said I. K. to appear before us, the said justices, this day at ——, in the said county, to answer unto the said complaint: And it appears to us, the said justices, upon the oath of I. S., constable of the parish of —— aforesaid, that he the said I. S. [did duly deliver the said summons to the said I. K. personally, on the —— day of —— instant, being seven days at the least before the time appointed for the hearing of the said complaint [*or* did use his best endeavours to deliver the said summons to the said I. K., and that in the absence of the said I. K. he the said I. S. did

448. *Return thereto (ante, 684).*

By virtue of the [above *or* within] warrant, I did on the —— day of
——, in the year of our Lord 18—, go to and cause possession of the premises in the said warrant mentioned to be delivered to ——, [one of] the
churchwardens and —— [one of] the overseers of the poor of the parish of
——, in the said warrant mentioned, pursuant to the statute in such case
made and provided.

The answer of
W. T.,
Chief constable of the hundred of ——,
or
Petty constable of the parish of ——,
Date.

---

449. *Declaration in Trespass for a Forcible Entry or Forcible Detainer, under 8 Hen. 6, c. 9, s. 6 (ante, 691).*

In the [Q. B., C. P. *or* Exch.]

The —— day of ——, A.D. 18—.

Venue (*u*), } A. B., by ——, his attorney, sues C. D.: For that at the
to wit. { time of the committing of the trespasses hereinafter next
mentioned, the plaintiff was seised (*x*) in his demesne [as of fee, *or* as of fee
tail, *or if of special entail say*, as of fee tail, (that is to say) to him and the
heirs lawfully issuing of the body of the plaintiff on the body of —— to be
begotten, *or* of the bodies of the plaintiff and of —— his wife, *or if for life
say*, as of freehold for the term of his natural life, *or* for the term of the
natural life of E. F.] of and in a certain dwelling-house [*or* close called
Greenacre, or describe it by abuttals as in an ordinary action of trespass, ante,
829], with the appurtenances, situate in [—— street, in] the parish
of ——, in the county of ——, [and known as No. —— in the said street]:
And the plaintiff being so seised thereof, the defendant not regarding the
statute passed in the eighth year of the reign of Henry the Sixth, late King
of England, intituled "The Duty of Justices of Peace where Land is
entered upon or detained with Force," unlawfully [and with strong hand,
and in a forcible manner (*y*)] broke and entered the said [messuage *or*
close] of the plaintiff, and then unlawfully, with strong hand and in a
forcible manner, put out and disseised the plaintiff thereof, and with strong
hand and in a forcible manner kept and continued the plaintiff so put out
and disseised for a long time : [And during that time the defendant, *here*

---

affix *or* cause to be affixed the said summons on the front door of the said
house *or* tenement, *or* dwelling, *as the case may be*, on the —— day of ——
instant, being seven days, at the least, before the time appointed for hearing
the said complaint :] But the said I. K. has neglected to appear according
to the said summons: We the said justices have proceeded to hear and
determine, [*&c., as above to the end*].

(*u*) The venue is local, and must be laid in the county or city wherein
the property is situate.

(*x*) It seems enough to say that the plaintiff was " seised" (without
more), because any seisin, even *pur autre vie*, is sufficient; *Rex* v. *Hoare*,
6 M. & S. 266; but the plaintiff must appear to be a freeholder, otherwise
he cannot have been *disseised ; Cole* v. *Eagle*, 8 B. & C. 409 (*ante*, 691).

(*y*) If the entry were peaceable, omit these words and complain only of
an *unlawful* entry and a *forcible detainer* (*ante*, 690).

state any special damage done to the property, 1 *Hawk. P. C., c.* 64; *but see* 2 *Chit. Pl.* 659, 7*th edit.*] And the plaintiff claims £——(*z*).

---

450. *Plea of Not Guilty by Statute (ante,* 691).

Same as ante, No. 60, *with the like marginal note.*

---

451. *Indictment at Common Law for a Forcible Entry and Detainer (ante,* 685).

Venue, } The jurors for our lady the Queen upon their oath present,
to wit. } That C. D., E. F., G. H. and I. K., together with divers other persons to the number of six or more, to the jurors aforesaid unknown, on the —— day of ——, A.D. 18—, with force and arms, and with strong hand, and in a violent and forcible manner, unlawfully did break and enter into a certain [dwelling-house *or* messuage, *or* barn *or* close of land called Greenacre, *or as the case may be*], with the appurtenances, situate and being in [—— street, in] the parish of ——, in the county aforesaid, [and called and known as No. —— in the said street], then and there being in the peaceable possession of one A. B. : And did then and there, with force and arms, and with strong hand and in a violent and forcible manner, unlawfully eject, expel, put out and amove the said A. B. from the peaceable possession of the said [dwelling-house], with the appurtenances : And did then and there, to wit, from the day and year aforesaid until the day of the taking of this inquisition, with force and arms and with strong hand, unlawfully and injuriously keep out the said A. B. from the possession of the said [dwelling-house], with the appurtenances, and still do so keep out the said A. B. therefrom : To the great damage of the said A. B., and against the peace of our said lady the Queen, her crown and dignity.

---

452. *Indictment under* 8 *Hen.* 6, *c.* 9, *or* 21 *Jac.* 1, *c.* 15, *for a Forcible Entry and Detainer, or for a Forcible Detainer after an Unlawful Entry (ante,* 691, 692).

Venue, } The jurors for our lady the Queen upon their oath present,
to wit. } That A. B., on the —— day of ——, A.D. 18—, was seised in his demesne [as of fee, *or* as of fee tail, *or if of special entail say,* as of fee tail, (that is to say) to him and the heirs lawfully issuing of the body of the said A. B. on the body of —— to be begotten, *or* of the bodies of the said A. B. and —— his wife, *or if for life only say,* as of freehold for the term of his natural life, *or* for the term of the natural life of E. F., *or if A. B. were only possessed for a term of years, omit the words* " seised in his demesne" *and say,* possessed for a term of years then and still unexpired and undetermined] of and in [*describe the property as in an ejectment, ex. gr.*] a certain messuage, with the appurtenances, situate and being in [—— street, in] the parish of ——, in the [county] aforesaid, [and called and known as No. —— in the said street] : And the said A. B. being so [seised *or* possessed] thereof, C. D., on the day and year aforesaid, with force and arms [and with strong hand and in a forcible manner (*a*)], unlawfully did break

---

(*z*) Claim enough to cover treble damages ; there is no harm in claiming too much, *ante,* 830, n. (*t*).

A second count in trespass *quare clausum fregit* (in the common form) may be added, if thought desirable ; but it may affect the plaintiff's right to treble damages and full costs, charges and expenses under the first count, unless care be taken to assess the damages separately (*ante,* 691).

(*a*) If C. D. entered in a peaceable manner omit these words. *Sir W. Fitzwilliam's case,* Cro. Jac. 19 ; *Ford's case,* id. 151.

and enter into the said [messuage], with the appurtenances, and then and there with strong hand and in a forcible manner unlawfully did eject, expel, put out and amove the said A. B. from the [seisin and (*b*)] peaceable possession of the said [messuage], with the appurtenances: And the said A. B. having been so unlawfully [disseised and (*b*)] dispossessed as aforesaid, the said C. D. thenceforth, to wit, from the day and year aforesaid until the day of the taking of this inquisition, with force and arms, [and with strong hand (*c*)], unlawfully and injuriously did keep out the said A. B. from the [seisin and (*b*)] possession of the said [messuage], with the appurtenances, and still doth so keep out the said A. B. therefrom: To the great damage of the said A. B., against the peace of our lady the Queen, and against the form of the statutes in such case made and provided.

---

453. *Writ or Warrant of Restitution upon the finding at Sessions of an Indictment for a Forcible Entry* (ante, 692).

County of ⎱   J. P., Esq., Q. R., Esq., and the Rev. S. T., clerk, [three]
—— ⎰   of the justices of our lady the Queen assigned to keep the peace in the said county, and also to hear and determine divers felonies, trespasses and other misdemeanors in the said county committed; To the sheriff of the said county, greeting: Whereas at the present general quarter sessions of the peace now being holden at —— in and for the said county, before us, the undersigned, and others, justices of our lady the Queen assigned to keep the peace in the said county, and also to hear and determine divers felonies, trespasses and other misdemeanors in the said county committed, upon the oaths of [*names of jurors*], good and lawful men of the said county, sworn and charged to inquire for our said lady the Queen and the body of the said county, it is presented as follows (that is to say), —— shire (to wit): The jurors for our lady the Queen upon their oath present, That [*here copy the indictment* (ante, No. 452), *then proceed thus* (*d*):] These are therefore to will and require, and in her Majesty's name to charge and command you the said sheriff, that, taking with you the power of the county (if it be needful), you go to the said [messuage, *or as the case may be*], situate in the said parish of ——, in the said county, in the above indictment mentioned and described, and the same, with the appurtenances, you cause to be [reseised *or* repossessed], and that you cause the said A. B. to be restored and put into full [seisin and] possession thereof, according as he before the entry aforesaid was [seised *or* possessed], according to the form of the statute in such case made and provided: And this you shall in

---

(*b*) If A. B. be not *seised*, but only possessed for a term of years, omit these words.

(*c*) If a forcible entry be charged the subsequent detainers may be unlawful without being forcible; *Andrews* v. *Lord Cromwell,* Cro. Jac. 31. If so, the words " with strong hand" may be omitted in this place; but it is usual to charge both a forcible entry and a forcible detainer, especially if the facts will support both.

(*d*) If defendants have been tried and convicted, here say, " And whereas such proceedings were afterwards had at the said general quarter sessions before us the undersigned and others, justices of our lady the Queen assigned to keep the peace in the said county, and also to hear and determine divers felonies, trespasses and other misdemeanors in the said county committed upon the said indictment, that the said [*defendants' names*], by a jury of the country taken between our said lady the Queen and the said [*defendants' names*], stand convicted of the premises in the said indictment above specified and charged upon [them] in manner and form as in and by the said indictment is above alleged against [them], as appears by the record of the said court of general quarter sessions."

nowise omit upon the peril that shall thereof ensue. Given under our hands and seals in open session at ——, in the said county, on the —— day of ——, in the year of our Lord 18—.

$$\begin{array}{c} \text{J. P. (L.s.)}\\ \text{Q. R. (L.s.)}\\ \text{S. T. (L.s.)} \end{array}$$

N.B.—This form should not be used without due consideration, as it is not to be found elsewhere, although the writ is mentioned in several works of authority (ante, 692). *See the form, post, No.* 460. *For forms of a writ of restitution in Q. B., after indictment for a forcible entry removed into that court by certiorari, and the defendant convicted, see* 2 *Gude's Crown Off. Prac.* 634.

---

454. *Record of a Conviction for a Forcible Detainer on View, and Commitment thereon* (ante, 693).

See 3 Burn's J., 93—95 (29th edit.); 1 Arch. J., 355, 356.

---

455. *Summons to Defendant to appear before Justices and a Jury* (ante, 693).

To C. D., of —— [labourer].

Whereas complaint hath this day been made before the undersigned, [one] of her Majesty's justices of the peace in and for the county of ——, for that A. B. on the —— day of ——, A.D. 18—, was seised [*state his seisin or possession as in an indictment, ante, No.* 452]: And the said A. B. being so [*seised or possessed*] thereof, you the said C. D. on the day and year aforesaid with force and arms [and with strong hand and in a forcible manner(*e*)] unlawfully did break and enter into the said [messuage], with the appurtenances, and then and there with strong hand and in a forcible manner unlawfully did eject, expel, put out and amove the said A. B. from the [seisin and] peaceable possession of the said [messuage], with the appurtenances: And the said A. B. having been so unlawfully [disseised and] dispossessed as aforesaid, you the said C. D. thenceforth, to wit, from the day and year last aforesaid until the making of the said complaint on this day, with force and arms and with strong hand unlawfully and injuriously did keep out the said A. B. from the [seisin and] possession of the said [messuage], with the appurtenances, and still do keep out the said A. B. therefrom: These are therefore to command you, in her Majesty's name, to be and appear on —— at —— o'clock in the forenoon at ——, before me or such justices of the peace for the said county as may then be there, and a jury of the said county, to answer to the said complaint, and to be further dealt with according to law.

Given under my hand and seal this —— day of ——, in the year of our Lord ——, at —— in the [county] aforesaid.

J. P. (L.s.)

---

456. *Precept of a Justice to the Sheriff to summon a Jury* (ante, 693).

County of } J. P., Esq., one of the justices of our lady the Queen as-
——. } signed to keep the peace in the said county, and also to hear and determine divers felonies, trespasses and other misdemeanors in the said county committed, to the sheriff of the said county, greeting: On behalf of our said lady the Queen I command you, that you cause to come before me at —— in the county aforesaid, on the —— day of —— [instant or next], twenty-four sufficient and indifferent men of the neighbourhood of ——, in the county aforesaid, every one of whom shall have lands or tenements of forty shillings yearly at the least, above reprises, to inquire upon

---

(*e*) If defendant entered peaceably, but unlawfully, omit the words within brackets.

their oaths for our said lady the Queen of a certain [entry with strong hand, *or* unlawful entry and detainer with strong hand] (as it is said) into the [dwelling-house, *or* messuage, *or* land, *as the case may be*] of one A. B. at —— aforesaid, in the county aforesaid, against the form of the statute in such case made and provided: And you are to return upon every of the jurors by you in this behalf to be impannelled twenty shillings of issues at the aforesaid day ; and have you then there this precept: And this you shall in nowise omit, upon the peril that shall thereof ensue.

Witness the said J. P., at ——, in the county aforesaid, the —— day of ——, A.D. 18—.   J. P.

---

457. *The Jurors' Oath (ante, 693).*
The Foreman's Oath.

You shall true inquiry and presentment make of all such things as shall come before you concerning [a forcible entry and detainer *or* an unlawful entry and forcible detainer] said to have been lately committed in the [dwelling-house, *or* messuage, *or* land] of A. B., at —— in this county : You shall spare no one for favour or affection, nor grieve any one for hatred or ill will, but proceed herein according to the best of your knowledge, and according to the evidence that shall be given to you : So help you God.

The other Jurors' Oath.

The oath that E. F., your foreman, hath taken on his part, you and every of you shall truly observe and keep on your parts : So help you God.

---

458. *The Inquisition or Finding of the Jury (ante, 694).*

County of⎰   An inquisition for our sovereign lady the Queen indented ——. ⎱ and taken at —— in the said county, on the —— day of ——, A.D. 18—, by the oaths of [*names of twelve or more jurors*], good and lawful men of the said county, before J. P., Esq., one [*or* J. P., Esq., and Q. R., Esq., two] of the justices of our said lady the Queen assigned to keep the peace in the said county, and also to hear and determine divers felonies, trespasses and other misdemeanors in the same county committed, who say upon their oaths severally, that A. B., on the —— day of ——, A.D. 18—, was [seised, &c., *here proceed exactly as in an indictment, ante*, No. 452, *to the end, then go on thus*] :—

We whose names are hereunto set, being the jurors aforesaid, do upon the evidence now produced before us find the inquisition aforesaid true.

Signatures of the Jury.

---

459. *Indorsement by Justices on the Inquisition (ante, 694).*

County of ⎰   Be it remembered, that J. P. and Q. R., Esqrs., justices ——. ⎱ [*or* J. P., Esq., one of the justices] in the within inquisition named, did on this —— day of ——, A.D. 18—, personally go to the [dwelling-house, *or* messuage, *or* land] and other the premises in the within written inquisition mentioned, and did [reseise *or* repossess], restore and put the within-named A. B. into full [seisin and] possession thereof, according as he before the [forcible entry and detainer, *or* unlawful entry and forcible detainer] thereof by C. D. in the said inquisition mentioned was [seised *or* possessed], according to the form of the statutes in such case made and provided.

Given at ——, in the county of ——, under [our hands and seals, *or* my hand and seal] the —— day of ——, A.D. 18—.

460. *Warrant to the Sheriff for Restitution* (*ante*, 694).

County of } J. P., Esq., one of the justices of our lady the Queen as-
———. { signed to keep the peace in the said county, and also to hear
and determine divers felonies, trespasses and other misdemeanors in the
said county committed, to the sheriff of the said county, greeting: Whereas
by an inquisition indented and taken before me the justice aforesaid [and
Q. R., Esq., one other of the said justices] at ——, in the county aforesaid,
on the —— day of ——, A.D. 18—, upon the oaths of [*names of jurors*] good,
and lawful men of the said county, and by virtue of the statutes made and
provided in cases of forcible entry and detainer, it is found that —*recite the
finding as in No.* 458, *in the past tense, to the words* "against the form of the
statutes in such case made and provided," *inclusive, then proceed thus :*—
Therefore on behalf of our sovereign lady the Queen I charge and command
you, that taking with you the power of the county (if it be needful) you go
to the said [dwelling-house, *or as the case may be*], and the same, with the
appurtenances, you cause to be [reseised *or* repossessed]; and that you
cause the said A. B. to be restored and put into full [seisin and] possession
thereof, according as he before the entry aforesaid was [seised *or* possessed]
according to the form of the said statutes: And this you shall in nowise
omit, upon the peril that shall thereof ensue.

Given under my hand and seal at — - , in the said county, on the ——
day of ——, in the year of our Lord 18—.

J. P. (L.S.)

*The sheriff's return to this warrant should agree in substance with the next
form, and see* ante, No. 430.

———

461. *Memorandum of Warrant, and what has been done under it* (*ante*, 694).

County of } Be it remembered, that on the —— day of ——, A.D. 18—,
———. { I. K., Esq., sheriff of the county aforesaid, did under and by
virtue of a warrant duly granted on the within inquisition, go to the [dwel-
ling-house, *or* messuage, *or* land], and other the premises in the within inquisition mentioned, and did [reseise *or* repossess], restore and put the
within-named A. B. into full [seisin and] possession thereof, according as
he before the [forcible entry and detainer, *or* unlawful entry and forcible
detainer] thereof by the said C. D. in the said inquisition mentioned was
[seised *or* possessed] according to the form of the statutes in such case made
and provided.

Given at —-, in the county of ——, under [our hands and seals, *or* my
hand and seal] (we *or* I being two *or* one of the justices within mentioned)
the —— day of ——, A.D. 18—.

Signatures and seals.

To be indorsed on the inquisition.

INDEX.

A.

Abatement of Suit—see "*Suggestions of Deaths*," &c. 350.

Abroad, service of writ when tenant abroad, 107.

Acceptance of subsequent Rent, waiver of notice to quit, 55; waiver of forfeiture, 408.

Acknowledgment of Title, to bar the Statute of Limitations, 17; form, 700.

Action without any Pleadings, special case stated, 65.

Acts of Occupiers, 231.

Acts of Ownership, 246.

Actual Ouster—when to be proved, 290; what amounts to, 291.

Actual Possession—legal right to, necessary to maintain ejectment, 66, 72, 287.

when and how it may be taken, 67.

Address and Description of Claimants—how obtained, 118.

Address for Service—by parties suing or defending in person, 97, 126; Reg. Prac. H. T. 1853, No. 166..126.

Adjournment of the Trial (17 & 18 Vict. c. 76, s. 19), 303.

Administrator de bonis non, 535.

Administrator with the Will annexed, 535.

Administrators—ejectment by, 533; evidence for plaintiffs, 535; evidence and points for defendant, 536; when the Statute of Limitations begins to run against them, 12; cannot sue before obtaining letters of administration, 534; but may claim from a prior day, 534; if not mentioned in a proviso of re-entry, cannot take advantage of it, 405.

Admissibility of Evidence, whether oral or written, to be decided by the judge, 168; evidence for and against such admissibility to be given *before* the document is read, 169.

Admission of Documents, pursuant to a notice to admit, 150; form, 758; affidavit of signature thereto, 153; forms, 758; effect of admission at the trial, 153; cannot be retracted, 153; primary evidence, 170; form of mutual admissions to save expense of proof of facts not disputed, 758.

Admittance to Copyholds, 621; how proved, 624.

Adverse Possession—doctrine of, abolished, 5, 8.

Advice on Evidence for Plaintiffs, 140; preliminary points to be considered before action commenced, 72.

Advowson—no ejectment for, 92.

Affirmation instead of Oath (17 & 18 Vict. c. 125, ss. 20, 21), 292; by Quakers, Moravians and Separatists, 293; form of affirmation in lieu of affidavit, 708.

C.

Canonry—not recoverable by ejectment, 91.

Case, for an injury to plaintiff's reversion, 64.   See *post*, " *Special Case.*"

Cattle-gates—ejectment for, 90.

Cause List, 275 ; must be watched, 279.

Cellar—ejectment for, 89.

Certainty, necessary in description of the property claimed, 85 ; in a notice
            to defend for part only, 122, 128 ; how objected to, 85 ; former
            modes, 85.

Certificates—for a special jury, 264 ; form, 771.
        to stay judgment or execution, 308.
        that refusal to admit documents was reasonable, 154 ; form, 759.

Cestui que trust—on entry becomes tenant at will to his trustee, 445 ; cannot
            maintain ejectment, 73 ; nor defend ejectment at the suit of his
            trustee, 73, 288 ; relief in equity, 373 ; Statute of Limitations, 14.

Challenges of Jurors, 255, 265—269 ; form of challenge to the array, 771.

Chamber—ejectment for, 88.

Chapel—ejectment for, 451, 604 ; how described in the writ, 89 ; service of
            the writ, 110 ; affidavit of service, 113.

Children, of tenants in possession should not be named in the writ as defend-
            ants, 84 ; service of writ on, 102 ; affidavit of such service, 113 ;
            form, 712.

Choses in Action—devise of, 494, 495.

Church—ejectment for, 601 ; how described in the writ, 89.

Churchwardens and Overseers—ejectment by, 605 ; how described in the
            writ, 94, 607.
        summary proceedings by, to recover parish houses or land, 681.
        may take actual possession when entitled to it, 67, 683.
        service of writ on them, 108.

Claimants or Plaintiffs—must be legally entitled to actual possession, 66, 72,
            73, 287 (see *post*, " *Title*") ; who should sue, 74 ; retainer of attor-
            ney for, 75 ; form, 700 ; how named in the writ, 93 ; title of, how
            to be stated, 93, 285 ; date of title, 94, 288 ; address and description
            of, how obtained, 118 ; forms, 725 ; how named and described in
            an affidavit, 703, n. (*p*), 704, n. (*s*) ; evidence for, generally, in an
            ejectment, 287 ; all may discontinue, 357 ; but not some or one of
            them without leave, 357.

Clear Days—how computed, 364.

Closes—how described in a writ, 89 ; if named the quantity need not be
            mentioned, 89 ; the word "close" or "closes" should not be used
            alone, 89 ; plea in trespass for mesne profits, that close not plain-
            tiff's, 63 ; form, 831.

Coal Mines—ejectment for, 90.

Committee of a Lunatic, 581.

Common Appurtenant may be recovered in ejectment, together with the land,
            but not separately, 91.

Companies—see *post*, " *Corporations ;*" notice to quit by or to, 39 ; ejectment
            by successors for a forfeiture, 406 ; ejectment against railway and
            other companies, 590 ; how described in the writ, 84, 94 ; service
            of the writ, 108 ; affidavit of such service, 113 ; form, 714.

Comparison of disputed Writing (17 & 18 Vict. c. 125, s. 25), 294.

Compensation, for lands taken or injuriously affected by a railway or other company, 590, 595; interests omitted to be purchased through mistake or inadvertence, 597.

Concurrent Rights (Statute of Limitations), 21.

Condition precedent—proof of performance of, 426.

Conditional Limitation of a Term, 402.

Conditions and Provisoes for Re-entry.

Generally, 400, 402; for breaches of covenant, 402; for other acts or events, 402; term sometimes limited conditionally, 402; a mere breach of covenant (not fortified by a proviso for re-entry), not sufficient to support ejectment, 403; how created, 403; to whom reserved, 404; by whom enforced, 405; by the lessor, 405; his heirs, executors or administrators, 405; assignee of reversion or part, 405, 406; remainderman after lease granted in pursuance of a power, 406; coparceners, 406; a company or their successors, 406; how construed, 407; impartially, 407; strictly, 407; "void or voidable," 408; waiver of forfeiture, 408; with knowledge thereof, 409; subsequent or continuing breach, 409; no waiver after ejectment brought, 410; merely lying by, no waiver, 410; particulars of breaches, 120, 410; inspection of lease, 120, 200, 410; relief in equity against forfeiture, 410; emblements after a forfeiture, 410.

In particular Cases—for non-payment of rent, 410; at common law, 400, 410; by statute (15 & 16 Vict. c. 76, s. 210), 401, 415; for not repairing, 401, 422; for waste, 401, 427; for not insuring, 401, 429; for exercising any prohibited trade or business, 401, 432; for assigning or underletting without licence, 401, 434; for impugning lessor's title, 439.

Confession, of action, 358; form, 812; judgment thereon, 358; form, 812.
of error in fact, and reversal of judgment by consent, 371; forms, 826.

Consent to Trial before the court or a judge without a jury, 143; forms, 751.

Construction, of conditions and provisoes for re-entry, 407; impartially, 407; strictly, 407; " void or voidable," 407.

Continual Claim, abolished, 16.

Continuance of Notice of Trial, in London or Middlesex, 148; form, 754.

Continuing Breaches of Covenant, 409; by non-repair, 425; by non-insurance, 430.

Contradictory Statements of an adverse Witness—proof of (17 & 18 Vict. c. 125, s. 23), 293.

Conviction of a Witness — proof of (17 & 18 Vict. c. 125, s. 25), 294.

Coparceners, ejectment by, 286; may sue jointly or severally, 286; except in ejectment for a forfeiture, 406; Statute of Limitations, 17.
appearance and defence by, 130; notice of such defence, 130; form, 734, 735; affidavit denying ouster, 130; form, 735; notice to be entered on the issue and record, 131; forms, 744, 745; actual ouster, when to be proved, 130, 290; what amounts to, 291; if not proved, judgment for defendant, 130, 290.

Copies, Duplicates and Counterparts, 252; attested copies, 252; examined copies, 252; office copies, 253; duplicates and counterparts, 253; copies of court rolls of a manor, 624; of documents to accompany briefs, 275.

Copyholds—ejectment for, 609.

By the Lord, for the whole manor, 611; for part of the demesnes or wastes, 611; for copyholds forfeited, 612; who may sue, 612; who

Forfeiture—continued.
> licence, 615 ; by waste, 616 ; by refusal of rent or services, or of a reasonable fine, 617 ; evidence for plaintiff, 618 ; evidence and points for defendant, 618 ; seizure quousque and ejectment thereon, 619 ; evidence for plaintiff, 620 ; evidence and points for defendant, 621.

> By *Attainder* for treason or felony. See " *Felons*," 875.

Forms of Proceedings, &c.—search under the proper title, ex. gr., affidavits, notices, writs, summonses and orders, rules, issues, judgments, executions, and the like.

Forthwith, meaning of, 116, 424.

Fraud—will procured by, may be avoided, 522.

Frauds—statute of. See *post*, " *Statutes cited*," 29 Car. 2, c. 3.

Fraudulent Conveyance (13 Eliz. c. 5), 544 ; valid as between the parties, 299, 545 ; void as against creditors, 299, 544 ; and purchasers, (27 Eliz. c. 4), 300 ; and assignees in bankruptcy, 543, 545 ; and assignees of an insolvent debtor, 558.

Fraudulent Preferences, 544, 558.

Freebench—ejectment for, 630.

Friendly Societies—now regulated by 18 & 19 Vict. c. 63..589.

Friends and Visitors, of tenants in possession should not be named as defendants in the writ, 76, 84.

Furze—ejectment for, 90.

G.

Garden or Garden Land—ejectment for, 90.

Gazette—when evidence of bankruptcy, &c., 547.

General Issue, " *By Statute* "—plea of, 117, 648, 650 ; form, 724.

Gorse and Furze—ejectment for, 90.

Grantee of Copyholds—ejectment by, 631.

Grass and Aftermath—ejectment for, 90.

Gravel Pits in a Manor, 612.

Growing Crops, 346. See " *Emblements*," 873.

Guardians—ejectment by, 582.

H.

Habeas Corpus for debtors to testify, 198 ; form, 762 ; precipe for, 763 ; affidavit for the writ, 762.

Habere Facias Possessionem. See " *Executions*," 874.

Hay, Grass and Aftermath—ejectment for, 90.

Hearsay, evidence of pedigree, 234.

Heath—ejectment for, 90.

Hedge and Ditch (Boundaries), 242 ; hedge with a ditch on each side, or hedge only, 243.

Heir at Law—ejectment by, 483 ; Inheritance Act (3 & 4 Will. 4, c. 106), 483.

Herbage—ejectment for, 90.

Highway or Road (Boundaries), 243 ; no objection to an ejectment for the land, 91 ; not affected by the execution of a writ of possession, 347.

Mesne Profits—continued.
  subsequent action of trespass for, 634.
  mesne profits pending error, 368, 636.
  form of declaration for mesne profits and costs, 829, 830 ; pleas thereto,
    830—832 ; replication joining issue, 832 ; or by way of estoppel,
    833—836 ; rejoinder, 836 ; demurrer, 836.

Messuage—ejectment for, 88, 89.

Mills—ejectment for, 89.

Mines—ejectment for, 90 ; in a manor, 612.

Minister of a Dissenting Congregation may be ejected by the trustees after a
  demand of possession, 451, 604.

Misnomer in Writ—consequences of, 83 ; amendment of, at the trial, 302.

Mixed Actions (except ejectment), abolished, 27.

Moor—ejectment for, 90.

Moravians—affirmation by, 293.

Mortgage—of copyholds, admittance necessary before the trial, 466.
  of toll-houses, toll-gates, &c., 91, 466 ; of the undertaking and tolls,
    &c., not sufficient, 91, 466.

Mortgagee v. Mortgagor, 462 ; before default, 462 ; after default, 465 ; Statute of Limitations (7 Will. 4 & 1 Vict. c. 28), 24 ; consequences
  of entry by mortgagee, 463 ; stay of proceedings upon payment of
  principal, interest and costs (15 & 16 Vict. c. 76, ss. 219, 220),
  467 ; evidence for plaintiff, 471 ; evidence and points for defendant, 472.
  v. Prior Tenants of Mortgagor, 473.
  v. Subsequent Tenants of Mortgagor, 475.
  v. Subsequent Mortgagee, 478.
  v. Strangers, 479.

Mortgagor v. Mortgagee, 481.
  v. Tenant, 481.
  v. Strangers, 482.

Mountain—ejectment for, 90 ; acts of ownership, evidence of boundaries,
  246.

N.

Names of Defendants, how to be mentioned in the writ, 83 ; titles of dignity,
  83 ; consequences of misnomer, 83 ; of improper omission or insertion of names, 84, 85 ; application to strike out names of defendants not served, 85, 135 ; nolle prosequi as to them, 135 ;
  form, 743 ; amendment of misnomers at the trial, 302.

Naturalized Persons, 576.

Ne Recipiatur, 273 ; form, 773.

New Trial—after verdict for defendant, 330 ; after verdict for plaintiff, 331 ;
  when to be moved for, 331 ; rule nisi to state grounds (17 & 18
  Vict. c. 125, s. 33), 332 ; appeal (s. 34), 332 ; costs of previous
  trial, 333.

Nisi Prius Record, 272 ; form, 769.

Non-adverse Possession—doctrine of, abolished, 6, 8.

Non-sane Memory—proof of, 522.

Nonsuit, 304 ; form of postea, 779.

Note of Exceptions at the Trial, 313 ; form, 773.

Notice—to quit, 29 ; forms, 697.
  to determine a lease at the end of the first seven or fourteen years, 398 ;
  form, 398, 698.

O.

Outer Doors, may be broken open to execute a writ of possession, 345.

Outstanding Term, sufficient to defeat an ejectment, 288, 298 ; even a tenancy from year to year is sufficient, 288 ; unless defendant estopped, 288 ; the court or a judge cannot restrain a defendant from setting up as a defence an outstanding term, 373, 374 ; when a court of equity will do so, 374 ; surrender of term, when presumed, 227.

Ownership—acts of, 246.

P.

Parcel or no Parcel, 240 ; identity of land claimed, 289 ; identity of property devised, 519.

Parish and County—to be mentioned in the writ, 92 ; mistakes as to, 92 ; amendment at the trial, 289, 302.

Parish Houses or Land—recovery of before justices, 681.

Parliament—error in, from Exchequer Chamber, 368.

Part of Property claimed may be recovered, 86, 285, 306 ; undivided parts how described in the writ, 87.

Particulars of plaintiff's address, &c., 119 ; form, 725 ; of land claimed, 119 ; form, 726 ; of land defended, 129 ; of breaches, 120, 410 ; form, 726.

Passage Room—ejectment for, 88.

Pease (acres of), ejectment for, 90.

Pedigree—how prepared, 489 ; proof of, 488 ; hearsay evidence admissible, 234.

Penal Action for not giving landlord due notice of writ in ejectment (15 & 16 Vict. c. 76, s. 209), 115 ; the like in county court, for not giving notice of summons out of that court (19 & 20 Vict. c. 108, s. 53), 661 ; penal or remedial, 646.

Penalty annexed to a proviso makes it only a covenant, 403.

Perambulations of a manor, 612.

Petition of Right, 62.

Piece of Land (this term should not be used *alone* in a writ), 89.

Piscary, 90, 91.

Pit of Water—ejectment for, 90 ; sand or gravel pits in a manor may be copyhold tenements, 612.

Plaintiffs. See " *Claimants*," 868.

Pleadings—none in ejectment, an equitable defence cannot be pleaded, 373.
plea in bar to assignment of error in law, 818 ; replication thereto, 818 ; assignment of error in fact, 824 ; plea thereto, 825.
declaration by landlord against tenant for a penalty of three years' improved or rack-rent for not forthwith giving notice of a writ of ejectment, 723 ; plea of the general issue (by statute), 724.
declaration in trespass for mesne profits and costs, 829, 830 ; pleas thereto, 830, 831, 832 ; replication "joining issue," 832 ; replication by way of estoppel, 833, 834, 835 ; rejoinder, 836 ; demurrer, 836.
declaration for double value, 838, 839 ; for double rent, 840, 841.
plea in trespass for an assault and battery, &c., justifying in defence of possession of a messuage, &c., 837 ; justification in trespass of an expulsion, &c., by one defendant as tenant from year to year, and by the others as his servants, 838.

Pluries—no alias or pluries writ of ejectment, 99.

Q.

Rent Charge—ejectment by owner of, 571.

Repairs—ejectment for not repairing, 401, 422 ; what repairs sufficient, 424.

Replevin—sometimes involves a question of title to land, 64.

Reply—evidence in, 300, 525.
    on further evidence of plaintiff, 301.
    general reply, 301.

Republication of Will by a codicil, 505, 513.

Reputation—evidence of, 241 ; as to boundaries of a manor or parish, 247 ;
    not of private estates, 241, 247.

Reputed Manor, 610.

Restitution of Possession after judgment set aside for irregularity, 349 ; form
    of writ, 796.
    the like, after judgment reversed in error, 349, 370 ; form of writ, 823.
    the like, by justices, after a forcible entry, &c. 693 ; forms, 858, 861.
    after an award, 797.

Retainer of attorney for claimants, 75 ; form, 700 ; the like, for defendants,
    700, 701.
    to counsel, 140 ; forms, 750.

Returns of Sheriffs to Writs of Execution—forms, 792, 793.

Reversioner—see "*Remainderman*," 885 ; cannot maintain ejectment until his
    estate falls into possession, 66, 287 ; except for a forfeiture—see
    "*Forfeiture*," 875 ; case for injury to reversion, 64 ; assignee of re-
    version, 405 ; of part of the reversion, 406 ; of the reversion in part
    of the land, 406 ; when the Statute of Limitations begins to run
    against him, 11 ; constructive admission of, to copyholds, 626.

Revival of Judgment, 338.

Revocation of a Will—by marriage, 503 ; not by other alteration of circum-
    stances, 503 ; by subsequent will or codicil, or destruction of the
    will, 503 ; by obliterations, interlineations and other alterations,
    504 ; by subsequent conveyance, 506.

Right to begin, 284.

River or Rivulet—ejectment for, 90, 91 ; boundaries, 245.

Road or Highway—ejectment for the soil, 91 ; not interfered with on exe-
    cuting a writ of possession, 347 ; boundaries, 243.

Rules of a Benefit Building Society—how proved, 588.

Rules of Court, cited.
    Practice Rules, H. T. 1853—No. 2..126 ; Nos. 15, 16..324 ; No. 29..
      150 ; No. 32..193 ; No. 34..147, 148 ; No. 35..147 ; No. 36..
      148 ; No. 41..144, 147 ; No. 42..273 ; No. 43..272 ; No. 44..
      261 ; No. 45..261 ; No. 47..260 ; No. 48..270 ; No. 49..270 ;
      No..50..331 ; Nos. 51, 52, 53..332 ; No. 54..333 ; Nos. 55, 56..
      337 ; No. 57..336 ; Nos. 64, 65..370 ; No. 66..371 ; Nos. 67,
      68..366 ; No. 69..369 ; Nos. 70 to 73..343 ; No. 76..343 ; Nos.
      91 to 96..385 ; Nos. 97 to 103..386 ; No. 112..131 ; No. 113..
      127 ; No. 114..281 ; No. 138..704 ; No. 139..706 ; No. 140..
      706 ; No. 141..707 ; Nos. 142, 143..707 ; No. 144..703 ; No.
      160..711 ; No. 161..146 ; No. 164 (*altered by Reg. Gen. E. T.* 1856),
      147 ; No. 166..126 ; No. 167..127 ; Nos. 174, 175, 176..145.
    Pleading Rules, H. T. 1853—No. 18..829 ; No. 21..117 ; No. 24..
      368 ; Nos. 25, 26..369 ; No. 27..362 ; No. 29..340 ; No. 30..281 ;
      No. 32..337.
    Other Rules—Mic. Vac. 1854, *No.* 2..704 ; *E. T.* 1856..147.

Rules of Court (Forms of)—see *post,* " *Summonses and Orders of a Judge.*"
    outline of rule nisi, 711 ; of rule absolute, 712.

Stamps—continued.

documents not produced in pursuance of a notice to produce, presumed to be stamped, 171 ; unless the contrary appear, 171.

on leases, 393 ; mortgages, 471 ; surrenders, 225 ; attested copies, 252 ; probates, 528, 535 ; none on mere attornments, 230.

Statutes cited.

I. *The Common Law Procedure Act,* 1852 (15 & 16 Vict. c. 76), s. 6..96 ; s. 7..118 ; s. 30..126 ; s. 31..125 ; s. 97..145 ; s. 98..148 ; s. 99..148, 339 ; s. 101..136 ; ss. 102, 103..272 ; ss. 104, 105.. 258 ; s. 106..259 ; ss. 107, 108..259 ; s. 109..260 ; s. 110..261 ; s. 111..263 ; ss. 112, 113..264 ; s. 114..269 ; s. 115..264 ; s. 116 ..273 ; ss. 117, 118..150 ; s. 119..151, 163 ; s. 121..136 ; s. 128 ..338 ; s. 141..372 ; ss. 146, 147..363 ; s. 148..362, 363 ; ss. 149, 150, 151..363 ; ss. 152, 153, 154..365 ; s. 155..367 ; s. 156.. 363 ; s. 157..368 ; s. 158..370 ; ss. 159 to 163..371 ; ss. 164 to 167..372 ; s. 168..83, 119 ; s. 169..93, 98, 118 ; s. 170..98 ; ss. 171 to 174..122 ; s. 175..85, 119 ; s. 176..123, 129 ; s. 177..123, 131 ; s. 178..134 ; s. 179..138 ; s. 180..140, 285 ; s. 181..289 ; s. 182..142 ; s. 183..280 ; s. 184..326 ; s. 185..336 ; s. 186.. 336, 341 ; s. 187..342 ; s. 188..130, 290 ; s. 189..290 ; s. 190.. 350 ; s. 191..352 ; ss. 192, 193..351 ; s. 194..352 ; ss. 195, 196 ..353 ; s. 197..354 ; ss. 198, 199..355 ; ss. 200, 201..357 ; s. 202 ..136 ; ss. 203, 204..358 ; s. 205..359 ; s. 206..337 ; s. 207..76 ; s. 208..361 ; s. 209..115 ; s. 210..415 ; s. 211..420 ; s. 212.. 421 ; s. 213..379 ; s. 214..387 ; s. 215..388 ; ss. 216, 217..389 ; s. 218..378 ; ss. 219, 220..467 ; s. 221..373 ; s. 222..302.

II. *The Common Law Procedure Act,* 1854 (17 & 18 Vict. c. 125), s. 1.. 143 ; s. 16..320 ; s. 18..284 ; s. 19..303 ; s. 20..292 ; ss. 21 to 24..293 ; ss. 25 to 27..294 ; ss. 28 to 31..295 ; s. 32..326, 362 ; s. 33..332 ; s. 34..321, 332 ; s. 35..332 ; ss. 36 to 44..333 ; s. 50..201 ; s. 51..202 ; s. 52..203 ; ss. 53, 54..205 ; ss. 55 to 57 ..206 ; s. 58..208 ; s. 59..264 ; s. 83..133 ; s. 92..355 ; s. 93.. 81, 121.

III. *Other Statutes.*

13 Edw. 1, c. 18 (elegits), 564.

18 Edw. 1, stat. 1 (quia emptores), 610.

5 Rich. 2, stat. 1, c. 8 (forcible entries), 686.

15 Rich. 2, c. 2 (forcible entries), 686.

4 Hen. 4, c. 8 (forcible entries), 686.

8 Hen. 6, c. 9 (forcible entries), 686.

32 Hen. 8, c. 7, s. 7 (tithes), 91.

32 Hen. 8, c. 16, s. 13 (leases to aliens), 578.

32 Hen. 8, c. 34 (grantees of reversions), 405.

5 Eliz. c. 9, s. 12 (subpœnas), 185.

13 Eliz. c. 5 (fraudulent conveyances), 299.

27 Eliz. c. 4 (voluntary settlements), 300.

29 Eliz. c. 5 (fraudulent conveyances), 299.

30 Eliz. c. 18 (voluntary settlements), 300.

31 Eliz. c. 11 (forcible entries), 688.

21 Jac. 1, c. 15 (forcible entries), 688.

21 Jac. 1, c. 16, ss. 1, 2 (limitations), 5.

13 Car. 2, stat. 2, c. 2, s. 10 (costs in error), 369.

16 & 17 Car. 2, c. 8, ss. 3, 4 (bail in error), 361.

29 Car. 2, c. 3 (frauds), ss. 1, 2 (leases), 222 ; s. 3 (assignments), 223 ; ss. 5, 6 (wills), 494 ; ss. 8, 9 (testamentary guardians), 582 ; s. 12 (special occupants), 494, 533 ; ss. 19 to 22 (wills), 494.

11 & 12 Will. 3, c. 6 (aliens), 576.

4 Geo. 2, c. 28, s. 1 (double value), 645.

London: printed by C. Roworth and Sons, Bell Yard, Temple Bar.